American Decades

Primary Sources, 2000–2009

American Decades
Primary Sources, 2000–2009

Rebecca Valentine

Lawrence W. Baker, Project Editor

GALE
CENGAGE Learning·

Detroit • New York • San Francisco • New Haven, Conn • Waterville, Maine • London

American Decades Primary Sources, 2000–2009

Project Editor: Lawrence W. Baker

Rights Acquisition and Management: Sheila Spencer

Composition: Evi Abou-El-Seoud

Manufacturing: Rita Wimberley

Imaging: John Watkins

Product Design: Kristine Julien

© 2013 Gale, Cengage Learning

For product information and technology assistance, contact us at
Gale Customer Support, 1-800-877-4253.
For permission to use material from this text or product,
submit all requests online at **www.cengage.com/permissions**.
Further permissions questions can be emailed to
permissionrequest@cengage.com

Cover photographs: New York City, September 11, 2001, © Reuters/Corbis; UGG boots, © Finnbarr Webster/Alamy; Hurricane Katrina, © NASA/Corbis; smartphone, © Mark Oleksiy/Shutterstock.com.

Library of Congress Control Number: 2013937149

Gale
27500 Drake Rd.
Farmington Hills, MI 48331-3535

ISBN-13: 978-1-4144-8602-4   ISBN-10: 1-4144-8602-2

This title will also be available as an e-book.
ISBN-13: 978-1-4144-3709-5 ISBN-10: 1-4144-3709-9
Contact your Gale, a part of Cengage Learning, sales representative for ordering information.

Printed in Mexico
1 2 3 4 5 6 7 17 16 15 14 13

Contents

1 THE ARTS

4 FASHION AND DESIGN

5 GOVERNMENT AND POLITICS

6 LAW AND JUSTICE

7 LIFESTYLES AND SOCIAL TRENDS

8 THE MEDIA

9 MEDICINE AND HEALTH

10 RELIGION

11 SCIENCE AND TECHNOLOGY

Acknowledgments

Following is a list of the copyright holders who have granted us permission to reproduce textual material in this volume of *American Decades Primary Sources, 2000–2009*. Credit information is sorted by subject category.

THE ARTS

"Maya Lin." Art21. Copyright © by Art21. Reproduced by permission of the publisher. — "Maya Lin: Grand Rapids Ice Rink and Park Project." Art21. Copyright © by Art21. Reproduced by permission of the publisher. — "Sally Mann." Art21. Copyright © by Art21. Reproduced by permission of the publisher. — "Ai Weiwei." Art21. Copyright © by Art21. Reproduced by permission of the publisher. — Miller, Laura. "Book Lovers' Quarrel." *Salon, 2001.* Copyright © 2001 by *Salon.* Reproduced by permission of the publisher. — Goodnow, Cecelia. "Teens Buying Books at Fastest Rate in Decades." *Seattle Post-Intelligencer,* 2007. Copyright © 2007 by *Seattle Post-Intelligencer.* Reproduced by permission of the publisher. — Rosenberg, Liz. "Where the Coolest Kids Are, Like, Undead." *Boston Globe,* 2009. Copyright © 2009 by *Boston Globe.* Reproduced by permission of the publisher.

BUSINESS AND THE ECONOMY

Securities and Exchange Commission. "Securities and Exchange Commission Complaint against Bernard L. Madoff." www.sec.gov, http://www.sec.gov/litigation/complaints/2008/comp-madoff121108.pdf, 2008. — Zellner, Wendy, Stephanie A. Forest, Emily Thornton, Peter Coy, Heather Timmons, Louis Lavelle, and David Henry. "The Fall of Enron." *Bloomberg Businessweek,* December 2001. Copyright © 2001 by *Bloomberg Businessweek.* Reproduced by permission of the publisher. — German, Kent. "Top 10 Dot-com Flops." CNET, November 2004. Copyright © 2004 by CNET. Reproduced by permission of the publisher. — Grossman, Lev. "The Apple of Your Ear." Time Inc., January 2007. Copyright © 2007 by Time Inc. Reproduced by permission of the publisher. — Stein, Sam. "Glass-Steagall Act: The Senators and Economists Who Got It Right." *Huffington Post,* June 2009. Copyright © 2009 by *Huffington Post.* Reproduced by permission of the publisher. — Foley, Stephen. "Crash of a Titan: The Inside Story of the Fall of Lehman Brothers." *The Independent,* September 2009. Copyright © 2009 by The Independent, Inc. Reproduced by permission of the publisher.

EDUCATION

U.S. Department of Education. "The No Child Left Behind Act of 2001, Executive Summary." U.S. Dept. of Education, http://www2.ed.gov/nclb/overview/intro/execsumm.html. — Kennedy, Angela. "True or False: No Child Left Behind Is Working." *Counseling Today,* June 2008. Copyright © 2008 by *Counseling Today.* Reproduced by permission of the publisher. — Rimer, Sara, and Karen W. Arenson. "Top Colleges Take More Blacks, but Which Ones?" *New York Times,* June 2004. Copyright © 2004 by *New York Times.* Reproduced by permission of the publisher. — Kamenetz, Anya. "The Profit Chase: For-profit Colleges Have Lots of Champions— and Lots of Problems." Slate.com, November 2004. Copyright © 2004 by Slate.com. Reproduced by permission of the publisher. — Jones, Judge John E., III. "Memorandum Opinion: *Kitzmiller v. Dover School District.*" National Center for Science Education, Public Domain, 2005. — Dillon, Sam. "Online Schooling Grows, Setting Off a Debate." *New York Times,* February 2008. Copyright © 2008 by *New York Times.* Reproduced by permission of the publisher. — Risen, Clay. "The Lightning Rod." *Atlantic,*

November 2008. Copyright © 2008 by *Atlantic*. Reproduced by permission of the publisher. — National Center for Education Statistics. "Home-schooled Students." *The Condition of Education 2009*. http://nces.ed.gov/programs/coe/pdf/coe_hsc.pdf, 2009. — Boonstra, Heather D. "Advocates Call for a New Approach After the Era of 'Abstinence-Only' Sex Eduation." *Guttmacher Policy Review*, 2009. Copyright © 2009 by Guttmacher Policy Review. Reproduced by permission of the publisher. — Cohen, Patricia. "In Tough Times, the Humanities Must Justify Their Worth." *New York Times*, February 2009. Copyright © 2009 by *New York Times*. Reproduced by permission of the publisher. — American Library Association. " New Report Shows Libraries Critical in Times of Crisis, but Funding Lags and Services Reduced." American Library Association, April 2009. Copyright © 2009 by American Library Association. Reproduced by permission of the publisher. — Leonhardt, David. "Colleges Are Failing in Gradua-tion Rates." *New York Times*, May 2009. Copyright © 2009 by *New York Times*. Reproduced by permission of the publisher.

FASHION AND DESIGN

Patteson, Jean. "Fashion Flip-flop: The Comfy Sandal Takes Upscale Turn." *Sun Sentinel*, May 2002. Copyright © 2002 by *Sun Sentinel*. Reproduced by permission of the publisher. — Grant, Lorrie. "UGG Boots a Fashion Kick." *USA Today*, November 2004. Copyright © 2004 by USA Today. Reproduced by permission of the publisher. — Ouroussoff, Nicolai. "The New New York Skyline." *New York Times*, September 2004. Copyright © 2004 by *New York Times*. Reproduced by permission of the publisher. — Manning-Schaffel, Vivian. "Metrosexuals: A Well-Groomed Market?" *Business Week*, May 2006. Copy-right © 2006 by *Business Week*. Reproduced by permission of the publisher. — Ellis, Kori. "Influence of *SATC* Fashion & Culture." sheknows.com, May 2008. Copyright © 2008 by sheknows.com. Repro-duced by permission of the publisher. — Pogrebin, Robin. "Architects Return to Class as Green Design Advances." *New York Times*, August 2009. Copyright © 2009 by *New York Times*. Reproduced by permission of the publisher.

GOVERNMENT AND POLITICS

Bush, George W. "Address to the Nation on the September 11 Attacks." whitehouse.gov. — Bush, George W. "Address to the Joint Session of the 107th Congress." whitehouse.gov. — CNN. "Septem-ber 11: Chronology of Terror." CNN, September 2001. Copyright © 2001 by CNN. Reproduced by permission of the publisher. — Fessenden, Ford, and John M. Broder. "Examining the Vote: The Overview; Study of Disputed Florida Ballots Finds Justices Did Not Cast the Deciding Vote." *New York Times*, November 2011. Copyright © 2011 by New York Times, Inc. Reproduced by permission of the pub-lisher. — Bush, George W. "State of the Union Address to the 107th Congress." whitehouse.gov. — Lynch, Timothy. "More Surveillance Equals Less Liberty: Patriot Act Reduces Privacy, Undercuts Judicial Review." CATO Institute, September 2003. Copyright © 2003 by CATO Institute. Reproduced by permission of the publisher. — American Library Association. "ALA Joins Challenge to Patriot Act in U.S. Supreme Court." American Library Association, October 2005. Copyright © 2005 by American Library Association. Reproduced by permission of the pub-lisher. — Carter, Graydon. "Green Is the New Black." *Vanity Fair*, May 2006. Copyright © 2006 by *Vanity Fair*. Reproduced by permission of the publisher. — MacFarquhar, Neil. "Saddam Hussein, Defiant Dictator Who Ruled Iraq with Violence and Fear, Dies." *New York Times*, December 2006. Copyright © 2006 by *New York Times*. Reproduced by permission of the publisher. — Obama, Barack H. "President Barack Obama's Inaugural Address." whitehouse.gov. http://www.whitehouse.gov/blog/inaugural-address/. — Ferrara, Peter. "The Tea Party Revolution." *American Spectator*, April 2009. Copyright © 2009 by *American Spectator*. Reproduced by permission of the publisher. — Broder, John M. "Social Causes Defined Kennedy, Even at the End of a 46-Year Career in the Senate." *New York Times*, August 2009. Copyright © 2009 by *New York Times*. Reproduced by permission of the publisher.

LAW AND JUSTICE

Krauthammer, Charles. "The Winner in *Bush v. Gore*?" *Time Magazine*, November 2004. Copyright © 2004 by *Time Magazine*. Reproduced by permission of the publisher. — 107th United States Congress. Uniting and Strengthening America by Providing Appropriate Tools Required to Intercept and Obstruct Terrorism Act of 2001. www.gpo.gov, Library of Congress, 2001. — Ashcroft, John. "The Proven Tactics in the Fight Against Crime." www.justice.gov, http://www.justice.gov/archive/ag/speeches/2003/ 091503nationalrestaurant.htm. — 107th United States Congress. Public Law 107-296, An Act to Establish the Department of Homeland Security, and for Other Purposes. dhs.gov, http://www.dhs.gov/xlibrary/assets/ hr_5005_enr.pdf,2002. — *Goodridge v. Department of Public Health*, 798 N.E. 2d 941, Mass. 2003. — Leung, Rebecca. "The Man Who Knew." CBS Interactive, Inc.,

February 2009. Copyright © 2009 by CBS Interactive, Inc. Reproduced by permission of the publisher. — "Summary of Emergency Economic Stabilization Act of 2008—Signed into Law Oct. 3, 2008." http://ag-marketcrisis.com/blog/2008/10/summary-ofstabilization-bill/. — "What Is TSA?" www.tsa.gov, http://www.tsa.gov/who_we_are/what_is_tsa.shtm. — Sterns, Olivia. "TSA Ramps Up Virtual 'Strip Searches'." ABC News, July 2008. Copyright © 2008 by ABC News. Reproduced by permission of the publisher.

LIFESTYLES AND SOCIAL TRENDS

Seymour, Lesley Jane. "Tweens 'R' Shoppers." *New York Times*, April 2007. Copyright © 2007 by *New York Times*. Reproduced by permission of the publisher. — Associated Press. "Harry Potter Is a Modern Phenomenon." MSNBC, July 2007. Copyright © 2007 by MSNBC. Reproduced by permission of the publisher. — McGregor, Jena. "Consumer Vigilantes." *Bloomberg Businessweek*, February 2008. Copyright © 2008 by *Bloomberg Businessweek*. Reproduced by permission of the publisher. — Stelter, Brian. "Guilty Verdict in Cyberbullying Case Provokes Many Questions Over Online Identity." *New York Times*, November 2004. Copyright © 2004 by *New York Times*. Reproduced by permission of the publisher. — Lopez, Mark Hugo, and Paul Taylor. "Dissecting the 2008 Electorate: Most Diverse in U.S. History." From *Most Diverse in U.S. History*. Pew Research Center, April 30, 2009. Copyright © Pew Research Center, 2009. Reproduced by permission of the publisher. — Chmielewski, Dawn C., and David Sarno. "How MySpace Fell Off the Pace." *Los Angeles Times*, June 2009. Copyright © 2009 by *Los Angeles Times*. Reproduced by permission of the publisher. — Morin, Rich, and Wendy Wang. "Home for the Holidays ... and Every Other Day." Pew Research Center, November 2004. Copyright © 2004 by Pew Research Center. Reproduced by permission of the publisher. — Johnson, Tom. "That's AOL Folks...." CNN Money.com, November 2004. Copyright © 2004 by CNN Money.com. Reproduced by permission of the publisher.

THE MEDIA

O'Connor, John. "'I'm the Guy They Called Deep Throat.'" *Vanity Fair*, 2007. Copyright © 2007 by *Vanity Fair*. Reproduced by permission of the publisher. — Cooper, Anderson. *Anderson Cooper 360° Special Edition: Katrina's Aftermath*. CNN, August 2005. Copyright © 2005 by CNN. Reproduced by permission of the publisher. — Ralli, Tania. "Who's a Looter? In Storm's Aftermath, Pictures Kick Up a Different Kind of Tempest." *New York Times*, November 2004. Copyright © 2004 by *New York Times*. Reproduced by permission of the publisher. — Tirella, Joseph V. "American Idolatry." Portfolio.com, May 2008. Copyright © 2008 by Portfolio.com. Reproduced by permission of the publisher. — "Tina Brown's *Daily Beast* Is Unleashed." *New York Times*, October 2008. Copyright © 2008 by *New York Times*. Reproduced by permission of the publisher. — McIntyre, Douglas A. "The Ten Major Newspapers That Will Fold Or Go Digital Next." *Wall Street Journal*, March 2009. Copyright © 2009 by *Wall Street Journal*. Reproduced by permission of the publisher. — Johnson, Steven. "How Twitter Will Change the Way We Live." Time, Inc., June 2009. Copyright © 2009 by Time, Inc. Reproduced by permission of the publisher. — Junod, Tom. "The Falling Man," by Tom Junod. Originally published in *Esquire Magazine*. 3 September 2003. Used by permission of the Author's Estate. — Salem, Rob. "Retirement Means More Oprah, Not Less." *The Star*, November 2004. Copyright © 2004 by *The Star*. Reproduced by permission of the publisher. — Mitchell, Robert L. "Y2K: The Good, the Bad and the Crazy." *Computerworld*, December 2009. Copyright © 2009 by *Computerworld*. Reproduced by permission of the publisher.

MEDICINE AND HEALTH

Angier, Natalie. "How Brain, and Spirit, Adapt to a 9/11 World." *New York Times*, September 2004. Copyright © 2002 by *New York Times*. Reproduced by permission of the publisher. — Saad, Lydia. "U.S. Smoking Rate Still Coming Down." Gallup Poll, July 2008. Copyright © 2008 by Gallup Poll. Reproduced by permission of the publisher. — "Obama Overturns Bush Policy on Stem Cells." CNN, March 2009. Copyright © 2009 by CNN. Reproduced by permission of the publisher. — Johns, Michael, and Atul Grover. "Health Care Reform 2009: Do We Know What We Don't Know?" *Roll Call*, July 2009. Copyright © 2009 by *Roll Call*. Reproduced by permission of the publisher. — Attkisson, Sharyl. "Swine Flu Cases Overestimated?" CBS Interactive, October 2009. Copyright © 2009 by CBS Interactive, Inc. Reproduced by permission of the publisher. — U.S. Department of Labor. "U.S. Department of Labor's OSHA Issues Record-breaking Fines to BP." osha.gov, http://www.osha.gov/pls/oshaweb/owadisp.show_document?p_table=NEWS_RELEASES&p_id=16674, 2009. — "2010 State Obesity Rates." cdc.gov, http://www.cdc.gov/obesity/data/trends.html. — White House. *National HIV/AIDS Strategy for the United States*. whitehouse.gov, http://www.whitehouse.gov/sites/default/files/uploads/NHAS.pdf, 2010.

RELIGION

Goodstein, Laurie. "A Day of Terror: The Ties; in U.S., Echoes of Rift of Muslims and Jews." *New York Times*, September 2001. Copyright © 2001 by *New York Times*. Reproduced by permission of the publisher. — United States Conference of Catholic Bishops. "Between Man and Woman: Questions and Answers About Marriage and Same-Sex Unions." United States Conference of Catholic Bishops, November 2004. Copyright © 2004 by United States Conference of Catholic Bishops. Reproduced by permission of the publisher. — Associated Press. "Fugitive Sect Leader Arrested Near Las Vegas." MSNBC, August 2006. Copyright © 2006 by MSNBC. Reproduced by permission of the publisher. — Gorski, Eric, Felisa Cardona, and Manny Gonzales. "Pastor Takes Leave Amid Allegations of Gay Sex." *Denver Post*, November 2004. Copyright © 2004 by *Denver Post*. Reproduced by permission of the publisher. — Bashir, Martin, and Deborah Apron. "Rick Warren and Purpose-Driven Strife." ABC News, March 2007. Copyright © 2007 by ABC News. Reproduced by permission of the publisher. — Pew Research Center. "Views About Abortion." Pew Research Center, November 2004. Copyright © 2004 by Pew Research Center. Reproduced by permission of the publisher. — Ross, Brian. "Obama's Pastor: God Damn America, U.S. to Blame for 9/11." ABC News, March 2008. Copyright © 2008 by ABC News. Reproduced by permission of the publisher. — Obama, Barack. "A More Perfect Union." *Huffington Post*, November 2004. Copyright © 2004 by *Huffington Post*. Reproduced by permission of the publisher. — "Religious Groups' Views on Global Warming." From the Pew Research Center's Forum on Religion & Public Life, © 2009, Pew Research Center. http://www.pewforum.org/Science-and-Bioethics/Religious-Groups-Views-on-Global-Warming.aspx.

SCIENCE AND TECHNOLOGY

Wade, Nicholas. "Once Again, Scientists Say Human Genome Is Complete." *New York Times*, April 2003. Copyright © 2003 by *New York Times*. Reproduced by permission of the publisher. — Wilford, John Noble. "Rover Unfurls, Opening New Stage in Exploration." *New York Times*, January 2004. Copyright © 2004 by *New York Times*. Reproduced by permission of the publisher. — Associated Press. "Hybrid Vehicle Registration Jumps." MSNBC, April 2004. Copyright © 2004 by MSNBC. Reproduced by permission of the publisher. — Drezner, Daniel W. "The Outsourcing Bogeyman." Council on Foreign Relations, May/June 2004. Copyright © 2004 by Council on Foreign Relations. Reproduced by permission of the publisher. — Associated Press. "Researchers Recover T. Rex Tissue." Wired.com, March 2005. Copyright © 2005 by Wired.com. Reproduced by permission of the publisher. — Penenberg, Adam L. "Cookie Monster." Slate.com, November 2004. Copyright © 2004 by Slate.com. Reproduced by permission of the publisher. — Thompson, Andrea. "'Significant Amount' of Water Found on Moon." Space.com, November 2004. Copyright © 2004 by Space.com. Reproduced by permission of the publisher.

SPORTS

"One More Title." *Sports Illustrated*, June 2000. Copyright © 2000 by *Sports Illustrated*. Reproduced by permission of the publisher. — Canseco, Jose. *Juiced: Wild Times, Rampant 'Roids, Smash Hits, and How Baseball Got Big*. William Morrow, 2005. Copyright © 2005 by William Morrow. Reproduced by permission of the publisher. — Caldwell, Dave. "Racing to Victory, and Leaving the Men and the Doubters Behind." *New York Times*, April 2008. Copyright © 2008 by *New York Times*. Reproduced by permission of the publisher. — Brinkley, Douglas. "Lance Armstrong Rides Again." *Vanity Fair*, September 2008. Copyright © 2008 by *Vanity Fair*. Reproduced by permission of the publisher. — Shipnuck, Alan. "Michael Phelps." *Sports Illustrated*, December 2008. Copyright © 2008 by *Sports Illustrated*. Reproduced by permission of the publisher. — Price, S. L. "The Takedown." *Sports Illustrated*, May 2009. Copyright © 2009 by *Sports Illustrated*. Reproduced by permission of the publisher. — Gross, Terry. "LeBron James Shoots for the 'Stars.'" National Public Radio, September 2009. Copyright © 2009 by National Public Radio. Reproduced by permission of the publisher. — Mandel, Stewart. "With Harsh USC Penalties, NCAA Sends Warning to All Elite Programs." *Sports Illustrated*, June 2010. Copyright © 2010 by *Sports Illustrated*. Reproduced by permission of the publisher.

About the Set

American Decades Primary Sources is an eleven-volume collection of more than two thousand primary sources on twentieth- and twenty-first-century American history and culture. Each volume comprises 150–200 primary sources. These documents are enhanced by informative context, with illustrative images—many of which are primary sources in their own right—adding perspective and a deeper understanding of both the primary sources and the milieu from which they originated.

Designed for students and teachers at the high school and undergraduate levels, as well as researchers and history buffs, *American Decades Primary Sources* meets the growing demand for primary source material.

Conceived as both a stand-alone reference and a companion to the popular *American Decades* set, *American Decades Primary Sources* is organized in the same subject-specific chapters for compatibility and ease of use.

PRIMARY SOURCES

To provide fresh insight into the key events and figures of the twentieth and twenty-first centuries, thirty historians and five advisors selected unique primary sources far beyond the typical speeches, government documents, and literary works. Screenplays, scrapbooks, sports box scores, patent applications, college course outlines, military codes of conduct, environmental sculptures, and CD liner notes are but a sampling of the more than seventy-five types of primary sources included.

Diversity is shown not only in the wide range of primary source types, but also in the range of subjects and opinions and the frequent combination of primary sources in entries. Multiple perspectives in religious, political, artistic, and scientific thought demonstrated the commitment of *American Decades Primary Sources* to diversity, in addition to the inclusion of considerable content displaying ethnic, racial, and gender diversity. *American Decades Primary Sources* presents a variety of perspectives on issues and events, encouraging the reader to consider subjects more fully and critically.

American Decades Primary Sources' innovative approach often presents related primary sources in an entry. The primary sources act as contextual material for each other—creating a unique opportunity to understand each and its place in history, as well as their relation to one another. These may be point-counterpoint arguments, a variety of diverse opinions, or direct responses to another primary source. One example is President Franklin Delano Roosevelt's letter to clergy at the height of the Great Depression, with responses by a diverse group of religious leaders from across the country.

Multiple primary sources created by particularly significant individuals—Dr. Martin Luther King Jr., for example—reside in *American Decades Primary Sources*. Multiple primary sources on particularly significant subjects are often presented in more than one chapter of a volume, or in more than one decade, providing opportunities to see the significance and impact of an event or figure from many angles and historical perspectives. For example, seven primary sources on the controversial Scopes "monkey" trial are found in five chapters of the 1920s volume. Primary sources on evolutionary theory may be found in earlier and later volumes, allowing the reader to see and analyze the development of thought across time.

ENTRY ORGANIZATION

Contextual material uses standardized rubrics that will soon become familiar to the reader, making the entries more accessible and allowing for easy comparison. Introduction and Significance essays—brief and focused—cover the historical background, contributing factors, importance, and impact of the primary source, encouraging the reader to think critically—not only about the primary source, but also about the way history is constructed. Key Facts and a Synopsis provide quick access and recognition of the primary sources, and the Further Resources are a stepping-stone to additional study.

ADDITIONAL FEATURES

Subject chronologies and thorough tables of contents (listing titles, authors, and dates) begin each chapter. The main table of contents assembles this information conveniently at the front of the book. An essay on using primary sources, a chronology of selected events outside the United States during the twentieth century (in the 1900s–1990s volumes) and the twenty-first century (in the 2000s volume), substantial general and subject resources, and primary source type and general indexes enrich *American Decades Primary Sources*.

The eleven volumes of *American Decades Primary Sources* provide a vast array of primary sources integrated with supporting content and user-friendly features. This value-laden set gives the reader an unparalleled opportunity to travel into the past, to relive important events, to encounter key figures, and to gain a deep and full understanding of America in the twentieth and twenty-first centuries.

About the Volume

The first decade of the twenty-first century was marked by globalization, and technology made that globalization possible. The 2000s saw some of the most influential technological advancements since the age of Thomas Edison as the Internet, cellular phones, and mp3 players came to dominate the American lifestyle and change the way society interacted not only within the boundaries of the United States, but across the world. Media and the way in which news was reported also contributed to the feeling of globalization throughout the decade. The United States experienced economic recession in the early part of the decade before enjoying a boom in real estate. As lenders found new—and ethically questionable—strategies to loan money to potential homebuyers, the housing market peaked mid-decade, then collapsed by 2008. Unemployment rates soared and people found themselves homeless. The 2000s claimed the highest rate of home foreclosures in a thirty-year history. The political arena offered no respite from the nation's economic woes. With three presidential elections, the decade was host to some of the most expensive, personally directed campaigns in political history. Whether natural or man-made, one disaster after another bombarded America in the 2000s, and by 2009, the country was exhausted, disheartened, and disenchanted. The following highlights represent a sample of what this volume has to offer.

HIGHLIGHTS OF PRIMARY SOURCES, 2000–2009
- An analysis of the Bush-Gore presidential election and outcome
- Text from the Patriot Act and public criticism of its impact
- An exposé on Mark Felt, aka Deep Throat, the FBI informant in the Watergate scandal
- A look back at the swine flu epidemic
- A history of the birth of the iPhone
- A look into green design and hybrid cars as America took environmentalism to a new level
- Profiles of athletes Lance Armstrong, LeBron James, and Michael Phelps
- Overview of trends in Young Adult literature, from *Harry Potter* to *Twilight* and everything in between
- Analysis of the fall of Enron
- Highlights of the No Child Left Behind Act and a hard look at its effectiveness
- Obituary of Senator Edward "Teddy" Kennedy
- First Inaugural Address given by President Barack Obama

VOLUME STRUCTURE AND CONTENT
Front matter
- Contents—lists primary sources, authors, and dates of origin, by chapter and chronologically within chapters.
- About the Set, About the Volume, About the Entry essays—guide the reader through the set and promote ease of use.
- Using Primary Sources—provides a crash course in reading and interpreting primary sources.
- Chronology of Selected World Events Outside the United States—lends additional context in which to place the decade's primary sources.

Chapters:

- The Arts
- Business and the Economy
- Education
- Fashion and Design
- Government and Politics
- Law and Justice
- Lifestyles and Social Trends
- The Media
- Medicine and Health
- Religion
- Science and Technology
- Sports

Chapter structure

- Chapter contents—lists primary sources, authors, and dates of origin chronologically, showing each source's place in the decade.

- Chapter chronology—highlights the decade's important events in the chapter's subject.

- Primary sources—displays sources surrounded by contextual material.

Back matter

- General Resources—promotes further inquiry with books, periodicals, websites, and audio and visual media, all organized into general and subject-specific sections.

- Primary Source Type Index—locates primary sources by category, giving readers an opportunity to easily analyze sources across genres.

- General Index—provides comprehensive access to primary sources, people, events, and subjects, and cross-referencing to enhance comparison and analysis.

About the Entry

The primary source is the centerpiece and main focus of each entry in *American Decades Primary Sources, 2000–2009*. In keeping with the philosophy that much of the benefit from using primary sources derives from the reader's own process of inquiry, the contextual material surrounding each entry provides access and ease of use, as well as giving the reader a springboard for delving into the primary source. Rubrics identify each section and enable the reader to navigate entries with ease.

ENTRY STRUCTURE

- Primary Source/Entry Title, Subtitle, Primary Source Type
- Key Facts—essential information about the primary source, including creator, date, source citation, and notes about the creator or source.
- Introduction—historical background and contributing factors for the primary source.
- Significance—importance and impact of the primary source, at the time and since.
- Primary Source—in text, text facsimile, or image format; full or excerpted.
- Further Resources—books, periodicals, websites, and audio and visual material.

NAVIGATING AN ENTRY

Entry elements are numbered and reproduced here, with an explanation of the data contained in these elements explained immediately thereafter according to the corresponding numeral.

Primary Source/Entry Title, Subtitle, Primary Source Type

[1] **"LeBron James Shoots for the 'Stars'"**

[2] High School Phenom-Turned-NBA Star

[3] **Radio transcript**

[1] **Primary Source/Entry Title:** The entry title is usually the primary source title, except in instances when an entry includes multiple primary sources. In those cases, a general title is provided, and the primary-source titles appear below the general title, directly above their individual Key Facts sections.

[2] **Subtitle:** Some entries contain subtitles.

[3] **Primary Source Type:** The type of primary source is listed just below the title.

Key Facts

[4] **By:** Terry Gross

[5] **Date:** September 9, 2009

[6] **Source:** Gross, Terry. "LeBron James Shoots for the 'Stars.'" *NPR*, September 9, 2009. www.npr.org/templates/transcript/transcript.php?storyId=112641310 (accessed on March 24, 2013).

[7] **About the Host:** Terry Gross was the host and producer of National Public Radio's *Fresh Air* program. Founded in 1975 as a daily three-hour show that aired locally in Philadelphia, *Fresh Air* was expanded in 1987 to an hour-long interview and music program that was broadcast nationally five days a week. Gross heavily researched the people she

interviewed ahead of time, and she earned a reputation as a thoughtful, attentive interviewer. Among her thousands of radio guests were Johnny Cash, Elie Wiesel, Nancy Reagan, Jimmy Carter, and Toni Morrison. In 1994, *Fresh Air* won the Peabody Award for its "probing questions, revelatory interviews, and unusual insights."

[4] **By:** The name of the primary source creator begins the Key Facts section.

[5] **Date:** The date of origin of the primary source appears in this field and may differ from the date of publication in the source citation below it; for example, speeches are often delivered before they are published.

[6] **Source:** The source citation is a full bibliographic citation, giving original publication data as well as reprint and/or online availability.

[7] **About the Author:** A brief biography of the author or originator of the primary source gives birth and death dates and a quick overview of the person's work. This rubric has been customized in some cases. If the primary source is a written document, the term "author" appears; however, if the primary source is a work of art, the term "artist" is used, showing the person's direct relationship to the primary source. For primary sources created by a group, "organization" may have been used instead of "author." Other terms may also be used to describe the creator or originator of the primary source. If an author is anonymous or unknown, a brief "About the Publication" sketch may appear.

Introduction

[8] **INTRODUCTION**

Born in 1984, LeBron James grew up in poverty in Akron, Ohio. He began playing basketball at the age of nine. By his senior year of high school, James had already been featured on the covers of *ESPN* magazine and *Sports Illustrated*. He also played football while still in high school, but a wrist injury cut short that career. Before that happened, he had been offered a football scholarship to the University of Notre Dame, but chose instead to remain dedicated to basketball....

[8] **Introduction:** The introduction is a brief essay on the contributing factors and historical context of the primary source. It is intended to promote understanding and equip the reader with essential facts to understand the context of the primary source.

Significance

[9] **SIGNIFICANCE**

"King James" became a free agent in 2010 and was courted by numerous teams. The star took a long time to decide what team he would sign with, and on a July 8, 2010, live televised special called *The Decision*, James announced he would sign with the Miami Heat. His decision was based in large part on the fact that two other free agents—Chris Bosh and Dwyane Wade— also signed with Miami. James reasoned that playing with these men as his teammates would give him a better chance of clinching a championship than if he had stayed with Cleveland. The decision caused an uproar in the world of basketball as James's former Cavs coach publicly denounced his choice. Fans were furious, and other players criticized the decision as cowardly because he was admittedly depending on teammates to shoulder the burden of winning. Many sports analysts condemned the athlete for waiting to make a decision until the last minute and keeping his decision a secret even to the interested coaches, who learned along with the rest of the country what team James had chosen. His free-agency period left James with a reputation as one of the most disliked athletes in professional sports, according to a 2012 public poll conducted by Nielsen and E-Poll Market Research. It was an about-face from the hero-worship that the Ohio native had experienced during his years with Cleveland....

[9] **Significance:** The Significance discusses the importance and impact of the primary source and the event it describes.

Primary Source Header, Synopsis, Primary Source

[10] "LeBron James Shoots for the 'Stars'"

[11] **SYNOPSIS**: LeBron James plugs his new memoir while reminiscing about his childhood and early NBA career.

[12] This is FRESH AIR. I'm Terry Gross. My guest, LeBron James, has been a sports star ever since he was on the cover of *Sports Illustrated* at the age of 17, when he was still in high school. He was the number one NBA draft pick out of high school. At 19, he became the youngest Rookie of the Year in NBA history. That was in the 2003–2004 season. At the end of last season, he was named the NBA's Most Valuable Player. He plays for the Cleveland Cavaliers.

James, who will turn 25 in December, grew up in Akron, and that's where his new memoir, "Shooting Stars," is set. It's about growing up poor, the son of a single mother. And it's about his friendship with the boys who became his teammates in junior high and how they managed to stick together, go to the same high school and become state champions. The book is co-written with Buzz Bissinger, who wrote "Friday Night Lights."

LeBron James, welcome to FRESH AIR. Do you remember the very first time that you dunked?

Mr. LeBRON JAMES (Basketball Player; Co-author, "Shooting Stars"): Yeah, I was in eighth grade, and my middle school every year has a teachers-versus-students game. You know, they play the basketball team. And in warm-ups, I have no idea what got into me, but it was so—it was so electric in this gym. I think this gym holds probably, like—oh, it holds probably, like, I'd say probably about 45 people in there. That's a lot, right, for an eighth-grade game, 45 people? . . .

[1 0] **Primary Source Headers:** The primary source header signals the beginning of the primary source.

[1 1] **Synopsis:** The synopsis gives a brief overview of the primary source.

[1 2] **Primary Source:** The majority of primary sources are reproduced as plain text. The primary source may appear excerpted or in full, and may appear as text, text facsimile (photographic reproduction of the original text), image, or graphic display (such as a table, chart, or graph). The font and leading of the primary sources are distinct from that of the context—to provide a visual clue to the change, as well as to facilitate ease of reading. As needed, the original formatting of the text

is preserved in order to more accurately represent the original (screenplays, for example). In order to respect the integrity of the primary sources, content some readers may consider sensitive (for example, the use of slang, ethnic or racial slurs, etc.) is retained when deemed to be integral to understanding the source and the context of its creation. Primary source images (whether photographs, text facsimiles, or graphic displays) are bordered with a distinctive double rule and include the header "Primary Source." The synopses for primary-source images are located in the captions associated with the images.

Further Resources

[1 3] **FURTHER RESOURCES**

Books

James, LeBron, and Buzz Bissinger. *Shooting Stars.* New York: Penguin Press, 2009.

Web Sites

Heitner, Darren. "LeBron James Reminds the World That He Is Not Michael Jordan." *Forbes*, February 13, 2013. www.forbes.com/sites/darrenheitner/2013/02/13/lebron-james-reminds-the-world-that-he-is-not-michael-jordan/ (accessed on March 24, 2013).

[1 3] **Further Resources:** A brief list of resources categorized as Books, Periodicals, and Web sites provides a stepping stone to further study.

Using Primary Sources

The definition of what constitutes a primary source is often the subject of scholarly debate and interpretation. Although primary sources come from a wide spectrum of resources, they are united by the fact that they individually provide insight into the historical *milieu* (context and environment) during which they were produced. Primary sources include materials such as newspaper articles, press dispatches, autobiographies, essays, letters, diaries, speeches, song lyrics, posters, and works of art that offer direct, firsthand insight or witness to events of their day.

Categories of primary sources include:

- Documents containing firsthand accounts of historic events by witnesses and participants. This category includes diary or journal entries, letters, newspaper articles, interviews, memoirs, and testimony in legal proceedings.

- Images, including (but certainly not limited to) works of art, photographs, songs, and advertisements.

- Secondary sources. In some cases, secondary sources or tertiary sources may be treated as primary sources, and they may be created many years after an event. Ordinarily, a historical retrospective published after the initial event is not considered a primary source. If, however, a resource contains statements or recollections of participants or witnesses to the original event, the source may be considered primary with regard to those statements and recollections.

ANALYSIS OF PRIMARY SOURCES

The material collected in this volume is not intended to provide a comprehensive overview of a topic or event. Rather, the primary sources are intended to generate interest and lay a foundation for further inquiry and study.

In order to properly analyze a primary source, readers should remain skeptical and develop probing questions about the source. As in reading a chemistry or algebra textbook, historical documents require readers to analyze them carefully and extract specific information. However, readers must also read "beyond the text" to garner larger clues about the social impact of the primary source.

In addition to providing information about their topics, primary sources may also supply a wealth of insight into their creator's viewpoint. For example, when reading a news article about an outbreak of disease, consider whether the reporter's words also indicate something about his or her origin, bias (an irrational disposition in favor of someone or something), prejudices (an irrational disposition against someone or something), or intended audience.

Students should remember that primary sources often contain information later proven to be false, or contain viewpoints and terms unacceptable to future generations. It is important to view the primary source within the historical and social context existing at its creation. If, for example, a newspaper article is written within hours or days of an event, later developments may reveal some assertions in the original article as false or misleading.

TEST NEW CONCLUSIONS AND IDEAS

Whatever opinion or working hypothesis the reader forms, it is critical that he or she then test that hypothesis against other facts and sources related to the incident. For example, it might be wrong to conclude that factual mistakes are deliberate unless evidence can be produced of a pattern and practice of such mistakes with an intent to promote a false idea.

The difference between sound reasoning and preposterous conspiracy theories (or the birth of urban legends) lies in the willingness to test new ideas against other sources, rather than rest on one piece of evidence such as a single primary source that may contain errors. Sound reasoning requires that arguments and assertions guard against argument fallacies that utilize the following:

- false dilemmas (only two choices are given when in fact there are three or more options)

- arguments from ignorance (*argumentum ad ignorantiam*; because something is not known to be true, it is assumed to be false)

- possibilist fallacies (a favorite among conspiracy theorists who attempt to demonstrate that a factual statement is true or false by establishing the possibility of its truth or falsity. An argument where "it could be" is usually followed by an unearned "therefore, it is.")

- slippery slope arguments or fallacies (a series of increasingly dramatic consequences is drawn from an initial fact or idea)

- begging the question (the truth of the conclusion is assumed by the premises)

- straw man arguments (the arguer mischaracterizes an argument or theory and then attacks the merits of his or her own false representations)

- appeals to pity or force (the argument attempts to persuade people to agree by sympathy or force)

- prejudicial language (values or moral judgments are attached to certain arguments or facts)

- personal attacks (*ad hominem*; an attack on a person's character or circumstances)

- anecdotal or testimonial evidence (stories that are unsupported by impartial information or data that is not reproducible)

- *post hoc* (after the fact) fallacies (because one thing follows another, it is held to cause the other)

- the fallacy of the appeal to authority (the argument rests upon the credentials of a person, not the evidence).

Despite the fact that some primary sources can contain false information or lead readers to false conclusions based on the "facts" presented, they remain an invaluable resource regarding past events. Primary sources allow readers and researchers to come as close as possible to understanding the perceptions and context of events and, thus, to more fully appreciate how and why misconceptions occur.

Chronology of Selected World Events
Outside the United States, 2000–2009

2000

In 2000, the world population is 6.08 billion people.

In 2000, Andrew Lloyd Webber's musical *Cats* ends its nineteen-year run in London and also closes on Broadway.

In 2000, J. K. Rowling publishes *Harry Potter and the Goblet of Fire*.

In 2000, outbreaks of Bovine Spongiform Encephalopathy, popularly known as mad cow disease, occur in Europe.

In 2000, Chinese author Gao Xingjian wins the Nobel Prize in Literature.

In 2000, Scottish film director Guy Ritchie marries singer Madonna.

In 2000, Chinese film *Crouching Tiger, Hidden Dragon* debuts.

In 2000, Sony introduces the PlayStation 2 video-game console.

In January, pressure mounts from around the world to return Elián González to his father in Cuba; the six-year-old boy had survived an escape attempt from the island to Florida that had claimed the lives of his mother and stepfather.

On January 1, predictions of widespread world-wide computer shutdowns due to the Y2K bug prove false as the new millennium begins.

On January 2, Muslims and Coptic Christians clash in southern Egypt.

On January 2, Israeli prime minister Ehud Barak and Syrian foreign minister Farouk al-Shara meet in Shepherdstown, New York, to discuss security and economic issues.

On January 3, the deposed president of Ivory Coast, Konan Bedie, arrives in France. His successor, military ruler Robert Guéï, will suspend payments on the foreign debt within the week.

On January 4, Israel agrees to begin giving land in the West Bank to the Palestinian Authority.

On January 4, Italy opens diplomatic relations with North Korea.

On January 5, a suicide bomber from the Liberation Tigers of Tamil Eelam strikes in Colombo, Sri Lanka, part of an ongoing struggle to gain a homeland for Tamils. In June of this year another attack will kill a government minister.

On January 5, the Dalai Lama welcomes the seventeenth lama of the Karmapa Buddhist order, Ogyen Trinley Dorje, to Dharmsala, India, after he leaves Tibet in opposition to Chinese oppression of the country.

On January 9, Chechen rebels attack Grozny, Russia.

On January 10, the UN Security Council convenes to discuss the spread of AIDS, especially in Africa.

On January 10, truck drivers in France block highways in protest against higher gas prices and fewer work hours.

On January 10, Islam Karimov wins a second term as president of Uzbekistan.

On January 12, Great Britain ends its ban on homosexuals in the military.

On January 15, Serbian paramilitary leader and accused war criminal Željko Ražnatović is assassinated in Belgrade.

On January 30, a Kenyan airliner crashes into the Atlantic Ocean near Ivory Coast.

On March 7, Bangladesh ratifies the Comprehensive Nuclear Test Ban Treaty (CNTBT).

On March 11, Socialist Ricardo Froilán Lagos Escobar becomes president of Chile, the country's first leftist leader since the death of Salvador Allende in 1973.

On March 17, more than seven hundred members of a religious cult called the Movement for the Restoration of the Ten Commandments of God in Uganda commit mass suicide.

On March 26, Vladimir Putin is elected president of Russia. One of his first official acts is to visit the troubled Republic of Chechnya.

On April 17, Morocco ratifies the CNTBT.

On May 24, Israeli troops withdraw from all of southern Lebanon except the Shebaa Farms area.

On May 28, Putin signs a Nuclear Test Ban law, opening the way for Russia to approve the CNTBT.

On June 13, South Korean president Kim Dae Jung visits North Korea, a first for a South Korean leader.

On June 26, the CNTBT is signed by representatives of Iceland and Portugal. Four days later Russia signs the treaty.

On June 28, Elián González is returned to Cuba to live with his father.

In July, Colombian president Andrés Pastrana initiates "Plan Colombia" to curtail drug trafficking; the United States will contribute $1.3 billion for helicopters and training.

On July 2, Mexicans elect Vicente Fox president of their country over the Partido Revolucionario Institucional (PRI), which has ruled for more than seven decades.

On July 10, more than 250 Nigerians die in a pipeline explosion.

On July 25, Air France's supersonic plane *Concorde* crashes while taking off from Paris, killing 114 people (four on the ground). Most of the passengers are German tourists.

On July 30, Hugo Chávez is reelected as president of Venezuela.

On August 12, the Russian nuclear submarine *Kursk* sinks in the Barents Sea. Allegations are made that some of the 118 sailors killed could have been saved with faster action by the navy and the acceptance of international aid, which was refused.

In September, Belarus and the United Arab Emirates (UAE) ratify the CNTBT.

On September 11, the World Economic Forum meets in Melbourne, Australia.

On September 15–October 1, the twenty-seventh Olympics are hosted by Sydney, Australia.

On September 26, International Monetary Fund and World Bank meetings in Prague are hampered by massive antiglobalization protests.

On September 26, the Greek ferry *Express Samina* sinks off the island of Páros, with the loss of 82 passengers and crew; more than 450 are saved.

On September 28, rock-throwing erupts as Israeli politician Ariel Sharon visits the Temple Mount in Jerusalem, igniting several days of clashes between Palestinians and Israelis. Termed the Second Intifada, actions by youthful protesters against Israeli rule are gradually taken over by militant groups.

On September 28, former Canadian prime minister Pierre Trudeau dies.

On October 5, Serbian president Slobodan Milošević is forced to step down as the leader of Yugoslavia.

On October 12, seventeen U.S. sailors perish in an al Qaeda suicide attack against the destroyer USS *Cole* in Aden, Yemen.

On October 26, Laurent Gbagbo becomes president of Ivory Coast, replacing Robert Guéï.

On November 2, two Russian cosmonauts and an American astronaut become the first crew to man the International Space Station in orbit.

On November 11, an Alpine cable-car fire in a tunnel in Kaprun, Austria, kills more than one hundred people.

On November 13, Philippine president Joseph Estrada is impeached.

On November 16, U.S. president Bill Clinton visits Vietnam.

On November 17, Peruvian president Alberto Fujimoro is removed from office on corruption charges. He will later be convicted for misuse of power and human-rights violations.

On November 24, a meeting is held in Zagreb, Croatia, between representatives of the European Union (EU) and former parts of Yugoslavia (Croatia, Bosnia and Herzegovina, Macedonia, and Albania) concerning regional stability and entry into the EU.

On December 10, former Pakistani prime minister Nawaz Sharif, who was overthrown by Pervez Musharraf, enters exile in Saudi Arabia.

On December 30, a string of bombs explode in Manila, killing more than twenty people.

On December 31, massive riots erupt in Algeria.

2001

In 2001, Wikipedia goes online.

In 2001, *Nature* magazine publishes the first map of the human genome.

In 2001, a self-contained artificial heart is invented.

In 2001, Canadian author Yann Martel publishes *Life of Pi.*

In 2001, Trinidadian novelist V. S. Naipaul wins the Nobel Prize in Literature.

In 2001, the movies *Harry Potter and the Sorcerer's Stone* and *The Fellowship of the Ring* debut.

In 2001, the Nintendo GameCube gaming system is introduced.

In January, Amr Moussa replaces Egyptian Ismat Abdel Meguid as secretary general of the Arab League.

On January 9, China launches an unmanned space vehicle.

On January 13, a strong earthquake hits El Salvador, taking nearly nine hundred lives.

On January 16, President Laurent-Désiré Kabila of the Democratic Republic of Congo is assassinated.

On January 20, Joseph Estrada is replaced as the president of the Philippines by Gloria Macapagal-Arroyo.

On January 23, Revolutionary Armed Forces of Colombia (FARC) rebels kidnap two American journalists.

On January 26, Gujarat, India, is destroyed by an earthquake that kills more than twenty thousand people.

On January 29, corruption charges against the president of Indonesia inspire thousands of students to storm the parliament building.

On February 6, Ariel Sharon is elected prime minister of Israel.

On February 7, Jean-Bertrand Aristide begins his third term as president of Haiti.

On February 9, a Japanese trawler is sunk off Hawaii after it is struck accidentally by an American submarine.

On February 12, a spacecraft (Near Earth Asteroid Rendezvous *Shoemaker*) lands for the first time on an asteroid.

On February 26, two huge Buddhist statues carved into the side of a mountain near Bamian are destroyed by the ruling Taliban in Afghanistan. The act is widely condemned.

In March, ethnic Albanians in Macedonia seek autonomy.

On March 4, a bomb, attributed to the Irish Republican Army, explodes in front of the BBC building in London.

On March 23, the Russian *Mir* space station falls back to Earth and is incinerated during atmospheric descent.

In April, Berbers protest in Kabylia, Algeria.

On April 1, Netherlands legalizes same-sex marriages.

On April 2, a U.S. spy plane and crew are forced down in China after a midair collision. The crew is released on April 11.

On May 6, Pope John Paul II visits a mosque in Syria.

On June 1, Nepalese crown prince Dipendra shoots and kills his parents and other members of the royal family before attempting to commit suicide; he dies three days later and the former king's brother Gyanendra becomes king.

On June 7, the Labour Party in Britain handily wins in the national elections. Tony Blair retains the post of prime minister.

On June 14, the Shanghai Cooperation Organization is formed (China, Kazakhstan, Kyrgyzstan, Russia, Tajikistan, and Uzbekistan).

On June 20, Musharraf assumes the presidency of Pakistan.

On June 23, Pope John Paul II visits Ukraine.

In July, in Sudan, the antigovernment Darfur Liberation Front is formed.

On July 16, Russia and China sign a treaty of cooperation and friendly relations.

On July 20, the members of the Group of Eight (G8) meet in Genoa, Italy, amid protests that cost at least one life.

On August 6, Brazilian author Jorge Amado de Faria dies.

On August 10, coalition jets strike Iraqi air-defense sites.

On August 21, NATO plans to send peacekeepers to Macedonia.

On September 2, South African surgeon Christiaan Barnard, who performed the first human heart transplant, dies.

On September 9, Taliban suicide bombers posing as journalists kill Afghanistan Northern Alliance leader Ahmad Shah Massoud.

On September 11, al Qaeda hijackers from Saudi Arabia, United Arab Emirates, Egypt, and Lebanon crash commercial airplanes into the World Trade Center towers in New York, the Pentagon in Arlington County, Virginia, and an empty field in Somerset County, Pennsylvania. Nations around the globe quickly condemn the terrorist attacks.

On September 18, Iranian leader Ayatollah Ali Khamenei denounces the World Trade Center's attack.

On September 22, Ukrainian-born violinist Isaac Stern dies.

On September 24, Taliban leaders respond defiantly to U.S. demands that Afghanistan turn over Osama bin Laden.

On September 25, Saudi Arabia, a major contributor to humanitarian and radical activities in Afghanistan, breaks ties with the Taliban.

On October 7, American and British planes bomb Taliban targets in Afghanistan. Protests against the attacks erupt in several Muslim countries, including Pakistan. Special forces are secretly inserted into the country, largely to link up with anti-Taliban factions in the Northern Alliance.

On October 19, an Indonesian ship sinks en route to Easter Island; more than 350 passengers perish.

On October 23, the Provisional Irish Republican Army begins disarmament.

On November 14, Kabul is captured by forces from the Northern Alliance.

On November 29, musician and former Beatles member George Harrison dies.

On December 11–17, Taliban forces withdraw from Qandahar. Many Taliban and al Qaeda fighters are trapped in the Tora Bora region and are routed by coalition troops. Reports surface that bin Laden has been wounded, but he escapes into the Pashtun-controlled region of Pakistan.

On December 13, terrorists attack the Indian parliament.

On December 19–20, riots caused by economic measures to shore up the banking system in Argentina force President Fernando de la Rua from office.

On December 22, Hamid Karzai is made interim president of Afghanistan.

On December 22, an al Qaeda sympathizer, Richard Reid, using a bomb hidden in his shoe, attempts to blow up an American Airways jet over the Atlantic Ocean as it travels from Britain to the United States.

On December 29, nearly three hundred people die in a shopping-complex fire in Lima, Peru.

2002

In 2002, the euro (currency of the European Union) begins circulation in coin and paper.

In 2002, Hungarian writer Imre Kertész wins the Nobel Prize in Literature.

In 2002, French archaeologists unearth the seven-million-year-old skull of a human ancestor in Chad.

On January 16, all assets of bin Laden, al Qaeda, and the Taliban are frozen by order of the UN Security Council.

On January 17, Spanish writer and Nobel Prize laureate Camilo José Cela dies.

On January 20, the FARC agrees to establish peace talks with the Colombia government.

On January 23, *Wall Street Journal* reporter Daniel Pearl is kidnapped and later brutally murdered in Pakistan.

On February 8–24, the Winter Olympics are held in Salt Lake City, Utah.

On February 9, Great Britain's Princess Margaret dies.

On February 10, Antar Zuabri, leader of the Islamic Army Group (blamed for killing thousands of civilians), is killed by Algerian antiterrorist forces.

On February 12, former Serbian leader Milošević goes on trial before a UN war-crimes tribunal at The Hague.

On February 22, Rebel leader Jonas Savimbi is killed in Angola.

On February 27, more than fifty Hindus are burned to death in a Muslim attack on a trainload of pilgrims in Godhra, India. Hindu mobs strike back, killing around sixty Muslims in Ahmadabad the following day.

On March 1, U.S. troops invade eastern Afghanistan. Operation Anaconda will eliminate approximately five hundred Taliban during two and a half weeks of battle.

On March 27, a Hamas suicide bomber attacks a Passover dinner in Netanya, Israel, killing twenty-eight attendees.

On March 30, Great Britain's Queen Mother, Elizabeth Bowes-Lyon, dies.

On April 2, Israel initiates Operation Defensive Shield in the West Bank.

On April 11, twenty-one tourists are killed in a suicide attack at the Ghriba Synagogue on the island of Jerba, Tunisia.

On April 12, a coup in Venezuela temporarily deposes President Chávez; he regains the leadership of the country two days later.

On May 5, Jacques Chirac is elected president of France.

On May 12, Cuban president Fidel Castro welcomes former U.S. president Jimmy Carter.

On May 20, East Timor becomes an independent country; it was formerly part of Indonesia.

On May 23, Iceland becomes the fifty-fifth country to ratify the Kyoto Accords, the UN convention on climate control.

On May 25, nearly two hundred people die in a train crash in Mozambique.

On May 25, a Chinese airliner crashes into the Taiwan Strait, leaving 225 passengers dead.

On June 22, western Iran is struck by a strong earthquake; more than 250 people perish.

On June 29, naval forces from North and South Korea exchange fire.

On June 30, Brazil defeats Germany in the World Cup, hosted by Japan and South Korea, earning its fifth crown.

On July 1, the UN International Criminal Court (established to prosecute individuals charged with war crimes and genocide) is formally established.

On July 2, the first nonstop balloon circumnavigation of the earth is completed by American Steve Fossett when he lands his vessel, *Spirit of Freedom*, in Australia.

On July 9, the African Union is formed.

On July 14, an assassination attempt is made on French president Jacques Chirac.

On July 22, Hamas military leader Salah Shahade is assassinated by Israeli forces.

On July 27, an accident at an air show held in L'viv, Ukraine, kills more than eighty spectators.

On August 7, Alvaro Uribe Velez assumes office as president of Colombia. His Patriot Plan steps up action against both leftist rebels and narcotics traffickers. FARC rebels mortar the inauguration.

On August 16, Palestinian terrorist Abu Nidal is assassinated in Iraq.

On August 20, the Iraqi embassy in Berlin is overrun by expatriate Iraqi dissidents.

On September 5, an assassination attempt is made against Afghan president Karzai; he survives, but around thirty others are killed.

On September 10, Switzerland joins the United Nations.

On September 12, before the UN Security Council, U.S. president George W. Bush claims Iraq has been sheltering terrorists and harboring weapons of mass destruction (WMD).

On September 19, a military rebellion in Ivory Coast results in half the country being controlled by rebel forces. French troops are requested to help the government and block rebel advances.

On September 26, more than one thousand passengers die when a ferry sinks off the coast of Gambia.

On September 27, East Timor joins the United Nations.

On October 12, terrorists explode bombs at popular nightclubs in Bali, killing more than two hundred people, many of them Australian tourists.

On October 23, fifty Chechen rebels take hostage more than seven hundred theatergoers in Moscow. Russian forces storm the building three days later, killing most of the rebels; more than a hundred hostages die.

On November 8, UN Resolution 1441 urges Iraq to disarm or face military consequences.

On November 21, Bulgaria, Estonia, Latvia, Lithuania, Romania, Slovakia, and Slovenia are invited to join NATO.

On November 22–27, Muslim rioting in Nigeria leads to more than one hundred deaths and forces the Miss World pageant to relocate to England.

On November 28, fifteen tourists and workers are killed in a terrorist attack against Israeli visitors at a hotel in Kenya.

On December 7, Iraq provides documentation to the United Nations supporting its claim that it does not have WMD.

On December 27, a government building in Chechnya is bombed, killing more than seventy people.

2003

In 2003, many countries struggle with outbreaks of Severe Acute Respiratory Syndrome (SARS) during the year, although the first incidents occurred as early as November 2002.

In 2003, Volkswagen ceases production of the traditional "Beetle" design.

In 2003, J. K. Rowling publishes *Harry Potter and the Order of the Phoenix.*

In 2003, Afghan author Khaled Hosseini publishes *The Kite Runner.*

In 2003, Iranian human-rights activist Shirin Ebadi wins the Nobel Peace Prize; South Africa writer J. M. Coetzee wins the Nobel Prize in Literature.

In 2003, a planet thought to be more than twelve billion years old is discovered by the Hubble telescope.

On January 31, a train derails in New South Wales, Australia, killing seven people.

On February 1, the space shuttle *Columbia* disintegrates upon reentry on its return trip to Earth; the first Israeli astronaut and an Indian American perish alongside five fellow crew members.

On February 5, U.S. secretary of state Colin Powell addresses the UN Security Council; he claims that the United States has "undeniable" evidence that Iraq has WMD. In the following weeks, millions of people throughout the world protest against possible war in Iraq.

On February 18, a subway fire in South Korea kills nearly two hundred people.

On March 1, British prime minister Tony Blair backs the U.S. claims against Iraq and calls for military action if Saddam Hussein does not comply with UN dictates.

On March 5, seventeen civilians are killed when a bomb destroys a bus in Haifa, Israel.

On March 12, Serbian prime minister Zoran Djindjic is assassinated.

On March 15, Hu Jintao becomes president of the People's Republic of China.

On March 19, the war against Iraq begins. British and American troops invade.

On March 23, a U.S. Army maintenance unit blunders into an ambush in An Nasiriyah. Lori Piestewa becomes the first Native American woman to die in battle while serving in the U.S. Army. Of seven soldiers captured by the Iraqis, Jessica Lynch becomes best known. Ten days later American commandos rescue the POWs.

On March 24, the Arab League calls for the removal of foreign troops from Iraq.

On April 7, Baghdad falls to U.S. forces.

On April 14, Palestinian terrorist Muhammed "Abu Abbas" Zaidan, mastermind of the *Achille Lauro* hijacking, is captured in Baghdad.

On April 25, soldiers of the Sudan Liberation Movement and Sudanese Liberation Army (SLM/SLA), which is formed out of the Darfur Liberation Front, attack Sudanese government garrisons.

On May 1, U.S. president Bush announces "mission accomplished" in Iraq in a ceremony aboard the USS *Abraham Lincoln* aircraft carrier.

On May 12, a powerful bomb explodes in a compound for foreign workers in Riyadh, Saudi Arabia, killing more than thirty people; al Qaeda claims responsibility.

On May 14, a suicide-bombing attempt is made against Chechen administrator Akhmad Kadyrov.

On May 16, thirty-three people are killed and more than a hundred wounded in terrorist attacks in Casablanca, Morocco.

On May 21, more than two thousand die in an earthquake in Algeria.

On May 25, Néstor Kirchner becomes president of Argentina.

On May 28, Israel accepts the U.S.-backed peace plan known as the "road map to peace."

On May 28, Peter Hollingworth resigns as governor-general of Australia.

On June 1, popular Myanmar (Burma) leader Aung San Suu Kyi is arrested by the ruling military.

On June 2, the European Space Agency launches a Mars probe from Kazakhstan.

On June 3, Zimbabwean opposition leader Morgan Tsvangirai (Movement for Democratic Change) is arrested. Strikes break out against President Robert Mugabe. Hundreds are arrested by the military.

On June 5, sixteen soldiers and civilians on a bus in Chechnya are killed in a suicide attack.

On June 18, the International Atomic Energy Agency (IAEA) claims that Iran is actively hiding its nuclear program.

On July 1, nearly half a million protesters in Hong Kong peacefully march against restrictive security measures.

On July 8, an airplane crash in Sudan takes the lives of 116, with only one survivor.

On July 22, Saddam Hussein's sons, Uday and Qusay, are killed in a firefight with U.S. troops.

In August, a heat wave in France leads to nearly fifteen thousand deaths, mostly in the first half of the month.

On August 1, a Russian military hospital in Chechnya is attacked; more than fifty perish.

On August 5, a car-bomb attack on a Marriott hotel in Jakarta, Indonesia, results in twelve deaths and hundreds of injuries.

On August 11, NATO takes over International Security Assistance Force (ISAF) operations in Afghanistan.

On August 13, Thai police and the CIA arrest Jemaah Islamiyah leader Hambali (Riduan Isamuddin), believed to be a top al Qaeda member.

On August 19, a massive bomb destroys the UN headquarters in Baghdad; among the dead is human-rights commissioner Sérgio Vieira de Mello of Brazil. More than twenty other employees also perish.

On August 26, Islamic militants set off two car bombs in Mumbai, India, killing more than fifty people.

On August 28, London is hit with a widespread electrical blackout.

On August 29, Shia leader Sayed Mohammed Baqir al-Hakim is assassinated in a bombing that also kills almost one hundred worshipers at a mosque in An Najaf, Iraq.

On September 10, Swedish foreign minister Anna Lindh is attacked by a mentally ill Swedish citizen originally from Yugoslavia. Lindh dies the following day.

On September 12, the United Nations lifts its sanctions against Libya; the restrictions had been placed in response to the 1988 Pan Am bombing.

On September 20, rioting erupts in Male, Maldives, after a prisoner dies in custody.

On October 2, North Korea announces successful plutonium extraction.

On October 2, Pakistan strikes al Qaeda militants within its borders, killing at least a dozen suspected terrorists.

On October 4, a suicide bomber attacks a restaurant in Haifa, Israel, killing twenty-one people.

On October 15, Yang Liwei pilots China's first manned space flight.

On October 17, Taipei finishes construction on Taipei 101, claimed to be the highest building in the world.

On October 18, Bolivian president Gonzalo Sánchez de Lozada resigns in the face of widespread protests by impoverished indigenous citizens.

On October 31, Malaysian prime minister Mahathir bin Mohamad resigns, ending more than two decades in office; he is replaced by Abdullah Ahmad Badawi.

On November 12, Italian troops are killed in a suicide bombing in An Nasiriyah, Iraq.

On November 15 and 20, terrorists carry out bombings in Istanbul, Turkey.

On November 23, Georgian president Eduard Shevardnadze resigns.

On December 9, a suicide bomber attacks the National Hotel in Moscow; five people die.

On December 13, Saddam Hussein is captured by American forces near Tikrit, Iraq.

14 and 25 December, Pakistan president Musharraf survives two assassination attempts.

On December 17, the privately financed rocket plane *SpaceShipOne* makes its first supersonic flight; on June 21, 2004, it makes its first trip into space.

On December 23, more than 230 people die in a natural-gas field explosion in Chongqing, China.

On December 26, thousands die in an earthquake centered around Bam, Iran.

2004

In 2004, Google introduces its Gmail electronic mail service.

In 2004, Kenyan environmental and political activist Wangari Maathai wins the Nobel Peace Prize; Austrian writer Elfriede Jelinek wins the Nobel Prize in Literature.

On January 1, President Musharraf wins a vote of confidence in Pakistan.

On January 3, an Egyptian airliner crashes into the Red Sea, killing all aboard.

On January 4, NASA rover *Spirit* lands on Mars and, along with companion vehicle *Opportunity* at another location, will far exceed expectations, supplying pictures and scientific data. Despite several small glitches, the rover will continue to operate into 2009.

On January 12, the RMS *Queen Mary 2*, the largest ocean liner in the world, begins her maiden voyage. On April 16, she will begin her first cross-Atlantic voyage.

On January 14, Libya ratifies the CNTBT.

On January 26, Afghanistan establishes a new constitution.

On February 1, hundreds are trampled at Mecca, Saudi Arabia, during the annual Hajj.

On February 1, some 124 members of Iran's parliament resign in protest of the refusal of the government to allow reformists to run for offices throughout the country.

On February 2, Israel plans to remove settlements from Gaza.

On February 2, Abdul Qadeer Kahn, a respected Pakistani nuclear scientist, admits to helping Iran, North Korea, and Libya develop nuclear technology.

On February 5, members of the Revolutionary Artibonite Resistance Front initiate a rebellion in Haiti.

On February 14, the collapse of a roof covering a water park in Moscow kills more than two dozen attendees.

On February 18, a train crash and explosion in Neyshabur, Iran, causes the deaths of nearly three hundred passengers and rescue personnel.

On February 26, Macedonian president Boris Trajkovski is killed in a plane crash.

On February 27, more than one hundred passengers are killed when the Philippine Islamic terrorist organization Abu Sayyaf bombs a ferry.

On February 28, President Aristide is deposed and forced to leave Haiti in a rightist coup.

On March 2, nearly two hundred die and five hundred are wounded in Karbala, Iraq, after terrorist bombings during celebrations of Ashura. Other attacks occur in Baghdad, mostly against Shia worshipers.

On March 11, nearly two hundred commuters are killed, and approximately seventeen hundred are wounded in coordinated terrorist bombings against commuter trains in Madrid, Spain.

On March 12, South Korean president Roh Moo Hyun is impeached, but the impeachment will later be overturned by the Supreme Court.

On March 17, José Luis Rodriguez Zapatero becomes Spanish prime minister, partly on his promise to remove soldiers from the Iraq conflict.

On March 19, Taiwanese president Chen Shui-bian survives an assassination attempt.

On March 22, an Israeli rocket attack kills Hamas cofounder Ahmed Yassin and his bodyguards in Gaza.

On March 29, Bulgaria, Estonia, Latvia, Lithuania, Romania, Slovakia, and Slovenia join NATO.

On March 29, smoking is banned in public places in Ireland, the first such nationwide ban to be instituted.

On March 31, four Blackwater contractors are murdered and publicly displayed in Al Fallujah, Iraq. U.S. forces will assault the city on April 5.

On April 6, Lithuanian president Rolandas Paksas is impeached and removed from office.

On April 8, a cease-fire is called in the troubled region of Darfur.

On April 22, hundreds are killed as a result of two trains colliding in Ryongchon, North Korea.

On April 24, South Waziristan leader Nek Mohammed agrees to stop fighting against the Pakistani army.

On April 30, the release of photographs revealing rampant abuse and humiliation of Iraqi prisoners in Abu Ghraib prison by American guards shocks the allies and sparks protests in the Islamic world.

On May 1, Cyprus, the Czech Republic, Estonia, Hungary, Latvia, Lithuania, Malta, Poland, Slovakia, and Slovenia join the European Union.

On May 2, a Christian mob in Yelwa, Nigeria, massacres more than six hundred Muslims. Muslims will retaliate by killing Christians and burning churches.

On May 9, Russian-backed Chechen president Akhmad Kadyrov is assassinated in Grozny.

On May 29, Islamic militants seize and kill more than twenty in an attack on a residential compound for foreigners in Al Khobar, Saudi Arabia.

On June 1, an interim government headed by Iyad Allawi is established in Iraq. The UN Security Council eventually recognizes the new government.

On June 18, Nek Mohammed is killed by a U.S. missile strike after reneging on his commitment to the Pakistani army.

On July 14, the Butler Review, which is critical of British intelligence-gathering leading up to the war in Iraq, is released.

On August 1, nearly four hundred people die in a supermarket fire in Asunción, Paraguay.

On August 12–29, the Olympic Games are held in Athens, Greece.

On August 14, Polish author and Nobel Prize laureate Czeslaw Milosz dies.

On August 22, Edvard Munch's paintings *The Scream* and *Madonna* are stolen from a museum in Oslo, Norway.

On August 24, Chechen suicide bombers bring down two commercial airplanes near Moscow, killing eighty-nine people.

On August 31, Hamas suicide bombers attack in Beersheba, Israel; sixteen people are killed, and more than sixty are wounded.

On August 31, a female Chechen suicide bomber strikes the subway in Moscow, taking ten lives.

On September 2, the UN Security Council calls for Syrian troops to withdraw from Lebanon.

On September 3, nearly 350 people, mostly children, die in a shoot-out with Russian forces after a two-day hostage incident orchestrated by Chechen rebels in Beslan, North Ossetia.

On September 7, Hurricane Ivan kills nearly forty people when it strikes Grenada.

On September 9, Australia's embassy in Jakarta, Indonesia, is attacked. Eleven die, and more than one hundred are wounded.

On September 10–13, Hurricane Ivan strikes Cuba, causing massive destruction but few deaths.

On September 15, UN secretary-general Kofi Annan criticizes the Iraq War.

On September 17, representatives from Japan and Mexico sign a free-trade agreement.

On September 23, floods caused by Hurricane Jeanne ravage Haiti, leaving at least one thousand dead.

On October 8, Algerian-French philosopher Jacques Derrida dies.

On October 23, Brazil launches a rocket into space from Alcântara Launch Center in Maranhão.

On October 23, northern Japan is struck by a strong earthquake; thirty-five are killed, and thousands are left homeless.

On November 2, filmmaker Theo van Gogh is assassinated in Amsterdam by a Muslim extremist upset about van Gogh's August release of a movie that depicted the mistreatment of women in Islam.

On November 8, American troops encircle and assault the insurgent stronghold of Al Fallujah, Iraq. An estimated fifteen hundred to sixteen hundred militants will be killed during the month-long battle.

On November 11, Palestinian leader and Nobel Peace Prize–winner Yasser Arafat dies of a blood disease. He is succeeded by Mahmoud Abbas.

On November 14, Burmese troops attack Karen villages.

On November 18, Russia ratifies the Kyoto Accords.

On November 21, Viktor Yanukovych wins the presidency of Ukraine. Opponents claim fraud, and in late December the Supreme Court annuls the election and orders a new one. The political unrest leads to the Orange Revolution.

On November 21, a strong earthquake strikes the northern half of the Caribbean island nation of Dominica.

On December 13, former Chilean president Augusto Pinochet is placed under house arrest.

On December 26, tsunamis triggered by a massive earthquake destroy coastal towns in Thailand and Indonesia, and cause death and damage as far away as Myanmar, Bangladesh, India, the Maldives, and the east African coast. More than two hundred thousand perish.

2005

In 2005, the video-sharing and -viewing Internet site called YouTube is launched.

In 2005, Boeing announces it will produce a stretched version of its popular 747 airliner.

In 2005, French doctors perform the first partial human-face transplant.

In 2005, J. K. Rowling publishes *Harry Potter and the Half-Blood Prince*.

In 2005, Swedish author Stieg Larsson's *Män som hatar kvinnor (The Girl with the Dragon Tattoo)* is posthumously published.

In 2005, Egyptian IAEA director Mohamed ElBaradei is awarded the Nobel Peace Prize; British writer Harold Pinter wins the Nobel Prize in Literature.

On January 9, Rawhi Fattouh is elected to head the Palestine Liberation Organization (PLO).

On January 13, militants from Gaza enter Israel and kill six people. Palestinian leader Mahmoud Abbas promises to control such attacks.

On January 17, the former premier of the People's Republic of China, Zhao Ziyang, dies.

On January 21, antitax protesters riot in Belize.

On January 25, more than two hundred die in a stampede at the Mandher Devi temple in India.

On January 29, China resumes commercial air traffic with Taiwan.

On January 30, Iraqis vote for representatives to a national assembly.

On February 2, German heavyweight-boxing champion Max Schmeling dies.

On February 10, municipal elections are held in Saudi Arabia for the first time. Only men are allowed to vote.

On February 14, former Lebanese prime minister Rafik Hariri is assassinated, allegedly by pro-Syrian elements within the country.

On February 14, three cities in the Philippines are bombed by al Qaeda–linked terrorists; at least eleven people are killed and 150 wounded.

On February 16, the Kyoto Protocol is now in force.

On February 23, U.S. president Bush and Russian president Putin visit Slovakia to attend a summit.

On February 25, Islamic Jihad stages attacks in Tel Aviv, Israel, killing five and wounding more than fifty.

On February 25, the founder of Amnesty International, Peter Benenson, dies.

On February 28, Lebanese prime minister Omar Karami resigns from office in response to anti-Syrian demonstrations.

On March 4, Italian journalist Giuliana Sgrena is accidentally wounded by American gunfire at a roadblock.

On March 7, women in Kuwait march for equal voting rights.

On March 14, a train derailment in Vietnam takes the lives of eleven passengers and injures hundreds of others.

On March 24, President Askar Alayev is overthrown in Kyrgyzstan in what becomes known as the Tulip Revolution.

On April 2, Pope John Paul II dies.

On April 6, Jalal Talabani, a Kurd, becomes the president of Iraq.

On April 9, Charles, Prince of Wales, marries Camilla Parker Bowles.

On April 19, the College of Cardinals in Rome elects German-born Joseph Ratzinger as pope; he chooses the name Benedict XVI.

On April 26, the last Syrian troops withdraw from Lebanon.

On May 4, more than sixty people are killed in a suicide-bombing attack against a police recruiting center in Arbil, Kurdish northern Iraq.

On May 10, an assassination attempt is made on President Bush during a state visit to Tbilisi, Georgia.

On May 25, Egyptian thugs in Cairo molest and beat women participating in protests against undemocratic elections. The actions by police who allowed the outrage lead to a movement to reform the political process in Egypt.

On June 14, Jamaican sprinter Asafa Powell sets the men's one-hundred-meter world record at 9.77 seconds.

On June 24, Mahmoud Ahmadinejad wins the presidency of Iran.

On June 30, Spain allows same-sex marriages.

On July 6, French writer and Nobel Prize laureate Claude Simon dies.

On July 7, suicide bombers, Muslim radicals with British backgrounds, attack the London subway and a bus; almost forty people are killed. Another coordinated bombing attempt against the transportation system fails two weeks later.

On July 10, Kurmanbek Bakiyev wins the presidency of Kyrgyzstan.

On July 12, Ethiopian raiders stage an attack across the Kenyan border, killing more than one hundred villagers.

On July 28, the Provisional Irish Republican Army ceases armed conflict with the British.

On August 3, Mauritanian president Maaouya Ould Sid'Ahmed Taya's rule is overthrown while he is on a state visit to Saudi Arabia.

On August 15–23, Israel removes more than eight thousand settlers from Gaza and the West Bank.

On September 7, Hosni Mubarak is reelected president of Egypt.

On September 19, North Korea asks for aid in return for stopping its nuclear program.

On September 25, news reporter May Chidiac is seriously wounded in a car bombing attributed to pro-Syrian elements in Lebanon.

On September 30, the Danish newspaper *Jyllands-Posten* publishes a cartoon with a physical depiction of the prophet Muhammad that sparks protests and threats of violence in the Islamic world.

On October 1, a bomb kills twenty-six people in Bali.

On October 2, the Arizona Cardinals and San Francisco 49ers of the National Football League play a regular season game for the first time outside the United States, in Mexico City.

On October 8, a massive earthquake in Kashmir, Pakistan, leads to the deaths of more than eighty thousand people.

On October 19, Saddam Hussein goes on trial.

On October 26, Iranian president Ahmadinejad calls for the elimination of Israel.

On October 27, weeks of rioting by young immigrant men from Africa and the Middle East begin in the underprivileged outskirts of Paris.

In November, Ellen Johnson-Sirleaf is elected president of Liberia. She is sworn in on January 16, 2006, as the first democratically elected female leader in Africa.

On November 9, more than sixty people are killed as three hotels in Amman, Jordan, are bombed by followers of Abu Musab al-Zarqawi.

On November 21, Ariel Sharon steps down as leader of the Likud Party in Israel.

On November 22, Germany elects its first female chancellor, Angela Merkel of the conservative Christian Democratic Union.

On November 28, the Canadian parliament is dissolved after a vote of no confidence.

On December 15, Iraqis elect their first parliament since Hussein's overthrow with more than a 70 percent turnout.

On December 18, war breaks out between Chad and Sudan.

2006

In 2006, the Internet social network Twitter is launched.

In 2006, the Svalbard Global Seed Vault, a project to preserve biodiversity, is established in Spitsbergen, Norway.

In 2006, Bangladeshi economist and banker Muhammad Yunus, who promotes the idea of microloans to entrepreneurs in developing countries, is awarded the Nobel Peace Prize; Turkish novelist Orhan Pamuk wins the Nobel Prize in Literature.

In 2006, the Nintendo Wii gaming system is introduced (the concept was revealed in 2005); Sony answers with the PlayStation 3.

On January 5, Ehud Olmert replaces Sharon as Israel's prime minister.

On January 12, more than 350 people are killed in a stampede at the Hajj in Mina, Saudi Arabia.

On January 15, Kuwaiti emir Jaber Al-Ahmad Al-Jaber Al-Sabah dies.

On January 22, Juan Evo Morales Ayma, a member of the Aymara nation, becomes Bolivia's first indigenous president.

In February, Muslims worldwide protest the depiction of Muhammad in cartoons originally published in a Danish newspaper in September 2005.

On February 4, a stampede in Manila kills more than seventy people.

On February 16, René Préval is elected president of Haiti; he is inaugurated on March 14.

On February 17, more than one thousand people are killed in a mudslide in Leyte, Philippines.

On February 22, in Samarra, Iraq, the famous Shia al-Askari mosque's dome is destroyed in sectarian violence.

On February 22, with a haul larger than $90 million, robbers in Great Britain pull off one of the largest bank heists in history in Tonbridge, Kent.

On February 24, the Philippines goes under martial law to counter a possible coup attempt.

On March 11, Socialist Michelle Bachelet Jeria becomes president of Chile.

On March 11, Slobodan Milošević is found dead at the UN Detention Center at The Hague.

On March 20, rebels slaughter more than 150 Chadian soldiers.

On March 21, immigrant workers riot in Dubai, causing millions of dollars of damage.

On March 28, workers in France riot over new employment laws.

On March 30, Brazilian astronaut Marcos Pontes becomes the first from his country to travel in space.

On April 11, Iran announces it has produced a small amount of enriched uranium.

On April 22, prodemocracy protestors in Nepal clash with police. Two days later, King Gyanendra restores the parliament. Within a month the country will have a secular government that will diminish the power of the king.

On May 1, Bolivia nationalizes its oil industry.

On May 12–15, prison riots and street attacks on police—believed to be coordinated by the criminal organization the First Command of the Capital (PCC)—erupt in the state of São Paulo in Brazil. More than eighty people die in widespread weekend violence.

On May 27, nearly six thousand people are killed in an earthquake in central Java.

On May 28, Uribe is reelected president of Colombia after restrictions against second presidential terms are overthrown.

On June 3, Montenegro becomes an independent state and on June 28 joins the United Nations. Serbia declares its independence on June 5.

On June 25, a Palestinian raid—in which two Israeli soldiers are killed and one, Gilad Shalit, is taken hostage—prompts an Israeli incursion into Gaza.

On July 4–5, North Korea tests several long-range missiles, sparking UN meetings on the potential threat.

On July 9, Italy defeats France in the World Cup, which is hosted by Germany.

On July 9, 124 of 203 people aboard a Russian airliner perish after a runway accident in Siberia.

On July 11, terrorist bombings in Mumbai kill more than two hundred people.

On July 12, Israel bombs Hezbollah targets in Lebanon. Hezbollah tries to bargain captured Israeli soldiers for the release of Israeli-held prisoners. On July 13, Haifa is struck by rockets, and the next day Israel responds by destroying sites in Beirut, Lebanon.

On July 24, nearly two hundred passengers and crew die, and more than eight hundred are wounded, in the bombing of a commuter train in Mumbai, India, allegedly by an extremist Islamic group.

On July 31, Raúl Castro is given presidential powers in Cuba by his brother, Fidel.

On August 3, German/Austrian/English opera star Elisabeth Schwarzkopf dies.

On August 14, the United Nations helps broker a truce between Israel and Hezbollah forces and establishes a peacekeeping presence along the southern border of Lebanon.

On August 22, all 169 people aboard a Russian airliner die in a crash in Ukraine. President Vladimir Putin orders an investigation into possible violation of air-safety rules.

On August 30, Egyptian author and Nobel Prize laureate Naguib Mahfouz dies.

On August 31, Munch's *The Scream* and *Madonna* are recovered.

On September 4, Australian naturalist Steve Irwin, who hosts the popular television show *The Crocodile Hunter*, is killed by a stingray-barb strike to his heart.

On September 10, Tongan king Taufa'ahau Tupou IV dies and is succeeded by his son, Tupou V.

On September 19, martial law is declared in Bangkok as a military coup overthrows the government.

On October 7, Russian journalist Anna Politkovskaya is murdered in Moscow, the thirteenth such killing of critics of Putin.

On October 9, North Korea tests a nuclear device.

On November 5, Saddam Hussein is convicted by an Iraqi court and later sentenced to death.

On November 12, Israel warns that it may be forced to strike Iran's nuclear facilities.

On November 15, Joseph Kabila is elected president of the Democratic Republic of Congo.

On November 21, Lebanese minister Pierre Amine Gemayel is assassinated.

On December 10, former Chilean president Augusto Pinochet dies; he had been indicted at home and in Europe on human-rights violations that occurred during his dictatorial rule (1973–1990) and was under house arrest.

On December 28, Ethiopian troops drive Muslim soldiers from Mogadishu, Somalia. Fighting will continue into January 2007, as rebels are pushed into Kenya.

On December 30, Saddam Hussein is executed by hanging.

2007

In 2007, Apple introduces the iPhone, a heavily hyped, full-featured cell phone and media player.

In 2007, the tomb of the first-century BCE Jewish king Herod is discovered by archaeologists.

In 2007, the last surviving clipper ship, the *Cutty Sark*, burns at its dock in London.

In 2007, J. K. Rowling's *Harry Potter and the Deathly Hallows*, the final volume in the *Harry Potter* series, is published.

In 2007, Khaled Hosseini publishes *A Thousand Splendid Suns*.

In 2007, the double-decked, wide-bodied European airliner, the *Airbus A380*, enters passenger service.

In 2007, British author Doris Lessing wins the Nobel Prize in Literature.

On January 1, Bulgaria and Romania join the European Union.

On January 1, more than one hundred people die in an Indonesian airliner crash.

On January 10, Venezuelan president Hugo Chávez begins his third term as president.

On January 10, former Sandinista leader Daniel Ortega is inaugurated president of Nicaragua.

On January 15, Saddam Hussein's half brother Barzan Ibrahim al-Tikriti and former Iraqi chief judge Awad Hamad al-Bandar are executed in Iraq.

On January 16, Rafael Correa becomes president of Ecuador.

On January 18, strong storms assault Europe, with damage and deaths ranging from the coast of England to Germany.

On January 19, journalist Hrant Dink is killed in Turkey by teenagers who allege he had insulted Islam.

On February 3, a bomb explosion in a Baghdad market kills more than 135 people.

On February 10–12, antigovernment protestors riot in Guinea.

On February 15, more than seventy members of the Muslim Brotherhood are arrested in Egypt.

On March 1, riots break out in Copenhagen, Denmark, after a popular building, the Ungdomshuset, is cleared for demolition.

On March 11, opposition leader Morgan Tsvangirai and fellow protestors are arrested and beaten by police in Harare, Zimbabwe. They are released by March 13.

On March 22, violence wracks the Democratic Republic of Congo as rebels led by Jean-Pierre Bemba protest their defeat in presidential elections. Bemba will seek sanctuary in the South African embassy, and his soldiers lay down their arms on March 28.

On March 23, fifteen British sailors are detained by Iran for straying into Iranian waters; they will be released on April 4.

On April 2, Sunni and Shia factions battle in Parachinar, Pakistan; more than forty people die.

On April 11, more than thirty people are killed in bombings in Algiers, Algeria.

On April 15, thousands of Pakistanis march against extremist violence in their country.

On April 18, three employees of a Christian publishing house are killed in Turkey.

On April 27, Abdullah Gul is elected president of Turkey, but without secular support. His election will be annulled on May 1.

On May 11, Samoan ruler Malietoa Tanumafili II dies.

On May 28, U.S. and Iranian officials meet in Baghdad to discuss the need for stability in Iraq.

On June 10–17, fighting erupts between Fatah and Hamas factions in Gaza.

On June 14, Austrian politician and former head of the United Nations Kurt Waldheim dies.

On June 17, author Salman Rushdie is knighted by Queen Elizabeth II, sparking demonstrations in Muslim countries.

On June 27, Brazilian military police battle with drug dealers in the *favelas* (slums) of Rio de Janeiro; approximately twenty people are killed.

On June 28, Egypt outlaws the practice of female circumcision.

In July, price controls are established in Zimbabwe to control high inflation. By October citizens are still finding it hard to buy necessities, such as bread.

On July 1, England bans smoking in public areas.

On July 16, a strong earthquake rattles Niigata, Japan.

On July 17, nearly two hundred people die in an airliner crash in São Paulo, Brazil.

On July 25, President Pratibha Patil is sworn in; she is the first woman to hold the position in India.

On August 6, Israeli prime minister Ehud Olmert meets with Palestinian president Mahmoud Abbas in Jericho in the West Bank.

On August 14, more than four hundred (some reports claim seven hundred) people perish in multiple suicide bombings in the Kurdish region of northern Iraq.

On August 15, a strong earthquake in Peru kills more than five hundred people and injures more than one thousand.

On September 6, famous Italian tenor Luciano Pavarotti dies.

On September 10, Nawaz Sharif returns to Pakistan.

On September 18, prodemocracy protesters in Myanmar are joined by Buddhist monks.

On October 2, South Korean president Moo Hyun holds a summit with North Korean leader Kim Jong Il.

On October 7, Musharraf is reelected president of Pakistan.

On October 10, Malaysia's first astronaut, Sheikh Muszaphar Shukor, travels to the International Space Station aboard a Russian rocket.

On October 17, Togo holds democratic elections.

On October 18, former prime minister Benazir Bhutto returns to Pakistan. Terrorist bombers attack crowds of well-wishers.

On October 21, growing anti-immigrant sentiment in Switzerland is expressed in increased representation by members of the Swiss People's Party in the National Council.

On October 28, Cristina Fernández de Kirchner is elected president of Argentina.

On November 3, Musharraf declares a state of emergency in Pakistan. Pakistani troops begin operations in the northeast, capturing and killing pro-Taliban forces—by early December, nearly three hundred have been killed.

On November 5, China positions its first lunar satellite.

On November 7, nine people are killed in a school shooting in Tuusula, Finland.

On November 13, a congressman and three others are killed in a bombing of the House of Representatives in Quezon City, Philippines.

On November 15, approximately five thousand people die in a cyclone that strikes Bangladesh.

On November 20, former Rhodesian prime minister Ian Smith dies.

On November 29, a mutiny in Manila is quickly defeated by Philippine forces.

On December 3, Australia signs the Kyoto Protocol.

On December 11, Algiers is again rocked by car bombs; more than forty people die.

On December 12, a UN agency is attacked in Algiers, with the death toll more than thirty.

On December 17, Saudi king Abdullah pardons a gang-rape victim who had been given a six-month jail sentence and two hundred lashes for being alone with a man with whom she was neither related nor married.

On December 20, paintings by Pablo Picasso and Candido Portinari are stolen from the São Paulo Museum of Art.

On December 27, former Pakistani prime minister and candidate Benazir Bhutto is assassinated, allegedly by supporters of Baitullah Mehsud of South Waziristan.

2008

In 2008, former Finnish president Martti Ahtisaari wins the Nobel Peace Prize; the Nobel Prize in Literature is awarded to French author J. M. G. Le Clézio.

In 2008, the European Organization for Nuclear Research (CERN) smashes two accelerated particle beams at the Large Hadron Collider (LHC) on the Swiss-French border.

In January, Kenya is wracked by serious rioting over contested presidential elections; more than eight hundred people will die.

On January 6, Georgian president Mikheil Saakashvili is reelected.

On January 7, riots break out in Kenya.

On January 11, New Zealand mountain climber and philanthropist Sir Edmund Hillary, the first person to summit Mount Everest (1953), dies.

On January 15, Uzbekistan president Islam Karimov starts his third term.

On January 21, stock markets worldwide experience major losses.

On January 27, former Indonesian dictator Suharto dies.

On February 4, Serbian president Boris Tadic wins reelection.

On February 5, Indian guru and founder of transcendental meditation Maharishi Mahesh Yogi dies.

On February 12, senior Hezbollah official Imad Fayez Mugniyah is assassinated.

On February 17, Kosovo declares its independence from Serbia.

On February 19, Fidel Castro permanently gives up power in Cuba.

On March 2, Dmitry Medvedev is elected president of Russia.

On March 14, Tibetan rioting against Chinese rule commences.

On March 24, Bhutan holds its first general elections.

In April, rising worldwide prices on food—caused in part by rising oil prices—spur rioting in many countries.

On April 11, Nepalese voters choose a new parliament to write a constitution.

On April 22, two female journalists are assassinated in Oaxaca Province, Mexico.

On April 22, Fernando Lugo wins the presidency of Paraguay.

On May 2, more than twenty thousand people die as Myanmar is hit by a cyclone.

On May 12, central China is struck by a massive earthquake. More than eighty-five thousand are killed.

On May 25, a U.S. spacecraft lands on Mars.

On May 25, Michel Suleiman is elected president of Lebanon.

On May 28, the Nepalese monarchy is abolished.

On May 30, Mexico initiates measures to counter the effects of rising food prices on the poor.

On July 2, Colombian soldiers free politician Ingrid Betancourt, who has been a hostage of leftist FARC rebels since 2002.

On July 14, the International Criminal Court charges Sudanese president Omar Hassan al-Bashir with acts of genocide.

On July 21, war criminal Radovan Karadžić is arrested in Serbia.

On August 6, Mohamed Ould Abdel Aziz overthrows President Sidi Ould Cheikh Abdallahi in Mauritania.

On August 7–11, troops from Georgia and Russia fight in South Ossetia.

On September 20, a car bomb outside the Marriott Hotel in Islamabad, Pakistan, kills more than fifty people.

On September 21, South African president Thabo Mbeki resigns (effective four days later).

On September 21, Israeli prime minister Olmert resigns his office.

On October 1, the Iraqi government begins taking control of its own military forces.

On November 10, South African singer and activist Miriam Makeba dies.

On November 26, a terrorist group based out of Pakistan attacks sites in Mumbai. More than 150 people are killed in the assault.

On December 14, an Iraqi reporter makes international headlines for throwing a shoe in protest at President Bush while he is making a speech in Baghdad.

On December 15, Abhisit Vejjajiva becomes the prime minister of Thailand.

On December 22, Guinean president Lansana Conté dies. Two days later a military coup places Moussa Camara in power.

2009

In 2009, German author Herta Müller wins the Nobel Prize in Literature.

In 2009, a vaccine against the AIDS virus shows some promise.

In 2009, the H1N1 (swine flu) virus causes international concerns.

On January 1, Slovakia begins using the euro.

On January 1, a nightclub fire in Bangkok, Thailand, takes the lives of more than sixty people.

On January 3, Israel invades Gaza.

On February 1, Iceland elects Jóhanna Sigurdardóttir, who becomes the first openly gay prime minister.

On February 7, wildfires in Australia kill more than 170 people.

On February 25–26, around seventy Bangladesh Rifles officers and family members are massacred by mutinous border guards possibly loyal to a militant Islamic group.

On March 3, a six-story historical archive building in Cologne, Germany, collapses, possibly due to nearby construction. Two other buildings collapse as well, with the loss of two lives. Many medieval records are destroyed.

On March 3, Pakistani gunmen attack a bus carrying cricket players from Sri Lanka; six policemen and the driver are killed.

On March 4, Sudanese president Omar Hassan al-Bashir is indicted by the International Criminal Court for war crimes committed in Darfur.

On April 1, Albania and Croatia join NATO.

On April 6, L'Aquila, Italy, is struck by an earthquake that kills more than 250 people.

On April 7, former Peruvian president Alberto Fujimori is sentenced to twenty-five years in prison.

On April 11, previously unknown Scottish singer Susan Boyle becomes a worldwide sensation following a broadcast of the television show *Britain's Got Talent*.

On April 12, U.S. naval forces free the captain of the *Maersk Alabama* from Somali pirates, who had taken him aboard a life vessel after the ship's crew initially thwarted the attack; three pirates are killed by sniper fire.

On April 28, Russian ballerina Ekaterina Maximova dies.

On May 1, Sweden allows same-sex marriages.

On May 10, Iranian American journalist Roxana Saberi is released from custody by Iran after being detained for months.

On May 18–19, the Sri Lankan civil war, which had lasted for twenty-seven years, comes to an end.

On June 1, a French airliner crashes into the Atlantic Ocean off Brazil with the loss of all aboard.

On June 13, Ahmadinejad retains the presidency of Iran, despite strong opposition by Mir Hossein Mousavi. Allegations of voter fraud are widespread, and protests continue for weeks before being quieted by government crackdown.

On June 20, an Iranian woman, Neda Agha-Soltan, is shot and killed during street demonstrations over Iran's disputed election results. Images of her death are posted worldwide and spark sympathy for the protesters.

On June 30, one passenger survives the crash of a Yemeni airliner off the coast of Comoros.

On July 17, the Marriott and Ritz-Carlton Hotels in Jakarta, Indonesia, are bombed by terrorists; nine people are killed.

On July 31, three American hikers are arrested along the Iran-Iraq border and are imprisoned. Some accounts claim Iranian forces crossed the border to apprehend the Americans.

On August 18, Kim Dae Jung, former South Korean president and winner of the Nobel Peace Prize, dies.

On September 26–30, Typhoon Ketsana sweeps through the Philippines, China, Vietnam, Cambodia, Laos, and Thailand; more than seven hundred people are killed.

On September 29, the Samoan Islands are struck by a strong earthquake.

On October 2, Rio de Janeiro is announced as the winner to host the 2016 Olympics.

On October 10, the border between Armenia and Turkey is officially opened.

On October 20, Pope Benedict approves rules that make it easier for Episcopalians, many angry at their church's acceptance of women and homosexual priests, to join the Roman Catholic Church.

On November 23, supporters of the Ampatuan clan in Maguindanao, Philippines, attack and kill nearly sixty political activists and media members.

On November 25, floods ravage Jedda, Saudi Arabia, killing more than 150 people.

1 | The Arts

Chronology

Important Events in The Arts, 2000–2009

2000

- On March 14, Stephen King publishes his ghost story *Riding the Bullet* exclusively in electronic form.
- On April 20, the heirs of a U.S. Army lieutenant who stole artwork while stationed in Germany during World War I agree to pay fines for nonpayment of taxes after owning and selling some of the works. Criminal charges for trafficking in stolen art were dismissed earlier.
- In May, the popular band Smashing Pumpkins announces they will disband.
- On October 26, the Broadway musical *The Full Monty* (based on a British movie) opens on Broadway.
- On November 17, the musical *Mamma Mia!* debuts in San Francisco and has a three-month run; it is produced in Los Angeles and Chicago before opening on 18 October 2001 on Broadway, where it becomes a major, long-running hit.
- On November 18, actors Michael Douglas and Catherine Zeta-Jones marry in New York City.

MOVIES: *All the Pretty Horses*, directed by Billy Bob Thornton and starring Penélope Cruz, Matt Damon, and Henry Thomas; *Almost Famous*, directed by Cameron Crowe and starring Billy Crudup, Kate Hudson, and Frances McDormand; *American Psycho*, directed by Mary Harron and starring Christian Bale, Josh Lucas, and Justin Theroux; *Bring It On*, directed by Peyton Reed and starring Jesse Bradford, Kirsten Dunst, and Eliza Dushku; *Cast Away*, directed by Robert Zemeckis and starring Tom Hanks, Helen Hunt, and Paul Sanchez; *The Cell*, directed by Tarsem Singh and starring Vincent D'Onofrio, Jennifer Lopez, and Vince Vaughn; *Dinosaur*, animated feature, directed by Eric Leighton and Ralph Zondag; *Dude, Where's My Car?*, directed by Danny Leiner and starring Jennifer Garner, Ashton Kutcher, and Seann William Scott; *The Emperor's New Groove*, animated feature, directed by Mark Dindal; *Erin Brockovich*, directed by Steven Soderbergh and starring Albert Finney and Julia Roberts; *Gladiator*, directed by Ridley Scott and starring Russell Crowe, Connie Nielsen, and Joaquin Phoenix; *High Fidelity*, directed by Stephen Frears and starring John Cusack, Iben Hjejle, and Todd Louiso; *How the Grinch Stole Christmas*, directed by Ron Howard and starring Jim Carrey; *Me, Myself & Irene*, directed by Bobby Farrelly and Peter Farrelly and starring Jim Carrey and Renée Zellweger; *Meet the Parents*, directed by Jay Roach and starring Robert De Niro and Ben Stiller; *Memento*, directed by Christopher Nolan and starring Carrie-Anne Moss, Guy Pearce, and Joe Pantoliano; *Mission: Impossible II*, directed by John Woo and starring Tom Cruise, Thandie Newton, and Dougray Scott; *Mission to Mars*, directed by Brian De Palma and starring Don Cheadle, Tim Robbins, and Gary Sinise; *Oh Brother, Where Art Thou?*, directed by Joel Coen and starring George Clooney, Tim Blake Nelson, and John Turturro; *The Patriot*, directed by Roland Emmerich and starring Mel Gibson, Heath Ledger, and Joely Richardson; *Pay It Forward*, directed by Mimi Leder and starring Helen Hunt, Haley Joel Osment, and Kevin Spacey; *The Perfect Storm*, directed by Wolfgang Petersen and starring George Clooney, Diane Lane, and Mark Wahlberg; *Pollock*, directed by Ed Harris and starring Harris and Marcia Gay Harden; *Remember the Titans*, directed by Boaz Yakin and starring Wood Harris, Will Patton, and Denzel Washington; *Requiem for a Dream*, directed by Darren Aronofsky and starring Ellen Burstyn, Jared Leto, and Jennifer Connelly; *Scream 3*, directed by Wes Craven and starring David Arquette, Neve Campbell, and Courteney Cox; *Sexy Beast*, directed by Jonathan Glazer and starring Ben Kingsley, Ian McShane, and Ray Winstone; *Snatch*, directed by Guy Ritchie and starring Benicio Del Toro, Brad Pitt, and Jason Statham; *Traffic*, directed by Steven Soderbergh and starring Benicio Del Toro, Michael Douglas, and Catherine Zeta-Jones; *Unbreakable*, directed by M. Night Shyamalan and starring Samuel L. Jackson, Bruce Willis, and Robin Wright; *Wonder Boys*, directed by Curtis Hanson and starring Michael Douglas, Tobey Maguire, and Frances

McDormand; *X-Men*, directed by Bryan Singer and starring Hugh Jackman, Ian McKellen, and Patrick Stewart.

NOVELS: Charles Baxter, *Feast of Love;* Michael Chabon, *The Amazing Adventures of Kavalier and Clay;* Tom Clancy, *The Bear and the Dragon;* Mary Higgins Clark, *Before I Say Goodbye;* Patricia Cornwell, *The Last Precinct;* Mark Z. Danielewski, *House of Leaves;* Tony Earley, *Jim the Boy;* Dave Eggers, *A Heartbreaking Work of Staggering Genius;* Janet Evanovich, *Hot Six;* Maureen Gibbon, *Swimming Sweet Arrow;* Myla Goldberg, *Bee Season;* John Grisham, *The Brethren;* Stephen Harrigan, *The Gates of the Alamo;* Joseph Heller, *Portrait of an Artist, as an Old Man;* Denis Johnson, *The Name of the World;* Robert Jordan, *Winter's Heart;* Heidi Julavits, *The Mineral Palace;* Dean Koontz, *From the Corner of His Eye;* Tim LaHaye and Jerry B. Jenkins, *The Indwelling: The Beast Takes Possession* and *The Mark: The Beast Rules the World;* Jhumpa Lahiri, *Interpreter of Maladies;* Jeffrey Lent, *In the Fall;* Joyce Carol Oates, *Blonde;* Rosamunde Pilcher, *Winter Solstice;* Tim Powers, *Declare;* Francine Prose, *Blue Angel;* Philip Roth, *The Human Stain;* John Sandford, *Easy Prey;* Christina Schwarz, *Drowning Ruth;* Nicholas Sparks, *The Rescue;* Danielle Steel, *The House on Hope Street* and *The Wedding;* Darin Strauss, *Chang and Eng;* James Welch, *The Heartsong of Charging Elk.*

POPULAR SONGS: Aaliyah, "Try Again"; Christina Aguilera, "What a Girl Wants"; Toni Braxton, "He Wasn't Man Enough"; Creed, "Higher"; Destiny's Child, "Jumpin', Jumpin'" and "Say My Name"; Faith Hill, "Breathe"; Janet Jackson, "Doesn't Really Matter"; Joe, "I Wanna Know"; Lonestar, "Amazed"; Madonna, "Music"; Matchbox Twenty, "Bent"; Pink, "There You Go"; Santana, featuring The Product G&B, "Maria Maria"; Santana, featuring Rob Thomas, "Smooth"; Savage Garden, "I Knew I Loved You"; Sisqo, "Thong Song"; 3 Doors Down, "Kryptonite"; Vertical Horizon, "Everything You Want."

2001

- In April, responding to complaints by construction workers and the Catholic League for Religious and Civil Rights, Deborah Masters paints a loincloth on a 12-inch image of a naked Christ, part of her three-hundred-foot-long mural of New York street life at Kennedy International Airport.

- On April 12, actor Steve Buscemi suffers stab wounds to his head and upper body outside a bar in Wilmington, North Carolina.

- On April 19, the Broadway hit musical *The Producers*, starring Matthew Broderick and Nathan Lane, opens.

- On July 3, the Screen Actors Guild and American Federation of Television and Radio Artists reach an agreement with studios that forestalls an actors guild strike.

- On August 25, popular singer and emerging actor Aaliyah and eight others die in the crash of an overloaded plane after takeoff from the Bahamas.

- On September 11, in addition to the thousands of lives lost in the terrorist attack on the World Trade Center, artwork valued in the tens of millions is destroyed, including a large tapestry by Joan Miró, sculptures by Auguste Rodin and Alexander Calder, and paintings by Pablo Picasso, Roy Lichtenstein, and David Hockney. Broadway shows are cancelled and many concerts are postponed.

- In November, the animated movie *Monster's, Inc.,* by Pixar, dominates the box office, earning approximately $63 million in its first weekend.

- On November 16, *Harry Potter and the Sorcerer's Stone* opens to large crowds in theaters across the United States.

- On November 20, the Andrew Mellon Foundation announces it will provide $50 million to assist New York City cultural and performing arts organizations affected by 9/11.

- On November 29, British superstar George Harrison, formerly lead guitarist for the Beatles, dies in Los Angeles.

- On December 19, Tony Kushner's play *Homebody/ Kabul* opens at the New York Theatre workshop.

- On December 20, Michael Hammond is confirmed as chairman of the National Endowment for the Arts. He dies one week after taking office.

MOVIES: *A.I.: Artificial Intelligence*, directed by Steven Spielberg and starring Jude Law, Frances O'Connor, and Haley Joel Osment; *Ali*, directed by Michael Mann and starring Jamie Foxx, Will Smith, and Jon Voight; *A Beautiful Mind*, directed by Ron Howard and starring Jennifer Connelly, Russell Crowe, and Ed Harris; *Black Hawk Down*, directed by Ridley Scott and starring Josh Hartnett, Ewan McGregor, and Tom Sizemore; *Blow*, directed by Ted Demme and starring Penélope Cruz and Johnny Depp; *Bridget Jones's Diary*, directed by Sharon Maguire and starring Colin Firth, Hugh Grant, and Renée Zellweger; *Donnie Darko*, directed by Richard Kelly and starring Jake Gyllenhaal, Jena Malone, and Mary McDonnell;

Enemy at the Gates, directed by Jean-Jacques Annaud and starring Joseph Fiennes, Ed Harris, and Jude Law; *The Fast and the Furious*, directed by Rob Cohen and starring Vin Diesel, Michelle Rodriguez, and Paul Walker; *Hannibal*, directed by Ridley Scott and starring Anthony Hopkins, Julianne Moore, and Gary Oldman; *Harry Potter and the Sorcerer's Stone*, directed by Chris Columbus and starring Rupert Grint, Richard Harris, and Daniel Radcliffe; *I Am Sam*, directed by Jessie Nelson and starring Dakota Fanning, Sean Penn, and Michelle Pfeiffer; *The Lord of the Rings: Fellowship of the Ring*, directed by Peter Jackson and starring Orlando Bloom, Ian McKellen, and Elijah Wood; *Monster's Ball*, directed by Marc Forster and starring Halle Berry, Taylor Simpson, and Billy Bob Thornton; *Monsters, Inc.*, animated feature, directed by Pete Docter and David Silverman; *Moulin Rouge!*, directed by Baz Luhrmann and starring Nicole Kidman, John Leguizamo, and Ewan McGregor; *Mulholland Dr.*, directed by David Lynch and starring Laura Harring, Justin Theroux, and Naomi Watts; *Ocean's Eleven*, directed by Steven Soderbergh and starring George Clooney, Brad Pitt, and Julia Roberts; *The Others*, directed by Alejandro Amenábar and starring Christopher Eccleston, Fionnula Flanagan, and Nicole Kidman; *The Royal Tenenbaums*, directed by Wes Anderson and starring Gene Hackman, Anjelica Huston, and Gwyneth Paltrow; *Shrek*, animated feature, directed by Andrew Adamson and Vicky Jenson; *Spy Game*, directed by Tony Scott and starring Brad Pitt and Robert Redford; *Swordfish*, directed by Dominic Sena and starring Halle Berry, Hugh Jackman, and John Travolta; *Training Day*, directed by Antoine Fuqua and starring Scott Glenn, Ethan Hawke, and Denzel Washington; *Vanilla Sky*, directed by Cameron Crowe and starring Tom Cruise, Penélope Cruz, and Cameron Diaz; *Zoolander*, directed by Ben Stiller and starring Stiller, Christine Taylor, and Owen Wilson.

NOVELS: Elizabeth Benedict, *Almost*; Mary Higgins Clark, *On the Street Where You Live*; Michael Connelly, *A Darkness More Than Night*; Clive Cussler, *Valhalla Rising*; Jennifer Egan, *Look at Me*; Louise Erdrich, *The Last Report on the Miracles at Little No Horse*; Janet Evanovich, *Seven Up*; Jonathan Franzen, *The Corrections*; Sue Grafton, *"P" Is for Peril*; John Grisham, *A Painted House* and *Skipping Christmas*; Charlaine Harris, *Dead Until Dark*; John Irving, *The Fourth Hand*; Jan Karon, *A Common Life*; Stephen King, *Dreamcatcher*; King and Peter Straub, *Black House*; Dean Koontz, *One*

Door Away from Heaven; Tim LaHaye and Jerry B. Jenkins, *Desecration*; Dennis Lehane, *Mystic River*; Heather McGowan, *Schooling*; Terry McMillan, *Day Late and a Dollar Short*; Alice Munro, *A Quiet Genius*; Ann Patchett, *Bel Canto*; James Patterson, *1st to Die* and *Suzanne's Diary for Nicholas*; Dawn Powell, *The Country and the City*; Nora Roberts, *Midnight Bayou*; Mary Robison, *Why Did I Ever*; Brian Ascalon Roley, *American Son*; Richard Russo, *Empire Falls*; John Sandford, *Chosen Prey*; W. G. Sebald, *Austerlitz*; Danielle Steel, *The Kiss* and *Leap of Faith*; Mattie J. T. Stepanek, *Journey Through Heartsongs*; Anne Tyler, *Ordinary People*; Brady Udall, *The Miracle Life of Edgar Mint*; Colson Whitehead, *John Henry Days*.

POPULAR SONGS: Aerosmith, "Jaded"; Christina Aguilera, Lil' Kim, Mýa, and Pink, "Lady Marmalade"; Mary J. Blige, "Family Affair"; Blu Cantrell, "Hit 'Em Up Style (Oops!)"; Crazy Town, "Butterfly"; Destiny's Child, "Survivor"; Dido, "Thank You"; Dream, "He Loves U Not"; Enrique Iglesias, "Hero"; Janet Jackson, "All for You"; Alicia Keys, "Fallin'"; Lifehouse, "Hanging By a Moment"; Jennifer Lopez, "I'm Real" and "Love Don't Cost a Thing"; Madonna, "Don't Tell Me"; *NSYNC, "Gone"; Shaggy, featuring Rayvon, "Angel"; Shaggy, featuring Ricardo "Rikrok" Ducent, "It Wasn't Me"; Train, "Drops of Jupiter"; Usher, "U Remind Me."

2002

- In April, a 1714 Stradivarius "Le Maurien" violin, worth more than $1.5 million, is stolen from Christophe Landon's rare violin workshop and instrument store on Broadway near Lincoln Center, New York.

- On May 3, the movie *Spider-Man* is released and by August grosses more than $400 million.

- On August 15, with Harvey Fierstein starring, the hit musical *Hairspray* debuts on Broadway.

MOVIES: *About Schmidt*, directed by Alexander Payne and starring Hope Davis, Dermot Mulroney, and Jack Nicholson; *Adaptation*, directed by Spike Jonze and starring Nicolas Cage, Chris Cooper, and Meryl Streep; *The Bourne Identity*, directed by Doug Liman and starring Chris Cooper, Matt Damon and Franka Potente; *Catch Me If You Can*, directed by Steven Spielberg and starring Leonardo DiCaprio, Tom Hanks, and Christopher Walken; *Chicago*, directed by Rob Marshall and starring Richard Gere, Renée Zellweger, and Catherine Zeta-Jones; *Collateral Damage*, directed by Andrew

Davis and starring John Leguizamo and Arnold Schwarzenegger; *Confessions of a Dangerous Mind*, directed by George Clooney and starring Drew Barrymore, Clooney, and Sam Rockwell; *Die Another Day*, directed by Lee Tamahori and starring Halle Berry, Pierce Brosnan, and Rosamund Pike; *8 Mile*, directed by Curtis Hanson and starring Kim Basinger, Eminem, and Brittany Murphy; *Equilibrium*, directed by Kurt Wimmer and starring Christian Bale, Sean Bean, and Emily Watson; *Gangs of New York*, directed by Martin Scorsese and starring Daniel Day-Lewis, Leonardo DiCaprio, and Cameron Diaz; *Harry Potter and the Chamber of Secrets*, directed by Chris Columbus and starring Rupert Grint, Daniel Radcliffe, and Emma Watson; *The Hours*, directed by Stephen Daldry and starring Nicole Kidman, Julianne Moore, and Meryl Streep; *Ice Age*, animated feature, directed by Carlos Saldanha and Chris Wedge; *Insomnia*, directed by Christopher Nolan and starring Al Pacino, Hilary Swank, and Robin Williams; *John Q*, directed by Nick Cassavetes and starring Robert Duvall and Denzel Washington; *The Lord of the Rings: The Two Towers*, directed by Peter Jackson and starring Ian McKellen, Viggo Mortensen, and Elijah Wood; *Minority Report*, directed by Steven Spielberg and starring Tom Cruise, Colin Farrell, and Samantha Morton; *My Big Fat Greek Wedding*, directed by Joel Zwick and starring Michael Constantine, John Corbett, and Nia Vardalos; *The Pianist*, directed by Roman Polanski and starring Adrien Brody, Frank Finlay, and Thomas Kretschmann; *Red Dragon*, directed by Brett Ratner and starring Ralph Fiennes, Anthony Hopkins, and Edward Norton; *The Ring*, directed by Gore Verbinski and starring Brian Cox, Martin Henderson, and Naomi Watts; *Road to Perdition*, directed by Sam Mendes and starring Tom Hanks, Jude Law, and Paul Newman; *Signs*, directed by M. Night Shyamalan and starring Rory Culkin, Mel Gibson, and Joaquin Phoenix; *Spider-Man*, directed by Sam Raimi and starring Willem Dafoe, Kirsten Dunst, and Tobey Maguire; *Star Trek: Nemesis*, directed by Stuart Baird and starring Jonathan Frakes, Brent Spiner, and Patrick Stewart; *Star Wars: Episode II—Attack of the Clones*, directed by George Lucas and starring Hayden Christensen, Ewan McGregor, and Natalie Portman; *The Transporter*, directed by Louis Leterrier and Corey Yuen and starring Matt Schulze, Jason Statham, and Qi Shu; *Tuck Everlasting*, directed by Jay Russell and starring Alexis Bledel, Jonathan Jackson, and Sissy Spacek; *A Walk to Remember*, directed by Adam Shankman and starring Peter Coyote, Mandy Moore, and Shane West; *We Were Soldiers*, directed by Randall Wallace and starring Mel Gibson, Greg Kinnear, and Madeleine Stowe; *Wind Talkers*, directed by John Woo and starring Adam Beach, Nicolas Cage, and Peter Stormare.

NOVELS: Jean M. Auel, *The Shelters of Stone*; James Lee Burke, *Jolie Blon's Bounce*; Tom Clancy, *Red Rabbit*; Mary Higgins Clark, *Daddy's Little Girl*; Michael Connelly, *City of Bones*; Michael Crichton, *Prey*; Jeffrey Eugenides, *Middlesex*; Janet Evanovich, *Hard Eight*; Michel Faber, *The Crimson Petal and the White*; Jonathan Safran Foer, *Everything Is Illuminated*; Alan Furst, *Blood of Victory*; Sue Grafton, *"Q" Is for Quarry*; John Grisham, *The Summons*; Jan Karon, *In This Mountain*; Stephen King, *Everything's Eventual* and *From a Buick 8*; Tim LaHaye and Jerry B. Jenkins, *The Remnant*; Robert Littell, *The Company: A Novel of the CIA*; Alice McDermott, *Child of My Heart*; Emma McLaughlin and Nicola Kraus, *The Nanny Diaries*; China Miéville, *Perdido Street Station*; Walter Mosley, *Bad Boy Brawley Brown*; James Patterson, *Four Blind Mice*; Patterson and Andrew Gross, *2nd Chance*; Patterson and Peter de Jonge, *The Beach House*; Nora Roberts, *Chesapeake Blue* and *Three Fates*; Alice Sebold, *The Lovely Bones*; Nicholas Sparks, *Nights in Rodanthe*; Danielle Steel, *Answered Prayers*; Donna Tratt, *The Little Friend*; William Trevor, *The Story of Lucy Gault*.

POPULAR SONGS: Michelle Branch, "All You Wanted"; The Calling, "Wherever You Will Go"; Vanessa Carlton, "A Thousand Miles"; Creed, "My Sacrifice"; Eminem, "Lose Yourself"; Jimmy Eat World, "The Middle"; Avril Lavigne, "Complicated"; Linkin Park, "In the End"; Jennifer Lopez, "Ain't It Funny"; Kylie Minogue, "Can't Get You out of My Head"; *NSYNC, "Girlfriend"; Nelly, "Hot in Here"; Nelly, featuring Kelly Rowland, "Dilemma"; No Doubt, "Hey Baby"; Pink, "Don't Let Me Get Me" and "Get the Party Started"; Santana, featuring Michelle Branch, "The Game of Love"; Justin Timberlake, "Like I Love You"; Usher, "U Don't Have to Call" and "U Got It Bad."

2003

- On January 22–March 30, the Metropolitan Museum of Art in New York hosts a major exhibit of drawings by Leonardo da Vinci.

- On September 9, twelve-year-old Brianna LaHara is among 261 people sued by the Recording Industry of America for illegally downloading music. LaHara's family paid a fee to belong to a music-swapping service, and the honor student did not realize she was doing anything wrong.

- On September 24, facing budget deficits, the musicians of the Pittsburgh Symphony Orchestra ratify a three-year contract in which they accept a 7.8 percent pay cut in the first two years before a major raise in the 2005–2006 season.

- On October 30, the musical *Wicked*, starring Kristin Chenoweth and Idina Menzel, opens on Broadway.

- On December 17, *The Lord of the Rings: The Return of the King* is released and by next year earns more than $1 billion worldwide.

MOVIES: *The Cat in the Hat*, directed by Bo Welch and starring Mike Myers; *Cheaper By the Dozen*, directed by Shawn Levy and starring Hilary Duff, Bonnie Hunt, and Steve Martin; *Cold Mountain*, directed by Anthony Minghella and starring Nicole Kidman, Jude Law, and Renée Zellweger; *Finding Nemo*, animated feature, directed by Andrew Stanton and Lee Unkrich; *Holes*, directed by Andrew Davis and starring Shia LaBeouf, Jon Voight, and Sigourney Weaver; *Hulk*, directed by Ang Lee and starring Eric Bana, Jennifer Connelly, and Sam Elliott; *Identity*, directed by James Mangold and starring John Cusack and Ray Liotta; *The Italian Job*, directed by F. Gary Gray and starring Edward Norton, Donald Sutherland, and Mark Wahlberg; *Kill Bill: Vol. 1*, directed by Quentin Tarantino and starring David Carradine, Daryl Hannah, and Uma Thurman; *The Last Samurai*, directed by Edward Zwick and starring Billy Connolly, Tom Cruise, and Ken Watanabe; *The Lord of the Rings: The Return of the King*, directed by Peter Jackson and starring Ian McKellen, Viggo Mortensen, and Elijah Wood; *Lost in Translation*, directed by Sofia Coppola and starring Scarlett Johansson, Bill Murray, and Giovanni Ribisi; *Love Actually*, directed by Richard Curtis and starring Hugh Grant, Martine McCutcheon, and Liam Neeson; *Master and Commander: The Far Side of the World*, directed by Peter Weir and starring Russell Crowe; *The Matrix Reloaded* and *The Matrix Revolutions*, directed by Andy Wachowski and Lana Wachowski and starring Laurence Fishburne, Carrie-Anne Moss, and Keanu Reeves; *Mystic River*, directed by Clint Eastwood and starring Kevin Bacon, Sean Penn, and Tim Robbins; *Pirates of the Caribbean: The Curse of the Black Pearl*, directed by Gore Verbinski and starring Orlando Bloom, Johnny Depp, and Geoffrey Rush; *Seabiscuit*, directed by Gary Ross and starring Elizabeth Banks, Jeff Bridges, and Tobey Maguire; *Shanghai Knights*, directed by David Dobkin and starring Jackie Chan and Owen Wilson; *Something's Gotta Give*, directed by Nancy Meyers and starring Diane Keaton, Jack Nicholson, and Keanu Reeves; *Terminator 3: Rise of the Machines*, directed by Jonathan Mostow and starring Arnold Schwarzenegger; *The Texas Chainsaw Massacre*, directed by Marcus Nispel and starring Jessica Biel, Andrew Bryniarski, and Jonathan Tucker; *Underworld*, directed by Len Wiseman and starring Kate Beckinsale, Shane Brolly, and Scott Speedman; *X2*, directed by Bryan Singer and starring Halle Berry, Hugh Jackman, and Patrick Stewart.

NOVELS: Mitch Albom, *The Five People You Meet In Heaven*; Jane Alison, *The Marriage of the Sea*; Paul Auster, *Oracle Night*; Nicholson Baker, *A Box of Matches*; Thomas Berger, *Best Friends*; T. C. Boyle, *Drop City*; Anita Brookner, *Making Things Better*; Dan Brown, *The Da Vinci Code*; John Burdett, *Bangkok 8*; Frederick Busch, *A Memory of War*; Jay Cantor, *Great Neck*; Tom Carson, *Gilligan's Wake*; Susan Choi, *American Woman*; Tom Clancy, *The Teeth of the Tiger*; Michael Connelly, *Lost Light*; Patricia Cornwell, *Blow Fly*; Meghan Daum, *The Quality of Life Report*; Don DeLillo, *Cosmopolis*; Pete Dexter, *Train*; Louise Erdrich, *The Master Butcher's Singing Club*; Janet Evanovich, *To the Nines*; Kinky Friedman, *Kill Two Birds and Get Stones*; Cristina García, *Monkey Hunting*; William Gibson, *Pattern of Recognition*; Neil Gordon, *The Company You Keep*; Katherine Govier, *Creation*; John Grisham, *Bleachers* and *The King of Torts*; David Guterson, *Our Lady of the Forest*; Khaled Hosseini, *The Kite Runner*; Michael Ignatieff, *Charlie Johnson in the Flames*; Pico Iyer, *Abandon*; Diane Johnson, *L'Affaire*; Edward P. Jones, *The Known World*; Robert Jordan, *Crossroads of Twilight*; Ken Kalfus, *The Commissariat of Enlightenment*; Garrison Keillor, *Love Me*; Thomas Keneally, *Office of Innocence*; Tim LaHaye and Jerry B. Jenkins, *Armageddon*; Jhumpa Lahiri, *The Namesake*; Chang-rae Lee, *Aloft*; Jonathan Lethem, *The Fortress of Solitude*; Jim Lewis, *The King Is Dead*; David Liss, *The Coffee Trader*; Simon Mawer, *The Fall*; Donald Miller, *Blue Like Jazz*; Thomas Moran, *Anja the Liar*; Toni Morrison, *Love*; Walter Mosley, *Six Easy Pieces: Easy Rawlins Stories*; Ruth Ozeki, *All Over Creation*; Carolyn Parkhurst, *The Dogs of Babel*; Suzan-Lori Parks, *Getting Mother's Body*; James Patterson, *The Lake House*; Patterson and Andrew Gross, *The Jester*; George P. Pelecanos, *Soul Circus*; Richard Powers, *The Time of Our Singing*; Richard Price, *Samaritan*; Sara Pritchard, *Crackpots*; Annie Proulx, *That Old Ace in the Hole*; Nora Roberts, *Birthright*; Norman Rush, *Mortals*; John Sandford, *Naked Prey*; Jane Smiley, *Good Faith*; Danielle Steel, *Johnny Angel*; Robert Stone, *Bay of Souls*; Ellen Ullman, *The Bug*; Vendela Vida, *And Now You Can*

Go; Marianne Wiggins, *Evidence of Things Unseen*; Tobias Wolff, *Old School*.

POPULAR SONGS: Christina Aguilera, "Beautiful"; Aguilera, featuring Lil' Kim, "Can't Hold Us Down"; Black Eyed Peas, featuring Justin Timberlake, "Where Is the Love?"; Kelly Clarkson, "Miss Independent"; Evanescence, "Bring Me to Life"; 50 Cent, "In da Club"; Kid Rock and Sheryl Crow, "Picture"; Beyoncé, featuring Jay-Z, "Crazy in Love"; Beyoncé, featuring Sean Paul, "Baby Boy"; Avril Lavigne, "I'm With You"; Jennifer Lopez, featuring LL Cool J, "All I Have"; Maroon 5, "Harder to Breathe"; Matchbox Twenty, "Unwell"; Nelly, P. Diddy, and Murphy Lee, "Shake Ya Tailfeather"; Outkast, "Hey Ya!"; Santana, featuring Alex Band, "Why Don't You and I"; 3 Doors Down, "Here without You" and "When I'm Gone"; Justin Timberlake, "Cry Me a River" and "Rock Your Body."

2004

* In February, Mel Gibson's movie *The Passion of the Christ*, a violent depiction of the death of Jesus Christ, is criticized as anti-Semitic but does well at the box office.

* In March, the New Museum of Contemporary Art in New York, Museum of Contemporary Art in Chicago, and U.C.L.A. Hammer Museum in Los Angeles combine resources to purchase works by emerging artists.

MOVIES: *Anchorman: The Legend of Ron Burgundy*, directed by Adam McKay and starring Christina Applegate, Steve Carell, and Will Ferrell; *The Aviator*, directed by Martin Scorsese and starring Kate Beckinsale, Cate Blanchett, and Leonardo DiCaprio; *The Bourne Supremacy*, directed by Paul Greengrass and starring Joan Allen, Matt Damon, and Franka Potente; *Collateral*, directed by Michael Mann and starring Tom Cruise, Jamie Foxx, and Jada Pinkett Smith; *Crash*, directed by Paul Haggis and starring Sandra Bullock, Don Cheadle, and Thandie Newton; *Dawn of the Dead*, directed by Zack Snyder and starring Mekhi Phifer, Sarah Polley, and Ving Rhames; *Dodgeball: A True Underdog Story*, directed by Rawson Marshall Thurber and starring Ben Stiller, Christine Taylor, and Vince Vaughn; *Eternal Sunshine of the Spotless Mind*, directed by Michel Gondry and starring Jim Carrey and Kate Winslet; *Friday Night Lights*, directed by Peter Berg and starring Derek Luke, Jay Hernandez, and Billy Bob Thornton; *Harry Potter and the Prisoner of Azkaban*, directed by Alfonso Cuarón and starring Rupert Grint, Daniel Radcliffe, and Emma Watson; *Hellboy*, directed by Guillermo del Toro and starring Selma Blair, Doug Jones, and Ron Perlman; *Hotel Rwanda*, directed by Terry George and starring Don Cheadle and Joaquin Phoenix; *The Incredibles*, animated feature, directed by Brad Bird; *Kill Bill: Vol. 2*, directed by Quentin Tarantino and starring David Carradine, Michael Madsen, and Uma Thurman; *Ladder 49*, directed by Jay Russell and starring Joaquin Phoenix and John Travolta; *Lemony Snicket's A Series of Unfortunate Events*, directed by Brad Silberling and starring Jim Carrey, Jude Law, and Meryl Streep; *Man on Fire*, directed by Tony Scott and starring Dakota Fanning, Christopher Walken, and Denzel Washington; *Mean Girls*, directed by Mark Waters and starring Jonathan Bennett, Lindsay Lohan, and Rachel McAdams; *Million Dollar Baby*, directed by Clint Eastwood and starring Eastwood, Morgan Freeman, and Hilary Swank; *The Notebook*, directed by Nick Cassavetes and starring James Garner, Rachel McAdams, and Gena Rowlands; *Ray*, directed by Taylor Hackford and starring Jamie Foxx, Regina King, and Kerry Washington; *Shark Tale*, animated feature, directed by Bibo Bergeron and Vicky Jenson; *Shrek 2*, animated feature, directed by Andrew Adamson and Kelly Asbury; *Sideways*, directed by Alexander Payne and starring Thomas Haden Church, Paul Giamatti, and Virginia Madsen; *Spider-Man 2*, directed by Sam Raimi and starring Kirsten Dunst, Tobey Maguire, and Alfred Molina; *The Stepford Wives*, directed by Frank Oz and starring Matthew Broderick, Nicole Kidman, and Bette Midler; *The Terminal*, directed by Steven Spielberg and starring Tom Hanks and Catherine Zeta-Jones; *Troy*, directed by Wolfgang Petersen and starring Eric Bana, Orlando Bloom, and Brad Pitt; *The Village*, directed by M. Night Shyamalan and starring William Hurt, Joaquin Phoenix, and Sigourney Weaver.

NOVELS: Jonathan Ames, *Wake Up, Sir!*; Kate Atkinson, *Case Histories*; David Baldacci, *Hour Game*; Russell Banks, *The Darling*; T. C. Boyle, *The Inner Circle*; Michael Connelly, *The Narrows*; Patricia Cornwell, *Trace*; Nelson DeMille, *Night Fall*; Janet Evanovich, *Metro Girl* and *Ten Big Ones*; Sue Grafton, *"R" Is For Ricochet*; John Grisham, *The Last Juror*; Thomas Keneally, *The Tyrant's Novel*; Stephen King, *The Dark Tower* and *Song of Susannah*; Tim LaHaye and Jerry B. Jenkins, *Glorious Appearing*; Walter Mosley, *Little Scarlet*; Joyce Carol Oates, *The Falls*; James Patterson, *London Bridges* and *Sam's Letters to Jennifer*; Patterson and Andrew Gross, *3rd Degree*; Tom Perrotta, *Little Children*; Nancy Reisman, *The*

First Desire; Nora Roberts, *Northern Lights*; Marilynne Robinson, *Gilead*; Philip Roth, *The Plot Against America*; John Updike, *Villages*; Kate Walbert, *Our Kind*; Tom Wolfe, *I Am Charlotte Simmons*.

POPULAR SONGS: Black Eyed Peas, "Hey Mama"; Kelly Clarkson, "Breakaway"; Evanescence, "My Immortal"; Hoobastank, "The Reason"; JoJo, "Leave (Get Out)"; Alicia Keys, "If I Ain't Got You"; Avril Lavigne, "My Happy Ending"; Maroon 5, "She Will Be Loved" and "This Love"; Christina Milian, "Dip It Low"; Nelly, featuring Tim McGraw, "Over and Over"; OutKast, "The Way You Move"; Ashlee Simpson, "Pieces of Me"; Jessica Simpson, "With You"; Britney Spears, "Toxic"; Switchfoot, "Dare You to Move" and "Meant to Live"; Usher, "Burn"; Usher, featuring Ludacris and Lil' Jon, "Yeah!"; Usher and Alicia Keys, "My Boo."

2005

- On February 1, conceptual artists Christo and Jeanne-Claude debut the two-week display called "The Gates," more than seven thousand individual saffron nylon sheets suspended from steel posts in Central Park in New York City.

- On March 17, the musical *Spamalot*, inspired by the zany antics of the comedy troupe Monty Python, debuts on Broadway. Two other blockbuster musicals debut during the year, *Jersey Boys* and *The Color Purple*.

- On June 13, singer Michael Jackson is acquitted of felony charges of child molestation, conspiracy, and alcohol charges by a California jury.

- On November 18, an oil painting by Jackson Pollock (valued at $11.6 million) and a silkscreen by Andy Warhol are stolen from the Everhart Museum in Scranton, Pennsylvania.

MOVIES: *Batman Begins*, directed by Christopher Nolan and starring Christian Bale, Michael Caine, and Ken Watanabe; *Brokeback Mountain*, directed by Ang Lee and starring Jake Gyllenhaal and Heath Ledger; *Capote*, directed by Bennett Miller and starring Philip Seymour Hoffman; *Charlie and the Chocolate Factory*, directed by Tim Burton and starring Johnny Depp; *The Chronicles of Narnia: The Lion, the Witch and the Wardrobe*, directed by Andrew Adamson and starring Georgie Henley, William Moseley, and Tilda Swinton; *Cinderella Man*, directed by Ron Howard and starring Russell Crowe and Renée Zellweger; *Coach Carter*, directed by Thomas Carter and starring Rick Gonzalez, Samuel L. Jackson, and Robert Ri'chard; *Fantastic Four*, directed by Tim Story and starring Jessica Alba, Michael Chiklis, and Chris Evans; *The 40 Year-Old Virgin*, directed by Judd Apatow and starring Steve Carell, Catherine Keener, and Paul Rudd; *Four Brothers*, directed by John Singleton and starring Tyrese Gibson, Garrett Hedlund, and Mark Wahlberg; *Good Night, and Good Luck*, directed by George Clooney and starring Patricia Clarkson, Clooney, and David Strathairn; *Harry Potter and the Goblet of Fire*, directed by Mike Newell and starring Rupert Grint, Daniel Radcliffe, and Emma Watson; *The Interpreter*, directed by Sydney Pollack and starring Catherine Keener, Nicole Kidman, and Sean Penn; *Jarhead*, directed by Sam Mendes and starring Lucas Black, Jamie Foxx, and Jake Gyllenhaal; *Kingdom of Heaven*, directed by Ridley Scott and starring Orlando Bloom, Eva Green, and Liam Neeson; *Madagascar*, animated feature, directed by Eric Darnell and Tom McGrath; *Memoirs of a Geisha*, directed by Rob Marshall and starring Ken Watanabe, Michelle Yeoh, and Ziyi Zhang; *Mr. & Mrs. Smith*, directed by Doug Liman and starring Angelina Jolie, Brad Pitt, and Vince Vaughn; *Munich*, directed by Steven Spielberg and starring Eric Bana, Daniel Craig, and Marie-Josée Croze; *Rent*, directed by Chris Columbus and starring Rosario Dawson, Taye Diggs, and Wilson Jermaine Heredia; *The Ring Two*, directed by Hideo Nakata and starring David Dorfman, Sissy Spacek, and Naomi Watts; *Serenity*, directed by Joss Whedon and starring Chiwetel Ejiofor, Nathan Fillion, and Gina Torres; *Sin City*, directed by Frank Miller and Robert Rodriguez and starring Mickey Rourke, Clive Owen, and Bruce Willis; *Star Wars Episode III: Revenge of the Sith*, directed by George Lucas and starring Hayden Christensen, Natalie Portman, and Ewan McGregor; *Syriana*, directed by Stephen Gaghan and starring George Clooney, Matt Damon, and Amanda Peet; *Walk the Line*, directed by James Mangold and starring Joaquin Phoenix and Reese Witherspoon; *War of the Worlds*, directed by Steven Spielberg and starring Tom Cruise, Dakota Fanning, and Tim Robbins; *Wedding Crashers*, directed by David Dobkin and starring Rachel McAdams, Vince Vaughn, and Owen Wilson; *White Noise*, directed by Geoffrey Sax and starring Michael Keaton.

NOVELS: Sandra Brown, *Chill Factor*; Mary Higgins Clark, *No Place Like Home*; Michael Connelly, *The Closers* and *The Lincoln Lawyer*; Patricia Cornwell, *Predator*; Catherine Coulter, *Point Blank*; Clive Cussler with Paul Kemprecos, *Polar Shift*; E. L. Doctorow, *The March*; Bret Easton Ellis, *Lunar Park*; Louise Erdrich, *The Painted Drum*; Janet

Evanovich, *Eleven on Top*; Diana Gabaldon, *A Breath of Snow and Ashes*; Sue Grafton, *"S" Is For Silence*; W. E. B. Griffin, *The Hostage*; John Grisham, *The Broker*; Kathryn Harrison, *Envy*; Robert Jordan, *Knife of Dreams*; Thomas Kelly, *Empire Rising*; Sue Monk Kidd, *The Mermaid Chair*; Elizabeth Kostova, *The Historian*; Tim LaHaye and Jerry B. Jenkins, *The Rising*; Elmore Leonard, *The Hot Kid*; Sam Lipsyte, *Home Land*; George R. R. Martin, *A Feast for Crows*; Cormac McCarthy, *No Country for Old Men*; Walter Mosley, *Cinnamon Kiss*; James Patterson, *Mary, Mary*; Patterson and Andrew Gross, *The Lifeguard*; Patterson and Maxine Paetro, *4th of July*; Patterson and Howard Roughan, *Honeymoon*; Francine Prose, *A Changed Man*; Nicholas Sparks, *At First Sight* and *True Believer*; William T. Vollman, *Europe Central*.

POPULAR SONGS: Black Eyed Peas, "Don't Phunk with My Heart"; Chris Brown, "Run It"; Mariah Carey, "Don't Forget about Us," "Shake It Off," and "We Belong Together"; Ciara featuring Missy Elliott, "One, Two Step"; Kelly Clarkson, "Because of You," "Behind These Hazel Eyes," and "Since U Been Gone"; Green Day, "Boulevard of Broken Dreams"; Alicia Keys, "Karma"; Lifehouse, "You and Me"; Mario, "Let Me Love You"; Nickelback, "Photograph"; Pussycat Dolls, featuring Busta Rhymes, "Don't Cha"; Rihanna, "Pon de Replay"; Gwen Stefani, "Hollaback Girl"; Usher, "Caught Up"; Weezer, "Beverly Hills"; Kanye West, featuring Jaime Foxx, "Gold Digger."

2006

- On July 7, *Pirates of the Caribbean: Dead Man's Chest* is released; the film earns more than $1 billion worldwide.

- On September 19–December 10, art photographs by Robert Polidori of the damage left by Hurricane Katrina in New Orleans are displayed at the Metropolitan Museum of Art.

- In November, David Geffen sells Jackson Pollock's painting *Number 5, 1948* (1948) for $140 million and Willem de Kooning's *Woman III* (1952–1953) for $137.5 million.

- On November 8, Francisco Goya's painting "Children With a Cart" is stolen in Pennsylvania during transport to a museum exhibition in Toledo, Ohio; the painting is recovered later in the month.

MOVIES: *Apocalypto*, directed by Mel Gibson and starring Dalia Hernández, Gerardo Taracena, and Raoul Trujillo; *Babel*, directed by Alejandro González Iñárritu and starring Gael García Bernal,

Cate Blanchett, and Brad Pitt; *Barnyard*, animated feature, directed by Steve Oedekerk; *Blood Diamond*, directed by Edward Zwick and starring Jennifer Connelly, Leonardo DiCaprio, and Djimon Hounsou; *Borat*, directed by Larry Charles and starring Sacha Baron Cohen; *Cars*, animated feature, directed by John Lasseter and Joe Ranft; *Casino Royale*, directed by Martin Campbell and starring Judi Dench, Daniel Craig, and Eva Green; *Charlotte's Web*, animated feature, directed by Gary Winick; *Children of Men*, directed by Alfonso Cuarón and starring Chiwetel Ejiofor, Julianne Moore, and Clive Owen; *The Da Vinci Code*, directed by Ron Howard and starring Tom Hanks, Jean Reno, and Audrey Tautou; *Déjà vu*, directed by Tony Scott and starring James Caviezel, Paula Patton, and Denzel Washington; *The Departed*, directed by Martin Scorsese and starring Matt Damon, Leonardo DiCaprio, and Jack Nicholson; *The Devil Wears Prada*, directed by David Frankel and starring Adrian Grenier, Anne Hathaway, and Meryl Streep; *Dreamgirls*, directed by Bill Condon and starring Jamie Foxx, Beyoncé Knowles, and Eddie Murphy; *Eragon*, directed by Stefen Fangmeier and starring Sienna Guillory, Jeremy Irons, and Ed Speleers; *Flags of Our Fathers*, directed by Clint Eastwood and starring Joseph Cross, Barry Pepper, and Ryan Phillippe; *Ice Age: The Meltdown*, animated feature, directed by Carlos Saldanha; *Inside Man*, directed by Spike Lee and starring Jodie Foster, Clive Owen, and Denzel Washington; *Little Miss Sunshine*, directed by Jonathan Dayton and Valerie Faris and starring Steve Carell, Toni Collette, and Greg Kinnear; *Mission: Impossible III*, directed by J. J. Abrams and starring Tom Cruise, Michelle Monaghan, and Ving Rhames; *Pirates of the Caribbean: Dead Man's Chest*, directed by Gore Verbinski and starring Orlando Bloom, Johnny Depp, and Keira Knightley; *The Prestige*, directed by Christopher Nolan and starring Christian Bale, Hugh Jackman, and Scarlett Johansson; *The Pursuit of Happyness*, directed by Gabriele Muccino and starring Thandie Newton, Jaden Smith, and Will Smith; *The Queen*, directed by Stephen Frears and starring James Cromwell, Helen Mirren, and Michael Sheen; *Superman Returns*, directed by Bryan Singer and starring Kate Bosworth, Brandon Routh, and Kevin Spacey; *Talladega Nights: The Ballad of Ricky Bobby*, directed by Adam McKay and starring Sacha Baron Cohen, Will Ferrell, and John C. Reilly; *300*, directed by Zack Snyder and starring Gerard Butler, Lena Headley, and David Wenham; *V for Vendetta*, directed by James McTeigue and starring Rupert Graves, Natalie

Portman, and Hugo Weaving; *World Trade Center*, directed by Oliver Stone and starring Maria Bello, Nicolas Cage, and Michael Peña; *X-Men: The Last Stand*, directed by Brett Ratner and starring Halle Berry, Hugh Jackman, and Patrick Stewart.

NOVELS: Mitch Albom, *For One More Day*; Monica Ali, *Alentejo Blue*; Howard Bahr, *The Judas Field*; Julian Barnes, *Arthur and George*; Mary Higgins Clark, *Two Little Girls in Blue*; Michael Connelly, *Echo Park*; Patricia Cornwell, *At Risk*; Ivan Doig, *The Whistling Season*; Jennifer Egan, *The Keep*; Janet Evanovich, *Twelve Sharp*; Richard Ford, *The Lay of the Land*; Nell Freudenberger, *The Dissident*; Terry Goodkind, *Phantom*; Allegra Goodman, *Intuition*; Ward Just, *Forgetfulness*; Ken Kalfus, *A Disorder Peculiar to the Country*; Jonathan Kellerman, *Gone*; Stephen King, *The Cell* and *Lisey's Story*; Dean Koontz, *The Husband*; David Long, *The Inhabited World*; Cormac McCarthy, *The Road*; Alice McDermott, *After This*; Brad Melzer, *The Book of Fate*; Claire Messud, *The Emperor's Children*; Stephenie Meyer, *New Moon*; David Mitchell, *Black Swan Green*; James Patterson, *Cross*; Patterson and Andrew Gross, *Judge & Jury*; Patterson and Peter de Jonge, *Beach Road*; Patterson and Maxine Paetro, *The 5th Horseman*; Marisha Pessl, *Special Topics in Calamity Physics*; Richard Powers, *The Echo Maker*; Thomas Pynchon, *Against the Day*; Anna Quindlen, *Rise and Shine*; Nora Roberts, *Angels Fall*; Philip Roth, *Everyman*; Diane Setterfield, *The Thirteenth Tale*; Gary Shetyngart, *Absurdistan*; Scott Smith, *The Ruins*; Nicholas Sparks, *Dear John*; Danielle Steel, *The House*; Anne Tyler, *Digging to America*; John Updike, *Terrorist*; Colson Whitehead, *Apex Hides the Hurt*; Daniel Woodrell, *Winter's Bone*.

POPULAR SONGS: Gnarls Barkley, "Crazy"; Natasha Bedingfield, "Unwritten"; Beyoncé, featuring Slim Thug, "Check on It"; Mary J. Blige, "Be Without You"; James Blunt, "You're Beautiful"; Chris Brown, "Run It"; Cassie, "Me & U"; Chamillionaire, featuring Krayzie Bone, "Ridin'"; The Fray, "Over My Head (Cable Car)"; Nelly, featuring Paul Wall, Ali & Gipp, "Grillz"; Nelly Furtado, featuring Timbaland, "Promiscuous"; Ne-Yo, "So Sick"; Panic! At The Disco, "I Write Sins Not Tragedies"; Sean Paul, "Temperature"; Daniel Powter, "Bad Day"; Pussycat Dolls, featuring Snoop Dogg, "Buttons"; Rihanna, "SOS"; Shakira, featuring Wyclef Jean, "Hips Don't Lie"; Justin Timberlake, "Sexy Back"; Yung Joc, "It's Goin' Down."

2007

- On January 17, on a Friday morning during rush hour, Joshua Bell performs incognito as a street

musician in the L'Enfant Plaza Metro Station in Washington, D.C.

- On September 18–January 6, 2008, the Metropolitan Museum of Art mounts a major exhibit of more than two hundred Dutch masterpieces from its collection, including works by Aelbert Cuyp, Rembrandt, and Johannes Vermeer.

MOVIES: *American Gangster*, directed by Ridley Scott and starring Russell Crowe, Chiwetel Ejiofor, and Denzel Washington; *Beowulf*, directed by Robert Zemeckis and starring Crispin Glover, Angelina Jolie, and Ray Winstoner; *The Bourne Ultimatum*, directed by Paul Greengrass and starring Joan Allen, Matt Damon, and Édgar Ramírez; *Charlie Wilson's War*, directed by Mike Nichols and starring Tom Hanks, Philip Seymour Hoffman, and Julia Roberts; *Enchanted*, directed by Kevin Lima and starring Amy Adams, James Marsden, and Susan Sarandon; *The Game Plan*, directed by Andy Fickman and starring Dwayne Johnson, Madison Pettis, and Kyra Sedgwick; *Ghost Rider*, directed by Mark Steven Johnson and starring Nicolas Cage, Sam Elliott, and Eva Mendes; *The Golden Compass*, directed by Chris Weitz and starring Daniel Craig, Nicole Kidman, and Dakota Blue Richards; *Hairspray*, directed by Adam Shankman and starring Nikki Blonsky, Queen Latifah, and John Travolta; *Halloween*, directed by Rob Zombie and starring Tyler Mane, Malcolm McDowell, and Scout Taylor-Compton; *Harry Potter and the Order of the Phoenix*, directed by David Yates and starring Rupert Grint, Daniel Radcliffe, and Emma Watson; *I Am Legend*, directed by Francis Lawrence and starring Alice Braga, Will Smith, and Charlie Tahan; *Into the Wild*, directed by Sean Penn and starring Emile Hirsch, Catherine Keener, and Vince Vaughn; *Juno*, directed by Jason Reitman and starring Michael Cera, Jennifer Garner, and Ellen Page; *Knocked Up*, directed by Judd Apatow and starring Katherine Heigl, Seth Rogen, and Paul Rudd; *Live Free or Die Hard*, directed by Len Wiseman and starring Justin Long, Timothy Olyphant, and Bruce Willis; *Meet the Robinsons*, animated feature, directed by Stephen J. Anderson; *Michael Clayton*, directed by Tony Gilroy and starring George Clooney, Tilda Swinton, and Tom Wilkinson; *No Country for Old Men*, directed by Ethan Coen and Joel Coen and starring Javier Bardem, Josh Brolin, and Tommy Lee Jones; *Pirates of the Caribbean: At World's End*, directed by Gore Verbinski and starring Orlando Bloom, Johnny Depp, and Keira Knightley; *Ratatouille*, animated feature, directed by Brad Bird and Jan Pinkava; *Shrek the Third*, animated feature, directed by Raman Hui and Chris Miller; *The Simpsons Movie*, animated feature, directed by David Silverman; *Spider-Man 3*, directed by Sam Raimi and starring Kirsten Dunst, Topher Grace, and Tobey Maguire; *There Will Be Blood*, directed by Paul Thomas Anderson and starring Paul Dano, Daniel Day-Lewis, and Ciarán Hinds; *Transformers*, directed by Michael Bay and starring Josh Duhamel, Megan Fox, and Shia LaBeouf.

NOVELS: Sherman Alexie, *The Absolutely True Diary of a Part-Time Indian*; Martin Amis, *House of Meetings*; David Baldacci, *Simple Genius* and *Stone Cold*; Michael Chabon, *The Yiddish Policeman's Union*; Mary Higgins Clark, *I Heard That Song Before*; Leah Hager Cohen, *House Lights*; Patricia Cornwell, *Book of the Dead*; Don DeLillio, *Falling Man*; Junot Diaz, *The Brief Wondrous Life of Oscar Wao*; Janet Evanovich, *Lean Mean Thirteen* and *Plum Lovin'*; Joshua Ferris, *Then We Came to the End*; Vince Flynn, *Protect and Defend*; Ken Follett, *World Without End*; Sue Grafton, *"T" Is for Trespass*; John Grisham, *Playing for Pizza*; Steven Hall, *The Raw Shark Texts*; Khaled Hosseini, *A Thousand Splendid Suns*; Denis Johnson, *Tree of Smoke*; Sophie Kinsella, *Shopaholic & Baby*; Thomas Mallon, *Fellow Travelers*; Stephenie Meyer, *Eclipse*; Walter Mosley, *Blonde Faith*; Alice Munro, *The View from Castle Rock*; James Patterson, *Double Cross*; Patterson and Michael Ledwidge, *Step on a Crack* and *The Quickie*; Patterson and Maxine Paetro, *The 6th Target*; Patterson and Howard Roughan, *You've Been Warned*; Tom Perrotta, *The Abstinence Teacher*; Jodi Picoult, *Nineteen Minutes*; J. D. Robb, *Innocent in Death*; Philip Roth, *Exit Ghost*; Richard Russo, *Bridge of Sighs*; William Trevor, *Cheating at Canasta*.

POPULAR SONGS: Akon, "Don't Matter"; Akon, featuring Eminem, "Smack That"; Akon, featuring Snoop Dogg, "I Wanna Love You"; Beyoncé, "Irreplaceable"; Daughtry, "It's Not Over"; Fergie, "Big Girls Don't Cry" and "Fergalicious"; Fergie, featuring Ludacris, "Glamorous"; Nelly Furtado, "Say It Right"; Avril Lavigne, "Girlfriend"; Maroon 5, "Makes Me Wonder"; Mims, "This Is Why I'm Hot"; Plain White T's, "Hey There Delilah"; Rihanna, featuring Jay-Z, "Umbrella"; Shop Boyz, "Party Like a Rock Star"; Soulja Boy, "Crank That"; Gwen Stefani, featuring Akon, "The Sweet Escape"; T-Pain, featuring Yung Joc, "Buy U a Drank (Shawty Snappin')"; Timbaland, featuring Keri Hilson, "The Way I Are"; Carrie Underwood, "Before He Cheats."

2008

- On September 7, Jonathan Larson's *Rent* ends its twelve-year run on Broadway.

- On October 16, the revival of Arthur Miller's *All My Sons*—starring John Lithgow, Dianne Wiest, Patrick Wilson, and Katie Holmes—opens on Broadway to brisk business.

- On November 8, the Taubman Museum of Art (formerly the Art Museum of Western Virginia), located in a modern building designed by Frank Gehry protégé Randall Stout, opens in Roanoke.

- On November 13, the musical *Billy Elliot*, about a young boy more interested in ballet than sports and based on a hit British film of the same name, debuts on Broadway.

MOVIES: *Appaloosa*, directed by Ed Harris and starring Harris, Viggo Mortensen, and Renée Zellweger; *Bolt*, animated feature, directed by Byron Howard and Chris Williams; *The Chronicles of Narnia: Prince Caspian*, directed by Andrew Adamson and starring Ben Barnes, Georgie Henley, and Skandar Keynes; *The Dark Knight*, directed by Christopher Nolan and starring Christian Bale, Aaron Eckhart, and Heath Ledger; *Eagle Eye*, directed by D. J. Caruso and starring Rosario Dawson, Shia LaBeouf, and Michelle Monaghan; *Gran Torino*, directed by Clint Eastwood and starring Christopher Carley, Eastwood, and Bee Vang; *Horton Hears a Who!*, animated feature, directed by Jimmy Hayward and Steve Martino; *The Hurt Locker*, directed by Kathryn Bigelow and starring Brian Geraghty, Anthony Mackie, and Jeremy Renner; *The Incredible Hulk*, directed by Louis Leterrier and starring Edward Norton, Tim Roth, and Liv Tyler; *Indiana Jones and the Kingdom of the Crystal Skull*, directed by Steven Spielberg and starring Cate Blanchett, Harrison Ford, and Shia LaBeouf; *Iron Man*, directed by Jon Favreau and starring Robert Downey Jr., Terrence Howard, and Gwyneth Paltrow; *Mamma Mia!*, directed by Phyllida Lloyd and starring Pierce Brosnan, Amanda Seyfried, and Meryl Streep; *Milk*, directed by Gus Van Sant and starring Josh Brolin, Emile Hirsch, and Sean Penn; *Pineapple Express*, directed by David Gordon Green and starring Gary Cole, James Franco, and Seth Rogen; *Quantum of Solace*, directed by Marc Forster and starring Mathieu Amalric, Daniel Craig, and Olga Kurylenko; *Sex and the City*, directed by Michael Patrick King and starring Kim Cattrall, Cynthia Nixon, and Sarah Jessica Parker; *Slumdog Millionaire*, directed by Danny Boyle and Loveleen Tandan and starring Dev Patel, Freida Pinto, and Saurabh Shukla; *The Spiderwick Chronicles*, directed by Mark Waters and starring Sarah Bolger, Freddie Highmore, and David Strathairn; *Taken*, directed by Pierre Morel and starring Maggie Grace, Famke Janssen, and Liam Neeson; *10,000 BC*, directed by Roland Emmerich and starring Camilla Belle, Marco Khan, and Steven Strait; *Tropic Thunder*, directed by Ben Stiller and starring Jack Black, Robert Downey Jr., and Stiller; *21*, directed by Robert Luketic and starring Kate Bosworth, Kevin Spacey, and Jim Sturgess; *Twilight*, directed by Catherine Hardwicke and starring Billy Burke, Robert Pattinson, and Kristen Stewart; *Valkyrie*, directed by Bryan Singer and starring Tom Cruise, Bill Nighy, and Carice Van Houten; *Vantage Point*, directed by Pete Travis and starring Matthew Fox, Dennis Quaid, and Forest Whitaker; *WALL-E*, animated feature, directed by Andrew Stanton; *The Wrestler*, directed by Darren Aronofsky and starring Mickey Rourke, Marisa Tomei, and Evan Rachel Wood.

NOVELS: Kate Atkinson, *When Will There Be Good News?*; David Baldacci, *Divine Justice* and *The Whole Truth*; Charles Bock, *Beautiful Children*; Sandra Brown, *Smoke Screen*; Shannon Burke, *Black Flies*; Lee Child, *Nothing to Lose*; Mary Higgins Clark, *Where Are You Now?*; Harlan Coben, *Hold Tight*; James Collins, *Beginner's Greek*; Michael Connelly, *The Brass Verdict*; Helene Cooper, *The House at Sugar Beach*; Patricia Cornwell, *Scarpetta*; Nelson DeMille, *The Gate House*; Tony Earley, *The Blue Star*; Janet Evanovich, *Fearless Fourteen* and *Plum Lucky*; Christine Feehan, *Dark Curse*; Vince Flynn, *Extreme Measures*; W. E. B. Griffin, *Black Ops*; John Grisham, *The Appeal*; Lauren Groff, *The Monsters of Templeton*; Laurell K. Hamilton, *Blood Noir*; Jonathan Kellerman, *Compulsion*; Sherrilyn Kenyon, *Acheron*; Stephen King, *Duma Key*; Chuck Klosterman, *Downtown Owl*; Dean Koontz, *Odd Hours*; Jhumpa Lahiri, *Unaccustomed Earth*; Dennis Lehane, *The Given Day*; Stephenie Meyer, *The Host*; Sue Miller, *The Senator's Wife*; James Patterson, *Cross Country*; Patterson and Gabrielle Charbonnet, *Sundays at Tiffany's*; Patterson and Howard Roughan, *Sail*; Jodi Picoult, *Change of Heart*; Richard Price, *Lush Life*; Kathy Reichs, *Devil Bones*; Nora Roberts, *Tribute*; Marilynne Robinson, *Home*; Philip Roth, *Indignation*; Daniel Silva, *Moscow Rules*; Curtis Sittenfeld, *American Wife*; Nicholas Sparks, *The Lucky One*; Neal Stephenson, *Anathem*; Brad Thor, *The Last Patriot*; John Updike, *The Widows of Eastwick*; Sean Williams, *The Force Unleashed*; Tobias Wolff, *Our Story Begins*; David Wroblewski, *The Story of Edgar Sawtelle*.

POPULAR SONGS: Sara Bareilles, "Love Song"; Natasha Bedingfield, "Pocketful of Sunshine"; Chris Brown,

"Forever" and "With You"; Chris Brown, featuring T-Pain, "Kiss Kiss"; Coldplay, "Viva la Vida"; Flo Rida, featuring T-Pain, "Low"; Alicia Keys, "No One"; Leona Lewis, "Bleeding Love"; Ne-Yo, "Closer"; Katy Perry, "I Kissed a Girl"; Ray J and Yung Berg, "Sexy Can I"; Rihanna, "Disturbia," "Don't Stop the Music," and "Take a Bow"; Jordin Sparks and Chris Brown, "No Air"; T.I, "Whatever You Like"; Timbaland, featuring One Republic, "Apologize"; Usher, featuring Young Jeezy, "Love in This Club"; Lil Wayne, featuring Static Major, "Lollipop."

2009

- On April 10, the Hearst Castle in California returns two sixteenth-century Venetian oil paintings to the heirs of a Jewish couple who had the pieces confiscated from them in Nazi Germany in 1935.

- In June, Geoffrey Naylor's fountain sculpture on the campus of the University of Florida, installed in 1975, is removed and scheduled for scrapping because of years of vandalism and rising costs for restoration.

- On July 7, using funds provided by the American Economic Recovery and Reinvestment Act, the National Endowment for the Arts announces direct grants worth $29,775,000 to more than six hundred arts groups.

- On August 7, Rocco Landesman is confirmed by the Senate as chairman of the National Endowment for the Arts.

- On September 10–November 19, the Metropolitan Museum of Art displays Vermeer's masterpiece *The Milkmaid*, the first time it has been shown in the United States since the 1939 World's Fair.

- On October 15, the Margot and Bill Winspear Opera House, supporting the Dallas Opera, opens in Texas.

- On November 11, Andy Warhol's "200 One Dollar Bills" is sold for $43.7 million at Sotheby's; later in the month newspapers report that in a private sale completed the previous year Warhol's "Eight Elvises" sold for $100 million.

- On December 18, *Avatar* is released and by next year becomes the highest grossing movie ever, earning worldwide box office receipts of more than $2 billion by the end of January.

MOVIES: *Angels & Demons*, directed by Ron Howard and starring Tom Hanks, Ewan McGregor, and Ayelet Zurer; *Avatar*, directed by James Cameron and starring Zoe Saldana, Sigourney Weaver, and Sam Worthington; *The Blind Side*, directed by John Lee

Hancock and starring Quinton Aaron, Sandra Bullock, and Tim McGraw; *A Christmas Carol*, animated feature, directed by Robert Zemeckis; *Coraline*, animated feature, directed by Henry Selick; *The Hangover*, directed by Todd Phillips and starring Justin Bartha, Bradley Cooper, and Zach Galifianakis; *Harry Potter and the Half-Blood Prince*, directed by David Yates and starring Rupert Grint, Daniel Radcliffe, and Emma Watson; *Ice Age: Dawn of the Dinosaurs*, animated feature, directed by Carlos Saldanha and Mike Thurmeier; *Inglourious Basterds*, directed by Quentin Tarantino and starring Diane Kruger, Brad Pitt, and Eli Roth; *Invictus*, directed by Clint Eastwood and starring Matt Damon and Morgan Freeman; *It's Complicated*, directed by Nancy Meyers and starring Alec Baldwin, Steve Martin, and Meryl Streep; *Julie & Julia*, directed by Nora Ephron and starring Amy Adams, Chris Messina, and Meryl Streep; *Knowing*, directed by Alex Proyas and starring Rose Byrne, Nicolas Cage, and Chandler Canterbury; *Law Abiding Citizen*, directed by F. Gary Gray and starring Gerard Butler and Jamie Foxx; *Night at the Museum: Battle of the Smithsonian*, directed by Shawn Levy and starring Amy Adams, Ben Stiller, and Owen Wilson; *Precious*, directed by Lee Daniels and starring Mo'Nique, Paula Patton, and Gabourey Sidibe; *The Princess and the Frog*, animated feature, directed by Ron Clements and John Musker; *The Proposal*, directed by Anne Fletcher and starring Sandra Bullock, Ryan Reynolds, and Mary Steenburgen; *Public Enemies*, directed by Michael Mann and starring Christian Bale, Johnny Depp, and James Russo; *Sherlock Holmes*, directed by Guy Ritchie and starring Robert Downey Jr., Jude Law, and Rachel McAdams; *The Soloist*, directed by Joe Wright and starring Robert Downey Jr., Jamie Foxx, and Catherine Keener; *Star Trek*, directed by J. J. Abrams and starring Simon Pegg, Chris Pine, and Zachary Quinto; *Surrogates*, directed by Jonathan Mostow and starring Radha Mitchell, Ving Rhames, and Bruce Willis; *The Taking of Pelham 1 2 3*, directed by Tony Scott and starring Luis Guzmán, John Travolta, and Denzel Washington; *Up*, animated feature, directed by Pete Docter and Bob Peterson; *Up in the Air*, directed by Jason Reitman and starring George Clooney and Vera Farmiga; *Watchmen*, animated feature, directed by Zack Snyder; *Where the Wild Things Are*, directed by Spike Jonze and starring Catherine O'Hara, Max Records, and Forest Whitaker; *X-Men Origins: Wolverine*, directed by Gavin Hood and starring Hugh Jackman, Ryan Reynolds, and Liev Schreiber; *Zombieland*, directed by Ruben Fleischer and starring Jesse Eisenberg, Woody Harrelson, and Emma Stone.

NOVELS: Paul Auster, *Invisible*; Nicholson Baker, *The Anthologist*; David Baldacci, *First Family*; Dan Brown, *The Lost Symbol*; Jim Butcher, *Turn Coat*; Lee Child, *Gone Tomorrow*; Mary Higgins Clark, *Just Take My Heart*; Chris Cleave, *Little Bee*; Harlan Coben, *Long Lost*; Michael Connelly, *Nine Dragons* and *The Scarecrow*; Pat Conroy, *South of Broad*; Catherine Coulter, *Knockout*; Guillermo Del Toro and Chuck Hogan, *The Strain*; Janet Evanovich, *Finger Lickin' Fifteen* and *Plum Spooky*; Christine Feehan, *Dark Slayer*; Sue Grafton, *"U" Is for Undertow*; John Grisham, *The Associate*; Laurell K. Hamilton, *Skin Trade*; Charlaine Harris, *Dead and Gone*; Robert Jordan and Brandon Sanderson, *The Gathering Storm*; Jonathan Kellerman, *True Detectives*; Sherrilyn Kenyon, *Bad Moon Rising*; Stephen King, *Under the Dome*; Barbara Kingsolver, *The Lacuna*; Dean Koontz, *Relentless*; Brad Leithauser, *The Art Student's War*; Jonathan Lethem, *Chronic City*; Penelope Lively, *Family Album*; Valerie Martin, *The Confessions of Edward Day*; Colum McCann, *Let the Great World Spin*; Maile Meloy, *Both Ways Is the Only Way I Want It*; Philipp Meyer, *American Rust*; Lonnie Moore, *A Gate at the Stars*; Alice Munro, *Too Much Happiness*; Audrey Niffenegger, *Her Fearful Symmetry*; James Patterson, *I, Alex Cross*; Patterson and Richard DiLallo, *Alex Cross's Trial*; Patterson and Maxine Paetro, *The 8th Confession* and *Swimsuit*; Jayne Anne Phillips, *Lark and Termite*; Jodi Picoult, *Handle with Care*; J. D. Robb, *Promises in Death*; Nora Roberts, *Black Hills*; John Sandford, *Wicked Prey*; Joanna Scott, *Follow Me*; Daniel Silva, *The Defector*; Nicholas Sparks, *The Last Song*; Kathryn Stockett, *The Help*; Colm Toibin, *Brooklyn*; Abraham Verghese, *Cutting for Stone*; Jennifer Weiner, *Best Friends Forever*; Colson Whitehead, *Sag Harbor*.

POPULAR SONGS: The All-American Rejects, "Gives You Hell"; Beyoncé, "Single Ladies (Put a Ring on It)"; The Black Eyed Peas, "Boom Boom Pow" and "I Gotta Feeling"; Flo Rida, "Right Round"; Jamie Foxx, featuring T-Pain, "Blame It"; The Fray, "You Found Me"; Keri Hilson, featuring Kanye West and Ne-Yo, "Knock You Down"; Kings of Leon, "Use Somebody"; Lady Gaga, "Poker Face"; Lady Gaga, featuring Colby O'Donis, "Just Dance"; Jason Mraz, "I'm Yours"; Pitbull, "I Know You Want Me (Calle Ocho)"; Jay Sean, featuring Lil Wayne, "Down"; Soulja Boy Tell 'Em, featuring Sammie, "Kiss Me thru the Phone"; Taylor Swift, "Love Story" and "You Belong with Me"; T.I., featuring Rihanna, "Live Your Life"; T.I., featuring Justin Timberlake, "Dead and Gone"; Kanye West, "Heartless."

The Sopranos

Photo

By: David Chase

Date: January 10, 1999–June 10, 2007

Source: Chase, David. *The Sopranos*, January 10, 1999–June 10, 2007. www.hbo.com/the-sopranos (accessed on February 22, 2013).

About the Creator: David Chase spent his early years in television as a producer and writer on hit series such as *Northern Exposure* and *The Rockford Files*. *The Sopranos* was his second original series and earned him seven Emmy Awards.

INTRODUCTION

Originally conceived as a feature film about a mobster seeking therapy for his "mother issues," *The Sopranos* was instead adapted into a television series, produced by television veteran David Chase, who also wrote thirty of the series' eighty-six episodes.

Admittedly autobiographical at least in part, the show revolved around Italian Mafia street boss Tony Soprano, whose character was rumored to have been based loosely on real-life mobster Vincent "Vinny Ocean" Palermo, the de facto head of the DeCavalcante crime family in New Jersey. Chase's

PRIMARY SOURCE

The Sopranos

SYNOPSIS: *The Sopranos* was an HBO series that ran from 1999 to 2007 and was the most financially successful cable television series of its generation. Series stars shown here are (left to right) Michael Imperioli, James Gandolfini, Tony Sirico, and Steven Van Zandt. © HBO/THE KOBAL COLLECTION/ART RESOURCE, NY

own life experiences were reflected in some of the characters and family dynamics, and his decision to create a show about an organized crime family stemmed from an early fascination with gangster films and television shows like *The Untouchables*.

Chase and producer Brad Grey shopped the series idea around to several networks without success. As Chase explained in a *Vanity Fair* interview, "Even though it's a Mob show, *The Sopranos* is based on members of my family. It's about as personal as you can get." And personal was not what was turning profits in the land of television in the late 1990s. Neither was cinematography, another aspect of Chase's show that set it apart. He may have changed his story from a movie to a series, but keeping a cinematic feel to it was a non-negotiable point.

HBO was Chase's last resort. Knowing that the cable network was just branching out into more original programming, Chase called HBO's programming president, Chris Albrecht, a man he'd known for year. Albrecht knew he had just been handed a gift. As he told *Vanity Fair*,

> This show is about a guy who's turning 40. He's inherited a business from his dad. He's trying to bring it into the modern age. He's got all the responsibilities that go along with that. He's got an overbearing mom that he's still trying to get out from under. Although he loves his wife, he's had an affair. He's got two teenage kids, and he's dealing with the realities of what that is. He's anxious; he's depressed; he starts to see a therapist because he's searching for the meaning of his own life. I thought: The only difference between him and everybody I know is he's the don of New Jersey. So, to me, the Mafia part was sort of the tickle for why you watched. The reason you stayed was because of the resonance and the relatability of all that other stuff.

HBO was not flush with money in those days, and the show was picked up via a standard contract.

SIGNIFICANCE

With James Gandolfini starring as Tony Soprano and a strong, if not necessarily well-known, cast hand-picked by Chase, the pilot episode was shot. No one was certain it would be picked up because it was the most expensive drama on cable television and because it violated too many unspoken rules of contemporary television. Even choosing the title proved to be a challenge. HBO did not like *The Sopranos* because they felt viewers would think it was about opera. Chase stuck to his guns even as HBO pushed to call it *Family Man*, and the show debuted on January 10, 1999, to instant acclaim. Within weeks, each episode was drawing ten-million-plus viewers, with a peak audience of eighteen million during Season Four.

The entire cast became an overnight sensation. Even Steven Van Zandt, who had achieved a high level of notoriety as a guitar player with Bruce Springsteen's E Street Band since 1975, was surprised at the impact of even the first episode as people stopped him on the street to praise the show and his role in it. For HBO, the series was its saving grace; *The Sopranos* put it on the map and saved it from being known primarily by boxing fans only. Although the network never provided a specific figure, it did reveal that the show was worth "tens of millions of dollars" to HBO. Critics repeatedly labeled it one of the most influential artistic works of the decade. Television storytelling would never be the same.

The acceptance and popularity of the show opened up the door for other hard-hitting dramas to stake a claim not only on cable television, but on the regular networks. It also raised the stakes and standards for script writing. As *Sopranos* actor and sometimes-writer Michael Imperioli put it, "The thing that I take away as a writer, the whole key to David and the show's success, is detail. Nothing is left generic."

The Sopranos ran for six seasons for a total of eighty-six episodes. It earned dozens of award nominations, including twenty-one for Outstanding Writing in a Drama Series, and won seven Emmy Awards. Although it was nominated for the Primetime Emmy Award for Outstanding Drama Series every year it was eligible, it won only in 2004 and 2007, making it the first series on cable network ever to win it. The entire season was released on DVD and the show was syndicated to run on A&E at a cost of $2.6 million per episode, though the episodes had to be "sanitized" before airing.

PRIMARY SOURCE

THE SOPRANOS

See primary source photo.

FURTHER RESOURCES
Web Sites

Biskind, Peter. "An American Family." *Vanity Fair*, April 2007. www.vanityfair.com/culture/features/2007/04/sopranos200704?currentPage=1 (accessed on February 22, 2013).

Susman, Gary. "Mob Mentality." *Entertainment Weekly*, February 1, 2005. www.ew.com/ew/article/0,,1023183,00.html (accessed on February 22, 2013).

Zennie, Michael. "Woman Claims Former New Jersey Mob Boss, Inspiration for Tony Soprano, Cheated Her Out of a Strip Club and $1.3M." *Daily Mail*, October 4, 2011. www.dailymail.co.uk/news/article-2045149/Woman-claims-New-Jersey-mob-boss-inspiration-Tony-Soprano-cheated-Houston-strip-club.html (accessed on February 22, 2013).

Art21 Artists

"Maya Lin"

Web site article

By: Art21

Date: 2001

Source: "Maya Lin." *Art21*. www.art21.org/artists/maya-lin?expand=1 (accessed on March 19, 2013).

"Maya Lin: Grand Rapids Ice Rink and Park Project"

Web site article

By: Art21

Date: 2001

Source: "Maya Lin: Grand Rapids Ice Rink and Park Project." *Art21*. www.art21.org/texts/maya-lin/interview-maya-lin-grand-rapids-ice-rink-and-park-project (accessed on March 19, 2013).

"Sally Mann"

Web site article

By: Art21

Date: 2001

Source: "Sally Mann." *Art21*. www.art21.org/artists/sally-mann?expand=1 (accessed on March 19, 2013).

"Ai Weiwei"

Web site article

By: Art21

Date: 2012

Source: "Ai Weiwei." *Art21*. www.art21.org/artists/ai-weiwei?expand=1 (accessed on March 19, 2013).

About the Organization: PBS, parent of the art organization Art21, is the well-known acronym for Public Broadcasting Service, a non-profit television network in the United States. Its 354 members hold collective ownership, and together they are the most prominent provider of programs to the country's public stations PBS launched in 1970 and it became known for its family-oriented, educational programming such as *"Sesame Street,* and *Mr. Rogers' Neighborhood* as well as reliable news shows like *Frontline* and *PBS NewsHour.* The network, though consistently voted America's most-trusted national institution since the mid-2000s, came under attack frequently by conservative special-interest and political groups for being too liberal.

INTRODUCTION

PBS, long an ambassador of the arts and education, launched Art21 in 2001. According to its Web site, it is "a nonprofit contemporary art organization dedicated to introducing broad public audiences to today's visual artists—stimulating critical reflection as well as conversation through the production of films, books, multimedia and Internet-based resources, education programs, and special events."

Art21 produces its own programs and films. Before the end of the decade, it had established itself as the premiere chronicler of contemporary art and artists, and it won the coveted Peabody Award for its biennial television series, *Art in the Twenty-First Century.* In addition to its digital projects, Art21 maintained a blog, and it earned a reputation as the preeminent supplier of ideas, lesson plans, and a vast array of learning/teaching materials to art teachers and schools across the world. It hosted a year-long professional development initiative called Art21 Educators, the purpose of which was to support K-12 teachers of media arts, humanities, social studies, language arts, and visual arts. The program was run on an application basis and was sponsored in part by the National Endowment for the Arts.

Each season of Art21's PBS series comprised four episodes, each with a different theme. Each theme featured artists that fit into that niche in one way or another. Then each artist was featured on Art21's Web site with a biography and essays, images of his or her work, and a videotaped interview.

Photographer Sally Mann was featured in the first episode of the first season under the theme of Place, while architect/sculptor Maya Lin appeared in the second episode—with the theme of Identity—of that 2001 season. Photographer/sculptor Ai Weiwei was not featured until the first episode of Season 6 (2012), under the theme of Change, but most of his groundbreaking work was created in the 2000s.

Maya Lin's *Wave Field* sculpture at the Storm King Art Center in Mountainville, New York. © BOB ELAM/ALAMY.

SIGNIFICANCE

In addition to the Peabody Award, Art21 won various film, television, and art festival awards. It was an effective vehicle for giving featured artists international exposure, and for making art accessible and understandable to the general public.

In an effort to remain in the spotlight and relevant in the ever-changing world of art, Art21 developed a Facebook page, and it can be found on Twitter as well as YouTube, where it posts featured video segments from its episodes.

In 2012, Art21 was nominated for Best Documentary Series for Online Film & Video in the sixteenth annual Webby Awards for its *New York Close Up* film series. The focus of the new series was artists in the first decade of their career working in New York City. David Michel Davies, executive director of the Webby Awards, praised Art21. "Nominees like Art21 are setting the standard for innovation and creativity on the Internet. It is an incredible achievement to be selected among the best from the nearly 10,000 entries we received this year."

PRIMARY SOURCE

"MAYA LIN"

SYNOPSIS: Artist biography.

Born in 1959 in Athens, Ohio, Maya Lin catapulted into the public eye when, as a senior at Yale University, she submitted the winning design in a national competition for a Vietnam Veterans Memorial to be built in Washington, DC. She was trained as an artist and architect, and her sculptures, parks, monuments, and architectural projects are linked by her ideal of making a place for individuals within the landscape. Lin, a Chinese-American, came from a cultivated and artistic home: her father was the Dean of Fine Arts at Ohio University, and her mother is a Professor of Literature at Ohio University. Lin remarks: "As the child of immigrants, you have that sense of 'Where are you? Where's home?' And trying to make a home." She draws inspiration for her sculpture and architecture from culturally diverse sources, including Japanese gardens, Hopewell Indian earthen mounds, and works by American earth-works artists of the 1960s and 1970s. Her most recognizable work, the Vietnam Veterans Memorial, allows the names of those lost in combat to speak for themselves, connecting a tragedy that happened on foreign soil with the soil of America's capital city, where it stands. Lin lives in New York and Colorado.

PRIMARY SOURCE

"MAYA LIN: GRAND RAPIDS ICE RINK AND PARK PROJECT"

SYNOPSIS: The artist talks about various projects and her artistic influences.

ART21: What was the initial concept you had in mind for the Grand Rapids park project? What was in your mind's eye?

LIN: It's funny, whenever I start—I have no idea why I end up creating each of these site-specific works. I think [what is] atypical is that—you might look at *Eclipsed Time*, you might then go visit *The Wave Field*, or *Groundswell*, or even what's going on in Grand Rapids—materially and formally, they're very different. The mediums I use range widely, from broken glass to water to granite. And I think, formally—each time out with these large-scale works—they can look very different. But there are some very strong, underlying ideas that go throughout the works. One of them is time; one of them is an idea about landscape and the earth, or natural states or phenomena. So I think,

for me, Grand Rapids is also very contextually site-specific; it's not just a reaction to a physical site, it's the cultural site.

So, with the *The Wave Field* in Michigan, it was for an aerospace engineering building, and I had no idea what I was going to do. My site could have been in the building they were building or outside. And I just read up on aerospace and flight for three months and then came up with the idea of *The Wave Field*, which is basically a book image of a naturally occurring water wave that came about because flight requires resistance, and that led to turbulence studies, which led to fluid dynamics.

For Grand Rapids, I think I started thinking about the city and its proximity—it's two blocks away from the river that gave it its name. The Army Corps of Engineers broke the rapids, so that the city would stop flooding. I just started thinking in the back of my head about water. I think I have used water in many of my pieces, and when I'm not using water, like *The Wave Field*, it's a recreation of a water wave. *Groundswell*—the definition of ground swell is the beginning swell in the ocean before it makes a wave. And the color of the glass—I deliberately mixed two colors to get a color like water.

So, for Grand Rapids, I just started with an intuition, and I started playing with it. I'd actually started with frozen waves of earth, kind of taking where I left off with *The Wave Field*, and that grew into an early Plasticine model that deals with water fountains: one liquid, one gas, one vapor. The ice-skating rink—which I always knew was going to be a large physical part of the site—I knew would become my focal point. So, that's probably what I would say is the initial underground, subconscious idea I might be toying with. I don't think you can say, "because of this, I did this; because of this, I did that." I think art is wonderful because it's everything you've ever known and everything you've ever done, somehow percolating up, working with ideas that you might want to explore. And then you can just wake up one morning and know what you want to do—the hissing of the heat.

ART21: How much were you influenced by the Ohio mound-builder culture?

LIN: I think they were always there; there were school trips. I think there are a few things dealing with landscape that have been a very strong influence on my work. One of them is my whole southeastern Ohio topography. There were these ancient mounds built, earth mounds, effigies. Some were ones called the Serpent Mound; it is this beautiful snake. Others were just whole cities, burial mounds. And the Hopewell and Adena [traditions] made and left these two to three thousand years ago. Some are still standing. They're in cow pastures, corn fields. As a child, you knew they were there. They'd show up in someone's corn field. But oddly enough, I think influential on me was the landscape itself

A visitor at the Reynolds Gallery in Richmond, Virginia, looks at the photography of Sally Mann. Mann's work has been controversial, and Virginia governor James Gilmore sought guidelines to prevent "outrageous displays" from being displayed on state property. © AP IMAGES/RICHMOND TIMES-DISPATCH/DEAN HOFFMEYER.

in southeastern Ohio. (When everyone thinks of Ohio—and they think northern—they think Cleveland.) It is incredibly hilly, and right where I grew up, the landscape just undulates beautifully. And you really do have a sense, always, of that ground plain rising up and rolling. It's the rolling hills, and they're quite, quite luscious and quite beautiful.

But as important would probably be the fact that my dad was a potter. And my brother and I, after school—because we were at the university lab school—we'd get out of school at three o'clock and we'd have two hours in my dad's pottery studio to wait, before he was ready to go home. So, just days, hours spent playing with clay. And I think I would say that so much of my work deals with the plastic medium of clay. Water, again, is a very plastic, fluid medium. My childhood is the '60s; and the notion of what plastic, fluid, design shapes were beginning to originate out of there, again, plays into the back of your head. But I think for me, it was probably my father's potting that I would watch. That's something I really, really played with as a child and was probably more of an influence.

ART21: Are there other material influences?

LIN: No, it should be the elements. Why do some materials interest me more than others? Water is an amazing element because it can occur in three states. It can be a solid (ice), a liquid, or it can be a gas (steam). And, again, going back to science, it's probably why I wanted to become a scientist early on. The ability for water to transform or transmute itself, the fact that it can constantly be in flux as to what it is, is probably why I'm drawn to it. So, that the Grand Rapids park uses ice, vapor, and liquid—water in all its three stages—is absolutely the core idea behind that piece.

PRIMARY SOURCE

"SALLY MANN"

SYNOPSIS: Artist biography.

Sally Mann was born in 1951 in Lexington, Virginia, where she continues to live and work. She received a BA from Hollins College in 1974, and an MA in writing from the same school in 1975. Her early series of photographs of her three children and husband resulted in a series called "Immediate Family." In her recent series of landscapes of Alabama, Mississippi, Virginia, and Georgia, Mann has stated that she "wanted to go right into the heart of the deep, dark South." Shot with damaged lenses and a camera that requires the artist to use her hand as a shutter, these photographs are marked by the scratches, light leaks, and shifts in focus that were part of the photographic process as it developed during the nineteenth century. Mann has won numerous awards, including Guggenheim and National Endowment for the Arts fellowships. Her books of photographs include "Immediate Family, At Twelve: Portraits of Young Women," and "Mother Land: Recent Landscapes of Georgia and Virginia." Her photographs are in the permanent collections of many museums, including the Museum of Modern Art and Whitney Museum of American Art in New York, and Smithsonian American Art Museum in Washington, DC.

PRIMARY SOURCE

AI WEIWEI

SYNOPSIS: Artist biography

Ai Weiwei was born in Beijing, China, in 1957. An outspoken human rights activist, Ai was arrested by Chinese authorities in April 2011 and held incommunicado for three months. Upon his release, he was prohibited from traveling abroad and engaging in public speech, and he was subjected to continued government surveillance. Ai's position as a provocateur and dissident artist informs the tenor and reception of much of his recent work. He infuses his sculptures, photographs, and public artworks with political conviction and personal poetry, often making use of recognizable and historic Chinese art forms in critical examinations of a host of contemporary Chinese political and social issues. In his sculptural works he often uses reclaimed materials—ancient pottery and wood from destroyed temples—in a conceptual gesture that connects tradition with contemporary social concerns. He also employs sarcasm, juxtaposition, and repetition to reinvigorate the potency and symbolism of traditional images and to reframe the familiar with minimal means. A writer and curator, Ai extends his practice across multiple disciplines and through social media to communicate with a global public and to engage fellow artists with projects on a massive scale. Ai Weiwei attended the Beijing Film Academy and the Parsons School of Design in New York. He has received an honorary doctorate from the Faculty of Politics and

Ai Weiwei's *Fountain of Light* sculpture at the Louisiana Museum of Modern Art in Denmark. © MARTIN BRINK/ALAMY.

Social Science, University of Ghent, Belgium (2010), as well as many awards, including the Skowhegan Medal (2011) and the Chinese Contemporary Art Award (2008). His work has appeared in major exhibitions at Kunsthaus Bregenz (2011); the Victoria & Albert Museum, London (2011); Asia Society Museum, New York (2011); Tate Modern, London (2010); São Paulo Bienal (2010); Haus der Kunst, Munich (2009); Mori Art Museum, Tokyo (2009); and Documenta XII (2007). Ai Weiwei lives and works in Beijing, China.

FURTHER RESOURCES
Books

Al Weiwei. *Ai Weiwei's Blog: Writings, Interviews, and Digital Rants, 2006–2009*. Boston: MIT Press, 2011.

Lin, Maya. *Boundaries*. New York: Simon & Schuster, 2006.

Mann, Sally. *What Remains*. New York: Bullfinch, 2003.

Web Sites

Art21. http://www.art21.org/ (accessed on March 19, 2013).

Lord of the Rings Trilogy

Poster

By: Peter Jackson

Date: 2001, 2002, 2003

Source: *Lord of the Rings* Trilogy. Directed by Peter Jackson. Newline Cinema, 2001, 2002, 2003.

About the Director: Peter Jackson is a New Zealand filmmaker, whose work is characterized by dazzling special effects and epic settings. Jackson's early films were standard horror-parody trope, for which he received little praise. *Heavenly Creatures*, a dramatic fictionalization of a recent murder case in Christchurch, was Jackson's first film to attract substantial attention, which he leveraged into a winning bid on the film rights to the *Lord of the Rings* franchise, which elevated him to the peak of public recognition. He also released a film adaptation of *The Lovely Bones* and a remake of *King Kong* during the 2000s.

INTRODUCTION

Peter Jackson's adaptation of J. R. R. Tolkien's seminal *Lord of the Rings* trilogy was divided into three films, each roughly following the events of the book for which it was named: *The Fellowship of the Ring* (2001), *The Two Towers* (2002), and *The Return of the King* (2003). The films were filmed exclusively in New Zealand.

The Fellowship of the Ring was mostly expository in nature, establishing the tone and setting for the following two films. The trilogy's main protagonist, a Hobbit (small humanoid creatures) named Frodo Baggins (Elijah Wood), is introduced, as is his native country—a bucolic sea of grassy hills called "The Shire," one of many unique geographical features of the fantastical world of "Middle-earth." Frodo's uncle, a jovial adventurer-Hobbit named Bilbo, gives his nephew a magical ring that allows its bearer to become invisible. Unbeknownst to either of them, the ring had previously been used by an evil being named Sauron to conquer Middle-earth, only to have his finger severed in battle and his spirit captured in the ring, where it would dwell for as long as the ring existed. A great wizard known as Gandalf (Ian McKellen) perceives the ring's capacity for evil and convinces Frodo to flee the Shire with his Hobbit friend Samwise Gamgee (Sean Astin), knowing that Sauron's minions will soon be searching for the ring.

After Frodo and Sam depart, Gandalf consults Saruman, a more powerful wizard who imprisons

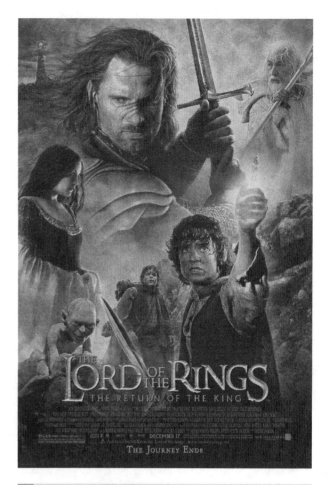

Gandalf and reveals himself to be an agent of Sauron, for whom he is assembling a massive army of Orcs (large, brutish humanoid creatures obsessed with violence) with plans of world conquest. Frodo and Sam, unexpectedly accompanied by two other Hobbits called Merry (Dominic Monaghan) and Pippin (Billy Boyd), are met by a mysterious man named Aragorn (Viggo Mortensen), who transports them to the Elven city of Rivendell, defending them from attack during the trip. Gandalf escapes his captor and convenes an emergency meeting of the governments of Middle-earth aligned against Sauron's forces of evil, where it is revealed that the ring borne by Frodo is called the One Ring, and that it must be destroyed to permanently erase Sauron's corrupting presence in Middle-earth. A group called the Fellowship of the Ring is assembled for this task, comprising the Hobbits, Gandalf,

Aragorn, an Elf named Legolas (Orlando Bloom), a man named Boromir (Sean Bean), and a Dwarf named Gimli (John Rhys-Davies).

The Fellowship sets off towards Mount Doom, a volcanic mountain in the blighted region of Mordor, home of the Orcs and the place the One Ring was forged (and thus the only place it can be destroyed). On the way, the group is attacked by a party of Orcs, followed by a fire-creature called a Balrog, which Gandalf sacrifices himself to defend the rest of the group from. Boromir attempts to convince the Fellowship that the One Ring should be used in battle against the Orcs, causing Frodo to flee with it, fearing the misappropriation of the Ring's powers. As another group of Orcs descends upon the travelers, Boromir is killed, Merry and Pippin are captured by Orcs, Samwise joins Frodo for his journey to Mount Doom, and the rest of the Fellowship follows the Orcs to rescue the captured Hobbits.

The Two Towers follows the three groups separately. Frodo and Sam, while traveling through Mordor, are beset by Gollum (Andy Serkis), a hideous creature that had once possessed the One Ring. His attempt to recover the Ring is averted, and the Hobbits convince him to guide them through the treacherous landscape of Mordor. Meanwhile, Gimli, Legolas, and Aragorn travel to the kingdom of Rohan in pursuit of the Orks holding Merry and Pippin, where they find a government torn by factional tensions and a king enchanted by one of Saruman's servants. One of the king's nephews is exiled from the country, to which he responds by rallying an army and attacking the group of Orcs holding Merry and Pippin as captives, allowing the Hobbits to escape into a forest. There they meet an ancient Ent, one of many such tree-people inhabiting the forest. While Merry and Pippin confer with the Ents, the other two Hobbits follow Gollum to a secret, unguarded entrance to the mountains of Mordor. Gollum schemes against the Hobbits, planning to kill them and reclaim his Ring.

Aragorn, Gimli, and Legolas, joined by a reincarnated Gandalf, free the people of Rohan from the control of Saruman's cohort. The king evacuates his people to Helm's Deep, a fortified city. Saruman duly sends an enormous force towards the stronghold, intent in wiping out the kingdom of Rohan. Sam, Frodo, and Gollum are captured by a group of men, who intend to transport them to a distant kingdom until Frodo demonstrates the powerful influence of the One Ring, at which point they release them. An incredible battle erupts at Helm's Deep, as Saruman's army descends upon the allied human and Elven forces

amassed there. The Ents, infuriated by the havoc wrought upon their ancient forest by Saruman's war effort, attack the Orcs from the rear, destroying a dam and drowning thousands of the creatures, leaving Saruman trapped in his tower. The allied soldiers at Helm's Deep succeed in rebuffing the siege, claiming final victory over Saruman.

The Return of the King concludes the *Lord of the Rings* saga dramatically. Gandalf proclaims that Sauron will respond to the defeat of his chief operative by attacking Gondor, a human kingdom. The reunited Fellowship (excepting Frodo and Samwise) assists in reclaiming a captured city after Sauron's evil Nazgul army overtakes it. One of the men of Gondor gives Aragorn the sword of Isildur, the man who first defeated Sauron by cutting off his finger, and to whom the ghostly Army of the Dead owes unswerving allegiance. Aragorn proves himself to be the heir of Isildur by brandishing the sword in front of the King of the Dead. At another battle in Gondor, the forces of good are saved from the brink of defeat by the arrival of the Army of the Dead, who repel the attacking Orcs.

Frodo, increasingly seduced by the power of the One Ring, abandons Sam. Sam overhears Gollum muttering about its plans to kill Frodo and reclaim the Ring, and follows the pair. Gollum tricks Frodo and leaves him to die at the hands of an enormous spider, which Sam repels, saving his friend's life. Frodo is captured by Orcs, but again rescued by Samwise, after which they continue their trek to Mount Doom. Aragorn and his followers launch an assault on the Gate of Mordor, drawing their enemies' focus away from the Hobbits as they make the final climb up Mount Doom. As they reach the mouth of the mountain, Frodo is overcome by the Ring, and refuses to destroy it until attacked by Gollum. The creature bites off Frodo's finger in an attempt to seize the ring, and they both fall towards the molten center of Mount Doom. Frodo catches a ledge and survives, but Gollum and the One Ring fall into the fire, destroying Sauron forever. The entire land of Mordor begins disintegrating.

Sam and Frodo return to The Shire after being rescued from the destruction of Mordor by a pair of giant eagles. Aragorn is crowned King of Men, and all is well in Middle-earth.

SIGNIFICANCE

Peter Jackson's *Lord of the Rings* films were among the most financially successful in the history of cinema, grossing a combined box-office total of $1,030,181,320 in the United States and $2,911,700,000 globally. Such success was to be expected, of course, considering that over $280 million were spent on the production of the films, which included hiring hundreds of extras for the huge battle scenes; constructing dozens of gigantic set-pieces, like castles and towns; digitized special effects of unprecedented scope, scale, and complexity; and shooting millions of miles of tape to create each of the three-hour-long films. All three of the films are ranked in the top 50 highest-earning movies in the world, with *The Return of the King* the highest at number six.

Fans and critics alike received the *Lord of the Rings* films favorably, despite some departures from J. R. R. Tolkien's treasured source material. The movies received overwhelmingly positive reviews, ranking among the most highly rated trilogies on both the Rotten Tomatoes and Metacritic review aggregators, along with such classics as the *Toy Story* and *Star Wars* trilogies. Casual filmgoers were wowed by the incredible special effects and massive, majestic battles, while Tolkien fans were taken with the films' high fidelity to their inspiration. The films were placed on a number of "best of" lists for the 2000s decade. *Time* magazine placed the trilogy second in its list of the decade's best films, lauding Peter Jackson's labor: "The New Zealander spent seven years on the project, chose and directed its perfect cast and orchestrated the luminous effects work, all to create a fantasy epic of tremendous scope, gravity and heart."

The *Lord of the Rings* trilogy received a total of thirty Academy Awards nominations, of which they won seventeen. *The Return of the King* was particularly well-received, winning all eleven Oscars for which it was nominated, including Best Directing, Best Picture, Best Visual Effects, and Best Editing. This achievement tied the film with *Ben-Hur* and *Titanic* for the most Academy Awards in history. Additionally, each film from the trilogy won dozens of awards from other organizations and film festivals.

Perhaps the most noteworthy aspect of the *Lord of the Rings* film trilogy was its effect of renewing popular interest in J. R. R. Tolkien's work, which had long stood among the most influential and important fantasy canons of the modern world. The movies made it more acceptable than ever for fans to discuss the exploits of elves and wizards, and to dress as such to attend the theater. The reinvigorated world of Tolkien fandom proved hugely profitable for merchandisers, who transformed the previously obscure work into one of popular culture's most prominent franchises, marketed similarly to *Star Wars* and *Harry Potter*.

PRIMARY SOURCE

LORD OF THE RINGS

See primary source photo.

FURTHER RESOURCES

Web Sites

Corliss, Richard. "Top 10 Movies of the 2000s: *The Lord of the Rings* Trilogy (2001–03)." *Time*, December 29, 2009. http://entertainment.time.com/2009/12/29/the-10-best-movies-of-the-decade/slide/the-lord-of-the-rings-trilogy-2001-03/ (accessed on March 15, 2013).

"The Lord of The Rings." *Box Office Mojo*. www.boxofficemojo.com/franchises/chart/?id=lordoftherings.htm (accessed on March 15, 2013).

"The Lord of The Rings: The Fellowship of the Ring." *IMDb: Internet Movie Database*. www.imdb.com/title/tt0120737/ (accessed on March 15, 2013).

"The Lord of The Rings: The Fellowship of the Ring." *Rotten Tomatoes*. www.rottentomatoes.com/m/the_lord_of_the_rings_the_fellowship_of_the_ring/ (accessed on March 15, 2013).

"The Lord of The Rings: The Return of the King." *IMDb: Internet Movie Database*. http://www.imdb.com/title/tt0167260/ (accessed on March 15, 2013).

"The Lord of The Rings: The Return of the King." *Rotten Tomatoes*. www.rottentomatoes.com/m/the_lord_of_the_rings_the_return_of_the_king/ (accessed on March 15, 2013).

"The Lord of The Rings: The Two Towers." *IMDb: Internet Movie Database*. www.imdb.com/title/tt0167261/ (accessed on March 15, 2013).

"The Lord of The Rings: The Two Towers." *Rotten Tomatoes*. www.rottentomatoes.com/m/the_lord_of_the_rings_the_two_towers/ (accessed on March 15, 2013).

"Book Lovers' Quarrel"

Jonathan Franzen's Dustup with Oprah Exposes the Deep Rift Between Devotees of the "Literary" and Fans of the "Popular."

Web site article

By: Laura Miller

Date: October 26, 2001

Source: Miller, Laura. "Book Lovers' Quarrel." *Salon*, October 26, 2001. www.salon.com/2001/10/26/franzen_winfrey/ (accessed on February 21, 2013).

About the Web site: *Salon* is a news site that launched in 1995. With a focus on politics and current affairs as well as reviews and articles regarding the arts, *Salon* boasts a readership of fifteen million unique visitors monthly. Its writing ranges from personal essays to bold investigative reporting, offering something for every literary taste.

INTRODUCTION

Media mogul Oprah Winfrey hosted a popular talk show—*The Oprah Winfrey Show*—that aired from September 1986 to May 2011. In 1996, she introduced Oprah's Book Club to the show. Each month for the first handful of years and then every quarter or so after that, she selected a book, almost exclusively a novel, for her viewing audience to read and discuss. In its fifteen-year run, Winfrey featured seventy books.

Having a book recommended by Winfrey practically guaranteed an immediate skyrocket in sales. Given that upwards of seven million viewers watched her talk show, it was no surprise when her recommendations increased sales sometimes by the millions. For example, when Winfrey featured the Tolstoy classic *Anna Karenina*, Penguin books immediately increased its press run by eight hundred thousand copies. In 2005, *Business Week* reported on Winfrey's clout. "Publishers estimate that her power to sell a book is anywhere from 20 to 100 times that of any other media personality."

Most authors were thrilled to hear that Winfrey was endorsing their work. Jonathan Franzen was an exception. When Winfrey chose his 2001 best-selling novel *The Corrections* for her book club, Franzen refused to let her feature it on the grounds that although she had chosen solid books with literary merit in the past, she had also been known to recommend schlock—books full of one-dimensional characters and contrived or trite plots. Another reason the author cited for not wanting to join the Oprah ranks was that his books would include the Oprah's Book Club seal on the cover.

SIGNIFICANCE

A surprised Winfrey did not let Franzen's criticism dampen her spirits, and she chose a replacement novel and moved on. Franzen apologized profusely, but in some ways, it was too late. His remarks had already painted him as a literary snob,

Jonathan Franzen, author of *The Corrections.* © AP IMAGES/ ERWIN ELSNER/PICTURE-ALLIANCE/DPA.

someone who believed the masses could not discern between pulp fiction and high-brow literature. His response to Winfrey's selection of his book opened up a firestorm of heated discussion on the purpose of literature between not only readers, but writers as well. According to a *People* magazine article, author Chris Bohjalian spoke out, saying, "I was angry on behalf of the book club. And I was appalled as a reader who appreciates the incredible amount that Oprah Winfrey has done for books." Bohjalian's own book, *Midwives*, became a Winfrey pick and sales soared from one hundred thousand copies to 1.6 million as a result.

Laura Miller's *Salon* article highlights the controversy and illustrates how divided the American reading public could be. Ironically, Winfrey eventually forgave Franzen and invited him to let her recommend his 2009 novel *Freedom*, for her club. This time, the author accepted.

According to Franzen's literary agency's Web site, *The Corrections* won the National Book Award and was translated into thirty-five languages. An international bestseller, the novel sold nearly one million hardcover copies in America alone.

"BOOK LOVERS' QUARREL"

SYNOPSIS: Jonathan Franzen's rejection of Oprah Winfrey's invitation to be an Oprah Book Club pick for his novel *The Corrections* stirred controversy among readers and writers alike.

Alas. That's the first word that came to mind when I heard that Oprah Winfrey had withdrawn her invitation to Jonathan Franzen, who was to have been the 42nd novelist to participate in her televised monthly book club.

Franzen, who had been traveling across country on a tour to promote "The Corrections," had left behind a trail of remarks made to members of the press asking how he felt to have his new novel chosen by the talk show host. Taken all together, those remarks suggest pretty strongly that Franzen considered selection for the Oprah book club to be a kind of stigma. He told the *Oregonian* that he had considered turning down the show. "She's picked some good books," Franzen said in an interview posted on Powells.com, "but she's picked enough schmaltzy, one-dimensional ones that I cringe, myself...." Although the rest of the quote read "even though I think she's really smart and she's really fighting the good fight," damage was done.

Franzen has apologized and clarified, blamed his own inexperience in handling the media and attributed his reservations to not wanting to see a "corporate logo" on the cover of his book—but it will be difficult for him to erase the impression that snobbishness caused him to diss Winfrey. And so, alas. Alas because "The Corrections" is a very fine book, one of the best I've read in several years, and Franzen is a well-intentioned, hardworking, serious and very talented writer whose work I've long admired (full disclosure: I know Franzen socially). "Oprah Winfrey is bent on demonstrating that estimates of the size of the audience for good books is too small," Franzen told the *New York Times* Wednesday, "and that is why it is so unfortunate that this is being cast as arrogant Franzen and popular Winfrey."

Fixing that bit of typecasting will be as hard as any of the "corrections" attempted by Franzen's characters, partly because there are so many people who are primed to believe the worst of him. His lapse hasn't occurred in a vacuum. America's book culture too often seems composed of two resentful camps, hunkered down in their foxholes, lobbing the occasional grenade at each other and nursing their grievances. One side sees itself as scorned by a snooty self-styled elite and the other sees itself as keepers of the literary flame, neglected by a vulgarian mainstream that would rather wallow in mediocrity and dreck. Each side remains exquisitely sensitive to perceived rejection from the other, and the fact that one is often characterized as female and the

other as male resonates with the edgy relations between the sexes of late.

This divide in the reading public is also a place where the submerged class anxieties of American life flare up. Conversations about books are often rife with silly agendas, each speaker intent on indicating just how high (or, in the case of contrarians, low) his or her brow can go. It's astonishing sometimes how dismissive and venomous readers can be when talking about authors they don't like, or think they don't like. Even if you do loathe the novels of, say, William Gass or Anne Tyler, unless you're a student you can hardly claim with any credibility that they're being thrust down your throat. Such nastiness is stupid and pointless. Film buffs got over this stuff years ago; thanks to critics like Pauline Kael, it's possible to like Bergman without having to badmouth the Farrelly brothers. In fact, it's entirely possible to enjoy both.

Furthermore, when a particular novel, like "The Corrections," comes out to almost universally positive reviews (the *New Republic*—which pursues a formulaic policy of waiting to see which novels everyone else likes so that it can run an essay about how all other critics are sadly misguided dupes—doesn't count), it and its author are regarded with not just suspicion but a kind of reflexive antipathy. Everyone's had the experience of disliking a book—or a movie, or a record—that some critic raved about; that's not what I mean. The more enthusiastic reviews a novel gets, the less convinced certain book people are that it has any merit.

You hear complaints about "hype," despite the fact that no mere novel (with the possible exception of "Hannibal") gets the kind of publicity and advertising accorded the average Hollywood movie (like, say, "Bandits"). This very invisibility is something, incidentally, that literary people always grouse about. A week after "The Corrections" debuted, a friend who works in publishing and admires the book explained, "People are sick of hearing about Franzen and will just be glad to read about something else for a change." Would those be the same people who perpetually bemoan the fact that American culture doesn't give enough weight and attention to novels? No doubt a goodly portion of the people who carped about the enthusiastic press for "The Corrections" will jump at the chance to knock Franzen for not wanting to seem too popular.

The sad and petty truth is that far too many book lovers don't really want a good book to reach a large audience because that would tarnish the aura of specialness they enjoy as connoisseurs of literary merit. I'm not just talking about egghead critics here, since there are just as many people who stand ready to condemn "hip and trendy" or "too clever" books they've never taken the trouble to read. Behind what a friend calls the "get him!

Syndrome"—that reflexive impulse to take pot shots at any author enjoying "too much" attention—lies the deeply unattractive tendency for book people to act like stingy trolls sitting atop a mound of treasure they don't want to share. If they did, it would be a lot harder to use their reading habits as a way of feeling better than other people.

What makes Franzen's gaffe so unfortunate is that "The Corrections" is the kind of book that bridges the gap between high- and middlebrow readers, between people who like brainiac puzzle novels and those who want stories of family and emotional life. Enid Lambert, the mother character in the novel, is the book's great achievement, a portrait of a sentimental Middle American woman that's smart and unflinching but ultimately sympathetic. Oprah trusted that the readers she sent to "The Corrections" would connect with that sympathy and at the same time be able to handle Franzen's sometimes savage take on contemporary life.

Franzen, by contrast, told Terry Gross on "Fresh Air" that he worried because some people at book signings (men, to be specific) had told him that they are "put off" by "Oprah books." I can't blame anyone who's heard the kind of withering jibes sometimes directed at "Oprah books" for wincing at the idea that his book might be subjected to the same. (Here's a suggestion: Only people who have never made such cracks are allowed to fulminate about Franzen's blunder.) But the truth is that you can't transcend the literary caste system while trying to cater discreetly to one faction.

Oprah's selection of "The Corrections" was a bold, generous choice for a book that is also bold and generous. If the author has on this occasion lacked the nerve and imagination of his creation, well, writers are human beings, too, and sometimes they screw up. The books are what matter, if we could just manage to remember that.

FURTHER RESOURCES
Web Sites

"Commentary: Why Oprah Opens Readers' Wallets." *BloombergBusinessweek*, October 9, 2005. http://www.businessweek.com/stories/2005-10-09/commentary-why-oprah-opens-readers-wallets (accessed on February 21, 2013).

"Jonathan Franzen." *Barclay Agency*. http://barclayagency.com/franzen.html (accessed February 21, 2013).

Schindehette, Susan. "Novel Approach." *People*, November 12, 2001. http://www.people.com/people/archive/article/0,,20135698,00.html (accessed on February 21, 2013).

Wyatt, Edward. "Tolstoy's Translators Experience Oprah's Effect." *New York Times*, June 7, 2004. http://www.nytimes.com/2004/06/07/books/tolstoy-s-translators-experience-oprah-s-effect.html (accessed on February 21, 2013).

Lost in Translation

Poster

By: Sofia Coppola

Date: 2003

Source: *Lost in Translation*. Directed by Sofia Coppola. Focus Features, 2003.

About the Director: Sofia Coppola was an American movie director, producer, screenwriter, and actress. She became the first American woman to be nominated for an Academy Award for Best Director in 2003, the same year she won the Academy Award for Best Original Screenplay for *Lost in Translation*. She was the only daughter of legendary film director Francis Ford Coppola and cousin of actor Nicolas Cage.

INTRODUCTION

Lost In Translation is the story of an unlikely friendship between two Americans who find themselves stuck in Tokyo, Japan. Bob, played by veteran actor Bill Murray, is an aging movie star who needs to make some quick cash and does so by shooting a few whiskey ads. Charlotte, played by a young Scarlett Johansson, recently graduated from college and is as uncertain of her future as she is her husband, played by Giovanni Ribisi. He leaves his wife to work on a photo shoot, which is why the couple is in Tokyo to begin with. Bob and Charlotte meet in the trendy bar of the Park Hyatt Hotel and immediately bond over a common sense of loneliness, cultural isolation and confusion, and general uncertainty.

Soon the duo is meeting every day and the platonic relationship develops as they wile away the hours at karaoke bars and find themselves on other grand adventures around the city. They seem to be falling in love with one another, though theirs is not a typical romance. In an interview with Indiewire.com, Coppola explained her decision to not make them intimate, crediting the power of the relationship in the (completely inaudible to the audience) in her ear, kisses her, and leaves.

SIGNIFICANCE

What did Bob say to Charlotte? That was the eternal question movie-goers were asking. American film critic Roger Ebert believed the movie ended just as it should. "We shouldn't be allowed to hear it. It's between them, and by this point in the movie, they've become real enough to deserve their privacy." Ebert gave the movie four stars and praised the performances of both Murray and Johansson. "I loved this movie.... I loved the way Bob and Charlotte didn't solve their problems but felt better anyway.... These are two wonderful performances. Bill Murray has never been better."

Most critics agreed with Ebert and determined *Lost in Translation* to be a subtle, successful comedy, though a handful condemned the movie for allegedly belittling the Asian culture and its people. Murray disagreed and told *The Guardian* as much, explaining that the clueless American was the true butt of the joke. "I know the Japanese are laughing more at the Americanisms than we are laughing at the Japanese-isms ... they love watching the stupidity of the foreigner in Tokyo. They're not offended at all."

Coppola would never reveal what the budget for her film was, but she made reference to it as a "couple million." Given that it earned a domestic gross in excess of $44 million in the box office, it was an impressive sophomore effort for the young director whose first film, *The Virgin Suicides*, earned her a reputation as a director to watch. Coppola was familiar with Tokyo and wanted to capture the chaos and many moods of the city. Using high-speed film to give the movie a homemade intimacy, Coppola shot the movie in twenty-seven days, sometimes without sound. Her style was to let the acting happen, not force it onto the screen. Explained Johansson to *Time* magazine, "She waited for us to have a moment instead of cutting to it. She knows what she wants, and she's not going to move on until she gets it. You're in the hands of someone who has a vision."

The vision paid off, as *Lost in Translation* won an Oscar for Best Original Screenplay in 2003. It was also nominated for Best Director, Best Picture, and Best Actor. It earned three of the five Golden Globes for which it was nominated, and earned three of the six British Academy of Film and Television Arts (BAFTA) film awards for which it was nominated. Coppola cemented her place in history as a screenwriter as well as a director as she won numerous film industry awards for Best Screenplay.

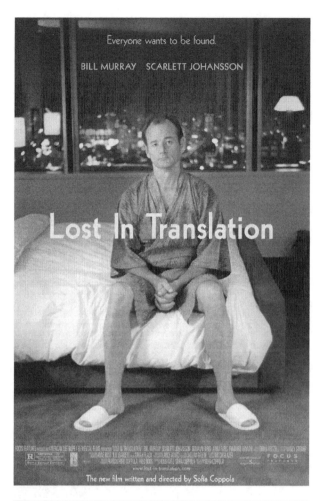

PRIMARY SOURCE

Lost in Translation

SYNOPSIS: Two lonely Americans meet by chance in a Tokyo hotel and form a unique friendship, made all the more valuable because it is destined to end. © FOCUS FEATURES/KOBAL COLLECTION/ART RESOURCE, NY

fact that it is fleeting. "I liked this relationship. I've had friends like that where you have a flirtation but you're just friends. I wanted it to be more innocent. If they slept together, that would bring in reality."

Bob ultimately meets the female vocalist of the bar and the two retreat to his room. When Charlotte arrives the next morning to ask him to have breakfast with her, she finds them and obviously feels a sense of jealousy and betrayal, despite the friends-only nature of their relationship. They reconcile later that evening, and Bob leaves for home the following morning. The two say goodbye in the hotel lobby, but while in the taxi on the way to the airport, Bob notices Charlotte on the sidewalk and tells the driver to stop. Bob goes to her, whispers something

LOST IN TRANSLATION

See primary source photo.

FURTHER RESOURCES

Web Sites

Betts, Kate. "Sofia's Choice." *Time*, September 15, 2003. www.time.com/time/magazine/article/0,9171,1005674-1,00.html (accessed on March 12, 2013).

Ebert, Roger. "Lost in Translation." *Chicago Sun-Times*, September 12, 2003. http://rogerebert.suntimes.com/apps/pbcs.dll/article?AID=/20030912/REVIEWS/309120302/1023 (accessed on March 12, 2013).

Macnab, Geoffrey. "'I Know How to Be Sour.'" *The Guardian*, December 31, 2003. www.guardian.co.uk/film/2004/jan/01/1 (accessed on March 12, 2013).

Mitchell, Wendy. "Sofia Coppola Talks About 'Lost in Translation,' Her Love Story That's Not 'Nerdy.'" *Indiewire*, February 4, 2004. www.indiewire.com/article/sofia_coppola_talks_about_lost_in_translation_her_love_story_thats_not_nerd (accessed on March 12, 2013).

A History of Violence

Poster

By: David Cronenberg

Date: 2005

Source: *A History of Violence*. Directed by David Cronenberg. 20th Century Fox.

About the Director: David Cronenberg is a Canadian filmmaker, known best for his exceptional screenwriting and directing. Cronenberg's early work is characterized as "body horror," a genre focusing on unsettling transformations or changes of its characters. Science fiction elements were frequently incorporated into such films as *The Fly*, *Naked Lunch*, and *Dead Ringers*, while Cronenberg's later work dealt more realistically with the concept of human change, through psychologically probing thrillers such as *A History of Violence*, *A Dangerous Method*, and *Cosmopolis*. Cronenberg is widely considered one of the best directors of his era, having received recognition from numerous film societies and even the government of

A History of Violence

SYNOPSIS: A man's act of righteous violence forces him to confront a hidden past. © NEW LINE PRODUCTIONS/KOBAL COLLECTION/ART RESOURCE, NY

his home country, which made him an Officer of the Order of Canada in 2002.

INTRODUCTION

Released in September 2005, *A History of Violence* was a critically acclaimed examination of violence as a means of conflict resolution and its role in human identity. The screenplay was loosely adopted from a 1997 graphic novel of the same name.

The film follows demure Tom Stall (Viggo Mortensen), who operates a diner in the rural town of Millbrook, Indiana. Millbrook is depicted as the idyllic manifestation of small-town U.S.A., inhabited by pleasant characters and free of tension or discontent. The placid atmosphere is disrupted by a pair of fugitive murderers, who enter Tom's diner as it is closing. When a waitress attempts to go home for the night, one of the men threatens her with a gun, expressing his intent to kill her and rob Tom's business. Tom reacts decisively, unexpectedly disarming the man with the gun and shooting both criminals to death. Although he is heralded as a hero, Tom does his best to avoid media attention and downplay the significance of his actions. He is unsuccessful in escaping all media exposure, however.

The day after the incident, three unfamiliar characters enter Tom's diner, addressing him as "Joey Cusack." A man named Fogarty (Ed Harris), apparently the leader of the group, makes increasingly ominous statements until Tom threatens to call the police, at which point the group departs. Following an encounter with the men, the town sheriff warns Tom that they appear to be involved in organized crime and that there is an influential mob boss named Richie Cusack in Philadelphia. While shopping, Tom's wife Edie (Maria Bello) is approached by the gangsters, who begin interrogating her about her husband and Richie Cusack (William Hurt), to whom they imply that Tom is related, although she is unable to answer any of their questions satisfactorily. The gangsters proceed to kidnap Tom's son Jack (Ashton Holmes), using the boy to lure Jack to their car. When one of them points a gun at Tom, he deftly breaks the man's arm, snatching the gun and using it to kill him and one of his companions. Fogarty shoots Tom in the chest before he has the chance to turn his weapon on the surviving gangster. As he prepares to kill Tom, Fogarty is fatally shot in the back by Jack, who had retrieved his father's shotgun from the house.

While her husband is in the hospital recovering from his gunshot wound, Edie demands the truth from Tom, who admits that when he was young he had been Joey Cusack, a hitman for an Irish criminal family in Philadelphia. He only quit, he says, when he crossed Fogarty and began fearing for his safety. Edie is visibly unsettled by the revelation, but still helps protect him from the scrutiny of the local sheriff. One night, as Tom lies in bed, he receives a phone call from Richie Cusack, who reveals that he is, in fact, Tom's brother, and beckons him to visit Philadelphia. Tom consents, departing immediately. Upon his arrival at his brother's mansion, he discovers that Richie had been penalized by the mob for Tom's youthful transgressions, and that the only way to make amends was for Richie to kill him. An accomplice attacks Tom, but is quickly foiled. Two more would-be assassins are neutralized by Tom, who then shoots Richie in the head, killing him. Tom returns home to find his family

preparing the table for dinner, which he eats with them in the last scene of the film.

SIGNIFICANCE

A History of Violence was lauded by critics as one of the best films of 2005, receiving particular praise for its character development and complexity. *Rolling Stone* film critic Peter Travers placed the movie fourth on his list of the top ten best films of the decade, while Roger Ebert applauded Cronenberg's execution of a complex message through simple methods. Many reviews highlighted the film's ability to expose the contradictions of violence in human culture while still managing to deliver excitement and traditional, theatrical suspense—as *New York Times* film critic Manohla Dargis put it, *A History of Violence* was "a masterpiece of indirection and pure visceral thrills ... the feel-good, feel-bad movie of the year." The film fared reasonably well at the box office, generating $31,504,633 in gross domestic revenue and $29,236,194 more internationally.

The film was one of the most popular and successful of director David Cronenberg's career, garnering not only critical acclaim but substantial public recognition. It was nominated for seventy-one total film industry awards—including two Oscars, one for screenwriter Josh Olson's adaptation script and another for William Hurt's portrayal of supporting character Richie Cusack—winning thirty-five of them, including Best Picture and Best Director awards at the 9th Toronto Film Critics Association Awards and *Village Voice* Film Poll. Cronenberg directed two other movies during the 2000s: *Spider* (2002) and *Eastern Promises* (2007), but neither of them managed to achieve the level of success reached by *A History of Violence*.

◼ PRIMARY SOURCE

A HISTORY OF VIOLENCE

See primary source photo.

◼

FURTHER RESOURCES
Web Sites

Ebert, Roger. "A History of Violence." *Chicago Sun-Times.* http://rogerebert.suntimes.com/apps/pbcs.dll/article?AID=/20050922/REVIEWS/50919002/1023 (accessed on March 14, 2013).

"A History of Violence." *Box Office Mojo.* www.boxofficemojo.com/movies/?id=historyofviolence.htm (accessed on March 14, 2013).

"A History of Violence." *Internet Movie Database.* IMDb. www.imdb.com/title/tt0399146 (accessed on March 14, 2013).

"A History of Violence." *Metacritic.* http://www.metacritic.com/movie/a-history-of-violence (accessed on March 14, 2013).

"Ten Best Movies of the Decade." *Rolling Stone.* www.rollingstone.com/movies/lists/10-best-movies-of-the-decade-19691231 (accessed on March 14, 2013).

There Will Be Blood

Poster

By: Paul Thomas Anderson

Date: 2007

Source: *There Will Be Blood.* Original release 2007. Paramount Vantage Miramax Films. Directed by Paul Thomas Anderson.

About the Director: Paul Thomas Anderson is an American film director, script writer, and producer. Of the six movies he has written and directed, three (*Boogie Nights*, *Magnolia*, and *There Will Be Blood* have been nominated for various Academy Awards, including Best Original Screenplay and Best Motion Picture of the Year. Anderson's name has been included on numerous "Best Director" lists, and in 2012, *The Guardian* hailed him as one of the best film directors in the world for his dedication to the craft and disdain for being in the spotlight.

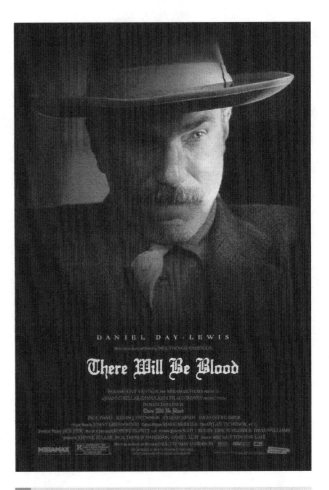

■ PRIMARY SOURCE

There Will Be Blood

SYNOPSIS: A rags-to-riches story of biblical proportions becomes a dark and twisted tale of greed and corruption. © PARAMOUNT/VANTAGE/THE KOBAL COLLECTION/ART RESOURCE, NY

INTRODUCTION

There Will Be Blood was a dark recasting, a sort of twisted transformation, of the age-old theme of the American Dream. Using the Southern California oil boom of the late 1800s and early 1900s, director Paul Thomas Anderson told a story of greed and envy based loosely on the 1926 Upton Sinclair novel *Oil!*

Award-winning actor Daniel Day Lewis portrays Daniel Plainview, the film's wicked, emotionally void oil speculator whose greed and unethical business practices wreak havoc on the majority of everyone he comes in contact with, including the son (H. W.) he adopts when one of his employees is killed in a drilling accident. Plainview's is a rags-to-riches story that begins in 1898 in the New Mexico wilderness, where he blasts a small mine and finds silver ore. Hiring his

own crew, Plainview then strikes oil and completely reinvents himself as an oil man. Nine years pass and he has numerous productive wells around New Mexico, where he travels with his son to buy drilling rights to private property.

A shady businessman, Plainview is basically run out of a small town when locals begin questioning his claims and promises, but he eventually meets with a reluctant couple and negotiates a contract to drill on their land, which proves to be oil-rich. Soon after, a young man named Paul Sunday (played by up-and-comer Paul Dano) approaches Plainview with information to sell. He tells Plainview of a California town called Little Boston, which he knows sits on a promising oil supply. Plainview consults with Sunday's father and twin brother, Eli, a local preacher and faith healer of questionable integrity. Eli agrees to take half of the $10,000 up front and the other half once the derrick proves viable. The money will be used to build a new church.

Plainview tries to buy all the land surrounding the Sunday ranch so that he can own all drilling rights as well as the option to build a pipeline to the ocean so as to circumvent the need to use the new railroads to ship his oil. Everyone agrees to sell except a man named William Bandy. Plainview takes what he can get and builds his first derrick, which strikes oil and causes an explosion that causes H. W. to lose his hearing. The boy becomes sullen, a condition worsened by the appearance of a man named Henry (played by Kevin O'Connor) who claims to be Plainview's half-brother. In a jealous retaliation, H. W. sets fire to the house where Plainview and Henry are sleeping. Both men escape and H. W. is sent away to boarding school.

In time, Plainview owns three successful oil wells in Little Boston, and Eli demands his $5,000, which gets him nothing but a beating at the hands of a vengeful Plainview. The two men irritated one another from their first meeting, primarily because Plainview is a godless man and views Eli with distrust. He mocks the defeated preacher and asks why, if he could truly heal others, he did nothing to restore H. W.'s hearing.

Plainview soon becomes suspicious of Henry's identity and murders him when the man confesses to be Henry's brother. He buries the dead man in Bandy's backyard, and the next day, Bandy tells Plainview that he knows what happened. Using this information, he blackmails Plainview into leasing Bandy's land on the condition that Plainview be baptized at Eli Sunday's church. Eli first humiliates the greedy Plainview and then announces to the congregation that the newest member has donated $5,000, thereby collecting the money Plainview had once promised but then refused to deliver.

Plainview succumbs to alcoholism, and the movie finishes with a shocking scene of violence between Plainview and Eli.

SIGNIFICANCE

There Will Be Blood garnered high praise from critics and viewers alike as it grossed over $40 million in theaters across the nation for a total gross in excess of $76 million worldwide.

The movie became a *New York Times* Critics' Pick, and reviewer Manohla Dargis credited director Anderson's professional growth for the film's success. "This is Mr. Anderson's fifth feature and it proves a breakthrough for him as a filmmaker.... *There Will Be*

Blood exhibits much the same qualities as Mr. Anderson's previous work—every shot seems exactly right—but its narrative form is more classical and less weighted down by the pressures of self-aware auteurism."

American film critic Roger Ebert described his movie-going experience this way: "Watching the movie is like viewing a natural disaster that you cannot turn away from.... It is a force beyond categories. It has scenes of terror and poignancy, scenes of ruthless chicanery, scenes awesome for their scope, moments echoing with whispers and an ending that in some peculiar way this material demands...." Ebert determined that while the film could easily be called great by many, he was not convinced of its greatness, though he gave the movie three-and-a-half out of four stars.

The hauntingly memorable film found its way onto many "best of 2007" lists, and it was included on the American Film Institute's Ten Movies of the Year list. The movie itself was nominated for dozens of awards and won many, as did Daniel Day-Lewis and Paul Thomas Anderson. Day-Lewis walked away with the year's Academy Award for Best Actor and the Golden Globe Award for Best Actor in a Motion Picture.

PRIMARY SOURCE

THERE WILL BE BLOOD

See primary source photo.

FURTHER RESOURCES
Books
Sinclair, Upton. *Oil!* New York: Albert & Charles Boni, 1926.

Web Sites
Catterall, Ali, Charlie Lyne, Gwilym Mumford, and Damon Wise. "The 23 Best Film Directors in the World Today." *The Guardian*, August 31, 2012. http://www.guardian.co.uk/film/2012/sep/01/best-film-directors-world-2012 (accessed on March 11, 2013).

Dargis, Manohla. "An American Primitive, Forged in a Crucible of Blood and Oil." *New York Times*, December 26, 2007. http://movies.nytimes.com/2007/12/26/movies/26bloo.html?pagewanted=all&_r=0 (accessed on March 11, 2013).

Ebert, Roger. "There Will Be Blood." *Roger Ebert Rogerebert.com*, January 4, 2008. http://www.rogerebert.com/apps/pbcs.dll/article?AID=/20080103/REVIEWS/801030301/1023 (accessed on March 11, 2013).

"Teens Buying Books at Fastest Rate in Decades"

New 'Golden Age of Young Adult Literature' Declared

Newspaper article

By: Cecelia Goodnow

Date: March 7, 2007

Source: Goodnow, Cecelia. "Teens Buying Books at Fastest Rate in Decades." *Seattle Post-Intelligencer*, March 7, 2007. www.seattlepi.com/ae/books/article/ Teens-buying-books-at-fastest-rate-in-decades-1230449. php#page-1 (accessed on February 27, 2013).

About the Author: Cecelia Goodnow was a reporter for the *Seattle Post-Intelligencer* from 1983 to 2009, where she produced more than twelve hundred bylined articles. Her reporting included Life and Arts, Parent and Family, Children's Book Reviews, and general topics with an emphasis on health, social issues, education, and cultural trends. Goodnow's May 2008 front-page article "Indiana Jones and the Legend of the Obsessed Fan" generated nearly thirty-eight thousand one-day page views, and this article on teen reading was among the top 10 emailed stories at *Seattle P-I* for two weeks, giving the newspaper uncharacteristic national exposure. The *Post-Intelligencer* started as a newspaper in 1863 and became an online-only medium on March 18, 2009.

INTRODUCTION

Given that the young adult literature market was a multi-billion dollar business by the beginning of the twenty-first century, it may be difficult to imagine that it was ever a struggling industry, or that it is, relatively speaking, a young one. As a genre, Young Adult (YA) was formally recognized in the 1950s, with J. D. Salinger's novel *The Catcher in the Rye* (1951) marking the transition. S. E. Hinton's groundbreaking novel *The Outsiders* (1966) and Paul Zindel's *The Pigman* (1968) further solidified the foundation of this new category of fiction. These were books written for and about adolescents, and they dealt with topics and issues modern teens continue to face: substance use, suicide, gangs, and self-identity crises.

YA literature largely consisted of coming-of-age novels, with authors like Judy Blume and Robert Cormier leading the way throughout the 1970s. Blume's controversial coming-of-age novel *Are You There God? It's Me, Margaret* (1970) was written for the nine-to-twelve-year-old market, but adult outcry over the book's frank discussion of sexuality, challenge to religion, and inappropriate behavior of characters landed the book on the American Library Association's list of the top one hundred most frequently challenged books. Her next novel, *Forever* (1975), was one of the most-banned books in history for its depiction of sexual intercourse and treatment of teen pregnancy and birth control. Likewise, Cormier's *The Chocolate War* (1974) had the honor of topping the ALA's list of most-censored books for two decades because of its language, violence, and a general disrespect for authority. In the novel, protagonist Jerry refuses to sell chocolates to raise money for his school and a violent series of events follows.

Problem novels gave way to romance in the YA genre in the early 1980s, but the end of the decade saw a rise in the interest of thriller, suspense, and mystery. Author R. L. Stine was the king of young adult horror/ thriller with his *Fear Street* and then *Goosebumps* series, which saturated the YA market from 1989 to 1998. Lois Lowry gave young readers something to think about when she debuted the first novel in her series about a dystopian society in 1994. *The Giver* was published to great acclaim, and sold more than five million copies by the end of 2012. In 1997, British author J. K. Rowling introduced the *Harry Potter* series with *Harry Potter and the Philosopher's Stone* and YA literature took an immediate turn as a relatively quiet decade for the genre exploded. The second book of the series was published in the United States in June 1999 and debuted at the top of three best-seller lists, including that of the *New York Times*. The third novel followed the same debut pattern in September of that year and it became official: America's young adults were reading again.

SIGNIFICANCE

As Rowling published the remaining four novels in the *Harry Potter* series, interest in magic and the supernatural remained strong. The novels were adapted to film, and by 2011, the *Harry Potter* brand was valued in excess of $15 million. In 2005, romance and the supernatural combined in the Stephenie Meyer series of *Twilight* books. So popular were her four novels—and their resulting movies—that vampire fantasy became its own subgenre in YA fiction. The common theme of fantasy and the supernatural ignited an instant and significant flame in the world of teen reading. Throughout the decade, supernatural fiction was the trend, whether characters be fairies, were-wolves, vampires, ghosts, or zombies. And for the most part, these fictitious tales involved romance and the inevitable result—sex.

Two teenagers make their selections at a bookstore. Young Adult readership increased in the first decade of the twenty-first century. © KEITH MORRIS/ALAMY.

In an interview with GreatSchools, San Francisco librarian Jennifer Collins explained that modern YA literature explores basically the same themes as it did in the 1960s and 1970s, but it does so in a more graphic and detailed manner. "In the past five years more books push the limit to explore themes of at-risk teens and teens on the edge." This has been the role of YA literature, historically, dating back as far as the premiere YA novel, *The Catcher in the Rye*. Has there ever been a character more angst-ridden and sexually obsessed than Holden Caulfield? Author Barbara Feinberg weighed in. "*The Catcher in the Rye* is beautiful and subtle.... Now, a lot of young adult books have a pared down quality. They feel more like TV. It's all about the issue." Powells Books bookseller Danielle Marshall agreed. "Some very adult topics are being presented to kids.... Explicit sex is pretty much something you don't want your middle-schooler reading about."

Not all in the book industry agreed. Bookseller Jill Saginaro admitted that YA fiction in the 2000s pushed the boundaries, but insisted that the majority of it was not scandalous. "Five to 10 years ago, YA was hampered by dark stuff, but now I'm proud of the direction it's going in," she told GreatSchools. "Many of the old books for boys were about sports ... they were shallow and perpetuated a stereotype of boys.... Now I'm seeing more complex characters."

Author David Levithan, who wrote the best-selling novel *Nick & Norah's Infinite Playlist*, celebrated the era as "the second golden age for young-adult books ... the most exciting time for young-adult literature since the late 1960s and 1970s...." Whatever the reason—a wider variety of topics and issues,

publishing houses that have finally recognized the value of the 12–18-year-old reader, edgier writing, securing its own space in public libraries—YA literature enjoyed a heyday at the end of the twentieth century, and it showed no signs of slowing down as the new millennium dawned.

PRIMARY SOURCE

"TEENS BUYING BOOKS AT FASTEST RATE IN DECADES"

SYNOPSIS: Young adult readers are reading more—and more sophisticated—literature after book sales experienced a slump in the 1990s.

Like a lot of teens, Leslie Cornaby has a crowded schedule—her days crammed with homework, hobbies and an array of techno diversions. When she's not checking e-mail, she's cruising YouTube or scrolling her iPod to tunes by Pink or Christina Aguilera.

She's also reading—just for the glorious fun of it—and says, "Most of my friends are readers, too."

The Shorecrest High School sophomore may not realize it, but she's enjoying the fruits of one of the most fertile periods in the history of young adult literature.

It's a time of strong writing and strong sales as readers in the 12-to-18 age group rock the marketplace.

"Kids are buying books in quantities we've never seen before," said *Booklist* magazine critic Michael Cart, a leading authority on young adult literature. "And publishers are courting young adults in ways we haven't seen since the 1940s."

Credit a bulging teen population, a surge of global talent and perhaps a bit of Harry Potter afterglow as the preteen Muggles of yesteryear carry an ingrained reading habit into later adolescence.

Not only are teen book sales booming—up by a quarter between 1999 and 2005, by one industry analysis—but the quality is soaring as well. Older teens in particular are enjoying a surge of sophisticated fare as young adult literature becomes a global phenomenon.

All of which leads Cart to declare, "We are right smack-dab in the new golden age of young adult literature."

REBIRTH BEGAN AFTER 1990S

It's a welcome development in a field that has seen ups and downs since the salad days of the 1970s—the era of greats such as Judy Blume ("Forever") and Robert Cormier ("The Chocolate War"). By the 1990s, critics said teen fiction had grown tired and formulaic.

Now comes the rebirth.

Fantasy and graphic novels are especially hot, and adventure, romance, humor and gritty coming-of-age tales remain perennial favorites. In addition, racy series such as "The Gossip Girls"—often likened to a teen "Sex and the City"—have created a buzz.

More notably, though, there's a new strain of sophistication and literary heft as publishers cater to the older end of the spectrum with books that straddle teen and adult markets.

King County librarian Holly Koelling has been tracking these trends as she writes an upcoming edition of "Best Books for Young Adults," an American Library Association reference book.

"There has been an increase in the age of the protagonist, the complexity of the plotting and the content—the gravity of the content," Koelling said. "I think it may be a reflection of a more sophisticated teenage population."

That's welcome news given the recent gloomy update from the National Assessment of Educational Progress, which found that 12th-graders nationally scored lower in reading in 2005 than in 1992, with scores virtually unchanged since 2002.

Declines were seen at all levels except the top 10th percentile of students—the teens who presumably make up a good share of the book-buying public.

The teens who *are* reading welcome the growing sophistication of young adult literature.

"Chick lit and a lot of the 'teen books' out there are great for vacation or a quick read," said Jennifer Schmidt, 15, part of the Shoreline library's Teen Advisory Group, "but I think there are a lot of teens out there who like reading stuff that's a little deeper."

Take a look at the *New York Times* children's bestseller list.

At No. 7, holding strong after 46 weeks, is "The Book Thief," a Holocaust tale narrated by Death and written with stunning beauty by a young Aussie author, Markus Zusak. It was published in Australia as an adult title.

At No. 5 is Ellen Hopkins' new novel, "Impulse," the tale of three suicidal teens who meet at a psychiatric hospital. Like her meth-addiction novel, "Crank," it's written in a challenging format—free-verse poetry.

Then there's "Octavian Nothing: Traitor to the Nation," the 2006 National Book Award winner for Young People's Literature.

Set in Revolutionary War–era Boston, it's a searing, audacious tale of racial experimentation that the author describes as part of "a 900-page, two-volume historical epic for teens, written in a kind of unintelligible 18th-century Johnsonian-Augustan prose."

Obviously, teen lit is fast outgrowing its bobby socks.

"It's not just 'Sweet Valley High' right now," said Hayden Bass, a librarian at the Seattle Public Library's downtown Teen Center. "The quality has been pushed way up."

TURNAROUND REASONS CITED

As for which came first—the surge in quality or the receptive audience—no one is entirely sure.

"It's both at once," said Nancy Hinkel, publishing director at Knopf Books for Young Readers. She likens the phenomenon to a "snake that's swallowing its tail."

Reflecting the field's growing stature, the National Book Foundation in 1996 expanded the National Book Award to include not only fiction, non-fiction and poetry, but also a category for Young People's Literature.

Four years later the American Library Association created the Michael L. Printz Award for Excellence in Young Adult Literature—big brother to the better-known Newbery and Caldecott medals for younger readers.

Pierce County librarian Judy Nelson, president of the national Young Adult Library Services Association, said the move reflects the "ever-increasing volume of excellent literature for teens."

Today's creative ferment is a sharp change from just a decade ago, when Cart warned that young adult literature was being gutted by chain-store marketers who were supplanting librarians and editors as arbiters of taste.

Horror and other pulp series prevailed, most titles were aimed at ages 11 to 14, and older teens were becoming an "endangered species" in the marketplace, Cart chided in his 1996 book, "From Realism to Romance: 50 Years of Change and Growth in Young Adult Literature."

Reached by phone in Indiana, Cart laughed softly and said, "That was then and this is now."

There are many reasons for the turnaround, not least the sheer size of the teen population—well over 30 million kids with ready cash in their pockets. Called Gen Y or Millennials, they trail only the baby boomers in number.

"The publishing world has recognized that teens have a lot of disposable income, and they're willing to spend it," Nelson said. "They buy books. They (especially) buy paperbacks."

They also visit the library. In the King County Library System, teen fiction now circulates at a higher rate than adult fiction.

"In the summertime, the shelves in my teen section are almost empty, which is great!" said librarian Rick Orsillo of King County's Shoreline branch.

The staying power of books is especially remarkable given the lure of YouTube, MySpace and other techie diversions. Shrewdly, the book world is meeting teens on their own turf, with libraries creating MySpace pages and publishers advertising on popular teen sites.

Noting that the Web has been used to "hype, announce and promote books," Cornaby, 16, the Shorecrest 10th-grader, said, "I don't have to go to my school's library anymore to find out what the latest books are, and I can also get a book on audio and put it on my iPod if I really want to."

SEEKING TEEN INPUT

Finally, teens are actively shaping the literary scene, as more libraries—including the Seattle Public Library—form teen advisory groups to attract young readers and help influence collections.

Publishers sometimes use them as focus groups, and the American Library Association solicits teen input before it votes on its annual list of Best Books for Young Adults.

In January, the Best Books panel, meeting at the ALA conference in Seattle, heard from about 40 Northwest teens—many of them from the Shoreline group led by Orsillo, a member of the panel.

Zeno Dellby, 16, with a gray watch cap pulled down around his ears, marched to the microphone to support crowd favorite "Octavian Nothing," saying, "I thought it was wonderfully grim and unusual."

Victor Li, 17, panned "Inside Delta Force," saying, "The writing was slow-paced. It just dragged on."

Feather Osborn, 15, pitched "Wintersmith," wooed by the humor of satirist Terry Pratchett. "Terry Pratchett," she said, "is simply a comic genius."

Their comments wowed Angelina Benedetti, a King County libraries manager and Printz Award panelist. She said later she was shocked the teens talked more about "Octavian Nothing" than stereotypical chick lit.

"They finally have something to challenge them," she said. "It is really a golden age."

FURTHER RESOURCES
Books
Cart, Michael. *Young Adult Literature: From Romance to Realism*. Chicago: ALA Editions, 2010.

Periodicals
Reno, Jamie. "Generation R (R Is for Reader)." *Newsweek*, May 13, 2008. *The Daily Beast* www.thedailybeast.com/

newsweek/2008/05/13/generation-r-r-is-for-reader. html (accessed on February 27, 2013).

Web Sites
"Cecelia Goodnow." *Goodnow Communications.* http://ceceliagoodnow.com/resume.html (accessed on February 27, 2013).

Kavner, Lucas. "Lois Lowry, 'Son' and 'The Giver' Author, Reflects on Dystopian Novels, Psychopaths, and Why Kids Make the Best Audiences." *Huffington Post*, October 5, 2012. www.huffingtonpost.com/2012/10/04/lois-lowry-the-giver-son_n_1940969.html (accessed on February 27, 2013).

"Panel Explores Trends in Young Adult Literature." *Fordham Notes*, November 30, 2012. http://fordham-notes.blogspot.com/2012/11/panel-explores-trends-in-young-adult.html (accessed on February 27, 2013).

Wilde, Marian. "Young Adult Lit Grows Up Fast." *Great-Schools.* www.greatschools.org/students/books/609-young-adult-fiction.gs (accessed on February 27, 2013).

"Young Adult Banned Books." *Marquette University.* www.marquette.edu/library/lor/banned-books-week/children.shtml (accessed on February 27, 2013).

The Hurt Locker

Poster

By: Mark Boal

Date: 2008

Source: *The Hurt Locker*. Directed by Kathryn Bigelow. Universal Studios, 2008.

About the Writer: Mark Boal is a freelance journalist whose articles have appeared in publications such as *Rolling Stone* and *Playboy*. An embedded journalist with the U.S. Army during the Iraq War, Boal wrote of the mysterious disappearance of war veteran Specialist Richard Davis in the article "Death and Dishonor." The piece served as the basis for the screenplay that eventually became the 2007 film, *In the Valley of Elah*. Boal wrote *The Hurt Locker* around a fictitious set of characters and events he created based on interviews and observations of Iraq.

INTRODUCTION
American film critic Roger Ebert began his review of *The Hurt Locker* with this: "A lot of movies begin with poetic quotations, but 'The Hurt Locker' opens

PRIMARY SOURCE

The Hurt Locker

SYNOPSIS: Written by an Iraq War journalist, this film depicted the experiences of a fictitious bomb disposal team during the war. © FIRST LIGHT PRODUCTIONS/KINGSGATE FILMS/THE KOBAL COLLECTION/ART RESOURCE, NY

with a statement presented as fact: 'War is a drug.'" Writer Mark Boal used his experiences as a war journalist to write a screenplay that paints a portrait of a group of three elite American bomb squad technicians whose job every day is to disarm roadside explosives in war-torn Baghdad. Although fictitious, the characters and events of *The Hurt Locker* are based on fact. And Boal explicitly demonstrates how, for some, the ever-present dangers and thrills of war can become addicting. It is that addiction—the danger of that addiction—that drives the film.

The term "hurt locker" is soldier vernacular for the place "you don't want to be," as writer Boal explained to BBC News. "If a bomb goes off, you're going to be in the hurt locker. That's how they used it in Baghdad. It means slightly different things to different people, but all the definitions point to the same idea." A simple film title, it in no way gave the viewer a hint of what was in store, for the film's violent action and tension were consistent and pervasive, setting the pace and maintaining it until the very end.

Although the movie had premiered in Venice in 2008, it did not hit American theaters until 2009. By that time, America had been fighting the war in Iraq for about six years. Everyone knew someone who was fighting, had fought, or had died. The war had divided the nation politically, and any movie about the war shown at that time ran the risk of increasing that divisiveness. But that was the surprise and allure of *The Hurt Locker*: It seemed to bring into question not the morality of war, or the justification for war, but the effects of war. Staff Sergeant William James, leader of the three-man bomb squad, lives for his job. He loves that one wrong move can mean the end; the thrill of that challenge is what drives him. It is that focus that director Kathryn Bigelow chose to emphasize. She asked the audience: Is James insane or just remarkably courageous? Is there a difference? Does it matter when it comes to war? The movie, as a result, though action-oriented, came off as a meditation on human nature, albeit one portrayed in the chaotic throes of combat.

SIGNIFICANCE

Film critic Richard Roeper hailed *The Hurt Locker* as "one of the best films of the year." Film critics ranked it in their Top 10 lists more often than any other movie of 2009, and it won in six of the nine categories—including Best Picture, Best Director, and Best Original Screenplay—for which it was nominated at the Academy Awards that year. Costing a mere $11 million to make, the movie had the honor of being, as of February 2013, the lowest-grossing film ever to win an Oscar for Best Picture. At the time of its nomination, it had grossed $12.6 million domestically. That number increased to $14.7 by the time the Oscar was awarded.

The movie made a name for director Kathryn Bigelow in particular. Hers was the first Oscar ever awarded to a female director; the Directors Guild of America honored her with the Award for Outstanding Achievement as well. Again, it was the first time a female director had ever won. Bigelow won the Washington DC Area Film Critics award for Best Director as well as Best Director award from the British Academy of Film and Television Arts. Like the movie itself, she received dozens of awards in recognition of her excellence.

By choosing to film the movie in Jordan, where the weather and geography is like that of Baghdad, Bigelow infused the project with authenticity. The heat was oppressive and made wearing bomb suits and camouflage a brutal experience. The cast and crew worked twelve-hour days, a grueling schedule under even the best circumstances. To give the viewing audience a sense of immediacy, Bigelow chose to capture multiple perspectives using Super 16 mm cameras. "That is how we experience reality: You look at the microcosm and the macrocosm simultaneously—in detail and in a bigger sweep," she explained in an *American Cinematographer* interview. This technique proved to be a double-edged sword. It gave the movie a documentary-like quality, but that fact caused many viewers to misinterpret what they were watching to be a documentary. So while film critics were nearly unanimous in their praise, war veterans were less enthusiastic. A review in the *Air Force Times* called the portrayal of a bomb expert "grossly exaggerated and not appropriate," while former war correspondent Christian Lowe criticized, "Some of the scenes are so disconnected with reality to be almost parody."

Writer Boal defended his protagonist's portrayal as a maverick. "He's a fictional character, but I did certainly meet soldiers who [were] willing to take extraordinary risks. And you have to realize that the film takes place in a very specific time, 2004. It's not representative of the entire war." Bigelow echoed his hope that viewers would come away from the movie with an appreciation of what was going on in Iraq. "Even though it's about a particular time, I hope it will remind people that there are still men in harm's way."

PRIMARY SOURCE

THE HURT LOCKER

See primary source photo.

FURTHER RESOURCES
Books
Castner, Brian. *The Long Walk: A Story of War and the Life That Follows.* New York: Doubleday, 2012.

Web Sites
"Academy Awards Best Picture Facts & Trivia." *Filmsite.org.* www.filmsite.org/bestpics1.html (accessed on February 27, 2013).

Carroll, Ward. "Hurt Locker Is a Blast Without the Spark." *Defense Tech,* July 10, 2009. http://defensetech.org/2009/07/10/hurt-locker-is-a-blast-without-the-spark/ (accessed on February 27, 2013).

Crane, Anita. "In 'Hurt Locker', Realism Is the Special Effect." *Spero News.* www.speroforum.com/a/19823/In-Hurt-Locker-realism-is-the-special-effect (accessed on February 27, 2013).

Ebert, Roger. "The Hurt Locker." *Sun Times*, July 8, 2009. http://rogerebert.suntimes.com/apps/pbcs.dll/article?AID=/20090708/REVIEWS/907089997 (accessed on February 27, 2013).

Ford, Matt. "Real Hurt Lockers in Iraq: Life is No Movie." *Air Force Times*, March 8, 2010. www.airforcetimes.com/news/2010/03/ap_hurtlocker_reallife_030810/ (accessed on February 27, 2013).

Roeper, Richard. "The Hurt Locker." *RichardRoeper.com.* www.richardroeper.com/reviews/thehurtlocker.aspx (accessed on February 27, 2013).

Thomson, Patricia. "Risk and Valor: The Hurt Locker." *American Cinematographer*, July 2009. www.patriciathomson.net/PatriciaThomson/AC-Hurt_Locker.html (accessed on February 26, 2013).

"What Is a 'Hurt Locker'?" *BBC News*, March 8, 2010. http://news.bbc.co.uk/2/hi/uk_news/magazine/8555318.stm (accessed on February 27, 2013).

Synecdoche, New York

Poster

By: Charlie Kaufman

Date: 2008

Source: *Synecdoche, New York.* Written and directed by Charlie Kaufman. Sony Pictures Classics, 2008.

About the Writer/Director: New York Film School graduate Charlie Kaufman was a writer of several critically acclaimed films, including *Being John Malkovich*, *Adaptation*, and *Eternal Sunshine of the Spotless Mind*. His movies have won dozens of awards for Best Screenplay and Best Writer from various film societies.

INTRODUCTION
Charlie Kaufman's on-screen male characters have always been men in the throes of despair, struggling with desolation and compulsion, even obsession. They want to matter—to the world in general, to a woman in particular. From that very simple desire were borne the movies that Kaufman is best known for writing. In 2008, that film was titled *Synecdoche, New York*.

"NO FILM WITH AN AMBITION THIS LARGE AND AN ACHIEVEMENT THIS IMPRESSIVE, CAN BE ANYTHING BUT EXHILARATING." THANKS IN LARGE PART TO A SUPERB CAST LED BY PHILIP SEYMOUR HOFFMAN'S UNSPARING, SYMPATHETIC, TOWERING PERFORMANCE, THE MOVIE SHOULD DELIGHT VIEWERS WHO BOTH WORK THE MOVIE OUT AND SURRENDER TO ITS SPELL.

A MIRACLE MOVIE.

PHILIP SEYMOUR HOFFMAN   SAMANTHA MORTON   MICHELLE WILLIAMS   CATHERINE KEENER   EMILY WATSON

DIANNE WIEST   JENNIFER JASON LEIGH   HOPE DAVIS   TOM NOONAN

SYNECDOCHE NEW YORK

PRIMARY SOURCE

Synecdoche, New York

SYNOPSIS: This postmodern movie is about a depressed theater director who struggles to create one lasting masterpiece into which he can pour himself before he dies. © SIDNEY KIMMEL ENTERTAINMENT /THE KOBAL COLLECTION/ART RESOURCE, NY

In a departure from some of his previous films, Kaufman did not choose Spike Jonze to direct *Synecdoche*, but chose instead to direct it himself. Wesley Morris, film critic for the *Boston Globe*, called the Jonze-less Kaufman "rawer, blunter, sadder, and crueler in his satire—a tad more soulful, too."

Synecdoche is a postmodern tale of an aging and hypochondriac theater director, named Caden Cotard (played by Philip Seymour Hoffman), whose latest production grows increasingly elaborate and confusing until the boundary between real life and drama are so blurred as to be rendered invisible. American film critic Roger Ebert described Cotard in his *Chicago Sun-Times* review: Cotard has "all the hangups and self-pity … the arrogance and fear, typical of his job.

In other words, he could be me. He could be you. The job, the name, the race, the gender, the environment, all change. The human remains pretty much the same."

Caden sets out to create a theatrical production of brutal realism, something he can completely devote himself to in an effort to stop thinking about the fact that his wife took their young daughter and left him to live in Berlin. To that end, he gathers a talented cast into a warehouse in Manhattan's theater district and tells them to live their lives as if the city existed inside that warehouse. The city grows as time passes, and as it does, Caden begins to lose his own sense of reality. He becomes romantically involved with a number of the actresses, but each relationship fails for its own unique reasons. As his life falters, so does his health, and by the time the production has grown so large as to be unwieldy and virtually meaningless—literally, decades have passed—Caden is nearly dead.

SIGNIFICANCE

Film critics were divided in their assessment of the movie. *The Guardian* reviewer Peter Bradshaw wrote, "The film is either a masterpiece or a massively dysfunctional act of self-indulgence and self-laceration. It has brilliance, either way...." Ebert echoed a sentiment commonly uttered by critics and regular viewers alike: "I think you have to see [it] twice. I watched it the first time and knew it was a great film and that I had not mastered it. The second time because I needed to. The third time because I will want to."

Synecdoche was not a simple film; it was not easy to watch and understand, partly because it was a production (movie) about a production (play) that progressed but never was fully realized. Ebert praised it for its depth. "This is a film with the richness of great fiction.... It's not that you have to return to understand it. It's that you have to return to realize how fine it really is. The surface may daunt you. The depths enfold you. The whole reveals itself." And that idea—the parts and the whole— is in itself an explored theme in the film. The title itself, while a twist of the New York city Schenectady, also stands alone as a figure of speech in which a term for a part or portion of something is used to refer to the entirety of something else. The opposite is also implied, that the whole of something could be used to refer to a part of it. For example, the word "head" is used to refer to cattle, and the word "police" can represent one or several officers.

Critic Manohla Dargis of the *New York Times* could not say enough positive things about *Synecdoche*, particularly its construction and the way it blurs the lines between time, space and narrative. "It's extravagantly conceptual but also tethered to the here and now, which is why, for all its flights of fancy, worlds within worlds and agonies upon agonies, it comes down hard for living in the world with real, breathing, embracing bodies pressed against other bodies. To be here now, alive in the world as it is rather than as we imagine it to be, seems a terribly simple idea, yet it's also the only idea worth the fuss...."

While Kaufman received accolades for his avant garde execution of the storyline, the cast was equally praised. In particular, critics appreciated the performances of Catherine Keener, who played Caden's ex-wife, Adele Lack, Dianne Weist, who played several roles in the film, and Michelle Williams, who played Claire Keen, an actress in the cast whom Caden eventually marries. Although the film appeared on many critics' top ten lists of 2008 and won numerous film industry awards, it did not perform remarkably at the box office. The film that cost an estimated $21 million to make had a total gross of just over $3 million in American theaters.

PRIMARY SOURCE

SYNECDOCHE, NEW YORK

See primary source photo.

FURTHER RESOURCES
Web Sites

Bradshaw, Peter. "Synecdoche, New York." *The Guardian*, May 14, 2009. www.guardian.co.uk/film/2009/may/15/synecdoche-new-york (accessed on March 11, 2013).

Dargas, Manohla. "Dreamer, Live in the Here and Now." *New York Times*, October 23, 2008. http://movies.nytimes.com/2008/10/24/movies/24syne.html (accessed on March 11, 2013).

Ebert, Roger. "Synecdoche, New York." *Rogerebert.com*, November 5, 2008. http://rogerebert.suntimes.com/apps/pbcs.dll/article?AID=/20081105/REVIEWS/811059995 (accessed on March 11, 2013).

Morris, Wesley. "Suffering for His Art." *Boston Globe*, November 7, 2008. www.boston.com/ae/movies/articles/2008/11/07/suffering_for_his_art/ (accessed on March 11, 2013).

"Synecdoche, New York." *BoxOffice.com*. www.boxoffice.com/statistics/movies/synecdoche-new-york-2008 (accessed on March 11, 2013).

"Where the Coolest Kids Are, Like, Undead"

Newspaper article

By: Liz Rosenberg

Date: June 28, 2009

Source: Rosenberg, Liz. "Where the Coolest Kids Are, Like, Undead." *Boston Globe*. June 28, 2009. www.boston.com/ae/books/articles/2009/06/28/young_adults_feel_affinity_with_supernatural_characters_in_books/?page=1 (accessed on March 15, 2013).

About the Author: Liz Rosenberg, a graduate of Bennington College, has written numerous children's picture books, and her reviews of other writers' children's books appear regularly in the *Boston Globe*. A teacher at New York's Binghamton University since 1979, Rosenberg has published several award-winning volumes of poetry and, by the end of the 2000s, three novels.

INTRODUCTION

As a genre, Young Adult (YA) was formally recognized in the 1950s, with J. D. Salinger's novel *The Catcher in the Rye* marking the transition. S. E. Hinton's groundbreaking novel *The Outsiders* (1966) and Paul Zindel's *The Pigman* (1968) further solidified the foundation of this new category of fiction. These were books written for and about adolescents, and they dealt with topics and issues modern teens continue to face: substance use, suicide, gangs, and self-identity crises.

YA literature largely consisted of coming-of-age novels, with authors like Judy Blume and Robert Cormier leading the way throughout the 1970s. Blume's controversial coming-of-age novel *Are You There God? It's Me, Margaret* (1970) was written for the nine-to-twelve-year-old market, but adult outcry over the book's frank discussion of sexuality, challenge to religion, and inappropriate behavior of characters landed the book on the American Library Association's list of the top one hundred most frequently challenged books. Her next novel, *Forever* (1975), was one of the most-banned books in history for its depiction of sexual intercourse and treatment of teen pregnancy and birth control. Likewise, Cormier's *The Chocolate War* (1974) had the honor of topping the ALA's list of most-censored books for two decades because of its language, violence, and a general disrespect for authority. In the novel, protagonist

A collection of vampire literature, a highly popular genre among Young Adult readers in the 2000s decade. © ALEX MASI/ CORBIS.

Jerry refuses to sell chocolates to raise money for his school and a violent series of events follows.

Problem novels gave way to romance in the YA genre in the early 1980s, but the end of the decade saw a rise in the interest of thriller, suspense, and mystery. Author R. L. Stine was the king of young adult horror/ thriller with his *Fear Street* and then *Goosebumps* series, which saturated the YA market from 1989 to 1998. Lois Lowry gave young readers something to think about when she debuted the first novel in her series about a dystopian (frightening) society in 1994. *The Giver* was published to great acclaim, and sold more than five million copies by the end of 2012. In 1997, British author J. K. Rowling introduced the *Harry Potter* series with *Harry Potter and the Philosopher's Stone*, and sales exceeded all expectations. The second book of the series was published in the United States in June 1999 and debuted at the top of three best-seller lists, including the *New York Times*. The third novel followed the same debut pattern in September of that year.

As Rowling published the remaining four novels in the *Harry Potter* series, interest in magic and the supernatural remained strong. The novels were adapted to film, and by 2011, the Harry Potter brand was valued in excess of $15 million. In 2005, romance and the supernatural combined in the Stephenie Meyer *Twilight* series. By the end of 2009, her four novels made up 9 percent of all book sales. Their popularity—and that of the movie adaptations— had a cultural impact so significant that vampire fantasy became its own subgenre in YA fiction. The common theme of fantasy and the supernatural ignited an instant and significant flame in the world of teen reading. Throughout the decade, supernatural fiction was the trend, whether characters be fairies, were-wolves, vampires, ghosts, or zombies.

Rosenberg's article provides some explanation for why the undead—vampires in particular—appealed so readily, and for so long, to teens.

SIGNIFICANCE

Vampires and other undeads continued to rule the Young Adult market into the next decade. Countless novels—some serialized, others stand-alone—featuring vampires appeared on bookshelves seemingly overnight. Supernatural romance crossed over into a new genre called New Adult, written for the eighteen-to-twenty-four-year-old reading audience. These romances involved the undead, but unlike their Young Adult counterparts, also included more—and more graphic—sex scenes. Authors and publishers knew they had a market that had outgrown YA but still enjoyed the same themes they were reading a year ago, and they packaged and repackaged books to sell to those readers.

By 2010, interest in vampires, while still strong, had decreased; 17 percent of all book sales in 2009 were vampire/paranormal books, a figure that dropped to 9 percent in 2010. Soon dystopian novels like Suzanne Collins's *The Hunger Games* became the hottest trend. Though the novel was published in 2008 to mostly positive reviews, it was not until 2012, when the movie adaptation hit the big screen, that the theme of dystopian societies really took hold for YA readers. Opening weekend was a box-office record (for a non-sequel film) at $152.5 million in North America. Scott Westerfield's *Uglies* series was another runaway best-selling series, popular among the YA crowd. The first and second novels in the series were published in 2005, and Westerfield continued to publish into the next decade. He took advantage of the trend of graphic novels and adapted some of his *Uglies* stories to that format.

◼ PRIMARY SOURCE

"WHERE THE COOLEST KIDS ARE, LIKE, UNDEAD"

SYNOPSIS: Vampire fiction saturates the Young Adult genre because it allows readers to consider ideas and concepts without having to engage in them.

It's impossible to talk about new trends in young-adult fiction without considering the wildly popular supernatural fiction—much of it terrible knock-offs of the "Twilight" series by Stephenie Meyer. One surprising fact remains: Meyer can write beautiful prose, and she creates characters that young people care passionately about.

But why vampires? Why so many books for teenagers about the dead and the undead—about ghosts, ghouls, fairies and werewolves?

Like all speculative fiction, that of the supernatural allows teenagers to grapple with ideas. In this it's kin to science fiction, though that genre tends to be social and political—"Stranger in a Strange Land" by Robert Heinlein or "A Clockwork Orange" by Anthony Burgess—while the supernatural inclines toward the psychological and personal. Not always, of course. The original "Dracula," published in 1897 by Bram Stoker, comprised

a socio-political commentary on the desiccated, blood-sucking upper class. Mary Shelley's 1816 "Frankenstein" is a work of philosophy and science far closer to Heinlein's work than to Meyer's series, though both came to the authors in dream form.

But in the 1960s, a TV show called "Dark Shadows" introduced a new kind of soap-opera vampire: sexy, darkly comic, and doomed. The notion of eternal love and desire entered in, while writers like Anne Rice and "Cirque Du Freak's" Darren Shan updated and refined vampire literature. Of course, vampires are great metaphorical teenagers anyway. They stay up all night and sleep all day. They hunger for what they can't have, and are never satisfied. They are the original emo-goths, dressing in black, going without sleep, exuding a brooding, outsider sexiness. Vampire literature allows teenagers to think about sex and violence without censorship. It appeals to young men, because vampires are dangerous, super-fast and super-strong. It appeals to the romantic in young women, though the passivity of many female characters in vampire literature is a bit troubling. But the newest supernatural teen books aim to end all that.

Consider Madison Avery, murdered on prom night—sort of. She's the feisty teenage heroine of "Once Dead, Twice Shy," (HarperCollins, $16.99, 240 pp.) by Kim Harrison, author of the best-selling "Hollows" series. Madison evades her dark reaper by stealing his amulet, and spends much of the novel bouncing between spheres, getting herself, her handsome prom date, and guardian angel into misadventures. "Once Dead, Twice Shy" has more plot holes than a slice of Swiss cheese, yet it's compelling reading. Harrison knows how to keep her story moving—with time-keepers and arch-angels, the fated and the doomed.

Like most paranormal young-adult literature, it ricochets between teenage realism and wild fantasy. Being mostly dead, Madison doesn't sleep much, doesn't eat much, but her perspicacious eye and sassy sense of humor teeter between laughter and grief. Here she looks with an outsider's eye at her own father's kitchen: "the white-and-yellow-tiled splashboard and the cream-colored walls looked tired ... There was a small lazy Susan with napkins, salt and pepper, and a dusty ashtray sitting right where it would be in my mom's kitchen—whispers of her still in my dad's life though she'd been gone for years."

Black wings cluster around the doomed, and dark reapers chase Madison all over town, but she prevails.

At the heart of "Once Dead, Twice Shy" is an argument about free will versus fate, yet it's the idea of the idea that takes center stage.

Much new supernatural literature toys with big ideas without fully engaging them. Marilyn Kaye's new paperback "Gifted" series (Kingfisher, $7.99) proves the point. Her heroes and heroines all possess special gifts—one reads minds, another sees the future, and a popular boy, injured in a car accident, now hears the dead speaking. Our heroine Amanda is a mean Queen Bee body-snatcher: Her gift and curse is literally to enter anyone she pities.

Like Harrison, Kaye knows how to tell a story and is the author of the updated fairy tale "Penelope," made into a popular movie. One can practically feel a "Gifted" TV series zooming around the corner. We could do worse. If the characters in the "Gifted" books are familiar types, they are nonetheless enlivened by Kaye's quick-paced plotting, her crisp prose, and blend of piquancy and humor: "There were 342 students at Meadowbrook Middle School," begins "Out of Sight Out of Mind," the first "Gifted" book, "and three lunch periods each day.... The noise and commotion, however, suggested that half the population of mainland China was eating lunch together."

Brushing lightly against the theme of the paranormal, "Nothing But Ghosts," (HarperCollins, 288 pp., $17.99) by Beth Kephart uses ghosts more as metaphors than central plot devices. Katie's much-adored mother has died, and Katie inhabits a house full of loss. No wonder she's out as early and late as possible: "My bike is the ten-speed, thin-wheeled kind, a perfect silver streak. If you were looking down on me and my bike from a cloud above, you'd think we were a zipper." She happens onto a local mystery and ghost story, and in unraveling it comes to terms with some of her own grief. Kephart's language is diamond-sharp and bright. The city of Barcelona, with its underground ghosts and tunnels, plays a part—so does art and French history, love and family. "How do you go from being a star to being a black hole?" the heroine asks, a question pertinent to the neighborhood heiress, her deceased mother, and life itself. If there's a taste of the paranormal here, there's also the sustenance and comfort that many teenagers are seeking in books.

FURTHER RESOURCES
Web Sites

Barnes, Brooks. "'Hunger Games' Ticket Sales Set Record." *New York Times*, March 25, 2012. www.nytimes.com/2012/03/26/movies/hunger-games-breaks-box-office-records.html (accessed on March 15, 2013).

Hess, Monica. "Katniss, Bella Vie for Literary Legacy." *USA Today*, March 26, 2012. http://usatoday30.usatoday.com/USCP/PNI/Features/2012-03-26-PNI0326liv-heroines_ST_U.htm (accessed on March 15, 2013).

Minzesheimer, Bob, and Anthony DeBarros. "2010 Saw a Frenzy for Fiction, Led by Stieg Larsson's 'Girl' Trilogy." *USA Today*, January 13, 2011. http://usatoday30.usatoday.com/life/books/news/2011-01-12-booktrends13_N.htm (accessed on March 15, 2013).

2 Business and the Economy

Chronology

Important Events in Business and the Economy, 2000–2009

2000

- On January 1, computer clocks turn over with only minor glitches, following $8.8 billion in government spending and $100 billion by private businesses to prepare for the "Y2K bug."

- On January 4, Alan Greenspan is nominated for his fourth term as chairman of the Federal Reserve Board.

- On January 10, America Online Inc. announces a deal to buy Time Warner Inc. for over $160 billion in stock and debt.

- On January 13, Bill Gates announces that he will step down as CEO of Microsoft Corp.

- On February 7, Pfizer Inc. announces deal to buy Warner-Lambert Co. for $90 billion in stock, forming the world's second-largest drug company.

- On March 13, *Chicago Tribune* publisher Tribune Co. announces an $8 billion deal to buy Times Mirror Co., publisher of the *Los Angeles Times*, *Baltimore Sun*, and *Newsday*.

- On August 9, Bridgestone-Firestone Inc. announces it is recalling 6.5 million tires following reports of blowouts and peeling treads on sport-utility vehicles and light trucks.

- On September 13, Chase Manhattan Corp. announces a $34.3 billion deal to buy J. P. Morgan & Co., uniting the third- and fifth-largest U.S. banks.

- On October 16, Chevron Corp. announces plan to buy Texaco Inc. for $36 billion, creating the world's fourth-largest oil company.

- On October 25, AT&T Corp. announces its split into four companies providing long-distance, wireless, cable television, and Internet services.

- On November 16, Coca-Cola Co. settles a racial-discrimination class-action suit for $192.5 million with about 2,000 current and former black employees.

2001

- On January 17, California utility Pacific Gas & Electric, squeezed by rising power prices and laws barring rate hikes, orders rolling blackouts cutting off two million electricity customers in Northern California. Governor Gray Davis declares state of emergency and orders the state Department of Water Resources to buy power for ratepayers.

- On January 20, President Bill Clinton pardons commodities trader Marc Rich, who had fled the United States in 1983 to avoid prosecution on conspiracy, tax evasion, racketeering, and illegal trading with Iran.

- On May 26, Congress approves $1.35 trillion tax cut spread over ten years. President George W. Bush signs the legislation on June 7.

- On June 28, a U.S. appeals court overturns a ruling ordering that Microsoft Corp. be broken up. The Justice Department abandons its case, demanding the dissolution on September 6.

- On September 11, the Federal Aviation Administration grounds all commercial flights following the disasters in New York, Washington, D.C., and Pennsylvania caused by planes hijacked by terrorists; international flights are diverted to Canada or sent back to their originating airports. The New York Stock Exchange (NYSE), the American Stock Exchange (ASE), and the National Association of Securities Dealers Automated Quotations (NASDAQ) do not open, remaining closed until September 17, when the Dow Jones Industrial Average falls 684 points, or 7.1 percent, the index's biggest one-day drop up to that time.

- On September 21, Congress approves a $15 billion bailout package for airlines, ailing from 9/11-related losses.

- On October 12, camera and film manufacturer Polaroid files for Chapter 11 bankruptcy protection.

- On October 26, the Pentagon chooses Lockheed Martin Corp. for a $200 billion contract to build more than 3,000 supersonic jet fighters.

- On December 2, Enron Corp. files for bankruptcy, its stock practically worthless following Dynegy's decision to back out of its planned acquisition.

- On December 28, President Bush formally grants permanent normal-trade status to China, effective January 1, 2002.

2002

- On January 11, Ford Motor Co. announces plans to lay off 35,000 workers, close four plants, and drop four vehicle models.

- On January 22, Kmart Corp. files for Chapter 11 protection from creditors in the nation's biggest retail bankruptcy, listing $16.29 billion in assets and $10.35 billion in debt.

- On March 5, President Bush imposes tariffs of up to 30 percent on steel imported from Europe, Asia, and South America.

- On March 14, the Justice Department indicts Enron accounting firm Arthur Andersen LLP, alleging it destroyed documents related to a fraud probe. The firm is convicted on June 15, but the Supreme Court overturns the conviction in 2005.

- On June 25, WorldCom Inc. announces it overstated cash flow by $3.8 billion over the past fifteen months and will lay off 17,000 of its 85,000 employees. The Securities and Exchange Commission (SEC) files fraud charges on 26 June, and the company declares bankruptcy on July 21.

- On July 15, the euro trades ahead of the dollar for the first time.

- On July 24, Adelphia Communications Corp. founder John Rigas is arrested on fraud charges following the company's bankruptcy filing.

- On July 30, President Bush signs into law the Sarbanes-Oxley Act, a package of corporate governance and accounting reforms.

- On August 7, federal authorities indict Samuel Waksal, founder and former chief of pharmaceutical company ImClone LLC, on charges of obstruction of justice and bank fraud.

- On November 5, SEC chairman Harvey Pitt resigns amid criticism over mounting accounting scandals.

- On December 6, Treasury secretary Paul O'Neill and National Economic Council chairman Lawrence Lindsey resign. CSX Corp. chief John Snow is nominated to succeed O'Neill and former Goldman Sachs Group Inc. chairman Stephen Friedman to succeed Lindsey.

2003

- On January 12, AOL-Time Warner Inc. chairman Steve M. Case announces his resignation, ahead of the decision to write down the value of his company's AOL division by $35 billion and its cable division by $10 billion.

- On April 28, ten of the nation's biggest investment banks reach a settlement with the SEC, National Association of Securities Dealers, and the NYSE to avoid prosecution over tainted research reports.

- On May 23, Congress approves the Jobs and Growth Tax Relief Reconciliation Act of 2003, providing $318 billion in tax cuts over eight years; President Bush signs the legislation a week later.

- On June 2, the Federal Communications Commission votes 3–2 to rescind a ruling barring any one media company from owning both a television station and a newspaper in the same market.

- On June 4, Martha Stewart is indicted in federal court on conspiracy, obstruction of justice, and securities fraud charges related to trades of ImClone stock. She pleads not guilty and steps down as chairwoman and chief of Martha Stewart Living Omnimedia Inc.

- On August 14, a blackout eventually blamed on Ohio utility FirstEnergy Corp. leaves 50 million people in the Northeast and Midwest without power, some for as long as two days.

- On September 3, New York attorney general Eliot Spitzer announces fraud charges against hedge fund Canary Capital Partners LLC, alleging improper trading of mutual-fund shares. The case initiates a wave of charges by Spitzer's office and the Securities and Exchange Commission against mutual-fund companies.

- On September 17, NYSE chairman and chief Richard Grasso resigns amid criticism of his compensation by SEC and several large pension funds.

- On November 4, HealthSouth CEO Richard Scrushy becomes the first executive indicted under the Sarbanes-Oxley Act.

- On December 18, California governor Arnold Schwarzenegger declares a fiscal crisis following downgrades of the state's bond ratings, allowing him to reduce government spending by $150 million without legislative approval.

2004

- On March 2, former WorldCom Inc. chief Bernard Ebbers is charged with securities fraud, conspiracy, and false regulatory filings; he pleads not guilty. The company's former chief financial officer, Scott Sullivan, pleads guilty on the same day to securities fraud and agrees to cooperate with prosecutors. Ebbers is convicted on March 15, 2005.

- On March 5, Martha Stewart is convicted on charges of conspiracy and obstruction. She will be sentenced to five months in prison, five months' house arrest, and nineteen months of probation and be ordered to pay a $30,000 fine, plus court fees.

- On April 2, the fraud trial of former Tyco International Ltd. executives ends in a mistrial. The executives are found guilty of conspiracy, grand larceny, securities fraud, and falsifying business records in a June 17, 2005 decision.

- On May 17, oil prices reach a twenty-one-year high of $41.85 per barrel of light sweet crude, reflecting Middle East tensions and surging demand from China.

- On May 18, President Bush nominates Alan Greenspan to an unprecedented fifth term as Federal Reserve chairman.

- On June 30, the Federal Reserve Board raises the benchmark interchange rate from 1 percent to 1.25 percent, the first hike in four years for the overnight-loans rate.

- On July 7, federal prosecutors indict former Enron chief Kenneth Lay on charges including conspiracy and bank, securities, and wire fraud. He is convicted on May 15, 2006.

- On July 8, Adelphia Communications Corp. founder John Rigas is convicted of conspiracy, bank fraud, and securities fraud.

2005

- On February 2, President Bush calls for a partial privatization of the Social Security program in his State of the Union Address.

- On June 1, William Donaldson announces his resignation as SEC chairman. He is succeeded by California congressman Christopher Cox.

- On June 7, General Motors Corp. announces it will cut 25,000 jobs by 2008.

- On June 23, the Supreme Court rules in *Kelo v. City of New London* that the city could invoke eminent domain to take private property in order for private developers to build office space and a hotel, expanding the justification of eminent domain beyond public works or transportation projects.

- On June 27, the Supreme Court rules in *MGM Studios v. Grokster Ltd.* that software companies producing Internet file-sharing software are liable to suits when they intend for customers to use the software in violation of copyright laws.

- On July 25, the Teamsters and Service Employees International Union announce their secession from the American Federation of Labor and Congress of Industrial Organizations (AFL-CIO) at the labor coalition's national convention.

- On July 28, Congress passes the Central American Free Trade Agreement. President Bush signs it into law on 5 August.

- On July 29, Congress passes energy legislation authorizing $12.3 billion in incentives for new technology, alternative fuels, and nuclear power. President Bush signs it into law on August 8.

- On August 29, Hurricane Katrina strikes the Gulf Coast, leaving 80 percent of New Orleans underwater and causing extensive damage in Gulfport and Biloxi, Mississippi, and Mobile, Alabama, while hobbling the Gulf's petrochemical, maritime cargo, fishing, sugarcane, rice, cotton, and tourism industries. Light sweet crude oil hits $71 per barrel on August 30 owing to Gulf shortages. Congress approves $62 billion in emergency spending for hurricane relief on September 8. The cost to private insurers tops $40 billion.

- On September 14, Delta Air Lines Inc. and Northwest Airlines Inc. file for bankruptcy protection, blaming high fuel costs.

- On December 20, New York City transit workers begin a three-day strike, halting bus and subway service.

2006

- On January 2, twelve miners die in a methane gas explosion at International Coal Group Inc.'s Sago Mine in Tallmansville, West Virginia.

- On January 24, Ford Motor Co. announces plans to cut up to 30,000 jobs over six years and close as many as fourteen factories.

- On February 1, Ben Bernanke is sworn in as chairman of the Federal Reserve Board.

- On May 1, amid national debate on legislation to curb illegal immigration, more than one million people take part in "Day Without Immigrants" demonstrations around the country to highlight the role of immigrant workers in the economy.

- On May 30, Treasury secretary John Snow announces his resignation; Goldman Sachs chief Henry Paulson is named as his successor.

- On July 6, Florida's Supreme Court rejects a $145 billion judgment in a class action against five tobacco companies, calling the award excessive.

2007

- On May 14, DaimlerChrysler AG announces it will sell 80.1 percent of its Chrysler division to private equity firm Cerberus Capital Management LP for $7.4 billion.

- On September 24, seventy-three thousand United Auto Workers union members take part in a strike of General Motors plants; a deal between labor and management ends the walkout on September 26.

- On October 9, the Dow Jones Industrial Average closes above 14,000 for the first time, hitting 14,164.53.

- On October 30, Merrill Lynch & Co. chief E. Stanley O'Neal announces his resignation less than a week after the company's disclosure of an $8.4 billion write-down on bad subprime mortgage investments. He is succeeded on November 14 by NYSE chief John A. Thain.

- On November 4, Citigroup Inc. reveals it is writing down $8 to $11 billion in assets owing to bad subprime mortgage investments, following a $5.9 billion write-down the previous month. Chairman and chief Charles O. Prince III also announces his resignation.

- On November 5, the Writers Guild of America's East and West unions strike as contract negotiations with the Alliance of Motion Picture and Television Producers break down. The walkout ceases production for all scripted television programming and lasts until February 12, 2008.

- On December 6, President Bush announces an agreement among major mortgage lenders to help cash-strapped homeowners with adjustable-rate subprime mortgages by placing temporary freezes on rate hikes and refinancing through the Federal Housing Administration.

- On December 18, Congress passes legislation requiring increases in automobile fuel economy standards to 35 miles per gallon by 2020. President Bush signs the bill into law the following day.

- On December 19, Morgan Stanley & Co. discloses a $9.4 billion write-down of subprime mortgage assets.

2008

- On February 12, General Motors Corp. announces losing $722 million in the fourth quarter and $38.7 billion for all of 2007.

- On March 16, the Federal Reserve approves the sale of Bear Stearns, which had been crippled by subprime-related losses, to J. P. Morgan Chase & Co. at $2 per share following a 47 percent plunge in the stock, to $30 per share.

- On March 16, the Federal Reserve begins letting securities dealers borrow from it on the same terms as banks.

- On May 12, immigration agents raid the Agriprocessors Inc. meatpacking plant in Postville, Iowa, arresting 389 in what the government describes as the biggest immigration enforcement action at a single U.S. workplace.

- On July 11, the Federal Deposit Insurance Corp. (FDIC) places IndyMac Bank in conservatorship following a run on assets triggered by losses on defaulted mortgages. Parent IndyMac Bancorp files for bankruptcy protection on July 31.

- On July 13, the Federal Reserve Board and the Treasury Department announce that they will request temporary authority from Congress to buy equity in the Federal National Mortgage Association (FNMA) and in the Federal Home Loan Mortgage Corporation (FHLMC), popularly known as Fannie Mae and Freddie Mac. They assume control of the quasi-public lending enterprises on September 7.

- On September 14, Bank of America Corp. reaches an agreement to buy Merrill Lynch & Co. for $50 billion.

- On September 15, Lehman Brothers Holdings Inc. declares bankruptcy.

- On September 16, the Federal Reserve takes a 79.9 percent equity stake in American International Group Inc. (AIG), also ailing from mortgage losses, and creates an $85 billion credit facility, subsequently expanding the line of credit to $144 billion by October 31.

- On September 20, the Treasury Department publicly proposes a $700 billion bailout plan to buy bad mortgage-backed securities. Companion legislation fails initially in the House of Representatives on September 29, but a revised version passes both chambers on October 3 and is signed by President Bush the same day.

- On September 21, the Federal Reserve announces that Goldman Sachs Group Inc. and Morgan Stanley & Co. will restructure as bank holding companies and submit to more government oversight.

- On September 25, federal regulators place Washington Mutual Bank, straining under subprime mortgage losses, into receivership following a ten-day run on the bank that drains $16.4 billion in deposits. The FDIC sells the banking subsidiaries to J.P. Morgan Chase & Co. for $1.9 billion.

- On September 29, the Dow Jones Industrial Average drops a record 777 points in one day of trading.

- On October 3, Wachovia Corp., under pressure from federal regulators to sell following a one-day $5 billion run on deposits, reaches a deal to be acquired by Wells Fargo & Co. for $15.4 billion.

- On November 10, electronics retailer Circuit City files for bankruptcy protection. The White House announces it will increase the AIG bailout from $123 billion to $150 billion. AIG discloses losses of $24.5 billion from July to September 2008.

- On November 12, Treasury secretary Henry Paulson announces that Troubled Asset Relief Program (TARP) funds will be spent on stabilizing and stimulating credit markets in part by buying shares in banks.

- On November 18–19, the chief executives of General Motors (GM), Chrysler, and Ford request a taxpayer-financed rescue in congressional hearings.

- On November 23, Citigroup finalizes its rescue plan with the Treasury Department, Federal Reserve, and FDIC providing for the government to invest $20 billion in the bank and to partially guarantee more than $300 billion in assets.

- On November 25, the Federal Reserve and the Treasury Department announce an $800 billion program to thaw frozen credit markets—$600 billion allocated to buying debt from Fannie Mae, Freddie Mac, and other mortgage financiers and $200 million to encourage investors to buy securities tied to car and student loans and other forms of consumer credit.

- On December 8, Tribune Co. files for bankruptcy protection.

- On December 11, federal agents arrest investment adviser Bernard Madoff in New York, charging him with operating a $50 million Ponzi scheme. The size of the fraud is subsequently estimated at $65 billion.

2009

- On February 17, President Barack Obama signs a $787 billion stimulus package, providing $212 billion in tax cuts and $575 billion in new federal spending.

- On February 18, President Obama orders that $275 billion be allocated to help homeowners avoid foreclosure.

- On February 25, bank "stress tests" mandated by the stimulus legislation begin. Ten banks are ordered in May to raise a combined $74.6 billion in new capital.

- On March 2, AIG posts a $61.7 billion loss for 2008's fourth quarter. The Treasury Department agrees to provide $30 billion more in financing.

- On March 12, Bernie Madoff pleads guilty to eleven counts of fraud, money laundering, perjury, and theft. On June 29 he is sentenced to 150 years in prison.

- On March 23, the Treasury Department announces the Public-Private Investment Program, in which the government will provide subsidies and other incentives to encourage private investors to buy up to $1 trillion in toxic loans and assets.

- On March 29, a White House task force studying aid for struggling automakers forces the resignation of GM chief Rick Wagoner.

- On March 30, President Obama, threatening to withdraw U.S. support to Chrysler and GM, issues a thirty-day deadline for Chrysler to merge with Fiat or find another suitable merger partner and a sixty-day deadline for GM to rework its business plan.

- On April 15, "Tea Party" demonstrations across the country protest the Obama administration's stimulus programs.

- On April 30, Chrysler files for bankruptcy protection after creditors reject a White House–brokered restructuring plan.

- On May 18, the Supreme Court agrees to hear a case challenging the 2002 Sarbanes-Oxley Act.

- On June 1, GM files for bankruptcy protection with $172.81 billion in debt and $82.29 billion in assets.

- On June 18, federal authorities arrest Texas banker R. Allen Stanford, founder of the Stanford Group Co., after a federal grand jury indicts him on charges of fraud involving the misallocation of certificate-of-deposit assets into private-equity investments.

- On July 10, GM emerges from bankruptcy.

- On July 24, the federal government begins offering refund vouchers of up to $4,500 on trade-ins of older, low-fuel-efficiency automobiles. The initial $1 billion funding of the so-called Cash for

Clunkers program runs out quickly, prompting Congress to pass a $2 billion extension.

- On September 16, Richard Trumka is elected president of the AFL-CIO, succeeding the retiring John Sweeney.

- On October 22, Christina Romer, head of the White House Council of Economic Advisers, predicts in congressional testimony that the unemployment rate will remain at or above 10 percent into 2010.

- On November 3, Warren Buffett's Berkshire Hathaway buys Burlington Northern Sante Fe railroad for $34 billion.

- On December 1, GM fires chief Fritz Henderson and names chairman Edward Whitacre as interim chief.

- On December 3, General Electric (GE) sells NBC Universal to Comcast in deal valued at $30 billion.

"Securities and Exchange Commission Complaint against Bernard L. Madoff"

Legal complaint

By: Securities and Exchange Commission

Date: December 1, 2000

Source: Securities and Exchange Commission. "Securities and Exchange Commission Complaint against Bernard L. Madoff," December 1, 2008. www.sec.gov/litigation/complaints/2008/comp-madoff121108.pdf (accessed on March 11, 2013).

About the Agency: The U.S. Securities and Exchange Commission (SEC) is an agency of the U.S. federal government responsible for regulating and monitoring the stock market and many aspects of the financial system. It was created in 1934, in reaction to the destructive behavior of Wall Street that caused the Great Depression. The SEC is authorized to enforce regulations judicially by investigating and monitoring entities operating within the U.S. investment banking sector and reporting malfeasance to law enforcement agencies. It is also tasked with creating and enforcing the ethics policies by which investment bankers are bound.

INTRODUCTION

Bernard L. Madoff, known to the public as "Bernie," was born in 1938 to a Jewish family living in New York. After obtaining a bachelor's degree in political science, Madoff used the money he had earned during college to start Bernard L. Madoff Investment Securities LLC in 1960. Initially trading in penny stocks, Madoff's eponymous company grew throughout the ensuing decades, becoming one of the most recognized and respected stock brokerage firms on Wall Street. Madoff became a notorious figure in the financial sector for his early contributions to the creation of the NASDAQ Stock Market, a digitized competitor to the New York Stock Exchange. Having demonstrated the viability of an off-the-floor stock exchange and helped test and develop the technology necessary to operate it, Madoff was appointed as the chairman of NASDAQ, a position he retained for several years.

In addition to the successful stock brokerage operated by Bernard L. Madoff Investment Securities, the company operated an unadvertised wealth-management service. Madoff's prestige and influence within the affluent social circles of high finance, politics, philanthropy, and the New York City Jewish community were enough to secure the confidence of investors, who entrusted hundreds of millions of dollars to his personal investment advisory divisions. Using an ambiguous investment strategy, Madoff reported perpetually rising dividends on the investments of his clients, never once reporting a quarter of net loss, even during the early-2000s recession. Madoff's unwavering profit reports attracted further investment in his wealth management business, much of which came from other personal investment firms that would invest the money in his company and profit immensely from the reported returns he achieved on their customers' capital. By the time of the 2008 subprime mortgage crisis and subsequent evaporation of available credit, Madoff's wealth management operation boasted a client list containing celebrities, numerous charities, and the personal pension funds of several wealthy individuals.

Unfortunately for all parties involved, however, Madoff was not the financial prodigy he pretended to be. The wealth-management division of his company was actually a classic Ponzi scheme, in which Madoff would report unrealistically high returns on the investments of his clients while secretly using the money of other clients to pay for redemption requests. In doing so, Madoff maintained the trust of his clients—dividends could be procured at request—even though he was not actually investing their money. Hundreds of millions of dollars were thus stored in a single account belonging to Madoff, even as he reported tens of billions in total client balances. His fraud was unable to sustain itself, though, when the 2008 recession caused clients to file for withdrawals en masse, requesting billions of dollars in fabricated returns when Madoff had only a fraction of the amount in available capital. The beleaguered financier, under extreme stress from the situation, confessed to his sons in December 2008 that his success was built on lies and that his fraud was on the brink of exposure. His sons, both employees of Madoff's company, reported their father to the authorities on December 11 of that year.

Madoff was quick to confess his deceit, pleading guilty to eleven federal felonies in March 2009 preliminary trials related to his fraud. He admitted to systematically defrauding investors of billions of dollars over the course of two decades, and to deliberately filing false reports with the SEC. Despite official suspicions to the contrary, Madoff maintained that he was the sole executor of his scheme and refused to implicate any accomplices. He was found guilty on all 11 counts with which he was charged and sentenced to the maximum 150 years in prison. He began serving his sentence in June 2009, with no hope of living to see his release.

SIGNIFICANCE

Bernie Madoff's Ponzi scheme represented the largest fraud in the history of the United States. Although exact numbers were impossible to ascertain because the perpetrator fabricated his earnings reports, estimates pinned the total amount Madoff stole from his clients at around $18 billion, with tens of billions more in lost *expected* earnings. In the midst of the financial crisis of the late 2000s, during which greedy Wall Street bankers and brokers were vilified for their role in the recession, Madoff arose as the figurehead of all the public opposed—he was depicted as a greedy, irresponsible banker willing to exploit charities, friends, and customers who had trusted him with caring for their wealth, unrepentant and unapologetic for the harm he had wrought. No one even attempted to justify or excuse his massive crime.

The SEC was also the target of extensive criticism for failing to detect Madoff's fraud, despite having conducted official investigations of his business in response to earlier complaints against him. It was alleged that Madoff was given easy treatment by the SEC because of his personal ties to the agency, which he had frequently assisted in updating and enforcing its policies. The Madoff affair was cited as evidence supporting broader accusations of general incompetence and negligence on the part of the SEC, which had recently had its flaws exposed by the rampant irresponsibility and corruption of the financial industry. The fact that Madoff, who had frequently been accused by analysts and accountants of illegal conduct, had eluded detection for a fraudulent scheme of such unprecedented scale until it collapsed on top of him indicated to legislators and the public that the regulatory infrastructure of the financial industry required substantial reforms.

Of the money stolen by Madoff, an unspecified amount was recovered by the SEC and the Federal Bureau of Investigation, and his $800 million estate was seized. Victims of his fraud had some of their losses recovered, although considerable amounts are suspected to have been transported overseas or laundered. Several personal investment services that had reinvested client money with Madoff's

Money manager Bernard Madoff walks near his home in New York City on December 17, 2008, during his trial for investment fraud. © DANIEL ACKER/BLOOMBERG VIA GETTY IMAGES.

company were bankrupted, as were a number of charities and other philanthropic organizations. Hundreds of individuals lost their life savings to Madoff, which resulted in lost homes and property. Madoff was remembered as one of the greatest villains of the 2000s decade, whose greed ruined lives and left incredible economic destruction in its wake.

PRIMARY SOURCE

"SECURITIES AND EXCHANGE COMMISSION COMPLAINT AGAINST BERNARD L. MADOFF"

SYNOPSIS: This complaint, signed by James Clarkson, associate regional director of the SEC, formerly registers the grievances of the SEC against Bernie Madoff. They contain a slew of allegations of illegal behavior related to the assets management arm of his Wall Street investment firm, amounting to a Ponzi scheme of unprecedented proportions.

SECURITIES AND EXCHANGE COMMISSION
Plaintiff,

- against -

BERNARD L. MADOFF,

BERNARD L. MADOFF INVESTMENT SECURITIES LLC,
Defendants.

COMPLAINT

Plaintiff Securities and Exchange Commission ("Commission"), for its Complaint against defendants Bernard L. Madoff ("Madoff ") and Bernard L. Madoff Investment Securities LLC ("BMIS"), alleges:

SUMMARY

1. The Commission brings this emergency action to halt ongoing fraudulent offerings of securities and investment advisory fraud by Madoff and BMIS, a broker dealer and investment adviser registered with the Commission. From an indeterminate period through the present, Madoff and BMSI has committed fraud through the investment adviser activities of BMIS. Yesterday, Madoff admitted to one or more employees of BMIS that for many years he has been conducting a Ponzi-scheme through the investment adviser activities of BMIS and that BMIS has liabilities of approximately $50 billion. Madoff told these employees that he intends to distribute any remaining funds at BMIS to employees and certain investors in the investment advisor business, such as family and friends. Such a distribution will be unfair and inequitable to other investors and creditors of BMIS.

2. Expedited relief is needed to halt the fraud and prevent the Defendants from unfairly distributing the remaining assets in an unfair and inequitable manner to employees, friend and relatives, at the expense of other customers.

3. To halt the ongoing fraud, maintain the status quo and preserve any assets for injured investors, the Commission seeks emergency relief, including temporary restraining orders and preliminary injunctions, and an order: (i) imposing asset freezes against the Defendants; (ii) appointing a receiver over BMIS; (iii) allowing expedited discovery and preventing the destruction of documents; and (iv) requiring the Defendants to provide verified accountings. The Commission also seeks permanent injunctions, disgorgement of ill-gotten gains, plus prejudgment interest and civil monetary penalties against all of the Defendants.

VIOLATIONS

4. By virtue of the conduct alleged herein:

    a. All Defendants directly or indirectly, singly or in concert, have engaged, and are engaging, in acts, practices,

schemes and courses of business that constitute violations of Sections 206(1) and 206(2) of the Advisers Act of 1940 ("Advisers Act") [15 U.S.C. §§ 80b-6(1), (2)], and Section 17(a) of the Securities Act of 1933 (the "Securities Act"), 15 U.S.C. § 77q(a) and Section 10(b) of the Securities Exchange Act of 1934 (the "Exchange Act"), 15 U.S.C. § 78j(b), and Rule l0b-5 thereunder, 17 C.F.R. § 240.10b-5.

NATURE OF THE PROCEEDINGS AND RELIEF SOUGHT

7. The Commission brings this action pursuant to the authority conferred upon it by Section 20(b) of the Securities Act, 15 U.S.C. § 77t(b), and Section 21(d)(1) of the Exchange Act, 15 U.S.C. § 78u(d)(1), seeking to restrain and enjoin permanently the Defendants from engaging in the acts, practices and courses of business alleged herein.

8. In addition to the injunctive and emergency relief recited above, the Commission seeks: (i) final judgments ordering Defendants to disgorge their ill-gotten gains with prejudgment interest thereon; and (ii) final judgments ordering the Defendants to pay civil penalties pursuant to Section 20(d) of the Securities Act, 15 U.S.C. § 77t(d), and Section 21(d)(3) of the Exchange Act, 15 U.S.C. § 78u(d)(3).

JURISDICTION AND VENUE

10. This Court has jurisdiction over this action pursuant to Section 214 of the Advisers Act [15 U.S.C. 5 80b-141, Section 22(a) of the Securities Act [15 U.S.C. § 77v(a)] and Sections 21(e) and 27 of the Exchange Act [15 U.S.C. §§ 78u(e) and 78aa].

11. Venue is proper in the Southern District of New York pursuant to 28 U.S.C. § 1391. The Defendants, directly and indirectly, have made use of the means and instrumentalities of interstate commerce, or of the mails, in connection with the transactions, acts, practices and courses of business alleged herein. A substantial part of the events comprising Defendants' fraudulent scheme that gives rise to the Commission's claims occurred in the Southern District of New York, including that BMIS is located and headquartered in this District and certain of Madoff and BMIS committed their fraudulent securities and adviser activities in this District.

THE DEFENDANTS

12. **Madoff** is a resident of New York City and is the sole owner of BMIS. BMIS' website indicates that Madoff founded BMIS in the early 1960s and that he is an

attorney. Madoff is a former Chairman of the board of directors of the NASDAQ stock market. BMIS is both a broker-dealer and investment adviser registered with the Commission. Madoff oversees and controls the investment adviser services at BMIS as well at the overall finances of BMIS.

13. **BMI** is a broker-dealer and investment advisor registered in both capacities with the Commission. BMIS engages in three different operations, which include investment adviser services, market making services and proprietary trading. BMIS' website states that it has been providing quality executions for broker-dealers, banks and financial institutions since its inception in 1960;" and that BMIS, "[w]ith more than $700 million in firm capital, Madoff currently ranks among the top 1% of US Securities firms." The most recent Form ADV for BMIS filed in January 2008 with the Commission stated that BMIS had over $17 billion in assets under management, and 23 clients. BMIS represented that its trading strategy for adviser accounts involved trading in baskets of equity securities and options thereon.

FACTS

14. From an indeterminate time to the present, Madoff and BMIS have been conducting a Ponzi-scheme through the investment adviser services of MIS.

15. Madoff conducts certain investment advisory business for clients that is separate from the BMIS' proprietary trading and market making activities.

16. Madoff ran his investment adviser business from a separate floor in the New York offices of BMIS.

17. Madoff kept the financial statements for the firm under lock and key, and was "cryptic" about the firm's investment advisory business when discussing the business with other employees of BMIS.

18. In or about the first week of December 2008, Madoff told a senior employee that there had been requests from clients for approximately $7 billion in redemptions, that he was struggling to obtain the liquidity necessary to meet those obligations, but that he thought that he would be able to do so. According to this senior employee, he had previously understood that the investment advisory business had assets under management on the order of between approximately $8-15 billion.

19. On or about December 9, 2008, Madoff informed another senior employee that he wanted to pay 2008 bonuses to employees of the firm in December, which was earlier than employee bonuses are usually paid.

20. Bonuses traditionally have been paid at BMIS in February of each year for the previous year's work.

21. On or about December 10, 2008, the two senior employees referenced above visited Madoff at the offices of BMIS to discuss the situation further, particularly because Madoff had appeared to these two senior employees to have been under great stress in the prior weeks.

22. At that time, Madoff informed the senior employees that he had recently made profits through business operations, and that now was a good time to distribute it. When the senior employee challenged his explanation, Madoff said that he did not want to talk to them at the office, and arranged a meeting at Madoff's apartment in Manhattan. At that meeting Madoff stated, in substance, that he "wasn't sure he would be able to hold it together" if they continued to discuss the issue at the office.

23. At Madoff's Manhattan apartment, Madoff informed the two senior employees, in substance, that his investment advisory business was a fraud. Madoff stated that he was "finished," that he had "absolutely nothing," that "it's all just one big lie," and that it was "basically, a giant Ponzi scheme." In substance, Madoff communicated to the senior employees that he had for years been paying returns to certain investors out of the principal received from other, different, investors. Madoff stated that the business was insolvent, and that it had been for years. Madoff also stated that he estimated the losses from this fraud to be approximately $50 billion. One of the senior employees has a personal account at BMIS in which several million had been invested under the management of Madoff.

24. At Madoff's Manhattan apartment, Madoff further informed the two senior employees referenced above that, in approximately one week, he planned to surrender to authorities, but before he did that, he had approximately $200-300 million left, and he planned to use that money to make payments to certain selected employees, family, and friends.

FIRST CLAIM FOR RELIEF
Violations of Sections 206(1) and 206(2) of the Advisers Act
(Against Madoff and BMIS)
(Fraud Upon Advisory Clients and Breach of Fiduciary Duty by Investment Adviser)

25. Paragraphs 1 through 24 are realleged and incorporated by reference as if set forth fully herein.

26. Madoff and BMIS at all relevant time were investment advisers within the meaning of Section 201(11) of the Advisers Act [15 U.S.C. § 80b-2(11)]

27. Madoff and BMIS directly or indirectly, singly or in concert, knowingly or recklessly, through the use of the mails or any means or instrumentality of interstate commerce, while acting as investment

advisers within the meaning of Section 202(11) of the Advisers Act [15 U.S.C. §80b-2(11)]: (a) have employed, are employing, or are about to employ devices, schemes, and artifices to defraud any client or prospective client; or (b) have engaged, are engaging, or are about to engage in acts, practices, or courses of business which operates as a fraud or deceit upon any client or prospective client.

28. As described in the paragraphs above, Madoff and BMIS violated Sections 206(1) and 206(2) of the Advisers Act [15 U.S.C. §§ 80b-6(1), (2)] and unless enjoined will continue to violate Sections 206(1) and 206(2) of the Advisers Act [15 U.S.C. §§ 80b-6(1), (2)].

SECOND CLAIM FOR RELIEF
Violations of Section 17(a)(I) of the Securities Act
(Against all Defendants)
(Antifraud violations)

29. Paragraphs 1 through 24 are realleged and incorporated by reference as if set forth fully herein.

30. From at least 2005 through the present, the Defendants, in the offer and sale of securities, by the use of the means and instruments of transportation and communication in interstate commerce or by the use of the mails, directly and indirectly, have employed and are employing devices, schemes and artifices to defraud.

31. The Defendants knew or were reckless in not knowing of the activities described above.

32. By reason of the activities herein described, the Defendants have violated and are violating Section 17(a)(1) of the Securities Act [15 U.S.C. §77q(a)(1)].

THIRD CLAIM FOR RELIEF
Violations of Section 17(a)(2) and 17(a)(3) of the Securities Act
(Against all Defendants)
Antifraud violations)

33. Paragraphs 1through 24 are realleged and incorporated by reference as if set forth fully herein.

34. From at least 2005, the Defendants, in the offer and sale of securities, by the use of the means and instruments of transportation and communication in interstate commerce or by the use of the mails, directly and indirectly, have obtained and are obtaining money and property by means of untrue statements of material fact or omissions to state material facts necessary in order to make the statements made, in light of the circumstances under which they were made, not misleading, and have engaged and are engaging in transactions, practices or courses of business which have operated and will operate as a fraud and deceit upon investors.

35. By reason of the activities herein described, the Defendants have violated and are violating Sections 17(a)(2) and 17(a)(3) of the Securities Act [15 U.S.C. §77q(a)(2) and §77q(a)(3)1.

FOURTH CLAIM FOR RELIEF
Violations of Section 10(b) of the Exchange Act and Rule 10b-5
(Against all Defendants)
(Antifraud violations)

36. Paragraphs 1through 24 are realleged and incorporated by reference as if set forth fully herein.

37. From at least 2005 through the present, the Defendants, in connection with the purchase and sale of securities, directly and indirectly, by the use of the means and instrumentalities of interstate commerce or of the mails, have employed and are employing devices, schemes and artifices to defraud; have made and are making untrue statements of material fact and have and are omitting to state material facts necessary in order to make the statements made, in light of the circumstances under which they were made, not misleading; and have engaged and are engaging in acts, practices and courses of business which operated as a fraud and deceit upon investors.

38. Defendants knew or were reckless in not knowing of the activities described above.

39. By reason of the activities herein described, the Defendants have violated and are violating Section 10(b) of the Exchange Act [15 U.S.C. §§78j(b)] and Rule 10b-5 [17 C.F.R. 4240.10b-51 promulgated thereunder.

PRAYER FOR RELIEF

WHEREFORE, the Commission respectfully requests that the Court grant the following relief:

I.

Enter judgment in favor of the Commission finding that the Defendants each violated the securities laws and rules promulgated thereunder as alleged herein;

II.

An Order temporarily and preliminarily, and Final Judgments permanently, restraining and permanently enjoining the Defendants, their agents, servants, employees and attorneys and all persons in active concert or participation with them who receive actual notice of the injunction by personal service or otherwise, and each of them, from committing future violations of Section Sections 206(1) and 206(2) of the Advisers Act [15 U.S.C. §§ 80b-6(1) and 80b-6(2)].

III.

An Order temporarily and preliminarily, and Final Judgments permanently, restraining and permanently enjoining the Defendants, their agents, servants, employees and attorneys and all persons in active concert or participation with them who receive actual notice of the injunction by personal service or otherwise, and each of them, from committing future violations of Section 17(a) of the Securities Act, 15 U.S.C. § 77q(a), Section 10(b) of the Exchange Act, 15 U.S.C. § 78j(b) and Rule 10b-5, 17 C.F.R. § 240.10b-5.

IV.

An order directing the Defendants to disgorge their ill-gotten gains, plus prejudgment interest thereon.

V.

Final Judgments directing the Defendants to pay civil money penalties pursuant to Section 209(e) of the Advisers Act [15 U.S.C. 5§ 80b-91, Section 20(d) of the Securities Act [15 U.S.C. § 77t(d)] and Section 21(d)(3) of the Exchange Act 115 U.S.C. § 78u(d)(3)].

VII.

Granting such other and further relief as to this Court seems just and proper.

FURTHER RESOURCES

Books

Kirtzman, Andrew. *Betrayal: The Life and Lies of Bernie Madoff.* New York: Harper Perennial, 2010.

Morgenson, Gretchen. *Reckless Endangerment: How Outsized Ambition, Greed, and Corruption Created the Worst Financial Crisis of Our Time.* New York: St. Martin's Griffin, 2012.

Web Sites

"Bernard L. Madoff News." *New York Times.* http://topics.nytimes.com/top/reference/timestopics/people/m/bernard_l_madoff/index.html (accessed on March 11, 2013).

"The Madoff Files: Bernie's Billions." *The Independent.* www.independent.co.uk/news/business/analysis-and-features/the-madoff-files-bernies-billions-1518939.html (accessed on March 11, 2013).

"The Madoff Investment Scandal." *NPR.* www.npr.org/series/98393250/the-madoff-investment-scandal (accessed on March 1, 2013).

"United States v. Bernard L. Madoff and Related Cases." *United States Department of Justice.* www.justice.gov/usao/nys/madoff.html (accessed on March 11, 2013).

"The Fall of Enron"

Magazine article

By: Wendy Zellner, Stephanie Anderson Forest, Emily Thornton, Peter Coy, Heather Timmons, Louis Lavelle, and David Henry

Date: December 2001

Source: Zellner, Wendy, Stephanie A. Forest, Emily Thornton, Peter Coy, Heather Timmons, Louis Lavelle, and David Henry. "The Fall of Enron." *Business Week*, December 16, 2001. www.businessweek.com/stories/2001-12-16/the-fall-of-enron (accessed on October 18, 2012).

About the Publication: *Business Week* is a weekly periodical that was founded in September 1929. The magazine's coverage of the American business realm—politics, practices, trends, marketing, and management, among other topics—was initially editorial in nature, but it transitioned gradually towards a more objective presentation of internationally relevant business news. At the time *The Fall of Enron* was published, *Business Week* was one of the world's leading business publications, along with *Forbes* and *Fortune*. It was later acquired by the Bloomberg publishing conglomerate, changing its name to *Businessweek*.

INTRODUCTION

Enron Corporation was founded in 1985, the result of several successive mergers between American energy companies. The company originally provided a diverse array of goods and services related to the energy and commodities markets, but soon it moved its headquarters from Omaha, Nebraska, to Houston, Texas, and reduced its business dealings to focus on the production and transmission of electricity and natural gas. Soon afterward, Enron hired finance wunderkind Andrew Fastow as an accountant. Recent deregulation of the energy industry, effected primarily through the Natural Gas Wellhead Decontrol Act of 1989 and the National Energy Policy Act of 1992, provided a stage for Fastow to engage in legally murky bookkeeping practices intended to bolster Enron's financial performance, at least on paper. Chief among these accounting tricks was the creation of several "limited liability special purpose entities," financial bodies that existed solely to assume the debts and liabilities of the parent company, thus artificially bolstering Enron's reported value and profitability.

Thanks largely to Fastow's "creative accounting" practices, Enron was able to attract droves of investors enticed by the company's favorable credit rating and ever-increasing stock price. Even amid costly missteps and failed ventures (kept secret by transferring losses to special purpose entities), Enron's available capital continued to climb, allowing it to develop pipelines, power plants, and water plants, and to expand into foreign markets such as Brazil, India, and England. In 1999, Enron started an ambitious online commodities trading endeavor, called EnronOnline, the world's first such service.

By the time EnronOnline was launched, the company's carefully maintained façade was beginning to crumble. Industry insiders began questioning Enron's fraudulent and fabricated earnings reports (which presented expected future revenue and returns as actual income), causing investment capital to start drying up. Executives who knew of Fastow's accounting practices, fearful of an impending collapse in the scheme, began selling their Enron stock in large quantities. The resulting decline in Enron's stock value caused panic among investors, who were urged not to dispense with their holdings. By August 2001, Enron's stock had fallen below half of its value the year prior. Heightened media scrutiny led the company to retroactively edit its financial reports for several years, at which point Enron's credit rating was downgraded. After failing to secure the billions of dollars in credit necessary to pay off debts incurred by its credit devaluation, Enron filed for bankruptcy on December 2, 2001, at the time the largest such filing in U.S. history.

SIGNIFICANCE

An investigation conducted by the U.S. Securities and Exchange Commission (SEC) in response to Enron's financial collapse discovered that company executives had knowingly misled investors and business partners. The extent of this deceit was revealed in January 2006 court proceedings, when Fastow, former Enron CEO and chairman Kenneth Lay, former president and COO Jeffrey Skilling, and sixteen others involved in the company's fraud were convicted on felony charges including fraud, money laundering, conspiracy, obstruction of justice, insider trading, and making false statements.

The American public was outraged at the deliberate, institutionalized corruption that Enron executives had perpetrated over the previous decade. Especially inflammatory was the fact that the executives responsible profited immensely from the fraud at the expense of regular employees, whose pensions,

healthcare plans, and even compensation were dispensed in the form of Enron stock, which was rendered worthless when the company went bankrupt (the company's image was not improved by the flagrant arrogance exhibited by Enron executives at their trials). Although it was not the decade's largest or most spectacular example of corporate misconduct, the Enron scandal came to represent the greed and corruption of corporate America as the nation's working class grew increasingly disillusioned and dissatisfied with its treatment at the hands of "Big Business."

PRIMARY SOURCE

"THE FALL OF ENRON"

SYNOPSIS: This article, published in one of the United States' most prominent business periodicals, details the Enron scandal as it was understood immediately after the company filed for bankruptcy. It discusses Enron history and the public's reaction to revelations of fraud, and it provides economic context for the company's demise.

To former Enron (ENE) CEO Jeffrey K. Skilling, there were two kinds of people in the world: those who got it and those who didn't. "It" was Enron's complex strategy for minting rich profits and returns from a trading and risk-management business built essentially on assets owned by others. Vertically integrated behemoths like ExxonMobil Corp. (XOM), whose balance sheet was rich with oil reserves, gas stations, and other assets, were dinosaurs to a contemptuous Skilling. "In the old days, people worked for the assets," Skilling mused in an interview last January. "We've turned it around—what we've said is the assets work for the people."

But who looks like Tyrannosaurus Rex now? As Enron Corp. struggles to salvage something from the nation's largest bankruptcy case, filed on Dec. 2, it's clear that the real Enron was a far cry from the nimble "asset light" market maker that Skilling proclaimed. And the financial maneuvering and off-balance-sheet partnerships that he and ex-Chief Financial Officer Andrew S. Fastow perfected to remove everything from telecom fiber to water companies from Enron's debt-heavy balance sheet helped spark the company's implosion. "Jeff's theory was assets were bad, intellectual capital was good," says one former senior executive. Employees readily embraced the rhetoric, the executive says, but they "didn't understand how it was funded."

Neither did many others. Bankers, stock analysts, auditors, and Enron's own board failed to comprehend the risks in this heavily leveraged trading giant. Enron's bankruptcy filings show $13.1 billion in debt for the

The Enron logo is displayed in front of the company's Houston, Texas, headquarters in January 2002. © JAMES NIELSEN/AFP/GETTY IMAGES.

parent company and an additional $18.1 billion for affiliates. But that doesn't include at least $20 billion more estimated to exist off the balance sheet. Kenneth L. Lay, 59, who had nurtured Skilling, 48, as his successor, sparked the first wave of panic when he revealed in an Oct. 16 conference call with analysts that deals involving partnerships run by his CFO would knock $1.2 billion off shareholder equity. Lay, who had been out of day-to-day management for years, was never able to clearly explain how the partnerships worked or why anyone shouldn't assume the worst—that they were set up to hide Enron's problems, inflate earnings, and personally benefit the executives who managed some of them.

That uncertainty ultimately scuttled Enron's best hope for a rescue: its deal to be acquired by its smaller but healthier rival, Dynegy Inc. (DYN). Now Enron is frantically seeking a rock-solid banking partner to help maintain some shred of its once-mighty trading empire. Already, 4,000 Enron workers in Houston have lost their jobs. And hundreds of creditors, from banks to telecoms to construction companies, are trying to recover part of the billions they're owed.

From the beginning, Lay had a vision for Enron that went far beyond that of a traditional energy company. When Lay formed Enron from the merger of two pipeline companies in 1985, he understood that deregulation of the business would offer vast new opportunities. To exploit them, he turned to Skilling, then a McKinsey & Co. consultant. Skilling was the chief nuts-and-bolts-operator from 1997 until his departure last summer, and the architect of an increasingly byzantine financial structure. After he abruptly quit in August, citing personal reasons, and his right-hand financier Fastow was ousted Oct. 24, there was no one left to explain it.

Much of the blame for Enron's collapse has focused on the partnerships, but the seeds of its destruction were planted well before the October surprises. According to former insiders and other sources close to Enron, it was already on shaky financial ground from a slew of bad investments, including overseas projects ranging from a water business in England to a power distributor in Brazil. "You make enough billion-dollar mistakes, and they add up," says one source close to Enron's top executives. In June, Standard & Poor's analysts put the company on notice that its underperforming international assets were of growing concern. But S&P, which like *BusinessWeek* is a unit of The McGraw-Hill companies, ultimately reaffirmed the credit ratings, based on Enron's apparent willingness to sell assets and take other steps.

Behind all the analyses of Enron was the assumption that the core energy business was thriving. It was still growing rapidly, but margins were inevitably coming down as the market matured. "Once that growth slowed, any weakness would start becoming more apparent," says Standard & Poor's Corp. director Todd A. Shipman. "They were not the best at watching their cost." Indeed, the tight risk controls that seemed to work well in the trading business apparently didn't apply to other parts of the company.

Skilling's answer to growing competition in energy trading was to push Enron's innovative techniques into new arenas, everything from broadband to metals, steel, and even advertising time and space. Skilling knew he had to find a way to finance his big growth plans and manage the international problems without killing the company's critical investment-grade credit rating. Without a clever solution, trading partners would flee, or the cost of doing deals would become insurmountable.

"He's Heartbroken"

No one ever disputed that Skilling was clever. The Pittsburgh-born son of a sales manager for an Illinois valve company, he took over as production director at a startup Aurora (Ill.) TV station at age 13 when an older staffer quit and he was the only one who knew how to operate the equipment. Skilling landed a full-tuition scholarship to Southern Methodist University in Dallas to study engineering, but quickly changed to business. After graduation, he went to work for a Houston bank. The bank later went bust while Skilling was at Harvard Business School. Skilling said that fiasco made him determined to keep strict risk controls on Enron's trading business. He once told *BusinessWeek* that "I've never not been successful in business or work, ever." Skilling now declines to comment, but his brother Tom, a Chicago TV weatherman, says of him: "He's heartbroken over what's going on there. ... We were not raised to look on these kinds of things absent emotion."

Enron's "intellectual capital" was Skilling's pride and joy. He recruited more than 250 newly minted MBAs each year from the nation's top business schools. Meteorologists and PhDs in math and economics helped analyze and model the vast amounts of data that Enron used in its trading operations. A forced ranking system weeded out the poor performers. "It was as competitive internally as it was externally," says one former executive.

It was no surprise then that Skilling would turn to a bright young finance wizard, Fastow, to help him find capital for his rapidly expanding empire. Boasting an MBA from Northwestern University, Fastow was recruited to Enron in 1990 from Continental Bank, where he worked on leveraged buyouts. Articulate, handsome, and mature beyond his years, he became Enron's CFO at age 36. In October, 1999, he earned *CFO Magazine*'s CFO Excellence Award for Capital Structure Management. An effusive Skilling crowed to the magazine: "We didn't want someone stuck in the past, since the industry of yesterday is no longer. Andy has the intelligence and the youthful exuberance to think in new ways."

But Skilling's fondness for the buttoned-down Fastow was not widely shared. Many colleagues considered him a prickly, even vindictive man, prone to attacking those he didn't like in Enron's group performance reviews. Fastow, through his attorney, declined to comment for this story. When he formed and took a personal stake in the LJM partnerships that blew up in October, the conflict of interest inherent in those deals only added to his colleagues' distaste for him. Enron admits Fastow earned more than $30 million from the partnerships. The Enron CFO wasn't any more popular on Wall Street, where investment bankers bristled at the finance group's "we're smarter than you guys" attitude. Indeed, that came back to haunt Enron when it needed capital commitments to stem the liquidity crisis. "It's the sort of organization about which people said, 'Screw them. We don't really owe them anything,'" says one investment banker.

While LJM—and Fastow's direct personal involvement and enrichment—shocked many, the deal was just the latest version of a financing strategy that Skilling and Fastow had used to good effect many times since the mid-'90s to fund investments with private equity while keeping assets and debt off the balance sheet. Keeping the debt off Enron's books depended on a steady or rising stock price and an investment-grade credit rating. "They were put together with good intentions to offset some risk," says S&P analyst Ron M. Barone. "It's conceivable that it got away from them."

Did it ever. The off-balance-sheet structures grew increasingly complex and risky, according to insiders and others who have studied the deals. Some, with names like Osprey, Whitewing, and Marlin, were revealed in Enron's financial filings and even rated by the big credit-rating agencies. But almost no one seemed to have a clear picture of Enron's total debt, what triggers might hasten repayment, or how some of the deals could dilute shareholder equity. "No one ever sat down and added up how many liabilities would come due if this company got downgraded," says one lender involved with Enron. Many investors were unaware of provisions in some deals that could essentially dump the debts back on Enron. In some cases, if Enron's stock fell below a certain price and the credit rating dropped below investment grade—once unimaginable—nearly $4 billion in partnership debt would have to be covered by Enron. At the same time, the value of the assets in many of these partnerships was dropping, making it even harder for Enron to cover the debt.

High Hopes

Skilling tried to accelerate the sale of international assets after becoming chief operating officer in 1997, but the efforts were arduous and time-consuming. Even as tech stocks melted down, Skilling was determined not to scale back his grandiose broadband trading dreams or the resulting price-to-earnings multiple of almost 60 that they helped create for Enron's stock. At its peak in August, 2000, about a third of the stock's $90 price was attributable to expectations for growth of broadband trading, executives estimate.

That rapidly rising stock price—up 55% in '99 and 87% in 2000—gave Skilling and Fastow a hot currency for luring investors into their off-balance-sheet deals. They quickly became dependent on such deals to finance their expansion efforts. "It was like crack," says a company insider. Trouble is, Enron's stock came tumbling back to earth when market valuations fell this year. By April, its price had fallen to about 55. And its far-flung operational troubles were taking their own toll. In its much-hyped broadband business, for instance, a capacity glut and financial meltdown made it hard to find creditworthy counterparties for trading. And after spending some $1.2 billion to build and operate a fiber-optic network, Enron found itself with an asset whose value was rapidly deteriorating. Even last year, company executives could see the need to cut back an operation that had 1,700 employees and a cash burn rate of $700 million a year.

"Something to Prove"

And the international problems weren't going away. Enron's 65% stake in the $3 billion Dabhol power plant in India was mired in a dispute with its largest customer, which refused to pay for electricity. Some Indian politicians have despised the deal for years, claiming that cunning and even corrupt Enron executives cut a deal that charged India too much for its power.

Enron's ill-fated 1998 investment in the water-services business was another drag on earnings. Many saw the purchase of Wessex Water in England as a "consolation prize" for Rebecca P. Mark, the hard-charging Enron executive who had negotiated the Dabhol deal and other investments around the world. With Skilling having won out as Lay's clear heir apparent, top executives wanted to move her out of the way, say former insiders. A narrowly split board approved the Wessex deal, which formed the core of Azurix Corp., to be run by Mark. But Enron was blindsided by British regulators who slashed the rates the utility could charge. Meanwhile, Mark piled on more high-priced water assets. "Once [Skilling] put her there, he let her go wild," says a former executive. "And she's going to go wild because she has something to prove." Mark spent too much on a water concession in Brazil and ran into political obstacles. She declined to comment for this story.

But if Azurix was a prime example of Enron's sketchy investment strategy, it also demonstrated how the company tried to disguise its problems with financial alchemy. To set up the company, Enron formed a partnership called the Atlantic Water Trust, in which it held a 50% stake. That kept Wessex off Enron's balance sheet. Enron's partner in the joint venture was Marlin Water Trust, which consisted of institutional investors. To help attract them, Enron promised to back up the debt with its own stock if necessary. But if Enron's credit rating fell below investment grade and the stock fell below a certain point, Enron could be on the hook for the partnership's $915 million in debt.

The end for Enron came when its murky finances and less-than-forthright disclosures spooked investors and Dynegy. The clincher came when Dynegy's bankers spent hours sifting through a supposedly final draft of Enron's about-to-be-released 10Q—only to discover two pages of damning new numbers when the quarterly statement was made publicly available. Debt coming due in the fourth quarter had leapt from under $1 billion to $2.8 billion. Even worse, cash on hand—to which Dynegy had recently contributed $1.5 billion—shrunk from $3 billion to $1.2 billion. Dynegy "had a two-hour meeting with the new treasurer of Enron, who had been in that seat for two weeks," said a source close to the deal. "He had no clue where the numbers came from."

Respect for Assets

Skilling and Fastow face most of the wrath of reeling employees. "Someone told me yesterday if they see Jeff Skilling on the street, they would scratch out his eyes," says a former executive. One of Fastow's lawyers, David B. Gerger, says his client has been the subject of death threats and anti-Semitic tirades in Internet chat rooms. "Naturally people look for scapegoats, but it would be wrong to scapegoat Mr. Fastow," says Gerger.

He confirms that Fastow has hired a big gun to handle his civil litigation: David Boies's firm, which represented the Justice Dept. in its suit against Microsoft Corp. On Dec. 5, Milberg Weiss Bershad Hynes & Lerach filed a suit against Fastow, Skilling, and 27 other Enron executives, saying they illegally made more than $1 billion off stock sales before Enron tanked. And a source at the Securities & Exchange Commission says four U.S. Attorney Offices are considering whether to pursue criminal charges against Enron and its officers.

Would the cash squeeze have caught up to Enron, even without Skilling's and Fastow's fancy financing? Credit analysts still argue that the debt would have been manageable, absent the crisis of confidence that dried up Enron's trading business and access to the capital markets. But even they have a new respect for old-fashioned, high-quality assets. "When things get really tough, hard assets are the kind you can depend upon," says S&P's Shipman. That's something Enron's whiz-kid financiers failed to appreciate.

FURTHER RESOURCES
Books

Bryce, Robert. *Pipe Dreams: Greed Ego, and the Death of Enron*. New York: Public Affairs, 2002.

Cruver, Brian. *Anatomy of Greed*. New York: Carroll & Graf, 2002.

MacLean, Beth, and Peter Elkind. *Smartest Guys in the Room: The Amazing Rise and Scandalous Fall of Enron*. London: Portfolio, 2003.

Web Sites

"Enron Legal News Archive." www.breakinglegalnews.com/search/enron (accessed on February 16, 2013).

"Public Domain Enron Email Corpus and Database." www.enron-mail.com/ (accessed on February 16, 2013).

"TIME Specials: Behind the Enron Scandal." *TIME*. www.time.com/time/specials/packages/0,28757,2021097,00.html (accessed on October 18, 2012).

"Top 10 Dot-com Flops"

Editorial

By: Kent German

Date: August 2005

Source: German, Kent. "Top 10 Dot-com Flops." August 2005. www.cnet.com/1990-11136_1-6278387-1. html (accessed on February 15, 2013).

About the Web site: CNET was created in 1994, originally existing as a television production company focused on consumer electronics and technology. The company expanded its holdings to include a Web site and radio station, as well as various technology sites and services. In the 2000s, CNET was one of the leading news sources concerned with electronics and technology, featuring interviews with industry personnel, product reviews, editorials, and product previews. The site and its subsidiaries were purchased by CBS Interactive in 2008, expanding the availability and profile of CNET and its network of affiliates.

INTRODUCTION

The term "speculative bubble" refers to a condition in which a commodity—which could be almost anything, from a valuable raw material to trading cards to stock options—is routinely exchanged at a significantly higher price than its actual value. Typically, the phenomenon arises because investors are encouraged to purchase a given commodity by seeing its traded price trend upward for a sustained period, with the expectation that the price will continue to rise in the future. As more and more people purchase units of the commodity in question, each successive investor expects to receive more per unit when selling the commodity than he or she paid for it, even though its real intrinsic value (the utility of the commodity) does not increase. Thus, a commodity that is the subject of a speculative bubble eventually ends up trading at a value significantly higher than its fundamental worth, artificially inflating the "on paper" assets of those that possess it.

Unfortunately for those who grow rich by investing in a commodity bubble, the condition is ultimately untenable. Eventually, the sale price required for an investor to profit by selling a commodity purchased at an inflated value will be higher than any buyer is willing to pay. Once this point is reached, the traded value of the commodity begins to plummet as investors scramble to unload their

holdings and minimize their losses. This process is known as the "bursting" of the bubble, characterized by the traded value of the commodity in question reverting to its equilibrium position. The bursting of a speculative bubble causes those unlucky enough to possess significant holdings in the relevant commodity to lose enormous amounts of money, as their on-paper value immediately plummets in reflection of the commodity's actual value.

The spectacular rise of Internet business in the United States is an example of a speculative bubble. During the final three years of the 1990s, the collective business world was abuzz with excitement over the Internet's potential to revolutionize the way humans lead their lives and conduct their business. Venture capitalists and options traders, eager to capitalize on the emerging (and barely understood) technology, threw billions of dollars into nearly any half-boiled startup with a semblance of a business plan, so long as that plan somehow incorporated the Internet. The companies that were founded in those early days of a commercialized Internet, known as "dot-coms," were most often staffed and founded by ambitious, idealistic young programmers and business students with little or no experience of real-world business operations and funded by venture capitalists who were clueless about the mechanisms and capabilities of the Internet.

Despite the numerous hazards of e-commerce, hundreds of seemingly viable dot-coms sprung up between 1997 and 1999, offering every conceivable online service. Because the market was so thoroughly saturated with competition, the standard business model of these companies was to spend as much money as possible advertising and cultivating public awareness, with little or no consideration given to producing revenue or making a profit. It was more important to establish the company's position in the eye of the public, the reasoning went, than to make money right out of the gate. Because of the hype surrounding the industry, Internet companies were able to command enormously inflated stock prices, turning early investors into overnight millionaires.

SIGNIFICANCE

However, the prosperity was not to last. The practice of spending millions of dollars—usually culled from IPOs and startup funds—on advertising and generating awareness instead of providing an appealing service, although vaunted by technology and business experts alike, proved to be a risky one. Only the most innovative and well-planned dot-coms, such as Google and Amazon, were able to withstand several years of incurred loss before beginning to earn money. The rest saw their stock values plummet as they ran out of capital, resulting in acquisition or liquidation for most. The NASDAQ Composite stock index reached the dot-com bubble's peak in March 2000, after which the bubble burst and the value of most Internet company stocks declined steadily throughout 2000 and 2001. Billions of dollars in equity were lost over this period, producing a minor recession that significantly thinned the number of active, publicly traded Internet companies.

The business atmosphere of the 2000s decade was largely a product of the seemingly ridiculous strategies and mindsets of the dot-com bubble, in that the surviving Internet companies were careful to avoid repeating the mistakes such thinking engenders. Investors, too, freshly burned by foolish dot-com executives and unfounded media hype, were duly cautioned against the dangers of excessive speculation, although the real-estate bubble of the late 2000s proves that this lesson was short-lived.

PRIMARY SOURCE

"TOP 10 DOT-COM FLOPS"

SYNOPSIS: In this article, the author lists ten of the most spectacular or otherwise noteworthy failures of the dot-com boom.

The most astounding thing about the dot-com boom was the obscene amount of money spent. Zealous venture capitalists fell over themselves to invest millions in start-ups; dot-coms blew millions on spectacular marketing campaigns; new college graduates became instant millionaires and rushed out to spend it; and companies with unproven business models executed massive IPOs with sky-high stock prices. We all know what eventually happened. Most of these start-ups died dramatic deaths. These are the celebrity victims of the new-economy bust.

1. Webvan (1999–2001): A core lesson from the dot-com boom is that even if you have a good idea, it's best not to grow too fast too soon. But online grocer Webvan was the poster child for doing just that, making the celebrated company our number one dot-com flop. In a mere 18 months, it raised $375 million in an IPO, expanded from the San Francisco Bay Area to eight U.S. cities, and built a gigantic infrastructure from the ground up (including a *$1 billion* order for a group of high-tech warehouses). Webvan came to be worth $1.2 billion (or $30 per share at its peak), and it touted a 26-city expansion plan. But considering that the grocery business has razor-thin margins to begin with, it was never able to

attract enough customers to justify its spending spree. The company closed in July 2001, putting 2,000 out of work and leaving San Francisco's new ballpark with a Webvan cup holder at every seat.

2. Pets.com (1998–2000): Another important dot-com lesson was that advertising, no matter how clever, cannot save you. Take online pet-supply store Pets.com. Its talking sock puppet mascot became so popular that it appeared in a multimillion-dollar Super Bowl commercial and as a balloon in the Macy's Thanksgiving Day Parade. But as cute—or possibly annoying—as the sock puppet was, Pets.com was never able to give pet owners a compelling reason to buy supplies online. After they ordered kitty litter, a customer had to wait a few days to actually get it. And let's face it, when you need kitty litter, you *need* kitty litter. Moreover, because the company had to undercharge for shipping costs to attract customers, it actually lost money on most of the items it sold. Amazon.com-backed Pets.com raised $82.5 million in an IPO in February 2000 before collapsing nine months later.

Pets.com's mascot, the talking sock-puppet dog. © CHRIS HONDROS/GETTY IMAGES.

3. Kozmo.com (1998–2001): The shining example of a good idea gone bad, online store and delivery service Kozmo.com made it on our list of the top 10 tech we miss. For urbanites, Kozmo.com was cool and convenient. You could order a wide variety of products, from movies to snack food, and get them delivered to your door for free within an hour. It was the perfect antidote to a rainy night, but Kozmo learned too late that its primary attraction of free delivery was also its undoing. After expanding to seven cities, it was clear that it cost too much to deliver a DVD and a pack of gum. Kozmo eventually initiated a $10 minimum charge, but that didn't stop it from closing in March 2001 and laying off 1,100 employees. Though it never had an IPO (one was planned), Kozmo raised about $280 million and even secured a $150 million promotion deal with Starbucks.

4. Flooz.com (1998–2001): For every good dot-com idea, there are a handful of really terrible ideas. Flooz.com was a perfect example of a "what the heck were they thinking?" business. Pushed by *Jumping Jack Flash* star and perennial *Hollywood Squares* center square Whoopi Goldberg, Flooz was meant to be online currency that would serve as an alternative to credit cards. After buying a certain amount of Flooz, you could then use it at a number of retail partners. While the concept is similar to a merchant's gift card, at least gift cards are tangible items that are backed by the merchant and not a third party. It boggles the mind why anyone would rather use an "online currency" than an actual credit card, but that didn't stop Flooz from raising a staggering $35 million from investors and signing up retail giants such as Tower Records, Barnes & Noble, and Restoration Hardware. Flooz went bankrupt in August 2001 along with its competitor Beenz.com.

5. eToys.com (1997–2001): eToys is now back in business, yet its original incarnation is another classic boom-to-bust story. The company raised $166 million in a May 1999 IPO, but in the course of 16 months, its stock went from a high of $84 per share in October 1999 to a low of just 9 cents per share in February 2001. Much like Pets.com, eToys spent millions on advertising, marketing, and technology and battled a host of competitors. And like many of its failed brethren, all that spending outweighed the company's income, and investors quickly jumped ship. eToys closed in March 2001, but after being owned for a period by KayBee Toys, it's now back for a second run.

6. Boo.com (1998–2000): Though Boo.com is another flop that has been given new life by Fashionmall.com, its original incarnation proved that dot-com flops were not restricted to U.S. shores. Founded in the United Kingdom as an online fashion store, Boo.com was beset with problems and mismanagement from the start. Its complicated Web site, which relied heavily on JavaScript and Flash, was very slow to load at a time when dial-up Internet usage was the norm. Boo spent wads of cash to market itself as a global company but then had to deal with different languages, pricing, and tax structures in all the countries it served. The company also mysteriously decided to pay postage on returns, but even more importantly, sales never reached expectations. Boo.com eventually burned through $160 million before liquidation in May 2000.

7. MVP.com (1999–2000): Like Planet Hollywood and Flooz.com, MVP.com proved that celebrity endorsements are worth nothing in the long run. Backed by sports greats John Elway, Michael Jordan, and Wayne Gretzky and $65 million, MVP sold sporting goods online. Founded in 1999, the company grew to more than 150 employees, but a high-profile partnership came to be a liability. A few months after its launch, MVP.com entered into an $85 million, four-year agreement with CBS in which the network would provide advertising in exchange for an equity stake in the e-tailer. Yet barely a year later, CBS and its online affiliate SportsLine.com killed the agreement because MVP.com failed to pay the network an agreed-upon $10 million per year. The game was over for MVP.com soon afterward, and SportsLine took over the domain.

8. Go.com (1998–2001): The Walt Disney Company felt the sting of the dot-com bust with its portal Go.com. Started in 1998, Go.com was a combination of Disney's online properties and Infoseek, in which the Mouse had previously acquired a controlling interest. Though it was meant to be a "destination site" much like Yahoo, Go.com had its own little quirks, such as content restrictions against adult material. Disney was never able to make Go.com popular enough to validate the millions spent on promotion. In January 2001, Go.com was shut down, and Disney took a write-off of $790 million. Go.com still exists, but it carries only feeds from other Disney Web properties.

9. Kibu.com (1999–2000): Unlike the other flops listed here, Kibu.com, an online community for teenage girls, didn't wait till the very end to wave the white flag. In fact, at the time of its October 2000 closing, the company had not run out of the $22 million it raised. And on a more bizarre note, the end came only 46 days after a flashy San Francisco launch party. Though Kibu had started to attract traffic from its target demographic (incidentally one of the fastest-growing segments of Web users), company officials said they decided to shut down because "Kibu's timing in financial markets could not have been worse." Kibu was backed by several Silicon Valley bigwigs, and they sent a strong message about the financial prospects of other dot-coms by bailing on Kibu so soon.

10. GovWorks.com (1999–2000): Last but certainly not least, the story of GovWorks.com was good enough to become the documentary Startup.com, which chronicles its brief life. Envisioned as a Web site for citizens to do business with municipal government, GovWorks was started by two childhood friends in 1999. One was the flashy salesman, while the other had the technical know-how. At first, the future seemed bright as they suddenly found themselves worth millions of dollars each and rubbing elbows with the politically powerful. But you can guess what happened—everything that could go wrong soon did. Personalities and egos clashed during long work hours, one partner was ousted, technology was stolen, and they never got the software to work as it should have. A competitor eventually took over GovWorks in 2000.

FURTHER RESOURCES

Books

Cassidy, John. *Dot.con: How America Lost Its Mind and Its Money in the Internet Era.* New York: HarperCollins, 2002.

Lowenstein, Roger. *Origins of the Crash: The Great Bubble and Its Undoing.* London: Penguin, 2004.

Wolff, Michael. *Burn Rate: How I Survived the Gold Rush Years on the Internet.* New York: Simon & Schuster, 1998.

Web Sites

"The Dot-Com Bubble Bursts" *New York Times.* www.nytimes.com/2000/12/24/opinion/the-dot-com-bubble-bursts.html (accessed on February 15, 2013).

"When Bubble Burst" *International Monetary Fund.* www.imf.org/external/pubs/ft/weo/2003/01/pdf/chapter2.pdf (accessed on February 15, 2013).

"The Apple of Your Ear"

Magazine article

By: Lev Grossman

Date: January 12, 2007

Source: Grossman, Lev. "The Apple of Your Ear." *Time Magazine*, January 12, 2007. www.time.com/time/magazine/article/0,9171,1576854,00.html (accessed on February 22, 2013).

About the Publication: *Time* magazine, often stylized as *TIME*, was the United States' first news magazine, founded in 1918. Since it was first published, the magazine has been a popular source of news for Americans, featuring interviews and original reporting on a variety of cultural and political current events, both domestic and global. Known for its editorials, columnists, guest contributors, and photo essays, *Time* has long been a cultural and journalistic staple in the United States and one of its most noteworthy publications. It has also expanded to include international editions, such as *Time Europe* and *Time Asia*. The magazine's most famous segment is its annual "Person of the Year" award, in which the most influential person of the year is recognized and given a cover story.

INTRODUCTION

The California-based consumer electronics company Apple Inc. was founded in 1976 by Steve Jobs and Steve Wozniak, a pair of technology enthusiasts who had both dropped out of college to pursue careers in the emerging personal-computer industry. Apple's first product was the Apple I home computer kit, followed in 1977 by the Apple II, an innovative personal computer designed with a plastic, self-containing case and a full-color Graphical User Interface. Apple II proved successful, allowing the company to expand rapidly during the early 1980s. The Macintosh personal computer system, released in 1984 under the guidance of Jobs, was incredibly popular, but it soon lost market share to more powerful machines being released by competitor IBM. Undeterred, Jobs continued expending significant company resources on personal projects, prompting his forced resignation imposed by Apple CEO John Sculley and the board of directors. Without the vision of Jobs or Wozniak, who had left the company after being injured in an airplane accident, Apple lost momentum. Although its Macintosh II computer and assorted compatible accessories were successful, the proliferation of the PC-exclusive Windows Operating System, made by Microsoft, cost Apple the opportunity to attract new customers. The company began losing money in the 1990s, posting an incredible $68 million loss in the final quarter of 1995 and an almost-crippling loss of $740 million in the first quarter of 1996.

Apple was pulled from the brink of collapse by its acquisition of software company NeXT, where Jobs had been employed since his departure from Apple. Jobs reclaimed leadership of Apple in 1997 and set about radically restructuring the company and redefining its aims. With the release of the iMac personal computer, an all-in-one, streamlined, user-friendly system with a distinctive, minimalist design (the work of engineer and product designer Jonathan Ive), Apple made a triumphant return to commercial prominence. In 2001, the company revolutionized consumer electronics marketing and sales by opening the first Apple Stores, retail spaces designed specifically for the sale, display, and maintenance of Apple electronics. In November of that year, Apple unveiled the innovative iPod personal media player, also designed by Ive. The pocket-sized iPod, which was capable of storing and playing MP3 audio files (and, in later iterations, other types of media, such as videos and games), was a runaway success, quickly becoming one of the most profitable consumer electronic devices in history. In 2003, Apple launched the iTunes store, an online marketplace for the sale of MP3s, which became responsible for the majority of the world's music downloads, reporting over five billion purchases by the end of 2008. The company also began selling the MacBook line of laptop computers, which became hugely popular for their streamlined, simple interface and operability.

At the same time Apple was reclaiming its prominent position in the consumer electronics market, mobile phones were developing into one of the fastest-growing sectors of the global economy. Although the technology for cellular phones had existed since the 1960s, and had been publicly available since the late 1980s, they did not become commercially viable until the late 1990s. As telecommunications companies recognized the potential market for mobile phones, the technology for providing wireless cellular service rapidly developed, and by the early 2000s they had become widely available and affordable. Cell phones were transformed from a novelty to a near-necessity in conjunction with the increasingly interconnected and constantly communicating society generated by the development of email and the Internet. In 2003, the BlackBerry mobile phone was released, establishing the popularity of "smartphones"—cell phones equipped with mobile operating systems, capable of providing functionality exceeding standard calling and text messaging services, such as Web browsing, email, personal organization, instant messaging, and other standalone applications that require considerable computing power.

Intrigued by the recent development of touchscreen technology, Jobs instructed a team of Apple engineers to investigate its potential in 2005, initially planning to create a personal computing device that replaced the traditional mouse-and-keypad interface with an interactive touchscreen. Upon reviewing the results of the project's research, however, Jobs realized the technology's potential application in the expanding mobile phone market. He tasked Ive with designing a cell phone that implemented a touchscreen. The final

The Apple iPhone was launched in the United States in June 2007. © ALAIN DENANTES/GAMMA-RAPHO/GETTY IMAGES.

result, called the iPhone, was a masterpiece of minimalist design, featuring a face comprised almost entirely of a multi-touch enabled screen and a single button, as well as a small, 2.0 megapixel camera, a speaker, and an ambient light sensor. The device was additionally equipped with headphone and computer-connection inputs, an accelerometer, Global Positioning System (GPS) hardware, and a powerful built-in processor. The iPhone ran on the proprietary iPhone Operating System (iOS), which allowed different tasks to be executed by a series of discrete applications (apps), each represented by its own icon. It was heavily customizable, versatile, and capable of storing and playing rich media files, such as videos, games, music, photos, and text documents.

When the iPhone was announced in January 2007, it created an immediate storm of speculation and anticipation among technophiles and devoted Apple consumers. Jobs presented the device as a revolution in the functionality of smartphones, an all-in-one package for conducting the communication, storage, organization, and entertainment needs of its owners— a simple, intuitive means for emailing, Web browsing, calling, texting, and planning. The iPhone was particularly unique in its relationship with cellular service carrier Cingular, which had made the unprecedented move of allowing Apple complete control over the design of its hardware and software rather than strictly regulating the technological specifications of the device, as carriers typically did with other handset-telephone manufacturers. Apple filed over two hundred patent applications for various design features of the iPhone in an attempt to ensure that it was not replicated by other manufacturers.

The night before the iPhone's U.S. launch on June 29, 2007, customers lined city blocks and camped in lines outside Apple Stores, eager to purchase the device on the day of its release. It was a massive success, selling over one million units within seventy-five days of being made commercially available. In November of that year, the iPhone was released in France, Germany, Ireland, Spain, Portugal, and the United Kingdom, followed by twenty-two more countries in July 2008. Upon its initial release, the iPhone was offered with two hard drive options: 4GB, retailing at $499, and 8GB, available for $599. Reviewers and industry experts were generally favorable of the iPhone, noting its aesthetic appeal and streamlined functionality, earning it the honor of being titled *Time* magazine's "invention of the year." Although the iPhone never approached the sales figures claimed by mobile phones manufactured by rivals like Samsung, Nokia, and Motorola, its high profit margin made it immensely profitable for Apple.

In February 2008, Apple discontinued the 4GB iPhone model and introduced a 16GB model. The next month, the company released a development kit, allowing third-party programmers to create their own apps for the iPhone. These apps were made available with the July launch of the iTunes App Store, which accompanied iOS 2.0, the first major update to the phone's operating system. The App Store launched with approximately five hundred available apps, but it quickly grew to include thousands of programs capable of performing a diverse range of tasks. Some apps were available for free, and others required a payment, typically of less than $10. By 2009, the App Store had generated $769 million in revenue for Apple. In June 2008, Apple announced the iPhone 3G, the successor to the original iPhone, which was to come equipped with 3G wireless functionality, software improvements, and upgraded hardware. When it began shipping on July 11, 2008, the original iPhone was officially discontinued, and its final compatible iOS upgrade, version 3.1.3, was published a year later.

SIGNIFICANCE

If Apple's refined approach to consumer electronics was the industry's most significant development of the 2000s decade, then the iPhone was the single most important product released during that time. Like the iPod and MacBook product line, the iPhone demonstrated the premium customers were willing to pay for simplicity in design and usability in function. Apple's products, culture, and commitment to customer satisfaction generated not only profitability but a veritable legion of devoted customers, whose willingness to purchase every new product the company released, and vocally advocate their merits, earned them the moniker "the Cult of Mac." This phenomenon demonstrated that Steve Jobs's acute attunement to the desires of consumers—who were often willing to sacrifice features in their technology in exchange for enhanced usability—was unrivaled, leading other companies to mimic Apple's every move.

The iPhone also had a monumental impact on the mobile phone industry. In addition to spawning dozens of knockoffs and imitations, the popularity of the iPhone's multi-touch design catalyzed the movement of cell phone manufacturers away from interfaces cluttered with keys, buttons, and switches towards more refined, touchscreen-focused designs. Likewise, the success of Apple's initiative to attract third-party app developers with the iTunes App Store prompted other companies to imitate its format, manifested as such digital marketplaces as Google's Android App Market, released in 2008, BlackBerry World, launched in 2009, and the Windows Phone Store, which debuted in 2010. Cellular service providers, threatened by Apple's exclusive contract with Cingular (later AT&T), scurried to respond to the iPhone by forming exclusivity deals with other phone designs, although none managed to approach the level of success achieved by Apple.

As the iPhone's successors proliferated the technology market, their success was somewhat tinged with tragedy—Steve Jobs, who had survived pancreatic cancer treatment in 2003, was forced to leave Apple for most of 2011 when he relapsed. Although not unforeseen, Jobs's death in October of that year represented the loss of one of the twenty-first century's most visionary, directed businessmen. Media retrospectives and tributes celebrated his contributions to contemporary society and culture in the United States, and they noted that he had at least had the fortune of seeing his final projects, the iPhone and iPad (an enlarged iPhone without phone-calling capabilities), reach fruition and incredible success.

More than anything, the popularity of the iPhone allowed U.S. society to grow increasingly connected and available, as users were given quick, easy access to every method of communication, including social media sites like Facebook and Twitter through proprietary apps, as well as video-calling services like Skype and Viber. The growing ubiquity of the iPhone and other Apple products among members of the younger generations harkened the arrival of a perpetually communicative, endlessly collaborative culture in which cell phones were scarcely used as telephones.

PRIMARY SOURCE

"THE APPLE OF YOUR EAR"

SYNOPSIS: This article describes Apple's foray into the mobile phone market with its release of the iPhone.

The iPhone started out the way a lot of cool things do: as something completely different. A few years ago, Steve Jobs noticed how many development dollars were being spent—particularly in the greater Seattle metropolitan area—on what are called tablet PCs: flat portable computers that work with a touch screen instead of a mouse and keyboard. Jobs, being Jobs, was curious. He had some Apple engineers noodle around with a touch screen. When they showed him what they came up with, he got excited.

So excited he forgot all about tablet computers. He had bigger game to hunt.

Jobs had just led Apple on a triumphant rampage through a new market sector, portable digital-music players, and he was looking around for more technology to conquer. He found the ideal target sitting on his hip. Consumers bought nearly a billion cell phones last year, 10 times the number of iPods in circulation. Break off just 1% of that, and you can buy yourself a lot of black turtlenecks. "It was unanimous that this should be it," Jobs says. "It wasn't even by a little, it was by a mile. It was the hardest one too." Apple's new iPhone, which will be available in June, could do to the cell-phone market what the iPod did to the portable-music-player market: crush it pitilessly beneath the weight of its own superiority. This is unfortunate for anybody else who makes cell phones, but it's good news for those of us who use them.

The game is a little different this time. With the iPod, Jobs essentially created a whole new product category. The cell-phone turf is already held by entrenched armies of phonemakers and service providers. They may not be as hip or innovative as Apple, but they will shred one another for nickels, and there are a lot of nickels on the ground. One point of market share in the handset business is worth $1.4 billion. Motorola, having sold more

than 50 million Razrs with not enough to show for it, will probably be reverse engineering the iPhone before it hits the stores. "We already have cell phones and smart phones, so the marketplace is already very competitive," says industry analyst Jeff Kagan. "We have not seen Apple compete in the insanely intense, competitive wireless marketplace."

But it wasn't just the money. Cell phones interested Jobs because even though they do all kinds of stuff—calling, text messaging, Web browsing, contact management, music playback, photos and video—they do it very badly, by forcing you to press lots of tiny buttons and navigate diverse heterogeneous interfaces and squint at a tiny screen. "Everybody hates their phone," Jobs says, "and that's not a good thing. And there's an opportunity there." To Jobs' perfectionist eyes, phones are broken. Jobs likes things that are broken. It means he can make something that isn't and sell it to you at a premium price.

That was why, 2½ years ago, Jobs sicced his wrecking crew of designers and engineers on the cell phone as we know—and hate— it. They began by melting the face off a video iPod. No clickwheel, no keypad. They sheared off the entire front and replaced it with a huge, bright, vivid screen—that touch screen Jobs got so excited about a few paragraphs ago. When you need to dial, it shows you a keypad; when you need other buttons, the screen serves them up. When you want to watch a video, the buttons disappear. Suddenly, the interface isn't fixed and rigid, it's fluid and molten. Software replaces hardware.

Into that iPod they stuffed a working version of Apple's operating system, OS X, so that the phone could handle real, nontoy applications like Web browsers and e-mail clients. They put in a cell antenna and two more antennas for wi-fi and Bluetooth, plus a bunch of sensors, so that the phone knows how bright its screen should be and whether it should display vertically or horizontally, and when it should turn off the touch screen so that you don't accidentally operate it with your ear.

Then Jonathan Ive, Apple's head of design—the Englishman who shaped the iMac and the iPod—squashed the case to less than half an inch thick and widened it to what looks like a bar of expensive chocolate wrapped in aluminum and stainless steel. The iPhone is a typical piece of Ive design: an austere, abstract, Platonic-looking form that somehow also manages to feel warm and organic and ergonomic. Unlike my phone. Ive picks it up and points out four little nubbins on the back. "Your phone's got feet on," he says, not unkindly. "Why would anybody put feet on a phone?" Ive has the answer, of course: "It raises the speaker on the back off the table. But the right solution is to put the speaker in the right place in the first place. That's why our speaker isn't on the bottom, so you can have it on the table and you don't need feet." Sure enough, no feet mar the iPhone's smooth lines.

O.K., so it's pretty. Now pick it up and make a call. A big friendly icon appears on that huge screen. Say a second call comes in while you're talking. Another icon appears. Tap that second icon, and you switch to the second call. Tap the "merge calls" icon, and you've got a three-way conference call. It's ridiculously simple.

Another example: voice mail. Until now you've had to grope through your v-mail by ear, blindly, like an eyeless cave creature. On the iPhone you see all your messages laid out visually, onscreen, labeled by caller. If you want to hear one, you touch it. Done. Now try a text message: instead of jumbling them all together in your In box, iPhone arranges your texts by recipient, as threaded conversations made of little jewel-like bubbles. And instead of "typing" on a three-by-four number keypad, you get a display of a full, usable QWERTY keyboard. You will never again have to hit the 7 key four times to type the letter s.

Now forget about phone calls. Look at the video, which is impressively crisp and sharp. This is the first time the hype about "rich media" on a phone has actually appeared plausible. Look at the e-mail client, which handles attachments, inline images and HTML e-mails as adroitly as a desktop client. Look at the Web browser, a modified version of Safari that displays actual Web pages, not a teensy, deformed version of the Web. There's a Google Maps application that's almost worth the price of admission on its own.

I do have nitpicks. You can't download songs onto iPhone directly from the iTunes store; you have to export them from a computer. And even though it has wi-fi and Bluetooth on it, you can't sync iPhone with a computer wirelessly. And there should be games on it. And you're required to use it as a phone—you can't use it without signing up for cellular service. Boo.

But these are quibbles. The fact is, the iPhone shatters two basic axioms of consumer technology. One, when you take an application and put it on a phone, that application must be reduced to a crippled and annoying version of itself. Two, when you take two devices—such as an iPod and a phone—and squish them into one, both devices must necessarily become lamer versions of themselves. The iPhone is a phone, an iPod and a mini-Internet computer all at once, and they all—contrary to basic physics—occupy the same space at the same time, but without taking a hit in performance. In a way, iPhone is the wrong name for it. (Indeed, Cisco is suing Apple, claiming it owns the trademark.) It's a handheld computing platform that just happens to contain a phone.

Why is Apple able to do things most other companies can't? Partly by charging for it: the iPhone will cost $499 for a 4-GB model, $599 for 8-GB. And partly because unlike most companies, Apple does its own hardware, its own software and its own industrial design. When it all takes place under one roof, you get a kind of collaborative synergy that makes unusual things happen.

Apple also places an unusual emphasis on interface design. It sweats the cosmetic details that don't seem very important until you really sweat them. "I actually have a photographer's loupe that I use to make sure every pixel is right," says Scott Forstall, Apple's vice president of Platform Experience. "We will argue over literally a single pixel." As a result, when you swipe your finger across the screen to unlock the iPhone, you're not just accessing a system of nested menus, you're entering a tiny universe in which data exist as bouncy, gemlike objects. You can actually pinch an image with two fingers and make it smaller. Because there's no mouse or keyboard, just that touch screen, there's a powerful illusion that you're physically handling data.

Of course, Apple's other secret weapon is the controlling hand of Steve Jobs, 51, for whom this is an almost mystically significant year. It has been five years since the iPod launched, 30 years since Jobs co-founded Apple (with Stephen Wozniak) and 10 since he returned there after having been fired. In that decade, Apple's stock has gone up more than 1,500%. Neither age nor success—nor cancer surgery in 2004—has significantly mellowed him, although some of the silver in his beard is creeping up into his hair. All technologists believe their products are better than other people's, or at least they say they do, but Jobs believes it a little more than most. He calls the iPhone "the most important product Apple has ever announced, with the possible exception of the Apple II and the Macintosh. It's also going to be an incredible revolution for the whole industry."

Jobs' zeal for product development—and enforcing his personal vision—remains as relentless as ever. He keeps Apple's management structure unusually flat for a 20,000-person company, so that he can see what's happening at ground level. There is just one committee in the whole of Apple, to establish prices. I can't think of a comparable company that does no—zero—market research with its customers before launching a product. Ironically, Jobs' personal style could not be more at odds with the brand he has created. If the motto for Apple's consumers is "Think different," the motto for Apple employees is "Think like Steve."

The same goes for Apple's partners. The last time Apple experimented with a phone, the largely unsuccessful ROKR, Jobs let Motorola make it. "What we learned was that we wouldn't be satisfied with glomming iTunes onto a regular phone," Jobs says. "We realized through that experience that for us to be happy, for us to be proud, we were going to have to do it all."

Apple's superiority complex can inspire resentment, which is one reason for some of the Silicon Valley schadenfreude over Jobs' current stock-options woes. An internal investigation has cleared Jobs, but a federal investigation and a shareholder lawsuit are still going forward. (Jobs declines to talk about the options issue.) Taking pleasure in seeing a special person knocked down to size is a great American pastime. But there's no point in pretending that Jobs isn't special. A college dropout whose biological parents gave him up for adoption, Jobs has presided over four major game-changing product launches: the Apple II, the Macintosh, the iPod and the iPhone; five if you count the release of Pixar's Toy Story, which I'm inclined to. He's like Willy Wonka and Harry Potter rolled up into one.

That doesn't mean Apple can operate beyond the boundaries of the Securities and Exchange Commission. But the iPhone wouldn't have happened without Apple's "we're special" attitude. One reason there's limited innovation in cell phones generally is that the cell carriers have stiff guidelines that the manufacturers have to follow. Carriers demand that all their handsets work the same way. "A lot of times, to be honest, there's some hubris, where they think they know better," Jobs says. "They dictate what's on the phone. That just wouldn't work for us because we want to innovate. Unless we could do that, it wasn't worth doing." Jobs demanded special treatment from his phone-service partner, Cingular, and he got it. He even forced Cingular to re-engineer its technical infrastructure to handle the iPhone's unique voice-mail scheme. "They broke all their typical process rules to make it happen," says Tony Fadell, who heads Apple's iPod division. "They were infected by this product, and they were like, 'We've gotta do this!'"

Now that the precedent has been set, it will be interesting to see if other cell-phone makers start demanding Apple-style treatment from wireless carriers. Stanley Sigman, Cingular's president and CEO, committed his company to the iPhone two years ago sight-unseen, but he appears understandably eager to play down the uniqueness of Apple's deal. "I think the interesting aspect of it is our willingness and ability to work together, to allow Cingular to be Cingular and Apple to be Apple," he says. "We have great relationships with other manufacturers. But he's clearly brought a product to market that's years ahead of anybody else." It will also be worth watching to see how successful

competitors will be in knocking off the iPhone's all-screen form factor, which will be tricky without Apple's touch-screen technology. Apple has filed for around 200 patents associated with the iPhone, building an imposing legal wall.

Will the iPhone succeed? Well, what's success? Apple will break the 100 million mark with iPods this year (it also passed 2 billion songs sold on iTunes). Jobs says he wants to move 10 million iPhones by the end of next year. That number is well in character as far as its ambition goes. The iPhone is exclusive to Cingular for now, and Cingular has only 58 million customers. Jobs hopes to launch in Europe late this year and Asia in 2008. The iPhone is too beautiful and too brilliant not to be a moneymaker, but it'll be a slow burn by iPod standards.

Perhaps it's not quite right to call the iPhone revolutionary. It won't create a new market or change the entertainment industry the way the iPod did. When you get right down to it, the device doesn't even have that many new features—it's not like Jobs invented voice mail, or text messaging, or conference calling or mobile Web browsing. He just noticed that they were broken, and he fixed them.

But that's important. When our tools don't work, we tend to blame ourselves, for being too stupid or not reading the manual or having too fat fingers. "I think there's almost a belligerence—people are frustrated with their manufactured environment," says Ive. "We tend to assume the problem is with us and not with the products we're trying to use." In other words, when our tools are broken, we feel broken. And when somebody fixes one, we feel a tiny bit more whole.

FURTHER RESOURCES
Books
Segall, Ken. *Insanely Simple: The Obsession That Drives Apple's Success.* New York: Portfolio, 2012.

Web Sites
"Apple History" *Apple-History.com.* http://apple-history.com/ (accessed on February 22, 2013).

"Apple Official Site: iPhone" *Apple.* http://www.apple.com/iphone/ (accessed on February 22, 2013).

"Apple's Rivals Battle for iOS Scraps as App Market Sales Grow to $2.2 Billion" *Apple Insider.* http://appleinsider.com/articles/11/02/18/rim_nokia_and_googles_android_battle_for_apples_ios_scraps_as_app_market_sales_grow_to_2_2_billion.html (accessed on February 22, 2013).

"Glass-Steagall Act: The Senators and Economists Who Got It Right"

Editorial

By: Sam Stein

Date: June 11, 2009

Source: Stein, Sam. "Glass-Steagall Act: The Senators and Economists Who Got It Right." *Huffington Post*, June 11, 2009. www.huffingtonpost.com/2009/05/11/glass-steagall-act-the-se_n_201557.html (accessed on March 2, 2013).

About the Web site: The *Huffington Post* is a popular news Web site, which was founded in May 2005 by Arianna Huffington. The site, which features original journalism, regular and guest columns, and news aggregation covering a variety of political and social topics pertaining to life in the United States, features a decidedly liberal tone and sympathies, acting as a counterpoint to its conservative equivalent, the *Drudge Report*. The *Huffington Post* has received a number of industry awards since its launch and attracted some of the best-known political bloggers and columnists to contribute content, making it one of the nation's most popular political Web sites. In addition to the main site, Arianna Huffington's Huffington Post Media Group operates a number of local and international pages, modeled after the original. In 2011, the site was acquired by AOL for $315 million. The following year, it made Internet history by becoming the first digital news source to receive a Pulitzer Prize.

INTRODUCTION

The Banking Act of 1933 was created in an attempt to better regulate the U.S. financial sector after the Great Depression exposed the perils of a self-governing banking industry concerned solely with profit maximization. In response to the bank runs that caused banks to lose all liquidity during the Depression, the Banking Act established the Federal Deposit Insurance Corporation (FDIC) to promote confidence in the security of funds deposited into federally insured banks. Four provisions of the Act—numbers 16, 20, 21, and 32, collectively known as the Glass-Steagall Act—were included to prohibit individual banks from engaging in both investment and commercial activities. Commercial banks, which were concerned primarily with extending credit and storing the money of customers, were subjected to federally set reserve

requirements and given access to the Fed's discount window. Investment banks, meanwhile, did not receive FDIC insurance, and they conducted stock-market investing and securities trading and sold insurance. Both investment and commercial banks were barred from underwriting securities and insurance, however. Advocates of the act claimed that, by subjecting the financial industry to stricter regulation and closer scrutiny, banks would convert into institutions facilitating the growth of the "real economy," rather than generating exorbitant profits by acting as intermediaries between producers and consumers.

American banks were, somewhat predictably, unhappy with the Glass-Steagall Act because it limited their abilities to generate profit. Commercial banks could not use money deposited by customers to invest in stocks, commodities, securities, and other volatile financial instruments; meanwhile, the funds available to investment banks were limited to those provided by individuals with surplus capital and interested in gambling it on the exchange market. Throughout the rest of the twentieth century, the financial industry launched a series of successful lobbying efforts, receiving ever-greater concessions from the U.S. Congress and federal economic regulatory entities regarding permissible conduct under the Glass-Steagall Act. Banks effectively argued that the separation of investment and commercial banks hampered competition between domestic banks and, more importantly, against international banks, which were subject to no such restrictions and thus grew increasingly larger and more profitable than their American counterparts.

By the 1990s, the Glass-Steagall Act had decayed into a shadow of its former self, maintaining only the clauses prohibiting investment banks from underwriting insurance policies. Commercial and investment banks had become mutually interdependent, although not explicitly consolidated. It came as little surprise, though, when the Citicorp commercial holding corporation was permitted by the Securities and Exchange Commission (SEC) and the U.S. Comptroller to acquire the insurance conglomerate Travelers Group in 1998, which resulted in the creation of the Citigroup corporation, the nation's first legal combination of an investment and commercial bank since the Great Depression. The following year, Congress passed the Financial Services Modernization Act of 1999 (commonly called the Gramm-Leach-Bliley Act), officially repealing the Glass-Steagall Act. Because the Glass-Steagall Act had been effectively unenforced for years, the only material change caused by Gramm-Leach-Bliley was the abolition of the requirement that executives, officers, and employees of financial firms work for only one such company in the industry, a statute that had been created to prevent potential conflicts of interest from arising.

SIGNIFICANCE

Almost immediately after the passage of the Gramm-Leach-Bliley Act, the U.S. economy experienced a recession caused by the burst of the dot-com stock bubble. The reaction among economists was split into two camps: those who believed that allowing banks to merge investment and commercial banking under a single roof would soften the impact of recessions, and those who believed that such combinations promoted risky behavior by banks that posed more potential risk to the broader economy that the possible return could justify. The former argued that, by allowing banks to diversify their interests, the blows caused by economic downturns would only harm isolated divisions of banks, rather than cripple the entire institution. The latter camp warned that consolidation of commercial and investment banks would cause bankers to take unnecessary risks with the money of their customers, and that the increasingly complex arrangements and financial instruments permitted under Gramm-Leach-Bliley would create a web of mutually interdependent banks in which the collapse or failure of any institution would have a devastating impact on the U.S. economy.

Opponents of Gramm-Leach-Bliley were vindicated in late 2006, when the artificially inflated housing market bubble burst, leaving the nation's largest banks—which had essentially caused the bubble through the unsafe, irresponsible practice of subprime mortgage lending and heavy speculative trading on mortgage-backed securities—in danger of collapse. The deregulation of the financial industry, said critics, allowed for the creation of enormous conglomerate banks that happily burdened the economy with tremendous risk in exchange for profits for executives and traders, and upon which the productive economy was so dependent that the federal government had no choice but to provide hundreds of billions of dollars in emergency funds to them. Joseph Stiglitz, a Nobel Prize–winning economist, likened the atmosphere of the post–Glass-Steagall American financial industry to that of pre-regulation banking that ultimately caused the Great Depression, characterized by excessive leveraging and dilution of assets and the perpetual repackaging of securities under the guise of increasingly innovative financial instruments.

Unfortunately for those who had predicted the outcome of repealing the Glass-Steagall Act, by 2008 it was too late to avert the consequences of irresponsible banking, and the nation's economy plummeted into the most serious recession in recent history. Recovery efforts by the federal government, informed by hindsight, made a point of stipulating that bailout funds were to be provided with the caveat that the banks receiving them had to submit to rigorous transparency and oversight protocol. Although the extent to which the new regulations were successful remained to be seen by the end of the 2000s decade, they were celebrated by progressive economists as a step towards a harmonious banking establishment in the United States.

PRIMARY SOURCE

"GLASS-STEAGALL ACT: THE SENATORS AND ECONOMISTS WHO GOT IT RIGHT"

SYNOPSIS: In this article, the author describes the Glass-Steagall Act and its effects and laments its repeal.

The footage of him speaking on the Senate floor has become something of a cult flick for the particularly wonky progressive. The date was November 4, 1999. Senator Byron Dorgan, in a patterned red tie, sharp dark suit and hair with slightly more color than it has today, was captured only by the cameras of CSPAN2.

"I want to sound a warning call today about this legislation," he declared, swaying ever so slightly right, then left, occasionally punching the air in front of him with a slightly closed fist. "I think this legislation is just fundamentally terrible."

The legislation was the repeal of the Glass-Steagall Act (alternatively known as Gramm Leach Bliley), which allowed banks to merge with insurance companies and investment houses. And Dorgan was, at the time, on a proverbial island with his concerns. Only eight senators would vote against the measure—lionized by its proponents, including senior staff in the Clinton administration and many now staffing President Obama, as the most important breakthrough in the worlds of finance and politics in decades.

"It was more like a tidal wave in 1999," the North Dakota Democrat recalled of that vote in an interview with the *Huffington Post*. "You've seen the roll call. We didn't really have to deal with push back because they had such a strong, strong body of support for what they call modernization that the vote was never in doubt.... The title of the bill was 'The Financial Modernization Act.' And so if you don't want to modernize, I guess you're considered hopelessly old fashioned."

Ten years later, Dorgan has been vindicated. His warning that banks would become "too big to fail" has proven basically true in the wake of the current financial crisis. He seems eerily prescient for claiming then that

U.S. senator Byron Dorgan of North Dakota, an opponent of the 1999 repeal of the Glass-Steagall Act. © AP IMAGES/ JEFF MCEVOY.

Congress would "look back ten years time and say we should not have done this." But he wasn't entirely alone. Sens. Barbara Boxer, Barbara Mikulski, Richard Shelby, Tom Harkin and Richard Bryan also cast nay votes.

As did Sen. Russ Feingold, who, in a statement from his office, recalled that "Gramm-Leach-Bliley was just one of several bad policies that helped lead to the credit market crisis and the severe recession it helped cause."

The late Sen. Paul Wellstone also opposed the bill, warning at the time that Congress was "about to repeal the economic stabilizer without putting any comparable safeguard in its place."

Outside government, doomsday-ing over the repeal of Glass-Steagall seemed far more palatable a position to take. Edward Kane, a finance professor at Boston College, warned that "nobody will be able to discipline a Citigroup" once the legislation passed, because the banks would be too big and the issues too complex.

"It made it possible for the very big firms to take risks in a way that would require a great deal of investment risk and time for regulatory agencies," Kane recalled ten years later. "You had people who could basically outplay the regulators."

Jeffrey Garten, who at the time had left his post as Undersecretary of Commerce for International Trade at the Clinton White House, wrote in the *New York Times* that if these new "megabanks" were to falter, "they could take down the entire global financial system with them."

"Sooner or later, perhaps starting with the next serious economic downturn," he wrote, "the US will have to confront one of the great challenges of our times: how does a sovereign nation govern itself effectively when politics are national and business is global?"

Consumer protection advocate Ralph Nader, meanwhile, was far more succinct in his skepticism. "We will look back at this and wonder how the country was so asleep," he said at the time. "It's just a nightmare."

When the Senate voted to pass Gramm-Leach-Bliley by a vote of 90–8, it reversed what was, for more than six decades, a framework that had governed the functions and reach of the nation's largest banks. No longer limited by laws and regulations, commercial and investment banks could now merge. Many had already begun the process, including, among others, J. P. Morgan and Citicorp. The new law allowed it to be permanent. The updated ground rules were low on oversight and heavy on risky ventures. Historically in the business of mortgages and credit cards, banks now would sell insurance and stock.

Nevertheless, the bill did not lack champions, many of whom declared that the original legislation—forged during the Great Depression—was both antiquated and cumbersome for the banking industry. Congress had tried 11 times to repeal Glass-Steagall. The twelfth was the charm.

"Today Congress voted to update the rules that have governed financial services since the Great Depression and replace them with a system for the 21st century," said then–Treasury Secretary Lawrence Summers. "This historic legislation will better enable American companies to compete in the new economy."

"I welcome this day as a day of success and triumph," said Sen. Christopher Dodd (D-Conn.).

"The concerns that we will have a meltdown like 1929 are dramatically overblown," said Sen. Bob Kerrey (D-Neb.).

"If we don't pass this bill, we could find London or Frankfurt or years down the road Shanghai becoming the financial capital of the world," said Sen. Chuck Schumer, D-N.Y. "There are many reasons for this bill, but first and foremost is to ensure that U.S. financial firms remain competitive."

Looking back, members of Congress have tried to downplay the significance of their support. One high-ranking Hill aide notes that his boss, who voted for the bill, did so because banks were already beginning to merge with investment houses. It should be noted, additionally, that Dodd and Schumer were able to hammer out, as part of the legislation, the Community Reinvestment Act, which required banks to extend lines of credit to predominantly minority areas.

Officials from the Clinton White House, meanwhile, shift between defensiveness and repentance. One former high-ranking official argued that while the legislation changed the balance between a bank's commercial and non-commercial activities, the problem was not necessarily the blurring of those lines. "What really brought the economy to its knees was the incredibly over-leveraged and unregulated risks taken by these non-commercial banks." In short: there wasn't enough oversight.

"The White House task force meetings covered a whole series of these issues," said the official. "A lot of people raised serious questions about how far we were going. And it wasn't just here. There were a whole series of issues around the same time in which the Treasury was always promoting the interest of big finance. It was true under [Bob] Rubin and at least as true under Larry [Summers]."

Not everyone looks back at that vote with regret. The repeal of the law, they argue, was responsible for the sharp growth that the market experienced in the subsequent years. Moreover, the argument goes, if not for the over-leveraging of credit in the housing market the gut shot that many major banks endured could have been avoided.

That said, the concept of regulation has, over the past decade, taken on a drastic shift in public perception, from being viewed as a hindrance to economic growth to a guardrail from future disaster. And spearheading that effort at revamping the regulatory system is the same senator who foresaw the problem in the first place.

"I'm from a little small town of 300 people in North Dakota," Dorgan told the *Huffington Post*. "Where I grew up, we have seen a history … of some of the larger banks and difficulties farmers have had in dealing with some of the larger banks over the last century or so. And so, my own view about these issues is that there needs to be, to the extent that you can, create a free market that works with price competition and product differentiation and so on, but there needs to be a referee with a whistle and a striped shirt, I mean the free market sometimes needs referees."

FURTHER RESOURCES
Web Sites
"The Alarming Parallels Between 1929 and 2007." *American Prospect*, October 2, 2007. http://prospect.org/article/alarming-parallels-between-1929-and-2007 (accessed on March 2, 2013).

"Capitalist Fools." *Vanity Fair*, January 2009. http://media.yoism.org/CapitalistFools-Stiglitz.pdf (accessed on March 2, 2013).

"Federal Reserve Bank of New York Circulars: June 22, 1933." *Federal Reserve Archives.* http://fraser.stlouisfed.org/publication-issue/?id=10671 (accessed on March 2, 2013).

"Gramm-Leach-Bliley Act Legal Resources." *Bureau of Consumer Protection Business Center.* http://business.ftc.gov/privacy-and-security/gramm-leach-bliley-act (accessed on March 2, 2013).

"Crash of a Titan: The Inside Story of the Fall of Lehman Brothers"

One year ago, the assembled brains of the Fed and Wall Street sealed the fate of one of its oldest banks. In this gripping account of that weekend last September, Stephen Foley counts the cost of high finance's darkest hour.

Newspaper article

By: Stephen Foley

Date: September 7, 2009

Source: Foley, Stephen. *Crash of a Titan: The Inside Story of the Fall of Lehman Brothers.* The Independent, September 7, 2009. www.independent.co.uk/news/business/analysis-and-features/crash-of-a-titan-the-inside-story-of-the-fall-of-lehman-brothers-1782714.html# (accessed on March 22, 2013).

About the Publication: *The Independent* is one of the United Kingdom's leading newspapers. Since beginning publication in 1986, the paper has gained popularity across the English-speaking world for its adherence to the principles of objective journalism, such as lack of political affiliation and unbiased coverage of current events. Its editors occasionally deviate from this practice on particularly polarizing issues, most notably the Iraq and Afghanistan wars and 2010 British general elections. *The Independent* is recognizable by its distinct cover format, which frequently employs unorthodox headline designs and image placement.

INTRODUCTION
Lehman Brothers, Inc. was founded in 1850 as a commodities trading firm in Montgomery, Alabama.

In subsequent generations it grew into one of the largest and most prestigious entities in the U.S. financial market, boasting branches across the world and operating brokerage services, investment banking, wealth management funds, and securities trading. By 2008, Lehman Brothers employed over twenty-five thousand people worldwide and reported more than $600 billion in assets, making it the fourth-largest investment bank in the nation.

Under the stewardship of CEO Richard Fuld, Lehman Brothers had been a leading advocate and issuer of mortgage-backed securities—publicly traded securities deriving their value from those of mortgages. This practice allowed the bank to quickly increase its revenue, especially as it was a leading provider of the loans upon the securities were based. Unfortunately, the housing market burst of 2006–2007 caused home values to spiral, sending many Lehman Brothers mortgages into delinquency and rapidly deflating the value of the mortgage-backed securities that constituted a considerable portion of the bank's reported value. As the subprime mortgage crisis came to a head in August 2007, it became apparent that Lehman Brothers was drastically over-leveraged, holding over thirty times more liabilities than equity (meaning that the bank held $30 in debt for every $1 in available reserve funds).

The sudden development of the 2008 credit crisis caught the entire financial industry off-guard, but none were more severely impacted than Lehman Brothers. As the bank began hemorrhaging money— posting $2.8 billion in losses for the second quarter of 2008, and a record-setting $3.9 billion loss after that— its board of directors scrambled to find a way to rescue the company. A series of banks, including Bank of America and the Korean Development Bank, ultimately rejected proposals to purchase the failing Lehman Brothers. The Federal Reserve Bank of the United States found it impossible to justify providing a "bailout" of the beleaguered bank, despite having recently nationalized Freddie Mac and Fannie Mae, as well as providing financial support to the American Insurance Group and investment bank Bear Stearns. On September 15, 2008, after selling off the majority of its assets, Lehman Brothers, Inc. filed for Chapter 11 bankruptcy protection.

SIGNIFICANCE

The Lehman Brothers bankruptcy, valued at over $600 billion, was the largest in U.S. history and sent the global financial industry reeling. Every major bank across the world was connected to the bankrupt firm through a complex web of trades, investments, deals, and securities, and they all suffered immediate losses from its collapse. Although it is impossible to gauge the total losses caused by Lehman Brothers' bankruptcy because of the interdependent nature of valuation, the amount certainly figures in the trillions of dollars. A number of prominent U.S. hedge funds and other personal investment funds reported substantial losses as a result of investing in the once-promising company. The Dow Jones Industrial Average Lost over 500 points the day after the collapse of Lehman Brothers, one of the largest single-day losses ever recorded.

Barclays, a United Kingdom–based bank, acquired the defunct central brokerage division of Lehman Brothers on September 22, as well as its towering Manhattan headquarters, for $1.36 billion. In what industry analysts called a windfall, Barclays assumed $47.4 billion in Lehman securities and $45.5 billion in trading liabilities as part of the deal. Namura Holdings, a Japanese investment bank, reached a deal on October 13 to acquire Lehman Brothers' Asia-Pacific, Middle East, and African operations, which consisted of investment banks and equities firms.

The most visceral significance of Lehman Brothers' bankruptcy was its effect on the U.S. government's response to the 2008 financial crisis. Lawmakers and Treasury officials, who had previously been hesitant to react to the increasingly desperate condition of the American banking industry, had no choice but to accept the necessity of preventing full-scale economic collapse when the extent and degree of destruction wrought by the collapse of a single bank was exposed. Thus, Lehman Brothers was regarded as a martyr to the cause of government intervention into the financial industry—although it caused considerable damage to the global banking infrastructure, it revealed the prudence of federal bailout programs.

■ PRIMARY SOURCE

"CRASH OF A TITAN: THE INSIDE STORY OF THE FALL OF LEHMAN BROTHERS"

SYNOPSIS: This article describes the events leading to and encompassing the collapse of Lehman Brothers, one of the largest and most prestigious firms in the U.S. financial sector.

Go home. It's no one famous. You're just looking at a whole bunch of people who lost their jobs. Police shouted into the crowd, hastily erecting barricades, but New Yorkers and tourists were moth-like in the face of camera flashbulbs and the spotlights of television crews. Even in the neon-lit stampede of humanity that is Times Square, this was a sight to remember.

Photographers take pictures of Lehman Brothers employees carrying boxes of personal effects as they leave the bankrupt investment bank's New York City headquarters on September 15, 2008. © AP IMAGES/MARY ALTAFFER.

For the first time since it began crackling and fizzing in the obscurest corners of Wall Street more than a year before, the credit crisis finally had a human face. Many human faces. One by one, Lehman employees stumbled outside, carrying duffel bags stuffed with personal effects. As that Sunday ground on, more and more employees decided that they would not wait to find out the fate of the 158-year old investment bank. Hope had ebbed away that it had any future at all. Mid-afternoon, a rumour had shot round: maybe the bankruptcy would be so chaotic, so catastrophic, that the authorities would seal off the headquarters entirely. Even more came to grab what they wanted to save, just in case.

By the time darkness fell it was running on all the news channels: Lehman Brothers was filing for bankruptcy.

Few emerging from the building would speak to reporters, but those that did expressed disbelief. Anger that Lehman had been driven to the ground. Sadness at the careers derailed and the livelihoods lost. But most of all, shock. By September 2008, America had already entered the age of the bailout, and despite a week of insisting there would be no government money to save

Lehman Brothers, no one could quite believe that Hank Paulson, Treasury secretary, and Federal Reserve chairman Ben Bernanke would let the bank go to the wall.

Lehman Brothers had 25,000 staff around the world, 4,500 at its European headquarters in Canary Wharf in London, where the scenes of bagging and boxing were repeated the next morning. It was the fourth largest of the Wall Street investment banks and the oldest. It had survived repeated financial panics around the turn of the 19th century and thrived during the Great Depression. It had over $600bn of assets and vast, untanglable trading relationships with every other major firm in finance. It was, almost everyone agreed, too big to fail.

And yet fail it did. In the small hours of the morning, on Monday, 15 September 2008, Lehman Brothers filed for bankruptcy, the biggest in American history by a factor of six.

It is no less extraordinary, one year on, to recall images from that weekend, probably the defining pictures of this great financial crisis. The NYPD officer shouting into the crowd was dead wrong. We weren't just looking at a bunch of people who lost their jobs. (And many, in the end, didn't.) We were looking at the symbolic end of a way of life on Wall Street and the start of very real economic horrors for the rest of us. We were looking—we can say this with confidence—at a terrible, terrible error.

"It's unconscionable what they did—or more accurately what they didn't do," says Joseph Stiglitz, Nobel prize-winning economist and professor at Columbia University. "They didn't do their homework. People were talking about the failure of Lehman Brothers from the moment of the failure of Bear Stearns in March, or before, and they didn't do a thing. If they knew there was systemic risk, why didn't they do anything about it?"

Paulson had been pushing Lehman to find a solution to its problems, to sell itself or to raise cash. He had not been preparing a government-sponsored contingency plan. There was none. That weekend, everyone was flying blind.

Lehman's fate was sealed not in the boardroom of that gaudy Manhattan headquarters. It was sealed downtown, in the gloomy grey building of the New York Federal Reserve, the Wall Street branch of the US central bank. Almost exactly 10 years previously, Dick Fuld, the scrappy Lehman boss, had sat in the Fed's wood-panelled conference room and hammered out with his fellow chief executives the deal that rescued Long-Term Capital Management (LTCM). On that occasion, when one of the largest hedge funds tottered and threatened to bring down the financial system, Wall Street's finest minds found a way to save it.

This was precisely the template that Paulson, Bernanke and the New York Fed chairman Tim Geithner had in mind when they summoned Wall Street bosses again on the Friday of Lehman's final weekend. One by one they got the call: Be here at 6pm. Only this time, Fuld was not invited. He would be left to rattle around the Times Square boardroom, awaiting his bank's fate. How had it come to this?

In 1850, Henry, Emanuel and Mayer Lehman, Bavarian immigrants to Alabama, began bartering for cotton as payment from customers at their store, and within a few years these original Lehman Brothers were full-blown commodities traders. Subsequent generations of Lehmans would take the firm into investment banking, backing America's great retail enterprises, from Woolworth's to Macy's, and then funding the first television manufacturers and broadcasters in the Thirties.

Richard Severin Fuld, son of a well-to-do New York family, came to Lehman in 1969 as a trader of commercial paper, and quickly proved himself boisterous, even by the standards of a Wall Street trading floor. Colleagues named him The Gorilla, and his brutality was legendary. He ruled by intimidation, and he conceived of Wall Street as a war,

his staff a great fighting force manning a battleship, its guns permanently trained on even bigger rivals. His "never surrender" attitude meant that he rejected offers from potential buyers for Lehman Brothers earlier in 2008, when outsiders were saying the bank was too weak to survive on its own. The great outpouring of anger against him has come not just from the public and politicians, but from Lehman staff. The New York artist Geoffrey Raymond set up camp outside the Lehman offices on the day after the bankruptcy, and handed green marker pens to employees to graffiti a portrait of Fuld. It is littered with sarcastic messages. "Nice trade," says one. Another: "Enjoy your old age, Prick Fuld."

Hauled before Congress in October, his only public outing since the fall of Lehman, Fuld blamed "rumours, speculation, misunderstandings and factual errors" for the collapse. "I want to be very clear. I take full responsibility for the decisions that I made and for the actions that I took based on the information we had at the time," he said, but there was nothing he would have done differently.

Like the bosses of other investment banks, Fuld had been salivating since the middle of the decade over the enormous profits on offer from slicing and dicing America's mortgages into securities for sale to investors around the world. Lehman rushed headlong into this business, ignoring warnings that the US housing market had become dangerously overheated and that mortgage brokers were doling out loans to people who could never repay them. The bank was also one of the biggest financiers of commercial property and had taken some pretty optimistic views of its portfolio's worth.

A reckoning was fast approaching and Lehman had put itself at more risk than most: to juice results and get ahead of the competition, it had pumped itself up on debt. The bank held less than a dollar in reserves for every $30 of its liabilities. As long as it had assets to match them, this was fine. But investors were increasingly sceptical about the value of the assets Lehman claimed.

In that final week, when Fuld announced a further $3.9bn loss, confidence collapsed. Clients fled. Jamie Dimon, head of the mighty JPMorgan Chase, another storied investment bank, phoned personally to demand that Lehman put up $5bn in collateral or he'd pull the bank's credit lines. Lehman scraped together the coin—just—and made it to the weekend, but it was clear it wasn't coming out the other side as an independent bank.

■   ■   ■

Henry Merritt Paulson, Hank to everyone, is a man of impeccable free market credentials. It is gobsmacking that he will go down in history as the Treasury secretary who ordered the biggest-ever government intervention in the US banking system. It is still gobsmacking to him, too.

Terrifying looking—totally bald, with the thick neck of the American football player that he was in college—Paulson had been both an obvious choice for Treasury secretary and an odd one. The $37m-a-year boss of Goldman Sachs had been wooed by President George Bush in 2006 with the promise of autonomy over economic policy, and he reluctantly accepted the call to service, becoming the latest in a long line of Goldman executives to pass through the revolving door into government. But he was not a natural politician, a tub-thumper in negotiation rather than a flatterer, and a tongue-tied mess in public speaking.

The best orator in the world would have had trouble explaining the Treasury's policy pirouettes as the credit crisis spiralled last year. In March, Paulson had orchestrated the sale of Bear Stearns to JPMorgan, financed with the loan of public money from the Federal Reserve. Just the weekend before Lehman collapsed, he had ordered the mother of all bailouts, the nationalisation of America's two mortgage finance giants, Fannie Mae and Freddie Mac, putting the Treasury on the hook for potentially hundreds of billions of dollars.

Yet in subsequent days, he had rediscovered his free market mojo. Capitalism must claim its scalps. Banks that take too much risk should be hoist on that petard. If the government were to guarantee nobody fails, then what's to stop bankers rolling the dice for higher and higher stakes—and higher and higher bonuses when the gambles pay off?

This was the line in the sand moment, Paulson figured. The time to "re-establish moral hazard". Lehman would get no money from the government. Wall Street would have to sort this one out itself. No bailout this weekend, he said.

It was a message delivered by the Fed's Tim Geithner, the quiet-spoken government apparatchik whose career was forged in the Asian debt crises of a decade earlier, when the chief executives piled in to the Fed that Friday evening. Some blame him for not delivering it forcefully enough. Paulson and Bernanke did deliver it forcefully, but all the way through that fraught weekend it hung there in the room: You did it for Bear Stearns. Few could really believe that there wouldn't somehow be taxpayer money, Fed loans or government guarantees—something—to smooth a rescue.

In a 48-hour blizzard of brainstorming and deal-doing, Wall Street was changed forever. But not in the way Paulson had hoped.

It was clear from that Saturday morning, when the titans of the industry reconvened, that Lehman was infinitely more complicated than LTCM before it. The chief executives were split into teams, some to examine how awful Lehman's property portfolio might be, others to try to untangle Lehman's trading relationships. No one doubted that the consequences of failing to do a deal could be catastrophic, but the bickering began immediately.

One plan was for the biggest banks to put up money to cover losses on the $85bn property portfolio, while freeing up the good bits of Lehman—its fiery bond trading business—for sale to one of the two suitors in the room, Bank of America or the UK's Barclays. John Mack spoke up against the idea. How was it fair that his firm, Morgan Stanley, should end up with a slice of a dodgy property portfolio while Barclays or BofA walks off with the Lehman jewels? Other firms pointed out that, after the credit crisis, they couldn't afford to rescue of someone else.

Nonetheless, talks continued. Bob Diamond, who runs Barclays' investment banking division, had made no secret of his desire to turn it into a global powerhouse, but had previously argued it was better to poach staff from rivals, rather than buy competitors outright and be saddled with reluctant employees. This weekend, though, he scented the chance for a bold move. Barclays advisers crawled all over Lehman's books, as Diamond barked orders.

No less ambitious was Ken Lewis, the bespectacled banker from North Carolina, whose Bank of America has long been an also-ran in investment banking. The company's bright-red branches dominated retail banking, but Lewis's attempts to build an investment bank to rival Goldman Sachs and its peers were always something of a laughing stock. When bad bets by its Wall Street traders had wiped out the profits from the retail banking side in 2007, Mr Lewis said he had had "all the fun I can stand in investment banking". But Lewis saw an opportunity to change his fortunes with an audacious bid for Lehman, and his staff had been sniffing around all week. By Friday, though, they knew they couldn't make the numbers work. His team of advisers flew back to North Carolina empty-handed on Saturday morning, only to be told to get straight back on the plane to New York. Now Lewis was flying in with them. The mission had changed. There was a new target. They touched down around lunchtime.

Early Saturday morning, Lewis had taken a call from John Thain, a protégé of Paulson from his Goldman Sachs days, who now ran Merrill Lynch. Thain was brainy in a way that didn't quite add up to smart. He would later lose his job at Merrill and his reputation when it was revealed he had spent squandered $1.2m of shareholders' cash on redecorating his office with a $35,000 "commode on legs", an $8,000 rug and a $1,400 "parchment waste can".

That morning, though, Thain had seen an important pattern in the credit crisis. With markets panicking, investors and clients were sucking their money away from whichever bank looked the most dangerous. After Bear Stearns in March it had been Lehman. After Lehman, it would be Merrill. Thain was determined not to do a Dick

Fuld—fight the market and lose. To salvage what he could of the 94-year old firm, he was willing to sell it. The next day, Merrill agreed to be taken over.

It is time to "spray foam on the runway", Tim Geithner told his sleep-deprived officials on Sunday afternoon. Lehman was going to crash.

Only then did the truth dawn. Paulson, Geithner and Bernanke had not been negotiating. There really would be no government guarantees, no taxpayer bailout. Bob Diamond at Barclays had come closest to a deal, but even he had come back to the Treasury demanding that it backstop Lehman's trading positions until he could arrange a vote of Barclays shareholders. When Barclays received a "no", the game was over for Lehman.

Dick Fuld, pacing uptown, had come to the same realisation by the middle of Sunday. Geithner was not returning his calls. He had telephoned Ken Lewis's home in North Carolina so often that Donna Lewis had to tell him to stop. If her husband wanted to call him back, he would.

Spraying foam on the runway meant doing whatever was possible to keep markets happy while the

unpredictable consequences of Lehman's failure played out. The Fed promised to pump money into the markets. The terrified Wall Street chief executives agreed to pay for a $70bn insurance fund that they could draw on if any turned out to have big exposure to Lehman losses. Meanwhile, Geithner shifted his attention to the insurance giant AIG, where he was trying to orchestrate another private-sector rescue.

There was not enough foam. When Lehman crashed, pieces flew off in all directions. On the Monday morning, an exhausted-looking Paulson began a tense press conference with an attempt at levity. "I hope you all had a good weekend," he said. He insisted that markets had had a long time to prepare for Lehman's collapse, and the banking system was "safe and sound". But it wasn't. Investment funds that had promised their savers they were the safest place for their money came forward to say they had lost money on Lehman, sparking panic.

The private sector pulled away from AIG, leaving the Fed no alternative but to nationalise it, and worry about untangling its vast sub-prime mortgage trades later. By Wednesday, the credit markets had seized up entirely. Big

On September 24, 2010, Christie's auction house employees carry a Lehman Brothers sign in preparation for an auction of items from the bankrupt company. © AP IMAGES/JOHN STILLWELL.

corporations were reporting difficulty getting funding to pay wages and invoices. The economy appeared in grave danger. By the middle of the week, Paulson would complain: "I feel like Butch Cassidy and the Sundance Kid. Who are these guys that just keep coming?"

On Thursday night, the Treasury went literally down on his knees before Nancy Pelosi, speaker of the House of Representatives, begging her to agree taxpayer money to bail out the financial system. Bernanke, a scholar of the financial panic that caused the Great Depression, told fearful lawmakers there wouldn't be a banking system in place by Monday morning if they didn't act. Paulson talked openly about planning for martial law, about how to feed the American people if banking and commerce collapsed. Despite this, it would take almost two weeks before Congress agreed—at the second attempt.

■ ■ ■

The best defence of the decision to let Lehman fail is that it shocked Congress into providing funds to recapitalise the banking system—something it might not have done without the scenes of Lehman staff carrying their boxes into the street. If the credit crisis had continued to play out slowly, largely hidden from public view, America's sclerotic political system may never have mustered the energy to react. But the consequences of those 48 hours, when Paulson's laissez-faire capitalism briefly reasserted itself, were severe. Ben Bernanke admits that Lehman's demise had consequences for the rest of the economy. "It was that shock to the financial system that led to the global recession that began last fall, which was probably the worst one since World War Two," he told public television. "When Lehman Brothers failed, the financial markets went into anaphylactic shock, basically."

"People argue that if it wasn't Lehman Brothers it would have been something else," says Alan Blinder, the former Federal Reserve board member and professor at Princeton University. "I don't buy that. I don't mean everything would have been great if we had bailed out Lehman. We were in a financial crisis before Lehman. But it had a shock value that just caused everything to fall off a cliff. If you look at data on almost anything—consumer spending, investment spending, car sales, employment—it just drops off the table at Lehman Brothers and I don't think we needed to have that."

Paulson's initial defence of letting Lehman fail, that he believed the market had had time to prepare, gave way to the one he uses today, echoed by Bernanke. This

is that there was simply no way the Fed or the Treasury could have intervened. There was no legal mechanism to provide funds to an insolvent company. It's an argument that still perplexes many. "That's their second line," says Joseph Stiglitz. "When their first line looked incredible, they decided they didn't have the legal authority. It should be viewed as an unacceptable. They didn't have legal authority to do Lehman Brothers, but two days later they had legal authority to do AIG, an insurance company? Nobody thought they had legal authority to do Bear Stearns, but they found a legal authority."

The Treasury—now run by Geithner, appointed by Barack Obama to succeed Paulson in January—and the Fed are pushing Congress for precisely the formal powers they say they need to seize and sort out future Lehmans. The proposal is part of a wider set of reforms designed to ensure Wall Street is never again allowed to run wild, gamble with so much borrowed money, or to allow firms to grow so big they can hold the economy to ransom when they get into trouble. But these reforms are bogged down in Congress, in the teeth of a resurgent lobbying effort from the finance industry.

One year older, one year wiser, and yet we still can't say with any certainty: never again.

. . .

FURTHER RESOURCES

Books

McDonald, Lawrence G. *A Colossal Failure of Common Sense: The Inside Story of the Collapse of Lehman Brothers.* New York: Crown Business, 2010.

Web Sites

"Lehman Brothers." *Bloomberg.* http://topics.bloomberg.com/lehman-brothers/ (accessed on March 22, 2013).

"Lehman Brothers Bankruptcy." *Huffington Post.* www.huffingtonpost.com/news/lehman-brothers-bankruptcy (accessed on March 22, 2013).

"Lehman Brothers Bankruptcy" *New York Times.* http://topics.nytimes.com/top/news/business/companies/lehman_brothers_holdings_inc/index.html (accessed on March 22, 2013).

"Lehman Brothers News." *Topix.* http://www.topix.com/com/lehman-brothers (accessed on March 22, 2013).

3 Education

Chronology

Important Events in Education, 2000–2009

2000

- In February, Florida's legislature approves Governor Jeb Bush's "One Florida" initiative that bans colleges and universities from considering race as a factor in admission.

- On February 29, a six-year-old boy in Mount Morris Township, Michigan, shoots and kills his classmate at their elementary school.

- On March 3, Bob Jones University, a fundamentalist Christian institution in Greenville, South Carolina, lifts its long-standing ban on interracial dating.

- On March 14, a Florida judge rules against vouchers, finding that the state constitution prohibits the use of public funds to send students to private schools, invalidating a school-voucher program begun eight months earlier.

- On May 8, the Philadelphia school board adopts a policy that requires all public-school students to wear a uniform to class, becoming the first major city to pass such a law.

- On June 19, in *Santa Fe Independent School District v. Doe*, the Supreme Court rules that the district should not be allowing student-led prayer prior to football games as it violates the establishment clause of the First Amendment. Prayers at any school-sponsored extracurricular activity are deemed unconstitutional.

- On June 28, the Supreme Court, by a six-to-three vote, rules in *Mitchell v. Helms* that a federal program (the Education Consolidation and Improvement Act of 1981) that provides computers and other equipment to private schools is constitutional.

- On August 1, Kansas voters oust two conservative members of the state school board who had voted to remove any mention of evolution from the state curriculum.

- On September 11, California enacts a plan to help needy students attend college: high-school students with good grades and financial need receive free tuition at public institutions or $10,000 a year toward tuition at a private school.

- On November 9, Ruth J. Simmons, president of Smith College, is chosen to lead Brown University, becoming the first African American to head an Ivy League institution. She is sworn in on July 3, 2001.

2001

- On February 2, William Michael Stankewicz attacks students and faculty with a machete at North Hopewell-Winterstown Elementary School in the Red Lion School District of York County, Pennsylvania. He is later convicted and sentenced to serve between 132 and 264 years in prison.

- On February 14, the Kansas State Board of Education reverses its 1999 decision to remove the theory of evolution from the state's science curriculum.

- On March 5, a freshman at Santana High School in Santee, California, opens fire with a handgun at school, killing two students and injuring thirteen others.

- In May, the William and Flora Hewlett Foundation pledges $400 million to Stanford University in the largest gift ever given to an institution of higher learning in the United States.

- On May 16, fourteen-year-old Nathaniel Brazill is convicted of second-degree murder and is later sentenced to twenty-eight years in prison for shooting a teacher at Lake Worth Middle School in Florida.

- On June 26, the Bush administration nominates Gerald A. Reynolds, a lawyer and affirmative-action opponent, to head the Education Department's Office of Civil Rights.

- On November 25, police foil a Columbine-style murder plot at a New Bedford, Massachusetts, high school after one of three students involved in the plan comes forward. The leader of the group is eventually sentenced to three years of probation.

- In December, after their original exams are quarantined in an anthrax scare, 7,500 students nationwide retake their Scholastic Aptitude Tests

(SATs). The original tests never reached the scoring center.

2002

- On January 8, the No Child Left Behind (NCLB) Act, which mandates that schools have to perform to new federal standards or face a range of penalties, is signed into law by President George W. Bush.

- On February 19, the Supreme Court votes unanimously that the practice of allowing students to grade fellow students' classroom assignments does not violate privacy laws.

- On April 11, the Walton Family Charitable Support Foundation, created by the family of Wal-Mart founder Sam Walton, donates $300 million to the University of Arkansas. It is the largest donation ever made to an American public university.

- On April 12, after publicly feuding with Harvard president Lawrence Summers, prominent African American professor Cornel West announces that he has accepted a job at Princeton University.

- On May 7, University of Wisconsin-Stout student Lucas John Helder admits that he planted eighteen pipe bombs in mailboxes across five states, earning the nickname "The Midwest Pipe Bomber."

- On June 12, the Accreditation Council for Graduate Medical Education approves new regulations in which a medical resident's hours are not to exceed eighty hours a week, and single shifts can be no longer than twenty-four hours.

- On June 20, in a seven-to-two vote, the Supreme Court rules that an individual student cannot sue a school under the Family Educational Rights and Privacy Act, a federal law that protects student privacy, for releasing personal information.

- On June 26, a federal appeals court in San Francisco rules that requiring students to recite the Pledge of Allegiance is unconstitutional because of the phrase "under God."

- On June 27, the Supreme Court, in a five-to-four ruling, approves drug testing as a possible requisite for participation in interscholastic, extracurricular competition.

- On October 18, poet Quincy Troupe resigns after only four months as California's first poet laureate, after admitting that he falsified his resume, which stated that he had graduated from a college that he had only attended. He later resigns from his teaching position at the University of California at San Diego.

2003

- On January 15, in a televised address, President Bush weighs in on the University of Michigan admissions controversy; he denounces the use of race in university admissions and plans to file a brief with the Supreme Court asking that they find the policy unconstitutional.

- On February 20, Sami Al-Arian, a suspended University of South Florida computer engineering professor, is charged with funding and advising a Palestinian terrorist organization. He is fired on February 26.

- On February 28, the Ninth Circuit Court of Appeals refuses a request from the federal government to reconsider its ruling that making children recite the Pledge of Allegiance is unconstitutional.

- On April 24, two years after a machete attack that injured fourteen people at a Red Lion School District elementary school in Pennsylvania, eighth-grader James Sheets brings multiple weapons into Red Lion Area Junior High School. After fatally shooting the principal, Sheets turns the gun on himself.

- On May 21, an explosion inside the Sterling Law School at Yale University damages two rooms. No injuries are reported, and investigators believe the explosion was caused by a pipe bomb.

- On June 23, the Supreme Court rules that University of Michigan's law school admissions policy, which considers race as a factor, is constitutional while its similar undergraduate system is not, in *Grutter v. Bollinger* and *Gratz v. Bollinger* respectively.

- In July, New York City officials announce plans for Harvey Milk High School, the first public school aimed at protecting gay students from discrimination.

- In July, evangelist Pat Robertson announces his massive prayer offensive called "Operation Supreme Court Freedom." Robertson asks his followers to pray that at least three Supreme Court justices retire so that conservative justices may take over and overturn rulings on school prayer.

- ON August 23, in Naples, Florida, Ave Maria University opens. Founded by Domino's Pizza owner Thomas S. Monaghan, it is the first Roman Catholic institution of higher learning established in the United States in forty years.

- On October 14, the Supreme Court agrees to hear *Elk Grove Unified School District v. Newdow*, which will consider the constitutionality of school Pledge of Allegiance recitations.

2004

- On February 23, Secretary of Education Rod Paige calls the National Education Association (NEA), the nation's largest teachers' union, a terrorist organization in reference to the group's persistent lobbying against No Child Left Behind reforms. Paige later apologizes.

- On February 25, in a seven-to-two vote, the Supreme Court rules that states are not violating the First Amendment if they choose not to subsidize, with taxpayer-funded scholarships, students studying for ministry.

- On May 17, President Bush and his presidential election opponent, Democratic senator John Kerry of Massachusetts, attend ceremonies in Topeka, Kansas, honoring the fiftieth anniversary of *Brown v. Board of Education* school desegregation.

- On June 14, in *Elk Grove Unified School District v. Newdow*, the Supreme Court rules unanimously that the words "under God" in the Pledge of Allegiance do not violate the establishment clause.

- On August 4, Mary Kay Letourneau is released from prison after serving a seven-year sentence for having sex with her thirteen-year-old student while she was a teacher in Des Moines, Washington. Letourneau has borne two children by the student and upon her release reunites with him. The two are married months later.

- On August 17, a survey conducted by the National Assessment of Educational Progress finds that the test scores of charter-school students are considerably lower than those of students in public schools.

- On November 10, the Association of International Educators reports that the number of foreign students enrolled in American graduate programs has declined.

- On November 15, Secretary of Education Paige resigns.

- On November 17, President Bush nominates White House special aide on domestic issues Margaret Spellings, one of the authors of No Child Left Behind, to become secretary of education. She assumes office January 20, 2005.

2005

- On January 7, conservative radio host Armstrong Williams admits that he accepted payments from the Department of Education to say favorable things about the Bush administration's education reform. Williams also admits an open-door policy with members of the administration, allowing them to come on his program whenever they chose.

- In February, a bipartisan task force of legislators argues that No Child Left Behind is unconstitutional and sets schools up for failure.

- On March 16, the *New England Journal of Medicine* predicts that if the childhood obesity epidemic continues, the current generation of children may have a life expectancy of two to five years shorter than adults today.

- On March 21, sixteen-year-old Jeff Weise shoots five fellow students (as well as a teacher and a security guard) at Red Lake High School in Minnesota before turning the gun on himself.

- On April 7, Secretary of Education Spellings announces revisions to No Child Left Behind and promises increased flexibility to states that are attempting to comply.

- On April 20, the NEA and school districts in Michigan, Texas, and Vermont file suit against the federal government for violation of No Child Left Behind; the plaintiffs argue that the government has not provided the proper funding for the mandates.

- In May, the documentary movie *Corridor of Shame: The Neglect of South Carolina's Rural Schools* debuts.

- On May 21, a third of the faculty of Calvin College protest President Bush's commencement speech. Their petition reads, "We believe your administration has launched an unjust and unjustified war in Iraq."

- On August 1, in response to a question on the teaching of so-called intelligent-design theories, which argue for the presence of a divine creator of the natural world, Bush says, "I think that part of education is to expose people to different schools of thought. You're asking me whether or not people ought to be exposed to different ideas, the answer is yes."

- On August 26, a federal bankruptcy judge rules that churches and schools of the Roman Catholic diocese of Spokane, Washington, can be liquidated to pay the claims of victims of sexual abuse at the hands of priests.

- On August 29, Hurricane Katrina makes landfall in southeast Louisiana; many schools are closed for weeks or longer.

- On September 26, a federal court hears opening arguments of *Kitzmiller v. Dover Area School District*, which challenges the teaching of intelligent design in a public-school curriculum.

- On September 30, the Government Accountability Office rules that the Bush administration engaged in the illegal dissemination of propaganda when it paid for favorable coverage of its education reform.

- On October 1, a bomb explodes outside the University of Oklahoma's memorial stadium during a football game. Bomber Joel Henry Hinrichs III is killed.

- On October 3, the Open Content Alliance announces their plan to digitize thousands of books and scholarly papers, making them available on the Internet.

- On November 15, students at the University of Tennessee interrupt a keynote speech given by Dick Cheney, heckling the vice president and calling for an end of the war in Iraq.

- On December 7, the Supreme Court rules that the government may hold a person's Social Security benefits in order to collect unpaid student loans.

- On December 20, Judge John E. Jones III rules in *Kitzmiller v. Dover Area School District* that it is unconstitutional to teach intelligent design as an alternative to the theory of evolution in a public school.

2006

- On January 31, President Bush calls for an increase in spending for science education in his State of the Union address.

- On February 21, Controversial Harvard president Lawrence Summers resigns.

- On March 6, the Supreme Court votes unanimously in *Rumsfeld v. Forum for Academic and Institutional Rights* to uphold a federal law that says colleges and universities must allow military recruiters the same access to students as they do other potential employers or else lose federal funds. A group of law schools had challenged the law, arguing that it violated their First-Amendment right to free speech and association. The schools objected to the military's exclusion of openly gay men and women.

- On May 3, the three largest soft-drink companies in the United States announce that they will remove sugary drinks such as soda and iced tea from cafeterias and vending machines in schools, replacing soft drinks with water, milk, and fruit juice.

- In August, the National Center for Education Statistics releases a report that finds charter-school students score considerably lower in math compared to students in public schools.

- On August 21, the Virginia Tech campus is closed and classes are canceled as police search for William C. Morva, suspected in the murder of a security guard and a police officer. Officials arrest and charge Morva a day and a half later. He is sentenced to receive the death penalty.

- On September 17, five Duquesne University basketball players are shot on campus after trying to calm a disturbed man at the student union. Three of the student athletes are hospitalized.

- On September 27, during a hostage situation at Platte Canyon High School in Colorado, the gunman sexually assaults several female students and mortally wounds another before shooting himself.

- On September 29, Eric Hainstock, a fifteen-year-old high-school student, fatally shoots his principal, John Klang, at Weston High School in Cazenovia, Wisconsin. He is given a life sentence in prison, with the possibility of parole in thirty years.

- On October 2, Charles Carl Roberts IV invades an Amish schoolhouse in Nickel Mines, Pennsylvania, with guns and restraints. After sending out all the boys and adults, he shoots the girls, killing five and wounding five. He then kills himself.

- On October 2, two schools in Las Vegas, Nevada, are locked down after a student brings an AK-47 assault rifle and other automatic weapons to school.

- On October 12, work begins on demolishing the one-room schoolhouse in Nickel Mines.

- On October 29, the board of trustees at the world's premier school for the deaf, Gallaudet University in Washington, D.C., terminates the contract of incoming president Jane K. Fernandes after weeks of protests by students.

- On November 20, a school bus careens from an Interstate 565 overpass in Huntsville, Alabama, killing four high-school girls.

- On December 5, the U.S. Court of Appeals for the Ninth Circuit rules that Kamehameha, a preparatory school in Hawaii, can favor native Hawaiians in its admissions policy.

- On December 22, rape charges are dropped against three Duke University lacrosse players accused of assaulting a stripper at an off-campus party.

2007

- On February 11, Harvard University announces that historian Drew Gilpin Faust will become the first female president in the school's 371-year history.

- On March 19, the Supreme Court hears arguments in *Morse v. Frederick*, the case of an Alaskan student who was suspended for displaying a banner reading "Bong Hits 4 Jesus" in front of his high school.

- On April 11, North Carolina attorney general Roy Cooper says the Duke University lacrosse players had been falsely accused and criticizes prosecutor Mike Nifong for his handling of the case, calling him a "rogue prosecutor."

- On April 11, Don Imus's popular radio show and television simulcasts are canceled after public outrage over racist comments Imus made about the Rutgers University women's basketball team. Imus later issues an apology: "I want to take a moment to apologize for an insensitive and ill-conceived remark we made the other morning regarding the Rutgers women's basketball team.... It was completely inappropriate and we can understand why people were offended. Our characterization was thoughtless and stupid, and we are sorry."

- On April 16, Virginia Tech student Seung-Hui Cho kills thirty-two people and wounds fifteen more on campus in Blacksburg. Cho, a senior, also kills himself following the most deadly shooting rampage on American soil.

- On April 19, university officials at Virginia Tech announce that students killed in the massacre will be posthumously awarded their degrees during the spring commencement ceremony.

- On June 15, facing disbarment, Nifong resigns his position as district attorney for Durham County, North Carolina.

- On June 25, the Supreme Court rules in *Morse v. Frederick* that school administrators can prohibit students from displaying pro-drug-use messages.

- On June 28, the Supreme Court rules five to four that programs in Seattle, Washington, and Louisville, Kentucky, which maintain racial integration by considering race when assigning students to schools, are unconstitutional.

- On July 11, the House of Representatives votes to cut $19 billion in federal subsidies to student lenders. The law also increases Pell Grants by $500 over five years and creates loan-forgiveness programs for public servants.

- On July 24, the University of Colorado dismisses controversial professor Ward Churchill for academic misconduct. Churchill insists that he is being fired because of his political outspokenness.

- On August 8, Barbara R. Morgan, a former teacher from Idaho, is aboard the space shuttle *Endeavour* as it lifts off. Morgan was the backup to Christa McAuliffe, the teacher who died in the 1986 *Challenger* explosion.

- On August 31, Nifong is found in contempt of court for lying to a judge in the Duke University lacrosse case and is sentenced to one day in jail.

- On September 20, more than 10,000 people march in Jena, Louisiana, to protest harsh measures taken against six black students for assaulting a white student. On hand are civil-rights activists Jesse Jackson, Al Sharpton, and Martin Luther King III.

- On September 21, freshman Loyer D. Braden shoots two female students (one fatally) on the Delaware State University campus.

- On October 10, a fourteen-year-old high-school student opens fire at his school in Cleveland, Ohio, injuring two students and two teachers before killing himself.

- On November 28, officials at Arlington High School in LaGrange, New York, announce that the state police have thwarted a Columbine-style attack on the school.

- In December, the Bush administration's abstinence-only sex education program's effectiveness is questioned when the birth rate for teens ages fifteen to nineteen rises 3 percent in 2006. It is the first time this statistic has risen since 1991.

2008

- On January 28, during his last State of the Union address, President Bush urges Congress to reauthorize No Child Left Behind.

- On February 8, a student shoots and kills two students and then kills herself at Louisiana Technical College in Baton Rouge, Louisiana.

- On February 14, alumnus Stephen P. Kazmierczak opens fire in a classroom at Northern Illinois University. He kills five students and wounds fifteen more before killing himself.

- On April 5, a bus transporting a high-school band overturns on Interstate 94, northwest of Minneapolis, Minnesota. One person is killed, and three more are critically injured.

- On April 25, students across the country participate in the thirteenth annual Day of Silence, which protests the silencing of homosexual students by harassment, bullying, and intimidation.

- On August 21, fifteen-year-old Jamar B. Siler shoots and kills a classmate in the cafeteria of his Knoxville, Tennessee, high school.

- On September 23, an effigy of presidential nominee Barack Obama is found hanging from a tree on the campus of George Fox University in Newberg, Oregon.

- On October 26, two students are killed on the campus of the University of Central Arkansas in Conway when a shooter opens fire from a passing car.

- On December 16, Obama nominates Chicago school superintendent Arne Duncan as secretary of education.

2009

- In April, the federal government declares the swine-flu outbreak a public-health emergency after confirming twenty cases in the United States. Schools across the country close in an attempt to isolate those who have been infected.

- On April 25, University of Georgia professor George M. Zinkhan III kills three people, including his former wife, in Athens. Zinkhan's body is later found in a ditch in the north Georgia wilderness.

- On July 16, prominent African American scholar and Harvard professor Henry Louis Gates Jr. is arrested and briefly jailed for disorderly conduct and resisting arrest. Gates had been locked out of his house, and a neighbor called the police, mistaking him for an intruder.

- On October 26, Richard Herman, chancellor of the University of Illinois at Urbana-Champaign, resigns as a result of an admissions scandal in which well-connected students were given preferential treatment.

- On December 4, American foreign-exchange student Amanda Knox is found guilty of murdering her British roommate in 2007 while studying in Italy. Both Knox and her former boyfriend receive lengthy prison sentences.

No Child Left Behind Act: What It Is and Is Not

The No Child Left Behind Act of 2001, Executive Summary

Law

By: U.S. Department of Education

Date: Signed into law January 8, 2002

Source: U.S. Department of Education. "The No Child Left Behind Act of 2001, Executive Summary." *U.S. Department of Education.* Last modified February 10, 2004. www2.ed.gov/nclb/overview/intro/execsumm.html (accessed on February 21, 2013).

About the Agency: The U.S. Department of Education was formed in 1980 by combining offices from a number of federal agencies. Its mission, according to its official Web site, is "to promote student achievement and preparation for global competitiveness by fostering educational excellence and ensuring equal access." In 2013, the department employed forty-four hundred staff and operated with a $68 billion budget.

"True or False: No Child Left Behind Is Working"

Magazine article

By: Angela Kennedy

Date: June 2008

Source: Kennedy, Angela. "True or False: No Child Left Behind Is Working." *Counseling Today,* June 2008. http://ct.counseling.org/2008/06/true-or-false-no-child-left-behind-is-working/ (accessed on February 21, 2013).

About the Magazine: *Counseling Today* is a publication of the American Counseling Association, a professional organization dedicated to helping counselors with resources, products, services, and information. Available as a print or online edition, the periodical is published monthly and covers all topics and issues pertinent to counselors.

INTRODUCTION

In 1965, under the Lyndon B. Johnson administration, the Elementary and Secondary Education Act (ESEA) was signed, marking the entrance of the federal government into the business of public education. It would never again *not* be involved in a regulatory manner again. The ESEA was a significant component of Johnson's War on Poverty, as its mission was to improve the quality of education for children in need in both public and parochial schools. It addressed the funding needs of parochial schools through the creation of Title I, a provision of ESEA that ensured these schools would receive monies from the funding granted to public schools. Title I remains in effect in the twenty-first century and continues to do what it was intended to do, although it has been reauthorized with modifications and the incorporation of new and additional objectives over the years.

A major reauthorization in 1994 overhauled the ESEA to include the mandate that each state would develop an individual standards-based system applicable to all students, even those who qualified for Title I funding. The motivation behind this rewrite was to improve efficiency of the system. To do that, there needed to be clear, measurable goals to track progress of student learning. Title I students would now be held to the same standards as students outside that needs-based funding. This new facet of ESEA was known as Goals 2000.

The No Child Left Behind Act (NCLB Act) was signed into law in January 2002 as a refinement and extension of Goals 2000; it is, in effect, the seventh reauthorization of the ESEA. The rationale behind the Act is to achieve and maintain equal education for all students, regardless of socioeconomic background and ability. Among other things, the NCLB Act further develops the accountability aspect of the ESEA by operating on one idea: States set achievement goals. Schools that meet those goals receive funding; those that don't, do not. And progress is measured by a standardized test.

SIGNIFICANCE

The Executive Summary of NCLB outlines the law's rigorous requirements. NCLB covers many federal education programs, but it was controversial before it ever passed into law for its testing, accountability, and school improvement demands.

Briefly stated, states determined their educational goals. These goals had to ensure that all students were proficient in grade-level math and reading by the year 2014, and each state defined grade-level performance. Every school was required to make what the act calls "adequate yearly progress" (AYP), and this progress was measured by standardized tests administered annually in grades 3–8, once in grades 10–12. Science must be tested once in grades 3–5, 6–8, and 10–12.

President George W. Bush signs into law the No Child Left Behind Act on January 8, 2002. Behind the president are two children, Tez Taylor (left) and Cecilia Pallcio. Behind them are (left to right) Rep. George Miller, D-CA, Sen. Ted Kennedy, D-MA, education secretary Rod Paige, Sen. Judd Gregg, R-NH, Rep. John Boehner, R-OH, and an unidentified woman. © AP IMAGES/RON EDMONDS.

Proficiency rates toward each school's goals were expected to increase each year leading up to 2014. To achieve AYP, the school had to achieve its targeted goals in reading and math within each specific subgroup. These subgroups were defined demographically and included English language learners, students with disabilities, low-income students, and major racial and ethnic groups.

If a school failed to meet its AYP for two consecutive years, the government identified it for "school improvement" and the school was required to develop an improvement plan and devote at least 10 percent of its Title I funds to teacher professional development. For each year a school failed to meet its AYP, the consequence was more grave and significant,

the worst-case scenario being that a school was subjected to a restructuring plan that completely overhauled the school's governance in one way or another.

The NCLB Act had far-reaching impact on the educational landscape and was controversial from the start. The idea that schools should be held accountable for the quality of education they gave students was admirable, but the execution of measuring progress and accountability—through standardized testing—angered and frustrated educators and policymakers. Angela Kennedy's interview with school counselors is an example of this, and her subject's concerns are an accurate representation of the general consensus.

As the decade passed, more and more schools failed to meet their AYP goals. Cries of "teaching to the test" arose not only from teachers, but also from parents who were concerned that the priority had become not to give their children well-rounded educations, but to teach them a specific set of skills designed to correctly answer a particular kind of test question. By 2010, 38 percent of schools failed to meet their AYP, a significant increase from 29 percent in 2006.

Although in the minority, the law had advocates among educational leaders. They praised NCLB for its transparency and inclusiveness and lauded the act's strict rules of accountability as necessary for the change public education needed.

The No Child Left Behind Act of 2001 expired in 2007. Although the U.S. Congress had attempted to rewrite and restructure the act, members missed new president Barack Obama's deadline for updating it. During his 2008 presidential campaign, Obama promised to offer states some relief from the act, and he followed through on that promise. Before the end of 2012, President Obama had offered waivers to thirty-three states, though some of those waivers came with conditions.

PRIMARY SOURCE

THE NO CHILD LEFT BEHIND ACT OF 2001, EXECUTIVE SUMMARY

SYNOPSIS: This executive summary provides an overview of the intentions behind the No Child Left Behind Act of 2001 and how it was expected to change the face of public education in the United States

These reforms express my deep belief in our public schools and their mission to build the mind and character of every child, from every background, in every part of America.

President George W. Bush

January 2001

Three days after taking office in January 2001 as the 43rd President of the United States, George W. Bush announced No Child Left Behind, his framework for bipartisan education reform that he described as "the cornerstone of my Administration." President Bush emphasized his deep belief in our public schools, but an even greater concern that "too many of our neediest children are being left behind," despite the nearly $200 billion in Federal spending since the passage of the Elementary and Secondary Education Act of 1965

(ESEA). The President called for bipartisan solutions based on accountability, choice, and flexibility in Federal education programs.

Less than a year later, despite the unprecedented challenges of engineering an economic recovery while leading the Nation in the war on terrorism following the events of September 11, President Bush secured passage of the landmark No Child Left Behind Act of 2001 (NCLB Act). The new law reflects a remarkable consensus—first articulated in the President's No Child Left Behind framework—on how to improve the performance of America's elementary and secondary schools while at the same time ensuring that no child is trapped in a failing school.

The NCLB Act, which reauthorizes the ESEA, incorporates the principles and strategies proposed by President Bush. These include increased accountability for States, school districts, and schools; greater choice for parents and students, particularly those attending low-performing schools; more flexibility for States and local educational agencies (LEAs) in the use of Federal education dollars; and a stronger emphasis on reading, especially for our youngest children.

Increased Accountability

The NCLB Act will strengthen Title I accountability by requiring States to implement statewide accountability systems covering all public schools and students. These systems must be based on challenging State standards in reading and mathematics, annual testing for all students in grades 3–8, and annual statewide progress objectives ensuring that all groups of students reach proficiency within 12 years. Assessment results and State progress objectives must be broken out by poverty, race, ethnicity, disability, and limited English proficiency to ensure that no group is left behind. School districts and schools that fail to make adequate yearly progress (AYP) toward statewide proficiency goals will, over time, be subject to improvement, corrective action, and restructuring measures aimed at getting them back on course to meet State standards. Schools that meet or exceed AYP objectives or close achievement gaps will be eligible for State Academic Achievement Awards.

More Choices for Parents and Students

The NCLB Act significantly increases the choices available to the parents of students attending Title I schools that fail to meet State standards, including immediate relief—beginning with the 2002–03 school year—for students in schools that were previously identified for improvement or corrective action under the 1994 ESEA reauthorization.

LEAs must give students attending schools identified for improvement, corrective action, or restructuring the opportunity to attend a better public school, which may include a public charter school, within the school district. The district must provide transportation to the new school, and must use at least 5 percent of its Title I funds for this purpose, if needed.

For students attending persistently failing schools (those that have failed to meet State standards for at least 3 of the 4 preceding years), LEAs must permit low-income students to use Title I funds to obtain supplemental educational services from the public- or private-sector provider selected by the students and their parents. Providers must meet State standards and offer services tailored to help participating students meet challenging State academic standards.

To help ensure that LEAs offer meaningful choices, the new law requires school districts to spend up to 20 percent of their Title I allocations to provide school choice and supplemental educational services to eligible students.

In addition to helping ensure that no child loses the opportunity for a quality education because he or she is trapped in a failing school, the choice and supplemental service requirements provide a substantial incentive for low-performing schools to improve. Schools that want to avoid losing students—along with the portion of their annual budgets typically associated with those students—will have to improve or, if they fail to make AYP for 5 years, run the risk of reconstitution under a restructuring plan.

GREATER FLEXIBILITY FOR STATES, SCHOOL DISTRICTS, AND SCHOOLS

One important goal of No Child Left Behind was to breathe new life into the "flexibility for accountability" bargain with States first struck by President George H. W. Bush during his historic 1989 education summit with the Nation's Governors at Charlottesville, Virginia. Prior flexibility efforts have focused on the waiver of program requirements; the NCLB Act moves beyond this limited approach to give States and school districts unprecedented flexibility in the use of Federal education funds in exchange for strong accountability for results.

New flexibility provisions in the NCLB Act include authority for States and LEAs to transfer up to 50 percent of the funding they receive under 4 major State grant programs to any one of the programs, or to Title I. The covered programs include Teacher Quality State Grants, Educational Technology, Innovative Programs, and Safe and Drug-Free Schools.

The new law also includes a competitive State Flexibility Demonstration Program that permits up to 7 States to consolidate the State share of nearly all Federal State grant programs—including Title I, Part A Grants to Local Educational Agencies—while providing additional flexibility in their use of Title V Innovation funds. Participating States must enter into 5-year performance agreements with the Secretary covering the use of the consolidated funds, which may be used for any educational purpose authorized under the ESEA. As part of their plans, States also must enter into up to 10 local performance agreements with LEAs, which will enjoy the same level of flexibility granted under the separate Local Flexibility Demonstration Program.

The new competitive Local Flexibility Demonstration Program would allow up to 80 LEAs, in addition to the 70 LEAs under the State Flexibility Demonstration Program, to consolidate funds received under Teacher Quality State Grants, Educational Technology State Grants, Innovative Programs, and Safe and Drug-Free Schools programs. Participating LEAs would enter into performance agreements with the Secretary of Education, and would be able to use the consolidated funds for any ESEA-authorized purpose.

PUTTING READING FIRST

No Child Left Behind stated President Bush's unequivocal commitment to ensuring that every child can read by the end of third grade. To accomplish this goal, the new Reading First initiative would significantly increase the Federal investment in scientifically based reading instruction programs in the early grades. One major benefit of this approach would be reduced identification of children for special education services due to a lack of appropriate reading instruction in their early years.

The NCLB Act fully implements the President's Reading First initiative. The new Reading First State Grant program will make 6-year grants to States, which will make competitive subgrants to local communities. Local recipients will administer screening and diagnostic assessments to determine which students in grades K–3 are at risk of reading failure, and provide professional development for K–3 teachers in the essential components of reading instruction.

The new Early Reading First program will make competitive 6-year awards to LEAs to support early language, literacy, and pre-reading development of preschool-age children, particularly those from low-income families. Recipients will use instructional strategies and professional development drawn from scientifically based reading research to help young children to attain the fundamental knowledge and skills they will need for optimal reading development in kindergarten and beyond.

First lady Laura Bush and President George W. Bush visit fourth and fifth graders at P.S. 76 in the Bronx, New York, on September 26, 2007, following a speech by the president about the No Child Left Behind Act. © AP IMAGES/CHARLES DHARAPAK.

OTHER MAJOR PROGRAM CHANGES

The No Child Left Behind Act of 2001 also put the principles of accountability, choice, and flexibility to work in its reauthorization of other major ESEA programs. For example, the new law combines the Eisenhower Professional Development and Class Size Reduction programs into a new Improving Teacher Quality State Grants program that focuses on using practices grounded in scientifically based research to prepare, train, and recruit high-quality teachers. The new program gives States and LEAs flexibility to select the strategies that best meet their particular needs for improved teaching that will help them raise student achievement in the core academic subjects. In return for this flexibility, LEAs are required to demonstrate annual progress in ensuring that all teachers teaching in core academic subjects within the State are highly qualified.

The NCLB Act also simplified Federal support for English language instruction by combining categorical bilingual and immigrant education grants that benefited a small percentage of limited English proficient students in relatively few schools into a State formula program. The new formula program will facilitate the comprehensive planning by States and school districts needed to ensure implementation of programs that benefit all limited English proficient students by helping them learn English and meet the same high academic standards as other students.

Other changes will support State and local efforts to keep our schools safe and drug-free, while at the same time ensuring that students—particularly those who have been victims of violent crimes on school grounds—are not trapped in persistently dangerous schools. As proposed in No Child Left Behind, States must allow students who attend a persistently dangerous school, or who are victims of violent crime at school, to transfer to a safe school. States also must report school safety statistics to the public on a school-by-school basis, and LEAs must use Federal Safe and Drug-Free Schools and Communities funding to implement drug and violence prevention programs of demonstrated effectiveness.

"TRUE OR FALSE: NO CHILD LEFT BEHIND IS WORKING"

SYNOPSIS: Several school counseling professionals give their opinions on the NCLB Act.

Mark Twain once said, "I have never let my schooling interfere with my education."

That very sentiment can easily be applied to the No Child Left Behind debate, as many school officials have questioned whether this legislation actually interferes with providing school students a well-rounded and quality curriculum.

Signed into law by President George W. Bush on Jan. 8, 2002, the No Child Left Behind Act significantly changed federal education policy for grades kindergarten through 12. Notably, it requires standardized testing for all students in English and math every year in grades 3 through 8, as well as once in high school. NCLB has put pressure on U.S. primary and secondary schools to improve the academic performance of all students, and many school districts have certainly progressed, but not without many opponents raising an important question: At what cost?

Large numbers of student advocates, including school counselors, have criticized NCLB's stringent accountability and strict testing requirements, claiming its implementation is too costly, narrows the curriculum and does not take into consideration the unique needs of every student. Proponents of education reform say the legislation has exposed the achievement gap between minority and nonminority students, as well as performance discrepancies between disadvantaged and affluent students.

NCLB is the name given to the most recent version of the Elementary and Secondary Education Act of 1965, which is due to expire this year. As Congress looks to "reauthorize"—extend or revise—the federal statute, school counseling professionals weigh in on what's working and what needs to change to ensure that, in fact, no child is left behind.

Ted Martinez

"(NCLB's) overall objective of trying to reach 100 percent proficiency in both reading and math by the year 2014 is not only unrealistic, but impossible to achieve. But I think it's typical of how politicians think, as opposed to education professionals," says Ted Martinez, an American Counseling Association member and school counselor with the New London Public School System in Connecticut. "Politicians have to have some end point, so they put 2014."

"(NCLB) has a strong emphasis on accountability and intense testing. I'm not for or against it, nor argue the merits of whether every grade should be tested, but I think it is unrealistic to subject kids from other countries to these high-stakes tests when they don't even know the language. It's really unfair and that's my biggest concern," says Martinez, who works with a large population of ELL (English language learner) students in his district.

"You have to be able to speak, read and write the English language if you are going to be able to negotiate your existence in this society. I think 98 percent of them absolutely want to do that. But to subject them to this kind of testing is incredibly frustrating. If you don't know the language, how are you going to measure something that they don't even have?"

Martinez adds that, in his opinion, the tests aren't student friendly, and he doesn't think that relying solely on test scores for accountability is an adequate gauge of a school's level of achievement with students. "The question is, do you want these kids to achieve or fail? If you don't supply them with the resources to acquire the skills that they need, testing them all the time isn't going to help them learn the English language."

Carolyn Stone

Carolyn Stone, past president of the American School Counselor Association, a division of ACA, is a school counselor educator at the University of North Florida. She has 22 years of experience in the field of education as a teacher, counselor and supervisor.

"Because I was an educator who was around before NCLB, and because I saw firsthand what happens to students when there is no accountability, I am a very strong supporter of standards for kids. It really holds the educators who are in charge of these young lives and their learning accountable for what happens. That said, high-stakes testing has really done a disservice in many respects to students."

Stone feels strongly that schools should be allowed to use different forms of assessments for students and that "success" shouldn't be defined by one test. "We know enough about assessments that we should be able, as a nation, to use different types of assessments and even multiple assessments to determine a student's grasp and competence within standards. Standards are good, but high-stakes testing is not necessarily (good)."

Paula Stanley

With 16 years of experience as a school counselor educator, ACA member Paula Stanley has a different perspective on the effects of NCLB. In working with her interns at Radford University in Virginia, she has noticed a change in the perceived roles of school counselors in the past few years. So much so, she says, that several individuals have entered the university's school counseling program only to change their specialty upon realizing that they may not get to work with students in the capacity they had assumed.

"There is just so much paperwork that they feel like they are not able to assist the students adequately, and it's really not what they went into counseling for. They want to have direct contact with students, and they are finding it really frustrating managing all the paperwork and also trying to fill their role as a counselor, as indicated by the ASCA standards. You have counselors who don't feel like they have the time to work with students on developmental needs. In most cases, the school counselors are in charge of managing the assessment, managing the success of students over time and working with special needs children. They are already overworked and not able to provide the counseling and services they want to. With NCLB, their role has become even more administrative."

Interns are also finding it increasingly difficult to meet the required 120 direct service hours per semester for their internship, Stanley notes. "Because NCLB (student test results are) tied to funding, teachers don't want students to leave the classrooms, so it gets more difficult for counselors to have access to the students who could benefit from their services." She adds that school counselors really do value students' academic success just as much as their social development and vocational aspirations, and school counselors are willing to work with teachers and administrations in becoming more accountable.

However, Stanley says, reducing the developmental role of school counselors ultimately works against student success. "The focus is just on making students pass this test, but some of the reasons why students aren't doing well on the tests are personal or social. They may have feelings of low self-worth or confidence, or they may have problems at home. They come to school with these problems burning inside of them, and it's hard for them to focus on their schoolwork." Given the chance and time, school counselors can help these children with coping skills and even encourage parents to get more involved with their child's academic success, she says.

Stanley admits the data gained from analyzing test scores can be beneficial as a means of proving the vital role of school counselors and their services. However, she says, "Someone with much less than a master's degree can count out tests. School counselors feel that their skills aren't being used, and much of the work (associated with administering the tests) can be done by clerical staff. The negative aspects of NCLB do seem to be more prominent in school counselors' minds."

"It's really affecting how we train counselors, the choices that students make in their counseling specialty and, ultimately, their choices once they have entered the school counseling profession. It's affecting all three points of that continuum."

Christopher Laudo

A school counselor at Salisbury Elementary in Gap, Pa., Christopher Laudo's perspective is that, although there are serious flaws in how NCLB is written, the legislation has ushered in a great opportunity for innovation and change. "By making the status quo unacceptable, the federal mandates of NCLB have served to create an unparalleled sense of urgency that has resulted in serious efforts to address equity and social justice. For school counselors, it has meant that we can no longer sit on the fence and debate whether we should be running a data-driven program. Because other professionals in the school setting are required to show their impact on student academic success, school counselors must hold themselves to the same standard." If school counselors fail to demonstrate their impact on student success or take a leadership role in helping to remove systemic barriers to student success, Laudo says, they run the risk of being perceived as unnecessary.

"This switch to more of a systems focus has resulted in having some very powerful conversations with my principal. Through the problem-solving process, as we share data and look to remove barriers to learning, we have formed an even stronger alliance. Before NCLB, such conversations might have been too uncomfortable or awkward to have. Now, thanks to NCLB, they are a necessary part of the growth process of the school."

Eric Sparks

Serving the Wake County Public School System in North Carolina for more than 13 years, ASCA President Eric Sparks says he has witnessed several positive aspects of NCLB. "It's helped us to focus on data and look to see which students are being successful and which students need help. It really fits in well with the ASCA model in terms of using data to identify students who aren't being successful academically or behaviorally. In that respect, it has helped school counselors show how they are contributing to the overall goals of the schools."

Sparks adds that there are some major dilemmas surrounding NCLB, the biggest being funding— or the lack thereof. "There are issues on how the formula is set up in terms of how schools are evaluated, so that has been a challenge to some of the schools." He says many schools don't think they have the resources they need to help all students achieve and meet the NCLB standards. He also notes that the number of subgroups as defined in NCLB, which takes into account minority students, English as a second language and socioeconomic status, can vary greatly between schools. "We have schools that range from four or five subgroups all the way up to 24 to 25 subgroups. The intent of NCLB is good in that you are looking at all of your students and making sure that all are progressing toward academic achievement, but keeping up with all the subgroups can be challenging for schools."

On the other hand, "The focus on data has really helped us to move from making decisions on what we think is best for students to making decisions that are based on the outcome data." Sparks adds that the data are essential when determining what is actually working to benefit student success. "We can look at the data and rethink our efforts and refocus our activities and programs."

The temptation for elementary and intermediate schools is to concentrate on the curriculum covered in the standardized tests ("teaching the test") and ignore other areas such as the arts, sciences and social studies, Sparks acknowledges. "We hear anecdotally, from teachers, counselors and administrators from around the country, that those areas aren't being emphasized as much as they have been in the past because more resources go toward language arts and math. That could have a negative impact on students in the long run if schools don't take measures to counteract that. If we aren't providing activities for students to participate in the arts, we are really missing out on opportunities to help the development of the overall student. Students who do participate in the arts, there's research that shows they do better in other areas, like math and language." He adds that nurturing talent and encouraging students in extra-curricular ventures promotes self-confidence and provides balance.

"We do hear also that the level of stress on students has increased. We are hearing that from teachers and counselors alike. As school counselors are working on their plans and programs for their schools, a lot of times they are adding in additional emphasis on ways to cope with stress, anxiety and providing workshops on test-taking skills. (But) while there are a lot of challenges to NCLB, before NCLB, it was easy to just look at school data as a whole and not really dig in and see who isn't being successful. Now we can help more students achieve in school."

Delores Curry

A high school counselor at Bloomington High School in California, Delores Curry says it's important for school counselors to advocate for themselves to be included in the rewriting/reauthorization of NCLB as a necessary component in student achievement. "One of the concerns we have as the school counseling profession is making sure that when the legislation talks about 'school

personnel,' school counselors are included within that group. As with any policy or legislation that must be followed, there's always going to be those who are happy and those who are not."

Overall, she believes NCLB has helped ensure that schools are making services and programs available to both subgroups of students and individual students who are struggling to meet NCLB standards. "With NCLB, you are identifying students and catching students that may have been tossed to the wayside before."

Organizations grade NCLB

According to the ASCA position statement on high-stakes testing, "High-stakes tests can penalize schools and students for factors over which they have no control, such as socioeconomic influences, naturally occurring yearly fluctuations or a student's state of readiness to perform on the day of the test. The scores resulting from high-stakes tests do not take into account important factors such as a school's adequacy of educational funding, lack of standardization of the test's administration, interpretation and scoring, potential errors in scoring or barriers to student performance. The testing results do not necessarily indicate student learning."

While ASCA supports the use of standardized tests as one of many measures of student and school achievement, it rejects the use of high-stakes tests or any other single measurement instrument. According to ASCA's position statement, "The professional school counselor encourages multiple measures when life-influencing decisions are being made."

In a recent survey conducted by Teachers Network, more than 5,600 public school teachers from all 50 states were questioned on the effectiveness of NCLB and its impact on schools. Only 37 percent found standardized testing "somewhat useful." Less than 1 percent agreed that it was an effective way to evaluate the quality of schools.

ACA Assistant Director of Public Policy and Legislation Chris Campbell says that, although not optimum, NCLB was a good start to education reform. "(ACA) strongly supports the main purpose of NCLB: to afford all children an equal opportunity to receive a quality education and, in doing so, to close the achievement gap between disadvantaged children and their more advantaged peers," Campbell says. "ACA believes that highly qualified teachers are critical to student achievement. However, if children are not physically and mentally prepared to learn, the best classroom instruction will not produce the desired results." . . .

FURTHER RESOURCES

Books

Rhodes, Jesse H. *An Education in Politics: The Origin and Evolution of No Child Left Behind.* Ithaca, NY: Cornell University Press, 2012.

Web Sites

"About ED: Overview and Mission Statement." *U.S. Department of Education.* http://www2.ed.gov/about/landing.jhtml (accessed on February 22, 2013).

Hanna, Julia. "The Elementary and Secondary Education Act." *Harvard Graduate School of Education,* Summer 2005. http://www.gse.harvard.edu/news_events/features/2005/08/esea0819.html (accessed on February 22, 2013).

"No Child Left Behind." *Education Week,* September 19, 2011. http://www.edweek.org/ew/issues/no-child-left-behind/ (accessed on February 22, 2013).

"No Child Left Behind—Overview." *New America Foundation,* September 12, 2012. http://febp.newamerica.net/background-analysis/no-child-left-behind-overview (accessed on February 22, 2013).

Resmovits, Joy. "No Child Left Behind Waivers Granted to 33 U.S. States, Some with String Attached." *Huffington Post,* August 13, 2012. http://www.huffingtonpost.com/2012/07/19/no-child-left-behind-waiver_n_1684504.html (accessed on February 22, 2013).

"Top Colleges Take More Blacks, but Which Ones?"

Newspaper article

By: Sara Rimer and Karen W. Arenson

Date: June 24, 2004

Source: Rimer, Sara, and Karen W. Arenson. "Top Colleges Take More Blacks, but Which Ones?" *New York Times,* June 24, 2004. www.nytimes.com/2004/06/24/us/top-colleges-take-more-blacks-but-which-ones.html (accessed on February 18, 2013).

About the Authors: Sara Rimer is the Boston University chief science and health media relations officer and a former *New York Times* reporter. Karen Arenson wrote about higher education, economics, finance, and non-profits for the *New York Times* for thirty years before becoming an M.I.T. Corporation executive committee member and a Woodrow Wilson Visiting Fellow with the Council of Independent Colleges.

INTRODUCTION

According to a paper published by sociologists in 2009, a greater proportion of immigrant black high school graduates attends elite American colleges and universities than both native-born black and white students. "How African American Is the Net Black Advantage? Differences in College Attendance among Immigrant Blacks, Native Blacks, and Whites" was published by Pamela R. Bennett of Johns Hopkins University and Amy Lutz of Syracuse University.

It compiled the results of the National Education Longitudinal Survey of Freshmen (NELS) begun in 1988, which followed a nationally representative cohort of 1,028 black eighth-grade graduates that year through the next twelve; generally what could be expected to encompass four years of high school, four years of college undergraduate studies and four years of graduate studies. The NELS concluded in 2000, and its results were examined by Bennett and Lutz.

They knew that a significant advantage was available to black college students through federally mandated and funded affirmative action programs. These were put in place after the 1960s civil rights movement to counter entrenched disadvantages caused by decades of racial segregation and "Jim Crow" laws. These laws intentionally disenfranchised Southern blacks and put opportunities out of reach of many descendants of slaves. The researchers wondered how much of the affirmative action advantage actually accrued to these American-born black students, who were the intended beneficiaries of these programs.

Previous studies had already shown that although a smaller proportion of black high school graduates than white high school graduates attended college overall, black high school graduates were more likely to attend college when their socioeconomic family background and academic performance were the same as those of white high school graduates. The 1988–2000 study revealed that, of those black high school graduates who did attend college, a greater percentage of those who enrolled at more elite schools tended to be immigrants rather than their American-born counterparts.

Lutz and Bennett found that among black students who either immigrated to the United States with their families or who were American-born children of immigrant parents, 9.2 percent were studying at selective colleges such as Ivy League schools, while only 2.4 percent of black students and 7.3 percent of white students born to descendants of several generations of native-born Americans were enrolled in these elite schools. The researchers wondered if these odds were affected by the generally higher levels of

Harvard University students celebrate graduation day in 2005. © PETER TURNLEY/CORBIS.

education and other factors among adult black immigrants to the United States.

SIGNIFICANCE

The Civil Rights Act of 1964 banned racial discrimination in American education. The following year, President Lyndon Johnson gave a speech at Howard University, outlining the justification for federal adoption of affirmative action in righting past wrongs, when black students were mostly excluded from elite colleges. He said:

> You do not wipe away the scars of centuries by saying: Now you are free to go where you want, and do as you desire, and choose the leaders you please. You do not take a person who, for years, has been hobbled by chains and liberate him, bring him up to the starting line of a race and then say, "You are free to compete with all the others," and still justly believe that you have been completely fair. Thus it is not enough just to open the gates of opportunity. All our citizens must have the ability to walk through those gates. This is the next and the more profound stage of the battle for civil rights. We seek not just freedom but opportunity.

> We seek not just legal equity but human ability, not just equality as a right and a theory, but equality as a fact and equality as a result.

Slowly, through the leadership and advocacy of President Johnson and others who believed the time had come for real racial equality in America, the tide began to turn. As other minority groups—women, the disabled, immigrants—also began to demand equal treatment under the law, affirmative action's original intent as restitution for the legacy of slavery broadened to include the representation of diversity for diversity's sake. This benefited all minority groups to some extent, but the NELS study showed that certain groups benefited more from affirmative action in higher education, namely immigrants. With the number of black immigrants doubling over the decade following the NELS study, their numbers were bound to have an impact on the disposition of college-bound black high school graduates.

The study revealed that where those immigrants originated was a significant factor in their choice of which colleges to attend. These origins tended to determine their attitudes toward education as a determinant of enhanced economic mobility, and their own ability to successfully navigate the rigor of elite schools. Regardless, by 2009, there was serious questioning of the ethical implications of immigrant black students benefiting more than African Americans from the results of affirmative action. A 2007 article in the *Journal of Blacks in Higher Education*, for instance, was headlined, "University Race-Sensitive Admissions Programs Are Not Helping Black Students Who Most Need Assistance." It ended with the report that "recently, many of the nation's most elite colleges and universities have shifted gears … a movement is under way to recruit students of all races from low-income families."

Part of that movement included a comprehensive look back at the issue in the context of the University of Texas-Austin from 1950—when a landmark court case mandated desegregated graduate and professional schools in America—through 2010, based on a sampling of results of the 1996 Texas law mandating that the top ten percent of each year's high school graduating class automatically receive access to any college in the state. The *Harvard Journal of African-American Policy* published "Actuating Equity: Historical and Contemporary Analyses of African-American Access to Selective Higher Education from Sweatt to the Top 10 Percent Law" in its "Policy: 2011" edition. Its conclusion was that although access to selective state universities for native-born black students continued to struggle to match that of immigrant blacks, there were signs that possibly "historic rifts are starting to heal."

A 2011 *Diverse Issues In Higher Education* journal article seemed to prove out this hopeful trend. "Poverty Not Destiny: Elite Colleges Team Up to Give Talented Yet Impoverished Youths the Skills Necessary to Apply, Get Accepted and Thrive at the Nation's Most Selective Higher Ed Institutions" profiled internal and external programs by several selective universities to reach out to students from the lowest socioeconomic sectors and prepare them for success in studies at these institutions through intensive skill- and confidence-building activities.

Henry Louis Gates Jr., Harvard history professor and director of the W. E. B. Du Bois Institute for African and African American Research. © AP IMAGES/STEVEN SENNE.

▮ PRIMARY SOURCE

"TOP COLLEGES TAKE MORE BLACKS, BUT WHICH ONES?"

SYNOPSIS: Harvard law professor Lani Guinier and Henry Louis Gates Jr., Harvard history professor and director of the W. E. B. Du Bois Institute for African and African American Research, point out that as many as two-thirds of Harvard's black undergraduates are children of immigrants or biracial couples. They are concerned that African American students—whose

families have been in America for generations and who are the originally intended beneficiaries of affirmative action—are being left behind in admissions to the country's most selective colleges.

At the most recent reunion of Harvard University's black alumni, there was lots of pleased talk about the increase in the number of black students at Harvard.

But the celebratory mood was broken in one forum, when some speakers brought up the thorny issue of exactly who those black students were.

While about 8 percent, or about 530, of Harvard's undergraduates were black, Lani Guinier, a Harvard law professor, and Henry Louis Gates Jr., the chairman of Harvard's African and African-American studies department, pointed out that the majority of them—perhaps as many as two-thirds—were West Indian and African immigrants or their children, or to a lesser extent, children of biracial couples.

They said that only about a third of the students were from families in which all four grandparents were born in this country, descendants of slaves. Many argue that it was students like these, disadvantaged by the legacy of Jim Crow laws, segregation and decades of racism, poverty and inferior schools, who were intended as principal beneficiaries of affirmative action in university admissions.

What concerned the two professors, they said, was that in the high-stakes world of admissions to the most selective colleges—and with it, entry into the country's inner circles of power, wealth and influence—African-American students whose families have been in America for generations were being left behind.

"I just want people to be honest enough to talk about it," Professor Gates, the Yale-educated son of a West Virginia paper-mill worker, said recently, reiterating the questions he has been raising since the black alumni weekend last fall. "What are the implications of this?"

Both Professor Gates and Professor Guinier emphasize that this is not about excluding immigrants, whom sociologists describe as a highly motivated, self-selected group. Blacks, who make up 13 percent of the United States population, are still underrepresented at Harvard and other selective colleges, they said.

The conversation that bubbled up that weekend has continued across campus here and beyond as these professors and others publicly raise painful and complicated questions about race and class and how they play out in elite university admissions, issues that some educators and black admissions officers have privately talked about for some time.

There is no consensus on the answers, and since most institutions say they do not look into the origins of their black students, the absence of hard data makes the discussion even more difficult.

Some educators, including the president of Harvard, Lawrence H. Summers, declined to comment on the issue; others are divided.

The president of Amherst College, Anthony W. Marx, says that colleges should care about the ethnicity of black students because in overlooking those with predominantly American roots, colleges are missing an "opportunity to correct a past injustice" and depriving their campuses "of voices that are particular to being African-American, with all the historical disadvantages that that entails."

But others say there is no reason to take the ancestry of black students into account.

"I don't think it should matter for purposes of admissions in higher education," said Lee C. Bollinger, the president of Columbia University, who as president of the University of Michigan fiercely defended its use of affirmative action. "The issue is not origin, but social practices. It matters in American society whether you

grow up black or white. It's that differential effect that really is the basis for affirmative action."

Professors Gates and Guinier cite various sources for their figures about Harvard's black students, including conversations with administrators and students, a recent Harvard undergraduate honors thesis based on extensive student interviews, and the "Black Guide to Life at Harvard," which surveyed 70 percent of the black undergraduates and was published last year by the Harvard Black Students Association.

Researchers at Princeton University and the University of Pennsylvania who have been studying the achievement of minority students at 28 selective colleges and universities (including theirs, as well as Yale, Columbia, Duke and the University of California at Berkeley), found that 41 percent of the black students identified themselves as immigrants, as children of immigrants or as mixed race.

Douglas S. Massey, a Princeton sociology professor who was one of the researchers, said the black students from immigrant families and the mixed-race students represented a larger proportion of the black students than that in the black population in the United States generally. Andrew A. Beveridge, a sociologist at Queens College, says that among 18- to 25-year-old blacks nationwide, about 9 percent describe themselves as of African or West Indian ancestry. Like the Gates and Guinier numbers, these tallies do not include foreign students.

In the 40 or so years since affirmative action began in higher education, the focus has been on increasing the numbers of black students at selective colleges, not on their family background. Professor Massey said that the admissions officials he talked to at these colleges seemed surprised by the findings about the black students. "They really didn't have a good idea of what they're getting," he said.

But few black students are surprised. Sheila Adams, a Harvard senior, was born in the South Bronx to a school security officer and a subway token seller, and her family has been in this country for generations. Ms. Adams said there were so few black students like her at Harvard that they had taken to referring to themselves as "the descendants."

The subject, however, remains taboo among some college administrators. Anthony Carnevale, a former vice president at the Educational Testing Service, which develops SAT tests, said colleges were happy to the take high-performing black students from immigrant families.

"They've found an easy way out," Mr. Carnevale said. "The truth is, the higher-education community is no longer connected to the civil rights movement. These immigrants represent Horatio Alger, not *Brown v. Board of Education* and America's race history."

Almost from its inception, following the civil rights struggles of the 1960s, affirmative action has been attacked and redefined. In its 1978 *Bakke* decision, the Supreme Court shifted the rationale away from issues of social justice to the educational value of diversity.

One black admissions official at a highly selective college said the reluctance of college officials to discuss these issues has helped obscure the scarcity of black students whose families have been in this country for generations.

"If somebody does not start paying attention to those who are not able to make it in, they're going to start drifting farther and farther behind," said the official, who declined to be identified because the subject is so charged. "You've got to say that the long-term blacks were either dealt a crooked hand, or something is innately wrong with them. And I simply won't accept that there is something wrong with them."

Mary C. Waters, the chairman of the sociology department at Harvard, who has studied West Indian immigrants, says they are initially more successful than many African-Americans for a number of reasons. Since they come from majority-black countries, they are less psychologically handicapped by the stigma of race. In addition, many arrive with higher levels of education and professional experience. And at first, they encounter less discrimination.

"You need a philosophical discussion about what are the aims of affirmative action," Professor Waters said. "If it's about getting black faces at Harvard, then you're doing fine. If it's about making up for 200 to 500 years of slavery in this country and its aftermath, then you're not doing well. And if it's about having diversity that includes African-Americans from the South or from inner-city high schools, then you're not doing well, either."

Even among black scholars there is disagreement on whether a discussion about the origins of black students is helpful. Orlando Patterson, a Harvard sociologist and West Indian native, said he wished others would "let sleeping dogs lie."

"The doors are wide open—as wide open as they ever will be—for native-born black middle-class kids to enter elite colleges," he wrote in an e-mail message.

There is also wide disagreement about what, if anything, should be done about the underrepresentation of African-American students whose families have been here for generations. Even Professor Gates, who can trace his ancestry back to slaves, and Professor Guinier,

whose mother is white and whose father immigrated from Jamaica, emphasize different ideas.

"This is about the kids of recent arrivals beating out the black indigenous middle-class kids," said Professor Gates, who plans to assemble a study group on the subject. "We need to learn what the immigrants' kids have so we can bottle it and sell it, because many members of the African-American community, particularly among the chronically poor, have lost that sense of purpose and values which produced our generation."

In Professor Guinier's view, there are plenty of other blacks who could also succeed at elite colleges, but the institutions are not doing enough to find them. She said they were overly reliant on measures like SAT scores, which correlate strongly with family wealth and parental education.

"Colleges and universities are defaulting on their obligation to train and educate a representative group of future leaders," said Professor Guinier, a Harvard graduate herself who has been studying college admissions practices for more than a decade. "And they are excluding poor and working-class whites, not just descendants of slaves."

Harvard admissions officials say that they, too, are concerned about attracting more lower-income students of all races. They plan to spend an additional $300,000 to $375,000 a year to recruit more low-income students and provide more financial aid to these students.

"This increases the chances that we will be able to reach into the communities that have not been reached," said William R. Fitzsimmons, dean of admissions and financial aid.

While Harvard officials ignore the ethnic distinctions among their black students, Harvard's black undergraduates are developing a body of literature in the form of student research papers.

Aisha Haynie, the undergraduate whose senior thesis Professor Guinier cited, said her research was prompted by the reaction from her black classmates when she told them that she was not from the West Indies or Africa, but from the Carolinas. "They would say, 'No, where are you really from?'" said Ms. Haynie, 26, who earned a master's degree in public policy at Princeton and is now in medical school.

Marques J. Redd, a 20-year-old from Macon, Ga., who graduated in June and was one of the editors of Harvard's black student guide, said that Harvard officials had discouraged them from collecting the data on who the black students were.

"But we thought it was one aspect of the black experience at Harvard that should be documented," he said. "The knowledge had power. It was something that needed to be out in the open instead of something that people whispered about."

FURTHER RESOURCES

Books

Massey, Douglas S., Camille Z. Charles, Garvey F. Lundy, and Mary J. Fischer. *The Source of the River: The Social Origins of Freshmen at America's Selective Colleges and Universities*. Princeton, NJ: Princeton University Press, 2003.

Periodicals

Bennett, Pamela R., and Amy Lutz. "How African American Is the Net Black Advantage? Differences in College Attendance Among Immigrant Blacks, Native Blacks, and Whites." *Sociology of Education* 82 (January 2009): 70–99.

Cooper, Kenneth J. "Poverty Not Destiny: Elite Colleges Team Up to Give Talented Yet Impoverished Youths the Skills Necessary to Apply, Get Accepted, and Thrive at the Nation's Most Selective Higher Ed Institutions." *Diverse Issues in Higher Education* 28, no. 18 (October 13, 2011): 18. www.thefreelibrary.com/Poverty+not+destiny%3A+elite+colleges+team+up+to+give+talented+yet...-a0271049071 (accessed on February 18, 2013).

Dietz, Laurel, Choquette Hamilton, Julian Vasquez Heilig, Richard J. Reddick, and Cristobal Rodriguez. "Actuating Equity: Historical and Contemporary Analyses of African American Access to Selective Higher Education from Sweatt to the Top 10 Percent Law." *Harvard Journal of African American Public Policy* 17 (Annual 2011).

Johnson, Jason B. "Shades of Gray in Black Enrollment: Immigrants' Rising Numbers Is a Concern to Some Activities." *San Francisco Chronicle*, February 22, 2005. www.sfgate.com/education/article/Shades-of-gray-in-black-enrollment-Immigrants-2728709.php (accessed on February 18, 2013).

Massey, Douglas S., Margarita Mooney, Kimberly C. Torres, and Camille Z. Charles. "Black Immigrants and Black Natives Attending Selective Colleges and Universities in the United States." *American Journal of Education* 113 (February 2007): pp. 243–271. www.umich.edu/~abpafs/blackimmgrants.pdf (accessed on February 18, 2013).

Web Sites

"Immigrant Blacks More Likely to Attend Elite Colleges." *Johns Hopkins University* 82 (January 2009): 70–100. www.jhu.edu/news/home09/aug09/net_black_advantage.html (accessed on February 18, 2013).

"University Race-Sensitive Admissions Programs Are Not Helping Black Students Who Most Need Assistance" *Journal of Blacks in Higher Education*, 2007. www.jbhe.com/news_views/56_race_sensitive_not_helping.html (accessed on February 18, 2013).

"The Profit Chase"

For-profit colleges have lots of champions—and lots of problems

Web site article

By: Anya Kamenetz

Date: November 16, 2005

Source: Kamenetz, Anya. "The Profit Chase: For-profit Colleges Have Lots of Champions—and Lots of Problems." *Slate*. www.slate.com/articles/news_and_politics/college_week/2005/11/the_profit_chase.html (accessed on February 18, 2013).

About the Author: Anya Kamenetz is a staff writer for *Fast Company* magazine and a columnist for Tribune Media. In 2009, she wrote a column called "How Web-Savvy Edupunks Are Transforming American Higher Education" and in 2010 a book on the subject titled *DIY U: Edupunks, Edupreneurs, and the Coming Transformation of Higher Education*. In 2010, she was named a Game Changer in Education by the *Huffington Post*. Her writing has also appeared in *New York Magazine*, the *New York Times*, the *Washington Post*, *Salon*, the *Nation*, the *Forward*, and *Vegetarian Times*.

INTRODUCTION

Most people are familiar with the concept of nonprofit public (state) universities and private colleges, but in the early 1990s, another type of school moved to prominence in post-secondary education: the for-profit college, also referred to as a "proprietary school." These schools gained cultural legitimacy through a piece of federal legislation passed in 1992 by the U.S. House of Representatives Committee on Education and the Workforce. Dubbed the "90-10 rule," this law revised the official definition of an "institution of higher education" to include these for-profit schools for the purpose of determining eligibility for federal aid in the form of low-interest student loans.

This rule held that a proprietary school, whose course offerings and delivery structure in some way filled a niche that traditional universities and non-profit private colleges did not, would provide enough value to attract at least 10 percent of students who would be willing to pay their own way, without needing student loans. These would be students who did not meet federal guidelines for receiving taxpayer-subsidized loans. That would be enough to qualify the remaining 90 percent of proprietary school students for student loan eligibility, a ratio traditional educational institutions met with regularity.

This ruling put proprietary schools on the radar of those seeking an alternative to traditional four-year universities, whose curricula includes a balance of applied disciplines and liberal arts knowledge believed to form a well-rounded person. While that type of education has been acknowledged as desirable for those with the time, money, and temperament to afford it, there was enough interest on the part of potential students for a legitimate course of study that would take half as long or less, and prepare them for specific careers they had already determined they wanted. The accelerated course of study would be limited to only those classes necessary to develop the basic knowledge and skill sets to enter the workforce prepared to be productive and to start earning a living.

Many people believed that this was a new concept, but in fact at that time, the idea had been tried and proven 160 years before. Most historians agree that Foster's Commercial School of Boston, Massachusetts, founded by Benjamin Franklin Foster in 1832, was the first established school in America with the mission of training students for commercial careers. Within a few years, up to twenty private career schools had sprung up to teach business subjects. Duff's Mercantile College was founded in Pittsburgh, Pennsylvania, in 1841, and is recognized today as the country's oldest private career school in continual operation, having evolved into the current Everest Institute. By the time of the American Civil War (1861–65), about fifty career schools were operating under the management of Bryant & Stratton, the country's first major chain of for-profit career colleges.

A combination of new technology and cultural revolutions drove the growth of these career colleges after the turn of the twentieth century. The invention of shorthand note-taking and high-efficiency machines such as typewriters and adding machines made offices far more productive, and someone had to teach workers to use them properly and to manage the increased workflow they were capable of processing. The appearance of the automobile sped things up even more, bringing a whole new skill set to be learned in their safe and efficient operation and logistical management. As social mores relaxed and women began to enter the workforce, they also needed training to move from domestic skills to those needed in the workplace.

So, for-profit business schools had already been around for quite some time before the 90-10 rule was established in 1992, but they had remained under the radar because they were not accepted by mainstream academics and many others as legitimate educational institutions. However, the owners of these for-profit schools organized themselves into trade associations, complete with lobbyists on Capitol Hill, whose job it was to put for-profit colleges on the radar. They did their jobs well enough to result in the 1992 ruling, and with this governmental recognition, proprietary post-secondary schools entered the realm of educational legitimacy.

SIGNIFICANCE

By 2005, a difficult economy and rising tuition rates put even more pressure on college students to get through their studies as quickly as possible and leave school with a job already waiting, or at least as prepared as possible for immediate employment in their field of study. This situation created an ideal climate for for-profit educational institutions offering accelerated diploma and certificate tracks that allow students to complete programs in about half the time of a traditional four-year degree at a non-profit college or university. These accelerated programs also began making accommodations for students who were already working part- or full-time.

The market responded positively to these proprietary schools, which ran saturation schedules of television and radio ads promising a quick degree available even to students who were already working, and often implying placement with high quality employers even before they graduated. Conservative legislators in Congress, viewing traditional non-profit colleges with their soaring tuitions and spendthrift ways as poorly managed institutions unworthy of federal support, saw proprietary schools as a market-based solution leveraging modern technology to get things done and deserving of their support.

One particularly attractive characteristic of these schools to legislators was their accessibility to traditionally underprivileged populations. With an economic recession in full swing, tax revenues were down and budgets from local to federal levels were being squeezed. Anything that held the promise of getting more people off of public welfare and into paying jobs was welcome in the eyes of those responsible for keeping the government solvent. It was a powerful incentive to legitimize proprietary schools.

However, as the years rolled by and for-profit colleges began to evince a startlingly large proportion of student loan defaults and legislators began hearing more than a few complaints about deceptive advertising practices, they decided to start taking a closer look into these schools. This article reveals some of what was found, including fuzzy outcome statistics and an unattractive link between proprietary school lobbyists and the campaigns of legislators who supported them. Combined with class-action lawsuits by disgruntled students and a less-than-stellar history of deceptive practices and even fraud, by the middle of the next decade proprietary schools would come under intensifying scrutiny from state and federal governments as well as the media, putting their future in question.

PRIMARY SOURCE

"THE PROFIT CHASE: FOR-PROFIT COLLEGES HAVE LOTS OF CHAMPIONS—AND LOTS OF PROBLEMS."

SYNOPSIS: As America's recession ground on into its fifth year and high school graduates faced dwindling hope of affording the time or expense of a four-year college, post-secondary schools like ITT and the University of Phoenix jumped into the education landscape with accelerated programs and high profile ads showing happy graduates with rosy futures. The result was a significant gain in enrollment momentum for these for-profit institutions, but their track record of graduate job placement measured against higher-than-average tuition rates prompted this article's look at the darker side of propriety schools' history and current troubles.

You've seen this ad before, on the subway or at a bus shelter: An attractive young ethnic type beams in three-quarter profile, against a background of blue sky and clouds, looking off at … his future. At the bottom appears an aspirational word like Apex or Phoenix or Capella. Despite appearances, the product is not a psychopharmaceutical; it's one of the nation's 2,000-odd for-profit colleges.

So-called proprietary schools, which rely on tuition to both cover their operating costs and turn a profit, enroll about 1.6 million of the 20 million students at all accredited colleges nationwide; they run 28 percent of all two-year colleges. Their enrollment is growing four times faster than the sector as a whole, about 8 percent a year. The largest is the Apollo Group, which operates the well-known University of Phoenix and three other colleges. In all, Apollo has 176 locations, plus many online programs, with a total enrollment of 307,400 students in the United States, Puerto Rico, and Canada, up there with the largest state university systems.

Conservatives have hailed the robust for-profit college phenomenon as a welcome infusion of free-market forces into an otherwise bloated higher-education sector. The top official at the Department of Education making decisions about higher education, Bush appointee Sally Stroup, was previously a lobbyist for the Apollo Group. A vigorous champion of proprietary schools, Richard Vedder of AEI was recently named to a blue-ribbon Department of Education commission on the future of higher education that aims to tackle, among other things, the issue of soaring costs. Proprietary schools, among the largest donors to higher-education committee members, not surprisingly also have many loyal Republican supporters in Congress.

The Austin, Texas, location of the University of Phoenix, one of the largest proprietary schools in the United States.
© EDITORIAL IMAGE, LLC/ALAMY.

But before we herald these institutions as the smarter, leaner future of higher education, it is worth scrutinizing their practices and their shady past. There is no question that they are adept at turning a profit. Yet commercial colleges' long history of ethical lapses and the highly uneven quality of their offerings make them a poor model for a higher-education field in crisis.

American "career colleges" date back to the 1850s, when H. B. Stratton and P. R. Bryant founded a chain of 50 schools starting in Buffalo, N.Y., to teach shorthand, bookkeeping, and the use of the newfangled mechanical typewriter primarily to women, who were not welcome at most traditional colleges. They occupied cheap rental space in downtown office buildings rather than spending money on leafy campuses. The industry also grew through correspondence courses, which acquired a checkered reputation over the years. For every reputable accounting program, there were hucksters like the bogus art schools that took out the famous "can you draw this?" matchbook ads.

As the liberal arts curriculum evolved (or devolved) from the classics, to the humanities, to today's critical-thinking courses and ethnic-studies departments, the need for vocational education remained, and commercial institutions were there to fill it. They attracted underserved students, especially low-income and working adults, by offering accelerated courses with flexible schedules and focusing their pitch on job placement. These schools commonly report placement rates of a credulity-straining 80 percent or 90 percent, no matter what the program; the Department of Education does not track or verify these numbers. Tuition is set far above the rates charged by public community colleges, for-profits' main competitors, yet below those at private nonprofits.

Today, according to the biggest for-profit lobbying group, these schools graduate about half of the "technically trained workers"—a fuzzy category—in the United States. Proprietary schools are the likeliest place to turn if you're interested in becoming a Microsoft Certified™ Systems Administrator, or a clerk processing the paperwork for an HMO. Many of these colleges do offer bona fide degrees, including advanced degrees, in established subjects like business or computer science. But the volume business is in non-degree programs, which are shorter and cheaper to produce; they can cost hundreds or thousands of dollars yet terminate in a certificate of dubious value. Some of the offerings are pure wish fulfillment, like video-game design, film directing, or fashion merchandising; others are so limited they barely deserve to be called postsecondary. At the University of Phoenix, for example, you can earn a master of arts in education or an MBA with a specialty in e-commerce. At the other end of the spectrum, an outfit called Allied Schools offers a home-study course in "medical report writing" that involves "basic keyboarding skills, with an emphasis on medical terminology." There is no *US News & World Report* ranking or other objective measure to guide prospective students, who must make do with marketing claims.

Proprietary schools have been eligible for federal student aid under Title IV of the Higher Education Act since 1972. Taxpayer money, $4.3 billion in 2004, in the form of guaranteed student loans and Pell Grants, remains the primary source of revenue for these schools. This makes it emphatically the public's business how good a job they're doing. Unfortunately, the enticement of unlimited federal cash led proprietary schools into their darkest era in the 1980s. With little federal oversight, unscrupulous recruiters haunted welfare offices to sign up unqualified and even homeless students, collected their aid money, and offered useless courses in return. Student loan defaults peaked in 1992 at 22 percent, and proprietary schools accounted for nearly half of all defaulters, although they were the source of just a fifth of all loans. Angry student advocates nearly succeeded in casting these schools out of the federal aid program altogether. Instead, 1,500 of the nation's then 4,000 trade

schools were disaccredited, and the 1992 reauthorization of the Higher Education Act added complicated funding rules to try to control fraud.

Since the mid-1990s, the industry has spruced up its public image. After a round of buy-ups and mergers, publicly traded companies now enroll nearly half of for-profit students. These companies are Wall Street darlings—the highest-earning stocks of any industry between 2000 and 2003. But the very characteristic that makes them so attractive to investors, the ability to enroll ever-increasing numbers of students, has been the continuing source of trouble. A rash of investigations and complaints has called into question both these schools' business practices and their educational results.

A Department of Education inspector testified in May 2005 that during the previous six years, 74 percent of the agency's institutional-fraud cases have involved proprietary schools. In the last few years, the SEC has probed or investigated three of the 10 biggest higher-education companies, ITT, Career Education Corporation, and Corinthian Colleges, for discrepancies in their financial reporting. In September 2004, the University of Phoenix received the largest fine ever levied by the Department of Education, $9.8 million, for linking enrollment to recruiters' financial incentives, a violation of agency rules. In January of 2005, *60 Minutes* aired an exposé on the Career Education Corporation, which has been sued by students who borrowed up to $80,000 for courses and were stuck working in retail. Frustrated students are increasingly turning to class-action lawsuits to make good on what they say are the colleges' false claims about job placement; such suits have been filed against Corinthian and ITT, among others.

All this bad publicity has hurt stock prices for the companies involved, but it hasn't diminished the industry's political capital. In the last year, Congress has moved toward relaxing all the restrictions of the '92 crackdown. Most important, the version of the Higher Education Act currently before the House would include proprietary schools in a single definition of "an institution of higher education." Right now, they are eligible for student aid but not other kinds of subsidies available to nonprofit colleges; the change would potentially allow them to compete for millions more in infrastructure and program-related grants.

Conservatives like Vedder embrace for-profit colleges precisely because they are businesses. They see them as more focused on cutting costs and raising productivity than state-supported universities, with their tenured professors and their money-losing philosophy departments. They have a point there. The cost of public higher education has been rising steeply for decades. Colleges are a common budget-balancer for states facing fiscal crises; institutions in turn raise tuition, with much of the bill ultimately going back to the federal government in the form of student aid. The prevailing sentiment in Washington is that it's time to turn off the spigot and force colleges to control their spending. The current budget-reconciliation bill, in fact, includes the largest cuts to student aid in the 40-year history of the program.

It's true that proprietary institutions have taken the lead in money-saving innovations like accelerated courses, distance learning, and the deprofessionalization of teaching (hiring only instructors); nonprofit schools, for better and for worse, are already following these examples. Yet pointing to proprietary schools as models of probity is wishful thinking. Experts like Vedder, praising the "highly profitable" for-profit schools, willfully ignore the reality that the big higher-education companies were built to suck up federal hand-outs, which provide the majority of their income; these schools grab a share of federal aid higher than their share of enrollment, while public community colleges receive less than their share. Even worse, the prevalence of fraud, waste, and abuse in these schools from their origins down to the present day is a clear signal that turning a profit, not serving students, is their top priority. When students equal revenue, the pressure is on to pack them in and charge them as much as the market will bear. When colleges have shareholders, decisions are going to be made with short-term profitability in mind, and the shiny images in those subway ads will displace honest assessments of performance. Or as a University of Phoenix enrollment director told recruiters, as quoted in a 2003 Department of Education report, "It's all about the numbers. It will always be about the numbers. But we need to show the Department of Education what they want to see."

FURTHER RESOURCES

Periodicals

Blumenstyk, Goldie. "Year-Old Code of Conduct Makes Slow Progress Among For-Profit Colleges." *Chronicle of Higher Education* 59, no. 8 (October 10, 2012).

Carlson, Scott, and Goldie Blumenstyk. "The False Promise of the Education Revolution." *Chronicle of Higher Education* 59, no. 17 (December 17, 2012).

Hayes, Dianne. "Reinventing Higher Education: Colleges and Universities Retool to Recruit, Retain S=students." *Diverse Issues in Higher Education* 29, no. 18 (October 11, 2012): 12.

Stratford, Michael. "For-Profit Colleges' Marketers Generate Leads, and Controversy." *Chronicle of Higher Education* 59, no. 9 (October 22, 2012).

Web Sites

Di Meglio, Francesca. "Investigators Probe Shuttered For-Profit Colleges." *Bloomberg Businessweek*, January 9, 2013. www.businessweek.com/articles/2013-01-09/investigators-probe-shuttered-for-profit-colleges (accessed on February 18, 2013).

George, Michael. "110 For-profit Colleges Accused of Lying, Defrauding Taxpayers." *ABC Action News WFTS-TV*, January 4, 2013. www.abcactionnews.com/dpp/news/local_news/investigations/i-team-110-for-profit-colleges-accused-of-lying-defrauding-taxpayers #ixzz2J7vct7Hr (accessed on February 18, 2013).

Greenblatt, Mark. "Whistle-Blower: For-Profit College Operator Allegedly Inflates Job Placement Rates." *ABC News*, November 26, 2012. www.abcnews.go.com/US/whistle-blower-profit-college-operator-allegedly-inflates-job/story?id=17810902 (accessed on February 18, 2013).

Harkin, Tom. "For-Profit College Investigation." *Tom Harkin, Iowa's Senator*, July 30, 2012. www.harkin.senate.gov/help/forprofitcolleges.cfm (accessed on February 18, 2013).

Kirkham, Chris. "For-Profit Colleges Manage Student Loan Default Rates, Senators Call For Investigation. " *Huffington Post*, December 27, 2012. www.huffingtonpost.com/2012/12/27/for-profit-colleges-student-loan-default_n_2371688.html (accessed on February 18, 2013).

Pavlus, Sarah. "Phoenix Takes a Nosedive: Major For-Profit College Accreditation in Jeopardy." *AlterNet*, January 9, 2013. www.alternet.org/education/phoenix-takes-nosedive-major-profit-college-accreditation-jeopardy (accessed on February 18, 2013).

Ramos-Chapman, Naima. "Screw U: Some For-profit Colleges Are Ripping Off Students and Taxpayers—and Denying Students Their Chance for a Better Future." *Campus Progress*, December 14, 2010. www.campusprogress.org/campaigns/issues/screw_u_for-profit_colleges_scamming_students_and_taxpayers_out_of_the/ (accessed on February 18, 2013).

Kitzmiller v. Dover School District

Court decision

By: Judge John E. Jones III

Date: December 20, 2005

Source: Jones, Judge John E., III. "Memorandum Opinion: *Kitzmiller v. Dover School District*." *United States District Court for the Middle District of Pennsylvania.* Case 4:04-cv-02688-JEJ, Document 342 (December 20, 2005). National Center for Science Education legal archives. www.ncse.com/files/pub/legal/kitzmiller/highlights/2005-12-20_Kitzmiller_decision.pdf (accessed on February 18, 2013).

About the Author: Judge John E. Jones III had been, at the time of this decision, a federal District Court justice for the Middle District of the state of Pennsylvania for three years. Prior to that position, he had been the chairman of the Pennsylvania Liquor Control Board (1995–2002), solicitor for the City of Pottsville (1994–96), and a Schuylkill County assistant public defender (1983–95), as well as having practiced privately as an attorney. He was a member of the American Bar Association, the Pennsylvania Bar Association, the Schuylkill County Bar, and the Federal Judges' Association. He received his law degree from Dickinson College School of Law.

INTRODUCTION

There has always been conflict between those who believe in the literal interpretation of the Christian Holy Bible as the word of God and the history of the world, and those who believe in the scientific view of how the world and nature came to be. As far back as 1633, Italian astronomer Galileo Galilei was excoriated by the Vatican Inquisition for publishing his five-hundred-page *Dialogue Concerning the Two Chief World Systems*, which supported Copernicus's belief that the Earth orbited around the sun, and not vice-versa. The result was the end of Galilei's brilliant scientific career and of the Italian Renaissance.

Science and theology would continue their rocky relationship into the future. Their respective American advocates clashed for the first time, at least publicly, over how to handle the origins of life in education in 1925. The state of Tennessee had passed a statute that forbid the teaching of Charles Darwin's Theory of Evolution in public school classrooms, and high school biology teacher John Scopes was charged with doing so. During the 1927 trial, one counsel for the defense referred to the Galileo inquisition in characterizing the current trial.

The guilty verdict of the great public spectacle that came to be known as the "Scopes Monkey Trial" was appealed to the Tennessee Supreme Court and overturned. However, it was done on a technicality and not on the grounds that being forced to teach Biblical creationism was unconstitutional, which was the verdict sought by defense attorney Clarence Darrow. Still, of fifteen states that had anti-evolution education bills pending at the time, only two were able to get them passed into law. The stage was set for a continuation of the science/religion schism.

One of those states was Arkansas, which took the original verdict of the Scopes trial before its appeal to confirm the constitutionality of an anti-evolution law. In 1928 it passed such a law, making it illegal for any state-supported school or university teacher "to teach the theory or doctrine that mankind ascended or descended from a lower order of animals," or "to adopt or use in any such institution a textbook that teaches" this theory. Educators found to be in violation were subject to termination and charged with a civil misdemeanor.

Accordingly, from that time, science textbooks in Arkansas did not reference the origins of man. In the 1965–66 academic year, however, biology teachers in the Little Rock school system recommended that the administration adopt a textbook that included reference to Darwin"s evolution theory, and they did so. A young teacher, Susan Epperson, found herself in a quandary when faced with teaching her tenth grade science class from the text, which she was required to use but which contained the banned material. Unwilling to jeopardize her teaching job, she brought suit in the state"s Chancery Court. Holding a degree in zoology, Epperson was not against the evolution theory and her suit sought to have the law overturned as unconstitutional.

She was successful, but it was a circuitous route to the final decision in 1968. Though the Chancery Court noted that the law could be construed as unconstitutional because it infringed on Epperson"s right to free speech as guaranteed by the First Amendment, ultimately it upheld the law as an exercise of the right of the state to determine public school curricula. The case was appealed to the Arkansas state Supreme Court. There, the vague language of the law was called into question, and arguments were made that it might go against the Fourteenth Amendment's Due Process clause. The state court equivocated about whether the language expressly forbid even mentioning the evolution theory, or simply prohibited teaching that the theory was true.

Ultimately, however, the outcome of *Epperson v. Arkansas* at the state Supreme Court level was that the law was, indeed, unconstitutional. Part of the judges' written decision said:

> In any event, we do not rest our decision upon the asserted vagueness of the statute. On either interpretation of its language, Arkansas' statute cannot stand. It is of no moment whether the law is deemed to prohibit mention of Darwin's theory, or to forbid any or all of the infinite varieties of communication embraced within the term "teaching." Under either interpretation, the law must be stricken because of its conflict with the constitutional prohibition of state laws respecting an establishment of religion or prohibiting the free exercise thereof. The overriding fact is that Arkansas' law selects from the body of knowledge a particular segment which it proscribes for the sole reason that it is deemed to conflict with a

Students gather in front of Dover High School in Dover, Pennsylvania. Dover High School was the subject of the "intelligent design" *Kitzmiller v. Dover School District* court case in 2005. © AP IMAGES/BRADLEY C. BOWER.

particular religious doctrine; that is, with a particular interpretation of the Book of Genesis by a particular religious group.

It was the first time an American court had expressly opined that requiring teachers to either include or avoid certain material solely because it ran counter to the theological tenets of any religion was unconstitutional. It was a huge blow for creationists, but it was not the end of the issue. A related 1987 case in Louisiana, *Edwards v. Aguillard*, struck down a law requiring teachers to give equal time to Christian creationism if they were going to teach Darwinism. The verdict rested on essentially the same argument that decided *Epperson*. And since 1999, there has been an ongoing tug-of-war between anti-evolution advocates and science-based supporters on the Kansas state Board of Education. That struggle continued right through and beyond the *Kitzmiller* trial.

SIGNIFICANCE

When the Dover Area school board in Pennsylvania voted to include the concept of "intelligent design" in its science curriculum alongside the teaching of natural selection based on Charles Darwin's theory of evolution, eleven parents of students in the district filed suit against the board. They claimed that this first-ever decision to give what supporters call "creation science" equal academic weight as long-accepted scientific concepts was unconstitutional, and they called it creationism in disguise.

With a history of repeated losses in several state-level court cases, believers in the Christian tenet of creationism according to a literal interpretation of the Bible' Book of Genesis realized that if they were to have any success getting their worldview into school curricula—a major tenet of the evangelism required by their faith—they would have to change their tactics.

Enter the Discovery Institute in Seattle, Washington. The Institute describes its mission as "to advance a culture of purpose, creativity and innovation." Its Web site describes the science and culture portion of its work as follows:

Scientific research and experimentation have produced staggering advances in our knowledge about the natural world, but they have also led to increasing abuse of science as the so-called "new atheists" have enlisted science to promote a materialistic worldview, to deny human freedom and dignity and to smother free inquiry. Our Center for Science and Culture works to defend free inquiry. It also seeks to counter the materialistic interpretation of science by demonstrating that life and the universe are the products of intelligent design and by challenging the materialistic conception of a self-existent, self-organizing universe and the Darwinian view that life developed through a blind and purposeless process.

Though the Institute has several articles on its Web site disclaiming that it originated the term "intelligent design," the term does not show up in common discussions found in periodicals or elsewhere until after the 1987 *Edwards v. Aguillard*, decision.

One of the first major appearances of the term is in the book *Of Pandas and People: The Central Question of Biological Origins*, edited by Charles B. Thaxton, a Fellow of the Discovery Institute. Though the Institute refutes accusations that the book was developed as a tool to promote religious concepts of human origins by circumventing resistance to the term "creationism" by using more scientific-sounding terms, it was published just two years after the *Edwards* trial, and is intended for use as a textbook. It figured prominently in the *Kitzmiller* trial, as it was offered as an alternative text to those commonly used in high school biology classes at the time.

Many news organizations and publications freely referred to intelligent design as a more socially acceptable term for creationism. Its concept was that living organisms are too complex to have been created by anything other than a force of higher intelligence. The term did not convince those allied against the Dover school board, however, and it certainly did not sway the judge. His sometimes pointed language in the 139-page opinion accused several board members of lying to conceal their true motive, which he said was to promote religion.

History shows that periodic revivals of fundamentalist beliefs such as creationism have arisen during times of immense or rapid cultural change, perhaps as a way for people to retreat to the familiar and comfortable in the face of unknown challenges wrought by such change. The Scopes trial took place in the wake of World War I, which swept away the vestiges of the more sedate, rigidly ordered Victorian Age. *Epperson* occurred on the heels of the American civil rights movement, amidst the upheaval of the Vietnam War protests, the hippie movement, and the arrival of the rock 'n roll music revolution. And *Edwards* happened just after the Chernobyl nuclear plant meltdown, the *Challenger* space shuttle disaster, the hijacking of several airplanes and a cruise ship, and amid the turmoil of the Iran-Contra scandal and the depth of the AIDS crisis in America.

Even after multiple defeats in some of the highest courts in the land, proponents of intelligent design—now also called creation science—have no intention of letting the matter rest. Even into the early 2010s, four states were considering similar legislation as that shot down in *Kitzmiller*, with more than forty such bills having been introduced in the previous decade.

Talking about these bills, Joshua Rosenau of the National Center for Science Education (NCSE) told the *Guardian* newspaper of London in January 2013, "Taken at face value, they sound innocuous and lovely: critical thinking, debate and analysis. It seems so innocent, so pure. But they chose to question only areas that religious conservatives are uncomfortable with. There is a religious agenda here." Barbara Forrest, a Southeastern Louisiana University philosophy professor and NCSE board of directors member, attributed the popularity of such bills to the outcome of the *Kitzmiller* case. In the same *Guardian* article, she was quoted as saying, "Creationists never give up. They never do. The language of these bills may be highly sanitized but it is creationist code."

■ PRIMARY SOURCE

"MEMORANDUM OPINION: *KITZMILLER V. DOVER SCHOOL DISTRICT*"

SYNOPSIS: A 2004 decision by a small town school district requiring high school science teachers to include discussion of the religious concept of "intelligent design" sparked a 2005 trial in Pennsylvania's federal District Court. After hearing six weeks of testimony, the judge declared the school board's decision unconstitutional, on the grounds that it violated the "Establishment Clause" of the First Amendment.

IN THE UNITED STATES DISTRICT COURT FOR THE MIDDLE DISTRICT OF PENNSYLVANIA

TAMMY KITZMILLER, *et al.*, Plaintiffs, v. DOVER AREA SCHOOL DISTRICT, *et al.* Defendants.

Case No. 04cv2688, Judge Jones.

MEMORANDUM OPINION

December 20, 2005

INTRODUCTION:

On October 18, 2004, the Defendant Dover Area School Board of Directors passed by a 6–3 vote the following resolution:

Students will be made aware of gaps/problems in Darwin's theory and of other theories of evolution including, but not limited to, intelligent design. Note: Origins of Life is not taught.

Plaintiff Tammy Kitzmiller and her attorney, Eric Rothschild, enter the U.S. District courthouse in Harrisburg, Pennsylvania, September 26, 2005, during the *Kitzmiller v. Dover School District* trial. © AP IMAGES/THE PATRIOT NEWS/CHRISTOPHER MILLETTE.

On November 19, 2004, the Defendant Dover Area School District announced by press release that, commencing in January 2005, teachers would be required to read the following statement to students in the ninth grade biology class at Dover High School:

> The Pennsylvania Academic Standards require students to learn about Darwin's Theory of Evolution and eventually to take a standardized test of which evolution is a part.
>
> Because Darwin's Theory is a theory, it continues to be tested as new evidence is discovered. The Theory is not a fact. Gaps in the Theory exist for which there is no evidence. A theory is defined as a well-tested explanation that unifies a broad range of observations.
>
> Intelligent Design is an explanation of the origin of life that differs from Darwin's view. The reference book, *Of Pandas and People*, is available for students who might be interested in gaining an understanding of what Intelligent Design actually involves.
>
> With respect to any theory, students are encouraged to keep an open mind. The school leaves the discussion of the Origins of Life to individual students and their families. As a Standards-driven district, class instruction focuses upon preparing students to achieve proficiency on Standards-based assessments.

A. Background and Procedural History

On December 14, 2004, Plaintiffs filed the instant suit challenging the constitutional validity of the October 18,

2004 resolution and November 19, 2004 press release (collectively, "the ID Policy"). It is contended that the ID Policy constitutes an establishment of religion prohibited by the First Amendment to the United States Constitution, which is made applicable to the states by the Fourteenth Amendment, as well as the Constitution of the Commonwealth of Pennsylvania. Plaintiffs seek declaratory and injunctive relief, nominal damages, costs, and attorneys' fees.

This Court's jurisdiction arises under 28 U.S.C. § § 1331, 1343, and 42 U.S.C. § 1983. In addition, the power to issue declaratory judgments is expressed in 28 U.S.C. § § 2201 and 2202. This Court has supplemental jurisdiction over Plaintiffs' cause of action arising under the Constitution of the Commonwealth of Pennsylvania pursuant to 28 U.S.C. § 1367. Venue is proper in this District under 28 U.S.C. § 1391(b) because one or more Defendants reside in this District, all Defendants reside in the Commonwealth of Pennsylvania, and the events or omissions giving rise to the claims at issue occurred in this District.

For the reasons that follow, we hold that the ID Policy is unconstitutional pursuant to the Establishment Clause of the First Amendment of the United States Constitution and Art. I, § 3 of the Pennsylvania Constitution.

. . .

FURTHER RESOURCES

Books

DeWolf, David, John West, Casey Luskin, and Jonathan Witt. *Traipsing Into Evolution: Intelligent Design and the Kitzmiller v. Dover Decision*. Seattle: Discovery Institute Press, 2006.

Lebo, Lauri. *The Devil in Dover: An Insider's Story of Dogma v. Darwin in Small-town America*. New York: The New Press, 2009.

Slack, Gordy. *The Battle Over the Meaning of Everything: Evolution, Intelligent Design, and a School Board in Dover, PA*. Hoboken, NJ: Jossey-Bass, 2008.

Web Sites

Cline, Austin. "*Kitzmiller v. Dover*, Intelligent Design Court Case: Summary and Analysis of the Decision Against Dover's Intelligent Design Policy." *About.com*, April 13, 2012. www.atheism.about.com/od/kitzmillervdover/a/AnalysisIndex.htm?rd=1 (accessed on February 18, 2013).

"The Evolution Controversy." *Exploring Constitutional Law*. law2.umkc.edu/faculty/projects/ftrials/conlaw/evolution.htm (accessed on February 18, 2013).

Rothschild, Eric, Stephen Harvey, Thomas Schmidt, Alfred Wilcox, Richard Katskee, Alex Luchenitser, Vic

Walczak, and Paula Knudsen. *"Kitzmiller v. Dover,* Intelligent Design Court Case: Summary and Analysis of the Decision Against Dover's Intelligent Design Policy." *Intelligent Design Case: Kitzmiller et al v. Dover Area School District.* American Civil Liberties Union of Pennsylvania. www.aclupa.org/legal/legaldocket/ intelligentdesigncase/ (accessed on February 18, 2013).

Tabb, Kathryn. "The Debate Over Intelligent Design: What Would Darwin Say?" *Forbes.com,* February 5, 2009. www.forbes.com/2009/02/05/intelligent-design-evolution-creation-opinions-darwin09_0205_kathryn_tabb.html (accessed on February 18, 2013).

"Online Schooling Grows, Setting Off a Debate"

Newspaper article

By: Sam Dillon

Date: February 1, 2008

Source: Dillon, Sam. "Online Schooling Grows, Setting Off a Debate." *New York Times.* February 1, 2008. www.nytimes.com/2008/02/01/education/01virtual.html? _r=1&scp=2&sq=online+education&st=nyt (accessed on February 17, 2013).

About the Author: Two-time Pulitzer Prize winner Sam Dillon was the national education correspondent for the *New York Times* and covered issues affecting America's public schools, colleges, and universities. This was his second educational assignment during his thirteen-year career at the *Times.* During the early 1990s, he covered the New York City school system.

INTRODUCTION

In 1988, faced with dropping test scores, increased dropout rates, and other signs of system failure, Albert Shanker, president of the American Federation of Teachers, called for the reform of public schools in the United States. He proposed establishing "schools of choice," which would remain public but be legally and financially autonomous. These schools would not require tuition, would be free of religious affiliation and selective student admission—anyone who wanted to attend would be welcome. This was intended to accommodate the needs of students who might be failing to thrive in a traditional public school environment.

These schools would also be unencumbered by many state laws and school district regulations, allowing them far more flexibility in their classroom approach and curriculum content. Ideally, their accountability would be measured more by student outcomes rather than how those outcomes came about.

There were already a few schools operating this way, but they were not called "charter schools." This term evolved based on the fact that such schools would exist by authorization of their specific "charters," or statements of purpose, procedures and processes contained in the application for authorization.

Each state would require its own charter school law to enable their creation. This law would have to define what constitutes a charter school, who is able to authorize a new school's charter that allows it to start up, who can teach in it, who is responsible for funding, administration, and oversight, and how the schools will be accountable for their performance and results. One of the main tenets of charter schools is freedom from all but the most basic, major laws and regulations governing traditional public schools. This allows charters to be innovative and flexible in their programs and processes, which in turn allows them to quickly adapt to changes in their surrounding communities and cultures. This freedom was seen as necessary to avoid the under-achievement plaguing too many traditional schools.

Minnesota was the first state to pass a charter school law in 1991, with California following next in 1992. By 2009, forty-one states and the District of Columbia had charter school laws.

Some charter schools focus on fundamentals like reading, writing, mathematics, and other basic subjects, and they design their curriculum for students who may be struggling with them in traditional schools. Other charters specialize in the arts and humanities, visual and performing arts, literature, or music. Essentially, these schools can be whatever their creators envision them to be, since they are not required to adhere to rigid bureaucracies, content, and delivery methods.

In theory, charter schools can deliver a higher quality of education because they have much more freedom to design their programs to fit the needs of the specific students they serve. In actuality, performance has been inconsistent, accountability has been difficult to enforce under current regulations, there have been high profile cases of mismanagement and fraud, and charter schools have proven to siphon off much-needed funding from already under-funded traditional public schools. By 2008, there was a growing rift between lawmakers, educators, and parents who thought charter schools were nothing but a front for scam artists, and those who believed the concept is sound but the implementation needs serious work.

SIGNIFICANCE

Initially, traditional schools saw charter schools as a threat. They realized the new schools would draw away some of their funding and might potentially also draw away their best and brightest students. They were also aware that if the new schools out-performed them in outcomes, it would cast the traditional schools in a bad light.

There has been no across-the-board consistency in such outcomes in the dozen years since charter schools first took off in America. Some charter schools have failed in reaching or sustaining their academic achievement goals, while others have succeeded admirably, similar to conventional schools. However, there have been some overall visible, positive results.

The Center for Education Reform, a pro-charter organization, says that charter schools remain popular with some constituencies because they have been a solution in the problem of making sure every child has access to a quality education. It says this is because the focus is on the students instead of on administration, rules, and other distractions that hold traditional public schools back.

The Center also reports that on a nationwide average, "charter schools are funded at 61 percent of their district counterparts, averaging $7,612 per pupil, compared to $10,441 per pupil at conventional district public schools." It claims that charter schools have had a discernible "ripple effect" on the communities where they are located, spurring improvement in traditional local schools that have been motivated by some of the charters' successes. "Increasingly, members of the traditional public school system are turning to charter schools for examples of 'best-practices' regarding everything from curriculum to staffing to teacher retention," it says.

Originally it was presumed that charters would find more of a home among rural communities whose public schools were isolated from many mainstream progressive education programs and resources. However, the U.S. Department of Education's First Year Report in 1997—part of a four-year national charter school study—found instead that most of them tended to locate in urban areas. They are predominantly small, with two hundred students or fewer, and more racially diverse but with fewer special needs students than average public schools.

The 2007 annual survey by the Center for Education Reform reported that 54 percent of charter

school students qualified for free or reduced lunches, a common figure used to determine how many low-income students are enrolled in a given school. It also said that half of all charter students belong to "at risk" demographic categories.

While a 2002 article from Arizona State University's Education Policy Analysis Archives suggested that charters in poorer areas may receive more funding than traditional public schools, a 2005 national report from the Thomas B. Fordham Institute found that urban charters actually receive, on average, 22 to 40 percent less funding than their conventional counterparts.

Along with funding issues, charters are plagued by concerns about sponsorship by their authorizing body, a cap on the number of charters allowed in any given region, regulatory waivers, fiscal and legal autonomy, performance, exploitation by for-profit businesses, and their exemption from collective bargaining. There have also been some claims that while charters started out as a progressive movement toward best educational practices, they are now shifting into a conservative movement to privatize education and attack teachers' unions.

While advocates remained committed to the idea of charter schools as entities with a unique ability to involve their entire communities in developing student-centered education, the jury was still out as the movement continued to evolve.

PRIMARY SOURCE

"ONLINE SCHOOLING GROWS, SETTING OFF A DEBATE"

SYNOPSIS: This *New York Times* article explores the dilemma facing American states that must decide whether online classes are appropriate for young students and how to fairly allocate public education funding among traditional schools and Internet-based virtual schools, which are growing in popularity due to their convenience and customizability.

MILWAUKEE—Weekday mornings, three of Tracie Weldie's children eat breakfast, make beds and trudge off to public school—in their case, downstairs to their basement in a suburb here, where their mother leads them through math and other lessons outlined by an Internet-based charter school.

Half a million American children take classes online, with a significant group, like the Weldies, getting all their schooling from virtual public schools. The rapid growth of these schools has provoked debates in courtrooms and legislatures over money, as the schools compete with local districts for millions in public dollars, and over issues

Twelve-year-old Marcy Thompson works on a science assignment in her bedroom in Cross Plains, Wisconsin, on January 14, 2008; she is one of eight hundred students in the Wisconsin Virtual Academy. © AP IMAGES/ANDY MANIS.

like whether online learning is appropriate for young children.

One of the sharpest debates has concerned the Weldies' school in Wisconsin, where last week the backers of online education persuaded state lawmakers to keep it and eleven other virtual schools open despite a court ruling against them and the opposition of the teachers union. John Watson, a consultant in Colorado who does an annual survey of education that is based on the Internet, said events in Wisconsin followed the pattern in other states where online schools have proliferated fast.

"Somebody says, 'What's going on, does this make sense?'" Mr. Watson said. "And after some inquiry most states have said, 'Yes, we like online learning, but these are such new ways of teaching children that we'll need to change some regulations and get some more oversight.'"

Two models of online schooling predominate. In Florida, Illinois and half a dozen other states, growth has been driven by a state-led, state-financed virtual school that does not give a diploma but offers courses that supplement regular work at a traditional school. Generally, these schools enroll only middle and high school students.

At the Florida Virtual School, the largest Internet public school in the country, more than 50,000 students are taking courses this year. School authorities in Traverse City, Mich., hope to use online courses provided by the Michigan Virtual School next fall to educate several hundred students in their homes, alleviating a classroom shortage.

The other model is a full-time online charter school like the Wisconsin Virtual Academy. About 90,000 children get their education from one of 185 such schools nationwide. They are publicly financed, mostly elementary and middle schools.

Many parents attracted to online charters have previously home-schooled their children, including Mrs. Weldie. Her children—Isabel, Harry and Eleanor, all in elementary school—download assignments and communicate intermittently with their certified teachers over the Internet, but they also read story books, write in workbooks and do arithmetic at a table in their basement. Legally, they are considered public school students, not home-schoolers, because their online schools are taxpayer-financed and subject to federal testing requirements.

Despite enthusiastic support from parents, the schools have met with opposition from some educators, who say elementary students may be too young for Internet learning, and from teachers, unions and school boards, partly because they divert state payments from the online student's home district.

Other opposition has arisen because many online charters contract with for-profit companies to provide their courses. The Wisconsin academy, for example, is run by the tiny Northern Ozaukee School District, north of Milwaukee, in close partnership with K12 Inc., which works with similar schools in seventeen states.

The district receives annual state payments of $6,050 for each of its 800 students, which it uses to pay teachers and buy its online curriculum from K12.

Saying he suspected "corporate profiteering" in online schooling, State Senator John Lehman, a Democrat who is chairman of the education committee, last month proposed cutting the payments to virtual schools to $3,000 per student. But during legislative negotiations that proposal was dropped.

Jeff Kwitowski, a K12 spokesman, said, "We are a vendor and no different from thousands of other companies that provide products and services to districts and schools."

Pennsylvania has also debated the financing of virtual charter schools. Saying such schools were draining them financially, districts filed suit in 2001, portraying online schools as little more than home schooling at taxpayer expense. The districts lost, but the debate has continued.

Last year, the state auditor found that several online charters had received reimbursements from students' home districts that surpassed actual education costs by more than $1 million. Now legislators are considering a bill that would in part standardize the payments at about $5,900 per child, said Michael Race, a spokesman for the State Department of Education.

The state auditor in Kansas last year raised a different concern, finding that the superintendent of a tiny prairie district running an online school had in recent years given 130 students, and with them $106,000 in per-pupil payments, to neighboring districts that used the students' names to pad enrollment counts. The auditor concluded that the superintendent had carried out the subterfuge to compensate the other districts for not opening their own online schools.

"Virtual education is a growing alternative to traditional schooling," Barbara J. Hinton, the Kansas auditor, said in a report. Ms. Hinton found that virtual education had great potential because students did not have to be physically present in a classroom. "Students can go to school at any time and in any place," she said.

But, she added, "this also creates certain risks to both the quality of the student's education and to the integrity of the public school system."

Rural Americans have been attracted to online schooling because it allows students even on remote ranches to enroll in arcane courses like Chinese.

In Colorado, school districts have lost thousands of students to virtual schools, and, in 2006, a state audit found that one school, run by a rural district, was using four licensed teachers to teach 1,500 students across the state. The legislature responded last year by establishing a new division of the Colorado Department of Education to tighten regulation of online schools.

The Wisconsin Virtual Academy has 20 certified, unionized teachers, and 800 students who communicate with one another over the Internet.

The school has consistently met federal testing requirements, and many parents, including Mrs. Weldie, expressed satisfaction with the K12 curriculum, which allows her children to move through lessons at their own pace, unlike traditional schools, where teachers often pause to take account of slower students. Isabel Weldie, 5, is in kindergarten, "But in math I'm in first grade," she said during a break in her school day recently.

"That's what I love most about this curriculum," Mrs. Weldie said. "There's no reason for Isabel to practice counting if she can already add."

In 2004, the teachers' union filed a lawsuit against the school, challenging the expansive role given to parents, who must spend four to five hours daily leading their children through lesson plans and overseeing their work. Teachers monitor student progress and answer questions in a couple of half-hour telephone conferences per month and in interactive online classes using conferencing software held several times monthly.

A state court dismissed the case, but in December an appeals court said the academy was violating a state law requiring that public school teachers be licensed.

The ruling infuriated parents like Bob Reber, an insurance salesman who lives in Fond du Lac and whose 8-year-old daughter is a student at the academy. "According to this ruling, if I want to teach my daughter to tie her shoes, I'd need a license," Mr. Reber said.

Not so, said Mary Bell, the union president: "The court did not say that parents cannot teach their children—it said parents cannot teach their children at taxpayers' expense."

Kristin Kipp, a high school teacher at Colorado's Virtual Academy, poses with her computer in Golden, Colorado. © AP IMAGES/ED ANDRIESKI.

The Weldies and 1,000 other parents and students from online schools rallied in Madison, the state capital, urging lawmakers to save their schools. Last week, legislators announced that they had agreed on a bipartisan bill that would allow the schools to stay open, while requiring online teachers to keep closely in touch with students and increasing state oversight.

FURTHER RESOURCES
Books

Christensen, C. M., M. B. Horn, and C. W. Johnson *Disrupting Class: How Disruptive Innovation Will Change the Way the World Learns.* New York: McGraw Hill, 2008.

Klein, Carol L. *Virtual Charter Schools and Home Schooling.* Amherst, NY: Cambria Press, 2006.

Peterson, Paul E. *Saving Schools: From Horace Mann to Virtual Learning.* Cambridge, MA: Belknap Press of Harvard University Press. Reprint ed., 2011.

Periodicals

Clark, Jim. "Collaboration Tools in Online Learning Environments." *ALN Magazine* 45, no. 3 (2006). Available online at www.nspnvt.org/jim/aln-colab.pdf (accessed on February 17, 2013).

Huerta, L. A., C. d'Entremont, and M. F. Gonzalez. "Cyber Charter Schools: Can Accountability Keep Pace with Innovation?" *Phi Delta Kappan* 88, no. 1 (2006): 23–30. Available online at www.pdkmembers.org/members_online/publications/Archive/pdf/k0609hue.pdf (accessed on February 17, 2013).

Web Sites

Ahn, June. "What's the Controversy around Cyber Charter Schools?" *Teachers College Record*, June 16, 2010. www.tcrecord.org/Content.asp?ContentID=16018 (accessed on February 17, 2013).

Luna, Kay. "The Online Learning Controversy." *Quad-City Times*, December 17, 2011. www.qctimes.com/the-online-learning-controversy/article_dfbdfc8e-2920-11e1-a27a-001871e3ce6c.html (accessed on February 17, 2013).

Pogash, Carol. "Public Financing Supports Growth of Online Charter Schools." *New York Times*, June 4, 2010. www.nytimes.com/2010/06/04/us/04bccharter.html (accessed on February 17, 2013).

Wojciechowska, Iza. "Continuing Debate Over Online Education." *Inside Higher Education*, July 16, 2010. www.insidehighered.com/news/2010/07/16/online (accessed on February 17, 2013).

"The Lightning Rod"

Magazine article

By: Clay Risen

Date: November 2008

Source: Risen, Clay. "The Lightning Rod." *The Atlantic*, November 2008. http://www.theatlantic.com/magazine/archive/2008/11/the-lightning-rod/307058/ (accessed on February 20, 2013).

About the Author: Clay Risen is a *New York Times* editor and journalist. His work has appeared in *Smithsonian* and *The New Republic*, among other places. Risen's book, *A Nation on Fire: America in the Wake of the King Assassination*, was published in 2009.

INTRODUCTION

The District of Columbia Public Schools (DCPS)—there were 168 individual schools in the system in 2008—have been in need of serious reform for several decades. In 1967, a federal judge ordered the mostly white school board to halt all practices that discriminated against African American students. Reformers hoped for a bright future; that future has yet to materialize, though it has not been for lack of trying.

In 2008, DCPS was 84.4 percent African American, 9.4 percent Hispanic, 4.6 percent white, and 1.6 percent other. Approximately 66 percent of the DCPS student population was classified as low income, and the district had a dropout rate higher than the national average, despite the fact that it enjoyed the nation''s third-highest per-pupil funding budget. Clearly, something had to be done, but every reform effort had failed. The District continued to score among the lowest rankings in math and reading across the nation.

Desperate measures were required, and newly elected Washington, D.C., mayor Adrian Fenty believed maverick reformer Michelle Rhee was exactly what DCPS needed to overhaul a broken system. Rhee was hired in 2007 to be the first-ever chancellor of DCPS.

SIGNIFICANCE

As Clay Risen's article explains, Rhee did not waste time. She closed schools and fired principals and cut office jobs in her first year alone. Her attempt to renegotiate teacher compensation in 2008 was rejected outright by teachers and their unions for Rhee's refusal to grant tenure. A believer in merit pay—pay commensurate with student achievement—Rhee refused to give up. In 2010, she and the unions agreed upon a new contract, one that offered 20 percent pay increases and bonuses for strong student performance. In addition, teacher tenure was suspended for one year, with seniority protections diminished. With this contract in place, Rhee fired almost 250 teachers and put more than 700 school workers on notice. While the chancellor was praised by many for her zero-tolerance policy, she had her share of critics who resented her aggressive style of reform.

By the end of the decade, D.C. schools saw an improvement in test scores at all levels. Graduation rates had also improved. But many people—educators, parents, labor unions—were not happy with Michelle Rhee. Amid the clamor and accusations of having a personal agenda that prevented her from working with anyone within the system, Rhee tendered her resignation in October 2010. Although offered jobs in school districts across the nation, Rhee declined them all and instead founded a reform advocacy group called StudentsFirst.

In March 2011, *USA Today* ran an article suggesting that the remarkable test score increases of one of Rhee's schools—Crosby S. Noyes Education Campus—were achieved by cheating. Just 10 percent of Noyes's students tested proficient in math in 2006; within two years, that number had jumped to 58 percent. Results in reading were similar. Teachers were awarded $8,000 bonuses in 2008 and 2010 as a reward for student achievement. The principal was given $10,000. It seemed too good to be true.

Perhaps it was. A full-blown *USA Today* investigation revealed that the tests from Noyes and 102 other district schools had "extraordinarily high numbers of erasures," which were easily detected by the electronic scanners. A federal investigation ensued, but in early 2013, investigators announced a lack of evidence of widespread cheating in DCPS. Rhee was officially exonerated of any wrongdoing, but many still doubted her tactics, especially the idea of merit pay.

PRIMARY SOURCE

THE LIGHTNING ROD

SYNOPSIS: *From original article:* Michelle Rhee charged in as chancellor of the Washington, D.C., public schools wielding blackberrys and data—and a giant axe. She has made a city with possibly the country's worst public schools ground zero for education reform, and attracted a cadre of young zealots some critics call "Rhee-bots." Now the changes that she insists schoolchildren need are colliding head-on with the political wants of adults.

Michelle Rhee is always on message and always on call. If she's not speaking, she's thumbing away on her BlackBerry, or working a cell phone, or flipping open a laptop. When I met with her recently, she sat at her desk clasping a BlackBerry and a cell phone in her right hand; in front of her was a sleek Sony Vaio laptop, which she monitored incessantly during our conversation, while off to her right was yet another computer, a desktop PC. Apparently there is a second BlackBerry somewhere. And it's not for show. "Every e-mail a parent sends me, I answer," she said, a boast that even her critics grudgingly concede.

BlackBerry-wielding type-A personalities out to shake up the system are a common sight in Washington. Until recently, their habitat consisted almost exclusively of the halls of Congress and the K Street corridor—the think tanks, lobby shops, and congressional staffs most of us talk about when we talk about the capital. Rarely would you find them in the "other" Washington, the one most Americans would prefer to forget: the perennially dysfunctional city of 580,000 people, many of them poor and black; the city of the Marion Barry machine, of sky-high murder rates and voter disenfranchisement and the 1968 King riots. And, of course, the city of abysmal schools.

But thanks to Rhee and her boss, the young and charismatic Mayor Adrian Fenty, the city government is awash with the sort of überprofessionals once found exclusively in congressional committee rooms and white-shoe law firms. Fenty is a big part of the rush. Like a number of young mayors—Newark's Cory Booker and, until he moved to the governor's office, Baltimore's Martin O'Malley—Fenty is a data-focused decision maker, less interested in politics as usual than a politics of results. Soon after taking office, in January of last year, Fenty focused his energy on wresting control of the city schools from the all-powerful school board, as New York's Michael Bloomberg did in 2002, a move that has gained the interest of many fellow mayors around the country. By last July, the city council had approved the mayor's appointment of Rhee as Washington's first schools chancellor.

Since her arrival, in the summer of 2007, Rhee, just 38 years old, has become the most controversial figure in American public education and the standard-bearer for a new type of schools leader nationwide. She and her cohort often seek to bypass the traditional forces of education schools and unions, instead embracing nontraditional reform mechanisms like charter schools, vouchers, and the No Child Left Behind Act. "They tend to be younger, and many didn't come through the traditional route," says Margaret Sullivan, a former education analyst at the Georgetown Public Policy Institute. And that often means going head-to-head with the people who did.

Rhee, responsible not to a school board but only to the mayor, went on a spree almost as soon as she arrived. She gained the right to fire central-office employees and then axed 98 of them. She canned 24 principals, 22 assistant principals, and, at the beginning of this summer, 250 teachers and 500 teaching aides. She announced plans to close 23 underused schools and set about restructuring 26 other schools (together, about a third of the system). And she began negotiating a radical performance-based compensation contract with the teachers union that could revolutionize the way teachers get paid.

Her quick action has brought Rhee laudatory profiles everywhere from *Newsweek* to the *Memphis Commercial-Appeal*, and appearances on *Charlie Rose* and at Allen & Company's annual Sun Valley conference. Washington is now ground zero for education reformers. "People are coming from across the country to work for her," says Andrew Rotherham, the co-director of Education Sector, a Washington think tank. "It's the thing to do." Rhee had Stanford and Harvard business-school students on her intern staff this summer, and she has received blank checks from reform-minded philanthropists at the Gates and Broad foundations to fund experimental programs. Businesses have flooded her with offers to help—providing supplies, mentoring, or just giving cash.

But a lot of people who live in long-neglected neighborhoods are nervous—particularly those who see her as the vanguard of a gentrified, post-black Washington. In this city, everything revolves around race, class, and neighborhoods, and it makes no small difference that Rhee is an upper-middle-class Korean American from suburban Ohio, overseeing a system that is more than 80 percent black and overwhelmingly poor. "One of the things I see Rhee's reform going hand in hand with," says Lee Glazer, a D.C. Public Schools mother and co-founder of Save Our Schools, an activist group that has opposed Rhee, "is a much larger gentrification plan that's been at work in the city for many years"—an understandable fear, given the rising cost of living in Washington and the condo developments pushing into formerly depressed parts of town. "It's hard to tell if they just don't know what the hell they're doing or they're evilly brilliant." Community pressure has, in turn, translated into political pressure from the city council, which is searching for ways to rein in the very chancellor it just empowered.

Washington, in other words, is a battlefield and national testing ground where upstart young reformers are pitted against an establishment unwilling to give ground to what it sees as reckless social experiments. "Anything that happens in D.C. tends to matter beyond D.C., because the school system is held up as an example for education," says Kevin Carey, the research and policy manager at Education Sector. In the past, the city's failure was taken as proof that urban public education wasn't working. Rhee's goal is to make Washington a showcase proving that view wrong. If she succeeds, she could have a stunning impact on American public education.

For decades, an establishment of Democratic politicians backed by union leaders has ruled the Washington public schools, which by almost any measure—test scores, attendance, safety—are among the worst in the country. All sides—unions, reformers, parents, and politicians—agree that substantial change is needed. What they can't agree on is the how. Reformers call for closing failing schools, deciding salaries on merit, and giving parents the choice of where students go to school.

Community activists may applaud these changes in the abstract, but they criticize the means, viewing reform plans as having been concocted by think tanks and nonprofits to be tested on disenfranchised poor minorities (they offer no dramatic proposals of their own). They fear that closing and consolidating schools will create administrative and security nightmares, as students from rival neighborhoods are thrust together. They worry that the new chancellor is cutting vital staff. "People are concerned, morale is low," says Candi Peterson, a board member of the Washington Teachers' Union, which engaged in a protracted struggle with Rhee over the new contract. But mostly, Rhee's opponents are coalescing around the charge that her reforms have run roughshod over the community—that she is less a chancellor than a dictator.

The problems Rhee faced when she arrived went beyond the classroom. Washington's $1 billion schools budget gave the system the third-highest per-pupil spending in the country, but much of the money fed a bureaucratic monstrosity that relied on disorganized paper files, kept paying ex-employees while missing paychecks to current teachers, let new textbooks and equipment languish in warehouses, and lacked even a firm enrollment count. "I'm not against reform," Peterson says. "I know we need reform."

Only 43 percent of students entering the ninth grade in a D.C. public school graduate within five years, and only 9 percent get a college degree within five years of leaving high school. In 2007, Washington ranked last among 11 urban school systems in math and second-to-last in reading on the National Assessment of Educational Progress. Not surprisingly, the system has hemorrhaged students: the current estimate of the student body, 46,000, is less than half what the 1960 total was. Many of those losses have come since Congress, which has oversight of the school system, approved charter schools for the District in the late 1990s.

Things weren't always so bad. Up to the mid-1960s, Washington had some of the country's best black public schools, including Dunbar High School, which produced Senator Edward Brooke, the civil-rights lawyer Charles Hamilton Houston, and D.C. Delegate Eleanor Holmes Norton. The schools were a magnet for middle-class black families who wanted a quality education but were largely shut out of white-majority schools, either by law or by residential segregation. By 1960, Washington was a center of black intellectual and cultural life. "People talk about Harlem, but in terms of a professional class and intelligentsia, Washington was on par," says NPR's Juan Williams, who covered education for *The Washington Post* in the 1970s.

Like many urban districts, Washington thrived because it could rely on a class of educators—in this case, African Americans—who were mostly kept out of other professions. But as barriers eroded in the 1950s and 1960s, experienced black teachers began leaving for better opportunities. At the same time, rising crime and the calamitous 1968 riots reversed the flow of black middle-class families, particularly after the 1968 Fair Housing Act encouraged them to decamp to the suburbs. Combined with the white flight that had by the late 1960s largely run its course, black flight left behind a core of socially isolated, desperately poor families, who suffered as the crime and joblessness rates climbed steeply through the 1970s.

Black flight also left behind a power vacuum, which was eagerly filled by a new generation of activists fronted by the civil-rights leader Marion Barry. Though he later became the butt of late-night-TV jokes, Barry is a political genius, and in the early 1970s he was one of the first in his generation to see the school system's political potential. Until Congress granted the city limited home rule in 1973, the D.C. school board was the only elected body in Washington, and thus one of the only paths of political ascent for the city's black leaders. In 1971, Barry won a landslide election for a seat on the board; he was so popular that his fellow members immediately made him president, a position he held until moving to the city council in 1974 and to the mayor's office four years later.

Barry quickly grasped that the school system could do more than just facilitate his own rise. With its thousands of well-paying jobs, it was an ideal way to rebuild the black middle class—and, not incidentally, it was a limitless source of patronage. Barry's climb coincided with that of William Simons, the fiery head of the Washington Teachers' Union. Simons was a sort of black equivalent to Albert Shanker, then the voluble head of New York's United Federation of Teachers, and he led his union in two lengthy, debilitating strikes during the 1970s. Through it all, Barry played the go-between, working the city and Congress around to Simons's position. A new political base was emerging, populated by teachers and led by Barry. "It's no longer about educating the best and brightest of black Washington but about establishing the schools as a place where blacks can get better jobs, higher salaries, and more benefits," Williams told me.

A generation later, the result was a system that was overstaffed, inefficient, and resistant to change, even as it got worse at its primary role of educating students. Into this mess stepped Adrian Fenty and Michelle Rhee.

Rhee's L-shaped desk sits just inside the door of a large, noisy room on the top floor of the D.C. Public Schools headquarters, a few blocks north of the Capitol. Three of her close aides have desks nearby, and a TV tuned to CNN blares from the opposite wall. The door is open, and people passing by poke their heads in to say hi. Only a change in carpet color, from mottled gray in the hall to off-pink, signals an executive presence. Rhee doesn't stand on ceremony, and she doesn't expect her guests to, either. During our interview, I sat on a chair crammed between her desk and the door.

Rhee is an obsessive worker, the type normally found in consulting firms and medical schools, up at 6 a.m. and often awake until after midnight. She rarely works from notes, and usually shows up at meetings without handlers, speaking with the rapid cadence of a high-school debater and peppering her sentences with words like *crappy* and *awesome*. And she does not suffer fools, gladly or otherwise. When I asked her how she would characterize her ideal relationship with parents, she replied, "That's a great question. So often reporters ask me stupid questions. I had one interview yesterday, and I was like, 'Okay, you are not smart.'"

On paper and in public, Rhee comes across as passionate and talented, armed with a casual, biting wit. Those qualities win her praise in newspaper profiles and applause at Sun Valley conferences. But as you get to know her, people say, it's easy to wonder whether there's anything besides the image. "There doesn't seem to be any difference between her on- and off-camera personas," says Kevin Carey, of Education Sector. I've heard some of Rhee's supporters call her and her staff "Rhee-volutionaries." Her opponents call them "Rhee-bots."

There is more to Rhee than that. She is intensely committed to her two daughters, something even her occasional adversaries in the community will readily point out. "She's a great mother," says Cherita Whiting, chair of the city's Ward 4 Education Council. Rhee's way of speaking with kids was frequently trotted out in my conversations as an example of her people skills: "She's very personable," says Claire Taylor, co-chair of a local PTA. "Whether you're a kindergartner or a student in a high school, she gets down to your level." (No one mentioned her ability to relate to adults, except in strictly business situations.)

Rhee is very close to her parents, both of them Korean immigrants—her father is a retired doctor and her mother owned a clothing store. They sent their daughter to a posh private school in Toledo, and also to spend a year living with relatives in Seoul. She excelled academically and majored in government at Cornell. Teaching was not in the picture. But during her senior year, she saw a show on PBS touting Teach for America, a then-new program that placed recent college graduates in low-income, low-performing schools. She applied and was accepted. The decision changed her life. She met Kevin Huffman, a fellow idealist and Ohio native, at a TFA summer training session in 1994, and they were married in 1996 (they are now separated).

After three years of teaching second and third grade in Baltimore, Rhee left to pursue a master's at Harvard's Kennedy School of Government with plans to return to education, though she didn't know where or how. She had made enough of an impression on Teach for America that its founder and president, Wendy Kopp, called her in the spring of 1997, just before graduation, to see if she would return to the fold. Kopp wanted her to quarterback the launch of a spin-off, the New Teacher Project, which would contract with school districts to find and train people looking to jump from their old jobs—scientists, journalists, lawyers—into education. "We brought her on to develop our business plan and get the project off the ground," Kopp told me over coffee at a downtown Starbucks, "but it soon became very clear that she could run the whole thing."

It's no surprise that Kopp likes Rhee. The two are almost identical in their zeal and relentless message delivery. They are both obsessive e-mailers. I got the feeling that they spend long hours prepping for every possible question. Not all reformers are so singularly focused—Andrew Rotherham's Education Sector blog often veers into discussions of fishing—but the movement is such that it attracts people who will build their lives around their jobs, and whose assessment of other people begins and ends with their work ethic. It's something they don't apologize for: personal sacrifice is necessary to any revolution. Relentless pursuit is a catchphrase at Teach for America, and the people who use it mean it. When people say that Rhee, Kopp, and others eat, breathe, and sleep education reform, the only doubt is whether they actually sleep.

Rhee's drive paid off. At its 10-year mark, the New Teacher Project had recruited some 28,000 new teachers, the bulk of them mid-career entrants, in more than 200 school districts, including in New York City and Washington. Today, the program operates in 25 U.S. cities, contributing in some up to 30 percent of all teachers hired annually. "She took something that could have operated at a lower level and turned it into something with real impact," Kopp told me.

She did all this long-distance: the New Teacher Project is headquartered in New York, but soon after its founding, Rhee moved back to Toledo (with Huffman, by then a lawyer) to be near her parents; later she followed them to Denver, where they moved after retirement. All the while she was flying weekly to New York or the project's client districts around the country. Somewhere in there she found time to give birth to two daughters.

Rhee might have maintained her marathon commutes indefinitely if it hadn't been for a commitment Adrian Fenty made in the spring of last year. Rhee had already been approached about the chancellor job by several people in his administration, and she had demurred each time, citing family commitments. But Fenty kept pushing, and eventually she laid out her real concern: she saw herself as a "change agent," and Washington as a graveyard for careers like hers. The school board was too powerful and too dominated by unions and special interests to give much of a chance to someone intent on closing schools and renegotiating contracts. Then Fenty laid out his vision: he would take control of the schools, and provide whatever political cover Rhee needed to completely overhaul them. The chancellor and the mayor would make the important decisions. The District's Office of the State Superintendent of Education would continue to manage the kinds of state-federal transactions handled by other state education departments, and would be headed by someone Fenty had already appointed. A few weeks after their meeting, she was scouting houses in Washington.

Now, Rhee is in a position to provide Fenty with political cover in return. She has become the focus of opponents' anger, while Fenty has reaped the political goodwill generated by the first signs of improvement in the schools, and by the relief that at last someone is doing something. Her charge-ahead manner may be essential to getting reform done. "The reality is, if you want to make changes, it's very hard to do that by committee," says Kristin Ehrgood, a board member of D.C. School Reform

Now, a group that has been generally supportive of Rhee's efforts. "While we certainly need every voice heard, it doesn't mean everyone is right." But, though Rhee can turn on the charm when she needs to, she has at times seemed reckless in provoking teachers and even parents.

A case in point is her own children's school. Last fall, Rhee and Huffman enrolled their two daughters, now 6 and 9, at Oyster-Adams, a bilingual public school. By all accounts, she kept a low profile, dropping off her kids three days a week (Rhee shares custody with Huffman, who has also relocated to Washington) and staying away from school politics.

She was, however, paying close attention to what she was hearing from other parents about the school's principal, Marta Guzman. Guzman was popular with many Hispanic parents, who saw her as a role model for minority success, and she had met most academic benchmarks. But she had also reportedly been unresponsive to various faculty and parent concerns, some of which Rhee heard at a November 2007 dinner with several parents. "There were some people who said this woman was the best thing since sliced bread, and others who said she was the worst thing that ever happened to the school, and lots in between," Rhee told me.

The following May, Guzman was among the 24 principals to receive nonrenewal notices from Rhee. "There was no reason given in the letter," Guzman told me. "It simply stated that the chancellor had decided not to renew my contract." Guzman accepted her termination, but dozens of parents didn't. The story exploded, with accusations of racism and classism popping up in e-mails, listservs, and the pages of The Washington Post. Mostly, though, parents complained about the lack of information coming from the chancellor's office. Oyster-Adams was, after all, their school, and they felt they should have a say in its direction. "People were upset with the way it was handled," said one pro-Rhee parent who asked to remain anonymous.

Rhee met with parents a couple of weeks later, and the controversy eventually died down (it helped that the teachers released a statement supporting her decision). "It's hard to convey how charismatic she is," Claire Taylor, the PTA leader, whose child attends Oyster-Adams, told me. "Her office will announce something to be done, like close a school. Everybody hates that. But when she goes and talks to the parents, many of them do a 180."

Rhee probably made the right decision, and she carried it out efficiently. But at least at first, she paid too little attention to anticipating the inevitable worries of parents, and did unnecessary damage to her own image.

Washington, D.C., mayor Adrian Fenty and D.C. Public Schools chancellor Michelle Rhee attend a screening of a film documentary about a Washington, D.C., high school band at the White House, October 11, 2007. © AP IMAGES/PABLO MARTINEZ MONSIVAIS.

Whether she recognizes it or not, her task is political as well as educational.

The reform camp, of which Rhee is the new hero, is shot through with divisions. But its members share a few common characteristics, and perhaps the most important is a belief in the primacy of teachers. This sounds banal, but it's actually quite controversial. Many people believe that teachers and the classroom are only one part of a vast web of relationships and environments that determine educational success. A high-profile proposal issued in June by the Economic Policy Institute and signed by a long list of boldfaced names recommended a laundry list of extracurricular efforts to boost student achievement.

Rhee's name doesn't appear among the signatures. In her opinion, external factors simply underline the need for better educators. And while she pays lip service to the realities of urban poverty outside school walls, she dismisses the impact that poverty and violence might have on achievement. "As a teacher in this system, you have to be willing to take personal responsibility for ensuring your children are successful despite obstacles," she told me. "You can't say, 'My students didn't get any breakfast today,' or 'No one put them to bed last night,' or 'Their electricity got cut off in the house, so they couldn't do their homework.'" This sort of moral certitude is exactly what turns off many veteran teachers in Washington. Even if Rhee is right, she seems to be asking for superhuman efforts, consistently, for decades to come. Making missionary zeal a job requirement is a tough way to build morale, not to mention support, among the teachers who have to confront the D.C. ghetto every day.

Rhee and her reform allies' response is to call for better teachers, and they want to work through Teach for America and other alternative programs to find them. This is another sticking point. Traditionally, a good teacher was considered to be someone who had trained in education schools, been certified by state boards, enlisted in unions, and committed to a lifetime career—elements tightly

Washington, D.C., Public Schools chancellor Michelle Rhee testifies at a House Education and Labor Committee hearing on July 17, 2008. © AP IMAGES/SUSAN WALSH.

interwoven with any district's political structure. Reformers criticize all those elements. One of Rhee's favorite anecdotes, which she has recounted in practically every speech I've seen her give, contrasts the hard work, creativity, and popularity of a newbie teacher named "Mr. Wallace"—who just happens to be part of Teach for America—with a hardened older teacher across the hall, who stands at the door flicking the light switch and saying "I'm waiting, I'm waiting" to get her students' attention. "Well, they're waiting too," Rhee invariably says. "They're waiting for her to teach them something." In Rhee's world, the educational system divides between the Mr. Wallaces and everyone else, and it's no coincidence that Mr. Wallace sounds an awful lot like Rhee herself.

Rhee advocates another controversial plank in the reformist agenda: merit pay. Vociferously opposed by the teachers unions—a National Education Association

convention audience booed Barack Obama when he told them he supported it—merit pay scales a teacher's salary based on student achievement. Proponents say this is the only way to make teachers want to improve their performance. Opponents say it will torpedo already low morale and drive a wedge through faculty solidarity, and that basing merit pay on student performance leaves out all sorts of nonquantifiable aspects of learning. Rhee is willing to risk it. "We have heroic figures out in the school district, people who work unbelievable hours," she told me. "I want to not only recognize them but reward them. I want to pay them a lot more money"—more than $100,000, compared with the national average salary of $47,600. Rhee's proposed contract with the Washington Teachers' Union would allow current teachers to choose between tenure based on seniority combined with a lower salary and at-will employment combined with a higher, performance-based salary. The contract would place all new teachers in the latter category, and give all teachers a raise—but would effectively phase out tenure over time and make D.C. the first major school district to go to a completely merit-based pay structure. As this article went to press, negotiations were ongoing, but it was clear that Rhee faced an uphill battle. She had a backup in case the rank and file voted down the contract. During negotiations, additional plans were announced by the Office of the State Superintendent to tie teacher licensing to student achievement, sidestepping the union and effectively giving Rhee the power to fire underperforming teachers.

Behind the fighting lie basic questions: What makes a good teacher? And how do you recognize one? For Rhee and her fellow reformers, the answer is data. Lots of data. There may be many unquantifiables in teacher quality, but most of the traits that matter to reformers can be put into numbers. It's an attitude born of Rhee's experience in Teach for America, which regularly assesses its teachers' effectiveness against in-house and state achievement levels. "TFA is a machine," says Jennifer Kirmes, who taught for the program in Washington and now works in its Chicago office. "Everything is done with data and analysis. Everything you do reflects back on how your students are doing." Rhee fully supports the accountability that underlies No Child Left Behind. Every week, she and her top staff members hold a "School Stat" meeting where they pore over data on everything from student performance to facilities' work orders.

This year, Washington was one of the top choices for incoming TFA corps members, drawn largely by Rhee. As one D.C.-bound TFA teacher, Stephanie Neves, wrote on her blog, "We are here during some crazy times in DC. We are here for the revolution. DC '08!"

The problem is that those immediately affected by Rhee's reforms—teachers and parents—can be less enamored of her get-tough posture. Many felt particularly put out earlier this year when Rhee refused to release a draft of her 2008–2009 budget in advance of a community budget hearing and her submitting it to the mayor—a position several residents said violated city law, and they filed a lawsuit to fight it. (The Fenty administration claimed that its takeover of the schools obviated the law, but a judge required the administration to provide a draft copy of the budget to the plaintiffs. Another judge later ruled for the Fenty administration; the plaintiffs have appealed.) To be fair, Rhee did meet several times with parents and once with activists to discuss school closings, but "most of us felt it was mostly for show," Marc Borbely, who attended the activist meeting and later led the budget-lawsuit effort, told me. "The things we said were mostly disregarded. When it comes to real decision-making, her philosophy is, 'I'll get input, but there are no partners here.'"

Rhee sees herself not as a politician but as a technocrat; a decider, not a negotiator. "Does that mean every decision is going to be right? No," she said to me in a measured pace that sounded well-practiced. "Have I made some wrong decisions? Yeah. But the bottom line is, the reason I can sleep at night, really soundly every night, is because I know that even if I didn't make the right call, I made it because I believed at that moment that it was the best thing for kids."

Listening to Rhee, it's hard to disagree. But even if she speaks cavalierly about eschewing city politics, that doesn't make city politics go away. Complaints are bubbling up to the city council. In one particularly testy exchange at an all-day meeting in April, Marion Barry, now the representative for the city's poorest ward, lectured Rhee on the political realities of her job. "Whether or not you and the mayor want to take it out of the political arena, you cannot, because education all over America has political implications," he told her. "Parents are also voters."

Rhee would have none of it. "I think part of the problem of how the district has been run in the past is that decisions have been made for political reasons, and based on what was going to placate and satisfy adults instead of what was in the best interests of children."

"Let me be succinct, because my time is running out," Barry retorted. "Talk to other people on this, because I think you're absolutely wrong ... I know you want to do it the right way, but I think that's causing us more problems than we need to have."

The comment was a warning, but it was also a reflection of the very political nature of education in the American inner city, and particularly in Washington. In a city largely excluded from national politics, it makes sense that residents would feel particularly slighted by an outsider, installed without their input, who is happy to bypass the few forums left where poor and working-class parents can engage with the political system—the parent-teacher associations, the ward-level education committees, and other unofficial bodies that long wielded influence against the elected school board and suddenly find themselves powerless against a mayorally appointed chancellor. "I'm sympathetic with the need to act decisively and quickly, but at the same time, what does that do to one of our last democratic institutions?" asks Celia Oyler, a professor at Columbia University's Teachers College. To a reformer, that sounds like a classic plea for putting grown-ups' interests first.

Arguably, mayoral control has clarified political accountability, by making Fenty, rather than assorted school-board members and ancillary committees, ultimately responsible for fixing the schools. Mayoral control is now the source of Rhee's power—Fenty is overwhelmingly popular, in part thanks to Rhee's work—but it is also another potential weakness. "Fenty has a set term, and he's on board with her," Sara Mead, a senior research fellow at the New America Foundation, says. "The downside of having the mayor in charge is that you tie your fate to the mayor."

And cracks in that shield are already beginning to show. Though the city council gave Fenty control of the schools and later endorsed Rhee's job cuts, its members have been pushing bills to allow more council oversight of school operations and to reapportion power between Rhee and the state superintendent. Most recently, Barry and the council chair, Vincent Gray, delayed approval of millions of dollars in school-renovation funds. And it could get worse. "For legislators, when they see reform coming, there is a tendency to overregulate," says former city councilman Kevin Chavous. "It's a huge challenge. It has the potential to be lethal to all reform efforts."

Rhee is confronting the great divide over American public-education reform—not between left and right but between two philosophies about education. To Rhee and her fellow reformers, schools can, by themselves, produce successful students. To her opponents (and they include liberals and conservatives), schools are not enough, however "successful" their students. They are an important, but hardly the only, means with which children are inculcated with the skills and mores of their community.

The divide means that Rhee's challenge is not just to reform one of the worst school systems in the country and, in effect, prove whether or not inner-city schools can be revived at all. It is to answer a basic question about the nature of urban governance, a question about two visions of big-city management. In one, city politics is a vibrant, messy, democratic exercise, in which both the process and the results have value. In the other, city politics is only a prelude, the way to install a technocratic elite that can carry out reforms in relative isolation from the give-and-take of city life. Rhee's tenure will answer whether these two positions are mutually exclusive—and, if they are, whether public-school reform is even possible.

FURTHER RESOURCES
Books

Darling-Hammond, Linda. *The Flat World and Education: How America's Commitment to Equity Will Determine Our Future*. New York: Teachers College Press, 2010.

Rhee, Michelle. *Radical: Fighting to Put Students First*. New York: Harper, 2013.

Whitmire, Richard. *The Bee Eater: Michelle Rhee Takes on the Nation's Worst School District*. San Francisco: Jossey-Bass, 2011

Web Sites

Brown, Emma. "Michelle Rhee Responds to Federal Investigation of Alleged DCPS Cheating." *Washington Post*, January 8, 2013. www.washingtonpost.com/blogs/dc-schools-insider/post/michelle-rhee-responds-to-federal-investigation-of-alleged-dcps-cheating/2013/01/08/4f53daae-59b9-11e2-9fa9-5fbdc9530eb9_blog.html (accessed on February 20, 2013).

Gillum, Jack, and Marisol Bello. "When Standardized Test Scores Soared in D.C., Were the Gains Real?" *USA Today*, March 30, 2011. http://usatoday30.usatoday.com/news/education/2011-03-28-1Aschooltesting28_CV_N.htm (accessed on February 20, 2013).

Stillman, Lauren, and Rolf K. Blank. "Key State Education Policies on PK-12 Education: 2008." *Council of Chief State School Officers*, 2009. www.ccsso.org/Documents/2008/Key_State_Education_Policies_2008.pdf (accessed on February 20, 2013).

Turque, Bill. "Has D.C. School Reform Hit Pothole or Wall?" *Washington Post*, April 2, 2011. http://articles.washingtonpost.com/2011-04-02/local/35261833_1_school-reform-growth-in-test-scores-round-of-standardized-tests (accessed on February 20, 2013).

The Condition of Education 2009: Homeschooled Students

Table

By: National Center for Education Statistics

Date: 2009

Source: National Center for Education Statistics. "Homeschooled Students." *The Condition of Education 2009*, 2009. http://nces.ed.gov/programs/coe/pdf/coe_hsc.pdf (accessed on February 22, 2013).

About the Organization: The National Center for Education Statistics (NCES) is the primary federal agency responsible for collecting and analyzing data related to education. It is part of the Department of Education and the Institute of Education Sciences. The NCES publishes numerous reports throughout the year, and its statistics are used by Congress, federal agencies, state and local officials, and educational organizations to determine areas of strength and need as well as funding potential.

Supplemental Tables to Indicator 6
Homeschooled Students

Table A-6-1. Number and percentage distribution of all school-age children who were homeschooled and homeschooling rate, by selected characteristics: 1999, 2003, and 2007

Characteristic	1999 Number	Percentage distribution	Home-schooling rate[1]	2003 Number	Percentage distribution	Home-schooling rate[1]	2007 Number	Percentage distribution	Home-schooling rate[1]
Total	850,000	100.0	1.7	1,096,000	100.0	2.2	1,508,000	100.0	2.9
Homeschooled entirely	697,000	82.0	100.0	898,000	82.0	100.0	1,266,000	84.0	100.0
Homeschooled and enrolled in school part time	153,000	18.0	100.0	198,000	18.0	100.0	242,000	16.0	100.0
Enrolled in school less than 9 hours per week	107,000	12.6	100.0	137,000	12.5	100.0	173,000	11.5	100.0
Enrolled in school 9-25 hours per week	46,000	5.4	100.0	61,000	5.6	100.0	69,000	4.6	100.0
Race/ethnicity[2]									
White	640,000	75.3	2.0	843,000	77.0	2.7	1,159,000	76.8	3.9
Black	84,000	9.9	1.0	103,000	9.4	1.3	61,000	4.0	0.8
Hispanic	77,000	9.1	1.1	59,000	5.3	0.7	147,000	9.8	1.5
Other	49,000	5.8	1.9	91,000	8.3	3.0	141,000	9.3	3.4
Sex									
Male	417,000	49.0	1.6	569,000	51.9	2.2	633,000	41.9	2.4
Female	434,000	51.0	1.8	527,000	48.1	2.1	875,000	58.1	3.5
Number of children in the household									
One child	120,000	14.1	1.5	110,000	10.1	1.4	187,000	12.4	2.2
Two children	207,000	24.4	1.0	306,000	28.0	1.5	412,000	27.3	2.0
Three or more children	523,000	61.6	2.4	679,000	62.0	3.1	909,000	60.3	4.1
Number of parents in the household									
Two parents	683,000	80.4	2.1	886,000	80.8	2.5	1,348,000	89.4	3.6
One parent	142,000	16.7	0.9	196,000	17.9	1.5	115,000	7.6	1.0
Nonparental guardians	25,000	2.9	1.4	14,000	1.3	0.9	45,000	3.0	2.1
Parents' participation in the labor force									
Two parents, one in labor force	444,000	52.2	4.6	594,000	54.2	5.6	808,000	53.6	7.5
Two parents, both in labor force	237,000	27.9	1.0	274,000	25.0	1.1	509,000	33.8	2.0
One parent in labor force	98,000	11.6	0.7	174,000	15.9	1.4	127,000	8.4	1.3
No parent in labor force	71,000	8.3	1.9	54,000	4.9	1.8	64,000	4.3	1.5
Household income									
$25,000 or less	262,000	30.9	1.6	283,000	25.8	2.3	239,000	15.9	2.1
$25,001-50,000	278,000	32.7	1.8	311,000	28.4	2.4	364,000	24.1	3.4
$50,001-75,000	162,000	19.1	1.9	264,000	24.1	2.4	405,000	26.8	3.9
$75,001 or more	148,000	17.4	1.5	238,000	21.7	1.7	501,000	33.2	2.7
Parents' education									
High school diploma or less	160,000	18.9	0.9	269,000	24.5	1.7	206,000	13.7	1.4
Some college or vocational/technical	287,000	33.7	1.9	338,000	30.8	2.1	549,000	36.4	3.8
Bachelor's degree	213,000	25.1	2.6	274,000	25.0	2.8	444,000	29.4	3.9
Graduate/professional degree	190,000	22.3	2.3	215,000	19.6	2.5	309,000	20.5	2.9

[1] The homeschooling rate is the percentage of the total subgroup that is homeschooled. For example, in 2007, some 2.4 percent of all school-age males were homeschooled.
[2] Race categories exclude persons of Hispanic ethnicity. For more information on race/ethnicity, see supplemental note 1.
NOTE: Detail may not sum to totals because of rounding. Homeschooled students are school-age children (ages 5–17) in a grade equivalent to at least kindergarten and not higher than 12th grade. Excludes students who were enrolled in public or private school more than 25 hours per week and students who were homeschooled only because of temporary illness. For more information on the National Household Education Surveys Program (NHES), see supplemental note 3.
SOURCE: U.S. Department of Education, National Center for Education Statistics, Parent Survey of the 1999 National Household Education Surveys Program (NHES), Parent and Family Involvement in Education Survey of the 2003 and 2007 NHES.

PRIMARY SOURCE

The Condition of Education 2009: Homeschooled Students, Table A-6-1

SYNOPSIS: This table illustrates the rise in the number of American children who were homeschooled throughout the 2000s. U.S. DEPARTMENT OF EDUCATION, NATIONAL CENTER FOR EDUCATION STATISTICS.

INTRODUCTION

Prior to the Industrial Revolution, homeschooling was the norm. Primarily an agrarian society, Americans lived a family-centered lifestyle, and education—like everything else—happened at home. Children learned life skills such as growing food and cooking, caring for animals and other children, sewing, construction, and all the household chores. Book learning was part of that lifestyle, but it was not a focal point. Rather, lessons were fit into the daily routine, taught by family members or friends. When the season required all hands working in the fields or crops, academics were temporarily set aside until time allowed a return to reading and writing.

Once America became industrialized and the modern educational system was developed, compulsory attendance laws were implemented, the first in Massachusetts in 1852. Other states followed, until eventually there were federal laws regarding school attendance. Although the laws have changed over the years, one thing has not: Children are expected to attend schooling of some sort, be it public, private, or home.

There has been a handful of education reformers known for their consistent support of and belief in homeschooling. Among them, John Holt was perhaps the most prominent. Holt, a disillusioned school teacher, initially hoped to reform education within the existing school system but soon grew to believe the task was impossible. He began to advocate for homeschooling, but cautioned parents not to simply remove their children from the classroom with the goal of recreating a similar environment in the home. His idea, that children learn naturally if left to follow their own interests, transformed into a particular style of homeschooling called unschooling. The rest of his life (Holt died in 1985) was dedicated to the unschooling movement, for which he wrote books and published a magazine and newsletter. His teachings and writings were highly influential on the homeschooling/unschooling movements. Other key homeschooling figures were Rousas John Rushdoony, and Raymond and Dorothy Moore.

Homeschooling as a movement gained momentum in the 1960s and 1970s as these educational reformers gained more respect and were considered not so much radical as visionary. A key concept to their success was the idea that homeschooling was not an alternative because the federal educational system had failed, but because learning at home is merely an extension of daily life. In the 1970s, many Christians became concerned about the secularization of public schools. As prayer in schools began to be discouraged and even outlawed, religious families looked to homeschooling as a way to give their children academics without sacrificing their personal values. Other specific groups such as the Amish and Mennonites, even the Mormons, had been targets of federal government attacks on their values, lifestyles, and choices. For these citizens, homeschooling seemed like the only reasonable choice. By the end of the 1980s, homeschooling, while not the norm, had become a more widely accepted form of education. This trend toward "mainstreaming" continued throughout the 1990s and into the new millennium.

SIGNIFICANCE

As homeschooling groups organized at local, state, and federal levels and the idea of schooling at home came to be seen as an educational option for reasons other than religion, more Americans took the leap and began exploring homeschool curricula and strategies that worked for them. The advent of the Internet and email also made networking and sharing information easier than it had ever been, and it changed homeschooling curricula by expanding options for learning without increasing costs.

The NCES table, which is excerpted from a longer report, shows the significant growth of homeschooling throughout the 2000s. According to NCES, 850,000 students were homeschooled in 1999; that figure rose to 1.5 million in 2007. By 2010, some researchers estimated that number to have increased to nearly two million. Homeschooling was an option preferred by whites more than any other race (76.8 percent of total homeschoolers in 2007). Among reasons given for choosing to homeschool were, in order of importance: religious or moral instruction, concern for school environment (safety, drugs, peer pressure), and dissatisfaction with academic instruction.

As homeschooling grew in popularity, many states developed laws outlining testing requirements, rules for working with local schools in regards to extra-curriculars and enrolling in specific classes, a la carte style. Homeschooling cooperatives, where families collaborate and school their children together, drawing on the various strengths of each adult, addressed the social aspects of education as they learned together and went on field trips or attended classes held in libraries, recreation departments, or other organizations.

Critics of homeschooling argued that many parents are not up to the challenge of providing their children with a well-rounded education because they lack training and knowledge. Others were concerned that homeschooled students did not have the opportunity to learn socialization and thus suffered throughout their lives from an inability to relate to others. Further, they claimed that individual state laws vary to the point of inconsistency, and all are difficult at best to enforce.

Research continued to show that homeschooled students tended to score higher than their traditional-schooled peers on standardized tests. A 2008 study showed that they scored 37 percentile points higher, and a 2009 study indicated that students schooled at home by a parent who was also a certified teacher scored one percentile lower than those schooled by a parent who was not a teacher. As for the socialization concern, a 2003 National Home Education Research Institute survey indicated that homeschool graduates were highly active in their communities (71 percent, compared to 37 percent of their peers from a traditional education background).

HOMESCHOOLED STUDENTS, TABLE A-6-1

See primary source table.

FURTHER RESOURCES

Books

Rivero, Lisa. *The Homeschooling Option: How to Decide When It's Right for Your Family.* New York: Palgrave MacMillan, 2008.

Weldon, Laura Grace. *Free Range Learning: How Homeschooling Changes Everything.* Chino Valley, AZ: Hohm Press, 2010.

Web Sites

Azuz, Carl. "Doing the Math Behind Homeschooling." *CNN*, August 28, 2012. http://schoolsofthought.blogs.cnn.com/2012/08/28/doing-the-math-behind-homeschooling/ (accessed on February 22, 2013).

Dobson, Linda. "A Brief History of Homeschooling." *Parent at the Helm.* http://www.parentatthehelm.com/1222/a-brief-history-of-american-homeschooling/ (accessed on February 22, 2013).

Home School Legal Defense Association. "New Study Shows Homeschoolers Excel Academically." *HSLDA*, August 10, 2009. http://www.hslda.org/docs/media/2009/200908100.asp (accessed on February 22, 2013).

Home School Legal Defense Association. "Homeschooling Grows Up." *HSLDA*. http://www.hslda.org/research/ray2003/ (accessed on February 22, 2013).

National Center for Education Statistics. www.nces.ed.gov/ (accessed on February 22, 2013).

"Advocates Call for a New Approach After the Era of 'Abstinence-Only' Sex Education"

Periodical article

By: Heather D. Boonstra

Date: Winter 2009

Source: Boonstra, Heather D. "Advocates Call for a New Approach After the Era of 'Abstinence-Only' Sex Education." *Guttmacher Policy Review* 12, no. 1

(Winter 2009). www.guttmacher.org/pubs/gpr/12/1/gpr120106.html (accessed on March 17, 2013).

About the Organization: Founded in 1968 as the Center for Family Planning Program Development, the Guttmacher Institute was originally a somewhat independent division of the Planned Parenthood Federation of America. It became autonomous when it was renamed in 1977 and operated as a nonprofit. Its mission, according to its Web site, is "to generate new ideas, encourage enlightened public debate and promote sound policy and program development. The institute's overarching goal is to ensure the highest standard of sexual and reproductive health for all people worldwide."

INTRODUCTION

The battle over sex education has been raging since the 1960s, though it was as far back as 1912 that the National Education Association mandated teacher training in sex education. The 1940s saw the U.S. Public Health Service urgently advocating for sex education in schools, and in 1953, the American School Health Association developed a family life education program. Public officials and educators supported these health programs from their inception, but there was no swaying detractors from their goal of barring any and all sex education from schools.

Conservative and religious groups became publicly vocal in the late 1960s and into the early 1980s, their outrage based in morality. They viewed any sex-related information dispersed in schools as immoral, and one ultra-conservative organization, the John Birch Society, labeled the effort to educate America's youth about sexuality a "filthy Communist plot." Despite the society's best efforts, comprehensive programs continued to be taught and, in fact, they increased in acceptance for a short time because emerging evidence showed that, contrary to right-wing claims, knowledge of sex did not promote it, but rather helped delay it.

Sex education in the early 1980s was taught as one facet of family life education and human development courses, so students learned about reproduction but also about the importance of making good choices, thinking toward the future, and developing self-esteem. And then the AIDS epidemic swept the country, changing forever the landscape of sex education. Surgeon General C. Everett Koop recommended age-appropriate sex education in schools, starting in the third grade. He emphasized a need to include accurate information on both heterosexual and homosexual relationships. Koop's directive supported comprehensive sex education, but it also forced those

in opposition to its teaching to take a hard-line stance because they could not ignore the existence of AIDS. Their response? Abstinence-only education. The debate began then and has never ceased, no matter what surveys and statistics support.

SIGNIFICANCE

Abstinence-only programs had fallen out of favor with medical experts, educators, and many parents by the end of the 2000s. The Sexuality Information and Education Council of the United States (SIECUS) never supported the federal funding of such programs. Its Web site reflected its values:

> For over two decades, the federal government has sunk millions of taxpayer dollars into abstinence-only-until-marriage programs. While these programs often replace more comprehensive sexuality education courses, they rarely provide information on even the most basic topics in human sexuality such as puberty, reproductive anatomy, and sexual health, and they have never been proven effective. Since their inception, SIECUS has been tracking abstinence-only-until-marriage programs, advocating for an end to federal funding for these programs, and helping educators and parents keep these harmful programs out of their schools.

A 2012 New York Civil Liberties Union study of 82 of the state's school districts found that the lack of binding state-wide sex education standards was only harming students by using materials that were inaccurate, biased, and incomplete about things as basic as anatomy. More disturbing was how genders were presented as stereotypes while lesbian-gay-bisexual-transgender (LGBT) students were further marginalized and stigmatized.

As always, there was a clear division between political parties, with conservatives generally backing abstinence-only education while liberals generally supported comprehensive sex education. Despite the overwhelming evidence that abstinence-only education has never been effective, U.S. representatives Randy Hultgren (R-IL) and Daniel Lipinski (D-IL) introduced the Abstinence Education Reallocation Act in February 2013, which sought to award $550 million in Affordable Care Act grants over five years to programs that provide teenagers with abstinence-only education. Twelve Republican co-sponsors supported the measure, and a companion bill was expected to be introduced in the Senate. Democrats countered the bill with the Real Education for Healthy Youth Act, a bill seeking to "expand comprehensive sex education programs in schools and ensure that federal funds are spent on effective, age-appropriate, medically accurate programs." The legislation further provided guidelines that stipulated funding for only those programs that included LGBT language and featured accurate information regarding HIV.

The sex education debate seemed to be similar to that of abortion in that it will likely continue forever because science and reality cannot be considered outside morality and personal values. Until it can be, the two opposing sides will likely fail to reach a compromise.

PRIMARY SOURCE

"ADVOCATES CALL FOR A NEW APPROACH AFTER THE ERA OF 'ABSTINENCE-ONLY' SEX EDUCATION"

SYNOPSIS: Research overwhelmingly supports the claim that abstinence-only sex education is failing our students.

In the weeks since he was sworn into office, speculation has continued around the new directions in which President Barack Obama, with the help of a more supportive Congress, might take the country. For opponents of sex education programs that focus exclusively on abstinence, there is already a feeling of the beginning of a new era. Under the Bush administration and with the strong support of congressional social conservatives, "abstinence-only-until-marriage" emerged as the sanctioned approach to reducing U.S. teen pregnancy and sexually transmitted infection (STI) rates. Since 1996, well over $1 billion in federal and mandatory state matching grants has been spent to promote premarital abstinence among young Americans, through highly restrictive programs that ignore or often actively denigrate the effectiveness of contraceptives and safer-sex behaviors.

At long last, however, the tide seems to be turning. Over the last several years, the case against abstinence-only education has mounted. Continued funding for federal abstinence-only programs was hotly debated during a hearing held before the House Committee on Oversight and Government Reform in April 2008. At this first-ever congressional hearing to examine the effectiveness of abstinence-only education, social conservatives were on the defensive against a wealth of evidence that such a highly restrictive educational approach does not work to stop or even materially delay teen sex. A panel of public health experts, including representatives of the American Public Health Association, the Academy of Pediatrics and the Institute of Medicine, testified that there is no evidence base to support the current massive federal investment in abstinence-only programs.

Later that year, Congress rejected President Bush's request for yet another significant increase for the abstinence-only program and declined to give it any increase. Now, opponents of abstinence-only education are taking the next step, calling on the Obama administration and Congress to end federal funding for such programs entirely. Instead, they say, policymakers should throw their support behind a more comprehensive approach to sex education that genuinely addresses the reality of young people's lives—education that helps youth to delay sexual activity, even as it equips them with the information and skills they will need to behave safely and responsibly when they do begin to have sex.

THE RISE OF ABSTINENCE-ONLY PROGRAMS . . .

Only a few decades ago, debate over sex education focused on whether public schools had a role at all in educating children and young people about sex-related matters or whether parents should be the sole transmitters of sexually related values and information to their children. However, as the level of concern over teenage pregnancy—and later AIDS—increased, so did public support for sex education in schools. Over a few years in the 1970s and 1980s, the number of states that had policies requiring or encouraging the teaching of sex education grew rapidly.

Having lost the debate over whether there should be sex education in schools, groups that once opposed school-based programs moved to a new strategy—one aimed at limiting the content of programs to the promotion of premarital abstinence. In 1981, the first grants for what later came to be called "abstinence-only" programs were authorized under the Adolescent Family Life Act (AFLA). Sponsored by congressional family planning opponents, AFLA was promoted as a "family-centered" alternative to contraceptive counseling and services to teenagers; instead, this program's stated goal was to promote premarital "chastity and self-discipline."

Although AFLA has supported hundreds of relatively small teenage pregnancy prevention programs over the years (as well as programs providing support for pregnant and parenting teens), its total funding for abstinence-only education—currently at $13 million—has never been large. However, a lasting contribution of the program was the early development under its auspices of so-called fear-based sex education curricula that use scare tactics about such things as STIs and the failure rates of condoms and have become models for abstinence-only programs nationwide. The "real" money for abstinence-only programs came after 1996, the year in which social conservatives in Congress quietly inserted authorization for a new program into massive legislation designed to overhaul the nation's welfare system. Title V of the Social Security Act includes an ongoing guarantee of $50 million annually to the states; because states must spend $3 for every $4 they receive, the total amount spent pursuant to this program became almost $90 million annually overnight. To qualify for funding, abstinence-only programs must adhere to the requirements of a rigid eight-point definition, including barring teachers from discussing contraceptive methods or

ABSTINENCE VS. SEX EDUCATION

Abstinence-only Education, as Defined by Current Federal Law

According to Title V of the Social Security Act, an eligible abstinence education program is a program that

A) has as its exclusive purpose, teaching the social, physiological, and health gains to be realized by abstaining from sexual activity;

B) teaches abstinence from sexual activity outside marriage as the expected standard for all school age children;

C) teaches that abstinence from sexual activity is the only certain way to avoid out-of-wedlock pregnancy, sexually transmitted diseases, and other associated health problems;

D) teaches that a mutually faithful monogamous relationship in context of marriage is the expected standard of human sexual activity;

E) teaches that sexual activity outside of the context of marriage is likely to have harmful psychological and physical effects;

F) teaches that bearing children out-of-wedlock is likely to have harmful consequences for the child, the child's parents, and society;

G) teaches young people how to reject sexual advances and how alcohol and drug use increases vulnerability to sexual advances; and

H) teaches the importance of attaining self-sufficiency before engaging in sexual activity.

Sex Education, as Defined by the Responsible Education About Life Act

According to the Responsible Education About Life Act, a sex education program is a program that

(1) is age-appropriate and medically accurate;

(2) stresses the value of abstinence while not ignoring those young people who have had or are having sexual intercourse;

(3) provides information about the health benefits and side effects of all contraceptive and barrier methods used (a) as a means to prevent pregnancy; and (b) to reduce the risk of contracting sexually transmitted disease, including HIV/AIDS;

(4) encourages family communication between parent and child about sexuality;

(5) teaches young people the skills to make responsible decisions about sexuality, including how to avoid unwanted verbal, physical, and sexual advances and how to avoid making verbal, physical, and sexual advances that are not wanted by the other party;

(6) develops healthy relationships, including the prevention of dating and sexual violence;

(7) teaches young people how alcohol and drug use can affect responsible decision making; and

(8) does not teach or promote religion.

---

safer-sex practices, other than to emphasize their shortcomings, and requiring them to teach that "sexual activity outside of the context of marriage is likely to have harmful psychological and physical effects" (see table above).

... AND THE EVIDENCE AGAINST THEM

From this considerable base, federal funding for abstinence-only programs accelerated under the Bush administration, especially since the creation in 2000 of a third funding stream also tied to the eight-point definition, the Community-Based Abstinence Education (CBAE) program. Yet, even as funding increased, so did evidence that the approach is ineffective. Ironically, early emanations came in a report issued in 1996, the same year Congress created the Title V abstinence program. An often underemphasized fact about the earlier AFLA program is that it technically is a "demonstration" effort, mandated to test and evaluate various program

interventions. The report, conducted by a team of university researchers and entitled *Federally Funded Adolescent Abstinence Promotion Programs: An Evaluation of Evaluations*, concluded that "the quality of the AFLA evaluations funded by the federal government vary from barely adequate to completely inadequate." Moreover, the researchers said, they were aware of "no methodologically sound studies that demonstrate the effectiveness" of abstinence-only curricula.

Over the next decade, however, several well-designed studies began to suggest just how difficult it can be for people to practice abstinence consistently over time. Notable among these is a series of studies examining the effectiveness of virginity pledges, which are the centerpiece of many abstinence education programs. The most recent study, published in the January 2009 issue of *Pediatrics*, found that teens who take virginity pledges are just as likely to have sex as those who do not, but they are less likely to use condoms or other forms of contraception when they become sexually active. This study builds on past research showing that although virginity pledges may help some teens to delay sexual activity, teens who break their pledge are less likely to use contraceptives, are less likely to get tested for STIs and may have STIs for longer periods of time than teens who do not pledge.

A major bombshell dropped two years earlier, however, when a systematic look at the federal abstinence-only effort concluded in 2007 that none of the programs it evaluated were effective in stopping or even delaying sex. The study, mandated by Congress and conducted by Mathematica Policy Research over nine years at a cost of almost $8 million, was initially criticized because it did not look at a nationally representative sample of abstinence-only programs. Instead, it closely examined four programs considered by state officials and abstinence education experts to be especially promising. Even so, after following more than 2,000 teens for as long as six years, the evaluation found that none of the four programs was able to demonstrate a statistically significant beneficial impact on young people's sexual behavior. Individuals who participated in the programs were no more likely to abstain than those who did not.

The Mathematica findings were in keeping with those of another comprehensive review of sex and HIV education programs published later that year. Conducted by Douglas Kirby for the nonpartisan National Campaign to Prevent Teen and Unplanned Pregnancy, *Emerging Answers 2007* concludes that despite improvements in the quality and quantity of evaluation research in this field, "there does not exist any strong evidence that any abstinence program delays the initiation of sex, hastens the return to abstinence, or reduces the number of sexual partners."

On top of this, abstinence-only programs have been sharply criticized by leading medical professional organizations for being, by their very nature, antithetical to the principles of science and medical ethics. As a matter of law, abstinence-only programs are required to promote ideas that are at best scientifically questionable, and to withhold health- and life-saving information; as such, they may not credibly assert that they are "medically accurate." Little wonder, then, that leading health professional groups—including the American Medical Association, the American Academy of Pediatrics, the Society of Adolescent Medicine, and the American Psychological Association—have raised serious ethical concerns about U.S. support for such programs. "Governments have an obligation to provide accurate

information to their citizens and to eschew the provision of misinformation in government-funded health education and health care services," says the American Public Health Association in its policy statement on abstinence-only education. "While good patient care is built upon notions of informed consent and free choice, [abstinence-only education] programs are inherently coercive by withholding information needed to make informed choices."

TOWARD A MORE 'COMMON SENSE' APPROACH

As the evidence base against abstinence-only programs grew, so did the number of states that decided to opt out of the Title V program. To date, 23 states and the District of Columbia have declined to apply for the annual abstinence education grants set aside for them under Title V (see table). The number of adolescents living in those states is substantial: Nearly 14 million young people aged 12–18—46% of those nationwide—reside in states that have passed up abstinence-only funding.

Title V Abstinence-only Education Programs

Alabama	accepting funds
Alaska	not accepting funds
Arizona	not accepting funds
Arkansas	accepting funds
California	not accepting funds
Colorado	not accepting funds
Connecticut	not accepting funds
Delaware	not accepting funds
District of Columbia	not accepting funds
Florida	accepting funds
Georgia	accepting funds
Hawaii	accepting funds
Idaho	not accepting funds
Illinois	accepting funds
Indiana	accepting funds
Iowa	not accepting funds
Kansas	not accepting funds
Kentucky	accepting funds
Louisiana	accepting funds
Maine	not accepting funds
Maryland	accepting funds
Massachusetts	not accepting funds
Michigan	accepting funds
Minnesota	not accepting funds
Mississippi	accepting funds
Missouri	accepting funds
Montana	not accepting funds
Nebraska	accepting funds
Nevada	accepting funds
New Hampshire	accepting funds
New Jersey	not accepting funds

New Mexico . . . . not accepting funds
New York . . . . not accepting funds
North Carolina . . . . accepting funds
North Dakota . . . . accepting funds
Ohio . . . . not accepting funds
Oklahoma . . . . accepting funds
Oregon . . . . accepting funds
Pennsylvania . . . . accepting funds
Rhode Island . . . . not accepting funds
South Carolina . . . . accepting funds
South Dakota . . . . accepting funds
Tennessee . . . . accepting funds
Texas . . . . accepting funds
Utah . . . . accepting funds
Vermont . . . . not accepting funds
Virginia . . . . not accepting funds
Washington . . . . not accepting funds
West Virginia . . . . accepting funds
Wisconsin . . . . not accepting funds
Wyoming . . . . not accepting funds

In 2007, policymakers on Capitol Hill at long last signaled that, at the very least, the era of big increases for abstinence-only education was over. After many years of expansion, Congress rejected the Bush administration's recommendation to increase funding for CBAE by $28 million and instead kept its funding for FY 2008 unchanged at $176 million. But the major reversal of political fortune for abstinence-only education came with the 2008 election cycle. President Obama entered the White House with a strong record of support for what he calls "common sense approaches" to preventing unintended pregnancy and HIV, namely "comprehensive sex education that teaches both abstinence and safe sex methods."

Advocates for more comprehensive sex education are now looking to the president and Congress, whose leadership in both houses is dominated by social progressives, to make a more significant break from the past. In light of the wealth of evidence that abstinence-only programs have no beneficial effect on young people's sexual behavior, they are calling on policymakers to stop funding abstinence-only programs altogether and, going further, to create a new funding stream to support programs that are more comprehensive in scope.

Focusing on more comprehensive approaches is both good policy and good politics. It is good policy because it is based on scientific considerations and takes into account the reality of teens' lives. In sharp contrast to abstinence-only programs, there is strong evidence that more comprehensive approaches do help young people both to withstand the pressures to have sex too soon and to have healthy, responsible and mutually protective relationships when they do become sexually

active. According to Kirby in *Emerging Answers 2007*, "two-thirds of the 48 comprehensive programs that supported both abstinence and the use of condoms and contraceptives for sexually active teens had positive behavioral effects." Many either delayed or reduced sexual activity, reduced the number of sexual partners or increased condom or contraceptive use. "What is particularly encouraging," said Kirby in a 2007 interview, "is that when some curricula that were found to be effective in one study were implemented by other educators in other states and evaluated by independent research teams, they remained effective if they were implemented with fidelity in the same type of setting and with similar youth."

Changing course is good politics, because it is in sync with what Americans say they want for their children. . . . There is far greater support for comprehensive sex education than for the abstinence-only approach.

Changing course is also good politics, because it is in sync with what Americans say they want for their children. According to the results of a 2005–2006 nationally representative survey of U.S. adults, published in the *Archives of Pediatrics and Adolescent Medicine*, there is far greater support for comprehensive sex education than for the abstinence-only approach, regardless of respondents' political leanings and frequency of attendance at religious services. Overall, 82% of those polled supported a comprehensive approach, and 68% favored instruction on how to use a condom; only 36% supported abstinence-only education.

As a practical matter, advocates for comprehensive approaches are looking to the Responsible Education About Life (REAL) Act as a model for federal sex education policy in the future. Introduced in slightly different forms in past years and reintroduced in 2009 in the House and Senate respectively by Rep. Barbara Lee (D-CA) and Sen. Frank Lautenberg (D-NJ), the REAL Act sets out a broad alternative vision for how U.S. policy might best meet the needs of young people. As currently drafted, the bill would authorize at least $50 million annually for five years to support state programs that operate under an eight-point definition of "responsible education," which stands in sharp contrast to the eight-point definition used for the federal abstinence-only funds. Similar to the abstinence-only approach, however, REAL provides a set of principles to guide the content of programs, but leaves curriculum development to local communities.

Of course, passage of the REAL Act is just one step in the larger campaign to support comprehensive sex education. Because sex education programs are guided by policies at multiple levels, from school board policies

U.S. representative Barbara Lee of California reintroduced the Responsible Education About Life (REAL) Act to the House of Representatives in 2009. © AP IMAGES.

U.S. senator Frank Lautenberg of New Jersey reintroduced the Responsible Education About Life (REAL) Act to the Senate in 2009. © AP IMAGES/MEL EVANS.

to city health department regulations to national and state-level laws, policies at each level need to support more comprehensive approaches. And because the REAL Act would direct its funds to state governments, questions remain about funding for Community-Based organizations and whether some states will decline to apply for the annual comprehensive sex education grants—as many have done under the Title V abstinence program. Moreover, policies and funding must be accompanied by efforts to address a host of other needs, including for teacher training, model programs, community assessment tools and program evaluation. Nonetheless, the leadership of the federal government in making sure that young people have the information and skills they will need to make healthy choices about sexual behavior—as teens now and as tomorrow's adults—is critical. In this respect, there is widespread agreement that improvement is both possible and imperative.

WHAT IS 'MEDICAL ACCURACY' IN SEX EDUCATION?

A number of reports have examined the medical accuracy of federally funded abstinence-only programs. According to a 2004 congressional review conducted by the minority staff of the House Committee on Government Reform, 11 of the 13 most popular abstinence-only curricula were rife with medical and scientific inaccuracies. For example, many grossly underestimated the effectiveness of condoms, made false claims about the risks of abortion or offered misinformation on the incidence and transmission of STIs. Two more recent reviews by the Government Accountability Office found similar problems, faulting the government for not keeping closer tabs on the medical accuracy of grantees' educational materials.

Apparently responding to these charges, the 2007 program guidelines for the CBAE program created a new requirement specifically pertaining to medical accuracy. "This is a welcome development," says John Santelli, department chair and professor of clinical population and family health at the Mailman School of Public Health, Columbia University, in an interview for this article. "But the fact that abstinence-only programs are required by law to provide biased information and withhold positive information about contraception raises serious questions about the ethics of these programs." Santelli continues:

"If adolescents are sexually active—or will be shortly—they need information to protect their health and lives. Where there is a need to know, medically incomplete is medically inaccurate."

Recognizing the importance of scientifically grounded health policies, Santelli suggests in a 2008 *American Journal of Public Health* article a definition of medically accurate information that incorporates an understanding of the scientific process. Medically accurate information, he says, is information "relevant to informed decision-making based on the weight of scientific evidence, consistent with generally recognized scientific theory, conducted under accepted scientific methods, published in peer-reviewed journals and recognized as accurate, objective and complete by mainstream professional organizations.... The deliberate withholding of information that is needed to protect life and health (and therefore relevant to informed decision-making) should be considered medically inaccurate." Santelli contends that each state and the federal government should adopt requirements for medical accuracy in health education. Although definitions will not end attempts to manipulate health policy-making, "they provide a clear standard in refuting such attempts."

FURTHER RESOURCES
Web Sites

"Abstinence Only Until Marriage Programs." *SIECUS.* http://www.siecus.org/index.cfm?fuseaction=page.view Page&pageId=523&parentID=477 (accessed on March 17, 2013).

Associated Press. "Sex Education Called Plot by Communists." *Spokane Daily Chronicle*, March 27, 1969. http://news.google.com/newspapers?nid=1338&dat=19690327& id=JWxYAAAAIBAJ&sjid=FfgDAAAAIBAJ&pg= 2972,3416651 (accessed on March 17, 2013).

Miller, Johanna. "Bird, Bees and Bias: How New York Schools Are Failing Our Young People." *ACLU*, September 14, 2012. http://www.aclu.org/blog/reproductive-freedom-lgbt-rights/bird-bees-and-bias-how-new-york-schools-are-failing-our-young (accessed on March 17, 2013).

"Mission." *Guttmacher Institute*. http://www.guttmacher.org/about/mission.html (accessed on March 17, 2013).

Pardini, Priscilla. "The History of Sexuality Education." *Rethinking Schools*. http://www.rethinkingschools.org/sex/sexhisto.shtml (accessed on March 17, 2013).

Wing, Nick. "Abstinence Education Reallocation Act Seeks $550 Million to Keep Teens from Having Sex." *Huffington Post*, March 4, 2013. http://www.huffington-post.com/2013/03/04/abstinence-education-reallocation-act_n_2807356.html (accessed on March 17, 2013).

"In Tough Times, the Humanities Must Justify Their Worth"

Newspaper article

By: Patricia Cohen

Date: February 25, 2009

Source: Cohen, Patricia. "In Tough Times, the Humanities Must Justify Their Worth." *New York Times*. www.nytimes.com/2009/02/25/books/25human.html (accessed on February 20, 2013).

About the Author: *Patricia Cohen* is a reporter who primarily covers the arts and humanities for the *New York Times*. She is the author of *In Our Prime: The Invention of Middle Age*, a book that takes readers from turn-of-the-century factories that refused to hire middle-aged men to high-tech laboratories where researchers are unraveling the secrets of the middle-aged mind and body. She traces how midlife has been depicted in film, television, advertisements, and literature. Cohen exposes the myths of the midlife crisis and empty nest syndrome and investigates anti-aging treatments like human growth hormones, estrogen, Viagra, Botox, and plastic surgery.

INTRODUCTION

By 2009, the United States had seen its share of economic ups and downs for nearly eight years. Economic conditions that had already been slowly declining took a precipitous dip in 2001 after the collapse of many dot-coms and the terrorist attacks of September 11. The Wall Street meltdown of September 2008 sent the country into freefall, and unemployment rates soared with massive layoffs at even top-tier companies that had always been bastions of financial strength.

Meanwhile, tuition costs for public and private colleges and universities continued to rise, variously attributed to rising faculty pay and benefits, luxury amenities such as richly appointed recreation centers and gourmet dining halls, falling state funding, and general inefficient management, among other factors. These ballooning tuitions—on average, doubling in the previous twenty-five years—forced many college students to work during their studies, lengthening the time it took to reach their degrees from an average of four years to six, and adding two more years of schooling costs. At the completion of their degrees, these students emerged, already carrying a crippling mound of debt into a job market so tight they often could not find employment in their chosen field, if they could find it at all. Within just a few years, student loan defaults would reach record rates.

While these students were in school, technology advanced at warp speed. Some who had struggled to afford and master a laptop computer for college work entered a world that was rapidly moving toward a largely mobile economy. They had to find ways to afford smartphones and data plans just to stay current with their peers or risk becoming anachronisms, sometimes before they even got their first full-time jobs.

This technological progress also changed the way many workers performed their jobs and significantly affected required skill sets. New technology invaded almost every sector of business, from education itself to standard office work, from home maintenance to healthcare. Much of what students had learned at the university was rapidly becoming dated, if not already obsolete. And driving it all were firms who develop said technology, and who were increasingly looking for graduates in the applied sciences.

This sparked a huge push by educators to pour resources into developing and staffing concentrated science/technology/engineering/math (STEM) study tracks, but they were already behind the curve. Ironically, in the midst of this tight job market, high-tech companies were forced to import top STEM talent from abroad, since American schools were not producing enough of these highly skilled graduates.

A public debate soon arose between those who saw the need for more home-grown technology workers whose studies had revolved around STEM and those who supported a classic liberal arts education. The argument was that the humanities, while a nice idea about education for its own sake, was becoming a luxury American students and their country could ill afford when it was not producing enough top-level minds to lead the United States into a science- and technology-based future. Liberal arts proponents fired back that all the hard science knowledge in the world is essentially useless without the ability to think and write clearly about its concepts with the power of an open, creative imagination and the analysis of a critical mind.

The debate would continue into the second decade of the twenty-first century. Many speculated that America was headed down a path of stratification between those who could afford the richness and future agility to adapt to a changing marketplace afforded by an education that included the humanities, and those whose economic situations limited them to two-year career colleges or certificates that would prepare their heads and hands for work but not for the

ability to move past the everyday operations into a future of fulfilling development and application of new ideas.

SIGNIFICANCE

In 1943, psychologist and researcher Abraham Maslow published his "Theory of Human Motivation," which has been generally accepted as an accurate representation of why people do the things they do. Better known as Maslow's Hierarchy of Needs, this theory posits that there are five levels of need that people move through, from the most primitive to the most exalted.

The lowest level is labeled Physiological, encompassing the need for the most basic bodily functions such as breathing, eating, drinking, sex, and excretion. The second level, Safety, speaks of people's need for security of their physical body, morality, health, family, resources, property, and employment. The next two levels—Love/Belonging and Esteem—deal with relationship to others and to oneself, moving from desire for friendship, family, and intimacy to feelings of self-esteem, confidence, achievement, and respect for oneself and others. The top level—Self-Actualization—represents the pinnacle of human endeavor and development, in response to the need for morality, creativity, spontaneity, acceptance of facts, and problem solving.

In the history of human development, mankind has moved from the primitive first level through the establishment of civilization to reach the security of the second. Once the ability to hunt, fish, farm and build took humans past those two levels at which actual physical safety is still in jeopardy, people could afford the relative luxury of turning their thoughts to the inner life of the mind and soul.

Mankind's collective ascent through these levels has been inextricably bound with—indeed, made possible by—various incarnations of education, both formal and informal. This ascent has occasionally reversed as societies engage in war, revolution, and other upheavals that threaten foundational physical safety. But overall, human trajectory has been upward, allowing most people to now enjoy the expectancy of a life that is about more than just the drudgery of providing for their physical needs.

From this perspective, it might appear that since the turn of the twenty-first century, society has been in one of those periods of upheaval—at least in the United States—that forces abandonment of pursuit of the sublime at least temporarily, while it attends to shoring up its sense of physical and psychological security. Wars, terrorist attacks, and economic contraction have all contributed to lack of a collective sense of well-being. This has turned immediate attention to solving the problems of reliably providing for basic needs, which stand in the way of a return to an atmosphere that enables people to occupy themselves with a higher order of attainment.

Once again, education is a key component of people's ability to reach this goal. For Americans, a comfortable level of security—at least as much as is within their control—has a great deal to do with returning to economic stability and growth. That return is predicated in large part on getting the majority of employable citizens back to work in reliable jobs that are both adequately remunerative and sufficiently fulfilling on an intellectual basis.

For this to happen, colleges and universities must prepare graduates with applied skills to be immediately productive when they enter the workforce, increasing the Gross Domestic Product and expanding the national economy. Graduates must also be prepared to help create new jobs where there are none, through both the application of technology and math skills and through growth into leadership positions that require critical analysis, innovative ideas, and the ability to communicate with clarity.

The challenge before schools now is whether or not the humanities will remain a supported part of how they achieve this preparation. The United States is not the only country facing such decisions. In 2010, the British government published a report, "Securing a Sustainable Future for Higher Education." Following its recommendations, post-secondary schools in the United Kingdom moved all humanities courses from main degree offerings to extra-curricular electives requiring students to pay for them separately, in addition to regular tuition. The long-term effect of this move remains to be seen, but the future of the United States as a world power may hang on the result of similar decisions to be made at home.

▮ PRIMARY SOURCE

"IN TOUGH TIMES, THE HUMANITIES MUST JUSTIFY THEIR WORTH"

SYNOPSIS: As the Great Recession lingers on, tuitions become more expensive, and a tight job market clamors for more employees skilled in the applied sciences, the *New York Times* looks at how humanities departments of many colleges and universities are feeling the pressure to justify the need for liberal arts degrees.

One idea that elite universities like Yale, sprawling public systems like Wisconsin and smaller private

colleges like Lewis and Clark have shared for generations is that a traditional liberal arts education is, by definition, not intended to prepare students for a specific vocation. Rather, the critical thinking, civic and historical knowledge, and ethical reasoning that the humanities develop have a different purpose: They are prerequisites for personal growth and participation in a free democracy, regardless of career choice.

But in this new era of lengthening unemployment lines and shrinking university endowments, questions about the importance of the humanities in a complex and technologically demanding world have taken on new urgency. Previous economic downturns have often led to decreased enrollment in the disciplines loosely grouped under the term "humanities"—which generally include languages, literature, the arts, history, cultural studies, philosophy, and religion. Many in the field worry that in this current crisis, those areas will be hit hardest.

Already scholars point to troubling signs. A December survey of 200 higher education institutions by *The Chronicle of Higher Education* and Moody's Investors Services found that 5 percent have imposed a total hiring freeze, and an additional 43 percent have imposed a partial freeze.

In the last three months, at least two dozen colleges have canceled or postponed faculty searches in religion and philosophy, according to a job postings page on Wikihost.org. The Modern Language Association's end-of-the-year job listings in English, literature, and foreign languages dropped 21 percent for 2008–09 from the previous year—the biggest decline in 34 years.

"Although people in humanities have always lamented the state of the field, they have never felt quite as much of a panic that their field is becoming irrelevant," said Andrew Delbanco, the director of American studies at Columbia University.

With additional painful cuts across the board a near certainty even as millions of federal stimulus dollars may be funneled to education, the humanities are under greater pressure than ever to justify their existence to administrators, policy makers, students, and parents. Technology executives, researchers and business leaders argue that producing enough trained engineers and scientists is essential to America's economic vitality, national defense, and health care. Some of the staunchest humanities advocates, however, admit that they have failed to make their case effectively.

This crisis of confidence has prompted a reassessment of what has long been considered the humanities' central and sacred mission: to explore, as one scholar put it, "what it means to be a human being."

Richard Freeland is introduced as Northwestern University's new president, May 29, 1996. He later served as the Massachusetts commissioner of higher education. © AP IMAGES/GAIL OSKIN.

The study of the humanities evolved during the twentieth century "to focus almost entirely on personal intellectual development," said Richard M. Freeland, the Massachusetts commissioner of higher education. "But what we haven't paid a lot of attention to is how students can put those abilities effectively to use in the world. We've created a disjunction between the liberal arts and sciences and our role as citizens and professionals."

Mr. Freeland is part of what he calls a revolutionary movement to close the "chasm in higher education between the liberal arts and sciences and professional programs." The Association of American Colleges and Universities recently issued a report arguing the humanities should abandon the "old Ivory Tower view of liberal education" and instead emphasize its practical and economic value.

Next month Mr. Freeland and the association are hosting a conference precisely on this subject at Clark University in Worcester, Mass. There is a lot of interest on the national leadership level in higher education, Mr. Freeland said, but the idea has not caught on among professors and department heads.

Baldly marketing the humanities makes some in the field uneasy.

Derek Bok, a former president of Harvard and the author of several books on higher education, argues, "The humanities has a lot to contribute to the preparation of students for their vocational lives." He said he was referring not only to writing and analytical skills but also to the type of ethical issues raised by new technology like stem-cell research. But he added: "There's a lot more to a liberal education than improving the economy. I think that is one of the worst mistakes that policy makers often make—not being able to see beyond that."

Anthony T. Kronman, a professor of law at Yale and the author of "Education's End: Why Our Colleges and Universities Have Given Up on the Meaning of Life," goes further. Summing up the benefits of exploring what's called "a life worth living" in a consumable sound bite is not easy, Mr. Kronman said.

But "the need for my older view of the humanities is, if anything, more urgent today," he added, referring to the widespread indictment of greed, irresponsibility and fraud that led to the financial meltdown. In his view, this is the time to re-examine "what we care about and what we value," a problem the humanities "are extremely well-equipped to address."

Anthony Kronman, dean of the Yale Law School, introduces U.S. secretary of the Treasury Robert Rubin (left) at Yale function, October 17, 1998. © AP IMAGES/DOUGLAS HEALEY.

To Mr. Delbanco of Columbia, the person who has done the best job of articulating the benefits is President Obama. "He does something academic humanists have not been doing well in recent years," he said of a president who invokes Shakespeare and Faulkner, Lincoln and W. E. B. Du Bois. "He makes people feel there is some kind of a common enterprise, that history, with its tragedies and travesties, belongs to all of us, that we have something in common as Americans."

During the second half of the twentieth century, as more and more Americans went on to college, a smaller and smaller percentage of those students devoted themselves to the humanities. The humanities' share of college degrees is less than half of what it was during the heyday in the mid- to late 1960s, according to the Humanities Indicators Prototype, a new database recently released by the American Academy of Arts & Sciences. Currently they account for about eight percent (about 110,000 students), a figure that has remained pretty stable for more than a decade. The low point for

humanities degrees occurred during the bitter recession of the early 1980s.

The humanities continue to thrive in elite liberal arts schools. But the divide between these private schools and others is widening. Some large state universities routinely turn away students who want to sign up for courses in the humanities, Francis C. Oakley, president emeritus and a professor of the history of ideas at Williams College, reported. At the University of Washington, for example, in recent years, as many as one-quarter of the students found they were unable to get into a humanities course.

As money tightens, the humanities may increasingly return to being what they were at the beginning of the last century, when only a minuscule portion of the population attended college: namely, the province of the wealthy.

That may be unfortunate but inevitable, Mr. Kronman said. The essence of a humanities education—reading the great literary and philosophical works and coming "to grips with the question of what living is for"—may become "a great luxury that many cannot afford."

FURTHER RESOURCES

Books

Kronman, Anthony T. *Education's End: Why Our Colleges and Universities Have Given Up on the Meaning of Life.* New Haven, CT: Yale University Press, 2007.

Nussbaum, Martha C. *Not for Profit: Why Democracy Needs the Humanities.* Princeton, NJ: Princeton University Press, Reprint ed., 2012.

Yunus, Muhammad. *Building Social Business: The New Kind of Capitalism That Serves Humanity's Most Pressing Needs.* New York: PublicAffairs Books, 2010.

Web Sites

Basu, Jackie, and Karmia Cao, Gregory Hertz, Julian Kusnadi, Miles Osgood, and Alex Romanczuk. "The Value of a Humanities Degree: Six Students' Views." *Chronicle of Higher Education*, June 5, 2011. www.chronicle.com/article/The-Value-of-a-Humanities/127758/ (accessed on February 20, 2013).

Bruni, Frank. "The Imperiled Promise of College" *New York Times Sunday Review*, April 28, 2012. www.nytimes.com/2012/04/29/opinion/sunday/bruni-the-imperiled-promise-of-college.html (accessed on February 20, 2013).

Churchwell, Sarah. "The Case for the Humanities." *Thought-Out*, October 22, 2012. www.thoughtoutproject.com/politics/how-ideas-work-the-humanism-of-humanities/#.UQcL0kpdcrK (accessed on February 20, 2013).

Fish, Stanley. "Bound for Academic Glory?" *New York Times*, December 23, 2007. www.opinionator.blogs.nytimes.com/2007/12/23/bound-for-academic-glory/ (accessed on February 20, 2013).

Fish, Stanley. "Will the Humanities Save Us?" *New York Times*, January 6, 2008. www.opinionator.blogs.nytimes.com/2008/01/06/will-the-humanities-save-us/ (accessed on February 20, 2013).

Mexal, Stephen J. "The Unintended Value of the Humanities" *Chronicle of Higher Education*, May 23, 2010. www.chronicle.com/article/The-Unintended-Value-of-the/65619/ (accessed on February 20, 2013).

Scott, Amy. "Why Has College Gotten So Expensive?" *American Public Media—Marketplace: Your Money*, August 10, 2012. www.marketplace.org/topics/your-money/why-has-college-gotten-so-expensive (accessed on January 29, 2013).

Summary. "Browne Review: Securing a Sustainable Future for Higher Education." *Guardian*, October 12, 2010. www.guardian.co.uk/education/interactive/2010/oct/12/browne-review-higher-education (accessed on February 20, 2013).

Sunday Dialogue: Studying the Humanities" *New York Times Sunday Review*, May 5, 2012. www.nytimes.com/2012/05/06/opinion/sunday/sunday-dialogue-studying-the-humanities.html (accessed on February 20, 2013).

Vasager, Jeevan, and Jessica Shepherd. "Tuition Fees: Heavy Debts Will Not Put Students Off University Prize—Browne." *Guardian*, October 12, 2010. www.guardian.co.uk/education/2010/oct/12/tuition-fees-debts-students-university-browne?intcmp=239 (accessed on February 20, 2013).

"New Report Shows Libraries Critical in Times of Crisis, but Funding Lags and Services Reduced"

Press release

By: American Library Association

Date: April 13, 2009

Source: American Library Association. "New Report Shows Libraries Critical in Times of Crisis, but Funding Lags and Services Reduced." *American Library Association*, April 13, 2009. http://www.ala.org/news/news/pressreleases2009/april2009/2009state (accessed on February 20, 2013).

About the Organization: The American Library Association (ALA) was founded as a non-profit in 1876 by a small group of librarians who recognized the need for a professional organization that would allow them to do their jobs more efficiently and effectively. According to the ALA's constitution, its mission is " to provide leadership for the development, promotion, and improvement of library and information services and the profession of librarianship in order to enhance learning and ensure access to information for all." The oldest library organization in the world, the ALA boasted a membership of around sixty-two thousand at the end of the first decade of the 2000s.

INTRODUCTION

The public library is as American as baseball and apple pie, literally. Although Europe had subscription libraries since the early 1700s, it was not until 1833 that the first free library was founded. Residents of

Peterborough, New Hampshire, believed that all townspeople had the right to access their community's stored knowledge. By 1910, every state boasted public libraries. The concept was based on the traditional values of cooperation and sharing. Regardless of socioeconomic status, every American citizen had the ability to procure a library card, and with it, access to a nearly endless wealth of information.

Public libraries remained one of the cornerstones of community life throughout the decades. In 1872, when the first library extended its hours to include Sundays so that all patrons could find time to visit, many citizens considered it sacrilege. But the very idea of the library—to serve the public when the public needed to be served—required such a bold move, and even in the late 1990s, Sunday was the busiest day for public libraries across the nation. Likewise, when times got tough, such as during the Great Depression, public libraries devised unique ways to keep their doors open. The Cleveland public library sponsored "overdue weeks," asking patrons who had the means to keep their books out until they were overdue so that the library could collect the twelve cents per week fine. By the mid-1930s, public libraries were serving 60 percent of the population. In fact, it is no coincidence that when the economy is in ill health, library use soars. Where else can one spend absolutely no money yet find hours of entertainment?

The irony is that, in times of economic recession or depression, local, state, and federal governments are forced to find ways to cut their spending. Public libraries are often among the first to feel the loss as funding is drastically cut or even eliminated. As America slid into economic despair toward the end of the 2000s, hundreds of public libraries saw their hours reduced while others had branches completely closed. Philadelphia's Free Library System was slated to be shut down entirely—all fifty-four of its libraries—on October 2, 2009, due to budget cuts. A massive letter and e-mail campaign saved the system from such doom as concerned citizens wrote to emphasize how pivotal a role their neighborhood libraries play in the lives of their families and schools.

SIGNIFICANCE

Given that the recession was still going strong through the end of the decade, the country's public libraries remained poised for budget cuts and closings. Factors other than the economy came into play, however, as technological advances became more commonplace.

A major factor in library use or lack thereof was the advent of the Internet. There was a time not long ago when patrons needed to seek the assistance of a reference librarian in order to conduct online research. This was necessary because of the research databases;

one mistake could be costly for a library, so it was more efficient and safer to have all searching done by a trained librarian. This is not the case any longer, as anyone with basic computer and Internet knowledge can conduct his or her own research. And if patrons have their own computer, they do not even need to go to the library for anything. The age of instant information-gathering has made some of the services offered by most public libraries obsolete, but not for everyone. There will always be patrons who do not own their own computer, or subscribe to an Internet service provider, or even know how to operate a computer.

Another electronic advance that has greatly affected libraries is the debut of the e-reader. Known as Nooks and Kindles by many, these e-readers make printed books analogous to dinosaurs for many readers. Several sites offer e-books for free or at very little charge, and once downloaded, they never have to be returned. The e-book era has changed not only the face of book publishing and marketing, but also libraries. The number of e-books purchased by libraries has increased; and because they are digital, they do not require physical storage space. The popularity of e-books has quickly escalated: for instance, the Seattle Public Library reported a 92 percent increase in e-book circulation in 2010 while the New York Public Library reported an 81 percent increase in 2011. And while this seems like a simple connect-the-dots scenario, the reality is far more challenging. Publishers and authors are generally not in favor of working with libraries because they worry that offering titles for free to borrowers will negatively impact sales of their books. So if libraries are to keep up with public reading habits, something will need to change so that they can stock what their patrons want to read, in the format they want.

Public libraries get most of their funding locally; they truly are grassroots, community-oriented organizations. But when giant retailers such as Amazon, Google, and Barnes and Noble developed the ability to give away more free e-book titles than most libraries hold in their print collection, it became clear that there is no easy resolution to the struggle to keep these community cornerstones up and running. And the scenario was not likely to change for the better any time soon.

▌ PRIMARY SOURCE

"NEW REPORT SHOWS LIBRARIES CRITICAL IN TIMES OF CRISIS, BUT FUNDING LAGS AND SERVICES REDUCED"

SYNOPSIS: Despite the fact that Americans rely upon their public libraries more during an economic recession, funding of libraries is often one of the first cuts to be made when budgets are reduced.

The value of libraries in communities across the country continued to grow in 2008—and accelerated dramatically as the national economy sank and people looked for cost effective resources in a time of crisis, according to the American Library Association's (ALA) annual State of America's Libraries report, released today as part of National Library Week, April 12–18, 2009.

U.S. libraries experienced a dramatic increase in library card registration as the public continues to turn to their local library for free services. More than 68 percent of Americans have a library card. This is the greatest number of Americans with library cards since the American Library Association (ALA) started to measure library card usage in 1990, according to a 2008 Web poll conducted by Harris Interactive.

The report also says library usage soared as Americans visited their libraries nearly 1.4 billion times and checked out more than 2 billion items in the past year, an increase of more than 10 percent in both checked out items and library visits, compared to data from the last economic downturn in 2001.

However, public funding did not keep pace with use, according to a survey conducted by the ALA. Forty-one percent of states report declining state funding for U.S. public libraries for fiscal year 2009. Twenty percent of these states anticipate an additional reduction in the current fiscal year.

While reductions have been seen from coast to coast, the southeastern section of the country has been the hardest hit, with declines as large as 30 percent in South Carolina and 23.4 percent in Florida in FY09 compared with FY08. Per capita state aid in South Carolina has fallen back to 2003 levels, at the same time inflation has averaged between 2.5 and 3.4 percent annually. Additionally:

The effects of the slumping economy on local libraries were often painful, and many community colleges began reducing library hours or staff just when enrollment was swollen by unemployed people seeking to acquire new skills.

Even as funding began to falter, the report shows that libraries continued to serve as excellent community resource offering users a goldmine of information, resources and support for those affected by the recession.

Libraries continue to report that job-related activities are a priority use of their computers and Internet services. Nationwide, libraries are offering programs tailored to meet local community economic needs, providing residents with guidance (including sessions with career advisers), training and workshops in resume writing and interviewing, job-search resources, and connections with outside agencies that offer training and job placement.

However, despite increased demand for library computers, libraries typically have not seen a corresponding increase in budgets, and many are challenged to provide enough computers or fast-enough connection speeds to meet demand.

ALA President Jim Rettig said, "As illustrated in the ALA's State of America's Libraries Report, in times of economic hardship, Americans turn to—and depend on—their libraries and librarians."

Other key findings in the 2009 State of America's Libraries report:

- Children are among the heaviest users of public-library resources. Children's materials accounted for 35 percent of all circulation transactions, and attendance at library-based children's programs was 57.8 million.
- Individual visits to school library media centers increased significantly at the schools that responded to both the 2007 and 2008 surveys: up 22.7 percent for the 50th percentile, up 12.5 percent for the 75th percentile, and up almost 25 percent for the 95th percentile. There were no major year-to-year differences in the responses with regard to the other variables.
- Academic libraries maintain their leading role in partnering to scan and digitize print book collections, with the potential to provide unprecedented access to millions of volumes. Large-scale digitization initiatives include Google Book Search, Microsoft Live Search Books, Open Content Alliance, and the Million Book Project.
- A survey of public, academic, school libraries and special libraries revealed that 40 percent of the 404 libraries that responded circulate games; PC games were the most frequently circulated type, offered by 25 percent, but the number of libraries circulating console and handheld games rose slightly from 2006 to 2007, while those circulating PC games and board/card games decreased slightly.
- The number of mobile library service vehicles continues to increase from more than 930 in 2008, vs. 825 nationwide in 2005.
- The library profession continued its active efforts in 2008 both to make its ranks more accessible to members of ethnic and racial minority groups and to strengthen its outreach efforts to underserved populations.

The ALA State of America's Libraries Report is produced annually and reports on key library trends and data.

The full text of the 2008 State of America's Libraries is available at www.ala.org/2009state.

FURTHER RESOURCES

Books

Murray, Stuart A. P. *The Library: An Illustrated History*. New York: Skyhorse, 2009.

Web Sites

Coffman, Steve. "The Decline and Fall of the Library Empires." *Information Today*, April 2012. www.infotoday. com/searcher/apr12/Coffman–The-Decline-and-Fall-of-the-Library-Empire.shtml (accessed on February 20, 2013).

Karas, David. "Libraries Fight to Stay Relevant in a Digital Age." *Christian Science Monitor*, June 27, 2011. www. csmonitor.com/USA/Society/2011/0627/Public-libraries-fight-to-stay-relevant-in-digital-age?nav=628693-csm_blog_post-bottomRelated (accessed on February 20, 2013).

Morris, David. "The Public Library Manifesto." *Yes! Magazine*, May 6, 2011. www.yesmagazine.org/happiness/the-public-library-manifesto (accessed on February 20, 2013).

OCLC. *From Awareness to Funding*, June 20, 2008. www.oclc. org/reports/funding/fullreport.pdf (accessed on February 20, 2013).

"Colleges Are Failing in Graduation Rates"

Newspaper article

By: David Leonhardt

Date: September 8, 2009

Source: Leonhardt, David. "Colleges Are Failing in Graduation Rates." *New York Times*. www.nytimes. com/2009/09/09/business/economy/09leonhardt.html (accessed on March 19, 2013).

About the Author: David Leonhardt has been the Washington bureau chief for the *New York Times* since September 6, 2011. He joined the *Times* in 1999, writing the "Economics Scene" column, from which this article is taken. He also wrote for the *Times Sunday Magazine*. Before that, he wrote for the *Washington Post* and *Business Week*. In April, 2011 he won a Pulitzer Prize in the "Commentary" category "for his

graceful penetration of America's complicated economic questions, from the federal budget deficit to health care reform."

INTRODUCTION

The National Center for Education Statistics (NCES) is the United States' primary federal entity for collecting and analyzing data related to education. Two primary indicators it measures regarding the status of post-secondary education in the country are the Graduation Completion Rate, which reflects how many students graduate with a degree, and the Drop-Out Rate, which measures the number of students who disengage with the educational institutions in which they are enrolled.

These measures are calculated by both the NCES and the U.S. Department of Education's Institute of Education Sciences to analyze the success or the failure of college-level students and of the American educational system.

High school and college level dropouts, as well as overall education system trends, affect the completion rate. Concern over the U.S. graduation rate has grown as completion has decreased over the past few decades, despite the fact that there has been a twenty-year decline in the percentage of dropouts among sixteen-to-twenty-four-year-olds and college enrollment among high school graduates has jumped substantially.

SIGNIFICANCE

Statistics show that graduation rates for college-level students are declining across the board. The Early College High School Initiative, begun in 2002, established a practice known as dual enrollment. This allows students to combine high school and college-level classes to obtain their high school diploma and an associate degree simultaneously. Community colleges' mission to provide better access to higher education and graduation for under-served populations is based on research indicating this is a primary factor in balancing income inequalities and increasing U.S. worker productivity. Public universities traditionally offered four-year degrees to mainstream post-secondary students. All of these institutions—some more than others—are seeing declining rates of program completion.

One 2009 study—"Understanding Decrease in Completion Rates and Increase in Time to Degree" by John Bound, Michael Lovenheim, and Sarah Turner—indicated that non-completion and a related trend in increased time to degree (now reaching six years instead of four) were, overall, a result of a combination of "rapid growth in the size of the college-age population and dilution in resources per student at many public colleges" outside the top tier of public and private institutions. This study produced evidence that the increased time to attainment of degree was "consistent with students working more to meet rising college costs thereby negatively affecting the length of time it takes them to complete college." In short, students who come to college ill-prepared and with fewer financial resources struggle more to stay in school long enough to get their degrees and take longer to get them if they do indeed graduate.

This situation in turn leads to the likelihood that students entering college as disadvantaged will remain so, at least on an economic basis, for the rest of their lives. The College Board, a non-profit association formerly known as the College Entrance Examination Board, in 2010 published a report titled "Education Pay." It shows that graduation level has significant bearing on lifetime ability to earn money, with a tendency for earnings to increase on par with increasing education level. At the time of the study, American workers with a master's degree had an average income of $67,300 and those with a bachelor's made an average of $55,700, while those lacking a high school diploma tended to make about $24,300.

Not only does graduation level affect how much money one can earn, it increasingly affects one's ability to get a job at all. According to the U.S. federal government's *College Completion Tool Kit*, published in 2010, by 2018 only 10 percent of all jobs will be available to those without a high school diploma, and 28 percent for those who do graduate high school but do not go to college. The next 12 percent of jobs will be attainable by those with some college but no degree, and college graduates with an associate degree will qualify for 17 percent. Those holding a baccalaureate will qualify for 23 percent of the remaining positions, with just 10 percent reserved for those with graduate degrees.

The long-term implications of this situation for the overall American economy and standard of living are clear.

PRIMARY SOURCE

"COLLEGES ARE FAILING IN GRADUATION RATES"

SYNOPSIS: The *New York Times* examines the growing rate of non-graduation at American public universities through the lens of a book by two established education professionals who believe the problem stems from a system that focuses on student enrollment rather than successful completion of

studies. David Leonhardt posits that a culture of failure has become entrenched and accepted in the majority of the nation's state post-secondary schools. He argues that this phenomenon is an economic issue that affects poor students to a far greater extent than rich ones, and that failure to address the issue at its root will have lasting negative effects on the entire American economy.

If you were going to come up with a list of organizations whose failures had done the most damage to the American economy in recent years, you'd probably have to start with the Wall Street firms and regulatory agencies that brought us the financial crisis. From there, you might move on to Wall Street's fellow bailout recipients in Detroit, the once-Big Three.

But I would suggest that the list should also include a less obvious nominee: public universities.

At its top levels, the American system of higher education may be the best in the world. Yet in terms of its core mission—turning teenagers into educated college graduates—much of the system is simply failing.

Only 33 percent of the freshmen who enter the University of Massachusetts, Boston, graduate within six years. Less than 41 percent graduate from the University of Montana, and 44 percent from the University of New Mexico. The economist Mark Schneider refers to colleges with such dropout rates as "failure factories," and they are the norm.

The United States does a good job enrolling teenagers in college, but only half of students who enroll end up with a bachelor's degree. Among rich countries, only Italy is worse. That's a big reason inequality has soared, and productivity growth has slowed. Economic growth in this decade was on pace to be slower than in any decade since World War II—even before the financial crisis started.

So identifying the causes of the college dropout crisis matters enormously, and a new book tries to do precisely that.

It is called "Crossing the Finish Line," and its findings are based on the records of about 200,000 students at 68 colleges. The authors were able to get their hands on that data because two of them are pillars of the education establishment: William Bowen (an economist and former Princeton president) and Michael McPherson (an economist and former Macalester College president).

For all the book's alarming statistics, its message is ultimately uplifting—or at least invigorating.

Yes, inadequate precollege education is a problem. But high schools still produce many students who have the skills to complete college and yet fail to do so. Turning them into college graduates should be a lot less difficult than fixing all of American education.

University of Michigan graduates celebrate their accomplishments at their commencement ceremony, April 26, 2008. Michigan's Ann Arbor campus has a graduation rate of 88 percent. © AP IMAGES/TONY DING.

"We could be doing a lot better with college completion just by working on our colleges," as Robert Shireman, an Education Department official who has read an early version of the book, says.

Congress and the Obama administration are now putting together an education bill that tries to deal with the problem. It would cancel about $9 billion in annual government subsidies for banks that lend to college students and use much of the money to increase financial aid. A small portion of the money would be set aside for promising pilot programs aimed at lifting the number of college graduates. All in all, the bill would help.

But it won't solve the system's biggest problems—the focus on enrollment rather than completion, the fact that colleges are not held to account for their failures. "Crossing the Finish Line" makes it clear that we can do better.

The first problem that Mr. Bowen, Mr. McPherson and the book's third author, Matthew Chingos, a doctoral candidate, diagnose is something they call under-matching. It refers to students who choose not to attend the best college they can get into. They instead go to a less selective one, perhaps one that's closer to home or, given the torturous financial aid process, less expensive.

About half of low-income students with a high school grade-point average of at least 3.5 and an SAT score of at least 1,200 do not attend the best college they could have. Many don't even apply. Some apply but don't enroll. "I was really astonished by the degree to which presumptively well-qualified students from poor families under-matched," Mr. Bowen told me.

They could have been admitted to Michigan's Ann Arbor campus (graduation rate: 88 percent, according to College Results Online) or Michigan State (74 percent), but they went, say, to Eastern Michigan (39 percent) or Western Michigan (54 percent). If they graduate, it would be hard to get upset about their choice. But large numbers do not. . . .

In effect, well-off students—many of whom will graduate no matter where they go—attend the colleges that do the best job of producing graduates. These are the places where many students live on campus (which raises graduation rates) and graduation is the norm. Meanwhile, lower-income students—even when they are better qualified—often go to colleges that excel in producing dropouts.

"It's really a waste," Mr. Bowen says, "and a big problem for the country." As the authors point out, the only way to lift the college graduation rate significantly is to lift it among poor and working-class students. Instead, it appears to have fallen somewhat since the 1970s.

What can be done?

Money is clearly part of the answer. Tellingly, net tuition has no impact on the graduation rates of high-income students. Yet it does affect low-income students. All else equal, they are less likely to make it through a more expensive state college than a less expensive one, the book shows. Conservatives are wrong to suggest affordability doesn't matter.

But they are right that more money isn't the whole answer. Higher education today also suffers from a deep cultural problem. Failure has become acceptable.

Students see no need to graduate in four years. Doing so, as one told the book's authors, is "like leaving the party at 10:30 p.m." Graduation delayed often becomes graduation denied. Administrators then make excuses for their graduation rates. And policy makers hand out money based on how many students a college enrolls rather than on what it does with those students.

There is a real parallel here to health care. We pay doctors and hospitals for more care instead of better care, and what do we get? More care, even if in many cases it doesn't make us healthier.

In education, the incentives can be truly perverse. Because large lecture classes are cheaper for a college than seminars, freshmen are cheaper than upperclassmen. So a college that allows many of its underclassmen to drop out may be helping its bottom line.

If you look closely, you can still find reasons for optimism. A few colleges, like the University of Maryland, Baltimore County, have intensive programs that have raised graduation rates. The State of West Virginia has begun tying student aid to academic progress, and graduation rates there have risen. *Washington Monthly* magazine has published a new college ranking based in part on graduation rates. (Kudos to Penn State, among others.) When students fill out an online form for federal financial aid, the Obama Education Department now informs them of the graduation rate at any college in which they express interest.

But an enormous amount of work remains, and it's hard to think of any work that's more important to the American economy.

Last year, even in the grip of a recession that has spared no group of workers, the gap between what a college graduate earned and what everyone else earned reached a record. Workers with bachelor's degrees made 54 percent more on average than those who attended college but didn't finish, according to the Labor Department. Fifty-four percent—just think about how that adds up over a lifetime. And then think about how many students never cross the college finish line.

FURTHER RESOURCES

Books

Arum, Richard, and Josipa Roksa. *Academically Adrift: Limited Learning on College Campuses.* Chicago: University of Chicago Press, 2010.

Bowen, William G., Matthew M. Chingos, and Michael S. McPherson. *Crossing the Finish Line.* Princeton, NJ: Princeton University Press, 2009.

Braxton, John, ed. *Reworking the Student Departure Puzzle.* Nashville: Taylor & Vanderbilt University Press, 2000.

Christensen, Clayton M., and Henry J. Eyring. *The Innovative University: Changing the DNA of Higher Education from the Inside Out.* Hoboken, NJ: Taylor & Jossey-Bass, 2011.

Pascarella, Ernest T., and Patrick T. Terenzini. *How College Affects Students: A Third Decade of Research.* Hoboken, NJ: Taylor & Jossey-Bass, 2005.

Web Sites

Bound, John, Michael Lovenheim, and Sarah Turner. "Why Have College Completion Rates Declined? An Analysis of Changing Student Preparation and Collegiate Resources." *National Bureau of Economic Research*, December 2009. www.nber.org/papers/w15566 (accessed on March 19, 2013).

Brainard, Jeffrey, and Andrea Fuller. "Graduation Rates Fall at One-Third of 4-Year Colleges." *Chronicle of Higher Education*, December 5, 2010. www.chronicle.com/article/Graduation-Rates-Fall-at/125614/ (accessed on March 19, 2013).

Lubrano, Alfred. "At Conference, Education, Labor Secretaries Warn about Declining College Graduation Rate." *Philadelphia Inquirer*, March 1, 2011. articles.philly.com/2011-03-01/news/28640500_1_education-arne-duncan-education-pipeline-community-college (accessed on March 19, 2013).

Nealy, Michelle J. "College Graduation Rates Could Dramatically Decline, If Minorities Don't Improve College Completion, Report Says." *Diverse Issues in Higher Education*, June 9, 2009. www.diverseeducation.com/article/12666/ (accessed on March 19, 2013).

4 | Fashion and Design

Chronology

Important Events in Fashion and Design, 2000–2009

2000

- In January, the "green" Adam Joseph Lewis Center for Environmental Studies on the Oberlin College campus in Ohio includes a greenhouse wastewater-purification system.

- On February 23, singer Jennifer Lopez makes a memorably revealing appearance at the Grammy Awards in a plunging sheer green Versace dress.

- On May 18, the *Victoria's Secret Fashion Show* is webcast from Cannes, France, to American viewers, marking the first time the event takes place outside of the United States. Organizers raise $3.5 million for AIDS research.

- In August, fashion notables Calvin Klein, Ralph Lauren, and Norman Norell are among the first inductees on the "Fashion Walk of Fame," on Seventh Avenue in New York City's garment district.

- In October, American fashion designer Tom Ford takes over as creative director of the French fashion house Yves Saint Laurent.

- On October 13, *Trading Spaces*, a television show that pitted two teams in redecorating a room in their rival's home, debuts on TLC.

2001

- On March 25, Icelandic pop star Björk turns heads in Los Angeles when she wears an unconventional swan-shaped dress on the red carpet at the seventy-third Academy Awards. Actress Julia Roberts wears a vintage Valentino black with white trim dress, considered by many to be the most beautiful on the red carpet for the decade.

- On June 22, clothing retailer Gap announces a 7 percent cut in its workforce.

- On September 28, directed by and starring Ben Stiller, the movie *Zoolander* premieres, spoofing the shallowness of the fashion industry.

- In November, the last issue of the women's magazine *Mademoiselle* is published.

- On November 15, the *Victoria's Secret Fashion Show* airs on television (ABC) for the first time.

- In December, sportswear designer Michael Kors launches his "leg shine" body-highlighting product.

2002

- Ford introduces a retro-style Thunderbird, which helps inspire a return to traditional car designs during the decade. Also introduced this year is the Hummer H2, a huge, boxy SUV, based on the military version; it is widely criticized as being energy inefficient and having poor gas mileage.

- In August, the Levi Strauss company, which makes denim jeans and pants, announces it will close six of its U.S. factories and lay off more than 3,000 workers.

2003

- Jennifer Lopez introduces a new line of women's clothing, called Sweetface.

- In February, the first issue of *Teen Vogue*, a fashion magazine for young women, is published with singer Gwen Stefani featured on the cover.

- In May, Cleveland, Ohio, opens its first annual fashion week. The event will grow to be the third largest in the country by the end of the decade.

- On May 20, *America's Next Top Model*, a reality-television show, premieres on UPN. Created and hosted by supermodel Tyra Banks, the program features young models who compete for a break in the modeling industry.

- On July 17, architect David Childs is chosen to design the Freedom Tower, which will rise on the site of the destroyed World Trade Center in New York City.

2004

- New York socialite and model Nicky Hilton launches her clothing line, Chick.

- On May 23, the Seattle Central Library building opens; a modernistic glass-covered set of geometric forms designed by architects Rem Koolhaas and Joshua Prince-Ramus of the radical Dutch architectural firm OMA, it is regarded as one of the most striking new structures in the United States.

- On May 26, the Louisiana State legislature rejects a proposed bill that would have outlawed low-riding pants.

- On July 4, the first stone of the Freedom Tower is laid at the former World Trade Center site.

- On September 28, designer Geoffrey Beene, famous for his minimalist designs and the popular men's fragrance Grey Flannel, dies in New York City.

- On December 1, the Bravo Network's fashion-based reality-television show *Project Runway* premieres. Hosted by German American supermodel Heidi Klum, the program pits aspiring fashion designers in a competition to win a $100,000 prize and an editorial feature in *Elle* magazine.

2005

- Ford introduces the retro-style Mustang S197, a sleek update of its classic "muscle" car.

- In the summer, the Boho Gypsy skirt sweeps the nation as a popular fashion statement.

- On September 6, the premier fall issue of *Men's Vogue* is released, with actor George Clooney featured on the cover.

2006

- In February, Renée Strauss (designer) and Martin Katz (jeweler) design a wedding dress featuring 150 carats of diamonds that is worth approximately $12 million.

- TOMS Shoes is founded by Blake Mycoskie. For every pair of shoes sold, the company donates a pair to a child in need.

- On June 30, *The Devil Wears Prada*, starring Meryl Streep and Anne Hathaway, premieres. In the film, Streep portrays a thinly veiled fictional version of *Vogue* editor Anna Wintour.

- On June 27, revisions to the design of the Freedom Tower are made in response to criticisms that some aspects of the proposed structure are not aesthetically pleasing.

- On September 28, the television sitcom *Ugly Betty*, starring America Ferrara and Vanessa Williams, debuts on ABC. The series revolves around the experiences of a frumpy secretary at a fashion magazine.

2007

- Ray-Ban reintroduces its classic sunglass design, the Wayfarer.

- On June 11, the town of Delcambre, Louisiana, bans the wearing of saggy pants that expose men's underwear. Other towns in Louisiana will follow suit and ban the display of undergarments.

- On June 26, iconic Belgian American fashion designer Liz Claiborne dies in New York City.

- On July 19, period drama *Mad Men* premieres on AMC. Set in the early 1960s, the show features period-correct set and costume design and helps to launch a national retro fascination with the clean, modern look of the 1960s.

- On August 3, American clothing retailer Aéropostale opens its first store in Canada, as it begins to expand into international markets.

- On August 19, style icons Mary-Kate and Ashley Olsen launch The Row, a high-end couture brand.

- In September, protesters from People for the Ethical Treatment of Animals (PETA), dressed in sexy outfits, hand out citations to people wearing fur who are attending New York Fashion Week events.

- In October, the first annual Portland, Oregon, fashion week showcases ecofriendly designs and products.

- In November, the Los Angeles–based clothing company American Apparel sparks controversy by running a billboard in Manhattan depicting a topless model bent against a wall, which critics and feminists claim is pornographic and incites violence against women.

- In December, public schools in Atlanta ban the wearing of "baggy oversize clothing."

2008

- In April, the cover of *Vogue*'s "Shape" issue, featuring basketball star LeBron James and Brazilian fashion model Gisele Bündchen, is criticized for allegedly playing on racial stereotypes.

- On May 13, U.S. District Judge Richard Smoak rules that a junior at Ponce De Leon High School in Florida was denied her First Amendment rights when she was prohibited from wearing gay-pride clothing.

- On August 7, anti-fur ads, sponsored by PETA, featuring Olympic swimmer Amanda Beard posing nude debut.

- In October, reports reveal that the Republican National Committee spent more than $150,000 on clothes for vice-presidential candidate Sarah Palin, including items purchased at Saks Fifth Avenue and Neiman Marcus.

- On October 30, Condé Nast publications announces it will cease publication of *Men's Vogue*.

- On December 22, Donna Karan announces that her fall 2009 clothing lines will not include fur, after protests from the organization PETA.

2009

- Chris Yura, a former model and football player, founds SustainU, a clothing line that uses only recycled materials and domestic labor to produce its products.

- In January, former competitive skater and fashion designer Vera Wang is inducted into the U.S. Figure Skating Hall of Fame for her costume designs.

- In January, First Lady Michelle Obama selects twenty-six-year-old Taiwanese American designer Jason Wu to make her gown for the presidential inaugural ball.

- On January 14, the foundation of the Freedom Tower, now known as the One World Trade Center, is completed.

- On March 11, during a possible high-speed automobile race on the streets of Newport Beach, California, TapouT brand cofounder Charles "Mask" Lewis dies in a crash. Along with partner Dan "Punkass" Caldwell, Lewis had built the company from a start-up in 1997 to yearly sales of more than $200 million.

- In June, Jennifer Lopez closes the Sweetface brand.

- In June, the new modernistic, "green" Cooper Union academic building, designed by Thom Mayne, opens in New York City.

- On June 17, clothing retailer Eddie Bauer files for Chapter 11 bankruptcy protection.

- On August 20, *Project Runway* moves from Bravo to the Lifetime Network.

- In November, *Glamour* magazine hosts a photo-shoot article on plus-size models. Several high-end fashion lines have begun to produce fashion for larger women.

Skinny Jeans

Photograph

By: Sean Murphy

Date: Undated

Source: Murphy, Sean. Getty Images.

INTRODUCTION

There was a time—back in 1873—when blue jeans were nothing more than workwear. Invented by tailor Jacob Davis and businessman Levi Strauss, waist overalls, as they were then called, were originally made of cotton "duck," a material that was strong but failed to soften up over time. The men chose instead to use denim, and to strengthen the pockets, they sewed metal rivets at the points of strain. Thus was born the basic Levi Strauss blue jeans.

Since that time, jeans have gone through a variety of transformations and a number of trends. One of those trends—the skinny jean—enjoyed a revival in the 2000s, though many teens of that generation believed they were the first to "discover" the style and turn it into a trend. In fact, skinny jeans have been around since the 1950s and 1960s. They were known by other names: drainpipes, stovepipes, pegs, cigarettes, slim-fit. And the fit and styles fluctuated, depending on the influence of movie stars and musicians, but one thing remained constant: skinny jeans were popular in subcultures. While boys and men of the 1950s primarily wore pants similar to uniforms, the counterculture of the day—greasers, bikers, musicians—wore skinny jeans. Rock and roll

PRIMARY SOURCE

Skinny jeans

SYNOPSIS: Skinny jeans became one of the hottest trends—for boys and girls—in the 2000s. © SEAN MURPHY/DIGITAL VISION/GETTY IMAGES.

idols like Elvis Presley and Jerry Lee Lewis wore them. Bad-boy actors like Marlon Brando and James Dean paired them with T-shirts for instant sex appeal and just a hint of danger.

Fast-forward to the 1970s punk rock subculture. While hippies were sporting bell-bottoms and flowing shirts reminiscent of Renaissance poets, punk rockers expressed their anti-authority attitudes by dressing in leather, T-shirts, and skinny jeans. Everything about them, from their music to their fashion sense, screamed rebel. In the 1980s, fashion continued to be impacted by films and the stars who made them. Blockbuster hit *Flashdance* gave America torn necklines that slid down the shoulder—and yes, Spandex. Manufacturers began making jeans with a percentage of Spandex mixed in with the cotton so that the skin-tight jeans could bend and remain comfortable. This fashion trend continued into the early 1990s, though again, skinnies were found primarily on the music scene. Influenced by hair bands like Poison and Guns N' Roses, musicians stuck to the fashion style that worked for them. By the end of the decade, boot-cut jeans had moved into the spotlight, and in urban areas, gangster-style blue jeans that were worn belted just below the buttocks were all the rage. Grunge music had risen to the forefront of the music culture, and suddenly the wrinkled, baggy style was in.

SIGNIFICANCE

Denim blue jeans continued to be the pants of choice particularly among America's youth in the 2000s. Boot cut and flares (welcome back, 1970s) were mainstream, but for the first time, so were skinny jeans. Fashion designers featured them on runways with models like Kate Moss wearing them long so that the bottoms scrunched up. As before, the music scene heavily influenced fashion, and as garage rock bands and indie rock became more central to the era's culture, so did the fashion styles the musicians wore.

In a new twist, skinny jeans were the choice of skateboarders and BMX bikers—two popular sport scenes—because they fit tight against the body yet allowed for easy movement. Scene kids and hipsters wore skinnies, and the fit was tighter than ever. A major change from previous generations was the fit: Skinny jeans were now made in a variety of styles ranging from low-rise to cropped to super skinny and everything in between. By the end of the 2000s, skinny jeans were available in nearly every color of the rainbow, and the decade closed with no sign of their popularity waning among males or females.

FURTHER RESOURCES
Web Sites

"Art of Denim: History of Skinny Jeans." *Over the Rainbow*, March 28, 2012. http://insiderainbow.com/art-of-denim-history-of-skinny-jeans/ (accessed on February 22, 2013).

Cocozza, Paula. "Skinny Jeans: The Fashion Trend hat Refuses to Die." *Guardian*, January 9, 2013. http://www.guardian.co.uk/fashion/2013/jan/09/skinny-jeans-fashion-trend-refuses-to-die (accessed on February 22, 2013).

Skinny Jeans. http://www.skinnyjeans.com/ (accessed on February 22, 2013).

Crocs

Photograph

By: Bernie Pearson

Date: 2002

Source: Pearson, Bernie. Alamy.

About the Company: Founded in 2002, Crocs became a billion-dollar company through sales of its 100 percent–recycled resin shoe. By 2012, the company had sold more than two hundred million pairs of shoes, which by that time had expanded to include not only the iconic clog but sneakers, sandals, fur-lined boots, and heels. Crocs developed a Crocs Cares program in 2007 and partnered with various relief organizations to donate and distribute shoes to impoverished populations both in the United States and abroad. By early 2013, Crocs had donated tens of thousands of shoes in more than forty countries.

INTRODUCTION

Once upon a time, three Boulder, Colorado, friends went sailing in the Caribbean. A foam clog one of them had bought in Canada gave them an idea for a business: Build a shoe made of odor-preventing

Crocs

SYNOPSIS: Introduced in 2002, the Croc became an instant sensation among people who valued utilitarianism and comfort over fashion. Adults and children alike clamored for the shoe to the extent that sales exceeded one billion dollars in 2011. © BERNIE PEARSON/ ALAMY.

material that is both comfortable and functional. Make it fun and affordable. And that is exactly what they did.

Lyndon "Duke" Hanson, Scott Seamans, and George Boedecker leased a warehouse in Florida and began selling their shoes to fellow sailing buffs. Word-of-mouth soon had other people who depend on their feet for work—doctors, restaurant staff, nurses—clamoring for the odd-looking clog with holes all over it.

The entrepreneurs needed a material that would be lightweight yet solid, comfortable, and odor-free. They hired scientists to develop a foam-like resin called Croslite that forms to the feet, and what began as a simple business soon became a worldwide phenomenon. In November 2002, the first style of Croc—the Beach—debuted at a boat show in Florida. The two hundred pairs on display sold out

immediately. Total sales in 2002 were $24,000; by 2007, sales exceeded $847 million.

SIGNIFICANCE

Everyone was wearing Crocs. President George W. Bush owned at least one pair; celebrities like George Clooney and Rihanna wore theirs in public. About two billion children around the world owned Crocs. The company came out with new styles, added more colors, bought out a home-based company that created bling to wear on the clog-sandal—the fashion world shuddered at the clunky, funky shoe, but no one bought Crocs in hopes of being fashionable. They bought them because they were fun, easy to wear, and comfortable both in and out of the water.

Crocs began touting its shoes as a healthy alternative to that forever-summer staple: the flip-flop.

Where the beloved flip-flop lacked a heel, thereby enabling the foot to roll inward and damage ligaments and tendons, Crocs had a slight heel as well as a strap to keep feet in place. U.S. Ergonomics tested the shoe in 2005 and recommended it as a healthy alternative footwear, and by 2009, the American Podiatric Medical Association endorsed it. Not all podiatrists agreed with the Crocs claim, but Crocs began making a line of "Rx" styles specifically aimed at consumers with circulation, back, or foot problems. One particular style—the Cloud Rx—was designed and manufactured specifically for diabetic wearers. The specialized line was also marketed at people who are on their feet all day, such as hospital workers.

Crocs received bad press in the mid-2000s as dozens of reports, from as far away as Japan, were filed of instances of children getting their Crocs-clad feet caught in escalators. Two of the major selling points of the shoes—their flexibility and grip—seemed to be the reason for foot entrapment on escalators. In some cases, children's feet were gashed; in others, toenails were ripped off. The most serious accidents involved completely mangled feet. Crocs responded to the allegations that their shoes were dangerous by pointing out that in many instances, accident reports included the phrase "rubber shoes," not particularly citing Crocs. But given that Crocs sold more of their shoes than the knock-off brands did altogether, it was only logical to assume that many of the culprit shoes involved were Crocs. Malls and subway systems began posting notices warning riders of the dangers of wearing Crocs on their equipment.

Crocs were blamed for another safety issue in the mid- to late-2000s. Hospitals around the world began banning Crocs after a hospital in Sweden suspected Crocs acted as isolators to electricity and caused medical equipment to malfunction. The ban caused outrage among hospital staff, many for whom Crocs were the footwear of choice based on comfort and ease of care (they are washable). Other hospitals banned the shoe for fear syringes and body fluids could fall through the holes on the top of the clog, putting staff at risk for infection. Crocs' Rx line addressed that issue, but the company refuted the static electricity accusation. A company press release read, "We know of no reason that Crocs would be any more susceptible to electricity than shoes such as sneakers and other types of footwear worn by medical professionals."

Such concerns did not seem to affect sales of Crocs. Like many companies, it went through a slump during the recession years of the late 2000s, and financial analysts and industry experts questioned whether Crocs were a flash in the pan, a company whose star burned so fast and so brilliantly that it burned itself out. These doubters were silenced when, in 2011, Crocs sales exceeded $1 billion.

PRIMARY SOURCE

CROCS

See primary source photograph.

FURTHER RESOURCES
Web Sites

Associated Press. "Crocs Clogs and Escalators May Be Risky Mix." *NBC News*, September 18, 2007. http://www.nbcnews.com/id/20837380/#.UR4T8Ge6WSo (accessed on February 22, 2013).

Gulli, Cathy. "The Shocking Truth About Crocs." *Macleans*, June 4, 2007. http://www.macleans.ca/science/health/article.jsp?content=20070604_106081_106081 (accessed on February 22, 2013).

Kelly, Tara. "Can Crocs Be More Than a One-Hit Wonder?" *Time*, October 9, 2009. http://www.time.com/time/business/article/0,8599,1928778,00.html (accessed on February 22, 2013).

Wellington, Elizabeth. "Fashion Attack." *Philly.com*, July 5, 2007. http://articles.philly.com/2007-07-05/news/24994606_1_crocs-soft-shoe-socks (accessed on February 22, 2013).

"Fashion Flip-flop: The Comfy Sandal Takes Upscale Turn"

Newspaper article

By: Jean Patteson

Date: May 27, 2002

Source: Patteson, Jean. "Fashion Flip-flop: The Comfy Sandal Takes Upscale Turn." *Sun Sentinel*, May 27, 2002. http://articles.sun-sentinel.com/2002-05-27/lifestyle/0205240586_1_flip-flops-thong-rubber (accessed on March 15, 2013).

About the Newspaper: In 1910, the *Fort Lauderdale Weekly Herald* debuted as the first newspaper in the area. It was soon followed by a local paper titled *Everglades Breeze*. The latter was renamed *Sentinel* in 1925, the same year the two papers were bought by an Ohio publisher and consolidated into one under the name *Daily News and Evening Sentinel.* After numerous owners and name changes, the paper finally became the *Sun Sentinel* and focused on reporting events and news related to South Florida. The newspaper has been nominated for the Pulitzer Prize numerous times, both for writing and for photography.

INTRODUCTION

Flip-flops, a term first coined in the 1960s, have been around in one form or another for about six thousand years. Archaeologists have even found hieroglyphs of them in Ancient Egyptian murals, and the simple shoe—constructed of papyrus and palm leaves—was the preference of royalty, as evidenced by the fact that a pair of primitive flip-flops was found in King Tutankhamen's tomb. Cross the sea to Japan, and the flip-flop prototype could be found on men and women alike. Traditional zori were made of rice straw and cloth, and American soldiers returning home from World War II brought them along as souvenirs. Soldiers serving during the Korean War again brought the flip-flop prototypes to America as well, where women were happy to wear them around the house.

Hong Kong–based entrepreneur John Cowie saw an opportunity and began manufacturing inexpensive rubber versions of the shoe in the 1940s, which became popular with the beach set in the 1950s and 1960s. As the American demand for zori-inspired flip-flops increased, so did production, which helped Japan get back on its feet after suffering through a wartime economy for years. The once-humble sandal now began showing up in five-and-dimes and other low-end retailers in bright colors that consumers wore with swim suits, shorts, and breezy summer dresses. And because they were priced so low, shoppers could purchase more than one pair. Inexpensive to make, manufacturers of flip-flops realized a large profit margin, and the flip-flop solidified its place in American culture.

Havaianas, a Brazilian company, quickly became the brand to buy after debuting a line of flip-flops in 1962 that were made of EVA- and PVC-free rubber. Unlike its cheaper competitors, Havaianas gives the soles of its shoes a textured pattern, a feature that has become the brand's signature. It is considered by industry experts to be the first upscale version of the flip-flop, and by 2010, the company was producing more than 150 million pairs annually.

SIGNIFICANCE

Flip-flops may have earned the honor of being the most comfortable shoe, but in 2005,

Northwestern University's national championship women's lacrosse team created a flip-flop controversy so newsworthy that it made headlines in *USA Today.* In a photograph of the team posing with President George W. Bush at the White House, four of the nine women standing in the front row were shown to be wearing flip-flops. Family members of the women were dismayed at the women's footwear choices, but during an appearance on NBC's *Today* show, player Aly Josephs defended the team. "Nobody was wearing old beach flip-flops." Teammate Kate Darmody agreed. "I tried to think of something that would go well with my outfit and at the same time not be that uncomfortable. But at the same time not disrespect the White House." Michael Wood, vice president at a marketing firm called Teen Research Unlimited shared his thoughts. "There used to be a day when people dressed up to ride on airplanes, or go to football games.... Is a trip to the White House special? You would hope that it would be ... special enough to get dressed up for." Other experts pointed out that Generation Y'ers such as these young lacrosse players have grown up in a climate where people in positions of power are not remote or necessarily deserving of reverence but have instead been humanized. It did not go unnoticed, either, that the president's daughter, Gen Y'er Jenna, wore black flip-flops to court to plead no contest to the charge of being a minor in possession of alcohol.

President Barack Obama made history when he was photographed on vacation in Hawaii in 2011 wearing flip-flops. The media had a field day, but Americans were reminded how odd Richard Nixon looked wearing wingtip shoes on the beach while he was president. The wearing of flip-flops did not seem out of line with Obama's image as a man of the people, and the frenzy soon passed.

Fashion trends aside, flip-flops may lead the way in comfort but prolonged use proved hazardous to foot health. Podiatrists reviled the shoe for its lack of arch and ankle support. While people with well-balanced feet could wear flip-flops without problems, the majority of Americans—78 percent, according to the National Foot Health Assessment of 2012—suffered from at least one foot problem. "If that foot is unbalanced or has a pronated or lower arch, that's a foot that is begging for support. It is begging for that person not to gain weight. It's begging for that person to keep their Achilles tendon stretched," foot and ankle surgeon David Levine told CBS News.

Levine was not alone in his concern for foot health. A study at Auburn University found that

Fashionable and multicolored flip-flops have become more common in the past couple decades. © MARTIN BARRAUD/TAXI/ GETTY IMAGES.

people who wore flip-flops tended to walk with their toes curled, which led to a shorter stride. This put excess force on the legs instead of sharing it with the feet. Left unchanged, such a shift led to injury and a permanent adjustment to one's gait that affected hips and ankles. The American Podiatric Medical Association recognized that not all flip-flops were created equal and published a list of acceptable brands and styles.

■ **PRIMARY SOURCE**

"FASHION FLIP-FLOP: THE COMFY SANDAL TAKES UPSCALE TURN"

SYNOPSIS: This article follows the transformation of the humble flip-flop into a high-fashion item.

Flip-flops are like dirty gym shoes, says Miami footwear designer Donald J. Pliner.

"They're not the nicest-looking things, but they're so easy to wear, so comfortable. You don't have to think about it. You just slip your feet into them and go," he says.

"Basically, people are lazy. No wonder flip-flops are popular."

The casual rubber slip-ons, so suited to beachside living, have always been a Florida favorite. But flip-flops have moved way beyond casual in recent seasons—particularly the women's styles. And they're no longer made just of rubber.

Now they come in leather, denim or rope, with heels or platform soles, and decorated with buckles, sequins or crystals.

The single identifying feature that remains unchanged is the double strap that comes up between the first and second toes. That thong is what separates flip-flops (no matter how embellished) from all other sandals.

Flip-flops are not the invention of American surf shops, although their association with those establishments might lead to that conclusion. Rather, they are copied from Japanese zori—sandals made with sponge-rubber soles and a thong between the first two toes.

It was back in the late 1990s that flip-flops made the leap from beach to city sidewalk, says Jen Mooney, fashion editor at *Footwear News*, a trade publication.

"In New York a few years ago, everyone started wearing cheap rubber flip-flops. They look great, they're easy to wear, they're really inexpensive—so why not? They became a huge trend overnight," she says.

Designers took note, and for a couple of seasons sent their models down the runway wearing flip-flops—even with ball gowns.

"They give an outfit a funky edge, a certain attitude, casual but chic," says Mooney. "Almost every company does them now."

That includes such style leaders as Ferragamo, Prada and Gucci, and trendy newcomers such as Kate Spade, Faryl Robin and Lisa Nadine. Even Chanel has put its famous double C's on flip-flops—which sell for a cool $405.

With such a high-priced stamp of approval, there's no doubt about it: The humble beach thong has morphed into a high-fashion phenomenon.

Pliner designs flip-flops with supportive orthotic footbeds, platform soles, 2-inch hourglass heels and straps of brightly colored suede or metallic leather.

They're beautiful and sensuous, he says. And they go with everything.

"Flip-flops are the easiest solution to summer footwear."

FURTHER RESOURCES
Books
DeMello, Margo. *Feet & Footwear: A Cultural Encyclopedia.* New York: Macmillan, 2009.

Web Sites
Associated Press. "NU's Lacrosse Team Sparks Flip-flop Flap at White House." *USA Today*, July 19, 2005. http://usatoday30.usatoday.com/news/nation/2005-07-19-flip-flops_x.htm (accessed on March 15, 2013).

Associated Press. "White House Footwear Fans Flip-flop Kerfuffle." *NBC News*, July 22, 2005. www.nbcnews.com/id/8670164/ns/us_news/t/white-house-footwear-fans-flip-flop-kerfuffle/#.UUDx0Fe9iSo (accessed on March 15, 2013).

Castillo, Michelle. "Lack of Arch Support in Flip-flops May Lead to Foot Problems, Experts Say." *CBS News*, July 18, 2012. www.cbsnews.com/8301-504763_162-57475215-10391704/lack-of-arch-support-in-flip-flops-may-lead-to-foot-problems-experts-say/ (accessed on March 15, 2013).

"Footwear, Flip Flops/Sandals." *American Podiatric Medical Association.* http://www.apma.org/learn/Company ProductsList.cfm (accessed on March 15, 2013).

Greve, Frank. "Flip-flops Have Place in History." *Free Republic*, April 30, 2006. www.freerepublic.com/focus/f-news/1624334/posts (accessed on March 15, 2013).

Hix, Lisa. "Flip-flops in the Office: Tragedy or Triumph?" *Collectors Weekly*, February 25, 2011. www.collectorsweekly.com/articles/flip-flops-in-the-office-tragedy-or-triumph/ (accessed on March 15, 2013).

"UGG Boots a Fashion Kick"

Newspaper article

By: Lorrie Grant

Date: December 10, 2003

Source: Grant, Lorrie. "UGG Boots a Fashion Kick." *USA Today*, December 10, 2003. www.usatoday.com/money/industries/retail/2003-12-10-ugg_x.htm (accessed on February 22, 2013).

About the Newspaper: *USA Today* launched in 1982 to much skepticism. With its abundant, colorful graphics and brief articles, detractors considered it gimmicky. Within one year, however, circulation had reached one million. By the 1990s, the newspaper had more than two million paid subscribers. An impressive statistic under any circumstance, this is made all the more remarkable by the fact that the 1990s was the beginning of the decline of print newspapers. By 2012, it had become the widest-circulated American newspaper in print.

INTRODUCTION

Fashion has never known rhyme or reason. Seemingly overnight, an accessory or item of apparel becomes the next "gotta have" for the season. This is exactly what happened with the boots known as Uggs.

Before the word *Ugg* was a brand name, its lowercase version was used to describe any boot made from sheepskin. Originally worn in Australia by ranchers in the nineteenth century, ugg boots were a staple of the wardrobe of the continent's working class. Australian surfer Brian Smith sewed his own uggs to keep warm and protect his feet from hot sand, and when he emigrated to California in 1978, he brought dozens of pairs along with him. Smith began selling his boots surfside and at trade shows, and soon he had created a demand far beyond what he could hand sew when he was not riding the waves. Having purchased the Ugg trademark in the meantime, Smith was ready to sell his design. It would be many years before he had a buyer.

Doug Otto, founder of Deckers, a parent company of several brands of apparel and outdoor gear including Teva, had had his eye on the ugg boot for years. An avid surfer, he knew firsthand the warmth of an ugg; the businessman side of him knew there was a market for such footwear and as yet, no product to fill it. Otto went public with Deckers in 1993 and approached his colleagues with the idea of buying out Smith, who by that time was manufacturing a slipper in addition to a boot. Smith was no businessman, however; he knew a great product but not how to sell or market it. Even so, sales had reached $18.3 million in 1995, and it was then that Deckers bought UGG.

Otto began shaping the UGG brand and targeting the affluent consumer. He expanded sales beyond California, added styles, and stopped selling UGG in discount retailers. Sales dropped significantly until 2000, when media mogul Oprah Winfrey featured a pair of UGG boots on her talk show and bought her staff 350 pairs. Sales jumped $3 million instantly, and celebrities all over began sporting the humble UGG. The talk-show maven would eventually include UGG a total of five times on her annual *Favorite Things* special.

SIGNIFICANCE

By 2010, UGG products counted for 87 percent of Deckers' revenue, a statistic that points to the boot's

The warm, comfortable, and popular UGG boots.
© FINNBARR WEBSTER/ALAMY.

staying power. Such a long run in the fickle world of fashion is nearly unheard of, and by the end of the first decade of the twenty-first century, the biggest challenge for Deckers was to find new ways to market and maintain its UGG customer base.

To that end, Deckers fought—and usually won—many trademark battles in court, some of them against mom-and-pop businesses based in Australia. Deckers did not want these smaller companies trading on the UGG reputation for quality and status, even if they were only selling on eBay or across the sea.

At the time the *USA Today* article was written, UGG was still on the upswing. It had secured its place in trendy fashion with the boot everyone knew on sight. Within a few years, the UGG brand would outsource its manufacturing to China and team up with fashion icon Jimmy Choo to broaden its product offering and customer base. The UGG had become a status symbol for children as well as adults, and even some of the most die-hard haters could not resist the clunky boot when Choo added his leopard print or bedazzling sequins.

"UGG BOOTS A FASHION KICK"

SYNOPSIS: A brief history of the UGG and an exploration into the mystery of its lasting appeal.

Just when it seemed the holiday shopping season would be devoid of a must-have item—the kind that builds shopping enthusiasm and drives retail traffic—along came UGG Australia boots for women....

Retailers didn't see it coming and are sold out nearly everywhere. There won't be more until February at the earliest—as late as June for the most popular styles and colors.

While the fleece-lined footwear has been around more than 25 years, UGGs increasingly have been seen this year on famous and fashion-forward feet—from Kate Hudson to Oprah Winfrey. Celebrity-driven trends often take off fast, leaving retailers scrambling to exploit them, but about the only place you'll find these $90-to-$185 boots is the gotta-have-it last resort: eBay (though bids for the popular pink have approached $400 in some cases).

There have been shoe rushes before: Timberland (TBL) boots—the yellow, waterproof, ankle-high variety—were for hikers and utility workers until rap artists started sporting them and rapping about them.

But the rush for UGGs is in a class of its own.

"I can't remember anything quite like this," says Michael Atmore, editorial director at *Footwear News*. And, he says, "Anything in limited supply has an extra appeal because you feel lucky to get your hands on it, which adds to the frenzy."

UGG Australia—a division of Goleta, Calif.-based Deckers Outdoor (DECK)—was named brand of the year by Atmore's trade publication for its retail success as well as for the boots' combination appeal as both a functional item and fashion trend.

Function gave them their start in the USA. They are a common style in Australia and known there generically as "Uggs." Aussie surfer Brian Smith began selling them under the UGG Australia brand on the West Coast in 1978. The boots' fleece lining breathes and wicks away heat and moisture to keep the feet dry and at body temperature. Surfers put them on to warm up from the water.

Now they are showing up on the feet of Sarah Jessica Parker, Hudson, Cameron Diaz and Sandra Bullock. Winfrey listed them among her favorite things, and ads showed up in *O* magazine. Magazine *InStyle* declared them in style.

While retailers seem to have been blindsided by the footwear's sudden fashion status, an industry expert stops short of calling that a retailing failure, saying it was impossible to anticipate the surge for such a shapeless (but oh so comfortable) boot for women.

"One photograph can 'metamorphosize' a brand from dead to great. The fashion industry today is following the celebrity, and when that happens, the retailer has no control or clue of what tomorrow's trend will be," says Marshal Cohen, co-president of researcher NPD Fashionworld.

Another expert says the boot's function helped fuel the trend. "No matter what the item is, if it has celebrity endorsement today, that's enough to move it," says David Wolfe at fashion consultant Doneger. "But Uggs are more than a fad because they are practical, and they are warm, and they are so funky."

Retailers big and small were caught flat-footed.

The baby pink and baby blue ones, $99 at Nordstrom, sold out in September. The chain is now taking orders for spring delivery.

Squires Family Clothing & Footwear in Katonah, N.Y., is logging 150 phone calls a day from all over but is turning down orders for future delivery from callers outside Westchester County.

Even half-priced knockoffs at teen girl retailer Delia's are gone (more to come in January), and Target's $25 tan version is out.

Nordstrom has carried the full line, which includes men's and women's boots and slippers, since 1990, but demand this year is through the roof.

"We had indications last spring that this fashion trend was starting and that led us to buy aggressively, but the kind of increases we're having is outstripping the aggressive buy," says Scott Meden, lead women's shoe buyer at Nordstrom.

He says everyone from the fashionista who has to have the latest look to a more mainstream customer is coming in for the boots. Hottest are the Ultra and Classic styles, as well as the Sundance, which is one of the main celebrity preferences.

"We're going to run out, and we're doing everything we can to get the bits available because someone has canceled an order," Meden adds. His next shipment is due in April. New orders on Nordstrom.com are not being promised until June.

In fact, the boots are so popular that Nordstrom had a traveling display Nov. 22 through Saturday of a collection of custom-trimmed UGGs with decoration by celebrities Lucy Liu, Britney Spears and Anjelica Huston. They are being auctioned to benefit the Michael J. Fox Foundation for Parkinson's Research and save-the-oceans effort Oceana.

Unfortunately for retailers, this out-of-nowhere hit is a double-edged sword. Sales momentum is being built by the buzz. But the lead time to make and deliver shoes—months longer than for apparel—means that demand can't be met anytime soon.

UGG Australia was taken aback, too.

"I was surprised that we sold out as early as we did. We usually sell out in November and December, but this craziness was so early," says UGG Australia President Connie Rishwain.

The boots are still made in Australia, source of all of the sheepskin, and in New Zealand and Asia. UGG now is booking orders for February, March and April delivery, when it usually doesn't handle the next year's orders until July or August.

"By the time we sold out of boots at the end of September, I couldn't get any more for Christmas," Rishwain says. "Now, we're selling them for spring, which is the first time that we're selling for first- and second-quarter" delivery.

FURTHER RESOURCES

Web Sites

Anderson, Christina. "Are Uggs Really That Bad?" *Huffington Post*, December 30, 2012. www.huffingtonpost.com/2012/12/30/uggs-boots-2012_n_2353613.html (accessed on February 23, 2013).

Conley, Lucas. "The Golden Fleece." *WSJ*, September 9, 2010. magazine.wsj.com/features/behind-the-brand/the-golden-fleece/ (accessed on February 23, 2013).

"The Love Begins, Southern California." *UGG Australia*. www.uggaustralia.com/the-story-of-ugg/story-ugg,default,pg.html (accessed on February 23, 2013).

"The New New York Skyline"

Newspaper article

By: Nicolai Ouroussoff

Date: September 5, 2004

Source: Ouroussoff, Nicolai. "The New New York Skyline." *New York Times*, September 5, 2004. www.nytimes.com/2004/09/05/arts/design/05OURO.html?scp=5&sq=Nicolai+Ouroussoff (accessed on March 17, 2013).

About the Publication: The *New York Times* was founded in 1851 as a concise, four-page summary of daily news items. News mogul Adolph S. Ochs acquired the paper in 1896, expanding its scope and size. By the turn of the twentieth century, the *New York Times* was the pre-eminent U.S. newspaper, acclaimed for its objective reporting of "All the News That's Fit to Print." In 1905, the popularity and importance of the paper was memorialized by the City of New York, which called its new public square "Times Square," in honor of the newspaper. The paper's investigative reporting on official and political affairs has always been a trademark, garnering the journalism staff more than one hundred Pulitzer Prizes for its coverage of wars and governments—most notably for its publication of the "Pentagon Papers," leaked documents attesting to the mishandling and uncertainty of the Vietnam War. The *New York Times* remains the nation's most prestigious and important newspaper, and continues to be owned and operated by descendants of Ochs.

INTRODUCTION

Since the city's early development, the skyline of New York City represented the diversity, enterprise, and ambition of the United States' cultural and commercial capital. As time wore on, an endless series of new buildings was added to the cityscape, concentrated in the neighborhoods of midtown and lower Manhattan. The decoupage of brick, glass, steel, and concrete formed a kaleidoscope of increasingly imposing and innovative structures representing every architectural style, school, and convention, from the stately Art Deco grandiloquence of the Empire State and Chrysler buildings to the sleek, abstract postmodernism of the United Nations headquarters and Sony Tower. New York was a celebrated focal point of architectural experimentation and display throughout most of the twentieth century.

By the onset of the 2000s decade, however, strict development restrictions, declining property values, waning economic centrality, and the recent expansion of other cities had left New York City relatively devoid of creative new buildings. Most major construction completed during the 1980s and 1990s was strictly functional in design, consisting of plain, utilitarian structures erected with the sole concern of housing business offices and unremarkable residential apartments. Acclaimed and experienced architects took work designing structures to be constructed in budding (or re-emerging) international hubs like Barcelona, Frankfurt, Shanghai, Hong Kong, Dubai, Singapore, and London, leaving New York City to fall behind the stylistic development of its contemporaries.

A panoramic view of the New York City skyline, August 9, 2002. © MELVIN LEVINE/TIME LIFE PICTURES/GETTY IMAGES.

After the September 11, 2001, terrorist attacks destroyed the World Trade Center's "Twin Towers," two of the tallest and most iconic buildings in New York, there was a renewed interest in the continued development of Manhattan. The first major project completed after September 11 was the Time Warner Center, a jutting, angular, mixed-use complex designed by David Childs. Completed in October 2003, the building consisted of two glass-covered, fifty-five-story residential towers connected by an atrium filled with retail shops, positioned desirably in front of Columbus Circle. Time Warner Center was followed in 2004 by Bloomberg Tower, an obtrusive, graduated tower that also stands fifty-five stories tall and was designed by Cesar Pelli & Associates. The building housed a number of luxury condominiums and retail outlets, as well as the headquarters for the Bloomberg media conglomerate.

In 2006, construction of the tessellated Hearst Tower was completed. The sharply geometric, steel-and-glass building stood forty-six stories tall and housed the Hearst Corporation headquarters, presiding prominently over Midtown. The New York Times building, designed by Renzo Piano and towering fifty-two stories above the West Side, was finished in 2007. Its chief tenants were newspaper offices, including the *New York Times* and the *Boston Globe*, among others. The $1 billion Bank of America Tower, the second-tallest building in New York City, was completed in 2009. It received praise for its environmentally friendly design and innovative, column-free interior office space.

SIGNIFICANCE

Although Manhattan saw increased development during the 2000s decade, concerns arose during the time that the New York City skyline would lose its iconic stature as it descended into miles of nondescript,

indistinct high-rises and skyscrapers. Such fears were none abated by the rapid growth of the boroughs surrounding Manhattan, particularly Queens and Brooklyn, from which large-scale structures had historically been restricted. As the predominant skyline of Manhattan blurred with those across the East River, some worried that Manhattan was being transformed into an inaccessible, elitist bastion of extreme wealth, from which all but the most affluent people and extraordinary businesses were excluded by real estate prices. Such a phenomenon was best demonstrated by Harlem—what had been a dilapidated, decaying neighborhood only decades earlier became one of the trendiest and most vibrant in New York City thanks to widespread urban renewal programs and community development.

Nonetheless, city officials approved increasingly ambitious and expensive projects, hoping that the city might reclaim its full majesty with the addition of recognizable, unique structures. Chief among these undertakings was One World Trade Center, the approbated replacement for the destroyed Twin Towers. The new structure, which began construction in 2006 and was scheduled for completion in 2013, was designed to stand 104 stories tall, towering above the rest of the New York skyline and covered in a reflective, octagonal-tapering facade. It was projected to stand as the tallest structure in the Western Hemisphere and the third-tallest building in the world.

PRIMARY SOURCE

"THE NEW NEW YORK SKYLINE"

SYNOPSIS: This article describes major architectural additions in New York City following the destruction of the World Trade Center "Twin Towers."

The skyline is back.

For the last three years, our collective focus has been on ground zero. Meanwhile, some of the world's most prominent architects have been quietly pressing ahead with plans that will remake the city's skyline on a level not seen since the World Trade Center was built in the 1970's. The most remarkable expression of that shift is a growing list of stunning residential towers designed by celebrated talents like Richard Meier, Santiago Calatrava, Christian Portzamparc and Enrique Norten. But it also includes visions of corporate gluttony: colossal mega-structures that are essentially hybrids of residential skyscrapers and suburban office parks. And it coincides with the slow but inevitable erosion of the boundaries that have defined the edges of the Manhattan skyline for a century.

For New Yorkers who still feel stirrings of nostalgia for the prewar city, such sweeping changes are apt to provoke mild hysteria. But cities derive their meaning from the influx of new ideas, and the flowering of the new skyline reaffirms that New York's creative energy has not yet been entirely spent.

A more legitimate reason for anxiety is that the majority of the towers built in New York in recent memory have been so dismal. Manhattan's skyline was once a monument to the relentless force of modernity, but for decades now the city's reputation as a center of architectural experimentation has been losing ground to London, Barcelona, Beijing, and Shanghai—cities whose civic leaders seem less frightened of the future. The best of the current crop of projects suggest an effort, however fitful, to break out of that creative malaise.

The roots of that malaise predate Sept. 11. They can be traced back to the late 1970's—to the fall of late Modernism and the subsequent rise of a view of history that often favored a mindless repetition of the past over confronting the anxieties of an uncertain future. What it mostly produced were buildings whose faux historical décor was used to cloak generic development formulas.

The low point may have come during the final year of Rudolph W. Giuliani's administration, when the Department of City Planning unveiled a proposal that would have forced most new building to conform to the scale of existing neighborhoods. Dubbed "uniform bulk," the proposal was conceived in response to projects like Donald Trump's 72-story residential high-rise at First Avenue between 47th and 48th Streets. The plan's intent was to force developers to respect the city's existing historical fabric. What it would have produced is a deadening uniformity, particularly in the skyline.

Fortunately, the plan was rejected after furious objections by local real estate developers. Meanwhile,

Mr. Trump's tower was built and the sky didn't fall. Designed by Costas Kondylis, the building's slender rectangular form could not be more benign. Its taut, tinted glass exterior plays off the blue-green glass of the United Nations Secretariat building and the repetitive grid of windows that decorate the twin 38-story towers of United Nations Plaza. Together, they form a graceful composition of transparent and reflective surfaces.

As it turns out, the future of the city's skyline may have as much to do with the increasingly cosmopolitan tastes of the city's affluent classes as with zoning issues. The first projects to capitalize on that trend were Richard Meier's Perry Street towers, completed in 2002. Mr. Meier's pristine glass-and-steel designs, which look out over the Hudson River esplanade, were ridiculed for construction problems and leaky roofs. But they also set a model of skyline architecture as a work of art, to be collected by the city's rich. A third tower a block away on Charles Street, which is currently under design, is a luxurious twist on the old Modernist notion of gesamt-kunstwerk—an environment conceived as a total work of art. In this version, Mr. Meier will design the interiors and furniture as well as the building itself.

That model has been pushed to its extreme with a new plan by the Spanish architect Santiago Calatrava for a building that would rise at 80 South Street, near the foot of the Brooklyn Bridge. The tower, which may be approved by the city planning department later this month, would be anchored by an 835-foot-tall concrete core, with 12 four-story cubes cantilevered off its sides, each of which would house a single 10,000-square-foot apartment. The design is reminiscent of a well-known proposal from the 1970's: the Japanese Metabolist towers, never built, in which entire housing blocks sprouted out of vertical columns like the branches of a tree. In Mr. Calatrava's hands, however, that vision is far more elegant. The apartments appear as crystalline glass town houses floating above the city. Their beauty stems as much from their aura of poetic isolation as from their structural purity.

But what's mind-boggling about the scheme are the economics that make it possible. Like Mr. Meier's Charles Street tower, each of Mr. Calatrava's apartments is conceived as a self-contained urban refuge, a $30,000,000 prestige object for the global elites. If they like, Mr. Calatrava will even custom design each of the apartments to suit them.

This notion—that architecture is a luxury to be consumed, like an Hermès bag or a private jet—may soon transform the skyline as much as the expansion of American corporate power did a generation ago. Several blocks west of the Calatrava tower, Frank Gehry is working on a luxury high-rise for the Ratner Development

Company, the same developer he is teamed with to design the proposed Nets stadium in Brooklyn.

Whatever the interiors are like, the public will most likely get the best view. Mr. Gehry's 75-story tower—which could not be shown here, because it is still in the earliest stages of design—is conceived as a series of undulating glass panels that hang down over the building's structural frame like flowing drapery. The curtain-like surfaces split apart at various points, then peel open at the top to create an almost classical crown. In its way, the tower is as elaborate as the nearby Woolworth Building, whose soaring neo-gothic stone facades set a standard of aesthetic excess and visual splendor nearly a century ago.

Even the building's location reflects the increasing value of such architectural status symbols. Historically, the reason the bulk of Manhattan's towers were concentrated near Wall Street and in Midtown was because the bedrock there is especially solid. Both Mr. Gehry's and Mr. Calatrava's towers would be built in an area just north of Wall Street, where the bedrock is less firm. To support them, engineers will have to drive pylons more than 150 feet into the earth, adding millions to construction costs.

Such considerations no longer seem to matter. The celebrated French architect Christian Portzamparc and Gary Handel, of New York, are currently completing a design for a luxury residential tower farther north at 28th Street and Lexington Avenue, overlooking Madison Square. The tower's faceted glass form will have the sharp edges of a cut diamond.

And in Harlem, similar projects are being used as tools for urban renewal. The Mexican architect Enrique Norten, for example, is now working on a proposal for an office, hotel and residential tower at 125th Street and Park Avenue. The structure's office space is a solid five-story container that rests on the more delicate glass-enclosed base of the two-story retail space, creating a palpable sense of compression. The hotel and residential tower rises another 38 stories above this base, overlooking the elevated tracks that run along Park Avenue.

The tower's design is meant to evoke the energy of the passing trains. Slender horizontal steel bands give shape to the facade's exterior, which bulges slightly at its center, as if the building were taking a deep breath of air. A series of thin, fin-like columns carry the tower down to the ground. Seen from Manhattan, the structure will conjure a fragment of Midtown that has somehow splintered off—an apt metaphor for a building that is being seen as a symbol of Harlem's rapid gentrification.

Taken as a whole, these projects represent a level of architectural creativity that the skyline hasn't seen in a generation. Despite their range of styles, their lightness suggests a more ephemeral city, a skyline whose delicacy would stand in sharp contrast to the muscular upward thrust of older skyscrapers. Just as important, they refuse to conform to the period styles of their neighbors. Instead, they offer a more sophisticated view of context, one that acknowledges that the city's beauty stems from the frictions that occur when competing visions of urbanity are allowed to coexist.

But they also connect to a tradition of social striving that may not have been so overt since the days of the robber barons. In their aesthetic purity, they speak of a world removed from the little miseries of everyday life. If they differ in spirit from the Vanderbilt mansions of the past, it is only in that they promise to be more conspicuous. They are paradises for aesthetes.

Not all the new high-rises are so delicately conceived. The new corporate paradise, by comparison, is more utilitarian, and brutal, in its expression. The demands of global corporations—what were once quaintly called multinationals—have created a new kind of superstructure, as imposing in its way as the commercial Superblocks that were one of the most maligned clichés of the 1970's. The enormous floor plates of these hulking new structures—some will stretch to the equivalent of two city blocks—are made to accommodate the need for increasingly open, free-flowing work spaces.

The most visible example is Bloomberg Media's new headquarters, designed by Cesar Pelli and currently under construction between 58th and 59th streets and Lexington and Third Avenues. Covering an entire city block, the building is shaped by the collision between the expanding scale of global corporations and the immense value of Manhattan air rights. Rising 85 feet, the base is a solid block of office space, with a womb-like oval atrium carved out of its core to allow public access to ground-floor retail shops. The offices will be vast, loft-like spaces, lined with hundreds of employees hunched over their computer screens. Designed for maximum efficiency, these spaces are the information age's answer to Ford's assembly line.

The building's exterior steps back as it rises, eventually forming a single residential tower along Lexington that will allow the developer to exploit the value of the air rights above the offices. But despite the public pretensions of its atrium, what the project resembles most is a suburban office park plunked down on the island of Manhattan. Its reflective glass envelope is the architectural equivalent of a generic wrapper.

By comparison, a similar proposal for Goldman Sachs at the northern edge of Battery Park City has the virtue of clarity. Designed by Harry Cobb of Pei Cobb Freed, the tower's 18-story trapezoidal base will include gargantuan 75,000-square-foot floor plates—significantly larger than

The Goldman Sachs headquarters in Battery Park in New York City. © TERESE KREUZER/ALAMY.

those on the Bloomberg building, and nearly twice the size of those in the former World Trade Center—to accommodate the hordes of Goldman Sachs employees. [A tower for office space] is set on top of this base, its curved facade overlooking the Hudson. But along West Street, the structure is a vast 55-story expanse of glass, its uniform surface interrupted only by a single vertical slot. . . .

This hybrid formula is now being adopted by the Department of City Planning, which sees it as a way to keep big corporations from fleeing for the suburbs. In its current zoning guidelines for the Hudson Yards, for example, the city agency is planning to propose the creation of two development corridors—one along 11th Avenue, the other extending west from Ninth Avenue—parts of which could accommodate structures with footprints between 40,000 and 80,000 square feet, or two entire city blocks. The plan, which will be presented to the city for certification later this month, will also create setbacks for residential towers to allow developers to take advantage of the valuable air rights.

The scale of such projects alone could significantly alter the city's character. Visually, they are reminiscent of the Metropolis imagined by the architectural renderer Hugh Ferriss at the end of the 1920's: a city of mountain-like

angular surfaces so dense and opaque it seems to be chiseled out of stone. At their most poetic, they evoke primordial caves illuminated by a few stray rays of light.

But the projects also reflect a deeper fear: that the urban pull of Manhattan is losing its ongoing battle with suburbia. That fear is rekindled whenever corporate executives threaten to escape to the safe, open spaces of Westchester County, Jersey City and Stamford, Conn. In recent years, it has been exacerbated by both the spiraling costs of Manhattan real estate and the insecurities caused by Sept. 11. The response is the creation of a kind architectural mongrel: a view of urbanity that is rooted in suburban notions of isolation and conformity.

The greatest threat to Manhattan's identity, however, may no longer be the suburbanization of the city but the urbanization of the outlying boroughs. And by far the most ambitious proposals for a new urban skyline today are in Queens. Together, they stretch along more than two miles of the East River waterfront, creating a dense ribbon of towers that could one day rival Manhattan's.

Of these, the design by the Miami-based Arquitectonica is the furthest along. Dubbed Queens West, the project would transform 22 acres of abandoned waterfront warehouses into a playful mix of high-rise and low-rise buildings, commercial development and waterfront parks. The project's residential towers, some of which would reach 45 stories, are lined up along the esplanade. The design would fit nicely in a department at Target: hip, affordable versions of high-concept buildings. The waterfront towers are a variety of heights and sizes, like boxes playfully stacked on top of each other. What's most disturbing about the project, in fact, is not its scale but its décor. In a bizarre effort to break down the composition's visual scale, the buildings are decorated with crisscrossing patterns of window mullions in a variety of colors: burgundy, blue, green and yellow. Together, the surfaces look like Scottish plaid.

Just to the south, the Los Angeles-based firm Morphosis is working on a less conventional housing development originally conceived as part of New York's bid for the 2012 Olympic games. It would include a series of low-rise housing complexes whose sinuous forms trace the water's edge and frame one side of a lush public park. Three rectangular towers anchor the complex's northern edge.

The development's snake-like forms vaguely evoke the work of the British group Archigram—the 1970's firm that once proposed the creation of machine-like "Walking Cities." But in urban planning terms, the proposal is a throwback to Le Corbusier's 1952 Unité d'Habitation in Marseille, a grid of apartments raised up on columns and set in a vast park—a rational antidote to the chaos and congestion of Manhattan. As such, the Morphosis project represents a kind of revenge by the great Swiss Modernist, who was famously tossed aside in the competition to design the United Nations headquarters nearly 50 years ago.

Morphosis' vision may soon be joined by Richard Rogers's design for Silvercup Studios at the foot of the 59th Street bridge, whose symmetrical high-tech towers are a more muscular take on similar themes. Mr. Rogers is best-known for his design of high-tech Modernist structures like Lloyd's Insurance Exchange in London and as the co-architect of the Pompidou Center in Paris. In Manhattan, he is currently working on a waterfront esplanade that would extend from the tip of Battery Park to the Manhattan Bridge.

It is only as one begins to consider these Queens developments as a single mass that their effect becomes clear. In obliterating the distinction between vertical and horizontal cities that once separated Manhattan from the outlying boroughs, the new skyline will shift the city's center. The East River will essentially be re-imagined as a spine, binding Manhattan to Brooklyn and Queens rather than defining Manhattan's outer limits.

Such a shift would mean the lowering of one of the city's most rigid psychological barriers. It is apt to raise other fears: the steady erosion of Manhattan's primacy as a center of cultural production, the fleeing of the city's creative class to Brooklyn, and the transformation of Manhattan into an enclave for the rich. But it could also reinvigorate the city's architecture. Instability is good for culture. And just as the Manhattan grid embodies the rational order of modernity, its skyline has always symbolized the urge to break free of those creative constraints. To regain its ascendancy, the city must summon that spirit of imaginative freedom once again.

FURTHER RESOURCES
Web Sites

"About." *The Shops at Columbus Circle: Time Warner Center.* www.theshopsatcolumbuscircle.com/about (accessed on March 17, 2013).

"Bank of America Tower at One Bryant Park." *Bank of America.* http://newsroom.bankofamerica.com/press-kit/bank-america-tower-one-bryant-park (accessed on March 17, 2013).

"Bloomberg Tower." *Emporis.* www.emporis.com/building/bloombergtower-newyorkcity-ny-usa (accessed on March 17, 2013).

"Hearst Tower." *Hearst Corporation.* www.hearst.com/real-estate/hearst-tower.php (accessed on March 17, 2013).

The New York Times Building. http://newyorktimesbuilding.com/ (accessed on March 17, 2013).

"World Trade Center." *The Port Authority of New York & New Jersey.* www.panynj.gov/wtcprogress/index.html (accessed on March 17, 2013).

"Metrosexuals: A Well-Groomed Market?"

Magazine article

By: Vivian Manning-Schaffel

Date: May 23, 2006

Source: Manning-Schaffel, Vivian. "Metrosexuals: A Well-Groomed Market?" *Bloomberg Businessweek*, May 23, 2006. www.businessweek.com/stories/2006-05-23/metrosexuals-a-well-groomed-market (accessed on February 28, 2013).

About the Magazine: What began as *BusinessWeek* in 1929 became *Bloomberg Businessweek* in 2009 when the magazine was purchased by Bloomberg, a multinational mass media corporation headquartered in New York City. Initially founded as a way to provide information and advice or opinions to the national business world, it became an aggressive magazine in the 1980s and 1990s with a focus on the economy and how it affected business. During that time, the magazine won numerous awards and added an international edition.

INTRODUCTION

After first using the term *metrosexual* in 1994 to no one's notice, journalist Mark Simpson used it a second time in a July 2002 *Salon* article to describe the fashion-conscious English soccer player David Beckham. Simpson's definition of metrosexual was as follows:

> The typical metrosexual is a young man with money to spend, living in or within easy reach of a metropolis—because that's where all the best shops, clubs, gyms and hairdressers are.... Particular professions, such as modeling, waiting tables, media, pop music and, nowadays, sport, seem to attract them but, truth be told, like male vanity products and herpes, they're pretty much everywhere.

Simpson continued to explain that while gay men provided the early prototype for metrosexuality in that they earnestly engaged in accessorizing their own idea of masculinity, the metrosexual of the 2000s was, for the most part, heterosexual. He was urban, primarily single, and dedicated to maintaining his physical appearance both in terms of fitness and fashion. The metrosexual—a combination of "metropolitan" and "sexual"—spent a great deal of money and time on things traditionally considered part of the female sphere: fashion and clothes, skincare, hygiene, haircare. He got manicures and pedicures, highlights and salon cuts. He used more hair product than his girlfriend and put great thought into making sure he was always well dressed, if not trendy. The metrosexual was in touch with his emotions and not ashamed to express them. In a society that developed its idea of masculinity on advertisements like the Marlboro Man, the metrosexual was the opposite of the tough, macho persona made famous by the American West.

The *Bloomberg Businessweek* article was published in 2006, around the same time that other articles about metrosexuality were appearing. Ironically, these articles were proclaiming the death of the metrosexual. One such article, published in June 2006 on ABC's *Good Morning America* site, quoted a 2005 global study of masculinity in which men revealed their uncertainty about their role in society. More than 70 percent accused advertising of being out of touch with men's reality. The debate became clear: Was the metrosexual representative of a truly natural shift in the cultural and societal expectation of what it means to be male, or was it the result of a major marketing campaign?

SIGNIFICANCE

As was obvious in the *Bloomberg Businessweek* article, marketing and advertising had a major impact on the mainstreaming of the metrosexual. According to Margaret C. Ervin, Ph.D, metrosexuality, in turn, impacted American culture. "Metrosexuality, often perceived as the queering of regular guys, continues to have an impact, whether or not the term itself is considered fashionable or current," she wrote in a contributing chapter to the 2011 book, *Performing American Masculinities: The 21st-Century Man in Popular Culture*. Ervin furthered her argument by pointing out that for many, the metrosexual was a threat to what they perceived as "real" masculinity. "The more reactionary responses there are to the metrosexual, the more this effect is realized. Attempts to legislate the demise of the metrosexual only serve as markers to locate it. Negation demonstrates presence."

And many did indeed attempt to refute the legitimacy of the metrosexual. Like the preppies of the 1980s—those men and women who sported Izod polo shirts tucked into Chinos and Sperry Topsiders on their sockless feet—metrosexuals became the fashion trendsetters that everyone loved to trash talk ... until athletes like New York Yankees legend Derek Jeter and Yankees hitter Alex Rodriguez joined the ranks. Jeter debuted and promoted his own fragrance collection for Avon in 2006 and, with a more subtle metrosexuality than soccer superstar Beckham, gave men—sports lovers, no less—permission to care about their appearance for appearance's sake. Popular television host Ryan Seacrest, with his highlighted hair and impeccable grooming habits, continued blazing the metrosexual path right into the next millennium. He was joined by Hollywood stars like Kanye West, Justin Timberlake, Tom Cruise, Brad Pitt, and Tyler Perry, and many others, proof the metro had gone mainstream.

The articles continued to publish, and people remained divided in their opinions of the metrosexual man. Was he more of a man because he gave his emotional life attention and was willing to challenge the traditional cultural norm of what it means to be masculine? Or was he less of a man because exfoliating, moussing, and waxing were behaviors only acceptable for women? A 2012 *Salon* article titled "Is the Metro Finally Dead?" reported that sociologist Erynn Masi de Casanova declared the death of the term certain, but the man who values grooming and fashion was alive and well and probably not going anywhere. Mark Simpson, considered the father of the metrosexual because he coined the term, admitted in *Salon*: "It might be said that metrosexuality represents a certain kind of liberation of the male, but I suspect it' another kind of enslavement, albeit a better-dressed variety."

PRIMARY SOURCE

"METROSEXUALS: A WELL-GROOMED MARKET?"

SYNOPSIS: Men's grooming and skincare products have become their own market segment as metrosexuality becomes more mainstream.

Since the advent of metrosexuality, companies have realized that they have a new market to capitalize on men who spend their money on grooming and appearance supplies. Walk through the aisles of any US drugstore, and you'll notice an abundance of male-targeted personal grooming products, such as anti-aging eye-creams, shower gels and formula facial cleansers, slowly monopolizing the shelves.

With so many brands clamoring for their slice of the pie, metrosexuals have out and out become their own market segment. And as sales figures roll in, there is clear evidence that the metrosexual market is indeed quite viable.

"With men becoming more involved with their grooming habits and the explosive growth in the men's segment (dollar volume +49% in 2005), we saw a huge opportunity to introduce the male consumer to a new proposition in skincare," says Carol J. Hamilton, president of the L'Oréal Paris division of L'Oréal USA, Inc., whose Men's Expert line was among the first to hit the mass market a few years ago.

According to L'Oréal Paris' 2005 annual report, men's skincare with its 11% growth in sales was L'Oréal Paris' fastest growing sector. And it's not just a US-based trend. There are numbers that quantify this as a global trend. The same report states only 4% of European men used a skincare product in 1990, compared to a whopping 20% in 2003.

Interestingly, younger men seem to be leading the charge, which points to a generational shift in thinking. In Europe, 24% of men under 30 use skincare products, compared with 20% of the population as a whole. In Japan, some 30% of men under 30 use a skincare product, and in South Korea the figure clocks in at over 80%.

The numbers do not lie. Younger men are clearly more interested in taking care of themselves than their

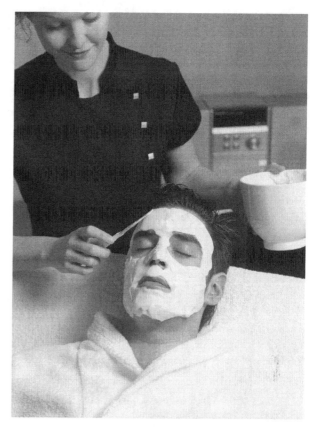

A woman applying a beauty mask to a man's face. Quality of skin care is one example of the concerns of a metrosexual. © PETER DAZELEY/GETTY IMAGES.

fathers or even their older brothers. But is it because metrosexuality has become more widely accepted by the masses or simply because of their generation's habits?

Edina Sultanik-Silver, owner of BrandPimps and Media Whores, a New York-based men's fashion public relations company, thinks metrosexual tendencies are a sign of the times.

"It's a generational thing. I think that Gen Y and millennial guys view all the creams and grooming preparations out there as OK and perfectly natural for them to use, rather than girly," says Sultanik-Silver. "The guys in these generations get their bodies waxed, work out, style their hair, go to tanning salons, etc., more than their predecessors. Possibly because they were raised on MTV, the Internet and reality shows, every minute of their lives is a photo-op, they always want to look like they're ready for their 15 minutes of fame, and don't think there's anything feminine about that."

So what liberated the inner metrosexual in these young men? Sultanik-Silver thinks it's the marriage between the media and consumerism, producing a sector that will continue to grow for some time.

"It (this trend) was mostly media driven, I believe, says Sultanik-Silver. "Everyone wants a piece of 'the next big thing.' Our popular culture is driven by image and consumerism right now. Word on the street was that men were interested in dressing up more, spending more on clothes, moisturizers, etc. Men's fashion and style were the hot buzz segment of the youth market and as a result, more brands began targeting young men as more retailers begin catering to them. To me, this signals the main-streamization of metrosexualism," says Sultanik-Silver. "And it's going to continue to grow."

As the success of Men's Expert bears testament, L'Oréal Paris has played an active role in the ongoing mainstreaming of metrosexuals. "In our first year, we brought a significant number of these 'men on the cusp' into the category and we will continue to do so," states Hamilton. "Our efforts, combined with other heavy activity in the category, will mean continued growth for many more years."

Although she agrees that the remaining stigma about men who are keen on grooming is dissolving rapidly, there is still a serious learning curve in regard to marketing to metrosexuals.

"Despite tremendous growth rates over the past several years, the men's treatment segment is still in its infancy," surmises Hamilton. "Today, less than 20% of men use a facial moisturizer. However, another 25% of men today say that they are interested in trying skincare treatments, but have not yet made the leap. On the whole, most men have moved away from any stigma associated with using what could be considered a more female product, but they are still not sure what to do and how to do it."

Young or old, metrosexuals apparently are here to stay. Eventually, the term "metrosexual" might even become dated. Then, metrosexuals simply would be known as men who enjoy their right to groom and shop for clothes.

FURTHER RESOURCES

Books

Flocker, Michael. *The Metrosexual Guide to Style: A Handbook for the Modern Man*. Boston: Da Capo Press, 2003.

Watson, Elwood and Marc E. Shaw. *Performing American Masculinities: The 21st-Century Man in Popular Culture* Bloomington: Indiana University Press, 2011.

Web Sites

"A Historical Perspective of BusinessWeek, Sold to Bloomberg." *Talking Biz News*, October 13, 2009. www.talkingbiznews.com/1/a-historical-perspective-of-businessweek-sold-to-bloomberg/ (accessed on February 28, 2013).

"Metrosexual Is Out, Macho Is In." *ABC Good Morning America*, June 19, 2006. http://abcnews.go.com/GMA/story?id=2092965&page=1 (accessed on February 28, 2013).

Simpson, Mark. "Meet the Metrosexual." *Salon*, July 22, 2002. www.salon.com/2002/07/22/metrosexual/ (accessed on February 28, 2013).

Simpson, Mark. "MetroDaddy Speaks!" *Salon*, January 5, 2004. www.salon.com/2004/01/05/metrosexual_ii/ (accessed on March 1, 2013).

"Hope"

Poster

By: Shepard Fairey

Date: 2008

Source: Fairey, Shepard. "Hope." AP Images.

About the Artist: Frank Shepard Fairey graduated from Rhode Island School of Design in 1992 with a Bachelors of Arts in illustration. His first art museum exhibition was held in 2009 at Boston's Institute of Contemporary Art, though he is most often described as a street artist. Fairey began his art career by screen printing and stenciling his own poster prints, which he would then hang throughout various urban areas using wheat paste (a mixture of vegetable starch and water). He has been arrested numerous times for his graffiti art and has a permanent criminal record as a result.

INTRODUCTION

In October 2007, former street artist Shepard Fairey had an informal discussion about U.S. presidential candidate Barack Obama with publicist Yosi Sergant. Fairey, who had a criminal record for illegally adorning buildings and walls with his art, knew he was a fringe artist whose name was synonymous with a sort of subculture in the art world, despite the fact that he was featured in legitimate art shows and exhibitions in Los Angeles. Although he had a desire to support Obama through his art, he admitted his reluctance in an interview with Ben Arnon of the *Huffington Post* in 2008. "An endorsement from someone like me might not actually be a welcome endorsement if it made Obama seem like the fringe, street-artist, radical types were his supporters. I really wanted to help and I didn't want to be that unwelcome endorsement or affiliation."

PRIMARY SOURCE

"Hope"

SYNOPSIS: Artist Shepard Fairey's poster became the iconic representation of Barack Obama's 2008 presidential campaign. © AP IMAGES/DAMIAN DOVARGANES.

Sergant encouraged Fairey to give the idea of creating a design for the Obama campaign more thought and even mentioned the idea to friends of his. One in particular, Hill Harper, knew Obama personally and mentioned Fairey's name to the presidential hopeful. Sergant took over managing the production of a design after getting permission for Fairey to put his creative energy to work. The artist found an Associated Press photo to use as a model for his image and set to work. In one day, he illustrated the image, and within twenty-four hours, the print was in production. A first run of seven hundred posters were screen printed in red, white, and blue, 350 of which were sold on the street and another 350 which Fairey hung up in strategic places around the city of Los Angeles. Unlike the poster that became known as "Hope," the first run included the word "Progress." While the campaign liked the poster, they told Sergant to push the "Hope" message, and so the rest were printed in the iconic way. Fairey also posted a printable version of the poster on his professional Web site, and the image immediately went viral. "It became very clear quickly that the demand for an image like that had not been supplied and that the Obama supporters were very hungry for it and also very motivated to spread it. ...there were a lot of people who were digging Obama but they didn't have any way to symbolically show their support." Fairey explained to Arnon.

Fairey began shipping the prints and posters nationwide and discovered that buyers were turning around and selling them for $2,000–$6,000 on the Internet. Sergant and Fairey also attended campaign rallies and handed out copies of the posters to attendees. Within weeks, the image was seen throughout the country and in the media. And while Sergant and Fairey were distributing the posters via more traditional channels such as online sales, much of the reason the image became a cultural phenomenon was because regular people—shopkeepers and teachers, municipal workers and grocery clerks—were motivated to get the message of hope out to the masses. It was a true grassroots movement, and it took on a life of its own.

SIGNIFICANCE

Soon the image could be found on stickers and apparel. Just as it was with distribution, so too was the proliferation of items featuring the "Hope" image a grassroots collaboration. For example, a clothing manufacturer called Upper Playground printed T-shirts and sweatshirts and donated them to be given out. The money they made from selling others went directly back into developing more shirts. Said Fairey, "When we did bus stop ads in Philadelphia, that was paid for with T-shirt money." Likewise, a friend of Fairey's and an Obama supporter was a sticker printer who sold sticker packs featuring the image. All money he made from the sales went back into producing more stickers. People who could afford to buy them, did. Those who could not were given them at no cost. And on and on it went.

In January 2009, the Smithsonian Institution acquired the poster for its National Portrait Gallery. Around that same time, a controversy arose over the photo Fairey used as the model for his print. Although he publicly denied it and even falsified documents meant to provide evidence that he used a different

photograph, Fairey eventually admitted that he used a 2006 file photo that had been taken by Associated Press photographer Mannie Garcia. Claiming his deceit as the worst thing he had ever done, Fairey settled in 2011 with the AP and agreed to pay $1.6 million for copyright infringement. In addition, he was required to share rights to all merchandise featuring the "Hope" image. For falsifying documents and contempt of court, the artist was sentenced in 2012 to a $25,000 fine, two years' probation, and three hundred hours of community service. Although the charge for contempt of court carried with it a potential six-month jail sentence, the judge in Fairey's case took into consideration the artist's considerable charity work performed over a period of years and chose not to send him to jail. "Punishment has been and will be in the form of public disgrace," said Magistrate judge Frank Maas.

Regardless of the copyright infringement controversy, the iconic "Hope" poster symbolizes grassroots effort at its best.

■ PRIMARY SOURCE

"HOPE"

See primary source photograph.

FURTHER RESOURCES
Books

Fairey, Shepard. *Obey: Supply & Demand: The Art of Shepard Fairey.* Berkeley, CA: Gingko Press, 2006.

Fairey, Shepard, and Jennifer Gross, eds. *Art for Obama: Designing Manifest Hope and the Campaign for Change.* New York: Abrams, 2009.

Gastman, Roger, and Caleb Neelon. *The History of American Graffiti.* New York: HarperCollins, 2011.

Library of Congress. *Presidential Campaign Posters: Two Hundred Years of Election Art.* Washington, DC: Library of Congress, 2012.

Web Sites

Arnon, Ben. "How the Obama 'Hope' Poster Reached a Tipping Point and Became a Cultural Phenomenon: An Interview with the Artist Shepard Fairey." *Huffington Post*, October 13, 2008. www.huffingtonpost.com/ben-arnon/how-the-obama-hope-poster_b_133874.html (accessed on February 23, 2013).

"Artists for Obama." *Barack Obama.* http://www.barackobama.com/art/portfolio#artists (accessed on February 23, 2013).

"The Best of the Obama Inaugural Merchandise." *Time.* www.time.com/time/specials/packages/completelist/ 0,29569,1872383,00.html (accessed on February 23, 2013).

Gearty, Robert. "Obama 'Hope' Poster Artist Dodges Jail Time, Socked with Community Service for Faking Records." *New York Daily News*, September 7, 2012. www.nydailynews.com/new-york/obama-hope-poster-artist-dodges-jail-time-socked-community-service-faking-records-article-1.1154233 (accessed on February 23, 2013).

Neumeister, Larry. "No Jail Time for Obama 'HOPE' Poster Artist in NY." *CNS News*, September 7, 2012. http://cnsnews.com/news/article/no-jail-time-obama-hope-poster-artist-ny (accessed on February 23, 2013).

"Influence of *SATC* Fashion & Culture"

Web site article

By: Kori Ellis

Date: May 20, 2008

Source: Ellis, Kori. "Influence of *SATC* Fashion & Culture." *She Knows*, May 20, 2008. http://www. sheknows.com/beauty-and-style/articles/803976/sex-and-the-city-fashion-as-character (accessed on March 8, 2013).

About the TV show's creator: Prior to creating the runaway hit television series *Sex and the City* in the 2000s, film producer Darren Starr created the 1990s hit series *Beverly Hills, 90210* and the primetime soap opera *Melrose Place*, also from the 1990s.

A movie poster from the 2010 film *Sex and the City 2*. Cast members are (left to right) Kristin Davis, Sarah Jessica Parker, Kim Cattrall, and Cynthia Nixon. © NEW LINE CINEMA/THE KOBAL COLLECTION/ART RESOURCE, NY

INTRODUCTION

In 1997, newspaper columnist Candace Bushnell published a collection of essays based on her real-life experiences—and those of her friends—under the title *Sex and the City*. The following year, film producer/ writer Darren Star debuted his HBO dramedy, *Sex and the City*, with a storyline based on Bushnell's book.

Set and filmed in New York City, the story revolves around four female friends who remain close despite the changing nature of their busy personal and professional lives.

Each episode was narrated by Carrie Bradshaw (Sarah Jessica Parker), a thirty-something columnist for a New York newspaper, and the action of each episode revolved around her train of thought while writing the column. Carrie was the main character of the series, which highlighted her many romantic entanglements and emotional breakdowns as well as those of her close friends Samantha Jones (Kim Cattrall), Charlotte York (Kristin Davis), and Miranda Hobbes (Cynthia Nixon). Each woman's continuing storyline was unique, yet they all shared three things: being female, a love of fashion, and living in Manhattan.

A scene from the 2008 film *Sex and the City*. Cast members displaying their fashion sense are (left to right) Kristin Davis, Sarah Jessica Parker, Cynthia Nixon, and Kim Cattrall. © NEW LINE CINEMA/THE KOBAL COLLECTION/CRAIG BLANKENHORN/ART RESOURCE, NY

It was the love of fashion that had the most significant impact on viewers. Other 1998 debuts included the sit-coms *Will & Grace* and *That '70s Show*, as well as the dramas *Dawson's Creek* and *Felicity*. Each series was phenomenally successful, but for reasons other than those that propelled the ratings of *Sex and the City*. Ellis's article highlights two key factors in the success of the show: each character's individuality and how fashion shaped the characters, so much so that *it* became a sort of fifth main character.

SIGNIFICANCE

Sex and the City influenced fashion in America from its first episode in 1998 through its 94th and final episode in 2004. The original series ran for six seasons and spawned two movies, *Sex and the City* (2008) and *Sex and the City 2* (2010). In 2013, another *SATC* spin-off, *The Carrie Diaries*, debuted, starring Anna Sophia Robb as a young Carrie Bradshaw. The show, which was set in 1984 and served as a prequel to *SATC*, received mixed reviews.

The success of *SATC* as a cultural influence can be credited to the show's stylist, Patricia Field. A native New Yorker herself, Field was responsible for making the wardrobe choices on the show that breathed life in fashion and made it come alive on screen. For her efforts, Field won four Costume Designers Guild Awards for Excellence in Costume Design for Television as well as a second Emmy for Outstanding Costumes for a Series.

Terri Pous, in an article for *Time* magazine, wrote, "The original series embodied fashion trends as much as it introduced them.... The show that streamed the latest from New York's sidewalks-cum-runways to anyone with a cable box and penchant for Cosmos from 1998–2004 started as a phenomenon and ended as a deep-running fold in turn-of-the-century culture." As Pous aptly pointed out, *SATC* was, at its core, a celebration of personal style, and it encouraged viewers to express their own self-identity through fashion choices. Each of the four main characters became known for their own kind of look, and fashion designers were ecstatic when one of them wore their brand because sales were guaranteed to skyrocket.

Narrator and protagonist Carrie Bradshaw horded shoes. Expensive shoes. Shoes that nearly every woman in America coveted. Her go-to brands were Jimmy Choo, Manolo Blahnik, and Uggs, and an entire episode was dedicated to shoes. Despite the obvious shallowness of such a plot, American women soon put their money where their mouths were and proudly became self-professed footwear fanatics, all because Carrie shamelessly spent more on shoes ($40,000) than she had on rent. As Paula Correri, accessory editor of a retail consultancy journal, explained, "Manolo Blahnik's success skyrocketed as a result of *Sex and the City*. The prices keep escalating, but women will starve themselves to score a pair of his shoes."

Upscale designer Fendi also benefitted from the popularity of *Sex and the City* when Carrie began carrying the Fendi handbag known as the Baguette. While the producers of the show were buying clothes and accessories from thrift stores in order to stay within budget, Fendi—then a relatively small designer in America—became the first vendor to loan them items. The kindness paid off as demand for the Baguette surpassed production, which was a win for Fendi, and it cemented Carrie's role as a trendsetter. Sarah Jessica Parker explained the phenomenon to the *Financial Times*: "Having the Fendi Baguette was a very big deal, and the gateway to everything else. It really opened the floodgates and influenced the storyline—especially Carrie's habit of spending more money on fashion than her home."

Accessories provided another outlet for personal expression for the *SATC* characters. Each had her own signature, and viewers tended to mimic the style of their favorite. Carrie was eclectic and wore gigantic flowers pinned to her dresses. She favored nameplate necklaces and bandanas, while the confident Samantha chose oversized brooches and zippy headscarves to reflect her larger-than-life attitude. Sensible Miranda wore suits for the most part and was rather minimalistic about her wardrobe, whereas classy Charlotte went for the feminine look with pearls and matching shoe-and-bag combinations.

By the time the series came to an end, it was nearly impossible to separate fashion from character. The seven-time Emmy-winning show also won eight Golden Globes, and *Entertainment Weekly* included it on its "best of" list. "A toast to the wonderful wardrobe from *Sex and the City*, which taught us that no flower is too big, no skirt too short, and no shoe too expensive."

PRIMARY SOURCE

INFLUENCE OF *SATC* FASHION & CULTURE

SYNOPSIS: This article asserts that the characters of the television show *Sex and the City* defined themselves through their fashion choices, which in turn impacted the American fashion scene.

Certainly the writing on "Sex and the City" was witty, smart and fun. However, the show utilized fashion as much as its great writing. Cynthia Nixon, who plays Miranda, told *People* magazine, "The clothes are like another character in the show. They help make it real."

Nothing could be more true. Each of the four main characters developed her own distinct style that we all grew to know and love.

SAMANTHA (KIM CATTRALL)

Everything that she does, says and wears exudes sex and confidence. Samantha is bold and outspoken in her opinions and her clothes. From bright red, skin-tight dresses to the latest designer bag to big hoop earrings, Samantha isn't afraid to make a statement.

CHARLOTTE (KRISTIN DAVIS)

Charlotte loves luxury, but she also thrives on order. She wouldn't be caught dead in shoes that don't match her bag. Her look is very preppy and proper with feminine and romantic touches.

MIRANDA (CYNTHIA NIXON)

Business-minded Miranda doesn't dress to flirt or attract men. Business suits by day and oversized T-shirts by night, Miranda is all about her corporate image at work and her comfort at home.

CARRIE (SARAH JESSICA PARKER)

Last but not least is Carrie Bradshaw. Carrie spends a bundle on high-end stilettos, such as Manolo Blahnik and Prada. However, she mixes designer pieces with quirky items that you might find at your local thrift shop. Her style is a little Bohemian, a little funk, a little feminine and a whole lot of fun.

From Charlotte's Badgley Mischka wedding dress when she married Harry to Carrie wearing bras to bed, and from Carrie's dozens upon dozens of stiletto heels to Samantha coveting the Hermes red "Birkin" bag, fashion was a focal point of every "Sex and the City" episode. Women around the world mimicked "Sex and the City" style.

For each show, the wardrobe designers produced more than 50 outfits. Designer Pat Fields revealed that the upcoming "Sex and the City" film required about 300 costume changes.

"We consider New York City and the fashion on the show interchangeably the fifth lady on the show, because they're as integral to the show in many respects as the women," said Sarah Jessica Parker.

When "Sex and the City: The Movie" hits theaters, there will undoubtedly be as much chatter about the fashions as there is about the plot.

FURTHER RESOURCES

Web Sites

Coster, Helen. "The Sex (and the City) Economy." *Forbes*, May 22, 2008. www.forbes.com/2008/05/22/twx-hbo-movies-biz-media-cz_hc_0522sexinc.html (accessed on March 8, 2013).

Long, Carola. "The First 'It' Bag." *Financial Times*, May 11, 2012. www.ft.com/cms/s/2/b0431e00-9601-11e1-a6a0-00144feab49a.html#axzz1upVUKhgm (accessed on March 8, 2013).

"Patricia Field: The Fashion Behind Sex and the City." *Female First*, May 7, 2008. www.femalefirst.co.uk/lifestyle-fashion/styletrends/satc-4867.html (accessed on March 8, 2013).

Pous, Terri. "Carrie's Return: Four Ways Sex and the City Changed Fashion." *Time*, January 14, 2013. http://style.time.com/2013/01/14/carries-return-four-ways-sex-and-the-city-changed-fashion/slide/how-sex-and-the-city-changed-fashion/ (accessed on March 8, 2013).

"Sex and the City." *HBO*. www.hbo.com/sex-and-the-city/index.html (accessed on March 8, 2013).

"Architects Return to Class as Green Design Advances"

Newspaper article

By: Robin Pogrebin

Date: August 19, 2009

Source: Pogrebin, Robin. "Architects Return to Class as Green Design Advances." *New York Times*, August 10, 2009. www.nytimes.com/2009/08/20/education/20BUILD.html?_r=0 (accessed on March 15, 2013).

About the Newspaper: The *New York Times* was founded in 1851 as a concise, four-page summary of daily news items. News mogul Adolph S. Ochs acquired the paper in 1896, expanding its scope and size. By the turn of the twentieth century, the *New York Times* was the preeminent U.S. newspaper, acclaimed for its objective reporting of "All the News That's Fit to Print." In 1905, the popularity and importance of the paper was memorialized by the City of New York, which called its new public square "Times Square" in honor of the journal. The paper's investigative reporting on official and political affairs has always been a trademark, garnering the journalism staff more than one hundred Pulitzer Prizes for its coverage of wars and governments—most notably for its publication of the "Pentagon Papers," leaked documents attesting to the mishandling and uncertainty of the Vietnam War. The *New York Times* remains the nation's most prestigious and important newspaper, and continues to be owned and operated by descendants of Ochs.

INTRODUCTION

Sustainable design was not a new concept in the late 2000s. The idea of environmentally aware design techniques in the broader effort to minimize the negative impact of buildings toward a more efficient and sustainable lifestyle had been around since the 1960s. The publication most representative of the sustainable living movement was the *Whole Earth Catalog*, which was published regularly between 1968 and 1972, and intermittently thereafter. It was a unique publication, with a philosophy that embraced, according to its Web site, "the rugged individualism and back-to-the-land movement of the Sixties counterculture" while striving to contribute to the nascent global community. Founded in 1968 by Stewart Brand, the catalog ignored politics and instead focused on the power of grassroots community. The function of the publication, according to Brand, was as an "evaluation and access device." Each item that appeared in the catalog was deemed to meet five criteria: useful as a tool; relevant to independent thought; high quality or low cost; not already common knowledge; and easily available by mail. It included photographs, diagrams, building plans, recipes, and other information relevant to living off the land and off the grid.

At a time when politics ruled the culture (prominent events were the Vietnam War; the assassinations of Martin Luther King Jr., John F. Kennedy, and Bobby Kennedy; civil rights demonstrations; and the Watergate scandal), the sustainable living movement seemed to many mainstream Americans to be little more than a hippie endeavor, a way to buck convention and drop out of society. That misperception continued through the decades even as the country began to witness the negative environmental impact of industry and urban development—and the resulting American lifestyles—that failed to take into account the health of an ever-more polluted planet.

In 1993, the World Congress of the International Union of Architects (UIA) adopted the Bill of Rights for the Planet. Developed by William McDonough Architects, the bill included principles of sustainable living as they relate to architecture and design. It encouraged the co-existence of humanity and nature, the elimination of the concept of waste, a reliance on natural energy flows, and an understanding of the limits of design, among other things. The UIA and the American Institute of Architects (AIA) further committed to work to change policies, regulations, and standards in both government and business so that sustainable design would become the norm rather than the exception. They agreed to educate the building industry as well as the public about the importance of a sustainable design, and—more difficult—bring existing buildings up to sustainable design standards.

Toward a similar end, the Interprofessional Council on Environmental Design (ICED) was a coalition of engineers, landscapers, and architects who vowed to work together to develop a vision statement so that all creators necessary for sustainable development were headed in the same direction. The statement stressed teamwork and recognized the endeavor as a multidisciplinary partnership.

Although there were experiments in sustainable living communities across the country in the early 2000s, it was not until later in the decade, as the public became more aware of global warming and its related natural resource/environmental issues, that sustainable architecture—also known as "green" architecture—became more than just fashionable or trendy. The *New York Times* article reports on the serious turn that the field of architecture has taken in terms of education of sustainable living and design.

SIGNIFICANCE

In an about-face of the trend toward "bigger is better" housing that dominated the 1990s and 2000s, America found itself not only embracing green architecture and design, with new construction using materials found locally and implementing more efficient and renewable systems for heating and cooling, but also doing more with less.

Small homes, once considered by many to be inferior, were suddenly in demand. Architect Sarah Susanka's best-selling book, *The Not So Big House*, celebrated small living quarters, as did Michelle Kodis's book, *Blueprint Small*. Susanka explained that at least a quarter of the population in America want

nothing to do with the suburbs and their large houses. "They have historically purchased houses in the inner ring of the suburbs. The reason they've done this is that the houses have character and the neighborhoods historically are strong." She claimed this segment of population—educated, progressive, with varying income levels—have "green" values.

Along with this shift to less square footage came a desire to have less impact, which is where green design and architecture came into play. As the decade came to a close, architecture graduates were able to earn master's degrees in Sustainability Management and know that they were likely to find steady work. An entirely underdeveloped sustainability industry grew rapidly as manufacturers of paints, glass, lighting, and other building materials introduced products made from sustainable resources. Technology and innovation had progressed enough that consumers no longer had to choose between affordability and sustainability.

PRIMARY SOURCE

"ARCHITECTS RETURN TO CLASS AS GREEN DESIGN ADVANCES"

SYNOPSIS: This article explains the new continuing education requirements regarding sustainable design for architects.

It seems like only yesterday that environmentally conscious building practices began making their way into the architecture profession.

How times have changed.

This year, the American Institute of Architects implemented a policy requiring all members to take four hours of continuing education courses in sustainable design every year.

The requirement, which extends through 2012, represents a response to a rapidly changing field and a recognition that architects must continue to refresh their knowledge of sustainable construction methods and building materials.

"This should be part of what all architects ought to know about," said Fredric M. Bell, the executive director of the New York chapter of the American Institute of Architects. "Education doesn't stop at architecture school. How do you ensure people stay abreast of changes in the profession?"

On its Web site, the A.I.A. explains the thinking behind the new continuing education requirement. "The issue of climate change and the impact of buildings on carbon emissions created a new expectation among clients and the public to look to the expertise of architects for solutions

Engineers install solar paneling on a roof, which will assist in using sunlight to heat the building. © SIMON BATTENSBY/
PHOTOGRAPHER'S CHOICE RF/GETTY IMAGES.

that can help them leave a greener footprint," it says. "The A.I.A. is responding to this growing demand for our members to assume greater leadership in addressing the challenges facing our planet."

The curriculum includes courses as diverse as "Ground Source Heating & Cooling for Commercial & Residential Properties," "How to Install—Successfully— New Wood Windows in Traditional Settings" and "Factory Preblended Mortar for Masonry Concrete."

"The technical design skills needed have increased substantially," said Michael Strogoff, the advisory group chair of the A.I.A.'s Practice Management Knowledge Community, which identifies and develops information on the business of architecture for use by the profession. "Bioclimatic design, energy usage, the sheer volume of sustainable materials and construction techniques require really focused learning."

Courses are offered at the A.I.A.'s national, regional and state conventions, where participants pay a

registration fee, and each local A.I.A. chapter holds sessions, some free and others costing up to $35 each. There are also private, registered providers that set their own fees, which vary widely. Licensed architects learn about subjects like building form, or how the shape of a building responds to the environment; energy modeling, including how much energy it takes to operate a building and ways to reduce the carbon footprint; how to reduce heat gain from sunlight; the most energy-efficient ways to position buildings relative to the sun, wind and other elements; ways to bring in natural light and reducing electricity consumption; and the preservation and reuse of existing buildings.

Courses are occasionally taught by building profes- sionals outside the architecture profession, like mechani- cal engineers, electrical engineers and landscaping experts. "Architects need to understand how the entire building comes together," Mr. Strogoff said.

This kind of expertise is now being applied to every aspect of design and construction, experts say, from how materials are transported to and disposed of at a work site, to the tools and machines used, to consideration of how a building will perform over the next half-century.

"How do we build buildings we can learn from so we can design higher-performance buildings?" Mr. Strogoff asked.

Whereas architects typically walk away from their projects after they are completed—perhaps visiting occasionally—now there is more emphasis on following the life of a building after it is occupied, studying how tenants use the structure and how its sustainable aspects hold up over time.

"Architects have been pushing for this, and now we have a receptive economy and a receptive clientele," Mr. Strogoff said.

While sustainable design used to come at a premium, costs are coming down as environmentally friendly materials become more common. In addition, people are increasingly willing to pay more to live and work in a green building.

"Private developers, leasing agents, they're beginning to understand that a highly sustainable building is good business and could be used to attract tenants," Mr. Strogoff said.

The mandatory A.I.A. credits are part of an 18-hour annual requirement that includes courses in health, safety and welfare. "Architects need to think holistically about water systems and air quality," Mr. Bell said. The continuing education courses are part of a growing national awareness about the importance of sustainable building. Indeed, there is a kind of informal continuing education going on across the architecture field, outside the boundaries of the professional requirements.

In April, the Center for Architecture in New York hosted a panel called "Safeguarding History and the Environment: Commonalities and Conflicts between Preservation and Sustainability."

"We have a lot to learn from historic buildings," said Chris Benedict, a sustainability architect and Pratt Institute faculty member who was part of the panel. "On the other hand, as we move forward, I think we all agree we need to be taking some things into consideration," particularly heating and cooling systems.

FURTHER RESOURCES
Books

Architecture for Humanity. *Design Like You Give a Damn [2]: Building Change from the Ground Up*. New York: Abrams, 2012.

Fairs, Marcus. *Green Design: Creative Sustainable Designs for the Twenty-First Century*. London: Carlton Books, 2009.

Web Sites

McDonough, William. "The Hannover Principles." *University of Virginia*. http://repo-nt.tcc.virginia.edu/classes/tcc315/Resources/ALM/Environment/hannover.html (accessed on March 15, 2013).

Solomon, Christopher. "For Many Homeowners, Less Is So Much More." *MSN Real Estate*. http://realestate.msn.com/article.aspx?cp-documentid=13107878 (accessed on March 15, 2013).

Whole Earth Catalog. http://www.wholeearth.com/back-issues.php (accessed on March 15, 2013).

<table>
<tr><td>5</td><td># Government and Politics</td></tr>
</table>

Chronology

Important Events in Government and Politics, 2000–2009

2000

- On April 22, Elián González, the young survivor of a tragic attempt to emigrate from Cuba to the United States in November 1999, is taken from his late mother's family in Miami. He is returned to Cuba to live with his father on June 28. The controversial decision to return González sparks tensions between Cuban immigrants and the federal government.

- On October 12, Al Qaeda terrorists attack the USS *Cole* at port in Yemen, killing seventeen U.S. sailors.

- On November 7, in the presidential election between the Democratic nominee, Vice President Al Gore, and his Republican opponent, Texas governor George W. Bush, the popular vote goes to Gore, but the electoral college tally is too close to call.

- On November 9, with the incomplete count giving Bush a lead of fewer than two thousand votes in Florida, a mandatory recount is ordered.

- On December 12, the U.S. Supreme Court decides in favor of Bush, overturning the Florida Supreme Court's decision to continue the recount of disputed ballots in Florida.

- On December 13, Gore concedes the election to Bush.

2001

- On January 20, Bush is inaugurated as the forty-third president of the United States.

- On May 26, Congress passes a major tax-relief bill in favor of large corporations.

- On September 11, terrorists hijack four American airliners. Both towers of the World Trade Center and the Pentagon are hit, and the fourth plane crashes in a field south of Pittsburgh, Pennsylvania.

- In mid-September through November, for several weeks anthrax spores are mailed to media centers in Florida and New York and congressional offices in Washington, D.C. Five people die as a result of the attacks. After a long and exhaustive investigation, the Federal Bureau of Investigation (FBI) traces the attacks to Dr. Bruce Edwards Ivins, a former biodefense scientist for the federal government, who kills himself in 2008 before charges can be filed.

- On September 20, Bush outlines his plan to confront worldwide terrorism.

- On October 7, U.S. and British forces begin air strikes (Operation Enduring Freedom) in Afghanistan. Hours after U.S. forces strike, Osama bin Laden releases a video praising the terrorist attacks on September 11, though he does not take credit for them.

- On October 26, Bush signs the Uniting and Strengthening America by Providing Appropriate Tools Required to Intercept and Obstruct Terrorism Act (USA PATRIOT Act), commonly known as the Patriot Act, into law, which expands the ability of law enforcement agencies to surveil private communication.

- On November 13, Bush signs an executive order authorizing military tribunals for terror suspects.

- On November 25, the first American casualty during hostilities in Operation Enduring Freedom is Central Intelligence Agency (CIA) agent John Micheal Spann, killed in a Taliban prisoner uprising in Afghanistan. American John Walker Lindh is among the prisoners.

- On December 2, the giant energy corporation Enron files for Chapter 11 bankruptcy, the largest filing in U.S. history.

- On December 9, U.S. forces capture Kandahar, a symbol of Taliban power.

- On December 18, Congress passes No Child Left Behind, Bush's education proposal to develop standardized tests to chart student development in all grades. Bush signs the act into law on January 8, 2002.

- On December 22, British citizen Richard Reid attempts to ignite a bomb packed in his shoes on board a flight from Paris, France, to Miami, Florida. The smell of a burning match alerts passengers and flight personnel, and the plane is diverted to Boston where Reid is arrested. Labeled the "Shoebomber," Reid admits to being a member of al Qaeda.

- On December 30, at Ground Zero, site of the fallen World Trade Center towers, a viewing platform opens for the public. Tickets are issued for crowd control.

2002

- On January 11, the first twenty detainees arrive at the detainment facility established on the U.S. Naval Base in Guantanamo Bay, Cuba. Labeled "enemy combatants" by Defense Secretary Donald Rumsfeld, these prisoners have no rights under the Geneva Convention.

- On January 29, Bush labels Iran, North Korea, and Iraq an "axis of evil" in his State of the Union address.

- On February 21, a video of the beheading of *Wall Street Journal* reporter Daniel Pearl, who had traveled to Pakistan to investigate the links between "Shoebomber" Richard Reid and al Qaeda, is released to the media.

- On June 1, in a speech at West Point, Bush clarifies the Bush Doctrine, his administration's case for preemptive war against terrorists and those countries that harbor them.

- On June 13, the United States withdraws from the thirty-year-old Anti-Ballistic Missile Treaty with Russia.

- On July 30, Bush signs corporate reform law creating a federal accounting board.

- On October 16, the Iraq War Resolution is passed, granting the Bush administration authorization to use military force in Iraq if diplomatic efforts fail.

- On November 5, in the midterm elections, Republicans win the Senate and expand their majority in the House.

- On November 25, the Department of Homeland Security is established. Pennsylvania governor Tom Ridge is tapped as the agency's first secretary.

- On December 5, at longtime senator Strom Thurmond's one-hundredth birthday celebration, Republican Senate majority leader Trent Lott observes that his state of Mississippi had proudly backed Thurmond's 1948 bid for the presidency. Running as a nominee of the States' Rights Party, Thurmond of South Carolina and a majority of southern congressmen had left the Democratic

Party, pledging to maintain segregation. Lott later apologizes for the insensitive nature of his remarks.

2003

- On February 5, Secretary of State Colin Powell addresses the United Nations to plead the U.S. case for an invasion in Iraq. Powell insists that evidence confirms biological and chemical weapons in Iraq.

- On March 20, the invasion of Iraq begins with the bombing of Baghdad's planning ministry.

- On April 1, Private First Class Jessica Lynch is rescued by U.S. Special Forces from a hospital in Iraq. Members of the Iraqi military had taken Lynch after nine of her fellow soldiers were killed in an ambush. Her rescue is videotaped by a military cameraman and edited footage is released to the media, portraying Lynch as a heroic prisoner of war. However, Lynch later testifies that she had not fought back when captured and accused the Pentagon of fabricating a story for war propaganda.

- On April 12, Congress approves $79 billion for military spending in Iraq, Homeland Security costs, and to provide aid to allies in the war on terrorism.

- On April 14, the Pentagon declares victory in Iraq.

- On May 1, Bush holds a press conference on the USS *Abraham Lincoln*, declaring an end to major military operations in Iraq. He stands before a banner that reads "Mission Accomplished." As violence escalates in Iraq, Bush is criticized for declaring the end to what could be a much longer war. In 2009 the president admits that the banner was a "mistake."

- On May 28, Bush signs a $350 billion tax cut, the third largest in American history.

- On June 2, in a three-to-two vote along political party lines, Republican commissioners of the Federal Communications Commission remove many restrictions that limit ownership of media within a local area, allowing for increased corporate media consolidation.

- On July 3, responding to a reporter's questions about increasing U.S. casualties in Iraq, Bush says, "There are some who feel like—that the conditions are such that they can attack us there. My answer is, bring 'em on. We've got the force necessary to deal with the security situation." Critics call the comments irresponsible.

- On July 14, in his *Washington Post* column, Robert Novak exposes Valerie Plame as an undercover CIA operative. The scandal surrounding the leak of

Plame's identity to Novak reaches the office of Vice President Dick Cheney.

- On October 7, former action-movie star Arnold Schwarzenegger is elected governor of California after Gray Davis is recalled.

- On November 5, Bush signs the Partial-Birth Abortion Ban Act.

- On December 8, Bush signs the Medicare Modernization bill into law, adding prescription benefits to the program, allowing for billions of dollars in subsidies to health-care and insurance providers and opening up competition from private plans.

- On December 14, after months of eluding U.S. troops, Saddam Hussein is discovered in a bunker on a farm near the Iraqi city of Tikrit.

2004

- On January 19, the presumed Democratic front-runner for the presidential nomination, Vermont governor Howard Dean, loses the Iowa primary, finishing third behind Massachusetts senator John Kerry and North Carolina senator John Edwards. During his concession speech, Dean screams loudly, delivering a passionate plea to his supporters. His flushed face and zeal make him a target for political pundits who criticize his speech as being too emotional. His campaign never recovers.

- On March 31, a crowd of Iraqis chanting anti-American slogans drag the burnt and mutilated bodies of four contractors employed by the U.S.-led coalition through the streets of Al Fallujah.

- On April 1, Bush signs the Unborn Victims of Violence bill into law. The law recognizes an unborn child, in any state of development, as a legal victim if injured or killed.

- On April 22, Patrick Daniel "Pat" Tillman, football star and Army Ranger, is killed in combat in Afghanistan. His death becomes an embarrassing scandal for the U.S. Army when it is revealed that military officials covered up his death by friendly fire in order to avoid bad publicity. He is posthumously awarded the Silver Star citation for valor by Lieutenant General Stanley McChrystal.

- In April–May, *New Yorker* journalist Seymour M. Hersh publishes articles revealing the Abu Ghraib prisoner-abuse scandal. Seventeen soldiers in Iraq are removed from duty for mistreating Iraqi prisoners after photographs of sexual, physical, and emotional abuse emerge.

- On June 5, former president Ronald Reagan dies at his home in Bel Air, California, at the age of ninety-three.

- On July 9, a Senate panel criticizes U.S. intelligence efforts preceding the war in Iraq.

- On July 22, the 9/11 Commission Report, formally the *Final Report of the National Commission on Terrorist Attacks upon the United States*, is released. The report, a nationwide best seller, is the conclusion of a much-publicized and politicized investigation of the attacks.

- On August 12, New Jersey governor Jim McGreevey declares that he is gay and has had an extramarital affair, and announces he will resign from office on November 15.

- On November 3, Bush is reelected to the presidency.

2005

- On January 20, Bush is sworn in for his second term as president.

- On February 2, in his State of the Union address, Bush calls for changes in the Social Security system, which he claims is headed for bankruptcy. Bush suggests that employees would benefit from private accounts that could be invested in the stock market.

- On March 17, Congress holds hearings on steroid use in baseball, hoping to prevent abuse and encourage more-stringent testing policies. Prominent players, including Jose Canseco and Mark McGwire, provide revealing testimony that suggests widespread abuse.

- On March 31, after a lengthy court battle and a passionate political debate, Terri Schiavo dies in hospice care at the age of forty-one. Schiavo became the center of national media attention when her husband successfully petitioned to have her feeding tube removed. Her parents appealed the decision and attracted the support of prominent politicians. However, when the federal appeals were exhausted, Schiavo's feeding tube was removed and she died of dehydration.

- On July 7, in a series of coordinated suicide bombings, terrorists affiliated with al Qaeda attack London's transit system, killing fifty-two civilians and wounding seven hundred. The bombers claim to be reacting to Britain's involvement in the U.S.-led war against Iraq.

- On July 28, the House narrowly passes the Central America Free Trade Agreement.

- On August 29, Hurricane Katrina strikes New Orleans. The storm and its aftermath devastates coastal regions in Louisiana, Mississippi, Alabama, and the Panhandle of Florida, killing 1,833 people and displacing hundreds of thousands. The Bush administration is severely criticized for perceived tardiness and ineptitude in responding to the catastrophe.

- On September 3, Chief Justice William Hubbs Rehnquist dies after serving on the Supreme Court for thirty-three years.

- On September 28, a Texas grand jury indicts Republican House majority leader Tom DeLay on charges of criminal conspiracy relating to the scandal associated with powerful Washington lobbyist Jack Abramoff. DeLay announces his resignation from Congress on April 4, 2006.

- On October 27, the Bush administration pulls back the nomination of Harriet Miers, White House legal counsel, to the vacant seat on the Supreme Court.

- On October 29, John Glover Roberts Jr. becomes the seventeenth chief justice of the U.S. Supreme Court.

2006

- On January 3, Abramoff pleads guilty to felony charges of corruption. A broad investigation reveals that he had defrauded his Native American clients with the help of several White House officials. He is also found guilty of trading expensive gifts, including trips and meals, for political favors. The scale of Abramoff's corruption rallies reformers in Congress against the influence of lobbyists in Washington, D.C.

- On May 3, Zacarias Moussaoui is sentenced to life in prison by a federal jury for conspiring to kill U.S. citizens in the September 11 terrorist attacks. He denies involvement, claiming that he belonged to a separate al Qaeda cell.

- On May 25, Kenneth Lay and Jeffrey Skilling, former Enron executives, are convicted of securities and wire fraud.

- On May 31, former FBI associate director W. Mark Felt Sr. admits that he is "Deep Throat," the key informant to *Washington Post* reporters Bob Woodward and Carl Bernstein, whose investigative journalism uncovered the Watergate scandal.

- On June 29, in a five-to-four decision, the Supreme Court rejects military tribunals for terrorism suspects, a significant component of Bush's war on terrorism. The ruling finds the tribunals to be in conflict with federal law and the rules of war established by the Geneva Convention.

- On July 19, Bush vetoes an embryonic stem-cell research bill.

- On November 7, in a major political shift, elections allow Democrats take the House of Representatives, the Senate, and a majority of governorships.

- On December 26, Gerald R. Ford, the thirty-eighth president of the United States, dies.

- On December 30, Saddam Hussein, after a much publicized 2004 trial, a conviction of crimes against humanity, and a death sentence, is hanged.

2007

- On January 4, Democratic representative Nancy Pelosi of California is elected the first female Speaker of the House.

- On January 10, Bush announces an escalation of troop deployment in Iraq. Later known as the "surge," the increase of military personnel becomes a hotly contested foreign-policy decision for the White House. By 2008 many pundits agree that the surge, along with growing support from Iraqis, had decreased violence.

- On January 20, New York Democratic senator Hillary Clinton announces her 2008 presidential candidacy, stating, "I'm in, and I'm in to win."

- On February 10, Illinois Democratic senator Barack Obama formally announces his 2008 presidential candidacy.

- On March 6, Vice President Cheney's former chief of staff Irving Lewis "Scooter" Libby is convicted of perjury and obstruction of justice in the Valerie Plame case. He is sentenced to thirty months in jail. Bush later commutes Libby's sentence.

- On April 18, in a five-to-four decision, the Supreme Court upholds a partial-birth abortion ban.

- On May 9, Bush signs the National Security and Homeland Security Presidential Directive that gives the president the power to direct all three branches of the government in case of a catastrophic disaster.

- On August 27, U.S. attorney general Alberto R. Gonzales resigns amid accusations of perjury before Congress, related to his testimony about the improper or illegal use of the Patriot Act to expose information about citizens.

- On August 31, a key advisor and close confidant of Bush, Karl Rove, resigns from his post as White House deputy chief of staff.

- On December 6, mortgage lenders reach an agreement with the Bush administration to freeze interest rates on subprime mortgages, high-interest home loans that were considered risky. While criticized by Democrats for not going far enough, the White House hopes to mitigate an increasingly dire mortgage crisis.

- On December 12, Bush vetoes Child Health Care Bill, legislation that would have expanded the State Children's Health Insurance program by $35 billion.

2008

- On January 14, Bush proposes a $145 billion stimulus package focused on tax breaks for consumers and businesses, in order to spur economic recovery in the face of increasing unemployment and home foreclosures.

- On March 8, Bush vetoes a bill that would ban the CIA from harsh interrogation tactics, including waterboarding.

- On March 12, New York Democratic governor Eliot Spitzer resigns in disgrace amid a sex scandal.

- On March 24, the death toll for American soldiers in Iraq reaches four thousand.

- On June 3, having won a majority of primary delegates, Obama becomes the presumptive Democratic nominee. Clinton ends her competitive run for the nomination.

- On June 27, the Supreme Court rejects a Washington, D.C., ban on handgun possession. The decision marks the first time in U.S. history that the Second Amendment is interpreted to affirm an individual's right to gun ownership.

- On July 10, Bush signs the Foreign Intelligence Surveillance Amendments Act (FISA), which loosens federal wiretapping restrictions regarding civilian surveillance involving terrorism and espionage.

- On July 14, Bush lifts the offshore oil drilling ban for the outer continental shelf, legislation implemented by his father, President George H. W. Bush.

- On August 8, John Edwards confesses to having had an extramarital affair with campaign photojournalist Rielle Hunter.

- On August 29, Republican presidential nominee John McCain chooses Alaska governor Sarah Palin as his running mate. She is the first woman on a Republican presidential ticket and proves to be an energizing force within the party.

- On September 15, lending giant Lehman Brothers Holdings Inc. files for Chapter 11 bankruptcy protection, becoming the largest bankruptcy filing in U.S. history.

- On September 29, the Dow Jones Industrial Average drops nearly 800 points, the biggest single-day point loss in stock market history. The loss marks the beginning of a long and damaging economic recession in the United States.

- On October 3, Bush signs the Emergency Economic Stabilization Act, a $700 billion bailout of the U.S. financial system, which establishes the Troubled Asset Relief Program (TARP).

- On November 4, Obama wins the presidential election.

- On December 19, Bush announces a $17.4 billion auto-industry rescue, with $13.4 billion in emergency loans to prevent General Motors and Chrysler from collapsing.

2009

- On January 20, Obama is inaugurated as the forty-fourth president of the United States.

- On January 29, Obama signs the Lilly Ledbetter Fair Pay Act, which supports equal pay regardless of race, sex, or age.

- On February 27, Tea (sometimes spelled out as "Taxed Enough Already") Party groups gather across the United States to protest TARP.

- On April 13, Obama signs a presidential memorandum removing restrictions that prevent Cuban Americans from visiting relatives in Cuba and sending remittances.

- On May 31, physician George Tiller is gunned down while serving as an usher during Sunday services at the Reformation Lutheran Church in Wichita, Kansas. The gunman, Scott Roeder, is an antiabortion activist, targeting Tiller for administering late-term abortions.

- On June 4, Obama gives a speech in Cairo, Egypt, reaching out to the Muslim world, thought to signal a dramatic shift in U.S. diplomacy.

- On June 24, South Carolina Republican governor Mark Sanford admits to and apologizes for an affair with an Argentine woman, during which time he disappeared from the country while his staff, based on Sanford's communication with them, claimed he was hiking in the Appalachian Mountains. Despite calls for his removal, he serves out his term.

- On August 6, Sonia Sotomayor is confirmed the first Hispanic woman on the Supreme Court.

- On August 25, Massachusetts Democratic senator Edward M. "Ted" Kennedy dies.

- On November 5, U.S. Army major Nidal Malik Hasan kills twelve fellow soldiers and a civilian in a shooting rampage at Fort Hood, Texas.

- On December 1, Obama announces an escalation of 30,000 troops in Afghanistan. The effort is designed to combat increased activity of Taliban fighters.

- On December 10, Obama is awarded the Nobel Peace Prize. Critics declare the award premature.

George W. Bush's 9/11-related Speeches

"Address to the Nation on the September 11 Attacks"

Speech

By: George W. Bush

Date: September 11, 2001

Source: Bush, George W. "Address to the Nation on the September 11 Attacks," September 11, 2001. http://georgewbush-whitehouse.archives.gov/infocus/bushrecord/documents/Selected_Speeches_George_W_Bush.pdf (accessed on February 23, 2013).

About the Speaker: George W. Bush, forty-third president of the United States, was born in 1946 to George H. W. Bush, the forty-first president, and Barbara Bush. An Ivy-League education from Yale and Harvard prepared him for success in the Texas oil industry, and a similarly prestigious pedigree prepared him for success in the state's high-stakes political atmosphere. The Republican Bush served as governor of Texas from 1994 until just after he narrowly defeated Vice President Al Gore in the national presidential election in 2000. Bush's eight years as president was defined by the September 11 terrorist attacks, the subsequent wars in Afghanistan and Iraq, and, later, the United States' mortgage and banking crises.

"Address to the Joint Session of the 107th Congress"

Speech

By: George W. Bush

Date: September 20, 2001

Source: Bush, George W. "Address to the Joint Session of the 107th Congress." Delivered September 20, 2001. http://georgewbush-whitehouse.archives.gov/infocus/bushrecord/documents/Selected_Speeches_George_W_Bush.pdf (accessed on February 23, 2013).

About the Speaker: See previous document.

INTRODUCTION

On September 11, 2001, less than one year into George W. Bush's first term as president of the United States, nineteen terrorists conducted an organized, concerted suicide attack against the nation. On the morning of 9/11, as the day is colloquially known, the terrorists, who were associated with the Islamist group al-Qaeda, hijacked four passenger jets traveling to and from various destinations in the United States. The planes were deliberately crashed by the hijackers into the "Twin Towers" of New York City's World Trade Center, the Pentagon in Arlington, Virginia, and a field in rural Pennsylvania, killing a total of 2,996 people (including the airplane passengers and the terrorists) and injuring 6,000 more.

The nation was devastated by the tragic attacks. President Bush, often the target of public ridicule for his frequent oratorical blunders, appeared on television the night of the attacks, delivering an unexpectedly poignant and heartfelt speech to soothe the frenzy of fear, anger, and sorrow that the attacks had catalyzed among the American public. Even Bush's harshest critics noted the deft elocution and reassuring effect of his emergency speech, which displayed the new leader's confidence and calm in the face of unanticipated adversity.

The Bush administration's response to the events of 9/11 was swift and confident. Following an immediate and massive emergency response effort and a few speeches related mostly to the nation's sadness and the tragedy itself, Bush's security and military officials definitively concluded that the al-Qaeda Islamist terrorist network was responsible for training, tasking, transporting, and supplying the hijackers, and constructed a reaction plan. This plan was presented to the U.S. public and government officials on September 20, in a televised address by President Bush to an emergency joint session of Congress.

In Bush's speech, al-Qaeda was blamed for the September 11 terrorist attacks and condemned for its contempt of Western democratic ideology. The rhetoric and political jargon that was to characterize U.S. political discourse about military involvement in the Middle East was first introduced, with Bush staging the conflict between al-Qaeda and the United States as a desperate, vital struggle between the forces of good and evil. America and its allies were depicted as the defenders of freedom, liberty, morality, and justice against the opposing force of radical Islamic fundamentalism and its disdain for civil liberties and human expression. Bush also noted in his speech that the United States would make no distinction between those who did not actively act to stop terrorism and those actually performing acts of violence.

Significantly, Bush used his speech to Congress to explain the formation of the Office of Homeland Security, a precursor to the Department of Homeland

President George W. Bush addresses the nation from the Oval Office of the White House on September 11, 2001, following terrorist attacks at the World Trade Center in New York City, at the Pentagon in Virginia, and in an airplane over Pennsylvania. © AP IMAGES/DOUG MILLS.

Security cabinet department that incorporated the duties of the previously disparate intelligence, emergency response, and domestic security agencies, with the stated mission of protecting the territory and people of the United States from external and internal threats. Bush alluded to the increasingly invasive federal conduct that is to accompany the new War on Terror at the end of his speech, describing the necessary sacrifices inherent to the investigation and prevention of terrorism and requesting that U.S. citizens cooperate with the program.

Most importantly, the speech presaged the impending invasion of Afghanistan—a Middle Eastern nation that had harbored, trained, and funded al-Qaeda leadership—by a coalition of governments led by the United States. The invasion was conducted with the stated goal of ousting the al-Qaeda–sympathetic Taliban government and thus eradicating a center of terrorist operations. Americans were informed of the tyranny of the Taliban regime and the importance of removing one of the primary actors in the Islamist terrorist movement.

SIGNIFICANCE

Bush's somber speech the evening of the attacks and his administration's authoritative response to one of the most trying disasters in U.S. history earned him immense support and trust from the nation's public, which the new president used as leverage to implement extensive new security measures and to gain popular support for the invasion of Afghanistan. Additionally, Bush's confident posture, epitomized in his speech to Congress, gave him the influence required to implement drastic and extensive measures in the fight to eradicate all of the terrorists on the planet. The Department of Homeland Security and the Travel Security Administration were both established as part of the Bush administration's zealous efforts to make the United States safe from any threat of any kind, and the Patriot Act, which granted far-reaching investigatory rights to federal agencies with almost no transparency, was enthusiastically adopted in keeping with Bush's "security" mantra.

To avenge the lives taken by the September 11 hijackers, the United States invaded Afghanistan on October 7, as Bush indicated it would. The Taliban government was quickly deposed and many al-Qaeda leaders and training camps were eliminated, but a local insurgency and ongoing sectarian conflicts caused the continued involvement of American troops long after the initial goals were accomplished. Osama bin Laden, the senior leader of al-Qaeda, managed to evade capture throughout the decade, until he was killed in a U.S. raid in Abbottabad, Pakistan, on May 2, 2011.

Much of the political and cultural substance of the 2000s decade was produced or influenced by 9/11 and the reaction it prompted from the U.S. government, characterizing the period as one of heightened suspicion, fear, and nationalism. Unfortunately for Bush, whose approval rating soared to over 90 percent in the immediate aftermath of the September 11 attacks, his steadfast demeanor and assuring leadership were eventually overshadowed by the financial and human cost of fighting the so-called War on Terror, the invasive measures authorized by the Patriot Act, and what many perceived to be the inefficiencies and questionable conduct of the Department of Homeland Security, all products of his administration's hard-line reaction to the attacks.

▊ PRIMARY SOURCE

"ADDRESS TO THE NATION ON THE SEPTEMBER 11 ATTACKS,"

SYNOPSIS: This speech explains the facts about the 9/11 terrorist attacks as they were understood immediately after they took place. Bush condemns the actions of the perpetrators and lauds the response of U.S. citizens to the attacks, as well as promising retributive justice against those responsible for taking American lives.

Good evening.

Today, our fellow citizens, our way of life, our very freedom came under attack in a series of deliberate and deadly terrorist acts.

The victims were in airplanes or in their offices—secretaries, businessmen and women, military and federal workers. Moms and dads. Friends and neighbors.

Thousands of lives were suddenly ended by evil, despicable acts of terror.

The pictures of airplanes flying into buildings, fires burning, huge structures collapsing, have filled us with disbelief, terrible sadness and a quiet, unyielding anger.

These acts of mass murder were intended to frighten our nation into chaos and retreat. But they have failed. Our country is strong. A great people has been moved to defend a great nation.

Terrorist attacks can shake the foundations of our biggest buildings, but they cannot touch the foundation of America. These acts shatter steel, but they cannot dent the steel of American resolve.

America was targeted for attack because we're the brightest beacon for freedom and opportunity in the world. And no one will keep that light from shining.

Today, our nation saw evil, the very worst of human nature, and we responded with the best of America, with the daring of our rescue workers, with the caring for strangers and neighbors who came to give blood and help in any way they could.

Immediately following the first attack, I implemented our government's emergency response plans. Our military is powerful, and it's prepared. Our emergency teams are working in New York City and Washington, D.C., to help with local rescue efforts.

Our first priority is to get help to those who have been injured and to take every precaution to protect our citizens at home and around the world from further attacks.

The functions of our government continue without interruption. Federal agencies in Washington which had to be evacuated today are reopening for essential personnel tonight and will be open for business tomorrow.

Our financial institutions remain strong, and the American economy will be open for business as well.

The search is underway for those who are behind these evil acts. I've directed the full resources for our intelligence and law enforcement communities to find those responsible and bring them to justice. We will make no distinction between the terrorists who committed these acts and those who harbor them.

I appreciate so very much the members of Congress who have joined me in strongly condemning these attacks. And on behalf of the American people, I thank the many world leaders who have called to offer their condolences and assistance.

America and our friends and allies join with all those who want peace and security in the world and we stand together to win the war against terrorism.

Tonight I ask for your prayers for all those who grieve, for the children whose worlds have been shattered, for all whose sense of safety and security has been threatened. And I pray they will be comforted by a power greater than any of us spoken through the ages in Psalm 23: "Even though I walk through the valley of the shadow of death, I fear no evil, for You are with me."

This is a day when all Americans from every walk of life unite in our resolve for justice and peace. America has stood down enemies before, and we will do so this time.

None of us will ever forget this day, yet we go forward to defend freedom and all that is good and just in our world.

Thank you. Good night and God bless America.

PRIMARY SOURCE

"ADDRESS TO THE JOINT SESSION OF THE 107TH CONGRESS"

SYNOPSIS: In this speech, President George W. Bush implicates the al-Qaeda terrorist network in the September 11, 2001, terrorist attacks and outlines the measures the U.S. government will take against it in revenge. The American people are implored to cooperate with the government's efforts and to tolerate its intrusions into their privacy and congratulated for their resilience after the greatest act of terrorism ever conducted against the United States.

Mr. Speaker, Mr. President Pro Tempore, members of Congress, and fellow Americans:

In the normal course of events, presidents come to this chamber to report on the state of the Union. Tonight, no such report is needed; it has already been delivered by the American people.

We have seen it in the courage of passengers who rushed terrorists to save others on the ground—passengers like an exceptional man named Todd Beamer. And would you please help me welcome his wife, Lisa Beamer, here tonight?

We have seen the state of our Union in the endurance of rescuers working past exhaustion. We have seen the unfurling of flags, the lighting of candles, the giving of blood, the saying of prayers—in English, Hebrew. and Arabic. We have seen the decency of a loving and giving people who have made the grief of strangers their own.

My fellow citizens, for the last nine days, the entire world has seen for itself the state of our Union—and it is strong.

Tonight we are a country awakened to danger and called to defend freedom. Our grief has turned to anger, and anger to resolution. Whether we bring our enemies to justice or bring justice to our enemies, justice will be done.

I thank the Congress for its leadership at such an important time. All of America was touched on the evening of the tragedy to see Republicans and Democrats joined together on the steps of this Capitol, singing "God Bless America." And you did more than sing; you acted, by delivering $40 billion to rebuild our communities and meet the needs of our military.

Speaker Hastert, Minority Leader Gephardt, Majority Leader Daschle and Senator Lott, I thank you for your friendship, for your leadership and for your service to our country.

And on behalf of the American people, I thank the world for its outpouring of support. America will never forget the sounds of our National Anthem playing at Buckingham Palace, on the streets of Paris and at Berlin's Brandenburg Gate.

We will not forget South Korean children gathering to pray outside our embassy in Seoul, or the prayers of sympathy offered at a mosque in Cairo. We will not forget moments of silence and days of mourning in Australia and Africa and Latin America.

Nor will we forget the citizens of 80 other nations who died with our own: dozens of Pakistanis; more than 130 Israelis; more than 250 citizens of India; men and women from El Salvador, Iran, Mexico and Japan; and hundreds of British citizens. America has no truer friend than Great Britain. Once again, we are joined together in a great cause—so honored the British prime minister has crossed an ocean to show his unity of purpose with America. Thank you for coming, friend.

On September the 11th, enemies of freedom committed an act of war against our country. Americans have known wars—but for the past 136 years they have been wars on foreign soil, except for one Sunday in 1941. Americans have known the casualties of war—but not at the center of a great city on a peaceful morning. Americans have known surprise attacks—but never before on thousands of civilians. All of this was brought upon us in a single day—and night fell on a different world, a world where freedom itself is under attack.

President George W. Bush speaks to the 107th Congress on September 20, 2001. Behind him are Speaker of the House Dennis Hastert (left) and Senate president pro tempore Robert Byrd. © WIN MCNAMEE/REUTERS/CORBIS.

Americans have many questions tonight. Americans are asking: Who attacked our country? The evidence we have gathered all points to a collection of loosely affiliated terrorist organizations known as al Qaeda. They are some of the murderers indicted for bombing American embassies in Tanzania and Kenya, and responsible for bombing the USS *Cole.*

Al Qaeda is to terror what the Mafia is to crime. But its goal is not making money; its goal is remaking the world—and imposing its radical beliefs on people everywhere.

The terrorists practice a fringe form of Islamic extremism that has been rejected by Muslim scholars and the vast majority of Muslim clerics—a fringe movement that perverts the peaceful teachings of Islam. The terrorists' directive commands them to kill Christians and Jews, to kill all Americans and make no distinctions among military and civilians, including women and children.

This group and its leader—a person named Osama bin Laden—are linked to many other organizations in different countries, including the Egyptian Islamic Jihad and the Islamic Movement of Uzbekistan. There are thousands of these terrorists in more than 60 countries. They are recruited from their own nations and neighborhoods and brought to camps in places like Afghanistan, where they are trained in the tactics of terror. They are sent back to their homes or sent to hide in countries around the world to plot evil and destruction.

The leadership of al Qaeda has great influence in Afghanistan and supports the Taliban regime in controlling most of that country. In Afghanistan we see al Qaeda's vision for the world.

Afghanistan's people have been brutalized—many are starving and many have fled. Women are not allowed to attend school. You can be jailed for owning a television. Religion can be practiced only as their leaders dictate. A man can be jailed in Afghanistan if his beard is not long enough.

The United States respects the people of Afghanistan—after all, we are currently its largest source of

A view inside the U.S. Capitol on the evening of September 20, 2001, during a special address to Congress by President George W. Bush regarding the events of September 11. © WIN MCNAMEE/REUTERS/CORBIS.

humanitarian aid—but we condemn the Taliban regime. It is not only repressing its own people, it is threatening people everywhere by sponsoring and sheltering and supplying terrorists. By aiding and abetting murder, the Taliban regime is committing murder.

And tonight, the United States of America makes the following demands on the Taliban: Deliver to United States authorities all of the leaders of Al Qaeda who hide in your land. Release all foreign nationals, including American citizens, you have unjustly imprisoned. Protect foreign journalists, diplomats and aid workers in your country. Close immediately and permanently every terrorist training camp in Afghanistan, and hand over every terrorist, and every person in their support structure, to appropriate authorities. Give the United States full access to terrorist training camps, so we can make sure they are no longer operating.

These demands are not open to negotiation or discussion. The Taliban must act, and act immediately. They will hand over the terrorists, or they will share in their fate.

I also want to speak tonight directly to Muslims throughout the world. We respect your faith. It's practiced freely by many millions of Americans, and by millions more in countries that America counts as friends. Its teachings are good and peaceful, and those who commit evil in the name of Allah blaspheme the name of Allah. The terrorists are traitors to their own faith, trying, in effect, to hijack Islam itself. The enemy of America is not our many Muslim friends; it is not our many Arab friends. Our enemy is a radical network of terrorists, and every government that supports them.

Our war on terror begins with al Qaeda, but it does not end there. It will not end until every terrorist group of global reach has been found, stopped and defeated.

Americans are asking, why do they hate us? They hate what they see right here in this chamber—a democratically elected government. Their leaders are self-appointed. They hate our freedoms—our freedom of religion, our freedom of speech, our freedom to vote and assemble and disagree with each other.

They want to overthrow existing governments in many Muslim countries such as Egypt, Saudi Arabia, and Jordan. They want to drive Israel out of the Middle East. They want to drive Christians and Jews out of vast regions of Asia and Africa.

These terrorists kill not merely to end lives, but to disrupt and end a way of life. With every atrocity, they hope that America grows fearful, retreating from the world and forsaking our friends. They stand against us because we stand in their way.

We are not deceived by their pretenses to piety. We have seen their kind before. They are the heirs of all the murderous ideologies of the 20th century. By sacrificing human life to serve their radical visions—by abandoning every value except the will to power— they follow in the path of fascism, Nazism, and totalitarianism. And they will follow that path all the way, to where it ends: in history's unmarked grave of discarded lies.

Americans are asking: How will we fight and win this war? We will direct every resource at our command— every means of diplomacy, every tool of intelligence, every instrument of law enforcement, every financial influence, and every necessary weapon of war—to the destruction and to the defeat of the global terror network.

This war will not be like the war against Iraq a decade ago, with a decisive liberation of territory and a swift conclusion. It will not look like the air war above Kosovo two years ago, where no ground troops were used and not a single American was lost in combat.

Our response involves far more than instant retaliation and isolated strikes. Americans should not expect one battle, but a lengthy campaign, unlike any other we have ever seen. It may include dramatic strikes, visible on TV, and covert operations, secret even in success. We will starve terrorists of funding, turn them one against another, drive them from place to place, until there is no refuge or no rest. And we will pursue nations that provide aid or safe haven to terrorism. Every nation, in every region, now has a decision to make. Either you are with us, or you are with the terrorists. From this day forward, any nation that continues to harbor or support terrorism will be regarded by the United States as a hostile regime.

Our nation has been put on notice: We are not immune from attack. We will take defensive measures against terrorism to protect Americans. Today, dozens of federal departments and agencies, as well as state and local governments, have responsibilities affecting homeland security. These efforts must be coordinated at the highest level. So tonight I announce the creation of a Cabinet-level position reporting directly to me, the Office of Homeland Security.

And tonight I also announce a distinguished American to lead this effort, to strengthen American security: a military veteran, an effective governor, a true patriot, a trusted friend—Pennsylvania's Tom Ridge. He will lead, oversee and coordinate a comprehensive national strategy to safeguard our country against terrorism, and respond to any attacks that may come.

These measures are essential. The only way to defeat terrorism as a threat to our way of life is to stop it, eliminate it and destroy it where it grows.

Many will be involved in this effort, from FBI agents to intelligence operatives to the reservists we have called to active duty. All deserve our thanks, and all have our prayers. And tonight, a few miles from the damaged Pentagon, I have a message for our military: Be ready. I've called the Armed Forces to alert, and there is a reason. The hour is coming when America will act, and you will make us proud.

This is not, however, just America's fight. And what is at stake is not just America's freedom. This is the world's fight. This is civilization's fight. This is the fight of all who believe in progress and pluralism, tolerance and freedom.

We ask every nation to join us. We will ask, and we will need, the help of police forces, intelligence services, and banking systems around the world. The United States is grateful that many nations and many international organizations have already responded—with sympathy and with support. Nations from Latin America, to Asia, to Africa, to Europe, to the Islamic world. Perhaps the NATO Charter reflects best the attitude of the world: An attack on one is an attack on all.

The civilized world is rallying to America's side. They understand that if this terror goes unpunished, their own cities, their own citizens may be next. Terror, unanswered, can not only bring down buildings, it can threaten the stability of legitimate governments. And you know what—we're not going to allow it.

Americans are asking: What is expected of us? I ask you to live your lives, and hug your children. I know many citizens have fears tonight, and I ask you to be calm and resolute, even in the face of a continuing threat.

I ask you to uphold the values of America and remember why so many have come here. We are in a fight for our principles, and our first responsibility is to live by them. No one should be singled out for unfair treatment or unkind words because of their ethnic background or religious faith.

I ask you to continue to support the victims of this tragedy with your contributions. Those who want to give can go to a central source of information, libertyunites.org, to find the names of groups providing direct help in New York, Pennsylvania, and Virginia.

The thousands of FBI agents who are now at work in this investigation may need your cooperation, and I ask you to give it.

I ask for your patience, with the delays and inconveniences that may accompany tighter security; and for your patience in what will be a long struggle.

I ask your continued participation and confidence in the American economy. Terrorists attacked a symbol of American prosperity. They did not touch its source. America is successful because of the hard work, and creativity, and enterprise of our people. These were the true strengths of our economy before September 11th, and they are our strengths today.

And finally, please continue praying for the victims of terror and their families, for those in uniform, and for our great country. Prayer has comforted us in sorrow, and will help strengthen us for the journey ahead.

Tonight I thank my fellow Americans for what you have already done and for what you will do. And ladies and gentlemen of the Congress, I thank you, their representatives, for what you have already done and for what we will do together. Tonight, we face new and sudden national challenges. We will come together to improve air safety, to dramatically expand the number of air marshals on domestic flights, and take new measures to prevent hijacking. We will come together to promote stability and keep our airlines flying, with direct assistance during this emergency.

We will come together to give law enforcement the additional tools it needs to track down terror here at home. We will come together to strengthen our intelligence capabilities to know the plans of terrorists before they act, and to find them before they strike.

We will come together to take active steps that strengthen America's economy, and put our people back to work.

Tonight, we welcome two leaders who embody the extraordinary spirit of all New Yorkers: Governor George Pataki, and Mayor Rudolph Giuliani. As a symbol of America's resolve, my administration will work with Congress, and these two leaders, to show the world that we will rebuild New York City.

After all that has just passed—all the lives taken, and all the possibilities and hopes that died with them—it is natural to wonder if America's future is one of fear. Some speak of an age of terror. I know there are struggles ahead, and dangers to face. But this country will define our times, not be defined by them. As long as the United States of America is determined and strong, this will not be an age of terror; this will be an age of liberty, here and across the world.

Great harm has been done to us. We have suffered great loss. And in our grief and anger we have found our mission and our moment. Freedom and fear are at war. The advance of human freedom—the great achievement of our time, and the great hope of every time—now depends on us. Our nation—this generation—will lift a dark threat of violence from our people and our future. We will rally the world to this cause by our efforts, by our courage. We will not tire, we will not falter, and we will not fail.

It is my hope that in the months and years ahead, life will return almost to normal. We'll go back to our lives and routines, and that is good. Even grief recedes with time and grace. But our resolve must not pass. Each of us will remember what happened that day and to whom it happened. We will remember the moment the news came—where we were and what we were doing. Some will remember an image of a fire, or a story of rescue. Some will carry memories of a face and a voice gone forever.

And I will carry this: It is the police shield of a man named George Howard, who died at the World Trade Center trying to save others. It was given to me by his mom, Arlene, as a proud memorial to her son. It is my reminder of lives that ended, and a task that does not end.

I will not forget the wound to our country and those who inflicted it. I will not yield; I will not rest; I will not relent in waging this struggle for freedom and security for the American people.

The course of this conflict is not known, yet its outcome is certain. Freedom and fear, justice and cruelty, have always been at war, and we know that God is not neutral between them.

Fellow citizens, we'll meet violence with patient justice—assured of the rightness of our cause, and confident of the victories to come. In all that lies before us, may God grant us wisdom, and may He watch over the United States of America.

FURTHER RESOURCES
Books
Bush, George W., and Jay Nordlinger. *We Will Prevail: President George W. Bush on War, Terrorism, and Freedom.* New York: Continuum, 2003.

Dolan, Chris J., and Betty Glad. *In War We Trust: The Bush Doctrine and the Pursuit of Just War.* New York: Ashgate, 2005.

Draper, Robert. *Dead Certain: The Presidency of George W. Bush.* New York: Free Press, 2007.

Gaddis, John Lewis. *Surprise, Security, and the American Experience.* Cambridge, MA: Harvard University Press, 2004.

Griffin, David R. *The New Pearl Harbor: Disturbing Questions About the Bush Administration and 9/11.* Northampton, MA: Interlink Publishing Group, 2004.

Meiertöns, Heiko. *The Doctrines of US Security Policy: An Evaluation under International Law.* Cambridge, MA: Cambridge University Press, 2010.

Shanahan, Timothy. *Philosophy 9/11: Thinking about the War on Terrorism.* Chicago: Open Court, 2005.

Web Sites

"The National Security Strategy." *The White House.* http://georgewbush-whitehouse.archives.gov/nsc/nss/2002/index.html (accessed on February 25, 2013).

"The September 11th Sourcebooks." www.gwu.edu/~nsarchiv/NSAEBB/sept11/index.html (accessed November 9, 2012).

Simon, Roger. "One Year After 9/11: A Nation Changed." www.usnews.com/usnews/9_11/articles/911opener.htm (accessed November 9, 2012).

"Understanding 9/11." http://archive.org/details/911 (accessed November 9, 2012).

"War on Terrorism FAQ." *The White House.* http://georgewbush-whitehouse.archives.gov/infocus/national-security/faq-what.html (accessed on February 25, 2013).

"September 11: Chronology of Terror"

A timeline listing the events of the September 11 terrorist attacks

Timeline

By: CNN

Date: September 12, 2001

Source: CNN. "September 11: Chronology of Terror." *CNN.com,* September 12, 2001. http://archives.cnn.com/2001/US/09/11/chronology.attack/index.html (accessed on February 23, 2013).

About the Publication: CNN, short for Cable News Network, was founded in 1980 as the first American network to provide continuous, twenty-four-hour news reporting and the first to offer no programming except for news. The network gained repute for its live, breaking coverage of the Space Shuttle *Challenger* disaster, the Gulf War, and the events of September 11, 2001. CNN expanded throughout the 1980s, establishing bureaus across the United States and much of the rest of the world, as well as acquiring affiliates and subsidiaries in several countries. By the end of the 2000s decade, CNN ranked among the largest news networks on the planet, with correspondents in almost every country and an enormous global audience.

INTRODUCTION

On the morning of September 11, 2001, nineteen men, affiliated with the al-Qaeda terrorist network, hijacked four U.S. passenger jets, in what would become the most destructive terrorist attack in the nation's history. At 8:45 AM Eastern Daylight Time, the first aircraft, American Airlines Flight 11, was piloted by its hijackers into the north tower of New York City's World Trade Center (WTC; also known as the Twin Towers), punching a hole in the building and immediately setting it ablaze. Eighteen minutes later, United Airlines Flight 175 was flown into the south tower of the WTC, causing an explosion and setting it on fire. At 9:43, American Airlines Flight 77 crashed into the Pentagon in Arlington County, Virginia, prompting immediate evacuation. At 10:10, the final aircraft, United Airlines Flight 93, plummeted into a field in rural Somerset County, Pennsylvania, after passengers successfully regained control of the plane and redirected it from its intended target (thought to be either the White House or the U.S. Capitol Building). All 227 passengers aboard the flights, as well as the 19 hijackers, were killed.

As news organizations scrambled to collect information on the details of the attacks, the nation reeled at initial reports. President George W. Bush appeared on television, issuing an emergency broadcast notifying the public that the events of the morning had been the work of terrorists. People around the world crowded around television sets and radios as it was reported that the south tower had collapsed, soon followed by the north, covering downtown New York in a haze of smoke and debris. As Washington, D.C., and New York City were evacuated, firefighters and emergency relief personnel flooded the impacted area, rushing into the burning towers in an attempt to rescue the thousands of people trapped inside. For the first time in the nation's history, all flights within the United States were grounded and an indefinite hold was placed on aviation. In the evening, fire from the burning Twin Towers spread to the nearby WTC Building 7, which proceeded to collapse around 5:00 PM.

A view of New York City on September 11, 2001, just as the second jetliner is about to crash into the South Tower of the World Trade Center. © ROBERT A. CUMINS/CORBIS.

President Bush addressed the nation at 8:30 PM EDT, expressing his condolences to the families of those killed by the attacks and assuring the public that those responsible for supporting the perpetrators would be brought to justice. The fire in the Pentagon continued throughout the night, as did the rescue efforts of New York City disaster workers, police officers, and firefighters. Although definitive casualty statistics were not available until the end of the month, CNN eventually confirmed a total of 2,977 deaths caused by the attacks, representing citizens of almost 100 nations. Of those killed, approximately two hundred died falling or jumping from the burning Twin Towers, and over four hundred of them were rescue workers killed by fire, smoke inhalation, or falling rubble. The rest were killed by the initial impact or were trapped inside the various structures damaged by the attacks, which included several buildings surrounding the World Trade Center.

SIGNIFICANCE

The events of September 11, 2001, came to define the political, social, and cultural atmosphere of the 2000s decade in the United States and had a resounding impact throughout the rest of the world. In the days immediately following the attacks, there was a profound outpouring of donations and sympathetic gestures to the victims and their families from people around the world, including thousands of volunteers traveling to New York to assist with cleanup and recovery efforts. American patriotism and national unity soared as the country shared the grief and anger produced by the devastating violation of its security. President Bush's popularity soared, especially after he appeared before a joint session of Congress to deliver a speech in which he outlined his planned response to the attacks, which included identifying, locating, and exacting justice upon the people and organizations responsible for planning the attacks.

By the morning of September 12, the Federal Bureau of Investigation (FBI) had identified all nineteen of the hijackers, thanks to the discovery of luggage that had not been placed aboard one of the aircraft used in the attacks. Fifteen of the men were determined to be Saudi Arabian nationals, two as citizens of the United Arab Emirates, one as an

Egyptian, and the last as a Jordanian. The ensuing investigation quickly linked the men to al-Qaeda, a radical Islamic terrorist organization operating in the Middle East. It was discovered that Osama bin Laden, founder and leader of al-Qaeda, had orchestrated the attacks, supplying the hijackers with training, supplies, and a coordinated task, as well as providing transportation and refuge across the world. Bin Laden had expressed vehemence towards the United States for decades and had issued a condemnation of the nation based on the principles of his interpretation of Islam. He claimed to his followers that the United States was trespassing on Islamic law by providing military, political, and financial support to Israel, and by maintaining a military presence in Saudi Arabia, home to Mecca and other Muslim holy sites.

Al-Qaeda was heavily involved with the Taliban, the fundamentalist Islamic government of Afghanistan, which had aided, supplied, and accommodated the terrorist organization since it claimed control of the nation. Bin Laden had resided in Afghanistan periodically throughout his life, and he was headquartered there at the time of the September 11 attacks. Because the Taliban refused to surrender bin Laden to the U.S. government, and because President Bush had pledged to respond with whatever means were required to bring the terrorists to justice, the United States committed itself to a military invasion of Afghanistan, which began on October 7, 2001. The War in Afghanistan, initially lauded as a success for its swift removal of the Taliban and destruction of al-Qaeda infrastructure and leadership, would end up lasting beyond the end of the decade, as the United States continued to combat a seemingly endless stream of insurgents sympathetic to the radical Islamic cause.

In addition to the invasion of Afghanistan, the U.S. government responded to the September 11 attacks with a global initiative to protect its citizens by seeking out and eradicating terrorism, known as the "War on Terror." To that effect, sweeping national defense reforms were made. The Department of Homeland Security (DHS), a cabinet department in the federal government, was created to consolidate the disparate branches of the state tasked with protecting the domestic security and safety of U.S. citizens from the threats of terrorism and disaster. The Transportation Security Administration (TSA) was created to transfer the role of patrolling and securing American travel, particularly air travel, from private entities to the federal government. Fears about the ability of the government to successfully protect against future terrorist plots led to the USA PATRIOT Act being passed in October 2001, granting enormously expanded investigatory powers to federal agencies, including provisions permitting warrantless searches, wiretaps, and property seizures.

September 11 also had a significant impact on the U.S. economy. The forced closure of the New York Stock Exchange and NASDAQ Stock Market that followed the attacks caused the markets to plummet upon reopening, and the U.S. dollar temporarily lost value in currency exchange markets. Reconstruction and cleanup costs to New York exceeded $10 billion, as did the tax revenue lost by the sudden elimination of over four hundred thousand jobs. The aviation industry, already financially troubled, was heavily hurt by the temporary stoppage of flight within the United States, necessitating government assistance to avoid collapse.

The September 11 terrorist attacks marked a permanent turning point in the history of the United States, prompting the nation to assume the role of global regulators. Citizens were confronted with immense tragedy as the country's vulnerability was exposed, and the horror of violence was brought to the public's doorstep. No other event of the 2000s decade had more influence over the condition of life in the United States than the destruction of the World Trade Center.

PRIMARY SOURCE

"SEPTEMBER 11: CHRONOLOGY OF TERROR"

SYNOPSIS: This timeline details the events of the September 11, 2001, terrorist attacks.

8:45 AM (all times are EDT): A hijacked passenger jet, American Airlines Flight 11 out of Boston, Massachusetts, crashes into the north tower of the World Trade Center, tearing a gaping hole in the building and setting it afire.

9:03 AM: A second hijacked airliner, United Airlines Flight 175 from Boston, crashes into the south tower of the World Trade Center and explodes. Both buildings are burning.

9:17 AM: The Federal Aviation Administration shuts down all New York City area airports.

9:21 AM: The Port Authority of New York and New Jersey orders all bridges and tunnels in the New York area closed.

9:30 AM: President Bush, speaking in Sarasota, Florida, says the country has suffered an "apparent terrorist attack."

9:40 AM: The FAA halts all flight operations at U.S. airports, the first time in U.S. history that air traffic nationwide has been halted.

9:43 AM: American Airlines Flight 77 crashes into the Pentagon, sending up a huge plume of smoke. Evacuation begins immediately.

Chief of Staff Andy Card informs President George W. Bush of the attacks on New York City's World Trade Center during a visit at an elementary school in Sarasota, Florida, September 11, 2001. © AP IMAGES/DOUG MILLS.

9:45 AM: The White House evacuates.

9:57 AM: Bush departs from Florida.

10:05 AM: The south tower of the World Trade Center collapses, plummeting into the streets below. A massive cloud of dust and debris forms and slowly drifts away from the building.

10:08 AM: Secret Service agents armed with automatic rifles are deployed into Lafayette Park across from the White House.

10:10 AM: A portion of the Pentagon collapses.

10:10 AM: United Airlines Flight 93, also hijacked, crashes in Somerset County, Pennsylvania, southeast of Pittsburgh.

10:13 AM: The United Nations building evacuates, including 4,700 people from the headquarters building and 7,000 total from UNICEF and U.N. development programs.

10:22 AM: In Washington, the State and Justice departments are evacuated, along with the World Bank.

10:24 AM: The FAA reports that all inbound transatlantic aircraft flying into the United States are being diverted to Canada.

10:28 AM: The World Trade Center's north tower collapses from the top down as if it were being peeled apart, releasing a tremendous cloud of debris and smoke.

10:45 AM: All federal office buildings in Washington are evacuated.

10:46 AM: U.S. Secretary of State Colin Powell cuts short his trip to Latin America to return to the United States.

10:48 AM: Police confirm the plane crash in Pennsylvania.

10:53 AM: New York's primary elections, scheduled for Tuesday, are postponed.

10:54 AM: Israel evacuates all diplomatic missions.

10:57 AM: New York Gov. George Pataki says all state government offices are closed.

11:02 AM: New York City Mayor Rudolph Giuliani urges New Yorkers to stay at home and orders an evacuation of the area south of Canal Street.

11:16 AM: CNN reports that the Centers for Disease Control and Prevention is preparing emergency-response teams in a precautionary move.

11:18 AM: American Airlines reports it has lost two aircraft. American Flight 11, a Boeing 767 flying from Boston to Los Angeles, had 81 passengers and 11 crew aboard. Flight 77, a Boeing 757 en route from Washington's Dulles International Airport to Los Angeles, had 58 passengers and six crew members aboard. Flight 11 slammed into the north tower of the World Trade Center. Flight 77 hit the Pentagon.

11:26 AM: United Airlines reports that United Flight 93, en route from Newark, New Jersey, to San Francisco, California, has crashed in Pennsylvania. The airline also says that it is "deeply concerned" about United Flight 175.

11:59 AM: United Airlines confirms that Flight 175, from Boston to Los Angeles, has crashed with 56 passengers and nine crew members aboard. It hit the World Trade Center's south tower.

12:04 PM: Los Angeles International Airport, the destination of three of the crashed airplanes, is evacuated.

12:15 PM: San Francisco International Airport is evacuated and shut down. The airport was the destination of United Airlines Flight 93, which crashed in Pennsylvania.

12:15 PM: The Immigration and Naturalization Service says U.S. borders with Canada and Mexico are on the highest state of alert, but no decision has been made about closing borders.

12:30 PM: The FAA says 50 flights are in U.S. airspace, but none are reporting any problems.

1:04 PM: Bush, speaking from Barksdale Air Force Base in Louisiana, says that all appropriate security measures are being taken, including putting the U.S. military on high alert worldwide. He asks for prayers for those killed or wounded in the attacks and says, "Make no mistake, the United States will hunt down and punish those responsible for these cowardly acts."

1:27 PM: A state of emergency is declared by the city of Washington.

1:44 PM: The Pentagon says five warships and two aircraft carriers will leave the U.S. Naval Station in Norfolk,

A painting by Gil Cohen shows a U.S. fighter jet flying over the burning Pentagon on September 11, 2001. © CORBIS.

Virginia, to protect the East Coast from further attack and to reduce the number of ships in port. The two carriers, the USS *George Washington* and the USS *John F. Kennedy*, are headed for the New York coast. The other ships headed to sea are frigates and guided missile destroyers capable of shooting down aircraft.

1:48 PM: Bush leaves Barksdale Air Force Base aboard *Air Force One* and flies to an Air Force base in Nebraska.

2 PM: Senior FBI sources tell CNN they are working on the assumption that the four airplanes that crashed were hijacked as part of a terrorist attack.

2:30 PM: The FAA announces there will be no U.S. commercial air traffic until noon EDT Wednesday at the earliest.

2:49 PM: At a news conference, Giuliani says that subway and bus service are partially restored in New York City. Asked about the number of people killed, Giuliani says, "I don't think we want to speculate about that—more than any of us can bear."

3:55 PM: Karen Hughes, a White House counselor, says the president is at an undisclosed location, later

revealed to be Offutt Air Force Base in Nebraska, and is conducting a National Security Council meeting by phone. Vice President Dick Cheney and National Security Adviser Condoleezza Rice are in a secure facility at the White House. Defense Secretary Donald Rumsfeld is at the Pentagon.

3:55 PM: Giuliani now says the number of critically injured in New York City is up to 200 with 2,100 total injuries reported.

4 p.m: CNN National Security Correspondent David Ensor reports that U.S. officials say there are "good indications" that Saudi militant Osama bin Laden, suspected of coordinating the bombings of two U.S. embassies in 1998, is involved in the attacks, based on "new and specific" information developed since the attacks.

4:06 PM: California Gov. Gray Davis dispatches urban search-and-rescue teams to New York.

4:10 PM: Building 7 of the World Trade Center complex is reported on fire.

4:20 PM: U.S. Sen. Bob Graham, D-Florida, chairman of the Senate Intelligence Committee, says he was "not surprised there was an attack (but) was surprised at the specificity." He says he was "shocked at what actually happened—the extent of it."

4:25 PM: The American Stock Exchange, the Nasdaq and the New York Stock Exchange say they will remain closed Wednesday.

4:30 PM: The president leaves Offutt Air Force Base in Nebraska aboard *Air Force One* to return to Washington.

5:15 PM: CNN Military Affairs Correspondent Jamie McIntyre reports fires are still burning in part of the Pentagon. No death figures have been released yet.

5:20 PM: The 47-story Building 7 of the World Trade Center complex collapses. The evacuated building is damaged when the twin towers across the street collapse earlier in the day. Other nearby buildings in the area remain ablaze.

5:30 PM: CNN Senior White House Correspondent John King reports that U.S. officials say the plane that crashed in Pennsylvania could have been headed for one of three possible targets: Camp David, the White House or the U.S. Capitol building.

6 PM: Explosions are heard in Kabul, Afghanistan, hours after terrorist attacks targeted financial and military centers in the United States. The attacks occurred at 2:30 AM local time. Afghanistan is believed to be where bin Laden, who U.S. officials say is possibly behind Tuesday's deadly attacks, is located. U.S. officials say later that the United States had no involvement in the incident whatsoever. The attack is credited to the Northern Alliance, a group fighting the Taliban in the country's ongoing civil war.

6:10 PM: Giuliani urges New Yorkers to stay home Wednesday if they can.

6:40 PM: Rumsfeld, the U.S. defense secretary, holds a news conference in the Pentagon, noting the building is operational. "It will be in business tomorrow," he says.

6:54 PM: Bush arrives back at the White House aboard *Marine One* and is scheduled to address the nation at 8:30 PM. The president earlier landed at Andrews Air Force Base in Maryland with a three-fighter jet escort. CNN's John King reports Laura Bush arrived earlier by motorcade from a "secure location."

7:17 PM: U.S. Attorney General John Ashcroft says the FBI is setting up a Web site for tips on the attacks: www.ifccfbi.gov. He also says family and friends of possible victims can leave contact information at 800-331-0075.

7:02 PM: CNN's Paula Zahn reports the Marriott Hotel near the World Trade Center is on the verge of collapse and says some New York bridges are now open to outbound traffic.

7:45 PM: The New York Police Department says that at least 78 officers are missing. The city also says that as

many as half of the first 400 firefighters on the scene were killed.

8:30 PM: President Bush addresses the nation, saying "thousands of lives were suddenly ended by evil" and asks for prayers for the families and friends of Tuesday's victims. "These acts shattered steel, but they cannot dent the steel of American resolve," he says. The president says the U.S. government will make no distinction between the terrorists who committed the acts and those who harbor them. He adds that government offices in Washington are reopening for essential personnel Tuesday night and for all workers Wednesday.

9:22 PM: CNN's McIntyre reports the fire at the Pentagon is still burning and is considered contained but not under control.

9:57 PM: Giuliani says New York City schools will be closed Wednesday and no more volunteers are needed for Tuesday evening's rescue efforts. He says there is hope that there are still people alive in rubble. He also says that power is out on the westside of Manhattan and that health department tests show there are no airborne chemical agents about which to worry.

10:49 PM: CNN Congressional Correspondent Jonathan Karl reports that Attorney General Ashcroft told members of Congress that there were three to five hijackers on each plane armed only with knives.

10:56 PM: CNN's Zahn reports that New York City police believe there are people alive in buildings near the World Trade Center.

11:54 PM: CNN Washington Bureau Chief Frank Sesno reports that a government official told him there was an open microphone on one of the hijacked planes and that sounds of discussion and "duress" were heard. Sesno also reports a source says law enforcement has "credible" information and leads and is confident about the investigation.

FURTHER RESOURCES

Books

Damico, Amy M., and Sara E. Quay. *September 11 in Popular Culture: A Guide.* Westport, CT: Greenwood, 2010.

LIFE Magazine. *One Nation: America Remembers September 11, 2001.* New York: Little, Brown, 2001.

Web Sites

"The 9/11 Commission Report." *National Commission on Terrorist Attacks Upon the United States.* http://govinfo. library.unt.edu/911/report/911Report.pdf (accessed on February 23, 2013).

"Report for Congress: The Economic Effects of 9/11: A Retrospective Assessment." *Congressional Research*

Service, via Federation of American Scientists. www.fas.org/irp/crs/RL31617.pdf (accessed on February 23, 2013).

"The September 11 Sourcebooks." *National Security Archive.* www.gwu.edu/~nsarchiv/NSAEBB/sept11/index.html (accessed on February 23, 2013).

"September 11, 2001, Web Archive." *Library of Congress Web Archives.* http://lcweb2.loc.gov/diglib/lcwa/html/sept11/sept11-overview.html (accessed on February 23, 2013).

2000 Presidential Election Disputes

"Examining the Vote: The Overview; Study of Disputed Florida Ballots Finds Justices Did Not Cast the Deciding Vote"

Newspaper article

By: Ford Fessenden and John M. Broder

Date: November 12, 2001

Source: Fessenden, Ford, and John M. Broder. "Examining the Vote: The Overview; Study of Disputed Florida Ballots Finds Justices Did Not Cast the Deciding Vote." *New York Times*, November 12, 2001. www.nytimes.com/2001/11/12/us/examining-vote-overview-study-disputed-florida-ballots-finds-justices-did-not.html (accessed on March 3, 2013).

About the Newspaper: The *New York Times* is one of the oldest and most reputable newspapers in the United States. Since being founded in 1851, the New York City–based *Times* has printed and run daily editions continuously, except for three periods of brief interruption due to labor disputes. Its hard-hitting, thorough, and topical coverage of "All the News That's Fit to Print" has made it a cornerstone of American journalism, garnering one of the nation's highest circulation rates and 108 Pulitzer Prizes. In recent decades, the *New York Times* has maintained its reputation through its refusal to compromise its reporting on politically and socially divisive topics, both domestic and international. In response to flagging print-edition subscription numbers and sales revenue, the paper implemented a pay-to-read online content scheme in 2005.

2000 Presidential Election Political Cartoon

Political cartoon

By: Ann Telnaes

Date: 2000

Source: Telnaes, Ann. 2000 Presidential Election Political Cartoon. *Carttonist Group.* www.cartoonistgroup.com/store/add.php?iid=50825 (accessed on March 5, 2013).

About the Cartoonist: Ann Telnaes began her editorial cartoonist career as a designer for Walt Disney Imagineering and contributed her design and animation skills to studios located throughout the world. She won the Pulitzer Prize for Editorial Cartooning in 2001 and her first book, *Humor's Edge*, was published in 2004. Her work has been exhibited in Paris, Jerusalem, Lisbon, and Washington, D.C. Telnaes's cartoons are posted weekly on the *Washington Post*'s Web site.

INTRODUCTION

The 2000 U.S. presidential election was the closest and most hotly contested in the nation's history. Following an uncommonly adversarial and divisive campaign, the Democratic Party's candidate, Vice President Al Gore, faced the Republican Party's nominee, Texas governor George W. Bush, at the polls. As results of the November 7 vote were tabulated, it became apparent that the ultimate victor would win only by a small margin. Bush won most of the Southern and Midwestern states, while Gore carried most of New England, the West Coast, and the Great Lakes states. In several states, the race was so close that exit poll statistics were rendered useless, leading several news organizations to erroneously report Gore as the winner or to repeatedly change their election-result predictions.

By the next day, it was evident that whichever candidate had claimed Florida's 25 electoral votes would attain the 270-vote victory requirement and become the forty-third president of the United States. On the morning of November 8, the final Florida tally had been completed, with Bush winning the popular vote by a margin of about two thousand votes. However, Bush's victory was not yet secure—his margin of victory was slight enough to require a mandatory recount under Florida state law. By the time the recount was complete, Bush's margin of victory over Gore had fallen to around three hundred votes, qualifying the vice president to challenge state results and request a manual recount in the counties of his choosing.

PRIMARY SOURCE

2000 Presidential Election Political Cartoon

SYNOPSIS: This cartoon pokes fun at the media's focus on the ongoing Election 2000 drama, while seemingly ignoring other world events. ANN TELNAES EDITORIAL CARTOON USED WITH THE PERMISSION OF ANN TELNAES AND THE CARTOONIST GROUP. ALL RIGHTS RESERVED.

Gore decided on four counties to conduct recounts, all of them historically liberal. Two of these counties failed to meet the November 26 recount deadline and submitted their initial results as final and official, and the other two reconfirmed Bush as their victor. Gore challenged these announcements, resulting in a Florida Supreme Court order that all ballots rejected by mechanical tabulation processes (amounting to some seventy thousand votes) be manually examined and counted. This procedure was immediately halted by the U.S. Supreme Court, which staged emergency proceedings to determine the proper course of action in identifying the true winner of the election.

On December 12, following hearings and examination of the unprecedented legal circumstances of the contested election results, the Supreme Court issued its ruling on the case of *Bush v. Gore*, in which it found the proposed Florida recount to be unconstitutional. Because no method of recounting all of the state's ballots could be designed and conducted before the date required by the governing U.S. law (the same day the Court made its decision), Bush's victory was upheld and he was awarded the presidency.

SIGNIFICANCE

George W. Bush's election prompted widespread objection from the American public. Some pundits and political commentators claimed that Bush had essentially been elected by the Supreme Court, noting that

Vice President Al Gore (right) welcomes President-elect George W. Bush to Gore's residence on December 19, 2000, shortly after the U.S. Supreme Court's decision officially gave Bush Florida's twenty-five electoral votes, resulting in Bush's election as president. © AP IMAGES/J. SCOTT APPLEWHITE.

the ruling on *Bush v. Gore* was split 7–2 along ideological lines, indicating the possibility that conservative justices had acted on a personal political basis rather than an objective interpretation of the law. Others pointed out that the Court's ruling was issued as a "one-off," specifically stating that it was not to be used as legal precedent in deciding the results of future contested elections. This curious caveat was seen by some as an acknowledgment of the decision's illegitimacy, since U.S. law is supposed to be a consistent application of constitutional principles, which should typically remain congruent and universal instead of applying only to a single incident. It was also frequently remarked that Bush had actually lost the popular vote to Gore by more than five hundred thousand votes, but still managed to win in the electoral college, a fact frequently lamented by those critical of the U.S. election system. (Only three other U.S. presidents— John Quincy Adams in 1824, Rutherford B. Hayes in

1876, and Benjamin Harrison in 1888—had been victorious in the same fashion.)

The 2000 presidential election's largest impact on U.S. voting procedures came in the form of voting reform, in response to the complications arising from complicated, outmoded, confusing, and non-uniform ballot-marking and ballot-counting requirements. Much of the controversy surrounding the Florida recount related to the exceptional number of votes in the state that went uncounted, due primarily to poor ballot design that caused voters to erroneously vote for too few or too many political candidates (both causes of immediate disqualification). Subsequent elections attempted to rectify this issue by employing more intuitive, simple ballots and electronic voting machines, which are theoretically incapable of error.

Although they were released a year after the election had been decided, the studies covered in "Examining the Vote: The Overview" cleared up some of the lingering disagreement and uncertainty about the effects of the Supreme Court's decision to prevent the Florida recount on the final election results.

PRIMARY SOURCE

"EXAMINING THE VOTE: THE OVERVIEW; STUDY OF DISPUTED FLORIDA BALLOTS FINDS JUSTICES DID NOT CAST THE DECIDING VOTE"

SYNOPSIS: This article presents the findings of an independent examination of all the Florida ballots, counted and uncounted, from the 2000 presidential election. It is concluded that, even using the most favorable method of interpreting and counting the votes, Gore would have lost with his bid to recount in only four counties. However, the study finds that had Gore requested a recount of every ballot submitted in Florida, it is likely that he would have won. The article also briefly discusses the impact of absentee ballots on the outcome of the election.

A comprehensive review of the uncounted Florida ballots from last year's presidential election reveals that George W. Bush would have won even if the United States Supreme Court had allowed the statewide manual recount of the votes that the Florida Supreme Court had ordered to go forward.

Contrary to what many partisans of former Vice President Al Gore have charged, the United States Supreme Court did not award an election to Mr. Bush that otherwise would have been won by Mr. Gore. A close examination of the ballots found that Mr. Bush would have retained a slender margin over Mr. Gore if the Florida court's order to recount more than 43,000 ballots had not been reversed by the United States Supreme Court.

Even under the strategy that Mr. Gore pursued at the beginning of the Florida standoff—filing suit to force hand recounts in four predominantly Democratic counties—Mr. Bush would have kept his lead, according to the ballot review conducted for a consortium of news organizations.

But the consortium, looking at a broader group of rejected ballots than those covered in the court decisions, 175,010 in all, found that Mr. Gore might have won if the courts had ordered a full statewide recount of all the rejected ballots. This also assumes that county canvassing boards would have reached the same conclusions about the disputed ballots that the consortium's independent observers did. The findings indicate that Mr. Gore might have eked out a victory if he had pursued in court a course like the one he publicly advocated when he called on the state to "count all the votes."

In addition, the review found statistical support for the complaints of many voters, particularly elderly Democrats in Palm Beach County, who said in interviews after the election that confusing ballot designs may have led them to spoil their ballots by voting for more than one candidate.

More than 113,000 voters cast ballots for two or more presidential candidates. Of those, 75,000 chose Mr. Gore and a minor candidate; 29,000 chose Mr. Bush and a minor candidate. Because there was no clear indication of what the voters intended, those numbers were not included in the consortium's final tabulations.

Thus the most thorough examination of Florida's uncounted ballots provides ammunition for both sides in what remains the most disputed and mystifying presidential election in modern times. It illuminates in detail the weaknesses of Florida's system that prevented many from voting as they intended to. But it also provides support for the result that county election officials and the courts ultimately arrived at—a Bush victory by the tiniest of margins.

The study, conducted over the last 10 months by a consortium of eight news organizations assisted by professional statisticians, examined numerous hypothetical ways of recounting the Florida ballots. Under some methods, Mr. Gore would have emerged the winner; in others, Mr. Bush. But in each one, the margin of victory was smaller than the 537-vote lead that state election officials ultimately awarded Mr. Bush.

Even so, the media ballot review, carried out under rigorous rules far removed from the chaos and partisan heat of the post-election dispute, is unlikely to end the argument over the outcome of the 2000 presidential election. The race was so close that it is possible to get different results simply by applying different hypothetical vote-counting methods to the thousands of uncounted ballots. And in every case, the ballot review produced a result that was even closer than the official count—a margin of perhaps four or five thousandths of one percent out of about six million ballots cast for president.

The consortium examined 175,010 ballots that vote-counting machines had rejected last November. Those included so-called undervotes, or ballots on which the machines could not discern a preference for president, and overvotes, those on which voters marked more than one candidate.

The examination then sought to judge what might have been considered a legal vote under various conditions—from the strictest interpretation (a clearly punched hole) to the most liberal (a small indentation, or dimple, that indicated the voter was trying to punch a hole in the card). But even under the most inclusive standards, the review found that at most, 24,619 ballots could have been interpreted as legal votes.

The numbers reveal the flaws in Mr. Gore's post-election tactics and, in retrospect, why the Bush strategy of resisting county-by-county recounts was ultimately successful.

In a finding rich with irony, the results show that even if Mr. Gore had succeeded in his effort to force recounts of undervotes in the four Democratic counties, Miami-Dade, Broward, Palm Beach and Volusia, he still would have lost, although by 225 votes rather than 537. An approach Mr. Gore and his lawyers rejected as impractical—a statewide recount—could have produced enough votes to tilt the election his way, no matter what standard was chosen to judge voter intent.

Another complicating factor in the effort to untangle the result is the overseas absentee ballots that arrived after Election Day. A *New York Times* investigation earlier this year showed that 680 of the late-arriving ballots did not meet Florida's standards yet were still counted. The vast majority of those flawed ballots were accepted in counties that favored Mr. Bush, after an aggressive effort by Bush strategists to pressure officials to accept them.

A statistical analysis conducted for *The Times* determined that if all counties had followed state law in reviewing the absentee ballots, Mr. Gore would have picked up as many as 290 additional votes, enough to tip the election in Mr. Gore's favor in some of the situations studied in the statewide ballot review.

But Mr. Gore chose not to challenge these ballots because many were from members of the military overseas, and Mr. Gore did not want to be accused of seeking to invalidate votes of men and women in uniform.

Democrats invested heavily in get-out-the-vote programs across Florida, particularly among minorities, recent immigrants and retirees from the Northeast. But their efforts were foiled by confusing ballot designs in crucial counties that resulted in tens of thousands of Democratic voters spoiling their ballots. More than 150,000 of those spoiled ballots did not show evidence of voter intent even after independent observers closely examined them and the most inclusive definition of what constituted a valid vote was applied.

The majority of those ballots were spoiled because multiple choices were made for president, often, apparently, because voters were confused by the ballots. All were invalidated by county election officials and were excluded from the consortium count because there was no clear proof of voter intent, unless there were other clear signs of the voter's choice, like a matching name on the line for a write-in candidate.

In Duval County, for example, 20 percent of the ballots from African-American areas that went heavily for Mr. Gore were thrown out because voters followed instructions to mark a vote on every page of the ballot. In 62 precincts with black majorities in Duval County alone, nearly 3,000 people voted for Mr. Gore and a candidate

Judge Robert Rosenberg, a Broward County, Florida, canvassing board member, uses a magnifying glass to examine a disputed ballot on November 24, 2000. © AP IMAGES/ALAN DIAZ.

whose name appeared on the second page of the ballot, thus spoiling their votes.

In Palm Beach County, 5,310 people, most of them probably confused by the infamous butterfly ballot, voted for Mr. Gore and Patrick J. Buchanan. The confusion affected Bush voters as well, but only 2,600 voted for Mr. Bush and another candidate.

The media consortium included *The Times, The Wall Street Journal,* The Tribune Company, *The Washington Post,* The Associated Press, *The St. Petersburg Times, The Palm Beach Post* and CNN. The group hired the National Opinion Research Center at the University of Chicago in January to examine the ballots. The research group employed teams of three workers they called coders to examine each undervoted ballot and mark down what they saw in detail. Three coders provided a bulwark against inaccuracy or bias in the coding. For overvotes, one coder was used because there was seldom disagreement among examiners in a trial run using three coders.

The data produced by the ballot review allows scrutiny of the disputed Florida vote under a large number of situations and using a variety of different standards that might have applied in a hand recount, including the appearance of a dimple, a chad dangling by one or more corners and a cleanly punched card.

The difficulty of perceiving dimples or detached chads can be measured by the number of coders who saw them, but most of the ballot counts here are based on what a simple majority—two out of three coders—recorded.

The different standards mostly involved competing notions of what expresses voter intent on a punch card. The 29,974 ballots using optical scanning equipment were mostly interpreted using a single standard—any unambiguous mark, whether a circle or a scribble or an X, on or near the candidate name was considered evidence of voter intent.

If all the ballots had been reviewed under any of seven single standards, and combined with the results of an examination of overvotes, Mr. Gore would have won, by a very narrow margin. For example, using the most permissive "dimpled chad" standard, nearly 25,000 additional votes would have been reaped, yielding 644 net new votes for Mr. Gore and giving him a 107-vote victory margin.

But the dimple standard was also the subject of the most disagreement among coders, and Mr. Bush fought the use of this standard in recounts in Palm Beach, Broward and Miami-Dade Counties. Many dimples were so light that only one coder saw them, and hundreds that were seen by two were not seen by three. In fact, counting dimples that three people saw would have given Mr. Gore a net of just 318 additional votes and kept Mr. Bush in the lead by 219.

Using the most restrictive standard—the fully punched ballot card—5,252 new votes would have been added to the Florida total, producing a net gain of 652 votes for Mr. Gore, and a 115-vote victory margin.

All the other combinations likewise produced additional votes for Mr. Gore, giving him a slight margin over Mr. Bush, when at least two of the three coders agreed.

While these are fascinating findings, they do not represent a real-world situation. There was no set of circumstances in the fevered days after the election that would have produced a hand recount of all 175,000 overvotes and undervotes.

The Florida Supreme Court urged a statewide recount and ordered the state's 67 counties to begin a manual re-examination of the undervotes in a ruling issued Dec. 8 that left Mr. Gore and his allies elated.

The Florida court's 4-to-3 ruling rejected Mr. Gore's plea for selective recounts in four Democratic counties, but also Mr. Bush's demand for no recounts at all. Justice Barbara Pariente, in her oral remarks, asked, "Why wouldn't it be proper for any court, if they were going to order any relief, to count the undervotes in all of the counties where, at the very least, punch-card systems were operating?"

The court ultimately adopted her view, although extending it to all counties, including those using ballots marked by pen and read by optical scanning. Many counties immediately began the effort, applying different standards and, in some cases, including overvotes.

The United States Supreme Court stepped in only hours after the counting began, issuing an injunction to halt. Three days later, the justices overturned the Florida court's ruling, sealing Mr. Bush's election.

But what if the recounts had gone forward, as Mr. Gore and his lawyers had demanded?

The consortium asked all 67 counties what standard they would have used and what ballots they would have manually recounted. Combining that information with the detailed ballot examination found that Mr. Bush would have won the election, by 493 votes if two of the three coders agreed on what was on the ballot; by 389 counting only those ballots on which all three agreed.

PRIMARY SOURCE

2000 PRESIDENTIAL ELECTION POLITICAL CARTOON

See primary source image.

FURTHER RESOURCES

Books

Brinkley, Douglas. *36 Days: The Complete Chronicle of the 2000 Presidential Election Crisis*. New York: Times Books, 2001.

Bugliosi, Vincent. *The Betrayal of America: How the Supreme Court Undermined the Constitution and Chose Our President*. New York, Thunder's Mouth Press, 2001.

Gillman, H. *The Votes That Counted: How the Court Decided the 2000 Presidential Election*. Chicago: University of Chicago Press, 2001.

Posner, Richard A. *Breaking the Deadlock: The 2000 Election, the Constitution, and the Courts*. Princeton, NJ: Princeton University Press, 2001.

Toobin, Jeffrey. *Too Close To Call: The Thirty-Six-Day Battle to Decide the 2000 Election*. New York: Random House, 2001.

Web Sites

"CBS News Coverage of Election Night 2000: Investigation, Analysis, Recommendations." *CBS News*. www.cbsnews.com/htdocs/c2k/pdf/REPFINAL.pdf (accessed on March 5, 2013).

"Election 2000." *NPR.org*. www.npr.org/news/national/election2000 (accessed March 5, 2013).

"Election 2000: The Postelection Events Day by Day." www.usnews.com/usnews/news/election/magtimeline.htm (accessed on March 5, 2013).

"State of the Union Address to the 107th Congress"

Speech

By: George W. Bush

Date: January 29, 2002

Source: Bush, George W. "State of the Union Address to the 107th Congress," January 29, 2002. http://georgewbush-whitehouse.archives.gov/infocus/bushrecord/documents/Selected_Speeches_George_W_Bush.pdf (accessed February 27, 2013).

About the Speaker: George W. Bush, forty-third president of the United States, was born in 1946 to George H. W. Bush, the forty-first president, and Barbara Bush. An Ivy-League education from Yale and Harvard prepared him for success in the Texas oil industry, and a similarly prestigious pedigree prepared him for success in the state's high-stakes political atmosphere. The Republican Bush served as governor of Texas from 1994 until just after he narrowly defeated Vice President Al Gore in the national presidential election in 2000. Bush's eight years as president was defined by the September 11 terrorist attacks, the subsequent wars in Afghanistan and Iraq, and, later, the United States' mortgage and banking crises.

INTRODUCTION

On September 11, 2001, less than one year into George W. Bush's first term as president of the United States, nineteen terrorists conducted an organized, concerted suicide attack against the nation. On the morning of 9/11, as the day is colloquially known, the terrorists, who were associated with the Islamist group al-Qaeda, hijacked four passenger jets traveling to and from various destinations in the United States. The planes were deliberately crashed by the hijackers into the "Twin Towers" of New York City's World Trade Center, the Pentagon in Arlington, Virginia, and a field in rural Pennsylvania, killing a total of 2,996 people (including the airplane passengers and the terrorists) and injuring 6,000 more.

The Bush administration's response to the events of 9/11 was swift and confident. Following an immediate and massive emergency response effort and a few speeches related mostly to the nation's sadness and the tragedy itself, Bush's security and military officials definitively concluded that the al-Qaeda Islamist terrorist network was responsible for training, tasking, transporting, and supplying the hijackers, and constructed reaction plan. This plan was presented to the U.S. public and government officials on September 20, in a televised address by President Bush to an emergency joint session of Congress.

To avenge the lives taken by the September 11 hijackers, the United States invaded Afghanistan on October 7, as Bush indicated it would. The Taliban government was quickly deposed and many al-Qaeda leaders and training camps were eliminated, but a local insurgency and ongoing sectarian conflicts caused the continued involvement of American troops long after the initial goals were accomplished. Osama bin Laden, the senior leader of al-Qaeda, managed to evade capture throughout the decade, until he was killed in a U.S. raid in Abbottabad, Pakistan, on May 2, 2011.

By the end of January 2002, America remained focused on terrorism. President Bush's State of the Union Address—his first—reflected that focus. The address emphasized Bush's vision of "three great goals for America": win the war on terrorism, strengthen homeland defense, and revitalize the economy.

SIGNIFICANCE

President Bush described a strategy to protect America that called for near-perpetual warfare if necessary and made clear that if countries did not act against terrorism, America would. Somber and, at times, menacing in tone, the president labeled North Korea, Iran, and Iraq the "Axis of Evil," a term that would haunt him throughout his presidency and which European Union foreign policy chief Chris Patten publicly doubted was a "well thought-through policy." The address itself became commonly referred to as the Axis of Evil speech, and by including Iran in that trio, some historians claimed that Bush virtually irrevocably altered the relationship between that country and America.

The United States had long considered Iran a potentially dangerous enemy in the Middle East. After the speech, Iran's leader, Ayatollah Ali Khamenei, requested that the Supreme National Security Council assess the pros and cons of entering into talks with the United States. By May 1, Khamenei dismissed the possibility of negotiations, stating, "The Islamic Republic of Iran will never succumb to America's bullying.... Negotiations with America are beneficial to the American government." Relations with Iran never improved, and on March 20, 2003, America led coalition forces in an invasion of Iraq. The resulting war would last eight years, eight months, three weeks, and four days.

In addition to announcing the largest increase in defense spending in two decades for the purpose of buying more weapons and raising military wages, President Bush proposed doubling the fund for homeland security, a goal that would increase homeland defense spending to almost $38 billion.

Promising to keep the deficit small if Congress acted responsibly, the president warned Americans that the cost of war and homeland security would also increase the federal deficit. He urged Congress to pass his economic stimulus program and make permanent tax cuts while urging Americans to volunteer four thousand hours or two years of service to help other Americans in need. A pared-down, $42 billion stimulus bill was signed in March 2002, but the economy was still in recession when the president ended his two-term stint in the White House in January 2009.

PRIMARY SOURCE

PRESIDENT BUSH'S 2002 STATE OF THE UNION ADDRESS

SYNOPSIS: President George W. talks about his plans for winning the war on terrorism, strengthening homeland defense, and revitalizing the economy. He also introduces the controversial term "Axis of Evil" in describing North Korea, Iran, and Iraq.

Mr. Speaker, Vice President Cheney, members of Congress, distinguished guests, fellow citizens, as we gather tonight, our nation is at war, our economy is in recession and the civilized world faces unprecedented dangers. Yet the state of our union has never been stronger.

We last met in an hour of shock and suffering. In four short months, our nation has comforted the victims, begun to rebuild New York and the Pentagon, rallied a great coalition, captured, arrested and rid the world of thousands of terrorists, destroyed Afghanistan's terrorist training camps, saved a people from starvation and freed a country from brutal oppression.

The American flag flies again over our embassy in Kabul. Terrorists who once occupied Afghanistan now occupy cells at Guantanamo Bay. And terrorist leaders who urged followers to sacrifice their lives are running for their own.

America and Afghanistan are now allies against terror. We will be partners in rebuilding that country. And this evening we welcomed the distinguished interim leader of a liberated Afghanistan: Chairman Hamid Karzai.

The last time we met in this chamber, the mothers and daughters of Afghanistan were captives in their own homes, forbidden from working or going to school. Today women are free, and are part of Afghanistan's new government. And we welcome the new minister of women's affairs, Dr. Sima Samar.

Our progress is a tribute to the spirit of the Afghan people, to the resolve of our coalition and to the might of the United States military.

When I called our troops into action, I did so with complete confidence in their courage and skill. And tonight, thanks to them, we are winning the war on terror. The men and women of our armed forces have delivered a message now clear to every enemy of the United States: Even 7,000 miles away, across oceans and continents, on mountaintops and in caves—you will not escape the justice of this nation.

For many Americans, these four months have brought sorrow and pain that will never completely go away. Every day a retired firefighter returns to Ground Zero to feel closer to his two sons who died there. At a memorial in New York, a little boy left his football with a note for his lost father: "Dear Daddy, please take this to Heaven. I don't want to play football until I can play with you again someday."

Last month, at the grave of her husband, Michael, a CIA officer and Marine who died in Mazur-e-Sharif, Shannon Spann said these words of farewell: "Semper fi, my love." Shannon is with us tonight.

Shannon, I assure you and all who have lost a loved one that our cause is just, and our country will never forget the debt we owe Michael and all who gave their lives for freedom. Our cause is just, and it continues. Our discoveries in Afghanistan confirmed our worst fears, and showed us the true scope of the task ahead. We have seen the depth of our enemies' hatred in videos, where they laugh about the loss of innocent life. And the depth of their hatred is equaled by the madness of the destruction they design. We have found diagrams of American nuclear power plants and public water facilities, detailed instructions for making chemical weapons, surveillance maps of American cities, and thorough descriptions of landmarks in America and throughout the world.

What we have found in Afghanistan confirms that, far from ending there, our war against terror is only beginning. Most of the 19 men who hijacked planes on September the 11th were trained in Afghanistan's camps. And so were tens of thousands of others. Thousands of dangerous killers, schooled in the methods of murder, often supported by outlaw regimes, are now spread throughout the world like ticking time bombs, set to go off without warning.

Thanks to the work of our law enforcement officials and coalition partners, hundreds of terrorists have been arrested, yet tens of thousands of trained terrorists are still at large. These enemies view the entire world as a battlefield, and we must pursue them wherever they are. So long as training camps operate, so long as nations harbor terrorists, freedom is at risk and America and our allies must not, and will not, allow it.

Our nation will continue to be steadfast, and patient and persistent in the pursuit of two great objectives. First, we will shut down terrorist camps, disrupt terrorist plans, and bring terrorists to justice. And second, we must prevent the terrorists and regimes who seek chemical, biological or nuclear weapons from threatening the United States and the world.

Our military has put the terror training camps of Afghanistan out of business, yet camps still exist in at least a dozen countries. A terrorist underworld—including groups like Hamas, Hezbollah, Islamic Jihad and Jaish-i-Mohammed—operates in remote jungles and deserts, and hides in the centers of large cities.

While the most visible military action is in Afghanistan, America is acting elsewhere. We now have troops in the Philippines, helping to train that country's armed forces to go after terrorist cells that have executed an American, and still hold hostages. Our soldiers, working with the Bosnian government, seized terrorists who were plotting to bomb our embassy. Our Navy is patrolling the coast of Africa to block the shipment of weapons and the establishment of terrorist camps in Somalia.

My hope is that all nations will heed our call and eliminate the terrorist parasites who threaten their countries and our own. Many nations are acting forcefully. Pakistan is now cracking down on terror, and I admire the strong leadership of President Musharraf.

But some governments will be timid in the face of terror. And make no mistake about it: If they do not act, America will.

Our second goal is to prevent regimes that sponsor terror from threatening America or our friends and allies with weapons of mass destruction. Some of these

President George W. Bush makes a point during his State of the Union address on January 29, 2002. © REUTERS/ CORBIS.

regimes have been pretty quiet since September the 11th. But we know their true nature. North Korea is a regime arming with missiles and weapons of mass destruction, while starving its citizens.

Iran aggressively pursues these weapons and exports terror, while an unelected few repress the Iranian people's hope for freedom.

Iraq continues to flaunt its hostility toward America and to support terror. The Iraqi regime has plotted to develop anthrax and nerve gas and nuclear weapons for over a decade. This is a regime that has already used poison gas to murder thousands of its own citizens—leaving the bodies of mothers huddled over their dead children. This is a regime that agreed to international inspections—then kicked out the inspectors. This is a regime that has something to hide from the civilized world. States like these, and their terrorist allies, constitute an axis of evil, arming to threaten the peace of the world. By seeking weapons of mass destruction, these regimes pose a grave and growing danger. They could provide these arms to terrorists, giving them the means to match their hatred. They could attack our allies or attempt to blackmail the United States. In any of these cases, the price of indifference would be catastrophic.

We will work closely with our coalition to deny terrorists and their state sponsors the materials, technology, and expertise to make and deliver weapons of mass destruction. We will develop and deploy effective missile defenses to protect America and our allies from sudden attack. And all nations should know: America will do what is necessary to ensure our nation's security.

We'll be deliberate, yet time is not on our side. I will not wait on events while dangers gather. I will not stand by as peril draws closer and closer. The United States of America will not permit the world's most dangerous regimes to threaten us with the world's most destructive weapons.

Our war on terror is well begun, but it is only begun. This campaign may not be finished on our watch—yet it must be and it will be waged on our watch.

We can't stop short. If we stopped now—leaving terror camps intact and terror states unchecked—our sense of security would be false and temporary. History has called America and our allies to action, and it is both our responsibility and our privilege to fight freedom's fight.

Our first priority must always be the security of our nation, and that will be reflected in the budget I send to Congress. My budget supports three great goals for America: We will win this war; we'll protect our homeland; and we will revive our economy.

September the 11th brought out the best in America, and the best in this Congress. And I join the American people in applauding your unity and resolve. Now Americans deserve to have this same spirit directed toward addressing problems here at home. I'm a proud member of my party—yet as we act to win the war, protect our people, and create jobs in America, we must act, first and foremost, not as Republicans, not as Democrats, but as Americans.

It costs a lot to fight this war. We have spent more than a billion dollars a month—over $30 million a day— and we must be prepared for future operations. Afghanistan proved that expensive precision weapons defeat the enemy and spare innocent lives, and we need more of them. We need to replace aging aircraft and make our military more agile, to put our troops anywhere in the world quickly and safely. Our men and women in uniform deserve the best weapons, the best equipment, the best training—and they also deserve another pay raise.

My budget includes the largest increase in defense spending in two decades—because while the price of freedom and security is high, it is never too high. Whatever it costs to defend our country, we will pay.

The next priority of my budget is to do everything possible to protect our citizens and strengthen our nation against the ongoing threat of another attack. Time and distance from the events of September the 11th will not make us safer unless we act on its lessons. America is no longer protected by vast oceans. We are protected from attack only by vigorous action abroad, and increased vigilance at home.

My budget nearly doubles funding for a sustained strategy of homeland security, focused on four key areas: bioterrorism, emergency response, airport and border security, and improved intelligence. We will develop vaccines to fight anthrax and other deadly diseases. We will increase funding to help states and communities train and equip our heroic police and firefighters. We will improve intelligence collection and sharing, expand patrols at our borders, strengthen the security of air travel, and use technology to track the arrivals and departures of visitors to the United States.

Homeland security will make America not only stronger, but, in many ways, better. Knowledge gained from bioterrorism research will improve public health. Stronger police and fire departments will mean safer neighborhoods. Stricter border enforcement will help combat illegal drugs. And as government works to better secure our homeland, America will continue to depend on the eyes and ears of alert citizens.

A few days before Christmas, an airline flight attendant spotted a passenger lighting a match. The crew and passengers quickly subdued the man, who had been trained by al Qaeda and was armed with explosives. The people on that airplane were alert and, as a result, likely saved nearly 200 lives. And tonight we welcome and thank flight attendants Hermis Moutardier and Christina Jones.

Once we have funded our national security and our homeland security, the final great priority of my budget is economic security for the American people. To achieve these great national objectives—to win the war, protect the homeland and revitalize our economy—our budget will run a deficit that will be small and short-term, so long as Congress restrains spending and acts in a fiscally responsible way. We have clear priorities and we must act at home with the same purpose and resolve we have shown overseas: We'll prevail in the war, and we will defeat this recession.

Americans who have lost their jobs need our help and I support extending unemployment benefits and direct assistance for health care coverage. Yet American workers want more than unemployment checks—they want a steady paycheck. When America works, America prospers, so my economic security plan can be summed up in one word: jobs.

Good jobs begin with good schools, and here we've made a fine start. Republicans and Democrats worked together to achieve historic education reform so that no child is left behind. I was proud to work with members of both parties, Chairman John Boehner and Congressman George Miller. Senator Judd Gregg. And I was so proud of our work, I even had nice things to say about my friend, Ted Kennedy. I know the folks at the Crawford coffee shop couldn't believe I'd say such a thing, but our work on this bill shows what is possible if we set aside posturing and focus on results.

There is more to do. We need to prepare our children to read and succeed in school with improved Head Start and early childhood development programs. We must upgrade our teacher colleges and teacher training and launch a major recruiting drive with a great goal for America: a quality teacher in every classroom.

Good jobs also depend on reliable and affordable energy. This Congress must act to encourage conservation, promote technology, build infrastructure, and it must act to increase energy production at home so America is less dependent on foreign oil.

Good jobs depend on expanded trade. Selling into new markets creates new jobs, so I ask Congress to finally approve trade promotion authority. On these two key issues, trade and energy, the House of Representatives has acted to create jobs, and I urge the Senate to pass this legislation.

Good jobs depend on sound tax policy. Last year, some in this hall thought my tax relief plan was too small; some thought it was too big. But when those checks arrived in the mail, most Americans thought tax relief was just about right. Congress listened to the people and responded by reducing tax rates, doubling the child credit, and ending the death tax. For the sake of long-term growth and to help Americans plan for the future, let's make these tax cuts permanent.

The way out of this recession, the way to create jobs, is to grow the economy by encouraging investment in factories and equipment, and by speeding up tax relief so people have more money to spend. For the sake of American workers, let's pass a stimulus package.

Good jobs must be the aim of welfare reform. As we reauthorize these important reforms, we must always remember the goal is to reduce dependency on government and offer every American the dignity of a job.

Americans know economic security can vanish in an instant without health security. I ask Congress to join me this year to enact a patients' bill of rights to give uninsured workers credits to help buy health coverage, to approve an historic increase in spending for veterans' health, and to give seniors a sound and modern Medicare system that includes coverage for prescription drugs.

A good job should lead to security in retirement. I ask Congress to enact new safeguards for 401K and pension plans. Employees who have worked hard and saved all their lives should not have to risk losing everything if their company fails. Through stricter accounting standards and tougher disclosure requirements, corporate America must be made more accountable to employees and shareholders and held to the highest standards of conduct.

Retirement security also depends upon keeping the commitments of Social Security, and we will. We must make Social Security financially stable and allow personal retirement accounts for younger workers who choose them.

Members, you and I will work together in the months ahead on other issues: productive farm policy, a cleaner environment, broader home ownership, especially among minorities, and ways to encourage the good work of charities and faith-based groups. I ask you to join me on these important domestic issues in the same spirit of cooperation we'e applied to our war against terrorism.

During these last few months, I've been humbled and privileged to see the true character of this country in a time of testing. Our enemies believed America was weak and materialistic, that we would splinter in fear and selfishness. They were as wrong as they are evil.

The American people have responded magnificently, with courage and compassion, strength and resolve. As I have met the heroes, hugged the families and looked into the tired faces of rescuers, I have stood in awe of the American people.

And I hope you will join me—I hope you will join me in expressing thanks to one American for the strength and calm and comfort she brings to our nation in crisis, our First Lady, Laura Bush.

None of us would ever wish the evil that was done on September the 11th, yet after America was attacked, it was as if our entire country looked into a mirror and saw our better selves. We were reminded that we are citizens, with obligations to each other, to our country, and to history. We began to think less of the goods we can accumulate, and more about the good we can do.

For too long our culture has said, "If it feels good, do it." Now America is embracing a new ethic and a new creed: "Let's roll." In the sacrifice of soldiers, the fierce brotherhood of firefighters, and the bravery and generosity of ordinary citizens, we have glimpsed what a new culture of responsibility could look like. We want to be a nation that serves goals larger than self. We've been offered a unique opportunity, and we must not let this moment pass.

My call tonight is for every American to commit at least two years—4,000 hours over the rest of your lifetime—to the service of your neighbors and your nation. Many are already serving, and I thank you. If you aren't sure how to help, I've got a good place to start. To sustain and extend the best that has emerged in America, I invite you to join the new USA Freedom Corps. The Freedom Corps will focus on three areas of need: responding in case of crisis at home; rebuilding our communities; and extending American compassion throughout the world.

One purpose of the USA Freedom Corps will be homeland security. America needs retired doctors and nurses who can be mobilized in major emergencies; volunteers to help police and fire departments; transportation and utility workers well trained in spotting danger.

Our country also needs citizens working to rebuild our communities. We need mentors to love children, especially children whose parents are in prison. And we need more talented teachers in troubled schools. USA Freedom Corps will expand and improve the good efforts of AmeriCorps and Senior Corps to recruit more than 200,000 new volunteers.

And America needs citizens to extend the compassion of our country to every part of the world, so we will renew the promise of the Peace Corps, double its volunteers over the next five years, and ask it to join a new effort to encourage development and education and opportunity in the Islamic world.

This time of adversity offers a unique moment of opportunity—a moment we must seize to change our culture. Through the gathering momentum of millions of acts of service and decency and kindness, I know we can overcome evil with greater good. And we have a great opportunity during this time of war to lead the world toward the values that will bring lasting peace.

All fathers and mothers, in all societies, want their children to be educated, and live free from poverty and violence. No people on Earth yearn to be oppressed, or aspire to servitude, or eagerly await the midnight knock of the secret police.

If anyone doubts this, let them look to Afghanistan, where the Islamic "street" greeted the fall of tyranny with song and celebration. Let the skeptics look to Islam's own rich history, with its centuries of learning and tolerance and progress. America will lead by defending liberty and justice because they are right and true and unchanging for all people everywhere.

No nation owns these aspirations, and no nation is exempt from them. We have no intention of imposing our culture. But America will always stand firm for the nonnegotiable demands of human dignity: the rule of law; limits on the power of the state; respect for women; private property; free speech; equal justice; and religious tolerance.

America will take the side of brave men and women who advocate these values around the world, including the Islamic world, because we have a greater objective than eliminating threats and containing resentment.

We seek a just and peaceful world beyond the war on terror.

In this moment of opportunity, a common danger is erasing old rivalries. America is working with Russia and China and India, in ways we never have before, to achieve peace and prosperity. In every region, free markets and free trade and free societies are proving their power to lift lives. Together with friends and allies from Europe to Asia, and Africa to Latin America, we will demonstrate that the forces of terror cannot stop the momentum of freedom.

The last time I spoke here, I expressed the hope that life would return to normal. In some ways, it has. In others, it never will. Those of us who have lived through these challenging times have been changed by them. We've come to know truths that we will never question: evil is real, and it must be opposed. Beyond all differences of race or creed, we are one country, mourning together and facing danger together. Deep in the American character, there is honor, and it is stronger than cynicism. And many have discovered again that even in tragedy—especially in tragedy—God is near.

In a single instant, we realized that this will be a decisive decade in the history of liberty, that we've been called to a unique role in human events. Rarely has the world faced a choice more clear or consequential.

Our enemies send other people's children on missions of suicide and murder. They embrace tyranny and death as a cause and a creed. We stand for a different choice, made long ago, on the day of our founding. We affirm it again today. We choose freedom and the dignity of every life.

Steadfast in our purpose, we now press on. We have known freedom's price. We have shown freedom's power. And in this great conflict, my fellow Americans, we will see freedom's victory.

Thank you all. May God bless.

FURTHER RESOURCES
Books
Knott, Stephen F. *Rush to Judgment: George W. Bush, the War on Terror, and His Critics.* Lawrence: University Press of Kansas, 2012.

Web Sites
"Frontline: How Iran Entered the 'Axis.'" *PBS.* www.pbs.org/wgbh/pages/frontline/shows/tehran/axis/map.html (accessed on February 27, 2013).

Wagner, Alex. "Bush Labels North Korea, Iran, Iraq an 'Axis of Evil.'" *Arms Control Association*, March 2002. www.armscontrol.org/act/2002_03/axismarch02 (accessed on February 27, 2013).

USA PATRIOT Act and Surrounding Controversy

"More Surveillance Equals Less Liberty: Patriot Act Reduces Privacy, Undercuts Judicial Review"

Newspaper editorial

By: Timothy Lynch

Date: September 10, 2003

Source: Lynch, Timothy. "More Surveillance Equals Less Liberty: Patriot Act Reduces Privacy, Undercuts Judicial Review." *The Hill*, September 10, 2003.

About the Publication: *The Hill* is a Washington, D.C., newspaper that reports on the activity of the U.S. Congress, its primary audience. The paper runs profiles, news about political developments and campaigns, arts and dining reviews, investigative pieces, and editorial pieces about Capitol Hill and its denizens. During the 2000s, *The Hill* was the most-read and highest-circulated Capitol Hill news publication.

"ALA Joins Challenge to Patriot Act in U.S. Supreme Court"

Press release

By: American Library Association

Date: October 4, 2005

Source: American Library Association. "ALA Joins Challenge to Patriot Act in U.S. Supreme Court." *ALA: American Library Association*. www.ala.org/news/news/pressreleases2005/october2005/alapatriotamicus (accessed on March 3, 2013).

About the organization: The American Library Association (ALA) was founded as a non-profit in 1876 by a small group of librarians who recognized the need for a professional organization that would allow them to do their jobs more efficiently and effectively. According to the ALA's constitution, its mission is "to provide

leadership for the development, promotion, and improvement of library and information services and the profession of librarianship in order to enhance learning and ensure access to information for all." The oldest library organization in the world, the ALA boasted a membership of around sixty-two thousand at the end of the first decade of the 2000s.

INTRODUCTION

During the period directly following the September 11, 2011, terrorist attacks, there was a pervasive sentiment, present among U.S. legislators and civilians alike, that the nation's stability and people were no longer secure from violence. The atmosphere of uncertainty, mistrust, and fear that arose from that unprecedented violation of U.S. security led Congress to pursue immediate action. During the month following 9/11, several anti-terrorism and heightened-security bills were proposed, which were consolidated into a single law under the Patriot Act. The Patriot Act incorporated measures proposed in its precursors, comprising changes and additions to an extensive array of policies regarding many facets of activity within the United States.

Both houses of Congress voted to approve the law eagerly, pushing it through the House of Representatives and the Senate in two days. On the third day, October 26, President George W. Bush signed the Patriot Act into law, to take effect on February 1, 2002. The act consists of ten titles, each including provisions related to a specific facet of the United States' new efforts to "deter and punish American terrorists in the United States and around the world, to enhance law enforcement investigatory tools, and for other purposes":

Title I—Enhancing Domestic Security against Terrorism: establishes funding for pursuing and investigating terrorists, as well as expanding the powers of the president in anti-terrorism capacities.

Title II—Enhanced Surveillance Procedures: authorizes a large expansion of the investigatory powers of federal agencies in relation to terrorism and foreign intelligence operations.

Title III—International Money Laundering Abatement and Financial Anti-terrorist Financing Act of 2001: provides measures against counterfeiting and international money laundering, and for improved financial record-keeping and transparency.

Title IV—Protecting the Border: expands the power of the Immigration and Naturalization Service and U.S. attorney general in enforcing immigration law and investigating immigrants.

Title V—Removing Obstacles to Investigating Terrorism: expedites and facilitates the investigation of terrorism by eliminating many of the requirements for federal acquisition of telephone and Internet records, among other things. Title V also grants the government the authority to issue financial rewards for assistance in combating terrorism.

Title VI—Providing for Victims of Terrorism, Public Safety Officers and Their Families: increases the availability, amount, and speed of compensation for the families of public safety officers killed in terrorist attacks.

Title VII—Increased Information Sharing for Critical Infrastructure Protection: allows the sharing of information and resources between law enforcement agencies regarding crimes that cross multiple jurisdictions.

Title VIII—Strengthening the Criminal Laws against Terrorism: establishes a legal definition of terrorism and the penalties associated with its assorted manifestations.

Title IX—Improved Intelligence: requires the establishment of standards, requirements, and priorities for foreign intelligence gathering, as well as guidelines for its use, transmission, and verification.

Title X—Miscellaneous: addresses various unsorted issues, such as the definition of electronic surveillance and the airing of grievances related to the Patriot Act, as well as officially condemning the September 11 terrorist attacks.

The Patriot Act represented one of the single largest changes to the Constitution in U.S. history, amending hundreds of laws. It was reauthorized three times after its initial implementation, and sections were expanded, changed, removed, and added entirely to reflect the changing priorities and perceptions of American efforts against terrorism. Since it entered into effect in 2002, the act consistently remained one of the most controversial and frequently discussed aspects of U.S. politics, continuing to influence the practices of the federal government in surveillance and investigation.

SIGNIFICANCE

Immediately after the Patriot Act was signed, it became the center of a fierce controversy that would continue throughout the decade. At the center of the debate surrounding the act lay a fundamental conflict between the necessity of adequately equipping and empowering the U.S. government to protect its citizens from internal and external threat, and the importance of maintaining the integrity of the Constitution and the privacies and protections it provides. Supporters of the law maintain its necessity in defending the nation against terrorism and subterfuge, while detractors claim that the Patriot Act unduly and unnecessarily violates the civil liberties of average citizens.

Probably the most inflammatory aspect of the Patriot Act was the federal investigatory behavior authorized by the law. Such behaviors included roving wiretaps, a special type of wiretap that does not require court approval to follow a target from one device to another; so-called "sneak and peek" warrants, which permitted law enforcement agents to access private premises without the knowledge or consent of their owner; the acquisition of personal records for tracking and analyzing private activity; and, most notably, the practice of invoking national security letters (NSLs) to circumvent the judicial approval requirements associated with criminal investigations. Under the Patriot Act, NSLs could be issued by any Federal Bureau of Investigation (FBI) agent with a rank of field supervisor or above, without a search warrant, probable cause, or even reasonable suspicion of probable cause, to authorize the acquisition of information pertinent to an investigation, such as telephone records, Internet usage records, email histories, and financial records. NSLs also included an indefinite gag order that prevented the people and organizations from which such information was gathered from disclosing that the NSL was ever conducted.

These NSLs were of particular concern to public libraries, organizations historically supportive of citizens' rights to privacy. If served with NSL orders, a library was prohibited from alerting the patron who was the person of interest that his or her library records were being scrutinized, as was any computer history he or she might have developed while using the library. This very act of secrecy went against the mission of public libraries, as did the violation without reason of a citizen's privacy.

Concerned citizens and politicians contended that these activities represented a violation of the First and Fourth Amendments and that they constituted unnecessarily intrusive conduct by the federal government. Commenters noted that no arrests leading from NSLs were ever disclosed, making the tens of thousands of NSLs issued during the decade seem completely unjustified. Critics attested that the Patriot Act was an example of post-9/11 opportunism, which exploited the fear and confusion that resulted from the attacks to expand the investigatory power of the U.S. government. It was frequently noted that "national security" and "fighting terrorism" were often cited as justification for what would otherwise have been illegal activity by federal agents and also invoked to avoid disclosing the details of criminal investigations.

Politicians throughout the decade were faced with the difficulty of defending the Patriot Act and maintaining the safety of the nation while being bombarded with complaints and lawsuits about the act's dubious legality. Despite much public dissatisfaction with the law, the effective strengthening of the U.S. security infrastructure permitted it to stay in place throughout the decade.

PRIMARY SOURCE

"MORE SURVEILLANCE EQUALS LESS LIBERTY: PATRIOT ACT REDUCES PRIVACY, UNDERCUTS JUDICIAL REVIEW"

SYNOPSIS: In this article, Lynch expresses concern that the Patriot Act authorizes excessively invasive behavior by federal agencies, specifically criticizing Section 215 and the alleged elimination of financial privacy produced by the act.

Now that two years have passed since the trauma of the Sept. 11 catastrophe, it is a good time to take a step back from the politics of the moment and take stock as to how our policymakers have responded to the threat posed by terrorism.

Sending American soldiers to Afghanistan was a decisive move by President Bush—because it was going right to the root of the problem, which is Osama bin Laden, his elite henchmen and his training camps.

The war on the home front also has been aggressive but in many ways misguided.

The assumption has been that there was simply too much liberty and privacy in America—and that federal law-enforcement agencies did not have enough power. To remedy that perceived problem, policymakers rushed the USA Patriot Act into law.

The Patriot Act was designed to reduce privacy and increase security. It has succeeded in at least reducing privacy.

Financial privacy is essentially gone. The feds have turned banks, brokerage houses, insurers and other financial institutions into state informers. Those firms must notify the Treasury Department about "suspicious" transactions, and the government can subpoena your

President George W. Bush and Attorney General John Ashcroft. © BOB E. DAEMMRICH/SYGMA/CORBIS.

checking-account records even if there is no evidence of wrongdoing.

Even though the feds were notified about several of hijacker Mohammed Atta's financial transactions before Sept. 11, no action was taken.

But in the logic of the public sector, that failure means the government was hobbled by insufficient money and insufficient power. Thus, the Treasury Department is now engaging in more surveillance.

Attorney General John Ashcroft says that all of the "safeguards of our Constitution" have been honored. But the Constitution's most vital safeguard is the principle of the separation of powers, and it has been undermined repeatedly.

One of the most odious provisions of the Patriot Act is known as Section 215.

That provision empowers FBI agents to demand things from people in terrorism-related investigations.

Judith Krug, director of intellectual freedom for the American Library Association, wears a button that shows indicating her position against certain aspects of the Patriot Act. The "hysteric" reference is to Attorney General John Ashcroft's statement that described claims that the FBI can monitor Americans' reading habits as "baseless hysteria." © AP IMAGES/ TED S. WARREN.

Ashcroft and conservative analysts claim that the Patriot Act operates in a similar fashion to ordinary search warrants so there is nothing to worry about. Heather MacDonald of the Manhattan Institute, for example, says, "The FBI can do nothing under Section 215 without the approval of a federal court."

In truth, the act creates a façade of judicial review. Here is the pertinent language: "Upon an application made pursuant to this section, the judge shall enter" the order.

That was crafty. Instead of enacting a law that says whenever an FBI agent wants to demand something from someone, he can do so as long as he is following leads in a terrorism investigation, the Patriot Act accomplishes the same end indirectly. The FBI can now use boilerplate forms and submit them to federal magistrates, who "shall" approve the applications.

The judicial check is not there. The judiciary cannot scrutinize the foundation for the Justice Department applications.

The impression is, in any event, false. The FBI can use Section 215 to obtain personal belongings—anything, really—directly from a person's home.

To top it all off, Section 215 has a gag provision that criminalizes speech about 215 orders. So if the CEO of a telecommunications firm finds that his company is spending a million dollars a year to comply with Section 215 orders and wants to complain to Congress, he better not make that call or send that letter. Leavenworth awaits such a move.

The courts are not likely to abide by that blatant restriction of free speech, but it may take years for a definitive ruling on the subject.

In the meantime, only the FBI knows how many people will have been cowed into silence by 215.

Too many conservatives have brushed aside grievances about civil-liberties violations in the mistaken belief that President Bush's political opponents are simply trying to dress up a partisan attack in noble-sounding rhetoric about liberty, privacy and the Constitution. The opposite is true.

President Bush and Attorney General Ashcroft have given their political opponents a just cause—namely, resisting the growth of a surveillance state.

PRIMARY SOURCE

"ALA JOINS CHALLENGE TO PATRIOT ACT IN U.S. SUPREME COURT."

SYNOPSIS: In direct response to the perceived unconstitutionality of the Patriot Act in general and NSLs in particular, the American Library Association joined several other book- and publishing-related organizations in filing an amicus brief in U.S. Supreme Court.

Today, the American Library Association (ALA) and the Freedom to Read Foundation joined with the Association of American Publishers and the American Booksellers Foundation for Free Expression to file an amicus brief before the U.S. Supreme Court supporting "John Doe," an ALA member who is challenging Section 505 of the USA PATRIOT Act with the support of the American Civil Liberties Union (ACLU).

The brief emphasizes the fact that a library already has been identified in a September 21 *New York Times* story, which stated: "A search of a court-operated Web site offered a pointer to the plaintiffs' identity. There, a case numbered 3:2005cv01256 is listed under the caption, "Library Connection Inc. v. Attorney General."

The ALA brief asserts: "The speculation highlights the absurdity of the permanent gag order, and puts an ALA member in an untenable bind. With this report in the public domain, the gag order both serves an even less important interest and causes even greater First Amendment harm that this Court must remedy."

The brief supports the ACLU motion before the U.S. Supreme Court seeking an emergency court order to lift the FBI gag order imposed on Doe so that the plaintiff, an actual recipient of a National Security Letter, can participate in the public debate as Congress prepares to reauthorize or amend the PATRIOT Act in the coming weeks.

"Doe is perhaps the most important voice in the current debate over the USA PATRIOT Act," said ALA President Michael Gorman. "It is essential that the Supreme Court vacate the stay barring Doe from speaking to Congress and the American people about his experience."

Section 505 authorizes the FBI to use National Security Letters, a form of administrative subpoena, to demand a wide range of personal records, including library records, without court approval or judicial supervision, permitting the FBI to demand a library user's records without showing that

the library user is suspected of wrongdoing. Those who receive an NSL are subject to an automatic, permanent gag order and are required to keep silent.

U.S. District Judge Janet C. Hall previously ruled that disclosure of the recipient's identity would jeopardize neither national security nor the investigation. The federal government has appealed to the 2nd U.S. Circuit Court of Appeals.

FURTHER RESOURCES
Books

Etzioni, Amitai. *How Patriotic Is the Patriot Act?: Freedom Versus Security in the Age of Terrorism.* London: Routledge, 2004.

Scheppler, Bill. *The USA PATRIOT Act: Antiterror Legislation in Response to 9/11 (Library of American Laws and Legal Principles).* New York: Rosen, 2005.

Smith, Cary S. *The Patriot Act: Issues and Controversies.* Springfield, IL: Charles C. Thomas, 2010.

Web Sites

Abramson, Larry, and Maria Godoy. "The Patriot Act: Key Controversies." *National Public Radio.* www.npr.org/news/specials/patriotact/patriotactdeal.html (accessed on March 7, 2013).

"The Patriot Act: What Is the Proper Balance Between National Security and Individual Rights?" *Constitutional Rights Foundation.* www.crf-usa.org/america-responds-to-terrorism/the-patriot-act.html (accessed on March 7, 2013).

"Reform the Patriot Act." *ACLU.* www.aclu.org/free-speech-national-security-technology-and-liberty/reform-patriot-act-section-215 (accessed on March 7, 2013).

"The USA PATRIOT Act." *American Library Association.* www.ala.org/advocacy/advleg/federallegislation/theusa-patriotact (accessed on March 7, 2013).

"The USA PATRIOT Act: Preserving Life and Liberty." *United States Department of Justice.* www.justice.gov/archive/ll/highlights.htm (accessed on March 7, 2013).

"Green Is the New Black"

Magazine article

By: Graydon Carter

Date: May 2006

Source: Carter, Graydon. "Green Is the New Black." *Vanity Fair,* May 2006. www.vanityfair.com/magazine/2006/05/graydon200605 (accessed on March 19, 2013).

About the Magazine: First published as a men's fashion magazine in 1913 under the name *Dress and Vanity Fair*, the periodical thrived throughout the 1920s until the Great Depression swept America and forced the publication to merge with *Vogue* in 1935. Condé Nast revived the magazine in 1983 and it became known for its controversial photography as well as hard-hitting journalism. In the twenty-first century, *Vanity Fair* publishes all things having to do with pop fashion and society.

INTRODUCTION

George W. Bush was elected president of the United States in 2000, and took office on January 20, 2001. Within a month of assuming the responsibilities of his new office, Bush drew the criticism of environmentalist and conservationist groups for his refusal to impose caps on the emission of carbon monoxide by power plants. Despite campaign assurances to the contrary, the new president contended that he was not obligated to limit the emission of the carcinogenic and ozone-depleting aerosol because doing so was not mandated by the Clean Air Act, although the prevailing scientific consensus suggested that carbon dioxide was a leading cause of atmospheric damage. In March 2001, Bush announced his refusal to implement the Kyoto Protocol, an international agreement to lower the emission of harmful chemicals and pollutants into the atmosphere, disregarding the fact that the United States had been a leading proponent of the treaty, which President Bill Clinton had signed in 1997. Bush reasoned that the United States did not have to honor its commitment because doing so would hinder its efforts to achieve energy independence and reduce the competitiveness of its national economy. By 2011, the United States was the only member of the United Nations not to recognize the Kyoto Protocol.

The Bush administration's environmental policy rested largely on servicing the interests of industry. During his presidency, the U.S. Forest Service saw massive budget cuts and restrictions of authority, leading to the allowance of oil drilling and excavation in and near previously protected areas, such as the Arctic National Wildlife Refuge in Alaska and the Arches State Park in Utah. Under Bush, the Environmental Protection Agency (EPA) removed protections against development, logging, and recreational activity in national forests. He was also responsible for dismantling wildlife protection policies, reducing the size of the protected species list and many of the legal protections afforded to endangered species and their habitats. Bush also reversed historical precedent by endorsing commercial whaling in American waters.

Bush and his advisers officially expressed uncertainty at the notion of global warming, ignoring the growing scientific consensus that human activity was responsible for the depletion of the Earth's atmosphere and consequential elevation of global temperatures. Philip A. Cooney, a former lobbyist for the oil industry and one of Bush's appointees to the White House Council on Environmental Equality, even admitted to actively censoring federal environmental reports to minimize the inclusion of scientific findings linking human activity to climate change. Bush's EPA permitted an increase in the use of toxic pesticides, harmful to both humans and the atmosphere. It also defunded programs to clean up hazards such as mercury, lead, and arsenic from the environment, as well as permitting a 6 percent decrease in the fuel economy of American automobiles, the nation's leading use of petrol.

In an attempt to convince the public that he had the best interests of the environment in mind, Bush passed the Clear Skies Act, an amendment of the long-standing Clean Air Act. The Clear Skies Act sought to reduce the emission of mercury, nitrogen oxide, sulfur dioxide, and carbon monoxide. However, the Natural Resources Defense Council and other environmentalist organizations objected to the law, noting that it was more lenient than its predecessor, and would contribute to global warming, weaken pollution-fighting efforts, and harm public health. The one action taken by Bush that was universally lauded by environmentalists was his designation of almost 200,000 square miles of Pacific coastal area as a national monument, prohibiting the destruction of the fragile marine ecosystem. During the same period, he also passed policies prohibiting the performance of environmental impact surveys on potential mining sites, disallowing research of the impact of global warming of protected species and habitats, and uniformly permitting oil drilling in national parks (although this measure was overturned in federal court).

SIGNIFICANCE

The Bush administration was condemned by scientists and environmental groups as the single most destructive in U.S. history. As with much of Bush's policy, both foreign and domestic, it was widely asserted that his environmental policy was designed to assist the interests of powerful industrial lobbies, particularly those involving manufacturing, energy production, and oil. Upon leaving office, Bush had created an extensive web of laws protecting pollution and the destruction of natural ecosystems, which would pose considerable obstacles for future administrations looking to curb the environmental impact of the United States.

Most significantly, the Bush administration's refusal to acknowledge global warming with any attitude but apprehension created a lasting debate about the effects of industry on the global environment. Despite overwhelming scientific evidence that human activity was having a directly adverse effect on the environment, official refutation of that point created a persistent sense of doubt that permitted lawmakers and industrialists to continue to pollute unabated. The Bush EPA's deliberate obfuscation of scientific findings also created a lasting debate among the American public about climate change, even though there were few environmental scientists willing to challenge the validity of humanity's contributions to global warming.

Bush's reluctance to impose any type of restriction on industrial activity led twenty-four state governments to implement their own emission caps and renewable energy policies. Individual states also passed legislation prohibiting the destruction of protected wildlife habitats and forests. The tension between environmentalists and the Bush administration brought the issue of global warming to the forefront of public discussion.

PRIMARY SOURCE

"GREEN IS THE NEW BLACK"

> SYNOPSIS: A letter from the editor introduces the first environmentally themed issue of *Vanity Fair* magazine with an indictment of President George W. Bush's environmental policy.

I'm confident that the environmental path that I announce will benefit the entire world.

—George W. Bush, February 2002

Like father, like son. In his 2004 State of the Union address, President Bush did not once mention global warming, clean air, clean water, pollution, or even the word "environment." The last president to go through an entire State of the Union address without mentioning the environment was Bush's father, George H. W. Bush, in 1992. The current Bush may have made a hash of everything he has turned his hand to as president, but in one area he has outperformed his father, and that is in dismantling the nation's environmental laws. Never before in American history has a president so willfully delivered the government departments and agencies responsible for safeguarding America's air, water, and public lands into the hands of anti-regulatory zealots, many of whom came from the same polluting industries they're charged with regulating. In most recent administrations, Congress provided a safety net when a president

went too far. The Republican-controlled Congress during the Bush years has done little in the way of providing a check on his anti-regulatory ideology.

In 2004, I wrote *What We've Lost*, a book about the Bush administration. It sold only reasonably well, in part, I think, because the book was a horrific downer, an unrelenting account of the administration's actions, bungles, deceptions, half-truths, untruths, and downright corruptions. I also think that for the first time in my entire life I was actually ahead of popular opinion. The book—still available in bookstores, by the way!—was simply too critical of the president and his administration, and Americans, being the generous people they are, were then still willing to give this collection of crooks and nincompoops the benefit of the doubt. The chapter on the environment was especially disheartening in that it set the template for much of what we have to look forward to during the final three years of the Bush administration.

The president did not waste time in his attack on the laws that protected the nation's air, water, and land. On January 20, 2001, his first day in office, Bush called in Chief of Staff Andrew Card and told him to send directives to every executive department with authority over environmental issues ordering them to immediately put on hold more than a dozen new regulations left over from the Clinton administration. These regulations included everything from one that lowered arsenic levels in drinking water to another that sought to reduce releases of raw sewage. There were rules setting limits on logging, drilling, and mining on public lands; increasing energy-efficiency standards; and banning snowmobiles in Yellowstone and Grand Teton National Parks. All were put on hold.

What Bush did on that first day as president came as no surprise to those who knew what he had left behind on December 21, 2000—his last day as governor of Texas. According to a 2000 report by the Republicans for Environmental Protection (REP), Texas was the worst state in the nation for emissions of toxic and ozone-causing chemicals, as well as for the discharge of carcinogens harmful to the brains and central nervous systems of small children. Texas had the highest number of hazardous-waste incinerators and released more airborne industrial toxins than any state in the nation. It was No. 1 in the production of cancer-causing benzene and vinyl chloride, in the release of toxic waste into underground wells, and in violations of clean-water discharge standards.

During Bush's six years in Austin, Houston passed Los Angeles as the city with the worst air quality in America; by the time he left office, a third of Texas's rivers were so polluted that they were unfit for recreational use. The REP study could find not a single initiative by Bush during his time as governor that sought to improve either the state's air or its water.

Two and a half years after the organization released its report on Bush's record in Texas, the same group produced an environmental report card on his term as president. The results were even worse than his grades at Yale: one B minus, six D's, and an F. This study, remember, wasn't done by a group of tree-hugging liberals—it was done by good old-fashioned Republicans. In 2004, when Bush was running for re-election, the REP Political Action Committee took the almost unprecedented step, for a G.O.P. group, of refusing to endorse the party's standard-bearer. It was "a simple and honest acknowledgement," the organization said, "that over the last four years, the Bush administration has compiled a deliberately anti-environmental, anti-conservation record that will result in lasting damage to public health and to America's natural heritage."

The president evidently felt otherwise. In his second presidential debate against Senator John Kerry, he declared, "I'm a good steward of the land. The quality of the air is cleaner since I've been the president. Fewer water complaints since I've been the president." But as the Natural Resources Defense Council reported in January 2005, "Over the course of the first term, this administration led the most thorough and destructive campaign against America's environmental safeguards in the past 40 years." According to Robert F. Kennedy Jr. and many others, Bush is without doubt the worst environmental president in U.S. history.

In this, *Vanity Fair*'s first "Green Issue," we begin our increased commitment to reporting on the threat to our precious environment. Of most pressing concern to all world citizens—or at least those not employed by the White House—is global warming. The administration has attempted to frame the danger with the softer-sounding "climate change." Veteran environmental writer Mark Hertsgaard, whose story on the current danger appears in this issue, argues that a more accurate phrasing, given the almost inarguable fact that global warming is upon us, is "climate crisis."

Michael Shnayerson, who wrote our story on mountaintop mining, has done numerous reports on the environment for us over the last few years and serves, I suppose, as *Vanity Fair*'s de facto environmental editor. Which is fitting, inasmuch as his father, Bob Shnayerson, was named *Time* magazine's first environmental editor back in 1969. Again, like father, like son.

FURTHER RESOURCES

Books

Kennedy, Robert F., Jr. *Crimes Against Nature: How George W. Bush and His Corporate Pals Are Plundering the Country and Hijacking Our Democracy.* New York: Harper Perennial, 2005.

Web Sites

Associated Press. "NASA Scientist rips Bush on Global Warming." *NBC News.* http://www.nbcnews.com/id/6341451/#.UUidMhwp-So (accessed on March 19, 2013).

"The Bush Record." *National Resources Defense Council.* http://www.nrdc.org/bushrecord/default.asp (accessed on March 19, 2013).

Goldenberg, Suzanne. "The Worst of Times: Bush's Environmental Legacy Examined." *Guardian.* www.guardian.co.uk/politics/2009/jan/16/greenpolitics-george-bush (accessed on March 19, 2013).

Hakim, Danny. "E.P.A. Holds Back Report on Car Fuel Efficiency." *New York Times,* July 28, 2005. www.nytimes.com/2005/07/28/business/28fuel.html (accessed on March 19, 2013).

Revkin, Andrew C. "Bush Aide Softened Greenhouse Gas Links to Global Warming." *New York Times,* June 8, 2005. www.nytimes.com/2005/06/08/politics/08climate.html?_r=2&scp=1&sq=Bush%20Aide%20Softened%20Greenhouse%20Gas%20Links%20to%20Global%20Warming&st=cse&oref=slogin& (accessed on March 19, 2013).

Abu Ghraib Inmate Photo

Photograph

By: Unidentified photographer

Date: June 13, 2006

Source: Unidentified photographer. AP Images. June 13, 2006.

About the photograph: This photograph is just one of hundreds of digital photographs and videos documented by U.S. Army personnel stationed at the Abu Ghraib prison in Baghdad, Iraq. Included in the images were depictions of sexual assault, physical abuse, sexual and psychological humiliation, simulated electroshock torture, and prison guards posing cheerfully next to the corpse of a murdered prisoner. The Department of Defense led an internal investigation into the matter, and *60 Minutes II* and the *New Yorker* magazine investigated reports of mistreatment of prisoners at Abu Ghraib.

INTRODUCTION

During his reign as president of Iraq, Saddam Hussein established a number of facilities across the country in which to imprison, torture, and sometimes execute political prisoners. Among these facilities was the Abu Ghraib prison, located in a suburb of Baghdad, the capital of Iraq and the scene of heavy fighting during the United States–led military invasion of the nation. Following the successful defeat of conventional Iraqi forces and the removal of Hussein's Ba'athist regime from power in April 2003, Coalition forces appropriated the country's infrastructure, including its prison complexes. Abu Ghraib prison was selected as a detention center for captured enemy combatants and suspected terrorists. U.S. military police personnel were tasked with caring for and extracting information from their captives.

Following President George W. Bush's declaration of victory in Iraq, fighting between U.S. troops and various elements of Iraqi society resistant to American rule increased dramatically. In an effort to overcome the unexpected challenge of maintaining the security and administrative functions of a foreign nation populated by armed, experienced, and opinionated religious and political factions, the architects of the American war effort pressured officials to authorize, and even encourage, extreme interrogation tactics. Controversially, the U.S. Department of Defense, headed by Secretary Donald Rumsfeld, approved of a series of "enhanced interrogation techniques" for quickly acquiring intelligence from captured resistance forces. These techniques, typically considered unlawful torture under international and U.S. laws, included waterboarding, the process of repeatedly simulating the experience of drowning to induce fear and psychological distress in a victim; extended periods of sensory and sleep deprivation; intimidation of prisoners with dogs and humiliation; binding captives in stress positions to induce fatigue and distress; exposure to extreme temperatures; prolonged exposure to harsh sounds at excessive volumes; and physical strikes to the body, known commonly as "beating."

Even such cruel interrogation proved unsatisfactory for the soldiers of the 320th Military Police Batallion, which was responsible for staffing and operating the seized Abu Ghraib prison (rechristened the "Baghdad Correctional Facility" by its captors). As captured enemy combatants and their alleged co-conspirators poured into Abu Ghraib, their overseers and interrogators subjected them to increasingly sadistic, inhumane methods of torture, documenting hundreds of instances of prisoner abuse in digital photographs and videos over the course of a year. In early 2004, the Department of Defense announced

that an ongoing internal investigation had discovered the misconduct of the U.S. Army personnel operating the Abu Ghraib prison, including instances of prisoner homicide, rape, torture, and psychological abuse. The official announcement received little reaction from the public until April of that year, when the CBS television-news program *60 Minutes II* and the *New Yorker* magazine both ran coverage of the treatment of prisoners at Abu Ghraib. The *60 Minutes II* exposé was particularly damning, due to its inclusion of several previously unreleased photos gathered by Abu Ghraib prison faculty.

SIGNIFICANCE

Once the popular media exposed the depravity of American Abu Ghraib prison staff, the public reacted with outrage, as did the international community. President Bush, Vice President Dick Cheney, and Secretary of Defense Rumsfeld attempted to depict the atrocities committed at Abu Ghraib as an isolated incident, not to be taken as representative of the U.S. military or its policies. However, as was revealed later in the decade with the publication of the "Torture Memos," attorneys employed by the federal government, including Assistant Attorney General John Yoo and future attorney general Alberto Gonzales, had formulated a justification of systemic prisoner abuse and torture prior to the invasion of Iraq, in reaction to the asymmetrical nature of terrorist operations. This justification relied on the designation of captured enemy operatives as "illegal combatants"—irregular, unconventional forces that, according to the Pentagon, were exempt from protection from torture and abuse as extended to all combatants under a traditional interpretation of U.S. and international law—and the opinion of senior advisors that the War on Terror granted sweeping expansion to the unilateral authority of the executive branch of the federal government, including the ability to disregard U.S. law when operating outside the nation's boundaries.

The U.S. Army ultimately removed a total of seventeen soldiers from duty for their involvement in the Abu Ghraib scandal. Eleven more were convicted in courts-martial on different charges, including maltreatment of prisoners, dereliction of duty, and assault, resulting in fines, imprisonment, demotions, and dishonorable discharges. Many public figures, politicians, and news publications called for Rumsfeld to resign, but he did not. The Abu Ghraib scandal prompted a national discussion about the increasingly questionable conduct of the U.S. forces occupying

■ **PRIMARY SOURCE**

Abu Ghraib Inmate Photo

SYNOPSIS: This photo depicts one of the many abuses inflicted upon detainees by their American captors at the Abu Ghraib military prison in Baghdad, Iraq. © AP IMAGES.

Iraq, with conservative pundits defending the extralegal tactics being employed as a necessary defense against the forces of terrorism, while liberal aspects of the public condemned the nation's perceived exclusion from laws and treaties that it had ratified.

Despite attempts by the Bush administration to downplay the significance of the abuse of prisoners at Abu Ghraib, subsequent investigations conducted by Amnesty International and other human rights groups revealed that prisoner abuse continued to plague U.S. military prisons in Iraq and Afghanistan. The United States instituted widespread protocol in response to such accusations, eventually resulting in the return of all prisons in Iraq to the country's national police in 2010. The Abu Ghraib scandal, and the attempts by U.S. officials to rationalize or dismiss it, widened the political rift between America and the governments of Middle Eastern nations, which perceived actions by U.S. forces to violate the human and sovereign rights of the Iraqi people.

PRIMARY SOURCE

"ABU GHRAIB INMATE PHOTO"

See primary source photo.

FURTHER RESOURCES

Books

Clemens, Michael. *The Secrets of Abu Ghraib Revealed: American Soldiers on Trial.* Herndon, VA: Potomac, 2010.

Web Sites

"Abu Ghraib." *NPR.* www.npr.org/templates/archives/archive.php?thingId=126953108 (accessed on March 6, 2013).

Follman, Mark. "Investigations and Other Resources." *Salon.* www.salon.com/2006/03/14/investigations_resources/ (accessed on March 6, 2013).

Hersh, Seymour M. "Chain of Command." *New Yorker*, May 17, 2004. www.newyorker.com/archive/2004/05/17/040517fa_fact2?currentPage=all (accessed on March 6, 2013).

"Iraq: Beyond Abu Ghraib: Detention and Torture in Iraq." *Amnesty International*, March 6, 2006. www.amnesty.org/en/library/info/MDE14/001/2006 (accessed on March 6, 2013).

Svensson, Birgit. "Iraqi Prisons: The Curse of Abu Ghraib." *Qantara.* http://en.qantara.de/wcsite.php?wc_c=8225 (accessed on March 6, 2013).

"Saddam Hussein, Defiant Dictator Who Ruled Iraq with Violence and Fear, Dies"

Newspaper article

By: Neil MacFarquhar

Date: December 30, 2006

Source: MacFarquhar, Neil. "Saddam Hussein, Defiant Dictator Who Ruled Iraq with Violence and Fear, Dies." *New York Times*, December 30, 2006. www.nytimes.com/2006/12/30/world/middleeast/30saddam.html?_r=2 (accessed on February 25, 2013).

About the Publication: The *New York Times* was founded in 1851 as a concise, four-page summary of daily news items. News mogul Adolph S. Ochs acquired the paper in 1896, expanding its scope and size. By the turn of the twentieth century, the *Times* was the pre-eminent U.S. newspaper, acclaimed for its objective reporting of "All the News That's Fit to Print." In 1905, the popularity and importance of the paper was memorialized by the City of New York, which called its new public square "Times Square," in honor of the publicaton. The paper's investigative reporting on official and political affairs has always been a trademark, garnering the journalism staff more than one hundred Pulitzer Prizes for its coverage of wars and governments—most notably for its publication of the "Pentagon Papers," leaked documents attesting to the mishandling and uncertainty of the Vietnam War. The *New York Times* remains the nation's most prestigious and important newspaper, and it continues to be owned and operated by descendants of Ochs.

INTRODUCTION

Saddam Hussein, the son in a poor tribal family in rural Iraq, exploited his nation's unstable political environment to establish supreme authority, in the process becoming one of the Arab world's most pivotal and polarizing figures. Hussein first gained influence in the late 1950s by attaching himself to the cause of the Ba'ath (Arabic for Renaissance) Party, a revolutionary group that promoted an amalgamated ideology containing strains of pan-Arabism, Arab nationalism, and socialism. Emboldened by a swell of anti-monarchy, anti-colonial sentiment in the Middle East, the people of Iraq staged a popular rebellion against King Faisal II and his Hashemite Dynasty on July 14, 1958, an event known as the 14 July Revolution. The revolutionaries replaced the deposed monarchy with an Iraqi Republic, headed primarily by members of the Ba'ath Party. Internal disputes between General Abd al-Karim Qasim, the nominal head of the new Republic, and Ba'ath Party officials led to a failed assassination attempt against the general, in which the young Saddam played an instrumental role.

After fleeing Iraq for the safety of Syria and Egypt, Saddam Hussein was awarded a position of authority within the Ba'ath Party for his loyalty to its cause. A series of purges, unstable alliances, and personal conflicts took place within the Iraqi government throughout the 1960s, ultimately producing a Ba'athist chokehold on politics in the country. In 1968, thanks to much bargaining and savvy, Saddam was appointed deputy of Ahmed Hassan al-Bakr's pseudo-socialist regime, a position he filled with much success. Although al-Bakr was ostensibly the leader of the Iraqi Ba'ath Party and government, Hussein was a more popular and influential figure, successfully implementing unification and modernization programs encouraging literacy, Iraqi nationalism, class destratification, and economic infrastructure development. Within five years of his appointment, Hussein had transformed Iraq from a disorganized society fractured by sectarian conflict to a progressive, economically advanced nation unified under a strong central government.

One of Hussein's most intelligent acts as al-Bakr's deputy was overseeing the nationalization of Iraq's immense oil reserves. By seizing the nation's underdeveloped oil fields, Hussein was able to generate significant income for infrastructure improvement, as well as creating hundreds of thousands of government jobs. Clever political maneuvering and fortuitous circumstances allowed Hussein to claim control of Iraq's military in 1976, a position he relished. His forceful political tactics and strict enforcement of Ba'athist legal principals, often through secret or private police units, made him a notorious figure among the Iraqi people, although not an unpopular one. In 1979, Hussein made a power grab, ousting the former president of the Republic and purging hundreds of political opponents from office. Many were executed after being put to farcical trial on charges of dissent or treason.

As Hussein was consolidating dominance of the Iraqi government, the neighboring nation of Iran was also undergoing a political transformation. Iran's secular Pahlavi dynasty was ousted by the nation's vocal Shia population, who installed a new, Islamic government, headed by the Ayatollah Khomeini. Saddam feared that his nation's under-represented Shia majority—although they accounted for only 20 percent of Iraq's government, Sunnis had complete control of the Ba'ath regime—would be inspired to attempt a similar coup, contrasting Hussein's pan-Arab aspirations with the wave of Islamist sentiment sweeping the Middle East. Threatened by the possibility of a Shia insurgency in Iraq, Hussein authorized a pre-emptive invasion of Iran in September 1980, initiating a conflict, known as the Iran-Iraq War, that would last eight years and cause approximately one million deaths between the two nations. It was during this conflict that the world first witnessed Saddam's possession of, and willingness to use, chemical weapons, both against enemy troops and unruly Iraqi Kurds, who saw the war with Iran as an opportunity to secede from Iraq to form an independent Kurdish state. State officials also revealed that Saddam was pursuing nuclear weapons research, although no success in the field was ever demonstrated.

Throughout the war, Iraq was depicted as the "good guy" by Western governments and media, receiving financial and military support from France, West Germany, the United States, and several Arab nations. When the war came to a UN-brokered standstill in 1988, neither side could be named the victor, although Iraq had accrued hundreds of billions of dollars in war debt and lost much of its oil-production infrastructure, whereas the Islamist Iranian government gained admiration and political traction for successfully fending off its hostile neighbor with little international support, lending credibility to the Shi'ite movement. Saddam attempted to pay back his country's enormous debt by colluding with other OPEC members to artificially limit the global availability of oil, thus raising the price Iraq could charge for petroleum exports. When Kuwait, among other nations, refused to comply with Hussein's demands for debt relief and oil-market manipulation, he grew incensed.

Claiming that Kuwait, a small emirate located on the southern border of Iraq, had been "slant drilling" into Iraqi territory and syphoning oil into its own fields, Hussein began amassing Iraqi troops near the perimeter of the country. Despite the warnings of U.S. officials, Hussein invaded Kuwait on August 2, 1990, alleging that the emirate was historically an important component of the territory of Iraq. The powerful Iraqi military had no difficulty seizing the capital and claiming the region as the nineteenth province of Iraq. On January 16, 1991, the United States and a coalition of allied militaries executed a continuous, devastating aerial campaign against Hussein's forces, quickly eliminating the Iraqi threat. In February, the coalition's ground divisions rolled into Kuwait, effortlessly routing the occupation and taking an estimated 175,000 prisoners.

As a penalty for Hussein's belligerence, noncompliance with military sanctions, and disregard for reparations demands, the UN imposed stiff economic embargoes on trade with Iraq, barring oil exports and food imports. These sanctions had a devastating effect on the Iraqi people, but strengthened Saddam's domestic power, as nepotism, cronyism, and strict adherence to the Ba'ath Party line became necessary for officials to garner access to food and resources. Discontent and starvation produced frequent revolts among Shia, Kurds, and political dissidents, each uprising met with swift, brutally violent suppression. Anyone who questioned or criticized Saddam or his administration disappeared or was tortured or killed. As Saddam aged, he became delusional and paranoid, frequently cycling through confidants, advisors, and favored officials, alienating Ba'ath Party members who became fearful for their personal safety.

While Saddam's officials and citizens grew wary of him, so did the international community. Saddam refused to permit UN inspectors into the country, fueling longstanding concern in the United States that Iraq was developing nuclear or biological weapons. The United Kingdom and United States occasionally conducted air and missile strikes against strategic targets within Iraq, hoping to encourage rebellion, but they were ultimately without effect. Political, personal, and religious oppression remained endemic under Hussein's increasingly despotic rule, and executions for minor or imaginary trespasses against the absolute Ba'ath law became an everyday occurrence.

SIGNIFICANCE

On March 20, 2003, a United States-led military coalition invaded Iraq, citing Saddam Hussein's well-documented human rights abuses and his regime's alleged possession of weapons of mass destruction (WMDs; chemical, biological, or nuclear weapons) as justification for the operation. Due largely to Saddam's paranoid insistence on personally directing the activity of the Iraqi Republican Guard, and also the fact that many of the former leaders of the Iraqi government and military had been killed and replaced with Hussein's family and sycophantic Ba'athist yes-men, the Iraqi military was quick to fall to the might of Western armed forces. Within a month, Hussein's tyrannical regime had been toppled, but the man himself had eluded capture and disappeared into the Iraqi countryside. An extensive manhunt ensued, lasting until December 13, when he was captured in a rural compound near Tikrit, where he was found lying in a trap-door-concealed hole outside a barn.

Following his capture and detention at a series of military bases and detention centers within Iraq, Saddam Hussein was put to trial by the newly installed provisional Iraqi government on June 30, 2004. The deposed president maintained his legitimate authority over the nation of Iraq throughout his hearing, during which he was charged with crimes against humanity in relation to his authorization of the murder and torture of hundreds of civilians. On November 5, 2006, the special tribunal assembled to determine Hussein's crimes found him guilty and sentenced him to death by hanging, a verdict that was carried out on December 30 of that year.

Saddam Hussein was personally responsible for the modernization of Iraq, one of the most destructive wars of the twentieth century, the marked division of Arab and Islamic cultural identities, the wrongful deaths of unknown numbers of innocent men, women, and children, and the United States' involvement in its bloodiest military conflict since Vietnam. Although the Iraqi people might prefer to forget the influence he had over their history, Saddam Hussein's historical importance cannot be denied.

PRIMARY SOURCE

"SADDAM HUSSEIN, DEFIANT DICTATOR WHO RULED IRAQ WITH VIOLENCE AND FEAR, DIES"

SYNOPSIS: In this obituary, the author chronicles the life and reign of Iraqi ex-president Saddam Hussein, as well as the circumstances surrounding his death.

The hanging of Saddam Hussein ended the life of one of the most brutal tyrants in recent history and negated the fiction that he himself maintained even as the gallows loomed—that he remained president of Iraq despite being toppled by the United States military and that his power and his palaces would be restored to him in time.

The despot, known as Saddam, had oppressed Iraq for more than 30 years, unleashing devastating regional wars and reducing his once promising, oil-rich nation to a claustrophobic police state.

For decades, it had seemed that his unflinching hold on Iraq would endure, particularly after he lasted through disastrous military adventures against first Iran and then Kuwait, where an American-led coalition routed his unexpectedly timid military in 1991.

His own conviction that he was destined by God to rule Iraq forever was such that he refused to accept that he would be overthrown in April 2003, even as American tanks penetrated the Iraqi capital, Baghdad, in a war that has become a bitterly contentious, bloody occupation.

After eluding capture for eight months, Mr. Hussein became the American military's High Value Detainee No. 1. But he heaped scorn on the Iraqi judge who referred to him as the "former" president after asking him to identify himself on the first day of his trial for crimes against humanity, which ultimately led to his execution.

"I didn't say 'former president,' I said 'president,' and I have rights according to the Constitution, among them immunity from prosecution," he growled from the docket. The outburst underscored the boundless egotism and self-delusion of a man who fostered such a fierce personality cult during the decades that he ran the Middle Eastern nation that joking about him or criticizing him in public could bring a death sentence.

If a man's life can be boiled down to one physical mark, Mr. Hussein's right wrist was tattooed with a line of three dark blue dots, commonly given to children in rural, tribal areas. Some urbanized Iraqis removed or at least bleached theirs, but Mr. Hussein's former confidants told *The Atlantic Monthly* that he never disguised his.

Ultimately, underneath all the socialist oratory, underneath the Koranic references, the tailored suits and the invocations of Iraq's glorious history, Mr. Hussein held onto the ethos of a village peasant who believed that the strongman was everything. He was trying to be a tribal leader on a grand scale. His rule was paramount, and sustaining it was his main goal behind all the talk of developing Iraq by harnessing its considerable wealth and manpower.

Mosques, airports, neighborhoods and entire cities were named after him. A military arch erected in Baghdad in 1989 was modeled on his forearms and then enlarged 40 times to hold two giant crossed swords. In school, pupils learned songs with lyrics like "Saddam, oh Saddam, you carry the nation's dawn in your eyes."

The entertainment at public events often consisted of outpourings of praise for Mr. Hussein. At the January 2003 inauguration of a recreational lake in Baghdad, poets spouted spontaneous verse and the official translators struggled to keep up with lines like, "We will stimulate ourselves by saying your name, Saddam Hussein, when we say Saddam Hussein, we stimulate ourselves."

While Mr. Hussein was in power, his statue guarded the entrance to every village, his portrait watched over each government office and he peered down from at least one wall in every home. His picture was so widespread that a joke quietly circulating among his detractors in 1988 put the country's population at 34 million—17 million people and 17 million portraits of Saddam.

BATTLES AND BLOODSHED

Throughout his rule, he unsettled the ranks of the Baath Party with bloody purges and packed his jails with political prisoners to defuse real or imagined plots. In one of his most brutal acts, he rained poison gas on the northern Kurdish village of Halabja in 1988, killing an estimated 5,000 of his own citizens suspected of being disloyal and wounding 10,000 more.

Even at the end, he showed no remorse. When four Iraqi politicians visited him after his capture in December 2003, they asked about his more brutal acts. He called the Halabja attack Iran's handiwork; he said that Kuwait was rightfully part of Iraq and that the mass graves were filled with thieves who fled the battlefields, according to Adnan Pachachi, a former Iraqi foreign minister. Mr. Hussein declared that he had been "just but firm" because Iraqis needed a tough ruler, Mr. Pachachi said.

It was a favorite theme, one even espoused in a novel attributed to Mr. Hussein called "Zabibah and the King."

At one point, the king asks the comely Zabibah whether the people needed strict measures from their leader. "Yes, Your Majesty," Zabibah replies. "The people need strict measures so that they can feel protected by this strictness."

Aside from his secret police, he held power by filling the government's upper ranks with members of his extended clan. Their Corleone-like feuds became the stuff of gory public soap operas. Mr. Hussein once sentenced his elder son, Uday, to be executed after he beat Mr. Hussein's food taster to death in front of scores of horrified party guests, but later rescinded the order. The husbands of his two eldest daughters, whom he had promoted to important military positions, were gunned down after they defected and then inexplicably returned to Iraq.

Continual wars sapped Iraq's wealth and decimated its people. In 1980, Mr. Hussein dragged his country into a disastrous attempt to overthrow the new Islamic government in neighboring Iran. By the time the war ended in stalemate in 1988, more than 200,000 Iraqis were dead and hundreds of thousands more wounded. Iran suffered a similar toll. Iraq's staggering war debt, pegged around $70 billion, soon had wealthy Arab neighbors demanding repayment. Enraged, he invaded Kuwait in August 1990, only to be expelled by an American-led coalition in the Persian Gulf war seven months later.

Yet in the language of his Orwellian government, Mr. Hussein never suffered a setback. After the gulf war ended with the deaths of an estimated 150,000 Iraqis, he called "the Mother of All Battles" his biggest victory and maintained that Iraq had actually repulsed an American attack.

"Iraq has punched a hole in the myth of American superiority and rubbed the nose of the United States in the dust," Mr. Hussein said.

His defeat in Kuwait, followed by more than a decade of tense confrontations with the West over his suspected weapons programs, ultimately led to his overthrow. The extended bloodbath that followed the invasion, with the monthly death toll of Iraqi civilians estimated roughly at 3,000 by the end of 2006, made some nostalgic for even the oppressive days of Mr. Hussein, when public security was not an issue. His repressive ways were credited with keeping the fractious population of 26 million—including 20 percent Sunni Muslims, who dominated; 55 percent Shiite Muslims; 20 percent Kurds plus several tiny minorities including Christians—from shattering along ethnic lines.

THE PATHWAY TO POLITICS

Saddam Hussein was born on April 28, 1937, in a mud hut on stilts near the banks of the Tigris River near the village of Tikrit, 100 miles northwest of Baghdad. He was raised by a clan of landless peasants, his father apparently deserting his mother before his birth. (Government accounts said the father died.)

"His birth was not a joyful occasion, and no roses or aromatic plants bedecked his cradle," his official biographer, Amir Iskander, wrote in "Saddam Hussein, the Fighter, the Thinker and the Man," published in 1981.

Mr. Hussein told his biographer that he did not miss his father growing up in an extended clan. But persistent stories suggest that Mr. Hussein's stepfather delighted in humiliating the boy and forced him to tend sheep. Eventually, he ran away to live with relatives who would let him go to school.

Mr. Hussein's first role in the rough world of Iraqi politics came in 1959, at age 22, when the Baath Party assigned him and nine others to assassinate Abdul Karim Kassem, the despotic general ruling Iraq. Violence was a quick way for a young man who grew up fatherless in an impoverished village to get ahead; bloodshed became the major theme of his life.

During the failed assassination, Mr. Hussein suffered a bullet wound to the leg. The official version portrayed him as a hero who dug the bullet out with a penknife, while the other version suggests that the plot failed because he opened fire prematurely.

He sought asylum in Egypt, where President Gamal Abdel Nasser nurtured the region's revolutionary movements. Soon after returning to Iraq, Mr. Hussein married his first cousin and the daughter of his political mentor, Sajida Khairallah Tulfah, on May 5, 1963. The couple had two sons, Uday and Qusay, and three daughters, Raghad, Rana and Hala. He had mistresses, including prominent Iraqi women, but never flaunted them.

His wife, three daughters and roughly a dozen grandchildren survive him. Uday and Qusay, along with Qusay's teenage son, Mustapha, died in July 2003 during a gun battle with American forces in a villa in the northern city of Mosul. Denounced by an informant, they had been the two most wanted men in Iraq after their father.

The first years of Saddam Hussein's marriage coincided with political tumult in Iraq, with at least six coups or attempted revolts erupting between the assassination of King Faisal II in 1958 and the July 1968 putsch that brought the Baath Party to power.

Mr. Hussein's main role while still in his early 30s was organizing the party's militia, the seed of the dreaded security apparatus. By November 1969, he had eliminated rivals and dissidents to the extent that President Ahmed Hassan al-Bakr appointed him vice president and deputy chairman of the Revolutionary Command Council, as the cabinet was known. Mr. Hussein remained head of the intelligence and internal security agencies, in effect controlling Iraq.

The Arab Baath Socialist Party, whose name means "renaissance" in Arabic, had been formed in the 1930s to push a secular, socialist creed as the ideal path to achieving Arab unity. But that dogma proved a sinister excuse for the imprisonment, exile or execution of all potential rivals.

No other Arab despot matched the savagery of Mr. Hussein as he went about bending all state institutions to his whim. His opening act, in January 1969, was hanging around 17 so-called spies for Israel in a downtown Baghdad square. Hundreds of arrests and executions followed as the civilian wing of the Baath Party gradually eclipsed the Iraqi military.

Mr. Hussein staged perhaps his most macabre purge in 1979, when at age 42 he consolidated his hold on Iraq. Having pushed aside President Bakr, he called a gathering of several hundred top Baathists.

One senior official stepped forward to confess to having been part of a widespread plot to allow a Syrian takeover. After guards dragged the man away, Mr. Hussein took to the podium, weeping at first as he began reading a list of dozens implicated. Guards dragged away each of the accused. Mr. Hussein paused from reading occasionally to light his cigar, while the room erupted in almost hysterical chanting demanding death to traitors. The entire dark spectacle, designed to leave no doubt as to who controlled Iraq, was filmed and copies distributed around the country.

Firing squads consisting of cabinet members and other top officials initially gunned down 21 men, including five ministers. Iraq's state radio said the officials executed their colleagues while "cheering for the long life of the

Party, the Revolution and the Leader, President, Struggler, Saddam Hussein."

Mr. Hussein invariably ensured that those around him were complicit in his bloody acts, which he masqueraded as patriotism, making certain that there would be no guiltless figure to rally opposition.

In an authoritative account of Mr. Hussein's government called "The Republic of Fear," the self-exiled Iraqi architect Kenaan Makiya (writing under the pseudonym Samir al-Khalil) estimated that at least 500 people died in the purge that consolidated Mr. Hussein's power.

Mr. Hussein's titles reflected his status as an absolute ruler modeled after one of his heroes, Josef Stalin of the former Soviet Union. They included president of the republic, commander in chief of the armed forces, field marshal and prime minister. In addition, the state-owned news media referred to him repeatedly as the Struggler, the Standard Bearer, the Knight of the Arab Nation and the Sword of the Arabs.

Mr. Hussein saw his first opportunity for Iraq to dominate the region in the turmoil that swept neighboring Iran immediately after its 1979 Islamic revolution. In September 1980, Mr. Hussein believed that by invading Iran he could both seize a disputed waterway along the border and inspire Iranians of Arab origin to revolt against their Persian rulers. Instead, they resisted fanatically. Mr. Hussein never acknowledged making a gross miscalculation; rather, he vilified the Iranian Arabs as traitors to the Arab cause.

Iraq fared badly in the war, not least because Mr. Hussein interfered in the battle plans despite a complete lack of military training, even issuing orders based on dreams. When strategies urged by Mr. Hussein failed, he often accused the commanders of betrayal, cowardice and incompetence and had them executed.

THE FIELD MARSHAL

Mr. Hussein adored the macho trappings of the armed forces, appointing himself field marshal and dressing his ministers in olive-green fatigues. If he was a poor military strategist, he was fortunate in his first choice of enemy. The fear that an Islamic revolution would spread to an oil producer with estimated reserves second only to Saudi Arabia tipped the United States and its allies toward Baghdad and they provided weapons, technology and, most important, secret satellite images of Iran's military positions and intercepted communications.

The war lasted for eight years until Iran accepted a cease-fire in July 1988, with both sides terrorizing each other's civilian populations by rocketing major cities. But the March 1988 mustard gas attack on the Iraqi village of Halabja by its own government was perhaps the most gruesome incident.

Mr. Hussein waged war while investing in massive development that markedly improved daily life. Rural villages were electrified and linked by modern highways. Iraq boasted some of the best universities and hospitals in the Arab world—all free. Its painters, musicians and other artists, helped by government subsidies, were also the most accomplished in the region. Mr. Hussein had his own development methods. Anyone who avoided mandatory adult literacy classes in rural areas faced three years in jail.

Official corruption was unknown in Iraq in the 1980s, and religious worship somewhat free. Mr. Hussein occasionally took populist measures to underscore the importance of the public welfare. Once, for example, he decided that his ministers were too fat and he demanded that they diet, publishing their real weights and their target weights in the news media. Mr. Hussein's own weight could fluctuate from chubby to relatively trim, although well tailored suits hid his paunch. Around six feet tall, he was stocky and wore a trademark moustache.

In keeping with a ruler who used violence to achieve and sustain power, Mr. Hussein's most widespread investments were in his military. He ended the Iran-Iraq war with one million men under arms.

By then Iraq had embarked on extensive projects to acquire a homegrown arsenal of nuclear, chemical and biological weapons. Iraq had also become a regional power, and Mr. Hussein expected to dominate the Arab world. In March 1990, he threatened to "burn half of Israel" if it ever acted against Iraq, even though the Israeli Air Force had humiliated the Iraqi leader by destroying his country's nuclear research center at Osirik in June 1981.

Mr. Hussein's next target was another neighbor, Kuwait, which Iraq had long considered part of Iraq and coveted for its deep-water port. On Aug. 2, 1990, his army swiftly occupied the tiny, immensely wealthy emirate, provoking an international crisis. Mr. Hussein declared the country Iraq's 19th province, installing a puppet government. Saudi Arabia and other conservative Arab states were shaken and outraged, while the United States and other Western countries feared for the oil fields ringing the Persian Gulf. The United Nations imposed a trade embargo and economic sanctions.

The United States and eventually 33 other nations deployed forces to the region and warned of a wider war if Mr. Hussein did not withdraw. He held onto Kuwait despite repeated threats from the United States, which dominated the military coalition by dispatching some 500,000 American soldiers. Mr. Hussein portrayed the invasion as the start of an Islamic holy war to liberate Jerusalem. He declared that the "throne dwarfs" of the gulf must be overthrown so their wealth could finance the Arab cause.

Iraqi president Saddam Hussein waves to supporters in Baghdad in October 1985. © AP IMAGES/INA.

His public aims resonated among many Arabs in Jordan, Yemen and elsewhere, particularly because the brutality of Mr. Hussein's government had never been detailed by the state-controlled media of other Arab states. In addition, Mr. Hussein's Scud missiles crashing into Tel Aviv, however ineffective, created a stir in the Arab world.

Washington and its coalition allies hoped that the war would bring Mr. Hussein's downfall. Even before the war ended, President George H. W. Bush encouraged the Iraqi people to overthrow him, but there was no coherent plan. The ground offensive against Iraq ended after 100 hours, partly out of concern that American troops not occupy an Arab capital, partly because Arab allies feared the disintegration of Iraq and partly because a "100-hour war" made a good sound bite. Dick Cheney, then secretary of defense, warned that sending American forces to Baghdad would get them stuck in a "quagmire."

This decision enabled much of the elite Republican Guard to escape with minimal losses. The first Bush administration did little to support Shiite and Kurdish uprisings that erupted immediately after the war. Mr. Hussein crushed them.

OIL, FOOD AND WEAPONS

For the next decade, Mr. Hussein repeatedly brought Iraq to the brink of renewed warfare by refusing United Nations weapons inspectors the access required to catalog and destroy Iraq's arsenal of unconventional weapons, as specified in the cease-fire agreement.

The United Nations maintained strict economic sanctions against Iraq until 1996, when some oil exports were allowed to pay for food, medicine and war reparations. The sanctions, devastating to Iraqis, proved a boon to Mr. Hussein and his subordinates. The Government Accountability Office in the United States Congress estimated that the Iraqi leader siphoned at least $10 billion from the program by making oil trades off the books and demanding kickbacks.

Still, in an effort to end sanctions, Baghdad over the years offered at least five "full, final and complete" weapons disclosures, which the United Nations dismissed as incomplete. Some of the most extensive revelations emerged after the astonishing August 1995 defection of Mr. Hussein's two sons-in-law and his two eldest daughters to Jordan. The Iraqi government was apparently worried that Lt. Gen. Hussein Kamel al-Majid, a son-in-law and the minister in charge of weapons development, would disclose all that he knew. Six months later, the general and his brother abruptly declared they had accepted amnesty and returned. Within days, Mr. Hussein's daughters divorced them, and they died in a violent shootout.

Although family feuds often descended into bloodshed, Mr. Hussein tried to maintain strict control of his own image. He dyed his hair black and refused to wear his reading glasses in public, according to interviews with exiles published in *The Atlantic Monthly* in March 2002. Because a slipped disc caused him to limp slightly, he was never filmed walking more than a few steps. Each of his 20 palaces was kept fully staffed, with meals prepared daily as if he were in residence to disguise his whereabouts. Delicacies like imported lobster were first dispatched to nuclear scientists to be tested for radiation and poison.

His wine of choice was Portuguese, Mateus Rosé, but he never drank in public to maintain the conceit that he was a strict Muslim. He even had genealogists draw a family tree that linked him to Fatima, the daughter of the Prophet Muhammad.

He kept an immaculate desk, with reports from all the ministries neatly stacked. He usually read only the executive summaries, but would occasionally dig deeper and always complained that he was being deceived. He often was, with even his son Qusay telling military commanders to lie if Mr. Hussein thought something had been accomplished that was not.

He was particularly phobic about germs. Even top generals summoned to meet him were often ordered to strip to their underwear and their clothes were then washed, ironed and X-rayed before they could get dressed to see him. Mr. Hussein's American jailers reported that he tried to maintain those precautions, using baby wipes to clean meal trays, his table and utensils before eating.

Rarely traveling abroad, and surrounded by often uneducated cousins, he had a limited worldview. He once reacted with wonder when an American reporter told him that the United States had no law against insulting the president. Former officials portrayed him as a vain, paranoid loner who no longer believed he was a normal person and considered compromise a sign of weakness.

Saad al-Bazzaz, an Iraqi writer and editor, said that Mr. Hussein, having risen so far beyond the village and cheated death so often, believed that God anointed him.

Mr. Bazzaz told *The Atlantic* that even Mr. Hussein's speeches echoed Koranic texts. "In the Koran, Allah says, 'If you thank me, I will give you more,'" Mr. Bazzaz said. "In the early '90s, Saddam was on TV, presenting awards to military officers, and he said, 'If you thank me, I will give you more.'"

CONTROLLING A NATION

Iraq under Mr. Hussein had a stifled quality. Imprisonment, torture, mutilation and execution were frequent occurrences, at least for those who chose to dabble in anything vaguely political. Simple information like the weather report was classified. There was no freedom of expression—even foreign newspapers were banned—and no freedom to travel. Contact with foreigners was proscribed.

There were widespread reports that Mr. Hussein himself periodically carried out the torture or even execution of those he felt had crossed him. In the summer of 1982, for example, Riyadh Ibrahim Hussein, the health minister, suggested during a cabinet meeting that Mr. Hussein step down to ease the negotiation of a cease-fire with Iran. Mr. Hussein recommended that the two retire to another room to discuss the proposal. When they did, a shot rang out. Mr. Hussein returned to the cabinet meeting alone, although in later interviews he denied killing anyone. The minister's widow was sent his dismembered corpse.

While assassinating Shiite Muslim religious leaders who opposed him, Mr. Hussein ordered mosques constructed around Baghdad on a scale not seen since it was the medieval capital of the Muslim caliphate. Perhaps the most striking was the Mother of All Battles mosque completed in 2001, the 10th anniversary of the Persian Gulf war. The minarets resembled Scud missiles, and the mosque held a Koran written with 28 gradually donated liters of Mr. Hussein's blood.

Evidence from inside Iraq after the invasion confirmed what United Nations weapons inspectors anticipated before—that Mr. Hussein abandoned the attempt to develop nuclear, biological and chemical weapons after his 1991 defeat. Orders from Mr. Hussein to destroy vestiges of the program, interpreted before the 2003 invasion as an attempt to hide their development, turned out to be an effort to comply with the ban.

The fatal controversy over whether Iraq was still developing unconventional weapons stemmed in part from Mr. Hussein's desire to convince different audiences of different things, a postwar study by the Defense

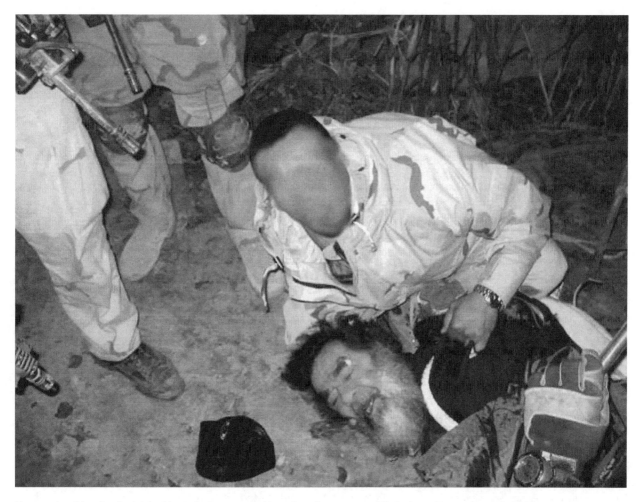

Former Iraqi leader Saddam Hussein is captured in a farmhouse near Tikrit, Iraq, December 14, 2003. © EPA/CORBIS.

Department concluded. He wanted the West to believe that he had abandoned the program, which he had. Yet he also wanted to instill fear in enemies like Iran and Israel, plus maintain the esteem of Arabs, by claiming that he possessed the weapons.

Some Bush administration critics argued that the accusations over unconventional weapons were a smoke screen, that government hawks were determined to topple Mr. Hussein as a way of reasserting American power. Richard Clarke, a former national security adviser to three presidents, described in his 2004 book "Against All Enemies" the scene in the White House in the immediate aftermath of the Sept. 11, 2001, attacks against the United States, with President Bush and other senior officials trying to link Mr. Hussein directly to Al Qaeda, Osama bin Laden's organization. No such link was ever established.

Just before the invasion, Mr. Hussein, cigar in hand, appeared on television almost nightly, belittling American forces to small groups of Republican Guard commanders.

Yet his main concern was preserving his government, which the United States military discovered in interviews with his captured aides. Some of the unclassified results were published in a 2006 article in *Foreign Affairs* titled "Saddam's Delusions: The View From the Inside."

By 2003, Iraq's military was anemic, weakened by sanctions and constant changes in command, not to mention the fact that Mr. Hussein, suspicious of coup attempts, barred any rigorous maneuvers and repeatedly created new popular militias. Commanders also constantly lied to him about their state of preparedness. The United States report quoted Mr. Hussein's personal interpreter as saying that the president thought that his "superior" forces would put up a "heroic resistance and inflict such enormous losses on the Americans that they would stop their advance."

Mr. Hussein cited both Vietnam and the hasty American withdrawal from Somalia in 1994 as evidence, and did not take the threat of regime change seriously. He

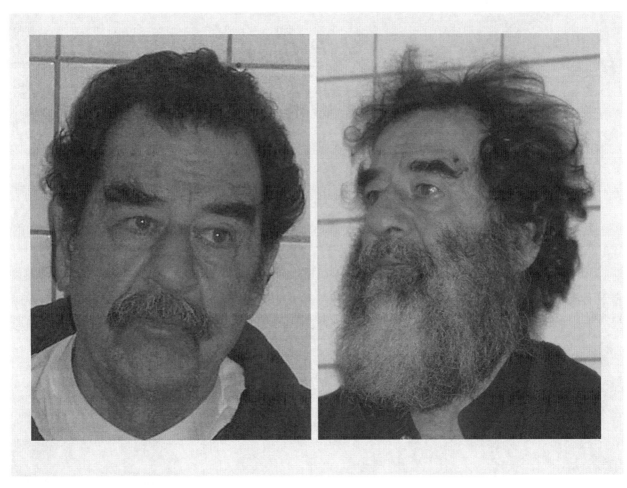

Saddam Hussein is shown after his capture in December 2003, before and after his beard was shaved. © AP IMAGES/U.S. ARMY HO.

so much believed his own publicity about his success in fighting the first gulf war that he used it as a blueprint for the second. Hence, his main worry during the invasion was to avoid repeating the Shiite and Kurdish internal rebellions of 1991. He did not blow up the bridges over the Tigris and Euphrates to slow the American advance, for example, out of concern that he would need to rush troops south to quell any uprising.

The war plan as described in the 2006 book "Cobra II: The Inside Story of the Invasion and Occupation of Iraq" states that while Republican Guard troops were supposed to seal off the approaches to Baghdad, only the Special Republican Guard was permitted inside the capital, again as insurance against a coup. The collapse came so quickly that Mr. Hussein was still issuing orders to units that had ceased to exist.

After an April 9 sighting in public, he disappeared, apparently using up to 30 hiding places and the aid of loyal tribesmen to escape capture despite a $25 million reward. He often traveled as he had during the first gulf war, in a

battered orange and white Baghdad taxi. He issued periodic messages encouraging the insurgency.

In a letter dated April 28 that was faxed to *Al Quds al Arabi*, an Arabic newspaper published in London, he blamed traitors for his ouster and urged Iraqis to rebel. "There are no priorities greater than expelling the infidel, criminal, cowardly occupier," he wrote.

A LEADER'S LEGACY

In December 2003, his location was divulged by a clan member captured in a raid on a Baghdad house. Less than 11 hours later, 600 American soldiers and Special Operations forces supported by tanks, artillery and Apache helicopter gunships surrounded two farmhouses near the banks of the Tigris in Ad Dwar, a village about nine miles southeast of Tikrit, the tribal seat. The soldiers—no Iraqis were involved—found nothing on the first sweep. But on the second, more intensive search, under a trap door, Mr. Hussein was discovered lying at the bottom of an eight-foot-deep hole.

His first words when he emerged, nervous and disoriented, were, "I am Saddam Hussein, president of Iraq, and I am willing to negotiate," in halting English.

A Special Operations soldier there shot back, "President Bush sends his regards," the military said later. The main indication that the filthy, dilapidated concrete hut close by had been used by the former Iraqi president was a battered green metal suitcase holding $750,000 in neatly bundled bills.

Mr. Hussein, sporting a bushy salt-and-pepper beard, was first shown on television undergoing a medical exam for head lice. The pictures electrified and shocked Iraqis and the larger Arab world, with some cheering and some appalled to see a captive Arab leader put on undignified display.

He was imprisoned at Camp Cropper, near the international airport some 10 miles from Baghdad, on the grounds of a former palace complex that the United States military turned into a prison for senior members of the government. The prison consisted of three rows of single-story buildings surrounded by a double ring of razor wire.

Mr. Hussein was kept in solitary confinement—letters and care packages including cigars sent via the Red Cross from his wife and daughters living in Qatar or Jordan were his main contact with the outside world. He lived in a relatively spartan cell consisting of a bed, a toilet, a chair, a towel, some books and a prayer rug.

Some of his former American guards, interviewed for a July 2005 story in GQ magazine, said he acted in a fatherly way, offering advice on finding a good wife—"neither too smart nor too dumb, not too old nor too young"—and invited them to hang out in one of his palaces after he was restored to power. He claimed that President Bush had always known he had no unconventional weapons. His favorite snack was Doritos corn chips, his guards said.

Mr. Hussein was combative throughout his trial, using it as a platform to encourage the insurgents. The proceedings frequently seemed to slide toward chaos, with the star defendant and the judges shouting at each other. The trial, held in one of the grandiose buildings erected not far from Mr. Hussein's former presidential palace, proved something of a security nightmare, with three defense lawyers assassinated.

At one point, something he said prompted guffaws from a spectator in an overhead gallery. Mr. Hussein turned and pointed a finger, saying, "The lion does not care about a monkey laughing at him from a tree."

Mr. Hussein often tried to draw parallels between himself and the famous leaders of Mesopotamia, the earliest civilization in the region, as well as Saladin, the 12th-century Kurdish Muslim military commander who expelled the crusaders from Jerusalem.

What preoccupied him, he said, was what people would be thinking about him in 500 years. To the horror of historic preservationists, he had the ancient walls of the former capital, Babylon, completely reconstructed using tens of thousands of newly fired bricks. An archaeologist had shown him bricks stamped with the name of Nebuchadnezzar II in 605 B.C.

After the reconstruction, the small Arabic script on thousands of bricks read in part, "In the reign of the victorious Saddam Hussein, the president of the Republic, may God keep him, the guardian of the great Iraq and the renovator of its renaissance and the builder of its great civilization, the rebuilding of the great city of Babylon was done."

FURTHER RESOURCES
Books

Coughlin, Con. *Saddam: His Rise and Fall.* New York: Harper Perennial: 2005.

Sada, Georges Hormuz. *Saddam's Secrets.* Nashville, TN: Thomas Nelson, 2009.

Sassoon, Joseph. *Saddam Hussein's Ba'ath Party: Inside an Authoritarian Regime.* Cambridge, UK: Cambridge University Press, 2011.

Web Sites

"Saddam Hussein Profile." *BBC News.* http://news.bbc.co.uk/2/hi/middle_east/1100529.stm (accessed on February 26, 2013).

"The Saddam Hussein Sourcebook." *The National Security Archive.* www.gwu.edu/~nsarchiv/special/iraq/index.htm (accessed on February 26, 2013).

Rod Blagojevich Political Cartoon

Political cartoon

By: Dave Granlund

Date: December 10, 2008

Source: Granlund, Dave. Rod Blagojevich Political Cartoon, December 10, 2008. *PoliticalCartoons.com.* http://www.politicalcartoons.com/cartoon/f481710b-8bff-4765-92b2-bac1bb292b6e.html (accessed on February 25, 2013).

About the Cartoonist: Dave Granlund is a widely circulated editorial cartoonist whose work has appeared in over

OBAMA'S SENATE SEAT

FOR SALE

HEY, IT'S NOT LIKE I POSTED IT ON EBAY!!

GUV

BLAGOJEVICH

FBI

DAVE GRANLUND © www.davegranlund.com

PRIMARY SOURCE

Rod Blagojevich Political Cartoon

SYNOPSIS: This cartoon satirizes Rod Blagojevich's attempts to solicit bribes in exchange for appointment to Barack Obama's vacated seat in the U.S. Senate. DAVE GRANLUND.

seven hundred newspapers and shown on several nationally syndicated television networks. His work has been published since 1977, and it deals primarily with current events and political satire. Granlund is a college graduate who served in the U.S. Air Force for eight years and tours the country as a guest speaker and lecturer in addition to creating cartoons.

INTRODUCTION

Rod Blagojevich was born in Chicago, Illinois, to a family of first-generation Serbian immigrants. After graduating from Northwestern University with a bachelor's degree in history, he obtained a legal degree from Pepperdine University School of Law in 1983. He entered practice as an assistant attorney to the Cook County, Illinois, state attorney and married Patricia Mell, the daughter of influential Chicago

alderman Richard Mell. In 1992, Blagojevich obtained the Democrat Party nomination in the race for the 33rd District of the Illinois State House of Representatives, which he won soundly on a platform based around crime reduction. He relinquished the seat in 1996 to pursue election to the U.S. House of Representatives in Illinois's 5th Congressional District. With the backing and financial support of his father-in-law, Blagojevich defeated the Republican incumbent, serving three terms before announcing his bid in the 2002 gubernatorial election. After narrowly winning the Democrat Party nomination, he defeated the Republican candidate, state attorney general Jim Ryan, and was thus elected governor of Illinois.

Blagojevich's tenure, although initially popular with Illinois citizens, quickly became dogged by criticism and controversy. His standoffish persona and heavily progressive policy proposals alienated both the Democrat and Republican elements of the state legislature, attracting public criticism for his inability to effectively pass new legislature or institute meaningful reform. State officials lamented the governor's lack of involvement in the day-to-day proceedings of the government he had been elected to direct, noting that he continued to live in his Chicago home despite being entitled to occupy the Executive Mansion in Springfield, where legislative sessions were conducted. Blagojevich's stubborn ways resulted in frequent public disagreements with members of his own administration, including his lieutenant governor, Pat Quinn, and Democrat officials like the state's comptroller, attorney general, secretary of state, and treasurer. However, the Illinois public was pleased enough with his success in passing key legislation—such as death penalty reform, a statewide smoking ban, anti-discrimination policies, and expanded health programs—that he was reelected to the position in 2006.

Blagojevich's second term as governor was plagued with scandal, federal investigation, and public discontent. In an effort to fund expansions of educational budgets without raising taxes, he constantly sought to cut state jobs and wages, upsetting the powerful state-government labor unions representing them. The state senate remained in a gridlock caused by his inability to effectively resolve political conflict. His habit of commuting daily via private jet, at the expense of Illinois taxpayers, drew considerable ire, although he continued to do so. Allegations of misconduct began to be leveled at the governor for his purported abuse of power and authority in appointing government positions and awarding state contracts and jobs, all of which he consistently denied. Then, in 2006, as part of an ongoing anti-corruption campaign headed by Patrick Fitzgerald, the U.S. attorney for the Northern District of Illinois, several close political allies of Blagojevich, including several members of his campaign and fundraising teams, were arrested on conspiracy charges.

In a highly publicized series of trials, Tony Rezko, one of Blagojevich's key campaign aides, was revealed to be guilty of conducting a series of kickback schemes in which individuals and businesses would exchange money for contracts from two state boards, among other illegal political favors. During the Rezko hearings, Blagojevich was frequently implicated as a complicit party to the illicit operations, although formal charges were not brought against him in relation to them. However, he was placed under federal investigation, including covert surveillance of his conduct and correspondences. As a result of evidence collected by the Federal Bureau of Investigation (FBI) as part of this investigation, which apparently revealed illegal

conduct, Blagojevich and his chief of staff John Harris were simultaneously arrested on the morning of December 9, 2008. They were held on numerous felony charges, detailed in a eventy-two-page affidavit, relating to crimes allegedly committed by the governor and several of his senior advisors.

Chief among Blagojevich's charges was the assertion that he had attempted to exploit his exclusive authority to designate a replacement for Barack Obama, who had just been elected president of the United States and thus vacated his seat in the U.S. Senate as a representative of Illinois. According to the FBI, which cited phone calls recorded by means of wiretaps placed in Blagojevich's home and campaign office, he had offered to exchange appointment to the Senate position for his own appointment to an influential political office or high-paying position within a company. He was also accused of extortion, for threatening to withhold public funds from the *Chicago Tribune* newspaper unless it agreed to fire certain writers who had been critical of his governance, and of graft, for leveraging the appropriation of public funds and contracts into contributions to his political campaigns. Blagojevich denied any guilt.

Although he was released from custody on bond, the embattled governor was almost immediately submitted to impeachment proceedings, which were concluded on July 29, 2009, when the Illinois State Senate voted unanimously to remove him from office and bar him permanently from holding state office. He was succeeded by Lieutenant Governor Pat Quinn. On April 29 of that year, Blagojevich was indicted by a federal grand jury on twenty-four felony counts, including extortion, conspiracy, graft, fraud, racketeering, and making false statements to federal investigators.

SIGNIFICANCE

After his first case was ruled a mistrial, Rod Blagojevich was found guilty of eighteen of the charges of which he was accused on June 27, 2011, and subsequently sentenced to serve fourteen years in a Colorado federal prison. Before his sentencing, the disgraced politician and his wife enjoyed a brief period of minor celebrity in the United States, appearing on talk shows, news programs, and even reality shows as contestants. His disastrous career as governor was destined to be remembered as one of the most corrupt in U.S. history. The Blagojevich scandal was one of the most publicized and extensive political controversies of the 2000s decade, noteworthy not only for the coverage it received but also for the sheer vitriol it generated towards the Illinois state government. Blagojevich was only the eighth governor to be impeached in the United States, and the first from Illinois to receive that dubious distinction.

Blagojevich's caustic legacy was largely reversed by his successor, who immediately set about instituting ethical reform and transparency regulation initiatives in Illinois government, as well as reversing some of his predecessor's more costly policies. However, before his impeachment, Blagojevich was able to appoint former state attorney general Roland Burris to Obama's vacated Senate seat, despite considerable opposition from the current attorney general. Burris, who was immediately scrutinized and ridiculed for his questionable involvement in Blagojevich's administration and political campaigns, was not reelected in 2010.

Although Blagojevich's corruption was not unique—a common problem among Illinois politicians, especially those from Chicago, where "pay to play" is practically a political motto—it was an important development in U.S. politics.

PRIMARY SOURCE

ROD BLAGOJEVICH POLITICAL CARTOON

See primary source cartoon.

FURTHER RESOURCES
Web Sites
"Affadavit Regarding Rod Blagojevich and John Harris." *United States Department of Justice.* www.justice.gov/usao/iln/pr/chicago/2008/pr1209_01a.pdf (accessed on February 25, 2013).

Bernstein, David. "Mr. Un-Popularity." *Chicago Magazine,* February 2008. www.chicagomag.com/Chicago-Magazine/February-2008/Mr-Un-Popularity/index.php?cp=1&cparticle=1&si=0&siarticle=0#artanc (accessed on February 25, 2013).

Davey, Monica. "Two Sides of a Troubled Governor, Sinking Deeper." *New York Times,* December 14, 2008. www.nytimes.com/2008/12/15/us/politics/15blagojevich.html?bl&ex=1229490000&en=b47302a032bc52ff&ei=5087%0A&_r=0 (accessed on February 25, 2013).

Davey, Monica, and Jack Healy. "Illinois Governor Charged in Scheme to Sell Obama's Seat." *New York Times,* December 9, 2008. www.nytimes.com/2008/12/09/us/politics/10Illinois.html (accessed on February 25, 2013).

Scherer, Michael. "Governor Gone Wild: The Blagojevich Scandal." *Time,* December 11, 2008. www.time.com/time/magazine/article/0,9171,1865954,00.html (accessed on February 25, 2013).

"President Barack Obama's Inaugural Address"

Speech

By: Barack Hussein Obama

Date: January 20, 2009

Source: Obama, Barack H. "President Barack Obama's Inaugural Address." Delivered January 20, 2009. www.whitehouse.gov/blog/inaugural-address/ (accessed on February 26, 2013).

About the Speaker: Barack Hussein Obama, the forty-fourth president of the United States, was born in Hawaii on August 4, 1961, and raised in Indonesia and the United States, the son of an American mother and Kenyan father. He graduated from Columbia University and completed graduate studies at Harvard Law School, an education he employed as a community organizer, professor of law, and civil rights attorney in Chicago, Illinois. His vocal belief in equal liberties and protection under the law for all U.S. citizens earned Obama an election to the Illinois state senate, where he continued to address civil rights issues by pursuing a social-liberal legislative agenda. Pleased with his success protecting racial and income equality in office, the citizens of Illinois voted him into a U.S. Senate position in 2004, from which Obama spring-boarded into a presidential bid on a Democrat Party platform. He successfully defeated Republican opponent John McCain in the 2008 general election to claim the presidency. His tenure during the final two years of the 2000s decade was characterized by an emphasis on international diplomacy and managing the impact of the subprime mortgage crisis, the near-collapse of the auto industry, the collapse of the housing market, and the resultant economic recession.

INTRODUCTION

Following a distinguished career in public service, Barack Obama sought the Democrat Party nomination for the presidency. Strong public support and clever campaign strategy made him the early favorite in the hotly contested race for the nomination. Unprecedented fundraising income, innovative grassroots and "new media" campaign techniques, and congeniality allowed Obama to secure the nomination over opponents including former first lady and U.S. senator Hillary Clinton of New York and former U.S. senator John Edwards of North Carolina, the 2004 Democratic vice presidential nominee. In keeping with his political rights work, Obama's campaign platform

Barack Obama is sworn in as the forty-fourth president of the United States by Supreme Court chief justice John Roberts on January 20, 2008. His wife, Michelle, and children, Malia and Sasha, are by his side. © RAIF-FINN HESTOFT/CORBIS.

focused on domestic issues like social welfare programs; gender, race, and socioeconomic equality; healthcare reform; and energy independence. He was also a vocal advocate of expedient U.S. military withdrawal from Afghanistan.

Compared to seventy-one-year-old U.S. senator John McCain, the Republican Party presidential nominee from Arizona, Obama appeared young, hip, and aware—many analysts cite McCain's "out of touch" personal and political positions as the key to his defeat. Others point out the polarizing effect of Alaska governor Sarah Palin, a staunch right-wing conservative whose frequent gaffes and abrasive demeanor may have pushed undecided voters away from the Republican ticket, on which she was the vice presidential nominee. Conversely, Obama's running

mate, U.S. senator Joe Biden of Delaware, was a generally inoffensive and likeable personality, who lent experience and articulate diction to Obama's platform.

Obama won the 2008 presidential election handily, becoming the first African American president of the United States of America. He delivered his Inaugural Address on January 20, 2009, the day he officially entered office. The event of Obama's inauguration was one of the most-attended and most-watched official events in U.S. history, and his Inaugural Address was one of the most-heard speeches ever made. In it, he invokes the hope and optimism expressed in his campaign, focusing on retaining and maintaining traditional American values while executing the changes necessary for a more perfect Union.

SIGNIFICANCE

In addition to the obviously monumental historical significance of being the first black man to assume the highest office in the United States, Obama and his campaign had several subtle impacts on the way presidential campaigns are conducted. His record-shattering campaign-fundraising income demonstrated the utility of small-scale, local contribution-gathering, and his ability to appeal to a broader demographic than the traditional "wealthy white male" presidential candidate is credited with his wins in traditionally Red states with high minority populations.

Of particular note is the Obama campaign's consistent use of branding to maintain a consistent, popular public image for its candidate. Iconic images such as the "Hope" poster and the signature "Rising Sun" logo, combined with high-profile endorsements and slogans like "Yes We Can" and "Change We Can Believe In," produced an identifiable, tangible "brand" that voters identified with and supported through endless merchandising.

PRIMARY SOURCE

"PRESIDENT BARACK OBAMA'S INAUGURAL ADDRESS"

SYNOPSIS: The new president talks about the country's hardships and outlines his ambitious goals for the next four years.

My fellow citizens: I stand here today humbled by the task before us, grateful for the trust you've bestowed, mindful of the sacrifices borne by our ancestors.

I thank President Bush for his service to our nation—as well as the generosity and cooperation he has shown throughout this transition.

Forty-four Americans have now taken the presidential oath. The words have been spoken during rising tides of prosperity and the still waters of peace. Yet, every so often, the oath is taken amidst gathering clouds and raging storms. At these moments, America has carried on not simply because of the skill or vision of those in high office, but because we, the people, have remained faithful to the ideals of our forebears and true to our founding documents.

So it has been; so it must be with this generation of Americans.

That we are in the midst of crisis is now well understood. Our nation is at war against a far-reaching network of violence and hatred. Our economy is badly weakened, a consequence of greed and irresponsibility on the part of some, but also our collective failure to make hard choices and prepare the nation for a new age. Homes have been lost, jobs shed, businesses shuttered. Our

health care is too costly, our schools fail too many—and each day brings further evidence that the ways we use energy strengthen our adversaries and threaten our planet.

These are the indicators of crisis, subject to data and statistics. Less measurable, but no less profound, is a sapping of confidence across our land; a nagging fear that America's decline is inevitable, that the next generation must lower its sights.

Today I say to you that the challenges we face are real. They are serious and they are many. They will not be met easily or in a short span of time. But know this America: They will be met.

On this day, we gather because we have chosen hope over fear, unity of purpose over conflict and discord. On this day, we come to proclaim an end to the petty grievances and false promises, the recriminations and worn-out dogmas that for far too long have strangled our politics. We remain a young nation. But in the words of Scripture, the time has come to set aside childish things. The time has come to reaffirm our enduring spirit; to choose our better history; to carry forward that precious gift, that noble idea passed on from generation to generation: the God-given promise that all are equal, all are free, and all deserve a chance to pursue their full measure of happiness.

In reaffirming the greatness of our nation we understand that greatness is never a given. It must be earned. Our journey has never been one of short-cuts or settling for less. It has not been the path for the faint-hearted, for those that prefer leisure over work, or seek only the pleasures of riches and fame. Rather, it has been the risk-takers, the doers, the makers of things—some celebrated, but more often men and women obscure in their labor—who have carried us up the long rugged path towards prosperity and freedom.

For us, they packed up their few worldly possessions and traveled across oceans in search of a new life. For us, they toiled in sweatshops, and settled the West, endured the lash of the whip, and plowed the hard earth. For us, they fought and died in places like Concord and Gettysburg, Normandy and Khe Sahn.

Time and again these men and women struggled and sacrificed and worked till their hands were raw so that we might live a better life. They saw America as bigger than the sum of our individual ambitions, greater than all the differences of birth or wealth or faction.

This is the journey we continue today. We remain the most prosperous, powerful nation on Earth. Our workers are no less productive than when this crisis began. Our minds are no less inventive, our goods and services no less needed than they were last week, or last month, or last year. Our capacity remains undiminished. But our

President Barack Obama speaks to the nation during his Inaugural Address on January 20, 2009. © RICK FRIEDMAN/ CORBIS.

time of standing pat, of protecting narrow interests and putting off unpleasant decisions—that time has surely passed. Starting today, we must pick ourselves up, dust ourselves off, and begin again the work of remaking America.

For everywhere we look, there is work to be done. The state of our economy calls for action, bold and swift. And we will act, not only to create new jobs, but to lay a new foundation for growth. We will build the roads and bridges, the electric grids and digital lines that feed our commerce and bind us together. We'll restore science to its rightful place, and wield technology's wonders to raise health care's quality and lower its cost. We will harness the sun and the winds and the soil to fuel our cars and run our factories. And we will transform our schools and colleges and universities to meet the demands of a new age. All this we can do. All this we will do.

Now, there are some who question the scale of our ambitions, who suggest that our system cannot tolerate too many big plans. Their memories are short, for they have forgotten what this country has already done, what free men and women can achieve when imagination is joined to common purpose, and necessity to courage. What the cynics fail to understand is that the ground has shifted beneath them, that the stale political arguments that have consumed us for so long no longer apply.

The question we ask today is not whether our government is too big or too small, but whether it works—whether it helps families find jobs at a decent wage, care they can afford, a retirement that is dignified. Where the answer is yes, we intend to move forward. Where the answer is no, programs will end. And those of us who manage the public's dollars will be held to account, to spend wisely, reform bad habits, and do our business in the light of day, because only then can we restore the vital trust between a people and their government.

Nor is the question before us whether the market is a force for good or ill. Its power to generate wealth and expand freedom is unmatched. But this crisis has reminded us that without a watchful eye, the market can spin out of control. The nation cannot prosper long when it favors only the prosperous. The success of our economy has always depended not just on the size of our gross domestic product, but on the reach of our prosperity, on the ability to extend opportunity to every willing heart—not out of charity, but because it is the surest route to our common good.

As for our common defense, we reject as false the choice between our safety and our ideals. Our Founding Fathers—our Founding Fathers, faced with perils that we can scarcely imagine, drafted a charter to assure the rule of law and the rights of man—a charter expanded by the blood of generations. Those ideals still light the world, and we will not give them up for expedience sake.

And so, to all the other peoples and governments who are watching today, from the grandest capitals to the small village where my father was born, know that America is a friend of each nation, and every man, woman and child who seeks a future of peace and dignity. And we are ready to lead once more.

Recall that earlier generations faced down fascism and communism not just with missiles and tanks, but with the sturdy alliances and enduring convictions. They understood that our power alone cannot protect us, nor does it entitle us to do as we please. Instead they knew that our power grows through its prudent use; our security emanates from the justness of our cause, the force of our example, the tempering qualities of humility and restraint.

We are the keepers of this legacy. Guided by these principles once more we can meet those new threats that demand even greater effort, even greater cooperation and understanding between nations. We will begin to responsibly leave Iraq to its people and forge a hard-earned peace in Afghanistan. With old friends and former foes, we'll work tirelessly to lessen the nuclear threat, and roll back the specter of a warming planet.

We will not apologize for our way of life, nor will we waver in its defense. And for those who seek to advance their aims by inducing terror and slaughtering innocents, we say to you now that our spirit is stronger and cannot be broken—you cannot outlast us, and we will defeat you.

For we know that our patchwork heritage is a strength, not a weakness. We are a nation of Christians and Muslims, Jews and Hindus, and non-believers. We are shaped by every language and culture, drawn from every end of this Earth; and because we have tasted the bitter swill of civil war and segregation, and emerged from that dark chapter stronger and more united, we cannot help but believe that the old hatreds shall someday pass; that the lines of tribe shall soon dissolve; that as the world grows smaller, our common humanity shall reveal itself; and that America must play its role in ushering in a new era of peace.

To the Muslim world, we seek a new way forward, based on mutual interest and mutual respect. To those leaders around the globe who seek to sow conflict, or blame their society's ills on the West, know that your people will judge you on what you can build, not what you destroy.

To those who cling to power through corruption and deceit and the silencing of dissent, know that you are on the wrong side of history, but that we will extend a hand if you are willing to unclench your fist.

To the people of poor nations, we pledge to work alongside you to make your farms flourish and let clean waters flow; to nourish starved bodies and feed hungry minds. And to those nations like ours that enjoy relative plenty, we say we can no longer afford indifference to the suffering outside our borders, nor can we consume the world's resources without regard to effect. For the world has changed, and we must change with it.

As we consider the role that unfolds before us, we remember with humble gratitude those brave Americans who at this very hour patrol far-off deserts and distant mountains. They have something to tell us, just as the fallen heroes who lie in Arlington whisper through the ages.

We honor them not only because they are the guardians of our liberty, but because they embody the spirit of service—a willingness to find meaning in something greater than themselves.

And yet at this moment, a moment that will define a generation, it is precisely this spirit that must inhabit us all. For as much as government can do, and must do, it is ultimately the faith and determination of the American people upon which this nation relies. It is the kindness to take in a stranger when the levees break, the selflessness of workers who would rather cut their hours than see a friend lose their job which sees us through our darkest hours. It is the firefighter's courage to storm a stairway filled with smoke, but also a parent's willingness to nurture a child that finally decides our fate.

Our challenges may be new. The instruments with which we meet them may be new. But those values upon which our success depends—honesty and hard work, courage and fair play, tolerance and curiosity, loyalty and patriotism—these things are old. These things are true. They have been the quiet force of progress throughout our history.

What is demanded, then, is a return to these truths. What is required of us now is a new era of responsibility— a recognition on the part of every American that we have duties to ourselves, our nation and the world; duties that we do not grudgingly accept, but rather seize gladly, firm in the knowledge that there is nothing so satisfying to the spirit, so defining of our character than giving our all to a difficult task.

This is the price and the promise of citizenship. This is the source of our confidence—the knowledge that God calls on us to shape an uncertain destiny. This is the meaning of our liberty and our creed, why men and women and children of every race and every faith can join in celebration across this magnificent mall; and why a man whose father less than 60 years ago might not have been served in a local restaurant can now stand before you to take a most sacred oath.

So let us mark this day with remembrance of who we are and how far we have traveled. In the year of America's birth, in the coldest of months, a small band of patriots huddled by dying campfires on the shores of an icy river. The capital was abandoned. The enemy was advancing. The snow was stained with blood. At the moment when the outcome of our revolution was most in doubt, the father of our nation ordered these words to be read to the people:

"Let it be told to the future world ... that in the depth of winter, when nothing but hope and virtue could survive ... that the city and the country, alarmed at one common danger, came forth to meet [it]."

America: In the face of our common dangers, in this winter of our hardship, let us remember these timeless words. With hope and virtue, let us brave once more the icy currents, and endure what storms may come. Let it be said by our children's children that when we were tested we refused to let this journey end, that we did not turn back nor did we falter; and with eyes fixed on the horizon and God's grace upon us, we carried forth that great gift of freedom and delivered it safely to future generations.

Thank you. God bless you. And God bless the United States of America.

■

FURTHER RESOURCES

Books

Maraniss, David. *Barack Obama: The Story.* New York: Simon & Schuster, 2012.

Mendell, David. *Obama: From Promise to Power.* New York: Amistad, 2007.

Tufankjian, Scout. *Yes We Can: Barack Obama's History-Making Presidential Campaign.* New York: powerHouse Books, 2008.

Web Sites

"Barack Obama Congressional Voting Record." *Washington Post.* http://projects.washingtonpost.com/congress/members/o000167 (accessed on February 26, 2013).

"Barack Obama News and Politics Coverage." *New York Times.* http://topics.nytimes.com/top/reference/timestopics/people/o/barack_obama/index.html (accessed on February 26, 2013).

"The Tea Party Revolution"

The fight for economic freedom begins in earnest today

Editorial

By: Peter Ferrara

Date: April 15, 2009

Source: Ferrara, Peter. "The Tea Party Revolution." *American Spectator*, April 15, 2009. http://spectator.org/archives/2009/04/15/the-tea-party-revolution (accessed on March 1, 2013).

About the Publication: The *American Spectator* was founded in 1924 by George Nathan and Truman Newberry. In 1967, the political opinion publication was acquired by the Indiana University Saturday Evening Club and retitled *The Alternative: An American Spectator*, under which title it published conservative political articles. In 1977, with the term *alternative* having fallen out of use in conservative rhetoric, the magazine reverted to its old name. The magazine's coverage of the Monica Lewinsky–Bill Clinton infidelity scandal propelled it briefly into the foreground of American political journalism, but a series of financial and personnel scandals left it without significant circulation or readership, fading into a jargon-heavy conservative echo chamber.

INTRODUCTION

The Tea Party was a political movement that rose to prominence in 2009, representing the diverse (and often conflicting) political aims of U.S. voters who had become dissatisfied and disillusioned with the state of the American democratic system. Although supporters of the Tea Party movement varied in their party allegiance, socioeconomic background, and motives, they held common several principal political tenets: reduced federal government, reduced taxes, opposition to healthcare reform, reduced government spending, opposition to entitlement programs, and market deregulation. Central to the Tea Party's platform was the belief that the federal government had overstepped its constitutional boundaries after the implementation of President Franklin D. Roosevelt's New Deal policies, and that it was the duty of the voters to force a return to constitutionally legitimate democracy.

The Tea Party moniker was drawn from the legendary Boston Tea Party, a symbolic political protest in which Massachusetts citizens dumped a shipment of tea into the Boston Harbor to protest the tax policy of the British Empire. Tea Party movement organizers used the name to draw parallels between the oppressive taxation imposed upon the American public by the tyrannical King George III and the contemporary internal revenue code of President Barack Obama, who was frequently portrayed as an equally insensitive, obtuse ruler. Symbolically comparing the aims of the Tea Party movement to those of the original American Revolutionaries was a tactic frequently employed by Tea Party rhetoricians, depicting the modern struggle for financial liberties as an analogy to the revolutionary fight for political and personal freedoms.

The Tea Party movement began as a series of independently organized, community-based protests against President Obama's "bailout package," the federal initiative to assist economic recovery from the 2008 mortgage and credit crises composed of the Emergency Economic Stabilization Act of 2008 and the American Recovery and Reinvestment Act of 2009. Local organizations and politicians in cities across the United States organized small protests in opposition to the passage of the bills, which allocated over $1 trillion in federal spending to help rescue homeowners and banks from debt. These protests attracted significant attention from conservative media, particularly Fox News, which lauded the grass-roots organization of political expression. Larger organizations, most notably the libertarian/populist/conservative activist group Americans for Prosperity, were inspired by the early Tea Party protests to organize their own demonstrations on a larger scale.

Implementing social media and online conservative communities to spread their message, local Tea Party groups sprang up across the country, each with its own separate, independent political agenda. From February 2009 onwards, hundreds of protests were staged across the country, some boasting thousands of participants, with speakers and demonstrators demanding a reduction of taxes and government spending. Although right-leaning news outlets, particularly Fox News, covered the protests feverishly, they received little press in most mainstream media, where they were met with a combination of puzzlement and derision.

Although the Tea Party movement began as a protest platform, local affiliates began issuing candidate endorsements for the upcoming 2010 congressional elections. Party-line Republicans and almost all Democrats were condemned by Tea Party activists, who professed a desire to install a new status quo consisting of fiscally conservative, socially liberal Republicans in Congress. Fervent demonstrations and campaign assistance from Tea Party groups, condemning Obama's proposed healthcare reform measures and the Democrat-held Congress's tax and budget hikes, became one of the major rallying points of the 2010 elections. Particularly inflammatory was the Tea Party–instigated conflict over the expansion of federal entitlement programs such as unemployment benefits, food stamps, welfare, and Social Security. Near the end of the campaign cycle, entitlement programs became the most polarizing issue in the election, with moderate Republicans losing favor to those strictly opposed to federally provided financial assistance.

SIGNIFICANCE

Thanks largely to the influence of the Tea Party movement, the 2010 elections saw a new wave of Republican politicians claim control of the House of Representatives and an increased footing in the Senate. Commentators noted that while these victors were invariably Republican, Tea Party–endorsed candidates represented a marked departure from traditional GOP politicians by endorsing a fiscally conscious, socially libertarian agenda, rather than one focused on promoting Christian social ideals (such as opposing same-sex marriage and limiting reproductive rights). The Tea Party's success in the 2010 elections is

frequently extolled as an example of triumphant citizen activism, although some critics have suggested that much of the party's achievement was due to wealthy corporate backers who helped the movement reach national prominence through selective reporting.

The Tea Party movement's greatest legacy was successfully obstructing almost every Democratic Party congressional initiative, particularly the Obama administration's attempts at healthcare reform. Tea Party activism was also instrumental in bringing about a new wave of Republican thought, one that rejected the necessity of alliance with the Christian Right and instead pursued more traditional Republican values, particularly minimal federal government authority. Although the movement waned somewhat after its initial national prominence, it demonstrated the potential effectiveness of political activism in the United States, and had a lasting impact on the composition of the Republican Party.

PRIMARY SOURCE

"THE TEA PARTY REVOLUTION"

SYNOPSIS: In this article, the author details the political ideology of the Tea Party movement and the circumstances surrounding it.

Congratulations to the hundreds of spontaneous grassroots organizers who have successfully organized the over 300 tea party events that will take place today across the country. Such events have already been widespread, and highly successful, with sudden big crowds: 2,000 in St. Louis, 3,000 in Cincinnati, 6,000 in Orlando, as recently reported by Peter Roff in a Fox News blog.

Because these events are highly decentralized, with no significant institutional organization or funding behind them, they represent a genuine outpouring of grassroots opinion with enormous political importance. For every person out in the streets today, there are undoubtedly many more who didn't make it who share the same opinions. The bigger the demonstrations today, the bigger the rest of the iceberg under water. Moreover, this movement represents genuine grassroots organization, as names and contact information are collected, and this will be valuable for future political activity.

These people are both against and for something. They are against the left-wing extremism of the current political leadership in Washington, from Barack Obama to Nancy Pelosi, to Barney Frank, to Henry Waxman, and on and on. No wonder *Newsweek* (soon going out of business) thinks we are a nation of socialists now, as it admitted in a recent cover story.

Former Speaker of the House Newt Gingrich addresses an audience at the John F. Kennedy School of Government at Harvard University, October 8, 2009. © AP IMAGES/STEVEN SENNE.

But even more, the tea party revelers are for a sophisticated vision of economic freedom. They recognize that the more resources the government takes out of the private sector, through taxes, borrowing and spending, the less freedom that average working people have left for the pursuit of happiness. Taxes as a percent of GDP, government spending as a percent of GDP, should be taken as reverse indicators of economic freedom. The higher they are, the less economic freedom people have. The lower they are, the more economic freedom we have. In other words, the more the government takes your money to spend on what *it* wants, the less freedom you have to choose to spend, or to save and invest, your own money as you want. And visa versa.

Let us review the already gruesome results of the Obama economic policy to see what has the people out in the streets. Obama's budget for this year increases federal spending by an extremist *34%* over the budget adopted for last year, *to a total of $4 trillion*, the highest ever! Since World War II, going back over 60 years now, federal spending as a percent of GDP has been stable, hovering around 20%. But federal spending for this year

under the Obama budget and economic policies will soar to a shocking *28.5% of GDP, an increase in the size of the federal government in Obama's first year of 42%* compared to the postwar average relative to GDP.

Over the longer run, because of exploding federal entitlements, federal spending will soar to 40% to 50% of GDP, depending on how much permanent damage Obama does. With state and local spending, the total will climb towards 60%, and we will no longer be a free country.

The Congressional Budget Office projects Obama's budget deficit for this year at a shocking *$1.845 trillion, the highest ever.* That would be more than seven times Reagan's largest deficit of $221 billion, which caused so much howling among liberals and Democrats. This Obama budget deficit will total an astounding *13.1% of GDP*, more than one-eighth of the entire U.S. economy, *for the federal deficit alone!*

Obama says that this is George Bush's budget deficit. But it wasn't George Bush who led adoption of a $1 trillion stimulus package in February, followed by a $410 billion supplemental spending bill the next week,

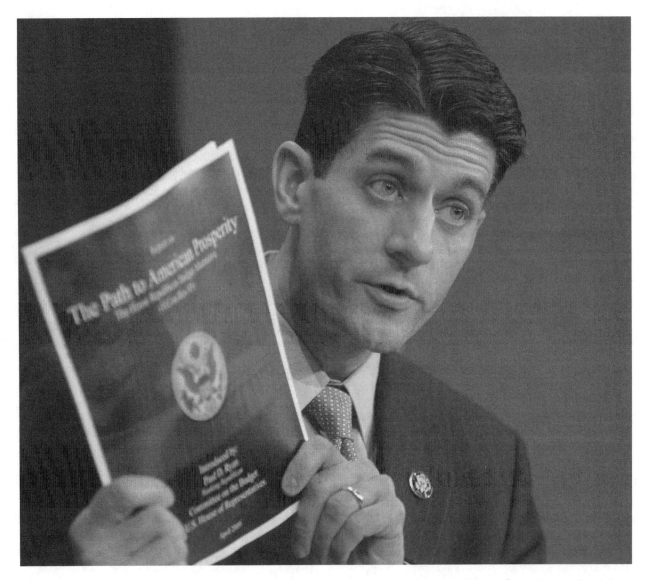

U.S. representative Paul Ryan of Wisconsin, the ranking Republican on the U.S. House Budget Committee, talks about a budget plan he was endorsing, April 1, 2009. Ryan was his party's vice presidential nominee in 2012. © AP IMAGES/J. SCOTT APPLEWHITE.

with a $275 billion housing bailout plan proposed the following week, $634 billion as a down payment on a new national health insurance entitlement adopted in the budget, and another $1 trillion bank bailout plan recently announced as well. (Note: The entire economy produces just $14 trillion a year, so $1 trillion is real money.)

Obama said in his national press conference on March 24, "We're doing everything we can to reduce that deficit." But do his actions recounted above look like he is "doing everything we can to reduce that deficit"?

The deficit for the last budget adopted when Congress was controlled by Republican majorities, for fiscal 2007, was $162 billion, or 1.2% of GDP. CBO

projects that by 2019 under Obama's budget, the deficit will still be well over $1 trillion.

Finally, under Obama's budget the national debt will double over the next five years, and triple over the next ten, to $17.3 trillion. The national debt as a percent of GDP will soar from 40% to a peacetime record of 82.4%, almost as large as the entire economy, and twice as high as when Reagan left office. If the economy does not recover permanently next year, as even the CBO assumes (not going to happen long term), Obama could even top the World War II record of national debt at 113% of GDP, spending mostly on welfare and entitlements, rather than on fighting the Nazis and Imperial Japan.

Does this sound like we're "moving from an era of borrow-and-spend to one where we save and invest," as Obama also said in his press conference last month?

Is this unfair to Obama, who needed to restore economic growth to a collapsing economy he inherited? After all, as Obama recently laughed, "What do you think a stimulus is?"

Well, ask yourself, will we restore growth through increased welfare, runaway federal spending, and record deficits and debt? Or does growth come from reducing tax rates, unnecessary regulatory burdens, and government spending, and maintaining a strong dollar? That's what Reagan did, and the result was a 25-year economic boom that spread across the entire planet, with "70 million people a year [worldwide] … joining the middle class," as Steve Forbes recently observed. What Obama is doing is the opposite of this proven formula, in every detail.

Oh, the economy will "recover" later this year, because it is still a powerful, capitalist economy that tends towards growth. But Obama's economic policies are taking America back on a long, slow, nostalgia tour to the glorious economy of Jimmy Carter, complete with gas and energy shortages, soaring inflation and interest rates, and persistent unemployment. Over the longer run, that road leads back to the liberal left glory days of the 1930s.

And I haven't even begun to talk about Obama's tax increases. By the end of next year, the top income tax rate will have risen by 20%, the top capital gains tax rate by 33%, and the tax on dividends by 33% as well, with the top death tax rate restored to 45%. Obama ran for President promising a tax cut for 95% of Americans, which turned out to be a miserable $400 per worker income tax credit, less than $8 a week, with no incentive effects to promote the economy. That will be more than offset by the $645 billion cap and trade tax Obama has proposed to combat non-existent global warming, which will be paid by everybody through higher prices for gas, electricity, home heating oil, coal, and everything produced with energy. Obviously, these sharp tax increases will trash the economy in the future, not promote growth. Higher energy costs in particular will chase remaining American manufacturing overseas.

All of this is why America will be in the streets today demanding a U-turn from Obama's road to oblivion, returning to Reagan's highway to prosperity, which Bush mistakenly exited.

But over the longer run, the tea party revelers are looking for an expanded vista of economic freedom, with less government control, lower taxes, reduced spending and debt, fewer unnecessary regulatory burdens, and sound money free from inflation. How can America achieve that?

Let me offer a few ideas. I am not claiming these as the agenda of today's tea parties. I am offering them as the best of the ideas that have been developed over recent decades, and the most promising for long-term freedom and prosperity, in the hope that many of those demonstrating today will support them in the future.

Newt Gingrich, who is speaking at the tea party in Atlanta today, has offered a 12-point economic recovery plan based on the principles of President Reagan's 1981 recovery plan. Gingrich proposes to reduce the 25% income tax rate paid by middle-income earners to 15%, which would effectively establish a flat tax of 15% for close to 90% of Americans. He would also reduce the federal corporate tax rate of 35%, the second highest in the industrialized world, to the 12.5% rate adopted 20 years ago in Ireland, which boosted that traditionally poor country to the second highest income in the EU. Our own Treasury Department says Ireland's 12.5% rate generates more corporate tax revenue as a percent of GDP than our 35% rate.

Gingrich also proposes to abolish the capital gains tax and the death tax, which both involve double taxation of savings and capital. He would also open up production of domestic U.S. energy across the board, ensuring plentiful, low cost energy supplies for the American economy. These policies would produce another generation-long economic boom.

Rep. Paul Ryan (R-WI) has offered a tax reform plan with just two rates, 10% applying to the first $100,000 in income each year, and 25% applying to all income above that. Generous personal exemptions would eliminate income taxes for a family of four on the first $40,000 earned each year.

For the payroll tax, Ryan has developed and introduced legislation that would allow workers the freedom to choose to save and invest half their Social Security taxes in their own personal accounts. To the extent each worker exercised this option, benefits from the account would replace future promised Social Security benefits on a proportional basis. Because over the long run market investment returns are so much higher than what Social Security can even promise, let alone pay, working people can gain enormously from this option. But Ryan's bill wisely retains the Social Security safety net, guaranteeing that each worker would still receive at least what they would have been paid in Social Security benefits under current law. So workers can gain, but they can't lose. Experience shows, however, that few if any workers would fall into that safety net over the long run.

Such personal savings, investment, and insurance accounts should be expanded over the long run to empower workers with the freedom to substitute the accounts for the entire payroll tax, with the accounts providing all of the benefits now financed by the payroll tax. This would produce an enormous reduction in the size of the federal government.

Another good idea is the national sales tax proposal. But the 23% sales tax rate is too high. The sales tax should substitute only for the income tax, not the payroll tax as well. Better to phase out the payroll tax under the personal account proposal above. The sales tax reform also does not need to be completely revenue neutral. It would work better providing a net tax cut. This may allow a sales tax rate of only 14%, particularly considering the boost to economic growth such reform would produce.

Another major reform would involve sending the hundreds of federal welfare programs back to the states based on the model of the highly successful 1996 reform of the old AFDC program. That reform replaced AFDC with a block grant of finite federal funds to each state for their own new, redesigned, welfare program based on work. The result surprised even the advocates of the idea, reducing the number of dependents on the old program by close to 60% nationwide. This same reform should now be extended to Medicaid, Food Stamps, housing subsidies, and the hundreds of other means-tested, federal welfare programs. This would also result in an enormous reduction in the size of the federal government.

The most important Obama initiative to stop now is health-care reform. Adding another huge entitlement program, ultimately the biggest of all, to our nation's debts will hasten the explosion of big government and the ultimate bankruptcy of our country. Obama's proposal inevitably involves the same government health-care rationing as in every other country that has adopted such a government-run health care system. That is because once such a system is adopted, there is no other way to control health costs.

Such government health-care rationing means a reduction in the standard of living for average Americans, as they suffer less timely and less effective health care. A huge reduction in America's standard of living would result as well from Obama's cap and trade global warming plan, as America must then suffer with less energy costing much more. That means smaller, weaker cars, less driving and other transportation, less consumption of energy-intensive meat and dairy products, colder homes, workplaces and stores in winter, hotter homes, workplaces and stores in summer, and less of everything that uses electricity.

A safety net assuring essential health-care services can be created without a government takeover of the entire health-care system. Broader use of reforms that extend patient power and choice, such as health savings accounts and interstate sales of health insurance, would best control costs.

These reforms and ideas would create a bright future for America of freedom and prosperity. Achieving them

requires active, widespread, grassroots support. That is the hope that today's tea parties across America raise.

FURTHER RESOURCES

Books

Foley, Elizabeth P. *The Tea Party: Three Principles.* Cambridge, UK: Cambridge University Press, 2012.

O'Hara, John M. *A New American Tea Party: The Counterrevolution Against Bailouts, Handouts, Reckless Spending, and More Taxes.* Hoboken, NJ: John Wiley & Sons, 2010.

Web Sites

"History News Network Hot Topics: The Tea Party Movement." *George Mason University.* http://hnn.us/articles/124391.html (accessed on March 1, 2013).

"National Survey of Tea Party Supporters." *New York Times/CBS News.* http://documents.nytimes.com/new-york-timescbs-news-poll-national-survey-of-tea-party-supporters?ref=politics (accessed on March 1, 2013).

"Official Home of the American Tea Party Movement." *Tea Party Patriots.* http://teapartypatriots.ning.com (accessed on March 1, 2013).

"Tea Party Movement." *New York Times.* http://topics.nytimes.com/top/reference/timestopics/subjects/t/tea_party_movement/index.html (accessed on March 1, 2013).

Tea Party Patriots. http://www.teapartypatriots.org/ (accessed on March 1, 2013).

"Social Causes Defined Kennedy, Even at the End of a 46-Year Career in the Senate"

Newspaper article

By: John M. Broder

Date: August 26, 2009

Source: Broder, John M. "Social Causes Defined Kennedy, Even at the End of a 46-Year Career in the Senate." *New York Times.* www.nytimes.com/2009/08/27/us/politics/27kennedy.html (accessed March 2, 2013).

About the publication: The *New York Times* was founded in 1851 as a concise, four-page summary of daily news items. News mogul Adolph S. Ochs acquired the paper in 1896, expanding its scope and size. By the turn of the twentieth century, the *New York Times* was the pre-eminent U.S. newspaper, acclaimed for its objective reporting of "All the News That's Fit to Print." In 1905, the popularity and importance of the paper was memorialized by the City of New York, which called its new public square "Times Square" in honor of the newspaper. The paper's investigative reporting on official and political affairs has always been a trademark, garnering the journalism staff more than one hundred Pulitzer Prizes for its coverage of wars and governments—most notably for its publication of the "Pentagon Papers," leaked documents attesting to the mishandling and uncertainty of the Vietnam War. The *New York Times* remains the nation's most prestigious and important newspaper, and it continues to be owned and operated by descendants of Ochs.

INTRODUCTION

When one considers the Kennedy family, the names most commonly recalled are John and Bobby. Both men were influential politicians, known as much for their behavior out of office as for what they accomplished while in office. And both died before reaching their professional peaks, victims of gunshot wounds inflicted by assassins whose crimes brought them their fifteen minutes of fame while bringing the rest of the country to its knees in shock. This unlikely pattern of early demise became known as "the Kennedy curse."

But if JFK and Bobby were the lead actors in the drama that was known as Camelot, younger brother Edward—known as Teddy—was that member of the supporting cast who eventually stole the show. Kennedy served in the U.S. Senate for 46 years, nine months, and 19 days (November 7, 1962–August 25, 2009); citizens of Massachusetts had elected him to represent their state nine times, a record bested by just one other senator. His was a political career that, though perhaps less glamorous than his older brothers', made a more profound, longer-lasting impact on the lives of Americans from all walks of life.

The youngest of nine children from a wealthy, old-money family from the East Coast, Kennedy lived his life, for a time, the way people often expect a privileged young man to live. Although he never let his personal habits interfere with his political message, he was inevitably compared to John and Bobby and by many accounts, found to be unworthy, if not incapable. His most infamous faux paux nearly derailed him in 1969, and there is a camp of historians who believe that the Chappaquiddick incident—in which

Kennedy's campaign aide, Mary Jo Kopechne, drowned—prevented the Senator from ever having a true chance to follow in his brother's footsteps as president of the United States. Other historians and people who knew Kennedy believe that the presidency was never a goal he truly wanted to attain, but rather felt obliged to chase. The Lion of the Senate, as he became known, recognized that he was more suited to a life in the Senate, where he was able to affect more—and more important—pieces of legislation.

SIGNIFICANCE

Throughout his political career, Kennedy cast 15,235 votes, about 27 votes for every month he served. A stalwart believer in civil rights and equal opportunities for all, the youngest Kennedy never backed down from a civil rights battle. His first speech as a senator, delivered just four months after the assassination of brother John, focused on the Civil Rights Act of 1964. In it, he said, "It is true, as has been said on this floor, that prejudice exists in the minds and hearts of men. It cannot be eradicated by law. But I firmly believe a sense of fairness and good will also exists in the minds and hearts of men side by side with the prejudice; a sense of fairness and good will which shows itself so often in acts of charity and kindness toward others. This noble characteristic wants to come out. It wants to, and often does, win out against the prejudice. Law, expressing as it does the moral conscience of the community, can help it come out in every person, so in the end the prejudice will be dissolved." This deep sense of morality never faded, and Kennedy was involved in every civil rights issue and legislation for five decades.

Education for all, but particularly for the disad-vantaged, was another cornerstone of Kennedy's political agenda. Always with an eye on the underdog and the voiceless, Kennedy also focused his political clout on supporting disabled Americans, protecting the environment, promoting democracy and human rights, and supporting the military. He sat on dozens of committees, and although clearly a committed Democrat, was known for his willingness to collaborate across party lines in an effort to reach a greater good.

Affordable health care for every individual was a life-long cause for Teddy Kennedy, and tens of millions of Americans have been the recipients of his tireless efforts. From his first term in the Senate, when he introduced an amendment to the Economic Opportunity Act that significantly increased medical care access to low-income communities, to his diligence and leadership that led to the groundwork for the 2009 health care reform legislation, Kennedy never ceased fighting for those who could not fight for themselves.

Broder's *New York Times* article provides a comprehensive overview of Kennedy's life, a fitting obituary for a political leader whose light may never have burned brightly, but which never completely burned out.

■ PRIMARY SOURCE

"SOCIAL CAUSES DEFINED KENNEDY, EVEN AT THE END OF A 46-YEAR CAREER IN THE SENATE"

SYNOPSIS: Despite a life often overshadowed by the personal and professional drama of his older brothers John F. Kennedy and Robert Kennedy, Edward "Teddy" Kennedy arguably had a greater impact on American politics during his forty-six years of service in the Senate than either of his siblings. He is remembered not only for his political legacy, but for his dynamic personality as well.

Senator Edward M. Kennedy of Massachusetts, a son of one of the most storied families in American politics, a man who knew acclaim and tragedy in near-equal measure and who will be remembered as one of the most effective lawmakers in the history of the Senate, died late Tuesday night. He was 77.

The death of Mr. Kennedy, who had been battling brain cancer, was announced Wednesday morning in a statement by the Kennedy family, which was already mourning the death of the senator's sister Eunice Kennedy Shriver two weeks earlier.

"Edward M. Kennedy—the husband, father, grandfather, brother and uncle we loved so deeply—died late Tuesday night at home in Hyannis Port," the statement said. "We've lost the irreplaceable center of our family and joyous light in our lives, but the inspiration of his faith, optimism and perseverance will live on in our hearts forever."

President Obama said Mr. Kennedy was one of the nation's greatest senators.

"His ideas and ideals are stamped on scores of laws and reflected in millions of lives—in seniors who know new dignity, in families that know new opportunity, in children who know education's promise, and in all who can pursue their dream in an America that is more equal and more just—including myself," he said. Mr. Obama is scheduled to speak at a funeral Mass for Mr. Kennedy on Saturday morning in Boston.

Mr. Kennedy had been in precarious health since he suffered a seizure in May 2008. His doctors determined the cause was a malignant glioma, a brain tumor that carries a grim prognosis.

As he underwent cancer treatment, Mr. Kennedy was little seen in Washington, appearing most recently at the White House in April as Mr. Obama signed a national service bill that bears the Kennedy name. In a letter last week, Mr. Kennedy urged Massachusetts lawmakers to change state law and let Gov. Deval Patrick appoint a temporary successor upon his death, to assure that the state's representation in Congress would not be interrupted.

While Mr. Kennedy was physically absent from the capital in recent months, his presence was deeply felt as Congress weighed the most sweeping revisions to America's health care system in decades, an effort Mr. Kennedy called "the cause of my life."

On July 15, the Senate Health, Education, Labor and Pensions Committee, which Mr. Kennedy headed, passed health care legislation, and the battle over the proposed overhaul is now consuming Capitol Hill.

Mr. Kennedy was the last surviving brother of a generation of Kennedys that dominated American politics in the 1960s and that came to embody glamour, political idealism and untimely death. The Kennedy mystique—some call it the Kennedy myth—has held the imagination of the world for decades, and it came to rest on the sometimes too-narrow shoulders of the brother known as Teddy.

Mr. Kennedy, who served 46 years as the most well-known Democrat in the Senate, longer than all but two other senators, was the only one of those brothers to reach old age. President John F. Kennedy and Senator Robert F. Kennedy were felled by assassins' bullets in their 40s. The eldest brother, Joseph P. Kennedy Jr., died in 1944 at the age of 29 while on a risky World War II bombing mission.

Mr. Kennedy ... electrified the opening night of the Democratic National Convention in Denver in August with an unscheduled appearance and a speech that had delegates on their feet. Many were in tears.

His gait was halting, but his voice was strong. "My fellow Democrats, my fellow Americans, it is so wonderful to be here, and nothing is going to keep me away from this special gathering tonight," Mr. Kennedy said. "I have come here tonight to stand with you to change America, to restore its future, to rise to our best ideals and to elect Barack Obama president of the United States."

Senator Kennedy was at or near the center of much of American history in the latter part of the 20th century and the early years of the 21st. For much of his adult life, he veered from victory to catastrophe, winning every Senate election he entered but failing in his only bid for the presidency; living through the sudden deaths of his brothers and three of his nephews; being responsible for the drowning death on Chappaquiddick Island of a young

U.S. senator Edward M. Kennedy speaks at the Democratic National Convention in Denver, Colorado, August 25, 2008, as he endorses Barack Obama for president. © AP IMAGES/RON EDMONDS.

woman, Mary Jo Kopechne, a former aide to his brother Robert. One of the nephews, John F. Kennedy Jr., who the family hoped would one day seek political office and keep the Kennedy tradition alive, died in a plane crash in 1999 at age 38....

Senator Robert C. Byrd, Democrat of West Virginia, one of the institution's most devoted students, said of his longtime colleague, "Ted Kennedy would have been a leader, an outstanding senator, at any period in the nation's history."

Mr. Byrd is one of only two senators to have served longer in the chamber than Mr. Kennedy; the other was Strom Thurmond of South Carolina. In May 2008, on learning of Mr. Kennedy's diagnosis of a lethal brain tumor, Mr. Byrd wept openly on the floor of the Senate.

MORE THAN A LEGISLATOR

Born to one of the wealthiest American families, Mr. Kennedy spoke for the downtrodden in his public life while living the heedless private life of a playboy and a

rake for many of his years. Dismissed early in his career as a lightweight and an unworthy successor to his revered brothers, he grew in stature over time by sheer longevity and by hewing to liberal principles while often crossing the partisan aisle to enact legislation. A man of unbridled appetites at times, he nevertheless brought a discipline to his public work that resulted in an impressive catalog of legislative achievement across a broad landscape of social policy.

Mr. Kennedy left his mark on legislation concerning civil rights, health care, education, voting rights and labor. He was chairman of the Senate Committee on Health, Education, Labor and Pensions at his death. But he was more than a legislator. He was a living legend whose presence ensured a crowd and whose hovering figure haunted many a president.

Although he was a leading spokesman for liberal issues and a favorite target of conservative fund-raising appeals, the hallmark of his legislative success was his ability to find Republican allies to get bills passed. Perhaps the last notable example was his work with President George W. Bush to pass No Child Left Behind, the education law pushed by Mr. Bush in 2001. He also co-sponsored immigration legislation with Senator John McCain, the 2008 Republican presidential nominee. One of his greatest friends and collaborators in the Senate was Orrin G. Hatch, the Utah Republican.

Mr. Kennedy had less impact on foreign policy than on domestic concerns, but when he spoke, his voice was influential. He led the Congressional effort to impose sanctions on South Africa over apartheid, pushed for peace in Northern Ireland, won a ban on arms sales to the dictatorship in Chile and denounced the Vietnam War. In 2002, he voted against authorizing the Iraq war; later, he called that opposition "the best vote I've made in my 44 years in the United States Senate."

At a pivotal moment in the 2008 Democratic presidential primaries, Mr. Kennedy endorsed Mr. Obama, then an Illinois senator, for president, saying he offered the country a chance for racial reconciliation and an opportunity to turn the page on the polarizing politics of the past several decades.

"He will be a president who refuses to be trapped in the patterns of the past," Mr. Kennedy said at an Obama rally in Washington on Jan. 28, 2008. "He is a leader who sees the world clearly, without being cynical. He is a fighter who cares passionately about the causes he believes in without demonizing those who hold a different view."

This month, Mr. Obama awarded Mr. Kennedy the Presidential Medal of Freedom, which his daughter, Kara, accepted on his behalf....

In December, Harvard granted Mr. Kennedy a special honorary degree. He referred to Mr. Obama's election as "not just a culmination, but a new beginning."

U.S. senator Edward M. Kennedy of Massachusetts speaks at the 1980 Democratic convention in New York City, following his loss to incumbent president Jimmy Carter. © DIEGO GOLDBERG/SYGMA/CORBIS.

He then spoke of his own life, and perhaps his legacy.

"We know the future will outlast all of us, but I believe that all of us will live on in the future we make," he said. "I have lived a blessed time."

Kennedy family courtiers and many other Democrats believed he would eventually win the White House and redeem the promise of his older brothers. In 1980, he took on the president of his own party, Jimmy Carter, but fell short because of Chappaquiddick, a divided party and his own weaknesses as a candidate, including an inability to articulate why he sought the office.

But as that race ended in August at the Democratic National Convention in New York, Mr. Kennedy delivered his most memorable words, wrapping his dedication to party principles in the gauzy cloak of Camelot.

"For me, a few hours ago, this campaign came to an end," Mr. Kennedy said in the coda to a speech before a rapt audience at Madison Square Garden and on television. "For all those whose cares have been our concern, the work goes on, the cause endures, the hope still lives and the dream shall never die."

A FAMILY STEEPED IN POLITICS

Born Feb. 22, 1932, in Boston, Edward Moore Kennedy grew up in a family of shrewd politicians. Both his father, Joseph P. Kennedy, and his mother, the former Rose Fitzgerald, came from prominent Irish-Catholic families with long involvement in the hurly-burly of Democratic politics in Boston and Massachusetts. His father, who made a fortune in real estate, movies and banking, served in President Franklin D. Roosevelt's administration, as the first chairman of the Securities and Exchange Commission and then as ambassador to Britain.

There were nine Kennedy children, four boys and five girls, with Edward the youngest. They grew up talking politics, power and influence because those were the things that preoccupied the mind of Joseph Kennedy. As Rose Kennedy, who took responsibility for the children's Roman Catholic upbringing, once put it, "My babies were rocked to political lullabies."

When Edward was born, President Herbert Hoover sent Rose a bouquet of flowers and a note of congratulations. The note came with 5 cents postage due; the framed envelope is a family heirloom. . . .

Although surrounded by the trappings of wealth—stately houses, servants and expensive cars—young Teddy did not enjoy a settled childhood. He bounced among the family homes in Boston, New York, London and Palm Beach, and by the time he was ready to enter college, he had attended 10 preparatory schools in the United States and England, finally finishing at Milton Academy, near Boston. He said that the constant moving had forced him to become more genial with strangers; indeed, he grew to be more of a natural politician than either John or Robert.

After graduating from Milton in 1950, where he showed a penchant for debating and sports but was otherwise an undistinguished student, Mr. Kennedy enrolled in Harvard, as had his father and brothers.

It was at Harvard, in his freshman year, that he ran into the first of several personal troubles that were to dog him for the rest of his life: He persuaded another student to take his Spanish examination, got caught and was forced to leave the university.

Suddenly draft-eligible during the Korean War, Mr. Kennedy enlisted in the Army and served two years, securing, with his father's help, a post at NATO headquarters in Paris. In 1953, he was discharged with the rank of private first class.

Re-enrolling in Harvard, he became a more serious student, majoring in government, excelling in public speaking and playing first-string end on the football team. He graduated in 1956 with a Bachelor of Arts degree, then enrolled in the University of Virginia School of Law, where Robert had studied. There, he ... took a degree in 1959. Later that year, he was admitted to the Massachusetts bar.

Mr. Kennedy's first foray into politics came in 1958, while still a law student, when he managed John's Senate re-election campaign. There was never any real doubt that Massachusetts voters would return John Kennedy to Washington, but it was a useful internship for his youngest brother.

That same year, Mr. Kennedy married Virginia Joan Bennett, a debutante from Bronxville, a New York suburb where the Kennedys had once lived. In 1960, when John Kennedy ran for president, Edward was assigned a relatively minor role, rustling up votes in Western states that usually voted Republican....

John Kennedy's election to the White House left vacant a Senate seat that the family considered its property. Robert Kennedy was next in line, but chose the post of attorney general instead (an act of nepotism that has since been outlawed). Edward was only 28, two years shy of the minimum age for Senate service.

So the Kennedys installed Benjamin A. Smith II, a family friend, as a seat-warmer until 1962, when a special election would be held and Edward would have turned 30. Edward used the time to travel the world and work as an assistant district attorney in Boston, waiving the $5,000 salary and serving instead for $1 a year.

As James Sterling Young, the director of a Kennedy Oral History Project at the University of Virginia, said the catchphrase of that era was: "Most people grow up and go into politics. The Kennedys go into politics and then they grow up."

Less than a month after turning 30 in 1962, Mr. Kennedy declared his candidacy for the remaining two years of his brother's Senate term. He entered the race with a tailwind of family money and political prominence. Nevertheless, Edward J. McCormack Jr., the state's attorney general and a nephew of John W. McCormack, then speaker of the United States House of Representatives, also decided to go after the seat....

But the Kennedys had ushered in an era of celebrity politics, which trumped qualifications in this case. Mr. Kennedy won the primary by a two-to-one ratio, then went on to easy victory in November against the Republican candidate, George Cabot Lodge, a member of an old-line Boston family that had clashed politically with the Kennedys through the years.

When Mr. Kennedy entered the Senate in 1962, he was aware that he might be seen as an upstart, with one brother in the White House and another in the cabinet. He sought guidance on the very first day from one of the Senate's most respected elders, Richard Russell of Georgia. "You go further if you go slow," Senator Russell advised.

Mr. Kennedy took things slowly, especially that first year. He did his homework, was seen more than he was heard and was deferential to veteran legislators.

On Friday, Nov. 22, 1963, he was presiding over the Senate when a wire service ticker in the lobby brought the news of John Kennedy's shooting in Dallas. Violence had claimed the second of Joseph Kennedy's sons.

Edward was sent to Hyannis Port to break the news to his father, who had been disabled by a stroke. He returned to Washington for the televised funeral and burial, the first many Americans had seen of him. He and Robert had planned to read excerpts from John's speeches at the Arlington burial service. At the last moment they chose not to.

A friend described him as "shattered—calm but shattered."

A DEADLY PLANE CRASH

Robert moved into the breach and was immediately discussed as a presidential prospect. Edward became a more prominent family spokesman.

The next year, he was up for re-election. A heavy favorite from the start, he was on his way to the state convention that was to renominate him when his light plane crashed in a storm near Westfield, Mass. The pilot and a Kennedy aide were killed, and Mr. Kennedy's back and several ribs were broken. Senator Birch Bayh of Indiana pulled Mr. Kennedy from the plane.

The senator was hospitalized for the next six months, suspended immobile in a frame that resembled a waffle iron. His wife, Joan, carried on his campaign, mainly by advising voters that he was steadily recovering. He won easily over a little-known Republican, Howard Whitmore Jr.

During his convalescence, Mr. Kennedy devoted himself to his legislative work. He was briefed by a parade of Harvard professors and began to develop his positions on immigration, health care and civil rights.

"I never thought the time was lost," he said later. "I had a lot of hours to think about what was important and what was not and about what I wanted to do with my life."

He returned to the Senate in 1965, joining his brother Robert, who had won a seat from New York. Edward promptly entered a major fight, his first. President Lyndon B. Johnson's Voting Rights Act was up for consideration, and Mr. Kennedy tried to strengthen it with an amendment that would have outlawed poll taxes. He lost by only four votes, serving lasting notice on his colleagues that he was a rapidly maturing legislator who could prepare a good case and argue it effectively.

Mr. Kennedy was slow to oppose the war in Vietnam, but in 1968, shortly after Robert decided to seek the presidency on an antiwar platform, Edward called the war a "monstrous outrage."

Robert Kennedy was shot on June 5, 1968, as he celebrated his victory in the California primary, becoming the third of Joseph Kennedy's sons to die a violent death. Edward was in San Francisco at a victory celebration. He commandeered an Air Force plane and flew to Los Angeles.

Frank Mankiewicz, Robert's press secretary, saw Edward "leaning over the sink with the most awful expression on his face."

"Much more than agony, more than anguish—I don't know if there's a word for it," Mr. Mankiewicz said, recalling the encounter in "Edward M. Kennedy: A Biography," by Adam Clymer (William Morrow, 1999).

Robert's death draped Edward in the Kennedy mantle long before he was ready for it and forced him to confront his own mortality. But he summoned himself to deliver an eloquent eulogy at St. Patrick's Cathedral in New York....

A NEW ROLE AS PATRIARCH

After the funeral, Edward Kennedy withdrew from public life and spent several months brooding, much of it while sailing off the New England coast.

Near the end of the summer of 1968, he emerged from seclusion, the sole survivor of Joseph Kennedy's boys, ready to take over as family patriarch and substitute father to John's and Robert's 13 children, seemingly eager to get on with what he called his "public responsibilities."

"There is no safety in hiding," he declared in August in a speech at College of the Holy Cross in Worcester, Mass. "Like my brothers before me, I pick up a fallen standard. Sustained by the memory of our priceless years together, I shall try to carry forward that special commitment to justice, excellence and courage that distinguished their lives."

There was some talk of his running for president at that point. But he ultimately endorsed Hubert H. Humphrey in his losing campaign to Richard M. Nixon.

Mr. Kennedy focused more on bringing the war in Vietnam to an end and on building his Senate career. Although only 36, he challenged Senator Russell B. Long of Louisiana, one of the shrewdest, most powerful legislators on Capitol Hill, for the post of deputy majority leader. Fellow liberals sided with him, and he edged Mr.

Long by five votes to become the youngest assistant majority leader, or whip, in Senate history.

He plunged into the new job with Kennedy enthusiasm. But fate, and the Kennedy recklessness, intervened on July 18, 1969. Mr. Kennedy was at a party with several women who had been aides to Robert. The party, a liquor-soaked barbecue, was held at a rented cottage on Chappaquiddick Island, off Martha's Vineyard. He left around midnight with Mary Jo Kopechne, 28, took a turn away from the ferry landing and drove the car off a narrow bridge on an isolated beach road. The car sank in eight feet of water, but he managed to escape. Miss Kopechne, a former campaign worker for Robert, drowned.

Mr. Kennedy did not report the accident to the authorities for almost 10 hours, explaining later that he had been so banged about by the crash that he had suffered a concussion, and that he had become so exhausted while trying to rescue Miss Kopechne that he had gone immediately to bed. A week later, he pleaded guilty to a charge of leaving the scene of an accident and was given a two-month suspended sentence.

But that was far from the end of the episode. Questions lingered in the minds of the Massachusetts authorities and of the general public. Why was the car on an isolated road? Had he been drinking? (Mr. Kennedy testified at an inquest that he had had two drinks.) What sort of relationship did Mr. Kennedy and Miss Kopechne have? Could she have been saved if he had sought help immediately? Why did the senator tell his political advisers about the accident before reporting it to the police?

The controversy became so intense that Mr. Kennedy went on television to ask Massachusetts voters whether he should resign from office. He conceded that his actions after the crash had been "indefensible." But he steadfastly denied any intentional wrongdoing.

His constituents sent word that he should remain in the Senate. And little more than a year later, he easily won re-election to a second full term, defeating a little-known Republican, Josiah A. Spaulding, by a three-to-two ratio. But his heart did not seem to be in his work any longer. He was sometimes absent from Senate sessions and neglected his whip duties. Senator Byrd, of West Virginia, took the job away from him by putting together a coalition of Southern and border-state Democrats to vote him out.

That loss shook Mr. Kennedy out of his lethargy. He rededicated himself to his role as a legislator. "It hurts like hell to lose," he said, "but now I can get around the country more. And it frees me to spend more time on issues I'm interested in." Many years later, he became friends with Mr. Byrd and told him the defeat had been the best thing that could have happened in his Senate career.

TURMOIL AT HOME

In the next decade, Mr. Kennedy expanded on his national reputation, first pushing to end the war in Vietnam, then concentrating on his favorite legislative issues, especially civil rights, health, taxes, criminal laws and deregulation of the airline and trucking industries. He traveled the country, making speeches that kept him in the public eye.

But when he was mentioned as a possible candidate for president in 1972, he demurred; and when the Democratic nominee, George McGovern, offered him the vice-presidential nomination, Mr. Kennedy again said no, not wanting to face the inevitable Chappaquiddick questions.

In 1973, his son Edward M. Kennedy Jr., then 12, developed a bone cancer that cost him a leg. The next year, Mr. Kennedy took himself out of the 1976 presidential race. Instead, he easily won a third full term in the Senate, and Jimmy Carter, a former one-term governor of Georgia, moved into the White House.

In early 1978, Mr. Kennedy's wife, Joan, moved out of their sprawling contemporary house overlooking the Potomac River near McLean, Va., a Washington suburb. She took up residence in an apartment of her own in Boston, saying she wanted to "explore options other than being a housewife and mother." But she also acknowledged a problem with alcohol, and conceded that she was increasingly uncomfortable with the pressure-cooker life that went with membership in the Kennedy clan. She began studying music and enrolled in a program for alcoholics.

The separation posed not only personal but also political problems for the senator. After Mrs. Kennedy left for Boston, there were rumors that linked the senator with other women. He maintained that he still loved his wife and indicated that the main reason for the separation was Mrs. Kennedy's desire to work out her alcohol problem. She subsequently campaigned for him in the 1980 race, but there was never any real reconciliation, and they eventually entered divorce proceedings.

Although Mr. Kennedy supported Mr. Carter in 1976, by late 1978 he was disenchanted. Polls indicated that the senator was becoming popular while the president was losing support. In December, at a midterm Democratic convention in Memphis, Mr. Kennedy could hold back no longer. He gave a thundering speech that, in retrospect, was the opening shot in the 1980 campaign.

"Sometimes a party must sail against the wind," he declared, referring to Mr. Carter's economic belt-tightening and political caution. "We cannot heed the call of those who say it is time to furl the sail. The party that tore itself apart over Vietnam in the 1960s cannot afford to tear itself apart today over budget cuts in basic social programs."

Mr. Kennedy did not then declare his candidacy. But draft-Kennedy groups began to form in early 1979, and some Democrats up for re-election in 1980 began to cast about for coattails that were longer than Mr. Carter's.

After consulting advisers and family members over the summer of 1979, Mr. Kennedy began speaking openly of challenging the president, and on Nov. 7, 1979, he announced officially that he would run. "Our leaders have resigned themselves to defeat," he said.

The campaign was a disaster, badly organized and appearing to lack a political or policy premise. His speeches were clumsy, and his delivery was frequently stumbling and bombastic. And in the background, Chappaquiddick always loomed. He won the New York and California primaries, but the victories were too little and came too late to unseat Mr. Carter. At the party's nominating convention in New York, however, he stole the show with his "dream shall never die" speech.

With the approach of the 1984 election, there was the inevitable speculation that Mr. Kennedy, who had easily won re-election to the Senate in 1982, would again seek the presidency. He prepared and planned a campaign. But in the end he chose not to run, saying he wanted to spare his family a repeat of the ordeal they went through in 1980. Skeptics said he also knew he could not fight the undertow of Chappaquiddick.

A FULL-ON SENATE FOCUS

Freed at last of the expectation that he should and would seek the White House, Mr. Kennedy devoted himself fully to his day job in the Senate, where he had already led the fight for the 18-year-old vote, the abolition of the draft, deregulation of the airline and trucking industries, and the post-Watergate campaign finance legislation. He was deeply involved in renewals of the Voting Rights Act and the Fair Housing law of 1968. He helped establish the Occupational Safety and Health Administration. He built federal support for community health care centers, increased cancer research financing and helped create the Meals on Wheels program. He was a major proponent of a health and nutrition program for pregnant women and infants.

When Republicans took over the Senate in 1981, Mr. Kennedy requested the ranking minority position on the Labor and Public Welfare Committee, asserting that the issues before the labor and welfare panel would be more important during the Reagan years.

In the years after his failed White House bid, Mr. Kennedy also established himself as someone who made "lawmaker" mean more than a word used in headlines to

U.S. senators Edward M. Kennedy of Massachusetts (left) and Robert Dole of Kansas hold a joint news conference to discuss a banking bill the two were working on in April 1983. © AP IMAGES/J. SCOTT APPLEWHITE.

describe any member of Congress. Though his personal life was a mess until his remarriage in the early 1990s, he never failed to show up prepared for a committee hearing or a floor debate.

His most notable focus was civil rights, "still the unfinished business of America," he often said. In 1982, he led a successful fight to defeat the Reagan administration's effort to weaken the Voting Rights Act.

In one of those bipartisan alliances that were hallmarks of his legislative successes, Mr. Kennedy worked with Senator Bob Dole, Republican of Kansas, to secure passage of the voting rights measure, and Mr. Dole got most of the credit.

Perhaps his greatest success on civil rights came in 1990 with passage of the Americans with Disabilities Act, which required employers and public facilities to make "reasonable accommodation" for the disabled.

When the bill was finally passed, Mr. Kennedy and others told how their views on the bill had been shaped by having relatives with disabilities. Mr. Kennedy cited his mentally disabled sister, Rosemary, and his son who had lost a leg to cancer.

Mr. Kennedy was one of Bill and Hillary Clinton's strongest allies in their failed 1994 effort to enact national health insurance, a measure the senator had been pushing, in one form or another, since 1969.

But he kept pushing incremental reforms, and in 1997, teaming with Senator Hatch, Mr. Kennedy helped enact a landmark health care program for children in low-income families, a program now known as the State Children's Health Insurance Program, or S-Chip.

He led efforts to increase aid for higher education and win passage of Mr. Bush's No Child Left Behind Act. He pushed for increases in the federal minimum wage. He helped win enactment of the Medicare prescription drug benefit, one of the largest expansions of government health aid.

He was a forceful and successful opponent of the confirmation of Robert H. Bork to the Supreme Court. In a speech delivered within minutes of President Ronald Reagan's nomination of Mr. Bork in 1987, Mr. Kennedy made an attack that even friendly commentators called demagogic.

Mr. Bork's "extremist view of the Constitution," Mr. Kennedy said, meant that "Robert Bork's America is a land in which women would be forced into back-alley abortions, blacks would sit at segregated lunch counters, rogue police could break down citizens' doors in midnight raids, and schoolchildren could not be taught about evolution, writers and artists could be censored at the whim of government, and the doors of the federal courts would be shut on the fingers of millions of Americans." Some of Mr. Kennedy's success as a legislator can be traced to the quality and loyalty of his staff, considered by his colleagues and outsiders alike to be the best on Capitol Hill....

A PLACE IN HISTORY

Mr. Kennedy "deserves recognition not just as the leading senator of his time, but as one of the greats in its history, wise in the workings of this singular institution, especially its demand to be more than partisan to accomplish much," Mr. Clymer wrote in his biography.

"The deaths and tragedies around him would have led others to withdraw. He never quits, but sails against the wind." ...

He reluctantly and at times awkwardly carried the Kennedy standard, with all it implied and all it required. And yet, some scholars contend, he may have proved himself the most worthy.

"He was a quintessential Kennedy, in the sense that he had all the warts as well as all the charisma and a lot of the strengths," said Norman J. Ornstein, a political scientist at the American Enterprise Institute.

"If his father, Joe, had surveyed, from an early age up to the time of his death, all of his children, his sons in particular, and asked to rank them on talents, effectiveness, likelihood to have an impact on the world, Ted would have been a very poor fourth. Joe, John, Bobby ... Ted.

"He was the survivor," Mr. Ornstein continued. "He was not a shining star that burned brightly and faded away. He had a long, steady glow. When you survey the impact of the Kennedys on American life and politics and policy, he will end up by far being the most significant."

FURTHER RESOURCES

Books

Kennedy, Edward M. *True Compass: A Memoir.* New York: Twelve, 2011.

Klein, Edward. *Ted Kennedy: The Dream That Never Died.* New York: Crown Archetype, 2009.

Web Sites

Edward M. Kennedy. www.tedkennedy.org (accessed March 2, 2013).

"Longest Serving Senators." *United States Senate.* www.senate.gov/senators/Biographical/longest_serving.htm (accessed March 2, 2013).

"Remembering Senator Edward M. Kennedy." *The White House.* www.whitehouse.gov/photos-and-video/photogallery/remembering-senator-edward-m-kennedy (accessed March 2, 2013).

6 Law and Justice

Chronology

Important Events in Law and Justice, 2000–2009

2000

- On March 21, in *FDA v. Brown & Williamson Tobacco Corp.* the U.S. Supreme Court rules 5–4 that the Food and Drug Administration does not have jurisdiction to regulate tobacco as a drug.

- On April 22, federal agents seize six-year-old Cuban refugee Elian González from the home of relatives in Miami.

- On April 26, following two rulings earlier in the week, the U.S. Supreme Court tells lower courts to increase opportunities for convicts to appeal their convictions.

- On June 7, U.S. District Court judge Thomas Penfield Jackson, who on 3 April had found software manufacturer Microsoft in violation of the nation's antitrust laws, orders the firm broken up into separate and competing companies—one for its Windows operating system and one for its other computer programs and Internet businesses.

- On June 19, prayers at school-sponsored extracurricular activities are deemed unconstitutional by the U.S. Supreme Court in *Santa Fe School District v. Doe.*

- On June 28, in *Mitchell v. Helms* the U.S. Supreme Court rules 6–1 that the Education Consolidation and Improvement Act (1981) allows federal monies to be used to provide computers and other equipment to private schools.

- On June 28, the U.S. Supreme Court rules in *Boy Scouts of America v. Dale* that the Boy Scouts did not discriminate by choosing to "forbid membership to homosexuals."

- On June 28, Elian González returns to Cuba with his father, Juan Miguel.

- On October 1, former president Bill Clinton is suspended from practice before the U.S. Supreme Court because of perjury he committed during the Monica Lewinsky affair; he resigns from the high-court bar in November.

- On December 12, in the controversial *Bush v. Gore* decision the U.S. Supreme Court orders an end to the recount of votes in Florida for the 2000 presidential election, handing the presidency to George W. Bush.

2001

- On January 20, Bush is inaugurated as the forty-third president of the United States.

- On February 2, former U.S. senator John David Ashcroft (R-Missouri) is sworn in as attorney general of the United States.

- On February 18, Robert Hanssen, a Federal Bureau of Investigation (FBI) agent, is charged with spying for the Soviet Union.

- On February 27, the U.S. Supreme Court unanimously rules that the Environmental Protection Agency has the power to set air-quality standards.

- On March 21, in *Ferguson v. Charleston* the U.S. Supreme Court rules that involuntary drug testing of women violates the Fourth Amendment protection against unreasonable search and seizure.

- On May 14, the U.S. Supreme Court rules in *United States v. Oakland Cannabis Buyers' Cooperative* that marijuana cannot be legally used for medical purposes.

- On June 11, the U.S. Supreme Court rules in *Good News Club, Inc. v. Milford Central School* that public schools must allow religious groups access to facilities for after-school activities.

- On June 11, Timothy McVeigh is executed for his role in the April 19, 1995 bombing of the Alfred P. Murrah Federal Building in Oklahoma City.

- On September 6, the U.S. Department of Justice drops its bid to break up Microsoft.

- On September 25, Deputy Assistant Attorney General John C. Yoo of the Office of Legal Counsel writes a memo that the White House uses to justify eavesdropping without warrants in the fight against terrorism.

- On October 23, Yoo and special counsel Robert J. Delahunty write a memo to White House counsel

Alberto R. Gonzales defending the use of military forces to fight terrorism domestically.

- On October 26, the Uniting and Strengthening America by Providing Appropriate Tools Required to Intercept and Obstruct Terrorism (USA PATRIOT) Act is signed into law by President Bush.

- On November 13, President Bush orders that foreigners suspected of involvement in terrorism against the United States be tried by military tribunals if captured.

- On November 30, Gary Ridgway, the "Green River Killer," is arrested. He later confesses to the murders of more than forty women.

- On December 11, Zacarias Moussaoui, a French citizen, is indicted for his alleged role in the September 11 terrorist attacks.

2002

- In January, the Justice Department begins its investigation of criminal proceedings at the failed energy conglomerate Enron.

- On January 8, the No Child Left Behind Act, an education-reform law, is signed by President Bush.

- On March 12, after a highly publicized trial, Andrea Yates of Houston, Texas, is found guilty of three counts of murder in the drownings of her five children. She is later sentenced to life in prison.

- On April 16, in a 6–3 decision, the U.S. Supreme Court strikes down the Child Pornography Prevention Act (1996) as a violation of the First Amendment.

- On May 10, Hanssen is sentenced to life in prison after he is found guilty of spying for the Soviet Union.

- On May 22, Former Klu Klux Klan member Bobby Frank Cherry is convicted of murder for his role in the 1963 16th Street Baptist Church bombing in Birmingham, Alabama, which killed four young girls who were attending Sunday School classes. The bombing was a major catalyst for federal intervention on civil rights.

- On June 20, the U.S. Supreme Court rules in *Atkins v. Virginia* that the execution of mentally handicapped convicts is cruel and unusual punishment.

- On June 27, in a 5–4 decision the U.S. Supreme Court approves random drug testing of public-school students as a prerequisite for participation in extracurricular interscholastic competitions.

- On October 24, after thirteen attacks (ten fatal) carried out over a twenty-two-day shooting spree in Washington, D.C., Maryland, and Virginia, the "Beltway Snipers" John Allen Muhammad and Lee Boyd Malvo are arrested.

- On November 25, the Homeland Security Act is signed into law, creating the cabinet-level Department of Homeland Security.

2003

- On January 21, the U.S. Supreme Court rules that individuals can be charged with conspiracy even if their arrests prevented the conspiracy from being carried out.

- On March 5, the U.S. Supreme Court rules 6–3 that states can continue to post the names and pictures of convicted sex offenders on the Internet.

- On April 7, the U.S. Supreme Court rules that cross burning with the intent of intimidation is not protected by the First Amendment, and that more than simply carrying out the act is needed to prosecute.

- On May 31, fugitive Eric Robert Rudolph, a suspect in the 1996 Centennial Olympic Park bombing in Atlanta, Georgia, is arrested in the mountain community of Murphy, North Carolina.

- On June 4, lifestyle guru Martha Stewart and her former stockbroker are indicted by a federal grand jury in New York City for allegedly lying to investigators in an insider-trading case.

- On June 23, in *Grutter v. Bollinger* the U.S. Supreme Court upholds (5–4) the University of Michigan Law School's affirmative-action admissions policy because it is narrowly tailored to promote diversity. On the same day, in *Gratz v. Bollinger* the court strikes down (6–3) the university's undergraduate affirmative-action policy, which awards twenty points to blacks, Hispanics, and Native Americans on an admissions rating scale.

- On June 23, the U.S. Supreme Court rules that libraries can install software that protects patrons, especially children, from gaining access to pornographic Internet websites.

- On June 26, the U.S. Supreme Court declares sodomy laws unconstitutional in *Lawrence v. Texas*.

- On October 7, California voters recall Democratic governor Joseph Graham "Gray" Davis Jr. from office and select Austrian-born movie actor and former bodybuilder Arnold Schwarzenegger, a Republican, over 134 other candidates to replace him.

- On November 5, President Bush signs into law the Partial Birth Abortion Ban Act.

- On November 12, Alabama chief justice Roy Moore is forced to step down from the bench for refusing to remove a monument of the Ten Commandments from the state's Judicial Building after it was ruled to violate the establishment clause of the First Amendment to the U.S. Constitution.

- On December 10, the U.S. Supreme Court in *McConnell v. Federal Election Commission* bans "soft money" contributions to political parties and overturns provisions restricting those under the age of eighteen from contributing to political campaigns.

2004

- On February 12, the city of San Francisco, California, begins issuing marriage licenses to homosexual couples.

- On February 25, in *Locke v. Davey* the U.S. Supreme Court rules 7–2 that states that offer taxpayer-funded scholarships to academically qualified low- and middle-income students do not have to give them to those who wish to study for the ministry.

- On April 1, President Bush signs the Unborn Victims of Violence law, which recognizes an unborn child, in any stage of development, as a legal victim if injured or killed.

- On May 19, U.S. Army specialist Jeremy Sivits pleads guilty in a court martial to his role in the Abu Ghraib prisoner abuse scandal in Iraq.

- On May 26, Terry Nichols is found guilty of murder for his role in the 1995 Oklahoma City bombing.

- On June 14, the U.S. Supreme Court rules unanimously in *Elk Grove v. Newdow* that the words "under God" in the Pledge of Allegiance do not violate the establishment clause of the First Amendment.

- On June 28, in *Rasul v. Bush* the U.S. Supreme Court rules that foreign nationals captured abroad and detained at Guantánamo Bay naval base in Cuba may challenge their detention in federal courts. In *Hamdi v. Rumsfeld* the court asserts that citizens held as enemy combatants have the right to contest their status.

- On September 13, the Assault Weapons Ban (1994) expires.

- On November 2, gay-marriage bans are passed in Arkansas, Georgia, Kentucky, Michigan, Mississippi, Montana, North Dakota, Oklahoma, Ohio, Utah, and Oregon.

- On November 9, the White House accepts the resignation of Attorney General Ashcroft, who will remain in the position until his replacement is selected.

2005

- On January 20, George W. Bush is sworn in as president for a second term.

- On February 3, Alberto Gonzales is appointed U.S. attorney general.

- On February 25, Dennis Lynn Rader, the "BTK" (Bind-Torture-Kill) serial killer alleged to have murdered ten people, is arrested in Wichita, Kansas.

- On March 1, in *Roper v. Simmons* the U.S. Supreme Court rules that the death penalty may not be imposed upon juvenile offenders.

- On May 31, former FBI agent W. Mark Felt reveals that he was "Deep Throat," a key source in the *Washington Post* coverage of the Watergate scandal that led to the resignation of President Richard M. Nixon in 1974.

- On June 13, the U.S. Supreme Court orders the conviction of Texas death-row inmate Thomas Miller-El thrown out because prosecutors had systematically excluded black jurors.

- On June 23, the U.S. Supreme Court decides in *Kelo v. City of New London, Connecticut* that governments can use eminent-domain laws for the purpose of economic development.

- On June 27, in *MGM v. Grokster* the U.S. Supreme Court rules that companies that actively and intentionally promote the illegal use of their software—in this case, for downloading copyrighted music and videos—can be sued.

- On June 27, in *McCreary County, Kentucky v. American Civil Liberties Union of Kentucky* the U.S. Supreme Court rules 5–4 that courthouse displays of the Ten Commandments are unconstitutional because they lack a primary secular purpose. In *Van Orden v. Perry*, however, it decides, also by a 5–4 majority, that a monument on the Texas state capitol grounds that depicts the commandments is permissible.

- On July 1, Associate Justice Sandra Day O'Connor announces plans to retire from the U.S. Supreme Court.

- On September 3, Chief Justice William H. Rehnquist dies.

- On September 26, Army reservist Lynndie England is convicted for her role in the Abu Ghraib prisoner-abuse scandal.

- On September 28, House majority leader Tom DeLay (R-Texas) is charged with criminal conspiracy for illegal campaign finance practices.

- On September 29, John G. Roberts Jr. is sworn in as the seventeenth chief justice of the U.S. Supreme Court.

- On October 3, President Bush nominates former White House deputy chief of staff Harriet Miers for the U.S. Supreme Court.

- On October 27, Miers withdraws from the Supreme Court nomination process after questions are raised about her qualifications for the post.

- On October 31, President Bush nominates Samuel Alito for the Supreme Court.

- On December 20, U.S. District judge John E. Jones III rules that teaching intelligent design in the classroom equates to teaching religion.

2006

- On January 17, in *Gonzales v. Oregon* the U.S. Supreme Court upholds the Oregon Death with Dignity Act (1997).

- On January 20, a state court rules Maryland's gay-marriage ban unconstitutional.

- On January 31, Alito is sworn in as an associate justice of the Supreme Court.

- On March 6, in *Rumsfeld v. Forum for Academic and Institutional Freedom* the U.S. Supreme Court decides that law schools must provide military recruiters with equal access to students on campuses.

- On May 22, the U.S. Supreme Court rules that police officers do not need a warrant to enter a home when individuals are fighting or someone is threatened with attack.

- On June 23, the "Liberty City Seven," members of the radical religious group Seeds of David, are arrested by FBI agents in Miami, Florida, for plotting to destroy the Sears Tower in Chicago.

- On June 29, the U.S. Supreme Court rejects military tribunals for terrorist suspects, finding the tribunals in conflict with federal law and the rules of war established by the Geneva Conventions.

- On October 20, in *Purcell v. Gonzalez* the U.S. Supreme Court unanimously overturns a lower court's injunction against an Arizona law requiring voters to provide proof of citizenship when they register and to present identification when they vote.

- On December 7, the Ohio ban against smoking in indoor public places goes into effect.

- On December 7, seven U.S. attorneys are fired by the Republican Bush administration, allegedly because they had failed to pursue investigations of Democratic officeholders. By mid-2007 many upper-level Justice Department officials, including Attorney General Gonzales, will resign their posts.

2007

- On january 4, White House legal counsel Harriet Miers announces her resignation, effective at the end of the month. She is replaced by Fred Fielding.

- On February 6, Deputy Attorney General Paul McNulty testifies before the Senate Judiciary Committee that the attorneys fired in 2006 were not relieved of their posts for political reasons. He later claims that he had been misled as to the reasons for the dismissals, because almost all of the attorneys had received high marks on job-performance evaluations.

- On February 12, five people are killed by a shooter at the Trolley Square Mall in Salt Lake City, Utah.

- On April 16, student Seung-Hui Cho shoots and kills thirty-two people and wounds dozens of others on the Virginia Tech campus before fatally shooting himself.

- On April 18, the U.S. Supreme Court upholds a partial-birth abortion ban.

- On April 25, Ohio congressman Dennis Kucinich attempts to introduce articles of impeachment against Vice President Dick Cheney.

- On May 29, in *Ledbetter v. Goodyear Tire and Rubber Company* the U.S. Supreme Court rules 5–4 that employees filing pay-discrimination complaints under Title VII of the Civil Rights Act must do so within 180 days of the adverse pay decision, even if they were not privy to information about their colleagues' compensation.

- On June 25, the U.S. Supreme Court rules in *Morse v. Frederick* that school administrators can prohibit students from displaying pro-drug-use messages.

- On August 27, Gonzales announces his resignation as U.S attorney general, effective September 17.

- On November 9, Michael B. Mukasey is installed as U.S. attorney general.

- On December 5, gunman Robert A. Hawkins kills eight at the Westroads Mall in Omaha, Nebraska, before committing suicide.

- On December 10, the U.S. Supreme Court decides in two cases that federal district court judges have latitude in determining sentences, instead of being forced to accept legislative standards.

2008

- On January 15, the Food and Drug Administration rules that food processed from cloned livestock is safe to eat.

- On April 16, the U.S. Supreme Court rules that states can continue to use lethal injection as their method of execution.

- On May 15, the California Supreme Court rules that the state's gay-marriage ban is unconstitutional.

- On June 25, in *Kennedy v. Louisiana* the U.S. Supreme Court rules that a sentence of death in cases of child rape is not proportional to a crime that leaves the victim alive. Part of their reasoning is that knowledge of a possible death sentence might push a rapist to kill his victim rather than leave a witness.

- On June 27, the U.S. Supreme Court rejects a Washington, D.C., ban on handgun possession, although it allows the district to ban certain individuals (criminals and the mentally ill) and weaponry (machine guns).

- On October 3, the Emergency Economic Stabilization Act is signed into law, appropriating funds for the Treasury Department to bail out failing banks.

- On November 4, Barack Obama is elected the forty-fourth president of the United States.

- On November 19, Judge Richard J. Leon of the federal district court in Washington, D.C., orders the release of five Algerian terrorist suspects who have been held at Guantánamo Bay for seven years because the government's secret evidence in the case was weak.

2009

- On January 20, Barack Obama is inaugurated as president; Chief Justice Roberts mistakenly rearranges the wording of the oath of office, and the oath is readministered two days later.

- On January 22, President Obama issues an executive order to close the detention camp at Guantánamo Bay within one year.

- On January 29, Illinois governor Rod Blagojevich, impeached by the state House of Representatives on corruption charges on 9 January, is unanimously convicted by the Senate and removed from office.

- On February 3, Eric Himpton Holder Jr. is sworn in as U.S. attorney general.

- On February 25, the U.S. Supreme Court rules unanimously in *Pleasant Grove City v. Summum* that a Utah city did not restrict the free speech of a religious sect when it did not allow the group to place a monument in a public park.

- On March 9, President Obama signs an executive order overturning the Bush-era ban on federal funding of research on embryonic stem-cell lines that were not in existence as of August 9, 2001.

- On April 3, the Iowa Supreme Court rules that a ban on gay marriage is unconstitutional.

- On May 19, President Obama implements stricter federal requirements for vehicle emissions and gas mileage.

- On June 3, New Hampshire legalizes gay marriage.

- On June 25, in *Safford Unified School Dist. #1 v. Redding* the U.S. Supreme Court rules 8–1 that a strip search of a public middle-school student suspected of distributing a prescription drug on campus violated her Fourth Amendment right to freedom from an unreasonable search.

- On June 29, in *Ricci v. DeStefano* the U.S. Supreme Court rules that New Haven, Connecticut, erred in throwing out the results of a firefighter promotion test because African American and Latino candidates had not performed as well as white candidates, arguing that race-conscious policies could only be used in cases of disparate-impact discrimination.

- On July 3, Alaska governor and former vice-presidential nominee Sarah Palin announces her resignation, citing "frivolous" ethics investigations.

- On August 8, Sonia Sotomayor is sworn in as associate justice, becoming the third woman to serve on the U.S. Supreme Court.

- On September 2, pharmaceutical giant Pfizer announces that it has finalized a $2.3 billion settlement over marketing its arthritis drug Bextra for unapproved uses and that its Pharmacia & Upjohn unit would plead guilty to one criminal count of violating the Food, Drug, and Cosmetic Act.

- On September 27, film director Roman Polanski is arrested in Switzerland on an outstanding U.S. warrant on statutory rape charges.

- On October 28, the Matthew Shepard and James Byrd Jr. Hate Crimes Prevention Act is signed into law. The provision extends federal hate-crimes law to include sexual orientation, gender identity, and disability.

- On November 6, the South Carolina Supreme Court orders a report by the State Ethics Commission into publicly funded travel by Governor Mark Sanford during an alleged affair with an Argentine woman be made public.

- On November 10, convicted gunman John Allen Muhammad is executed for his role in the 2002 "Beltway Sniper" attacks.

- On December 1, Virginia's public-smoking ban is implemented.

2000 Presidential Election

"The Winner in *Bush v. Gore*?"

Magazine article

By: Charles Krauthammer

Date: December 18, 2000

Source: Krauthammer, Charles. "The Winner in *Bush v. Gore*?" *Time*, December 18, 2000. www.time.com/time/magazine/article/0,9171,998788,00.html (accessed on March 7, 2013).

About the Magazine: First published in 1918, *Time* magazine was the first weekly newsmagazine to appear in the United States. Co-founders Briton Hadden and Henry Luce had previously worked together on the *Yale Daily News* and continued their collaboration until Hadden's death in 1929. Luce remained a key figure at the magazine until his death in 1967. His stock in the successful magazine venture brought him a yearly dividend in excess of $2.4 million at the time of his death. *Time* saw a number of editorial changes throughout its decades, and circulation has ebbed and flowed, with a relatively steady paid circulation of around 4.1 million until 2004, when it dropped to 4.0 million and then down to 3.4 million from 2007 to 2009. *Time* has struggled to stay relevant in an era where print news magazines have been largely replaced by online news sites, and it continues to focus on in-depth coverage of special events and history-making figures.

"Stu's Views"

Political cartoon

By: Maddy Dodson and Stu Rees

Date: Undated

Source: Dodson, Maddy, and Stu Rees. "Stu's Views." *Stu's.com*. www.stus.com/stus-category.php?cat=CAS&sub=CON (accessed on March 7, 2013).

About the Artists: Maddy Dodson practiced criminal law and then employee law before becoming a full-time cartoonist. Husband Stu Rees divides his time between a solo legal practice and cartooning. Rees won the Silver T-Square Award from the National Cartoonists Society in 2007. Both husband and wife graduated from Harvard Law School, and their cartoons have appeared the world over since 2002.

■ PRIMARY SOURCE

2000 Presidential Election Editorial Cartoon

SYNOPSIS: This cartoon illustrates the public's view that the role of the U.S. Supreme Court had lost its definition during the case involving presidential contenders Al Gore and George W. Bush. STU'S VIEWS.

INTRODUCTION

The 2000 U.S. presidential election was the closest and most hotly contested in the nation's history. Following an uncommonly adversarial and divisive campaign, the Democratic Party's candidate, Vice President Al Gore, faced the Republican Party's nominee, Texas governor George W. Bush, at the polls. As results of the November 7 vote were tabulated, it became apparent that the ultimate victor would win only by a small margin. Bush won most of the Southern and Midwestern states, while Gore carried most of New England, the West Coast, and the Great Lakes states. In several states, the race was so close that exit poll statistics were rendered useless, leading several news organizations to erroneously report Gore as the winner or to repeatedly change their election-result predictions.

By the next day, it was evident that whichever candidate had claimed Florida's 25 electoral votes would attain the 270-vote victory requirement and become the forty-third president of the United States. On the morning of November 8, the final Florida tally had been completed, with Bush winning the popular vote by a margin of about two thousand votes. However, Bush's victory was not yet secure—his margin of victory was slight enough to require a mandatory recount under Florida state law. By the time the recount was complete, Bush's margin of victory over Gore had fallen to around three hundred votes, qualifying the vice president to challenge state results and request a manual recount in the counties of his choosing.

Gore decided on four counties to conduct recounts, all of them historically liberal. Two of these counties failed to meet the November 26 recount deadline and submitted their initial results as final and official, and the other two reconfirmed Bush as their victor. Gore challenged these announcements, resulting in a Florida Supreme Court order that all ballots rejected by mechanical tabulation processes (amounting to some seventy thousand votes) be manually examined and counted. This procedure was immediately halted by the U.S. Supreme Court, which staged emergency proceedings to determine the proper course of action in identifying the true winner of the election.

On December 12, following hearings and examination of the unprecedented legal circumstances of the contested election results, the Supreme Court issued its ruling on the case of *Bush v. Gore*, in which it found the proposed Florida recount to be unconstitutional. Because no method of recounting all of the state's ballots could be designed and conducted before the date required by the governing U.S. law (the same day the Court made its decision), Bush's victory was upheld and he was awarded the presidency.

SIGNIFICANCE

George W. Bush's election prompted widespread objection from the American public. Some pundits and political commentators claimed that Bush had essentially been elected by the Supreme Court, noting that the ruling on *Bush v. Gore* was split 7–2 along ideological lines, indicating the possibility that conservative justices had acted on a personal political basis rather than an objective interpretation of the law. Others pointed out that the Court's ruling was issued as a "one-off," specifically stating that it was not to be used as legal precedent in deciding the results of future contested elections. This curious caveat was seen by some as an acknowledgment of the decision's illegitimacy, since U.S. law is supposed to be a consistent application of constitutional principles, which should typically remain congruent and universal instead of applying only to a single incident. It was also

frequently remarked that Bush had actually lost the popular vote to Gore by more than five hundred thousand votes, but still managed to win in the electoral college, a fact frequently lamented by those critical of the U.S. election system. (Only three other U.S. presidents—John Quincy Adams in 1824, Rutherford B. Hayes in 1876, and Benjamin Harrison in 1888—had been victorious in the same fashion.)

Criticism of the U.S. Supreme Court's role—some say interference—in the landmark election was vehement and was not relegated to the Court itself, but to media coverage of the proceedings. The line between law and politics had been blurred, and many questioned which held more sway in the Court's ultimate decision as a conservative chief justice and the other four conservative justices voted 5–4 to declare the recount unconstitutional, thereby ushering in a Republican president.

Although journalist Charles Krauthammer pondered the motivation for Chief Justice William Rehnquist to deny media coverage of the Court hearings and determined his reasoning to be a desire to maintain a modicum of mystery in the courtroom, his conclusion may be inaccurate. Having died in 2005, Rehnquist could not speak for himself on the topic, but one of his longtime personal friends, Herman Obermayer, ventured an explanation in his 2010 *ABA Journal* article, "The William Rehnquist You Didn't Know."

At dinner that night, Bill and I discussed what would have been the pros and cons of filming the oral arguments in his court five days earlier. Almost every major media organization in the world was signatory to a petition to allow TV coverage. While the justices turned down the request for live TV coverage, they did allow an audio feed and a typed transcript of *Bush v. Gore* to be released a few minutes after the arguments ended.

That evening Bill told me that he had begun wondering whether the intensity of the passions aroused by the court's involvement in the presidential election justified approaching live TV coverage with even more skepticism. He had a new concern, he said. It was one I had never thought about. I do not know whether the notion had been buried in his psyche for a long time, or if he had learned about it from one of his colleagues when they discussed the hateful and vicious way they were being described in the press.

His new reason for opposing videotaping the Supreme Court was that after several years of taping oral arguments, hundreds of tapes would be in the public domain. They could easily be aggregated and manipulated to demean and denigrate particular justices or to diminish the stature and legitimacy of the Supreme Court itself. A TV producer could easily cobble together a program in which a group of justices were shown repeatedly picking their noses, cleaning their teeth, dozing off, scratching their behinds, popping pills, doodling erotic obscenities, winking at old friends or asking foolish questions during an oral argument. In the course of a decade or two on the Supreme Court bench, it was inevitable that a sizable number of unflattering, silly and demeaning poses would have been recorded for each justice. . . .

Bill saw this post-*Bush v. Gore* scenario as a threat to the Supreme Court's stature and status.

PRIMARY SOURCE

"THE WINNER IN *BUSH V. GORE*?"

SYNOPSIS: Charles Krauthammer muses that Chief Justice William Rehnquist's refusal to let media cover the *Bush v. Gore* hearing is motivated by a desire to maintain an air of mystery.

The postelection stage groaned with a menagerie of personages vying for attention: politicians, judges, lawyers, talking heads. Yet who proved himself—once again—the craftiest, the savviest pol of them all? Chief Justice William H. Rehnquist.

It began with the unanimous first opinion he coaxed out of a court deeply and obviously divided on the matter of *Bush v. Gore*. Its beauty was its subtlety. Indeed, it was so subtle that it took three days for the TV mavens to figure it out. At first, they thought the court had merely ducked. In fact, it had issued a veiled but devastating rebuke to the Florida Supreme Court for creating a new deadline for certifying Florida's presidential election.

By vacating that decision with a mere query, the Rehnquist court strained to keep from humiliating its Florida subordinate. But the query—Could you kindly provide justification for a decision that appears baseless?—sent a pointed message to the willful Florida justices.

That chastisement had its effect on some of the Florida supremes. At oral argument, you could almost see Chief Justice Charles Wells and a few of his colleagues looking over their shoulder wondering whether Rehnquist & Co. would approve of their behavior.

But a willful majority of four justices decided to take Rehnquist up on his challenge. Despite Wells' warning that by ordering a partial statewide recount—something with "no foundation in the law of Florida"—they were inviting rebuke and reversal by the U.S. Supreme Court, they forged ahead and opened up yet another chapter in the recount saga.

But this one threatened a constitutional crisis: the collision of legislatures and courts of a kind unseen in

U.S. Supreme Court chief justice William Rehnquist. © AP IMAGES/HILLERY SMITH GARRISON.

more than a century. Re-enter the Rehnquist court. Amid the chaos, somebody had to play Daddy. Its earlier admonition having been ignored, the Supreme Court eschewed subtlety this time and bluntly stopped the Florida Supreme Court in its tracks—and stayed its willfulness. By 5-4, mind you, and Rehnquist doesn't like 5-4 in questions of this magnitude. But to avoid a constitutional train wreck, he was ready for the court to assert itself and thus bring a welcome finality to the postelection madness.

It was a high moment—first deft, then bold—that served to reinforce the high court's supremacy. But Rehnquist could only do so because for nearly two decades he has, against the odds, maintained the Supreme Court's prestige and mystique. This week he cashed in, but he had been building the capital for years. At a time when respect for every other institution of government has declined precipitously, the country still looks to the Supreme Court for authority and finality.

Polls routinely show trust in the Supreme Court exceeding that of Congress and the presidency, to say nothing of the press, which ranks down there with lawyers. Asked who should be involved in deciding this election, 60% said the Supreme Court, and only 38% said either Congress or the Florida legislature.

How does Rehnquist do it? There are many answers. One, often overlooked, is paramount. Rehnquist has been relentless in resisting the vanity and the flattery of television in the courtroom.

It has not been easy. The agitation for television is constant. When *Bush v. Gore* reached the high court and the networks demanded entry with cameras, the chorus grew particularly loud. Rehnquist said no. His denial seems anachronistic, but it represents a deep under-standing of the modern sensibility. Like Machiavelli, he knows how important an air of mystery is for maintaining authority. And TV's very essence is to demystify. Everything it touches becomes familiar and ordinary, ripe for irony and camp.

Had the Supreme Court allowed cameras in for the Florida case, is there any doubt that all nine Justices would have led *Saturday Night Live* the very next night? Rehnquist got a taste of television's capacity for leveling when he and the gold stripes on his robe became the subject of much media mirth during the Clinton impeachment trial.

The camera is unfailing in reducing whatever it observes. Nearly everyone in this constantly televised drama has been diminished: the Florida Supreme Court, the state legislature, the lawyers, the candidates. Why, after 24/7 TV coverage of chad counting by microscope and horoscope, even the belief in the very process of counting votes has been irreparably damaged.

Some things are best left unseen. In the television age, the way to avoid trivialization is to remain veiled. Rehnquist has brilliantly managed the politics of invisibil-ity. The very opaqueness of its workings has helped the court maintain its unmatched authority and supremacy. People tremble before it. Quite an achievement in an age in which people tremble before very little.

PRIMARY SOURCE

STU'S VIEWS

See primary source cartoon.

FURTHER RESOURCES
Books

Gillman, Howard. *The Votes That Counted: How the Court Decided the 2000 Presidential Election.* Chicago: University of Chicago Press, 2003.

Toobin, Jeffrey. *Too Close to Call: The Thirty-Six Day Battle to Decide the 2000 Election.* New York: Random House, 2002.

Web Sites

Cole, David. "The Liberal Legacy of *Bush v. Gore.*" *Georgetown University Law Center*, July 2006. http://scholarship.law.georgetown.edu/cgi/viewcontent.cgi?article=1417&context=facpub (accessed on March 7, 2013).

Obermayer, Herman. "The William Rehnquist You Didn't Know." *ABA Journal*, March 1, 2010. www.abajournal.com/magazine/article/the_william_rehnquist_you_didnt_know/ (accessed on March 7, 2013).

"Records of the Supreme Court of the United States." *National Archives.* www.archives.gov/research/guide-fed-records/groups/267.html (accessed on March 7, 2013).

The PATRIOT Act and Attorney General Ashcroft's Defense of It

H.R. 3162 (USA PATRIOT Act), Section 215

Law

By: 107th United States Congress

Date: Effective February 1, 2002

Source: 107th United States Congress. *Uniting and Strengthening America by Providing Appropriate Tools Required to Intercept and Obstruct Terrorism Act of 2001.* Signed October 26, 2001. www.gpo.gov/fdsys/pkg/BILLS-107hr3162enr/pdf/BILLS-107hr3162enr.pdf (accessed on February 25, 2013).

About the Act: The PATRIOT (or Patriot) Act was introduced by Rep. Jim Sensenbrenner Jr., a Republi-can from Wisconsin, as House Rule 3162 on October 23, 2001. It was passed in the House the next day and passed in the Senate the day after that. President George W. Bush signed the bill into law on October 26, and it entered force on February 1, 2002. The official, full name of the law is the Uniting and Strengthening America by Providing Appropriate Tools Required to Intercept and Obstruct Terrorism Act of 2001, abbreviated under the acronym PATRIOT (hence the law's common name). Many provisions of the law that were set to expire at the end of 2005, known as sunset provisions, were reauthorized in an updated version of the Patriot Act passed in 2006.

"The Proven Tactics in the Fight Against Crime"

Speech

By: John Ashcroft

Date: September 15, 2003

Source: Ashcroft, John. "The Proven Tactics in the Fight Against Crime." *The United States Department of Justice* September 15, 2003. www.justice.gov/archive/ag/speeches/2003/091503nationalrestaurant.htm (accessed on February 25, 2013).

About the Speaker: A former governor and senator from Missouri, John Ashcroft was the seventy-ninth attorney general and served in the George W. Bush administration from February 2001 to February 2005. His primary goal while in office was to fight the war on terror, and to that end he was a staunch proponent of the USA Patriot Act. A conservative by political standards, his emphatic focus on counteracting terrorism led him to call for measures that, at times, concerned even his traditionally like-minded peers. After having been involved in several controversies, Ashcroft resigned from office in November 2004, after Bush was reelected for a second term. His resignation took effect on February 3, 2005, at which time he set to work developing a business plan for his strategic consulting firm, The Ashcroft Group.

INTRODUCTION

During the period directly following the September 11, 2001, terrorist attacks, there was a pervasive sentiment, present among U.S. legislators and civilians alike, that the nation's stability and people were no longer secure from violence. The atmosphere of uncertainty, mistrust, and fear that arose from that unprecedented violation of U.S. security led Congress to pursue immediate action. During the month following 9/11, several anti-terrorism and heightened security bills were proposed, which were consolidated into a single law under the USA Patriot Act. The Patriot Act incorporated measures proposed in its precursors, comprising changes and additions to an extensive array of policies regarding many facets of activity within the United States.

Both houses of Congress voted to approve the law eagerly, pushing it through the House of Representatives and the Senate in two days. On the third day,

October 26, President George W. Bush signed the Patriot Act into law, to take effect on February 1, 2002. The act consists of ten titles, each including provisions related to a specific facet of the United States's new efforts to "deter and punish American terrorists in the United States and around the world..."

Among other things, the act drastically reduced restrictions on law enforcement's ability to search private records, including telephone, medical, financial, and e-mail/Internet. It loosened restrictions on detaining and deporting immigrants suspected of terrorism or related acts, thereby making it possible for nearly anyone to be detained with little cause or reason. Under the Patriot Act, the very definition of terrorism was significantly broadened, which in turn expanded authorities' power to apply the laws of the Act to a greater extent.

The Patriot Act represented one of the single largest changes to the Constitution in U.S. history, amending hundreds of laws. It was reauthorized three times after its initial implementation, and sections were expanded, changed, removed, and added entirely to reflect the changing priorities and perceptions of American efforts against terrorism. Since it entered into effect in 2002, the act consistently remained one of the most controversial and frequently discussed aspects of U.S. politics, continuing to influence the practices of the federal government in surveillance and investigation.

SIGNIFICANCE

Immediately after the Patriot Act was signed, it became the center of a fierce controversy that would continue throughout the decade. At the center of the debate surrounding the act lay a fundamental conflict between the necessity of adequately equipping and empowering the U.S. government to protect its citizens from internal and external threat, and the importance of maintaining the integrity of the Constitution and the privacies and protections it provides. Supporters of the law maintain its necessity in defending the nation against terrorism and subterfuge, while detractors claim that the Patriot Act unduly and unnecessarily violated the civil liberties of average citizens.

Probably the most inflammatory aspect of the Patriot Act was the federal investigatory behavior authorized by the law. Such behaviors included roving wiretaps, a special type of wiretap that did not require court approval to follow a target from one device to another; so-called "sneak and peek" warrants, which permitted law enforcement agents to access private premises without the knowledge or consent of their

U.S. attorney general John Ashcroft holds a report on the Patriot Act during an appearance in front of the U.S. House Judiciary Committee on July 13, 2004. © AP IMAGES/EVAN VUCCI.

owner; the acquisition of personal records for tracking and analyzing private activity; and, most notably, the practice of invoking national security letters (NSLs) to circumvent the judicial approval requirements associated with criminal investigations. Under the Patriot Act, NSLs could be issued by any Federal Bureau of Investigation (FBI) agent with a rank of field supervisor or above, without a search warrant, probable cause, or even reasonable suspicion of probable cause, to authorize the acquisition of information pertinent to an investigation, such as telephone records, Internet usage records, email histories, and financial records. NSLs also included an indefinite gag order that prevented the people and organizations from which such information was gathered from disclosing that the NSL was ever conducted.

Concerned citizens and politicians contended that these activities represented a violation of the First and Fourth Amendments, and that they constituted unnecessarily intrusive conduct by the federal government. Commenters noted that no arrests leading from NSLs were ever disclosed, making the tens of thousands of NSLs issued during the decade seem completely unjustified. Critics attested that the Patriot Act was an example of post-9/11 opportunism, which exploited the fear and confusion that resulted from the attacks to expand the investigatory power of the U.S. government. It was frequently noted that "national security" and "fighting terrorism" were cited as justification for what would otherwise have been illegal activity by federal agents and also invoked to avoid disclosing the details of criminal investigations.

Politicians throughout the decade were faced with the difficulty of defending the Patriot Act and maintaining the safety of the nation while being bombarded with complaints and lawsuits about the act's dubious legality. Among the act's staunchest defenders was Attorney General John Ashcroft. Although prior to the events of September 11, 2001,

Ashcroft chose not to make counterterrorism a priority, he focused on little else after. Critics contend he was merely interested in strengthening the power of the executive branch while diminishing the powers of Congress and the judiciary branch. Ashcroft's appointment to his post was confirmed with just 58 votes, the fewest in the history of the office. His critics accused him of using his power—and then his much-expanded power, thanks to the Patriot Act—to advance his own political and ideological goals.

Despite much public dissatisfaction with the law, the effective strengthening of the U.S. security infrastructure permitted the law to stay in place throughout the decade.

PRIMARY SOURCE

USA PATRIOT ACT, SECTION 215

SYNOPSIS: Section 215 of the Patriot Act describes the new authority of the federal government to access a wide range of personal material without notification, provided said information is collected as part of an investigation about terrorism or foreign spy operations. It includes a "gag order" expressly prohibiting the disclosure of materials sought or obtained under the authorization of Section 215.

H.R. 3162—UNITING AND STRENGTHENING AMERICA BY PROVIDING APPROPRIATE TOOLS REQUIRED TO INTERCEPT AND OBSTRUCT TERRORISM (USA PATRIOT ACT) ACT OF 2001, SECTION 215

SEC. 215. ACCESS TO RECORDS AND OTHER ITEMS UNDER THE FOREIGN INTELLIGENCE SURVEILLANCE ACT.

Title V of the Foreign Intelligence Surveillance Act of 1978 (50 U.S.C. 1861 et seq.) is amended by striking sections 501 through 503 and inserting the following:

SEC. 501. ACCESS TO CERTAIN BUSINESS RECORDS FOR FOREIGN INTELLIGENCE AND INTERNATIONAL TERRORISM INVESTIGATIONS.

(a) (1) The Director of the Federal Bureau of Investigation or a designee of the Director (whose rank shall be no lower than Assistant Special Agent in Charge) may make an application for an order requiring the production of any tangible things (including books, records, papers, documents, and other items) for an investigation to protect against international terrorism or clandestine intelligence activities, provided that such investigation of a United States person is not conducted solely upon the basis of activities protected by the first amendment to the Constitution.

(2) An investigation conducted under this section shall—

(A) be conducted under guidelines approved by the Attorney General under Executive Order 12333 (or a successor order); and

(B) not be conducted of a United States person solely upon the basis of activities protected by the first amendment to the Constitution of the United States.

(b) Each application under this section—

(1) shall be made to—

(A) a judge of the court established by section 103(a); or

(B) a United States Magistrate Judge under chapter 43 of title 28, United States Code, who is publicly designated by the Chief Justice of the United States to have the power to hear applications and grant orders for the production of tangible things under this section on behalf of a judge of that court; and

(2) shall specify that the records concerned are sought for an authorized investigation conducted in accordance with subsection (a)(2) to obtain foreign intelligence information not concerning a United States person or to protect against international terrorism or clandestine intelligence activities.

(c) (1) Upon an application made pursuant to this section, the judge shall enter an ex parte order as requested, or as modified, approving the release of records if the judge finds that the application meets the requirements of this section.

(2) An order under this subsection shall not disclose that it is issued for purposes of an investigation described in subsection (a).

(d) No person shall disclose to any other person (other than those persons necessary to produce the tangible things under this section) that the Federal Bureau of Investigation has sought or obtained tangible things under this section.

(e) A person who, in good faith, produces tangible things under an order pursuant to this section shall not be liable to any other person for such production. Such production shall not be deemed to constitute a waiver of any privilege in any other proceeding or context.

SEC. 502. CONGRESSIONAL OVERSIGHT.

(a) On a semiannual basis, the Attorney General shall fully inform the Permanent Select Committee on Intelligence of the House of Representatives and the Select Committee on Intelligence of the Senate concerning all requests for the production of tangible things under section 402.

(b) On a semiannual basis, the Attorney General shall provide to the Committees on the Judiciary of the House of Representatives and the Senate a report setting forth with respect to the preceding 6-month period—

(1) the total number of applications made for orders approving requests for the production of tangible things under section 402; and

(2) the total number of such orders either granted, modified, or denied.

PRIMARY SOURCE

"THE PROVEN TACTICS IN THE FIGHT AGAINST CRIME"

SYNOPSIS: Attorney General John Ashcroft defends the USA PATRIOT Act.

Good afternoon. Thank you for that introduction, Skip.

It is a pleasure to be here at the National Restaurant Association. I thank all of you for coming to Washington.

The genius of our system of government is that in America, we believe that it is the people who grant the government its powers. We believe that it is the people's values that should be imposed on Washington—not Washington's values on the people.

Your willingness to visit this city is a valuable reminder of the patriotism and entrepreneurship that make this nation great. These are the values that should sustain our hearts and inform our actions in these perilous times.

Of course, Washington is often known as a town filled with debates where people lose sight of the issues most important to the citizens. Your visits and your voices remind this city of the values of the people—the values that are truly important.

Unfortunately, at this moment, Washington is involved in a debate where hysteria threatens to obscure the most important issues.

If you were to listen to some in Washington, you might believe the hysteria behind this claim: "Your local library has been surrounded by the FBI." Agents are working round-the-clock. Like the X-Files, they are dressed in raincoats, dark suits, and sporting sunglasses. They stop patrons and librarians and interrogate everyone like Joe Friday. In a dull monotone they ask every person exiting the library, "Why were you at the library? What were you reading? Did you see anything suspicious?"

According to these breathless reports and baseless hysteria, some have convinced the American Library Association that under the bipartisan Patriot Act, the FBI is not fighting terrorism. Instead, agents are checking how far you have gotten on the latest Tom Clancy novel.

Now you may have thought with all this hysteria and hyperbole, something had to be wrong. Do we at the Justice Department really care what you are reading? No.

The law enforcement community has no interest in your reading habits. Tracking reading habits would betray our high regard for the First Amendment. And even if someone in the government wanted to do so, it would represent an impossible workload and a waste of law enforcement resources.

The fact is that our laws are very particular and very demanding. There are strict legal requirements. A federal judge must first determine that there is an existing investigation of an international terrorist or spy, or a foreign intelligence investigation into a non-U.S. person, and that the business records being sought are relevant to that investigation. Without meeting these legal requirements, obtaining business records, including library records, is not even an option.

With only 11,000 FBI agents in the entire country, it is simply ridiculous to think we could or would track what citizens are reading. I am not in a position to know, but according to the American Library Association there are more than 117,400 libraries in the United States. The American Library Association tells me that Americans visit our nation's libraries more than one billion times a year—1,146,284,000, to be exact. While there, they check out nearly two billion books a year—1,713,967,000, to be precise.

The hysteria is ridiculous. Our job is not.

It is the solemn belief of the United States Department of Justice that the first and primary responsibility of government is: to preserve the lives and protect the liberty of the people.

No one believes in our First Amendment civil liberties more than this administration. It is what we are fighting for in this war against tyranny. On my watch, we seek a war for justice that reflects the noblest ideals and highest standards set by the United States Constitution. I would not support or invite any change that might restructure or endanger our individual liberties and personal freedoms.

It would be a tragedy if the hysteria surrounding certain aspects of our war against terror were to obscure the important evidence that the Department of Justice has protected the lives and liberties of the citizenry, and not just in the very real world of anti-terrorism.

The American people deserve to know that violent crime has plunged to its lowest point in 30 years.

Thanks to this President's leadership and the work of the justice community, these numbers almost speak for themselves. But for the crime rate to hit a 30-year low, we

U.S. attorney general John Ashcroft addresses the National Restaurant Association on September 15, 2003. © AP IMAGES/
SUSAN WALSH.

had to focus on and drive down almost every category of crime.

The results of our new tactics are impressive and undeniable. Over the past two years according to the Bureau of Justice Statistics:

- Robberies are down 27 percent.
- Assaults are down 20 percent.
- Rapes and sexual assault are down 25 percent. But that is not enough. That is why President Bush supports $1 billion for the DNA technology initiative to ensure that every rapist and sexual predator is caught and sent to prison.

To put all these numbers in perspective, we must remember how lives are changed when law enforcement focuses on catching and prosecuting criminals. In fact, this 30-year low in violent crime means 981,320 fewer violent crimes in 2002 than in 2000. That is nearly one million fewer instances when citizens did not feel scared, victimized, lost and alien in their own communities.

- This means 219,290 fewer robberies;
- 748,820 fewer assaults; and
- 13,320 fewer instances of the devastating crimes of rape and sexual assault.

With such drops in violent crime, lives are not the only thing changed. The landscape of America is changed. When crime is fought at every juncture, citizens can walk their neighborhoods with confidence. They can shop freely, attend plays, and visit restaurants. Families can grow closer and communities can become more tightly knit.

People are not just safer on the street because violent crime is at an historic low; they are safer in their homes, too:

Attempted forcible entry is down 24 percent, since 2000; and overall crimes against property are down 13 percent, since 2000.

The first and primary responsibility of government is to preserve the lives and protect the liberties of the people. In the view of this department, that does not mean some of the people. It does not mean most of the people. It means all of the people.

And we are succeeding. This 30-year low in crime and the results of the last two years indicate that the violent crime victimization rate has fallen for all racial and ethnic groups across all income levels in every part of the country. In our view, equality under the law means equal protection, safety, and justice for every citizen—regardless of race, ethnicity, or income.

These new numbers show that our crime-fighting strategies are working on every level.

Another major reason for the historic 30-year lows in violent crime stem from the cooperation of the American people. We have seen a renewed sense of civic responsibility strengthen the cause of justice:

- Public trust in law enforcement has grown with more people reporting crimes and cooperating with law enforcement than ever before.
- Working with the National Sheriffs Association, we have almost doubled the number of Neighborhood Watch programs across the country, from 7,500 to more than 13,000. These are grassroots groups that are looking out for their neighbors and their nation.

We have applied these proven tactics from the past 10 years—tough laws, tough penalties, and cooperation at every level—to the fight against gun crime.

From Day One, this administration established a new and assertive strategy of gun-crime prevention. We sought to direct new thinking and new tactics toward one end: protecting citizens by prosecuting violent offenders and locking them up.

The President believes that if you use a gun in a crime, you should do hard time. This strategy works:

- Federal gun prosecutions increased by 36 percent.
- In fact, last year alone, federal gun crime charges rose over 20 percent—the largest annual increase ever.
- Because of such efforts, the number of violent crimes in which the offender was armed with a firearm fell over 31 percent from 2000 to 2002. And robberies committed with a firearm plummeted over 45 percent during this time period.
- In fact, in 2002, just seven percent of violent crimes were committed with a firearm. This is the lowest number ever recorded.

These numbers are no accident. They are not some freak luck of the draw. They are not a twist of fate. Thanks in no small part to the federal judiciary, we have been able to give maximum sentences to criminals—resulting in the maximum public good for the citizen.

New York Governor George Pataki once joked he had discovered the "root cause" of crime. When asked, he answered simply, "Criminals."

The lawless. The predatory. The habitual, repeat offenders. These are the real sources of crime. And we must target and remove the source of violence, intimidation, and criminal behavior.

Simply put, violent crime is at its lowest level in 30 years and continues to fall because our nation has chosen to fight crime at every opportunity. Violent crime is at record lows because we are locking up the violent, the lawless, and the predatory.

- Since the 1960s, we have known a small minority of criminals commit the vast number of crimes. Three decades ago, Marvin Wolfgang of the University of Pennsylvania found that six percent of criminals committed roughly 52 percent of all criminal offenses.
- Since 1995, violent offenders accounted for 63 percent of the growth in state prison populations.

Our simple, well-focused rules work.

Preventing crime by punishing criminals gets results. By enhancing cooperation, passing tougher laws, and enacting tough penalties, we have driven down crime. These same tactics have been deployed in the war on terror and they are the reason we prevented any terrorist attack over the past two years.

In every corner of the nation and at every level of government, the justice community has worked together, shared information, and struck at terrorist cells who would do us harm. Law enforcement has embraced the tools and spirit of the Patriot Act by communicating information, coordinating their efforts, and cooperating toward our integrated strategy of preventing terrorism. This has meant smarter, better-focused law enforcement—law enforcement that targets terrorists and secures our borders, letting hard-working immigrants and free trade prosper in a nation blessed by freedom.

In fact, the results of our anti-terrorism efforts are just as impressive and just as undeniable as our success in driving crime to a 30-year low.

All told, two-thirds of Al Qaeda's senior leadership have been captured or killed. And more than 3,000 suspected terrorists have been arrested in countries around the world. Many more have met a different fate.

Specifically:

- We have dismantled terrorist operations in New York, Michigan, Washington State, Oregon, and North Carolina;
- We have brought criminal charges against 262 individuals;
- 143 individuals have been convicted or pled guilty, including shoe-bomber Richard Reid, "American Taliban" John Walker Lindh, six members of the Buffalo cell, and two members of the Detroit cell;
- We have deported more than 515 individuals with links to the September 11th investigation; and
- We have stopped more than $200 million from funding terrorist groups.

This nation has never asked more of the men and women of law enforcement. And law enforcement has never achieved more than these past few years.

At every level of law enforcement, in every area of fighting crime, we have committed ourselves to a new strategy—a strategy of prevention. It is rooted in our Constitutional liberties, built on communication and cooperation and driven by the courage and integrity of the men and women of law enforcement. From the FBI in Washington to the local cop with his feet on the street, we owe our thanks for their hard work and respect for freedom and the law.

By attacking crime and terrorist operations at every point of vulnerability, we have communicated to the lawful and the lawless that in America we will fight to preserve lives and protect liberty.

For almost two decades, some in Washington have preached defeatism and surrender in the battle against the drug smugglers, the criminal, and the lawless. At one time, elite opinion held that law enforcement and citizens could not do anything. They believed we were doomed to live with rising crime. They argued that criminals were driven by circumstance and root causes beyond our control. They said that locking up the violent would not lead to lower crime or saved lives.

The ideological critics were proven wrong. You do not have to move to live in a safer neighborhood. We have proven that a free people and free society have the will and the resolve to overcome great challenges and create equal protection under the law. We have proven that the right ideas—tough laws, tough sentences, and constant cooperation—are stronger than the criminal or the terrorist cell.

Yet, despite these successes, some people in Washington and so-called experts urge us to return to a time when we did not treat every crime seriously and when parks and public spaces were hunting grounds for predators, instead of monuments to safety and peace.

That is why those who value the rule of law and liberty must respond with reason, with facts, and with the evidence that our proven tactics work.

We point to a simple equation: hardened criminals + prison + tough sentences = fewer criminals = less crime.

We have seen what works. At this moment in history, our challenge is to speak clearly and act boldly, so we can build an America where every life is held precious, every liberty is preserved, and every citizen is protected by justice.

Thank you.

FURTHER RESOURCES

Books

Finn, Christopher. *From the Palmer Raids to the Patriot Act: A History of the Fight for Free Speech in America.* Boston: Beacon Press, 2008.

Malek, Alia. *Patriot Acts: Narratives of Post-9/11 Injustice.* San Francisco: McSweeney's, 2011.

Web Sites

"Ashcroft, John David." *Biographical Directory of the United States Congress.* http://bioguide.congress.gov/scripts/biodisplay.pl?index=A000356 (accessed on February 25, 2013).

Talanian, Nancy. "John Ashcrof's Legacy." *Common Dreams,* February 16, 2005. www.commondreams.org/views05/0216-31.htm (accessed on February 25, 2013).

"USA PATRIOT Act." *Financial Crimes Enforcement Network.* www.fincen.gov/statutes_regs/patriot/ (accessed on February 26, 2013).

Title I—Department of Homeland Security

Law

By: 107th United States Congress

Date: November 25, 2002

Source: 107th United States Congress. *Public Law 107-296, An Act to Establish the Department of Homeland Security, and for Other Purposes.* Signed November 25, 2002. www.dhs.gov/xlibrary/assets/hr_5005_enr.pdf (accessed on March 7, 2013).

About the Act: The Homeland Security Act of 2002 was introduced while America was still reeling in the aftermath of the terrorist attacks of September 11, 2001. The act created the Department of Homeland Security, which assumed many services and organizations that had been conducted in other departments of the federal government. It was the largest reorganization of the government since the Department of Defense was established in 1949.

INTRODUCTION

On September 11, 2001, less than one year into George W. Bush's first term as president of the United States, nineteen terrorists conducted an organized, concerted suicide attack against the nation. On the morning of 9/11, as the day is colloquially known, the terrorists, who were associated with the Islamist group al-Qaeda, hijacked four passenger jets traveling to and from various destinations in the United States. The planes were deliberately crashed by the hijackers into the "Twin Towers" of New York City's World Trade Center, the Pentagon in Arlington, Virginia, and a field in rural Pennsylvania, killing a total of 2,996 people (including the airplane passengers and the terrorists) and injuring 6,000 more.

The nation was devastated by the tragic attacks. President Bush, often the target of public ridicule for his frequent oratorical blunders, appeared on television the night of the attacks, delivering an unexpectedly poignant and heartfelt speech to soothe the frenzy of fear, anger, and sorrow that the attacks had catalyzed among the American public. Even Bush's harshest critics noted the deft elocution and reassuring effect of his emergency speech, which displayed the new leader's confidence and calm in the face of unanticipated adversity.

The Bush administration's response to the events of 9/11 was swift and confident. Following an immediate and massive emergency response effort and a few speeches related mostly to the nation's sadness and the tragedy itself, Bush's security and military officials definitively concluded that the al-Qaeda Islamist terrorist network was responsible for training, tasking, transporting, and supplying the hijackers, and constructed reaction plan. This plan was presented to the U.S. public and government officials on September 20, in a televised address by President Bush to an emergency joint session of Congress.

In that speech, the president announced the establishment of, among other things, the Office of Homeland Security, a precursor to the Department of Homeland Security (DHS), which would incorporate the duties of the previously disparate intelligence, emergency response, and domestic security agencies, with the stated mission of protecting the territory and people of the United States from external and internal threats. Bush alluded to the increasingly invasive federal conduct that was to accompany the new "War against Terror," described the necessary sacrifices inherent to the investigation and prevention of terrorism, and requested that U.S. citizens cooperate with the program.

A Homeland Security Strategy published in July 2002 outlined the department's primary objectives: Guard the country's borders, prevent domestic terrorist attacks, establish a national defense strategy, and reduce damage resulting from natural disasters and terrorist acts.

In accordance with the act, the Department of Homeland Security employed 180,000 workers from 22 existing federal agencies, each responsible for performing security-related duties. The department consisted initially of four sub-agencies, which included border and transportation security, emergency preparedness, technology, and intelligence. Within a short time, a fifth agency—management—was added to handle personnel and human resources issues as well as budget-related matters. Although the department was

functioning on March 1, 2003, the plan was to have it entirely consolidated by September 30.

SIGNIFICANCE

In October 2001, Pennsylvania governor Tom Ridge—the president's domestic security advisor—was appointed the first Secretary of the Office of Homeland Security. Ironically, when Senators Arlen Specter and Joe Lieberman introduced a bill to establish a Homeland Security Department earlier that month, President Bush and his advisors were not in support of it. Ridge himself publicly stated that he would have most likely recommended that the president veto the bill. By 2002, however, as the response to 9/11 became more politicized, sentiments had changed, and the Homeland Security Act was passed.

Reorganizing the government proved to be more difficult and costly than anyone initially estimated. Ridge and his team of leaders needed to reconsider how the DHS was organized and made changes to the infrastructure. Even so, the department was inundated from the beginning with criticism for alleged waste, ineffectiveness, pervasive bureaucracy, and a lack of transparency. One particular media-saturated event was a congressional audit conducted in 2006. The audit report accused DHS employees of credit card fraud as it uncovered countless questionable purchases made using government-issued cards. Among the findings were $68,500 worth of unused dog booties and a $227 beer brewing kit. According to the audit report and as published in the *New York Times*, more than nine thousand employees spent $420 million in 2005 using their DHS credit cards. Nearly half of the purchases made in a randomly chosen five-month window were not preauthorized by supervisors, and 63 percent lacked supporting documentation as to whether or not the goods or services had ever been received. Congressional leaders publicly expressed disappointment over the lack of leadership and discipline in the DHS, an understatement given that the department had been blamed for wasting nearly $2 billion in response to the hurricane disasters of 2005.

The situation did not improve much as the years passed, as in 2008 the DHS was found to have overseen approximately $15 billion in failed contracts during the five years of its existence. The contracts—which accounted for one-third of the organization's spending—were either cancelled, delayed, or over-budget. The government continued to be plagued with management problems almost relentlessly. Before the end of the decade, the DHS was on its third secretary. By 2008, it employed two hundred thousand people and operated on an annual budget of $50 billion.

Homeland Security secretary Tom Ridge answers questions at a news conference on February 2, 2004. © AP IMAGES/
GERALD L. NINO.

Criticism of DHS was not relegated to outsiders. The Office of Personnel Management conducted a survey of federal employees in July 2006. All thirty-six federal agencies were polled. DHS had low scores across the board and ranked thirty-third on the talent management index, dead last on the job satisfaction index, and thirty-fifth on the leadership and knowledge management index. Clark Kent Ervin, former inspector general of the Homeland Security Department, emphasized the potential problem rife with unhappy employees. "Dysfunction equals danger. The less good people feel about their jobs, the less likely they are to be attentive and alert. It is still the case that the department is just a collection of disparate, dysfunctional agencies. There is yet to be an integrated, cohesive whole," he said in an interview reported on CBS News.

Despite promises from DHS leadership to improve workplace attitude and function, a 2012 survey of large federal agencies found that the DHS, which by then employed 240,000 people, ranked last

for "effective leadership," "training and development," and "support for diversity," among other things.

It has not been all bad at the DHS. The 2011 report from the Government Accountability Office concluded that although they still had far to go in terms of management of programs and other aspects, the consolidated agencies that conduct business as the DHS had improved airport passenger screening, security at the Mexico-America border, and cyber infrastructure. In addition, several programs had been implemented to help raise public awareness, including the national terrorism advisory system and the "If You See Something, Say Something" campaign.

PRIMARY SOURCE

TITLE I—DEPARTMENT OF HOMELAND SECURITY ACT

SYNOPSIS: This is legislation that established the Department of Homeland Security in 2002.

SEC. 101. EXECUTIVE DEPARTMENT; MISSION.

(a) ESTABLISHMENT.—There is established a Department of Homeland Security, as an executive department of the United States within the meaning of title 5, United States Code.

(b) MISSION.—

(1) IN GENERAL.—The primary mission of the Department is to—

(A) prevent terrorist attacks within the United States;

(B) reduce the vulnerability of the United States to terrorism;

(C) minimize the damage, and assist in the recovery, from terrorist attacks that do occur within the United States;

(D) carry out all functions of entities transferred to the Department, including by acting as a focal point regarding natural and manmade crises and emergency planning;

(E) ensure that the functions of the agencies and subdivisions within the Department that are not related directly to securing the homeland are not diminished or neglected except by a specific explicit Act of Congress;

(F) ensure that the overall economic security of the United States is not diminished by efforts, activities, and programs aimed at securing the homeland; and

(G) monitor connections between illegal drug trafficking and terrorism, coordinate efforts to sever such connections, and otherwise contribute to efforts to interdict illegal drug trafficking.

(2) RESPONSIBILITY FOR INVESTIGATING AND PROSECUTING TERRORISM.—Except as specifically provided by law with respect to entities transferred to the Department under this Act, primary responsibility for investigating and prosecuting acts of terrorism shall be vested not in the Department, but rather in Federal, State, and local law enforcement agencies with jurisdiction over the acts in question.

SEC. 102. SECRETARY; FUNCTIONS.

(a) SECRETARY.—

(1) IN GENERAL.—There is a Secretary of Homeland Security, appointed by the President, by and with the advice and consent of the Senate.

(2) HEAD OF DEPARTMENT.—The Secretary is the head of the Department and shall have direction, authority, and control over it.

(3) FUNCTIONS VESTED IN SECRETARY.—All functions of all officers, employees, and organizational units of the Department are vested in the Secretary.

(b) FUNCTIONS.—The Secretary—

(1) except as otherwise provided by this Act, may delegate any of the Secretary's functions to any officer, employee, or organizational unit of the Department;

(2) shall have the authority to make contracts, grants, and cooperative agreements, and to enter into agreements with other executive agencies, as may be necessary and proper to carry out the Secretary's responsibilities under this Act or otherwise provided by law; and

(3) shall take reasonable steps to ensure that information systems and databases of the Department are compatible with each other and with appropriate databases of other Departments.

(c) COORDINATION WITH NON-FEDERAL ENTITIES.—With respect to homeland security, the Secretary shall coordinate through the Office of State and Local Coordination (established under section 801) (including the provision of training and equipment) with State and local government personnel, agencies, and authorities, with the private sector, and with other entities, including by—

(1) coordinating with State and local government personnel, agencies, and authorities, and with the private sector, to ensure adequate planning, equipment, training, and exercise activities;

(2) coordinating and, as appropriate, consolidating, the Federal Government's communications and systems of communications relating to homeland security with State and local government personnel, agencies, and authorities, the private sector, other entities, and the public; and

(3) distributing or, as appropriate, coordinating the distribution of, warnings and information to State and local government personnel, agencies, and authorities and to the public.

(d) MEETINGS OF NATIONAL SECURITY COUNCIL.—The Secretary may, subject to the direction of the President, attend and participate in meetings of the National Security Council.

(e) ISSUANCE OF REGULATIONS.—The issuance of regulations by the Secretary shall be governed by the provisions of chapter 5 of title 5, United States Code, except as specifically provided in this Act, in laws granting regulatory authorities that are transferred by this Act, and in laws enacted after the date of enactment of this Act.

(f) SPECIAL ASSISTANT TO THE SECRETARY.— The Secretary shall appoint a Special Assistant to the Secretary who shall be responsible for—

(1) creating and fostering strategic communications with the private sector to enhance the primary mission of the Department to protect the American homeland;

(2) advising the Secretary on the impact of the Department's policies, regulations, processes, and actions on the private sector;

(3) interfacing with other relevant Federal agencies with homeland security missions to assess the impact of these agencies' actions on the private sector;

(4) creating and managing private sector advisory councils composed of representatives of industries and associations designated by the Secretary to—

(A) advise the Secretary on private sector products, applications, and solutions as they relate to homeland security challenges; and

(B) advise the Secretary on homeland security policies, regulations, processes, and actions that affect the participating industries and associations;

(5) working with Federal laboratories, federally funded research and development centers, other federally funded organizations, academia, and the private sector to develop innovative approaches to address homeland security challenges to produce and deploy the best available technologies for homeland security missions;

(6) promoting existing public-private partnerships and developing new public-private partnerships to provide for collaboration and mutual support to address homeland security challenges; and

(7) assisting in the development and promotion of private sector best practices to secure critical infrastructure.

(g) STANDARDS POLICY.—All standards activities of the Department shall be conducted in accordance with section 12(d) of the National Technology Transfer Advancement Act of 1995 (15 U.S.C. 272 note) and Office of Management and Budget Circular A-119.

SEC. 103. OTHER OFFICERS.

(a) DEPUTY SECRETARY; UNDER SECRETARIES.— There are the following officers, appointed by the President, by and with the advice and consent of the Senate:

(1) A Deputy Secretary of Homeland Security, who shall be the Secretary's first assistant for purposes of subchapter III of chapter 33 of title 5, United States Code.

(2) An Under Secretary for Information Analysis and Infrastructure Protection.

(3) An Under Secretary for Science and Technology.

(4) An Under Secretary for Border and Transportation Security.

(5) An Under Secretary for Emergency Preparedness and Response.

(6) A Director of the Bureau of Citizenship and Immigration Services.

(7) An Under Secretary for Management.

(8) Not more than 12 Assistant Secretaries.

(9) A General Counsel, who shall be the chief legal officer of the Department.

(b) INSPECTOR GENERAL.—There is an Inspector General, who shall be appointed as provided in section 3(a) of the Inspector General Act of 1978.

(c) COMMANDANT OF THE COAST GUARD.—To assist the Secretary in the performance of the Secretary's functions, there is a Commandant of the Coast Guard, who shall be appointed as provided in section 44 of title 14, United States Code, and who shall report directly to the Secretary. In addition to such duties as may be provided in this Act and as assigned to the Commandant by the Secretary, the duties of the Commandant shall include those required by section 2 of title 14, United States Code.6 USC 113.

(d) OTHER OFFICERS.—To assist the Secretary in the performance of the Secretary's functions, there are the following officers, appointed by the President:

(1) A Director of the Secret Service.

(2) A Chief Information Officer.

(3) A Chief Human Capital Officer.

(4) A Chief Financial Officer.

(5) An Officer for Civil Rights and Civil Liberties.

(e) PERFORMANCE OF SPECIFIC FUNCTIONS.— Subject to the provisions of this Act, every officer of the Department shall perform the functions specified by law for the official's office or prescribed by the Secretary.

FURTHER RESOURCES
Books
Faddis, Charles. *Willful Neglect: The Dangerous Illusion of Homeland Security*. Guildford, CT: Lyons Press, 2010.

National Commission on Terrorist Attacks. *The 9/11 Commission Report*. New York: Norton, 2004.

Web Sites
Caldwell, Alicia A. "Report: 10 Years Later, DHS Still Has Work to Do." *Associated Press*, September 7, 2011. www.sltrib.com/sltrib/world/52537125-68/department-security-dhs-homeland.html.csp (accessed on March 7, 2013).

Flock, Elizabeth. "Homeland Security Named Worst Big Place to Work of Federal Agencies." *U.S. News & World Report*, December 13, 2012. www.usnews.com/news/blogs/washington-whispers/2012/12/13/homeland-security-named-worst-big-place-to-work-of-federal-agencies (accessed on March 7, 2013).

Hedgpeth, Dana. "Congress Says DHS Oversaw $15 Billion in Failed Contracts." *Washington Post*, September 7, 2008. www.washingtonpost.com/wp-dyn/content/article/2008/09/16/AR2008091603200_pf.html (accessed on March 7, 2013).

"The Homeland Security Act." *PBS NewsHour*, May 15, 2003. www.pbs.org/newshour/indepth_coverage/terrorism/homeland/securityact.html (accessed on March 7, 2013).

"Homeland Security Department." *Washington Post*. www.washingtonpost.com/politics/homeland-security-department/gIQALxPx4O_topic.html (accessed on March 7, 2013).

"Homeland Security Employees Rank Last in Job Satisfaction." *ABC News*, February 8, 2007. http://abclocal.go.com/wls/story?section=news/national_world&id=5017688 (accessed on March 7, 2013).

Lipton, Eric. "Homeland Security Department Is Accused of Credit Card Misuse." *New York Times*, July 19, 2006. www.nytimes.com/2006/07/19/washington/19cards.html?ei=5088&en=5e9000b0261c5602&ex=1310961600&adxnnl=1&partner=rssnyt&emc=rss&adxnnlx=1164294012-DXvgXm9ImuoTtQCqwkhFjA&_r=0 (accessed on March 7, 2013).

Van Bergen, Jennifer. "Homeland Security Act: The Rise of the American Police State, Part I." *Scoop Independent News*, December 2–4, 2002. Originally published December 2–4 at Truthout.com. www.scoop.co.nz/stories/HL0212/S00017.htm (accessed on March 7, 2013).

Grutter v. Bollinger

Court decision

By: U.S. Supreme Court

Date: June 23, 2003

Source: *Grutter v. Bollinger*. U.S. Supreme Court, June 23, 2003. http://www.law.cornell.edu/supct/html/02-241.ZS.html (accessed on March 21, 2013).

About the Justice Who Authored the Opinion: Sandra Day O'Connor served as an associate justice of the U.S. Supreme Court from 1981 until her retirement in 2006. Before her appointment by President Ronald Reagan, O'Connor was a judge in Arizona, where she typically ruled with a conservative interpretation of the law. She departed from this practice during her service with the Supreme Court, establishing a reputation as an unpredictable voter. She is most famous for being the first woman appointed to the Supreme Court, an ardent supporter of federalism, and her persistent opposition to laws perceived to infringe the Fourth Amendment rights of U.S. citizens.

INTRODUCTION

Grutter v. Bollinger was first brought to court in 2000. The case was filed by Barbara Grutter, a Michigan resident whose application to the University of Michigan Law School had been rejected despite her 3.8 college grade point average (GPA) and excellent score of 161 on the Law School Admission Test (LSAT). Grutter alleged that the university's admissions policy, which gave preferential treatment to ethnic minorities (particularly African American, Native American, and Hispanic applicants), violated the Equal Protection Clause of the Fourteenth Amendment to the U.S. Constitution and the Civil Rights Act of 1964, which collectively prohibit discriminatory provision of services based on race or ethnicity. The school argued that their admissions selection policy was constitutionally protected under *Regents of the University of California v. Bakke*, in which the U.S. Supreme Court found that racial considerations can be made in school admissions if they serve a valid, compelling public interest (although the criteria for determining such legitimate interests remained unclear).

The District Court in which *Grutter v. Bollinger* was first heard found in favor of the plaintiff, claiming all considerations of race in determining the allocation of services, such as merit-based education, to be unconstitutional. On appeal, the Sixth Circuit reversed the lower court's ruling. The U.S. Supreme Court granted the case *certiorari* in 2003, agreeing to settle the matter once and for all. The Court found in favor of the University of Michigan, 5–4, with Justices Sandra Day O'Connor, John Paul Stevens, Ruth Bader Ginsburg, Stephen Breyer, and David Souter concurring, and Chief Justice William Rehnquist and Justices Antonin Scalia, Anthony Kennedy, and Clarence Thomas dissenting. In the majority opinion, Justice O'Connor stated that the school's admission policy served a narrow and legitimate public interest in providing a diverse learning environment for students and thus forcing them to critically examine the stereotypes on which racial discrimination depended. It was also noted that, in providing preferential acceptance for racial minorities, those accepted would not be compelled to feel burdened by acting as representatives of their race or isolated. Justice O'Connor stated that such affirmative action policies, if effective, would eventually become unnecessary, and thus unconstitutional.

The dissenting opinions, published independently by Justice Thomas and Chief Justice Rehnquist, opposed the majority on the grounds that any admissions policy that took race or ethnicity into consideration constituted discrimination under the Constitution. They pointed to the Berkeley School of Law in California, where the state legislature had deliberately prohibited admission policies giving special attention based on race, yet still maintained a diverse student body. It was also noted that affirmative action programs were designed to correct historical inequalities, not to promulgate diverse educational environments.

SIGNIFICANCE

The Supreme Court's opinion in *Grutter v. Bollinger* established the legality of the University of Michigan Law School's policy of giving preference in admissions to racial minorities over whites. The opinion was popular among affirmative action groups and liberal activism organizations. However, it was heavily criticized by conservatives and equal rights advocates, who accused the Supreme Court of judicial activism. While *Grutter* further solidified the practice, as established in *Bakke* years earlier, a case called *Gratz v. Bollinger*, decided concurrently with *Grutter*, struck down the practice of quota-based admissions policies, which were found not to give individual consideration to each applicant.

Until the undefined goals of affirmative action are achieved, *Grutter v. Bollinger* provided the legal basis for the continued use of race-based admissions policies in U.S. colleges and universities.

PRIMARY SOURCE

GRUTTER V. BOLLINGER

SYNOPSIS: In this decision, the U.S. Supreme Court issues its majority opinion in the case of *Grutter v. Bollinger*, ruling that racially motivated university admissions policies do not violate the Fourteenth Amendment anti-discrimination clauses, so long as they favor racial minorities rather than whites.

The University of Michigan Law School (Law School), one of the Nation's top law schools, follows an official admissions policy that seeks to achieve student body diversity through compliance with *Regents of Univ. of Cal. v. Bakke*, 438 U.S. 265. Focusing on students' academic ability coupled with a flexible assessment of their talents, experiences, and potential, the policy requires admissions officials to evaluate each applicant based on all the information available in the file, including a personal statement, letters of recommendation, an essay describing how the applicant will contribute to Law School life and diversity, and the applicant's undergraduate grade point average (GPA) and Law School Admissions Test (LSAT) score. Additionally, officials must look beyond grades and scores to so-called "soft variables," such as recommenders' enthusiasm, the quality of the undergraduate institution and the applicant's essay, and the areas and difficulty of undergraduate course selection. The policy does not define diversity solely in terms of racial and ethnic status and does not restrict the types of diversity contributions eligible for "substantial weight," but it does reaffirm the Law School's commitment to diversity with special reference to the inclusion of African-American, Hispanic, and Native-American students, who otherwise might not be represented in the student body in meaningful numbers. By enrolling a "critical mass" of underrepresented minority students, the policy seeks to ensure their ability to contribute to the Law School's character and to the legal profession.

When the Law School denied admission to petitioner Grutter, a white Michigan resident with a 3.8 GPA and 161 LSAT score, she filed this suit, alleging that respondents had discriminated against her on the basis of race in violation of the Fourteenth Amendment, Title VI of the Civil Rights Act of 1964, and 42 U.S.C. § 1981; that she was rejected because the Law School uses race as a "predominant" factor, giving applicants belonging to certain minority groups a significantly greater chance of admission than students with similar credentials from disfavored racial groups; and that respondents had no compelling interest to justify that use of race. The District

Barbara Grutter (left) and Jennifer Gratz (center) talk to reporters outside the U.S. Supreme Court building in Washington, D.C., April 1, 2003. They were plaintiffs in two separate affirmative action cases against the University of Michigan. © AP IMAGES/SUSAN WALSH.

Court found the Law School's use of race as an admissions factor unlawful. The Sixth Circuit reversed, holding that Justice Powell's opinion in *Bakke* was binding precedent establishing diversity as a compelling state interest, and that the Law School's use of race was narrowly tailored because race was merely a "potential 'plus' factor" and because the Law School's program was virtually identical to the Harvard admissions program described approvingly by Justice Powell and appended to his *Bakke* opinion.

Held: The Law School's narrowly tailored use of race in admissions decisions to further a compelling interest in obtaining the educational benefits that flow from a diverse student body is not prohibited by the Equal Protection Clause, Title VI, or § 1981. Pp. 9–32.

(a) In the landmark *Bakke* case, this Court reviewed a medical school's racial set-aside program that reserved 16 out of 100 seats for members of certain minority groups. The decision produced six separate opinions, none of which commanded a majority. Four Justices would have upheld the program on the ground that the government can use race to remedy disadvantages cast on minorities by past racial prejudice. ... Four other Justices would have struck the program down on statutory grounds. ... Justice Powell, announcing the Court's judgment, provided a fifth vote not only for invalidating the program, but also for reversing the state court's injunction against any use of race whatsoever. In a part of his opinion that was joined by no other Justice, Justice Powell expressed his view that attaining a diverse student body was the only interest asserted by the university that survived scrutiny. ... Grounding his analysis in the academic freedom that "long has been viewed as a special concern of the First Amendment," ... Justice Powell emphasized that the "'nation's future depends upon leaders trained through wide exposure' to the ideas and mores of students as diverse as this Nation." ... However, he also emphasized that "[i]t is not an interest in simple ethnic diversity, in which a specified percentage of the student body is in effect guaranteed to be members of selected ethnic groups," that can justify using race. ... Rather, "[t]he diversity that furthers a compelling state interest encompasses a far broader array of qualifications and characteristics of which racial or ethnic origin is but a single though important element." ... Since *Bakke*, Justice Powell's opinion has been the touchstone for constitutional analysis of race-conscious admissions policies. Public and private universities across the Nation have modeled their own admissions programs on Justice Powell's views. Courts, however, have struggled to discern whether Justice Powell's diversity rationale is binding precedent. The Court finds it unnecessary to decide this issue because the Court endorses Justice Powell's view that student body diversity is a compelling state interest in the context of university admissions....

(b) All government racial classifications must be analyzed by a reviewing court under strict scrutiny. ... But not all such uses are invalidated by strict scrutiny. Race-based action necessary to further a compelling governmental interest does not violate the Equal Protection Clause so long as it is narrowly tailored to further that interest. ... Context matters when reviewing such action. ... Not every decision influenced by race is equally objectionable, and strict scrutiny is designed to provide a framework for carefully examining the importance and the sincerity of the government's reasons for using race in a particular context.

(c) The Court endorses Justice Powell's view that student body diversity is a compelling state interest that can justify using race in university admissions. The Court defers to the Law School's educational judgment that diversity is essential to its educational mission. The Court's scrutiny of that interest is no less strict for taking into account complex educational judgments in an area that lies primarily within the university's expertise. ... Attaining a diverse student body is at the heart of the Law School's proper institutional mission, and its "good faith" is "presumed" absent "a showing to the contrary." ... Enrolling a "critical mass" of minority students simply to assure some specified percentage of a particular group merely because of its race or ethnic origin would be patently unconstitutional. ... But the Law School defines its critical mass concept by reference to the substantial, important, and laudable educational benefits that diversity is designed to produce, including cross-racial understanding and the breaking down of racial stereotypes. The Law School's claim is further bolstered by numerous expert studies and reports showing that such diversity promotes learning outcomes and better prepares students for an

increasingly diverse workforce, for society, and for the legal profession. Major American businesses have made clear that the skills needed in today's increasingly global marketplace can only be developed through exposure to widely diverse people, cultures, ideas, and viewpoints. High-ranking retired officers and civilian military leaders assert that a highly qualified, racially diverse officer corps is essential to national security. Moreover, because universities, and in particular, law schools, represent the training ground for a large number of the Nation's leaders, ... the path to leadership must be visibly open to talented and qualified individuals of every race and ethnicity. Thus, the Law School has a compelling interest in attaining a diverse student body....

(d) The Law School's admissions program bears the hallmarks of a narrowly tailored plan. To be narrowly tailored, a race-conscious admissions program cannot "insulat[e] each category of applicants with certain desired qualifications from competition with all other applicants." ... Instead, it may consider race or ethnicity only as a "'plus' in a particular applicant's file"; *i.e.*, it must be "flexible enough to consider all pertinent elements of diversity in light of the particular qualifications of each applicant, and to place them on the same footing for consideration, although not necessarily according them the same weight," ... It follows that universities cannot establish quotas for members of certain racial or ethnic groups or put them on separate admissions tracks. ... The Law School's admissions program, like the Harvard plan approved by Justice Powell, satisfies these requirements. Moreover, the program is flexible enough to ensure that each applicant is evaluated as an individual and not in a way that makes race or ethnicity the defining feature of the application. See *Bakke, supra,* at 317 (opinion of Powell, J.). The Law School engages in a highly individualized, holistic review of each applicant's file, giving serious consideration to all the ways an applicant might contribute to a diverse educational environment. There is no policy, either *de jure* or *de facto,* of automatic acceptance or rejection based on any single "soft" variable. ... Also, the program adequately ensures that all factors that may contribute to diversity are meaningfully considered alongside race. Moreover, the Law School frequently accepts nonminority applicants with grades and test scores lower than underrepresented minority applicants (and other nonminority applicants) who are rejected. The Court rejects the argument that the Law School should have used other race-neutral means to obtain the educational benefits of student body diversity, *e.g.*, a lottery system or decreasing the emphasis on GPA and LSAT scores. Narrow tailoring does not require exhaustion of every conceivable race-neutral alternative or mandate that a university choose between maintaining a reputation for excellence or fulfilling a commitment to provide educational opportunities to members of all racial groups. ... The Court is satisfied that the Law School adequately considered the available alternatives. The Court is also satisfied that, in the context of individualized consideration of the possible diversity contributions of each applicant, the Law School's race-conscious admissions program does not unduly harm nonminority applicants. Finally, race-conscious admissions policies must be limited in time. The Court takes the Law School at its word that it would like nothing better than to find a race-neutral admissions formula and will terminate its use of racial preferences as soon as practicable. The Court expects that 25 years from now, the use of racial preferences will no longer be necessary to further the interest approved today. ...

(e) Because the Law School's use of race in admissions decisions is not prohibited by Equal Protection Clause, petitioner's statutory claims based on Title VI and §1981 also fail. ...

FURTHER RESOURCES

Web Sites

"Grutter v. Bollinger." *American Civil Liberties Union*. www. aclu.org/racial-justice/grutter-v-bollinger (accessed on March 21, 2013).

"Grutter v. Bollinger." *CaseBriefs*. www.casebriefs.com/blog/law/ethics/ethics-keyed-to-hazard/the-structure-of-legal-practice/grutter-v-bollinger/ (accessed on March 21, 2013).

"Grutter v. Bollinger." *Chicago-Kent College of Law*. www. oyez.org/cases/2000-2009/2002/2002_02_241/ (accessed on March 21, 2013).

"Grutter v. Bollinger." *FindLaw*. http://caselaw.lp.findlaw. com/scripts/getcase.pl?court=us&vol=000&invol=02-241 (accessed on March 21, 2013).

Goodridge v. Department of Public Health

Court decision

By: Massachusetts chief justice Margaret Marshall

Date: November 18, 2003

Source: *Goodridge v. Department of Public Health*, 798 N.E. 2d 941 (Mass. 2003). Decided on November 18, 2003. news.findlaw.com/wp/docs/conlaw/goodridge 111803opn.pdf (accessed on March 20, 2013).

About the Appellant: The plaintiffs in the case of *Goodrich v. Department of Public Health* issued their litigation under the representation of Gay and Lesbian Advocates and Defenders (GLAD), a legal-rights nonprofit group "dedicated to ending discrimination based on sexual orientation, HIV status and gender identity and expression." Since its inception in 1978, the organization has successfully represented those affected by such discrimination in several related cases, as well as performing political advocacy and awareness campaigns.

INTRODUCTION

Gay and lesbian marriage was one of the most contentious and important political issues of the 2000s decade. Arguments in favor of legalizing same-sex marriage in the United States had gained traction in the 1990s as the general public became definitively aware of the gay community's efforts to escape political and civil discrimination, although laws prohibiting same-sex marriage had been formally contested since the 1970s. By 2000, civil unions between gay and lesbian couples had earned legal recognition across most of the nation, but gay-rights advocates objected that such unions did not carry the same legal and economic benefits as heterosexual marriages.

The heightened public support of gay rights cultivated in the 1990s resulted in judicial reconsideration of legislation prohibiting same-sex marriage, first evidenced on March 4, 2003, when hearings for the case of *Goodridge v. Department of Public Health* began in the Massachusetts Supreme Judicial Court, the state's highest court. The case dated back to April 2001, when seven same-sex couples (named in the court docket), represented by GLAD, sued the Massachusetts Department of Health because they had been denied marriage licenses in the state (the Department of Health is the office responsible for applying marriage and partnership law in Massachusetts). In the initial hearing, the Massachusetts Superior Court had upheld the prohibition of same-sex marriage, but GLAD's appeal to the state's highest court was met with an agreement to examine the case.

In court, GLAD argued that the state's practice of refusing to give marriage certificates to same-sex couples was unjust and unconstitutional because it was based purely on prejudice against homosexuals, rather than a necessary or prudent protection of the legal establishment of marriage. The plaintiffs noted that each of the gay couples represented had a stable, happy relationship, and that several of them had successfully adopted and raised children. The defendant argued that same-sex couples should not be permitted to marry because they cannot naturally procreate, which the Massachusetts Department of Public Health maintained to be the primary purpose of the institution of marriage.

In a 4–3 decision, the Massachusetts Supreme Judicial Court reversed the lower court's ruling, legalizing same-sex marriage in the state. The majority opinion stated that, by creating an arbitrary distinction between gay "civil unions" and heterosexual marriages, the state had relegated homosexuals to a "second-class citizen" status in express violation of the Constitution. The state of Massachusetts began issuing marriage certificates to same-sex couples 180 days after the ruling was issued, making it the first state in the Union to do so.

SIGNIFICANCE

As a direct result of *Goodridge v. Department of Public Health*, over ten thousand same-sex marriage certificates were awarded in Massachusetts over the following five years. By the end of the decade, the states of Connecticut, Iowa, New Hampshire, and Vermont had also abolished their policies denying same-sex couples the right to marry. Other states passed laws recognizing the legitimacy of gay marriage licenses, although the majority continue to consider them unofficial.

Gay marriage remained a volatile issue in U.S. politics, complicated by the inability of activists to successfully repeal the Defense of Marriage Act, a 1996 federal law defining marriage as including one woman and one man. Other states in which proposed measures recognizing the legitimacy of same-sex marriages were put to vote saw such efforts soundly defeated, ensuring that gay rights in the United States remained a point of contention into the 2010s.

PRIMARY SOURCE

GOODRIDGE V. DEPARTMENT OF PUBLIC HEALTH
MAJORITY OPINION

SYNOPSIS: In this decision, Chief Justice Margaret H. Marshall lays out the legal foundation of the Court's decision against the ban on gay marriage and addresses the social importance of equality in the United States. (*Note:* Footnotes have been removed here, due to their technical legal nature.)

MARSHALL, C.J.

Marriage is a vital social institution. The exclusive commitment of two individuals to each other nurtures love and mutual support; it brings stability to our society. For those who choose to marry, and for their children, marriage provides an abundance of legal, financial, and social benefits. In return it imposes weighty legal, financial, and social obligations. The question before us is whether, consistent with the Massachusetts Constitution, the Commonwealth may deny the protections, benefits, and obligations conferred by civil marriage to two individuals of the same sex who wish to marry. We conclude that it may not. The Massachusetts Constitution affirms the dignity and equality of all individuals. It forbids the creation of second-class citizens. In reaching our conclusion we have given full deference to the arguments made by the Commonwealth. But it has failed to identify any constitutionally adequate reason for denying civil marriage to same-sex couples.

We are mindful that our decision marks a change in the history of our marriage law. Many people hold deep-seated religious, moral, and ethical convictions that marriage should be limited to the union of one man and one woman, and that homosexual conduct is immoral. Many hold equally strong religious, moral, and ethical convictions that same-sex couples are entitled to be married, and that homosexual persons should be treated no differently than their heterosexual neighbors. Neither view answers the question before us. Our concern is with the Massachusetts Constitution as a charter of governance for every person properly within its reach. "Our obligation is to define the liberty of all, not to mandate our own moral code." *Lawrence v. Texas*, 123 S.Ct. 2472, 2480 (2003) (*Lawrence*), quoting *Planned Parenthood of Southeastern Pa. v. Casey*, 505 U.S. 833, 850 (1992).

Whether the Commonwealth may use its formidable regulatory authority to bar same-sex couples from civil marriage is a question not previously addressed by a Massachusetts appellate court. It is a question the United States Supreme Court left open as a matter of Federal law in *Lawrence, supra* at 2484, where it was not an issue. There, the Court affirmed that the core concept of common human dignity protected by the Fourteenth Amendment to the United States Constitution precludes government intrusion into the deeply personal realms of consensual adult expressions of intimacy and one's choice of an intimate partner. The Court also reaffirmed the central role that decisions whether to marry or have children bear in shaping one's identity. *Id.* at 2481. The Massachusetts Constitution is, if anything, more protective of individual liberty and equality than the Federal Constitution; it may demand broader protection for fundamental rights; and it is less tolerant of government intrusion into the protected spheres of private life.

Barred access to the protections, benefits, and obligations of civil marriage, a person who enters into an

Co-plaintiffs David Wilson (left) and his partner, Robert Compton, celebrate the decision in the *Goodridge v. Public Health Department* case that allowed same-sex marriages in Massachusetts. © DEANNE FITZMAURICE/SAN FRANCISCO CHRONICLE/CORBIS.

intimate, exclusive union with another of the same sex is arbitrarily deprived of membership in one of our community's most rewarding and cherished institutions. That exclusion is incompatible with the constitutional principles of respect for individual autonomy and equality under law.

I.

The plaintiffs are fourteen individuals from five Massachusetts counties. As of April 11, 2001, the date they filed their complaint, the plaintiffs Gloria Bailey, sixty years old, and Linda Davies, fifty-five years old, had been in a committed relationship for thirty years; the plaintiffs Maureen Brodoff, forty-nine years old, and Ellen Wade, fifty-two years old, had been in a committed relationship for twenty years and lived with their twelve year old daughter; the plaintiffs Hillary Goodridge, forty-four years old, and Julie Goodridge, forty-three years old, had been in a committed relationship for thirteen years and lived with their five year old daughter; the plaintiffs Gary Chalmers, thirty-five years old, and Richard Linnell, thirty-seven years old, had been in a committed relationship for thirteen years and lived with their eight year old daughter and Richard's mother; the plaintiffs Heidi Norton, thirty-six

years old, and Gina Smith, thirty-six years old, had been in a committed relationship for eleven years and lived with their two sons, ages five years and one year; the plaintiffs Michael Horgan, forty-one years old, and David Balmelli, forty-one years old, had been in a committed relationship for seven years; and the plaintiffs David Wilson, fifty-seven years old, and Robert Compton, fifty-one years old, had been in a committed relationship for four years and had cared for David's mother in their home after a serious illness until she died.

The plaintiffs include business executives, lawyers, an investment banker, educators, therapists, and a computer engineer. Many are active in church, community, and school groups. They have employed such legal means as are available to them—for example, joint adoption, powers of attorney, and joint ownership of real property—to secure aspects of their relationships. Each plaintiff attests a desire to marry his or her partner in order to affirm publicly their commitment to each other and to secure the legal protections and benefits afforded to married people....

In March and April, 2001, each of the plaintiff couples attempted to obtain a marriage license from a city or town clerk's office. As required under G.L. c. 207, they completed notices of intention to marry on forms provided by the registry, see G.L. c. 207, § 20, and presented these forms to a Massachusetts town or city clerk, together with the required health forms and marriage license fees. See G.L. c. 207, § 19. In each case, the clerk either refused to accept the notice of intention to marry or denied a marriage license to the couple on the ground that Massachusetts does not recognize same-sex marriage. Because obtaining a marriage license is a necessary prerequisite to civil marriage in Massachusetts, denying marriage licenses to the plaintiffs was tantamount to denying them access to civil marriage itself, with its appurtenant social and legal protections, benefits, and obligations.

On April 11, 2001, the plaintiffs filed suit in the Superior Court against the department and the commissioner seeking a judgment that "the exclusion of the [p]laintiff couples and other qualified same-sex couples from access to marriage licenses, and the legal and social status of civil marriage, as well as the protections, benefits and obligations of marriage, violates Massachusetts law." See G.L. c. 231A. The plaintiffs alleged violation of the laws of the Commonwealth, including but not limited to their rights under arts. 1, 6, 7, 10, 12, and 16, and Part II, c. 1, § 1, art. 4, of the Massachusetts Constitution.

The department, represented by the Attorney General, admitted to a policy and practice of denying marriage licenses to same-sex couples. It denied that its actions violated any law or that the plaintiffs were entitled to relief. The parties filed cross motions for summary judgment.

A Superior Court judge ruled for the department. In a memorandum of decision and order dated May 7, 2002, he dismissed the plaintiffs' claim that the marriage statutes should be construed to permit marriage between persons of the same sex, holding that the plain wording of G.L. c. 207, as well as the wording of other marriage statutes, precluded that interpretation. Turning to the constitutional claims, he held that the marriage exclusion does not offend the liberty, freedom, equality, or due process provisions of the Massachusetts Constitution, and that the Massachusetts Declaration of Rights does not guarantee "the fundamental right to marry a person of the same sex." He concluded that prohibiting same-sex marriage rationally furthers the Legislature's legitimate interest in safeguarding the "primary purpose" of marriage, "procreation." The Legislature may rationally limit marriage to opposite-sex couples, he concluded, because those couples are "theoretically ... capable of procreation," they do not rely on "inherently more cumbersome" noncoital means of reproduction, and they are more likely than same-sex couples to have children, or more children.

After the complaint was dismissed and summary judgment entered for the defendants, the plaintiffs appealed. Both parties requested direct appellate review, which we granted.

II.

Although the plaintiffs refer in passing to "the marriage statutes," they focus, quite properly, on G.L. c. 207, the marriage licensing statute, which controls entry into civil marriage. As a preliminary matter, we summarize the provisions of that law.

General Laws c. 207 is both a gatekeeping and a public records statute. It sets minimum qualifications for obtaining a marriage license and directs city and town clerks, the registrar, and the department to keep and maintain certain "vital records" of civil marriages. The gatekeeping provisions of G.L. c. 207 are minimal. They forbid marriage of individuals within certain degrees of consanguinity, §§ 1 and 2, and polygamous marriages. See G.L. c. 207, § 4. See also G.L. c. 207, § 8 (marriages solemnized in violation of §§ 1, 2, and 4, are void ab initio). They prohibit marriage if one of the parties has communicable syphilis, see G.L. c. 207, § 28A, and restrict the circumstances in which a person under eighteen years of age may marry. See G.L. c. 207, §§ 7, 25, and 27. The statute requires that civil marriage be solemnized only by those so authorized. See G.L. c. 207, §§ 38-40.

The record-keeping provisions of G.L. c. 207 are more extensive. Marriage applicants file standard information forms and a medical certificate in any Massachusetts city or town clerk's office and tender a filing fee. G.L. c. 207, §§ 19-20, 28A. The clerk issues the marriage license, and when the marriage is solemnized, the individual authorized to solemnize the marriage adds additional information to the form and returns it (or a copy) to the clerk's office. G.L. c. 207, §§ 28, 30, 38-40 (this completed form is commonly known as the "marriage certificate"). The clerk sends a copy of the information to the registrar, and that information becomes a public record. See G.L. c. 17, § 4; G.L. c. 66, § 10.

In short, for all the joy and solemnity that normally attend a marriage, G.L. c. 207, governing entrance to marriage, is a licensing law. The plaintiffs argue that because nothing in that licensing law specifically prohibits marriages between persons of the same sex, we may interpret the statute to permit "qualified same sex couples" to obtain marriage licenses, thereby avoiding the question whether the law is constitutional. See *School Comm. of Greenfield v. Greenfield Educ. Ass'n*, 385 Mass. 70, 79 (1982), and cases cited. This claim lacks merit.

We interpret statutes to carry out the Legislature's intent, determined by the words of a statute interpreted according to "the ordinary and approved usage of the language." *Hanlon v. Rollins*, 286 Mass. 444, 447 (1934).

The everyday meaning of "marriage" is "[t]he legal union of a man and woman as husband and wife," Black's Law Dictionary 986 (7th ed.1999), and the plaintiffs do not argue that the term "marriage" has ever had a different meaning under Massachusetts law. See, e.g., *Milford v. Worcester*, 7 Mass. 48, 52 (1810) (marriage "is an engagement, by which a single man and a single woman, of sufficient discretion, take each other for husband and wife"). This definition of marriage, as both the department and the Superior Court judge point out, derives from the common law. See *Commonwealth v. Knowlton*, 2 Mass. 530, 535 (1807) (Massachusetts common law derives from English common law except as otherwise altered by Massachusetts statutes and Constitution). See also *Commonwealth v. Lane*, 113 Mass. 458, 462-463 (1873) ("when the statutes are silent, questions of the validity of marriages are to be determined by the jus gentium, the common law of nations"); C. P. Kindregan, Jr., & M. L. Inker, Family Law and Practice § 1.2 (3d ed.2002). Far from being ambiguous, the undefined word "marriage," as used in G.L. c. 207, confirms the General Court's intent to hew to the term's common-law and quotidian meaning concerning the genders of the marriage partners.

The intended scope of G.L. c. 207 is also evident in its consanguinity provisions. See *Chandler v. County Comm'rs of Nantucket County*, 437 Mass. 430, 435 (2002) (statute's various provisions may offer insight into legislative intent). Sections 1 and 2 of G.L. c. 207 prohibit marriages between a man and certain female relatives and a woman and certain male relatives, but are silent as to the consanguinity of male-male or female-female marriage applicants. See G.L. c. 207, §§ 1-2. The only reasonable explanation is that the Legislature did not intend that same-sex couples be licensed to marry. We conclude, as did the judge, that G.L. c. 207 may not be construed to permit same-sex couples to marry.

III.

A.

The larger question is whether, as the department claims, government action that bars same-sex couples from civil marriage constitutes a legitimate exercise of the State's authority to regulate conduct, or whether, as the plaintiffs claim, this categorical marriage exclusion violates the Massachusetts Constitution. We have recognized the long-standing statutory understanding, derived from the common law, that "marriage" means the lawful union of a woman and a man. But that history cannot and does not foreclose the constitutional question.

The plaintiffs' claim that the marriage restriction violates the Massachusetts Constitution can be analyzed in two ways. Does it offend the Constitution's guarantees of equality before the law? Or do the liberty and due process provisions of the Massachusetts Constitution secure the plaintiffs' right to marry their chosen partner?

In matters implicating marriage, family life, and the upbringing of children, the two constitutional concepts frequently overlap, as they do here. See, e.g., *M.L.B. v. S. L.J.*, 519 U.S. 102, 120 (1996) (noting convergence of due process and equal protection principles in cases concerning parent-child relationships); *Perez v. Sharp*, 32 Cal.2d 711, 728 (1948) (analyzing statutory ban on interracial marriage as equal protection violation concerning regulation of fundamental right). See also *Lawrence, supra* at 2482 ("Equality of treatment and the due process right to demand respect for conduct protected by the substantive guarantee of liberty are linked in important respects, and a decision on the latter point advances both interests"); *Bolling v. Sharpe*, 347 U.S. 497 (1954) (racial segregation in District of Columbia public schools violates the due process clause of the Fifth Amendment to the United States Constitution), decided the same day as *Brown v. Board of Educ. of Topeka*, 347 U.S. 483 (1954) (holding that segregation of public schools in the States violates the equal protection clause of the Fourteenth Amendment). Much of what we say concerning one standard applies to the other.

We begin by considering the nature of civil marriage itself. Simply put, the government creates civil marriage. In Massachusetts, civil marriage is, and since pre-Colonial days has been, precisely what its name implies: a wholly secular institution. See *Commonwealth v. Munson*, 127 Mass. 459, 460-466 (1879) (noting that "[i]n Massachusetts, from very early times, the requisites of a valid marriage have been regulated by statutes of the Colony, Province, and Commonwealth," and surveying marriage statutes from 1639 through 1834). No religious ceremony has ever been required to validate a Massachusetts marriage. *Id.*

In a real sense, there are three partners to every civil marriage: two willing spouses and an approving State. See *DeMatteo v. DeMatteo*, 436 Mass. 18, 31 (2002) ("Marriage is not a mere contract between two parties but a legal status from which certain rights and obligations arise"); *Smith v. Smith*, 171 Mass. 404, 409 (1898) (on marriage, the parties "assume[ ] new relations to each other and to the State"). See also *French v. McAnarney*, 290 Mass. 544, 546 (1935). While only the parties can mutually assent to marriage, the terms of the marriage—who may marry and what obligations, benefits, and liabilities attach to civil marriage—are set by the Commonwealth. Conversely, while only the parties can agree to end the marriage (absent the death of one of them or a marriage void ab initio), the Commonwealth defines the exit terms. See G.L. c. 208.

Civil marriage is created and regulated through exercise of the police power. See *Commonwealth v. Stowell*, 389 Mass. 171, 175 (1983) (regulation of marriage is properly within the scope of the police power).

"Police power" (now more commonly termed the State's regulatory authority) is an old-fashioned term for the Commonwealth's lawmaking authority, as bounded by the liberty and equality guarantees of the Massachusetts Constitution and its express delegation of power from the people to their government. In broad terms, it is the Legislature's power to enact rules to regulate conduct, to the extent that such laws are "necessary to secure the health, safety, good order, comfort, or general welfare of the community" (citations omitted). Opinion of the Justices, 341 Mass. 760, 785 (1960). [FN12] See *Commonwealth v. Alger*, 7 Cush. 53, 85 (1851).

Without question, civil marriage enhances the "welfare of the community." It is a "social institution of the highest importance." *French v. McAnarney, supra.* Civil marriage anchors an ordered society by encouraging stable relationships over transient ones. It is central to the way the Commonwealth identifies individuals, provides for the orderly distribution of property, ensures that children and adults are cared for and supported whenever possible from private rather than public funds, and tracks important epidemiological and demographic data.

Marriage also bestows enormous private and social advantages on those who choose to marry. Civil marriage is at once a deeply personal commitment to another human being and a highly public celebration of the ideals of mutuality, companionship, intimacy, fidelity, and family. "It is an association that promotes a way of life, not causes; a harmony in living, not political faiths; a bilateral loyalty, not commercial or social projects." *Griswold v. Connecticut*, 381 U.S. 479, 486 (1965). Because it fulfills yearnings for security, safe haven, and connection that express our common humanity, civil marriage is an esteemed institution, and the decision whether and whom to marry is among life's momentous acts of self-definition.

Tangible as well as intangible benefits flow from marriage. The marriage license grants valuable property rights to those who meet the entry requirements, and who agree to what might otherwise be a burdensome degree of government regulation of their activities. See *Leduc v. Commonwealth*, 421 Mass. 433, 435 (1995), cert. denied, 519 U.S. 827 (1996) ("The historical aim of licensure generally is preservation of public health, safety, and welfare by extending the public trust only to those with proven qualifications"). The Legislature has conferred on "each party [in a civil marriage] substantial rights concerning the assets of the other which unmarried cohabitants do not have." *Wilcox v. Trautz*, 427 Mass. 326, 334 (1998). See *Collins v. Guggenheim*, 417 Mass. 615, 618 (1994) (rejecting claim for equitable distribution of property where plaintiff cohabited with but did not marry defendant); *Feliciano v. Rosemar Silver Co.*, 401 Mass. 141, 142 (1987) (government interest in promoting

marriage would be "subverted" by recognition of "a right to recover for loss of consortium by a person who has not accepted the correlative responsibilities of marriage"); *Davis v. Misiano*, 373 Mass. 261, 263 (1977) (unmarried partners not entitled to rights of separate support or alimony). See generally *Attorney Gen. v. Desilets*, 418 Mass. 316, 327-328 & nn. 10, 11 (1994).

The benefits accessible only by way of a marriage license are enormous, touching nearly every aspect of life and death. The department states that "hundreds of statutes" are related to marriage and to marital benefits. With no attempt to be comprehensive, we note that some of the statutory benefits conferred by the Legislature on those who enter into civil marriage include, as to property: joint Massachusetts income tax filing (G.L. c. 62C, § 6); tenancy by the entirety (a form of ownership that provides certain protections against creditors and allows for the automatic descent of property to the surviving spouse without probate) (G.L. c. 184, § 7); extension of the benefit of the homestead protection (securing up to $300,000 in equity from creditors) to one's spouse and children (G.L. c. 188, § 1); automatic rights to inherit the property of a deceased spouse who does not leave a will (G.L. c. 190, § 1); the rights of elective share and of dower (which allow surviving spouses certain property rights where the decedent spouse has not made adequate provision for the survivor in a will) (G.L. c. 191, § 15, and G.L. c. 189); entitlement to wages owed to a deceased employee (G.L. c. 149, § 178A [general] and G.L. c. 149, § 178C [public employees]); eligibility to continue certain businesses of a deceased spouse (e.g., G.L. c. 112, § 53 [dentist]); the right to share the medical policy of one's spouse (e.g., G.L. c. 175, § 108, Second [a] [3] [defining an insured's "dependent" to include one's spouse), see *Connors v. Boston*, 430 Mass. 31, 43 (1999) [domestic partners of city employees not included within the term "dependent" as used in G.L. c. 32B, § 2]); thirty-nine week continuation of health coverage for the spouse of a person who is laid off or dies (e.g., G.L. c. 175, § 110G); preferential options under the Commonwealth's pension system (see G.L. c. 32, § 12[2] ["Joint and Last Survivor Allowance"]); preferential benefits in the Commonwealth's medical program, MassHealth (e.g., 130 Code Mass. Regs. § 515.012[A] prohibiting placing a lien on long-term care patient's former home if spouse still lives there); access to veterans' spousal benefits and preferences (e.g., G.L. c. 115, § 1 [defining "dependents"] and G.L. c. 31, § 26 [State employment] and § 28 [municipal employees]); financial protections for spouses of certain Commonwealth employees (fire fighters, police officers, prosecutors, among others) killed in the performance of duty (e.g., G.L. c. 32, §§ 100-103); the equitable division of marital property on divorce (G.L. c. 208, § 34); temporary and permanent alimony rights (G.L. c. 208, §§ 17 and 34);

the right to separate support on separation of the parties that does not result in divorce (G.L. c. 209, § 32); and the right to bring claims for wrongful death and loss of consortium, and for funeral and burial expenses and punitive damages resulting from tort actions (G.L. c. 229, §§ 1 and 2; G.L. c. 228, § 1. See *Feliciano v. Rosemar Silver Co., supra*).

Exclusive marital benefits that are not directly tied to property rights include the presumptions of legitimacy and parentage of children born to a married couple (G.L. c. 209C, § 6, and G.L. c. 46, § 4B); and evidentiary rights, such as the prohibition against spouses testifying against one another about their private conversations, applicable in both civil and criminal cases (G.L. c. 233, § 20). Other statutory benefits of a personal nature available only to married individuals include qualification for bereavement or medical leave to care for individuals related by blood or marriage (G.L. c. 149, § 52D); an automatic "family member" preference to make medical decisions for an incompetent or disabled spouse who does not have a contrary health care proxy, see *Shine v. Vega*, 429 Mass. 456, 466 (1999); the application of predictable rules of child custody, visitation, support, and removal out-of-State when married parents divorce (e.g., G.L. c. 208, § 19 [temporary custody], § 20 [temporary support], § 28 [custody and support on judgment of divorce], § 30 [removal from Commonwealth], and § 31 [shared custody plan]; priority rights to administer the estate of a deceased spouse who dies without a will, and requirement that surviving spouse must consent to the appointment of any other person as administrator (G.L. c. 38, § 13 [disposition of body], and G.L. c. 113, § 8 [anatomical gifts]); and the right to interment in the lot or tomb owned by one's deceased spouse (G.L. c. 114, §§ 29-33). Where a married couple has children, their children are also directly or indirectly, but no less auspiciously, the recipients of the special legal and economic protections obtained by civil marriage. Notwithstanding the Commonwealth's strong public policy to abolish legal distinctions between marital and nonmarital children in providing for the support and care of minors, see *Department of Revenue v. Mason M.*, 439 Mass. 665 (2003); *Woodward v. Commissioner of Social Sec.*, 435 Mass. 536, 546 (2002), the fact remains that marital children reap a measure of family stability and economic security based on their parents' legally privileged status that is largely inaccessible, or not as readily accessible, to nonmarital children. Some of these benefits are social, such as the enhanced approval that still attends the status of being a marital child. Others are material, such as the greater ease of access to family-based State and Federal benefits that attend the presumptions of one's parentage.

It is undoubtedly for these concrete reasons, as well as for its intimately personal significance, that civil marriage has long been termed a "civil right." See, e.g., *Loving v. Virginia*, 388 U.S. 1, 12 (1967) ("Marriage is one of the 'basic civil rights of man,' fundamental to our very existence and survival"), quoting *Skinner v. Oklahoma*, 316 U.S. 535, 541 (1942); *Milford v. Worcester*, 7 Mass. 48, 56 (1810) (referring to "civil rights incident to marriages"). See also *Baehr v. Lewin*, 74 Haw. 530, 561 (1993) (identifying marriage as a "civil right[ ]"); *Baker v. State*, 170 Vt. 194, 242 (1999) (Johnson, J., concurring in part and dissenting in part) (same). The United States Supreme Court has described the right to marry as "of fundamental importance for all individuals" and as "part of the fundamental 'right of privacy' implicit in the Fourteenth Amendment's Due Process Clause." *Zablocki v. Redhail*, 434 U.S. 374, 384 (1978). See *Loving v. Virginia, supra* ("The freedom to marry has long been recognized as one of the vital personal rights essential to the orderly pursuit of happiness by free men").

Without the right to marry—or more properly, the right to choose to marry—one is excluded from the full range of human experience and denied full protection of the laws for one's "avowed commitment to an intimate and lasting human relationship." *Baker v. State, supra* at 229. Because civil marriage is central to the lives of individuals and the welfare of the community, our laws assiduously protect the individual's right to marry against undue government incursion. Laws may not "interfere directly and substantially with the right to marry." *Zablocki v. Redhail, supra* at 387. See *Perez v. Sharp*, 32 Cal.2d 711, 714 (1948) ("There can be no prohibition of marriage except for an important social objective and reasonable means").

Unquestionably, the regulatory power of the Commonwealth over civil marriage is broad, as is the Commonwealth's discretion to award public benefits. See *Commonwealth v. Stowell*, 389 Mass. 171, 175 (1983) (marriage); *Moe v. Secretary of Admin. & Fin.*, 382 Mass. 629, 652 (1981) (Medicaid benefits). Individuals who have the choice to marry each other and nevertheless choose not to may properly be denied the legal benefits of marriage. See *Wilcox v. Trautz*, 427 Mass. 326, 334 (1998); *Collins v. Guggenheim*, 417 Mass. 615, 618 (1994); *Feliciano v. Rosemar Silver Co.*, 401 Mass. 141, 142 (1987). But that same logic cannot hold for a qualified individual who would marry if she or he only could.

B.

For decades, indeed centuries, in much of this country (including Massachusetts) no lawful marriage was possible between white and black Americans. That long history availed not when the Supreme Court of California held in 1948 that a legislative prohibition against interracial marriage violated the due process and equality guarantees of the Fourteenth Amendment, *Perez v.*

Sharp, 32 Cal.2d 711, 728 (1948), or when, nineteen years later, the United States Supreme Court also held that a statutory bar to interracial marriage violated the Fourteenth Amendment, *Loving v. Virginia*, 388 U.S. 1 (1967). As both *Perez* and *Loving* make clear, the right to marry means little if it does not include the right to marry the person of one's choice, subject to appropriate government restrictions in the interests of public health, safety, and welfare. See *Perez v. Sharp, supra* at 717 ("the essence of the right to marry is freedom to join in marriage with the person of one's choice"). See also *Loving v. Virginia, supra* at 12. In this case, as in Perez and Loving, a statute deprives individuals of access to an institution of fundamental legal, personal, and social significance—the institution of marriage—because of a single trait: skin color in Perez and Loving, sexual orientation here. As it did in Perez and Loving, history must yield to a more fully developed understanding of the invidious quality of the discrimination.

The Massachusetts Constitution protects matters of personal liberty against government incursion as zealously, and often more so, than does the Federal Constitution, even where both Constitutions employ essentially the same language. See *Planned Parenthood League of Mass., Inc. v. Attorney Gen.* , 424 Mass. 586, 590 (1997); *Corning Glass Works v. Ann & Hope, Inc. of Danvers*, 363 Mass. 409, 416 (1973). That the Massachusetts Constitution is in some instances more protective of individual liberty interests than is the Federal Constitution is not surprising. Fundamental to the vigor of our Federal system of government is that "state courts are absolutely free to interpret state constitutional provisions to accord greater protection to individual rights than do similar provisions of the United States Constitution." *Arizona v. Evans*, 514 U.S. 1, 8 (1995).

The individual liberty and equality safeguards of the Massachusetts Constitution protect both "freedom from" unwarranted government intrusion into protected spheres of life and "freedom to" partake in benefits created by the State for the common good. See *Bachrach v. Secretary of the Commonwealth*, 382 Mass. 268, 273 (1981); *Dalli v. Board of Educ.* , 358 Mass. 753, 759 (1971). Both freedoms are involved here. Whether and whom to marry, how to express sexual intimacy, and whether and how to establish a family—these are among the most basic of every individual's liberty and due process rights. See, e.g., *Lawrence, supra* at 2481; *Planned Parenthood of Southeastern Pa. v. Casey*, 505 U.S. 833, 851 (1992); *Zablocki v. Redhail*, 434 U.S. 374, 384 (1978); *Roe v. Wade*, 410 U.S. 113, 152-153 (1973); *Eisenstadt v. Baird*, 405 U.S. 438, 453 (1972); *Loving v. Virginia*, supra. And central to personal freedom and security is the assurance that the laws will apply equally to persons in similar situations. "Absolute equality before the law is a

fundamental principle of our own Constitution." Opinion of the Justices, 211 Mass. 618, 619 (1912). The liberty interest in choosing whether and whom to marry would be hollow if the Commonwealth could, without sufficient justification, foreclose an individual from freely choosing the person with whom to share an exclusive commitment in the unique institution of civil marriage.

The Massachusetts Constitution requires, at a minimum, that the exercise of the State's regulatory authority not be "arbitrary or capricious." *Commonwealth v. Henry's Drywall Co.*, 366 Mass. 539, 542 (1974). Under both the equality and liberty guarantees, regulatory authority must, at very least, serve "a legitimate purpose in a rational way"; a statute must "bear a reasonable relation to a permissible legislative objective." *Rushworth v. Registrar of Motor Vehicles*, 413 Mass. 265, 270 (1992). See, e.g., *Massachusetts Fed'n of Teachers v. Board of Educ.* , 436 Mass. 763, 778 (2002) (equal protection); *Coffee-Rich, Inc. v. Commissioner of Pub. Health*, 348 Mass. 414, 422 (1965) (due process). Any law failing to satisfy the basic standards of rationality is void.

The plaintiffs challenge the marriage statute on both equal protection and due process grounds. With respect to each such claim, we must first determine the appropriate standard of review. Where a statute implicates a fundamental right or uses a suspect classification, we employ "strict judicial scrutiny." *Lowell v. Kowalski*, 380 Mass. 663, 666 (1980). For all other statutes, we employ the " 'rational basis' test." *English v. New England Med. Ctr.*, 405 Mass. 423, 428 (1989). For due process claims, rational basis analysis requires that statutes "bear[ ] a real and substantial relation to the public health, safety, morals, or some other phase of the general welfare." *Coffee-Rich, Inc. v. Commissioner of Pub. Health, supra*, quoting *Sperry & Hutchinson Co. v. Director of the Div. on the Necessaries of Life*, 307 Mass. 408, 418 (1940). For equal protection challenges, the rational basis test requires that "an impartial lawmaker could logically believe that the classification would serve a legitimate public purpose that transcends the harm to the members of the disadvantaged class." *English v. New England Med. Ctr., supra* at 429, quoting *Cleburne v. Cleburne Living Ctr., Inc.*, 473 U.S. 432, 452 (1985) (Stevens, J., concurring).

The department argues that no fundamental right or "suspect" class is at issue here, and rational basis is the appropriate standard of review. For the reasons we explain below, we conclude that the marriage ban does not meet the rational basis test for either due process or equal protection. Because the statute does not survive rational basis review, we do not consider the plaintiffs' arguments that this case merits strict judicial scrutiny.

The department posits three legislative rationales for prohibiting same-sex couples from marrying: (1) providing

Co-plaintiff Ellen Wade (left, center) holds hands with her partner, Maureen Brodoff, following the decision in *Goodridge v. Public Health Department* case that allowed same-sex marriages in Massachusetts. © AP IMAGES/JIM ROGASH.

a "favorable setting for procreation"; (2) ensuring the optimal setting for child rearing, which the department defines as "a two-parent family with one parent of each sex"; and (3) preserving scarce State and private financial resources. We consider each in turn.

The judge in the Superior Court endorsed the first rationale, holding that "the state's interest in regulating marriage is based on the traditional concept that marriage's primary purpose is procreation." This is incorrect. Our laws of civil marriage do not privilege procreative heterosexual intercourse between married people above every other form of adult intimacy and every other means of creating a family. General Laws c. 207 contains no requirement that the applicants for a marriage license attest to their ability or intention to conceive children by coitus. Fertility is not a condition of marriage, nor is it grounds for divorce. People who have never consummated their marriage, and never plan to, may be and stay married. See *Franklin v. Franklin*, 154 Mass. 515, 516 (1891) ("The consummation of a marriage by coition is not necessary to its validity"). People who cannot stir

from their deathbed may marry. See G.L. c. 207, § 28A. While it is certainly true that many, perhaps most, married couples have children together (assisted or unassisted), it is the exclusive and permanent commitment of the marriage partners to one another, not the begetting of children, that is the sine qua non of civil marriage.

Moreover, the Commonwealth affirmatively facilitates bringing children into a family regardless of whether the intended parent is married or unmarried, whether the child is adopted or born into a family, whether assistive technology was used to conceive the child, and whether the parent or her partner is heterosexual, homosexual, or bisexual. If procreation were a necessary component of civil marriage, our statutes would draw a tighter circle around the permissible bounds of nonmarital child bearing and the creation of families by noncoital means. The attempt to isolate procreation as "the source of a fundamental right to marry," post at (Cordy, J., dissenting), overlooks the integrated way in which courts have examined the complex and overlapping realms of personal autonomy, marriage, family life, and child rearing. Our jurisprudence recognizes that, in these nuanced and fundamentally private areas of life, such a narrow focus is inappropriate.

The "marriage is procreation" argument singles out the one unbridgeable difference between same-sex and opposite-sex couples, and transforms that difference into the essence of legal marriage. Like "Amendment 2" to the Constitution of Colorado, which effectively denied homosexual persons equality under the law and full access to the political process, the marriage restriction impermissibly "identifies persons by a single trait and then denies them protection across the board." *Romer v. Evans*, 517 U.S. 620, 633 (1996). In so doing, the State's action confers an official stamp of approval on the destructive stereotype that same-sex relationships are inherently unstable and inferior to opposite-sex relationships and are not worthy of respect.

The department's first stated rationale, equating marriage with unassisted heterosexual procreation, shades imperceptibly into its second: that confining marriage to opposite-sex couples ensures that children are raised in the "optimal" setting. Protecting the welfare of children is a paramount State policy. Restricting marriage to opposite-sex couples, however, cannot plausibly further this policy. "The demographic changes of the past century make it difficult to speak of an average American family. The composition of families varies greatly from household to household." *Troxel v. Granville*, 530 U.S. 57, 63 (2000). Massachusetts has responded supportively to "the changing realities of the American family," *id.* at 64, and has moved vigorously to strengthen the modern family in its many variations. See, e.g., G.L. c. 209C (paternity statute); G.L. c. 119, § 39D (grandparent visitation statute); *Blixt v. Blixt*, 437 Mass. 649 (2002), cert. denied, 537 U.S. 1189 (2003) (same); *E.N.O. v. L.M.M.*, 429 Mass. 824, cert. denied, 528 U.S. 1005 (1999) (de facto parent); *Youmans v. Ramos*, 429 Mass. 774, 782 (1999) (same); and Adoption of Tammy, 416 Mass. 205 (1993) (coparent adoption). Moreover, we have repudiated the common-law power of the State to provide varying levels of protection to children based on the circumstances of birth. See G.L. c. 209C (paternity statute); *Powers v. Wilkinson*, 399 Mass. 650, 661 (1987) ("Ours is an era in which logic and compassion have impelled the law toward unburdening children from the stigma and the disadvantages heretofore attendant upon the status of illegitimacy"). The "best interests of the child" standard does not turn on a parent's sexual orientation or marital status. See e.g., *Doe v. Doe*, 16 Mass.App.Ct. 499, 503 (1983) (parent's sexual orientation insufficient ground to deny custody of child in divorce action). See also *E.N.O. v. L.M.M.*, *supra* at 829-830 (best interests of child determined by considering child's relationship with biological and de facto same-sex parents); *Silvia v. Silvia*, 9 Mass.

App.Ct. 339, 341 & n. 3 (1980) (collecting support and custody statutes containing no gender distinction).

The department has offered no evidence that forbidding marriage to people of the same sex will increase the number of couples choosing to enter into opposite-sex marriages in order to have and raise children. There is thus no rational relationship between the marriage statute and the Commonwealth's proffered goal of protecting the "optimal" child rearing unit. Moreover, the department readily concedes that people in same-sex couples may be "excellent" parents. These couples (including four of the plaintiff couples) have children for the reasons others do—to love them, to care for them, to nurture them. But the task of child rearing for same-sex couples is made infinitely harder by their status as outliers to the marriage laws. While establishing the parentage of children as soon as possible is crucial to the safety and welfare of children, see *Culliton v. Beth Israel Deaconness Med. Ctr.*, 435 Mass. 285, 292 (2001), same-sex couples must undergo the sometimes lengthy and intrusive process of second-parent adoption to establish their joint parentage. While the enhanced income provided by marital benefits is an important source of security and stability for married couples and their children, those benefits are denied to families headed by same-sex couples. See, e.g., note 6, supra. While the laws of divorce provide clear and reasonably predictable guidelines for child support, child custody, and property division on dissolution of a marriage, same-sex couples who dissolve their relationships find themselves and their children in the highly unpredictable terrain of equity jurisdiction. See *E.N.O. v. L.M.M.*, *supra*. Given the wide range of public benefits reserved only for married couples, we do not credit the department's contention that the absence of access to civil marriage amounts to little more than an inconvenience to same-sex couples and their children. Excluding same-sex couples from civil marriage will not make children of opposite-sex marriages more secure, but it does prevent children of same-sex couples from enjoying the immeasurable advantages that flow from the assurance of "a stable family structure in which children will be reared, educated, and socialized." Post at (Cordy, J., dissenting).

No one disputes that the plaintiff couples are families, that many are parents, and that the children they are raising, like all children, need and should have the fullest opportunity to grow up in a secure, protected family unit. Similarly, no one disputes that, under the rubric of marriage, the State provides a cornucopia of substantial benefits to married parents and their children. The preferential treatment of civil marriage reflects the Legislature's conclusion that marriage "is the foremost setting for the education and socialization of children" precisely because it "encourages parents to remain committed to each other and to their children as they grow." Post at (Cordy, J., dissenting).

In this case, we are confronted with an entire, sizeable class of parents raising children who have absolutely no access to civil marriage and its protections because they are forbidden from procuring a marriage license. It cannot be rational under our laws, and indeed it is not permitted, to penalize children by depriving them of State benefits because the State disapproves of their parents' sexual orientation.

The third rationale advanced by the department is that limiting marriage to opposite-sex couples furthers the Legislature's interest in conserving scarce State and private financial resources. The marriage restriction is rational, it argues, because the General Court logically could assume that same-sex couples are more financially independent than married couples and thus less needy of public marital benefits, such as tax advantages, or private marital benefits, such as employer-financed health plans that include spouses in their coverage.

An absolute statutory ban on same-sex marriage bears no rational relationship to the goal of economy. First, the department's conclusory generalization—that same-sex couples are less financially dependent on each other than opposite-sex couples—ignores that many same-sex couples, such as many of the plaintiffs in this case, have children and other dependents (here, aged parents) in their care. The department does not contend, nor could it, that these dependents are less needy or deserving than the dependents of married couples. Second, Massachusetts marriage laws do not condition receipt of public and private financial benefits to married individuals on a demonstration of financial dependence on each other; the benefits are available to married couples regardless of whether they mingle their finances or actually depend on each other for support.

The department suggests additional rationales for prohibiting same-sex couples from marrying, which are developed by some amici. It argues that broadening civil marriage to include same-sex couples will trivialize or destroy the institution of marriage as it has historically been fashioned. Certainly our decision today marks a significant change in the definition of marriage as it has been inherited from the common law, and understood by many societies for centuries. But it does not disturb the fundamental value of marriage in our society.

Here, the plaintiffs seek only to be married, not to undermine the institution of civil marriage. They do not want marriage abolished. They do not attack the binary nature of marriage, the consanguinity provisions, or any of the other gate-keeping provisions of the marriage licensing law. Recognizing the right of an individual to marry a person of the same sex will not diminish the validity or

dignity of opposite-sex marriage, any more than recognizing the right of an individual to marry a person of a different race devalues the marriage of a person who marries someone of her own race. If anything, extending civil marriage to same-sex couples reinforces the importance of marriage to individuals and communities. That same-sex couples are willing to embrace marriage's solemn obligations of exclusivity, mutual support, and commitment to one another is a testament to the enduring place of marriage in our laws and in the human spirit.

It has been argued that, due to the State's strong interest in the institution of marriage as a stabilizing social structure, only the Legislature can control and define its boundaries. Accordingly, our elected representatives legitimately may choose to exclude same-sex couples from civil marriage in order to assure all citizens of the Commonwealth that (1) the benefits of our marriage laws are available explicitly to create and support a family setting that is, in the Legislature's view, optimal for child rearing, and (2) the State does not endorse gay and lesbian parenthood as the equivalent of being raised by one's married biological parents. These arguments miss the point. The Massachusetts Constitution requires that legislation meet certain criteria and not extend beyond certain limits. It is the function of courts to determine whether these criteria are met and whether these limits are exceeded. In most instances, these limits are defined by whether a rational basis exists to conclude that legislation will bring about a rational result. The Legislature in the first instance, and the courts in the last instance, must ascertain whether such a rational basis exists. To label the court's role as usurping that of the Legislature, see, e.g., *post* at (Cordy, J., dissenting), is to misunderstand the nature and purpose of judicial review. We owe great deference to the Legislature to decide social and policy issues, but it is the traditional and settled role of courts to decide constitutional issues.

The history of constitutional law "is the story of the extension of constitutional rights and protections to people once ignored or excluded." *United States v. Virginia*, 518 U.S. 515, 557 (1996) (construing equal protection clause of the Fourteenth Amendment to prohibit categorical exclusion of women from public military institute). This statement is as true in the area of civil marriage as in any other area of civil rights. See, e.g., *Turner v. Safley*, 482 U.S. 78 (1987); *Loving v. Virginia*, 388 U.S. 1 (1967); *Perez v. Sharp*, 32 Cal.2d 711 (1948). As a public institution and a right of fundamental importance, civil marriage is an evolving paradigm. The common law was exceptionally harsh toward women who became wives: a woman's legal identity all but evaporated into that of her husband. See generally C. P. Kindregan, Jr., & M. L. Inker, Family Law and Practice §§ 1.9 and 1.10

(3d ed.2002). Thus, one early Nineteenth Century jurist could observe matter of factly that, prior to the abolition of slavery in Massachusetts, "the condition of a slave resembled the connection of a wife with her husband, and of infant children with their father. He is obliged to maintain them, and they cannot be separated from him." *Winchendon v. Hatfield*, 4 Mass. 123, 129 (1808). But since at least the middle of the Nineteenth Century, both the courts and the Legislature have acted to ameliorate the harshness of the common-law regime. In *Bradford v. Worcester*, 184 Mass. 557, 562 (1904), we refused to apply the common-law rule that the wife's legal residence was that of her husband to defeat her claim to a municipal "settlement of paupers." In *Lewis v. Lewis*, 370 Mass. 619, 629 (1976), we abrogated the common-law doctrine immunizing a husband against certain suits because the common-law rule was predicated on "antediluvian assumptions concerning the role and status of women in marriage and in society." *Id.* at 621. Alarms about the imminent erosion of the "natural" order of marriage were sounded over the demise of antimiscegenation laws, the expansion of the rights of married women, and the introduction of "no-fault" divorce. Marriage has survived all of these transformations, and we have no doubt that marriage will continue to be a vibrant and revered institution.

We also reject the argument suggested by the department, and elaborated by some amici, that expanding the institution of civil marriage in Massachusetts to include same-sex couples will lead to interstate conflict. We would not presume to dictate how another State should respond to today's decision. But neither should considerations of comity prevent us from according Massachusetts residents the full measure of protection available under the Massachusetts Constitution. The genius of our Federal system is that each State's Constitution has vitality specific to its own traditions, and that, subject to the minimum requirements of the Fourteenth Amendment, each State is free to address difficult issues of individual liberty in the manner its own Constitution demands.

Several amici suggest that prohibiting marriage by same-sex couples reflects community consensus that homosexual conduct is immoral. Yet Massachusetts has a strong affirmative policy of preventing discrimination on the basis of sexual orientation. See G.L. c. 151B (employment, housing, credit, services); G.L. c. 265, § 39 (hate crimes); G.L. c. 272, § 98 (public accommodation); G.L. c. 76, § 5 (public education). See also, e.g., *Commonwealth v. Balthazar*, 366 Mass. 298 (1974) (decriminalization of private consensual adult conduct); *Doe v. Doe*, 16 Mass.App.Ct. 499, 503 (1983) (custody to homosexual parent not per se prohibited).

The department has had more than ample opportunity to articulate a constitutionally adequate justification for limiting civil marriage to opposite-sex unions. It has failed to do so. The department has offered purported justifications for the civil marriage restriction that are starkly at odds with the comprehensive network of vigorous, gender-neutral laws promoting stable families and the best interests of children. It has failed to identify any relevant characteristic that would justify shutting the door to civil marriage to a person who wishes to marry someone of the same sex.

The marriage ban works a deep and scarring hardship on a very real segment of the community for no rational reason. The absence of any reasonable relationship between, on the one hand, an absolute disqualification of same-sex couples who wish to enter into civil marriage and, on the other, protection of public health, safety, or general welfare, suggests that the marriage restriction is rooted in persistent prejudices against persons who are (or who are believed to be) homosexual. "The Constitution cannot control such prejudices but neither can it tolerate them. Private biases may be outside the reach of the law, but the law cannot, directly or indirectly, give them effect." *Palmore v. Sidoti*, 466 U.S. 429, 433 (1984) (construing Fourteenth Amendment). Limiting the protections, benefits, and obligations of civil marriage to opposite-sex couples violates the basic premises of individual liberty and equality under law protected by the Massachusetts Constitution.

IV.

We consider next the plaintiffs' request for relief. We preserve as much of the statute as may be preserved in the face of the successful constitutional challenge. See *Mayor of Boston v. Treasure & Receiver Gen.*, 384 Mass. 718, 725 (1981); *Dalli v. Board of Educ.*, 358 Mass. 753, 759 (1971). See also G.L. c. 4, § 6, Eleventh.

Here, no one argues that striking down the marriage laws is an appropriate form of relief. Eliminating civil marriage would be wholly inconsistent with the Legislature's deep commitment to fostering stable families and would dismantle a vital organizing principle of our society. We face a problem similar to one that recently confronted the Court of Appeal for Ontario, the highest court of that Canadian province, when it considered the constitutionality of the same-sex marriage ban under Canada's Federal Constitution, the Charter of Rights and Freedoms (Charter). See *Halpern v. Toronto (City)*, 172 O.A.C. 276 (2003). Canada, like the United States, adopted the common law of England that civil marriage is "the voluntary union for life of one man and one woman, to the exclusion of all others." *Id.* at, quoting *Hyde v. Hyde*, [1861-1873] All E.R. 175 (1866). In holding that the limitation of civil marriage to opposite- sex couples violated the Charter, the Court of Appeal refined the common-law meaning of marriage. We concur with this remedy, which is entirely consonant with established principles of jurisprudence empowering a court to refine a common-law principle in light of evolving constitutional standards. See *Powers v. Wilkinson*, 399 Mass. 650, 661-662 (1987) (reforming the common-law rule of construction of "issue"); *Lewis v. Lewis*, 370 Mass. 619, 629 (1976) (abolishing common-law rule of certain interspousal immunity).

We construe civil marriage to mean the voluntary union of two persons as spouses, to the exclusion of all others. This reformulation redresses the plaintiffs' constitutional injury and furthers the aim of marriage to promote stable, exclusive relationships. It advances the two legitimate State interests the department has identified: providing a stable setting for child rearing and conserving State resources. It leaves intact the Legislature's broad discretion to regulate marriage. See *Commonwealth v. Stowell*, 389 Mass. 171, 175 (1983).

In their complaint the plaintiffs request only a declaration that their exclusion and the exclusion of other qualified same-sex couples from access to civil marriage violates Massachusetts law. We declare that barring an individual from the protections, benefits, and obligations of civil marriage solely because that person would marry a person of the same sex violates the Massachusetts Constitution. We vacate the summary judgment for the department. We remand this case to the Superior Court for entry of judgment consistent with this opinion. Entry of judgment shall be stayed for 180 days to permit the Legislature to take such action as it may deem appropriate in light of this opinion. See, e.g., *Michaud v. Sheriff of Essex County*, 390 Mass. 523, 535-536 (1983). *So ordered.* GREANEY, J.

FURTHER RESOURCES

Books

Chauncey, George. *Why Marriage: The History Shaping Today's Debate Over Gay Equality*. New York: Basic Books, 2005.

Corvino, John, and Maggie Gallagher. *Debating Same-Sex Marriage (Point/Counterpoint)*. Oxford, UK: Oxford University Press, 2012.

Gerstmann, Evan. *Same-Sex Marriage and the Constitution*. Cambridge, UK: Cambridge University Press, 2008.

Web Sites

"Gay Marriage." *ProCon.org*. http://gaymarriage.procon.org/ (accessed on March 20, 2013).

"Gay Rights in the US, State by State." *The Guardian*. www.guardian.co.uk/world/interactive/2012/may/08/gay-rights-united-states (accessed on March 20, 2013).

"Same-Sex Marriage, Civil Unions, and Domestic Partnerships." *New York Times*. http://topics.nytimes.com/top/reference/timestopics/subjects/s/same_sex_marriage/index.html (accessed on March 20, 2013).

"The Man Who Knew"

Web site article

By: Rebecca Leung

Date: February 4, 2004

Source: Leung, Rebecca. "The Man Who Knew." *CBS News*, February 4, 2004. www.cbsnews.com/stories/2003/10/14/60II/main577975.shtml (accessed on March 7, 2013).

About the News Agency: In 1934, the radio broadcasting upstart Columbia Broadcasting System (CBS) launched CBS News, the first full-coverage, live radio news division in the United States. The reporting agency gained popularity and repute among American listeners for the charisma of its news reporters and its reliable coverage of global events like World War II. CBS transitioned profitably into the television market in the 1940s, becoming the nation's largest television network by the 2000s. The broadcaster's ubiquity helped maintain the popularity of CBS News, which became one of the leading news sources in the world, reporting on a variety of national, local, and international topics in several formats across the globe.

INTRODUCTION

Following the Gulf War (August 1990–February 1991), in which the country of Iraq had acted as the aggressor against neighboring Kuwait, the United Nations Security Council passed a series of resolutions prohibiting Iraq from possessing, producing, or acquiring the materials necessary to produce weapons of mass destruction (WMDs), a category of exceptionally deadly armaments that includes chemical, biological, and nuclear weapons. Iraq's oft-belligerent leader, President Saddam Hussein, was publicly compliant with the UN measures, but was suspected by members of the international political community to be covertly acting in defiance of the clauses prohibiting nuclear and chemical weapons development. These concerns culminated in the establishment of a special UN committee to monitor Iraq's weapons and military programs through on-site inspection and document analysis, which was known as the United Nations Special Commission (UNSCOM).

As the 1990s decade progressed, it became apparent that Hussein had no intention of complying with the UN disarmament resolutions or permitting

UNSCOM investigators full, unfettered access to suspect facilities and documents. Escalating tensions between Iraq and international officials hoping to prevent war crimes or genocide led to military intervention (and almost full-scale conflict) several times, creating a lingering atmosphere of mutual distrust. By the end of the 1990s, the UNSCOM initiative had given up hope and left Iraq altogether, citing Hussein's constant attempts to frustrate their investigations. All subsequent proposals to reinstate a disarmament oversight process in Iraq were met with unequivocal rejection.

In 2002, as the United States began preparing for its armed invasion of Iraq, it presented the public and the United Nations with a litany of assertions intended to justify military action. Chief among these justifications was the claim that Saddam Hussein and his regime were in possession of WMDs and thus posed a grave, certain threat to international stability, a statement made with such frequency and assuredness that it became accepted as fact. In truth, however, Iraq had never developed or possessed WMDs, as Coalition forces were to discover after thoroughly ravaging the nation.

SIGNIFICANCE

The revelation that the violation of Iraq's sovereignty was carried out under false pretenses outraged some members of the American public and vindicated others, but had little impact on the conduct of the U.S. military, which continued to occupy the nation until December 2011. Experts and policy officials involved in investigating Iraq prior to the invasion stated that they had repeatedly discredited the information used as evidence of Iraq's possession of WMDs, which included falsified reports, inaccurate intelligence, and misinterpreted satellite photos, but that the U.S. government ignored their objections.

Military insiders and government personnel indicated that the United States may have been aware of the faults in its intelligence on Iraq but deliberately concealed them to lend legitimacy to the decision to invade. Some even went so far as to claim that the United States wholly fabricated information to create a favorable international opinion on its hostile military action in Iraq. Whatever the case, the administration was able to sidestep the issue by shifting the focus of its rhetoric from its claims of diffusing a threat to international peace and towards claims of defending the people of Iraq from oppression at the hands of Saddam Hussein and his authoritarian Ba'ath regime.

PRIMARY SOURCE

"THE MAN WHO KNEW"

SYNOPSIS: This report explains the reaction of U.S. secretary of state Colin Powell to the absence of WMDs in Iraq, as well as detailing inaccuracies in the intelligence used by the United States to justify its invasion of Iraq.

In February, Secretary of State Colin Powell made a surprising admission.

He told *The Washington Post* that he doesn't know whether he would have recommended the invasion of Iraq if he had been told at the time that there were no stockpiles of banned weapons.

Powell said that when he made the case for war before the United Nations one year ago, he used evidence that reflected the best judgments of the intelligence agencies.

But long before the war started, there was plenty of doubt among intelligence analysts about Saddam's weapons.

One analyst, Greg Thielmann, told Correspondent Scott Pelley last October that key evidence cited by the administration was misrepresented to the public.

Thielmann should know. He had been in charge of analyzing the Iraqi weapons threat for Powell's own intelligence bureau.

"I had a couple of initial reactions. Then I had a more mature reaction," says Thielmann, commenting on Powell's presentation to the United Nations last February.

"I think my conclusion now is that it's probably one of the low points in his long, distinguished service to the nation."

Thielmann was a foreign service officer for 25 years. His last job at the State Department was acting director of the Office of Strategic Proliferation and Military Affairs, which was responsible for analyzing the Iraqi weapons threat.

He and his staff had the highest security clearances, and saw virtually everything—whether it came into the CIA or the Defense Department.

Thielmann was admired at the State Department. One high-ranking official called him honorable, knowledgeable, and very experienced. Thielmann had planned to retire just four months before Powell's big moment before the U.N. Security Council.

On Feb. 5, 2003, Secretary Powell presented evidence against Saddam: "The gravity of this moment is matched by the gravity of the threat that Iraq's weapons of mass destruction pose to the world."

At the time, Thielmann says that Iraq didn't pose an imminent threat to the U.S.: "I think it didn't even

U.S. secretary of state Colin Powell address the United Nations Security Council on the topic of weapons inspections in Iraq on February 14, 2003. © AP IMAGES/KATHY WILLENS.

constitute an imminent threat to its neighbors at the time we went to war."

And Thielmann says that's what the intelligence really showed. For example, he points to the evidence behind Powell's charge that Iraq was importing aluminum tubes to use in a program to build nuclear weapons.

Powell said: "Saddam Hussein is determined to get his hands on a nuclear bomb. He is so determined that he has made repeated covert attempts to acquire high-specification aluminum tubes from 11 different countries even after inspections resumed."

"This is one of the most disturbing parts of Secretary Powell's speech for us," says Thielmann.

Intelligence agents intercepted the tubes in 2001, and the CIA said they were parts for a centrifuge to enrich uranium—fuel for an atom bomb. But Thielmann wasn't so sure.

Experts at the Oak Ridge National Laboratory, the scientists who enriched uranium for American bombs, advised that the tubes were all wrong for a bomb program. At about the same time, Thielmann's office was working on another explanation. It turned out the tubes' dimensions perfectly matched an Iraqi conventional rocket.

"The aluminum was exactly, I think, what the Iraqis wanted for artillery," recalls Thielmann, who says he sent that word up to the Secretary of State months before.

Houston Wood was a consultant who worked on the Oak Ridge analysis of the tubes. He watched Powell's speech, too.

"I guess I was angry, that's the best way to describe my emotions. I was angry at that," says Wood, who is among the world's authorities on uranium enrichment by centrifuge. He found the tubes couldn't be what the CIA thought they were. They were too heavy, three times too thick and certain to leak.

"Wasn't going to work. They would have failed," says Wood, who reached that conclusion back in 2001.

Thielmann reported to Secretary Powell's office that they were confident the tubes were not for a nuclear program. Then, about a year later, when the administration was building a case for war, the tubes were resurrected on the front page of The New York Times.

"I thought when I read that there must be some other tubes that people were talking about. I just was flabbergasted that people were still pushing that those might be centrifuges," says Wood.

The New York Times reported that senior administration officials insisted the tubes were for an atom-bomb program.

"Science was not pushing this forward. Scientists had made their determination, their evaluation, and now we didn't know what was happening," says Wood.

In his U.N. speech, Secretary Powell acknowledged there was disagreement about the tubes, but he said most experts agreed with the nuclear theory.

"There is controversy about what these tubes are for. Most U.S. experts think they are intended to serve as rotors in centrifuges used to enrich uranium," said Powell.

"Most experts are located at Oak Ridge and that was not the position there," says Wood, who claims he doesn't know anyone in academia or foreign government who would disagree with his appraisal. "I don't know a single one anywhere." . . .

In his State of the Union address, the president said: "The British government has learned that Saddam Hussein recently sought significant quantities of uranium from Africa. Our intelligence sources tell us that he has attempted to purchase high-strength aluminum tubes suitable for nuclear-weapons production."

After the war, the White House said the African uranium claim was false and shouldn't have been in the president's address. But at the time, it was part of a campaign that painted the intelligence as irrefutable.

"There is no doubt that Saddam Hussein now has weapons of mass destruction. There is no doubt he is amassing them to use against our friends, against our allies, and against us," said Vice President Dick Cheney.

Powell said: "My colleagues, every statement I make today is backed up by sources, solid sources. These are not assertions. What we are giving you are facts and conclusions based on solid intelligence."

It was solid intelligence, Powell said, that proved Saddam had amassed chemical and biological weapons: "Our conservative estimate is that Iraq today has a stockpile of between 100 and 500 tons of chemical-weapons agent." . . .

Satellite photos were also notoriously misleading, according to Steve Allinson, a U.N. inspector in Iraq in the months leading up to war.

Was there ever a time when American satellite intelligence provided Allinson with something that was truly useful?

"No. No, not to me. Not on inspections that I participated in," says Allinson, whose team was sent to find decontamination vehicles that turned out to be fire trucks.

Another time, a satellite spotted what they thought were trucks used for biological weapons.

"We were told we were going to the site to look for refrigerated trucks specifically linked to biological agents," says Allinson. "We found 7 or 8 of them, I think, in total. And they had cobwebs in them. Some samples were taken and nothing was found."

If Allinson doubted the satellite evidence, Thielmann watched with worry as Secretary Powell told the Security Council that human intelligence provided conclusive proof.

Thielmann says that many of the human sources were defectors who came forward with an ax to grind. But how reliable was the defector information they received

"I guess I would say, frequently we got bad information," says Thielmann.

Some of it came from defectors supplied by the Iraqi National Congress, the leading exile group headed by Ahmed Chalabi.

"You had the Iraqi National Congress with a clear motive for presenting the worst possible picture of what was happening in Iraq to the American government," says Thielmann.

But there was a good deal more in Secretary Powell's speech that bothered the analysts. Powell claimed Saddam still had a few dozen Scud missiles.

"I wondered what he was talking about," says Thielmann. "We did not have evidence that the Iraqis had those missiles, pure and simple."

Last week, David Kay, the former chief U.S. arms inspector, said his team found no stockpiles of banned weapons. His assessment of 12 years of U.S. intelligence was this: "Let me begin by saying we were almost all wrong and I certainly include myself here.... My view was that the best evidence that I had seen was that Iraq indeed had weapons of mass destruction."

Secretary Powell declined an interview for this broadcast. But as *60 Minutes II* mentioned earlier, Powell told *The Washington Post* this week that he doesn't know if he would have recommended invasion if he'd know(n) then that there were no stockpiles of weapons.

But Tuesday, he added this: "The bottom line is this. The president made the right decision. He made the right decision based on the history of this regime, the intention that this terrible leader, terrible despotic leader had the capabilities on a variety of levels. The delivery systems were there, and nobody's debating that, the infrastructure that was there, the technical know-how that was there. The only thing we are debating are the stockpiles."

Thursday marks one year since Secretary Powell's U. N. speech. In that time, Thielmann has come to his own conclusion about the presentation. He believes the decision to go to war was made - and intelligence was interpreted to fit that conclusion.

"There's plenty of blame to go around. The main problem was that the senior administration officials have what I call faith-based intelligence. They knew what they wanted the intelligence to show," says Thielmann....

FURTHER RESOURCES

Books

Auerswald, Philip E.. *Iraq, 1990–2006: A Diplomatic History Through Documents.* Cambridge, UK: Cambridge University Press, 2009.

Blix, Hans. *Disarming Iraq.* Ann Arbor, MI: Pantheon, 2004.

Whitney, Craig R. *The WMD Mirage: Iraq's Decade of Deception and America's False Premise for War.* New York: PublicAffairs, 2005.

Web Sites

"Iraq WMD Timeline: How the Mystery Unraveled." NPR News. www.npr.org/templates/story/story.php?storyId= 4996218 (accessed on March 7, 2013).

"Report to the President of the United States." Commission on the Intelligence Capabilities of the United States Regarding Weapons of Mass Destruction. www. nytimes.com/packages/pdf/politics/20050331_wmd_ report.pdf (accessed on March 7, 2013).

"U.S Secretary of State Colin Powell Addresses the U.N. Security Council." georgewbush-whitehouse.archives. gov/news/releases/2003/02/20030205-1.html (accessed on March 7, 2013).

"Summary of Emergency Economic Stabilization Act of 2008—Signed into Law Oct. 3, 2008"

Law

By: Financial Markets Crisis Resource Center

Date: 2009

Source: "Summary of Emergency Economic Stabilization Act of 2008—Signed into Law Oct. 3, 2008." *Financial Markets Crisis Resource Center*, 2009. http://ag-marketcrisis.com/blog/2008/10/summary-of-stabilization-bill/ (accessed on March 6, 2013).

About the Organization: The Financial Markets Crisis Resource Center was a temporary service created by the Akin Gump Strauss Hauer & Feld law firm, with the purpose of providing free legal information about the laws implemented in response to the subprime mortgage crisis of 2008. Akin Gump Strauss Hauer & Feld is one of the world's most prestigious corporate law firms, operating in eight U.S. cities, as well as in China, Russia, the United Kingdom, Switzerland, and the United Arab Emirates.

INTRODUCTION

The 2008 economic recession, sometimes called the "Great Recession" in recognition of its unrivaled severity, was among the most troubled economic periods in U.S. history. Although the recession was produced by an incomprehensibly complex series of events, economists agree that its fundamental cause was the bursting of the U.S. mortgage bubble. Housing values had grown rapidly through the first half of the 2000s decade, partially inflated by the practice of trading mortgage-backed securities (MBS)—financial instruments that derived their value from mortgage debt owed to lending institutions, which allowed speculative trading on housing prices, similar to trading on stock options and commodities. Eventually, the artificially inflated housing market rebounded, causing home values to decline sharply. American mortgage recipients, many of whom had agreed to adjustable-rate mortgages (ARMs)—in which the interest rate on the loan is adjusted relative to the value of the property it was being used to purchase—were suddenly faced with houses worth less than the value of the mortgage and interest rates several times higher than they had expected. Such conditions forced large numbers of Americans, unable to make increased payments or unwilling to spend more on their loan than their home was worth, into foreclosure.

Lending institutions, whose income had grown heavily reliant on MBS trading, were devastated by the rash of foreclosures that started after home values peaked in 2006. By 2007, U.S. banks had lost billions of dollars in liquidity due to the sudden devaluation of their securities, causing the availability of credit offered by these banks to fall drastically. International banks, many of whom invested and traded in the U.S. MBS market, grew worried of a potential credit crisis and responded by tightening the availability of their own lending, causing global economic activity to slow. Consumers were consequentially unable to purchase at the same rate as they had during the first half of the decade, causing spending to decrease and further exacerbating the decreasing activity of the U.S. economy. By early 2008, these factors had combined to create a rapidly worsening economic recession, bringing the nation to the brink of financial collapse.

As the economic situation worsened, the financial sector was the hardest-hit. All five of the largest U.S. investment banks faced insolvency by the end of 2008. Recognizing the gravity of the situation, the federal government decided to act decisively to avert the total collapse of the nation's financial industry, which was essentially the engine that drove the rest of the economy by disbursing and disseminating its capital, as well as generating the majority of its gross domestic product (GDP). After the bankruptcy of Lehman Brothers and the forced acquisition of Goldman Sachs and Merrill Lynch by smaller institutions, the U.S. Congress hastily passed the Emergency Economic Stabilization Act of 2008 (EESA), which was signed into law by President George W. Bush on October 3, 2008. The central provision of the act, called the Troubled Assets Relief Program (TARP), authorized the appropriation of up to $700 billion to be used for the direct acquisition of near-worthless assets, particularly MBSs, from lenders, essentially rescuing them from suffering the consequences of their ill-advised lending practices. Commonly referred to as "the bank bailout," the rationale behind TARP was that, by rescuing the central components of the economy from certain destruction, it would prevent further decline in employment and national productivity, as well as inject much-needed credit and liquidity into the market.

In addition to TARP, EESA included a number of other items intended to facilitate the economy's smooth and expedient recovery. The mortgages acquired by the U.S. Treasury Department as assistance to the entities holding them were to be permitted for later sale, in order to recover taxpayer money used to finance the rescue of the financial industry. Firms that received assistance from the program were expressly prohibited from using financial incentives to encourage further risky behavior from executives, and extensive oversight measures were implemented to ensure transparency regarding the use and reinvestment of capital awarded in exchange for troubled assets relief. Finally, the Federal Deposit Insurance Corporation (FDIC) insurance available for deposit was increased from $100,000 to $250,000 until the end of 2009.

SIGNIFICANCE

EESA was met with both celebration and objection. Fiscal conservatives and liberal opponents of corporate welfare criticized TARP as a taxpayer-funded subsidization of an industry plagued by irresponsible and self-destructive practices. Such critics noted that the majority of foreclosures stemmed from subprime mortgages—home loans granted to parties that did not meet the standard criteria required to receive such loans, but given them anyway at heightened interest rates—and claimed that the banks were suffering the consequences of such myopic, greedy conduct. Others protested that EESA did nothing to assist in broad economic recovery or help rescue Americans from having their homes foreclosed upon, but was rather a taxpayer gift to the banks that had caused the recession in the first place. The primary objection to EESA among members of Congress was that the bill was passed too quickly, without giving proper consideration to other means by which to legislatively assist economic recovery.

Despite these objections, by most accounts TARP was reasonably successful in achieving its aim of averting the collapse of the U.S. financial industry. As of 2012, a total of $165.33 billion in bailout funds had been dispensed directly to financial institutions worth over $10 billion each. Only $4.47 billion of that money was still unpaid, and an additional $16 billion was earned for taxpayers as accrued interest and dividends gained by federal investments through TARP. The Obama administration was able to cut the program's expenditures by over $200 billion, thanks to the resilience of the stock market and financial sector after receiving bailout money. However, the broader economy was not able to rebound as quickly. Employment rates remained depressed throughout the end of the decade, as did housing prices.

The Emergency Economic Stabilization Act represented one of the largest national economic interventions in the world's history. Although some condemned it as an attempt to move the United States towards a centralized, state-controlled society, most economists and policy experts recognized it as a necessary action to prevent the disintegration of international commerce and the United States' role as a financial leader. It represented the first in a number of efforts by the federal legislature to alleviate the effects of the 2008 recession and restore the U.S. economy to its full potential.

■ PRIMARY SOURCE

"SUMMARY OF EMERGENCY ECONOMIC STABILIZATION ACT OF 2008—SIGNED INTO LAW OCT. 3, 2008"

SYNOPSIS: This article summarizes the text and purpose of the Emergency Economic Stabilization Bill of 2008.

… The Emergency Economic Stabilization Act of 2008 (the "Act"), … after being passed by the Senate on October 1, 2008, was passed by the House and signed by President Bush on October 3, 2008. The Act will, among other things, "immediately provide authority and facilities that the Secretary of the Treasury can use to restore liquidity and stability to the financial system of the United States." Section 2(1).

General Provisions

The Act grants the Secretary of the Treasury (the "Secretary") authority to establish a troubled asset relief program (the "program") to purchase, and to make and fund commitments to purchase, "troubled assets" from any "financial institution." Section 101(a)(1). "Troubled assets" include "residential or commercial mortgages and any securities, obligations, or other instruments that are based on or related to such mortgages, that in each case was originated or issued on or before March 14, 2008," as well as any other financial instrument that the Secretary, in consultation with the Chairman of the Board of Governors of the Federal Reserve System, deems "necessary to promote financial market stability," so long as such determination is transmitted in writing to certain congressional committees. Section 3(9). A "financial institution" is "any institution, including, but not limited to, any bank, savings association, credit union, security broker or dealer, or insurance company, established and regulated under the laws of the United States or any State … and having significant operations in the United States, but excluding any central bank of, or institution owned by, a foreign government." Section 3(5).

The Act grants the Secretary authority to purchase up to $700 billion of troubled assets under the program. The authority to spend $250 billion goes into effect immediately. Section 115(a)(1). The President may increase the limit to $350 billion at any time by submitting a written certification to Congress. Section 115(a)(2). Authority to spend the final $350 billion goes into effect if the President submits to Congress a written report detailing the Secretary's plan to spend it, unless Congress enacts a joint resolution disapproving of the plan within fifteen days of such submission. Section 115(a)(3), (c)(1). …

Mechanics of the Program

The Secretary must implement the program through a newly created Office of Financial Stability (within the Treasury Department's Office of Domestic Finance), which will be headed by an Assistant Secretary of the Treasury appointed by the President with the advice and consent of the Senate. Section 101(a)(3)(A). The Secretary may take such actions as he deems necessary to carry out his authority under the program, including designating financial institutions as agents of the federal government and establishing vehicles authorized to purchase, hold, and sell troubled assets and issue obligations. Section 101(c). …

The Secretary must make purchases using, where appropriate, "market mechanisms, including auctions or reverse auctions." Section 113(b)(2). The Secretary may not purchase or make a commitment to purchase troubled assets from a financial institution unless he receives stock warrants or senior debt instruments in the financial institution. Section 113(d)(1). The Secretary may, however, make de minimis exceptions for financial institutions from which less than $100 million of troubled assets are purchased. Section 113(d)(3)(A).

The Act imposes limits on executive compensation of participating financial institutions in some circumstances. First, if the Secretary makes direct purchases of troubled assets from a financial institution without using market mechanisms and receives in return a "meaningful equity or debt position," then the financial institution must satisfy "appropriate standards for executive compensation and corporate governance." Section 111(b)(1). Such standards include "limits on compensation that exclude incentives for senior executive officers of a financial institution to take unnecessary and excessive risks that threaten the value of the financial institution during the period that the Secretary holds an equity position in the financial institution," "a provision for the recovery by the financial institution of any bonus or incentive compensation paid to a senior executive officer based on statements of earnings, gains, or other criteria that are later proven to be materially inaccurate," and "a prohibition on the financial institution making any golden parachute payment to its senior executive officer during the period that the Secretary holds an equity or debt position in the financial institution." Section 111(b)(2). Second, if the Secretary makes over $300 million in auction purchases from a financial institution, that institution may not enter "any new employment contract with a senior executive officer that provides a golden parachute in the event of an involuntary termination, bankruptcy filing, insolvency, or receivership." Section 111(c). These two provisions only apply, however, to the five highest-paid executives of a financial institution. Section 111(b)(3). Third, in some limited circumstances, the Act caps the income tax deductions participating financial institutions may take with respect to executive compensation. Section 302.

The Secretary has authority to exercise all rights with respect to the purchased assets. Section 106(a). The Secretary may hold the assets to maturity or until "such time as the Secretary determines that the market is optimal for selling such assets, in order to maximize the value for taxpayers." Section 113(a)(2)(A). The Secretary may sell the assets at a price that he determines will, based on "available financial analysis, ... maximize return on investment for the Federal Government." Section 113(a)(2)(B). All proceeds from the program must be paid into the general fund of the Treasury for reduction of the public debt. Section 106(d).

The Act also establishes a Troubled Assets Insurance Financing Fund and authorizes the Secretary to establish a program to guarantee troubled assets. Section 102(a)(1), (d)(2). Under this program, the Secretary will collect premiums from financial institutions seeking such guarantees; these funds will then be used to fulfill obligations of the guarantees. Section 102(c), (d)(1), (3).

Oversight and Reporting

The Act sets out several oversight mechanisms to monitor the Secretary's activities under the program.

First, the Act vests principal oversight responsibility in the Comptroller General. *See* Section 116(a)(1). ... Section 116(a)(2)(A)-(B). The Comptroller General must submit reports on the program at least every two months to certain congressional committees and the Special Inspector General (see below). Section 116(a)(3).

Second, the Act establishes several new entities with oversight responsibilities:

- The Congressional Oversight Panel (COP) is responsible for "review[ing] the current state of the financial markets and the regulatory system." Section 125(b), (b). The COP must submit to Congress monthly reports on the program and, by January 20, 2009, a special report on regulatory reform of the financial system. Section 125(b)(1)-(2). The COP is to be comprised of five members appointed by the Speaker and minority leader of the House of Representatives and the majority and minority leaders of the Senate. Section 125(c)(1).

- The Financial Stability Oversight Board (FSOB) is responsible for, among other things, reviewing and making recommendations regarding the Secretary's exercise of authority under the program. Section 104(a). The FSOB, which must meet monthly, is to be comprised of five members: the Secretary, the Chairman of the Board of Governors of the Federal Reserve System, the Director of the Federal Housing Finance Agency, the Chairman of the Securities and Exchange Commission, and the Secretary of Housing and Urban Development. Section 104(b), (d). The FSOB has the authority to "ensure" that the program is consistent with the purposes of the Act, the economic interests of the United States, and the protection of taxpayers. Section 104(e). The FSOB must report at least quarterly to certain congressional committees and the COP. Section 104(g).

- The Office of the Special Inspector General for the Troubled Asset Program is responsible for, among other things, conducting "audits and investigations" of the program. Section 121(a), (c). The Special Inspector General is appointed by the President with the advice and consent of the Senate. Section 121(b)(1). Starting no later than sixty days after his confirmation to the position, the Special Inspector

General must submit quarterly reports of his activities to several congressional committees. Section 121(f)(1).

Third, the Act directs the Secretary to make various reports to Congress and the public (in addition to those already described above):

- The Secretary must submit to several congressional committees monthly reports, including detailed financial statements, explaining the actions taken pursuant to the program. Section 105(a)....
- The Secretary must prepare and submit to Congress annual financial statements audited by the Comptroller General. Section 116(b).
- *Finally*, the Act provides for judicial review of the Secretary's actions under the program pursuant to the Administrative Procedure Act. Section 119(a)(1)....

Homeowner Protection

The Act contains several provisions designed to protect homeowners. For example, with respect to any mortgages, mortgage-backed securities, and other assets secured by residential real estate purchased under the program, the Secretary must "implement a plan that seeks to maximize assistance for homeowners and use the authority of the Secretary to encourage the servicers of the underlying mortgages ... to take advantage of ... available programs to minimize foreclosures." Section 109(a). The Secretary must also "consent, where appropriate, and considering net present value to the taxpayer, to reasonable requests for loss mitigation measures," *i.e.*, loan modification requests. Section 109(c).... The final Act does, however, contain a new provision temporarily increasing—until December 31, 2009—the FDIC's

deposit insurance limit from $100,000 to $250,000 per account. Section 136(a).

FURTHER RESOURCES
Books
Fried, Joseph. *Who Really Drove the Economy into the Ditch?* New York: Algora, 2012.

Web Sites
"Emergency Economic Stabilization Act." *Wall Street Journal.* http://online.wsj.com/public/resources/documents/senatebillAYO08C32_xml.pdf (accessed on March 6, 2013).

"The Financial Crisis Inquiry Report." *Financial Crisis Inquiry Commission.* www.gpo.gov/fdsys/pkg/GPO-FCIC/pdf/GPO-FCIC.pdf (accessed on March 6, 2013).

"Financial Stability." *U.S. Department of the Treasury.* www.treasury.gov/initiatives/financial-stability/Pages/default.aspx (accessed on March 6, 2013).

"Money, Power & Wall Street." *PBS Frontline*, April 20, 2012. www.pbs.org/wgbh/pages/frontline/business-economy-financial-crisis/money-power-wall-street/dig-deeper-what-you-need-to-know-about-the-financial-crisis/ (accessed on March 6, 2013).

Reeves, Jeff. "2008 TARP Funds—Where Are They Now?" *InvestorPlace*, May 23, 2012. http://investorplace.com/2012/05/2008-tarp-funds-where-are-they-now/ (accessed on March 6, 2013).

Solomon, Deborah. "Estimated TARP Cost Is Cut by $200 Billion." *Wall Street Journal*, December 7, 2009. http://online.wsj.com/article/SB126015764384079549.html (accessed on March 6, 2013).

Lifestyles and Social Trends

Chronology

Important Events in Lifestyles and Social Trends, 2000–2009

2000

- Toyota introduces its hybrid-model, Prius, as a 2001 model year in the United States and immediately generates long waiting lists, evidence of evolving interest in eco-consciousness and climate change.

- On January 1, the so-called Y2K bug does not result in widespread computer malfunctions, inaugurating a decade dominated by digital technology.

- On March 10, the Nasdaq closes at a record high in the frenzy surrounding the Internet bubble. The next day the financial success of Internet start-up companies takes a significant downturn, in what the media call the "dot com bust."

- On April 3, the Supreme Court fines Microsoft Corporation under antitrust laws in a ruling some critics warn might set the precedent for more regulation of the Internet.

- On April 16, Discovery Channel's broadcast of the British series *Walking with Dinosaurs* becomes the most-watched documentary show in cable history.

- On April 19, Oprah Winfrey debuts *O: The Oprah Magazine*.

- On October 26, Sony launches its popular PlayStation 2 video-game console.

- On November 7, the presidential election is too close to call, leading to an extended recount in Florida and a Supreme Court decision (December 12) awarding the office to George W. Bush.

2001

- Bratz, a line of ten-inch multicultural dolls with enlarged heads and modern clothing and makeup, is released in the United States and becomes a favorite toy for young girls. Annual sales reach $500 million in 2008.

- Valerie Gibson publishes *Cougar: A Guide for Older Women Dating Younger Men*, popularizing the use of the word "cougar."

- On January 15, the online encyclopedia Wikipedia is launched with completely user-generated content.

- In June, the Nintendo handheld gaming system, Game Boy Advance, is released for sale in the United States.

- On June 11, comedian Joe Rogan hosts the reality-competition series *Fear Factor*.

- On August 25, popular R&B singer and actress Aaliyah dies in a plane crash in the Bahamas.

- On September 11, suicide bombers hijack four airplanes, crashing two of them into New York City's World Trade Center and one into the Pentagon. The fourth plane crashes in Shanksville, Pennsylvania, killing all forty passengers and airflight crew and the four hijackers aboard.

- On October 23, Apple debuts its handheld MP3 music-file-storing device, the iPod, which quickly becomes one of the most sought-after personal electronic devices.

2002

- Media attention turns to allegations of widespread sexual abuse in the Catholic Church, sparking a crisis that reverberates throughout the decade.

- The BlackBerry smartphone hits the market.

- On January 8, President Bush signs the No Child Left Behind Act.

- In February, merchandise featuring Disney character Lizzie McGuire (played by Hilary Duff) is heavily marketed to pre- and early-teen girls.

- On February 8–24, the Olympic Winter Games are held in Salt Lake City, Utah, and extreme-sports stars such as snowboarders compete for the first time.

- On May 19, the popular science-fiction/thriller series *The X-Files* broadcasts its final episode.

- On June 11, the first season of *American Idol* premieres; the season ends with Kelly Clarkson winning the title in September.

- On October 21, the U.S. Department of Agriculture (USDA) organic label is issued.

2003

- In March, the World Health Organization releases a warning on the respiratory disease SARS (Severe Acute Respiratory Syndrome), sparking worldwide concern and an increase in the use of surgical masks.

- In April, Apple opens its online music-downloading service, iTunes.

- In May, the first "flash mob" occurs in Manhattan; groups of individuals gather suddenly at a location and perform a song or dance, often captured on video, and then the participants quickly disperse.

- On July 15, *Queer Eye for the Straight Guy* premieres on cable network Bravo.

- On October 10, popular conservative talk-radio host Rush Limbaugh admits he has an addiction to painkillers.

- On November 18, the Massachusetts Supreme Court rules anti-same-sex marriage laws unconstitutional; the state legalizes gay marriage in 2004.

2004

- In February, the online social-networking site Facebook debuts.

- On April 29, the World War II Memorial opens on the National Mall. "Honor Flights" are commissioned to enable veterans to attend the dedication, held on May 29.

- In July–August, the major party conventions offer press credentials to bloggers, demonstrating the growing presence of amateur online journalism in mainstream politics.

- On September 22, ABC airs the pilot of *Lost*, which generates devoted followers and demonstrates how television can employ the Internet by linking viewers to several sites related to a program.

- On November 4, eleven states ban gay marriage in local elections as voters report in exit polls that "moral values" are the most important issue on the ballot. President Bush wins reelection, defeating Democratic candidate John Kerry.

- On November 21, the handheld Nintendo DS gaming system is released for sale in the United States.

2005

- A wave of online identity theft plagues Internet users, exposing the danger posed to privacy by the ubiquity of the Internet.

- The Sony PlayStation Portable (PSP) handheld gaming system is released for sale in North America.

- On February 16, the Kyoto Protocol, an international agreement aimed at fighting climate change, goes into effect without the support of the United States.

- In March, YouTube, a video-sharing website, is launched.

- On March 3, millionaire Steve Fossett completes a nonstop solo flight around the globe, breaking a world record.

- In May, the political blog and news aggregator, *The Huffington Post*, is launched.

- On May 19, the final installment of the six-movie *Star Wars* series, *Revenge of the Sith*, opens.

- On July 2, a series of ten simultaneous concerts, known as Live 8, takes place across the world, including one in Philadelphia, to call attention to global poverty.

- On August 29, Hurricane Katrina makes landfall in New Orleans, Louisiana, resulting in a massive storm surge that overcomes the city's levees, leaving much of the town underwater for weeks. Portions of Mississippi and Alabama are also devastated.

2006

- A national survey reveals that nearly one out of every four American adults from the age of eighteen to fifty has at least one tattoo.

- Bakugan Battle Brawlers, a game (based on a Japanese anime series) that employs cards and little magnet-embedded spheres that pop open, becomes popular, especially with young boys.

- On January 24, *An Inconvenient Truth* opens at the Sundance Film Festival. The documentary featuring Al Gore and his mission to educate the American public about climate change becomes one of the most popular documentaries of all time.

- On March 24, the Disney Channel debuts the *Hannah Montana* series, featuring Miley Cyrus in the lead role. The show influences music and style choices of children.

- On April 10, massive protests take place in cities across the country, protesting proposed changes in immigration policy that would make aiding and abetting illegal immigration a felony and rallying for a comprehensive immigration reform.

- In July, microblogging platform Twitter is launched. "Tweeting" quickly becomes a trendy way to publicize events, keep up with celebrities, and break and follow news stories before major media outlets arrive at the scene.

- In August, a major transatlantic terrorist highjacking plot is foiled, leading to new policies for airline passengers, including a ban on bringing liquids through security.

- In November, Democrats gain a majority in Congress, reflecting frustration with the war in Iraq, the mishandling of Hurricane Katrina, and a series of scandals involving Republican politicians.

- On November 20, comedian Michael Richards, best known for his role as "Kramer" on *Seinfeld*, makes racist comments during a stand-up routine and is heavily criticized in the media. He later apologizes.

2007

- Many items made in China—including children's toys, pet food, and makeup—are pulled from U.S. shelves because of health and safety concerns.

- In January, Apple enters the smartphone market with the debut of the iPhone, which quickly becomes the trendsetter in cell-phone design and technology.

- In March, comic character Captain America, who first appeared in print during World War II, is killed off in a story line by Marvel Comics.

- On April 4, radio personality Don Imus makes a racial slur against members of the Rutgers University women's basketball team; he is later fired.

- On April 16, a disturbed student at Virginia Tech goes on a shooting rampage, killing thirty-two people and injuring twenty in the deadliest campus shooting incident in U.S. history. The tragedy leads to upgraded security measures on college campuses nationwide, a close look at mental-health services and safeguards for students, and questions about gun regulation.

- On July 19, the cable drama *Mad Men* premieres. The popularity of the program prompts a resurgence in 1960s-era style in clothing and accessories.

- On September 20, thousands travel to Jena, Louisiana, to protest what they feel is the unfair arrest and harsh sentencing of six young black men for assault in an incident stoked by racial animosity following the display of a noose from a tree in front of the Jena High School.

- In November, the first signs of a major meltdown in the previously robust housing market emerge. The real-estate bust sparks the economic downturn of the latter part of the decade.

- On November 19, the Amazon Kindle ereader debuts. It is soon followed by handheld reading devices designed by Sony, Barnes & Noble, and Apple.

2008

- Rising gas prices lead many Americans to consider trading large vehicles for fuel-efficient or hybrid models, and to make use of public transportation and car-pooling.

- On April 30, the independent Dutton's Bookstore in Los Angeles closes.

- In May, more than six million copies of the video game *Grand Theft Auto IV* are sold in one week.

- In June, California courts legalize same-sex marriage; voters repeal the law in the November elections.

- In July, YouTube cohosts with CNN a two-part presidential debate.

- On July 1, California orders that phone devices in cars must be hands-free. Many states and localities struggle with the phenomena of drivers making cell-phone calls or texting while on the road.

- On July 12, the Harley-Davidson Museum, honoring the motorcycle company that was founded 105 years previously, opens in Milwaukee, Wisconsin.

- On September 13, comedian Tina Fey spoofs Republican vice presidential candidate Sarah Palin on *Saturday Night Live*.

- On November 4, America elects its first African American president, Barack Obama.

- On November 13, millions of fans of the online game *World of Warcraft* line up to buy the latest update.

- On November 21, the Smithsonian Institution's National Museum of American History reopens after a two-year renovation, including a permanent display of the restored Star Spangled Banner.

2009

- In February, the final installment in Neil Gaiman's graphic novel series, *Sandman*, is published.

- On June 11, H1N1 flu, popularly known as "swine flu," is declared a pandemic, putting a high demand on vaccines and leading to the proliferation of hand-sanitizing products in schools and businesses.

- On June 25, pop icon Michael Jackson dies at his home in Los Angeles.

- In July, a national debate over racial profiling is provoked when Harvard English professor Henry

Louis Gates Jr. is accused of breaking into a house (which turns out to be his own home) by a white Cambridge, Massachusetts, police officer. President Obama, who initially criticized the officer, invites both men to the White House for a "beer summit" on July 30 to discuss the issue informally, an incident that tests the "post-racial" climate some hoped the election of an African American president signaled.

- On July 4, radio personality Casey Kasem, host of *American Top Forty*, signs off the air for his last broadcast.

- On September 9, President Obama addresses Congress on the topic of health care, making health-care reform a major element of his domestic agenda and laying the groundwork to transform the way insurance and health care operate.

- On September 13, rapper Kanye West interrupts singer Taylor Swift while she is giving an acceptance speech at the MTV Video Music Awards ceremony, grabbing the microphone to proclaim that Beyonce Knowles should have won the best female music video award.

- In October, major retailers Wal-Mart, Target, and online-store Amazon engage in a major price war over best-selling holiday books, indicating the predominance of online shopping.

- On October 15, a Colorado couple stages a hoax in which they claim one of their sons has drifted off attached to a helium balloon. They will plead guilty in November to charges stemming from the incident.

- In November, *Gourmet* magazine publishes its final issue.

- On November 24, Tareq and Michaela Salahi "crash" a White House dinner and pose for pictures with President Obama and other attendees.

Transportation Security Administration Documents

"What Is TSA?"

Fact sheet

By: Transportation Security Administration

Date: Department formed November 19, 2001; document revised February 6, 2013

Source: "What Is TSA?" *Transportation Security Administration*, February 6, 2013. http://www.tsa.gov/about-tsa/what-tsa (accessed on March 12, 2013).

About the Department: The Transportation Security Administration (TSA) was founded on November 19, 2001, following the September 11, 2001, terrorist attacks. As an arm of the Department of Homeland Security, TSA operations focus heavily on preventing terrorist attacks on American travelers by screening luggage and persons for bombs or weapons, which might be used to carry out such attacks.

"TSA Ramps Up Virtual 'Strip Searches'"

Web site article

By: Olivia Sterns

Date: July 17, 2008

Source: Sterns, Olivia. "TSA Ramps Up Virtual 'Strip Searches'." *ABC News*, July 17, 2008. abcnews.go.com/Travel/BusinessTravel/story?id=5380042&page=1#.T8jApcWTLE0 (accessed on March 12, 2013).

About the News Organization: Compared to its direct competitors, ABC News got a late start in the U.S. news environment. The organization was founded as a division of the American Broadcasting Company in 1945, two years after the company's formation, and it immediately initiated a regular radio news schedule. ABC News consistently placed third in listenership and income after rivals NBC and CBS, which both enjoyed the benefits of having been established a decade earlier. This trend persisted after the transition to television news programs until the late 1970s, when ABC debuted several highly popular, untraditional news programs, including *20/20*, *Nightline*, and *This Week*, which experienced enduring popularity from the moment of inception. Since then, ABC News has remained one of the top three news

departments in the United States, vying for supremacy over NBC and CBS with television, radio, and online news programs.

INTRODUCTION

The Transportation Security Administration (TSA) was founded on November 19, 2001, as part of the U.S. government's response to the terrorist attacks that occurred two months earlier. The agency was formed as a central body for regulating the nation's public transportation, particularly air travel. It is tasked with protecting the security of travelers and transportation infrastructure by enforcing regulations designed to prevent smuggling, hijackings, and attacks on public transportation systems, claiming jurisdiction over nautical, air, and land travel, including highways, bus and subway systems, docks and bays, and airports.

The TSA's most important and visible role is implementing and enforcing strict airport security measures, which involves the establishment of standardized, rigorous passenger screening protocol at airport checkpoints. Part of the TSA's efforts to prevent terrorism is the maintenance of a "No Fly List" containing the names of every person barred from air travel because they are considered potential security threats. TSA agents are also tasked with using X-ray scans and physical pat-downs to ensure that no combustible, explosive, or otherwise dangerous materials are being transported on commercial passenger flights.

SIGNIFICANCE

According to the Department of Justice, the TSA has been highly successful in achieving its goal of protecting American travelers. Since its inception, the agency has intercepted thousands of dangerous weapons, arrested hundreds of drug traffickers, and foiled multiple plots to stage attacks on flights in the United States. Few are willing to debate the necessity of the agency's existence, but many raised objections to the TSA's methods throughout the 2000s decade. In its first eight years of operation, thousands of complaints were filed against the TSA for the inappropriate behavior of its agents and the allegedly invasive practices it employed as policy.

Many air passengers were upset by the increasingly strict security measures enforced by the TSA, such as the prohibition of liquids and gels in carry-on luggage. They grew significantly more upset as the agency implemented new screening procedures, most notably enhanced pat-down protocol that required

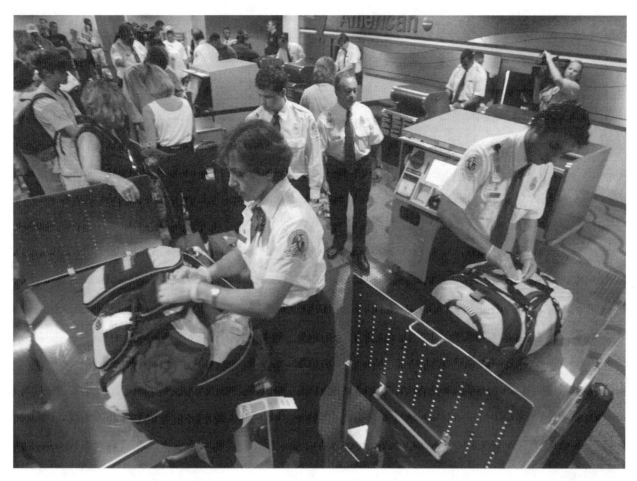

Transportation Security Agency employees at Miami International Airport screen passenger luggage. © AP IMAGES/RICHARD PATTERSON.

agents to touch the breasts and genital areas of all passengers and the installation of millimeter wave scanners at security checkpoints, which produce naked images of scanned subjects to ensure that they are not carrying restricted materials. The American Civil Liberties Union was among the multiple entities to legally challenge the constitutionality of the TSA's practices on the grounds that they violated the Fourth Amendment's protection against unreasonable searches and seizures.

The TSA also came under intense criticism for its alleged ineffectuality and the frequent misbehavior of its employees. News media frequently reported on the malfeasances and abuses of TSA agents, whose illegal behavior included stealing money and valuables from passengers' luggage, inappropriately groping or sexually assaulting people subjected to pat-downs, conducting unauthorized strip searches, and accepting bribes. Hundreds of TSA agents were fired over the course of the 2000s decade for various

contract violations and illegal acts. Another major criticism of the TSA was its purported lack of effectiveness in preventing the transportation of illegal or unsafe goods, with security experts likening the agency's practices to an elaborate, costly ruse. Politicians and pundits called for the disestablishment of the agency, which many considered to be nothing more than an act, soothing the concerns of worried travelers without actually making transportation any safer.

Despite the unpopularity of the TSA among the American public, the agency continued operation throughout the 2000s decade.

PRIMARY SOURCE

"WHAT IS TSA?"

SYNOPSIS: In this fact sheet, the stated goals and operational statistics of the Transportation Security Administration are presented.

The Transportation Security Administration (TSA) was created in the wake of 9/11 to strengthen the security of the nation's transportation systems while ensuring the freedom of movement for people and commerce. Within a year, TSA assumed responsibility for security at the nation's airports and deployed a federal workforce to screen all commercial airline passengers and baggage. In March 2003, TSA moved from the Department of Transportation to the Department of Homeland Security.

Today, TSA employs a risk-based strategy to secure U.S. transportation systems and works closely with stakeholders in aviation, rail, transit, highway, and pipeline sectors, as well as the partners in the law enforcement and intelligence community. The agency continuously sets the standard for excellence in transportation security through its people, processes, technologies and use of intelligence to drive operations.

TSA is committed to evolving its systems to enhance the safety of the traveling public as well as individual passenger experiences whenever possible.

WHO WE ARE

- TSA's nearly 50,000 Transportation Security Officers screen more than 1.8 million passengers each day at more than 450 airports nationwide.
- TSA deploys approximately 2,800 Behavior Detection Officers at airports across the country, leading to more than 2,200 arrests to date.
- TSA utilizes more than 400 TSA explosives specialists in aviation and multimodal environments.
- Thousands of Federal Air Marshals are deployed every day on domestic and international flights.
- TSA has trained and deployed approximately 800 explosives detection canine teams to airports and mass transit systems nationwide.

WHAT WE DO

- Screen more than 1.87 million passengers a day, preventing thousands of guns from getting on planes. Nationwide, TSA detected over 1,500 guns in 2012 alone.
- Deploy advanced imaging technology machines at airports nationwide, leading to the detection of prohibited, illegal or dangerous items.
- Installed new software on millimeter wave units that automatically detects potential threats using the same outline of a person for all passengers.
- Conduct 100 percent air cargo screening on domestic and international-outbound passenger aircraft, implementing a key security requirement of the 9/11 Act.

- Since the agency's inception, TSA has screened more than 4 billion checked bags for explosives.
- Conduct 100 percent terrorist watch list matching of passengers on domestic and international airline flights to, from, and within the United States, which fulfills a key recommendation of the 9/11 Commission Report.
- Continually evolve our risk-based, intelligence-driven approach to security to further enhance the safety of the traveling public.
- Expand the TSA PreCheck expedited screening initiative to airports across the country for eligible participants.
- Change screening procedures for passengers ages 12 and younger so officers can better focus on passengers who pose a higher risk to transportation security.
- Conduct daily background checks on over 15 million transportation-related employees working in or seeking access to the nation's transportation system.
- Support the allocation of $2 billion to mass transit security in federal grant money, including system security enhancements for Amtrak since 2005.
- To date, TSA has conducted thousands of Visible Intermodal Prevention and Response operations—utilizing teams who work in collaboration with local law enforcement and other security officials to keep travelers safe.
- Provide over 2 million maritime workers unescorted access to secure areas of ships and maritime facilities with a biometric Transportation Worker Identification Credential.

PRIMARY SOURCE

"TSA RAMPS UP VIRTUAL 'STRIP SEARCHES'"

SYNOPSIS: In this article, the author reports on the increasingly invasive practices of the TSA and the public's reaction to them.

The Transportation Security Administration announced this week that security checkpoints at 21 of the nation's busiest airports will be getting scanners that take near-naked photos of passengers.

After placing embarrassing liquids in see-through baggies and exposing unsightly bare feet, what's a little more humiliation in the name of safety in the skies?

According to some people, it's a violation of your rights.

"It's a virtual strip search," American Civil Liberties Union director of technology and liberty Barry Steinhardt said. "If *Playboy* published these pictures, there would be members of Congress calling them pornography."

Transportation Security Administration program analyst and instructor Sherrie Soto demonstrates the new millimeter wave unit to TSA security officers, March 10, 2009. © AP IMAGES/THE SALT LAKE TRIBUNE, LEAH HOGSTEN.

Within just a few seconds of stepping inside, the portal uses millimeter wave technology to generate a graphic 3-D image that outlines the nude contours of passengers' bodies. In doing so, it also detects any explosives, metallic or non-metallic weapons, and other objects carried anywhere on the body.

According to TSA spokeswoman Lara Uselding, the new technology in the L3 portals represents the "first huge advancement" over the ubiquitous metal detectors first deployed in the 1970s. She said that checks are in place to ensure passengers' privacy.

PRIVACY VIOLATION?

Multiple procedures, including the blurring of the face and automatic deletion of images, protect passengers' privacy, Uselding said.

Most importantly, she added, "the officer who directs you into the portal never sees the image." Instead, a second officer who is "off in a remote location" reads the image and "never makes eye contact" with the scanned passenger, she said.

The L3 portals have been tested for the past few months in 10 airports across the country, where they were used as an alternative to a personal pat-down search, as a secondary screening procedure. According to Uselding, 96 percent of the passengers at John F. Kennedy and Los Angeles airports who were given the option, chose the portal over the pat-down.

The privacy procedures are not good enough for Steinhardt, however, who called TSA's new rollout "security theater."

"Almost no passengers know that once you go through this portal, they're displaying their body," he said. He wants the TSA to show passengers an example of what the image looks like before they get scanned, which they currently do not do.

"TSA does what it can to screen the modesty of passengers going through. People can complain, but this is the world we live in now. Like it or not, it has to be done," said *Aviation Week* writer Benet Wilson.

SECURITY OR FOR SHOW?

Like Wilson, many passengers say anything is worth it for safety, and millimeter wave technology portals have already proved effective in several courtrooms across the country, and at diamond mines worldwide, where they are used to scan employees for concealed stones.

"This major step-up in technology, coupled with our enhanced security training for our officers, will elevate security across the board ... [and] will greatly enhance our ability to find small IED components made of common items, which remain the greatest threat," TSA administrator Kip Hawley said.

The expansion of wave technology portals comes along with a rollout of advanced technology X-ray machines to screen baggage, which Steinhardt said should be the greater priority.

"It's high time that TSA actually screens luggage, and I hope that this works," he said.

"The dirty little secret here is that this is mostly for show," Steinhardt added. "TSA already did the single most important thing in terms of aircraft safety, and that was ordering that the cockpit doors be secured.... Most of what has gone on since has been security theater, rather than real security."

Wilson expressed relief, though, that TSA was finally stepping up technology, with both the passenger imaging portals and the new X-ray machines.

"I think they need to start rolling them out," she said. "I would like to see them in more airports."

For better or worse, the new portals are also expected to cut down on wait time in security lines, by trimming the time officers spend on manual pat-downs. For some people, that just might be worth the indecent exposure.

FURTHER RESOURCES

Books

Means, Nathan, and Kip Hawley. *Permanent Emergency: Inside the TSA and the Fight for the Future of American Security*. New York: Palgrave Macmillan, 2012.

Molotch, Harvey. *Against Security: How We Go Wrong at Airports, Subways, and Other Sites of Ambiguous Danger*. Princeton, NJ: Princeton University Press, 2012.

Web Sites

Transportation Security Administration. http://www.tsa.gov (accessed on March 12, 2013).

"Transportation Security Administration News." *New York Times.* http://topics.nytimes.com/top/reference/timestopics/organizations/t/transportation_security_administration/index.html (accessed on March 12, 2013).

"TSA." *Huffington Post.* http://www.huffingtonpost.com/news/tsa (accessed on March 12, 2013).

The Joy of Tech Editorial Cartoon

Editorial cartoon

By: Nitrozac & Snaggy

Date: 2007

Source: Schmalcel, Liza (Nitrozac), and Bruce Evans (Snaggy). *The Joy of Tech.* 2007. http://www.geekculture.com/joyoftech/joyarchives/1041.html (accessed on March 8, 2013.)

About the Comic: *Joy of Tech* is a Web comic about technology and pop culture, released three times a week since its creation in 2000. Its Canadian authors, Liza Schmalcel and Bruce Evans, are known by the aliases Nitrozac and Snaggy, and are known for their previous work on *After Y2K*, a different comic. Schmalcel is also the founder of the Web site GeekCulture.com, and Evans is also a multimedia artist.

INTRODUCTION

The second half of the 2000s decade saw the American public grow enamored with social networking services like Facebook, Myspace, and Twitter. As more and more people signed up for such services, an unexpected problem arose—personal information shared on social networks, such as political opinions and illegal activity, began landing users in trouble. Police, alert to the growing prevalence of social media, routinely employed digital investigators to gather evidence of drug use or trafficking, monitoring the Facebook profiles of suspected criminals for professions of illegal activity. Employers exploited people's naïve tendency to share their personal beliefs and hobbies on social networking sites, inspecting the profiles of prospective employees to identify the most well-behaved candidates when hiring. A single errant drunken rant or nude photo, previously embarrassing but not permanently damaging to a person's

The Joy of Tech™

by Nitrozac & Snaggy

Signs of the social networking times.

©2007 Geek Culture

joyoftech.com

PRIMARY SOURCE

The Joy of Tech Editorial Cartoon

SYNOPSIS: This cartoon makes light of the increasing connection between the Internet and "real life," parodying the oft-repeated warnings that employers investigate prospective employees on the Internet when hiring. GEEK CULTURE.

---

reputation, could be used in the age of social networking sites and Google searches to destroy the public standing and financial well-being of an individual.

SIGNIFICANCE

The users of social networking services were surprisingly slow to recognize the importance of monitoring their online activity. News media frequently issued reports on people who lost their jobs or spouses due to social media indiscretions, and numerous arrests were made on the basis of ill-advised sharing. One of the most significant social developments of the 2000s decade was the ever-increasing connectivity between the Internet and the exterior world, which forced U.S. citizens to more closely monitor their activity both online and off.

PRIMARY SOURCE

THE JOY OF TECH EDITORIAL CARTOON

See primary source cartoon.

FURTHER RESOURCES
Web Sites

Fitzgerald, Britney. "Facebook Overshare: 7 Things You Might Not Realize You're Telling the World." *Huffington Post*, September 17, 2012. www.huffingtonpost.com/2012/09/17/facebook-overshare_n_1844606.html (accessed on March 7, 2013).

"Social Network Sites: Block or Not?" *Network World*. www.networkworld.com/community/tech-debate-block-social-networks (accessed on March 7, 2013).

"Tweens 'R' Shoppers"

Newspaper article

By: Lesley Jane Seymour

Date: April 22, 2007

Source: Seymour, Lesley Jane. "Tweens 'R' Shoppers." *New York Times*, April 22, 2007. www.nytimes.com/2007/04/22/nyregion/nyregionspecial2/22RSHOP.html?_r=2&scp=7&sq=Tweens&st=cse& (accessed on March 8, 2013).

About the Author: Lesley Jane Seymour served as editor-in-chief of *Marie Claire* magazine for about five years before accepting the editor-in-chief position of *More* magazine in 2008. Under her leadership, *Marie Claire* was recognized with a National Magazine Award for General Excellence in 2006, and she used her clout to spearhead several cause-related programs, including one to raise awareness of domestic violence and another to campaign for the world organization, Save the Children. Prior to her stint at *Marie Claire*, Seymour worked at *Redbook*, *YM*, *Glamour* and *Vogue*.

INTRODUCTION

There was a time when the primary consumer of the typical American family was either the mother (for items such as groceries, sundries, and clothing) or the father (for big-ticket items such as vehicles, homes, and the like). By 1995, nearly every consumer goods industry was marketing toward children. And according to James McNeal, author of the 1999 book *The Kids Market: Myths and Realities*, "They are a market with more market potential than any other demographic group." McNeal claims that in the 1980s, only one-third of retail chains marketed toward children, but by the time his book hit the shelves, that figure had increased to two-thirds and was on the rise. Clearly, marketers had discovered a gold mine, and things were only going to get better.

As McNeal points out, kids (his term) are more like three distinct markets: a primary (spending their money on their own wants and needs), an influence (determining in large part how their parents spend money), and a future (inevitably they will continue to consume and spend). This realization changed the direction of advertising in America, and perhaps in no more significant way than the marketing aimed at the "tween" group—those consumers between the ages of seven and twelve. In a society that has become undeniably youth-oriented, parents have gradually shifted their focus from traditional parenting to treating their children more like friends. This emphasis on youth culture, according to psychologist Kit Yarrow, encourages tweens to make their wants and desires known. The author of *Gen BuY: How Tweens, Teens and Twenty-Somethings Are Revolutionizing Retail*, Yarrow attributes tween influence on parents to a refusal to embrace the old adage, "Children are to be seen and not heard." "Parents are much more likely to think of their tweens as having valid and valuable opinions. Therein lies the influence. They talk, listen and care about each other's opinions."

Youth Trends Research co-founder Josh Weil credits the online shopping boom for having an effect on the tween-led shopping revolution. Even though most tweens do not have access to credit cards whenever they want them, a Cotton Incorporated Lifestyle Monitor survey published in 2012 revealed that 53 percent of tweens browse for apparel online. Weil explains, "Online is important from a 'click to mortar' standpoint. Tweens might peruse Crewcuts for J.Crew—and that's leading up to a purchase they want to make that weekend."

SIGNIFICANCE

This increase in the spending of tween consumers changed the culture of shopping dramatically. Malls as they appeared in the early twenty-first century clearly catered to the retail-savvy tween with their bass-heavy pop music and touch-screen computer cameras. Multi-age stores like Gap and Limited had been replaced with tween-focused chains like Justice, P.S., and abercrombie kids. Those who graduated from these early-tweenage stores headed straight to their sibling stores: Aeropostale, dELiA's, Pacsun, and others.

Retailers called this phenomenon responsible for tween influence "age compression," when kids get older at a younger age. According to NPD Group, a consumer market research company, seven- to fourteen-year old girls spent $11.5 billion in 2007, a $1.0 billion increase from 2004. But tween influence was felt in the skin care and makeup industries as well. Yarrow tried to make sense of the idea of age compression as it related to the sexualization of children who sought to grow up quicker in terms of their physical appearance. "For tweens and teens, it's not so much sexual as attention-getting. They just don't compute sexy the way adults do. It's a dress-up game."

The reality of tween shoppers, who along with teens and twenty-somethings are what Yarrow calls "Gen Y," is that they have forever changed the shopping landscape. Because of their savvy influence, retail Web sites are more creative and technically

Michelle Silonuk of Columbus, Ohio, a mother of two daughters, shops at Justice, a store that caters to the tween market in August 2006. © AP IMAGES/JAY LAPRETE.

advanced. In fact, 50 percent of retailers redesigned their sites in 2008 in an effort to keep up with Gen Y. These shoppers are responsible for writing half of all online customer reviews, and because they lose interest quickly, retailers introduce new products in an effort to prevent Gen Yers from becoming bored.

PRIMARY SOURCE

"TWEENS 'R' SHOPPERS"

SYNOPSIS: In the world of retail, the tween population rises to the top of the spending heap as modern pre-adolescents put their money where their mouths are.

It is 11:15 a.m. The kids have the day off from school and I'm mall crawling The Westchester in White Plains, with my posse: my 11-year-old daughter, Lake, and two of her friends, Annabelle Kirk, 11, and Eve Wulf, 12.

They are identically (though they would say individually) decked out in the suburban tween girl uniform,

almost head-to-toe Abercrombie: skin-tight jeans and layered T-shirts, as well as ballet flats, Uggs, or Michael Kors boots. Eve wears a Juicy Couture bracelet with a $60 charm that her mother bought for her for Valentine's Day, which the others fawn over longingly.

Shortly after we enter the mall, my perfectly coiffed and lip-glossed group of girls step into Louis Vuitton and gaze at a white mink stole covered with colorful logos in a plastic case. "I have to have this!" exclaims Lake.

"That will take your babysitting money," replies a surprisingly playful saleswoman, "for-ever!"

"Oh!" Lake says. "I didn't know it was real!"

Back in the main hall, the girls spot a man carrying two giant pink Juicy Couture bags, and they start hissing like snakes, cheering, "Ju-i-ccc-y! Ju-i-ccc-y!" as if the brand was their favorite member of the Mamaroneck High School football team.

When we pull up in front of Abercrombie, the preteen version of Abercrombie & Fitch, silence falls over my crowd. With its cloying overspritzed air, loud thumping music, blowup posters of young girls and boys, this is ground zero for tween fashion worship: collared shirts in sorbet colors, tanks so thin they often come with holes already in them and skin-tight jeans that curvier teenagers can't squeeze into.

It's a place where I have been held hostage so often that I have coined a name for that vacant look of resignation women get when setting foot inside the store: Dead mom walking.

But on this day I've come not to bury Abercrombie. I am here to observe my daughter and her two friends make their way around a suburban mall to help me understand why shopping seems to have become an acceptable hobby, even an obsession, among some young girls. And to see how stores like Abercrombie and American Eagle Outfitters, as well as luxury brands, successfully court these young girls and turn them into customers.

After 28 years in the fashion business, the last four running *Marie Claire* magazine, I am well acquainted with the pleasures of shopping and how the fashion industry is always trying to focus on new audiences. What was surprising about watching these girls move around the mall was their depth of knowledge of even the most sophisticated brands and their brand loyalty.

For them, going to the mall is no longer about looking. The concept of window shopping no longer exists. Going home without a bag is unthinkable. Shopping has become about buying.

"The idea of recreational shopping is not new," said Juliet B. Schor, a professor of sociology at Boston College and author of "Born to Buy: The Commercialized Child and the New Consumer Culture" (Scribner). "Think back on stereotypes of women of leisure at the turn of the century who spent all their time shopping."

What is new, she said, "is there is less of a cultural taboo on materialism."

Ms. Schor said this increase in materialistic values has been reflected in several recent studies, including a Pew Research Center poll of adults 18 to 25 in 2006 that found a majority of those surveyed said that "getting rich" was their main goal.

Combine this new emphasis on consumerism with the influence of celebrities, like Paris Hilton, and you can see where the younger set is getting its notions of fashion, style and culture. There is also TV, with its fashion shows aimed at younger viewers, from "America's Next Top Model" to "Project Runway."

And there are the celebrity magazines, which count young girls as a significant chunk of their readership.

"We know these readers love to see what celebs are wearing on their arms, carrying on their backs and shopping for," said Bonnie Fuller, editorial director for American Media, which owns *Star* magazine, one of the weeklies that has helped raise the image of celebrity shopping to iconic status. "They see them as fashion role models, no question."

And it's not just tweens who have become fashion obsessed. "They're reflecting adult women who are more interested in fashion and logos than when we grew up," Ms. Fuller said. "American society was not as style- and fashion-oriented 30 years ago."

Several luxury brands and retail apparel companies, like Abercrombie & Fitch, began singling out tweens about a decade ago.

Originally a clothing manufacturer's term to describe adolescents who have outgrown children's styles, but could not yet wear teenage looks (remember the old "preteen"?), a tween is described variously as ages 8 to 15, 9 to 12 or 8 to 12.

It also describes perfectly the way my posse ricochets between childlike abandon and adult composure—by the minute. As we walked past the Brookstone store, they threw themselves onto the massage chairs and jumped up and down, just like children. They are caught between two worlds and that is perhaps why stores like the Limited Too, which my group no longer considers "cool," carry such a schizophrenic mix of bubblegum and bras.

The reason behind the intense focus on tweens and teens is their phenomenal purchasing power.

"The teen market has exploded in terms of size and direct spending power," said Michael Wood, vice president of Teenage Research Unlimited, who estimated that today's teenage population stood at 33.5 million. "The fastest growing power is the younger market, 12 to 15, accounting for 50 percent of the overall teen market."

Mr. Wood said that stores like Abercrombie, with its walls plastered with photos of all-American girls and boys who do not seem to have a care in the world, offer a safe haven, a kind of new American backyard.

"Being a kid today is really tough," said Mr. Wood, pointing out that this generation of children is growing up with security detectors at their schools. "In a world of worry, what a breath of fresh air."

While my daughter and two friends tried on their skinny jeans and T-shirts in Abercrombie's fitting rooms, I chatted with another mother, Sally Conrad, from Katonah, N.Y. She was shopping with her daughter Julia, 13, and I asked her why Abercrombie was their favorite store.

"It's not really about clothes," Ms. Conrad said. "At this age it's important for them to feel like they're part of a larger club. And this does it."

Daniel T. Cook, an associate professor of advertising at the University of Illinois, said that clothes shopping gives tweens a safe place in which to do some of the heavy lifting of adolescence.

"They get to select and survey a world of identities and selves that are presented out there," he said. "It almost has a sense of ritualistic or magical timeout."

For that reason, stores catering to this age group, in particular, have pulsating lights and kaleidoscopic colors. "They're designed to evoke fantasy," he said.

They are also designed to grab the billions of dollars that tweens independently spend and have sway over. According to 360 Youth, an advertising and marketing company that focuses on young people, tweens independently spend $51 billion annually and have "considerable sway" over another $170 billion annually spent on them by parents and family.

That "sway" is what made even more marketers interested. Wendy Liebmann, president and founder of WSL Strategic Retail, has studied consumer behavior in retail stores for 17 years for her How America Shops survey.

Two years ago, she said, she began noticing a change in young consumers. "You'd see parents saying to very young children, 'What flavor toothpaste do you want?'" she said.

In 2005, Ms. Liebmann quantified that impact and was "astounded" to find that parents said 75 percent of their children under 13 had some say—always or occasionally—on the purchases of home décor for their own room. Forty percent had some say in the skin care products they used, 45 percent on hair care products, 65 percent on sneakers and 58 percent on jeans.

"And you say to yourself, 'O.K., this is what parents are admitting!'" Ms. Liebmann said, laughing. "It's not surprising that by the time this child is 12 they feel they have every right to make decisions and think they have a legitimate opinion that should be paid attention to."

The sociological move away from authoritarian parents to parents-as-friends has given rise to a generation of children that was born to shop. The result?

"We have this incredibly sophisticated, thoughtful, opinionated consumer," Ms. Liebmann said. "And parents have created it."

Out of necessity, those time-pressed parents also began to integrate shopping into their lives. "They got into the minivan with the family and said, 'We're off to Best Buy or Target' or other places," Ms. Liebmann said. The idea of a store "as a meeting place became part of the vernacular," she said. Struggling malls began to offer food, ice-skating and spas to entice consumers to linger longer, and the separation between shopping and entertainment began to blur.

Sharon Zukin, a sociology professor at Brooklyn College and author of "Point of Purchase" (Routledge), does not deride tweens for wanting to shop because she claims it is the modern form of hunting and gathering.

"How many people bake their own bread, sew their own clothes?" she asked. "We're not self-sufficient anymore. You have to buy things today. In a way, learning how to shop is crucial today for how to survive."

Mother-daughter shopping can be a bonding experience. "In a traditional society you would have spent the whole day gathering food supplies and cooked tortillas together," Ms. Zukin said. "But we don't do that."

It can even be an important steppingstone toward adult independence. While interviewing people for her book, Ms. Zukin asked people whether they remembered their first shopping experience. "They all did," she said. "Shopping on your own is a rite of passage."

FURTHER RESOURCES

Books

McNeal, James U. *The Kids Market: Myths and Realities*, Ithaca, NY: Paramount Market Publishing, 1999.

Yarrow, Kit, and Jayne O'Donnell. *Gen BuY: How Tweens, Teens and Twenty-Somethings Are Revolutionizing Retail.* San Francisco: Jossey-Bass, 2009.

Web Sites

Cotton Incorporated. "Tween Spirit: Post-Recession Tween Shoppers Remain Force at Retail." *WWD.com*, April 10, 2012. www.wwd.com/markets-news/textiles/the-power-of-youth-post-recession-tween-shoppers-remain-force-at-retail-5849340 (accessed on March 8, 2013).

Diskin, Colleen. "Stores for Savvy Tween Shoppers Make It Easier—and Harder—on Parents." *NorthJersey.com*, January 30, 2011. www.northjersey.com/shopping/114888629_Stores_for_savvy_tween_shoppers_make_it_easier___and_harder___on_parents.html?c=y&page=1 (accessed on March 8, 2013).

Eisenberg, Richard. "Gen Y Forces Retailers to Keep Up with Technology, New Stuff." *USA Today*, September 30, 2009. http://usatoday30.usatoday.com/money/books/2009-09-13-tweens-teens-retail_N.htm (accessed on March 8, 20130.

"Lesley Jane Seymour." *Huffington Post.* www.huffingtonpost.com/lesley-jane-seymour/ (accessed on March 8, 2013).

O'Donnell, Jayne. "As Kids Get Savvy, Marketers Move Down the Age Scale." *USA Today*, April 13, 2007. http://usatoday30.usatoday.com/money/advertising/2007-04-11-tween-usat_n.htm (accessed on March 8, 2013).

"*Harry Potter* Is a Modern Phenomenon"

Web site article

By: Associated Press

Date: July 2, 2007

Source: Associated Press. "Harry Potter Is a Modern Phenomenon." *NBC News: Today*, July 2, 2007. www.today.com/id/19491516/ns/today-entertainment/t/harry-potter-modern-phenomenon/#.UUSUR1eweqh (accessed on March 16, 2013).

About the Featured Author: J. K. Rowling took five years to outline the plots for her seven-book *Harry Potter* series, which she began writing during a delayed train journey from Manchester to London. The British author was a single mother who struggled to make ends meet when her first book in the award-winning series was published. Rowling remarried and moved to Edinburgh, Scotland, with her husband and three children, where she continued to write. Rowling published her first novel for adults in 2012.

INTRODUCTION

Every once in a while, a story or fictitious character—or both—comes along that captures the attention of an entire culture, and the phenomenon that ensues becomes much larger than the story or character that incited it. The *Star Wars* films and the stories they told developed into one such phenomenon; *Star Trek* was another. These movies and the stories they told gave birth to an entire subculture, a microsociety of fans. Cultural reaction goes beyond branding, it is more than a matter of buying T-shirts and school supplies, posters and action figures. The "It" involves dressing up in costumes of favorite characters, standing in endless lines to get into the latest movie in the series, or to be one of the first to buy the book when it hits the shelves. There are conventions to attend, book signings, themed parties … the list of activities is a long one.

British author J. K. Rowling published the first *Harry Potter* book—*Harry Potter and the Sorcerer's Stone*—in London, in 1997. It had been a long while since any book had created a stir to the degree that Rowling's did. An edition under the title *Harry Potter and the Philosopher's Stone* was published in America the following year and reached the number one spot on the *New York Times* bestseller list in August 1999. It remained at or near the top for the rest of that year and most of the next. By the end of 2001, the book had sold more than five million hardbacks and 6.6 million paperbacks, making it a record-breaker. And that award-winning first novel was only the beginning.

SIGNIFICANCE

By the end of 2007, the year of the Associated Press article, Rowling had earned $300 million, which was six times more than the next-highest earning writer, James Patterson. Third in line was popular horror writer Stephen King, at $45 million. A spokesman for *Forbes* was quoted by *BBC News* as saying, "It was wizardry that transformed J. K. Rowling from a destitute single mother on welfare into a best-selling billionaire." By that time, all seven of her *Harry Potter* novels had been published and sold more than four hundred million copies in sixty-seven languages. Her final book, *Harry Potter and the Deathly Hallows*, had sold forty-four million copies worldwide, including fifteen million in the first twenty-four hours of its release.

Rowling's books were adapted to screen, and even before the final three saw opening night, the *Potter* franchise had generated $4.5 billion at the box office. By the time the final film was released, the series adaptation had grossed more than $7 billion and had the honor of highest-grossing film series in history. Warner Brothers, which produced all eight (the final book was split into two movies) films, called it a "stunning achievement." The series, both in book and film format, became the standard against which everyone began to compare popularity and profit.

America has not seen another phenomenon quite like *Harry Potter*. Stephenie Meyer's *Twilight* book series, featuring love, vampires, and vampire love, created its own phenomenon, but it was not as significant as Rowling's creation. Again, books were adapted to film, but even though they enjoyed success at the box office (to the tune of more than $3 million), they never impacted culture quite like *Harry Potter*. The same can be said of Suzanne Collins's *Hunger Games* books and subsequent movies. Popular, yes. Profitable, to be certain. But nothing comes close to capturing the consumer quite like *Harry Potter*.

Hundreds of *Harry Potter and the Deathly Hallows* books sit in a stack at a Swiss bookstore in July 2007. © AP IMAGES/ EDDY RISCH.

PRIMARY SOURCE

"*HARRY POTTER* IS A MODERN PHENOMENON"

SYNOPSIS: A single novel led to six more books, eight films, numerous video games, action figures, clothing, and a turning point in the reading habits of young people everywhere.

As the *Harry Potter* series wraps up this summer, we can look back at two remarkable narratives: Potter the boy wizard and Potter the cultural phenomenon.

Potter the wizard's fate will be known July 21 with the release of "Harry Potter and Deathly Hallows," Book 7 of J. K. Rowling's fantasy epic. Worldwide sales of the first six books already top 325 million copies and the first printing for "Deathly Hallows" is 12 million in the United States alone.

Potter the phenomenon doesn't compare for suspense, but like the wizard's tale, it is unique and extraordinary and well placed in tradition. Like "Star

Wars" and "Star Trek," it is the story of how a work of popular art becomes a world of its own—imitated, merchandised and analyzed, immortalized not by the marketers, but by the fans.

"Every phenomenon is a kind of myth unto itself, a myth about how a phenomenon becomes a phenomenon. The story of how the public embraced Potter only gives more momentum to Potter in our culture," says Neal Gabler, an author and cultural critic whose books include "Walt Disney" and "Life the Movie: How Entertainment Conquered Reality."

True phenomena are never planned. Not "Star Trek," a series canceled after three seasons by NBC; or "Star Wars," rejected throughout Hollywood before taken on by 20th Century Fox, which didn't bother pushing for merchandising or sequel rights. The public knew better—the young people who screamed for the Beatles or watched "Star Wars" dozens of times or carried on for years about "Star Trek" after its cancellation.

Several Publishers Rejected Book

In the beginning, "Harry Potter" simply needed a home. Several British publishers turned down Rowling, believing her manuscript too long and/or too slow, before the Bloomsbury Press signed her up in 1996, for $4,000 and a warning not to expect to get rich from writing children's books. An American publisher had bigger ideas: Scholastic editor Arthur A. Levine acquired U.S. rights for $105,000.

"I can vividly remember reading the manuscript and thinking, 'This reminds me of Roald Dahl,' an author of such skill, an author with a unique ability to be funny and cutting and exciting at the same time," Levine says.

"But I could not possibly have had the expectation we would be printing 12 million copies for one book ('Deathly Hallows'). That's beyond anyone's experience. I would have had to be literally insane."

For the media, the biggest news at first was Rowling herself: an unemployed, single English mother who gets the idea for a fantasy series while stuck on a train between Manchester and London, finishes the manuscript in the cafes of Edinburgh, Scotland, and finds herself compared, in more than one publication, to Dahl.

"In fact, if there is a downside to Rowling's story it is the distinct danger she will be called 'The New Roald Dahl,' which would be an albatross around her slender shoulders," the Glasgow-based *The Herald* warned in June 1997 with publication of "Harry Potter and the Philosopher's Stone," the first Potter book.

"Philosopher's Stone" was released in England during business hours with a tiny first printing. Bloomsbury suggested that Rowling use initials instead of her real name, Joanne, out of fear that boys wouldn't read a book by a woman.

The book quickly became a commercial and critical favorite and just kept selling. In July 1998, the *Guardian* in London noted that Rowling was more popular than John Grisham and declared "The Harry Potter books have become a phenomenon." At the time, "Philosopher's Stone" had sold 70,000 copies.

The first book came out in the United States in September 1998, renamed "Harry Potter and the Sorcerer's Stone" for young Americans and promoted by "Meet Harry Potter" buttons. Potter was first mentioned by The Associated Press that November, when Rowling was interviewed in New York during a five-city U.S. tour. Potter appeared a month later in *The New York Times*, cited well down in a roundup of holiday favorites.

"When the Potter books first came out, we didn't know they would sell millions of copies, but we all read them and loved them and we thought they were the kinds of books that would really grab a child. We hand-sold the heck out of them, the same way we would with any book that was so well written," says Beth Puffer, manager of the Bank Street Bookstore in New York City.

By January 1999, the AP was calling Potter a sensation, noting in a brief item that "Joanne Rowling has gone from hard-up single mother to literary phenomenon." In July 1999, the "p-word" appeared in long articles in the *Los Angeles Times*, *Publishers Weekly* and the *Times*, which observed that "Hannibal Lecter and Harry Potter are shaping up as the summer's must reads," but then added, with a bit of a wink, "Harry who?"

By 2000, Harry was a friend to millions, the toast of midnight book parties around the world. For a time, the first three *Potter* books held the top positions on the *Times'* hardcover fiction list of best sellers, leading the newspaper to create a separate category for children's books. The fourth work, "Harry Potter and the Goblet of Fire," had a first printing of 3.8 million in the United States alone. The release date became 12:01 a.m., sharp, "so everyone could come to it at the same time—no spoilers!" according to Scholastic spokeswoman Kyle Good.

Potter was pulling in all ages. Rene Kirkpatrick, a buyer for All for Kids Books & Music, an independent store based in Seattle, says the appeal to grown-ups set *Potter* apart. She began noticing that adults not only read Rowling, but would browse through other titles in the children's fantasy section.

"People were beginning to realize that there was some extraordinary literature written for people under 19," she says. "It doesn't feel odd anymore for adults to be seen reading children's books.... *Potter* has made a big difference."

"*Potter* has greatly expanded the real estate for young adult fiction," says Doug Whiteman, president of the Penguin Young Readers Group, a division of Penguin Group (USA). "The teen section of a bookstore is now quite a substantial area, shopped in not only by teens, but by parents."

Internet Explosion

Meanwhile, *Potter* was alive and breeding on the Internet, thanks to fan sites such as http://www.the-leaky-cauldron.org/ and http://www.mugglenet.com. *Potter* Web masters Emerson Spartz of Leaky Cauldron and Melissa Anelli of Mugglenet agree that between 2000 and 2003 the *Potter* galaxy exploded again, from publishing phenomenon to cultural phenomenon. Spartz notes the release of the first *Potter* movie, in 2001. Anelli refers to the three-year wait for book five, "Harry Potter and the Order of the Phoenix."

"Around 2000, message boards, mailing lists, blogs were starting to form into the community hubs we have now. So the fans, who were desperately awaiting word on the fifth book ... obsessed together on the Internet, writing their own fan fiction, having huge discussions picking every last piece of the canon apart and finding whatever way possible to make the wait tolerable," says Anelli, who is writing a history of *Potter*, due out in 2008.

"This built on itself exponentially until, by the time the fifth book came out in 2003, there was a rabid, active, flourishing online community that was spilling off the Net and into bookstores."

No longer was Rowling called the new Dahl. Now, publishers looked for the next J. K. Rowling. Countless works, from Cornelia Funke's "The Thief Lord" to Christopher Paolini's "Eragon," were compared to *Potter*. Again, a common symptom, like all the "new Bob Dylans" or the science fiction projects that followed "Star Wars," including the first "Star Trek" movie.

Along with imitators come the products: Beatle wigs, "Star Wars" sabers, "Star Trek" clocks, Harry Potter glasses. And along with the products come the spinoffs, whether business books such as Tom Morris' "If Harry Potter Ran General Electric," or Neil Mulholland's "The Psychology of Harry Potter" or John Granger's "Looking for God in Harry Potter."

"I think the reason that authors write books about J. K. Rowling's works and readers buy them is because being a fan of *Potter* is about much more than just reading and enjoying Ms. Rowling's book series," says Jennifer

Trek" produced a string of popular TV spin-offs and was adapted into a series of hit films, video games and novels, just as "Star Wars" inspired its own line of best-selling books and games. A live-action TV series is planned for 2009.

"Harry Potter and the Order of the Phoenix," the fifth *Potter* film, is a guaranteed blockbuster. The first four *Potter* movies have grossed more than $3 billion worldwide, and sales for the soundtracks top 1 million copies, according to Nielsen SoundScan, which tracks the retail market. *Potter* is the rare literary series to inspire a video game and is expected to have a theme park, in Orlando, Fla., by 2010.

While fads fade out, phenomena last, thanks to the same folks who got them started: the fans, the people who hold "Star Wars" conventions, play Beatles songs for their children, post their own "Star Trek" videos online or the *Potter* fans around the world already vowing to continue.

"I think we'll always have *Harry Potter* conventions-conferences, and the appeal won't end once it's off the 'new releases' shelf," Anelli says. "The mania will never be this intense again but this series will have life in the real world for a very long time."

When something has staying power, it's because it strikes some kind of fundamental chord," Gabler, the cultural critic, says. "Kids identify with Harry Potter and his adventures; they identify with his empowerment. It's all very circular. We feel empowered by making a phenomenon out of something like *Potter* and *Potter* itself addresses the very idea of empowerment."

Author J. K. Rowling signs copies of her new book *Harry Potter and the Deathly Hallows* in a New Orleans, Louisiana, bookstore, October 18, 2007. © AP IMAGES/BILL HABER.

FURTHER RESOURCES
Books
Rowling, J. K. *Harry Potter Schoolbooks: Fantastic Beasts and Where to Find Them/Quidditch Through the Ages.* New York: Scholastic, 2001.

Web Sites
"Biography." *J.K.Rowling.com.* http://www.jkrowling.com/en_US/#/about-jk-rowling/ (accessed on March 16,2013).

"Harry Potter Films Cross $7 Billion Box Office Mark." *Reuters,* July 22, 2011. www.reuters.com/article/2011/07/22/us-harrypotter-record-idUSTRE76L1I920110722 (accessed on March 16, 2013).

"Rowling 'Makes £5 Every Second.'" *BBC News,* October 3, 2008. http://news.bbc.co.uk/2/hi/entertainment/7649962.stm (accessed on March 16, 2013).

Heddle, an editor at Pocket Books, a division of Simon & Schuster that is publishing Anelli and has released more than 100 "Star Trek" related titles.

"I think it is similar to 'Star Trek' in that it takes place in a richly imagined world that invites fans to immerse themselves in every aspect. I think it's even closer to 'Star Wars' because it's also a very mythic story that appeals to a broad audience that crosses all age and gender lines."

Unbounded by age or format, phenomena are amphibious creatures: The Beatles were sensations on television and film and in books, which continue to come out, and sell, more than 30 years after their breakup. "Star

"Consumer Vigilantes"

Memo to Corporate America: Hell Now Hath No Fury Like a Customer Scorned

Magazine article

By: Jena McGregor

Date: February 21, 2008

Source: McGregor, Jena. "Consumer Vigilantes." *Business Week*, February 21, 2008. www.businessweek.com/magazine/content/08_09/b4073038437662.htm (accessed on March 8, 2013).

About the Publication: *Business Week* is a weekly periodical that was founded in September 1929. The magazine's coverage of the American business realm—politics, practices, trends, marketing, and management, among other topics—was initially editorial in nature, but it transitioned gradually towards a more objective presentation of internationally relevant business news. At the time "Consumer Vigilantes" was published, *Business Week* was one of the world's leading business publications, along with *Forbes* and *Fortune*. It was later acquired by the Bloomberg publishing conglomerate, changing its name to *Businessweek*.

INTRODUCTION

Vigilante consumerism is a sort of "consumer activism lite," in which consumers defend their rights as customers through non-litigious means. Instead of waging court battles to secure the right to reliable, safe products, vigilante consumers were more likely to leave a negative online review or circulate a horror story about a company that did not satisfy their expectations, slowly compelling corporate America to better consider the needs of its revenue source. The term was popularized by a 2007 *Business Week* cover article called "Consumer Vigilantes," which proclaimed that a new breed of customer, armed with a keyboard and video camera, was conquering the forces of inadequate customer service and disrespect one online post at a time.

As the Internet continued to expand its reach into society, many dissatisfied consumers were emboldened by the ability to reach massive audiences easily and without cost. They took to blogs, social media services, content aggregators, and message boards to express their qualms with the companies that had slighted them with inadequate customer service or a faulty product. Online review sites like Yelp and Angie's List emerged during the 2000s decade, providing a

platform for consumers to air their grievances with or profess their approval of businesses and products. Vigilante consumers also used the Internet to share tips and tricks for bypassing automated customer service systems and reaching human assistance directly. America's corporate world was put on notice that the nation's consumers were no longer willing to suffer abuse any longer.

SIGNIFICANCE

Businesses were quick to respond to the rise of vigilante consumerism. Recognizing the potential PR devastation that could be caused by a high-profile complaint campaign, such as a YouTube video decrying a product or a Facebook page disparaging a company, many large businesses hired dedicated customer service operatives, whose sole responsibility was pacifying the online tirades of unhappy customers. The importance of customer satisfaction was magnified in the Internet age, as it was no longer adequate for a company to feign concern for the happiness of the consumer—a vocally unhappy customer could cause a significant decline in the reputation and income of a company. Accordingly, corporations in the United States heightened their efforts to provide exceptional experiences for their customers, producing a more equitable supplier-consumer relationship.

PRIMARY SOURCE

"CONSUMER VIGILANTES"

SYNOPSIS: In this article, the author reports on the growing prevalence and influence of vigilante consumers, listing several successful examples of the trend.

In the annals of customer service, 2007 will go down as the year fed-up consumers finally dropped the hammer. In August a 76-year-old retired nurse named Mona Shaw smashed up a keyboard and a telephone in a Manassas (Va.) Comcast office after she says the cable operator failed to install her service properly. During her first visit to the branch outlet, the AARP secretary says she was left sitting on a bench in the hallway for two hours waiting for a manager. She returned, armed with a hammer, and let loose the rallying cry "Have I got your attention now?" Afterward, she was arrested, fined $345, and became a media sensation, capturing the hearts of frustrated consumers everywhere. (Says Comcast: "We apologize for any customer service issues that Ms. Shaw experienced.")

Three months earlier, in May, Michael Whitford uploaded a video in which he chooses among a golf club, an ax, and a sword before deciding on a sledgehammer as his weapon of choice for bashing his nonfunctioning Macbook to smithereens. In the video, Whitford, a systems engineer from Chandler, Ariz., says that Apple declined to cover the repair under warranty, citing damage from a spilled liquid. More than 340,000 people have viewed the black-and-white smash-up on YouTube. Whitford, whom *BusinessWeek* was not able to reach for comment, denies in the video that he spilled anything. In early July, he wrote on his blog that Apple had replaced his laptop. "I'm very happy now," he wrote. "Apple has regained my loyalty."

Meet today's consumer vigilantes. Even if they're not all wielding hammers, many are arming themselves with video cameras, computer keyboards, and mobile devices to launch their own personal forms of insurrection. Frustrated by the usual fix-it options—obediently waiting on hold with Bangalore, gamely chatting online with a scripted robot—more consumers are rebelling against company-prescribed service channels. After getting no-where with the call center, they're sending "e-mail carpet bombs" to the C-suite, cc-ing the top layer of manage-ment with their complaints. When all else fails, a plucky few are going straight to the top after uncovering direct numbers to executive customer-service teams not easily found by mere mortals.

And of course, they're filling up the Web with blogs and videos, leaving behind venom-spewed tales of woe. "There's a certain degree of extremism that's popping up, [a sense of] 'I'm going to get results, whatever means necessary,'" says Pete Blackshaw, executive vice-presi-dent of Nielsen Online Strategic Services, which mea-sures consumer-generated media. "Companies can brush these off as being atypical, mutant consumers, or they can say there's a very important insight in [their] emotions."

Behind the guerrilla tactics is a growing disconnect between the experience companies promise and custo-mers' perceptions of what they actually get. Consumers already pushed to the brink by evaporating home equity, job insecurity, and rising prices are more apt to snap when hit with long hold times and impenetrable phone trees. Just ask those who responded to our second annual ranking of the best companies for customer service, which uses data from J. D. Power & Associates. The average service scores for the brands in our study dipped slightly this year, and about two-thirds of the names that were in both years' studies were lower. (Like *BusinessWeek*, J. D. Power is owned by The McGraw-Hill Companies.)

EMPOWERED CUSTOMERS

A swell of corporate distrust—exacerbated by high executive pay, accounting lapses, and the offshoring of jobs—has people feeling more at odds with companies than ever before. "[That] has a visceral effect on how customers approach more day-to-day transactions," says Scott Broetzmann, president of Alexandria (Va.) Customer Care Measurement & Consulting. Meanwhile, he says, companies are responding with tighter return policies and increased focus on potential fraud. "You'd have to go back a long way to see the kind of acrimony that you're seeing now."

Technology is aiding the uprising, empowering consumers to do much more to make themselves heard. Now, with the proliferation of online video, they can be seen as well. "You could only get the point across so much with text," says Blackshaw. "As soon as you start adding sight, sound, and motion, you've got a whole other level of [emotion]." More consumers are equipped with mobile Web devices that can find executive e-mail addresses and phone numbers anytime, from any place. At the same time, customer angst sites are no longer just shouting "YourCompanySucks" into the cyberdarkness, but acting as gathering spots for sharing call-center secrets and trouble-shooting tips. And as the audience for more blogs and social-media sites such as Digg reach critical mass, it's easier than ever for consumers to wallpaper the Web with their customer-service nightmares.

Add a powerful media voice and a provocative site title to a blog, and it can have extraordinary impact. Bob Garfield, an *Advertising Age* columnist and National Public Radio host, lit up the blogosphere in October with a site cheekily called ComcastMustDie.com, one of the salvos in what he called his "consumer jihad" against the cable company. After repeated delays with his own service, Garfield, who has hosted a podcast on the site (special guest star Mona "The Hammer Lady" Shaw!), suggested that customers post their account numbers on the blog. Activity on the blog has slowed, but not before dozens of customers followed Garfield's suggestion; many report back, he says, that Comcast called them soon after they posted their account numbers and rants. Garfield can't help but point out the irony. "They've outsourced their worst-case customer-service issues to a blog dedicated to wiping them off the face of the earth."

Marcelo Salup credits Garfield's blog for finally getting Comcast to show up on time when his Internet and cable connections failed. Years of dialing the call center for a technician yielded at least eight missed appointments by Comcast, he says, but a post on ComcastMustDie brought a phone call the next morning and, later, a lead technician who showed up on time. Now, Salup says: "Anytime I have a problem, I also post it on the blog."

Other Comcast customers have used blogs, too. Dan Ortiz says he called the cable provider at least 20 times during his first month as a subscriber to fix dropped Web access and screen-image problems. Then the 26-year-old bike messenger logged on to *The Consumerist*, a blog with more than 2 million unique visitors a month that's part of Gawker Media's digital empire of snark. There he found a consumer vigilante's gold mine: a list of e-mail addresses for more than 75 Comcast executives and employees, along with instructions for launching what the blog calls its "executive e-mail carpet bomb."

Ortiz got lucky. After firing off a note copying all those names the day before Thanksgiving, he quickly had an inbox full of out-of-office replies, complete with contact information containing direct numbers. He called a Chicago manager at home, who put his lead technician on the case. Ortiz says a swarm of eight trucks showed up on his block. "Once you get ahold of [executives], they bend over backward for you," he says. He adds that Comcast sent him a tin of gourmet popcorn for Christmas and more than $700 in credits. Even better, he now has the mobile numbers for the lead technician in his area. "I'm not calling customer service ever again," he says.

The unenviable task of responding to such digital vitriol falls to Rick Germano, Comcast's senior vice-president for customer operations, who took over the role just as Garfield's "revolution" got under way. Germano says reading blogs "is very new, at least to Comcast" and that he's expanding the number of "e-care" representatives to help track and respond to blog comments and e-mails that come in through a new link to his office on Comcast's site. "We're servicing a million customers a day," he says. "An extra hundred doesn't really faze us." A Comcast spokesperson says the company is making efforts to improve customer satisfaction and that it's reacting to other blogs besides Garfield's. Scenarios like Salup and Ortiz's are "not the type of experiences that we want our customers to be having. We're going to respond to our customers wherever and however they have voiced their experiences. Ideally, we'd prefer it to be in the traditional ways."

GOING TO THE TOP

For consumers who really want gold-plated service, little compares to a resolution from "executive customer service." These "Valhallas of customer service," as Ben Popken, editor of *The Consumerist*, has called them, are powerful support reps who may sit at corporate headquarters or even in call centers. Typically, they respond to complaints that first come in to executives; these specialists may also respond to high-profile customers who pose legal or P.R. threats. *The Consumerist*, which instructs customers to try regular support numbers first, has been active in outing such numbers at a couple dozen companies.

Although executive customer service has been around for years, many companies are reluctant to talk about it. "They're usually stealth," says consultant Broetzmann. "Obviously, you don't publish the phone numbers. You don't even tell people they exist." Washington Mutual and Circuit City declined to provide details to *BusinessWeek* about their executive customer support; Bank of America wouldn't say more "because of operating and security purposes."

Consulting firms that help companies manage call centers and train employees say the online posting of these numbers is having an effect. Baker Communications, a Houston training firm, started up a course 18 months ago to prepare more people for such executive-service teams. More than 25 companies have sent employees, says Baker CEO Walter Rogers.

The biggest challenges in customer service may be dealing with consumers who are hard to mollify. For some, the sting of a bad experience cuts so deep that it transforms them from a merely upset customer into an activist no longer just looking for a refund. Take Justin Callaway, a Portland (Ore.) freelance video editor. He started his campaign against the wireless company Cingular—now AT&T—in 2006 after a technical glitch that he believes ruined one of his computer speakers. He had the speakers, which contained an amplifier, turned up full blast. When his cell phone rang, he says the speaker next to it made a loud noise and then went dead.

Callaway didn't call customer service right away. But when he looked into the issue for a grad school project months later, he learned more about GSM networks, which Cingular uses, and radio frequency interference, which he believes caused the damage. "I really felt irked that they didn't disclose [it]." He got some friends together to record a tune about Cingular. One of them helped him animate an angry bandit in the shape of the carrier's orange trademark, complete with an AT&T blue-and-white pirate's bandanna and an eye patch shaped like Apple's logo. (Cingular/AT&T is the only wireless provider that offers the iPhone.) His video, "Feeling Cingular," has been viewed more than 37,000 times on YouTube.

About a month after posting the video, Callaway got an e-mail from Bob Steelhammer, then a vice-president for e-commerce at AT&T. "Justin, in the spirit of goodwill, I would like to replace the $100 computer speakers on your home video-editing system," Steelhammer wrote. "Please let me know what brand and model [they] are." Callaway, who works with video equipment, says that even if there's not damage the phone causes an irritating buzz, and feels AT&T should do more to make consumers aware of the issue. That's why he didn't accept the offer. "It wasn't about the speakers anymore," he says. He's not stopping with the video, either: Callaway is seeking

A U.S. Airways jet sits on a runway. Irate passengers have taken to using their smart phones to track down airline executives' phone numbers and e-mail addresses when stranded on runways during delays. © B. CHRISTOPHER/ALAMY.

class-action status for a suit against Cingular over subscribers' inability to use their phones in some settings without interference. An AT&T spokesperson says that, due to the proposed litigation, it could not comment, but it works to resolve consumers' issues promptly.

FLIGHT OR FIGHT

Most customers, of course, don't have the time or energy to go that far in their service insurgencies. They want an apology, a human being who answers the phone, or simply some bottled water after a few hours sitting on the airport tarmac. But that doesn't mean they aren't above a few digs at executives' expense or a call to a cell phone after hours. That's especially true when a direct line to the CEO is the BlackBerry sitting right there in their laps.

The US Airways plane Ron Dee was on last October had just pulled away from the gate when the pilot came on the loudspeaker to tell the Cleveland-bound passengers that they were 42nd in line for takeoff, Dee recalls. A one- to two-hour delay was expected. Later, thunderstorms delayed the flight even more, prompting another

warning: The crew was coming up on its allowable flying time.

Dee, who develops real estate for a restaurant company, flies 100 times a year and is used to delays. That wasn't what upset him so much. "About three hours into the wait on the runway, there's no water left on the plane," he recalls. (A spokesperson for Republic Airways, which operated the regional jet for US Airways, says that records from its vendor show the flight was fully catered and that other beverages would have been available.)

After a quick search on his BlackBerry, Dee found e-mail addresses for Doug Parker, US Airways' CEO; Robert Isom, its COO; and Henri Dawes, its director of customer relations. His first missive, time-stamped 5:59 p.m., fired this shot: "If you get a chance, please call me and we can discuss how we handle customer service in our restaurants. Maybe that would help your company." The next, at 6:40, invoked the JetBlue Airways incident last February, a weather-induced operational snafu that was followed closely by CEO David Neeleman's departure. "What is that CEO's name from JetBlue [who] resigned? I am going to call information and get his home phone number.

Maybe he can get us back to the gate." Says Dee, whose flight was delayed more than four hours: "I probably sent an e-mail every 15 minutes or so for the last two and a half hours" he was on the plane.

He had nothing better to do: The flight was brought back to the gate, and Dee spent the night in a Philadelphia hotel he paid for himself. He never spoke to Dawes, but he did get three vouchers totaling $425. Would he use the BlackBerry as a stalking device the next time he's stuck on the runway? "Absolutely," he says. "You guys as a company, regardless of who you are, exist because of me and my fellow paying passengers."

FURTHER RESOURCES

Web Sites

Angie's List. http://www.angieslist.com (accessed on March 8, 2013).

"Consumer Protection: Major Issues & Resources" *Poli-Source.* www.polisource.com/consumer-protection.shtml (accessed on March 8, 2013).

Yelp. http://www.yelp.com (accessed on March 8, 2013).

"Guilty Verdict in Cyberbullying Case Provokes Many Questions Over Online Identity"

Newspaper article

By: Brian Stelter

Date: November 8, 2008

Source: Stelter, Brian. "Guilty Verdict in Cyberbullying Case Provokes Many Questions Over Online Identity." *New York Times*, November 8, 2008. www.nytimes.com/2008/11/28/us/28internet.html (accessed on March 16, 2013).

About the Newspaper: The *New York Times* was founded in 1851 as a concise, four-page summary of daily news items. News mogul Adolph S. Ochs acquired the paper in 1896, expanding its scope and size. By the turn of the twentieth century, the *New York Times* was the pre-eminent U.S. newspaper, acclaimed for its objective reporting of "All the News That's Fit to Print." In 1905, the popularity and importance of the paper was memorialized by the City of New York, which called

its new public square "Times Square" in honor of the newspaper. The paper's investigative reporting on official and political affairs has always been a trademark, garnering the journalism staff more than one hundred Pulitzer Prizes for its coverage of wars and governments—most notably for its publication of the "Pentagon Papers," leaked documents attesting to the mishandling and uncertainty of the Vietnam War. The *New York Times* remains the nation's most prestigious and important newspaper, and it continues to be owned and operated by descendants of Ochs.

INTRODUCTION

The advent of social sites like MySpace and Facebook made it possible for users to create entirely new worlds, separate from their physical realities. The absence of face-to-face communication gave anonymity, and visitors had to rely on an inherent assumption that other visitors were being truthful, that they were who they claimed to be.

But just as people lie in their face-to-face communication, so do they lie online. Lying is a natural human behavior; everyone lies about something. Published studies show that social media users lie more often; other published studies show that they tell fewer lies. The hard-and-fast conclusion: People lie, regardless.

While social media had been used to find old friends, locate family members, and even land marriage partners, its dark side arguably had more far-reaching effect. Cyberbullying—the use of electronic communication to deliberately harass, threaten, or support hostile behavior toward another person—became a buzzword in twenty-first-century culture, its prevalence a disturbing trend. According to a 2007 data memo published by Pew Research, 32 percent, nearly one-third of all teenage Internet users claimed to have been the targets of cyberbullying. The most common form of this behavior was having someone take a private email, instant message, or text message and post it online, but it was not the only, or most severe, form. That same report indicated that girls were more likely to be the victims of cyberbullying, particularly those ages fifteen to seventeen (41 percent compared to 29 percent of boys in the same age range).

Although some instances of cyberbullying were more annoying than anything, others were genuinely threatening. Again, older teen girls were the most frequent victims of this type of bullying. In the case of Lori Drew, the victim was in the younger age bracket, and the perpetrator was much older than usual. That fact was one of the aspects of this case that made it unique and all the more tragic.

Thirteen-year-old Megan Meier committed suicide in October 2006 after being cyberbullied. © AP IMAGES.

SIGNIFICANCE

Federal judge George H. Wu tentatively dismissed the conviction of Drew on July 2, 2009, on the grounds that the federal statute was too vague when applied to this case. Wu explained that "one could literally prosecute anyone who violates a terms of service agreement" in any way. Former federal prosecutor Matthew L. Levine agreed with Wu's decision to reconsider the case. "This law was designed to criminalize computer hacking, not people going to a Web site and violating terms of service that can be obscure and frankly arbitrary. This sets a very bad precedent of using this law for that purpose," he was quoted as saying in the *New York Times*. On August 28, 2009, Wu formally overturned Drew's guilty verdict.

While many irate citizens felt that justice had not been served in the Megan Meier case, legal experts agreed that despite the heinous outcome of Drew's behavior, which resulted in the suicide of the thirteen-year-old Meier, to prosecute and find her guilty of a computer crime would only lead to the violation of civil liberties for every Internet user. The case did have one positive impact: Cyberbullying was thrust into the spotlight.

As of 2012, forty-eight states had enacted bullying laws; thirty-eight of them included electronic harassment laws. Additionally, all forty-eight state laws include mandatory school policies against such cyberbullying. As for identity fraud, it remained a separate issue. Facebook, aware of the increase in identity fraud, provided specific reporting instructions for users who are concerned about bullying, harassment, and fraud. Even so, cyberbullying continued to make headlines into the next decade as parents and schools struggled to make children understand the importance of vigilant attention to private information as well as appropriate online behavior.

PRIMARY SOURCE

"GUILTY VERDICT IN CYBERBULLYING CASE PROVOKES MANY QUESTIONS OVER ONLINE IDENTITY"

SYNOPSIS: A woman is convicted of computer fraud in a case where the teenage victim committed suicide as a result of cyberbullying.

Is lying about one's identity on the Internet now a crime?

The verdict Wednesday in the MySpace cyberbullying case raised a variety of questions about the terms that users agree to when they log on to Web sites.

The defendant in the case, a Missouri woman, was convicted by a federal jury in Los Angeles on three misdemeanor counts of computer fraud for having misrepresented herself on the popular social network MySpace. The woman, Lori Drew, posed as a teenage boy in using the account to send first friendly and then menacing messages to Megan Meier, 13, who killed herself shortly after receiving a message in October 2006 that said in part, "The world would be a better place without you."

MySpace's terms of service require users to submit "truthful and accurate" registration information. Ms. Drew's creation of a phony profile amounted to "unauthorized access" to the site, prosecutors said, a violation of the Computer Fraud and Abuse Act of 1986, which until now has been used almost exclusively to prosecute hacker crimes.

While the Internet's anonymity was used in this case as a cloak to bully Megan, other users say they have perfectly good reasons to construct false identities online, if only to help protect against the theft of personal information, for example.

"It will be interesting to see if issues of safety and security will eventually trump the hallmark ideology of free, largely anonymous or pseudonymous participation in cyberspace," said Sameer Hinduja, a professor of criminology and criminal justice at Florida Atlantic University.

Andrew M. Grossman, senior legal policy analyst for the Heritage Foundation, said the possibility of being prosecuted for online misrepresentation, while remote, should worry users nonetheless.

"If this verdict stands," Mr. Grossman said, "it means that every site on the Internet gets to define the criminal law. That's a radical change. What used to be small-stakes contracts become high-stakes criminal prohibitions."

The judge in the Los Angeles case, George H. Wu, is to hear motions next month for its dismissal. Ms. Drew's defense asserts among other things, as it did at trial, that she never read MySpace's terms of service in detail.

"The reality, recognized by almost everyone, is that the vast majority of Internet users do not read Web site terms of service carefully or at all," said Phil Malone, director of the Cyberlaw Clinic at Harvard Law School.

Representatives of MySpace declined to make any executives available for interviews about the case. In a statement, the site said that it did not tolerate cyberbullying and would continue to work with industry experts to raise awareness of the "harm it can potentially cause."

Mr. Hinduja, who writes for the research site CyberBullying.us, said there had been a handful of cases involving teenagers who were "driven to suicide in part because of cyberbullying by peers." What drew the greatest attention to Megan's death, he said, was that it involved the actions of an adult, Ms. Drew, now 49, whose daughter's friendship with Megan had soured.

It remains easy to create a fraudulent account on social networking sites like MySpace and Facebook, though a witness at Ms. Drew's trial, Jae Sung, a MySpace vice president for customer care, said "impostor profiles" were deleted when they were flagged by users or discovered by the Web site's employees.

A number of corporations are competing to develop age verification software for Web sites. But relying on technology to confirm a user's identity is not without drawbacks. There are legitimate reasons to hide one's name and other information online, be it concern about identity theft or a need for comfort when asking for advice or help.

"We've been telling our kids to lie about ID information for a long time now," said Danah Boyd, a fellow at the Berkman Center for Internet and Society, at Harvard.

Ms. Boyd said forms of digital street outreach were needed.

"There are lots of kids hurting badly online," she said. "And guess what? They're hurting badly offline, too. Because it's more visible online, people are blaming technology rather than trying to solve the underlying problems of the kids that are hurting."

FURTHER RESOURCES

Web Sites

Cathcart, Rebecca. "Judge Throws Out Conviction in Cyberbullying Case." *New York Times*, July 2, 2009. www.nytimes.com/2009/07/03/us/03bully.html?ref=loridrew&_r=0 (accessed on March 15, 2013).

"Fact Sheet." *Cyberbullying Research Center*, January 2012. www.cyberbullying.us/cyberbullying_state_laws.php (accessed on March 16, 2013).

Lenhart, Amanda. "Data Memo: Cyberbullying and Online Teens." *Yello Dyno*, June 27, 2007. www.yellodyno.com/pdf/PEW_Report_Cyberbullying_2007.pdf (accessed on March 16, 2013).

"The Evolution of Communication" Editorial Cartoon

Editorial cartoon

By: Mike Keefe

Date: March 27, 2009

Source: Keefe, Mike. "The Evolution of Communication." © Cagle Cartoons, March 27, 2009. http://www.intoon.com/cartoons.cfm/id/68559 (accessed on March 11, 2013).

About the Artist: Mike Keefe was the editorial cartoonist for the *Denver Post* from 1975 until late 2011, and his work continues to be nationally syndicated. A Pulitzer Prize winner, Keefe's work has been honored with numerous other awards and has appeared in *USA Today*, the *Washington Post*, the *New York Times*, and most major news magazines across the country.

INTRODUCTION

The earliest forms of communication were in no way uniform, but rather, unique to each individual. It took three million years after the dawn of civilization for communication to take on an intentional format. Cave paintings created with pigments from the juices of berries and fruits as well as colored minerals illustrated various scenes of daily primitive life. In some cases, these murals and renderings told stories. Scholars agree, for the most part, that cave paintings were used primarily to communicate to others what animals were safe to eat. Other methods included smoke signals and drums, but neither of these were ideal, as they could attract unwanted attention and be easily misinterpreted.

Written communication progressed with the introduction of vellum (animal skin). Handwritten books, written almost exclusively for religious texts, were not readily available to the masses for two reasons: Only the wealthy and some religious populations had the opportunity to learn to read, and most people did not have time to read. It was not until the thirteenth century that books not related to religion began circulating, primarily due to the increase in the number of universities in Italy and the fact that the Crusaders were returning from their adventures. Their stories gave way to the Renaissance period, an era rich in culture and the arts.

Johann Gutenberg's printing press is credited with making literature accessible to the average peasant, though the typical peasant remained illiterate. Even so, books could be mass-produced, and at a fraction of the cost. As the literacy rate improved, so did the printing process. Mass publication of all printed materials— books, newspapers, magazines— made it possible for Americans to get their hands on reading material, regardless of their preferences.

Communication made a giant leap with the advent of e-mail, or electronic mail. Although e-mail as users know it in the twenty-first century was a work in progress since the 1960s, a man named Ray Tomlinson is credited with inventing it in 1972. It was he who

MASS
PUBLICATION

MOVABLE
TYPE

Mike Keefe THE DENVER POST 03·27·09

FIRST
WRITTEN
WORD

EMAIL

TWITTER

140
CHARACTERS.
WHAT MORE
IS THERE
TO SAY?

Tweet
Tweet

THE EVOLUTION OF
COMMUNICATION

www.caglecartoons.com

PRIMARY SOURCE

"The Evolution of Communication" Editorial Cartoon

SYNOPSIS: Cartoonist Mike Keefe illustrates the timeline of communication, emphasizing the advent of mass publication as the pinnacle, and the embrace of Twitter as regression comparable to the Stone Age. CAGLE CARTOONS.

randomly chose the @ character that is used today in every e-mail address. According to a 2009 study conducted by Pew Research, more than 90 percent of Internet users between the ages of 18 and 72 reported sending and receiving email, which made it the number one online activity at that time. Its popularity would decrease within two years as social media sites like Facebook and Twitter appeared and became a central force in communication not only between friends, but business-to-consumer as well.

SIGNIFICANCE

While Facebook and Twitter admittedly secured their place in the daily lifestyles of young people, the constant flow of (sometimes useless) information did not come without a price. Between the shorthand of cell phone texting and Tweeting, modern youth are growing up in a society that rarely rests and is never silent. As the popularity of social media and instant communication, albeit in short form and often-incomplete thoughts, increased, so did concern for

the latest generation's ability to truly communicate on a deeper, more meaningful level.

Educators complained that students struggled more than past generations to spell and speak properly. Texting and Tweeting abbreviations such as LOL (laugh out loud) and OMG (oh my god) became commonplace in written school assignments. The 2009 Pew study found that 86 percent of girls and 64 percent of boys between the ages of 12 and 17 texted friends several times a day, to the tune of thousands of texts sent and received on an individual basis each month. That same year, 2009, saw a significant increase in the use of Twitter. A whopping 72.5 percent of all users had joined during the first five months of the year, thanks primarily to the endorsement of celebrities like Ashton Kutcher and Oprah Winfrey.

Critics were not impressed, and many considered the electronic age of communication to be a major step backwards in the progress of relationships, be they personal or professional. Where once the country struggled to develop an effective and meaningful standard of communication, it now took that method and edited it down to 140 characters. Mike Keefe's cartoon illustrates this idea as he shows what he considers to be America's slow descent back into the Stone Age.

PRIMARY SOURCE

"THE EVOLUTION OF COMMUNICATION" EDITORIAL CARTOON

See primary source cartoon.

FURTHER RESOURCES

Books

Kovarik, Bill. *Revolutions in Communication: Media History from Gutenberg to the Digital Age.* New York: Continuum, 2011.

O'Reilly, Tim, and Sarah Milstein. *The Twitter Book.* Sebastopal, CA: O'Reilly Media, 2011.

Web Sites

Cheng, Alex, and Mark Evans. "Inside Twitter." *Sysomos.com.* www.sysomos.com/insidetwitter/ (accessed on March 11, 2013).

"Email Statistics." *PowerProDirect.* www.powerprodirect. com/index.php?option=com_content&view=article&id=132:email-statistics&catid=63:blog&Itemid=50 (accessed on March 11, 2013).

"History of Communication from Cave Drawings to the Web." *Creative Displays Now!* www.creativedisplaysnow. com/articles/history-of-communication-from-cave-drawings-to-the-web.htm (accessed on March 11, 2013).

"Mike Keefe." *The Association of American Editorial Cartoonists.* http://editorialcartoonists.com/cartoonist/profile. cfm/KeefeM/ (accessed on March 11, 2013).

"Mike Keefe: Biography." *inToon.* www.intoon.com/about. cfm (accessed on March 11, 2013).

"Dissecting the 2008 Electorate: Most Diverse in U.S. History"

Web site article

By: Mark Hugo Lopez and Paul Taylor

Date: April 30, 2009

Source: Lopez, Mark Hugo, and Paul Taylor. "Dissecting the 2008 Electorate: Most Diverse in U.S.

History." *Pew Research Center*, April 30, 2009. www.pewhispanic.org/2009/04/30/dissecting-the-2008-electorate-most-diverse-in-us-history/ (accessed on March 17, 2013).

About the Organization: The Pew Research Center, established in 2004, is one of the leading American polling organizations. It conducts hundreds of different polls and surveys annually to determine public opinion on political and social issues and to identify prevailing trends in behavior within the United States. Pew also conducts international surveys, known as the Pew Global Attitudes Project, to record and analyze worldwide opinions about a range of social and political issues. The organization is esteemed for its commitment to non-partisan, objective data collection, which is permitted by its status as a non-profit, publicly funded operation.

INTRODUCTION

The U.S. Census Bureau conducts a Current Population Survey (CPS), a survey that collects extensive demographic data, on a monthly basis. According to the CPS, the percentage of black Americans who have voted in presidential elections has historically totaled below the percentage of all citizens who voted. For example, in 1964, approximately 69 percent of all eligible Americans voted in the election, compared to about 58 percent of all black citizens. The largest difference (10.9 percent) was in 1972, and by the year 2000, the gap was just 1.2 percent. In 2008 and for the first time in history, black Americans cast their vote for president at a higher rate than the larger population, 2.6 percent higher. And black women had the highest voter turnout rate of any population segment.

The election itself was historical: America was potentially going to vote in its first woman (Hillary Clinton) or first African American president. The Republican party historically captured the African American vote—primarily because blacks were not welcome to attend the Democratic conventions in any capacity until 1924. Even that concession did not have great impact, given that most blacks lived in the South, where they had no voting rights at all until President Lyndon B. Johnson signed the 1965 Voting Rights Act. From that historic milestone on, no Republican president had ever garnered more than 15 percent of the black vote. The 2008 election eventually came down to a choice of Democrat Barack Obama or Republican John McCain, a self-proclaimed maverick.

The cornerstone of Obama's campaign was hope. He promised America—all of America, not just the wealthy or fortunate—that together, change could be achieved. "Yes we can" became his campaign slogan. By using Internet forums and social Web sites such as Facebook and MySpace, the presidential hopeful was able to forge relationships with supporters and inspire them to believe that something better was possible. Black voters—voters of all minorities, in fact—saw Obama as their chance to be heard, and they turned out in record numbers to cast their votes.

SIGNIFICANCE

The obvious reason for such a high minority voter turnout was that Obama was black. But he not only inspired a record-breaking number of minorities to vote, he also inspired a remarkable increase in voter turnout, period. According to the U.S. Census Bureau, 131 million people voted in the 2008 presidential election, an increase of five million from 2004. This figure included about two million more black voters, two million more Hispanic voters, and six hundred thousand more Asian voters. Additionally, 49 percent of votes were in the 18 to 24 age range, an increase of two percentage points over 2004. Young voters preferred Obama to McCain by a two-to-one ratio, and Erika Johansson of the nonpartisan initiative Declare Yourself noted, "Young people absolutely made the difference in this election. Without them, he would have lost the election." Notably, women exercised their right to vote (66 percent) more than men (62 percent).

When it came time to re-elect President Obama in 2012, blacks voted at a higher rate than any other minority for the first time in history. Again, experts cited reasons other than the president's skin color for such a turnout. The electorate itself had become more racially and ethnically diverse than ever before, so there was an increase in the number of minorities who could vote. Add to that the fact that fewer whites were voting than in the past, and the data takes on a different meaning. According to Pew Research, the white electorate had been falling for decades, and that fact combined with a lower turnout rate clearly reversed the gap whites and blacks once experienced.

◼ PRIMARY SOURCE

"DISSECTING THE 2008 ELECTORATE: MOST DIVERSE IN U.S. HISTORY"

SYNOPSIS: Black, Hispanic, and Asian voter turnout was greater in the 2008 presidential election than ever before.

The electorate in last year's presidential election was the most racially and ethnically diverse in U.S. history,

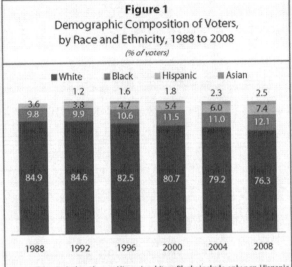

Figure 1
Demographic Composition of Voters, by Race and Ethnicity, 1988 to 2008
(% of voters)

◼ White ◼ Black ◼ Hispanic ◼ Asian

	1988	1992	1996	2000	2004	2008
Asian		1.2	1.6	1.8	2.3	2.5
Hispanic	3.6	3.8	4.7	5.4	6.0	7.4
Black	9.8	9.9	10.6	11.5	11.0	12.1
White	84.9	84.6	82.5	80.7	79.2	76.3

Note: Whites include only non-Hispanic whites. Blacks include only non-Hispanic blacks. Asians include only non-Hispanic Asians. Native Americans and mixed-race groups not shown. Asian share not available prior to 1990.
Source: Pew Research Center tabulations from the Current Population Survey, November Supplements data

with nearly one-in-four votes cast by non-whites, according to a new analysis of Census Bureau data by the Pew Research Center. The nation's three biggest minority groups—blacks, Hispanics and Asians—each accounted for unprecedented shares of the presidential vote in 2008.

Overall, whites made up 76.3% of the record 131 million people who voted in November's presidential election, while blacks made up 12.1%, Hispanics 7.4% and Asians 2.5%. The white share is the lowest ever, yet is still higher than the 65.8% white share of the total U.S. population.

The unprecedented diversity of the electorate last year was driven by increases both in the number and in the turnout rates of minority eligible voters.

The levels of participation by black, Hispanic and Asian eligible voters all increased from 2004 to 2008, reducing the voter participation gap between themselves and white eligible voters. This was particularly true for black eligible voters. Their voter turnout rate increased 4.9 percentage points, from 60.3% in 2004 to 65.3% in 2008, nearly matching the voter turnout rate of white eligible voters (66.1%). For Hispanics, participation levels also increased, with the voter turnout rate rising 2.7 percentage points, from 47.2% in 2004 to 49.9% in 2008. Among Asians, voter participation rates increased from 44.6% in 2004 to 47.0% in 2008. Meanwhile, among white eligible voters, the voter turnout rate fell slightly, from 67.2% in 2004 to 66.1% in 2008.

Much of the surge in black voter participation in 2008 was driven by increased participation among black women and younger voters. The voter turnout rate among

Table 1
Change in Voter Turnout Rates Among Eligible Voters, 2008 and 2004
(%)

	2008	2004	Change (% points)
All	63.6	63.8	-0.2
White	66.1	67.2	-1.1
Black	65.2	60.3	4.9
Hispanic	49.9	47.2	2.7
Asian	47.0	44.6	2.4

Note: Whites include only non-Hispanic whites. Blacks include only non-Hispanic blacks. Asians include only non-Hispanic Asians. Native Americans and mixed-race groups not shown.

Source: Pew Research Center tabulations from the Current Population Survey, November Supplements data

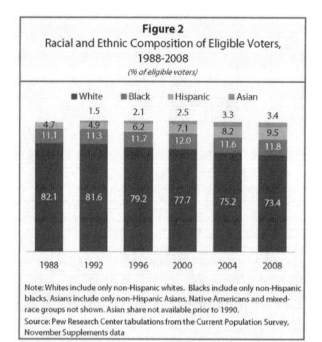

Figure 2
Racial and Ethnic Composition of Eligible Voters, 1988-2008
(% of eligible voters)

Note: Whites include only non-Hispanic whites. Blacks include only non-Hispanic blacks. Asians include only non-Hispanic Asians. Native Americans and mixed-race groups not shown. Asian share not available prior to 1990.

Source: Pew Research Center tabulations from the Current Population Survey, November Supplements data

eligible black female voters increased 5.1 percentage points, from 63.7% in 2004 to 68.8% in 2008. Overall, among all racial, ethnic and gender groups, black women had the highest voter turnout rate in November's election—a first.

Blacks ages 18 to 29 increased their voter turnout rate by 8.7 percentage points, from 49.5% in 2004 to 58.2% in 2008, according to an analysis by the Center for Information and Research on Civic Learning and Engagement (CIRCLE) at Tufts University, The voter turnout rate among young black eligible voters was higher than that of young eligible voters of any other racial and ethnic group in 2008. This, too, was a first.

Population Definitions Based on the Current Population Survey, November Supplement

Voting Age Population: The population of persons ages 18 and older.

Voting Eligible Population: Persons ages 18 and older who are U.S. citizens.

Registered Voter Population: Persons who say they were registered to vote in their state in the 2008 election.

Voter Population or Voter Turnout: Persons who say they voted in the November 2008 election.

Voter Turnout Rate: Share of the voting eligible population who say they voted.

The increased diversity of the electorate was also driven by population growth, especially among Latinos. Between 2004 and 2008, the number of Latino eligible voters rose from 16.1 million in 2004 to 19.5 million in 2008, or 21.4%. In comparison, among the general population, the total number of eligible voters increased by just 4.6%.

In 2008, Latino eligible voters accounted for 9.5% of all eligible voters, up from 8.2% in 2004. Similarly, the share of eligible voters who were black increased from 11.6% in 2004 to 11.8% in 2008. The share of eligible voters who were Asian also increased, from 3.3% in 2004 to 3.4% in 2008. In contrast, the share of eligible voters who were white fell from 75.2% in 2004 to 73.4% in 2008.

With population growth and increased voter participation among blacks, Latinos and Asians, members of all three groups cast more votes in 2008 than in 2004. Two million more blacks and 2 million more Latinos reported voting in 2008 than said the same in 2004. Among Asians, 338,000 more votes were reported cast in 2008 than in 2004. The number of white voters in 2008 was also up, but only slightly—increasing from 99.6 million in 2004 to 100 million in 2008.

The Pew Research Center analysis of Census Bureau data also finds a distinct regional pattern in the state-by-state increases in turnout. From 2004 to 2008, the greatest increases were in Southern states with large black eligible voter populations: Mississippi (where the voter turnout rate was up 8 percentage points), Georgia (7.5 points), North Carolina (6.1 points) and Louisiana (6.0 points). It also increased in the District of Columbia (6.9 points).

According to the exit polls in last year's presidential election, the candidate preference of non-white voters was distinctly different from that of white voters. Nearly all (95%) black voters cast their ballot for Democrat

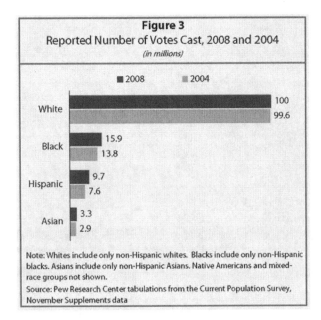

Figure 3
Reported Number of Votes Cast, 2008 and 2004
(in millions)

■ 2008   ■ 2004

White — 100 / 99.6
Black — 15.9 / 13.8
Hispanic — 9.7 / 7.6
Asian — 3.3 / 2.9

Note: Whites include only non-Hispanic whites. Blacks include only non-Hispanic blacks. Asians include only non-Hispanic Asians. Native Americans and mixed-race groups not shown.
Source: Pew Research Center tabulations from the Current Population Survey, November Supplements data

Barack Obama. Among Latino voters, 67% voted for Obama while 31% voted for Republican John McCain. Among Asian voters, 62% supported Obama and 35% voted for McCain. In contrast, white voters supported McCain (55%) over Obama (43%).

This report summarizes the participation of voters in the 2008 presidential election and follows reports from the Pew Hispanic Center, a project of the Pew Research Center, on the Latino vote and Latino public opinion about the election and the candidates.

The data for this report are derived from the November Voting and Registration Supplement of the Current Population Survey (CPS). The CPS is a monthly survey of about 55,000 households conducted by the Census Bureau for the Bureau of Labor Statistics. The November Voting and Registration Supplement is one of the richest sources available of information about the characteristics of voters. It is conducted after Election Day and relies on survey respondent self-reports of voting and voter registration....

FURTHER RESOURCES

Web Sites

Morgenstern, Claire. "Election 2008: Second-Largest Youth Voter Turnout in American History." *The Tartan*, November 10, 2008. http://thetartan.org/2008/11/10/news/elections (accessed on March 17, 2013).

Taylor, Paul. "The Growing Electoral Clout of Blacks Is Driven by Turnout, Not Demographics." *Pew Research* December 26, 2012. www.pewsocialtrends.org/2012/12/26/the-growing-electoral-clout-of-blacks-is-driven-by-turnout-not-demographics/ (accessed on March 17, 2013).

"Voter Turnout." *Social Science Data Analysis Network.* www.ssdan.net/content/voter-turnout (accessed on March 17, 2013).

"Voter Turnout Increases by 5 Million in 2008 Presidential Election, U.S. Census Bureau Reports." *U.S. Census Bureau*, July 20, 2009. www.census.gov/newsroom/releases/archives/voting/cb09-110.html (accessed on March 17, 2013).

"How MySpace Fell Off the Pace"

Newspaper article

By: Dawn C. Chmielewski and David Sarno

Date: June 17, 2009

Source: Chmielewski, Dawn C., and David Sarno. "How MySpace Fell Off the Pace." *Los Angeles Times*, June 17, 2009. http://articles.latimes.com/2009/jun/17/business/fi-ct-myspace17 (accessed on March 12, 2013).

About the Newspaper: The *Los Angeles Times* was first published in 1881, under the name *Los Angeles Daily Times*. It quickly rose to prominence as one of the premiere newspapers of the American West, primarily reporting on the merits and happenings of its titular city. The paper maintained a steady prominence through several successive ownership and management cycles, but failed to gain a major audience outside of the West until the 1960s, when it was reinvented to focus on issues of national and global importance through increased attention on field reporting and breaking news. Financial mismanagement and frequent staff changes resulted in the *Times* declaring bankruptcy and subsequently being acquired by the Tribune Company, owner of the *Chicago Tribune*. Throughout the 2000s decade, the *Los Angeles Times* remained one of the United States' most widely circulated and prominent newspapers, receiving recognition for its journalism with several Pulitzer Prizes.

INTRODUCTION

The rise and fall of Myspace was one of the 2000s decade's epic sagas, perfectly capturing the fickle and fleeting nature of success in the emerging world of social media. Founded in August 2003 as an attempt to refine the social networking and media sharing features of Friendster, one of the first Web sites to offer such services, the site name was initially stylized MySpace. Because the people who conceived the project were already employed by eUniverse, a large Internet marketing company, the site was able to develop from a concept to a fully realized business within the span of a month. MySpace quickly amassed users by tapping unto eUniverse's enormous user base, which consisted primarily of teenagers and young adults.

Thanks to the savvy of founding CEO Chris DeWolfe and company president Tom Anderson, MySpace established a significant online presence and a thriving user culture in its first year. Recognizing the potential profitability of commanding such an influential presence in the fledgling social networking scene, international news conglomerate News Corporation acquired the company in July 2005 for $580 million, providing the additional funding and resources necessary to boost MySpace to the forefront of popular culture. Features such as instant messaging, multiplayer games, streamlined media sharing, and enhanced profile customization options, implemented over the following two years, attracted a constantly expanding group of users to the service, which boasted its one hundred millionth account by August 2006. That same year, a $900 million, three-year advertising deal was struck between the social networking site and Internet giant Google, which became MySpace's exclusive provider of advertisements through its Google AdSense program.

Having changed its name to Myspace, the service was undeniably the most successful of its kind by the end of 2007, consistently ranking among the most-trafficked Web sites in the world. However, cracks in the company's business strategy were beginning to show. Bogged down by the strain and clutter of Google ads, which Myspace was contractually obligated to display in large volume, the site ran and loaded slowly. The same contract required Myspace to generate a certain number of unique visitors each month in order to receive its advertising stipend from Google, preventing the service from experimenting with significant design, layout, or functionality changes out of fear of even a temporary dip in traffic. Security on the site became notoriously ineffective, with user profiles frequently being hacked or deleted and rampant scammers and computer viruses. Worst of all, Myspace developed a reputation, largely caused by media sensationalism, as a seedy location populated by the less savory denizens of the Internet—the site was frequently depicted in the media as a hangout for political nuts, religious fanatics, drug manufacturers, pornographers, scammers, hackers, criminals, perverts, and every other sort of maniac or deviant.

By mid-2008, the sun began to set on Myspace, which started steadily losing members and revenue. In April, competitor Facebook surpassed Myspace as the most-visited social networking service on the Internet. News Corporation cycled through executives in an attempt to rescue Myspace from decline, but no amount of reorganization was enough to prevent the company from laying off more than a third of its employees in June 2009. By the end of the decade, the site had gone from the premiere social networking service to a barely inhabited, frequently derided relic.

SIGNIFICANCE

The meteoric rise and rapid descent of Myspace can be seen to represent the transience of success in the digital age and a testament to the importance of flexibility and innovation for the long-term viability of Internet businesses. Facebook's comparatively nimble but resource-light team was able to overcome Myspace, its leading competitor, by frequently updating and refining its features in response to user evaluations. Myspace, restricted by the bureaucracy of News Corporation and its burdensome advertising agreement with Google, was slow to respond to user feedback, only implementing improvements incrementally. Chief among Myspace user complaints was the site's poor security features, but the company was so slow to respond that many of its members elected to get their social networking services from a safer, more professional source.

The most common explanation of Myspace's decline is that the site clung too tightly to the strategy of using the site as a "portal," with users directing one another to various media or news items. As traversing the Web became easier and more intuitive, people no longer required a content aggregator or content-recommendation service to discover new media, but instead wanted their social networking services to specialize in facilitating interaction between users, an emphasis of Facebook and other Myspace competitors like Orkut and Twitter. Myspace, analysts contend, misapprehended the desires of its users and thus lost them to other social networking sites that were more closely attuned to the demands of the market.

Although Myspace did not cease operation completely—it rebranded itself as a music-oriented sharing and marketplace service—it never regained the luster it possessed before 2009, becoming an industry punch line that would persist into the following decade.

A screen shot of Myspace. © DIGITALLIFE/ALAMY.

■ **PRIMARY SOURCE**

"HOW MYSPACE FELL OFF THE PACE"

SYNOPSIS: In this article, the authors describe MySpace's faltering performance and falling popularity and the reasons behind the company's decline.

MySpace is looking to do an about-face.

The once-red-hot social networking site acquired three years ago by septuagenarian mogul Rupert Murdoch, which landed him on the cover of *Wired* magazine and won News Corp. praise for embracing the Internet ahead of its old-media rivals, has cooled considerably.

New statistics released this week show MySpace has been surpassed by rival Facebook in the U.S. market, where it once dominated, and ad revenue for the site is projected to decline.

Signaling the depth of its problems, MySpace on Tuesday said it was laying off 420 people—nearly one out of every three employees—as part of an aggressive restructuring that seeks to make the company smaller and more agile. The action follows a management shake-up in April, in which MySpace founder Chris DeWolfe was replaced as chief executive by Facebook's former chief operating officer, Owen Van Natta.

"Simply put, our staffing levels were bloated and hindered our ability to be an efficient and nimble team-oriented company," Van Natta said in a statement. "I understand that these changes are painful for many. They are also necessary for the long-term health and culture of MySpace."

Van Natta's comments underscore just how troubled Murdoch's big Internet gamble has become in the rapidly changing world of social media. Highly touted initiatives, such as MySpace Music, failed to live up to expectations, even as the site's developers constantly play catch-up to the technological innovations of others.

"MySpace ended up not being the leader that it wanted to be in the social-networking realm, on the tech front, on the ad front—and now on the usage front," said Debra Aho Williamson, an analyst with researcher eMarketer.

The perceived missteps are numerous. Some observers say it clung too long to a "portal strategy," in which it sought to amass an audience around entertainment content. By contrast, Facebook maintained its focus on features that enhance the social-networking experience, such as the "News Feed" that matches the immediacy of Twitter's staccato updates.

"The speed with which a company like Facebook is able to innovate and keep things fresh is the key to survival in this space," said Charlene Li, founder of Altimeter Group, a research firm specializing in social networking. "There are new things like Twitter that come along. What does Facebook do? It does Twitter ... and it does it better."

MySpace's miscalculations have cost it ground in its competition against Facebook.

Online audience measurement firm ComScore reported MySpace attracted 70.25 million users in May—a loss of 3.4 million people from the same period a year earlier. Meanwhile, Facebook nearly doubled the number of users over the same period and overtook MySpace in the U.S., with 70.28 million users.

Still, as Microsoft Research ethnographer Danah Boyd points out, with 70 million users, MySpace has hardly disappeared. "They are still as large as they were a year ago. And a year ago we were in awe of their size."

As the number of MySpace users declines, so does advertising revenue. EMarketer projects that U.S. revenue will fall 15% to $495 million in 2009 from $585 million last year.

Although News Corp. doesn't break out financial details for MySpace, revenue for the media giant's Fox Interactive Media division was down 11% in the most recent quarter from a year earlier, reflecting a double-digit drop in advertising. FIM also includes IGN Entertainment and the movie review site Rotten Tomatoes, although contributions from those businesses are modest compared with those from MySpace.

Murdoch tried to reassure investors about MySpace's direction during the company's earnings call last month, declaring that the management changes at MySpace "will help it regain its momentum."

That task may be harder than it looks. The history of social networks suggests that these sites have the fleeting popularity of a trendy nightclub. The site that's recognized as the birthplace of online communities, the Well, gave way to the more broadly available America Online, which was eclipsed by Friendster—which itself became passe.

"Each of these services supplants the one before. It takes the golden ring and everyone loves that, and they forget about the last one," said Roger L. Kay, president of research firm Endpoint Technologies Associates. "MySpace made sense at a particular date, that might have been 2003. At that moment, it was the place to

be.... Now, they have to do some major spade work on the quality of the site if they want to maintain the eyeballs."

FURTHER RESOURCES

Books

Angwin, Julia. *Stealing MySpace: The Battle to Control the Most Popular Website in America*. New York: Random House, 2009.

Lacy, Sarah. *The Stories of Facebook, Youtube and Myspace*. New York: Crimson, 2008.

Web Sites

Myspace. www.myspace.com (accessed on March 12, 2013).

"Myspace Site Information." *Alexa*. www.alexa.com/siteinfo/myspace.com (accessed on March 12, 2013).

"Special Report: How News Corp Got Lost in Myspace." *Reuters*. http://www.reuters.com/article/2011/04/07/us-myspace-idUSTRE7364G420110407 (accessed on March 12, 2013).

"Website Profile: Myspace." *Google*. https://www.google.com/adplanner/planning/site_profile#siteDetails?identifier=myspace.com&geo=001&trait_type=1&lp=true (accessed on November 26, 2012).

"Home for the Holidays ... and Every Other Day"

Poll

By: Wendy Wang and Rich Morin

Date: November 24, 2009

Source: Morin, Rich, and Wendy Wang. "Home for the Holidays ... and Every Other Day." *Pew Research Social & Demographic Trends*, November 24, 2009. www.pewsocialtrends.org/2009/11/24/home-for-the-holidays-and-every-other-day (accessed on March 12, 2013).

About the Organization: The Pew Research Center, established in 2004, is one of the leading American polling organizations. It conducts hundreds of different polls and surveys annually to determine public opinion on political and social issues and to identify prevailing trends in behavior within the United States. Pew also conducts international surveys, known as the Pew Global Attitudes Project, to record and analyze worldwide opinions about a range of social and political issues. The organization is esteemed for its commitment to non-partisan, objective data collection, which is permitted by its status as a non-profit, publicly funded operation.

INTRODUCTION

In December 2007, due to the sudden near-collapse of the U.S. financial sector, the federal rescue of the automobile industry, the bursting of the housing-market bubble, and the consequential global credit crisis, the nation's economy officially entered a period of recession. Soon dubbed the "Great Recession" in recognition of the severity of the economic decline, the recession had a devastating impact on American society. The unemployment rate sky-rocketed above 8 percent, peaking at 10 percent in October 2009, a level not seen in the country since the Great Depression of the 1930s. Median income levels plummeted, and millions of U.S. citizens lost their homes to mortgage foreclosures. The hardest-hit portion of the population was composed of middle-income workers, whose income was between $14 and $21 per hour—such jobs comprised approximately 60 percent of those eliminated in response to the recession.

Most middle-income jobs were held by young adults (ages 18–24), who had either recently graduated from college or started work immediately after high school and ascended to middle-income positions. This fact, combined with the scarcity of affordable housing and the enormous debt incurred through student loans, produced a phenomenon typical to economic recession: an exodus of young adults from their independent living situations back to the safety of their parents' homes. As employment opportunities dried up or were claimed by older, more experienced workers, a full 10 percent of adults moved back in with their families to save on living expenses. Many of those who did not were forced to consolidate their housing costs by moving in with one or more roommates. This trend ran counter to that present in U.S. society since the 1950s, in which Americans increasingly chose to live alone.

SIGNIFICANCE

The rising prevalence of cohabitation among adults, especially those who were forced to move back into their parents's homes, was contrary to the prevailing ethic of independence and self-reliance that so defines U.S. society and culture. Although some commenters lamented the growing tendency of young adults to "give up" and move back home, the majority of Americans recognized the necessity of financial security in such an uncertain economic climate. With little hope for gainful employment or homeownership, and burdened by college debt, young adults were forced to adopt a different mindset about the importance of independent living from that engendered in previous generations.

Dubbed "boomerang kids," those young adults who had ventured into the world of living alone only to return to the auspices of their childhood homes were presented with the dilemma of facing down the stigma associated with moving back in with their parents. Although the circumstances that caused them to move back home were neither produced nor influenced by their own shortcomings, boomerang kids had to deal with being called lazy and overly cautious. As *Huffington Post* editor Anthonia Akitunde opined, "At the heart of it all is this idea of independence. I feel like American culture is all about striking out on your own and following the American dream. I think it has more to do with the idea that [boomerang kids are] failing at meeting this idea of independence by going back home more than anything else." Although some parents expressed exasperation at the return of their young-adult children, most were sympathetic to the economic conditions that had forced them back—given the choice, most young adults would obviously have preferred living independently to relying on their parents.

It was not all bad for boomerang kids, however. In a poll conducted by the Pew Research Center, 24 percent of respondents who had moved back into their parents' homes said that doing so had improved their relationships with their family. Seventy-eight percent claimed to be satisfied with their living arrangements, and 77 percent expressed optimism about the future of their financial situations. Especially for full-time students, the availability of financial refuge provided by their parents was a blessing, allowing them to finish their studies without the distraction and stress of having to work forty hours a week in addition to doing coursework and attending class. Parents also benefited financially from the return of their adult children, in addition to the joy of being reunited with their offspring. The Pew study found that 48 percent of boomerang kids had paid rent to their parents in exchange for the provision of living accommodations, and that 89 percent had helped with household expenses.

It is possible that the extended, severe recession produced a shift in sentiment regarding living with family in the United States. The nation's young adults may have abandoned the traditional Western notion of disparate families in favor of the safety provided by large, cohabitational extended family units, as practiced by much of the non-Western world. What is certain is that the generation most affected by the Great Recession has been forced to reassess the traditional values of the United States in light of an economic mire they were hopeless to control.

PRIMARY SOURCE

"HOME FOR THE HOLIDAYS . . . AND EVERY OTHER DAY"

SYNOPSIS: In this article, the author describes the 2008 recession's impact on the rate of adults living independently in the United States.

The journey home for Thanksgiving won't be quite so far this year for many young adults. Instead of traveling across country or across town, many grown sons and daughters will be coming to dinner from their old bedroom down the hall, which now doubles as their recession-era refuge.

A recent survey by the Pew Research Center finds that 13% of parents with grown children say one of their adult sons or daughters has moved back home in the past year. Social scientists call them "boomerangers"—young adults who move in with parents after living away from home. This recession has produced a bumper crop.

Census Bureau data confirm that proportionately fewer young adults are living solo now than before the recession. Overall, the proportion of adults ages 18 to 29 who live alone declined from 7.9% in 2007 to 7.3% in 2009. Similar drops in the proportion of young people who

Changes in Share of Adults Who Live Alone: 2007-2009

	2007 %	2009 %	Change %
All	14.0	13.9	-0.1
Age Groups			
18-29	7.9	7.3	-0.6
30-49	9.5	9.5	—
50-64	15.7	15.6	-0.1
65+	30.2	30.1	-0.1

Source: Pew Research Center tabulations of Annual Social and Economic Supplement to the Current Population Survey, 2007 and 2009, U.S. Census Bureau.

live by themselves occurred during or immediately after the recessions of 1982 and 2001.

The current decline has been particularly steep among young women; the proportion who live by themselves fell by a full percentage point to 6.1%. Among young men, the share living on their own fell 0.2 percentage points to 8.4%, a statistically insignificant change.

While the recession has touched Americans of all ages, it has been particularly hard on young adults. According to the Bureau of Labor Statistics, a smaller share of 16- to 24-year-olds are currently employed—46.1%—than at any time since the government began collecting such data in 1948.

At the same time, college enrollment has soared to an all-time high. Taken together, record unemployment and growing college enrollments help explain why proportionately fewer young people today are living by themselves.

The Pew Research Center survey also asked all respondents if they had moved back home because of the recession. Fully one-in-ten adults ages 18 to 34 (10%) say the poor economy has forced them to move back in with Mom and Dad. [Note: Because different questions were asked of each group, the percentage of parents who report children moved back and the percentage of adult children who report moving back do not have to be identical. Parents were asked whether any child had moved back, while adult children were asked only if they personally moved in with their parents. Also, parents of adult children were not asked if the children who returned did so because of the recession.] An additional 12% say they acquired a roommate. Hard times are leading young adults to put their lives on hold in other ways as well. For example, some 15% of adults younger than 35 say they have postponed getting married because of the recession; an additional 14% say they have delayed having a baby.

Data from two different but complementary sources are used in this analysis to estimate the impact of the recession on living arrangements and family formation. The Annual Social and Economic Supplement to the Current Population Survey, conducted each March by the Census Bureau, was used to estimate the proportion of adults who lived alone in 2007 and in 2009. (The recession officially began in December 2007.)

These data are supplemented by a nationally representative survey of 1,028 adults by the Pew Research Center conducted Oct. 21–25, 2009. Results from this survey are used to produce estimates of changes in living arrangements and other actions taken by individuals in response to the recession.

Moving Back

To measure changes in household arrangements, the Pew Research survey asked all adults if they lived in their

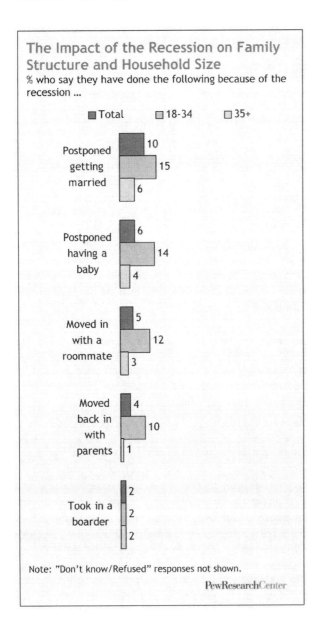

The Impact of the Recession on Family Structure and Household Size
% who say they have done the following because of the recession ...

■ Total   ▨ 18-34   ☐ 35+

Postponed getting married
10
15
6

Postponed having a baby
6
14
4

Moved in with a roommate
5
12
3

Moved back in with parents
4
10
1

Took in a boarder
2
2
2

Note: "Don't know/Refused" responses not shown.

PewResearchCenter

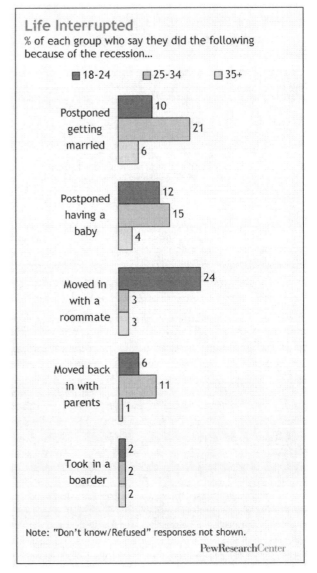

Life Interrupted
% of each group who say they did the following because of the recession...

■ 18-24   ▨ 25-34   ☐ 35+

Postponed getting married
10
21
6

Postponed having a baby
12
15
4

Moved in with a roommate
24
3
3

Moved back in with parents
6
11
1

Took in a boarder
2
2
2

Note: "Don't know/Refused" responses not shown.

PewResearchCenter

own home or with one or both parents in the parents' home. The survey further asked all adults if they had moved back in with their parents "as a result of the recession." Overall, about 11% of all adults 18 or older live with their parents in their home and 4% of all adults say they were forced to move back with their parents because of the recession, a proportion that rises to 10% among those ages 18 to 34.

About seven-in-ten grown children who live with their parents are younger than 30. About half work full- or part-time, while a quarter are unemployed and two-in-ten are full-time students. Of all adults who report they currently live in their parents' home, about a third (35%) say they had lived independently at some point in their lives before returning home. While the sample is small, roughly equal proportions of adult men and women live with their parents, while a somewhat larger proportion of Hispanics and blacks than whites live with their parents.

When the focus shifts to parents, a similar story emerges. According to the survey, nearly half of all adults (46%) have children ages 18 or older. Among these parents of adult children, some 13% say at least one of their grown sons or daughters had returned home in the past year for any reason.

The proportion of "boomeranged parents" increases to 19% among those ages 45 to 54 and declines sharply in later age groups.

Putting Life on Hold

The survey also found that the recession has altered the lives of young adults in several other important ways. For example, fully 15% of single adults younger than 35 say they have postponed getting married because of the recession, while an additional 14% of all young adults delayed having a baby. [Note: This survey did not determine how long individuals delayed getting married or having a child. Some may have delayed marriage or a family for a few weeks or months, while others may have decided to put them off for a year or more.]

The proportion of those who postponed their wedding because of the recession increases to 21% if the sample of young adults is limited to those 25 to 34— the age range in which most people get married.

At the same time, the bad economy has sent many of the youngest adults in the sample—those ages 18 to 24—scurrying to find a roommate. About one-in-four in that age group say they have moved in with a roommate because of the recession, eight times the proportion of 25- to 34-year-olds who have taken a similar step (24% vs. 3%).

But young adults are not the only ones whose lives have been changed by economic hard times. For example, about one-in-eight (12%) of all single adults between the ages of 35 and 54 have delayed marriage because of the recession.

At the same time, few Americans of any age have been forced by hard times to take in a boarder (2% of all adults) or postpone a divorce (1% among married respondents).

Fewer Young Adults Are Living Alone

In a departure from an upward trend over many decades, the share of adults in the United States who live by themselves was largely unchanged between March 2007 and March 2009. However, the story is quite different for adults ages 18 to 29.

About 7.3% of young adults lived by themselves in March 2009, a 0.6 percentage point decline from 2007. Similar declines occurred during or after the recessions of 1982 and 2001; in both periods the proportion of adults 18 to 29 who lived alone fell by 0.5 points.

In particular, young women are less likely to be living alone in 2009 than in 2007. According to the Census Bureau, the share of young women living alone has declined from 7.1% in 2007 to 6.1% this year. The drop in the share of young men who live by themselves was a statistically insignificant 0.2 percentage points.

Among adults of all ages, the percentage living alone fell during this period by 0.1 points to 13.9%. If the calculation is based on households rather than individuals,

Changes in Share of People Who Live Alone: 2007-2009

	2007 %	2009 %	Change %
Total	14.0	13.9	-0.1
Men	12.5	12.5	*
Women	15.3	15.3	*
18-29	7.9	7.3	-0.6
30-49	9.5	9.5	*
50-64	15.7	15.6	-0.1
65+	30.2	30.1	-0.1
Men			
18-29	8.6	8.4	-0.2
30-49	11.5	11.4	-0.1
50-64	14.2	14.3	+0.1
65+	19.0	18.7	-0.3
Women			
18-29	7.1	6.1	-1.0
30-49	7.7	7.6	-0.1
50-64	17.1	16.9	-0.2
65+	38.6	38.8	+0.2

Source: Pew Research Center tabulations of Annual Social and Economic Supplement, 2007 and 2009, U.S. Census Bureau.

individuals living alone currently make up slightly more than a quarter of all American households (27%).

Trends in Living Alone

The proportion of Americans who live alone has risen more or less steadily since 1950, with the most rapid growth occurring roughly between 1950 and 1980.

According to the Census Bureau, less than 5% of the population lived by themselves in 1950. By 2000 this share had climbed to more than 13%, and it reached its historic high of 14.3% in 2008. Most recently, there has been a slight drop in the overall share of adults living alone. While the proportion is largely unchanged from two years ago, it did drop 0.4 percentage points in the past year.

Although this change may seem trivial, year-by-year CPS data collected since the 1970s suggest that a decline of 0.4 percentage points is rare. It only happened twice in more than three decades: once between 1982 and 1983, when the live-alone percentage dropped to 11.5% from 11.8% in 1982, and again in 1992 to 1993 when it also fell

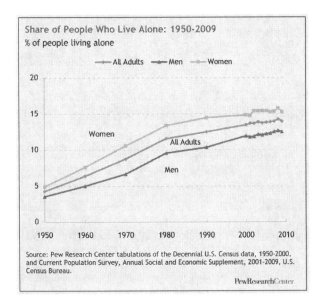

Share of People Who Live Alone: 1950-2009
% of people living alone

Source: Pew Research Center tabulations of the Decennial U.S. Census data, 1950-2000, and Current Population Survey, Annual Social and Economic Supplement, 2001-2009, U.S. Census Bureau.

PewResearchCenter

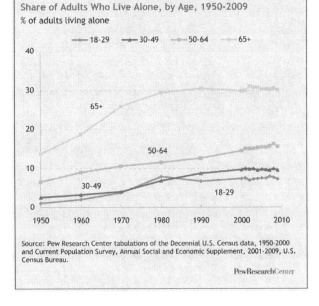

Share of Adults Who Live Alone, by Age, 1950-2009
% of adults living alone

Source: Pew Research Center tabulations of the Decennial U.S. Census data, 1950-2000 and Current Population Survey, Annual Social and Economic Supplement, 2001-2009, U.S. Census Bureau.

PewResearchCenter

0.4 percentage points. Notably, both periods were during or immediately after a recession.

The Demographics of Adults Who Live Alone

Women are more likely than men to live by themselves. Currently 15.3% of women and 12.5% of men live alone. The gap between the genders has expanded and narrowed over the years, with the smallest gap of 1.4 percentage points occurring in 1950 and the peak of 4.1 points recorded in 1990. Since 2000, the difference has stayed around 3 percentage points.

Living alone is closely related to age. In general, the older you get, the more likely you will live by yourself. Trends in the share of adults who live alone suggest a steady growth for all age groups since 1950, although the patterns are somewhat different for each group.

Only 1% of young adults ages 18 to 29 lived by themselves in 1950. That proportion increased rapidly to 7.5% by 1980 but then declined and has remained around 7.0% since 1990. In fact, the proportion of young adults living by themselves in 1980 was larger than it was for the 30–49 age group (7.5% vs. 6.5%). Today, the opposite is true, with those ages 30 to 49 more likely to be living alone than younger adults (9.5% vs. 7.3%).

Adults ages 65 and older are the most likely of any age group to be living alone. For this older group, the percentage of people who live alone sharply increased from 1950 to 1980 (13.7% to 29.4%) before leveling off. It now stands at 30.1%.

In particular, women ages 65 and older are much more likely than men of similar age to live alone, in large

part because wives tend to outlive husbands, leaving more widows than widowers. Currently, nearly four-in-ten older women live by themselves; that's more than double the proportion of older men (38.8% vs. 18.7%).

Among those younger than 50, the opposite pattern occurs. In this age group, the percentage of men who live alone outpaces the share of women. For example, 11.4% of men ages 30 to 49 live by themselves, compared with 7.6% of women.

About the Survey

Results for this survey are based on telephone interviews conducted with a nationally representative sample of 1,028 respondents ages 18 and older living in the continental United States. A combination of landline and cellular random digit dial (RDD) samples was used to represent all adults in the continental United States who have access to either a landline or cellular telephone. A total of 877 interviews were completed with respondents contacted by landline telephone and 151 with those contacted on their cellular phone. The data are weighted to produce a final sample that is representative of the general population of adults in the continental United States.

- Interviews conducted Oct. 21–25, 2009
- 1,028 interviews
- Margin of sampling error is plus or minus 3.9 percentage points for results based on the total sample at the 95% confidence level.
- Survey interviews were conducted under the direction of SSRS/Social Science Research Solutions. Interviews were conducted in English or Spanish.

*Paul Taylor, director of Pew Research Center's Social & Demographic Trends project, edited the report. Senior writer D'Vera Cohn provided editorial suggestions and Marcia Kramer copy-edited the report.

FURTHER RESOURCES
Web Sites

"Boomerang Kids: Bad for the Economy or Good for Families?" *Huffington Post*, August 15, 2012. www.huffingtonpost.com/2012/08/15/boomerang-kids_n_1777141.html (accessed on February 13, 2013).

El Nasser, Haya. "Adult Kids Living at Home on the Rise across the Board." *USA Today*, July 31, 2012. usatoday30.usatoday.com/news/nation/story/2012-08-01/boomerang-adults-recession-kids-at-home/56623746/1 (accessed on February 13, 2013).

Owens, Cassie. "My Life as a Boomeranger." *CNN*, April 12, 2012. www.cnn.com/2012/04/12/opinion/owens-boomerang-generation (accessed on February 13, 2013).

Parker, Kim. "The Boomerang Generation: Feeling OK about Living with Mom and Dad." *Pew Research Center*, March 15, 2012. www.pewsocialtrends.org/2012/03/15/the-boomerang-generation (accessed on February 14, 2013).

Plumer, Brad. "Low Wage Jobs Are Dominating the U.S. Recovery." *Washington Post*, August 31, 2012. www.washingtonpost.com/blogs/wonkblog/wp/2012/08/31/low-wage-jobs-are-dominating-the-u-s-recovery (accessed on February 13, 2013).

Chronology

Important Events in The Media, 2000–2009

2000

- Nightly network news attracts fewer than 30 million regular viewers, down almost half since 1980. More people are turning to the Internet and cable news programs.

- On February 2, *The Daily Show* on Comedy Central begins its popular satirical election coverage with a series of episodes titled "Indecision 2000," focusing on the primary in New Hampshire.

- On March 13, the Tribune Company announces it will purchase the *Los Angeles Times, Baltimore Sun, Newsday*, and several other media outlets.

- On April 19, *O: The Oprah Magazine*, headed by Oprah Winfrey, is launched.

- On May 31, *Survivor* (Borneo), a competition reality program, premieres on CBS.

- On June 11, a Pew Research Center report notes that one-third of Americans use the Internet for news, while viewership of national news broadcasts falls.

- On July 5, CBS debuts the competition reality series *Big Brother*.

- On October 6, CBS's *CSI: Crime Scene Investigation* debuts; the forensics-based crime show will spawn similar programs on this and other networks.

- On December 3, Showtime's *Queer as Folk* debuts; the drama, based on an earlier British series, follows the lives of five gay men in Pittsburgh and quickly becomes one of Showtime's most-watched programs.

- On December 14, AOL and Time Warner merge.

2001

- *The New Yorker* launches *newyorker.com*, an editorial website.

- More than half of U.S. households use at least one cell phone.

- On January 15, the online encyclopedia site Wikipedia debuts.

- In March, *George*, a magazine founded by John F. Kennedy Jr. (who died in a plane crash in 1999), ends publication.

- On March 5, Bethany McLean's article for *Fortune* questioning Enron's stock price ultimately leads to the unmasking of illegal business dealings and the collapse of the company.

- On April 3, comedian and talk-show host Rosie O'Donnell's magazine *Rosie* hits newsstands.

- On June 25, the Supreme Court rules that publishers must obtain copyright consent before posting freelancers' work online.

- On September 11, viewers watch in horror as the World Trade Center towers collapse on live television after terrorist attacks.

- On September 17, Bill Maher, comedian, political pundit, and host of ABC's *Politically Incorrect*, says that the World Trade Center terrorists were not "cowards"; he is fired in 2002, but reemerges on HBO with a program with a similar format.

- On September 24, the XM Satellite Radio service is launched, providing news, music, and other entertainment.

- On October 23, Apple releases the iPod.

- On November 6, the television program *24* premieres on the Fox network.

- On November 6, more than 400 million people regularly use the Internet.

2002

- On January 1, the term "blogosphere" (first coined by Brad Graham in 1999) is popularized by William Quick when he uses it on his blog "Daily Pundit" to describe the rise in blogging.

- On January 21, Tina Brown's *Talk* magazine folds.

- On Jananury 22, AOL/Time Warner launches an antitrust lawsuit against Microsoft.

- On January 23, *Wall Street Journal* reporter Daniel Pearl is kidnapped in Karachi, Pakistan. He is murdered by al-Qaeda on February 1.

- In March, the social network Friendster is founded; membership is strongest in Asian countries.

- On March 25, ABC debuts the romance reality show *The Bachelor*.

- On June 11, *American Idol*, a talent-competition show, premieres on Fox.

- On July 1, the satellite radio service Sirius is launched, providing uncensored, twenty-four-hour news, sports, music, and other entertainment.

2003

- In February, *Teen Vogue*, a fashion magazine aimed at young girls, begins publication.

- In March, the social-networking website MySpace launches.

- On March 20, the invasion of Iraq begins; hundreds of journalists have been "embedded" with individual units in the field.

- On April 3, Michael Kelly of the *Washington Post* is the first American reporter killed in Iraq.

- On April 9, images of Iraqis toppling the statue of Saddam Hussein make international news.

- On May 11, the *New York Times* publishes an explanation and apology for the plagiarism and fabricated stories of reporter Jayson Blair.

- On May 20, supermodel Tyra Banks hosts the first episode of the reality competition show *America's Next Top Model*.

- In October, the *New York Times* names Daniel Okrent its first public editor (an ombudsman tasked with being a watchdog on reporting by the paper).

2004

- On January 8, real-estate mogul Donald Trump debuts his reality show *The Apprentice*.

- On January 23, Robert Keeshan, better known from 1955 to 1984 as Captain Kangaroo (as well as Clarabel the Clown on the *Howdy Doody Show*, 1948–1953), dies.

- In February, photo-sharing website Flickr is launched.

- On February 1, viewers of the Superbowl Halftime Show witness Janet Jackson's "wardrobe malfunction," in which a portion of her costume is ripped off by fellow performer Justin Timberlake and her breast is exposed. The Federal Communications Commission later fines Viacom $27,500 for each of the twenty CBS-owned television stations for a total of $550,000.

- On February 4, social-networking site Facebook is launched for Harvard students only.

- On February 22, HBO's popular television series *Sex and the City*, which began in 1998, comes to an end.

- On March 21, *Deadwood*, a historical drama about a late-nineteenth-century South Dakota town, premieres on HBO.

- On May 10, *New Yorker* investigative reporter Seymour Hersh publishes an article on abuses of prisoners by U.S. troops at Abu Ghraib in Iraq.

- On June 2, Ken Jennings begins his record-setting winning streak on *Jeopardy!*

- On September 22, television program *Lost* premieres on ABC.

- On October 6, radio "shock jock" Howard Stern signs a five-year, $500 million deal with Sirius satellite radio.

- On October 8, Martha Stewart begins serving a five-month prison sentence for conspiracy, obstruction of justice, and making false statements.

- On October 19, *The Biggest Loser*, a reality show based on weight loss, debuts.

- On November 2, bloggers post early results from the polling stations in the national election.

- On November 9, the Mozilla Firefox web browser, an open source, free alternative to Internet Explorer, is released.

- On November 30, Jennings ends his winning streak on *Jeopardy!*, the longest-running in program history. He competed in seventy-four episodes and won more than $2.5 million.

- On December 1, longtime *NBC Nightly News* anchorman Tom Brokaw retires.

- On December 14, Google announces it will scan and post books in the public domain from five major libraries.

2005

- On January 15, *Tsunami Aid: A Concert of Hope*, a telethon organized to provide relief for victims of the 26 December Indonesian tsunami, airs on NBC and affiliate networks.

- On February 15, YouTube, a video-sharing website, launches.

- On March 24, the U.S. version of the British situation comedy *The Office* premieres on NBC.

- On April 23, the first YouTube video is uploaded.

- On May 9, the progressive news and blogging website Huffington Post debuts.

- On May 31, NBC launches the blog *The Daily Nightly*.

- On June 1, ABC debuts *Dancing with the Stars*, a competition show that pairs professional ballroom dancers with celebrities.

- On June 28, the three-dimensional mapping site Google Earth is launched.

- In July, *Vanity Fair* reveals that Mark Felt was "Deep Throat," the FBI officer who helped reporters uncover the Watergate affair and President Richard Nixon's involvement.

- On September 12, CBS News launches its blog *Public Eye*.

2006

- On January 3, *ABC World News Tonight* launches a blog, *The World Newser*.

- In March, Twitter, a messaging and social-networking website, is launched.

- In March, the McClatchy Company purchases Knight Ridder, making it the second largest newspaper corporation in the United States.

- On June 21, NBC debuts its challenge to Fox's *American Idol*, with *America's Got Talent*.

- In August, Twitter is made available to the public.

- On August 31, the documentary film *An Inconvenient Truth*, featuring Al Gore, is released, bolstering the growing green trend in the United States.

- In September, Sony Corporation issues its first portable tablet ebook device, the Sony Reader.

- On September 5, Katie Couric joins *CBS Evening News* as the first solo female evening anchor. The network also begins simulcasting the show on the World Wide Web.

- On September 26, Facebook is made available to users over the age of thirteen with a valid email address.

- On September 28, the popular comedy *Ugly Betty* premieres on ABC.

- On October 4, Wikileaks, a website created to reveal secret government documents, debuts.

- On October 9, Google buys YouTube for $1.65 billion.

- On October 11, Tina Fey's situation comedy *30 Rock*, about running a late-night comedy show, premieres on NBC.

2007

- On January 9, Apple unveils the iPhone. It will officially be released to the public in June.

- On April 11, CBS fires popular radio host Don Imus after he makes a racist comment about the Rutgers University women's basketball team.

- On June 10, HBO's hit drama *The Sopranos*, which began in 1999, airs its controversial series finale.

- On July 19, AMC's period drama *Mad Men*, about Madison Avenue advertising executives in the 1960s, premieres.

- On July 23, CNN and YouTube jointly host a presidential debate.

- On November 5, a Writers Guild of America strike halts production of scripted television and leads to a rise in "reality television" shows.

- On November 19, Amazon releases the Kindle, which allows users to purchase and read digital versions of books and magazines.

2008

- In January, the White House begins a blog.

- On January 5, ABC and Facebook cosponsor presidential debates.

- On February 8, negotiations with the Writers Guild of America are successfully completed, ending the Hollywood writers' strike.

- In August, more than 100 million people use Facebook.

- On December 16, the *Detroit Free Press* and *Detroit News* announce that they will end home delivery except on Thursdays, Fridays, and Sundays.

2009

- On January 15, pilot Chesley "Sully" Sullenberger safely lands U.S. Airways flight 1549 on the Hudson River after the plane is critically damaged by a bird strike. Media outlets dub the event "Miracle on the Hudson."

- On March 27, the *Christian Science Monitor* shifts its efforts to the Internet and publishes its last paper edition.

- On May 19, Fox's television musical *Glee*, which follows a group of glee-club misfits, premieres after *American Idol*.

- On June 12, all television stations are required to shift from analog to digital broadcasting.

- On July 17, "the most trusted man in America," news anchor Walter Cronkite, dies at age 92.

- On September 14, Jay Leno leaves the *Tonight Show* but remains with NBC for a five-nights-a-week 10:00 PM program, which lasts for only ninety-five episodes.

- On October 19, the *New York Times* announces it will cut one hundred newsroom jobs.

- In November, the final issue of *Gourmet*, a magazine for food lovers, is released.

- On November 20, Oprah announces her retirement (to occur in 2011) from the *Oprah Winfrey Show*.

- In December, a consortium of large American newspaper and magazine publishers announce plans to build a new Internet platform to allow future devices to access their products.

- On December 3, GE announces the sale of NBC to Comcast.

- On December 18, the Sony eReader allows subscribers to get the *Wall Street Journal* and *New York Post*.

"That's AOL Folks … "

Internet Leader and Entertainment Firm to Join Forces; New Company Worth $350B

Magazine article

By: Tom Johnson

Date: January 10, 2000

Source: Johnson, Tom. "That's AOL Folks … " *CNN Money*, January 10, 2000. http://money.cnn.com/2000/01/10/deals/aol_warner (accessed on March 19, 2013.)

About the Publication: CNN, short for Cable News Network, was founded in 1980 as the first American network to provide continuous, twenty-four-hour news reporting, and the first to offer no programming except for news. The network gained repute for its live, breaking coverage of the Space Shuttle *Challenger* disaster, the Gulf War, and the events of September 11, 2001. CNN expanded throughout the 1980s, establishing bureaus across the United States and much of the rest of the world, as well as acquiring affiliates and subsidiaries in several countries. By the end of the 2000s decade, CNN ranked among the largest news networks on the planet, with correspondents in almost every country and an enormous global audience.

INTRODUCTION

Time Warner Inc. was founded as part of a rebranding effort of conglomerate Kinney National Company's entertainment-industry assets. Starting in 1972, Warner Communications Inc., as the company was initially known, operated a diverse array of film, television, and music holdings, including the Warner Music Group and Warner Bros. Pictures. The company rose to prominence in the mid-1970s for its televised media offerings, operating popular cable and satellite channels such as the Movie Channel, MTV, and Nickelodeon. From 1975 to 1985, Warner also owned Atari, producer of Atari computational systems and the wildly successful Atari 2600 video game console. By the end of the 1980s, Warner was a household name, representing one of the largest media conglomerates in the United States. In addition to its ever-growing television offerings, the company held stake in a professional sports franchise, several film studios, a private manufacturing business, and several animation studios.

In January 1990, following a year of litigation intended to block the sale, brought by rival media purveyor Paramount Communications, Warner was acquired by Time Inc., one of the nation's largest print-media companies, for a total of $14.9 billion in cash and stock. The new company, known as Time Warner, continued to expand and diversify its products throughout the 1990s. In 1996, the company had the fortune of acquiring the Turner Broadcasting System, the nation's largest basic cable television provider, which operated such popular channels as CNN, TNT, and the Cartoon Network, in addition to owning the licenses to MGM's film catalogue and several film studios. This merger solidified Time Warner's position as a major force within the media industry, allowing expansion into international broadcasting markets.

As Time Warner was developing into one of the world's largest cable companies, America Online was pioneering the personal Internet business. America Online was founded in 1983 as Control Video Corporation, producing a short-lived system for online video gaming designed for Warner's Atari 2600 console. Two years after its inception, the company was renamed Quantum Computer Technologies, and it began marketing some of the world's first online protocols for use with personal computers—most notably Quantum Link for the Commodore Operating System (OS), AppleLink for the Apple II and Macintosh computers, and PC Link for IBM PCs. In 1989 the company changed its name to America Online and began offering its own proprietary online services, including email, gaming, and digital chat rooms. This first manifestation of America Online was revolutionary in that it included a graphical user interface (GUI), rather than a complex text-based interface, allowing computer-owners without advanced technical knowledge to navigate and operate Internet services.

In 1991, America Online released AOL for the Disk Operating System (DOS), the first of many online service suites produced by the company, including AOL for Windows Operating System and Apple/Mac Operating Systems. The AOL service suites quickly surpassed competing online service packages in popularity, thanks largely to the relative speed and ease of use offered by AOL's PlayNet software system, which hosted group chat rooms, online gaming, instant messaging, and email. AOL was periodically issued upgrades throughout the decade, offering users of the subscription-based service improved features, services, user interface, and Internet speed. Thanks to the success of AOL, America Online was contracted to design online services for the Library of Congress, the Smithsonian Museum, National Public Radio, and several educational organizations, cementing its status as the de facto leading Internet provider. By the end of the decade, the AOL system was on its fifth major update (version 5.0) and boasted over ten million subscribers, and America Online had officially adopted AOL as its company name. Use of AOL features cost a flat rate of $19.99 per month and could not be accessed through other Internet service providers.

On February 11, 2000, AOL and Time Warner filed a merger proposition with the Federal Trade Commission (FTC) and Federal Communication Commission (FCC). Under the conditions of the proposition, AOL would acquire Time Warner for $182 billion in stock and debt assumption, creating a digital-media behemoth valued at $350 billion—the largest company in U.S. business history. The merger was vaunted by financial and media industry commentators as a revolution in media provision, in which AOL would enjoy the increased speed and availability of Time Warner's extensive, high-capacity cable lines—used to offer dialup Internet access—while Time Warner would use AOL's enormous user population to market and sell its diverse range of branded products, such as music, television, comic books, films, and magazines. When the merger was approved by both regulatory agencies on January 11, 2001, the merger was officially completed. Although AOL, because of its larger market capitalization, owned 55 percent of the newly created AOL Time Warner, Inc., both companies were represented equally within the board of directors, representing their shared aims.

SIGNIFICANCE

Unfortunately for investors, nothing good came of the AOL–Time Warner consolidation. By 2001, the burst of the dot-com bubble had sent Internet technology stocks into sharp decline, causing a drop in AOL's market value. The recession caused by the September 11 terrorist attacks further injured the company's stock price, as financial concerns among distressed consumers reduced the rate at which AOL services attracted new subscriptions. Compounding AOL's problems was the rapid development of broadband Internet access, which was significantly faster than AOL's dialup service at little to no extra cost to the consumer. Were it not for the popularity of AOL's proprietary services, such as its instant messaging (IM) and gaming platforms, the company might have gone under in the face of such adverse conditions.

Meanwhile, AOL Time Warner's administration became caught up in an increasingly inimical series of resignations, demotions, reassignments, and public feuds stemming from executive infighting. Employees expressed difficulty reconciling the disparate corporate cultures of AOL and Time Warner, particularly because of Time Warner hostilities towards AOL for its dogged performance, which negatively impacted the earnings and bonuses of Time Warner employees. In 2002 it was revealed that AOL had been reporting deceptive revenue and production figures, causing a Securities and Exchange Commission (SEC)–mandated stock revaluation for the company, dropping its market value by $200 billion. By 2003, users were abandoning AOL services in droves, and the company was renamed Time Warner, with Time-Life spinning off into a separate corporate entity concerned exclusively with book and magazine publishing.

As the 2000s decade wore on, it became apparent that Time Warner had made a disastrous error in judgment by allying themselves with AOL. By 2006, the service had lost approximately 30 percent of the subscribers it had in 2003, due largely to heightened competition from companies such as Google and Yahoo, which offered services that AOL charged for—particularly email, instant messaging, video storage and sharing, and news coverage— prompting them to belatedly offer those services for free. This measure proved to be too little, too late, owing to AOL's late arrival to the free services sector, where other companies had already secured the majority of the market share. In 2008, AOL was divided into two departments, one offering its traditional online services suite and the other focused on developing advertising revenue. The next year, Time Warner officially disavowed its relationship with AOL, splitting the beleaguered Internet business off into an independent company.

The Time Warner–AOL partnership, for all its theoretical promise, turned out to be among the most ill-fated ventures in the history of American business. The merger is now a standard example in business classes, used to demonstrate that even the most promising plans can lead to huge financial loss if improperly executed. Although Time Warner was able to survive the losses incurred from its foray into "synergistic product cross-integration" on the strength of its traditional media divisions, AOL was not so lucky, fading into the obscurity shared by hundreds of once-great Internet companies. It will remain one of the 2000s decade's greatest ironies that the nation's biggest business deal turned out not to be a very big deal at all.

New Yorkers pass by the AOL Time Warner building in midtown Manhattan on September 18, 2003. © AP IMAGES/RICH KARECKAS.

PRIMARY SOURCE

"THAT'S AOL FOLKS ..."

SYNOPSIS: In this article, the author discusses the details, circumstances, and significance of the AOL–Time Warner merger.

In a stunning development, America Online Inc. announced plans to acquire Time Warner Inc. for roughly $182 billion in stock and debt Monday, creating a digital media powerhouse with the potential to reach every American in one form or another.

With dominating positions in the music, publishing, news, entertainment, cable and Internet industries, the combined company, called AOL Time Warner, will boast unrivaled assets among other media and online companies.

The merger, the largest deal in history, combines the nation's top Internet service provider with the world's top media conglomerate. The deal also validates the Internet's role as a leader in the new world economy, while redefining what the next generation of digital-based leaders will look like.

"Together, they represent an unprecedented power-house," said Scott Ehrens, a media analyst with Bear Stearns. "If their mantra is content, this alliance is unbeatable. Now they have this great platform they can cross-fertilize with content and redistribute."

The deal, if approved, calls for Time Warner shareholders to receive 1.5 shares of the new company for every share of Time Warner stock they own. AOL shareholders will receive one share of the new company for every AOL share they hold.

The new company will be 55 percent owned by AOL and 45 percent owned by Time Warner. The combination will immediately boast a market capitalization of $350 billion and an annual revenue stream topping $30 billion.

More importantly, it provides AOL, which already boasts more than 20 million subscribers through its AOL and Compuserve Internet services, high-speed broadband access to Time Warner's more than 13 million cable subscribers, further reinforcing its position as the nation's top online provider.

In return, Time Warner—parent company of a broad range of media outlets, including Warner Bros. Studios, HBO, CNN, Warner Music, *Time* magazine and CNNfn.com—gains a powerful national and growing international platform upon which to distribute and promote its sizable products.

"I don't think this is too much to say this really is a historic merger; a time when we've transformed the landscape of media and the Internet," said Steve Case, AOL's chairman and chief executive officer. "AOL-Time Warner will offer an incomparable portfolio of global brands that encompass the full spectrum of media and content."

In fact, Case said it's hard to imagine a home in the United States that is not touched by Time Warner or AOL in some way, be it television, movies, music or the Internet.

Analysts noted the deal also represents a fundamental shift in not only how content providers will be structured in the new digital economy, but how online companies are valued in the future.

The deal is significant in that although AOL—a company formed by Case after he grew tired of developing new pizzas for Pizza Hut—just recently began turning a profit, it boasted a much higher market capitalization than Time Warner, formed exactly 10 years ago through the merger of Time Inc. and Warner Communications.

So while Time Warner will initially provide roughly 70 percent of the combined company's profit stream, AOL actually will control a greater stake of its stock because of how highly Wall Street values the growth potential of the Internet.

"Today's announcement really does change the tectonic plates in this world," said Christopher Dixon, media analyst with PaineWebber.

"This really underscores the strength of the Internet," he said. "The Internet is here and it's no longer just about techs. It's about broadband, it's about streaming video, it's about streaming music and it's about coming up with all kinds of ways to use your computer in a very TV-like experience."

A DIGITAL MEDIA GIANT

The offer from AOL, which entered Monday with a market value of more than $163 billion, values Time Warner at $164.75 billion, about double the company's $83 billion market capitalization at the close of market trading Friday.

When roughly $17.2 billion in Time Warner debt is added to the equity value, the $181.95 billion offer ranks as the most expensive buyout in corporate history, far surpassing Vodaphone Airtouch's $148.6 billion cash and stock offer for Mannesmann late last year.

Time Warner shares soared on the news, climbing as high as 102 Monday before settling in up 23-3/8 at 93-1/8 by mid-afternoon.

AOL shareholders provided a more mixed reaction, bouncing the stock from positive to negative territory all day. By mid-afternoon, AOL shares lost 3/8 to 73-3/8.

The deal also pushed several other media and technology companies' shares up, as investors began guessing where the next mega-deal might take place.

"How you're delivering content and what you're doing to reach your customers, that's changing daily, and I think it would be foolish not to expect a lot more merger activity going forward," Doug Cliggott, a technology analyst with J. P. Morgan, told CNN.

Time Warner boss Gerald Levin is slated to become chief executive of the new company, while Case, who said he first approached Levin about such a merger in October, will serve as its chairman.

The companies said both boards already voted unanimously in favor of the deal, which company officials hope to finalize by the end of the year.

Ted Turner, Time Warner's vice chairman, will serve in the same capacity in the new company. Turner, who currently controls 9 percent of Time Warner's stock, has agreed to vote in favor of the deal.

While some experts speculated it may be difficult for Time Warner and AOL to merge their corporate cultures, Case, Turner and Levin expressed confidence they can overcome any obstacles.

Wearing a tweed jacket without a tie, the normally button-down Levin even joked about the different cultures. "It gives me great pleasure to welcome the 'suits' from Virginia here to New York."

Case, wearing a dark suit, said the areas of responsibility are clear.

"Gerry and I worked out very early what our relative responsibilities will be," Case said. "I'll focus more on the strategic issues, I'll manage the board, I'll focus on policy issues, I'll focus on technology issues, I'll focus on investments, I'll focus on philanthropy, the things that I said at the beginning I think I do well and I really care about. He'll be CEO running the company."

A Time Warner source said the two sides entered serious negotiations about two weeks ago before striking a deal over the weekend at Cravath, Swaine & Moore, Time Warner's law firm.

Neither side expects significant regulatory opposition to the deal, although each municipality served by Time Warner's cable system will have to approve the deal because there is a change in ownership.

Analysts did question how regulators would view any attempts by Time Warner to give AOL exclusive access to its cable lines, but press officials from the Federal Communications Commission, U.S. Department of Justice and Federal Trade Commission all declined comment on the deal.

Company officials emphasized the deal's ability to accelerate the combined company's revenue stream while generating significant efficiencies on the advertising and marketing end.

"So to me, I saw the power of that combination and as I looked around and looked at other companies and other opportunities, it really came down to there's only one combination," Levin said. "So I concluded that either we would do something with AOL or we would build ourselves, but this is infinitely preferable."

AOL Chief Financial Officer J. Michael Kelly said the company would generate annual revenue of $40 billion in its first full year of operation, while achieving $1 billion in "EBITA (earnings before interest and tax appreciation) synergies."

To highlight the point, AOL and Time Warner also announced several joint initiatives Monday.

AOL will now feature Time Warner's CNN.com, Entertaindom.com and InStyle magazine content on its service in addition to providing access to a wide range of Time Warner promotional clips.

In exchange, Time Warner plans to make a number of promotional offers available to only AOL members in addition to dramatically expanding the cross-promotion of AOL in a number of its offline media properties.

Analysts said the merger could immediately plant the seeds for future mega-deals among media companies and a growing number of online service providers.

"This is the first major combination of an online company and a bricks-and-mortar media company,"

said Ben Rogoff, manager of Aberdeen Asset Management's technology fund in London, which has more than 1 billion pounds ($1.6 billion) in assets, and holds America Online stock. "It's the deal that everyone will have to follow."

Ehrens said the company most likely to deal next is Yahoo! Inc., which draws more than 35 million visitors to its site each month, offering media firms unparalleled access to the online world.

Microsoft Corp. also will feel some heat from this deal as it struggles to encompass significant media content into its range of technology products.

"If Microsoft really wants to be a player in the media space, they are going to have to respond," Ehrens said. "This [deal] just pushes AOL/Time Warner into the stratosphere ahead of them."

FURTHER RESOURCES
Web Sites

Arango, Tim. "How the AOL-Time Warner Merger Went So Wrong." *New York Times*, January 10, 2010. http://www.nytimes.com/2010/01/11/business/media/11merger.html?pagewanted=all&_r=0 (accessed on March 19, 2013).

Li, Kenneth. "AOL Expected to Scrap Changes." *Reuters*, July 27, 2006. http://web.archive.org/web/20060818100420/http://news.yahoo.com/s/nm/20060727/wr_nm/media_timewarner_aol_dc_7 (accessed on March 19, 2013).

"The 2000s: A History of the FCC's Internet Policy Deregulation." *Media Access Project*, August 27, 2010. http://www.mediaaccess.org/2010/08/the-2000s-a-history-of-the-fcc%E2%80%99s-internet-policy-deregulation (accessed on March 19, 2013).

Feeding Tube Editorial Cartoon

Editorial Cartoon

By: Mike Peters

Date: April 2, 2005

Source: Peters, Mike. Feeding Tube Editorial Cartoon, April 2, 2005. Cartoonist Group.com. www.cartoonistgroup.com/store/add.php?iid=10081 (accessed on March 17, 2013.)

cartoonistgroup.com

THE FEEDING TUBE WAS REMOVED

THE MEDIA

SCHIAVO CASE

grimmy.com

© 2005 DAYTON DAILY NEWS KINGFEATURES SYN

PRIMARY SOURCE

Feeding Tube Editorial Cartoon

SYNOPSIS: This cartoon lampoons the frenzied coverage of the Terry Schiavo case in U.S. media. MIKE PETERS EDITORIAL CARTOON USED WITH THE PERMISSION OF GRIMMY, INC. AND THE CARTOONIST GROUP. ALL RIGHTS RESERVED.

About the Cartoonist: Mike Peters is a cartoonist who is best known for his comic strip *Mother Goose and Grimm*. After graduating from Washington University with an art degree and spending two years in the U.S. military, Peters began working as an editorial cartoonist in 1968. In 1984, having established himself as a popular and successful cartoonist, he departed from the realm of political cartooning to publish *Mother Goose and Grimm*, a daily comic strip featuring the antics of a dog, a goose, and an assortment of secondary characters from the animal kingdom. The strip's style, revolving heavily around pop culture and political references, proved successful, garnering its author industry accolades and eventually being published in over five hundred newspapers around the world. At the end of the 2000s decade, Peters's strip and editorial cartoons were a staple of U.S. newspapers' "funny pages."

INTRODUCTION

During the final quarter of the twentieth century, one of the most politically and legally contentious issues faced by U.S. legislatures and courts was the "right to die"; that is, determining the circumstances under which it was constitutionally and ethically acceptable for healthcare practitioners to deny or remove measures artificially sustaining the lives of patients with terminal conditions, or those with conditions preventing viable self-sufficiency with no chance of recovery. Debate over the right to die also dealt with the legal ability of patients to refuse medical care, and of physicians to assist in the death of wards who expressed a desire to end their own lives. Support for the legal recognition of the right of mentally incapacitated patients to die typically came from the liberal elements of American society, which argued that keeping people alive when they could not conduct themselves at a normal level of functionality and could not hope to recover from their disorder was an indignity and unnecessary waste of limited medical resources. Opponents of the right to die asserted that human life is inherently valuable and should not be allowed to expire if it could be reasonably sustained, and some voiced religious objections to any permission of human death.

A series of cases heard in the U.S. Supreme Court during this period established several legal principles regarding the right to die. People experiencing irreversible conditions that made them dependent on artificial methods of survival, such as ventilators, life-support machines, respirators, and feeding tubes, who had created living wills indicating their desire not to have their lives prolonged under such circumstances prior to the onset of their debilitation, could legally have the mechanisms extending their lives withdrawn. Those who had not left living wills, but had designated someone to assume power of attorney over themselves and their estates should they lose the cognitive capacity to conduct their own affairs, could have life-support measures removed if their designated guardian requested it. Those who had neither designated a legal custodian nor left a will could, if it was demonstrated in court that they would have wanted to die if reliant on artificial means of survival, have life-support systems and ventilators removed. Furthermore, the states of Washington and Oregon passed legislation legalizing the practice of physician-assisted suicide in terminally ill patients who expressed a desire to avert the suffering and degradation of life functions that would inevitably accompany the progression of their condition.

In the first half of the 2000s decade, the issue of the right to die was again brought to the attention of the American public, this time pertaining to the case of Teresa Marie "Terri" Schiavo. In February 1990, Shiavo, then twenty-seven years old, had suffered a heart attack while at home in St. Petersburg, Florida. Her husband, Michael Schiavo, called emergency services upon discovering her collapsed body, and responders found her without a pulse or respiration. The cardiac arrest, most likely the result of an electrolyte imbalance brought on by Schiavo's self-administered weight-control diet, put the young woman in a coma for two weeks. After her emergence, it was determined that Schiavo had suffered extensive brain damage due to oxygen deprivation, which caused her to lose motor control and coordination, response to external stimuli, and most cognitive function. Although her autonomic processes, such as breathing, digestion, and heart rate, were not substantially impaired by the brain damage, Schiavo's inability to

direct movement or swallow required that she be kept alive through the insertion of an abdominal feeding tube, through which nutrients and water were inserted directly into her stomach. Schiavo had neither left a living will indicating her wishes regarding treatment under the circumstances of her impairment nor designated a legal custodian, so her husband was appointed as her legal guardian.

Independent examinations conducted during the year following her heart attack by two physicians both concluded that Schiavo was in a persistent vegetative state, meaning that her brain damage had put her in a protracted condition of minor cognitive arousal and that she was incapable of cognizant awareness. Although she could occasionally produce sounds, facial expressions, and unsynchronized movements, Schiavo was determined not to possess full consciousness. Despite this grim diagnosis, Michael Schiavo spent the first three years after his wife's heart attack submitting her to multiple rehabilitation programs, hoping that one treatment or procedure might provide the key to her recovery. Having exhausted the available medical options, Michael Schiavo requested that a "do not resuscitate" order be granted to his wife, preventing the administration of any procedure to revive her should her heart or breathing cease. This request was submitted based on Michael's judgment, supported by the neurologists consulted about her situation, that Terri was not capable of recovery. Terri's parents, Robert and Mary Schindler, opposed Michael's acceptance of his wife's death and willingness to allow its expedited arrival, prompting what would become one of the most prolonged, scrutinized legal battles in recent U.S. history.

In May 1998, Michael Schiavo petitioned to have his wife's feeding tube removed, which would effectively result in her death from starvation and dehydration. He cited her declining condition, the absence of medical procedures capable of restoring her mental faculties, and the expenses incurred as a result of artificially extending her life as the reasons in favor of allowing her to die. The Schindlers filed an official opposition to this petition, resulting in the appointment of an objective, second legal guardian for Terri, who was to investigate the situation and relay his findings to the court. This guardian, named Richard Pearse, reported that there was a medical consensus supporting the diagnosis that Terri was in a persistent vegetative state, noting her inability to communicate or perform any task independently and that there was no possibility of her recovery. However, Pearse recommended that the court not issue the requested order to remove Shiavo's feeding tube, as Michael's motivation in doing so could potentially have been influenced by the fact that, if he remained married to Terri, he stood to inherit her estate upon her death. Also, because there was no evidence at the time that Terri would not have wanted to continue living, such as a will, it was in the court's best interest not to terminate the mechanism of her survival.

In January 2000, Michael and the Schindlers faced each other in a Florida state court to determine what Terri would have wanted to be done with her, had she been capable of expression or coherent thought. Michael testified that his wife would not have wanted her life to be artificially prolonged, claiming that she had mentioned it as a hypothetical in a conversation before the heart attack. Her parents responded by stating that Terri had been a loyal member of the Roman Catholic Church, and that she would not have wanted to violate her church's teachings regarding the sanctity of human life by refusing to receive nutrition and water. Several witnesses were called upon to testify for both parties in the case. George Greer, the judge presiding over the hearings, ruled in February of that year in favor of Michael, ordering the removal of Terri Schiavo's feeding tube. The Schindlers appealed to the Florida Second District Court of Appeals, where Greer's decision was upheld. Additionally, the Court maintained Michael's status as Terri's guardian, despite attempts by the Schindlers to force him to relinquish it. In March 2000, Terri's parents blocked the removal of her feeding tube by filing a motion requesting permission to attempt feeding of their daughter orally, which was rejected on the grounds that she was unable to swallow and thus would not be able to derive sufficient nutrition from manual food consumption to survive. Greer assigned April 24, 2001, as the day on which Terri's feeding tube was to be removed.

The next tactic employed by the Schindlers to delay the death of their daughter was to file suit against Michael Schiavo on the day the tube was removed, alleging that he had committed perjury during the previous series of trials. The judge assigned to the suit issued an injunction against the order to remove Terri's feeding tube until the new case could be resolved, and it was reinserted two days after it had been taken out. Michael's motion to have the tube re-removed was declined, pending the conclusion of the civil suit brought against him by the Schindlers. By this time, the Terry Schiavo case had begun generating publicity and attracting attention from the media, although coverage had not started to approach the level it would in the ensuing years. Michael Schiavo was found innocent of the charges against him, and the fate of Terri was placed back into the court of Judge Greer.

In August 2001, Greer heard a motion from the Schindlers requesting a stay on the order to remove their daughter's feeding tube so that they could pursue new, experimental treatment options with the potential to restore her mental function to a point sufficient for her to decide whether or not to allow her to die. The motion was dismissed, along with another request to remove Michael's guardianship of his wife. Hoping to reach a conclusive end to the battle over Terri's feeding tube, the Florida Second District Court of Appeals mandated an evidence-based trial, in which both parties were to support their claims by providing two expert witnesses, with a third, court-appointed neurologist to evaluate Schiavo's condition and deliver his finding at the trial. The trial, which took place over the course of several months during 2002, revealed that Terri had experienced significant cerebral atrophy and displayed no brain activity other than that regulating her autonomic functions. Greer reaffirmed his initial ruling, again finding Schiavo to be in a persistent vegetative state, with no hope for recovery, a decision upheld again in the Court of Appeals. The Schindlers began lobbying publicly for the cause of keeping their daughter alive, enlisting the support of Christian and disability rights activist groups to advocate on their behalf. More media outlets began covering the ongoing event, leading politicians to publicly state their positions on the case.

On October 15, 2003, Schiavo's feeding tube was removed for a second time, prompting the heavily conservative Florida legislature to respond with the quick passage of "Terri's Law," which authorized Governor Jeb Bush, brother of President George W. Bush, to intervene in the case. Florida state law enforcement seized Terri and transported her from the hospice at which she had been living to a state hospital, where her feeding tube was reinserted, then returned her. Michael filed a suit against the state government challenging its interference with the execution of the courts' rulings, which he won in May 2004, when "Terri's Law" was found unconstitutional and struck down. On appeal, the Florida Supreme Court upheld the law's rejection, which resulted in the removal of Schiavo's feeding tube on March 18, 2005.

The Schiavo case had by this point moved to the forefront of U.S. news, receiving constant, often sensationalist coverage. It was also heavily politicized, with officials and representatives of every inclination exploiting the situation to appeal to their various target voter demographics. Republicans in the U.S. Congress attempted to subpoena both Terri and Michael Schiavo to delay the removal of the feeding tube, but the effort was overturned by Judge Greer. After that failed, and Schiavo's feeding tube was removed for the third time,

Congress rushed to pass a bill, known commonly as the "Palm Sunday Compromise," that transferred jurisdiction over the case from Florida to federal courts. It was signed by President Bush on March 21, although all movements to have Schiavo's feeding tube reinserted were summarily rejected by the courts in which they were requested. Once the U.S. Supreme Court declined to hear the case, the Schindlers and their allies were left without further legal recourse, and on March 31, 2005, Terri Schiavo died.

SIGNIFICANCE

Schiavo's autopsy revealed extensive damage to the tissue and function of her brain, consistent with earlier appraisals that she would never be able to recover normal functionality. Her exact cause of death was never determined, because her body was in such an advanced state of disrepair that any of a number of factors related to the cessation of nutrient and water delivery could reasonably have been implicated in her death. Michael was celebrated by the advocates of the right to die, such as the American Civil Liberties Union, for his dedicated pursuit to allow his wife to die, and demonized by opponents of the right to die, consisting primarily of Christian organizations. The Schaivo case was considered a landmark in legal ethics, often presented as a case study in the role of the U.S. judiciary in relation to that of the legislature. It was also heralded as a triumph of civil liberty activism by liberal ethicists and theorists.

Perhaps the most noteworthy aspect of the Terry Schiavo saga was the amount of attention it attracted from U.S. media—the vigor with which news agencies and television stations pursued every avenue of conjecture and investigation into the case was rivaled only by the coverage devoted to the O. J. Simpson murder trial a decade earlier. Due to the sensitive and controversial nature of right to die debate, audiences eagerly awaited every new angle and piece of evidence supplied by the media, resulting in boosted ratings and readership for news outlets. The case also drew significant attention from politicians, who used it as an opportunity to publicly pander to audiences by professing their support of, or opposition to, the removal of Schiavo's feeding tube. As the case gained prominence, so too did public discourse regarding the rights of American citizens to end their lives.

Both the Schindler family and Michael Schiavo remained as public figures after Terri's death, releasing books and staging public appearances to argue their sides of the debate. The Schindlers created the Terri Schindler Schiavo Foundation, an activist organization that continues to provide legal support, advice, and advocacy for opponents of the right to die.

Terri Schiavo's place in U.S. history was cemented in the form of memorials and tributes bearing her name, albeit primarily by those who considered her death to have been wrongful. Although her case ended, it left a legacy in the continuing ethical, medical, political, religious, and philosophical debate over the right to die in the United States, which continued through the end of the 2000s decade.

PRIMARY SOURCE

FEEDING TUBE EDITORIAL CARTOON

See primary source cartoon.

FURTHER RESOURCES

Books

Caplan, Arthur L., James J. McCartney, and Dominic A. Sisti. *The Case of Terri Schiavo: Ethics at the End of Life*. Amherst, NY: Prometheus Books, 2006.

Web Sites

"A Report to Governor Jeb Bush and the 6th Judicial Circuit in the Matter of Theresa Marie Schiavo." *Abstract Appeal*. http://abstractappeal.com/schiavo/WolfsonReport.pdf (accessed on March 17, 2013).

"Terri Schiavo Case: Legal Issues Involving Healthcare Directives, Death, and Dying." *FindLaw*. http://news.findlaw.com/legalnews/lit/schiavo/ (accessed on March 17, 2013).

"The Terri Schiavo Information Page." *Abstract Appeal*. http://abstractappeal.com/schiavo/infopage.html (accessed on March 17, 2013).

"Terri Schiavo Timeline." *ABC News*. http://abcnews.go.com/Health/Schiavo/story?id=531632&page=1 (accessed on March 17, 2013).

"'I'm the Guy They Called Deep Throat'"

Magazine article

By: John D. O'Connor

Date: July 2005

Source: O'Connor, John. "'I'm the Guy They Called Deep Throat.'" *Vanity Fair*, July 2005. www.vanityfair.com/politics/features/2005/07/deepthroat200507 (accessed on March 17, 2013).

About the Magazine: First published as a men's fashion magazine in 1913 under the name *Dress and Vanity Fair*, the periodical thrived throughout the 1920s until the Great Depression swept America and forced the publication to merge with *Vogue* in 1935. Condé Nast revived the magazine in 1983 and it became known for its controversial photography as well as hard-hitting journalism. In the twenty-first century, *Vanity Fair* publishes all things having to do with pop fashion and society.

INTRODUCTION

Republican Richard M. Nixon was elected America's thirty-seventh president in 1968 and re-elected in 1972 in a landslide vote. Winning forty-nine of fifty states, it was the beginning of what would be the president's most politically successful year, at least from a public perspective. Behind the scenes, however, a scandal was brewing, one on such a grand scale that it would topple Nixon's administration and leave his name marred in history books as the only president ever to resign.

President Nixon was known in political circles for his paranoia. He was a believer in conspiracies, particularly those he surmised were against him. More than anything, Nixon wanted to be re-elected in the 1972 election, and he did not have qualms about breaking the law on his way to victory. To that end, he hired former FBI agent G. Gordon Liddy, who helped organize and lead several unethical and illegal activities on behalf of President Nixon. Liddy met with Attorney General John Mitchell, who became Nixon's campaign manager and confidante, in early 1972. Liddy provided Mitchell with a $1 million plan to spy on the Democrats and sabotage their campaign. He called the plan Gemstone and had every detail worked out. Liddy outlined several other plans aimed at discrediting the Democrats. Operation Sapphire would station a wired yacht filled with prostitutes off Miami Beach during the Democratic National Convention. Operation Opal would employ illegal electronic surveillance against a number of key Democrats, including presidential candidates Edmund Muskie and George McGovern. Operation Diamond would silence antiwar (Vietnam) protesters with organized kidnappings and muggings. Mitchell rejected the plans, and Liddy returned within three weeks, only to be sent away again. Eventually, Mitchell allegedly approved a scaled-back ($250,000) version that included spying on the Democratic National Committee (DNC) in its headquarters at the Watergate Complex in Washington, D.C., via illegal wiretaps and burglaries.

On June 17, 1972, five men were arrested inside the DNC headquarters. Virgilio González, Bernard Barker, Eugenio Martínez, James McCord, and Frank Sturgis were charged with attempted burglary and interception of telephone and other communications. At the time of their arrest, they had on their persons $2,300 in hundred-dollar bills with serial numbers in sequence, forty rolls of unused film, tear-gas guns, equipment used to pick locks, and a variety of sophisticated electronic recording devices. To further complicate matters for the men, McCord claimed to be a retired CIA officer and was currently involved in Nixon's Committee to Re-elect the President (CREEP) as a security man. Among their possessions were notebooks with contact information for former CIA officer E. Howard Hunt and G. Gordon Liddy. As days, weeks, and months passed, more—and more incriminating—evidence was uncovered, and so began the final days of the Nixon administration.

As was to be expected, the media immediately began scrutinizing the scandal, which came to be known simply as "Watergate." Two *Washington Post* reporters—Bob Woodward and Carl Bernstein—covered the scandal for two years. Their news articles contained details and information suspiciously close to what FBI investigators were able to uncover, and it became clear that they were getting inside information from someone with elite status and government connections. That someone was FBI deputy-director Mark Felt, whose code name was Deep Throat.

SIGNIFICANCE

As John O'Connor's article points out, the White House and the FBI were at odds even before the Watergate scandal, but President Nixon was convinced of the existence of a conspiracy against him and, for a number of reasons, specifically wanted Felt out of the picture. Felt struggled with the idea of being an informant, but in the end, his loyalty to his country and sense of justice outweighed his loyalty to an administration he viewed—quite correctly—as increasingly corrupt.

Thanks in large part to Deep Throat, Woodward and Bernstein were able to uncover and report on the scandal in a way no one else could. It was they who revealed on September 29, 1972, that John Mitchell, while acting attorney general, controlled a clandestine Republican fund used to finance far-reaching intelligence-gathering operations against the Democrats. On October 10, they reported that FBI agents had determined that the Watergate burglary was just one aspect of a massive campaign of political sabotage on the part of the Nixon re-election effort. Despite these

Washington Post reporters Carl Bernstein, left, and Bob Woodward, shown here in May 1973, gained prominence for their investigative reporting into the Watergate scandal. © AP IMAGES.

revelations, Nixon won the 1972 presidential election by beating U.S. senator George McGovern of South Dakota with 60 percent of the vote. But the story was still unraveling.

Throughout 1973, Watergate continued to be investigated, and a Senate Watergate Committee was established, with its hearings televised. Members of Nixon's administration began to resign, one by one, and White House counsel John Dean was fired. Within two months, he swore under oath that he discussed the Watergate cover-up at least thirty-five times with the president, who at the time was still denying having any knowledge of what was going on. Nixon was ordered (and refused) to turn over the White House tapes, which were made in secret and involved "alleged conversations between Mr. Nixon and various of his assistants on matters relating to the Watergate break-ins and the subsequent efforts to

cover up that crime," according to a July 24, 1973, *Washington Post* article. Instead, the president handed over individual tapes, here and there, as he saw fit, citing "executive privilege" as his reason for withholding the others. On November 17, Nixon infamously maintained his innocence on national television in a question-and-answer session with four hundred Associated Press managing editors. "I am not a crook," he insisted. When investigators found an eighteen-and-a-half-minute gap of silence on one of the Nixon tapes, the White House played dumb, and Chief of Staff Alexander Haig suggested that some "sinister force" erased the segment. On July 24, 1974, the U.S. Supreme Court ruled unanimously that Nixon would turn in all tape recordings of sixty-four conversations; they rejected his claims of executive privilege. Within three days, the House Judiciary Committee passed one of three articles of impeachment and charged the president with obstruction of justice. On August 8, Nixon became the first president in history to resign, and Vice President Gerald Ford took over the presidency the next day. The new president eventually pardoned Nixon of all Watergate-related charges. The five men found in the Watergate complex that June night in 1972, along with Hunt and Liddy, were indicted for conspiracy, burglary, and violation of federal wiretapping laws.

As decades passed, the Watergate record continued to expand to include transcription of hundreds of hours of Nixon's secret tapes, trials, and guilty pleas of about forty people related to Nixon's time in the White House, and memoirs of key players in the administration. In a 2012 *Washington Post* article, Woodward and Bernstein detailed their conclusion: Richard M. Nixon had launched and led five overlapping "wars" while in the White House—against peace activists, the media, Democrats, the justice system, and even history itself. They included in their summary a point of great irony: In the end, it was not the Democrats who ushered in the demise of Nixon's political career, but his own Republican party. A group of them, led by U.S. senator Barry Goldwater of Arizona, the 1964 Republican presidential nominee, visited Nixon at the White House on August 7, 1974. Nixon, knowing impeachment was a certainty in the U.S. House of Representatives, was counting on at least a shred of hope in the Senate. When asked how many votes he would get in a Senate trial, Goldwater replied, "I took a kind of nose count today and I couldn't find more than four very firm votes, and those would be from older Southerners. Some are very worried about what's been going on, and are undecided, and I'm one of them."

Nixon appeared on national television the next day with the announcement that he would resign.

Bob Woodward and Carl Bernstein won the Pulitzer Prize for their role in uncovering the Watergate scandal, an honor they achieved with the help of a man America knew only as Deep Throat.

▓ PRIMARY SOURCE

"'I'M THE GUY THEY CALLED DEEP THROAT'"

SYNOPSIS: A history of the FBI informer who gave journalists Bob Woodward and Carl Bernstein pertinent intelligence related to President Richard Nixon's cover-up of the Watergate scandal.

On a sunny California morning in August 1999, Joan Felt, a busy college Spanish professor and single mother, was completing chores before leaving for class. She stopped when she heard an unexpected knock at the front door. Upon answering it, she was met by a courteous, 50-ish man, who introduced himself as a journalist from *The Washington Post*. He asked if he could see her father, W. Mark Felt, who lived with her in her suburban Santa Rosa home. The man said his name was Bob Woodward.

Woodward's name did not register with Joan, and she assumed he was no different from a number of other reporters, who had called that week. This was, after all, the 25th anniversary of the resignation of President Richard Nixon, disgraced in the scandal known as Watergate, and hounded from office in 1974. The journalists had all been asking whether her father—the number-two man in the F.B.I. during the Watergate years—was "Deep Throat," the legendary inside informant who, on the condition of anonymity, had systematically passed along clues about White House misdeeds to two young reporters. Joan figured that similar phone calls were probably being placed to a handful of other Deep Throat candidates.

These names, over the years, had become part of a parlor game among historians: Who in the top echelons of government had mustered the courage to leak secrets to the press? Who had sought to expose the Nixon administration's conspiracy to obstruct justice through its massive campaign of political espionage and its subsequent cover-up? Who, indeed, had helped bring about the most serious constitutional crisis since the 1868 impeachment trial of Andrew Johnson—and, in the process, changed the fate of the nation?

Joan was suddenly curious. Unlike the others, this reporter had come by in person. What's more, he claimed to be a friend of her father's. Joan excused herself and spoke to her dad. He was 86 at the time, alert though clearly diminished by the years. Joan told him about the stranger at the door and was surprised when he readily agreed to see "Bob."

She ushered him in, excused herself, and the two men talked for half an hour, Joan recalls. Then she invited them to join her for a drive to the market nearby. "Bob sat in the backseat," she says. "I asked him about his life, his job. He said he'd been out here on the West Coast covering [Arizona senator] John McCain's [presidential] campaign and was in Sacramento or Fresno"—four hours away—"and thought he'd stop by. He looked about my age. I thought, Gee, [he's] attractive. Pleasant too. Too bad this guy isn't single."

Woodward and Felt waited in the car while Joan popped into the grocery store. On the way home, Joan remembers, Woodward asked her, "Would it be all right to take your dad to lunch and have a drink?" She agreed. And so, once back at the house, Woodward left to get his car.

The Watergate figure known as the secret "Deep Throat," Mark Felt, and his daughter, Joan Felt, on May 31, 2005.
© AP IMAGES/BEN MARGOT.

Joan, always looking after her dad's health, realized she should probably caution Woodward to limit her father to one or two drinks. Yet when she opened the front door, she could find neither the reporter nor his car. Puzzled, she decided to drive around the neighborhood, only to discover him outside the Felts' subdivision, walking into a parking lot of a junior high school some eight blocks from the house. He was just about to enter a chauffeured limousine. Joan, however, was too polite to ask Woodward why he had chosen to park there. Or why, for that matter, he had come in a limo.

That night her father was ebullient about the lunch, recounting how "Bob" and he had downed martinis. Joan found it all a bit odd. Her father had been dodging reporters all week, but had seemed totally comfortable with this one. And why had Woodward taken such precautions? Joan trusted her instincts. Though she still hadn't made the connection between Woodward, *The Washington Post*, and the Watergate scandal, she was convinced that this was a less than serendipitous visit.

Sure enough, in the years to follow, Mark Felt and his daughter, along with Joan's brother, Mark junior, and her son Nick, would continue to communicate with Woodward by phone (and in several e-mail exchanges) as Felt progressed into his 90s. Felt suffered a mild stroke in 2001. His mental faculties began to deteriorate a bit. But

he kept his spirit and sense of humor. And always, say Joan, aged 61, and Mark junior, 58, Woodward remained gracious and friendly, occasionally inquiring about Felt's health. "As you may recall," Woodward e-mailed Joan in August of 2004, "my father [is] also approaching 91. [He] seems happy—the goal for all of us. Best to everyone, Bob."

Three years after Woodward's visit, my wife, Jan, and I happened to be hosting a rather lively dinner for my daughter Christy, a college junior, and seven of her friends from Stanford. The atmosphere had the levity and intensity of a reunion, as several of the students had just returned from sabbaticals in South America. Jan served her typical Italian-style feast with large platters of pasta, grilled chicken, and vegetables, and plenty of beer and wine. Our house, in Marin County, overlooks the San Rafael Hills, and the setting that spring evening was perfect for trading stories about faraway trips.

Nick Jones, a friend of Christy's whom I had known for three years, listened as I related a story about my father, an attorney who had begun his career in Rio during World War II by serving as an undercover F.B.I. agent. When talk turned to the allure and intrigue of Rio in the 40s, Nick mentioned that his grandfather, also a lawyer, had joined the bureau around that time and had gone on to become a career agent. "What's his name?," I asked.

"You may have heard of him," he said. "He was a pretty senior guy in the F.B.I. ... Mark Felt."

I was blown away. Here was an enterprising kid who was working his way through school. He reminded me of myself in a way: an energetic overachiever whose father, like Nick's grandfather, had served as an intelligence agent. (Nick and I were both good high-school athletes. I went to Notre Dame, the University of Michigan Law School, class of '72, then joined the U.S. Attorney's Office in San Francisco, ultimately landing at a highly respected Bay Area law firm.) I had taken Nick under my wing, encouraging him to consider studying to become a lawyer. And yet I had no idea that his grandfather was the same guy—long rumored as the infamous Deep Throat—whom I'd heard about for years from my days as a federal prosecutor. Felt had even worked with my early mentor, William Ruckelshaus, most famous for his role in the so-called Saturday Night Massacre, of 1973. (When Watergate special prosecutor Archibald Cox subpoenaed nine Nixon tape recordings that he had secretly made in the Oval Office, the president insisted that Cox be fired. Rather than dismiss Cox, Nixon's attorney general, Elliot Richardson, and his deputy, Ruckelshaus, resigned in protest, becoming national heroes.)

Deep Throat, in fact, had been the hero who started it all—along with the two reporters he assisted, Bob Woodward and Carl Bernstein (both of whom would go on to make their journalistic reputations, and riches, through their Watergate revelations). And my daughter's friend, I suspected, was the famous source's grandson. "Mark Felt!," I exclaimed. "You're kidding me. Your granddad is Deep Throat! Did you know that?"

Nick answered calmly, and maybe with an air of uncertainty, "You know, Big John, I've heard that for a long time. Just recently we've started to think maybe it's him."

We let the subject drop that night, turning to other matters. But a few days later Nick phoned and asked me, in my role as an attorney, to come over and meet his grandfather. Nick and his mother wanted to discuss the wisdom of Felt's coming forward. Felt, Nick said, had recently admitted his secret identity, privately, to intimates, after years of hiding the truth even from his family. But Felt was adamant about remaining silent on the subject—until his death—thinking his past disclosures somehow dishonorable.

Joan and Nick, however, considered him a true patriot. They were beginning to realize that it might make sense to enlist someone from the outside to help him tell his story, his way, *before* he passed away, unheralded and forgotten.

I agreed to see Mark Felt later that week.

The identity of Deep Throat is modern journalism's greatest unsolved mystery. It has been said that he may be the most famous anonymous person in U.S. history. But, regardless of his notoriety, American society today owes a considerable debt to the government official who decided, at great personal risk, to help Woodward and Bernstein as they pursued the hidden truths of Watergate.

First, some background. In the early-morning hours of June 17, 1972, five "burglars" were caught breaking into the headquarters of the Democratic National Committee at the Watergate complex, along the Potomac River. Two members of the team were found to have address books with scribbles "W. House" and "W.H." They were operating, as it turned out, on the orders of E. Howard Hunt, a onetime C.I.A. agent who had recently worked in the White House, and G. Gordon Liddy, an ex-F.B.I. agent who was on the payroll of the Committee to Re-elect the President (CRP, pronounced Creep, which was organizing Nixon's run against Senator George McGovern, the South Dakota Democrat).

Funds for the break-in, laundered through a Mexican bank account, had actually come from the coffers of CRP, headed by John Mitchell, who had been attorney general during Nixon's first term. Following the break-in, suspicions were raised throughout Washington: What were five men with Republican connections doing with gloves, cameras, large amounts of cash, and bugging equipment in the Democrats' top campaign office?

The case remained in the headlines thanks to the dogged reporting of an unlikely team of journalists, both in their late 20s: Carl Bernstein, a scruffy college dropout and six-year veteran of the *Post* (now a writer, lecturer, and *Vanity Fair* contributor), and Bob Woodward, an ex-navy officer and Yale man (now a celebrated author and *Post* assistant managing editor). The heat was also kept on because of a continuing F.B.I. investigation, headed by the bureau's acting associate director, Mark Felt, whose teams interviewed 86 administration and CRP staffers. These sessions, however, were quickly undermined. The White House and CRP had ordered that their lawyers be present at every meeting. Felt believed that the C.I.A. deliberately gave the F.B.I. false leads. And most of the bureau's "write-ups" of the interviews were being secretly passed on to Nixon counsel John Dean—by none other than Felt's new boss, L. Patrick Gray. (Gray, the acting F.B.I. director, had taken over after J. Edgar Hoover's death, six weeks before the break-in.) Throughout this period, the Nixon camp denied any White House or CRP involvement in the Watergate affair. And after a three-month "investigation" there was no evidence to implicate any White House staffers.

The Watergate probe appeared to be at an impasse, the break-in having been explained away as a private extortion scheme that didn't extend beyond the suspects in custody. McGovern couldn't gain campaign traction with the issue, and the president was re-elected in November 1972 by an overwhelming majority.

But during that fateful summer and fall, at least one government official was determined not to let Watergate fade away. That man was Woodward's well-placed source. In an effort to keep the Watergate affair in the news, Deep Throat had been consistently confirming or denying confidential information for the reporter, which he and Bernstein would weave into their frequent stories, often on the *Post*'s front page.

Ever cautious, Woodward and Deep Throat devised cloak-and-dagger methods to avoid tails and eavesdroppers during their numerous rendezvous. If Woodward needed to initiate a meeting, he would position an empty flowerpot (which contained a red construction flag) to the rear of his apartment balcony. If Deep Throat was the instigator, the hands of a clock would mysteriously appear on page 20 of Woodward's copy of *The New York Times*, which was delivered before seven each morning. Then they would connect at the appointed hour in an underground parking garage. (Woodward would always take two cabs and then walk a short distance to their meetings.) The garage afforded Deep Throat a darkened venue for hushed conversation, a clear view of any potential intruders, and a quick escape route.

Whoever Deep Throat might have been, he was certainly a public official in private turmoil. As the two *Post* reporters would explain in their 1974 behind-the-scenes book about Watergate, *All the President's Men*, Deep Throat lived in solitary dread, under the constant threat of being summarily fired or even indicted, with no colleagues in whom he could confide. He was justifiably suspicious that phones had been wiretapped, rooms bugged, and papers rifled. He was completely isolated, having placed his career and his institution in jeopardy. Eventually, Deep Throat would even warn Woodward and Bernstein that he had reason to believe "everyone's life is in danger"— meaning Woodward's, Bernstein's, and, presumably, his own.

In the months that followed, the *Post*'s exposés continued unabated in the face of mounting White House pressure and protest. Deep Throat, having become more enraged with the administration, grew more bold. Instead of merely corroborating facts that the two reporters obtained from other sources, he began providing leads and outlining an administration-sanctioned conspiracy. (In the film version of the book, Robert Redford and Dustin Hoffman would portray Woodward and Bernstein, while Hal Holbrook assumed the Deep Throat role.)

Soon public outcry grew. Other media outlets began to investigate in earnest. The Senate convened riveting televised hearings in 1973, and when key players such as John Dean cut immunity deals, the entire plot unraveled. President Nixon, it turned out, had tape-recorded many of the meetings where strategies had been hashed out— and the cover-up discussed (in violation of obstruction-of-justice laws). On August 8, 1974, with the House of Representatives clearly moving toward impeachment, the president announced his resignation, and more than 30 government and campaign officials in and around the Nixon White House would ultimately plead guilty to or be convicted of crimes. In brief, Watergate had reaffirmed that no person, not even the president of the United States, is above the law.

Due in no small part to the secrets revealed by the *Post*, sometimes in consort with Deep Throat, the courts and the Congress have been loath to grant a sitting president free rein, and are generally wary of administrations that might try to impede access to White House documents in the name of "executive privilege." Watergate helped set in motion what would become known as the "independent counsel" law (for investigating top federal officials) and helped make whistle-blowing (on wrongdoings in business and government) a legally sanctioned, if still risky and courageous, act. Watergate invigorated an independent press, virtually spawning a generation of investigative journalists.

And yet, ever since the political maelstrom of Nixon's second term, Deep Throat has declined to reveal himself. He has kept quiet through seven presidencies and despite an anticipated fortune that might have come his way from a tell-all book, film, or television special. Woodward has said that Deep Throat wished to remain anonymous until death, and he pledged to keep his source's confidence, as he has for more than a generation. (Officially, Deep Throat's identity has been known only to Woodward, Bernstein, their former editor Ben Bradlee—and to Deep Throat himself.)

In *All the President's Men*, the authors described their source as a man of passion and contradiction: "Aware of his own weaknesses, he readily conceded his flaws. He was, incongruously, an incurable gossip, careful to label rumor for what it was, but fascinated by it. . . . He could be rowdy, drink too much, overreach. He was not good at concealing his feelings, hardly ideal for a man in his position." Even though he was a Washington creature he was "worn out" by years of bureaucratic battles, a man disenchanted with the "switchblade mentality" of the Nixon White House and its tactics of politicizing governmental agencies. Deep Throat was someone in an "extremely sensitive" position, possessing "an aggregate of hard information flowing in and out of many stations," while at the same time quite wary of his role as a confidential source. "Deep Throat," noted Woodward in a lecture in 2003, "lied to his family, to his friends, and colleagues, denying that he had helped us."

And as the years went on, Joan Felt had really begun to wonder whether her father might just be this courageous but tortured man.

Born in Twin Falls, Idaho, in 1913, Mark Felt came of age at a time when the F.B.I. agent was an archetypal patriot—a crime-fighter in a land that had been torn by war, the Depression, and Mob violence. Raised in modest circumstances, the outgoing, take-charge Felt worked his way through the University of Idaho (where he was head of his fraternity) and the George Washington University Law School, married another Idaho grad, Audrey Robinson, then joined the bureau in 1942.

Dapper, charming, and handsome, with a full head of sandy hair that grayed attractively over the years, Felt resembled actor Lloyd Bridges. He was a registered Democrat (who turned Republican during the Reagan years) with a conservative bent and a common man's law-and-order streak. Often relocating his family, he would come to speak at each new school that Joan Felt attended—wearing a shoulder holster, hidden under his pinstripes. In the bureau, he was popular with supervisors and underlings alike, and enjoyed both scotch and bourbon, though he was ever mindful of Hoover's edicts about his agents' sobriety. Felt helped curb the Kansas City Mob as that city's special agent in charge, using tactics both aggressive and innovative, then was named second-in-command of the bureau's training division in

1962. Felt mastered the art of succinct, just-the-facts-ma'am memo writing, which appealed to the meticulous Hoover, who made him one of his closest protégés. In 1971, in a move to rein in his power-seeking head of domestic intelligence, William C. Sullivan, Hoover promoted Felt to a newly created position overseeing Sullivan, vaulting Felt to prominence.

While Felt rose through the ranks, his daughter, Joan, became decidedly anti-Establishment. As Joan's lifestyle changed, her father quietly but strongly disapproved, telling her that she and her peers reminded him of radical Weather Underground members—a faction he happened to be in the process of hunting down. Joan cut off contact with her parents for a time (she has been reconciled with her dad for more than 25 years now), retreating to a commune where, with a movie camera rolling, she gave birth to her first son, Ludi (Nick's brother, now called Will), a scene used in the 1974 documentary *The Birth of Ludi*. On one occasion her parents arrived at Joan's farm for a visit, only to find her and a friend sitting naked in the sun, breast-feeding their babies.

Joan's brother, Mark junior, a commercial pilot and retired air-force lieutenant colonel, says that at that stage their father was utterly absorbed in his work. "By the time he'd got to Washington," Mark recalls, "he worked six days a week, got home, had dinner, and went to bed. He believed in the F.B.I. more than anything else he believed in in his life." For a time, Mark says, his dad also served as an unpaid technical adviser to the popular 60s TV program *The F.B.I.*, occasionally going onto the set with Efrem Zimbalist Jr., who played an agent with responsibilities similar to Felt's. "He was a cool character," says the younger Felt, "willing to take risks and go outside of the rule book to get the job done."

In his little-known 1979 memoir, *The F.B.I. Pyramid*, co-written with Ralph de Toledano, Felt comes across as a down-to-earth counterpart to the imperious Hoover—a man Felt deeply respected. Hoover, in Felt's view, was "charismatic, feisty, charming, petty, giant, grandiose, brilliant, egotistical, industrious, formidable, compassionate, domineering"; he possessed a "puritanical" streak, the bearing of an "inflexible martinet," and obsessive habits. ("Hoover insisted on the same seats in the plane, the same rooms in the same hotels. [He had an] immaculate appearance ... as if he had shaved, showered, and put on a freshly pressed suit for [every] occasion.") Felt, a more sociable figure, was still a man in the Hoover mold: disciplined, fiercely loyal to the men under his command, and resistant to any force that tried to compromise the bureau. Felt came to see himself, in fact, as something of a conscience of the F.B.I.

Well before Hoover's death, relations between the Nixon camp and the F.B.I. deteriorated. In 1971, Felt was

Former CIA associate director and Watergate "Deep Throat" figure Mark Felt appears on CBS-TV's *Face the Nation*. © BETTMANN/CORBIS.

called to 1600 Pennsylvania Avenue. The president, Felt was told, had begun "climbing the walls" because someone (a government insider, Nixon believed) was leaking details to *The New York Times* about the administration's strategy for upcoming arms talks with the Soviets. Nixon's aides wanted the bureau to find the culprits, either through wiretaps or by insisting that suspects submit to lie-detector tests. Such leaks led the White House to begin employing ex-C.I.A. types to do their own, homespun spying, creating its nefarious "Plumbers" unit, to which the Watergate cadre belonged.

Felt arrived at the White House to confront an odd gathering. Egil "Bud" Krogh Jr., deputy assistant for domestic affairs, presided, and attendees included ex-spy E. Howard Hunt and Robert Mardian, an assistant attorney general—"a balding little man," Felt recalled, "dressed in what looked like work clothes and dirty tennis shoes ... shuffling about the room, arranging the chairs and I [first] took him to be a member of the cleaning staff." (Mardian had been summoned to the West Wing from a weekend tennis game.) According to Felt, once the meeting began, Felt expressed resistance to the idea of wiretapping suspected leakers without a court order.

After the session, which ended with no clear resolution, Krogh's group began to have reason to suspect a single Pentagon employee. Nixon, nonetheless, demanded that "four or five hundred people in State, Defense, and so forth [also be polygraphed] so that we can immediately scare the bastards." Two days later, as Felt wrote in his book, he was relieved when Krogh told him that the administration had decided to let "the Agency," not the F.B.I., "handle the polygraph interviews.... Obviously, John Ehrlichman [Krogh's boss, Nixon's top domestic-policy adviser, and the head of the Plumbers unit] had decided to 'punish' the Bureau for what he saw as its lack of cooperation and its refusal to get involved in the work which the 'Plumbers' later undertook."

In 1972, tensions between the institutions deepened when Hoover and Felt resisted White House pressure to have the F.B.I. forensics lab declare a particularly damning memo a forgery—as a way of exonerating the administration in a corruption scandal. Believing that trumped-up forgery findings were improper, and trying to sustain the reputation of the F.B.I. lab, Felt claimed to have refused entreaties by John Dean. (The episode took on elements of the absurd when Hunt, wearing an ill-fitting red wig, showed up in Denver in an effort to extract information from Dita Beard, the communications lobbyist who had supposedly written the memo.)

Clearly, Felt harbored increasing contempt for this curious crew at the White House, whom he saw as intent on utilizing the Justice Department for their political ends. What's more, Hoover, who had died that May, was no longer around to protect Felt or the bureau's Old Guard, the F.B.I. chief having been replaced by an interim successor, L. Patrick Gray, a Republican lawyer who hoped to permanently land Hoover's job. Gray, with his eyes on that prize, chose to leave an increasingly frustrated Felt in charge of the F.B.I.'s day-to-day operations. Then came the break-in, and a pitched battle began. "We seemed to be continually at odds with the White House about almost everything," Felt wrote, regarding the dark days of 1972. He soon came to believe that he was fighting an all-out war for the soul of the bureau.

As the F.B.I. pushed on with its Watergate investigation, the White House threw up more and more barriers. When Felt and his team believed they could "trace the source of the money that had been in the possession of the Watergate 'burglars'" to a bank in Mexico City, Gray, according to Felt, "flatly ordered [Felt] to call off any interviews" in Mexico because they "might upset" a

C.I.A. operation there. Felt and his key deputies sought a meeting with Gray. "Look," Felt recalled telling his boss, "the reputation of the FBI is at stake.... Unless we get a request in writing [from the C.I.A.] to forgo the [Mexico] interview, we're going ahead anyway!

"That's not all," Felt supposedly added. "We must do something about the complete lack of cooperation from John Dean and the Committee to Reelect the President. It's obvious they're holding back—delaying and leading us astray in every way they know. We expect this sort of thing when we are investigating organized crime.... The whole thing is going to explode right in the President's face."

At a subsequent meeting, according to Felt, Gray asked whether the investigation could be confined to "these seven subjects," referring to the five burglars, plus Hunt and Liddy. Felt responded, "We will be going much higher than these seven. These men are the pawns. We want the ones who moved the pawns." Agreeing with his team, Gray chose to stay the course and continue the probe.

Felt's book gives no indication that during this same period he decided to go outside the bounds of government to expose the corruption within Nixon's team—or to overcome the impediments they were placing on his ability to do his job. There are only scant clues that he might have decided to pass along secrets to *The Washington Post*; in fact, Felt makes a point of categorically denying he is Deep Throat. But, in truth, the White House had begun asking for Felt's head, even though Gray adamantly defended his deputy. Felt would write:

> Gray confided to me, "You know, Mark, [Attorney General] Dick Kleindienst told me that I might have to get rid of you. He says White House staff members are convinced that you are the FBI source of leaks to Woodward and Bernstein." ...
>
> I said, "Pat, I haven't leaked anything to anybody. They are wrong!" ...
>
> "I believe you," Gray answered, "but the White House doesn't. Kleindienst has told me on three or four occasions to get rid of you but I refused. He didn't say this came from higher up but I am convinced that it did."

It is clear from the Watergate tapes that Felt was indeed one of the targets of Nixon's wrath. In October 1972, Nixon insisted he would "fire the whole Goddamn Bureau," and singled out Felt, whom he thought to be part of a plot to undermine him through frequent press leaks. "Is he a Catholic?" he asked his trusted adviser H. R. Haldeman, who replied that Felt was Jewish. (Felt, of Irish descent, is not Jewish and claims no religious affiliation.) Nixon, who sometimes suggested that a

Jewish conspiracy might be at the root of his problems, seemed surprised. "Christ," he said, "[the bureau] put a Jew in there?... It could be the Jewish thing. I don't know. It's always a possibility."

It was Gray, however, not Felt, who became the fall guy. At Gray's confirmation hearings, in February 1973, he was abandoned by his onetime allies in the West Wing and was left to "twist slowly, slowly in the wind," in the words of Nixon aide John Ehrlichman. With Gray now gone, Felt had lost his last sponsor and protector. Next up was interim F.B.I. director Ruckelshaus, who ultimately resigned as assistant attorney general in Nixon's Saturday Night Massacre. Felt left the bureau that same year and went on the lecture circuit.

Then, in 1978, Felt was indicted on charges of having authorized illegal F.B.I. break-ins earlier in the decade, in which agents without warrants entered the residences of associates and family members of suspected bombers believed to be involved with the Weather Underground. The career agent was arraigned as hundreds of F.B.I. colleagues, outside the courthouse, demonstrated on his behalf. Felt, over the strong objections of his lawyers that the jury had been improperly instructed, claimed that he was following established law-enforcement procedures for break-ins when national security was at stake. Even so, Felt was convicted two years later. Then, in a stroke of good fortune while his case was on appeal, Ronald Reagan was elected president and, in 1981, gave Felt a full pardon.

Felt and his wife had always looked forward to a retirement where they could live comfortably and bask proudly in his accomplishments. But as he endured years of courtroom travails, they both felt betrayed by the country he had served. Audrey, always an intense person, suffered profound stress, anxiety, and nervous exhaustion, which both of them bitterly blamed on his legal troubles. Long after her early passing, in 1984, Felt continued to cite the strain of his prosecution as a major factor in the death of his wife.

A week after our festive dinner in 2002, Nick Jones introduced me to his mother, Joan Felt—dynamic and open-minded, high-strung and overworked, proud and protective of her father, slim and attractive (she had been an actress for a time)—and to his grandfather. Felt, then 88, was a chipper, easygoing man with a hearty laugh and an enviable shock of white hair. His eyes sparkled and his handshake was firm. Though he required the assistance of a metal walker on his daily rounds, having sustained a stroke the year before, he was nonetheless engaged and engaging.

I soon realized the urgency behind Nick's request. A few weeks before—possibly in anticipation of the 30th anniversary of the Watergate break-in—a reporter for the *Globe* tabloid, Dawna Kaufmann, had called Joan to ask

Watergate investigative reports Bob Woodward, left, and Carl Bernstein appear together at the University of Texas at Austin in March 2007. © AP IMAGES/DAILY TEXAN/PETER FRANKLIN.

whether her father was actually Deep Throat. Joan talked briefly about Woodward's mysterious visit three years before. Kaufmann then wrote a piece headlined DEEP THROAT EXPOSED! In her story she quoted a young man by the name of Chase Culeman-Beckman. He had claimed, in a 1999 *Hartford Courant* article, that while attending summer camp in 1988 a young friend of his named Jacob Bernstein—the son of Carl Bernstein and writer Nora Ephron—had divulged a secret, mentioning that his father had told him that a man named Mark Felt was the infamous Deep Throat. Ephron and Bernstein, divorced by 1999, both asserted that Felt was the favorite suspect of Ephron's, and that Bernstein had never disclosed Deep Throat's identity. According to Bernstein's response at the time, their son was simply repeating his mother's guess. (When approached by reporters speculating about Deep Throat's identity, Woodward and Bernstein have consistently refused to divulge it.)

Soon after the *Globe* article appeared, Joan Felt received a frantic phone call from Yvette La Garde. During the late 1980s, following his wife's death, Felt and La Garde had become close friends and frequent social companions. "Why is he announcing it now?" a worried La Garde asked Joan. "I thought he wouldn't be revealed until he was dead."

Joan pounced. "Announcing what?" she wanted to know.

La Garde, apparently sensing that Joan did not know the truth, pulled back, then finally owned up to the secret she had kept for years. Felt, La Garde said, had confided to her that he had indeed been Woodward's source, but had sworn her to silence. Joan then confronted her father, who initially denied it. "I know now that you're Deep Throat," she remembers telling him, explaining La Garde's disclosure. His response: "Since that's the case, well, yes, I am." Then and there, she pleaded with him to announce his role immediately so that he could have some closure, and accolades, while he was still alive. Felt reluctantly agreed, then changed his mind. He seemed determined to take his secret with him to the grave.

But it turned out that Yvette La Garde had also told others. A decade before, she had shared her secret with her eldest son, Mickey, now retired—a fortunate confidant, given his work as an army lieutenant colonel based at NATO military headquarters (requiring a top-secret security clearance). Mickey La Garde says he has remained mum about the revelation ever since: "My mom's condo unit was in Watergate and I'd see Mark," he recalls. "In one of those visits, in 1987 or '88, she confided to [my wife] Dee and I that Mark had, in fact, been the Deep Throat that brought down the Nixon administration. I don't think Mom's ever told anyone else."

Dee La Garde, a C.P.A. and government auditor, corroborates her husband's account. "She confessed it," Dee recalls. "The three of us might have been at the kitchen table in her apartment. There's no question in my mind that she identified him. You're the first person I've discussed this with besides my husband."

The day of her father's grand admission, Joan left for class, and Felt went for a ride with Atama Batisaresare, an assisted-living aide. Felt, as a rule, exhibited a calm demeanor, letting his thoughts wander from one topic to another. On this trip, however, so Batisaresare later told Joan and me, Felt became highly agitated and focused on one subject, which sort of came out of the blue. The caregiver now recalls, in his thick Fijian accent, "He did tell me, 'An F.B.I. man should have loyalty to the department.' He talked about loyalty. He didn't mention he was a Deep Throat. He told me he didn't want to do it, but 'it was my duty to do it, regarding Nixon.'" (Felt would frequently return to this theme. While watching a

Watergate TV special that month, he and Joan heard his name come up as a Deep Throat candidate. Joan, trying to elicit a response, deliberately questioned her father in the third person: "Do you think Deep Throat wanted to get rid of Nixon?" Joan says that Felt replied, "No, I wasn't trying to bring him down." He claimed, instead, that he was "only doing his duty.")

On that Sunday in May when I first met Mark Felt, he was particularly concerned about how bureau personnel, then and now, had come to regard Deep Throat. He seemed to be struggling inside with whether he would be seen as a decent man or a turncoat. I stressed that F.B.I. agents and prosecutors now thought Deep Throat a patriot, not a rogue. And I emphasized that one of the reasons he might want to announce his identity would be for the very purpose of telling the story from his point of view.

Still, I could see he was equivocating. "He was amenable at first," his grandson Nick recalls. "Then he was wavering. He was concerned about bringing dishonor to our family. We thought it was totally cool. It was more about honor than about any kind of shame [to] Grandpa.... To this day, he feels he did the right thing."

At the end of our conversation, Felt seemed inclined to reveal himself, but refused to commit. "I'll think about what you have said, and I'll let you know of my decision," he told me very firmly that day. In the meantime, I told him, I would take on his cause pro bono, helping him find a reputable publisher if he decided to go that route. (I have written this piece, in fact, after witnessing the decline of Felt's health and mental acuity, and after receiving his and Joan's permission to reveal this information, normally protected by provisions of lawyer-client privilege. The Felts were not paid for cooperating with this story.)

Our talks dragged on, however. Felt told Joan that he had other worries. He wondered "what the judge would think" (meaning: were he to expose his past, might he leave himself open to prosecution for his actions?). He seemed genuinely conflicted. Joan took to discussing the issue in a circumspect way, sometimes referring to Deep Throat by yet another code name, Joe Camel. Nevertheless, the more we talked, the more forthright Felt became. On several occasions he confided to me, "I'm the guy they used to call Deep Throat."

He also opened up to his son. In previous years, when Felt's name had come up as a Deep Throat suspect, Felt had always bristled. "His attitude was: I don't think [being Deep Throat] was anything to be *proud* of," Mark junior says. "You [should] not leak information to *any*one." Now his father was admitting he had done just that. "Making the decision [to go to the press] would have been difficult, painful, and excruciating, and outside the bounds of his life's work. He would not have done it if he didn't feel it was the *only* way to get around the corruption in the White House and Justice Department. He was tortured inside, but never would show it. He was not this Hal Holbrook character. He was not an edgy person. [Even though] it would be the most difficult decision of his life, he wouldn't have pined over it."

At one lunch at a scenic restaurant overlooking the Pacific, Joan and Mark sat their father down to lay out the case for full, public disclosure. Felt argued with them, according to his son, warning them not to betray him. "I don't want this out," Felt said. "And if it got in the papers, I'd guess I'd know who put it there." But they persisted. They explained that they wanted their father's legacy to be heroic and permanent, not anonymous. And beyond their main motive—posterity—they thought that there might eventually be some profit in it. "Bob Woodward's gonna get all the glory for this, but we could make at least enough money to pay some bills, like the debt I've run up for the kids' education," Joan recalls saying. "Let's do it for the family." With that, both children remember, he finally agreed. "He wasn't particularly interested," Mark says, "but he said, 'That's a good reason.'"

Felt had come to an interim decision: he would "cooperate," but only with the assistance of Bob Woodward. Acceding to his wishes, Joan and I spoke to Woodward by phone on a half-dozen occasions over a period of months about whether to make a joint revelation, possibly in the form of a book or an article. Woodward would sometimes begin these conversations with a caveat, saying, more or less, "Just because I'm talking to you, I'm not admitting that he is who you think he is." Then he'd express his chief concerns, which were twofold, as I recall. First, was this something that Joan and I were pushing on Felt, or did he actually want to reveal himself of his own accord? (I interpreted this to mean: was he changing the long-standing agreement the men had kept for three decades?) Second, was Felt actually in a clear mental state? To make his own assessment, Woodward told Joan and me, he wanted to come out and sit down with her father again, not having seen him since their lunch.

"We went through a period where he did call a bit," Joan says of her discussions with Woodward. (Nick says he sometimes answered the phone and spoke with him, too.) "He's always been very gracious. We talked about doing a book with Dad, and I think he was considering. That was my understanding. He didn't say no at first. . . . Then he kept kind of putting me off on this book, saying, 'Joan, don't press me.' . . . For him the issue was competency: was Dad competent to release him from the agreement the two of them had made not to say anything until after Dad died? At one point I said, 'Bob, just between you and me, off the record, I want you to

confirm: was Deep Throat my dad?' He wouldn't do that. I said, 'If he's not, you can at least tell me that. We could put this to rest.' And he said, 'I can't do that.'"

Joan says that during this period Woodward had at least two phone conversations with Felt "without anyone else listening. Dad's memory gradually has deteriorated since the original lunch they had, [but] Dad remembered Bob whenever he called. . . . I said, 'Bob, it's unusual for Dad to remember someone as clearly as you.'" She says that Woodward responded, "He has good reason to remember me."

Woodward spoke with Mark junior at his home in Florida, as well. "He called me and discussed whether or not, and when, to visit Dad," he says. "I asked him briefly, 'Are you ever going to put this Deep Throat issue public?' And he said, essentially, that he made promises to my dad or someone that he wouldn't reveal this. . . . I can't imagine another reason why Woodward would have any interest in Dad or me or Joan if Dad wasn't Deep Throat. His questions were about Dad's present condition. Why would he care so much about Dad's health?"

According to Joan, Woodward scheduled two visits to come and see her father and, so she hoped, to talk about a possible collaborative venture. But he had to cancel both times, she says, then never rescheduled. "That was disappointing," she says. "Maybe [he was] just hoping that I would forget about it."

Today, Joan Felt has only positive things to say about Bob Woodward. "He's so reassuring and top-notch," she insists. They still stay in touch by e-mail, exchanging good wishes, their relationship engendered by a bond her father had forged in troubled times.

Nowadays, Mark Felt watches TV sitting beneath a large oil painting of his late wife, Audrey, and goes for car rides with a new caregiver. Felt is 91 and his memory for details seems to wax and wane. Joan allows him two glasses of wine each evening, and on occasion the two harmonize in a rendition of "The Star-Spangled Banner." While Felt is a humorous and mellow man, his spine stiffens and his jaw tightens when he talks about the integrity of his dear F.B.I.

I believe that Mark Felt is one of America's greatest secret heroes. Deep in his psyche, it is clear to me, he still has qualms about his actions, but he also knows that historic events compelled him to behave as he did: standing up to an executive branch intent on obstructing his agency's pursuit of the truth. Felt, having long harbored the ambivalent emotions of pride and self-reproach, has lived for more than 30 years in a prison of his own making, a prison built upon his strong moral principles and his unwavering loyalty to country and cause. But now, buoyed by his family's revelations and support, he need feel imprisoned no more.

FURTHER RESOURCES

Books

Bernstein, Carl, and Bob Woodward. *All the President's Men* New York: Simon & Schuster, 1974.

Holland, Max. *Leak: Why Mark Felt Became Deep Throat.* Lawrence: University Press of Kansas, 2012.

Washington Post Company. *The Original Watergate Stories.* New York: Diversion Books, 2012.

Woodward, Bob. *The Secret Man: The Story of Watergate's Deep Throat.* New York: Simon & Schuster, 2006.

Web Sites

Kilpatrick, Carroll. "President Refuses to Turn Over Tapes; Ervin Committee, Cox Issue Subpoenas." *Washington Post*, July 24, 1973. http://www.washingtonpost.com/politics/president-refuses-to-turn-over-tapes-ervin-committee-cox-issue-subpoenas/2012/06/04/gJQAWfG9IV_story.html (accessed on March 18, 2013).

"The Watergate Story: Timeline." *Washington Post.* www.washingtonpost.com/wp-srv/politics/special/watergate/timeline.html (accessed on March 18, 2013).

Woodward, Bob, and Carl Bernstein. "Woodward and Bernstein: 40 Years After Watergate, Nixon Was Far Worse Than We Thought." *Washington Post*, June 8, 2012. www.washingtonpost.com/opinions/woodward-and-bernstein-40-years-after-watergate-nixon-was-far-worse-than-we-thought/2012/06/08/gJQAlsi0NV_story.html (accessed on March 18, 2013).

Anderson Cooper 360° Special Edition: Katrina's Aftermath

Television broadcast

By: Anderson Cooper

Date: August 30, 2005

Source: Cooper, Anderson. *Anderson Cooper 360° Special Edition: Katrina's Aftermath*, August 30, 2005. http://transcripts.cnn.com/TRANSCRIPTS/0508/30/acd.01.html (accessed on March 17, 2013).

About the Author: Anderson Cooper, the son of Gloria Vanderbilt, heiress to the Vanderbilt fortune, was born in New York City in 1967. He earned a degree in political science from Yale University, although he never pursued a career in politics, instead opting to travel to the world's most violent and war-torn areas and reporting on their respective conflicts. He became a correspondent for ABC News in 1995 and then contracted as an anchor for CNN News in 2001, gaining recognition as the annual host of the CNN New Year's Eve special broadcast. His honest, straightforward, and personal approach to television reporting earned him popularity among American audiences, which CNN recognized in 2003 by making him the host and primary anchor of his eponymous news program, *Anderson Cooper 360°*. Cooper's on-site coverage of Hurricane Katrina and its aftermath earned him and the program several journalism awards and unprecedented public visibility, which he used to bring attention to international issues. *Anderson Cooper 360°* continued airing throughout the 2000s decade, becoming one of CNN's premiere programs.

INTRODUCTION

Hurricane Katrina was the most destructive natural disaster in the United States, as well as one of the deadliest. Katrina began as a tropical storm in the Atlantic Ocean on August 23, 2005, and made initial contact with the Florida coast two days later. The storm defied meteorological projections and crossed into the Gulf of Mexico, where fortuitous conditions allowed it to quickly grow in size and wind speed. By August 28, Katrina had developed into a Category 5 hurricane, with maximum recorded wind speeds of 175 mph, and was bearing down on the coastal states of Mississippi, Alabama, and Louisiana. The U.S. government initiated emergency protocol in response to the storm's approach, issuing evacuation orders for the predicted impact area and authorizing a state of emergency in the region. Despite urgent official appeals, thousands of citizens ignored the threat of the storm and elected to stay in the impact zone.

Katrina made landfall again on August 29, having been slowed by shallower waters to a Category 3 hurricane, with maximum sustained wind speeds of 125 mph. The coastal regions of Mississippi and Alabama were torn asunder by the storm's winds and elevated water levels, and southern Florida sustained a good deal of property damage, but the most devastating effects of Katrina were experienced in Louisiana's southeastern quadrant, particularly in the city of New Orleans. Surging water caused by the hurricane obliterated the levees surrounding New Orleans, flooding the city with torrential waters that would then stand and not be drained for weeks. Electricity and water distribution went down immediately, and all avenues of escape were

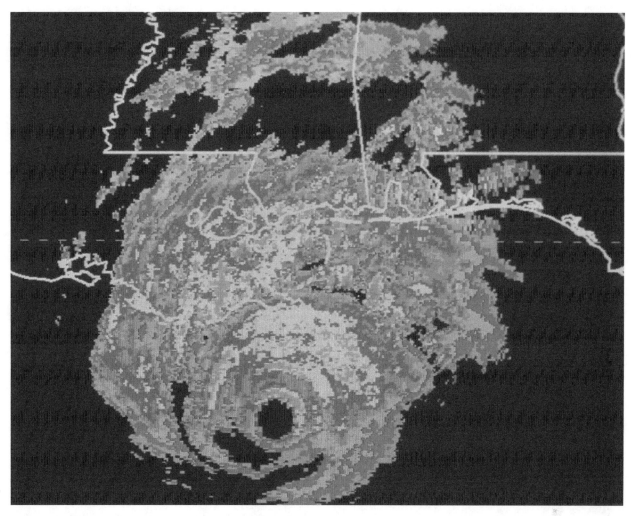

A radar image from the National Oceanic and Atmospheric Administration shows the path of Hurricane Katrina in late August 2005. © AP IMAGES/NATIONAL OCEANIC AND ADMINISTRATION ADMINISTRATION.

destroyed by water. Houses and other buildings took significant damage, leaving tens of thousands stranded without access to heat, food, clean water, sanitation, or communication equipment.

In response to reports of looting, theft, vandalism, and violence in New Orleans, thousands of National Guard and federal disaster relief agents were mobilized in the city the day after Katrina hit the Gulf Coast. Thousands of residents were evacuated to the area surrounding the city, many of them temporarily housed in the Superdome arena. The storm caused approximately $81 billion in total property damage to the affected area, as well as inestimable economic loss related to relief and volunteer efforts and the halt of oil industry operations in the Gulf. A total of 1,833 people are verified to have died as a result of the storm, and hundreds more disappeared but did not have their bodies recovered.

Media played a crucial role in organizing relief efforts and maintaining communication between stranded sectors of the impacted population and the authorities. News reporters are credited with providing up-to-date information to relief operations and authorities, as well as assisting disaster victims in reaching safety and relief provisions. Constant, ethos-fueled information relayed from television news reporters such as CNN's Anderson Cooper and Fox News's Geraldo Rivera kept the U.S. public connected with and sympathetic to the plight of New Orleans residents, helping attract volunteers and charitable contributions for emergency relief organizations.

SIGNIFICANCE

Hurricane Katrina became one of the biggest political mires of the 2000s decade for several agencies and individuals. A chief problem for the federal government arose when it was revealed that the levees surrounding New Orleans, which had been constructed by the U.S. Army Corps of Engineers, had failed primarily due to massive engineering flaws. The government was the target of heated public criticism for its apparent disregard of the safety of New Orleans and its citizens, for whom the levees were the only defense against floodwaters. Many local and state governments were criticized for the insufficient disaster provisions and preparation taken before the storm, which were implicated in the problems with evacuating, supplying, and housing those affected by the storm.

An array of commentators, ranging from politicians and activists to pundits and entertainers, raised concerns about the perceived failures of the federal government to adequately and appropriately respond to Hurricane Katrina's aftermath in New Orleans. Delayed response and lack of clear leadership were the chief complaints against President George W. Bush and upper administration, prompting years of finger-pointing, accusation, posturing, and blame-avoidance among politicians and agency heads associated with the controversy. The public was also incensed by media reports of misconduct by emergency police and relief workers during Katrina, particularly the Danziger Bridge shootings, in which police opened fire on unarmed civilians, killing two and wounding four, and then attempted to cover up the incident.

Ultimately, Hurricane Katrina exposed a weakness in the U.S. emergency response infrastructure, allowing it to be addressed. More stringent disaster mitigation and relief programs were instituted at all levels of government, and citizens were made more fully aware of the importance of complying with them.

CNN anchor and reporter Anderson Cooper. © AP IMAGES/ JENNIFER GRAYLOCK.

PRIMARY SOURCE

ANDERSON COOPER 360° SPECIAL EDITION: KATRINA'S AFTERMATH (EXCERPT TRANSCRIPT)

SYNOPSIS: Anderson Cooper and other news correspondents report live from New Orleans, Louisiana, Gulfport, Mississippi, and other southern areas immediately following the flooding caused by Hurricane Katrina. Interviews and eyewitness accounts depict the extent of the damage to the region and the problems experienced by residents.

ANDERSON COOPER, CNN ANCHOR: I am live in Gulfport, a city just devastated in Mississippi, one of many cities you'll be seeing tonight in this special edition of *360*. It is 7:00 p.m. on the East Coast, 6:00 p.m. here in Gulfport, and 4:00 p.m. in the West. *360* starts now.

(BEGIN VIDEO CLIP)

ANNOUNCER: Hundreds feared dead in Mississippi. Shreds of cities remain. Hurricane Katrina spares nothing.

UNIDENTIFIED MALE: We watched houses just disappear, you know, the water level get up over the roof. And then when the water receded, the houses just weren't there anymore.

ANNOUNCER: Tonight, we're live from Gulfport, Mississippi, Ground Zero for Katrina.

When the levee breaks. In New Orleans, from nightmare to nightmare. A day after Katrina, a levee built to protect the city ruptures. What about pressure on other levees? Will the giant lake swallow New Orleans?

When the Superdome transforms into a super home. Temperatures near 90. No power, no air conditioning, no way out for 30,000 people—three times the number there yesterday—taking shelter.

By air and by boat. More than 1,000 daring rescues in 24 hours. Tonight, how they saved the lucky ones and how many more need to hold on.

Downed power lines, chemical spills, wild animals. Tonight, what else Katrina unleashed.

This is a special edition of *ANDERSON COOPER 360*, "Hurricane Katrina: The Aftermath."

(END VIDEO CLIP)

COOPER: Welcome back to this live edition of *360*. We are in Gulfport, Mississippi, on the coast of Mississippi. And to say that this is a city stunned, a city on its knees, would not be an overstatement.

We just arrived in this city about two hours ago, and we have never seen things that we have seen over the last two hours. And we're going to be bringing you that in the next hour on this special edition of *360*.

Gulfport is on the south coast of Mississippi. It is just west of Biloxi. It is east of New Orleans. It is a city that has become a destination city for tourists, for people coming to casinos. All of that is destroyed at this point.

In New Orleans, we have seen all day long—there's a helicopter now passing over. It's an Army helicopter. We've been seeing that all day long.

And in New Orleans, we have been seeing scenes of just incredible rescues. People, literally, their lives hanging in the balance, being plucked from the roofs of their homes. It is a chaotic scene in New Orleans. We're going to take you there live in this next hour, as well.

There's so much to talk about. I-10, the highway which goes along the coast, is completely broken up in some places, collapsed, destroyed, in pieces. It is virtually impossible to get from one point to another. All of that will be covered in this next hour.

First, let's show you what the last 24 hours have been like. Here's CNN's Wolf Blitzer.

(BEGIN VIDEOTAPE)

WOLF BLITZER, CNN ANCHOR (voice-over): In the evening hours, after Hurricane Katrina struck, we still were getting close-ups of the crisis. Mere hints at that point of the devastation, the loss, and the struggle to survive.

UNIDENTIFIED MALE: Do you have any animals, broken bones?

UNIDENTIFIED MALE: No.

BLITZER: Into the night, it started to become evident. This truly is a disaster beyond what many people had imagined.

So many rescues. The Coast Guard carrying at least 100 people from one community, boatload after boatload to safety.

So many stories to tell.

UNIDENTIFIED MALE: Horrific. It was horrific. I kept what I think a cool head, told my wife we were going to survive, but she was panicking.

BLITZER: The morning after, 80 percent of New Orleans was under water, up to 20 feet in some places. The flooding made worse by a break in the 17th Street Canal, unleashing a gusher that swallowed homes and entire communities.

UNIDENTIFIED MALE: The city's like a bowl. It's like a bathtub with large parts below sea level. The estimates are it would take, you know, three months, 90 days, to get rid of that water.

BLITZER: A city in ruins, from the vast cavern of the Superdome to downtown hotels, and so many homes, and so many people who live there trapped.

UNIDENTIFIED MALE: We've got a rescue in progress.

BLITZER: Or worse.

HARVEY JACKSON, LOST WIFE IN HURRICANE: We got up in the roof, all the way to the roof, and water came. And the house just opened up and divided.

JENNIFER MAYERLE, CORRESPONDENT, WKRG-TV: Who was at your house with you?

JACKSON: My wife.

MAYERLE: Where is she now?

JACKSON: Can't find her body. She's gone.

BLITZER: In Mississippi, dozens are believed dead, up to 30 of them killed in one beachfront apartment complex alone. The casinos of Biloxi, once luxurious, now ravaged. A church split wide open.

In Alabama, a major bridge in Mobile closed because Katrina jammed a loose oil rig under it.

All across the disaster zone, more than two million people have no electricity. The water isn't drinkable. Power lines are down. Danger is everywhere. The tens of thousands of people still in shelters are being told to stay there.

The enormity of it all seems overwhelming. But still, there is hope.

GOV. HALEY BARBOUR, MISSISSIPPI: We're not going to solve that with a snap of a finger. But little by little, we'll get back to where it's tolerable. And then we'll rebuild. And the coast will be better than it ever was.

BLITZER: Wolf Blitzer, CNN, Washington.

(END VIDEOTAPE)

COOPER: It has been such a difficult day for people here in Mississippi, for people in Louisiana, in New Orleans. In a moment, we're going to take you to New Orleans, because what is happening there, well, it's just hard to imagine, frankly. But we'll bring you there live in a moment.

First, I just want to show you what downtown Gulfport, Mississippi, looks like right now. Over my shoulder, first of all, you see a semi truck, a tractor-trailer. And behind it—I don't know if you can make that out—there are just dozens of tractor- trailer trucks piled on top of each other. Now, those aren't supposed to be there. That's not a parking lot. All those have been swept just hundreds of yards into what is now just a burial ground for these trucks.

You might see that bird there. There are animals—there's wildlife just kind of stunned. That bird has been unable to fly, just walking around. And if you zoom out, that bird is standing in front of this casino. It says "CPA Casino."

You know, when I first saw that, I thought, OK, you know, that building's got some wreckage. Let me tell you. That building was not there 48 hours ago. That building was about half a mile or so to the east. That has been picked up by this storm and deposited over there intact. It is an extraordinary sight that is simply hard to wrap your mind around.

We are seeing people here just kind of stunned, wandering through the wreckage, just unable to kind of piece together what has happened to them in the last 24 hours. And more and more, we are hearing just tales of anguish.

And we are seeing anguish and hearing it from the people who lived through this storm. This is one man, his experience in New Orleans. Just listen to what this man has to say, what happened to him.

(BEGIN VIDEOTAPE)

JENNIFER MAYERLE, CORRESPONDENT, WKRG-TV: How are you doing, sir?

JACKSON: I'm not doing good.

MAYERLE: What happened?

JACKSON: The house just split in half.

MAYERLE: Your house split it half?

JACKSON: We got up in the roof, all the way to the roof, and water came. And the house just opened up and divided.

MAYERLE: Who was at your house with you?

JACKSON: My wife.

MAYERLE: Where is she now?

JACKSON: Can't find her body. She's gone.

MAYERLE: You can't find your wife?

JACKSON: No, she told—I tried. I hold her hand tight as I could. And she told me, "You can't hold me." She said, "Take care of the kids and the grandkids."

MAYERLE: What's your wife's name, in case we can put this out there?

JACKSON: Tonette Jackson.

MAYERLE: And, OK, and what's your name?

JACKSON: Harvey Jackson.

MAYERLE: Where are you guys going?

JACKSON: We ain't got nowhere to go. I'm lost. That's all I had. That's all I had. This is all a horrible joke.

(END VIDEOTAPE)

COOPER: It is really hard to imagine what people are going through right now. And I know we keep saying this over and over again, but our hearts go out to them, because there's just not help to be had right now for the people who are suffering.

Yes, there are people working hard trying to get relief to them, trying to save them, doing search-and-rescue operations. And they're doing tremendous jobs and saving lives.

But there are people who are desperately in need right now. You know, they have no place to go right now. They've got no water. They're just kind of wandering around.

Captain Bruce Jones is with the U.S. Coast Guard. He has taken part in some just remarkable rescues, saving, without a doubt, dozens, if not hundreds and thousands of people.

Captain, does anything prepare you for something like this?

CAPT. BRUCE JONES, COMMANDING OFFICER, COAST GUARD AIR STATION: No, we've never seen anything like this. The devastation is really overwhelming. Never seen flooding like this. Never seen so many people stranded, so many people needing assistance.

Our crews have been working through the night. Immediately after the hurricane passed New Orleans yesterday, we were on scene with the Coast Guard helicopters.

We've got 11 H-65 helicopters, three Coast Guard H-60 helicopters. They've been performing rescues the last 24 hours nonstop, night vision goggles throughout the night and now the daytime, and preparing to go out again tonight.

We've rescued hundreds, and there are hundreds more still stranded.

COOPER: Thank God for the U.S. Coast Guard. I mean, what you guys have been doing, just extraordinary in the last 24 hours. What are some of the rescues that you have seen? Who have you gotten? What kind of conditions are they in?

JONES: We're arriving in the flooded areas where we're finding—we're seeing handkerchiefs waving through cracks in roofs. We're seeing holes where people who made it up to the attic as the waters rose were able to take axes or other tools and knock holes in the roof and stick their arms through.

We're dropping our rescue swimmers down with hatchets to enlarge the holes and pull people through. We're seeing people in the water. We're seeing people in windows. We're seeing many children, many elderly people.

This morning, we hoisted a woman who weighed in excess of 400 pounds who had recently had very major surgery. She had gangrene. She'd been in the home unattended for two days.

People in all conditions. It's been very difficult, very dangerous and demanding rescue conditions for all of our personnel. And all of our men and women out there are doing a good job, without regard for the fact that their own homes may be flooded and destroyed and their own family's futures in jeopardy.

COOPER: That's the thing so many people don't realize. I mean, these members of the Coast Guard, they live in these communities. They have their own problems, their homes, as you said, their friends, their family in jeopardy. And yet they're still out there doing this job.

I mean, it's an extraordinary work that they are doing. How do people call the Coast Guard? I mean, the cell phones aren't working. So is it just you happen to be flying by, you're looking for people, and they're waving that handkerchief?

JONES: It's really as simple as that. Our helicopters are out there scouring the areas that are flooded, and they're seeing signs of distress, waving hands, waving T-shirts.

Last night, I was out on scene when it got dark. And as soon as it got dark, we put on the night vision goggles. And immediately, hundreds of flashlights flashing at us from people on rooftops who we couldn't see during the day.

They're making their way through their attics to the roofs. Just in the last half-hour, our last crew came and landed and said there's at least 200 people out to the east, south of Chalmette, where they were operating.

So it seems as though more people are coming out of the woodwork, coming out of their attics over the last 24 hours, as they get overheated, they're hungry, they're thirsty. It's been almost 100 degrees here today. And those who are elderly or sick already are beginning to deteriorate.

So we're throwing everything at it that we can. And not only our Coast Guard helicopters, we have National Guard helicopters from Florida, Texas, and Louisiana. And we have local officials in small boats, sheriff's boats, fire department boats, good Samaritans who are out going between the streets, looking for people in distress …

(CROSSTALK) COOPER: Well, Captain, I know you got to go. I appreciate all the hard work. And Godspeed to you and the men and women of the Coast Guard. Thank you very much.

I want to talk with David Mattingly who is on I-10. Parts of that highway just completely destroyed, by the way. David, what are you seeing where you are?

DAVID MATTINGLY, CNN CORRESPONDENT: Anderson, because this is high ground, so many people have sought refuge here after they had to exit their homes when the flood waters started rolling in.

In some cases, they escaped from their homes by walking, wading through the water. And they said the water was chest-high, sometimes up to their chin, as they tried to get out of here. Adults were carrying children on their shoulders, walking to the expressway, trying to get away from those flood waters.

They managed to do that in large numbers. There are hundreds of people up here. But they were fully expecting someone to come along to give them a ride to some kind of shelter. And that ride has not come along.

So we've had hundreds of people, elderly people, people in need of medicine, some in need of medical attention, children, all of them out here all day long with no shade in the blazing sun. It has been oppressively hot today.

Tempers are wearing thin, I can tell you that. People want to know, where is the ride that they've heard is coming but so far hasn't showed up?

Earlier today, we went out with some state officials in boats as they continue to rescue people from their homes. There are still people in their attics here in the eastern parts of New Orleans who are still calling for help. And that help is arriving very, very slowly.

Anderson?

COOPER: David Mattingly, we'll check in with you a little bit later. Dave Mattingly, one of the CNN reporters who has been covering this storm from the beginning, working really just around the clock. David, thank you for that.

We're getting a lot of e-mails, thousands of e-mails from viewers, asking how they can help. If you would like to help in any way, we're putting some numbers on the screen, some organizations that are doing work here.

CNN anchor Anderson Cooper reports from a house in New Orleans, Louisiana, during televised coverage of the one-year anniversary of Hurricane Katrina, August 28, 2006. © AP IMAGES.

We're also going to show you some of the animals affected by this storm. There are thousands of them. No doubt many have been killed. Well, there are snakes here in the water. There are birds walking around. There are even seals which have been left in parking lots. We'll have their story when we return.

(BEGIN VIDEO CLIP)

UNIDENTIFIED MALE: I've got family all around. And maybe they're seeing this and I'm OK, but I can't get out, call anybody. There's no way to let anybody know that, you know, I'm OK. But, yes, we're fine. And everybody lost everything, but we're, I guess, pretty resilient. We're going to make it and possibly move away from here. I don't know.

(END VIDEO CLIP)

COOPER: Well, right now in New Orleans, there are tens of thousands of people stuck in the Superdome. There's no electricity. Parts of the roof have broken. Water has been coming in. The bathrooms have stopped functioning.

I mean, imagine for a moment—I know a lot of you are probably sitting in your homes right now elsewhere in the country. And hopefully, you are dry. And hopefully, you are safe.

But, you know, as you go to sleep tonight, just think about those people in the Superdome right now and what they must be going through. And there are thousands and thousands of stories of people stuck in their homes right now.

No electricity. No ice. Nothing cool to drink. They don't know where to go. They don't know what to do. And they don't really have any information. And that's one of the things.

And we keep hearing from people, everywhere we go—I was in a Wal-Mart earlier in the day. And people just come up to you at the Wal-Mart and they're like, "Have you heard about my town? Do you know what's happening in my town?" And we don't know the information, you know? We just drove down here ourselves to see for ourselves what Gulfport was like. And, I mean, there was no description that could have prepared us for what we have seen and what you're going to see over the course of the next hour. I want to talk, though, a little bit about New Orleans and what is happening there and the levees there. That is a city which is under sea level, as you all know by now. So the levees are key in protecting that city, and they have been for decades now.

A levee broke yesterday. Another levee broke today. Water is still pouring into that city. It is just getting worse.

You can also go to the CNN web page, CNN.com, for more information on who is working here, what groups are working here, what they're doing. And if you want to help them in any way, you can.

I also just want to show you something just very briefly. Over my shoulder, as this light is going down, there is a Dole truck, pickup truck, one of the many—it's not a pickup, it's a tractor-trailer—that has just slammed into a hotel about 100 feet from here.

It just shows you the force of this storm. And it's so surreal in Gulfport right now. I mean, you see these images of things you don't expect. I mean, a truck in the lobby of a hotel.

We're also seeing all these—well, we all know about the levees in New Orleans, which have been a major point of concern, trying to keep that water out. Water continues to come in, flooding New Orleans. It's just getting worse, as a matter of fact right now. It's not getting better. We're going to talk about that a little bit later on after this break.

Tom Foreman takes a look at the levees and how important they are.

(BEGIN VIDEOTAPE)

TOM FOREMAN, CNN CORRESPONDENT (voice-over): The rain stopped falling, but the water kept rising. In New Orleans and its immediate suburbs, areas are now flooding that were largely clear at the storm's height.

JOHN ZARRELLA, CNN CORRESPONDENT: The water is also, if we can take a look now, creeping up the sides of the buildings here. Earlier today, none of this was standing here. So it is continuing to rise.

FOREMAN: To understand why at least two of the levees around the city have failed, think of New Orleans as a fortress protected against water on all sides by walls, levees, which are large, earthen dams.

Officials say the first failure, likely caused by water flowing over the levee and eroding it, happened on a boat canal at the east end of town. That's a low-lying area. So that flooding was contained.

The second levee failed in the same way. However, it was on a drainage canal in the north, near Lake Pontchartrain. This is critical. A side view of the city with the lake on the right, the Mississippi River on the left, shows almost the entire town is below lake level.

So unless the levee is plugged, water will flow until its level in much of the city is the same as the level of the lake. Only a small part of the French Quarter, which is at a higher level, and other areas with natural protection might stay dry.

UNIDENTIFIED MALE: But right now, our first primary emphasis is try to get that closure so we can stop the water flow and so we can start getting the water out of the city.

QUESTION: Do you have any idea how long that will take?

UNIDENTIFIED MALE: Don't have any idea.

FOREMAN: For now, officials say, until the levees are fixed and the massive pumps that failed during the storm are restarted, the water is going nowhere.

(END VIDEOTAPE)

FOREMAN: Big difference here between New Orleans and any other city in this country. Most other cities' drainage systems are set up so that naturally, if you leave water alone, it wants to leave town. It flows downhill and goes somewhere is else.

New Orleans is downhill. Without the pumps working, without the levees fixed, the water will just sit there, a health hazard, a menace to travel, a problem in every single way. These are top priorities right now.

They're trying to figure out how to do it in a place where you can barely move and you can barely get information.

Anderson?

COOPER: Yes, Tom, the information is such a hard thing to get. I appreciate that report.

And Tom brings up a good point, which is the health hazards of this water. There are so many things you don't think about in normal life. I mean, when there's all this standing water around, bacteria, germs, disease—we're all carrying around anti-bacterials that we're putting on our hands, because you just don't know what is out there. It's a potent mix.

We're going to talk to Elizabeth Cohen, a medical correspondent, a little bit later on about that.

There are also animals in the water. I mean, snakes, all sorts of animals to watch out for. So you've got to really be careful. We're going to talk about that, coming up.

We're also going to show you some just remarkable rescue efforts in New Orleans and elsewhere. And also, in Biloxi, we're going to take you to an apartment complex where 30 people in this one complex, 30 people were killed in the blink of an eye. We'll be right back.

(BEGIN AUDIO CLIP)

UNIDENTIFIED MALE: You've got a lot of people that we can't get back in town. The roads are bad. We don't know if we're going to be able to buy gasoline to come back. It really would be nice just to have the local officials of Louisiana, Mississippi, try to tell us a little more. What are we going to do about gasoline and the routes to get back home? I'm sure you all will give us the information as soon as you can, but we sure would like to know something now, thank you.

(END AUDIO CLIP)

COOPER: That's just some of our viewers who called in to tell us their experiences, their concerns, and their thoughts about this storm after they survived it.

Just want to show what—I mean, there are so many things that are happening right now, even here in Gulfport, as night has fallen. We've been smelling gas for the last hour or so, which has obviously been a concern.

Some officials have come up and are now—they found the source of the gas leak. They're trying to get a handle on it right now, trying to fix it. They are working—I mean, it's just so surreal here. I've got to tell you. They're working in front of this Dole truck, it's a banana truck, that has just been picked up, moved hundreds and hundreds of yards by the force of the water, and just slammed into a hotel.

There are literally dozens of these pickup trucks, of these tractor-trailer trucks, which have just been tossed like a child's toy. And you see that block, after block, after block here in Gulfport. It is just surreal. And it's hard to describe for you.

Just another quick note—and I know I'm sort of rambling—but there are so many people out there who are desperate for information. And there's been a lot of frustration that I've been hearing on the radio and talking to people. Why aren't you telling us about Pass Christian, Mississippi? Why aren't you telling us about some of these smaller towns?

And to be honest, we would if we could. We are very limited in just moving around. It took us, you know, about five hours of driving down from Philadelphia, Mississippi, just to get here to Gulfport.

And, you know, basically, we're going through what everyone else is going through, in terms of limited supplies. You know, we're low on gas. So it's tough for us to get to these places.

Gary Tuchman, our reporter, has been there throughout the day moving around on this coast as few have. We're going to talk to him in just a little bit.

But I want to talk to CNN's Elizabeth Cohen for a little bit, because there are so many dangers you don't think about. In all this water that is just laying around, bacteria, disease, and animals. Elizabeth Cohen takes a look at some of the dangers you might not realize in the debris and in the wreckage of this storm.

(BEGIN VIDEOTAPE)

ELIZABETH COHEN, CNN CORRESPONDENT (voice–over): It's not just the rising water. It's not just the devastated homes. A big part of Katrina's legacy will be the health problems she leaves behind for a very long time. Many people have no clean water to drink and no safe food to eat. Mosquitoes will breed West Nile virus in the pools of water. People have already died of carbon monoxide poisoning because they lost electricity and tried to use generators in their homes.

MICHAEL CHERTOFF, HOMELAND SECURITY SECRETARY: We're always racing the clock. We're racing the clock in terms of possible injury. We're racing the clock in terms of illness. We're racing the clock in terms of food and water.

COHEN: In a conference call Tuesday morning, officials from states pummeled by Katrina pleaded for assistance from the federal government and from neighboring states.

Mississippi asked Florida to get food and water to people in Biloxi near the border. Florida responded that it already had sent emergency workers who'd found people completely out of contact with the outside world, desperate for food and water.

An Alabama official warned about a significant hazardous material situation in Mobile Bay. A Mississippi official put it bluntly. He said, people will be dying not because the water is coming up, but because we can't get them medical treatment.

MIKE LEAVITT, HHS SECRETARY: We have several dozen public health officers who are currently on the ground. We have several hundred additional ones on standby and on the way. We have dozens of pallets of supplies, first-aid material, medical supplies, basic things being shipped to the region.

COHEN: One of the biggest problems, contaminated water.

IVOR VAN HEERDON, LOUISIANA STATE UNIVERSITY: It's all the chemicals within the city, from the gasoline storage facilities, storage plants, and, of course, coffins. We will have a large number of coffins released. This whole mix together in New Orleans is what we term this toxic gumbo.

COHEN: Another, contaminated food.

DR. JULIE GERBERDING, CDC DIRECTOR: Don't eat any perishable food that's been without refrigeration for more than four hours.

COHEN: Of course, for the millions without power, those four hours passed a long time ago, leaving many people without food, without clean water, without medical care, and officials trying to figure out how to get it to them.

Elizabeth Cohen, CNN, Atlanta.

(END VIDEOTAPE)

COOPER: Well, it's just not disease you've got to worry about. It's also animals in this wreckage, because there's stuff you just can't see, snakes, a lot of wildlife out there. A little while ago, Kyra Phillips talked to wildlife expert Tim Williams about some of the dangerous critters which are out there in the wreckage. Listen.

(BEGIN VIDEOTAPE)

KYRA PHILLIPS, CNN CORRESPONDENT: It's gators like this that you're concerned about out in these rising waters, right?

TIM WILLIAMS, GATOR WRANGLER, GATORLAND: Oh, my gracious. Those poor folks out there have got so many problems. And part of that's going to be these wild animals that are washed out of their homes. They don't have any place to go. They're going to see animals turning up in backyards and porches and underneath houses that they never thought they'd see out there.

PHILLIPS: What about snakes, Tim?

WILLIAMS: Oh. We've got some great snakes. I brought one of the prettiest ones that we had. This little guy here is a representative of some of the other snakes that could be out there. This is a rat snake. They have rat snakes throughout the Gulf states. And this snake likes to climb. So with the waters coming through, these types of snakes and rattlesnakes, cottonmouth, water moccasins, copperheads, all these different types of snakes will be flooded out of their dens and boroughs. There's a chance you could see those up in trees, bushes. They could swim into houses and, as the water recedes, be up inside some of the homes.

You know, people need to take caution for all the downed power lines and all the things we'd normally think of. And a lot of times we forget that these animals are out there crawling around. And we really need to be careful.

PHILLIPS: Well, Tim, you're holding this rat snake like it's no big deal. How lethal is a snake like this?

WILLIAMS: This snake's not. This snake is actually a constrictor. Eats mice and rats. It doesn't have venom. But the rattlesnakes and cottonmouths have very big fangs and some very potent venom. And if you're going to be out around these areas, especially cleaning up, watch what you're doing. You have trash and debris, snakes will get up in there. Use rakes, shovels, hoes to turn this stuff over. Wear gloves. Don't walk around barefoot. Wear shoes or boots, so in case someone unfortunately gets a bite from one of these animals, they have some—a little bit of protection there.

PHILLIPS: What are the things that we hear time and time again that simply, they're just not true?

WILLIAMS: Well don't suck the venom out. Don't put on tourniquets. Don't cut it. Don't put on ice. The best thing to do is seek professional medical attention as quickly as you can.

PHILLIPS: It's not just gators, it's not just snakes. There are other animals out there too, right, that individuals need to be aware of?

WILLIAMS: Yes. They're going to find raccoons, possums, and nutria, and skunks, and fox, and all kinds of animals running around. Again, hurt, injured, displaced, lost, hungry. So be very, very cautious of these animals. And just leave the things alone and let things as quickly as you can get back to normal.

PHILLIPS: Yes. Those people have so much to worry about, this is just one more thing.

WILLIAMS: Our hearts go out to them. We know what they went through, down here in Florida. And it wasn't as bad as what they're having right now. And we really have our thoughts and prayers with all those folks out there.

(END VIDEOTAPE)

COOPER: Well they certainly do. We came across an animal a little bit ago, a seal just here in Gulfport, just about 100 yards from where I'm standing right now. This, I mean, just one of those surreal things you see. The seal has been there since the storm. It was basically carried out on the water from this marina, from this, sort of, animal park, seal park, that's about a half mile away or so. And it was left in this parking lot. People have been trying to save this animal, pouring water on it, trying to keep it hydrated. We'll tell you a little bit later on what is going on with the seal right now.

A lot more ahead.

Jonathan Freed is going to take you to an apartment complex in Biloxi, Mississippi, where 30 people in this one apartment complex were killed in the blink of an eye. We'll be right back.

(COMMERCIAL BREAK)

(BEGIN VIDEO CLIP)

UNIDENTIFIED MALE: I'm a truck driver. My name is Dave. And I'm headed north down on 75 in Florida. I just wanted the people over there to know that the cavalry is on the way. Electric company trucks and tree removal trucks, firefighters, and rescue trucks on the way up. So they're coming, just hold on.

(END VIDEO CLIP)

COOPER: Some of our 360 viewers who have called in to talk about their experiences during Hurricane Katrina.

We have just gotten some news in to CNN from the Homeland Security Chief Michael Chernoff who has announced that there will be an involuntary call-up of Coast Guard Reserves in order to help in the search and rescue efforts. That just in to CNN. Homeland Security saying there will be an involuntary call-up of Coast Guard Reserves to help in these rescue efforts.

I just want to show you if you're just joining us, we're in Gulfport, Mississippi, a town very hard-hit. And we're still trying to assess the damage. Behind me, this casino barge, which as you know in Mississippi there's a state law, all casinos have to be on the water on these barges. So that barge, you can still see some of the slots inside it. That barge is now on the land. And it's moved several hundred yards. It was just picked up by this storm and deposited right here now on the land. It is extraordinary. You know, when I first saw it, I thought it got a little bit of damage just on the ground. I didn't realize the whole thing had been picked up and deposited right here.

There has been loss of life here in Mississippi. Perhaps the most in one spot that we know of at this point—and it is still early days—was in Biloxi, Mississippi, where 30 people were killed in one location.

CNN's Jonathan Freed has their story.

JONATHAN FREED, CNN CORRESPONDENT: Anderson, I can tell you that I had an opportunity to take a walk along the beach today here in Biloxi. And that walk has changed the way—it has forever changed the way that I will think about these storms. That—that is how extensive the devastation was today.

I would call it total devastation. I felt like I was walking on the set of a disaster movie. It was truly surreal. And it has forever changed me.

We took a left turn, and we came upon the apartment complex that you just spoke about, where we are told as many as 30 people could have been killed during the storm surge and the raging winds the other day.

Now, the damage is so extensive, though, officials are saying that that number could be higher as well. They say it could be lower. They think that they're comfortable with that roughly 30 figure. It could even be significantly larger for the general area of Biloxi as well.

But so twisted was all of this wreckage, it's so difficult to distinguish what you're looking at, that they say it's going to be a long time for them to really properly comb through all of the debris, to try to get a handle on who's missing—who is simply missing, for example, who actually got out of the way and because of the problems we're having with communication and cell phones, Anderson, who are simply missing—and who is actually dead.

One of the things that I wanted to know—I was walking around, and I kept asking myself, what did this look like when it happened? What—what was the nature of the force that could possibly do this? And I found myself asking, what did it sound like?

Well, we had a chance to talk to a couple of the people who actually experienced it today, and I made some notes for you. They told me that the water was loaded with debris. So much wood from all the broken-up homes, Anderson, they say that it looked like a moving and rolling floor, which—it's such a vivid image. And I can see it. When you look at that debris, you can just see how the water could have been loaded with that.

And when I asked them what it sounded like, some of them said it just sounded like a roar. And it just chilled them right to the bones. And they knew that they simply had to get out of the way, and that they had made a big mistake in deciding to stay.

Anderson.

COOPER: Jonathan, have the families of the people who have died there, have they been notified? I mean, do we know their identities at this point?

FREED: No. Officials are not even going that far. And it's somewhat frustrating for us and it's frustrating for them. They want to give us more specific information, but because of the nature of the destruction, they say it's just too soon. I think they really need to start crunching data as much as sifting through debris, to start matching up who's missing and who's just simply not around and unable to contact people to let them know that they're OK, and who's actually dead.

COOPER: That is just such a horrible thing. Jonathan Freed, we'll check in with you a little bit later on, as our prime-time coverage continues.

Again, we are getting so many e-mails from viewers asking how they can help, what they can do—because I know sitting in your home, it's frustrating seeing all this—and wanting to do something. You can check out—we're putting some information on the screen that might be able to give you some help on that. You can also check out our Web site, CNN.com. That will have more information about what groups are doing work here, and how you can help them in some ways.

We have a lot more ahead. Some remarkable search and rescue efforts that are still under way. We'll show you some of the efforts, people being taken, plucked from their attics, from the roofs of their homes.

A lot more ahead on this special edition of *360*.

COOPER: We are in Gulfport, Mississippi, live. I'm with Commander Alfred Sexton with the Gulfport Police. What can you tell us about—I mean, what are the search and rescue operations going on right now?

ALFRED SEXTON, COMMANDER, GULFPORT POLICE DEPARTMENT: You know, basically, again, everything's being coordinated through our Harrison County Civil Defense and Emergency Management. They're out there responding, trying to check areas. They have a plan in place to go across our area and to ensure that we still check every point that we can to ensure, you know, the safety and the rescue of those individuals.

COOPER: There's so many people around the country and especially in Mississippi watching this, wondering what's happened to their communities, to their loved ones. How do people find out information?

SEXTON: You know, again, you know, the best thing is the media outlets. You all have been doing a good job getting out there. Unfortunately you've had to show the bad side to get the seriousness out there. The radio stations, the Web sites.

There's plans in place that are going into effect. You know, again, we're just coming out of this. We're still in the recovery mode. So there's going to be things in place that, unfortunately, our state has learned from Florida. The things that they went through in the last year, that hopefully will save us some time. The key thing is that if you don't really need to be in the area, you don't need to be here. And you may want to, but just let us do our jobs.

COOPER: Right. Because if you're on the roads, you're taking up space that a rescue vehicle could be using. What a lot of people don't realize about the police is, I mean, you guys have gone through this storm yourselves. You've got homes which are damaged, loved ones affected as well. How bad is it here? I mean, it looks terrible.

SEXTON: Well you know, it is. And you're right. You brought up a unique point, about the second side of this coin is that we're emergency personnel first, but we have families, we have a lot of officers that don't have homes. But they're out here, they're doing their jobs, and they're proud of what was they're doing. And you can see it in their faces, as they're doing these 18 hours, and these 20 plus hours, on out there. On every call that they go on it's important to them to try to do what they have to do, and working with their fellow law enforcement. With the highway patrol coming in, and everybody coming in to help us, you know it was like a star in the night.

COOPER: Yes. Well, Commander, we appreciate you joining us. I know you've got a lot of work to do. Good luck to you and God speed.

SEXTON: I appreciate it.

COOPER: Thank you very much. So much work to be done here tonight. We appreciate all their efforts.

We have a lot left on this special edition of 360. We're going to show you some just extraordinary rescue efforts.

Also, we've been—we came across a seal, if you can believe it, of all things, just about 100 yards behind me, a little bit earlier on. We're going to show you what has happened. It's just one of those things you come across here that you don't really expect.

You know, we just got to Gulfport about two hours ago, and I have simply been stunned by what we saw. When we come back from this break, we're going to show you, sort of, my reporter's notebook of, kind of, walking around downtown Gulfport. Because what we saw was just truly extraordinary.

But first, I want to check in with CNN's Adaora Udoji who is in New Orleans with some breaking news. Adaora? Adaora, what can you tell us? Adaora, it's Anderson, you're on the air? What can you tell us?

We're trying to get communication with Adaora Udoji working out—Adaora, this is Anderson, you're on the air. What can you tell us?

ADAORA UDOJI, CNN CORRESPONDENT: Hi, Anderson, hello.

COOPER: Go ahead, Adaora. What can you tell us?

UDOJI: We're in downtown New Orleans, Anderson, right outside of the Superdome. And we ran into police officers who are telling us that there's a massive looting going on in the downtown area, particularly in those areas that have been flooded. They tell us that the water has continually been rising, that at some points it is up to 12 feet. They say it was in the last couple of hours that there have been a couple of shootings in the area. And they're very concerned that the situation could deteriorate as we move into nighttime.

It's actually also begun to rain. They told us that there have been a couple of reported incidents of various people, some of these I guess you could call them Katrina refugees, who are packed along the highway, trying to take others' cars because they're trying to get out of town. They were certainly advising us to be very careful. Really, they advise us not to go in the downtown area.

Anderson.

COOPER: Adaora, just, you know, there are so many people listening to this, and desperate for any kind of information. We don't want to alarm people in any way. Do you have any sense of how extensive this looting is? How many people have been shot or arrested?

UDOJI: They told us there have been three different shootings, and they were in and around the Superdome area. They were not all at one particular location. At least two of them, we were told, were in apartment buildings or near apartment buildings. When they talked about the looting, they said Canal, which is one of the main arteries in downtown New Orleans, that there had been massive—a lot of looting going on in that area, which is right—very close to where many of the hotels are. And again, they were just expressing concern of the possibility of things deteriorating overnight.

Anderson.

COOPER: All right, Adaora, appreciate that. This is the first information we've gotten on that. We will continue to follow it over the course of this evening and bring you any updates as warranted. We have a lot ahead in this continuing hour, this special edition of 360, live from Gulfport, Mississippi, one of the hardest-hit towns. We'll be right back.

(COMMERCIAL BREAK)

COOPER: A woman came up to me in Wal-Mart earlier today and said, please tell us about what is going on in Bay St. Louis. We're not getting any information out of there.

CNN's Gary Tuchman has been there and has a remarkable rescue that took place. Here's his piece.

(BEGIN VIDEOTAPE)

GARY TUCHMAN, CNN CORRESPONDENT (voice-over): A small Mississippi town in ruins. Bay St. Louis, which suffered catastrophic damage from Hurricane Camille in 1969, was hit even harder this time.

Nicky Nichelson moved here two years ago.

NICKY NICHELSON, HURRICANE KATRINA SURVIVOR: Here is my dream. I came here from New Orleans two-and-a-half years ago with a wonderful dream to have a B & B on the beach and I did for a very short period of time.

TUCHMAN (on camera): And Nicky, I can't even see where it was anymore. Where was it?

NICKELSON: I know. It was right here. This beautiful tree was in my front yard.

TUCHMAN (voice-over): Her bed and breakfast is now rubble, just like many of the homes and businesses on Main Street, just like the mile-long bridge which is part of U.S. 90 across the St. Louis Bay. Each of the stories is unique, but Nicky's is harrowing as well as lucky.

NICKELSON: This house had withstood Camille and withstood the huge wind of 1947. And—so, I felt we were safe. I felt safe in the house.

TUCHMAN: So she and six other people remained in the bed and breakfast. But a tidal surge came in. And then—

NICKELSON: My house literally crumbled.

TUCHMAN (on camera): While you were in it?

NICKELSON: While we were in it. Crumbled, just crumbled.

TUCHMAN (voice-over): And that's where this tree comes into the story. The seven were propelled by the storm surge to the tree. As the winds whipped and the torrents of rain fell, they grabbed on to a limb, literally for dear life.

NICKELSON: We held on, it was amazing, for almost three hours. And it just finally, finally slowed down. But I mean, it was washing over our heads—over our heads.

TUCHMAN: One of the employees of the B & B, Kevin McNeil, was next to Nicky on the limb.

(on camera): So, Nicky was here. You were where, Kevin?

KEVIN MCNEIL, HURRICANE KATRINA SURVIVOR: Right up there.

TUCHMAN: You were up there and the waves were hitting the branch. And what were you thinking?

NICKELSON: I started to pray a lot. I truly didn't know if we'd make it. I really didn't.

TUCHMAN: You must have been terrified.

NICKELSON: Absolutely.

MCNEIL: I was just trying to keep her calm.

NICKELSON: You know, and every once in a while we'd look at each other and touch, you know, a finger to each other.

MCNEIL: It was stinging so bad with the rain.

NICKELSON: It was awful.

TUCHMAN (voice-over): Minutes later, four of the seven, including a couple in their 80s, lost their grips and floated away. The three left on the tree were despondent.

(on camera): Did you think you were going to die?

NICKELSON: Yes. Yes, I did.

TUCHMAN (on camera): No doubt about it?

NICKELSON: No. No doubt about it. No doubt.

TUCHMAN (voice-over): But the water started to recede. Nicky and her friends were safe. And the four who floated away were later rescued.

(on camera): What were you thinking while that water was climbing the tree and you were on it?

NICKELSON: That I would be a little bit more religious; have a little more faith.

TUCHMAN: Have more faith?

NICKELSON: Yes.

TUCHMAN: If you lived?

NICKELSON: Yes. And my brother's a priest. He'll be very happy with that.

TUCHMAN (voice-over): Kevin hadn't been able to contact his nervous mother in Louisiana to say he was all right. We let him use our satellite telephone to do that.

MCNEIL: Love you. Love you. Bye. Bye.

TUCHMAN: And Nicky is now mulling the future with her faithful friend, Mattie the Scottish terrier, who by the way, was on that tree branch with Nicky.

(END VIDEOTAPE)

COOPER: Unbelievable, Gary. Has anyone died in— do we know, has anyone died in that town?

TUCHMAN: In Hancock County, where Bay St. Louis is, authorities are telling us they've had a number of deaths. They won't say the exact number, but what they're doing is they're putting red paint on the houses of those who have died—most of those houses in the water—so they can go back and get the bodies with refrigerated trucks that aren't there just yet.

COOPER: So at this point, they're not even able to get the bodies out? They're just leaving them in the ruins.

TUCHMAN: They've gotten some of them. They haven't been able to get all of them.

COOPER: That's so horrible. Gary Tuchman, thanks. Amazing reporting over the last 24 hours. Thanks very much.

A lot ahead. We've been following the story of this seal who we found a couple of hours ago in this parking lot. It has been swept hundreds of yards. It has not ended well for this seal. So many animals in need right now and of course, so many people desperately in need as well. We'll be right back.

COOPER: We are still live in Gulfport, Mississippi. Three seals were washed from the aquarium where they were—have been living—washed hundreds of yards. They were deposited in a parking lot. For the last 24 hours people have been trying to keep at least one of these seals alive.

We found a woman pouring water over the seal. Sadly, we need to tell you that just in the last hour or so, police shot that seal to death twice in the head to put it out of its misery because simply there is no—there was no place to bring that seal. Nothing to do.

So many animals in need, so many people in need. If you want to help in some way, here's how you can do it. On the screen, some information. You can also log on to the Web site, CNN.com—a lot more information.

FURTHER RESOURCES

Books

Brennan, Virginia. *Natural Disasters and Public Health: Hurricane Katrina, Rita, and Wilma.* Baltimore, MD: Johns Hopkins University Press, 2009.

Brinkley, Douglas. *The Great Deluge: Hurricane Katrina, New Orleans, and the Mississippi Gulf Coast.* New York: Harper Perennial, 2007.

Horne, Jed. *Breach of Faith: Hurricane Katrina and the Near Death of a Great American City.* New York: Random House, 2008.

Van Heerden, Ivor, and Bryan, Mike. *The Storm: What Went Wrong and Why During Hurricane Katrina—the Inside Story from One Louisiana Scientist.* New York: Penguin, 2007.

Web Sites

"Hurricane Katrina & Rita Web Archive." *Internet Archive* http://websearch.archive.org/katrina/ (accessed on November 10, 2012).

"Hurricane Katrina Archive." *NASA.* www.nasa.gov/vision/earth/lookingatearth/h2005_katrina.html (accessed on November 10, 2012).

Levees.org (accessed on November 10, 2012).

"Who's a Looter? In Storm's Aftermath, Pictures Kick Up a Different Kind of Tempest"

Newspaper article

By: Tania Ralli

Date: September 5, 2005

Source: Ralli, Tania. "Who's a Looter? In Storm's Aftermath, Pictures Kick Up a Different Kind of Tempest." *New York Times*, September 5, 2005. www.nytimes.com/2005/09/05/business/05caption.html (accessed on March 17, 2013).

About the Publication: The *New York Times* was founded in 1851 as a concise, four-page summary of daily news items. News mogul Adolph S. Ochs acquired the paper in 1896, expanding its scope and size. By the turn of the twentieth century, the *New York Times* was the pre-eminent U.S. newspaper, acclaimed for its objective reporting of "All the News That's Fit to Print." In 1905, the popularity and importance of the paper was memorialized by the City of New York, which called its new public square "Times Square," in honor of the newspaper. The paper's investigative reporting on official and political affairs has always been a trademark, garnering the journalism staff more than one hundred Pulitzer Prizes for its coverage of wars and governments—most notably for its publication of the "Pentagon Papers," leaked documents attesting to the mishandling and uncertainty of the Vietnam War. The *New York Times* remains the nation's most prestigious and important newspaper, and it continues to be owned and operated by descendants of Ochs.

INTRODUCTION

On the whole, media reportage in Hurricane Katrina's immediate aftermath made for gripping watching, listening, and reading. For many, it supplanted regular programs and activities, so compelling was its immediacy and the intensity of its narrative. The problem was that many of those stories were just plain wrong, and the erroneous reporting was not just the product of rookie reporters in a stressful situation. Some of the most venerable and respected news organizations around the world got caught up in the wave of less-than-accurate journalism due to numerous factors.

Even as the storm was still battering the Gulf Coast, pre-staged media crews were on scene, moving into the most affected areas to get their requisite live shots. However, it was not until after the cyclone moved away over land and the pressure of too much water volume burst the levees in New Orleans' Lower Ninth Ward that the true destruction began. Reporters rushed in, searching for knowledgeable authorities to provide reliable facts, figures, and plans of action to evacuate affected people and animals, repair the levee breach, and get the city pumped out and back to normal.

What they found instead was a lack of access to informed government officials, and the ones they could locate appeared as clueless as their questioners. Even those who seemed to have some kind of handle on the realities of the situation were largely ineffectual in doing anything about it. Without their mainstay disaster information sources on the ground, reporters turned to technology to connect them with alternate sources. They found that the storm had knocked out cell phone towers and Internet connections. Some even experienced failure of satellite phones. Without the ability to corroborate stories and check facts, and with the relentless hunger of the 24/7 news cycle to feed, reporters were often forced to rely on "man on the street" accounts and unsubstantiated rumor as the basis of their stories.

Meanwhile, a truly epic tragedy was unfolding around them. Astonishing levels of water now surrounded homes and businesses in the Ninth Ward, populated typically by the poor and elderly who lacked the means to leave before the storm arrived. Power was out to the entire area and there were no sources of clean water or food. There was no immediate means to evacuate the thousands of people stranded in hot attics and on blistering rooftops, and government officials at every level failed to respond in a timely manner to the needs of their constituents. People were suffering from thirst, heat exhaustion, hunger, and all manner of illness, with supplies rapidly dwindling. The sick and infirm were unable to get themselves to safety and many were dying preventable deaths. Human and animal bodies bobbed out into the flooded streets, and the floodwaters became dangerously tainted—a miasma of toxic chemicals and unpleasant floating cargo.

Some journalists became enraged at the apparent abandonment of the helpless residents. Subject to much of the same squalor and privations, these reporters realized they might have the power to move authorities to needed action by shedding their traditional role of objective reporting. They adopted an emotionally charged blend of on-the-scene reportage and outspoken advocacy for those whose misery they were reporting. The continuous repetition of these reports to fill the round-the-clock news cycle created the perception that New Orleans was in the midst of complete social breakdown. Though it ultimately did achieve some of the hoped-for pressure on authorities to act, this reporting approach also arguably reinforced the appearance of rampant lawlessness taking over one of America's most beloved cities as the world looked on.

SIGNIFICANCE

In the chaos of an ongoing emergency, interested parties are scraping for every bit of information they can get, and in a hyper-connected world, the major source of that information is usually the news media. People outside the affected area depend on the media for facts that shape their initial and ongoing perceptions of what is happening, so how that information is presented can have tremendous ramifications.

Residents in the impact zone led to be overly concerned about potential looting might choose to stay to protect their property and fail to evacuate, putting their lives at unnecessary risk. A media-intensified atmosphere of lawlessness might bias law enforcement officers into seeing some storm victims as dangerous and respond accordingly, with grave consequences. Officials may reallocate resources needed by victims if reports convince them that law enforcement or other authorities need them more, increasing the very real misery of those suffering. And the public might perceive anarchy that requires a National Guard presence more akin to a heavy-handed military occupation that oppresses suffering victims rather than a strong, friendly presence that ensures security while helping get things back to normal.

After Hurricane Katrina, the job of journalists to analyze what was true and what was not—which can be challenging even under normal circumstances—was made that much more difficult under the inarguable duress of a trying situation. But that duress made the need for accuracy, if anything, more important than ever, given that most storm survivors shown by the media were African American and poor, creating a situation rife with explosive racist potential.

A prime example of this dilemma is the furor caused when two photographs appeared on the Internet following Hurricane Katrina, which resulted in much discussion about the media and race.

When the two photographs were taken after New Orleans' Ninth Ward had flooded from a failed levee, electrical power was off, there were no accessible public sources of food or clean water, and there were widespread media reports of looting.

A black man holds groceries as he wades in flood water caused by Hurricane Katrina. The original caption in the photo following its release described the man as looting. © AP IMAGES/DAVE MARTIN.

Though the photographs are nearly identical, showing people leaving a grocery store with food and other necessities, the photo of white people identifies them as having "found bread and soda," implying a necessary act of foraging to survive, while the photo showing a young black man doing essentially the same thing describes him as having "just looted a grocery store."

Perhaps the most compelling argument for the need to maintain journalistic accuracy above all else is the fact that, years after the storm, countless people still believe those initial reports of rape, murder, and thugs attacking rescuers that have since been proven untrue.

■ PRIMARY SOURCE

"WHO'S A LOOTER? IN STORM'S AFTERMATH, PICTURES KICK UP A DIFFERENT KIND OF TEMPEST"

SYNOPSIS: A reporter for the *New York Times* compares and analyzes the meaning behind captions accompanying two photographs taken during Hurricane Katrina's aftermath, when New Orleans's Ninth Ward was underwater.

Two news photographs ricocheted through the Internet last week and set off a debate about race and the news media in the aftermath of Hurricane Katrina.

The first photo, taken by Dave Martin, an Associated Press photographer in New Orleans, shows a young black man wading through water that has risen to his chest. He is clutching a case of soda and pulling a floating bag. The caption provided by The A.P. says he has just been "looting a grocery store."

The second photo, also from New Orleans, was taken by Chris Graythen for Getty Images and distributed by Agence France-Presse. It shows a white couple up to their chests in the same murky water. The woman is holding some bags of food. This caption says they are shown "after finding bread and soda from a local grocery store."

Both photos turned up Tuesday on Yahoo News, which posts automatic feeds of articles and photos from wire services. Soon after, a user of the photo-sharing site Flickr juxtaposed the images and captions on a single page, which attracted links from many blogs. The left-leaning blog Daily Kos linked to the page with the comment, "It's not looting if you're white."

A white man and woman carry goods through flood water following Hurricane Katrina. The original caption in the photo following its release described them as "finding" the groceries. © CHRIS GRAYTHEN/GETTY IMAGES.

The contrast of the two photo captions, which to many indicated a double standard at work, generated widespread anger toward the news media that quickly spread beyond the Web.

On Friday night, the rapper Kanye West ignored the teleprompter during NBC's live broadcast of "A Concert for Hurricane Relief," using the opportunity to lambaste President Bush and criticize the press. "I hate the way they portray us in the media," he said. "You see a black family, it says they're looting. You see a white family, it says they're looking for food."

Many bloggers were quick to point out that the photos came from two different agencies, and so could not reflect the prejudice of a single media outlet. A writer on the blog BoingBoing wrote: "Perhaps there's more factual substantiation behind each copywriter's choice of words than we know. But to some, the difference in tone suggests racial bias, implicit or otherwise."

According to the agencies, each photographer captioned his own photograph. Jack Stokes, a spokesman for The A.P., said that photographers are told to describe what they have seen when they write a caption.

Mr. Stokes said The A.P. had guidelines in place before Hurricane Katrina struck to distinguish between "looting" and "carrying." If a photographer sees a person enter a business and emerge with goods, it is described as looting. Otherwise The A.P. calls it carrying.

Mr. Stokes said that Mr. Martin had seen the man in his photograph wade into a grocery store and come out with the sodas and bag, so by A.P.'s definition, the man had looted.

The photographer for Getty Images, Mr. Graythen, said in an e-mail message that he had also stuck to what he had seen to write his caption, and had actually given the wording a great deal of thought. Mr. Graythen described seeing the couple near a corner store from an elevated expressway. The door to the shop was open, and things had floated out to the street. He was not able to talk to the couple, "so I had to draw my own conclusions," he said.

In the extreme conditions of New Orleans, Mr. Graythen said, taking necessities like food and water to survive could not be considered stealing. He said that had he seen people coming out of stores with computers and DVD players, he would have considered that looting.

"If you're taking something that runs solely from a wall outlet that requires power from the electric company—when we are not going to have power for weeks, even months—that's inexcusable," he said.

Since the photo was published last Tuesday Mr. Graythen has received more than 500 e-mail messages, most of them supportive, he said.

Within three hours of the photo's publication online, editors at Agence France-Presse rewrote Mr. Graythen's caption. But the original caption remained online as part of a Yahoo News slide show. Under pressure to keep up with the news, and lacking the time for a discussion about word choice, Olivier Calas, the agency's director of multimedia, asked Yahoo to remove the photo last Thursday.

Now, in its place, when readers seek the picture of the couple, a statement from Neil Budde, the general manager of Yahoo News, appears in its place. The statement emphasizes that Yahoo News did not write the photo captions and that it did not edit the captions, so that the photos can be made available as quickly as possible.

Mr. Calas said Agence France-Presse was bombarded with e-mail messages complaining about the caption. He said the caption was unclear and should have been reworded earlier. "This was a consequence of a series of negligences, not ill intent," he said.

For Mr. Graythen, whose parents and grandparents lost their homes in the disaster, the fate of the survivors was the most important thing. In his e-mail message he wrote: "Now is no time to pass judgment on those trying to stay alive. Now is no time to argue semantics about finding versus looting. Now is no time to argue if this is a white versus black issue."

FURTHER RESOURCES

Periodicals

Giudici, M. "Hurricane Katrina: The Ethical Responsibility of the Media in Their Coverage of the Recovery Process." *Media Psychology Review* 1, no. 1 (2008). http://mprcenter.org/mpr/index.php?option=com_content&view=article&id=63&Itemid=122 (accessed on March 17, 2013).

Powers, Shawn. "Media Coverage of Hurricane Katrina: Implications and Developments in Public Diplomacy." *PD News – Media Monitor Reports*, September 8, 2005. http://uscpublicdiplomacy.org/index.php/newswire/media_monitor_reports_detail/050909_media_coverage_of_hurricane_katrina/ (accessed on March 17, 2013).

Sommers, Samuel R., Evan P. Apfelbaum, Kristin N. Dukes, Negin Toosi, and Elsie J. Wang, eds. "Race and Media Coverage of Hurricane Katrina: Analysis, Implications, and Future Research Questions." *Analyses of Social Issues and Public Policy* 6, no. 1 (2006), 1–17. http://www.columbia.edu/~nt2334/Sommers2006HurricaneKatrina.pdf (accessed on March 17, 2013).

Web Sites

Bressers, Bonnie. "Media coverage of Hurricane Katrina: Why the Message Matters." *K-State Libraries*. http://ksulib.typepad.com/ksbn/2011/09/bressers.html (accessed on March 17, 2013).

"Katrina Media Coverage: Transcript." *PBS NewsHour*. www.pbs.org/newshour/bb/weather/july-dec05/media_9-29.html (accessed on March 17, 2013).

"American Idolatry"

Magazine article

By: Joseph V. Tirella

Date: May 19, 2008

Source: Tirella, Joseph V. "American Idolatry." *Upstart Business Journal*, May 19, 2008. http://upstart.bizjournals.com/culture-lifestyle/culture-inc/arts/2008/05/19/American-Idol-by-the-Numbers.html (accessed on March 18, 2013).

About the Journal: *Upstart Business Journal* is owned by American City Business Journals, the North Carolina–based media company that publishes weekly newspapers in forty metropolitan areas. *Upstart* reports on the people and ideas behind the most dynamic and unique businesses in an effort to connect those businesses with other entrepreneurial risk takers. The journal's core editorial team works out of New York City and Charlotte but has a stable of reporters and editors across the nation.

INTRODUCTION

In 2001, a reality talent show debuted on British television. *Pop Idol* invited singers to audition and compete. Participants would perform for a panel of judges, but the ultimate winner would be chosen by votes cast by the viewing audience. The show was an instant hit but was put on hiatus after the second season because judge and music executive Simon Cowell wanted to create another show in the UK.

The interactive format had proven its worth, and soon Cowell and *Pop Idol* creator Simon Fuller pitched a similar show to television executives in the United States. The offer was met with poor response from everyone except Fox Network head Rupert Murdoch. The show was called *American Idol: The Search for a Superstar* and it broadcast its first episode in the summer of 2002. The combination of contestants with remarkable talent, those with absolutely no talent, and the acid-tongued Cowell as judge proved to be just what America was in the mood for; by 2004, *American Idol* was the most popular show on national television, a position it held for seven consecutive years. Millions of viewers tuned in weekly to watch—and vote for—contestants who vie for the title of American Idol, an honor that would guarantee them a record deal with a major recording label as well as a variety of contracts that would earn them hundreds of thousands of dollars—minimum—as well as untold publicity.

Idol judges for the first eight seasons included Cowell, dancer-singer Paula Abdul, and music industry personality Randy Jackson. The trio was a blend of personalities: Cowell was direct in his criticism and often perceived to be unjustly cruel. Abdul was quick to praise and made efforts to break bad news gently when she had nothing good to say. Jackson was the

Kelly Clarkson performs on September 3, 2002, during the first season of *American Idol* on her way to being the show's first winner. © AP IMAGES/LUCY NICHOLSON.

cool one who called contestants "Dawg" and seemed more like a friend than a judge. Together they created a balance while individually developing loyal fan bases.

The first season of *Idol* was co-hosted by two personalities: Ryan Seacrest and Brian Dunkelman. The latter quit after that initial run, leaving Seacrest the sole host. His enthusiasm was contagious, and contestants and viewers appreciated him equally. So integral to the success of the show was he that in 2009, Seacrest signed a three-year, $45 million contract to continue his hosting duties on *Idol*, earning him the title of highest paid reality television host to date, according to the *Hollywood Reporter*.

SIGNIFICANCE

American Idol launched the careers of several successful recording artists, including Kelly Clarkson (winner of Season 1), Jennifer Hudson (contestant in Season 3), Carrie Underwood (winner of Season 4), Jordin Sparks (winner of Season 6), Scotty McCreery

(winner of Season 10), and Phillip Phillips (winner of Season 11).

While the majority of those who go on to enjoy success are the actual winners of the show, the Top 10 finalists also find themselves in the spotlight as they travel the country performing in that season's *American Idol* tour. The *New York Times* reported that the Top 5 finalists in the 2010 season likely earned $100,000 from their participation in the show itself and could expect to earn three to four times more if the show's producers gave them a record deal. What began as a way to merely entertain America turned out to be a legitimate stepping stone for those truly talented enough to make it in the cutthroat music industry.

Beginning in Season 4, *American Idol* became the most expensive series on broadcast networks for advertisers. According to Adweek.com, a 30-second commercial in Season 5 cost advertisers $705,000, a "record-high price tag." And while later seasons saw a turnover of judges—Simon Cowell himself departed from the panel in Season 10—and were consistently plagued by criticism over voting methods and results, the show remained popular, a bedrock for the Fox Network. It is credited with inspiring other competitive singing shows like *The Voice* and *The X Factor*, each popular in its own way but nowhere near matching the success of the original interactive reality show.

PRIMARY SOURCE

"AMERICAN IDOLATRY"

SYNOPSIS: In a culture of reality television shows, *American Idol* reigns.

Editor's Note: *On May 21, David Cook became the latest winner of American Idol, taking the prize by a margin of 12 million votes out of a record 97.5 million cast.*

American Idol, which is wrapping up its season finale on May 22, is the most successful television show of this short century. Let that statement sink in for a moment. Yes, the show that gave us Clay Aiken and William Hung and Ryan Seacrest is the pop-cultural phenomenon of the post-9/11 world.

Idol launched in June 2002, and its first episode was watched by a mere 9.9 million viewers. But in time, the numbers would grow significantly—to more than triple that. *American Idol* is, to today's iPod-listening and iPhone-yapping adolescents, the equivalent of the Beatles, as painful as that might be for a certain generation to accept. On February 9, 1964, a reported 73 million people watched the Fab Four's introduction to America on *The Ed Sullivan Show*—like *Idol*, a top-rated variety program with some memorable acts and some not-so-memorable acts. That's one million fewer than the number of votes cast during the season finale of *American Idol* last year—not bad in an era when there are a zillion channel choices, not the three of *Sullivan's* day.

Yet in the beginning, plenty of television insiders, including executives at three major networks, ABC, CBS and NBC, all passed on their chance to buy the show. Rupert Murdoch, chairman and C.E.O. of News Corp., the Fox Network's corporate parent, said yes (though some have said it was actually Mike Darnell, Fox's reality chief, who gave the go-ahead). Now, in an era of endless cable stations and diminishing returns for networks, *American Idol* dominates television, and Murdoch's News Corp. reaps the financial benefits.

But ratings are down a bit this year, and *Idol*-haters are predicting the show's demise. Not Murdoch, of course, who last year said: "I think it's got years and years of life." Here's the tally on *Idol* to date:

- Total number of *American Idol* episodes since its debut in 2002 (as of May 19): 270
- Number of seasons *American Idol* has been ranked the No. 1 show on television: 3 (2005–2007)
- Value of the *American Idol* franchise, as estimated by *Advertising Age:* $2.5 billion
- Number of Oscar- or Golden Globe–winning performances by *American Idol* winners: 0
- Number of Oscar- or Golden Globe–winning performances by *American Idol* contestants: 2 (Jennifer Hudson, who finished seventh in season three, won both for her role in *Dreamgirls*)
- Worldwide box-office total for *Dreamgirls*: $154,852,975
- Worldwide box-office total of *From Justin to Kelly*, starring the first season's winner, Kelly Clarkson, and runner-up Justin Guarini: $4,928,883
- Total number of product placements during the 2007 season: 4,349
- Number of product placements during the first three months of the 2008 season: 3,291
- Estimated cost of a 30-second advertisement on the finale episode of *American Idol* each of the last three seasons: $1.3 million
- Approximate number of CDs sold by *American Idol* winners: 24.5 million
- Approximate number of CDs sold by *American Idol* runners-up: 6.5 million
- Highest number of CDs sold by an *American Idol* winner: 9,455,000 (Kelly Clarkson)
- Number of CDs sold by Justin Guarini, season one's runner-up: 143,000

- Number of CDs sold by William Hung, whose rendition of Ricky Martin's "She Bangs" was rejected during the audition phase of season three: 295,000
- Estimated number of viewers who watched the season premiere of *American Idol* on January 15, 2008: 33.2 million
- Percentage of decline this represents from the previous season's premiere: 13 percent
- Estimated number of Americans who watched the April 16 Democratic primary debate between Senator Hillary Clinton and Senator Barack Obama, the highest-rated debate this year: 10.7 million
- Number of votes cast during the season finale of *American Idol* last year: 74 million (*Idol* allows up to 10 votes per phone number)
- Number of people who voted for George W. Bush in the 2004 election: 62 million
- Percentage of Americans who believe their vote in *American Idol* is just as important as their vote for president, according to Fox News: 35 percent

FURTHER RESOURCES

Books

People Magazine editors. *People American Idol.* New York: People, 2012.

Rushfield, Richard. *American Idol: The Untold Story.* New York: Hyperion, 2011.

Web Sites

American Idol. www.americanidol.com/ (accessed on March 18, 2013).

"American Idol." *Reality TV Magazine.* http://realitytvmagazine.sheknows.com/category/american-idol/ (accessed on March 18, 2013).

Belloni, Matthew, and Nellie Andreeva. "Ryan Seacrest Closes Deal Worth $45 Mil." *Hollywood Reporter*, July 12, 2009. www.hollywoodreporter.com/news/ryan-seacrest-closes-deal-worth-86395 (accessed on March 18, 2013).

"The Lowdown on Upstart." *Upstart Business Journal.* http://upstart.bizjournals.com/about/ (accessed on March 18, 2013, 2013).

Mcclellan, Steve. "'Idol' Spots Going for a Song (Plus $700,000)." *Adweek*, September 12, 2005. www.adweek.com/news/advertising/idol-spots-going-song-plus-700000-81477 (accessed on March 18, 2013).

Wyatt, Edward. "'Idol' Winners: Not Just Fame but Big Bucks." *New York Times*, February 23, 2010. www.nytimes.com/2010/02/24/arts/television/24idol.html?_r=0 (accessed on March 18, 2013).

"Tina Brown's *Daily Beast* Is Unleashed"

Newspaper article

By: DealBook

Date: October 8, 2008

Source: "Tina Brown's *Daily Beast* Is Unleashed. *DealBook*, October 8, 2008. http://dealbook.nytimes. com/2008/10/08/tina-browns-daily-beast-is-unleashed/ ?scp=3&sq=daily+beast&st=nyt (accessed on March 19, 2013.)

About the Web site: DealBook is a business Web site that provides coverage of the financial sector and high-profile acquisitions, mergers, and dissolutions. It was created in 2006 as an extension of Andrew Ross Sorkin's popular column of the same name, published in the *New York Times*. The digital version is widely read among industry insiders, earning it several awards for online business reporting.

INTRODUCTION

The *Daily Beast* is a news aggregator and editorial site launched in October 2008. It is distinguished from other, highly similar sites—such as *Talking Points Memo*, *Drudge Report*, and the *Huffington Post*—by its founder and publisher, Tina Brown. Brown is known for her witty, topical consideration of diverse matters, exemplified by her successful career as editor of magazines like *Vanity Fair* and the *New Yorker*. Brown is also known for the exceptional quality of the company she keeps—a renown socialite and opinion-maker, Brown's acumen attracted immediate attention to the *Daily Beast*, both from journalists and writers hoping to have their work appear on Brown's newest production, and from cyber-pundits curious to see what she would be producing next. Noteworthy contributors to the *Daily Beast* include novelist Christopher Buckley, former UK prime minister Tony Blair, former U.S. secretary of state Condoleezza Rice, and journalist Eric Alterman, among others.

The site's launch caused a significant stir in the online community when it was released, garnering awards and accolades for the site and its curator, including a 2009 OMMA Award for News Reporting and a 2009 Online Journalism Award for Online Commentary. A popular feature of the *Daily Beast* since its creation has been the "Cheat Sheet," a series of articles selected each day by the site's staff for being the most important or noteworthy stories of that day.

Besides offering summaries of and links to articles posted on other news sites, the *Daily Beast* also features occasional pieces of original journalism, as well as social commentary, satire, sports coverage, literary and culinary reviews, and cultural works. The Web site's reporting carries a distinct liberal slant, frequently presenting sympathetic coverage of the Democrat Party and its attendant initiative.

The site's most-lauded contribution to the world of information was its "Book Beast" project. Book Beast was an imprint, started by Brown in conjunction with Perseus Books Group, which drastically increased the speed of the book publishing process. Using short books written by the *Daily Beast* contributors, the imprint cut the publishing cycle from its typical pace of two years to around three months by offering a digital version of the manuscript—known as an e-book—within a month of its submission, and a print version two to four months later. By doing so, readers were given access to a current-events piece while it was still relevant, allowing topical information to disseminate while it was still capable of informing the public discourse on a subject.

Upon its inception, Book Beast was heralded as an intermediary between the rapid-fire, cursory news provided by news aggregators and print newsmagazines, and the weighty, dense contents of analytic academic books. As subscriptions and ad revenue for American newsmagazines like *Newsweek*, the *Atlantic*, *Mother Jones*, and *Time* dwindled, Book Beast aimed to replace their role in providing concise, quick, accurate news to those looking to stay informed.

SIGNIFICANCE

Brown's news media has fared well since its inception, although its success tapered somewhat after the initial buzz subsided. The *Daily Beast* failed to generate the influence enjoyed by the *Huffington Post* and *Talking Points Memo*, the other news aggregators vying for the liberal-leaning audience, and it never had a shot at attracting readers from their conservative counterpart, *Drudge Report*. Likewise, those looking for objective, unbiased news aggregation are better served by Google News.

The *Daily Beast* has demonstrated that, as the world turned away from traditional sources (newspapers and television) for consuming news media, it was increasingly important to consumers that their news source fit a specific niche and supply a specific experience, one catered to its audience. Despite a theoretically sound and deftly executed concept, the *Daily Beast* failed to generate a profit by the end of the decade. Part of the site's unsatisfactory financial

Daily Beast founder Tina Brown. © AP IMAGES/EVAN AGOSTINI.

performance can be attributed to the difficulty of monetizing new-media services like news aggregators, which as a rule cannot hope to attract a significant audience if they charge visitors a subscription or usage fee. Even as such services caused the decline of traditional newsmagazines, they often struggled to earn substantial ad revenue. The *Huffington Post* worked around this problem by subsidizing its staff with unpaid opinion bloggers, but the *Daily Beast*'s approach—highly specialized banner and video advertisements customized to target each individual viewer—failed to attract high-paying advertisers, especially considering its small audience.

PRIMARY SOURCE

"TINA BROWN'S DAILY BEAST IS UNLEASHED"

SYNOPSIS: In this article, the author describes the *Daily Beast* and the hype surrounding the website's launch.

A new Web site had its debut this week, thedailybeast.com. But with more than 180 million of the things now online by some estimates, a new one would seem like just another digital drop in an ocean of zeroes and ones. Yawn.

Unless it's Tina Brown doing the dropping, *The New York Times*'s David Carr says. On Monday, *The Daily Beast* used Ms. Brown's gilded e-Rolodex—hey, look, her pal President Clinton is recommending books on the economic meltdown! And her chum Christopher Buckley's cracking wise!—to stick its head above the fray.

The Daily Beast, backed by Barry Diller's IAC/InterActiveCorp, is an aggregation of the trivial and the momentous, the original and the borrowed. With a slogan splashed across its home page promising rigorous editing of the culture for complicated times—"Read This Skip That"—the *Beast* is aiming to be a smaller, less chaotic version of the World Wide Web itself.

This being a Tina Brown enterprise, there is, of course, something called The Buzz Board. And the design, with its grids of links, articles and videos, brings to mind the look of the front of a glossy magazine. Some of the features are tricky, or nicely tricked up, depending on your view of technology, including moving headlines that chase the reader's eyes down the page. News features sit beside the digital catnip of "charticles." Opinions abound.

In greeting readers on Monday, Ms. Brown used the site to ask and answer an obvious question at a time of towering informational clutter: "Why should I visit you when there's already *Slate/Drudge/Huffington Post/TPM/Google News* and every other magazine and newspaper?"

Her answer: "Sensibility, darling."

Ah, yes, Darling: sensibility is Ms. Brown's game. *The Daily Beast*—named after the newspaper in Evelyn Waugh's Fleet Street satire, "Scoop"—is relying heavily on Ms. Brown's range of interests (from high to low, from powerful to incredibly powerful) to remain relevant enough to merit daily, even hourly, clicking. Given Ms. Brown's reputation for frantically changing everything in the final hours of closing every magazine she has edited, perhaps a medium that absorbs—indeed, requires—constant reiteration will suit her.

Even in the anarchic environs of the Web, Ms. Brown's efforts merit notice, partly because she has landed with a flurry of impact in all her endeavors (give or take a ratings-deprived talk show on CNBC). She first came to attention in 1979 as editor of *Tatler*, a British magazine, and came to America in 1983 to become the editor of *Vanity Fair*. In 1992 she was named editor of *The New Yorker*, where her mixing of high and low, earnest and frothy became a serial hit, altering the landscape of serious magazines and bringing celebrity into broad swaths of the culture.

She followed up those successes by leaving *The New Yorker* to found *Talk*, a much-discussed general-interest magazine that lasted three years and was eventually closed in the advertising recession after the attacks of Sept. 11. The magazine's every wiggle and wobble was drenched in hype, which may explain why *The Daily Beast* appeared on Monday with a minimum of it. The site still hit the radar, though.

"The design is lively," Nick Denton, founder of Gawker Media, told *The Times*. But, he added, citing Google's home page, among others, "it has to be simpler to work."

Mr. Denton said that graphic clutter or not, he would be among the people looking in. "I'll definitely read *The Daily Beast*," he said, continuing, "but I don't think there are that many of me."

Ms. Brown would beg to differ. "We have heard from a lot of people who love what we came up with, but we are tweaking and refining even as we speak," she said in a phone interview on Tuesday, sounding relieved to be free of interminable print deadlines. "That's the nice part about doing something on the Web."

Recalling her days in the crosshairs at *Talk*, she added, "the trouble with starting monthly magazines is that you have to go around trying to gather advertising, and the only thing you have to sell is the editor."

Edward Felsenthal, a former *Wall Street Journal* editor and *The Daily Beast*'s editor in chief, said that for the time being, there would be no ads. "We are working on getting the tone and content right, and then we will worry about selling ads," he told *The Times*. "This is a soft launch."

If it is, it resembles something of the tone Ms. Brown's friend Arianna Huffington set when she began huffingtonpost.com in 2005: a digital salon for all her show business friends. But *The Huffington Post* has since morphed—and found remarkable success—by tacking to the left and relying on a legion of unpaid bloggers to kick up political content during the most interesting election in years.

Some have suggested that Ms. Brown is merely going down a path of electronic publishing pioneered by Ms. Huffington, but neither woman buys it.

"I have known Tina since she was at Oxford, and I was at Cambridge, and I think she has a wonderful eye with a very clear point of view that will make for a very interesting, highly curated site," Ms. Huffington told *The Times*. "The great thing about new media is that it is not a zero-sum game. The more compelling content there is on the Web, the more people will be habituated to going there."

Ms. Brown noted that Ms. Huffington had already contributed to *The Daily Beast*—a Tuesday

recommendation to see "War Inc." with John Cusack—and said that talk of that kind of competition was rubbish.

"That is such a binary way of looking at media, and we don't see it that way," she said.

Postbinary or not, Ms. Brown does not appear to have lost her touch for creating a stir. On Tuesday, the site's second day of existence, Ms. Brown published an interview with Jennifer Lopez by Kevin Sessums, a longtime celebrity profiler—an article killed by an unnamed women's fashion magazine, in which he asks her about Scientology, breast feeding, a nervous breakdown and selling pictures of her twins. Those old magazine connections can come in mighty handy.

Within hours gawker.com was speculating about which magazine had spiked the piece; *New York* magazine's site, nymag.com, had teased apart Ms. Lopez's "breakdown"; and popsugar.com was drooling over the interview's naughtier bits. After a long time on the sidelines, Ms. Brown was back in the middle of the game, or at least the conversation.

FURTHER RESOURCES
Web Sites

"The Daily Beast." *Encyclo*. www.niemanlab.org/encyclo/daily-beast (accessed on March 19, 2013).

Daily Beast. www.thedailybeast.com (accessed on March 19, 2013).

Rich, Motoko. "Daily Beast Seeks to Publish Faster." *New York Times*, September 28, 2009. www.nytimes.com/2009/09/29/books/29beas.html?_r=2&scp=1&sq=The%20Daily%20Beast&st=cse& (accessed on March 19, 2013).

"The Ten Major Newspapers That Will Fold Or Go Digital Next"

Web site article

By: Douglas A. McIntyre

Date: March 9, 2009

Source: McIntyre, Douglas A. "The Ten Major Newspapers That Will Fold Or Go Digital Next." *24/7 Wall Street*, March 9, 2009. http://247wallst.com/2009/03/

09/the-ten-major-newspapers-that-will-fold-or-go-digital-next/ (accessed on March 19, 2013).

About the Author: Douglas A. McIntyre edits *24/7 Wall St.*, a free, daily digital newsletter comprising more than fifty articles per day about financial news and opinion. The publication has readers throughout North America, Asia, the Middle East, and Africa. Its articles are republished by many of the largest news sites and portals, including AOL DailyFinance, MarketWatch, MSNBC, MSN Money, Yahoo! Finance, Comcast, and the Huffington Post.

INTRODUCTION

Though people have informally shared news throughout history, newspapers are one of the most time-honored channels of public information. China's Han dynasty likely produced newspapers' earliest precursors, information sheets called *tipao*, which contained political news, military campaign reports, and execution notices, as early as 202 BCE. However, the *Acta Diurna*, published in Rome in 59 BCE, is generally acknowledged as the first real newspaper.

The first movable type-printed newspapers came from Germany in 1609, and the first American newspaper, *Public Occurrences,*, was printed in Boston in 1690. Newspapers' immediacy, ease of production, and relative affordability made them extremely popular with the general public. Periodic advances in pre-press technology, printing, and distribution continued through the years to make them more affordable to the average reader. From helping foment the American Revolution in the mid-1770s through keeping the masses informed of relentless technological advances near the turn of the twenty-first century, printed newspapers and their more in-depth cousins—magazines—remained staples of news reporting the world over.

With the coming of the Internet and other digital age technologies, however, print publications of all kinds saw a steep decline in readership in the twenty-first century. Many readers were now turning to far more immediate online news sources, whose content and delivery they could tailor to their tastes. This created decreasing support from advertisers, who saw their audiences migrating away from print and moved much of their budgets online.

Digital technology also introduced a relatively low bar to entry into the online news reporting business, since a computer and an Internet connection were essentially all that was needed to start up such an enterprise, which could be run by a very small staff. By contrast, the equipment and staff needed to curate content, produce and print paper pages, then distribute them physically to newsstands and other outlets remained far more expensive and required backing by a well-financed organization.

For a while, larger newspapers remained secure in their experience and expertise, as their digital competitors experimented with various business models and technologies. By the middle of the first decade of the twenty-first century, however, digital had found its rhythm and even major city daily newspapers were under pressure to adapt or die. By 2007, the number of U.S. print newspapers being published had fallen to 1,456. (In 1870, that number had been 5,091.)

SIGNIFICANCE

As the twenty-first century approached its second decade, the newspaper industry was in free-fall. Once a bastion of profitability and stability for its owners and employees, the industry was now reeling from technological innovations that had significantly changed the way people chose to consume their news, the content of the news itself, and what they were willing to pay for the information.

Since 1904, when the first school of journalism was founded at the University of Missouri, and 1923, when the American Society of Newspaper Editors drafted the "Canons of Journalism" that stated that "news reports should be free from opinion or bias of any kind," newspapers had begun building a high level of credibility and professionalism in the minds of readers. Absolute objectivity was the goal for professional reportage, but in the face of human imperfection, relative objectivity with at least the appearance of unassailability became the standard.

Over the years, newspapers withstood the threat of newer technologies such as radio and television that were continually expected to replace them. Instead, newspaper editors and publishers would return to the strengths of the form to shore up newspapers against new media. They would emphasize the ability of papers to exercise long form, in-depth reporting and connect findings as much as possible to local readers. This was possible because the entrance of radio and television into the media markets was relatively gradual, giving newspapers time to react positively. Both technologies were rather primitive when they first came on the scene, and they took decades to reach maturity and widespread usefulness and adoption. The arrival and maturation period of the Internet and related digital technologies, however, was anything but gradual.

Unlike TV and radio, which had military applications but were primarily developed for the public, the Internet was primarily developed by U.S. defense contractors for use by the military and its related entities. This meant that typical roadblocks to rapid development and deployment that Internet technology might have encountered from uncooperative private developers who felt threatened by it were almost nonexistent. The deep pockets of defense funding sources virtually ensured that the technology would be fast-tracked to adoption by the military and related educational entities such as universities and think tanks. From there, it was a short step to widespread public adoption and rapid private development of other digital technologies that would work with and extend the functionality of the Internet.

The history of newspapers as an industry that grew immense, then cannibalized itself through extensive mergers and consolidations to achieve economies of scale, made it particularly vulnerable to the rapid rise of digital media competition. By the time this new technology arrived in the private sector, thousands of newspapers were held by just a few companies, many of which remained top-heavy from a lack of staff-pruning following mergers. They also required, due to the nature of the work and their product, a huge capital investment in physical infrastructure, equipment, and labor. The need to continue servicing this overhead made the papers less than nimble in responding to the rapidly growing threat from digital media. They simply could not move fast enough to match the timeliness, interactivity, and customization with which online-based organizations could deliver the news.

Eventually, newspapers realized they must co-opt the new technology to help them remain relevant in news reportage. They reluctantly launched digital editions of their print products and leveraged electronic tools to help create content for both formats. Many of the more venerable papers boasted the most experienced staff, often meaning those staff were older and less adaptable to an electronic workflow, so some of the largest and strongest papers felt the pain first. For years, many of these organizations found themselves clumsily trying to shoehorn a new format into an old production process and failed. All the while, smart young startups piloted by "digital natives" and unencumbered by any allegiances to old technologies gained journalism experience and rapidly moved up the ladder in achievement, visibility, and respectability.

"Old school" papers that survive have done so at great cost to their staffs, some of which have been halved in round after round of layoffs, as management seeks to cut costs and return to profitability. Some have taken a tip from popular "reality TV" and turned more toward "infotainment" and sensationalism to revive public interest in their products. Though the most successful of these publishers seem to be those who have committed to a healthy print/digital hybrid model, it remains to be seen whether they will be able to survive in the long run.

PRIMARY SOURCE

"THE TEN MAJOR NEWSPAPERS THAT WILL FOLD OR GO DIGITAL NEXT"

SYNOPSIS: Newspapers were in trouble at the end of the first decade of the twenty-first century, having major difficulty competing with new online news reporting services. This article from a daily online newsletter, *24/7 Wall St.*, conjectures which of the largest newspapers will be the next to succumb to the rapidly changing news media landscape.

Over the last few weeks, the newspaper industry has entered a new period of decline. The parent of the papers in Philadelphia declared bankruptcy as did the Journal Register chain. *The Rocky Mountain News* closed and the *Seattle Post-Intelligencer*, owned by Hearst, will almost certainly close or only publish online. Hearst has said it will also close *The San Francisco Chronicle* if it cannot make massive cuts at the paper. The most recent rumor is that the company will fire half of the editorial staff. That action still may not be enough to make the property profitable.

24/7 Wall St. has created its list of the ten major daily papers that are most likely to fold or shut their print operations and only publish online. The properties were chosen based on the financial strength of their parent companies, the amount of direct competition that they face in their markets, and industry information on how much money they are losing. Based on this analysis, it is possible that eight of the fifty largest daily newspapers in the United States could cease publication in the next eighteen months.

1. *The Philadelphia Daily News.* The smaller of the two papers owned by The Philadelphia Newspapers LLC, which recently filed for bankruptcy. The parent company says it will make money this year, but with newspaper advertising still falling sharply, the city cannot support two papers and the *Daily News* has a daily circulation of only about 100,000. The tabloid has a small staff, most of whom could probably stay on at Philly.com, the web operation for both of the city dailies.

2. *The Minneapolis Star Tribune* has filed for Chapter 11. The paper may not make money this year even without the costs of debt coverage. The company said it made $26 million last year, about half of what it made in 2007. The odds are that the *Star Tribune* will lose money this year if its ad revenue drops another 20 percent. There is no point for creditors to keep the paper open if it cannot generate cash. It could become an all-digital property, but supporting a daily circulation of over 300,000 is too much of a burden. It could survive if its rival the *St. Paul Pioneer Press* folds. A grim race.

The final edition of the *Seattle Post-Intelligencer* print edition on March 17, 2009. © MARCUS DONNER/REUTERS/CORBIS.

3. *The Miami Herald*, which has a daily circulation of about 220,000. It is owned by McClatchy, a publicly traded company which could be the next chain to go into Chapter 11. The *Herald* has been on the market since December, but no serious bidders have emerged. Newspaper advertising has been especially hard hit in Florida because of the tremendous loss in real estate advertising. The online version of the paper is already well-read in the Miami area and Latin America and the Caribbean. The *Herald* has strong competition north of it in Fort Lauderdale. There is a very small chance it could merge with the *Sun-Sentinel*, but it is more likely that the *Herald* will go online-only with two editions, one for English-speaking readers and one for Spanish.

4. *The Detroit News* is one of two daily papers in the big American city badly hit by the economic downturn. It is unlikely that it can merge with the larger *Detroit Free Press* which is owned by Gannett. It is hard to see what would be in it for Gannett. With the fortunes of Detroit getting worse each day, cutting back the number of days that the paper is delivered will not save enough money to keep the paper open.

5. *The Boston Globe* is, based on several accounts, losing $1 million a week. One investment bank recently said that the paper is only worth $20 million. The paper is the flagship of what the Globe's parent, *The New York Times*, calls the New England Media Group. *NYT* has substantial financial problems of its own. Last year, ad revenue for the New England properties was down 18%. That is likely to continue or get worse this year. Supporting larger losses at the *Globe* will become nearly impossible. Boston.com, the online site that includes the digital aspects of the *Globe*, will probably be all that will be left of the operation.

6. *The San Francisco Chronicle*. Parent company Hearst has already set a deadline for shutting the paper if it cannot make tremendous cost cuts. The *Chronicle* lost as much as $70 million last year. Even if the company could lower its costs, the northern California economy is in bad shape. The online version of the paper could be the only version by the middle of the 2009.

7. *The Chicago Sun Times* is the smaller of two newspapers in the city. Its parent company, Sun-Times Media Group, trades for $.03 a share. Davidson Kempner, a large shareholder in the firm, has dumped the CEO and most of the board. The paper has no chance of competing with *The Chicago Tribune*.

8. *NY Daily News* is one of several large papers fighting for circulation and advertising in the New York City area. Unlike *The New York Times, New York Post, Newsday*, and *Newark Star Ledger*, the *Daily News* is not owned by a larger organization. Real estate billionaire Mort Zuckerman owns the paper. Based on figures from other big dailies it could easily lose $60 million or $70 million and has no chance of recovering from that level.

9. *The Fort Worth Star Telegram* is another one of the big dailies that competes with a larger paper in a neighboring market—Dallas. The parent of *The Dallas Morning News*, Belo, is arguably a stronger company than the *Star Telegram's* parent, McClatchy. The *Morning News* has a circulation of about 350,000 and the *Star Telegram* has just over 200,000. The *Star Telegram* will have to shut down or become an edition of its rival. Putting them together would save tens of millions of dollars a year.

10. *The Cleveland Plain Dealer* is in one of the economically weakest markets in the country. Its parent, Advance Publications, has already threatened to close its paper in Newark. Employees gave up enough in terms of concessions to keep the paper open. Advance, owned by the Newhouse family, is carrying the burden of its paper plus Conde Nast, its magazine group which is losing advertising revenue. The *Plain Dealer* will be shut or go digital by the end of next year.

FURTHER RESOURCES

Books

Emery, Michael C. and Edwin Emery, eds. *The Press and America: An Interpretive History of the Mass Media.* Upper Saddle River, NJ: Prentice Hall, 1992.

Flink, Stanley E. *Sentinel Under Siege: The Triumphs and Troubles of America's Free Press.* Boulder, CO: Westview Press, 1998.

Vaughn, Stephen L., ed. *Encyclopedia of American Journalism.* New York: Taylor & Francis, 2009.

Web Sites

"A Brief History of Newspapers." *Historic Newspapers and Early Imprints.* www.historicpages.com/nprhist.htm (accessed on March 19, 2013).

McIntyre, Douglas A. "Ten Major Newspapers That Will Fold Or Go Digital, An Update." *24/7 Wall Street*, March 24, 2009. www.247wallst.com/2009/03/24/ten-major-newspapers-that-will-fold-or-go-digital-an-update/ (accessed on March 19, 2013).

Newspaper Death Watch. www.newspaperdeathwatch.com/ (accessed on March 19, 2013).

Stephens, Mitchell. "History of Newspapers." *Collier's Encyclopedia.* www.nyu.edu/classes/stephens/Collier's%20page.htm (accessed on March 19, 2013).

"How Twitter Will Change the Way We Live"

Magazine article

By: Steven Johnson

Date: June 5, 2009

Source: Johnson, Steven. "How Twitter Will Change the Way We Live." *Time*, June 5, 2009. www.time. com/time/magazine/article/0,9171,1902818,00.html (accessed on March 19, 2013).

About the Publication: *Time* magazine, often stylized as *TIME*, was the United States' first news magazine, founded in 1918. Since it was first published, the magazine has been a popular source of news for Americans, featuring interviews and original reporting on a variety of cultural and political current events, both domestic and global. Known for its editorials, columnists, guest contributors, and photo essays, *Time* has long been a cultural and journalistic staple in the United States, and one of its most noteworthy publications. It has also expanded to include international editions, such as *Time Europe* and *Time Asia*. The magazine's most famous segment is its annual "Person of the Year" award, in which the most influential person of the year is recognized and given a cover story.

INTRODUCTION

Twitter was a Web-based social networking service that allowed users to issue and read text-based messages, called "tweets," restricted to a maximum length of 140 characters. The service was created in 2006, the brainchild of New York University student Jack Dorsey, who envisioned it as the digital equivalent to mobile-phone text messaging, but shared between groups rather than individuals. Twitter users were able to subscribe to other users's feeds, called "following" them, thus receiving updates whenever they issued new tweets. Tweets could be assigned to a specific group or relevant topic through the use of "hashtags"—words or phrases prefixed with the pound symbol. Likewise, the "@" symbol was used to mention or respond to other Twitter accounts. For instance, a tweet about the 2007 Super Bowl might appear as: "I hope @IndianapolisColts defeat @ChicagoBears tonight at #SuperBowlXLI." Twitter was vaunted as a simple, versatile, and concise means of group communication.

After its public release on July 15, 2006, Twitter almost immediately generated interest from technology media and investors, attracting several million dollars in growth seeding during its first venture capital round. Twitter's big break came at the 2007 South by Southwest Interactive (SXSWI) conference, a showcase for emerging communication services and products, where the service's popularity among bloggers and attendees was enough to garner its creators the coveted Web Award prize. Thanks largely to the hype generated by its strong showing at SXSWI, the service expanded rapidly, from approximately 475,000 unique visitors in the month of

February 2008 to over 7 million in February 2009—making it the fastest-growing social media platform in the world, at a rate of 1,382 percent annual growth. In 2007, there was an average of five thousand tweets posted each day. In 2008, that number rose to three hundred thousand per day. By 2009, there were approximately thirty-five million tweets being sent each day, about sixty-six tweets per minute for the entire year.

Much of Twitter's success was attributed to its devotion to open-source software, which allowed third-party programmers and users to develop applications for streamlining and customizing its use. Many avid Twitter users used such programs to sort and search through the otherwise-impenetrable stream of followers, tweets, and trending hashtags. Another boost to the service's usability was the release of applications for smartphones and tablet computers that allowed users to broadcast and read tweets on the go, without requiring them to access the Twitter Web site directly. One of Twitter's most beneficial innovations was its introduction of a program that allowed celebrities and popular figures to set up certified accounts, preventing imitations and allowing direct communication with the public.

Little was known about Twitter's financial performance, about which the company's employees were almost invariably silent. Although the service's terms of use agreement gave Twitter the rights to collect information and photos shared on the site, it did not sell them to third-party advertisers. It also did not display advertisements on its Web site, except for paid "sponsored tweets." Twitter was even free to use, not requiring a subscription fee or selling enhanced features. It was assumed by industry speculators that Twitter operated at a loss for most of its existence.

SIGNIFICANCE

Twitter had an enormous impact on American society, revolutionizing communication to almost the same degree as its social media predecessors, like Facebook and MySpace. The key to Twitter's popularity was its versatility. It provided a means of instantaneous communication between large groups of people, best exemplified by its use as a real-time emergency communication system during disasters, like the 2007 California wildfires, the 2008 Mumbai train bombings, and the 2009 Australian bush fires. Similarly, Twitter was frequently employed to coordinate movement and broadcast developments during the 2009 Iranian election protests and Moldovan civil uprising, when protesters used the service to communicate the movement of police forces and organize their efforts.

Another promising function of Twitter was its ability to encourage increased involvement between users in a variety of contexts. College and university professors set up Twitter accounts so that students could help one another and continue discussing curriculum outside of class. Law enforcement agencies used Twitter to provide real-time information about criminal activity or dangerous driving conditions. News media outlets culled information about breaking stories from information posted using the service. Twitter also facilitated interaction between celebrities and their fans, as well as politicians and voters—Barack Obama's 2008 campaign featured heavy use of Twitter, which exposed him to younger demographics than his technology-averse opponent, John McCain. Even fundraising and awareness programs found ways to use Twitter in the form of the #12for12 hashtag, which spotlighted various charities and allowed users to donate towards a $12,000 fundraising goal over 12-hour periods.

Businesses benefited tremendously from Twitter's unique ability to reach broad, diverse audiences. Large corporations took advantage of the ability to poll their consumer base and interact directly with customers, rather than try to establish good will through impersonal advertisements and spokespeople. Small companies were aided by Twitter's capacity to put them on equal footing with their larger competitors, as both could reach out to enormous quantities of consumers. Businesses of all sizes were able to improve public relations by responding quickly and directly to customer complaints and questions. Even NASA, threatened by budget cuts to the U.S. space program, benefited from Twitter, as astronauts aboard the International Space Station used the service to communicate in real time with the American public and appeal for increased funding.

Although Twitter was sometimes criticized for allegedly oversimplifying public discourse by limiting communication to minute, 140-character blurbs, it was also celebrated for allowing the instantaneous dissemination of ideas and information. Its capacity as an instrument of social change was best demonstrated in 2011, when Egyptian protesters used it to communicate with one another and the outside world as their government attempted to suppress their ability to speak freely. The successful rebellion against Egyptian president Hosni Mubarak's authoritarian regime was directly linked to Twitter's availability. In the United States, Twitter served to revolutionize not the government, but the ways in which groups interacted and exchanged information.

PRIMARY SOURCE

"HOW TWITTER WILL CHANGE THE WAY WE LIVE"

SYNOPSIS: In this article, the author describes Twitter's features and its potential impact on society, culture, and communication

The one thing you can say for certain about Twitter is that it makes a terrible first impression. You hear about this new service that lets you send 140-character updates to your "followers," and you think, Why does the world need this, exactly? It's not as if we were all sitting around four years ago scratching our heads and saying, "If only there were a technology that would allow me to send a message to my 50 friends, alerting them in real time about my choice of breakfast cereal."

I, too, was skeptical at first. I had met Evan Williams, Twitter's co-creator, a couple of times in the dotcom '90s when he was launching Blogger.com. Back then, what people worried about was the threat that blogging posed to our attention span, with telegraphic, two-paragraph blog posts replacing long-format articles and books. With Twitter, Williams was launching a communications platform that limited you to a couple of sentences at most. What was next? Software that let you send a single punctuation mark to describe your mood?

And yet as millions of devotees have discovered, Twitter turns out to have unsuspected depth. In part this is because hearing about what your friends had for breakfast is actually more interesting than it sounds. The technology writer Clive Thompson calls this "ambient awareness": by following these quick, abbreviated status reports from members of your extended social network, you get a strangely satisfying glimpse of their daily routines. We don't think it at all moronic to start a phone call with a friend by asking how her day is going. Twitter gives you the same information without your even having to ask.

The social warmth of all those stray details shouldn't be taken lightly. But I think there is something even more profound in what has happened to Twitter over the past two years, something that says more about the culture that has embraced and expanded Twitter at such extraordinary speed. Yes, the breakfast-status updates turned out to be more interesting than we thought. But the key development with Twitter is how we've jury-rigged the system to do things that its creators never dreamed of.

In short, the most fascinating thing about Twitter is not what it's doing to us. It's what we're doing to it.

The Open Conversation

Earlier this year I attended a daylong conference in Manhattan devoted to education reform. Called Hacking Education, it was a small, private affair: 40-odd educators, entrepreneurs, scholars, philanthropists and venture capitalists, all engaged in a sprawling six-hour conversation about the future of schools. Twenty years ago, the ideas exchanged in that conversation would have been confined to the minds of the participants. Ten years ago, a transcript might have been published weeks or months later on the Web. Five years ago, a handful of participants might have blogged about their experiences after the fact.

But this event was happening in 2009, so trailing behind the real-time, real-world conversation was an equally real-time conversation on Twitter. At the outset of the conference, our hosts announced that anyone who wanted to post live commentary about the event via Twitter should include the word #hackedu in his 140 characters. In the room, a large display screen showed a running feed of tweets. Then we all started talking, and as we did, a shadow conversation unfolded on the screen: summaries of someone's argument, the occasional joke, suggested links for further reading. At one point, a brief argument flared up between two participants in the room—a tense back-and-forth that transpired silently on the screen as the rest of us conversed in friendly tones.

At first, all these tweets came from inside the room and were created exclusively by conference participants tapping away on their laptops or BlackBerrys. But within half an hour or so, word began to seep out into the Twittersphere that an interesting conversation about the future of schools was happening at #hackedu. A few tweets appeared on the screen from strangers announcing that they were following the #hackedu thread. Then others joined the conversation, adding their observations or proposing topics for further exploration. A few experts grumbled publicly about how they hadn't been invited to the conference. Back in the room, we pulled interesting ideas and questions from the screen and integrated them into our face-to-face conversation.

When the conference wrapped up at the end of the day, there was a public record of hundreds of tweets documenting the conversation. And the conversation continued—if you search Twitter for #hackedu, you'll find dozens of new comments posted over the past few weeks, even though the conference happened in early March.

Injecting Twitter into that conversation fundamentally changed the rules of engagement. It added a second layer of discussion and brought a wider audience into what would have been a private exchange. And it gave the event an afterlife on the Web. Yes, it was built entirely out of 140-character messages, but the sum total of those tweets added up to something truly substantive, like a suspension bridge made of pebbles.

The Super-Fresh Web

The basic mechanics of Twitter are remarkably simple. Users publish tweets—those 140-character messages—from a computer or mobile device. (The character limit allows tweets to be created and circulated via the SMS platform used by most mobile phones.) As a social network, Twitter revolves around the principle of followers. When you choose to follow another Twitter user, that user's tweets appear in reverse chronological order on your main Twitter page. If you follow 20 people, you'll see a mix of tweets scrolling down the page: breakfast-cereal updates, interesting new links, music recommendations, even musings on the future of education. Some celebrity Twitterers—most famously Ashton Kutcher—have crossed the million-follower mark, effectively giving them a broadcast-size audience. The average Twitter profile seems to be somewhere in the dozens: a collage of friends, colleagues and a handful of celebrities. The mix creates a media experience quite unlike anything that has come before it, strangely intimate and at the same time celebrity-obsessed. You glance at your Twitter feed over that first cup of coffee, and in a few seconds you find out that your nephew got into med school and Shaquille O'Neal just finished a cardio workout in Phoenix.

In the past month, Twitter has added a search box that gives you a real-time view onto the chatter of just about any topic imaginable. You can see conversations people are having about a presidential debate or the *American Idol* finale or Tiger Woods—or a conference in New York City on education reform. For as long as we've had the Internet in our homes, critics have bemoaned the demise of shared national experiences, like moon landings and "Who Shot J.R." cliff hangers—the folkloric American living room, all of us signing off in unison with Walter Cronkite, shattered into a million isolation booths. But watch a live mass-media event with Twitter open on your laptop and you'll see that the futurists had it wrong. We still have national events, but now when we have them, we're actually having a genuine, public conversation with a group that extends far beyond our nuclear family and our next-door neighbors. Some of that conversation is juvenile, of course, just as it was in our living room when we heckled Richard Nixon's Checkers speech. But some of it is moving, witty, observant, subversive.

Skeptics might wonder just how much subversion and wit is conveyable via 140-character updates. But in recent months Twitter users have begun to find a route around that limitation by employing Twitter as a pointing device instead of a communications channel: sharing links to longer articles, discussions, posts, videos—anything that lives behind a URL. Websites that once saw their traffic dominated by Google search queries are seeing a growing number of new visitors coming from "passed links" at social networks like Twitter and Facebook. This is what the naysayers fail to understand: it's just as easy to use Twitter to spread the word about a brilliant 10,000-word *New Yorker* article as it is to spread the word about your Lucky Charms habit.

Put those three elements together—social networks, live searching and link-sharing—and you have a cocktail that poses what may amount to the most interesting alternative to Google's near monopoly in searching. At its heart, Google's system is built around the slow, anonymous accumulation of authority: pages rise to the top of Google's search results according to, in part, how many links point to them, which tends to favor older pages that have had time to build an audience. That's a fantastic solution for finding high-quality needles in the immense, spam-plagued haystack that is the contemporary Web. But it's not a particularly useful solution for finding out what people are saying *right now*, the in-the-moment conversation that industry pioneer John Battelle calls the "super fresh" Web. Even in its toddlerhood, Twitter is a more efficient supplier of the super-fresh Web than Google. If you're looking for interesting articles or sites devoted to Kobe Bryant, you search Google. If you're looking for interesting comments from your extended social network about the three-pointer Kobe just made 30 seconds ago, you go to Twitter.

From Toasters to Microwaves

Because Twitter's co-founders—Evan Williams, Biz Stone and Jack Dorsey—are such a central-casting vision of start-up savvy (they're quotable and charming and have the extra glamour of using a loft in San Francisco's SoMa district as a headquarters instead of a bland office park in Silicon Valley) much of the media interest in Twitter has focused on the company. Will Ev and Biz sell to Google early or play long ball? (They have already turned down a reported $500 million from Facebook.) It's an interesting question but not exactly a new plotline. Focusing on it makes you lose sight of the much more significant point about the Twitter platform: the fact that many of its core features and applications have been developed by people who are not on the Twitter payroll.

This is not just a matter of people finding a new use for a tool designed to do something else. In Twitter's case, the users have been redesigning the tool itself. The convention of grouping a topic or event by the "hashtag"—#hackedu or #inauguration—was spontaneously invented by the Twitter user base (as was the convention of replying to another user with the @ symbol). The ability to search a live stream of tweets was developed by another start-up altogether, Summize, which Twitter purchased last year. (Full disclosure: I am an adviser to one of the minority investors in Summize.) Thanks to these innovations, following a live feed of tweets about an

Twitter founders (left to right) Evan Williams, Biz Stone, and Jack Dorsey in their San Francisco offices in February 2005. © AURORA PHOTOS/ALAMY.

event—political debates or *Lost* episodes—has become a central part of the Twitter experience. But just 12 months ago, that mode of interaction would have been technically impossible using Twitter. It's like inventing a toaster oven and then looking around a year later and seeing that your customers have of their own accord figured out a way to turn it into a microwave.

One of the most telling facts about the Twitter platform is that the vast majority of its users interact with the service via software created by third parties. There are dozens of iPhone and BlackBerry applications—all created by enterprising amateur coders or small start-ups—that let you manage Twitter feeds. There are services that help you upload photos and link to them from your tweets, and programs that map other Twitizens who are near you geographically. Ironically, the tools you're offered if you visit Twitter.com have changed very little in the past two years. But there's an entire Home Depot of Twitter tools available everywhere else.

As the tools have multiplied, we're discovering extraordinary new things to do with them. Last month an anticommunist uprising in Moldova was organized via Twitter. Twitter has become so widely used among political activists in China that the government recently blocked access to it, in an attempt to censor discussion of the 20th anniversary of the Tiananmen Square massacre. A service called SickCity scans the Twitter feeds from multiple urban areas, tracking references to flu and fever. Celebrity Twitterers like Kutcher have directed their vast followings toward charitable causes (in Kutcher's case, the Malaria No More organization).

Social networks are notoriously vulnerable to the fickle tastes of teens and 20-somethings (remember Friendster?), so it's entirely possible that three or four years from now, we'll have moved on to some Twitter successor. But the key elements of the Twitter platform—the follower structure, link-sharing, real-time searching—will persevere regardless of Twitter's fortunes, just as Web conventions like links, posts and feeds have endured over the past decade. In fact, every major channel of information will be Twitterfied in one way or another in the coming years:

News and opinion. Increasingly, the stories that come across our radar—news about a plane crash, a feisty Op-Ed, a gossip item—will arrive via the passed links of the people we follow. Instead of being built by some kind of artificially intelligent software algorithm, a customized newspaper will be compiled from all the articles being read that morning by your social network. This will lead to more news diversity and polarization at the same time: your networked front page will be more eclectic than any traditional-newspaper front page, but political partisans looking to enhance their own private echo chamber will be able to tune out opposing viewpoints more easily.

Searching. As the archive of links shared by Twitter users grows, the value of searching for information via your extended social network will start to rival Google's approach to the search. If you're looking for information on Benjamin Franklin, an essay shared by one of your favorite historians might well be more valuable than the top result on Google; if you're looking for advice on sibling rivalry, an article recommended by a friend of a friend might well be the best place to start.

Advertising. Today the language of advertising is dominated by the notion of impressions: how many times an advertiser can get its brand in front of a potential customer's eyeballs, whether on a billboard, a Web page or a NASCAR hood. But impressions are fleeting things, especially compared with the enduring relationships of followers. Successful businesses will have millions of Twitter followers (and will pay good money to attract

A user is about to tweet on Twitter using his iPhone. © M4OS PHOTOS/ALAMY.

them), and a whole new language of tweet-based customer interaction will evolve to keep those followers engaged: early access to new products or deals, live customer service, customer involvement in brainstorming for new products.

Not all these developments will be entirely positive. Most of us have learned firsthand how addictive the micro-events of our personal e-mail inbox can be. But with the ambient awareness of status updates from Twitter and Facebook, an entire new empire of distraction has opened up. It used to be that you compulsively checked your BlackBerry to see if anything new had happened in your personal life or career: e-mail from the boss, a reply from last night's date. Now you're compulsively checking your BlackBerry for news from other people's lives. And because, on Twitter at least, some of those people happen to be celebrities, the Twitter platform is likely to expand that strangely delusional relationship that we have to fame. When Oprah tweets a question about getting ticks off her dog, as she did recently, anyone can send an @ reply to her, and in that exchange, there is the semblance of a normal, everyday conversation between equals. But of course, Oprah has more than a million followers, and that

isolated query probably elicited thousands of responses. Who knows what small fraction of her @ replies she has time to read? But from the fan's perspective, it feels refreshingly intimate: "As I was explaining to Oprah last night, when she asked about dog ticks ... "

End-User Innovation

The rapid-fire innovation we're seeing around Twitter is not new, of course. Facebook, whose audience is still several times as large as Twitter's, went from being a way to scope out the most attractive college freshmen to the Social Operating System of the Internet, supporting a vast ecosystem of new applications created by major media companies, individual hackers, game creators, political groups and charities. The Apple iPhone's long-term competitive advantage may well prove to be the more than 15,000 new applications that have been developed for the device, expanding its functionality in countless ingenious ways.

The history of the Web followed a similar pattern. A platform originally designed to help scholars share academic documents, it now lets you watch television shows, play poker with strangers around the world, publish your own newspaper, rediscover your high school girlfriend—and, yes, tell the world what you had for breakfast. Twitter serves as the best poster child for this new model of social creativity in part because these innovations have flowered at such breathtaking speed and in part because the platform is so simple. It's as if Twitter's creators dared us to do something interesting by giving us a platform with such draconian restrictions. And sure enough, we accepted the dare with relish. Just 140 characters? I wonder if I could use that to start a political uprising.

The speed with which users have extended Twitter's platform points to a larger truth about modern innovation. When we talk about innovation and global competitiveness, we tend to fall back on the easy metric of patents and Ph.D.s. It turns out the U.S. share of both has been in steady decline since peaking in the early '70s. (In 1970, more than 50% of the world's graduate degrees in science and engineering were issued by U.S. universities.) Since the mid-'80s, a long progression of doomsayers have warned that our declining market share in the patents-and-Ph.D.s business augurs dark times for American innovation. The specific threats have changed. It was the Japanese who would destroy us in the '80s; now it's China and India.

But what actually happened to American innovation during that period? We came up with America Online, Netscape, Amazon, Google, Blogger, Wikipedia, Craigslist, TiVo, Netflix, eBay, the iPod and iPhone, Xbox, Facebook and Twitter itself. Sure, we didn't build the Prius or the Wii, but if you measure global innovation in terms of actual lifestyle-changing hit products and not just grad students, the U.S. has been lapping the field for the past 20 years.

How could the forecasts have been so wrong? The answer is that we've been tracking only part of the innovation story. If I go to grad school and invent a better mousetrap, I've created value, which I can protect with a patent and capitalize on by selling my invention to consumers. But if someone else figures out a way to use my mousetrap to replace his much more expensive washing machine, he's created value as well. We tend to put the emphasis on the first kind of value creation because there are a small number of inventors who earn giant paydays from their mousetraps and thus become celebrities. But there are hundreds of millions of consumers and small businesses that find value in these innovations by figuring out new ways to put them to use.

There are several varieties of this kind of innovation, and they go by different technical names. MIT professor Eric von Hippel calls one "end-user innovation," in which consumers actively modify a product to adapt it to their needs. In its short life, Twitter has been a hothouse of end-user innovation: the hashtag; searching; its 11,000 third-party applications; all those creative new uses of Twitter—some of them banal, some of them spam and

some of them sublime. Think about the community invention of the @ reply. It took a service that was essentially a series of isolated microbroadcasts, each individual tweet an island, and turned Twitter into a truly conversational medium. All of these adoptions create new kinds of value in the wider economy, and none of them actually originated at Twitter HQ. You don't need patents or Ph.D.s to build on this kind of platform.

This is what I ultimately find most inspiring about the Twitter phenomenon. We are living through the worst economic crisis in generations, with apocalyptic headlines threatening the end of capitalism as we know it, and yet in the middle of this chaos, the engineers at Twitter headquarters are scrambling to keep the servers up, application developers are releasing their latest builds, and ordinary users are figuring out all the ingenious ways to put these tools to use. There's a kind of resilience here that is worth savoring. The weather reports keep announcing that the sky is falling, but here we are—millions of us—sitting around trying to invent new ways to talk to one another.

FURTHER RESOURCES
Web Sites

"How One Man Used Social Media to Raise $91,000 for Charity." *Social Media Examiner*, March 2, 2010. www.socialmediaexaminer.com/how-one-man-used-social-media-to-raise-91000-for-charity/#more-1971 (accessed on March 19, 2013).

"Twitter: About." *Twitter*. https://twitter.com/about (accessed on March 19, 2013).

"Twitter Users Send 50 Million Tweets Per Day." *The Telegraph*, February 23, 2010. www.telegraph.co.uk/technology/twitter/7297541/Twitter-users-send-50-million-tweets-per-day.html (accessed on February 22, 2013).

"Twitter's Tweet Smell Of Success." *Nielsen Newswire*. http://blog.nielsen.com/nielsenwire/online_mobile/twitters-tweet-smell-of-success/ (accessed on March 19, 2013).

"The Falling Man"

Magazine article

By: Tom Junod

Date: September 8, 2009

Source: Junod, Tom. "The Falling Man." *Esquire*, September 8, 2003. http://www.esquire.com/features/

ESQ0903-SEP_FALLINGMAN (accessed on March 20, 2013).

About the Author: Tom Junod is an American journalist who worked at *GQ* magazine before taking a job with *Esquire* in 1997. A ten-time finalist for the National Magazine Award from the American Society of Magazine Editors, Junod won twice, once for his profile of abortion doctor John Britton and again for a profile of a rapist undergoing controversial therapy.

INTRODUCTION

On the morning of September 11, 2001, nineteen men, affiliated with the al-Qaeda terrorist network, hijacked four U.S. passenger jets, in what would become the most destructive terrorist attack in the nation's history. At 8:45 AM Eastern Daylight Time, the first aircraft, American Airlines Flight 11, was piloted by its hijackers into the north tower of New York City's World Trade Center (WTC; also known as the Twin Towers), punching a hole in the building and immediately setting it ablaze. Eighteen minutes later, United Airlines Flight 175 was flown into the south tower of the World Trade Center, causing an explosion and setting it on fire. At 9:43, American Airlines Flight 77 crashed into the Pentagon in Arlington County, Virginia, prompting immediate evacuation. At 10:10, the final aircraft, United Airlines Flight 93, plummeted into a field in rural Somerset County, Pennsylvania, after passengers successfully regained control of the plane and redirected it from its intended target (thought to be either the White House or U.S. Capitol Building). All 227 passengers aboard the flights, as well as the nineteen hijackers, were killed.

The fire in the Pentagon continued throughout the night, as did the rescue efforts of New York City disaster workers, policemen, and firefighters. Although definitive casualty statistics were not available until the end of the month, CNN eventually confirmed a total of 2,977 deaths caused by the attacks, representing citizens of almost one hundred nations. Of those killed, approximately two hundred died falling or jumping from the burning Twin Towers, and over four hundred of them were rescue workers killed by fire, smoke inhalation, or falling rubble. The rest were killed by the initial impact or were trapped inside the various structures damaged by the attacks, which included several buildings surrounding the World Trade Center.

Associated Press photographer Richard Drew happened to be in New York City that morning, covering a fashion shoot. After taking some backstage photos, he was walking the runway in search of the best angles and perspectives from which to take his snapshots of the models when a call came in. His editor told him to leave the show and head to the World Trade Center. He got there just before 9:00 AM. "I immediately started photographing people.... We noticed people coming down [jumping] from the building. We don't know whether they were overcome by smoke. I was photographing several people coming down from the building and I have a sequence of photographs of this guy coming down," Drew explained in an interview with *The Daily Beast*.

One of the photographs in that sequence is featured here and came to be known, thanks to the 2003 *Esquire* article written by journalist Tom Junod, as "The Falling Man." Instantly, it became the iconic photo of the worst terrorist attack in history, and just as instantly, it stirred great controversy. Junod provides an in-depth history not only of the taking of the photo, but of the mixed emotional responses it elicited.

SIGNIFICANCE

Although early suggestions seemed to indicate that the Falling Man was a man named Norberto Hernandez—a chef at the Windows on the World restaurant at the top of the World Trade Center—as it turned out, it was not. His wife, who was absolutely positive that the man in the photo that captured his last seconds of life was not her husband, was correct. Hernandez did indeed die in the terrorist attacks, but the man in the iconic photo was possibly forty-three-year-old Jonathan Briley, also an employee at Windows on the World. Briley's body was buried in Mt. Kisco, but the horrendous fate that was his lives on forever. Junod wrote a follow-up article in 2011 for which he interviewed Briley's sister, Gwendolyn. She expressed a wish for people to see the haunting photo as she saw it. "People have to get over wondering who this man was. He's everybody. We're so stuck on who he was that we can't see what's right there in front of us. The photo's so much bigger than any man, because the man in the photo is clearly in God's hands. And it's God who gives us the grace to go on."

Photographer Richard Drew agreed that the photo is one man, but he is one man representative of so very many Drew witnessed that day. When asked to reflect on how he felt while taking the photo and the ensuing controversy, Drew told CNN,

> We've seen AP photographer's Nick Ut's picture of the little girl running from the napalm in Vietnam, we've seen AP photographer Eddie

Adams's picture of the Saigon police chief executing the man on the street; then we see the AP photographer John Filo's picture of the girl bending over the fallen student at Kent State. Those are all images that we all thought we didn't want to see, and there was controversy about them all, but it's part of the story. You have to tell the story. You can't just turn your head and stop. I don't think I captured this man's death; I think I captured part of his life.

More than a decade later, Americans remained divided as to whether or not the media should have ever published Drew's photo. Some found it sensational, insensitive, offensive, an intrusion into a personal moment. Many found it disconcerting because it represented a defining moment, that moment that one man chose to leap to his death rather than to perish in flames and smoke. Drew disagreed and explained to the *Daily Beast*, "For me, it's a very quiet moment. It's not a violent picture in any way.... I'm not haunted by it. I'm just interested that people still want to talk about it.... I'm very humbled that people think of it as such an iconic photograph and that it will be part of my photographic legacy."

Regardless of the jumper's identity, "even if people don't want to see my photograph, that man did fall out of the building," Drew told Yahoo! News. "To me, he'll always remain the unknown soldier."

▉ PRIMARY SOURCE

"THE FALLING MAN"

SYNOPSIS: This article looks at one of a sequence of frames depicting a victim of the September 11, 2001, terrorist attacks on the World Trade Center as he plunges one thousand feet to his death.

In the picture, he departs from this earth like an arrow. Although he has not chosen his fate, he appears to have, in his last instants of life, embraced it. If he were not falling, he might very well be flying. He appears relaxed, hurtling through the air. He appears comfortable in the grip of unimaginable motion. He does not appear intimidated by gravity's divine suction or by what awaits him. His arms are by his side, only slightly outriggered. His left leg is bent at the knee, almost casually. His white shirt, or jacket, or frock, is billowing free of his black pants. His black high-tops are still on his feet. In all the other pictures, the people who did what he did—who jumped—appear to be struggling against horrific discrepancies of scale. They are made puny by the backdrop of the towers, which loom like colossi, and then by the event itself. Some of them are shirtless; their shoes fly off as they flail

and fall; they look confused, as though trying to swim down the side of a mountain. The man in the picture, by contrast, is perfectly vertical, and so is in accord with the lines of the buildings behind him. He splits them, bisects them: Everything to the left of him in the picture is the North Tower; everything to the right, the South. Though oblivious to the geometric balance he has achieved, he is the essential element in the creation of a new flag, a banner composed entirely of steel bars shining in the sun. Some people who look at the picture see stoicism, willpower, a portrait of resignation; others see something else—something discordant and therefore terrible: freedom. There is something almost rebellious in the man's posture, as though once faced with the inevitability of death, he decided to get on with it; as though he were a missile, a spear, bent on attaining his own end. He is, fifteen seconds past 9:41 a.m. EST, the moment the picture is taken, in the clutches of pure physics, accelerating at a rate of thirty-two feet per second squared. He will soon be traveling at upwards of 150 miles per hour, and he is upside down. In the picture, he is frozen; in his life outside the frame, he drops and keeps dropping until he disappears.

▉ ▉ ▉

The photographer is no stranger to history; he knows it is something that happens later. In the actual moment history is made, it is usually made in terror and confusion, and so it is up to people like him—paid witnesses—to have the presence of mind to attend to its manufacture. The photographer has that presence of mind and has had it since he was a young man. When he was twenty-one years old, he was standing right behind Bobby Kennedy when Bobby Kennedy was shot in the head. His jacket was spattered with Kennedy's blood, but he jumped on a table and shot pictures of Kennedy's open and ebbing eyes, and then of Ethel Kennedy crouching over her husband and begging photographers—begging him—not to take pictures.

Richard Drew has never done that. Although he has preserved the jacket patterned with Kennedy's blood, he has never not taken a picture, never averted his eye. He works for the Associated Press. He is a journalist. It is not up to him to reject the images that fill his frame, because one never knows when history is made until one makes it. It is not even up to him to distinguish if a body is alive or dead, because the camera makes no such distinctions, and he is in the business of shooting bodies, as all photographers are, unless they are Ansel Adams. Indeed, he was shooting bodies on the morning of September 11, 2001. On assignment for the AP, he was shooting a maternity fashion show in Bryant Park, notable, he says, "because it featured actual pregnant models." He was fifty-four years old. He wore glasses. He was sparse in the

Photographer Richard Drew captures the collapse of the south tower of the World Trade Center on September 11, 2001. © AP IMAGES/RICHARD DREW.

scalp, gray in the beard, hard in the head. In a lifetime of taking pictures, he has found a way to be both mild-mannered and brusque, patient and very, very quick. He was doing what he always does at fashion shows—"staking out real estate"—when a CNN cameraman with an earpiece said that a plane had crashed into the North Tower, and Drew's editor rang his cell phone. He packed his equipment into a bag and gambled on taking the subway downtown. Although it was still running, he was the only one on it. He got out at the Chambers Street station and saw that both towers had been turned into smokestacks. Staking out his real estate, he walked west, to where ambulances were gathering, because rescue workers "usually won't throw you out." Then he heard people gasping. People on the ground were gasping because people in the building were jumping. He started shooting pictures through a 200mm lens. He was standing between a cop and an emergency technician, and each time one of them cried, "There goes another," his camera found a falling body and followed it down for a

nine- or twelve-shot sequence. He shot ten or fifteen of them before he heard the rumbling of the South Tower and witnessed, through the winnowing exclusivity of his lens, its collapse. He was engulfed in a mobile ruin, but he grabbed a mask from an ambulance and photographed the top of the North Tower "exploding like a mushroom" and raining debris. He discovered that there is such a thing as being too close, and, deciding that he had fulfilled his professional obligations, Richard Drew joined the throng of ashen humanity heading north, walking until he reached his office at Rockefeller Center.

There was no terror or confusion at the Associated Press. There was, instead, that feeling of history being manufactured; although the office was as crowded as he'd ever seen it, there was, instead, "the wonderful calm that comes into play when people are really doing their jobs." So Drew did his: He inserted the disc from his digital camera into his laptop and recognized, instantly, what only his camera had seen—something iconic in the extended annihilation of a falling man. He didn't look at any of the other pictures in the sequence; he didn't have to. "You learn in photo editing to look for the frame," he says. "You have to recognize it. That picture just jumped off the screen because of its verticality and symmetry. It just had that look."

He sent the image to the AP's server. The next morning, it appeared on page seven of *The New York Times*. It appeared in hundreds of newspapers, all over the country, all over the world. The man inside the frame—the Falling Man—was not identified.

■ ■ ■

They began jumping not long after the first plane hit the North Tower, not long after the fire started. They kept jumping until the tower fell. They jumped through windows already broken and then, later, through windows they broke themselves. They jumped to escape the smoke and the fire; they jumped when the ceilings fell and the floors collapsed; they jumped just to breathe once more before they died. They jumped continually, from all four sides of the building, and from all floors above and around the building's fatal wound. They jumped from the offices of Marsh & McLennan, the insurance company; from the offices of Cantor Fitzgerald, the bond-trading company; from Windows on the World, the restaurant on the 106th and 107th floors—the top. For more than an hour and a half, they streamed from the building, one after another, consecutively rather than en masse, as if each individual required the sight of another individual jumping before mustering the courage to jump himself or herself. One photograph, taken at a distance, shows people jumping in perfect sequence, like parachutists, forming an arc composed of three plummeting people, evenly spaced. Indeed, there were reports that some tried parachuting, before the force generated by their fall ripped the drapes, the tablecloths, the desperately gathered fabric, from their hands. They were all, obviously, very much alive on their way down, and their way down lasted an approximate count of ten seconds. They were all, obviously, not just killed when they landed but destroyed, in body though not, one prays, in soul. One hit a fireman on the ground and killed him; the fireman's body was anointed by Father Mychal Judge, whose own death, shortly thereafter, was embraced as an example of martyrdom after the photograph—the redemptive tableau—of firefighters carrying his body from the rubble made its way around the world.

From the beginning, the spectacle of doomed people jumping from the upper floors of the World Trade Center resisted redemption. They were called "jumpers" or "the jumpers," as though they represented a new lemminglike class. The trial that hundreds endured in the building and then in the air became its own kind of trial for the thousands watching them from the ground. No one ever got used to it; no one who saw it wished to see it again, although, of course, many saw it again. Each jumper, no matter how many there were, brought fresh horror, elicited shock, tested the spirit, struck a lasting blow. Those tumbling through the air remained, by all accounts, eerily silent; those on the ground screamed. It was the sight of the jumpers that prompted Rudy Giuliani to say to his police commissioner, "We're in uncharted waters now." It was the sight of the jumpers that prompted a woman to wail, "God! Save their souls! They're jumping! Oh, please God! Save their souls!" And it was, at last, the sight of the jumpers that provided the corrective to those who insisted on saying that what they were witnessing was "like a movie," for this was an ending as unimaginable as it was unbearable: Americans responding to the worst terrorist attack in the history of the world with acts of heroism, with acts of sacrifice, with acts of generosity, with acts of martyrdom, and, by terrible necessity, with one prolonged act of—if these words can be applied to mass murder—mass suicide.

■ ■ ■

In most American newspapers, the photograph that Richard Drew took of the Falling Man ran once and never again. Papers all over the country, from the *Fort Worth Star-Telegram* to the *Memphis Commercial Appeal* to *The Denver Post*, were forced to defend themselves against charges that they exploited a man's death, stripped him of his dignity, invaded his privacy, turned tragedy into leering pornography. Most letters of complaint stated the obvious: that someone seeing the picture had to know who it was. Still, even as Drew's photograph became at once iconic and impermissible, its subject remained unnamed. An editor at the *Toronto Globe and Mail* assigned a reporter

named Peter Cheney to solve the mystery. Cheney at first despaired of his task; the entire city, after all, was wallpapered with Kinkoed flyers advertising the faces of the missing and the lost and the dead. Then he applied himself, sending the digital photograph to a shop that clarified and enhanced it. Now information emerged: It appeared to him that the man was most likely not black but dark-skinned, probably Latino. He wore a goatee. And the white shirt billowing from his black pants was not a shirt but rather appeared to be a tunic of some sort, the kind of jacket a restaurant worker wears. Windows on the World, the restaurant at the top of the North Tower, lost seventy-nine of its employees on September 11, as well as ninety-one of its patrons. It was likely that the Falling Man numbered among them. But which one was he? Over dinner, Cheney spent an evening discussing this question with friends, then said goodnight and walked through Times Square. It was after midnight, eight days after the attacks. The missing posters were still everywhere, but Cheney was able to focus on one that seemed to present itself to him—a poster portraying a man who worked at Windows as a pastry chef, who was dressed in a white tunic, who wore a goatee, who was Latino. His name was Norberto Hernandez. He lived in Queens. Cheney took the enhanced print of the Richard Drew photograph to the family, in particular to Norberto Hernandez's brother Tino and sister Milagros. They said yes, that was Norberto. Milagros had watched footage of the people jumping on that terrible morning, before the television stations stopped showing it. She had seen one of the jumpers distinguished by the grace of his fall—by his resemblance to an Olympic diver—and surmised that he had to be her brother. Now she saw, and she knew. All that remained was for Peter Cheney to confirm the identification with Norberto's wife and his three daughters. They did not want to talk to him, especially after Norberto's remains were found and identified by the stamp of his DNA—a torso, an arm. So he went to the funeral. He brought his print of Drew's photograph with him and showed it to Jacqueline Hernandez, the oldest of Norberto's three daughters. She looked briefly at the picture, then at Cheney, and ordered him to leave.

What Cheney remembers her saying, in her anger, in her offended grief: "That piece of shit is not my father."

■ ■ ■

The resistance to the image—to the images—started early, started immediately, started on the ground. A mother whispering to her distraught child a consoling lie: "Maybe they're just birds, honey." Bill Feehan, second in command at the fire department, chasing a bystander who was panning the jumpers with his video camera, demanding that he turn it off, bellowing, "Don't you have any human decency?" before dying himself when the

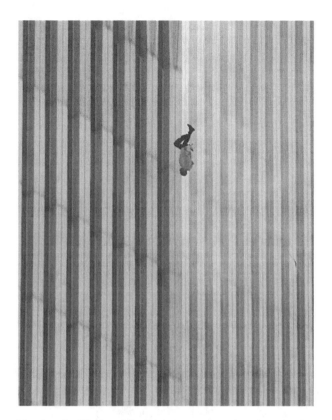

The iconic "Falling Man" photograph, taken by veteran Associated Press photographer Richard Drew, shows a man plummeting to his death after an airliner slammed into the World Trade Center on September 11, 2001. © AP IMAGES/RICHARD DREW.

building came down. In the most photographed and videotaped day in the history of the world, the images of people jumping were the only images that became, by consensus, taboo—the only images from which Americans were proud to avert their eyes. All over the world, people saw the human stream debouch from the top of the North Tower, but here in the United States, we saw these images only until the networks decided not to allow such a harrowing view, out of respect for the families of those so publicly dying. At CNN, the footage was shown live, before people working in the newsroom knew what was happening; then, after what Walter Isaacson, who was then chairman of the network's news bureau, calls "agonized discussions" with the "standards guy," it was shown only if people in it were blurred and unidentifiable; then it was not shown at all.

And so it went. In 9/11, the documentary extracted from videotape shot by French brothers Jules and Gedeon Naudet, the filmmakers included a sonic sampling of the booming, rattling explosions the jumpers made upon impact but edited out the most disturbing thing about the sounds: the sheer frequency with which they occurred. In

Rudy, the docudrama starring James Woods in the role of Mayor Giuliani, archival footage of the jumpers was first included, then cut out. In Here Is New York, an extensive exhibition of 9/11 images culled from the work of photographers both amateur and professional, there was, in the section titled "Victims," but one picture of the jumpers, taken at a respectful distance; attached to it, on the Here Is New York Website, a visitor offers this commentary: "This image is what made me glad for censuring [sic] in the endless pursuant media coverage." More and more, the jumpers—and their images—were relegated to the Internet underbelly, where they became the provenance of the shock sites that also traffic in the autopsy photos of Nicole Brown Simpson and the videotape of Daniel Pearl's execution, and where it is impossible to look at them without attendant feelings of shame and guilt. In a nation of voyeurs, the desire to face the most disturbing aspects of our most disturbing day was somehow ascribed to voyeurism, as though the jumpers' experience, instead of being central to the horror, was tangential to it, a sideshow best forgotten.

It was no sideshow. The two most reputable estimates of the number of people who jumped to their deaths were prepared by The New York Times and USA Today. They differed dramatically. The Times, admittedly conservative, decided to count only what its reporters actually saw in the footage they collected, and it arrived at a figure of fifty. USA Today, whose editors used eyewitness accounts and forensic evidence in addition to what they found on video, came to the conclusion that at least two hundred people died by jumping—a count that the newspaper said authorities did not dispute. Both are intolerable estimates of human loss, but if the number provided by USA Today is accurate, then between 7 and 8 percent of those who died in New York City on September 11, 2001, died by jumping out of the buildings; it means that if we consider only the North Tower, where the vast majority of jumpers came from, the ratio is more like one in six.

And yet if one calls the New York Medical Examiner's Office to learn its own estimate of how many people might have jumped, one does not get an answer but an admonition: "We don't like to say they jumped. They didn't jump. Nobody jumped. They were forced out, or blown out." And if one Googles the words "how many jumped on 9/11," one falls into some blogger's trap, slugged "Go Away, No Jumpers Here," where the bait is one's own need to know: "I've got at least three entries in my referrer logs that show someone is doing a search on Google for 'how many people jumped from WTC.' My September 11 post had made mention of that terrible occurance [sic], so now any pervert looking for that will get my site's URL. I'm disgusted. I tried, but cannot find any reason someone would want to know something like

Associated Press photographer Richard Drew took many pictures of debris-filled streets following the collapse of New York City's Twin Towers on September 11, 2001. © AP IMAGES/RICHARD DREW.

that.... Whatever. If that's why you're here—you're busted. Now go away."

▪ ▪ ▪

Eric Fischl did not go away. Neither did he turn away or avert his eyes. A year before September 11, he had taken photographs of a model tumbling around on the floor of a studio. He had thought of using the photographs as the basis of a sculpture. Now, though, he had lost a friend who had been trapped on the 106th floor of the North Tower. Now, as he worked on his sculpture, he sought to express the extremity of his feelings by making a monument to what he calls the "extremity of choice" faced by the people who jumped. He worked nine months on the larger-than-life bronze he called *Tumbling Woman*, and as he transformed a woman tumbling on the floor into a woman tumbling through eternity, he succeeded in transfiguring the very local horror of the jumpers into something universal—in redeeming an image many regarded as irredeemable. Indeed, *Tumbling Woman* was perhaps the redemptive image of 9/11—and yet it was not merely resisted; it was rejected. The day after

Tumbling Woman was exhibited in New York's Rockefeller Center, Andrea Peyser of the *New York Post* denounced it in a column titled "Shameful Art Attack," in which she argued that Fischl had no right to ambush grieving New Yorkers with the very distillation of their own sadness ... in which she essentially argued the right to look away. Because it was based on a model rolling on the floor, the statue was treated as an evocation of impact—as a portrayal of literal, rather than figurative, violence.

"I was trying to say something about the way we all feel," Fischl says, "but people thought I was trying to say something about the way they feel—that I was trying to take away something only they possessed. They thought that I was trying to say something about the people they lost. 'That image is not my father. You don't even know my father. How dare you try telling me how I feel about my father?'" Fischl wound up apologizing—"I was ashamed to have added to anybody's pain"—but it didn't matter.

Jerry Speyer, a trustee of the Museum of Modern Art who runs Rockefeller Center, ended the exhibition of

Tumbling Woman after a week. "I pleaded with him not to do it," Fischl says. "I thought that if we could wait it out, other voices would pipe up and carry the day. He said, 'You don't understand. I'm getting bomb threats.' I said, 'People who just lost loved ones to terrorism are not going to bomb somebody.' He said, 'I can't take that chance.'"

■ ■ ■

Photographs lie. Even great photographs. Especially great photographs. The Falling Man in Richard Drew's picture fell in the manner suggested by the photograph for only a fraction of a second, and then kept falling. The photograph functioned as a study of doomed verticality, a fantasia of straight lines, with a human being slivered at the center, like a spike. In truth, however, the Falling Man fell with neither the precision of an arrow nor the grace of an Olympic diver. He fell like everyone else, like all the other jumpers—trying to hold on to the life he was leaving, which is to say that he fell desperately, inelegantly. In Drew's famous photograph, his humanity is in accord with the lines of the buildings. In the rest of the sequence—the eleven outtakes—his humanity stands apart. He is not augmented by aesthetics; he is merely human, and his humanity, startled and in some cases horizontal, obliterates everything else in the frame.

In the complete sequence of photographs, truth is subordinate to the facts that emerge slowly, pitilessly, frame by frame. In the sequence, the Falling Man shows his face to the camera in the two frames before the published one, and after that there is an unveiling, nearly an unpeeling, as the force generated by the fall rips the white jacket off his back. The facts that emerge from the entire sequence suggest that the Toronto reporter, Peter Cheney, got some things right in his effort to solve the mystery presented by Drew's published photo. The Falling Man has a dark cast to his skin and wears a goatee. He is probably a food-service worker. He seems lanky, with the length and narrowness of his face—like that of a medieval Christ—possibly accentuated by the push of the wind and the pull of gravity. But seventy-nine people died on the morning of September 11 after going to work at Windows on the World. Another twenty-one died while in the employ of Forte Food, a catering service that fed the traders at Cantor Fitzgerald. Many of the dead were Latino, or light-skinned black men, or Indian, or Arab. Many had dark hair cut short. Many had mustaches and goatees. Indeed, to anyone trying to figure out the identity of the Falling Man, the few salient characteristics that can be discerned in the original series of photographs raise as many possibilities as they exclude. There is, however, one fact that is decisive. Whoever the Falling Man may be, he was wearing a bright-orange shirt under his white top. It is the one inarguable fact that the brute force of the fall reveals. No one can know if the tunic or shirt, open at the back, is being pulled away from him, or if the fall is simply tearing the white fabric to pieces. But anyone can see he is wearing an orange shirt. If they saw these pictures, members of his family would be able to see that he is wearing an orange shirt. They might even be able to remember if he owned an orange shirt, if he was the kind of guy who would own an orange shirt, if he wore an orange shirt to work that morning. Surely they would; surely someone would remember what he was wearing when he went to work on the last morning of his life....

But now the Falling Man is falling through more than the blank blue sky. He is falling through the vast spaces of memory and picking up speed.

■ ■ ■

Neil Levin, executive director of the Port Authority of New York and New Jersey, had breakfast at Windows on the World, on the 106th floor of the World Trade Center's North Tower, on the morning of September 11. He never came home. His wife, Christy Ferer, won't talk about any of the particulars of his death. She works for New York mayor Mike Bloomberg as the liaison between the mayor's office and the 9/11 families and has poured the energy aroused by her grief into her work, which, before the first anniversary of the attack, called for her to visit television executives and ask them not to use the most disturbing footage—including the footage of the jumpers—in their memorial broadcasts. She is a close friend of Eric Fischl's, as was her husband, so when the artist asked, she agreed to take a look at *Tumbling Woman*. It, in her words, "hit me in the gut," but she felt that Fischl had the right to create and exhibit it. Now she's come to the conclusion that the controversy may have been largely a matter of timing. Maybe it was just too soon to show something like that. After all, not long before her husband died, she traveled with him to Auschwitz, where piles of confiscated eyeglasses and extracted tooth fillings are on exhibit. "They can show that now," she says. "But that was a long time ago. They couldn't show things like that then...."

In fact, they did, at least in photographic form, and the pictures that came out of the death camps of Europe were treated as essential acts of witness, without particular regard to the sensitivities of those who appeared in them or the surviving families of the dead. They were shown, as Richard Drew's photographs of the freshly assassinated Robert Kennedy were shown. They were shown, as the photographs of Ethel Kennedy pleading with photographers not to take photographs were shown. They were shown as the photograph of the little Vietnamese girl running naked after a napalm attack was shown. They were shown as the photograph of Father Mychal Judge, graphically and unmistakably dead, was shown, and accepted as a kind of testament. They were shown as everything is shown, for, like the lens of a camera, history is a force that does not discriminate. What distinguishes the pictures of the jumpers from the pictures that have come before is that we—we Americans—are being asked to discriminate on their behalf. What distinguishes them, historically, is that we, as patriotic Americans, have agreed not to look at them. Dozens, scores, maybe hundreds of people died by leaping from a burning building, and we have somehow taken it upon ourselves to deem their deaths unworthy of witness—because we have somehow deemed the act of witness, in this one regard, unworthy of us.

■ ■ ■

Catherine Hernandez never saw the photo the reporter carried under his arm at her father's funeral. Neither did her mother, Eulogia. Her sister Jacqueline did, and her outrage assured that the reporter left—was forcibly evicted—before he did any more damage. But the picture has followed Catherine and Eulogia and the entire Hernandez family. There was nothing more important to Norberto Hernandez than family. His motto: "Together Forever." But the Hernandezes are not together anymore. The picture split them. Those who knew, right away, that the picture was not Norberto—his wife and his daughters—have become estranged from those who pondered the possibility that it was him for the benefit of a reporter's notepad. With Norberto alive, the extended family all lived in the same neighborhood in Queens. Now Eulogia and her daughters have moved to a house on Long Island because Tatiana—who is now sixteen and who bears a resemblance to Norberto Hernandez: the wide face, the dark brows, the thick dark lips, thinly smiling—kept seeing visions of her father in the house and kept hearing the whispered suggestions that he died by jumping out a window.

He could not have died by jumping out a window.

All over the world, people who read Peter Cheney's story believe that Norberto died by jumping out a window. People have written poems about Norberto jumping out a window. People have called the Hernandezes with offers of money—either charity or payment for interviews—because they read about Norberto jumping out a window. But he couldn't have jumped out a window, his family knows, because he wouldn't have jumped out a window: not Papi. "He was trying to come home," Catherine says one morning, in a living room primarily decorated with framed photographs of her father. "He was trying to come home to us, and he knew he wasn't going to make it by jumping out a window." She is a lovely, dark-skinned, brown-eyed girl, twenty-two years old, dressed in a T-shirt and sweats and sandals. She is sitting on a couch next to her mother, who is caramel-colored, with coppery hair tied close to her scalp, and who is wearing a cotton dress checked with the color of the sky. Eulogia speaks half the time in determined English, and then, when she gets frustrated with the rate of revelation, pours rapid-fire Spanish into the ear of her daughter, who translates. "My mother says she knows that when he died, he was thinking about us. She says that she could see him thinking about us. I know that sounds strange, but she knew him. They were together since they were fifteen." The Norberto Hernandez Eulogia knew would not have been deterred by smoke or by fire in his effort to come home to her. The Norberto Hernandez she knew would have endured any pain before he jumped out of a window. When the Norberto Hernandez she knew died, his eyes were fixed on what he saw in his heart—the faces of his wife and his daughters—and not on the terrible beauty of an empty sky.

How well did she know him? "I dressed him," Eulogia says in English, a smile appearing on her face at the same time as a shiny coat of tears. "Every morning. That morning, I remember. He wore Old Navy underwear. Green. He wore black socks. He wore blue pants: jeans. He wore a Casio watch. He wore an Old Navy shirt. Blue. With checks." What did he wear after she drove him, as she always did, to the subway station and watched him wave to her as he disappeared down the stairs? "He changed clothes at the restaurant," says Catherine, who worked with her father at Windows on the World. "He was a pastry chef, so he wore white pants, or chef's pants—you know, black-and-white check. He wore a white jacket. Under that, he had to wear a white T-shirt." What about an orange shirt? "No," Eulogia says. "My husband did not have an orange shirt."

There are pictures. There are pictures of the Falling Man as he fell. Do they want to see them? Catherine says no, on her mother's behalf—"My mother should not see"—but then, when she steps outside and sits down on the steps of the front porch, she says, "Please—show me. Hurry. Before my mother comes." When she sees the twelve-frame sequence, she lets out a gasping, muted call for her mother, but Eulogia is already over her shoulder, reaching for the pictures. She looks at them one after another, and then her face fixes itself into an expression of triumph and scorn. "That is not my husband," she says, handing the photographs back. "You see? Only I know Norberto." She reaches for the photographs again, and then, after studying them, shakes her head with a vehement finality. "The man in this picture is a black man." She asks for copies of the pictures so that she can show them to the people who believed that Norberto jumped out a window, while Catherine sits on the step with her palm spread over her heart. "They said my father was going to hell because he jumped," she says. "On the Internet. They said my father was taken to hell with the devil. I don't know what I would have done if it was him. I would have had a nervous breakdown, I guess. They would have found me in a mental ward somewhere. . . . "

Her mother is standing at the front door, about to go back inside her house. Her face has already lost its belligerent pride and has turned once again into a mask of composed, almost wistful sadness. "Please," she says as she closes the door in a stain of morning sunlight. "Please clear my husband's name."

■ ■ ■

A phone rings in Connecticut. A woman answers. A man on the other end is looking to identify a photo that ran in *The New York Times* on September 12, 2001. "Tell me what the photo looks like," she says. It's a famous picture, the man says—the famous picture of a man falling. "Is it the one called 'Swan Dive' on Rotten.com?" the woman asks. It may be, the man says. "Yes, that might have been my son," the woman says.

She lost both her sons on September 11. They worked together at Cantor Fitzgerald. They worked on the equities desk. They worked back-to-back. No, the man on the phone says, the man in the photograph is probably a food-service worker. He's wearing a white jacket. He's upside down. "Then that's not my son," she says. "My son was wearing a dark shirt and khaki pants."

She knows what he was wearing because of her determination to know what happened to her sons on that day—because of her determination to look and to see. She did not start with that determination. She stopped reading the newspaper after September 11, stopped watching TV. Then, on New Year's Eve, she picked up a copy of *The New York Times* and saw, in a year-end review, a picture of Cantor Fitzgerald employees crowding the edge of the cliff formed by a dying building. In the posture—the attitude—of one of them, she thought she recognized the habits of her son. So she called the photographer and asked him to enlarge and clarify the picture. Demanded that he do it. And then she knew, or knew as much as it was possible to know. Both of her sons were in the picture. One was standing in the window, almost brazenly. The other was sitting inside. She does not need to say what may have happened next.

"The thing I hold was that both of my sons were together," she says, her instantaneous tears lifting her voice an octave. "But I sometimes wonder how long they knew. They're puzzled, they're uncertain, they're scared—but when did they know? When did the moment come when they lost hope? Maybe it came so quick. . . . "

The man on the phone does not ask if she thinks her sons jumped. He does not have it in him, and anyway, she has given him an answer.

The Hernandezes looked at the decision to jump as a betrayal of love—as something Norberto was being accused of. The woman in Connecticut looks at the decision to jump as a loss of hope—as an absence that we, the living, now have to live with. She chooses to live with it by looking, by seeing, by trying to know—by making an act of private witness. She could have chosen to keep her eyes closed. And so now the man on the phone asks the question that he called to ask in the first place: Did she make the right choice?

"I made the only choice I could have made," the woman answers. "I could never have made the choice not to know."

Catherine Hernandez thought she knew who the Falling Man was as soon as she saw the series of pictures, but she wouldn't say his name. "He had a sister who was with him that morning," she said, "and he told his mother that he would take care of her. He would never have left her alone by jumping." She did say, however, that the man was Indian, so it was easy to figure out that his name was Sean Singh. But Sean was too small to be the Falling Man. He was clean-shaven. He worked at Windows on the World in the audiovisual department, so he probably would have been wearing a shirt and tie instead of a white chef's coat. None of the former Windows employees who were interviewed believe the Falling Man looks anything like Sean Singh.

Besides, he had a sister. He never would have left her alone.

A manager at Windows looked at the pictures once and said the Falling Man was Wilder Gomez. Then a few days later he studied them closely and changed his mind. Wrong hair. Wrong clothes. Wrong body type. It was the same with Charlie Mauro. It was the same with Junior Jimenez. Junior worked in the kitchen and would have been wearing checked pants. Charlie worked in purchasing and had no cause to wear a white jacket. Besides, Charlie was a very large man. The Falling Man appears fairly stout in Richard Drew's published photo but almost elongated in the rest of the sequence.

The rest of the kitchen workers were, like Norberto Hernandez, eliminated from consideration by their outfits. The banquet servers may have been wearing white and black, but no one remembered any banquet server who looked anything like the Falling Man.

Forte Food was the other food-service company that lost people on September 11, 2001. But all of its male employees worked in the kitchen, which means that they wore either checked or white pants. And nobody would have been allowed to wear an orange shirt under the white serving coat.

Veteran Associated Press photographer Richard Drew, center, at the New York Stock Exchange in October 2008. Drew took the iconic "Falling Man" photograph and was also present when Robert Kennedy was assassinated in 1968. © AP IMAGES/BERNADETTE TUAZON.

But someone who used to work for Forte remembers a guy who used to come around and get food for the Cantor executives. Black guy. Tall, with a mustache and a goatee. Wore a chef's coat, open, with a loud shirt underneath.

Nobody at Cantor remembers anyone like that.

Of course, the only way to find out the identity of the Falling Man is to call the families of anyone who might be the Falling Man and ask what they know about their son's or husband's or father's last day on earth. Ask if he went to work wearing an orange shirt.

But should those calls be made? Should those questions be asked? Would they only heap pain upon the already anguished? Would they be regarded as an insult to the memory of the dead, the way the Hernandez family regarded the imputation that Norberto Hernandez was the Falling Man? Or would they be regarded as steps to some act of redemptive witness?

Jonathan Briley worked at Windows on the World. Some of his coworkers, when they saw Richard Drew's photographs, thought he might be the Falling Man. He

was a light-skinned black man. He was over six five. He was forty-three. He had a mustache and a goatee and close-cropped hair. He had a wife named Hillary.

Jonathan Briley's father is a preacher, a man who has devoted his whole life to serving the Lord. After September 11, he gathered his family together to ask God to tell him where his son was. No: He demanded it. He used these words: "Lord, I demand to know where my son is." For three hours straight, he prayed in his deep voice, until he spent the grace he had accumulated over a lifetime in the insistence of his appeal.

The next day, the FBI called. They'd found his son's body. It was, miraculously, intact.

The preacher's youngest son, Timothy, went to identify his brother. He recognized him by his shoes: He was wearing black high-tops. Timothy removed one of them and took it home and put it in his garage, as a kind of memorial.

Timothy knew all about the Falling Man. He is a cop in Mount Vernon, New York, and in the week after his brother died, someone had left a September 12 newspaper open in the locker room. He saw the photograph of the Falling Man and, in anger, he refused to look at it again. But he couldn't throw it away. Instead, he stuffed it in the bottom of his locker, where—like the black shoe in his garage—it became permanent.

Jonathan's sister Gwendolyn knew about the Falling Man, too. She saw the picture the day it was published. She knew that Jonathan had asthma, and in the smoke and the heat would have done anything just to breathe....

The both of them, Timothy and Gwendolyn, knew what Jonathan wore to work on most days. He wore a white shirt and black pants, along with the high-top black shoes. Timothy also knew what Jonathan sometimes wore under his shirt: an orange T-shirt. Jonathan wore that orange T-shirt everywhere. He wore that shirt all the time. He wore it so often that Timothy used to make fun of him: When are you gonna get rid of that orange T-shirt, Slim?

But when Timothy identified his brother's body, none of his clothes were recognizable except the black shoes. And when Jonathan went to work on the morning of September 11, 2001, he'd left early and kissed his wife goodbye while she was still sleeping. She never saw the clothes he was wearing. After she learned that he was dead, she packed his clothes away and never inventoried what specific articles of clothing might be missing.

Is Jonathan Briley the Falling Man? He might be. But maybe he didn't jump from the window as a betrayal of love or because he lost hope. Maybe he jumped to fulfill the terms of a miracle. Maybe he jumped to come home to his family. Maybe he didn't jump at all, because no one can jump into the arms of God.

Oh, no. You have to fall.

Yes, Jonathan Briley might be the Falling Man. But the only certainty we have is the certainty we had at the start: At fifteen seconds after 9:41 a.m., on September 11, 2001, a photographer named Richard Drew took a picture of a man falling through the sky—falling through time as well as through space. The picture went all around the world, and then disappeared, as if we willed it away. One of the most famous photographs in human history became an unmarked grave, and the man buried inside its frame—the Falling Man—became the Unknown Soldier in a war whose end we have not yet seen. Richard Drew's photograph is all we know of him, and yet all we know of him becomes a measure of what we know of ourselves. The picture is his cenotaph, and like the monuments dedicated to the memory of unknown soldiers everywhere, it asks that we look at it, and make one simple acknowledgment.

That we have known who the Falling Man is all along.

FURTHER RESOURCES

Books

DiMarco, Damon. *Tower Stories: An Oral History of 9/11.* Santa Monica, CA: Santa Monica Press, 2007.

Web Sites

Junod, Tom. "Surviving the Fall." *Esquire*, September 9, 2011. http://www.esquire.com/the-side/feature/the-falling-man-10-years-later-6406030 (accessed on March 20, 2013).

Pompeo, Joe. "Photographer Behind 9/11 'Falling Man' Retraces Steps, Recalls 'Unknown Soldier.'" *Yahoo! News*, August 29, 2011. http://news.yahoo.com/photographer-behind-9-11-falling-man-retraces-steps-recalls-unknown-soldier.html (accessed on March 20, 2013).

Stern, Marlow. "9/11's Iconic 'Falling Man.'" *Daily Beast*, September 8, 2011. http://www.thedailybeast.com/articles/2011/09/08/richard-drew-s-the-falling-man-ap-photographer-on-his-iconic-9-11-photo.html (accessed on March 20, 2013).

Zahn, Paula. "Changed in a Moment: Interview of Photographer Richard Drew." *CNN*, October 11, 2001. http://transcripts.cnn.com/TRANSCRIPTS/0110/11/ltm.06.html (accessed on March 20, 2013).

"Retirement Means More Oprah, Not Less"

Newspaper article

By: Rob Salem

Date: November 23, 2009

Source: Salem, Rob. "Retirement Means More Oprah, Not Less." *Toronto Star*, November 23, 2009. www.thestar.com/entertainment/2009/11/23/salem_retirement_means_more_oprah_not_less.html (accessed on March 19, 2013).

About the Newspaper: The *Toronto Star* was first published in 1892, originally called the *Evening Star*. The paper gained a reputation for advocating political change and championing the rights of the common Canadian citizen. Renamed the *Toronto Star* in 1971, it retained its traditional status as the city's largest and most widely circulated news source, focusing on domestic news and social issues. In accordance with the government and culture of Ontario, the paper is among the most liberal and overtly political publications in Canada, frequently calling for recognition of social issues and supporting welfare and union causes.

INTRODUCTION

Oprah Winfrey was born to a poor single mother in rural Kosciusko, Mississippi, in 1954. After a difficult childhood, fraught with frequent moves and school changes, a young Winfrey won a full scholarship to Tennessee State University for her victory in a speaking competition. Winfrey graduated with a degree in communication and immediately secured a job as a news anchor on a Nashville television news station, then cycled through several successive positions with different television stations before moving to Chicago in 1983. There she took control of the city's least-popular talk show, which she quickly transformed into the most-watched and best-rated program of its type in the city. Her earnest, emotional, congenial demeanor, which attracted and scintillated viewers like no talk show host before her, earned Winfrey a full-hour, eponymous talk program, which aired its first episode on September 8, 1986.

The Oprah Winfrey Show was a phenomenal success. The charismatic host, in a marked departure from the traditional style of the talk-show format, dealt frequently with controversial and significant social issues by dedicating entire episodes to in-depth interviews with multiple relevant guests. Oprah connected to audiences like no television personality before by genuinely sympathizing with the misfortunes and triumphs of her guests, tearing up at tender moments and beaming during joyous ones. Ratings were also assisted by the caliber of Winfrey's guests—the show boasted appearances by high-profile interviewees from every realm of American culture, including musicians, actors, politicians, artists, athletes, performers, religious figures, authors, and more.

As Winfrey's public presence expanded, so did her influence. In 1996 she unveiled a new segment on her show, called Oprah's Book Club. By the beginning of the 2000s decade, almost every book selected for the Book Club—meaning that it had received the personal endorsement of Winfrey herself—became an instant best-seller, making her arguably the most influential literary figure of the new millennium. Social causes advocated by the trendsetting host, including such diverse concerns as the right of gays to marry, international disaster relief, and combating racism, benefited immensely from her support, which often equated to increased support among the U.S. public.

Consistently ranking among the most-watched and highest-rated programs on American television throughout the decade, *The Oprah Winfrey Show* was a veritable institution, commanding enormous cultural sway among U.S. citizens. Winfrey herself was undeniably the most successful and powerful woman in the nation and perhaps its most well-loved public figure. That is why it caused fans and followers of the icon so much consternation when, on November 20, 2009, Winfrey announced on-air that she would be ceasing production of the show after its twenty-fifth season, scheduled for 2011. The collective American psyche brimmed with dismay at the thought of losing the beloved Oprah Winfrey.

SIGNIFICANCE

Fortunately for those worried about losing Winfrey's steady-handed guidance, her so-called "retirement" was not really anything of the sort. Winfrey's savvy was not restricted to coaxing her audience—she had spent her career developing a diverse and profitable business empire, with a portfolio that included *O, The Oprah Magazine*; *Oprah.com*; film company Harpo Productions; and the Oxygen television channel. She also produced and/or starred in more than thirty films, television documentaries, and television series, and also co-authored five books. By the time the show aired its final episode in May 2011, Winfrey had laid the groundwork for appearances in every medium and indicated an intention to do so. So while the end of *The Oprah Winfrey Show* may have worried many, their concerns were unfounded. If anything, the end of the show would prove to allow Winfrey more freedom to spread her inspirational presence through every channel of the media.

PRIMARY SOURCE

"RETIREMENT MEANS MORE OPRAH, NOT LESS"

SYNOPSIS: In this article, the author briefly recounts Oprah Winfrey's career and the circumstances of her popularity, as well as assuring worried readers that the icon's retirement from television does not signal her retreat from public life.

It's Oprah's world; we just live in it.

I don't know why everyone seems so surprised. Oprah Winfrey calling it quits with her syndicated talk show became inevitable as the beloved billionaire moved up the food chain to mogul-hood, from afternoon icon to magazine publisher *(O)* to Broadway impresario *(The Color Purple)* to movie producer *(Precious)*.

Virtually every Oprah-endorsed expert has been spun off into his or her own series. She has merely to mention a

Oprah Winfrey announces new programming for her Oprah Winfrey Network on April 8, 2010. © AP IMAGES/MARY ALTAFFER.

book on the air and it becomes an instant bestseller. Hard-to-get celebrities from Tom Cruise to Sarah Palin feel comfortable enough in her earnest on-air embrace to freely humiliate themselves before a national audience.

Let's face it: was it not Oprah Winfrey who almost single-handedly got Barack Obama elected president of the United States? Presumably, this was because she was too otherwise occupied to take on the job herself.

So leaving syndicated daytime behind to start up her own network is the next logical step on Oprah's road to world domination.

Again ... she has been down this particular road before. No one seems to remember that, a little more than a decade ago, Winfrey was involved in the start-up of the Oxygen channel, later pulling out after disagreements on direction.

And now she is getting ready to blow Oxygen right off the American cable tier, rebranding the former

Discovery Health into the Oprah-centric OWN, as in Oprah Winfrey Network, though I prefer to take the title literally.

I mean, this is the same woman who only recently went to court over proprietary rights to the phrase "aha moment"—essentially attempting to buy actual words right out of the English language.

As it is, she already all but owns the letter "O."

I'm not saying she's not entitled. The woman is both a virtual saint and a canny entrepeneur—becoming a universally adored household name on the sheer strength of her emotional integrity and boundless empathy, while also possessing the foresight and business savvy to retain ownership and creative control of her brand.

Concerns to the contrary, Oprah hasn't forsaken us. Though she's hedging on making an on-air commitment at this early stage—why undermine her last syndicated season-and-a-half?—there can be no doubt she will resurface on OWN, if not quite perhaps in the same daily format.

But Oprah the mogul knows better than anyone that Oprah the icon is her greatest asset.

The public shock and horror will eventually abate, the more it becomes clear that this means more Oprah, not less.

As far as I can determine, her faithful staff were the first to find out, though given Winfrey's famously hands-on hiring practices, I would imagine that she'll be taking a lot of them with her.

The official announcement went out online soon after, around the same time Winfrey apparently put in a personal call to Ellen DeGeneres, her soon-to-be former competitor and likely dominant successor, with whom she recently posed for the Christmas cover of the December issue of O.

DeGeneres received the call just as she was wrapping up her own Thursday show taping and immediately broke the news to her studio audience.

"She is an amazing woman," DeGeneres said. "She will always be the queen of daytime television.

"She also said she is leaving me all of her money. And I was, like, 'Thanks Oprah, thank you.'"

Oprah tearfully told her own audience on air Friday morning, promising a memorable final 18 months before the move to cable.

"We are going to knock your socks off," she promised. "The countdown to the end of The Oprah Winfrey Show starts now."

And then, the Oprah Winfrey Network. To be followed, perhaps, by the United States of Oprah? And, eventually, Winfrey World?

I don't know about you, but I could think of worse places to live.

FURTHER RESOURCES

Books

Cooper, Irene. *Oprah Winfrey.* New York: Viking, 2007.

Kelley, Kitty. *Oprah: A Biography.* New York: Crown, 2010.

Mair, George. *Oprah Winfrey: The Real Story.* New York: Citadel, 2001.

Web Sites

Mask, Mia. "Oprah: The Billionaire Everywoman." *NPR.* www.npr.org/templates/story/story.php?storyId=124285 128 (accessed on March 19, 2013).

Oprah. www.oprah.com/index.html (accessed on March 19, 2013).

"Oprah Winfrey." *Internet Movie Database.* www.imdb.com/ name/nm0001856/ (accessed on March 19, 2013).

"Y2K: The Good, the Bad and the Crazy"

It's been 10 years since the infamous 'Year 2000 bug' crashed the millennium party; here's what we learned

Magazine article

By: Robert L. Mitchell

Date: December 28, 2009

Source: Mitchell, Robert L. "Y2K: The Good, the Bad and the Crazy." *Computerworld*, December 28, 2009. www.computerworld.com/s/article/9142555/Y2K_The_ good_the_bad_and_the_crazy?taxonomyId=14&page Number=1 (accessed on March 20, 2013).

About the Publication: *Computerworld* was first published in Framingham, Massachusetts, in 1967, and has been headquartered there ever since. The magazine covers a variety of topics related to computer and information technology (IT) sectors, such as industry news and technological innovations. *Computerworld* is circulated in many countries around the world, releasing two issues each month.

INTRODUCTION

As the change of the calendar from 1999 to 2000 drew closer, the American public was aware of the potential for a mysterious menace to their well being: the so-called "Y2K bug," an allegedly fatal flaw in the design of the world's computing infrastructure that threatened to cause the collapse of every digital or automated system in the world. Also known as the "Year 2000 problem," this purported glitch was said to arise from the practice, common in computer and software programming, of using only two digits to represent years in digital computation. For instance, a bank's digital accounts might record transactions from the year 1969 as having taken place in the year "69," and those from 1970 as "70," and so on. When the world's clocks turned to 12:00 AM on January 1, 2000, experts warned, computer systems that employed this simplified date system—a category that included nearly every digital system on the planet, ranging from automated traffic lights to financial records to official census information—would see the year flip from "99" to "00," causing computing errors and unforeseeable chaos as computers misinterpreted the year as being 1900.

News of the Y2K bug was abundant. During the final months of 1999, the American public was inundated with ominous statements from public officials and technology issues, cautioning citizens to prepare for the worst in case major computing glitches caused the collapse of society and plunged the world into chaos and anarchy. Dozens of survival guides were published, informing citizens about how best to prepare for a post-computer age in which there was no electricity, government records, or automated infrastructure. As the first minute of the new millennium approached, the United States—and the rest of the world—held its collective breath in nervous anticipation.

Then, on New Year's Day, 2000, contrary to the dire warnings projected by the media, the people of the United States awoke to discover that the severity of the Year 2000 problem had been vastly overstated. Almost no computing problems caused by the transition from 1999 to 2000 were reported, and most of those that did occur were trivial. The day passed largely without incident, and the panic that preceded it quickly faded from public memory.

SIGNIFICANCE

Although media sensationalism can be implicated in exaggerating the danger to society posed by the Y2K bug, much of the reason it had little impact on computing operations was that the programming community had recognized it as a potential threat to stability years prior, and had been steadily working to fix affected systems before the turn of the twenty-first

President Bill Clinton talks about the Y2K problem at a National Academy of Science gathering, July 14, 1998. © RICHARD ELLIS/ALAMY.

century. An international effort was mounted in 1997 to prevent any major computing failures or malfunctions through systematically modifying computer code to account for more than two-digit representations of years, which was highly successful. In the United States, both government employees and private-sector programmers and engineers spent millions of man-hours pre-emptively addressing the Y2K bug. As the 2000s decade progressed, the episode was remembered as a triumph of the computing industry and an example of the American news media's lurid, alarmist tendencies.

PRIMARY SOURCE

"Y2K: THE GOOD, THE BAD AND THE CRAZY"

SYNOPSIS: In this article, the author discusses some of the under-recognized effects of the Y2K scare on business and IT in the United States.

Ten years ago this week, the much-hyped Y2K crisis—which had come in with a long, sustained roar—went out with a whimper.

In the years and months leading up to the new millennium, IT organizations spent billions patching systems and replacing hardware and software that had infamously been designed to support only a two-digit year—a problem dubbed the Year 2000 bug, the Millennium bug, or simply Y2K.

While the world pondered dire predictions of massive global infrastructure failures—everything from elevators to air traffic control systems was rumored to be vulnerable—the specter of a total paralysis of business operations resulting from cascading Y2K failures galvanized organizations into a frenzy of activity. For many CIOs [chief information officers], the unprecedented size and scope of addressing Y2K problems was the biggest project of their careers.

And then it was over. On Dec. 31, 1999, the world held its breath—and nothing happened. Jan. 1, 2000 came in just like any other day. There were no major failures to report anywhere.

In the aftermath, or non-aftermath, some pundits said all the preparation had been overkill. Others maintained that only the hard work of IT pros, many of whom did not sleep that night, kept the information systems of the world on track.

Many of the IT professionals and CIOs who lived through that ordeal still carry those experiences, and painful lessons learned, with them to this day. On the eve of Y2K's 10-year anniversary, *Computerworld* asked a few veterans to recall the good and bad that came from the whole Year 2000 experience, and to share some of the crazy things that happened as the hype built up and the millennium closed in.

We start with "Y2K: The good"—read on for veterans' opinions on the ways Y2K changed IT for the better. Then read "Y2K: The bad" (and there was lots of bad) and the thrilling conclusion, "Y2K, the Crazy" (there was plenty of crazy, too). In the meantime, take a moment to share stories of how you spent Millennium Eve.

But first, the good.

IT Became a Player

"Y2K put IT on the map," says Paul Ingevaldson, who, as senior vice president of technology, oversaw Y2K preparations for Ace Hardware Corp.'s global operations.

For the first time, companies realized just how critical IT was to business operations. At retailers such as Ace Hardware, for example, the rise of e-commerce had forged a direct link between downtime and lost revenue. "There was no way they could not understand how important IT was to the company. That was the positive side," says Ingevaldson, who has since retired and now writes a regular column for *Computerworld*.

Y2K was a wake-up call for executive management in particular, says Benny Lasiter, who was a senior data management analyst and lead database administrator for a real-time trading floor application at Texaco Natural Gas, a division of Texaco U.S., which is now part of Chevron Products Co.

Starting in 1998, when remediation work for Y2K began in earnest, "the importance of IT across the organization was better understood at the highest levels of the company," says Lasiter, who is now an IT strategy consultant in Houston.

IT had top management's full attention, so much so that some CEOs were interested in the CIO's every step—even on New Year's Eve. "One of my roles was to keep the president and board chairman apprised," recalls Ingevaldson. "It was the only time I've received that kind of concern, that I would [be asked to] call them on New Year's morning," Ingevaldson says.

When It Came to IT Spending, the Sky Was the Limit

It's hard to say definitively how much Y2K cost the corporate world overall. In November of 1999, the U.S. Department of Commerce put the total cost of Y2K remediation at $100 billion.

By 2006, the number had climbed. IDC published a report that year calculating that the preparation and New

Year's Eve costs in the U.S. totaled $134 billion, with an additional $13 billion spent fixing minor problems in 2000 and 2001, according to analyst John Gantz. Worldwide, organizations were estimated to have spent $308 billion before the millennium on remediation efforts. That's a lot of cash.

For IT, the millennium bug represented an unprecedented opportunity to modernize. "I don't think we'll ever again get that opportunity to say, 'Hey, we need a blank check to get everything up to date.' We put a lot of fear into the CEOs back then," says Michael Israel, who, as chief operating officer at IT services provider AMC Computer Corp. oversaw the Y2K remediation work at Continuum Health Partners and its affiliated hospitals in and around New York City.

Before Y2K, an "if it ain't broke, don't fix it" mentality had kept outdated equipment, like the 285 original IBM PC AT computers at Continuum, in service. Now they finally had to go. "It was a once-in-a-lifetime opportunity to clean up and standardize," Israel says.

Dick Hudson, CIO at offshore drilling company Global Marine Inc. in Houston in the late '90s, experienced a similar kind of windfall. "Systems were antiquated, but for cost reasons you could never get management to appropriate the money to clean them up," he recalls. "[Y2K] scared the bejabbers out of CFOs and CEOs, so IT was able to clean up a lot of the garbage. It was a cathartic time, one of the best things that ever happened to IT."

Continuum's CFO didn't hesitate to sign off on the $20 million tab for Y2K preparedness, says Israel, now senior vice president of information services at Six Flags Theme Parks Inc.

The two-year project occupied 37 full-time staffers and required updates to 37,000 systems, including 7,000 PCs and between 500 and 600 servers. And even that was a drop in the bucket compared with efforts at large corporations like General Motors, which spent hundreds of millions of dollars on remediation efforts.

Y2K Put Software and Services Markets on the Map

Y2K wasn't just an opportunity to modernize; it also drove a huge payday for IT product and services vendors, says Dale Vecchio, an analyst at Gartner Inc. who consulted with clients on Y2K issues and now works with its application strategy and governance team.

Y2K remediation, in tandem with the emerging dot-com boom, became "one of the single biggest drivers for packaged software," Vecchio says. Venture-capital-driven dot-coms were on a buying spree, telecom companies were building out their networks to meet the demand for bandwidth, and IT organizations, as part of their Y2K remediation, were modernizing much of their software and hardware infrastructure and migrating many main-frame applications onto client/server systems. In that climate, third-party software and services were "an easy sell," Vecchio says.

At AMC Computer, salespeople were suddenly making money hand over fist. The Y2K spending bubble made many people rich. "We made a lot of money on it. A lot of folks thought the gravy train would never end," Israel says.

Portfolio management became the new mantra

To solve the Y2K problem, CIOs needed to know what applications they actually had. IT finally came to grips with the need to get its portfolio in order.

"The very reason why Y2K was a problem was that most CIOs couldn't put their hands on the application portfolio in the first place," says Stuart McGill, then VP of Y2K business at Micro Focus in Rockville, Md., which sold development environments used for client/server and mainframe Y2K remediation work. "They didn't have any discipline around the application portfolio."

"This was a time for [IT] to do discovery and documentation," Israel agrees, and it was a lesson that he took to heart. "That became the foundation for how I manage an IT environment today." From Y2K came a clearer understanding of the need to standardize workers' roles and to thoroughly document systems, he says.

Going forward, Y2K also prompted IT to think more strategically. "It really raised awareness of how some-thing as simple as a two-digit year can impact you down the road," Lasiter says. That led to better planning. "It opened up that thinking of what might happen in the future that we can avert now." After Y2K, he says, his staff was much more thorough in testing programs for every conceivable contingency before deploying them.

Y2K Was a 'Kumbaya' Moment

In tackling the millennium bug, many departments within distributed organizations worked together, some-times for the first time, to face a common enemy. "Y2K was an interesting phenomenon, in that it knew no industry or global bounds," says Vecchio.

The scope of the problem touched every part of the organization, in every country worldwide, Lasiter points out. That meant that in the run-up to Y2K, IT had a golden opportunity to build relationships with every part of the business, as well as with other areas of distributed IT organizations. And those connections would pay off later, during future projects.

Texaco had a distributed IT organization at the time. Initially, Lasiter didn't know many people outside of his own group. "Y2K brought a lot of unity within the IT community. For this project, we were all one," he says. After that, he says, cross-functional, cross-departmental projects became much easier to coordinate.

IT Saved the Day—and Millennium Eve

When the millennium came, IT was ready. Many IT managers and staff had to forgo New Year's parties, since they were either on call or standing by at work as the new year rolled in. But if the media, the public and even celebrities fretted over what might happen, most IT organizations were feeling good.

"We were confident that we wouldn't have any major outages," says Lasiter. And Texaco didn't. "The fact that we didn't have any major problems was a huge success." Still, it wasn't until later in the day on Jan. 1, after everything had been fully checked out, that IT began openly celebrating.

Tech support at Micro Focus stayed open but received no calls, remembers McGill, who is now chief technology officer for Micro Focus. In Stamford, Conn., Gartner analysts were on call. A few calls came in, says Vecchio, but most of the Y2K issues were minor inconveniences. "There was nobody who had a cata-strophic failure," he says.

In New York, Israel sat with his team in one of Continuum Health Partners' facilities. "We sat in the data center eating lasagna and ziti and watched the clock," he recalls. "Y2K was a quiet and anticlimactic event."

FURTHER RESOURCES
Books
Hyatt, Michael S. *The Y2K Personal Survival Guide.* New York: Regnery, 1998.

Web Sites
"Y2K Bug." *National Geographic.* http://education.national-geographic.com/education/encyclopedia/Y2K-bug/?ar_a=1 (accessed on March 20, 2013).

"Y2K Coverage." *BBC.* http://news.bbc.co.uk/2/hi/science/nature/585013.stm (accessed on March 20, 2013).

"The Year 2000 Scare." *NPR.* http://www.npr.org/templates/archives/archive.php?thingId=5055064 (accessed on March 20, 2013).

9 Medicine and Health

Chronology

Important Events in Medicine and Health, 2000–2009

2000

- On January 17, the Clinton administration calls for Food and Drug Administration (FDA) regulation of online pharmaceutical sales.

- On January 18, Michael J. Fox announces his retirement as an actor from the hit television series *Spin City* due to the effects of Parkinson's disease, a condition that he had disclosed to the press in 1998. He will continue to appear in guest roles and launches the Michael J. Fox Foundation for Parkinson's Research.

- On January 21, the FDA closes down gene-therapy experiments at the University of Pennsylvania following the death of patient Jesse Gelsinger on September 17, 1999. The FDA discovered that federal guidelines were not being followed.

- On February 17, the University of Pennsylvania fires medical school dean William Kelley.

- On March 7, Katie Couric, television news personality and cohost of *Today*, undergoes a colonoscopy procedure live on television.

- On April 19, ten-year-old North Carolinian Candace Newmaker, diagnosed with mental health and learning problems, dies in Colorado one day after undergoing a "rebirthing" program of intense breathing exercises (meant to be therapeutic and to foster a bond with her adoptive mother). Charges are brought against her mother and the therapists.

- On April 24, Adam David Litwin is discovered to be impersonating a resident in surgery after nearly six months at UCLA Medical Center. The incident highlights security concerns at this and other medical facilities.

- On April 27, Mayor Rudolph Giuliani of New York City announces he is undergoing treatment for prostate cancer, and later decides not to challenge Hillary Clinton for the New York senate seat.

- On May 11, the FDA approves use of saline-filled breast implants.

- On May 15, the San Francisco Department of Public Health offers free Tower Records gift certificates and condoms to individuals who agree to be tested for gonorrhea and chlamydia while at the Cat Club in an effort to combat the spread of sexually transmitted diseases.

- On May 22, two U.S. drug companies (Merck and Bristol-Myers Squibb) and three European drug companies announce they will provide AIDS drugs to poor nations at deep discounts, following intense pressure from the World Health Organization (WHO) and the Clinton administration.

- On August 7, the West Nile virus is reported in Boston, and alerts soon spread to seventeen states.

2001

- At the Rehabilitation Institute of Chicago a new nerve-cell operation allows a double amputee to control his robotic arms.

- On January 11, the Oregon Regional Primate Research Center announces the creation of the first genetically altered primate, a rhesus monkey named ANDi. It is hoped this will be useful in research into diseases such as Alzheimer's.

- On January 13, former president Ronald Reagan, who is eighty-nine and suffers from Alzheimer's disease, undergoes surgery to repair a broken right hip.

- On February 2, former Wisconsin governor Tommy Thompson takes over as secretary of the Department of Health and Human Services (HHS), replacing Donna Shalala.

- On March 21, the Supreme Court rules in *Ferguson v. Charleston* that involuntary drug testing of women violates Fourth Amendment protection against unreasonable search and seizure because of the right to privacy.

- On April 25, a National Institute of Child Health and Human Development report cited in the *Journal of the American Medical Association* claims that 16 percent of schoolchildren experience bullying.

- On April 30, psychological therapist Connell Watkins and associate Julie Ponder are convicted of reckless child abuse in the death of Candace Newmaker and are given sixteen-year sentences; the mother and two assistant therapists are sentenced to probation. The governor of Colorado, Bill Owens, signs a bill banning the so-called rebirthing breathing therapy that led to the death.

- On May 14, the Supreme Court rules unanimously in *United States v. Oakland Cannabis Buyers' Cooperative* that marijuana cannot be legally used for medical purposes.

- On May 29, disabled golfer Casey Martin, suffering from Klippel-Trenaunay-Weber syndrome, a progressive and untreatable circulatory disorder in his right leg, wins a ruling by the Supreme Court that he can participate on the professional tour using a motorized cart.

- On July 2, Robert Tools, fifty-nine, receives the first fully implantable, battery-powered artificial heart, at Jewish Hospital in Louisville, Kentucky. The surgery is performed by Laman A. Gray Jr. and Robert D. Dowling.

- In August, President Bush restricts federal support of stem-cell research on surplus embryos obtained from fertility clinics.

- On August 1, Minnesota Vikings offensive lineman Korey Stringer dies from heatstroke during practice; his death leads to discussions and changes in athletic practices held during periods of extreme heat.

- On November 6, Attorney General John Ashcroft issues a directive that physicians prescribing controlled substances for use in the Oregon Death with Dignity Act are in violation of the Controlled Substances Act (1970). The U.S. District Court quickly issues an injunction against Ashcroft's directive.

- On November 27, the National Cancer Institute announces that cigarettes labeled as "light" or "mild" are no safer than regular cigarettes.

2002

- Nearly 4,200 cases of West Nile virus infection are reported during the year; 284 people die from the disease.

- On February 28, the FDA approves new cost-effective plasma-screening tests to protect the nation's blood supply from AIDS and hepatitis.

- On March 26, Elias A. Zerhouni is appointed head of the National Institutes of Health (NIH).

- On July 18, the California Supreme Court upholds Proposition 215, which allows the use of medical marijuana for seriously ill patients.

- On August 5, Richard H. Carmona becomes the seventeenth surgeon general of the United States, replacing acting-general Kenneth P. Moritsugu (who later serves again in the acting position from 2006 to 2007).

- On October 29, the San Francisco federal court of appeals rules that doctors cannot have their licenses revoked for prescribing marijuana.

2003

- Nearly ninety-nine hundred cases of West Nile virus infection are reported during the year; 264 people die from the disease.

- In January, the FDA bans gene-therapy research involving retroviral vectors in blood stem cells. The ban will be relaxed in April.

- On January 22, federal judge Robert Sweet dismisses a suit brought by Samuel Hirsch against McDonald's fast-food restaurants on behalf of obese teenagers.

- On February 17, Baltimore Orioles pitcher Steve Bechler dies in Florida of heatstroke. He had been taking the weight-loss pill Xenadrine RFA-1 (containing ephedra).

- In July, beaches in New Jersey are closed after medical waste (vials and syringes) wash up onshore.

- On July 9, the FDA announces it will begin requiring makers of snack foods to indicate levels of trans fats on nutritional labels.

- On July 14, the *Archives of Internal Medicine* publishes a report that notes the beneficial effects that Katie Couric's 2000 live television colonoscopy and colon-cancer awareness effort has had in increasing testing and early detection.

- On October 21, the U.S. Senate passes legislation banning "partial-birth" abortions; President Bush signs the legislation on 5 November.

- On December 8, President Bush signs the Medicare Prescription Drug Improvement and Modernization Act into law.

- On December 30, the FDA bans dietary supplements that include ephedra.

2004

- The bodies of servicemen and -women killed in Afghanistan or Iraq are autopsied and given full CAT scans in order to build databases used in developing new techniques, procedures, and equipment to save lives in the future. One immediate change is lengthening the tube used to reinflate collapsed lungs.

- On March 29–30, the NIH holds the first National Sleep Conference to address sleep disorders.

- On April 12, the FDA bans dietary supplements containing ephedrine alkaloids.

- On June 5, former president Ronald Reagan dies after deteriorating health due to Alzheimer's disease. His family publicly supports stem-cell research as an avenue for potential cures.

- On August 2, President Bush signs the Food Allergen Labeling and Consumer Protection Act, which requires food labels to list potential allergens for consumers.

- On October 8, Congress passes the Anabolic Steroid Control Act, which reclassifies some performance-enhancing drugs as controlled substances and stiffens penalties for companies trying to work around steroid laws.

2005

- On January 26, Tommy Thompson is replaced as head of HHS by Mike Leavitt, former Utah governor and administrator with the Environmental Protection Agency.

- In February, University of Michigan researchers make advances in registering sound by delivering genes to guinea pigs that promote growth of hair cells in the cochlea.

- In February, the U.S. Supreme Court refuses to hear a case brought by Norma McCorvey (the "Jane Roe" of the 1973 *Roe v. Wade* decision) to overturn the original ruling.

- On March 18, in Florida, patient Terri Schiavo's feeding tube is removed, following approval from the U.S. Supreme Court. Schiavo, who suffered from severe brain damage, was in a coma for fifteen years, and dies on March 31.

- On August 31, emergency-power generators fail at Memorial Medical Center in New Orleans, as floodwaters caused by damage inflicted by Hurricane Katrina (which hit the city forty-eight hours earlier) inundate the lower floors, trapping patients and staff in the stifling-hot building (temperatures remained above 100 degrees for ten days). Critically ill patients with the least chance of survival were placed last on the evacuation list. Some patients on ventilators begin to die. On September 1 hospital staff administer drugs to patients deemed beyond

saving and leave the facility. On September 11 forty-five bodies were removed from the shuttered hospital.

2006

- On January 17, the Supreme Court rules in *Gonzales v. Oregon* that the Controlled Substances Act does not authorize the U.S. attorney general to regulate state standards of practice for medicine or allow the attorney general to declare a medical practice authorized under state law to be illegal. The ruling means that the Oregon Death with Dignity Act (1997) stands.

- On February 16, the last Mobile Army Surgical Hospital (MASH) is decommissioned, as mobile combat medical units are deployed in war zones.

- In March, gene therapy proves effective in treating two adult patients with blood myeloid disorders.

- On June 8, the FDA approves Gardasil, touted as the first-ever cervical-cancer vaccine, for blocking infections associated with the human papilloma virus.

- On July 17, Anna Pou and two nurses are arrested for their part in hastening the deaths of patients trapped in Memorial Medical Center in New Orleans during Hurricane Katrina.

- In August, seventeen patients under the care of the National Cancer Institute show regression of advanced melanoma due to the use of genetically engineered white blood cells.

- On August 24, the FDA approves nonprescription use of the Plan B "morning-after pill," which is taken within seventy-two hours after intercourse to prevent pregnancy.

- On December 5, New York City becomes the first major city to ban the use of trans fats in restaurants.

- On December 8, researchers at the University of Michigan announce the development of a bioengineered heart muscle.

- On December 19, President Bush signs a bill promoting public awareness of autism and funding research into the condition.

2007

- On January 15, the University of Texas M. D. Anderson Cancer Center and Southwestern Medical Center announce that tumor-suppressing genes with lipid-based nano-particles have reduced the number and size of human lung-cancer tumors in test mice.

- On April 9, New Mexico legalizes medical marijuana; the state will oversee production and distribution.

- On May 12–28, attorney Andrew Speaker flies to Europe on his honeymoon and then back to the United States via Canada, with "extremely drug-resistant tuberculosis (XDRTB)," claiming he was never told he could not fly but was simply "advised" not to do so.

- On June 1, right-to-death advocate Dr. Jack Kevorkian, who was serving a ten-to-twenty-five-year sentence for a 1999 second-degree murder conviction for assisting in a suicide, is released from prison on parole.

- On July 24, a grand jury refuses to indict Pou on any of the charges stemming from the deaths of hospital patients during Hurricane Katrina.

2008

- In May, Senator Edward M. "Ted" Kennedy (D-Mass.) is diagnosed with brain cancer.

- In December, Cleveland (Ohio) Clinic doctors perform the world's first near-total facial transplant surgery.

2009

- On January 26, Nadya Suleman (known derisively in the media as "Octomom"), an unemployed single mother, gives birth to eight children after fertility treatments (she already had six). She is accused of wishing to become famous, misusing fertility treatments, and wanting to "cash in" on the birth of her children.

- In March, New York City establishes a Bedbug Advisory Board to deal with an infestation of the pests.

- On March 9, President Barack Obama overturns his predecessor's stem-cell policy and allows the National Institutes of Health to fund research on embryonic stem cells beyond previous restrictions.

- On April 28, Kathleen Sebelius is sworn in as secretary of HHS.

- On April 29, Speaker is informed that his initial diagnosis was incorrect, and files suit against the Centers for Disease Control and Prevention (CDC).

- On June 22, President Obama signs the Family Smoking Prevention and Tobacco Control Act; it seeks to protect children by banning flavored cigarettes, advertisement near playgrounds and on sporting logos, and the use of terms "light," "low tar," or "mild."

- On October 24, President Obama declares the swine-flu pandemic (H1N1) a national emergency.

- On November 3, Regina Benjamin becomes the eighteenth surgeon general of the United States.

- In December, federal health officials estimate that approximately ten thousand Americans have died since April from the recent swine-flu outbreak.

"How Brain, and Spirit, Adapt to a 9/11 World"

Newspaper article

By: Natalie Angier

Date: September 10, 2002

Source: Angier, Natalie. "How Brain, and Spirit, Adapt to a 9/11 World." *New York Times*, September 10, 2002. www.nytimes.com/2002/09/10/science/how-brain-and-spirit-adapt-to-a-9-11-world.html?pagewanted=all&src=pm (accessed on March 20, 2013).

About the Newspaper: The *New York Times* was founded in 1851 as a concise, four-page summary of daily news items. News mogul Adolph S. Ochs acquired the paper in 1896, expanding its scope and size. By the turn of the twentieth century, the *New York Times* was the pre-eminent U.S. newspaper, acclaimed for its objective reporting of "All the News That's Fit to Print." In 1905, the popularity and importance of the paper was memorialized by the City of New York, which called its new public square "Times Square," in honor of the journal. The paper's investigative reporting on official and political affairs has always been a trademark, garnering the journalism staff more than one hundred Pulitzer Prizes for its coverage of wars and governments—most notably for its publication of the "Pentagon Papers," leaked documents attesting to the mishandling and uncertainty of the Vietnam War. The *New York Times* remains the nation's most prestigious and important newspaper, and continues to be owned and operated by descendants of Ochs.

INTRODUCTION

On the morning of September 11, 2001, nineteen men, affiliated with the al-Qaeda terrorist network, hijacked four U.S. passenger jets, in what would become the most destructive terrorist attack in the nation's history. At 8:45 AM Eastern Daylight Time, the first aircraft, American Airlines Flight 11, was piloted by its hijackers into the north tower of New York City's World Trade Center (WTC; also known as the Twin Towers), punching a hole in the building and immediately setting it ablaze. Eighteen minutes later, United Airlines Flight 175 was flown into the south tower of the WTC, causing an explosion and setting it on fire. At 9:43, American Airlines Flight 77 crashed into the Pentagon in Arlington County, Virginia, prompting immediate evacuation. At 10:10, the final aircraft, United Airlines Flight 93, plummeted

into a field in rural Somerset County, Pennsylvania, after passengers successfully regained control of the plane and redirected it from its intended target (thought to be either the White House or United States Capitol Building). All 227 passengers aboard the flights, as well as the nineteen hijackers, were killed.

As news organizations scrambled to collect information on the details of the attacks, the nation reeled at initial reports. President George W. Bush appeared on television, issuing an emergency broadcast notifying the public that the events of the morning had been the work of terrorists. People around the world crowded around television sets and radios as it was reported that the south tower had collapsed, soon followed by the north, covering downtown New York in a haze of smoke and debris. As Washington, D.C., and New York City were evacuated, firefighters and emergency relief personnel flooded the impacted area, rushing into the burning towers in an attempt to rescue the thousands of people trapped inside. For the first time in the nation's history, all flights within the United States were grounded and an indefinite hold was placed on aviation. In the evening, fire from the burning Twin Towers spread to the nearby WTC Building 7, which proceeded to collapse around 5:00 PM. The fire in the Pentagon continued throughout the night, as did the rescue efforts of New York City disaster workers, policemen, and firefighters. Although definitive casualty statistics were not available until the end of the month, CNN eventually confirmed a total of 2,977 deaths caused by the attacks, representing citizens of almost one hundred nations. Of those killed, approximately two hundred died falling or jumping from the burning Twin Towers, and over four hundred of them were rescue workers killed by fire, smoke inhalation, or falling rubble. The rest were killed by the initial impact or were trapped inside the various structures damaged by the attacks, which included several buildings surrounding the World Trade Center.

The events of September 11 caused more damage than was visible to the naked eye, and as days became weeks and months, Americans staggered through their grief and emerged from the shock, some able to carry on, others with lingering fear and confusion, anger and sadness. As the *New York Times* article posits, humans respond to monumental tragedy and grief with a process called habituation, the body's natural coping mechanism. For some, this ability to carry on was enough to move forward, beyond and into the days of recovery and renewal. For others, the suffering continued, was named, and recognized as a symptom that life was forever changed.

SIGNIFICANCE

The events of September 11, 2001, came to define the political, social, and cultural atmosphere of the 2000s decade in the United States, and they had a resounding impact throughout the rest of the world. In the days immediately following the attacks, there was a profound outpouring of donations and sympathetic gestures to the victims and their families from people around the world, including thousands of volunteers traveling to New York to assist with cleanup and recovery efforts. American patriotism and national unity soared as the nation shared the grief and anger produced by the devastating violation of its security.

As 2001 became 2002, which became 2003 and so forth, America found ways to heal. Annual memorial services were held to honor those who lost their lives in the attacks, but the ritual was as much for the surviving loved ones as anyone. Media continued to cover human interest stories of the event, and magazines such as *People* ran articles about 9/11 babies while news stations like ABC News aired segments following the babies from birth to their second birthdays, then returned to interview them in kindergarten and again on their tenth birthdays. Coverage of these children and their families' lives reminded Americans that life goes on and is valuable, that hope lives on in this next generation, that tragedy, while devastating, is not the end. Support groups at local, state, and national levels formed to help survivors as well as families and friends of victims process their feelings and sort through the haze of grief and disbelief. Some of these groups continued to meet long after the terrorist attacks. Families for Peaceful Tomorrows was one such group. Founded in 2002 by family members of those killed in the attacks, the mission of Peaceful Tomorrows was to develop and advocate nonviolent options and actions in the pursuit of justice. Members collaborated to work on large-scope projects, but many also put their efforts into local projects to foster multicultural understanding.

The projects were varied. One member, a Brooklyn-based educator, created a program in 2004 called 1-2-1 Contact. American and Iraqi students began corresponding through letters with a two-fold purpose in mind: "Educate American youth about the realities and consequences of choosing violence as a means to political ends" and "to lend social and material support to those directly affected by political violence." Another project, called The F Word: Images of Forgiveness, was developed by journalist Marina Cantacuzino and photographer Brian Moody. The duo travelled the globe to collect stories and photograph people whose lives had been permanently altered by violence and tragedy, but who had chosen forgiveness over retribution. The project was exhibited in various places along the New Hampshire seacoast.

The tenth anniversary of the event was particularly saturated in the media. New York City psychologist Sharon Brennan told *USA Today* that reaction to the intense coverage would be highly individualized. "Certainly, it can be a national vicarious group therapy, in terms of sharing the memories, the sadness, the strength and the empowerment."

According to a *New York Times* 2011 article, at least ten thousand firefighters, police officers, and civilians exposed to the attacks continued to suffer post-traumatic stress disorder. Health and well-being of the post-9/11 world remained a national concern, and in December 2010, Congress passed the James Zadroga 9/11 Health and Compensation Act, which provided $4.3 billion to treat people with illnesses and disorders related to the terrorist attacks.

The rubble of the attacks was cleared away. The New York skyline was rebuilt. The memorial services were held and anniversaries were celebrated. But America—and Americans—were forever changed on September 11, 2001.

PRIMARY SOURCE

"HOW BRAIN, AND SPIRIT, ADAPT TO A 9/11 WORLD"

SYNOPSIS: Scientists explain how the process of habituation allowed Americans to move forward with their daily lives after the terrorist attacks of September 11, 2001.

These days at the National Air and Space Museum in Washington, before visitors can see the Wright Brothers' 1903 *Flier*, Charles A. Lindbergh's *Spirit of St. Louis*, a touchable sample of lunar rock or any other souvenir of humanity's bounce toward the heavens, they first have to pass through a reminder of that morning the sky fell to earth.

The family-friendly museum now has visitors pass through a metal detector, open backpacks and diaper bags for inspection and, if need be, step aside for a brief pat down or a few waves of the beeping wand.

The reaction of the crowd outside to yet another gantlet of Big Brothers and Bossy Older Sisters in uniform? "Mom, this is so boring," a girl of about 6 grumbled.

After all, sanctioned nosiness and an almost aerosolized military spirit have become the humdrum standard, as expected as rush-hour traffic jams. Anybody who flies has the opportunity to feel like a war correspondent, as one's effects are searched and visibly armed officers wander airport corridors.

Long lines at airports, full of people going through security checks, have become the norm in U.S. society since the September 11, 2001, terrorist attacks. © AP IMAGES/ELAINE THOMPSON.

The National Institutes of Health in Bethesda, Md., used to be an open complex, a symbol of the free spirit that is the essence of the scientific enterprise. But with the temptations the laboratories hold for potential bioterrorists, vehicles are inspected from trunk to hood and even underneath with a mirror on a stick. A lake that will be a protective moat against car bombers is being built on the southern side of the site.

The Bush administration is talking about vaccinating hundreds of thousands of Americans, if not more, against smallpox, a menace thought to have been eradicated from the earth.

And though a few people blink, tremble or grumble, many find the signs of official vigilance comforting.

"I travel a lot, and when I'm waiting on line at the airport I have a lot more patience than I used to," said Dr. Dennis S. Charney, chief of the mood and anxiety disorder research program at the National Institute of Mental Health. "We're all doing what we have to do."

In sum, the abnormal has been normalized, integrated into the bristling, blaring ecosystem through which Americans navigate every day. And it is because human beings are so good at adapting to change, including to stimuli that would under many circumstances be considered negative and to updating their world view as readily as they hyperlink from Web page to Web page, that it sometimes looks as if the predictions of last fall have failed to come true and that, gee, we have not really changed at all. . . .

As scientists who study learning and memory see it, though, we have changed in numerous, subtle ways, from a newfound interest in world affairs and the inner workings of the once-reviled United Nations, to a barely conscious but unshakable expectation that the terrorists, whoever and wherever they are, will surely strike again. Yet we hardly notice these changes, any more than our skin expresses its disturbance at being encased in long sleeves one day and short the next.

The mechanism responsible for humanity's capacity to adjust and, in former Mayor Rudolph W. Giuliani's phrase, to "get on with life," is called habituation, and it is essential to the functioning of the brain and the construction of a life.

"Habituation is really important and fascinating in its details," said Dr. Thomas J. Carew, chairman of the department of neurobiology and behavior at the University of California at Irvine. "Typically what you habituate to are stimuli of no proven consequence like the clothes on your body or the ticking of the clock. It's adaptive to not pay attention to everything."

The ease with which one can habituate to even the most striking of stimuli became clear to him when he and his wife were driving through the mountains of Canada.

"My wife coined the phrase, 'Oh look, another breathtaking view,'" Dr. Carew said. "That sums up how the bar needs to be raised higher and higher for you to keep paying attention."

Through studying laboratory animals and patients with brain lesions, researchers have put together a rough model of how the brain habituates, said Dr. Joseph E. LeDoux, a professor at the Center for Neural Science at New York University. When a rat is exposed to a sound followed by a nasty shock, for example, the rat quickly learns to associate the sound with pain, a reinforcement carried out by the amygdala, an almond-shaped structure in the brain's limbic system, the seat of emotions and emotional memories.

If over time, however, the rat hears the sound and is not given a shock, another region of the brain, the frontal cortex, sends signals to the amygdala to inhibit the fear response. The frontal cortex, it seems, strives constantly to shift as much information as possible from "amygdala alert" to the polite yawn. Paying constant attention is resource-intensive and exhausting.

Moreover, said Dr. Terrence J. Sejnowski, a theoretical brain scientist at the Salk Institute in San Diego, maintaining perpetual alertness, particularly of the anxious, fearful variety, requires a chronic release of stress-related hormones like the corticosteroids, which can eventually break down muscle tissue, bone tissue and the neurons in some of the more fragile parts of the brain like the hippocampus.

There is also a strong tendency in all biological systems to return to a state of so-called homeostasis, or equilibrium. The body has an array of mechanisms to maintain the blood in a very narrow pH level, for example, as close to the ideal of 7.4 as possible, because that is the balance of acidity and alkalinity at which hemoglobin is best at grabbing oxygen.

By the same token, said Dr. Steven R. Quartz, director of the Social Cognitive Neuroscience Laboratory at the California Institute of Technology in Pasadena, the brain has a deep need to return to homeostasis, to its particular mix of signaling molecules like serotonin and dopamine, whenever a powerful event has thrown it out of biochemical whack. A tragedy like Sept. 11, Dr. Quartz said, "triggers massive chemical reactions in the emotional structures of the brain."

A result, he added, "is bereavement, the inability to focus on everyday tasks or follow a routine and social withdrawal."

But within days, weeks or months, depending on the person, the brain generally returns to its chemical set point.

"Thus," Dr. Quartz said, "paraplegics report themselves as basically happy in a matter of months after their accident. Lottery winners also report themselves as being at their same old level of happiness within a year after they hit the jackpot."

A return to equilibrium is by no means guaranteed, and great shocks can leave deep plangent scars on a subset of people, particularly those who experienced the collapse of the World Trade Center directly. Some have suffered from the terrible syndrome called post-traumatic stress disorder, with its symptoms of nightmares and flashbacks, chronic hyperanxiety and a tendency to detach from the world.

Dr. Charney, who studies the syndrome, said various interventions, including intense psychotherapy and the right cocktail of antidepressants, had been shown to ease the symptoms. And doctors emphasized that few of the many millions who watched the attacks on television were likely to have fallen into its vise.

As Dr. Quartz sees it, the nation has been eased back to emotional homeostasis through the display of exactly those symbols and actions that would in more ordinary circumstances seem obtrusive and disturbing, the armed guards, the metal detectors and the ID cards dangling around every employee's neck. Large, intricate and impersonal though contemporary society may appear to be, he said, it holds elements of ancient human needs—for the comforts of family, the strength of the tribe.

"We see familial metaphors all around us," Dr. Quartz said. "The White House as the national family home, the first family and so forth."

When disaster struck, laying waste the figment of our invulnerability, we needed symbols that the family and tribe still held, and we needed them quickly.

"It was imperative that protective symbols like armed guards and heightened bag searches be put in place," Dr. Quartz said. "Had they not, I wonder if there might have been a major crisis of identity and statehood."

Even though many people may suspect that such measures are largely useless—knives and guns still manage to pass through airport security gates—they serve the same consolidating, totemic purpose, Dr. Quartz said, "as the ritual spear a tribal chief might carry."

Children, who have no choice but to be very good at accepting change (their bodies are doing it to them every day), likewise know the power of symbols, rituals, rules, the Word.

Dr. Ellen R. DeVoe, an assistant professor of social work at Columbia, who with Dr. Tovah Klein of Barnard has been studying the reactions of young children in Lower Manhattan to the trade center collapse, said children had a remarkable capacity to create stories that reconstruct from the sorrow they see around them a safe and bearable world. She described two children who suggested that the towers be rebuilt, but this time with a billboard on them saying, "No airplanes can come here."

That sign would stop nothing, of course, except, perhaps, a grown-up's tears.

FURTHER RESOURCES
Books
Faludi, Susan. *The Terror Dream.* New York: Metropolitan Books, 2007.

Web Sites
Jayson, Sharon. "9/11 Anniversary News: Too Much or 'National Group Therapy'?" *USA Today*, September 7, 2011. http://usatoday30.usatoday.com/news/health/medical/health/medical/mentalhealth/story/2011-09-04/

9-11-anniversary-news-Too-much-or-national-group-therapy/50256412/1 (accessed on March 20, 2013).

9/11 Memorial. http://www.911memorial.org/ (accessed on March 20, 2013).

Peaceful Tomorrows. www.peacefultomorrows.org/ (accessed on March 20, 2013).

"U.S. Smoking Rate Still Coming Down"

About one in five American adults now smoke

Poll

By: Lydia Saad

Date: July 24, 2008

Source: Saad, Lydia. "U.S. Smoking Rate Still Coming Down." *Gallup*, July 24, 2008. www.gallup.com/poll/109048/us-smoking-rate-still-coming-down.aspx (accessed on March 20, 2013).

About the Organization: The Gallup Poll is a division of Gallup, Inc., a company dedicated to gathering and analyzing statistics on practically every facet of human life. The company, which was founded in 1958 by George Gallup, is considered one of the world's leading sources of opinion and behavior polls. Gallup researchers conduct hundreds of interviews a day, generating some of the most-cited and most-accurate results of any polling organization. Gallup is famous for successfully predicting the winner of every U.S. presidential election from 1936 to 2008 except for two. The company makes money by conducting audience and market research, allowing it to continue funding independent polls.

INTRODUCTION

Tobacco use has a long and influential history in North America, far predating the establishment of the United States. The plant was revered by Native Americans for its psychoactive and medicinal properties, being used ceremonially in religious and social rites, as well as implemented in healing balms and medicated poultices. European explorers were introduced to tobacco upon their earliest contact with the native inhabitants of North America, where they observed its effects of elation and fortification against fatigue when smoked or orally consumed. When the Virginia Colony was permanently established by English settlers in 1607, its administrators immediately

perceived the commercial potential of tobacco and set about developing extensive agricultural cultivation of the crop. The economic viability of Virginia, as well as the later-established Carolina Colony, was largely dependent on the growth and exportation of tobacco to Western Europe, where it became fashionable to consume the plant through a variety of means. Demand for tobacco was so high that it led to the importation of the first African slaves to America, to be put to work on plantations dedicated to the plant's cultivation.

By the seventeenth century, tobacco was a ubiquitous component of life in the colonies of North America, so much so that it was regularly used as currency in small transactions. Settlers of every class and profession consumed the drug daily, typically in the form of chewing or dipping tobacco. Plantations offered a large portion of the employment opportunities in the southern colonies, where the economy was dominated by the growth, collection, treatment, storage, and transport of tobacco. In 1881, the tobacco industry was revolutionized by the invention of the cigarette machine, which was capable of cutting and rolling tobacco into small tubes, bound by paper, to be smoked in a single instance. Cigarettes quickly became the standard method of tobacco consumption, much to the benefit of tobacco producers—whereas previously a person might consume in a day one or two "plugs" of chewing tobacco, or a pipe bowl of smoked tobacco, the cigarette made it simple and affordable to smoke frequently (or even constantly) throughout the day, increasing the demand for the plant.

Since its establishment, the U.S. government had drawn much of its income from excise taxes placed on tobacco, making the industry a favorable pursuit for both agriculturalists and the government. During the early twentieth century, cigarette consumption throughout the world increased at an explosive rate, owing largely to the highly addictive properties of nicotine, the active chemical in tobacco. The growing prevalence of cigarette smoking was accompanied by a proportional increase in lung cancer, lung diseases, and heart diseases, leading several prominent doctors and medical researchers to issue the first proclamations about the relationship between smoking and health problems. Such warnings were summarily ignored by the government, tobacco companies, and general public, however, and the U.S. smoking rate reached a peak of approximately 43 percent in the 1940s.

As more and more medical professionals began suggesting a relationship between smoking and lung cancer, the U.S. government started to take notice. In 1964, the U.S. surgeon general published the definitive "Report on Smoking and Health," firmly

The smoking rate in the United States at the end of the 2000s decade fell to 24 percent. © DBURKE/ALAMY.

establishing a causal link between cigarette smoking and a variety of diseases, particularly lung cancer. The report led to a series of regulations being imposed on the tobacco industry, restricting its advertising capabilities and mandating the inclusion of health warning labels on cigarette packaging. Millions of Americans responded by quitting cigarettes, and consumption continued to decline sharply from the 1960s onward. Increasingly restrictive regulations were placed on the advertisement and sale of tobacco products throughout the rest of the century, supported by progressively more damning research linking cigarettes to all manner of health problems.

In the 1990s, studies of the effects of second-hand smoke revealed that cigarette smoke was toxic not only to smokers, but also to those who indirectly ingested exhaled smoke. These findings led to a widespread ban on smoking in public buildings, such as restaurants, bars, government buildings, and places children were present. During the latter half of the 1990s, a series of high-profile lawsuits were brought against tobacco companies and cigarette manufacturers, dealing with a variety of alleged crimes including negligence, manslaughter, concealing or suppressing scientific evidence that cigarettes were dangerous and addictive, and deceptive advertising. Most of such litigation was resolved in the 2000s, with courts and juries finding almost unerringly in favor of the plaintiffs. The

smoking rate continued to decline throughout the decade, as tobacco companies were fined hundreds of millions of dollars for contributing to the deaths of their customers. By the end of the 2000s, the smoking rate had fallen by almost half to approximately 24 percent.

SIGNIFICANCE

In addition to the obvious benefits to the well-being of U.S. citizens, the decreased prevalence of cigarette smoking in the 2000s had other, more far-reaching implications. The declining occurrence of smoking-related diseases, including a dozen forms of cancer, scores of heart and lung diseases, and arterial disorders, was predicted to significantly reduce the public cost of healthcare required to treat such diseases. Tobacco lobbyists, one of the most influential special-interest groups in the United States, increased spending considerably in an attempt to combat the unfavorable impact of anti-tobacco lawsuits and legislation, although the effects of the elevated spending have yet to be determined. Declining sales in the United States led tobacco companies to more aggressively pursue markets in the developing world, where relaxed regulations and enforcement allowed the companies to advertise and sell to younger, less-educated consumers who are unaware of the serious health impact of smoking.

The anti-smoking movement continued to accelerate during the 2000s, resulting in most states banning public smoking altogether, with some cities going so far as to prohibit smoking in outdoor public places. In 2009, President Barack Obama signed the Family Smoking Prevention and Tobacco Control Act, further impeding the ability of tobacco companies to advertise and giving the Food and Drug Administration the authority to regulate tobacco sales. The law also banned the sale of flavored cigarettes (explicitly exempting menthol cigarettes from this ban) and required the placement of graphic warnings on tobacco products depicting the health problems they could cause, although this statute was later repealed as a violation of the free speech of tobacco manufacturers.

■ PRIMARY SOURCE

"U.S. SMOKING RATE STILL COMING DOWN"

SYNOPSIS: In this excerpted article, the author briefly describes the declining trend in U.S. tobacco-smoking rates.

The percentage of U.S. adults saying they smoked cigarettes in the past week, now 21%, is similar to what Gallup found in 2007. However, it represents a decline from earlier this decade, when between 22% and 28% said they smoked, and is among the lowest figures Gallup has recorded in more than six decades of polling on tobacco use in America.

Question: Have You, Yourself, Smoked Any Cigarettes in the Past Week?

November 13–15, 2000	Yes: 25% / No: 75%
July 19–22, 2001	Yes: 28% / No: 72%
July 9–11, 2002	Yes: 24% / No: 76%
July 7–9, 2003	Yes: 25% / No: 75%
November 3–5, 2003	Yes: 26% / No: 74%
July 8–11, 2004	Yes: 25% / No: 75%
November 7–10, 2000	Yes: 22% / No: 78%
July 7–10, 2005	Yes: 25% / No: 75%
November 7–10, 2005	Yes: 25% / No: 75%
July 16–9, 2006	Yes: 25% / No: 75%
November 9–12, 2006	Yes: 23% / No: 77%
July 12–15, 2007	Yes: 21% / No: 79%
August 3–5, 2007	Yes: 24% / No: 76%
November 11–14, 2007	Yes: 20% / No: 80%
July 10–13, 2008	Yes: 21% / No: 79%

More specifically, in three of the past four Gallup smoking measurements (conducted between July 2007 and today), only 20% or 21% of American adults have said they smoked cigarettes in the past week. Compared with the average of 25% who said they smoked from 2000 through 2006, this suggests a recent decline in U.S. smoking. . . .

The latest result comes from Gallup's annual Consumption Habits survey, conducted July 10–13, 2008.

Self-reported adult smoking peaked in 1954 at 45%, and remained at 40% or more through the early 1970s, but has since gradually declined. The average rate of smoking across the decades fell from 40% in the 1970s to 32% in the 1980s, 26% in the 1990s, and 24% since 2000.

Average Percentage of Cigarette Smokers, by Decade

1940s	43%
1950s	44%
1960s	40%
1970s	40%
1980s	32%
1990s	26%
2000s	24%

. . .

FURTHER RESOURCES

Books

Brandt, Allen. *The Cigarette Century: The Rise, Fall, and Deadly Persistence of the Product That Defined America.* New York: Basic Books, 2009.

Gately, Iain. *Tobacco: A Cultural History of How an Exotic Plant Seduced Civilization.* New York: Grove Press, 2003.

Web Sites

"A Brief History of Tobacco." *CNN.* www.cnn.com/US/9705/tobacco/history/index.html (accessed on March 20, 2013).

"From the First to the Last Ash: The History, Economics & Hazards of Tobacco." *Health Literacy Special Collection.* healthliteracy.worlded.org/docs/tobacco/Unit1/introduction.html (accessed on March 20, 2013).

"Smoking & Tobacco Use." *Centers for Disease Control and Prevention.* www.cdc.gov/tobacco/data_statistics/index.htm (accessed on March 20, 2013).

"Obama Overturns Bush Policy on Stem Cells"

Web site article

By: CNN

Date: March 9, 2009

Source: "Obama Overturns Bush Policy on Stem Cells." *CNN,* March 9, 2009. http://articles.cnn.com/2009-03-09/politics/obama.stem.cells_1_cancer-and-spinal-cord-embryonic-cell-research?_s=PM:POLITICS (accessed on March 21, 2013).

About the Web site: CNN.com is one of the global leaders in online news and information dissemination. Headquartered in Atlanta, Georgia, CNN offices are staffed around the clock, 365 days of the year. With bureaus throughout the world, CNN.com employs a professional team of four thousand newspeople. The online news service is a natural extension of CNN, the world's first twenty-four-hour television news network, which debuted on June 1, 1980.

INTRODUCTION

Scientists have been using human cells in their research since the early 1950s. Those whose efforts led to the development of the polio vaccine were awarded the Nobel Prize in 1954. There has never been a doubt that human cells were valuable in scientific and medical research. Stem cell research, however, has never been anything but controversial because it has involved fetuses and embryos. Opponents claim that such research devalues human life in its most essential or basic form; proponents believe the cells hold such potential promise that disorders and diseases that afflict humans today could quite possibly be eradicated. It is a controversy that has no clear or simple resolution. The inability to find common ground in the ethical and moral dilemma led, of course, to a need for regulations. Policymakers, including Congress, administration, and scientific and medical expert panels, got involved as far back as the 1970s.

Research at that point involved fetuses in utero as scientists strived to develop procedures like amniocentesis. Such research also helped doctors and scientists understand conditions such as congenital heart disease. Tissue from aborted fetuses was also used in research, as it was of the same type that led to the development of the polio vaccine. Initially these research projects were federally funded, but as opponents grew more vocal, funding was halted and expert panels were organized to help develop safeguards and, eventually, federal laws of restriction.

Research continued throughout the 1980s as scientists transplanted fetal tissue into adults suffering from major disease and disorders such as diabetes, Parkinson's, and spinal cord injuries. The material used in these procedures came from aborted fetuses, and public outcry intensified. Republican president Ronald Reagan halted all research in 1988, but the ban was lifted by an executive order signed by Democratic president Bill Clinton in 1993. Congress then passed legislation to codify federal guidelines for such research, and it continued uninterrupted.

The first embryonic stem cells were isolated in 1998, but scientists had long been interested in them because they, unlike any other cells, are pluripotent, capable of generating any kind of tissue in the body. Adult stem cells are multipotent, which means they can generate only a limited number of types of cells and tissues. Embryonic stem cells hold much greater potential for success in treating disease and in procedures like stem cell transplants. A committee established by the National Academy of Sciences (NAS) believes in the powerful potential of these stem cells to "offer hope for the millions who suffer from spinal-cord injuries, cardiovascular disease, autoimmune disease, diabetes, osteoporosis, cancer, Alzheimer's disease, Parkinson's disease and other disorders."

Initially, the cells used in embryonic stem cell research were derived from "extra" embryos that had been created in the process of infertility treatments but had not been needed and so were marked to be discarded. Recognizing the potential in the cells, scientists wanted to create embryos solely for the purpose of research, but the controversy over that idea was intense and endless. Do embryos have rights? Are they considered human beings or do they merely have the potential for human life? Is growing embryos for the purpose of destroying them—even in the quest to improve the quality of and save lives—playing God? After much deliberation and political upheaval, the Department of Health and Human Services determined in 1999 that federal funding could be used for stem cell research as long as derivation of the cells, which results in the embryo's destruction, was privately funded. Final guidelines were released on August 25, 2000, by the National Institutes of Health (NIH), and applications for research grants began pouring in.

It looked like scientists could finally begin their stem cell research unencumbered, but in his 2000 presidential campaign, Republican George W. Bush made it clear that he opposed federal funding for stem cell research that involved the destruction of living human embryos. Once elected, he stood firm in his belief but was not willing to overturn the NIH guidelines. Amidst strong lobbying from special interest groups on both sides of the issue, he instructed his secretary of Health and Human Services, Tommy Thompson, to review the guidelines. On August 9, 2001, Bush announced that research could continue, but only using the sixty-four cell lines already in existence. It was a compromise, and true to the nature of compromise, neither side was truly satisfied. Opponents of research had wanted a total ban; proponents were glad to be able to at least use the cell lines already in existence, but given that they were located around the globe, they had concerns. Were the cell colonies hardy and robust? Had they all been created in a manner consistent with high ethical standards? Was

President Barack Obama signs an Executive Order on stem cell research on March 9, 2009. Behind the president (left to right) are Energy secretary Stephen Chu, Dr. Harold Varmus, Dr. Patricia Bath, Dr. Michael Bishop, Rep. Diana DeGette of Colorado, Rep. Henry Waxman of California, and Speaker of the House Nancy Pelosi. © BILL O'LEARY/THE WASHINGTON POST/ GETTY IMAGES.

their genetic diversity sufficient to complete extensive research? Were all lines safe for human implantation? Would cell owners make them available to researchers in a timely and affordable way?

SIGNIFICANCE

Thompson acknowledged on September 5, 2001, that only twenty-four to twenty-five of the cell lines were established embryonic stem cell lines. The rest were derivations, and some were in early stages of development. All of the concerns researchers had were valid. In November, the NIH developed the Human Embryonic Stem Cell Registry, which listed all cell lines eligible for federally funded research. Important information regarding each line was included. Hopes for research were squelched when a report was released by the National Academy of Sciences just one month after Bush's announcement. In order for

research to continue, scientists needed more stem cell lines. By 2004, just fifteen stem cell lines were available to federally funded researchers. The restrictions placed on research by the Bush administration forced research into the private sector both in America and beyond, which posed a problem: The controlling factor would be profit, not good science. The bottom line was, federal funding through the NIH is what fuels biomedical research. Without it, progress is impeded.

In 2004, a bipartisan group of 206 House members and 58 senators—including a number of staunch antiabortionists—wrote letters to President Bush urging him to ease restrictions on research. But it was not until former president Ronald Reagan died that year in June from Alzheimer's disease that a shift in perception was noticed. Former first lady Nancy Reagan had privately supported stem cell research but publicly shared her opinion for the first time. That August, a Harris poll determined that 73 percent of Americans supported stem cell research. Still, the administration held its position.

In 2006, two research-related bills ended up on the president's desk, awaiting his signature. He signed one that forbid the establishment of farms in which embryos would be harvested solely for the purpose of research. And then, for the first time in his five years in office, President Bush vetoed a bill that had passed in Congress, the Stem Cell Research Enhancement Act (H.R. 810). He vetoed more stem cell legislation in 2007.

With the overturning of the restrictive policy by President Barack Obama in 2009, stem cell research was able to continue. But it did not happen without controversy. Two researchers who worked on adult stem cells filed a lawsuit against the federal government, stating that if embryos were destroyed in the process of obtaining stem cells, then the research could not be federally funded. The lower courts made conflicting rulings, after which a federal appeals court dismissed the case based on its perception that the way the administration interpreted the law was permissible. In January 2013, the Supreme Court effectively ended the case by refusing to hear an appeal. Although this was not the first lawsuit filed against the Obama administration for its decision to reverse Bush's executive order, it was the first one to reach the U.S. Supreme Court.

Since overturning many of the restrictions on embryonic stem cell research, scientists have made progress, particularly in treating degenerative eye disease. They have also had success in treating patients with spinal cord injuries and neurodegenerative diseases. New embryo stem cell lines have been created, all available for federal funding. After decades of intense controversy and media saturation, scientists are able to continue their work. Much of it has been a collaboration of researchers working with adult stem cells and those working with embryonic stem cells. Stephen Huhn, vice president of StemCells, Inc., a company that works with adult stem cells, was quoted in the *Atlantic* in 2012: "The field is advancing, and like everything in medicine, it takes time.... I think that expectations about how quickly we can do things have been raised."

PRIMARY SOURCE

"OBAMA OVERTURNS BUSH POLICY ON STEM CELLS."

SYNOPSIS: President Obama repeals the policy limiting federal funding for embryonic stem cell

research, claiming that science and faith are not inherently mutually exclusive.

President Obama signed an executive order Monday repealing a Bush-era policy that limited federal tax dollars for embryonic stem cell research.

Obama's move overturns an order signed by President Bush in 2001 that barred the National Institutes of Health from funding research on embryonic stem cells beyond using 60 cell lines that existed at that time.

Obama also signed a presidential memorandum establishing greater independence for federal science policies and programs.

"In recent years, when it comes to stem cell research, rather than furthering discovery, our government has forced what I believe is a false choice between sound science and moral values," Obama said at the White House.

"In this case, I believe the two are not inconsistent. As a person of faith, I believe we are called to care for each other and work to ease human suffering. I believe we have been given the capacity and will to pursue this research—and the humanity and conscience to do so responsibly."

The president pledged to develop "strict guidelines" to ensure that such research "never opens the door to the use of cloning for human reproduction."

Such a possibility, he maintained, is "dangerous, profoundly wrong and has no place in our society or any society."

Obama's order directs the NIH to develop revised guidelines on federal funding for embryonic stem cell research within 120 days, according to Dr. Harold Varmus, president of Memorial Sloan-Kettering Cancer Center and co-chairman of Obama's science advisory council.

"The president is, in effect, allowing federal funding of human embryonic stem cell research to the extent that it's permitted by law—that is, work with stem cells themselves, not the derivation of stem cells," Varmus said in a conference call with reporters Sunday.

While conceding that "the full promise of stem cell research remains unknown" and "should not be over-stated," Obama nevertheless expressed hope that the order will help spur faster progress in the search for cures to afflictions such as Parkinson's disease, cancer and spinal cord injuries. Researchers highly value embryonic stem cells because of their potential to turn into any organ or tissue cell in the body. Stem cells have this ability for a short time. A few days before the embryo would implant in the uterus, it starts to develop into specific cells that will turn into skin or eyes or other parts of a developing fetus.

When the embryo is 4 or 5 days old, scientists extract the stem cells and put them in a petri dish. With the removal of these stem cells—of which there may be about 30—the embryo is destroyed.

Twenty-one of the 60 stem cell lines authorized for research under the Bush policy have proven useful to researchers. Bush twice vetoed legislation—in July 2006 and June 2007—that would have expanded federally funded embryonic stem cell research.

At the time, Bush maintained that scientific advances allowed researchers to conduct groundbreaking research without destroying human embryos.

Conservative leaders echoed Bush's rationale in their criticism of Obama's decision.

"Advancements in science and research have moved faster than the debates among politicians in Washington, D.C., and breakthroughs announced in recent years confirm the full potential of stem cell research can be realized without the destruction of living human embryos," House Minority Leader John Boehner, R-Ohio, said Sunday.

Sen. Richard Shelby, R-Alabama, said the Bush policy imposed proper ethical limits on science.

"My basic tenet here is I don't think we should create life to enhance life and to do research and so forth," Shelby said Sunday. "I know that people argue there are other ways. I think we should continue our biomedical research everywhere we can, but we should have some ethics about it."

The issue of whether to lift the ban on federal funding for embryonic stem cell research has, however, exposed a clear rift between the more moderate and conservative factions of the GOP.

In February, a group of six moderate GOP congressmen sent a letter to Obama urging him to lift the funding ban.

Former first lady Nancy Reagan also issued a statement Monday thanking Obama for lifting the ban.

"These new rules will now make it possible for scientists to move forward," Reagan said. "Countless people, suffering from many different diseases, stand to benefit from the answers stem cell research can provide. We owe it to ourselves and to our children to do everything in our power to find cures for these diseases."

President Reagan was diagnosed with Alzheimer's disease after leaving office—an affliction that many scientists say eventually may be cured with the help of embryonic stem cell research.

Obama's presidential memorandum, however, may turn out to have a broader impact than his executive order.

The memorandum is expected to create a clear change of tone from the Bush administration on a broad range of scientific issues.

Bush's critics argued the former president allowed political factors improperly to influence funding decisions for science initiatives as well as to skew official government findings on issues such as global warming.

Obama's memorandum directs the White House Office of Science and Technology Policy "to develop a strategy for restoring scientific integrity to government decision-making."

In a thinly veiled criticism of his predecessor, Obama reiterated a promise to base "public policies on the soundest science" as well as to "appoint scientific advisers based on their credentials and experience, not their politics or ideology."

FURTHER RESOURCES

Books

Park, Alice. *The Stem Cell Hope: How Stem Cell Medicine Can Change Our Lives.* New York: Penguin, 2011.

Ruse, Michael, and Christopher A. Pynes. *The Stem Cell Controversy: Debating the Issue.* Amherst, NY: Prometheus, 2006.

Web Sites

"AAAS Policy Brief: Stem Cell Research." *AAAS.* www.aaas.org/spp/cstc/briefs/stemcells/ (accessed on March 21, 2013).

Abrams, Lindsay. "2013: Year of the Stem Cell." *The Atlantic,* December 28, 2012. www.theatlantic.com/health/archive/2012/12/2013-year-of-the-stem-cell/266574/ (accessed on March 21, 2013).

Fox, Maggie. "Court Rules Controversial Stem Cell Research Is Legal." *NBC News,* August 24, 2012. http://vitals.nbcnews.com/_news/2012/08/24/13458821-court-rules-controversial-stem-cell-research-is-legal?lite (accessed on March 21, 2013).

Gold, Rachel Benson. "Embryonic Stem Cell Research—Old Controversy; New Debate." *Guttmacher Report on Public Policy,* October 2004. www.guttmacher.org/pubs/tgr/07/4/gr070404.html (accessed on March 21, 2013).

Reaves, Jessica. "The Great Debate Over Stem Cell Research." *Time,* July 11, 2001. www.time.com/time/nation/article/0,8599,167245,00.html (accessed on March 21, 2013).

"Stem Cell Research FAQs." *Research America.* www.researchamerica.org/stemcell_faqs#substitution (accessed on March 21, 2013).

"Health Care Reform 2009: Do We Know What We Don't Know?"

Web site article

By: Michael Johns and Atul Grover

Date: July 27, 2009

Source: Johns, Michael, and Atul Grover. "Health Care Reform 2009: Do We Know What We Don't Know?" *Roll Call*, July 27, 2009. www.rollcall.com/news/-37230-1.html?pg=1 (accessed on March 21, 2013).

About the Web site: The tag line for *Roll Call* reads "The Source for News on Capitol Hill Since 1955," and that neatly sums up the role of this privately owned newspaper. Launched by Sid Yudain, the paper delivers "breaking news and behind-the-scenes intelligence on the people, politics, and personalities of Capitol Hill," according to its Web site. The publication also runs features written by reputable Washington analysts like Morton Kondracke and Norman Ornstein.

INTRODUCTION

The history of health care in America is long and storied. As far back as 1916, economists were lamenting the nation's poor track record in health care. Yale economist Irving Fisher was quoted in a speech saying, "At present the United States has the unenviable distinction of being the only great industrial nation without compulsory health insurance." He believed that what he perceived to be a cultural wrong would be righted within six months of his lecture, but more than nine decades would pass before the country managed to implement that lofty goal.

The debate raged then, and it continued to rage on and off through numerous presidential administrations. Dates changed, as did leadership and hot topics of the day, but one pattern emerged: Americans struggled to accept compulsory health insurance because it seemed by its very nature to be a socialist concept. In 1919, a Brooklyn physician called universal health coverage "UnAmerican." Fast-forward to 1965, and the American Medical Association (AMA) referred to government involvement in health care a matter of "creeping socialism." In the 2000s, it was referred to at different times and by different people as Fascist, Communist, Bolshevik, and, in 2009, "an audacious effort to Europeanize the country," according to Senate minority leader Mitch McConnell.

Democrat Barack Obama made health care reform one of his major presidential campaign issues in 2008. It was considered one of the lynchpins of his campaign, an issue—and a promise—that attracted members of the electorate who did not have a habit of voting. His healthcare plan involved mandatory insurance coverage for all Americans, an appealing vision for the estimated 40–46 million (nearly one of every six or seven) uninsured. True to his word, one of the first major initiatives the president instigated once in office was healthcare reform. On March 5, 2009, the White House held its first health care summit. The initial legislation was developed and passed on July 15 as the Affordable Health Choices Act. The bipartisan bill included in its final form more than 160 Republican amendments and took an entire month to discuss, edit, negotiate, and revise. This was one of the longest mark-up periods in congressional history.

Michael Johns, chancellor at Emory University, and Atul Grover, chief advocacy officer for Association of American Medical colleges, responded to the act in this article, published just twelve days after passage.

SIGNIFICANCE

On November 7, 2009, the House of Representatives passed a version of the health care bill in a 220–214 vote. Getting to that point was not smooth sailing, as Democrats lost arguably the staunchest supporter of health care reform when U.S. senator Edward "Teddy" Kennedy of Massachusetts died on August 26. Kennedy had a reputation for crossing party lines and ignoring voting history when it came to controversial issues like health care reform. Youngest brother in the famed Kennedy family, Teddy was respected for his social ideals and intentions in both the Democratic and Republican parties.

On December 19, conservative Democrat senator Ben Nelson of Nebraska became the sixtieth vote required to pass the Senate version of the health care bill. The battle was not over yet, as further revisions were made. Obama televised a health care summit with leaders from both parties on hand to explain the health care bill. On March 23, 2010, Obama signed the bill into law.

In August 2011, the Patient Protection and Affordable Care Act, commonly known as Obamacare, went to the federal Supreme Court to determine the constitutionality of the central provision that stipulated that individuals must purchase health care. Twenty-six states petitioned the high court to hear their claims, and the proceedings lasted three days. On June 28, 2012, Obamacare was found to be constitutional with a 5–4 vote, an outcome that surprised many. The controversial provision was allowed to stand as a tax rather than a mandate, so individuals could willingly forego purchasing health insurance, but they would be required to pay a tax for doing so. U.S. Supreme Court chief justice John Roberts wrote in his majority opinion, "The federal government does not have the power to order people to buy health insurance.... The federal government does have the power to impose a tax on those without health insurance." The law, which was set to be put into place in 2014, continued to polarize America at all levels.

▮ PRIMARY SOURCE

"HEALTH CARE REFORM 2009: DO WE KNOW WHAT WE DON'T KNOW?"

SYNOPSIS: This article succinctly analyzes Barack Obama's health care reform bill and questions whether it truly addresses the reforms required to improve the overall health index of America.

The most significant discussion of health care reform in the United States in nearly two decades has reached a critical stage with the focus of attention on expanding access to care while at the same time reducing costs and improving outcomes. Ensuring access to care through workable, comprehensive insurance reforms is indeed a worthy goal. But lost in the policy discussion is how best to improve the overall health of Americans.

If the U.S wants to achieve the health indicators of other nations, we need to have an honest discussion about what would get us there. As a nation, we spend far more of our gross domestic product (16 percent) on health care than any other country. Yet we lag far behind in health outcomes. Why?

Let's start with that data from the Organization for Economic Cooperation and Development. International comparisons of developed nations show that the next-highest investment in health care is by Norway, which devotes 9.1 percent of its GDP once all payers are considered. In real U.S. dollars, that's less than $5,000 per person, per year. Hardly a bargain, but consider what they get for that spending: Better life expectancy at birth, lower infant mortality, lower obesity rates. But is it Norway's health care spending and what it buys that leads to better health? Obesity has a stronger link to education than it does to health care spending.

If education affects health status, what about other factors? Accounting for such spending yields a very different picture of return on investment by nation; when other public spending is added to health care spending, the U.S. investment in building health falls far below that

of Norway and other OECD countries. The same variations can be seen within the U.S.

America is far more heterogeneous than most other developed nations, which also plays a role in health and health care. Significant variations in Medicare spending exist per capita by state, particularly at the end of life. But these simple comparisons hide the variations in total health spending and social factors across American communities.

Poverty, which greatly increases the chance of illness, plays an important role in these variations. According to the Census Bureau, 13 percent of Americans (children and adults) live in poverty. In Louisiana and Mississippi, where poverty rates are 19 percent and 21 percent respectively, both states spend less on health care per capita than the U.S. average, while spending more on Medicare beneficiaries than the U.S. average of $7,439.

Why is it then that the health of citizens in these two states lags far behind the nation as a whole? Could it be that once given health insurance and other benefits—by way of reaching the dual entitlements of Medicare and Social Security—when they turn 65 years of age, Louisianans and Mississippians must eventually pay a heavier price for a lifetime of neglected health needs?

In Texas, 16 percent of the population lives in poverty, and per capita health care spending is far below the U.S. average ($4,601 vs. $5,283). Yet Medicare per capita spending in Texas is far greater ($8,292) than the U.S. average.

Babies in all three states have among the lowest life expectancy at birth—not because of what's invested at the age of 65 and beyond, but rather because of what is not invested in children and young adults all of their lives.

States that have low poverty rates and relatively stable investments in health care throughout the lifetime of their citizens often show a very different picture. Vermont, smaller and far less diverse than its southern counterparts, has a poverty rate of 10 percent and spends about $6,000 a year on all patients, including Medicare beneficiaries.

Consider again how all of this matches up against the comparisons to other developed nations. On average, child poverty in OECD nations is 13 percent compared with more than 21 percent in the U.S. (and 5 percent in Norway). In single-parent households in the U.S., child poverty rates come close to 50 percent. While most discussions in the current debate have focused on the cost of clinical care, insurance rates and primary vs. specialty care, we may be missing the bigger picture.

Consider the classic epidemiologic example of matches and lung cancer. People who carry matches are far more likely to develop lung cancer than those who don't. Similarly, nations with mechanisms to ensure access to health care have better health status. However, in both cases, elements may be necessary but not sufficient to lead to the conclusions in question.

None of this argues against reducing waste, expanding insurance coverage or building a system with more primary care providers, all of which are characteristics of healthier nations. What it does indicate is the fallacy of looking at Medicare data as a proxy for health and the importance of a sustained investment in health throughout one's life, not just beginning at age 65 to improve health outcomes.

Whether looking within the U.S. or across OECD countries, the focus of our discussion must go beyond the narrow focus of health care spending in the last decades of life and more closely examine the relationship of health status indicators against investments in health over the lifetimes of individuals. If "reform" ignores these facts, and we only improve access and reduce costs, we are likely to look back in another 20 years and wonder why our nation hasn't become healthier.

FURTHER RESOURCES
Books
Jacobs, Lawrence R., and Theda Skocpol. *Health Care Reform and American Politics: What Everyone Needs to Know*. Rev. ed. New York: Oxford University Press, 2012.

Web Sites
Erbe, Bonnie. "What Is the Actual Number of Americans Without Health Insurance?" *US News & World Report*, August 20, 2009. http://www.usnews.com/opinion/blogs/erbe/2009/08/20/what-is-the-actual-number-of-americans-without-health-insurance (accessed on March 21, 2013).

Lepore, Jill. "Preëxisting Condition." *New Yorker*, December 7, 2009. www.newyorker.com/talk/comment/2009/12/07/091207taco_talk_lepore (accessed on March 21, 2013).

Mears, Bill, and Tom Cohen. "Emotions High After Supreme Court Upholds Health Care Law." *CNN*, June 28, 2012. www.cnn.com/2012/06/28/politics/supreme-court-health-ruling (accessed on March 21, 2013).

"Our History." *Roll Call*. http://corporate.cqrollcall.com/content/54/en/History (accessed on March 21, 2013).

Smith, Emily. "Timeline of the Health Care Law." *CNN*, June 17, 2012. http://www.cnn.com/2012/06/17/politics/health-care-timeline (accessed on March 21, 2013).

"Swine Flu Cases Overestimated?"

Web site article

By: Sharyl Attkisson

Date: October 27, 2009

Source: Attkisson, Sharyl. "Swine Flu Cases Overestimated?" *CBS News*, October 27, 2009. http://www.cbsnews.com/2100-500690_162-5404829.html (accessed on March 21, 2013).

About the Organization: CBS is the acronym for Columbia Broadcasting System, the second largest broadcaster in the world (behind the BBC). Initially a radio broadcasting company, it began making a profit as a television network in 1953. It dominated the top spots of television from 1955 to 1976 with shows like *M*A*S*H* and *All in the Family*. CBS began broadcasting news reports periodically throughout World War II, but it was not until 1948 that the first official nightly newscast was aired. The network launched several award-winning news programs, including *Sixty Minutes*, *48 Hours*, and *Face the Nation*.

INTRODUCTION

On March 28, 2009, four-year-old Edgar Hernandez was diagnosed with swine flu in Mexico. According to the Centers for Disease Control and Prevention (CDC), that is believed to be the same date the first case was diagnosed in the United States. Swine flu refers to a disease that exists in pigs but which can be transmitted to people. The human respiratory infection caused by the H1N1 virus, commonly known as the swine flu, was characterized by the same symptoms as any other flu: fever, cough, sore throat, head and body aches, chills, fatigue, diarrhea, and vomiting. More severe cases experienced symptoms including pneumonia, respiratory failure, and neurological issues such as seizures. Those patients who lived with chronic conditions like asthma and heart disease found their health in rapid decline as these conditions worsened.

The reason this particular strain of flu created a pandemic was because it contained genetic material from human, pig, and bird flu. As such, it was a variety of flu that had never been seen, and humans did not have much natural resistance to it. This lack of immunity leads to quick and easy contagion, with the possibility of symptoms more severe than those caused by common flu strains.

By April 13, 2009, the first known casualty from the swine flu was recorded in Mexico. Eight days later, health officials alerted American doctors about a dangerous, never-before-seen strain of swine flu. Within three days, eight more cases in the United States were confirmed, but concern is limited because the strain responded to two different medications. On April 26, the number of confirmed cases in the United States rose to twenty, and a public health state of emergency was declared. One day later, the World Health Organization raised the alert higher, to two steps below full-blown pandemic. The virus is now believed to be the cause of death in up to 149 cases in Mexico, and dozens of other cases across the globe are confirmed. On April 28, President Barack Obama sought $1.5 billion in emergency funds, and the alert level was raised to five. More cases were confirmed. A Mexican child visiting Texas became the first casualty on U.S. soil on April 29, and the next day, nearly three hundred schools across the country closed to help stall the spread of infection. On May 5, nearly six hundred cases were confirmed in thirty-nine states; within two days, that number increased to more than one thousand.

By May 20, there were more than ten thousand cases of swine flu worldwide, and a pandemic was declared on June 11. It was the first global flu epidemic in forty-one years.

SIGNIFICANCE

By the end of 2009, approximately forty-seven million Americans had contracted swine flu. One of the early estimates of the number of patients with that strain of flu was five million, as reported by the CDC. Within eight months, that number increased by forty-two million. Some health officials believed the outbreak could have been less severe had the H1N1 vaccine been made available sooner and had communication from the CDC to the public been clearer and more direct.

For reasons that remain unclear, the pandemic, which lasted from June 2009 to August 2010, claimed about fifteen times as many lives globally as initially believed. Experts conjecture that the final estimation of deaths—as high as 579,000—was significantly higher than the initial estimate of 18,500 (as reported by the World Health Organization) because the only deaths that can be counted with absolute certainty are those confirmed by lab testing. Many people do not have healthcare, and once a victim dies, evidence of the disease is undetectable. According to the June 26, 2012, issue of the *Lancet Infectious Diseases* journal, researchers confirmed that 80 percent of all confirmed

deaths occurred in people under the age of sixty-five; 30 percent of those victims were healthy prior to contracting the swine flu.

Before the publication of these findings in the *Lancet*, Joseph Kim of Inovio Pharmaceuticals told *U.S. News & World Report* that the world was due for a flu pandemic that could be significantly deadlier than the 2009 outbreak. "I really believe we were lucky in 2009 because the strain that won out was not particularly lethal. Bird flu kills over 60 percent of people that it infects, regardless of health or age. It is a phenomenal killing machine."

Between inaccurate estimates and a lack of health records for all people, there will never be a way to truly know without a doubt just how high the death toll was from the 2009 swine flu pandemic.

PRIMARY SOURCE

"SWINE FLU CASES OVERESTIMATED?"

SYNOPSIS: This article questions the accuracy of cases reported during the swine flu pandemic of 2009.

If you've been diagnosed "probable" or "presumed" 2009 H1N1 or "swine flu" in recent months, you may be surprised to know this: odds are you didn't have H1N1 flu.

In fact, you probably didn't have flu at all. That's according to state-by-state test results obtained in a three-month-long CBS News investigation.

The ramifications of this finding are important. According to the Centers for Disease Control and Prevention (CDC) and Britain's National Health Service, once you have H1N1 flu, you're immune from future outbreaks of the same virus. Those who think they've had H1N1 flu—but haven't—might mistakenly presume they're immune. As a result, they might skip taking a vaccine that could help them, and expose themselves to others with H1N1 flu under the mistaken belief they won't catch it. Parents might not keep sick children home from school, mistakenly believing they've already had H1N1 flu.

Why the uncertainty about who has and who hasn't had H1N1 flu?

In late July, the CDC abruptly advised states to stop testing for H1N1 flu, and stopped counting individual cases. The rationale given for the CDC guidance to forego testing and tracking individual cases was: why waste resources testing for H1N1 flu when the government has already confirmed there's an epidemic?

Some public health officials privately disagreed with the decision to stop testing and counting, telling CBS News that continued tracking of this new and possibly changing virus was important because H1N1 has a different epidemiology, affects younger people more than seasonal flu and has been shown to have a higher case fatality rate than other flu virus strains.

CBS News learned that the decision to stop counting H1N1 flu cases was made so hastily that states weren't given the opportunity to provide input. Instead, on July 24, the Council for State and Territorial Epidemiologists, CSTE, issued the following notice to state public health officials on behalf of the CDC:

"Attached are the Q&As that will be posted on the CDC website tomorrow explaining why CDC is no longer reporting case counts for novel H1N1. CDC would have liked to have run these by you for input but unfortunately there was not enough time before these needed to be posted."

When CDC did not provide us with the material, we filed a Freedom of Information request with the Department of Health and Human Services (HHS). More than two months later, the request has not been fulfilled. We also asked CDC for state-by-state test results prior to halting of testing and tracking, but CDC was again, initially, unresponsive.

While we waited for CDC to provide the data, which it eventually did, we asked all 50 states for their statistics on state lab-confirmed H1N1 prior to the halt of individual testing and counting in July. The results reveal a pattern that surprised a number of health care professionals we consulted. The vast majority of cases were negative for H1N1 as well as seasonal flu, despite the fact that many states were specifically testing patients deemed to be most likely to have H1N1 flu, based on symptoms and risk factors, such as travel to Mexico.

It's unknown what patients who tested negative for flu were actually afflicted with since the illness was not otherwise determined. Health experts say it's assumed the patients had some sort of cold or upper respiratory infection that is just not influenza.

With most cases diagnosed solely on symptoms and risk factors, the H1N1 flu epidemic may seem worse than it is. For example, on Sept. 22, this alarming headline came from Georgetown University in Washington D.C.: "H1N1 Flu Infects Over 250 Georgetown Students."

H1N1 flu can be deadly and an outbreak of 250 students would be an especially troubling cluster. However, the number of sick students came not from lab-confirmed tests but from "estimates" made by counting "students who went to the Student Health Center with flu symptoms, students who called the H1N1 hotline or the Health Center's doctor-on-call, and students who went to the hospital's emergency room."

Without lab testing, it's impossible to know how many of the students actually had H1N1 flu. But the statistical trend indicates it was likely much fewer than 250.

CDC continues to monitor flu in general and H1N1 through "sentinels," which basically act as spot-checks to detect trends around the nation. But at least one state, California, has found value in tracking H1N1 flu in greater detail.

"What we are doing is much more detailed and expensive than what CDC wants," said Dr. Bela Matyas, California's Acting Chief of Emergency Preparedness and Response. "We're gathering data better to answer how severe is the illness. With CDC's fallback position, there are so many uncertainties with who's being counted, it's hard to know how much we're seeing is due to H1N1 flu rather than a mix of influenza diseases generally. We can tell that apart but they can't."

After our conversation with Dr. Matyas, public affairs officials with the California Department of Public Health emphasized to CBS News that they support CDC policy to stop counting individual cases, maintaining that the state has the resources to gather more specific testing data than the CDC.

Because of the uncertainties, the CDC advises even those who were told they had H1N1 to get vaccinated unless they had lab confirmation. "Persons who are uncertain about how they were diagnosed should get the 2009 H1N1 vaccine." ...

However, the CDC recommendation for those who had "probable" or "presumed" H1N1 flu to go ahead and get vaccinated anyway means the relatively small proportion of those who actually did have H1N1 flu will be getting the vaccine unnecessarily. This exposes them to rare but significant side effects, such as paralysis from Guillain-Barre syndrome.

It also uses up vaccine, which is said to be in short supply. The CDC was hoping to have shipped 40 million doses by the end of October, but only about 30 million doses will be available this month.

The CDC did not response to questions from CBS News for this report.

FURTHER RESOURCES
Web Sites

Koebler, Jason. "Global Flu Pandemic 'Inevitable,' Expert Warns." *U.S. News & World Report*, December 24, 2012. www.usnews.com/news/articles/2012/12/24/global-flu-pandemic-inevitable-expert-warns (accessed on March 17, 2013).

LeBlond, Lawrence. "2009 Swine Flu Pandemic Death Toll Much Worse Than Originally Believed." *Red Orbit*, June 26, 2012. www.redorbit.com/news/health/1112645712/2009-swine-flu-pandemic-death-toll-much-worse-than-originally-believed/ (accessed on March 22, 2013).

Shedden, Mary. "Swine Flu Outlook for 2010 Is Slightly Better." *Tampa Bay Online*, December 24, 2009. www2.tbo.com/news/swine-flu/2009/dec/24/swine-flu-outlook-2010-slightly-better-ar-62168/ (accessed on March 22, 2013).

"Timeline: 2009 Swine Flu Outbreak." *NBC News*. www.nbcnews.com/id/30624302/#.UUYz31eweqh (accessed on March 22, 2013).

"U.S. Department of Labor's OSHA Issues Record-breaking Fines to BP"

Press release

By: U.S. Department of Labor

Date: October 30, 2009

Source: U.S. Department of Labor. "U.S. Department of Labor's OSHA Issues Record-breaking Fines to BP." *United States Department of Labor*, October 30, 2009. www.osha.gov/pls/oshaweb/owadisp.show_document?p_table=NEWS_RELEASES&p_id=16674 (accessed on March 22, 2013).

About the Office: The U.S. Department of Labor was established in 1888 as the Bureau of Labor, an office of the Department of the Interior. In 1913, President William Howard Taft elevated the bureau to its current status as a Cabinet department. The agency's responsibilities gradually increased over the course of the twentieth century to include the enforcement of worker safety and rights provisions, the administration of employment services and unemployment relief, and the regulation of labor unions.

INTRODUCTION

The Occupational Safety and Health Administration (OSHA) was established in April 1971 by President Richard Nixon's signing of the Occupational Safety and Health Act of 1970. The agency was created in recognition of the United States' need for an organization to provide comprehensive protection of the nation's workers from the inherent hazards of industry. Under the authority of the U.S. Department of Labor, OSHA was tasked with issuing and enforcing workplace health and safety standards, such as requirements for the use of personal protective equipment, procedures and limits for dangerous chemical exposure, and safe vehicle operation; it also was in charge of administering twenty-one different employee whistleblower statutes, even those not directly related to occupational health and safety. This task was accomplished through the deployment of compliance safety and health officers to the approximately seven million workplaces regulated by OSHA. Compliance officers made routine inspection of work facilities known to present significant danger to their employees—like construction sites, manufacturing plants, and any location that handles or processes volatile chemicals—in addition to surprise inspections of other sites in response to accidents or employee complaints.

OSHA and its representatives were authorized to impose fines on companies found not to be compliant with the agency's safety standards and to assess criminal charges for deliberately or excessively negligent employers. However, these fines were frequently criticized for allegedly being too small to seriously influence the safety measures implemented by large companies, which could cost hundreds of times more than the fines. During the 2000s, the efficacy of OSHA was often called into question by lawmakers as its role as a regulatory agency declined. OSHA was successful in passing only five new safety regulations during the 2000s, one of which was repealed by Congress in 2002. Much of the agency's work during the decade related to protecting disaster relief workers and volunteers by providing safety training and equipment following the September 11, 2001, terrorist attacks, Hurricane Katrina, and other major disaster recovery operations.

OSHA was given the opportunity to change its reputation as a pesky-but-ineffective office on March 23, 2005. That day, the Texas City, Texas, oil refinery, owned by BP Products North America Inc., experienced an explosion and fire that killed 15 workers and injured at least 170 more. The refinery was the third-largest in the world, employing thousands of people and providing a sizable portion of the United States' oil production. Following an investigation, OSHA determined that the explosion was caused by the ignition of combustible liquid that had flowed from a pressurized silo onto the ground. Investigators identified over three hundred safety violations, including failures in equipment maintenance and inspection, risk management procedures, staff training, and safety culture at the refinery, assessing a total fine of $21 million against BP (a record at the time).

Four years later, follow-up inspection conducted by OSHA revealed that BP had not taken sufficient measures to fix the safety code violations identified at the Texas City refinery, resulting in the imposition of an additional $87.43 million in fines. This enormous, record-setting fine carried a condemnation from OSHA officials, decrying the negligence of BP even after its disregard for safety regulations resulted in fifteen deaths. BP was to be handed additional fines for each day that the more than seven hundred safety violations remained unaddressed.

SIGNIFICANCE

Although the unprecedented $87.43 million fine against BP was depicted by OSHA officials as damning and sure to promote compliance with safety regulations, observers noted that the company generated tens of billions of dollars in annual profits, and that the fine thus represented a minimal loss. Still, BP appeared to take decisive action to align its safety policies with those promulgated by OSHA. The company also launched an independent investigation into the source of the 2005 explosion and found that the ultimate cause of the Texas City refinery's relaxed safety culture was caused by an emphasis on occupational safety (individual protection measures like wearing proper safety equipment and proper vehicle operation) over the equally important observance of process safety (procedural protection measures, such as equipment inspection and machine maintenance). OSHA adapted the findings from the independent commission to provide better safety training to other employers.

OSHA continued to receive criticism for not pursuing jail sentences for BP officials, but the controversy was soon overshadowed by accusations that the agency had bent to the desires of food-industry lobbyists in its decision not to regulate worker exposure to diacetyl, a chemical used in the manufacture of artificial butter flavoring. Agency officials responded by asserting that their regulatory power was unduly limited by Congress and the Environmental Protection Agency, producing a minor public debate. BP continued to own and operate the Texas City refinery, albeit in an ostensibly safer manner.

▌ PRIMARY SOURCE

"U.S. DEPARTMENT OF LABOR'S OSHA ISSUES RECORD-BREAKING FINES TO BP"

SYNOPSIS: In this press release, the author describes the fines assessed against the BP oil company for its infractions of OSHA safety requirements.

The U.S. Department of Labor's Occupational Safety and Health Administration (OSHA) today announced it is issuing $87,430,000 in proposed penalties to BP Products North America Inc. for the company's failure to correct potential hazards faced by employees. The fine is the largest in OSHA's history. The prior largest total penalty, $21 million, was issued in 2005, also against BP.

Safety violations at BP's Texas City, Texas, refinery resulted in a massive explosion—with 15 deaths and 170 people injured—in March of 2005. BP entered into a settlement agreement with OSHA in September of that year, under which the company agreed to corrective actions to eliminate potential hazards similar to those that caused the 2005 tragedy. Today's announcement comes at the conclusion of a six-month inspection by OSHA, designed to evaluate the extent to which BP has complied with its obligations under the 2005 agreement and OSHA standards.

"When BP signed the OSHA settlement from the March 2005 explosion, it agreed to take comprehensive action to protect employees. Instead of living up to that commitment, BP has allowed hundreds of potential hazards to continue unabated," said Secretary of Labor Hilda L. Solis. "Fifteen people lost their lives as a result of the 2005 tragedy, and 170 others were injured. An $87 million fine won't restore those lives, but we can't let this happen again. Workplace safety is more than a slogan. It's the law. The U.S. Department of Labor will not tolerate the preventable exposure of workers to hazardous conditions."

For noncompliance with the terms of the settlement agreement, the BP Texas City Refinery has been issued 270 "notifications of failure to abate" with fines totaling $56.7 million. Each notification represents a penalty of $7,000 times 30 days, the period that the conditions have remained unabated. OSHA also identified 439 new willful violations for failures to follow industry-accepted controls on the pressure relief safety systems and other process safety management violations with penalties totaling $30.7 million.

"BP was given four years to correct the safety issues identified pursuant to the settlement agreement, yet OSHA has found hundreds of violations of the agreement and hundreds of new violations. BP still has a great deal of work to do to assure the safety and health of the employees who work at this refinery," said acting Assistant Secretary of Labor for OSHA Jordan Barab.

The BP Texas City Refinery is the third largest refinery in the United States with a refining capacity of 475,000 barrels of crude per day. It is located on a 1,200-acre facility in Texas City, southeast of Houston in Galveston County.

A willful violation exists where an employer has knowledge of a violation and demonstrates either an intentional disregard for the requirements of the Occupational Safety and Health (OSH) Act of 1970, or shows plain indifference to employee safety and health. A penalty of up to $70,000 may be assessed for each willful violation.

A notification of failure to abate can be issued if an employer fails to correct a cited condition and the citation is a final order of the Occupational Safety and Health Review Commission. A penalty of up to $7,000 may be assessed for each day that the violation remains uncorrected.

Under the OSH Act, OSHA's role is to promote safe and healthful working conditions for America's working men and women by setting and enforcing standards, and providing training, outreach and education. For more information, visit http://www.osha.gov.

FURTHER RESOURCES

Books

Moran, Mark. *The OSHA Answer Book*. Orange Park, FL: Safetycertified.com Inc, 2005.

Web Sites

Lyall, Sarah. "At BP, a History of Boldness and Costly Blunders." *New York Times*, July 12, 2010. www.nytimes. com/2010/07/13/business/energy-environment/13bprisk. html?_r=0 (accessed on March 22, 2013).

"Occupational Safety & Health Administration." *United States Department of Labor*. www.osha.gov (accessed on March 22, 2013).

"Reflections on OSHA's History." *United States Department of Labor*. www.osha.gov/history/OSHA_HISTORY_ 3360s.pdf (accessed on March 22, 2013).

"Special Report: 2005 Texas City Explosion." *Houston Chronicle*, 2005. 130.80.29.3/content/chronicle/special/ 05/blast/index.html (accessed on March 22, 2013).

"2010 State Obesity Rates"

Table

By: Centers for Disease Control and Prevention

Date: 2010

Source: "2010 State Obesity Rates." *Centers for Disease Control and Prevention*. http://www.cdc.gov/obesity/ data/trends.html (accessed on March 22, 2013).

About the Organization: Founded in 1946 as the Communicable Diseases Center and renamed in 1967 and again in 1970, the Centers for Disease Control and

Prevention (CDC) is a federal agency under the Department of Health and Human Services that works to protect public health through education, enhancing public awareness, and promoting partnerships between health organizations at all levels of governance. The CDC pledges to the American public to base its decisions on "the highest quality scientific data, openly and objectively derived" and employs approximately fifteen thousand staff. According to its Web site, the CDC focuses on five areas: supporting state and local health departments, improving global health, reforming health policies, strengthening surveillance and epidemiology, and implementing measures to decrease the leading causes of death.

INTRODUCTION

By the 2000s, health officials considered obesity to be epidemic, and with good reason. Obesity—weighing thirty or more pounds over a healthy weight—in America's adult population more than doubled between the 1970s and the 2000s, from 15 percent to 31 percent. That equates to more than seventy-two million people. Childhood obesity also drastically increased: 5 percent of all American children ages two to nineteen were obese in the 1970s; that figure more than tripled to 17 percent in 2008. The World Health Organization called childhood obesity "one of the most serious public health challenges of the twenty-first century."

Obesity, which is measured by a person's body mass index—a weight-to-height ratio—became a major health concern for a number of reasons. As decades passed, there has been a global shift in diet, one that has moved away from whole, healthy foods in favor of a diet consisting of foods high in fat and sugar but low in vitamins, minerals, and micro-nutrients—all things the body needs to be balanced and healthy. Furthermore, people gradually have adopted more sedentary lifestyles. Even children do not get as much physical activity as they once did, many preferring instead to occupy their free time with technology like computers and video games. The advent of the Internet and the World Wide Web made it possible for consumers to shop from their sofas or beds, a computer in their laps. There was very little activity that did not transfer to an online virtual reality.

Obesity had once been associated only with high-income, developed countries, but by the late 2000s, it was prevalent in low- and middle-income countries as well. This trend was particularly concerning because obesity leads to increased risk of heart disease, diabetes, cancer, and other illnesses as it reduces life expectancy and increases health care costs. One government-sponsored study revealed that in 2008, weight-related medical bills cost the United States $147 billion. The CDC table for 2010 obesity rates indicates that no state had an obesity rate lower than 20 percent.

SIGNIFICANCE

Organizations like the CDC continued to follow and study obesity trends in an effort to curb their growth and help Americans choose healthier food and lifestyle alternatives. The challenge with dealing with obesity as a public health issue lay in its abstractness. James Greenberg, an associate professor at the Department of Health and Nutrition Sciences at Brooklyn College of the City University of New York, published an article in 2013 in the medical journal *Obesity*. His research showed that mortality is likely to occur 9.44 years earlier for young and middle-aged obese adults. "There are few reliable measures of its health hazards in the U.S. My objective was to estimate how much earlier mortality is likely to occur for Americans who are overweight and obese, with the end goal of improving awareness of the impact that excess weight has on longevity."

First lady Michelle Obama took her personal interest in health and fitness one step further when she launched the White House's "Let's Move!" initiative on February 9, 2010. The purpose of the program was to disseminate valuable information to parents, school authorities and staff, and other people who work with children. Let's Move! aimed to foster environments that support healthy choices both at home and beyond through national competitions, activities, and challenges. The first lady explained her goal: "This isn't just a policy issue for me. This is a passion. This is my mission. I am determined to work with folks across the country to change the way a generation of kids thinks about food and nutrition." The first lady's husband, President Barack Obama, created the Task Force on Childhood Obesity, the first of its kind, to review every individual policy and program relating to child nutrition and activity as part of the effort to develop a national plan of action for maximizing federal resources.

PRIMARY SOURCE

"2010 STATE OBESITY RATES"

SYNOPSIS: This table indicates the obesity trend in the United States and proves that no state has an obesity rate lower than 20 percent.

2010 State Obesity Rates

Alabama	32.2%
Alaska	24.5%
Arizona	24.3%
Arkansas	30.1%
California	24.0%
Colorado	21.0%
Connecticut	22.5%
Delaware	28.0%
District of Columbia	22.2%
Florida	26.6%
Georgia	29.6%
Hawaii	22.7%
Idaho	26.5%
Illinois	28.2%
Indiana	29.6%
Iowa	28.4%
Kansas	29.4%
Kentucky	31.3%
Louisiana	31.0%
Maine	26.8%
Maryland	27.1%
Massachusetts	23.0%
Michigan	30.9%
Minnesota	24.8%
Mississippi	34.0%
Missouri	30.5%
Montana	23.0%
Nebraska	26.9%
Nevada	22.4%
New Hampshire	25.0%
New Jersey	23.8%
New Mexico	25.1%
New York	23.9%
North Carolina	27.8%
North Dakota	27.2%
Ohio	29.2%
Oklahoma	30.4%
Oregon	26.8%
Pennsylvania	28.6%
Rhode Island	25.5%
South Carolina	31.5%
South Dakota	27.3%
Tennessee	30.8%
Texas	31.0%
Utah	22.5%
Vermont	23.2%
Virginia	26.0%
Washington	25.5%
West Virginia	32.5%
Wisconsin	26.3%
Wyoming	25.1%

FURTHER RESOURCES

Web Sites

"About CDC." *Centers for Disease Control and Prevention.* www.cdc.gov/about/history/ourstory.htm (accessed on March 22, 2013).

"About Let's Move." *Let's Move!* www.letsmove.gov/about (accessed on March 20, 2013).

"Global Strategy on Diet, Physical Activity, and Health: Childhood and Obesity." *World Health Organization.* www.who.int/dietphysicalactivity/childhood/en/ (accessed on March 22, 2013).

Hellmich, Nanci. "Percentage of Overweight Americans Stable." *USA Today,* October 3, 2005. http://usatoday30.usatoday.com/news/health/2005-10-03-weight-trends_x.htm (accessed on March 22, 2013).

Obesity Society. "Obesity Likely to Shorten Life by Nearly 10 Years for Americans." *Herald Online,* March 19, 2013. www.heraldonline.com/2013/03/19/4705597/obesity-likely-to-shorten-life.html (accessed on March 22, 2013).

Executive Summary of the *National HIV/AIDS Strategy for the United States*

Government social policy

By: White House

Date: July 2010

Source: White House. *National HIV/AIDS Strategy for the United States,* July 2010. http://www.whitehouse.gov/sites/default/files/uploads/NHAS.pdf (accessed on March 22, 2013).

About the Organization: The Office of National AIDS Policy (ONAP) was created as a component of the Domestic Policy Council under the George W. Bush administration with the purpose of providing broad policy guidelines and leadership on the government's response to the HIV/AIDS crisis. It works to coordinate a globally integrated approach to the prevention, care, and treatment of HIV/AIDS, and it was directly responsible for developing the 2010 *National HIV/AIDS Strategy for the United States.*

INTRODUCTION

History reveals that by the time the first cases of AIDS were diagnosed in the 1981, some 250,000 Americans were already infected. Acquired Immune Deficiency Syndrome—a disease of the immune system caused by the human immunodeficiency virus (HIV)—was initially believed to be a disease that affected only gay men because everyone with the diagnosis had been gay and male. The press initially referred to AIDS as GRID, an acronym that stood for "gay-related immune deficiency." Within months, patients of Haitian descent as well as women and drug users were being diagnosed not only in the United States, but across the globe, particularly in France and Africa. Clearly the disease was not relegated to gay men, and by 1982, the AIDS name had been assigned to it. Within the boundaries of the United States, the two primary target populations for AIDS were gay men and intravenous drug users. Given this fact, AIDS carried with it a social stigma and left victims feeling alone and without support. America at the time was led by a conservative presidential administration under Republican Ronald Reagan, and a prevailing attitude of intolerance of and prejudice against AIDS patients seriously impeded both scientific progress and public awareness. No one—not private citizens or public officials and politicians—wanted to talk about this frightening, fatal disease that seemed to have infected its victims overnight.

Americans mistakenly believed that only people who engaged in the same activities of gay men and intravenous drug users could be stricken with AIDS, and there was a general consensus that these people got what they deserved. Conservative right-wing religious leaders like Jerry Falwell and Pat Robertson publicly denounced AIDS patients. Falwell, known for his fire-and-brimstone sermons, told his congregation and anyone else who would listen that "AIDS is not just God's punishment for homosexuals, it is God's punishment for the society that tolerates homosexuals." Although this sentiment was not embraced by all Americans, it was certainly the belief of a vocal majority.

But then a newborn baby was diagnosed with AIDS. And then scores of hemophiliacs who had received blood transfusions were infected and diagnosed. And AIDS could no longer be ignored as a punishment. America's blood supply was infected with HIV, but no one in a position of power was willing to take on the public relations nightmare that would ensue, and so thirty-five thousand Americans were infected with HIV through blood transfusions before dealing with the AIDS epidemic became an obvious necessity.

Budget cuts mandated by the Reagan administration virtually tied the hands of the Centers for Disease

Control and Prevention (CDC). Figuring out the origin of AIDS so that scientists could better understand the disease in an effort to prevent and cure it required money at a time when the government cut the budget of the CDC by 25 percent. As the AIDS crisis worsened in Africa in 1984, scientists did what they could with the funding they had and developed an antibody test to determine if a patient had the virus. Around the same time, the first case of virus transmission through breast milk was reported, and by 1987, the antiretroviral drug azidothymidine (AZT) was approved by the Food and Drug Administration (FDA). AZT slowed the development or progress of the disease. That same year, the CDC launched its first AIDS public relations campaign, called "America Responds to AIDS."

The World Health Organization (WHO) declared December 1 to be World AIDS Day in 1988, and in 1990, Congress passed the Americans with Disabilities Act, which protected individuals with disabilities, including those infected or suspected of being infected with HIV or AIDS, from discrimination in the workplace and public places. By 1990, twice as many Americans had died of AIDS as had died in the Vietnam War. By 1991, the tenth anniversary of the discovery of the disease, the CDC reported that one million Americans were infected with HIV and 156,143 deaths had been reported.

Despite increased public awareness, funding, and education, AIDS was reported in the *New York Times* as the leading cause of death among all Americans ages twenty-five to forty-four in 1995. The following year saw much-needed advancement. As new medications were developed and approved by the FDA, doctors were able to treat HIV/AIDS with combination therapy—more than one drug—for the first time, resulting in a drastic decline in the number of AIDS-related deaths. Even so, AIDS was the fourth leading cause of death worldwide in 1999, and the infection rate had doubled in three years.

AIDS research continued to receive funding, but the disease was brutal in scope and death toll. By 2000, the Joint United Nations Programme on HIV/AIDS (UNAIDS) reported that 36.1 million people across the globe were living with HIV/AIDS, and almost 22 million had died of AIDS-related causes since the epidemic began in the early 1980s. Thirteen million children had lost one or both parents to the disease. The medications, while helpful, caused debilitating side effects, and studies showed that 14 percent of newly infected HIV cases in America were already exhibiting resistance to at least one of the antiviral drugs. President George W. Bush used his 2003 State

of the Union Address to announce his Emergency Plan for AIDS Relief (PEPFAR), a five-year, $15 billion initiative to fight HIV/AIDS. A major breakthrough occurred in 2006, when the FDA approved the first anti-HIV drug that could be taken once daily, in the form of a single pill. UNAIDS statistics estimate that thirty-three million people were living with HIV/AIDS by the end of 2007, and the CDC revealed that they had underestimated the number of new HIV infections in 2006 by 40 percent.

The battle against AIDS had seemed more like a dance: one step forward, two steps back. In 2007, hundreds of organizations formally demanded a more accountable, coordinated approach to fighting the disease. It was not a case of apathy or lack of effort; many people, both individuals and organized groups, were working tirelessly to combat the spread of AIDS. The problem lay in the fact that the effort was not collaborative or collective; there was no formal focus. This pressing situation was just one of many inherited by Barack Obama when he was voted into office in November 2008 as America's forty-fourth president.

The White House did not shy away from dealing with the AIDS crisis. In July 2008, *POZ* magazine reported that "the Senate Appropriations Committee voted to allocate $1.4 million earlier this month for the development of a National AIDS Strategy.... A similar provision was included in a bill passed by the House of Representatives Appropriations Committee in June. The funding would support staff, expenses and regional communications to develop and oversee the implementation of an AIDS strategy in the United States." The "Executive Summary" provides a general overview of the resulting strategy that the Obama administration implemented in July 2010.

SIGNIFICANCE

The National Strategy was met with general praise. In a 2012 *Huffington Post* article, journalist Chris Collins credited Obama with opening the lines of communication about a frightening topic. "The strategy changed—and in a way, restarted—the conversation about HIV in the United States. Five years ago, the domestic epidemic seemed invisible, and President Obama should be applauded for making it a priority in policy and funding."

Collins pointed out that while the original principles of the strategy remained immovable and important, the context of the document had changed drastically in within the two years it had since its development. The federal government had already shown that it could coordinate multiple efforts in the very creation of the strategy itself. Improvements in

President Barack Obama delivers remarks on the National HIV/AIDS Strategy at the White House on July 14, 2010. © AP IMAGES/CAROLYN KASTER.

health care made a significant improvement in places like Massachusetts. Health reform legislation in that state made it possible for more than 98 percent of its residents to have health insurance. As a result, HIV infection rates had decreased by 45 percent between 2000 and 2009. It was one of the metropolitan areas where syringe exchange programs were reinstated after a twenty-year ban. These changes had measurable outcomes; they were evidence based. San Francisco experienced much the same change because funding was aimed at prevention, stigma was lessened if not erased, and testing was ramped up so that treatment could start earlier. It was a win-win for everyone.

The National Strategy empowered state and local leadership by letting them make decisions about things like Medicaid participation and investment in HIV services, including treatment access and testing.

As of 2013, there were still facets of the strategy that had yet to be realized, such as full-scale media campaigns to fight prejudice and misinformation, but the initiative was written to leave room for growth and amendment. In addition to the National Strategy, a PEPFAR initiative called the Blueprint for an

AIDS-Free Generation, was released in January 2013 by Secretary of State Hillary Clinton. Battling the AIDS pandemic continued to be a priority in the second decade of the century, but success and victory were at the mercy of yet more budget cuts. Global health was an investment that needed to be made sooner rather than later, but with the risk of funding cuts to PEPFAR, the outcome was uncertain.

PRIMARY SOURCE

EXECUTIVE SUMMARY OF THE *NATIONAL HIV/AIDS STRATEGY FOR THE UNITED STATES*

SYNOPSIS: This document provides an overview of the major points of President Obama's strategy for combating HIV/AIDS.

When one of our fellow citizens becomes infected with the human immunodeficiency virus (HIV) every nine-and-a-half minutes, the epidemic affects all Americans. It has been nearly thirty years since the first cases of HIV garnered the world's attention. Without treatment, the virus slowly debilitates a person's immune system until they succumb to illness. The epidemic has claimed the lives of nearly 600,000 Americans and affects many more. Our Nation is at a crossroads. We have the knowledge and tools needed to slow the spread of HIV infection and improve the health of people living with HIV. Despite this potential, however, the public's sense of urgency associated with combating the epidemic appears to be declining. In 1995, 44 percent of the general public indicated that HIV/AIDS was the most urgent health problem facing the Nation, compared to only 6 percent in March 2009. While HIV transmission rates have been reduced substantially over time and people with HIV are living longer and more productive lives, approximately 56,000 people become infected each year and more Americans are living with HIV than ever before. Unless we take bold actions, we face a new era of rising infections, greater challenges in serving people living with HIV, and higher health care costs.

President Obama committed to developing a *National HIV/AIDS Strategy* with three primary goals: 1) reducing the number of people who become infected with HIV, 2) increasing access to care and optimizing health outcomes for people living with HIV, and 3) reducing HIV-related health disparities. To accomplish these goals, we must undertake a more coordinated national response to the HIV epidemic. The Strategy is intended to be a concise plan that will identify a set of priorities and strategic action steps tied to measurable outcomes. Accompanying the Strategy is a Federal Implementation Plan that outlines the specific steps to be taken by various Federal agencies to support the high-level priorities outlined in the Strategy. This is an ambitious plan that will challenge us to meet all of the goals that we set. The job, however, does not fall to the Federal Government alone, nor should it. Success will require the commitment of all parts of society, including State, tribal and local governments, businesses, faith communities, philanthropy, the scientific and medical communities, educational institutions, people living with HIV, and others. The vision for the *National HIV/AIDS Strategy* is simple:

> The United States will become a place where new HIV infections are rare and when they do occur, every person, regardless of age, gender, race/ethnicity, sexual orientation, gender identity or socio-economic circumstance, will have un-fettered access to high quality, life-extending care, free from stigma and discrimination.

Reducing New HIV Infections

More must be done to ensure that new prevention methods are identified and that prevention resources are more strategically concentrated in specific communities at high risk for HIV infection. Almost half of all Americans know someone living with HIV (43 percent in 2009). Our national commitment to ending the HIV epidemic, however,

cannot be tied only to our own perception of how closely HIV affects us personally. Just as we mobilize the country to support cancer prevention and research whether or not we believe that we are at high risk of cancer, or just as we support investments in public education whether or not we have children, success at fighting HIV calls on all Americans to help us sustain a long-term effort against HIV. While anyone can become infected with HIV, some Americans are at greater risk than others. This includes gay and bisexual men of all races and ethnicities, Black men and women, Latinos and Latinas, people struggling with addiction, including injection drug users, and people in geographic hot spots, including the United States South and Northeast, as well as Puerto Rico and the U.S. Virgin Islands. By focusing our efforts in communities where HIV is concentrated, we can have the biggest impact in lowering all communities' collective risk of acquiring HIV.

We must also move away from thinking that one approach to HIV prevention will work, whether it is condoms, pills, or information. Instead, we need to develop, evaluate, and implement effective prevention strategies and combinations of approaches including efforts such as expanded HIV testing (since people who know their status are less likely to transmit HIV), education and support to encourage people to reduce risky behaviors, the strategic use of medications and biomedical interventions (which have allowed us, for example, to nearly eliminate HIV transmission to newborns), the development of vaccines and microbicides, and the expansion of evidence-based mental health and substance abuse prevention and treatment programs. It is essential that all Americans have access to a shared base of factual information about HIV. The Strategy also provides an opportunity for working together to advance a public health approach to sexual health that includes HIV prevention as one component. To successfully reduce the number of new HIV infections, there must be a concerted effort by the public and private sectors, including government at all levels, individuals, and communities, to:

- Intensify HIV prevention efforts in communities where HIV is most heavily concentrated.
- Expand targeted efforts to prevent HIV infection using a combination of effective, evidence-based approaches.
- Educate all Americans about the threat of HIV and how to prevent it.

Increasing Access to Care and Improving Health Outcomes for People Living with HIV

As a result of our ongoing investments in research and years of clinical experience, people living with HIV can enjoy long and healthy lives. To make this a reality for everyone, it is important to get people with HIV into care early after infection to protect their health and reduce their potential of transmitting the virus to others. For these reasons, it is important that all people living with HIV are well supported in a regular system of care. The *Affordable Care Act*, which will greatly expand access to insurance coverage for people living with HIV, will provide a platform for improvements in health care coverage and quality. High risk pools are available immediately. High risk pools will be established in every state to provide coverage to uninsured people with chronic conditions. In 2014, Medicaid will be expanded to all lower income individuals (below 133% of the Federal poverty level, or about $15,000 for a single individual in 2010) under age 65. Uninsured people with incomes up to 400% of the Federal poverty level (about $43,000 for a single individual in 2010) will have access to Federal tax credits and the opportunity to purchase private insurance coverage through competitive insurance exchanges. New consumer protections will better protect people with private insurance coverage by ending discrimination based on health status and pre-existing conditions. Gaps in essential care and services for people living with HIV will continue to need to be addressed along with the unique biological, psychological, and social effects of living with HIV. Therefore, the Ryan White HIV/AIDS Program and other Federal and State HIV-focused programs will continue to be necessary after the law is implemented. Additionally, improving health outcomes requires continued investments in research to develop safer, cheaper, and more effective treatments. Both public and private sector entities must take the following steps to improve service delivery for people living with HIV:

- Establish a seamless system to immediately link people to continuous and coordinated quality care when they are diagnosed with HIV.
- Take deliberate steps to increase the number and diversity of available providers of clinical care and related services for people living with HIV.
- Support people living with HIV with co-occurring health conditions and those who have challenges meeting their basic needs, such as housing.

Reducing HIV-Related Health Disparities

The stigma associated with HIV remains extremely high and fear of discrimination causes some Americans to avoid learning their HIV status, disclosing their status, or accessing medical care. Data indicate that HIV disproportionately affects the most vulnerable in our society—those Americans who have less access to prevention and treatment services and, as a result, often have poorer health outcomes. Further, in some heavily affected communities, HIV may not be viewed as a primary concern, such as in communities experiencing problems with crime, unemployment, lack of housing, and other pressing issues. Therefore, to successfully

address HIV, we need more and better community-level approaches that integrate HIV prevention and care with more comprehensive responses to social service needs. Key steps for the public and private sector to take to reduce HIV-related health disparities are:

- Reduce HIV-related mortality in communities at high risk for HIV infection.
- Adopt community-level approaches to reduce HIV infection in high-risk communities.
- Reduce stigma and discrimination against people living with HIV.

Achieving a More Coordinated National Response to the HIV Epidemic in the United States

The Nation can succeed at meeting the President's goals. It will require the Federal Government and State, tribal and local governments, however, to do some things differently. Foremost is the need for an unprecedented commitment to collaboration, efficiency, and innovation. We also must be prepared to adjust course as needed. This Strategy is intended to complement other related efforts across the Administration. For example, the *President's Emergency Plan for AIDS Relief (PEPFAR)* has taught us valuable lessons about fighting HIV and scaling up efforts around the world that can be applied to the domestic epidemic. The *President's National Drug Control Strategy* serves as a blueprint for reducing drug use and its consequences, and the *Federal Strategic Plan to Prevent and End Homelessness* focuses efforts to reduce homelessness and increase housing security. The White House Office of National AIDS Policy (ONAP) will work collaboratively with the Office of National Drug Control Policy and other White House offices, as well as relevant agencies to further the goals of the Strategy. The Strategy is intended to promote greater investment in HIV/AIDS, but this is not a budget document. Nonetheless, it will inform the Federal budget development process within the context of the fiscal goals that the President has articulated. The United States currently provides more than $19 billion in annual funding for domestic HIV prevention, care, and research, and there are constraints on the magnitude of any potential new investments in the Federal budget. The Strategy should be used to refocus our existing efforts and deliver better results to the American people within current funding levels, as well as to highlight the need for additional investments. Our national progress will require sustaining broader public commitment to HIV, and this calls for more regular communications to ensure transparency about whether we are meeting national goals. Key steps are to:

- Increase the coordination of HIV programs across the Federal government and between federal agencies and state, territorial, tribal, and local governments.

- Develop improved mechanisms to monitor and report on progress toward achieving national goals.

This Strategy provides a basic framework for moving forward. With government at all levels doing its part, a committed private sector, and leadership from people living with HIV and affected communities, the United States can dramatically reduce HIV transmission and better support people living with HIV and their families.

FURTHER RESOURCES

Books

Barnett, Tony, and Alan Whiteside. *AIDS in the Twenty-First Century: Disease and Globalization.* New York: Palgrave Macmillan, 2002.

Harden, Victoria. *AIDS at 30.* Dulles, VA: Potomac Books, 2012.

Web Sites

Collins, Chris. "That National HIV/AIDS Strategy at Two: The Beginnings of Reform, and a Glimpse of Success." *Huffington Post,* July 12, 2012. www.huffingtonpost. com/chris-collins/hiv-america_b_1666335.html (accessed on March 22, 2013).

Press, Bill. "Press: The Sad Legacy of Jerry Falwell." *Milford Daily News,* May 18, 2007. www.milforddailynews.com/ opinion/x1987843539 (accessed on March 22, 2013).

"Senate Committee Approves Funding for National AIDS Strategy." *POZ,* July 21, 2008. www.poz.com/articles/ senate_aids_strategy_1_14947.shtml (accessed on March 22, 2013).

"Thirty Year of HIV/AIDS: Snapshots of an Epidemic." *amfAR.* www.amfar.org/thirty-years-of-hiv/aids-snap-shots-of-an-epidemic/ (accessed on March 22, 2013).

10 Religion

Chronology

Important Events in Religion, 2000–2009

2000

- On March 29, the Central Conference of American Rabbis (Reform Judaism) votes to allow rabbis to perform a marriage ritual between people of the same sex.

- On June 19, the Supreme Court rules 6–3 in *Santa Fe Independent School District v. Doe* to disallow student-led prayer, such as in opening invocations, at public school-sanctioned sporting events.

- On June 28, the Supreme Court rules 5–4 in *Boy Scouts of America v. Dale* that the Boy Scouts of America was not discriminating by choosing to "forbid membership to homosexuals."

- On June 28, the Supreme Court rules 6–3 in *Mitchell v. Helms* that a government-funded program can lend computers to parochial schools.

- On August 6, Democratic presidential candidate Al Gore of Tennessee selects Connecticut senator Joseph Lieberman to be his running mate, the first Jewish candidate to run on a major national presidential ticket.

- On October 12, the USS *Cole* is attacked by al Qaeda operatives in the Yemeni port of Aden. Seventeen sailors are killed and thirty-nine injured.

- On October 20, former president Jimmy Carter announces that he is renouncing his membership in the Southern Baptist Convention (SBC) because of its increasingly conservative shift.

- On October 30, delegates at the Baptist General Convention of Texas vote to shift more than $5 million in funding away from SBC and into Texas seminaries.

2001

- On January 20, after contentious recounts and court appeals, George W. Bush is inaugurated as the forty-third president of the United States, having been elected largely with the support of the Christian Coalition and evangelical Christians.

- On January 26, *Left Behind: The Movie*, a Christian film about the "rapture" based on a series of books of the same title by Tim LaHaye and Jerry Jenkins, premieres in select theaters.

- On January 29, President Bush creates the White House Office of Faith-Based and Community Initiatives by executive order, committing tax dollars to social programs led by religious and nonprofit organizations.

- On March 12, five leaders of the extremist antigovernment Greater Ministries International (Tampa, Florida) are convicted of federal conspiracy and fraud for a Ponzi scheme that amassed more than $500 million, starting in 1993, and swindled nearly 18,000 people.

- On March 13, the Hartford Seminary in Connecticut releases the survey Faith Communities in the United States Today, a study of 14,301 congregations, the largest-ever study of congregational activity up to that point; it concludes that most congregations maintain allegiance to their denominations.

- On June 11, the Supreme Court rules 6–3 in *Good News Club, Inc. v. Milford Central School* that public schools must allow religious groups access to facilities for the purpose of after-school activities.

- On August 9, President Bush agrees to allow federal funding for limited stem-cell research on previously extracted embryos but maintains a ban on any new extractions.

- On August 11, Mark S. Hanson is elected presiding bishop of the Evangelical Lutheran Church in America (ELCA).

- On September 11, nineteen al Qaeda operatives hijack four planes, committing the largest terrorist attack in U.S. history. Two airplanes, one leaving out of Newark and the other from Boston, were redirected and struck the World Trade Center towers, destroying both. A third was redirected to the Pentagon where it crashed, while the fourth, believed to have been en route to Washington, D.C., was brought down by passengers midflight over Shanksville, Pennsylvania.

- On October 22, the American Religious Identification Survey is released by the Graduate Center of the City University of New York, a phone survey of 50,281 American households between February and

June of 2001. The study is a follow-up to the 1990 National Survey of Religious Identification.

- On November 14, aid workers Dayna Curry and Heather Mercer (along with two aid workers from Australia and four from Germany) are freed from the Taliban by troops of the Northern Alliance in Afghanistan after one hundred days of captivity; they were charged with having violated Taliban law by promoting Christianity.

2002

- In June, the United States Conference of Catholic Bishops releases the *Charter for the Protection of Children & Young People*, a "zero tolerance" policy that ends the former policy of rehabilitation and reassignment of clergy accused of sexual abuse of minors. The body also releases a list of *Essential Norms for Diocesan/Eparchial Policies Dealing with Allegations of Sexual Abuse of Minors by Priests or Deacons.*

- On June 27, the Supreme Court decides 5–4 in *Zelman v. Simmons-Harris* that a Cleveland school district is not in violation of the establishment clause by allowing state-subsidized voucher money to go to private schools run by religious organizations.

- On November 1, Rick Warren's best seller *The Purpose Driven Life* is published; more than 30 million copies will be sold.

- On November 5, spurred by religious conservatives, Republicans gain control of Congress by winning a majority in the Senate and expanding their majority in the House.

- On December 13, Bernard Francis Law resigns as archbishop of the Catholic Diocese of Boston.

2003

- On March 18, Dan Brown's novel *The Da Vinci Code* is released in hardback. The book is controversial because it raises questions about the possibility that Jesus had married Mary Magdalene and fathered children.

- On April 27, after nine seasons on the air, the television series *Touched by an Angel* airs its final episode.

- On June 26, the Supreme Court rules 6–3 in *Lawrence v. Texas* that a ban on sodomy in Texas is unconstitutional.

- On August 5, the Reverend Gene Robinson, an openly practicing homosexual, is elected bishop of the Episcopal Church in New Hampshire.

- On August 23, Joseph L. Druce murders defrocked pedophile priest John J. Geoghan, plaintiff in the Boston Catholic Church sex scandal, in his prison cell.

- On September 9, the Catholic Diocese of Boston settles with victims in the Geoghan sexual-abuse case for $85 million.

- On September 26, the television series *Joan of Arcadia* premieres on CBS and runs for two seasons.

- On November 5, President Bush signs a ban on partial-birth abortions, after Congress attempted to pass a similar measure twice under President Bill Clinton, who vetoed it both times.

- On November 12, an ethics panel removes Alabama chief justice Roy Moore from office for refusing to remove a monument to the Ten Commandments from Alabama's judicial building after it was ruled to be a violation of the establishment clause of the constitution.

2004

- On January 21, *Saved!* debuts at the Sundance Film Festival.

- In February, Bishop Roger Mahoney of the Orange County Diocese in Los Angeles, California, issues the *Report to the People of God: Clergy Sexual Abuse in the Archdiocese of Los Angeles, 1930–2003*. He also begins the Safeguard the Children program.

- On February 25, Mel Gibson's *The Passion of the Christ* is released in theaters.

- On July 14, the U.S. Senate defeats 50–48 a proposed ban on gay marriage.

- In October, Joel Osteen's book *Your Best Life Now* is released, and his ministry, Lakewood Church, moves to the Compaq Center, former arena for the NBA's Houston Rockets.

- On November 5, Phyllis B. Anderson is elected president of Pacific Lutheran Theological Seminary, the first woman to head a Lutheran seminary in the United States.

- On December 26, a magnitude-nine earthquake erupts in the Indian Ocean, causing a tsunami that eventually kills more than 200,000 in Sri Lanka, India, Indonesia, and Thailand. Relief efforts from people of all faiths around the world pour into the devastated region.

- On December 31, William Tyndale College, a private Christian school in Michigan, announces it will have to close its doors, citing lack of enrollment.

2005

- On January 3, the Catholic Diocese of Orange County, California, settles with eighty-seven plaintiffs in a church sexual-abuse case for $100 million.

- On February 7, *Time* publishes its list of the "25 Most Influential Evangelicals."

- On February 11, Robert D. Fay, Kelvin Iguabita, Bernard Lane, and Robert Ward are defrocked by the Vatican for their individual involvement in sexual-abuse scandals.

- On March 18, after years of living in a persistent vegetative state, doctors remove Terri Schiavo's feeding tube after Circuit Judge George Greer rules against last-minute efforts by Florida congressional officials to keep her on life support contrary to the wishes of Schiavo's husband, Michael. The case garnered media attention nationwide and divided people from all across the religious spectrum over the right to life.

- On April 2, Pope John Paul II dies.

- On April 19, Cardinal Joseph Ratzinger is elected pope, taking the name Benedict XVI.

- On June 22, Billy Graham announces that his three-day event (June 24–26) at Flushing Meadows Corona Park will be his final crusade in America.

- On June 27, in two similar cases, *McCreary County v. ACLU of Kentucky* and *Van Orden v. Perry*, the Supreme Court issues seemingly opposing decisions on the display of the Ten Commandments in courthouses.

- In July, the Antiochian Orthodox Christian Archdiocese of North America leaves the National Council of Churches (NCC) over policies and statements by other NCC denominations regarding homosexuality.

- On July 28, the Fiqh Council of North America, backed by several other major Muslim organizations, issues a general fatwa against terrorism and extremism.

- On August 29, Hurricane Katrina, one of the five deadliest hurricanes in U.S. history, strikes the coast of the Gulf of Mexico, causing record destruction in New Orleans, Louisiana. People of all faiths dedicate relief efforts to the region.

- On September 17, Rick Warren launches his "P.E.A.C.E. Plan," an international missionary effort.

- On December 9, the movie *The Chronicles of Narnia: The Lion, the Witch, and the Wardrobe*, based on the Christian allegory by C. S. Lewis, is released in theaters.

2006

- On February 8, eighty-six leaders of Evangelical churches sign a letter—"Climate Change: An Evangelical Call for Action"—aimed at the National Association of Evangelicals and Congress to address issues of climate change. The letter is part of the larger "Evangelical Climate Initiative."

- On March 12, the television series *Big Love* premieres on Home Box Office (HBO) and runs for five seasons, winning a Golden Globe, Writer's Guild Award, and BMI Film & Television Award.

- On April 6, the National Geographic Society announces the translation and release of an ancient Coptic manuscript found in the 1970s that features the "Gospel of Judas." Written by a Gnostic sect of Christianity in the second or third century, the Gospel provides an alternate view of Jesus' crucifixion, in which Christ asks Judas to betray him and gives him prominence among apostles.

- On April 29, delegates from the Pacific Southwest region of American Baptist Churches (ABC), USA, vote to withdraw from the ABC, mostly due to differences over the issue of homosexuality.

- On May 19, the film *The Da Vinci Code*, based on Dan Brown's best-selling novel, is released in theaters.

- In October, Joel Osteen's *Become a Better You* is published.

- On November 2, Ted Haggard is accused by prostitute Mike Jones of homosexual relations and drug use. Haggard resigns as head of the National Association of Evangelicals and is subsequently fired from New Life Church in Colorado Springs.

- On November 4, Katharine Jefferts Schori is invested as presiding bishop of the Episcopal Church.

- On November 7, Keith Maurice Ellison wins Minnesota's fifth district House seat, becoming the first Muslim (having converted from Catholicism) to serve in Congress in the United States.

- On December 6, the Committee on Jewish Law and Standards (Conservative Judaism) approves the responsum "Homosexuality, Human Dignity, and Halakha," making it officially legal for a Jewish rabbi to officiate a marriage between same-sex partners.

2007

- On March 10, the Board of Directors of the National Association of Evangelicals affirms its support for Vice President Richard Cizik, responding to a letter signed by Christian conservatives such as James Dobson, Gary Bauer, and Tony Perkins that criticized Cizik's position of "creation care," which supports the view that humans are contributing to global warming.

- On March 13, Toba Spitzer is elected president of the Reconstructionist Rabbinical Assembly; she is the first openly gay person to head a rabbinical organization.

- On April 18, the Supreme Court rules 5–4 in *Gonzales v. Carhart* that the Partial-Birth Abortion Ban Act (2003) is constitutional.

- On May 31, the Billy Graham Library is dedicated in Charlotte, North Carolina.

- On July 27, the Mormon Church posts on its website the contents of a new pamphlet, "God Loveth His Children," that addresses the condition of homosexuality. While it maintains the distinction between same-sex attraction and acts, it softens the language used to describe homosexual tendencies, emphasizing a renewed commitment to the church and God.

- On September 24, four streets in Brooklyn, New York, are plastered with anti-Semitic fliers and graffiti.

- On September 25, Warren Jeffs, leader of the Fundamentalist Church of Jesus Christ of Latter-Day Saints in Salt Lake City, is found guilty on two counts of being an accomplice to rape. He is subsequently sentenced to two consecutive sentences of five years to life in prison.

- On October 13, the declaration "A Common Word between Us and You" is issued from 138 clerics of the Muslim faith in the United States, making a call for open dialogue and mutual understanding between leaders of Islam and Christianity.

- On November 23, Richard Roberts resigns as chancellor of Oral Roberts University over allegations of misuse of university funds.

2008

- On February 8, Thomas S. Monson is named president of the Church of Jesus Christ of Latter-Day Saints, replacing Gordon B. Hinckley, who had died the week before.

- On February 25, the Pew Forum on Religion & Public Life releases the results of its U.S. Religious Landscape Survey, compiled from interviews with more than 35,000 adults from May 8 to August 13.

- On March 14, in response to media scrutiny of controversial Reverend Jeremiah Wright, then-presidential candidate Barack Obama removes him

from his campaign staff and denounces his incendiary statements, while still affirming his support of Wright, who had ministered to Obama at Chicago's Trinity United Church of Christ.

- On April 3, Texas authorities enter the Yearning for Zion Ranch, part of the Fundamentalist Church of Jesus Christ of Latter-day Saints, in response to an anonymous phone call from a sixteen-year-old girl claiming to have been sexually abused by a fifty-year-old man; officials subsequently remove all 416 children, citing a dangerous environment.

- On April 14–19, Pope Benedict XVI visits the United States, making stops in Washington, D.C., and New York City for open-air masses at Nationals Park and Yankee Stadium, respectively.

- On May 15, in response to a lengthy lawsuit brought forth by gay-marriage advocates against the state, the California Supreme Court rules Proposition 22 (2000), which defines marriage as only being between a man and a woman, unconstitutional.

- On May 16, *The Chronicles of Narnia: Prince Caspian* is released in theaters.

- On May 22, Arizona senator John McCain repudiates Reverend John Hagee's endorsement of McCain in the presidential race, in response to the release of a sermon that attributes the Holocaust to God's plan.

- On July 29, Yale hosts the conference "Loving God and Neighbor in Word and Deed," the first of the "Common Word" meetings aimed at improving dialogue between Muslims and Christians.

- On August 16, Rick Warren hosts the "Civil Forum on the Presidency" at his Saddleback Church, where presidential candidates Barack Obama and John McCain speak on social issues and faith.

- On October 1, Bill Maher's documentary *Religulous* (a comedic mocking of organized religion) is released in theaters.

- On October 12–15, the second "Common Word" conference for Muslim-Christian dialogue is held at Cambridge University, featuring seventeen Muslim and nineteen Christian theologians.

- On November 4, voters in California ratify Proposition 8, which repeals California's decision to legalize same-sex marriage. The Mormon Church is credited with the majority of the financial support for Proposition 8 and its subsequent passage.

- On November 13, Doug Lockhart is appointed president and CEO of the International Bible Society and Send the Light (IBS-STL) North America, and

Scott Bolinder is appointed president of IBS-STL Global.

- On November 17, due to the economic recession, the Christian ministry Focus on the Family announces that it will have to lay off 149 people and cut an additional 53 vacant positions.

2009

- On January 20, Rick Warren, an opponent of gay marriage, delivers the invocation at President Obama's inauguration, upsetting many gay-rights activists. One week prior to the inauguration, Obama had asked openly homosexual Episcopal bishop Gene Robinson to deliver the invocation at an inaugural celebration in front of the Lincoln Memorial, a move seen as a concession to gay-rights groups.

- On February 5, at the National Prayer Breakfast, President Obama announces he will continue the White House Office of Faith-Based Initiatives instituted by President Bush, broadening its scope and renaming it the White House Office of Faith-Based and Neighborhood Partnerships.

- On February 25, the Supreme Court rules unanimously in *Pleasant Grove City v. Summum* that a city in Utah did not restrict the free speech of a religious sect (Summum) when it was denied placement of a new monument next to a monument of the Ten Commandments in a public park.

- On March 9, President Obama lifts the ban on federal funding of stem-cell research.

- On March 9, Trinity College in Hartford, Connecticut, releases the American Religious Identification Survey 2008, a study of 54,461 Americans carried out between February and November of 2008.

- On June 24, the Anglican Church of North America, a new province of the Anglican Communion led by conservatives who want to break from the Episcopal Church, installs Reverend Robert Duncan as its first archbishop.

- On July 14–15, the 76th General Convention of the Episcopal Church votes to allow ordination and marriage of homosexuals, further straining relations with its parent body, the Global Anglican Communion.

- On August 7, the American Jewish Congress criticizes conservative commentator Rush Limbaugh for comparing President Obama to Adolf Hitler.

- On August 21, the ELCA votes to allow "monogamous" partners in a committed same-sex relationship to be ordained as ministers. It is the largest mainstream Protestant denomination to make such a decision. One result of the decision is the intent of the Lutheran Coalition for Renewal (CORE), conservative Lutherans who are dissatisfied with the ELCA's decisions on homosexuality, to form the North American Lutheran Church.

- On September 1, Biblica, the publishing company that owns the copyright to the New International Version of the Bible, and Zondervan announce that a new translation will debut in 2011, incorporating changes in English-language use, gender-neutral pronouns, and scholarship on biblical history.

- On October 7, Georgetown University hosts the fourth "Common Word" conference that serves as a forum for interfaith dialogue between Christians and Muslims.

- On November 5, U.S. Army major Nidal Malik Hasan kills thirteen people and injures thirty-one in a shooting spree at Fort Hood, Texas.

"A Day of Terror: The Ties; in U.S., Echoes of Rift of Muslims and Jews"

Newspaper article

By: Laurie Goodstein

Date: September 12, 2001

Source: Goodstein, Laurie. "A Day of Terror: The Ties; in U.S., Echoes of Rift of Muslims and Jews." *New York Times*, September 12, 2001. www.nytimes. com/2001/09/12/us/a-day-of-terror-the-ties-in-us-echoes-of-rift-of-muslims-and-jews.html?scp=27& sq=muslims&st=nyt (accessed on March 22, 2013).

About the Newspaper: The *New York Times* was founded in 1851 as a concise, four-page summary of daily news items. News mogul Adolph S. Ochs acquired the paper in 1896, expanding its scope and size. By the turn of the twentieth century, the *New York Times* was the pre-eminent U.S. newspaper, acclaimed for its objective reporting of "All the News That's Fit to Print." In 1905, the popularity and importance of the paper was memorialized by the City of New York, which called its new public square "Times Square," in honor of the newspaper. The paper's investigative reporting on official and political affairs has always been a trademark, garnering the journalism staff more than one hundred Pulitzer Prizes for its coverage of wars and governments—most notably for its publication of the "Pentagon Papers," leaked documents attesting to the mishandling and uncertainty of the Vietnam War. The *New York Times* remains the nation's most prestigious and important newspaper, and continues to be owned and operated by descendants of Ochs.

INTRODUCTION

On the morning of September 11, 2001, nineteen men, affiliated with the al-Qaeda terrorist network, hijacked four U.S. passenger jets, in what would become the most destructive terrorist attack in the nation's history. At 8:45 AM Eastern Daylight Time, the first aircraft, American Airlines Flight 11, was piloted by its hijackers into the north tower of New York City's World Trade Center (WTC; also known as the Twin Towers), punching a hole in the building and immediately setting it ablaze. Eighteen minutes later, United Airlines Flight 175 was flown into the south tower of the WTC, causing an explosion and setting it on fire. At 9:43, American Airlines Flight 77 crashed into the Pentagon in Arlington County,

Virginia, prompting immediate evacuation. At 10:10, the final aircraft, United Airlines Flight 93, plummeted into a field in rural Somerset County, Pennsylvania, after passengers successfully regained control of the plane and redirected it from its intended target (thought to be either the White House or U.S. Capitol Building). All 227 passengers aboard the flights, as well as the 19 hijackers, were killed.

As news organizations scrambled to collect information on the details of the attacks, the nation reeled at initial reports. President George W. Bush appeared on television, issuing an emergency broadcast notifying the public that the events of the morning had been the work of terrorists. People around the world crowded around televisions and radios as it was reported that the south tower had collapsed, soon followed by the north, covering downtown New York in a haze of smoke and debris. As Washington, D.C., and New York City were evacuated, firefighters and emergency relief personnel flooded the impacted area, rushing into the burning towers in an attempt to rescue the thousands of people trapped inside. For the first time in the nation's history, all flights within the United States were grounded and an indefinite hold was placed on aviation. In the evening, fire from the burning Twin Towers spread to the nearby WTC Building 7, which proceeded to collapse around 5:00 PM. The fire in the Pentagon continued throughout the night, as did the rescue efforts of New York City disaster workers, policemen, and firefighters. Although definitive casualty statistics were not available until the end of the month, CNN eventually confirmed a total of 2,977 deaths caused by the attacks, representing citizens of almost one hundred nations. Of those killed, approximately two hundred died falling or jumping from the burning Twin Towers, and over four hundred of them were rescue workers killed by fire, smoke inhalation, or falling rubble. The rest were killed by the initial impact or were trapped inside the various structures damaged by the attacks, which included several buildings surrounding the World Trade Center.

In the wake of the attacks, while smoke still hung in the air and thousands of people were still searching for their loved ones, fear and panic eclipsed common sense and decency. Laurie Goodstein's *New York Times* article captured the spirit of the city just hours after the Towers tumbled.

SIGNIFICANCE

By the morning of September 12, the Federal Bureau of Investigation (FBI) had identified all nineteen of the hijackers, thanks to the discovery of luggage that had not been placed aboard one of the aircraft used in the attacks. Fifteen of the men were determined to be Saudi Arabian nationals, two as citizens of the United Arab Emirates, one as an Egyptian, and the last as a Jordanian. The ensuing investigation quickly linked the men to al-Qaeda, a radical Islamic terrorist organization operating in the Middle East. It was discovered that Osama bin Laden, founder and leader of al-Qaeda, had orchestrated the attacks, supplying the hijackers with training, supplies, and a coordinated task, as well as providing transportation and refuge across the world. Bin Laden had expressed vehemence towards the United States for decades and had issued a condemnation of the nation based on the principles of his interpretation of Islam. He claimed to his followers that the United States was trespassing on Islamic law by providing military, political, and financial support to Israel, and by maintaining a military presence in Saudi Arabia, home to Mecca and other Muslim holy sites.

During the period following the September 11 terrorist attacks, there was a pervasive sentiment, present among U.S. legislators and civilians alike, that the nation's stability and people were no longer secure from violence. The atmosphere of uncertainty, mistrust, and fear that arose from that unprecedented violation of U.S. security led Congress to pursue immediate action. During the month following 9/11, several anti-terrorism and heightened-security bills were proposed, which were consolidated into a single law under the Patriot Act. The Patriot Act incorporated measures proposed in its precursors, comprising changes and additions to an extensive array of policies regarding many facets of activity within the United States.

Both houses of Congress voted to approve the law eagerly, pushing it through the House of Representatives and the Senate in two days. On the third day, October 26, President George W. Bush signed the Patriot Act into law, to take effect on February 1, 2002. The act consists of ten titles, each including provisions related to a specific facet of the United States' new efforts to "deter and punish American terrorists in the United States and around the world, to enhance law enforcement investigatory tools, and ... other purposes."

The Patriot Act represented one of the single largest changes to the Constitution in U.S. history, amending hundreds of laws. It was reauthorized three times after its initial implementation, and sections were expanded, changed, removed, and added entirely to reflect the changing priorities and perceptions of American efforts against terrorism. Since it entered

into effect in 2002, the act consistently remained one of the most controversial and frequently discussed aspects of U.S. politics, continuing to influence the practices of the federal government in surveillance and investigation. At the center of the debate surrounding the act lay a fundamental conflict between the necessity of adequately equipping and empowering the U.S. government to protect its citizens from internal and external threats, and the importance of maintaining the integrity of the Constitution and the privacies and protections it provides. Supporters of the law maintain its necessity in defending the nation against terrorism and subterfuge, while detractors claim that the Patriot Act unduly and unnecessarily violates the civil liberties of average citizens.

Inherently problematic is the ambiguous language used in the Patriot Act. According to the Justice Department's inspector general, most complaints about the law were from Muslim Americans and Americans of Arab descent. They claimed physical and verbal abuse while being detained by government officials, and incidents of racial profiling in airports led to harassment and physical assault by security guards. Racial profiling—a form of discrimination by which law enforcement uses a person's race or cultural background as the primary reason to suspect him or her guilty of criminal activity—became a major issue with the passage of the Patriot Act. A prime example of racial profiling was revealed in 2011, when the Associated Press uncovered secret intelligence operations developed by the New York Police Department in which undercover officers infiltrated minority neighborhoods in 2006 as part of a human mapping program. According to the Associated Press Web site, "police subjected entire neighborhoods to surveillance and scrutiny, often because of the ethnicity of the residents, not because of any accusations of crimes. Hundreds of mosques and Muslim student groups were investigated and dozens were infiltrated." The operations were masterminded with help from the Central Intelligence Agency (CIA), despite the fact that the CIA is prohibited from spying on Americans. The Associated Press won the Pulitzer Prize for its investigations and resulting reports, which were published in the *New York Times*.

According to a 2004 report issued by the Institute for Social Policy and Understanding, the law was directly responsible for the significant increase in the number of hate crimes committed against Arabs and Muslims. "According to the FBI's Uniform Crime Reporting Program, 481 hate crimes were documented against Muslim Americans and Arab Americans in 2001. This is a massive increase from the 28 cases reported in 2000." Each subsequent year saw fewer reported hate crimes against this population, but in 2010, a disturbing fact was revealed by the FBI: Anti-Muslim hate crimes increased by a remarkable 50 percent over 2009's reported figure (160 vs. 107 incidents). This was the highest level of anti-Muslim hate crime since 2001. Although the reason for the spike in incidents was probably attributable to several factors, one of them, according to the FBI, was the vitriolic rhetoric among politicians and citizens alike regarding the plan to build Park51, a thirteen-story Islamic community center just two blocks from Ground Zero. The center would include a Muslim prayer space, and opponents referred to it as the "Ground Zero Mosque," a nonsensical term since it was neither a mosque nor was it to be located at Ground Zero, where the Twin Towers once stood.

■ PRIMARY SOURCE

"A DAY OF TERROR: THE TIES; IN U.S., ECHOES OF RIFT OF MUSLIMS AND JEWS"

SYNOPSIS: Muslim and Arab Americans, as well as Jews, faced hateful backlash in the wake of the terrorist attacks of September 11, 2001.

Muslim women in headscarves were advised to stay indoors. Mosques and Muslim schools in Los Angeles were shut down, and Muslim leaders in Michigan and other states reported receiving telephone threats.

Even though there was no definitive information yet about who was behind the terrorist attacks that struck New York City and Washington yesterday, Muslims and Arab-Americans in the New York region and across the country immediately braced for the backlash with the grim panic of students rehearsing a duck-and-cover air-raid drill.

A terrorist attack on the United States detonates particular repercussions here among both Muslims and Jews, whose kin in the Middle East are locked in a bitter battle that many people immediately assume has now arrived like an unwelcome immigrant on American shores.

In the face of suspicion and discrimination, Muslims struggled to assert their identities as loyal American citizens and to say that their religion does not approve of violence against innocents. Jews, meanwhile, could not help linking the victimization of Americans to that of Jews in Israel.

Yasser Ahmed, manager of an Arab-owned candy and grocery store on Broadway in Upper Manhattan, said about 10 people had come in shouting, "You guys did it!" and other accusations.

At an Arab-owned grocery store on West 177 Street, a shouting match erupted among customers when a Palestinian woman blamed American support of Israel for the terrorism.

"I'm Arabic and Palestinian and I have just one thing to say," said Yasmeen Hindi, 19, a customer at Uptown Deli Grocery. "I feel bad, but Americans have to understand something: If we're going to get killed, they're going to get killed back. Stop supporting the Israelis."

As several customers berated her, the store owner, Ahmed Naqi Mater, said: "Maybe it's not Arabs. Remember Oklahoma."

The news revived fresh memories among Muslims and Arab-Americans of the aftermath of the Oklahoma City bombing in 1995, when snap judgment blamed Muslim terrorists, and mosques were defaced, Muslim travelers detained in airports, and families harassed in their homes.

Yesterday in Dearborn, Mich., where one of nearly every three residents is Arab-American, Osama Siblani, the publisher of the *Arab American News*, said he and his colleagues had already received several hostile phone calls, including a death threat. One caller said, "Is this Osama Siblani?" Mr. Siblani recalled, sitting at his desk with a large blue bottle of Mylanta that he had brought with him for the ulcer he anticipated would act up. "I said it was, and they said, 'Pray to God that this wasn't Arabs'" because if it was, repercussions would follow.

American Muslim and Arab organizations rushed to condemn the attack in strongly worded news releases, some issued less than two and a half hours after the first plane hit the World Trade Center.

"American Muslims utterly condemn what are apparently vicious and cowardly acts of terrorism against innocent civilians," the American Muslim Political Coordination Council said in a statement. "We join with all Americans in calling for the swift apprehension and punishment of the perpetrators."

The group's members had been scheduled to meet at the White House yesterday with President Bush, whom they had endorsed in the presidential election last year.

For many Jewish leaders, the wail of sirens and the ensuing panic was all too reminiscent of the suicide bombings that have recently paralyzed Israel.

Yesterday morning, from their picture windows overlooking the World Trade Center, the staff members of United Jewish Communities, the umbrella group of Jewish charitable federations, looked on dumbfounded as smoke billowed from the first tower. When the second tower was hit by a second plane, some staff members shrieked and burst into tears, said Gail Hyman, vice president for public affairs.

As they were evacuating the building, Ms. Hyman said, one of the Israelis on the group's security staff said, "It's an awful thing to say, but it will deepen the understanding of what Israelis live with day in and day out."

Yet several leaders, like Abraham Foxman of the Anti-Defamation League, were uncomfortable suggesting that terrorism in the United States will lead Americans to have more compassion for Israelis.

"On the one hand it brings us closer, but it is a high price to pay for that realization of what we share as two peoples," said Mr. Foxman, stranded in a Queens hotel when his morning shuttle flight was unable to leave La Guardia Airport. "So people will now understand, but at what price? It's not worth it." . . .

For both Jewish and Muslim Americans, some of the most disturbing television images broadcast came not from New York City or Washington, but from Palestinians in the occupied territories who were celebrating joyously, honking horns and tossing sweets in the air.

"Does that mean they were behind this? I have no way of knowing," said David A. Harris, executive director of the American Jewish Committee. "But the fact that they are celebrating means they become our enemy. If they celebrate our tragedy, it speaks volumes of who they are and who we are. Those who find joy in this day are not friends of the United States."

Though they were aware of such images from Palestinian towns and refugee camps, Muslim and Arab leaders in the New York area emphasized that they were reacting to the emergency first and foremost as Americans. They urged their colleagues to donate blood, and their doctors to volunteer at the site.

"We have to show them we are part of the community," said Ahmed Shedeed, director of the Islamic Center of Jersey City. "This affects me as much as my neighbor. This is our country."

Mr. Shedeed said he had spent the day helping five teachers at his center whose husbands or relatives had worked in or near the towers.

People should not blame Arab-Americans for the attacks, said Sam Meheidli, a data processing supervisor in Dearborn.

"We're proud to be American, we haven't had any problems, we're doing our duty as American citizens," Mr. Meheidli said outside a polling place as he distributed flyers endorsing Abed Hammoud, an Arab-American candidate in the Dearborn mayoral primary yesterday, which was held as scheduled.

Across the nation, prominent Muslims reported receiving phone calls from worried men and women in their communities. "One of the people who called me said, 'Are they going to put us in concentration camps like the Japanese?'" said Mohamad el-Behairy, a retired college professor in Buffalo. In response, he told the caller not to worry, that such a thing as the internment of Japanese-Americans during World War II was unthinkable.

And Mr. Behairy said he reminded all who called that the destruction was "a tragic situation that has to be condemned by everyone who has an iota of decency."

FURTHER RESOURCES
Books
Peek, Lori. *Behind the Backlash: Muslim Americans After 9/11.* Ambler, PA: Temple University, 2011.

Web Sites
"FBI: Dramatic Spike in Hate Crimes Targeting Muslims." *Intelligence Report*, Spring 2012. www.splcenter.org/get-informed/intelligence-report/browse-all-issues/2012/spring/fbi-dramatic-spike-in-hate-crimes-targetin (accessed on March 22, 2013).

"Highlights of AP's Pulitzer Prize-winning Probe into Intelligence Operations." *Associated Press.* www.ap.org/media-center/nypd/investigation (accessed on March 22, 2013).

Senazi, Farid. "The U.S. Patriot Act: The Impact on the Arab and Muslim American Community: Executive Summary." *Institute for Social Policy and Understanding*, April 1, 2004. http://www.ispu.org/GetReports/35/1901/Publications.aspx (accessed on March 22, 2013).

"Between Man and Woman: Questions and Answers About Marriage and Same-Sex Unions"

Press release

By: United States Conference of Catholic Bishops

Date: 2003

Source: United States Conference of Catholic Bishops. "Between Man and Woman: Questions and Answers About Marriage and Same-Sex Unions," 2003. *United States Conference of Catholic Bishops.* www.usccb.org/issues-and-action/marriage-and-family/marriage/promotion-and-defense-of-marriage/questions-and-answers-about-marriage-and-same-sex-unions.cfm (accessed on March 23, 2013).

About the Organization: The United States Conference of Catholic Bishops is the governing body of the Catholic

Church's operations within the United States. It is composed of all members of the Catholic hierarchy in the country, both retired and active, of all ranks. Founded in 1966, the United States Conference of Catholic Bishops is tasked with administering the functions, teachings, and initiatives of the Catholic religion in the United States by overseeing the operation of all its Catholic churches. The organization has grown increasingly political in recent years, pursuing political activism against alleged infringements of the church's religious freedoms propagated by the U.S. government in the form of obligatory healthcare statutes and pursuit of criminal charges for widespread allegations of church officials sexually assaulting underage boys.

INTRODUCTION

The institution of marriage in the United States has historically been restricted to include only heterosexual couples. This custom excluded homosexual couples from receiving the federal and state benefits conferred by marriage, such as insurance benefits, the ability to file joint tax returns, tax incentives for the creation of a family, Social Security survivor's benefits, and legal immigration for non-citizens married to legal residents of the country. Although it has been a political issue in the United States since the early 1970s, the movement to legalize same-sex marriages only rose to national prominence in 1993, when the Supreme Court of Hawaii ruled in the case of *Baehr v. Miike* that the state was required to demonstrate a compelling legal interest in order to justify the prohibition of such marriages. Fearing that such a ruling would compel Hawaii and other states to legislate the express permission of same-sex marriage, the conservative-controlled 104th Congress, under President Bill Clinton, passed the Defense of Marriage Act (DOMA) in 1996. DOMA officially established the federal definition of marriage as a union consisting of one man and one woman (although it still allowed states to determine individually whether or not to permit same-sex marriages), and it exempted state governments from being required to recognize marriage certificates given to same-sex couples in other states and jurisdictions.

By the start of the 2000s decade, there was an increasingly popular movement in the United States for the recognition of equal rights and protection under the law for its lesbian, gay, bisexual, and transgender citizens (commonly called the LGBT movement). Contention over the legal status of the LGBT community developed into one of the decade's most polarizing public and political debates, with many prominent figures endorsing both sides of the argument—those in favor of legal recognition of same-sex marriage and those opposed to it. The opposition voiced three primary objections to the legalization of same-sex marriage: religious, social, and legal.

The most prominent, and common, objection to same-sex marriage, advocated most enthusiastically by the Catholic Church, was founded in religion. According to most denominations of Christianity, the institution of marriage was created by God as the fundamental unit of the family and society, with the fundamental purpose of facilitating reproduction and childrearing. The facts that same-sex couples cannot reproduce without external assistance; do not provide traditional, complimentary gender roles to their offspring; and that the Bible condemns homosexuality as a sin, combined to form the basis of the religious argument against same-sex marriage. The social objection to such unions claimed that children raised outside of the customary male-female parental unit would not be provided correct examples of gender roles or would not receive the necessary aspects of socialization and personal development provided by the presence of both a male and female parent. This, it was asserted, would cause children raised by same-sex parents to demonstrate a proclivity for deviant, illegal, non-traditional, or anti-social behavior. The legal argument against same-sex marriage alleged that the legalization of such would produce a "domino effect," leading to the official recognition of other non-traditional marital arrangements, such as polygamy, incestuous marriages, or object/animal–human marriages.

Advocates of same-sex marriage used a range of tactics in appealing for public support. To the religious objection, they responded that the religious opinions of some Americans should not be imposed on others at the expense of legal, social, and economic equality. A number of studies, notably those produced by the American Psychological Association and the American Medical Association, were proffered as a scientific contradiction to concerns that children raised by same-sex couples turned out maladjusted, emotionally unstable, or socially underdeveloped. Supporters of same-sex marriage noted that the claim that legalization would lead to that of other types of marriage was the same argument offered in opposition to legalizing interracial marriage in the 1960s, and that such concerns proved to be unfounded. Perhaps the most compelling argument offered by advocates of same-sex marriage was the contention that homosexuality was not an attribute deliberately selected, but rather conferred at birth. As such, it was asserted, sexual orientation was no different from race or gender, and using it as a basis for the denial of access to the civil benefits of marriage amounted to discrimination in direct violation of the Equal Protection Clause of the Fourteenth Amendment to the U.S. Constitution.

SIGNIFICANCE

The 2000s decade witnessed the LGBT movement attract growing publicity and support, leading to the establishment of same-sex civil unions and domestic partnerships in California, Maine, New Jersey, Nevada, Oregon, Washington, and Washington, D.C. Although not legally equivalent to marriage, such unions conferred almost all the same benefits provided by the states in which they were recognized. However, same-sex couples who entered into civil unions or domestic partnerships were still denied the federal benefits of marriage, causing continued discontent among the LGBT community. By 2009, the states of Connecticut, Iowa, Massachusetts, New Hampshire, and Vermont had legalized the performance of same-sex marriages, either through state court rulings in which the prohibition of such marriages were found to be illegal, or through the passage of state laws officially recognizing them. Additionally, California and Rhode Island passed legislation recognizing same-sex marriages performed in other states but did not legalize the issuance of same-sex marriage licenses themselves.

Opposition to same-sex marriage was particularly strong in the Southern and Western United States, where the standard tactic used to prevent its institution was the passage of amendments to state constitutions officially defining marriage as existing between one man and one woman. This tactic had the effect of preventing state legislatures from justifying the passage of laws recognizing same-sex marriage and of preventing state courts from interpreting their governing constitutions as allowing or requiring such marriages. By the end of the 2000s decade, the states of Alabama, Alaska, Arizona, Arkansas, California, Colorado, Florida, Georgia, Idaho, Kansas, Kentucky, Louisiana, Michigan, Mississippi, Missouri, Montana, Nebraska, Nevada, North Dakota, Ohio, Oklahoma, Oregon, South Carolina, South Dakota, Tennessee, Texas, Utah, Virginia, and Wisconsin had thus amended their constitutions. Additionally, the states of Delaware, Hawaii, Illinois, Indiana, Maine, Maryland, Minnesota, North Carolina, Pennsylvania, Washington, West Virginia, and Wyoming all maintained laws banning the performance or recognition of same-sex marriages.

The debate over same-sex marriage came to represent the central issue of the campaign for LGBT rights in the United States, and it showed no sign of reaching a conclusion as the 2000s decade drew to a close. It became a central issue in the 2008 public elections, with candidates of all political inclinations vocally proclaiming their posture on the topic. More importantly, the movement to legalize same-sex marriage in the United States became one of the defining social issues of the decade, which was sure to be remembered as crucial to its resolution.

■ PRIMARY SOURCE

"BETWEEN MAN AND WOMAN: QUESTIONS AND ANSWERS ABOUT MARRIAGE AND SAME-SEX UNIONS"

SYNOPSIS: In this article, the authors explain the Catholic objection to the legalization of same-sex marriage in the United States.

INTRODUCTION

A growing movement today favors making those relationships commonly called same-sex unions the legal equivalent of marriage. This situation challenges Catholics—and all who seek the truth—to think deeply about the meaning of marriage, its purposes, and its value to individuals, families, and society. This kind of reflection, using reason and faith, is an appropriate starting point and framework for the current debate.

We, the Catholic bishops of the United States, offer here some basic truths to assist people in understanding Catholic teaching about marriage and to enable them to promote marriage and its sacredness.

1. What is marriage?

Marriage, as instituted by God, is a faithful, exclusive, lifelong union of a man and a woman joined in an intimate community of life and love. They commit themselves completely to each other and to the wondrous responsibility of bringing children into the world and caring for them. The call to marriage is woven deeply into the human spirit. Man and woman are equal. However, as created, they are different from but made for each other. This complementarity, including sexual difference, draws them together in a mutually loving union that should be always open to the procreation of children (see *Catechism of the Catholic Church* [CCC], nos. 1602–1605). These truths about marriage are present in the order of nature and can be perceived by the light of human reason. They have been confirmed by divine Revelation in Sacred Scripture.

2. What does our faith tell us about marriage?

Marriage comes from the loving hand of God, who fashioned both male and female in the divine image (see Gn 1:27). A man "leaves his father and mother and clings

American Roman Catholic bishops, who are members of the United States Conference of Catholic Bishops, enter Washington Nationals Park in Washington, D.C., on April 17, 2008, to greet Pope Benedict XVI. © LARRY DOWNING/CORBIS.

to his wife, and the two of them become one body" (Gn 2:24). The man recognizes the woman as "bone of my bones and flesh of my flesh" (Gn 2:23). God blesses the man and woman and commands them to "be fertile and multiply" (Gn 1:28). Jesus reiterates these teachings from Genesis, saying, "But from the beginning of creation, 'God made them male and female. For this reason a man shall leave his father and mother [and be joined to his wife], and the two shall become one flesh'" (Mk 10:6–8).

These biblical passages help us to appreciate God's plan for marriage. It is an intimate union in which the spouses give themselves, as equal persons, completely and lovingly to one another. By their mutual gift of self, they cooperate with God in bringing children to life and in caring for them.

Marriage is both a natural institution and a sacred union because it is rooted in the divine plan for creation. In addition, the Church teaches that the valid marriage of baptized Christians is a sacrament—a saving reality. Jesus Christ made marriage a symbol of his love for his Church (see Eph 5:25–33). This means that a sacramental marriage lets the world see, in human terms, something

of the faithful, creative, abundant, and self-emptying love of Christ. A true marriage in the Lord with his grace will bring the spouses to holiness. Their love, manifested in fidelity, passion, fertility, generosity, sacrifice, forgiveness, and healing, makes known God's love in their family, communities, and society. This Christian meaning confirms and strengthens the human value of a marital union (see CCC, nos. 1612–1617; 1641–1642).

3. Why can marriage exist only between a man and a woman?

The natural structure of human sexuality makes man and woman complementary partners for the transmission of human life. Only a union of male and female can express the sexual complementarity willed by God for marriage. The permanent and exclusive commitment of marriage is the necessary context for the expression of sexual love intended by God both to serve the transmission of human life and to build up the bond between husband and wife (see CCC, nos. 1639–1640).

In marriage, husband and wife give themselves totally to each other in their masculinity and femininity (see CCC, no. 1643). They are equal as human beings but different as man and woman, fulfilling each other through this natural difference. This unique complementarity makes possible the conjugal bond that is the core of marriage.

4. Why is a same-sex union not equivalent to a marriage?

For several reasons a same-sex union contradicts the nature of marriage: It is not based on the natural complementarity of male and female; it cannot cooperate with God to create new life; and the natural purpose of sexual union cannot be achieved by a same-sex union. Persons in same-sex unions cannot enter into a true conjugal union. Therefore, it is wrong to equate their relationship to a marriage.

5. Why is it so important to society that marriage be preserved as the exclusive union of a man and a woman?

Across times, cultures, and very different religious beliefs, marriage is the foundation of the family. The family, in turn, is the basic unit of society. Thus, marriage is a personal relationship with public significance. Marriage is the fundamental pattern for male-female relationships. It contributes to society because it models the way in which women and men live interdependently and commit, for the whole of life, to seek the good of each other.

The marital union also provides the best conditions for raising children: namely, the stable, loving relationship of a mother and father present only in marriage. The state rightly recognizes this relationship as a public institution in its laws because the relationship makes a unique and essential contribution to the common good.

Laws play an educational role insofar as they shape patterns of thought and behavior, particularly about what is socially permissible and acceptable. In effect, giving same-sex unions the legal status of marriage would grant official public approval to homosexual activity and would treat it as if it were morally neutral.

When marriage is redefined so as to make other relationships equivalent to it, the institution of marriage is devalued and further weakened. The weakening of this basic institution at all levels and by various forces has already exacted too high a social cost.

6. Does denying marriage to homosexual persons demonstrate unjust discrimination and a lack of respect for them as persons?

It is not unjust to deny legal status to same-sex unions because marriage and same-sex unions are essentially different realities. In fact, justice requires society to do so. To uphold God's intent for marriage, in which sexual relations have their proper and exclusive place, is not to offend the dignity of homosexual persons. Christians must give witness to the whole moral truth and oppose as immoral both homosexual acts and unjust discrimination against homosexual persons. The *Catechism of the*

Catholic Church urges that homosexual persons "be accepted with respect, compassion, and sensitivity" (no. 2358). It also encourages chaste friendships. "Chastity is expressed notably in *friendship with one's neighbor.* Whether it develops between persons of the same or opposite sex, friendship represents a great good for all" (no. 2347).

7. Should persons who live in same-sex relationships be entitled to some of the same social and economic benefits given to married couples?

The state has an obligation to promote the family, which is rooted in marriage. Therefore, it can justly give married couples rights and benefits it does not extend to others. Ultimately, the stability and flourishing of society is dependent on the stability and flourishing of healthy family life. The legal recognition of marriage, including the benefits associated with it, is not only about personal commitment, but also about the social commitment that husband and wife make to the well-being of society. It would be wrong to redefine marriage for the sake of providing benefits to those who cannot rightfully enter into marriage. Some benefits currently sought by persons in homosexual unions can already be obtained without regard to marital status. For example, individuals can agree to own property jointly with another, and they can generally designate anyone they choose to be a beneficiary of their will or to make health care decisions in case they become incompetent.

8. In light of the Church's teaching about the truth and beauty of marriage, what should Catholics do?

There is to be no separation between one's faith and life in either public or private realms. All Catholics should act on their beliefs with a well-formed conscience based on Sacred Scripture and Tradition. They should be a community of conscience within society. By their voice and their vote, they should contribute to society's welfare and test its public life by the standards of right reason and Gospel truth. Responsible citizenship is a virtue. Participation in the political process is a moral obligation. This is particularly urgent in light of the need to defend marriage and to oppose the legalization of same-sex unions as marriages. Married couples themselves, by the witness of their faithful, life-giving love, are the best advocates for marriage. By their example, they are the first teachers of the next generation about the dignity of marriage and the need to uphold it. As leaders of their family—which the Second Vatican Council called a "domestic church" (*Lumen Gentium*, no. 11)—couples should bring their gifts as well as their needs to the larger Church. There, with the help of other couples and their pastors and collaborators, they can strengthen their commitment and sustain their sacrament over a lifetime.

CONCLUSION

Marriage is a basic human and social institution. Though it is regulated by civil laws and church laws, it did not originate from either the church or state, but from God. Therefore, neither church nor state can alter the basic meaning and structure of marriage. Marriage, whose nature and purposes are established by God, can only be the union of a man and a woman and must remain such in law. In a manner unlike any other relationship, marriage makes a unique and irreplaceable contribution to the common good of society, especially through the procreation and education of children. The union of husband and wife becomes, over a lifetime, a great good for themselves, their family, communities, and society. Marriage is a gift to be cherished and protected.

FURTHER RESOURCES

Books

Catholic Church. *Catechism of the Catholic Church*. New York: Image, 1995.

Corvino, John. *Debating Same-Sex Marriage (Point/Counterpoint)*. New York: Oxford University Press, 2012.

United States Conference of Catholic Bishops. *New American Bible Revised Edition*. Charlotte, NC: Saint Benedict Press, 2011.

Web Sites

"Archive: Same-Sex Marriage." *NPR*. www.npr.org/templates/archives/archive.php?thingId=125937705 (accessed on March 23, 2013).

"Brief of the American Psychological Association, the Massachusetts Psychological Association, the American Psychiatric Association, the National Association of Social Workers and Its Massachusetts Chapter, the American Medical Association, and the American Academy of Pediatrics as *Amici Curiae* in Support of Plaintiffs-Appellees and in Support of Affirmance." *American Psychological Association*. www.apa.org/about/offices/ogc/amicus/gill.pdf (accessed on March 23, 2013).

"Gay Rights in the States: Public Opinion and Policy Responsiveness." *American Political Science Review* 103, no. 3 (August 2009). www.columbia.edu/~jrl2124/Lax_Phillips_Gay_Policy_Responsiveness_2009.pdf (accessed on March 23, 2013).

"Same-sex Marriage, Gay Rights." *PollingReport*. www.pollingreport.com/civil.htm (accessed on March 23, 2013).

"Same-sex Marriage in the United States." *Greg Stoll*. gregstoll.dyndns.org/marriagemap (accessed on March 23, 2013).

"Statewide Marriage Prohibitions." *Human Rights Campaign*. web.archive.org/web/20110726161614/http://www.hrc.org/documents/marriage_prohibitions_2009.pdf (accessed on March 23, 2013).

"Topic: Same-Sex Marriage, Civil Unions, and Domestic Partnerships." *New York Times*. topics.nytimes.com/top/reference/timestopics/subjects/s/same_sex_marriage/index.html (accessed on March 23, 2013).

"Fugitive Sect Leader Arrested near Las Vegas"

Polygamist Warren Steed Jeffs was on FBI's most wanted list

Web site article

By: Associated Press

Date: August 29, 2006

Source: Associated Press. "Fugitive Sect Leader Arrested near Las Vegas," August 29, 2006. www.nbcnews.com/id/14569632/ns/us_news-crime_and_courts/t/fugitive-sect-leader-arrested-near-las-vegas/#; (accessed on March 22, 2013).

About the News Agency: NBC News was founded in February 1940 to provide news programming for the NBC television network. It was responsible for the United States' first televised news broadcast and would pioneer the format throughout its development. NBC News was the dominant American television news agency until the 1980s, thanks to its breaking coverage of contemporary issues such as the civil rights movement and space exploration, as well as its long string of congenial news anchors. NBC News ranked highly in viewership and ratings throughout the 2000s decade, vying with CBS and ABC for television news supremacy.

INTRODUCTION

Polygamy, the practice of marriage that includes more than two partners, has a long and contentious history in the United States. As early as 1830, Joseph Smith, founder of the Church of Jesus Christ of Latter-day Saints (LDS; known commonly as Mormonism), was advocating "plural marriages" between the members of his congregation. Mormon polygamous relationships involved a single man and multiple wives, an arrangement that Smith claimed was encouraged by God. Despite the United States' strict prohibition of bigamy, the Mormons continued to practice polygamy until 1890, when, under threat of the church's disincorporation and legal penalties, LDS president Wilford Woodruff issued a decree banning the establishment of new plural marriages. When the church officially disavowed polygamy and declared the dissolution of all existing plural marriages in 1904, several groups intent on maintaining the custom diverged from LDS, migrating to secluded portions of the American Southwest to avoid persecution and prosecution. These devoted polygamists maintained the teachings of the Mormon faith, but cited an alleged divine revelation delivered to LDS president John Taylor in 1886 as justification for rejecting the church's disavowal of polygamy.

These apostates formed their largest community in Short Creek, Arizona, where they were free from public and official scrutiny and could continue to practice polygamy in security. In 1935, the LDS Church declared the excommunication of all Mormons who still possessed multiple wives. Officially abandoned by their church, the residents of Short Creek formed the Fundamentalist Church of Jesus Christ of Latter-day Saints (FLDS), which professed fidelity to the true teachings of Mormonism. FLDS soon attracted the attention of the government of Arizona for its observance of polygamy, resulting in a police raid of the community in 1944 and another in 1953. These raids backfired, producing a swell of favorable public sentiment towards FLDS that ultimately prevented further government intervention and allowed FLDS to conduct itself without interference for the rest of the century.

The town of Short Creek was owned almost entirely by a public trust controlled by FLDS, including land, businesses, homes, and factories. The church reincorporated the community into two separate towns, the "twin cities" of Colorado City, Arizona, and Hildale, Utah, as membership grew. FLDS taught its adherents that polygamy was a practice ordained by God, and that it was the duty of devout men to obtain at least three wives in order to achieve eternal salvation—the more wives a man possessed, the more exalted he was in the eyes of Heaven. Church members practiced "Celestial Marriage," in which the leader of FLDS, through divine guidance, was tasked with assigning wives to men on the basis of piety and virtue, and authorized to reassign wives, property, and even children to other men as retribution for errant conduct. This system produced rampant inbreeding and underage marriage, as the demand for wives far exceeded the legally eligible supply of women. Many young men were expelled from the community to reduce competition for brides for older members of the church.

In 2002, FLDS leader and president Rulon Jeffs died and was replaced by his son, Warren, who adopted the official titles of "President and Prophet, Seer and Revelator" and "President of the Priesthood." In these capacities, Jeffs had absolute authority over the members and clergy of FLDS, and he was tasked with communicating with God to direct Celestial Marriages. In addition to controlling the assignment of wives and property to members of his congregation, Jeffs was given custodianship of the $100 million trust that owned most of Hildale and Colorado City, granting him practical ownership of both towns. His reign was brief, however. FLDS came under legal investigation in 2003 for its routine administration of underage marriages and the resultant sexual conduct of adults with girls as young as twelve years old. Jeffs was then subjected to the scrutiny of the U.S. government when the investigation revealed the extent of his church's polygamous practices.

In 2004, Jeffs was accused by three of his nephews of sexually assaulting them when they were children, prompting him to begin circulating throughout the Southwest to avoid formal charges. In June 2005, charges were filed against Jeffs in Mojave County, Arizona, for the sexual assault of a minor and conspiracy to commit sexual misconduct with a minor stemming from his arrangement of a marriage between a fourteen-year-old girl and her nineteen-year-old first cousin. A bounty of $10,000 was offered for information leading to his arrest and conviction. Later that year, Jeffs was placed on the FBI's wanted fugitive list, raising the reward to $60,000. In May 2006, Jeffs was featured on the television program *America's Most Wanted.* He continued to act as spiritual leader of FLDS even as he fled the authorities, conducting polygamous and underage marriages from a trailer that had been converted into a makeshift chapel.

In April 2006, the State of Utah issued an arrest warrant for Jeffs on two felony charges of accomplice rape of a minor for his involvement in the arranged marriage of two teenage girls to adult members of FLDS. The next month, he was placed on the FBI's Top Ten Most Wanted Fugitives list for committing unlawful flight to avoid prosecution on the charges levied against him, and the bounty for his capture was raised to $100,000. That same month, the accountant appointed to manage the FLDS trust fund filed charges against Jeffs for allegedly embezzling from the trust and defrauding its contributors. Jeffs was finally arrested on August 28, 2006, following a routine traffic stop in Clark County, Nevada. In addition to his brother and one of his many wives, the car in which Jeffs was captured contained over $50,000 in cash, numerous cell phones and computers, a police scanner, and several different disguises.

Fundamentalist Church of Jesus Christ of Latter-day Saints leader Warren Jeffs appears in a Las Vegas, Nevada, courtroom on August 31, 2006. He was transferred to Utah, where he received multiple charges, including polygamy. © AP IMAGES/LAURA RAUCH.

He was transported back to Utah to face trial on the accomplice rape charges. While awaiting his court date, he was indicted in Arizona on eight felony charges, including incest and sexual conduct with a minor.

SIGNIFICANCE

Jeffs's first trial was held September 11–25, 2007. He was found guilty on both counts of accomplice rape and sentenced to serve ten years to life in prison. He was transferred into the custody of Arizona authorities in February 2008, where he pleaded not guilty on all eight charges. While Jeffs was in Arizona, Texas law enforcement conducted a search of an FLDS compound in Eldorado, Texas, where they discovered evidence of unlawful sexual contact between Jeffs and underage girls, one twelve and the other fifteen years old, resulting in the filing of two felony sexual assault charges. He was held in prison in

Arizona until June 2010, when all charges against him were dismissed on the grounds that he was facing extradition to Texas. He was convicted on both of the charges in Texas in 2011, and he was sentenced to life in prison plus twenty years.

The Fundamentalist Church of Jesus Christ of Latter-day Saints stayed active throughout the tribulations of its pedophilic leader, despite receiving a storm of attention from the media and public condemnation for its practices. The church's headquarters were apparently shifted to Eldorado, Texas, with the estimated six thousand to ten thousand members continuing to receive spiritual instruction from Jeffs even while he was incarcerated and undergoing trial. No new charges were brought against FLDS leadership after Jeffs's conviction, although it is suspected that the sect continues to practice polygamy and ordain arranged marriages between underage girls and adult men. The chronicles of Warren Jeffs have served to illustrate the limits of free religious expression in the United States and provided one of the most-discussed public spectacles of the 2000s decade.

PRIMARY SOURCE

"FUGITIVE SECT LEADER ARRESTED NEAR LAS VEGAS"

SYNOPSIS: In this article, the author describes the crimes and capture of Warren Jeffs, leader of the Fundamentalist Church of Jesus Christ of Latter-day Saints.

The leader of a polygamist breakaway sect who was on the FBI's Most Wanted List has been arrested and faces sexual misconduct charges for allegedly arranging marriages between underage girls and older men, authorities said Tuesday.

Warren Steed Jeffs, 50, was taken into custody after he and two other people were pulled over late Monday by a Nevada Highway Patrol trooper on Interstate 15 just north of Las Vegas, FBI spokesman David Staretz said.

Jeffs leads the Fundamentalist Church of Jesus Christ of Latter-day Saints, a group that broke away from the Mormon church a century ago. He is said to have at least 40 wives and nearly 60 children.

He was wanted in Utah and Arizona on suspicion of sexual misconduct for allegedly arranging marriages between underage girls and older men.

He assumed leadership of the sect in 2002 after the death of his 98-year-old father, Rulon Jeffs, who had 65 children by several women. Jeffs took nearly all his father's widows as his own wives.

Since May, Jeffs has been on the FBI's Ten Most Wanted list, with a $100,000 reward offered for information leading to his capture.

Wife, Brother Also in Car

The other two people in the vehicle were identified as one of Warren Jeffs' wives, Naomi Jeffs, and a brother, Isaac Steed Jeffs, both 32, Staretz said. They were being interviewed by the FBI in Las Vegas but were not arrested.

Isaac Jeffs was driving a red Cadillac Escalade that was stopped for having no visible registration, said state Trooper Kevin Honea. An FBI agent was summoned to confirm Jeffs' identity, Honea said.

Warren Jeffs was in federal custody in Las Vegas awaiting a court hearing on a federal charge of unlawful flight to avoid prosecution, Staretz said.

FBI officials said at a press conference Tuesday that Jeffs was found with $54,000 in cash, numerous gift cards worth an additional $10,000, 15 cell phones, four portable radios, four laptop computers, a global positioning system device, a police scanner, several pairs of sunglasses and three wigs.

'Beginning of the End'

Arizona Attorney General Terry Goddard told KTAR-AM of Phoenix that Jeffs' arrest is "the beginning of the end of ... the tyrannical rule of a small group of people over the practically 10,000 followers of the FLDS sect." He predicted that it will inspire more people to come forward with allegations of sexual abuse.

Most of the church's members live in Hildale, Utah, and nearby Colorado City, Ariz.

Jeffs was indicted in June 2005 on an Arizona charge of arranging a marriage between a 16-year-old girl and a married man, and unlawful flight to avoid prosecution. He is charged in Utah with two felony counts of rape as an accomplice, for allegedly arranging the marriage of a teenage girl to an older man in Nevada.

The FLDS Church split from the Church of Jesus Christ of Latter-day Saints when the mainstream Mormon Church disavowed plural marriage more than 100 years ago.

Allegations from within Church

Jeffs has been called a religious zealot and dangerous extremist by those familiar with his church.

During his four-year rule, the number of underage marriages—some involving girls as young as 13—escalated into the hundreds, church dissidents said. They said that although the sect has long practiced the custom of arranged marriages, young girls were rarely married off until Warren Jeffs came to power.

People expelled from the community said young men were sent away to avoid competition for brides. Older men were cast out for alleged disobedience, and their wives and children were reassigned by Jeffs to new husbands and fathers, the former members said.

"If this will bring an end to that, that will be a good thing," said Ward Jeffs, an older half brother of Warren. "We're excited for the people down there, but we're very concerned about who might step up and take the leadership role."

It remained unclear Tuesday what would happen to the leadership of the church while Jeffs was incarcerated.

Federal and state law enforcement agencies will determine whether Jeffs should be extradited first to Utah or Arizona, said Steve Sorenson, a federal prosecutor in Salt Lake City. Utah's charges are more serious, and the federal unlawful flight charge was for leaving Utah, which could influence the decision, Sorenson said.

FURTHER RESOURCES

Books

Brower, Sam. *Prophet's Prey: My Seven-Year Investigation into Warren Jeffs and the Fundamentalist Church of Latter-Day Saints.* New York: Bloomsbury USA, 2011.

Singular, Stephen. *When Men Become Gods: Mormon Polygamist Warren Jeffs, His Cult of Fear, and the Women Who Fought Back.* New York: St. Martin's Griffin, 2009.

Web Sites

"A Brief History of the Polygamists in Colorado City, Arizona and Hildale, Utah." *Rick A. Ross Institute of New Jersey.* www.rickross.com/reference/polygamy/polygamy4.html (accessed on March 23, 2013).

"Polygamist Charged with Felony Accomplice Rape of a Minor." *FindLaw.* news.findlaw.com/hdocs/docs/polygamy/utjeffs40506crinf.html (accessed on March 23, 2013).

"Sect Leader Indicted on Sexual Conduct with Minor, Incest Charges." *CNN*, July 12, 2007. //www.cnn.com/2007/US/07/12/polygamy.charges/index.html (accessed on March 23, 2013).

"Warren Jeffs Gets Life in Prison for Sex with Underage Girls." *Salt Lake Tribune*, August 10, 2011. www.sltrib.com/sltrib/news/52354441-78/jeffs-sexual-child-jurors.html.csp (accessed on March 22, 2013).

"Warren Jeffs Resigns as Leader of the FLDS Church." *Deseret News*, December 5, 2007. www.deseretnews.com/article/695233512/Warren-Jeffs-resigns-as-leader-of-the-FLDS-Church.html (accessed on March 23, 2013).

"Pastor Takes Leave Amid Allegations of Gay Sex"

New Life Church's Ted Haggard, a backer of Amendment 43 to ban gay marriage in Colorado, says he could "not continue to minister under the cloud" of accusations.

Newspaper article

By: Eric Gorski, Felisa Cardona, and Manny Gonzales

Date: November 3, 2006

Source: Gorski, Eric, Felisa Cardona, and Manny Gonzales. "Pastor Takes Leave Amid Allegations of Gay Sex." *Denver Post*, November 3, 2006. www. denverpost.com/ci_4588998 (accessed on March 23, 2013).

About the Newspaper: The *Denver Post* was first published in 1892 as the *Evening Post*, a Democratic Party newspaper intended to cull favor for presidential candidate Grover Cleveland, who was unpopular in the region. After briefly ceasing publication, the paper was reborn as a daily news journal in 1894. In the 1930s, the paper debuted its iconic "Open Forum" page, one of the most acclaimed editorial sections of any U.S. newspaper. Recognized for its objective journalism and accurate reporting, the paper maintained high circulation numbers and received four Pulitzer Prizes throughout the remainder of the twentieth century. During the 2000s decade, although the paper struggled financially due to flagging readership and declining advertising prices, it received a Pulitzer Prize and developed one of the largest web presences among newspaper sites.

INTRODUCTION

Ted Haggard, a born-again Evangelical Christian from Indiana, founded the non-denominational New Life Church in Colorado Springs, Colorado, in 1984. Having received word from a friend of a prophetic dream depicting Haggard founding a church in the city, the Oral Roberts University–educated pastor moved there and began hosting independent prayers and church functions in his home, but he quickly expanded the size of his congregation and worship space. By the 1990s, the church was operating from a continually developing compound, which helped establish Colorado Springs as a center of the new conservative Christian movement. Haggard acted as head pastor throughout the church's rise, preaching in the evangelical charismatic tradition by employing vivid metaphors and a witty, eloquent persona to

encourage Christian behavior. In 2003, the pastor's popularity and theology earned him the position of president of the National Association of Evangelicals, one of the largest Christian fellowship organizations in the United States.

By 2006, the New Life Church was a veritable megachurch, boasting fourteen thousand members in its congregation and several large buildings for daily and Sunday services, outreach programs, and even a structure known as the "World Prayer Center," a landmark in the Global Prayer Movement. Haggard was one of the most politically influential and outspoken religious leaders in the United States, who publicly endorsed Amendment 43, a proposed addition to the Constitution of the State of Colorado that codified the definition of marriage as existing exclusively between heterosexual couples. Ironically, despite his public condemnation of homosexual activity as explicitly forbidden in the Bible, Haggard himself was not precisely heterosexual. For instance, in a February 2011 *GQ* article, he said that if he were "21 in this society, I would identify myself as a bisexual." Haggard has been married to Gayle Alcorn since 1978, and they have five children.

During the first two days of November 2006, a man named Mike Jones issued public allegations that he had been hired repeatedly by Haggard to engage in sexual activity for pay over the three years prior and also that the pastor had purchased and used crystal methamphetamine on multiple occasions. The story immediately attracted significant attention from the media, forcing Haggard to make a public response. In his initial statement to the press, Haggard denied having ever met Jones, having engaged in sexual activity with a man, and purchasing or using drugs. In accordance with the bylaws of the New Life Church, he resigned from his leadership position so that the accusations of improper conduct could be investigated. When Jones released a voicemail from Haggard in which he requests that Jones bring him meth, the pastor admitted to having received a massage from Jones and buying the drug, but he denied having used it.

During the course of a private investigation into Haggard's conduct performed by his church, it became apparent that Jones's claims were true, a fact that he eventually admitted publicly. Haggard was permanently released from his duties at the church and removed from his positions at various religious organizations, including the National Association of Evangelicals. As part of his pension agreement with the New Life Church, Haggard left the state of Colorado to attend college in Arizona. He was replaced as the church's senior pastor by Brady Coyd.

A portrait of New Life Church pastor Ted Haggard hangs in the world prayer center at the church's headquarters in Colorado Springs, Colorado, on November 2, 2006. Haggard soon left the church amidst gay sex and drug allegations. © AP IMAGES/DAVID ZALUBOWSKI.

SIGNIFICANCE

The episode of Ted Haggard's homosexual affair was among the most high-profile of the numerous scandals that plagued the various Christian institutions in the United States throughout the 2000s decade. Public perception and opinion of the Catholic Church and many Protestant sects incurred significant damage during the period, a result of perpetual controversy arising from a seemingly constant stream of fresh accusations of misconduct committed by religious leaders. The New Life Church saw a significant decline in membership in the aftermath of the Haggard scandal, especially once it was discovered that he had engaged in homosexual activity on at least one other occasion, with a member of his congregation. Haggard's church remained active in the Colorado Springs area after the disgraced departure of its founder, who made frequent television appearances on secular television programs, most notably in the HBO special *The Trials of Ted Haggard*, a documentary chronicling the pastor's scandal.

PRIMARY SOURCE

"PASTOR TAKES LEAVE AMID ALLEGATIONS OF GAY SEX"

SYNOPSIS: In this article, the authors report on allegations that Pastor Ted Haggard of the New Life Church in Colorado Springs routinely engaged in sex with a male prostitute over the course of three years.

New Life Church's Ted Haggard, a backer of Amendment 43 to ban gay marriage in Colorado, says he could "not continue to minister under the cloud" of accusations.

Facing shocking allegations that he paid a gay prostitute for sex, prominent Colorado Springs pastor Ted Haggard placed himself on administrative leave Thursday from his church position and resigned as president of the National Association of Evangelicals, a platform that made him a rising star in conservative politics.

Haggard, 50, said in a statement released by his 14,000-member New Life Church that he could "not continue to minister under the cloud created by the accusations made on Denver talk radio this morning."

In interviews over the past two days with KHOW talk radio, 9News and *The Denver Post*, Michael Forest Jones, 49, of Denver alleges he had sex on a monthly basis with Haggard over three years. Jones claimed Haggard used the name "Art," admitted he was married and used meth before the two had sex.

In an interview Wednesday with 9News, Haggard denied he'd used drugs or had gay sex, saying he's been faithful to his wife. Haggard, who has five children, could not be reached for comment Thursday.

Late Thursday, The Associated Press reported that the acting senior pastor at New Life, Ross Parsley, told KKTV-TV of Colorado Springs that Haggard admitted some of the accusations were true, but Parsley didn't elaborate.

The timing of the disclosure has stirred controversy, coming days before Colorado voters will decide on two measures related to gay rights and marriage. Haggard is a chief supporter of Amendment 43, which would define marriage as only between a man and a woman, and he has taken no position on Referendum I, which would grant domestic-partnership rights to same-sex couples.

Haggard is unquestionably a national figure. Since founding New Life Church in his basement in the 1980s, the son of an Indiana veterinarian has ascended the ranks of evangelical leaders, taking part in White House conference calls, counseling foreign leaders and being named by *Time* magazine as one of the nation's 25 most influential evangelicals.

Martin Nussbaum, New Life Church's attorney, emphasized that Haggard's leave and an imminent inquiry into the matter by an outside church board should not be construed as an admission of guilt but rather in keeping with church policies.

Under church bylaws, an outside "board of over-seers" investigates allegations of immorality, financial misdealings or teaching heresy, Nussbaum said. The board has authority to discipline the senior pastor, remove him or restore him to ministry.

"I am voluntarily stepping aside from leadership so that the overseer process can be allowed to proceed with integrity," Haggard said in his statement. "I hope to be able to discuss this matter in more detail at a later date."

The overseers board is made up of the Rev. Larry Stockstill of Bethany World Prayer Center in Baker, La., where Haggard worked as a youth pastor more than two decades ago; the Rev. Mark Cowart of Church For All Nations in Colorado Springs; the Rev. Tim Ralph of New Covenant Fellowship in Larkspur; and the Rev. Michael Ware of Victory Church in Westminster.

"We want to know the real truth," Ware said. "We obviously hope it's not true. We want to be open, independent. There's always two sides to a story."

Ware said the group has not met and has no timetable, and it's unclear what exactly the inquiry will involve.

Haggard was replaced on an interim basis by Parsley, who has worked in senior ministry in the church for 15 years. "People need to be patient and allow this process to unfold as it was designed to," Parsley said in a statement....

For 2 1/2 hours Thursday night, church elders met to discuss the situation. One man, who did not identify himself, said the congregation expects Haggard will address them during weekend services.

At Haggard's home just a short drive from the church, a gate blocking the driveway was locked, and television crews set up across the road.

Jones told *The Post* that Haggard contacted him about three years ago through an ad Jones placed in a gay newspaper or on the website Rentboy.com.

Jones said Haggard introduced himself as being from Kansas City, but Jones said he later knew otherwise because his caller ID showed the calls as coming from Colorado Springs pay phones. But he said he didn't confront him because Haggard was a client.

They met at least once a month at Jones' Denver apartment, and Haggard paid cash, Jones said. "He was very nice and very soft-spoken," Jones said. "We never talked about anything heavy-duty."

Jones alleged Haggard snorted a small amount of methamphetamine that he brought with him at least a dozen times to enhance the sexual pleasure. Haggard told 9News he's never done drugs.

About six months ago, Jones said, he was watching TV when he saw a History Channel program on the Antichrist that included Haggard as an expert. He researched Haggard on the Internet. "Once I pulled him up, I'm going, 'He's big.'"

Rob Brendle, an associate New Life pastor, said Haggard fought to make Amendment 43 only define marriage, breaking with other evangelical leaders who favored a broader measure barring domestic partnerships. Haggard has said marriage deserves special status, while civil protections should be a separate issue.

"He has been the person within the evangelical community in Colorado Springs, more than any other leader, been the defender of the rights of homosexuals with his work on the language of the amendment," Brendle said. "If there is a hammer who has been driving this nail, it's not Ted."

As for Jones' allegations, Brendle said, "I have no question in my mind that everything this man says is false. I know Ted to be a man of the utmost integrity and the highest moral character."

FURTHER RESOURCES

Books

Haggard, Gayle, and Angela E. Hunt. *Why I Stayed: The Choices I Made in My Darkest Hour*. Carol Stream, IL: Tyndale House, 2010.

Haggard, Ted. *The Life-Giving Church*. Ventura, CA: Regal Books, 2001.

Jones, Mike, and Sam Gallegos. *I Had to Say Something: The Art of Ted Haggard's Fall*. New York: Seven Stories Press, 2007.

Web Sites

Roose, Kevin. "The Last Temptation of Ted." *GQ*, February 2011. www.gq.com/news-politics/newsmakers/201102/pastor-ted-haggard?printable=true (accessed on March 23, 2013).

"Ted Haggard Dossier." *NNDB*. www.nndb.com/people/234/000120871/ (accessed on March 23, 2013).

"The Trials of Ted Haggard." *Internet Movie Database*. www.imdb.com/title/tt1364306/ (accessed on March 23, 2013).

"Rick Warren and Purpose-Driven Strife"

Pastor's Unconventional Approach Inspires Some, Alienates Others

Web site article

By: Martin Bashir and Deborah Apton

Date: March 7, 2007

Source: Bashir, Martin, and Deborah Apron. "Rick Warren and Purpose-Driven Strife." *ABC News*, March 7, 2007. http://abcnews.go.com/print?id=2914953 (accessed on March 24, 2013.)

About the News Organization: Compared to its direct competitors, ABC News got a late start in the U.S. news environment. The organization was founded as a division of the American Broadcasting Company in 1945, two years after the company's formation, and immediately initiated a regular radio news schedule.

ABC News consistently placed third in listenership and income after rivals NBC and CBS, which both enjoyed the benefits of having been established a decade earlier. This trend persisted after the transition to television news programs until the late 1970s, when ABC debuted several highly popular, untraditional news programs, including *20/20*, *Nightline*, and *This Week*, which experienced enduring popularity from the moment of inception. Since then, ABC News has remained one of the top three news departments in the United States, vying for supremacy over NBC and CBS with television, radio, and online news programs.

INTRODUCTION

Rick Warren founded the Saddleback Church in Lake Forest, California, in 1980. As head pastor, Warren adhered to the tenets of the Southern Baptist evangelical tradition, and his updated take on the Gospel helped attract droves of followers to his congregation. By the end of the 2000s decade, Saddleback Church reported an average of over twenty thousand attendees at Sunday services. In 1995, Warren published *The Purpose Driven Church*, an exposition of his theories on the Bible and the role of churches in contemporary American life. The book was well-received by the Christian literary and theoretical establishment, leading Warren to pen another book, titled *The Purpose Driven Life*. Divided into forty small chapters, *The Purpose Driven Life* was intended to be read over the course of forty days, with each corresponding chapter containing a Bible verse around which readers were meant to focus their thoughts and actions for that day. The chapters were divided into six broader lessons, which together comprised Warren's theological philosophy (covering five concepts) for the purpose of human life on Earth: worship, fellowship, discipleship, ministry, and evangelism.

Upon completing the book, the reader was intended to feel the inspiration and justification for a life devoted to Christian God. Warren's simple, concise summarization of the Bible's overarching messages helped his followers understand and embrace the position of religion in the chaotic, fast-paced twenty-first century. The fundamental message of *The Purpose Driven Life* was that humanity exists to serve and please God, and that only in doing so can people find true fulfillment, happiness, and satisfaction.

SIGNIFICANCE

The Purpose Driven Life was among the best-selling self-help books of the 2000s decade, appearing on the *New York Times* and *Wall Street Journal* best-seller lists as well as an extended appearance on the *Publisher's*

Saddleback Church pastor and successful author Rick Warren. © KRISTIN CALLAHAN/EVERETT COLLECTION INC./ALAMY.

Weekly chart. The book sold over thirty million copies within the first five years of its release and was translated into dozens of languages.

Warren's works had considerable impact on the practice of Christianity during the 2000s decade. They were credited with renewing public interest in the faith by providing context and understandability to the Bible's teachings. Churches across the United States adopted the suggestions contained in both *The Purpose Driven Life* and *The Purpose Driven Church* to accommodate younger members of their congregations and to help make their teachings seem relevant by giving concrete, "real-world" examples of how to apply the precepts of Christianity to everyday life. Some Christian traditionalists objected to this practice, however, arguing that it obscured the original teachings of the Bible behind popular psychology and self-help.

The congenial Warren was so well-received by the general American public that, despite his conservative political ideology, he was invited to perform the invocation at the inauguration ceremony of President Barack Obama in 2009.

■ PRIMARY SOURCE

"RICK WARREN AND PURPOSE-DRIVEN STRIFE"

SYNOPSIS: This article describes the controversy surrounding the adoption of Rick Warren's *Purpose Driven Life* in churches.

Pastor Rick Warren of Saddleback Church in California may be the best-known pastor on the planet. His book, "The Purpose Driven Life," has been translated into 56 languages and has sold 30 million copies.

However, the idea behind "purpose driven" is not something Pastor Warren takes credit for creating.

"The history of this idea—'purpose driven'—is not something I thought up in the first place," Warren explains. "There have been hundreds of books throughout history that talked about worship, fellowship, discipleship, ministry and evangelism."

But while these five purposes are biblically based, there is no denying that Warren has popularized these purposes around the world. He says he has trained 400,000 pastors worldwide to start purpose-driven churches. But it's Warren's untraditional use of the Christian language that may be the reason for his enormous following.

"I like to teach theology to people without telling them it's theology and without using theological terms," he said. "Simple does not mean simplistic. Simple does not mean superficial. Simple means it's clear."

But Warren's "outside in" approach to church growth is now causing rumblings. This past fall, *The Wall Street Journal* published an article titled "'Purpose driven' methods divide: Some evangelicals object to 'Madison Avenue' marketing of churches that follow author's advice." In North Wilkesboro, N.C., one church exemplifies this schism.

Tom Bartlett is the pastor of Celebration Church—now a purpose-driven church. When he arrived in 2004, the church was more traditional and was in a poor state.

Contemporary Worship

Bartlett said that when he first came to Celebration Church, the congregation was small and shrinking.

"There were 40 people my first Sunday, and I think the church had gotten down to about ... 25 to 30 in attendance."

It was a small showing. But then Bartlett began to apply Warren's five strategies for church growth. He started with contemporary worship and, like in hundreds of other purpose-driven churches nationwide, out went the hymns and in came the drums and guitars. Within two years, the congregation at Celebration Church grew from 30 congregants to 300.

"We've taken a particular style that we think reaches the people that we're trying to reach," Bartlett said. "There's a generation of people that we're not reaching by and large. And predominantly, they're younger, and we see them leaving the church in droves."

But not everybody in Bartlett's congregation was excited about the change. One of the first people to leave Bartlett's church was a retired pastor, Joe Owings.

"Their music took on a much more contemporary effect—pop music," said Owings. "[Bartlett] began to use, basically, the 'Saddleback Valley approach' to church growth and so forth. It was during that time that we began to get uncomfortable with the music. The emphasis seemed to be more on younger people and a new generation, and we just felt like we did not fit in."

'Self-Help Ministry'

Warren says on his Web site that "Purpose driven is not about a particular worship style." But many who follow Warren's approach tend to jettison traditional forms of worship.

And what about those people who don't want to hear guitar music, who prefer a quiet, reverent worship?

"Well, that's why there's different churches for different folks," said Bartlett. "And we realize that we're probably not going to reach every person."

But beyond ageism, there's more serious criticism that's now leveled at Warren and his purpose-driven churches: that the fundamental doctrines of Christianity are being mixed with popular psychology to help produce an evangelical version of "self-help."

"Well, the preaching was very much topical preaching," Owings said about the church he parted from in North Carolina. "It tended to deal with how to have a better marriage, or how to do this or how to do this. It was more self-help type ministry."

When asked if he believed that some churches had become pop psychology centers focusing too much on self-esteem and well-being, Owings said, "Yes. It's merchandising. . . . It tends to use psychological techniques. And it quotes more Freud, maybe, than it does the Bible."

It's Not About You?

Warren said that there is a danger in merging Christianity with psychology.

"Absolutely, there's a danger," he said. "Because what it does is feed this self-centeredness . . . I say, it's not about you. It's all about God. And one of the biggest myths is that all mega churches are alike. Well, they're not."

Warren also admitted that it can be difficult to strike a balance between the concerns of modern life and a focus on the Bible.

"When you're preaching and teaching the good news, you walk a very fine line where you're taking the world of the Bible and the world of today, and you're building a bridge between those [worlds]," he explained. "Now, it's easy to be biblical if you don't care about being relevant . . . And it's easy to be relevant if you don't care about being biblical. I happen to want to be both."

And so does Bartlett, who, at a recent church service, preached practically about love and giving out life skills to married couples. Bartlett firmly believes in using modern methods to convey old truths—that God wants us to live an abundant life.

"I think the problem most theologians have [with us] is that we don't use the big theological words. But we talk about the terms of repentance, we talk about the terms of justification and sanctification," he said. "And so we may not use the theological terms, but the concepts are conveyed in a way that people can understand."

Paying the Price

So the debate goes on: Is the purpose-driven method simplifying Christianity in exchange for church growth? The founder of the movement says the conflicts and divisions are inevitable costs.

"You know, I wouldn't intentionally want to cause pain to any person or to anyone," Warren said. "Am I willing to put up with pain so the people [that] Jesus Christ died for can come to know him? Absolutely."

Warren said that if some churches may suffer as a result of applying some of those principles, then "that's the price."

"Every church has to make the decision. . . . Is it going to live for itself, or is it going to live for the world that Jesus died for?"

When asked if he thinks that some of these splits are actually because Christians themselves are indulgent and refusing to change, Warren said, "Oh, without a doubt."

And when asked if he blames them, he replied, "I do blame them."

FURTHER RESOURCES

Books

Warren, Rick. *The Purpose Driven Church*. Grand Rapids, MI: Zondervan, 1995.

Warren, Rick. *The Purpose Driven Life*. Grand Rapids, MI: Zondervan, 2002.

Web Sites

"Ashley Smith's 'Unlikely Angel.'" *CBS News*, February 11, 2009. www.cbsnews.com/stories/2005/10/04/earlyshow/leisure/books/main910559.shtml (accessed on March 24, 2013).

Hagerty, Barbara Bradley. "Rick Warren: The Purpose-Driven Pastor." *NPR*. www.npr.org/templates/story/story.php?storyId=99529977 (accessed on March 24, 2013).

Purpose Driven. http://purposedriven.com/ (accessed on March 24, 2013).

"Views About Abortion"

Table

By: Pew Research Center

Date: 2008

Source: Pew Research Center. "Views About Abortion." *U.S. Religious Landscape Survey*, 2008. http://religions.pewforum.org/pdf/comparison-Views%20About%20Abortion.pdf (accessed on March 23, 2013).

About the Organization: The nonprofit Pew Research Center is, according to its Web site, "a nonpartisan fact tank that informs the public about the issues, attitudes and trends shaping America and the world." To that end, Pew conducts public polls, media analysis, and research. The organization achieves its goals through the efforts of seven research projects it has developed over time: Center for the People and the Press, Project for Excellence in Journalism, Forum on Religion and Public Life, Hispanic Center, Global Attitudes Project, Social and Demographic Trends, and Administration and Publishing.

INTRODUCTION

Induced abortion—the termination of pregnancy by the removal from the uterus of a fetus or embryo prior to viability—has been a contentious social and political issue for decades. History indicates that induced abortion had been used to terminate pregnancies dating as far back as c. 2700 BCE in China. Ancient Egyptians and citizens of the Roman Empire used numerous methods to induce unwanted pregnancies. As technology improved, so did abortion techniques, but moral and ethical issues prevented the procedure from being legalized throughout the world. Although some countries passed laws allowing for abortion under any or sometimes certain circumstances in the first half of

U.S. RELIGIOUS LANDSCAPE SURVEY

Views About Abortion

U.S. Religious Traditions	Legal in all cases	Legal in most cases	Illegal in most cases	Illegal in all cases	Don't know/ refused	Sample Size
National Total	18%	33%	27%	16%	6%	35556
Evangelical Churches	9%	24%	36%	25%	6%	9472
Mainline Churches	20%	42%	23%	7%	7%	7470
Historically Black Churches	18%	29%	23%	23%	8%	1995
Catholics	18%	32%	27%	16%	7%	8054
Mormons	8%	19%	61%	9%	4%	581
Orthodox	24%	38%	20%	10%	8%	363
Jehovah's Witnesses	5%	11%	25%	52%	7%	215
Other Christians	33%	42%	13%	6%	7%	129
Jews	40%	44%	9%	5%	2%	682
Muslims	13%	35%	35%	13%	4%	116
Buddhists	35%	46%	10%	3%	6%	411
Hindus	23%	46%	19%	5%	7%	257
Other Faiths	36%	41%	13%	4%	6%	449
Unaffiliated	29%	41%	16%	8%	6%	5048

Question wording: On another subject, do you think abortion should be (READ CATEGORIES IN ORDER TO HALF SAMPLE; IN REVERSE ORDER TO OTHER HALF OF SAMPLE) legal in all cases, legal in most cases, illegal in most cases, or illegal in all cases?

PRIMARY SOURCE

"Views About Abortion"

SYNOPSIS: This table illustrates views about abortion by religious affiliation in 2008. © PEW FORUM ON RELIGION AND PUBLIC LIFE.

the twentieth century, it was not until after 1950 that it became more widely accepted and the right to have one, protected. In the United States, this right was upheld in the famous 1973 court case, *Roe v. Wade*.

Religious views have directly affected individuals' beliefs about abortion. The Catholic Church, a vocal opponent of abortion, was not always so. Until the 1800s, the Church was divided in its stance on the procedure. Prior to that time, some religious leaders, such as Pope Gregory XIII (1572–1585), believed an embryo younger than forty days was not human, and so abortion before that time was not homicide. Pope Sixtus V (1575–1590) was the first pope to equate abortion with homicide, no matter what stage of pregnancy the mother was in. But his successor, Gregory XIV (1535–1591), deemed Sixtus V's views as too strict and ordered his edicts to be treated as if they had never existed. Abortion was a see-saw issue, one that depended wholly upon the personal views and beliefs of leaders.

The Pew Forum on Religion and Public Life's table here shows that, toward the end of the 2000s,

Americans were just as divided as they had ever been, regardless of religion. The only religion that forbade abortion under any circumstance was Catholicism, and yet, 48 percent of those Catholics surveyed believed abortion should be legal in all or most cases.

SIGNIFICANCE

By the end of the 2000s, most religions allowed for abortion in cases of rape or incest, or when keeping the pregnancy endangered the mother's life. According to Pew, surveys conducted in 2012 indicated that 54 percent of all Americans believed abortion should be legal in all or most cases. This statistic had remained relatively stable since the mid-1990s. Aside from religion, factors like political party, age, gender, and level of education played a role in determining individual opinion on the topic of abortion. For example, 58 percent of Republicans believed the procedure should be illegal in all or most cases, while 66 percent of Democrats believed it should be legal in all or most cases. Independents voted more along the lines of Democrats on the issue, with 55 percent believing abortion should be legal in all or most cases.

Each year seemed to have its surprises in the ongoing abortion debate. In 2012, a media frenzy ensued when the Susan G. Komen for the Cure, a prominent breast cancer research nonprofit, announced its plan to revoke $680,000 in grants to Planned Parenthood. The grants allowed Planned Parenthood, the nation's largest abortion provider, to fund breast screenings and education programs. Planned Parenthood—along with many American women—saw the revocation of grant monies as Komen's giving in to pressure from anti-abortion groups like LifeWay Christian Resources, a group owned by the Southern Baptist Convention. Komen denied the allegation and quickly reinstated the grants, but public outrage was not quelled. A 2012 Harris Interactive study indicated that Komen's "brand health" score fell 21 percent from 2011. It was the second-largest decline in the twenty-three years Harris had conducted the study.

▮ PRIMARY SOURCE

"VIEWS ABOUT ABORTION"

See primary source table.

▮▮

FURTHER RESOURCES
Books

Wicklund, Susan. *This Common Secret: My Journey as an Abortion Doctor.* Philadelphia: PublicAffairs, 2007.

Web Sites

"Abortion." *Pew Forum on Religion & Public Life*, January 2013. www.pewforum.org/Topics/Issues/Abortion/ (accessed on March 23, 2013).

Belluck, Pam. "Cancer Group Halts Financing to Planned Parenthood." *New York Times*, January 31, 2012. www.nytimes.com/2012/02/01/us/cancer-group-halts-financing-to-planned-parenthood.html (accessed on March 23, 2013).

"Historical Attitudes to Abortion." *BBC*. www.bbc.co.uk/ethics/abortion/legal/history_1.shtml (accessed on March 23, 2013).

Pew Research Center. www.pewresearch.org/ (accessed on March 23, 2013).

Barack Obama and His Controversial Pastor

"Obama's Pastor: God Damn America, U.S. to Blame for 9/11"

Web site article

By: Brian Ross

Date: March 13, 2008

Source: Ross, Brian. "Obama's Pastor: God Damn America, U.S. to Blame for 9/11." *ABC News*, March 13, 2008. http://abcnews.go.com/Blotter/DemocraticDebate/story?id=4443788&page=1#.ULUVJoc1mSp (accessed on March 23, 2013).

About the News Organization: Compared to its direct competitors, ABC News got a late start in the U.S. news environment. The organization was founded as a division of the American Broadcasting Company in 1945, two years after the company's formation, and immediately initiated a regular radio news schedule. ABC News consistently placed third in listenership and income after rivals NBC and CBS, which both enjoyed the benefits of having been established a decade earlier. This trend persisted after the transition to television news programs until the late 1970s, when ABC debuted several highly popular, untraditional news programs, including *20/20*, *Nightline*, and *This Week*, which experienced enduring popularity from the moment of inception. Since then, ABC News has remained one of the top three news departments in the United States, vying for supremacy over NBC and CBS with television, radio, and online news programs.

"A More Perfect Union"

Speech

By: Barack Obama

Date: March 18, 2008

Source: Obama, Barack. "A More Perfect Union." *Huffington Post*, March 18, 2008. www.huffingtonpost. com/2008/03/18/obama-race-speech-read-th_n_92077. html (accessed on March 23, 2013).

About the Author: Democrat Barack Obama served in the Illinois state senate from 1997 to 2004 and in the U.S. Senate from 2005 to 2008 before being elected as the forty-fourth president of the United States in 2008. Obama won the Nobel Peace Prize in 2009 and was re-elected to the White House in 2012.

INTRODUCTION

In March 2008, in the midst of the intense U.S. presidential contest, ABC News published and analyzed excerpts from the sermons of Pastor Jeremiah Wright, the retired former head of Chicago's Trinity United Church of Christ, of which presidential candidate Barack Obama had been a member since the 1980s. The excerpts published by ABC originated primarily from two of Wright's sermons—the first, titled "The Day of Jerusalem's Fall," was a response to the September 11, 2001, terrorist attacks, delivered on September 16, 2001; the second, "Confusing God and Government," was concerned with the distinction between morality and legality, and was delivered on April 13, 2003. The excerpts, which included statements that the U.S. government perpetrates terrorism across the globe and condemnations of its conduct regarding minorities, were highly inflammatory, sparking considerable controversy immediately following their publication.

Obama's long relationship with Wright, who had performed the future president's wedding ceremony and the baptisms of his children, was transformed into a political liability. Public officials and news media alike condemned the allegedly anti-American pastor, whose sermons and public speeches frequently expressed unpopular opinions on race relations, Zionist Judaism, and the actions of the U.S. government and military, which resulted in him being labeled a racist and an agitator. Obama's initial reaction to the controversy was not to condemn Wright or the Trinity United Church, but only to disavow the sentiments contained in the published excerpts. As the debate over Wright's sermons grew, however, the candidate came under attack for his connection to the pastor and his radical beliefs, prompting Obama to deliver a speech, titled "A More Perfect Union," on March 18, publicly dissociating himself from Wright's ideology.

SIGNIFICANCE

Wright responded to this perceived betrayal by embarking on a series of public appearances, defending his position by claiming that the excerpts from his sermons had been taken out of context and that his general position had been mischaracterized by the media. It was widely speculated at the time that Wright made deliberately divisive and controversial remarks during this media tour in an effort to damage Obama's campaign in revenge for the candidate's lack of support. On April 29, after attempting to placate the pastor in private, Obama became angry with Wright for his continued belligerence. The presidential candidate appeared on television to publicly state his disavowal of the pastor, and he left the Trinity United Church the following month. This did little to calm the media, however, as the rest of the campaign would involve commentary from politicians, academicians, and pundits alike about Wright and his connection to Obama.

The Jeremiah Wright episode was one of the most-discussed issues of the 2008 presidential race and probably the most politically damaging to Obama's campaign, although he was able to overcome the controversy to ultimately win the election and become president of the United States. The controversy was not materially dissimilar from any other of its type in the nation's electoral history, in that it involved intense scrutiny of a single inflammatory figure associated with a candidate and subsequent public posturing. The central issues of the controversy—minority rights, the role of religion in government, and federal conduct—are as old as the notion of democracy and have been analyzed and discussed seemingly infinitely. Likewise, Wright's invective, directed at the United States and its treatment of minorities, will likely be remembered as one more example of how a candidate's religious affiliations can affect his or her success in American politics.

■ PRIMARY SOURCE

"OBAMA'S PASTOR: GOD DAMN AMERICA, U.S. TO BLAME FOR 9/11"

SYNOPSIS: In this article, ABC News correspondent Brian Ross catalyzes the Jeremiah Wright controversy by publishing several quotations from the pastor's sermons.

Sen. Barack Obama's pastor says blacks should not sing "God Bless America" but "God damn America."

The Rev. Jeremiah Wright, Obama's pastor for the last 20 years at the Trinity United Church of Christ on

Chicago's south side, has a long history of what even Obama's campaign aides concede is "inflammatory rhetoric," including the assertion that the United States brought on the 9/11 attacks with its own "terrorism."

In a campaign appearance earlier this month, Sen. Obama said, "I don't think my church is actually particularly controversial." He said Rev. Wright "is like an old uncle who says things I don't always agree with," telling a Jewish group that everyone has someone like that in their family.

Rev. Wright married Obama and his wife Michelle, baptized their two daughters and is credited by Obama for the title of his book, "The Audacity of Hope."

An ABC News review of dozens of Rev. Wright's sermons, offered for sale by the church, found repeated denunciations of the U.S. based on what he described as his reading of the Gospels and the treatment of black Americans.

"The government gives them the drugs, builds bigger prisons, passes a three-strike law and then wants us to sing 'God Bless America.' No, no, no, God damn America, that's in the Bible for killing innocent people," he said in a 2003 sermon. "God damn America for treating our citizens as less than human. God damn America for as long as she acts like she is God and she is supreme."

In addition to damning America, he told his congregation on the Sunday after Sept. 11, 2001 that the United States had brought on al Qaeda's attacks because of its own terrorism.

"We bombed Hiroshima, we bombed Nagasaki, and we nuked far more than the thousands in New York and the Pentagon, and we never batted an eye," Rev. Wright said in a sermon on Sept. 16, 2001.

"We have supported state terrorism against the Palestinians and black South Africans, and now we are indignant because the stuff we have done overseas is now brought right back to our own front yards. America's chickens are coming home to roost," he told his congregation.

Sen. Obama told the *New York Times* he was not at the church on the day of Rev. Wright's 9/11 sermon. "The violence of 9/11 was inexcusable and without justification," Obama said in a recent interview. "It sounds like he was trying to be provocative," Obama told the paper....

"I wouldn't call it radical. I call it being black in America," said one congregation member outside the church last Sunday....

Rev. Wright, who declined to be interviewed by ABC News, is considered one of the country's 10 most influential black pastors, according to members of the Obama campaign.

Obama has praised at least one aspect of Rev. Wright's approach, referring to his "social gospel" and his focus on Africa, "and I agree with him on that." ...

In a statement to ABCNews.com, Obama's press spokesman Bill Burton said, "Sen. Obama has said repeatedly that personal attacks such as this have no place in this campaign or our politics, whether they're offered from a platform at a rally or the pulpit of a church. Sen. Obama does not think of the pastor of his church in political terms. Like a member of his family, there are things he says with which Sen. Obama deeply disagrees. But now that he is retired, that doesn't detract from Sen. Obama's affection for Rev. Wright or his appreciation for the good works he has done."

PRIMARY SOURCE

"A MORE PERFECT UNION"

SYNOPSIS: Democrat presidential candidate Barack Obama responds to Reverend Jeremiah Wright's fiery sermons in a speech that discussed issues of race in a way that no other presidential candidate before him ever had.

"We the people, in order to form a more perfect union."

Two hundred and twenty one years ago, in a hall that still stands across the street, a group of men gathered and, with these simple words, launched America's improbable experiment in democracy. Farmers and scholars; statesmen and patriots who had traveled across an ocean to escape tyranny and persecution finally made real their declaration of independence at a Philadelphia convention that lasted through the spring of 1787.

The document they produced was eventually signed but ultimately unfinished. It was stained by this nation's original sin of slavery, a question that divided the colonies and brought the convention to a stalemate until the founders chose to allow the slave trade to continue for at least twenty more years, and to leave any final resolution to future generations.

Of course, the answer to the slavery question was already embedded within our Constitution—a Constitution that had at its very core the ideal of equal citizenship under the law; a Constitution that promised its people liberty, and justice, and a union that could be and should be perfected over time.

And yet words on a parchment would not be enough to deliver slaves from bondage, or provide men and women of every color and creed their full rights and obligations as citizens of the United States. What would be needed were Americans in successive generations who were willing to do their part—through protests and struggle, on the streets and in the courts, through a civil war and civil disobedience and always at great risk—to

Rev. Jeremiah Wright Jr., the former pastor of Barack Obama, whose controversial comments in 2008 caused a stir during Obama's presidential campaign. © JEFF KOWALSKY/EPA/CORBIS.

narrow that gap between the promise of our ideals and the reality of their time.

This was one of the tasks we set forth at the beginning of this campaign—to continue the long march of those who came before us, a march for a more just, more equal, more free, more caring and more prosperous America. I chose to run for the presidency at this moment in history because I believe deeply that we cannot solve the challenges of our time unless we solve them together—unless we perfect our union by understanding that we may have different stories, but we hold common hopes; that we may not look the same and we may not have come from the same place, but we all want to move in the same direction—towards a better future for our children and our grandchildren.

This belief comes from my unyielding faith in the decency and generosity of the American people. But it also comes from my own American story.

I am the son of a black man from Kenya and a white woman from Kansas. I was raised with the help of a white grandfather who survived a Depression to serve in Patton's Army during World War II and a white grandmother who worked on a bomber assembly line at Fort Leavenworth while he was overseas. I've gone to some of the best schools in America and lived in one of the world's poorest nations. I am married to a black American who carries within her the blood of slaves and slave owners—an inheritance we pass on to our two precious daughters. I have brothers, sisters, nieces, nephews, uncles and cousins, of every race and every hue, scattered across three continents, and for as long as I live, I will never forget that in no other country on Earth is my story even possible.

It's a story that hasn't made me the most conventional candidate. But it is a story that has seared into my genetic makeup the idea that this nation is more than the sum of its parts—that out of many, we are truly one.

Throughout the first year of this campaign, against all predictions to the contrary, we saw how hungry the American people were for this message of unity. Despite the temptation to view my candidacy through a purely racial lens, we won commanding victories in states with some of the whitest populations in the country. In South Carolina, where the Confederate Flag still flies, we built a powerful coalition of African Americans and white Americans.

This is not to say that race has not been an issue in the campaign. At various stages in the campaign, some commentators have deemed me either "too black" or "not black enough." We saw racial tensions bubble to the surface during the week before the South Carolina primary. The press has scoured every exit poll for the latest evidence of racial polarization, not just in terms of white and black, but black and brown as well.

And yet, it has only been in the last couple of weeks that the discussion of race in this campaign has taken a particularly divisive turn.

On one end of the spectrum, we've heard the implication that my candidacy is somehow an exercise in affirmative action; that it's based solely on the desire of wide-eyed liberals to purchase racial reconciliation on the cheap. On the other end, we've heard my former pastor, Reverend Jeremiah Wright, use incendiary language to express views that have the potential not only to widen the racial divide, but views that denigrate both the greatness and the goodness of our nation; that rightly offend white and black alike.

I have already condemned, in unequivocal terms, the statements of Reverend Wright that have caused such controversy. For some, nagging questions remain. Did I know him to be an occasionally fierce critic of American domestic and foreign policy? Of course. Did I ever hear him make remarks that could be considered controversial while I sat in church? Yes. Did I strongly disagree with many of his political views? Absolutely—just as I'm sure many of you have heard remarks from your pastors, priests, or rabbis with which you strongly disagreed.

But the remarks that have caused this recent firestorm weren't simply controversial. They weren't simply a religious leader's effort to speak out against perceived injustice. Instead, they expressed a profoundly distorted view of this country—a view that sees white racism as endemic, and that elevates what is wrong with America above all that we know is right with America; a view that sees the conflicts in the Middle East as rooted primarily in the actions of stalwart allies like Israel, instead of emanating from the perverse and hateful ideologies of radical Islam.

As such, Reverend Wright's comments were not only wrong but divisive, divisive at a time when we need unity; racially charged at a time when we need to come together to solve a set of monumental problems—two wars, a terrorist threat, a falling economy, a chronic health care crisis and potentially devastating climate change; problems that are neither black or white or Latino or Asian, but rather problems that confront us all.

Given my background, my politics, and my professed values and ideals, there will no doubt be those for whom my statements of condemnation are not enough. Why associate myself with Reverend Wright in the first place, they may ask? Why not join another church? And I confess that if all that I knew of Reverend Wright were the snippets of those sermons that have run in an endless loop on the television and You Tube, or if Trinity United Church of Christ conformed to the caricatures being peddled by some commentators, there is no doubt that I would react in much the same way.

But the truth is, that isn't all that I know of the man. The man I met more than twenty years ago is a man who helped introduce me to my Christian faith, a man who spoke to me about our obligations to love one another; to care for the sick and lift up the poor. He is a man who served his country as a U.S. Marine; who has studied and lectured at some of the finest universities and seminaries in the country, and who for over thirty years led a church that serves the community by doing God's work here on Earth—by housing the homeless, ministering to the needy, providing day care services and scholarships and prison ministries, and reaching out to those suffering from HIV/AIDS.

In my first book, *Dreams from My Father*, I described the experience of my first service at Trinity:

> People began to shout, to rise from their seats and clap and cry out, a forceful wind carrying the reverend's voice up into the rafters.... And in that single note—hope!—I heard something else; at the foot of that cross, inside the thousands of churches across the city, I imagined the stories of ordinary black people merging with the stories of David and Goliath, Moses and Pharaoh, the Christians in the lion's den, Ezekiel's field of dry bones. Those stories—of survival, and freedom, and hope—became our story, my story; the blood that had spilled was our blood, the tears our tears; until this black church, on this bright day, seemed once more a vessel carrying the story of a people into future generations and into a larger world. Our trials and triumphs became at once unique and universal, black and more than black; in

Then-U.S. senator Barack Obama of Illinois prays during services at Trinity United Church of Christ in Chicago on October 31, 2004. © AP IMAGES/NAM Y. HUH.

chronicling our journey, the stories and songs gave us a means to reclaim memories that we didn't need to feel shame about ... memories that all people might study and cherish—and with which we could start to rebuild.

That has been my experience at Trinity. Like other predominantly black churches across the country, Trinity embodies the black community in its entirety—the doctor and the welfare mom, the model student and the former gang-banger. Like other black churches, Trinity's services are full of raucous laughter and sometimes bawdy humor. They are full of dancing, clapping, screaming and shouting that may seem jarring to the untrained ear. The church contains in full the kindness and cruelty, the fierce intelligence and the shocking ignorance, the struggles and successes, the love and yes, the bitterness and bias that make up the black experience in America.

And this helps explain, perhaps, my relationship with Reverend Wright. As imperfect as he may be, he has been like family to me. He strengthened my faith, officiated my wedding, and baptized my children. Not once in my conversations with him have I heard him talk about any ethnic group in derogatory terms, or treat whites with whom he interacted with anything but courtesy and respect. He contains within him the contradictions—the good and the bad—of the community that he has served diligently for so many years.

I can no more disown him than I can disown the black community. I can no more disown him than I can my white grandmother—a woman who helped raise me, a woman who sacrificed again and again for me, a woman who loves me as much as she loves anything in this world, but a woman who once confessed her fear of black men who passed by her on the street, and who on more than one occasion has uttered racial or ethnic stereotypes that made me cringe.

These people are a part of me. And they are a part of America, this country that I love.

Some will see this as an attempt to justify or excuse comments that are simply inexcusable. I can assure you it is not. I suppose the politically safe thing would be to move on from this episode and just hope that it fades into the woodwork. We can dismiss Reverend Wright as a crank or a demagogue, just as some have dismissed Geraldine Ferraro, in the aftermath of her recent statements, as harboring some deep-seated racial bias.

But race is an issue that I believe this nation cannot afford to ignore right now. We would be making the same mistake that Reverend Wright made in his offending sermons about America—to simplify and stereotype and amplify the negative to the point that it distorts reality.

The fact is that the comments that have been made and the issues that have surfaced over the last few weeks reflect the complexities of race in this country that we've never really worked through—a part of our union that we have yet to perfect. And if we walk away now, if we simply retreat into our respective corners, we will never be able to come together and solve challenges like health care, or education, or the need to find good jobs for every American.

Understanding this reality requires a reminder of how we arrived at this point. As William Faulkner once wrote, "The past isn't dead and buried. In fact, it isn't even past." We do not need to recite here the history of racial injustice in this country. But we do need to remind ourselves that so many of the disparities that exist in the African-American community today can be directly traced to inequalities passed on from an earlier generation that suffered under the brutal legacy of slavery and Jim Crow.

Segregated schools were, and are, inferior schools; we still haven't fixed them, fifty years after *Brown v. Board of Education*, and the inferior education they provided, then and now, helps explain the pervasive achievement gap between today's black and white students.

Legalized discrimination—where blacks were prevented, often through violence, from owning property, or loans were not granted to African-American business owners, or black homeowners could not access FHA mortgages, or blacks were excluded from unions, or the police force, or fire departments—meant that black families could not amass any meaningful wealth to bequeath to future generations. That history helps explain the wealth and income gap between black and white, and the concentrated pockets of poverty that persists in so many of today's urban and rural communities.

A lack of economic opportunity among black men, and the shame and frustration that came from not being able to provide for one's family, contributed to the erosion of black families—a problem that welfare policies for many years may have worsened. And the lack of basic services in so many urban black neighborhoods—parks for kids to play in, police walking the beat, regular garbage pick-up and building code enforcement—all helped create a cycle of violence, blight and neglect that continue to haunt us.

This is the reality in which Reverend Wright and other African-Americans of his generation grew up. They came of age in the late fifties and early sixties, a time when segregation was still the law of the land and opportunity was systematically constricted. What's remarkable is not how many failed in the face of discrimination, but rather how many men and women overcame the odds; how many were able to make a way out of no way for those like me who would come after them.

But for all those who scratched and clawed their way to get a piece of the American Dream, there were many who didn't make it—those who were ultimately defeated, in one way or another, by discrimination. That legacy of defeat was passed on to future generations—those young men and increasingly young women who we see standing on street corners or languishing in our prisons, without hope or prospects for the future. Even for those blacks who did make it, questions of race, and racism, continue to define their worldview in fundamental ways. For the men and women of Reverend Wright's generation, the memories of humiliation and doubt and fear have not gone away; nor has the anger and the bitterness of those years. That anger may not get expressed in public, in front of white co-workers or white friends. But it does find voice in the barbershop or around the kitchen table. At times, that anger is exploited by politicians, to gin up votes along racial lines, or to make up for a politician's own failings.

And occasionally it finds voice in the church on Sunday morning, in the pulpit and in the pews. The fact that so many people are surprised to hear that anger in some of Reverend Wright's sermons simply reminds us of the old truism that the most segregated hour in American life occurs on Sunday morning. That anger is not always productive; indeed, all too often it distracts attention from solving real problems; it keeps us from squarely facing our own complicity in our condition, and prevents the African-American community from forging the alliances it needs to bring about real change. But the anger is real; it is powerful; and to simply wish it away, to condemn it without understanding its roots, only serves to widen the chasm of misunderstanding that exists between the races.

In fact, a similar anger exists within segments of the white community. Most working- and middle-class white Americans don't feel that they have been particularly privileged by their race. Their experience is the immigrant experience—as far as they're concerned, no one's handed them anything, they've built it from scratch. They've worked hard all their lives, many times only to see their jobs shipped overseas or their pension dumped after a lifetime of labor. They are anxious about their futures, and feel their dreams slipping away; in an era of stagnant wages and global competition, opportunity comes to be seen as a zero sum game, in which your dreams come at my expense. So when they are told to bus their children to a school across town; when they hear that an African American is getting an advantage in landing a good job or a spot in a good college because of an injustice that they themselves never committed; when they're told that their fears about crime in urban neighborhoods are somehow prejudiced, resentment builds over time.

Like the anger within the black community, these resentments aren't always expressed in polite company. But they have helped shape the political landscape for at least a generation. Anger over welfare and affirmative action helped forge the Reagan Coalition. Politicians routinely exploited fears of crime for their own electoral ends. Talk show hosts and conservative commentators built entire careers unmasking bogus claims of racism while dismissing legitimate discussions of racial injustice and inequality as mere political correctness or reverse racism.

Just as black anger often proved counterproductive, so have these white resentments distracted attention from the real culprits of the middle class squeeze—a corporate culture rife with inside dealing, questionable accounting practices, and short-term greed; a Washington dominated by lobbyists and special interests; economic policies that favor the few over the many. And yet, to wish away the resentments of white Americans, to label them as misguided or even racist, without recognizing they are grounded in legitimate concerns—this too widens the racial divide, and blocks the path to understanding.

This is where we are right now. It's a racial stalemate we've been stuck in for years. Contrary to the claims of some of my critics, black and white, I have never been so naïve as to believe that we can get beyond our racial divisions in a single election cycle, or with a single candidacy—particularly a candidacy as imperfect as my own.

But I have asserted a firm conviction—a conviction rooted in my faith in God and my faith in the American people—that working together we can move beyond some of our old racial wounds, and that in fact we have no choice if we are to continue on the path of a more perfect union.

For the African-American community, that path means embracing the burdens of our past without becoming victims of our past. It means continuing to insist on a full measure of justice in every aspect of American life. But it also means binding our particular grievances—for better health care, and better schools, and better jobs—to the larger aspirations of all Americans—the white woman struggling to break the glass ceiling, the white man whose been laid off, the immigrant trying to feed his family. And it means taking full responsibility for our own lives—by demanding more from our fathers, and spending more time with our children, and reading to them, and teaching them that while they may face challenges and discrimination in their own lives, they must never succumb to despair or cynicism; they must always believe that they can write their own destiny.

Ironically, this quintessentially American—and yes, conservative—notion of self-help found frequent expression in Reverend Wright's sermons. But what my former pastor too often failed to understand is that embarking on a program of self-help also requires a belief that society can change.

The profound mistake of Reverend Wright's sermons is not that he spoke about racism in our society. It's that he spoke as if our society was static; as if no progress has been made; as if this country—a country that has made it possible for one of his own members to run for the highest office in the land and build a coalition of white and black; Latino and Asian, rich and poor, young and old—is still irrevocably bound to a tragic past. But what we know—what we have seen—is that America can change. That is true genius of this nation. What we have already achieved gives us hope—the audacity to hope—for what we can and must achieve tomorrow.

In the white community, the path to a more perfect union means acknowledging that what ails the African-American community does not just exist in the minds of black people; that the legacy of discrimination—and current incidents of discrimination, while less overt than in the past—are real and must be addressed. Not just with words, but with deeds—by investing in our schools and our communities; by enforcing our civil rights laws and ensuring fairness in our criminal justice system; by providing this generation with ladders of opportunity that were unavailable for previous generations. It requires all Americans to realize that your dreams do not have to come at the expense of my dreams; that investing in the health, welfare, and education of black and brown and white children will ultimately help all of America prosper.

In the end, then, what is called for is nothing more, and nothing less, than what all the world's great religions demand—that we do unto others as we would have them do unto us. Let us be our brother's keeper, Scripture tells us. Let us be our sister's keeper. Let us find that common stake we all have in one another, and let our politics reflect that spirit as well.

For we have a choice in this country. We can accept a politics that breeds division, and conflict, and cynicism. We can tackle race only as spectacle—as we did in the O.J. trial—or in the wake of tragedy, as we did in the aftermath of Katrina—or as fodder for the nightly news. We can play Reverend Wright's sermons on every channel, every day and talk about them from now until the election, and make the only question in this campaign whether or not the American people think that I somehow believe or sympathize with his most offensive words. We can pounce on some gaffe by a Hillary supporter as evidence that she's playing the race card, or we can speculate on whether white men will all flock to John McCain in the general election regardless of his policies.

We can do that.

But if we do, I can tell you that in the next election, we'll be talking about some other distraction. And then another one. And then another one. And nothing will change.

That is one option. Or, at this moment, in this election, we can come together and say, "Not this time." This time we want to talk about the crumbling schools that are stealing the future of black children and white children and Asian children and Hispanic children and Native American children. This time we want to reject the cynicism that tells us that these kids can't learn; that those kids who don't look like us are somebody else's problem. The children of America are not those kids, they are our kids, and we will not let them fall behind in a 21st century economy. Not this time.

This time we want to talk about how the lines in the Emergency Room are filled with whites and blacks and Hispanics who do not have health care; who don't have the power on their own to overcome the special interests in Washington, but who can take them on if we do it together.

This time we want to talk about the shuttered mills that once provided a decent life for men and women of every race, and the homes for sale that once belonged to Americans from every religion, every region, every walk of life. This time we want to talk about the fact that the real problem is not that someone who doesn't look like you might take your job; it's that the corporation you work for will ship it overseas for nothing more than a profit.

This time we want to talk about the men and women of every color and creed who serve together, and fight together, and bleed together under the same proud flag. We want to talk about how to bring them home from a war that never should've been authorized and never should've been waged, and we want to talk about how we'll show our patriotism by caring for them, and their families, and giving them the benefits they have earned.

I would not be running for President if I didn't believe with all my heart that this is what the vast majority of Americans want for this country. This union may never be perfect, but generation after generation has shown that it can always be perfected. And today, whenever I find myself feeling doubtful or cynical about this possibility, what gives me the most hope is the next generation—the young people whose attitudes and beliefs and openness to change have already made history in this election.

There is one story in particularly that I'd like to leave you with today—a story I told when I had the great honor of speaking on Dr. King's birthday at his home church, Ebenezer Baptist, in Atlanta.

There is a young, twenty-three-year old white woman named Ashley Baia who organized for our campaign in Florence, South Carolina. She had been working to organize a mostly African-American community since the beginning of this campaign, and one day she was at a roundtable discussion where everyone went around telling their story and why they were there.

And Ashley said that when she was nine years old, her mother got cancer. And because she had to miss days of work, she was let go and lost her health care. They had to file for bankruptcy, and that's when Ashley decided that she had to do something to help her mom.

She knew that food was one of their most expensive costs, and so Ashley convinced her mother that what she really liked and really wanted to eat more than anything else was mustard and relish sandwiches. Because that was the cheapest way to eat.

She did this for a year until her mom got better, and she told everyone at the roundtable that the reason she joined our campaign was so that she could help the millions of other children in the country who want and need to help their parents too.

Now Ashley might have made a different choice. Perhaps somebody told her along the way that the source of her mother's problems were blacks who were on welfare and too lazy to work, or Hispanics who were coming into the country illegally. But she didn't. She sought out allies in her fight against injustice.

Anyway, Ashley finishes her story and then goes around the room and asks everyone else why they're supporting the campaign. They all have different stories and reasons. Many bring up a specific issue. And finally they come to this elderly black man who's been sitting there quietly the entire time. And Ashley asks him why he's there. And he does not bring up a specific issue. He does not say health care or the economy. He does not say education or the war. He does not say that he was there because of Barack Obama. He simply says to everyone in the room, "I am here because of Ashley."

"I'm here because of Ashley." By itself, that single moment of recognition between that young white girl, the jobless, or education to our children.

But it is where we start. It is where our union grows stronger. And as so many generations have come to realize over the course of the two-hundred and twenty one years since a band of patriots signed that document in Philadelphia, that is where the perfection begins.

FURTHER RESOURCES

Books

Obama, Barack H. *The Audacity of Hope: Thoughts on Reclaiming the American Dream.* New York: Crown Publishers, 2006.

Wright, Jeremiah A., Jr. *What Makes You So Strong?: Sermons of Joy and Strength from Jeremiah A. Wright, Jr.* Chicago: Judson, 1993.

Web Sites

"Bill Moyers Journal," April 25, 2008. *PBS.* www.pbs.org/moyers/journal/04252008/watch.html (accessed on March 23, 2013).

"'The Day of Jerusalem's Fall'." *The Guardian*, March 27, 2008. www.guardian.co.uk/commentisfree/2008/mar/27/thedayofjerusalemsfall (accessed on March 23, 2013).

"Religious Groups' Views on Global Warming"

Poll

By: Pew Research Center

Date: April 16, 2009

Source: "Religious Groups' Views on Global Warming." *Pew Research Center*, April 16, 2009. www.pewforum.org/Science-and-Bioethics/Religious-Groups-Views-on-Global-Warming.aspx (accessed on March 23, 2013).

About the Organization: The nonprofit Pew Research Center is, according to its Web site, "a nonpartisan fact tank that informs the public about the issues, attitudes and trends shaping America and the world." To that end, Pew conducts public polls, media analysis, and research. The organization achieves its goals through the efforts of seven research projects it has developed over time: Center for the People and the Press, Project for Excellence in Journalism, Forum on Religion and Public Life, Hispanic Center, Global Attitudes Project, Social and Demographic Trends, and Administration and Publishing.

INTRODUCTION

According to *National Geographic*, global warming is the increase in temperature of the Earth's surface, caused by melting glaciers, rising sea levels, disappearing cloud forests, and struggling wildlife populations. Greenhouse gases, caused by human lifestyles and behaviors, are existing at higher levels than they have in the last 650,000 years. The "greenhouse effect" is the warming that occurs as gases in the Earth's atmosphere are trapped. The gases allow light in, but do not permit heat to escape, just like the glass walls of a greenhouse.

The concept of global warming is not new; scientists were aware of the greenhouse effect since 1824. Without the effect, Earth would be uninhabitable. But scientists now claim that until recently, the Earth's average temperature has remained relatively unchanged. Humans, however, are warming Earth with the burning of fossil fuels and other GHG emissions. As a result, climate changes are happening too fast for some living things; they cannot adapt. Global warming is also causing Greenland and Antarctica to melt, which could potentially raise sea levels too drastically. Another obvious and consistent change due to global warming is the occurrence of unpredictable, extreme weather conditions—intense heatwaves, hurricanes, droughts, storms, etc.

Scientists of yesteryear anticipated a global warming phenomenon, but media and weather experts and researchers have been warning Americans that it is happening more rapidly than ever expected. Eleven of the hottest years since thermometer readings have been available took place between 1995 and 2006.

The concept of global warming is taken seriously by some, scoffed at by others. In 2011, Yale University and George Mason University published a study of global warming beliefs based on political affiliation. Of respondents, 78 percent of Democrats agreed that global warming was happening in the here and now, compared to 53 percent of Republicans, 71 percent of Independents, and 34 percent of Tea Party members. The majority of Democrats (62 percent) believed global warming was being caused primarily because of human activity, compared to 36 percent of Republicans, 43 percent of Independents, and 18 percent of Tea Partiers.

The Pew Forum on Religion and Public Life conducted a survey as well, in 2009, which evidenced beliefs regarding global warming according to religious affiliation.

SIGNIFICANCE

As is true in how beliefs were expressed according to political affiliation, the more conservative or traditional the religion, the less likely a person was to believe in the concept of global warming. But the threat of global warming is quite real. Six thousand years ago, Nebraska—America's agricultural hub—was a desert. The Earth was one degree warmer then, than it is in the twenty-first century. The era known as the Dust Bowl? When topsoil literally blew away and the Earth refused to yield crops, causing hundreds of thousands of people to become starving refugees? The Earth was one degree warmer than it is in the twenty-first century. Scientists promise that global warming effects will be significantly more intense the next time they happen. Entire towns will be buried in sand, and Nebraska will return to its desert-like state, but so will eastern Montana, Wyoming, and several other states.

Even by the end of the 2000s, mountains like the Alps were coming apart. Sea ice, once believed to be permanent, was melting. Extreme weather conditions caused numerous hurricanes, earthquakes, and floods. All of these changes occurred with a rise of just one degree in the Earth's surface. More changes are expected before the end of the century: diseases like malaria will increase in incidence, ecosystems will change as animals become extinct, and sea levels are expected to rise between seven and twenty-three inches, among other phenomena.

There have been outspoken critics of the critics. Former U.S. vice president Al Gore wrote and starred in an Oscar-winning documentary about global warming in 2006. *An Inconvenient Truth* warned viewers of the environmental crisis at hand. The documentary has been credited with not only giving the environmental movement a much-needed boost of energy, but also for raising international awareness of climate change.

Americans, at least those who believe that global warming does indeed exist, have already begun taking steps to reduce carbon emissions and leave a smaller footprint. The manufacturing of hybrid cars, solar and wind energy, and energy-efficient lightbulbs; recycling; composting; consuming products made and packaged responsibly—some efforts are major, others less so. Activists agree: all are necessary.

Where once the global warming skeptics existed in both the scientific and the private community, as of 2013, there is no disagreement among scientific bodies of national or international standing: Global surfaces have increased as a direct result of human activity. Media and some private-interest groups may still fuel the controversy, but in scientific circles, the issue as to whether it exists or not has been resolved. As the *New York Times* reported, "The world is paying more attention than ever."

PRIMARY SOURCE

"RELIGIOUS GROUPS' VIEWS ON GLOBAL WARMING"

SYNOPSIS: This table shows how people of various religious affiliations perceive the concept of global warming.

Earth Day takes place on April 22 each year. One issue at the center of public discussions about the environment is global warming: whether it is occurring and what its causes might be. An analysis by the Pew Research Center's Forum on Religion & Public Life of a 2008 survey conducted by the Pew Research Center for the People & the Press examines views on global warming among major religious traditions in the U.S.

IS THERE SOLID EVIDENCE THE EARTH IS WARMING?
Total U.S. population

Yes, because of human activity: 47%
Yes, because of natural patterns: 18%
Yes, but don't know cause: 6%
No: 21%
Mixed evidence/Some evidence/Don't know: 8%

Unaffiliated

Yes, because of human activity: 58%
Yes, because of natural patterns: 11%
Yes, but don't know cause: 6%
No: 18%
Mixed evidence/Some evidence/Don't know: 7%

White mainline Protestants

Yes, because of human activity: 48%
Yes, because of natural patterns: 19%
Yes, but don't know cause: 6%
No: 19%
Mixed evidence/Some evidence/Don't know: 8%

White non-Hispanic Catholics

Yes, because of human activity: 44%
Yes, because of natural patterns: 20%
Yes, but don't know cause: 6%
No: 22%
Mixed evidence/Some evidence/Don't know: 8%

Black Protestants

Yes, because of human activity: 39%
Yes, because of natural patterns: 36%
Yes, but don't know cause: 5%
No: 15%
Mixed evidence/Some evidence/Don't know: 5%

White evangelical Protestants

Yes, because of human activity: 34%
Yes, because of natural patterns: 17%
Yes, but don't know cause: 7%
No: 31%
Mixed evidence/Some evidence/Don't know: 11%

FURTHER RESOURCES

Books

McKibben, Bill. *The Global Warming Reader*. New York: Penguin, 2011.

Web Sites

Leiserowitz, A., E. Maibach, C. Roser-Renouf, and J. D. Hmielowski. *Politics & Global Warming: Democrats, Republicans, Independents, and the Tea Party*. New Haven, CT: Yale Project on Climate Change Communication and George Mason University Center for Climate Change Communication, 2011. http://environment. yale.edu/climate/files/PoliticsGlobalWarming2011. pdf?utm_source=Yale+Project+on+Climate+Change+ Communication&utm_campaign=b83a63aa7a-Politics_ and_Global_Warming9_6_2011&utm_medium=email (accessed on March 23, 2013).

Revkin, Andrew C. "Arctic Melt Unnerves the Experts." *New York Times*, October 2, 2007. www.nytimes.com/2007/ 10/02/science/earth/02arct.html (accessed on March 23, 2013).

"What Is Global Warming?" *National Geographic*. http:// environment.nationalgeographic.com/environment/global- warming/gw-overview (accessed on March 23, 2013).

11 Science and Technology

Chronology

Important Events in Science and Technology, 2000–2009

2000

- Toyota begins marketing the hybrid car Prius in the United States; the manufacturer claims it has more power, better acceleration, and lower emissions than the previous model sold in Japan.

- Google begins selling advertisements associated with search keywords with bids starting at $.05 per click.

- The Society for Information Display gives Larry F. Weber its highest award for his contributions to plasma displays.

- Trek Technology and IBM begin selling the first Universal Serial Bus (USB) flash drives commercially.

- Researchers at the Duke University Medical Center implant electrodes in monkeys' brains and train them to reach for food using a robotic arm operated by those electrodes.

- Paleontologist John R. Horner and his team discover the Tyrannosaurus rex skeleton, designated MOR 1125, in the Hell Creek Formation in a remote corner of the Charles M. Russell National Wildlife Refuge in Montana.

- On May 1, under the executive order of President Bill Clinton, the "selective availability" restriction for the civilian use of the Global Positioning System (GPS) is lifted.

- On June 7, U.S. District Court judge Thomas Penfield Jackson finds that Microsoft is a monopoly and orders the company to release some of its intellectual property.

- On June 26, scientists produce the first draft of the Human Genome Sequence.

- In July, the search engine Google indexes one billion pages.

- In October, a public-private consortium announces plans to speed research on the sequencing of the complete genome of a laboratory mouse.

- In October, Sony and Pioneer unveil prototypes of what will become Blu-ray Disc players at the Combined Exhibition of Advanced Technologies (CEATEC) in Japan.

2001

- The United Nations Intergovernmental Panel on Climate Change (UNIPCC) issues a report stating that human activity is the "likely" cause of global warming.

- Scientists successfully clone the endangered gaur, a species of wild ox, but the clone dies two days after birth.

- Scientists in Italy report the successful cloning of a healthy baby mouflon, an endangered wild sheep.

- Jesse Sullivan, a double amputee, controls both of his robotic arms using a method of nerve-cell operation developed at the Rehabilitation Institute of Chicago.

- On January 20, President Clinton leaves the presidency with the best conservation record since Theodore Roosevelt.

- In March, President George W. Bush announces that the United States will not ratify the Kyoto Protocol because it would be detrimental to its economic interests.

- In August, President Bush restricts federally supported research to a limited number of stem-cell lines that had been previously obtained from surplus embryos at fertility clinics.

- On October 23, Apple launches the iPod music player.

- In November, scientists with the biotechnology company Advanced Cell Technology (ACT) report that they have cloned the first human embryos. The only embryo to survive the process stopped developing after dividing into six cells.

- In December, in a report titled "Abrupt Climate Change: Inevitable Surprises" the U.S. National Research Council announces that climate change may arrive quickly and have catastrophic effects.

2002

- Honda introduces the Accord Hybrid. Hybrids, particularly Toyota's Prius, start to take hold in the American marketplace.

- A British biotechnology company, PPL Therapeutics, announces that it has produced genetically modified pigs that can potentially be used to grow organs for human transplants.

- The *Odyssey* spacecraft spots what appear to be vast quantities of underground ice in the polar regions of Mars.

- The U.S. wind-energy industry wins passage of an extended production tax credit for electricity generated by wind power.

- On February 19, the Blu-ray Disc project is officially announced.

- In February–March, the Larson B ice shelf breaks off from the Antarctic Peninsula and floats away.

- On March 26, Elias A. Zerhouni is appointed to the National Institutes of Health by President Bush.

- In October, the television industry awards Donald Bitzer, Gene Slottow, and Robert Wilson an Emmy for technological achievement in plasma displays.

2003

- The third-generation Prius earns several awards and becomes one of the hottest-selling cars in Toyota's line of vehicles.

- The first 3G wireless network is launched.

- In January, the Food and Drug Administration (FDA) orders a pause in gene-therapy research involving retroviral vectors in blood stem cells.

- In February, the FDA's Biological Response Modifiers Advisory Committee meets to discuss measures that would allow some retroviral gene-therapy trials for the treatment of life-threatening diseases.

- On February 1, the space shuttle *Columbia* disintegrates upon reentry over Texas at approximately 9:00 AM, killing all seven astronauts—Commander Rick D. Husband, Pilot William McCool, Payload Commander Michael Anderson, Mission Specialist Kalpana Chawla, Mission Specialist David Brown, Mission Specialist Laurel Clark, and Payload Specialist Ilan Ramon, Israel's first astronaut.

- On February 2, National Aeronautics and Space Administration (NASA) administrator Sean O'Keefe appoints retired U.S. Navy admiral Harold Gelman Jr. to head the *Columbia* Accident Investigation Board.

- In April, the FDA eases the ban on gene-therapy trials that use retroviral vectors in blood stem cells.

- In April, the Human Genome Project is completed.

- On May 9, NASA announces that Bill Parsons will replace Ron Dittemore as shuttle program manager.

- On July 28, U.S. senator James Inhofe of Oklahoma claims global warming is a hoax.

- In August, the social-networking site MySpace is launched and soon experiences exponential growth.

- On October 21, the first images of the new planetary body Eris are taken.

2004

- Ford introduces the first hybrid sport utility vehicle (SUV), the Ford Escape.

- Google handles upward of 84.7 percent of all search requests on the World Wide Web.

- On June 21, the first privately funded rocket ship to carry a human into space, *SpaceShipOne*, makes its maiden voyage to the edges of space.

- On August 19, Google goes public, offering a total of 19,605,052 shares at $85.00 a share. At the end of the trading day, it closes at $100.34 a share.

- In November, Google indexes eight billion web pages.

- On December 26, an earthquake with a magnitude of between 9.1 and 9.3 on the Richter scale occurs in the Indian Ocean, causing a massive tsunami that takes the lives of more than 230,000 people in fourteen different countries.

2005

- Nicholas Negroponte, cofounder and director of the Media Lab at Massachusetts Institute of Technology (MIT), announces his plan to develop a laptop computer that costs only $100. The final product costs $199.

- On January 5, Mike Brown, Chad Trujillo, and David Rabinowitz are recognized for discovering a new planet orbiting the Sun that is larger than Pluto.

- In February, a research team at the University of Michigan is able to cure deafness in guinea pigs by delivering genes that promote growth of hair cells in the cochlea, the part of the inner ear that registers sound.

- On February 15, Steve Chen, Chad Hurley, and Jawed Karim register the domain name YouTube.com for their video-sharing website.

- On February 16, the Kyoto Protocol goes into effect. Notably, the United States and Australia do not ratify the treaty.

- In March, researchers announce the discovery of soft tissue inside the 68-million-year-old thighbone of a Tyrannosaurus rex.

- On April 23, the first video gets posted on YouTube titled "Me at the Zoo."

- In May, YouTube's viewership surpasses that of CNN.com.

- On June 7, Google is valued at nearly $52 million, making it one of the world's biggest media companies by stock-market value.

- On August 29, Hurricane Katrina ravages the U.S. Gulf Coast, causing more than eighteen hundred deaths and $100 million in damage to Louisiana alone.

- In December, more than one hundred thousand people in more than thirty nations hold marches as part of the first worldwide demonstration calling for action against global warming.

- On December 20, U.S. District judge John E. Jones III rules that teaching intelligent design in the classroom equates to teaching religion. Proponents of evolution see the ruling as an important victory.

- On December 20, members of the International Astronomical Union (IAU) meet in Prague to discuss the cultural and scientific fate of Eris and Pluto. They decide to assign Pluto, Eris, and the former asteroid Ceres the newly created status of dwarf planets.

- On December 20, "Google" officially becomes a verb meaning to use the Google search engine to obtain information on the World Wide Web.

2006

- YouTube is the fourth-most-viewed website in the world and is named *Time* magazine's invention of the year.

- The first Blu-ray Disc players hit the market. A format war with High-Definition/Density (HD-DVD) begins.

- Evan Williams, Biz Stone, and Jack Dorsey launch the microblogging service Twitter.

- In January, YouTube users watch approximately twenty-five million videos a day.

- On February 8, eighty-six Christian leaders form the Evangelical Climate Initiative, demanding that Congress regulate greenhouse-gas emissions.

- In March, gene therapy is effectively used to treat two adult patients for a myeloid disorder, a disease that affects white blood cells.

- In May, researchers involved with the Human Genome Project announce the completion of the DNA sequence for the last twenty-four human chromosomes.

- On May 28, *An Inconvenient Truth*, a documentary on climate change starring Al Gore, opens in theaters.

- On June 8, the FDA announces the approval of Gardasil, a vaccine for the human papillomavirus (HPV).

- In August, a team of researchers at the National Cancer Institute demonstrates a regression of advanced melanoma in seventeen patients whose white blood cells had been genetically engineered to recognize and attack cancer cells.

- On August 21, Marusa Bradac of the Kavli Institute for Particle Astrophysics and Cosmology at the Stanford Linear Accelerator Center makes the first landmark observation of dark matter in the Bullet Cluster.

- On September 13, Object 2003 UB313 and its satellite, which had been informally referred to as Xena and Gabrielle, respectively, are officially named Eris and Dysnomia.

- On October 9, Google acquires YouTube for $1.65 billion in Google stock. The deal is finalized in November.

- In November, Microsoft launches Vista along with Office 2007 and Exchange 2007. Customers soon complain that the system is slow and has multiple programming issues.

2007

- Experts estimate that YouTube consumes as much bandwidth space as the entire World Wide Web did in 2000.

- In January, Chevrolet introduces its Volt series hybrid sedan at the North American International Auto Show.

- On January 11, researchers at the University of Texas M. D. Anderson Cancer Center and the University of Texas Southwestern Medical Center deliver a combination of two tumor-suppressing genes with lipid-based nanoparticles, causing a drastic reduction in the number and size of human lung-cancer tumors in mice.

- In February, the UNIPCC issues a report stating that global warming is "unequivocal" and human activity is "very likely" the cause.

- On April 2, the U.S. Supreme Court rules that the Environmental Protection Agency has the authority to regulate heat-trapping gases in automobile emissions.

- In June, the 3G network claims its 200-millionth customer.

- In September, ice melt from the Arctic Ice Cap is so severe that the Northwest Passage, a shipping shortcut from Europe to Asia around the top of North America, opens for the first time since satellite records began in 1978.

- In October, Facebook sells $240 million in shares to Microsoft, solidifying the importance of social-networking sites in the marketplace.

- On October 12, Al Gore and the UNIPCC win the Nobel Peace Prize for disseminating greater knowledge about the man-made catastrophe of global warming and for proposing measures needed to counteract the crisis.

2008

- After years of debate, the FDA rules that meat and milk from cloned livestock are safe for consumption.

- MySpace cedes the social-networking crown to Facebook.

- YouTube is awarded the George Foster Peabody Award. *Entertainment Weekly* puts YouTube on its "best-of" list.

- Toshiba officially stops producing HD-DVD players, ending a three-year format war with Blu-ray Disc.

- Astronomers announce that they have obtained a visual picture of exoplanets—alien planets—orbiting distant stars.

- On January 24, a team of seventeen scientists from the J. Craig Venter Institute announces that it was able to completely synthesize and assemble 582,970 base pairs of the genome of the bacterium *mycoplasma genitalium*.

- On May 12, the Great Sichuan Earthquake occurs in the Sichuan province of China, measuring 8.5 on the Richter magnitude scale. It claims an estimated 68,000 lives.

- On May 15, due to pressure from environmental groups such as Greenpeace, the polar bear is finally listed as a threatened species under the Endangered Species Act.

- On May 21, President Bush signs the Genetic Nondiscrimination Act prohibiting U.S. insurance companies and employers from discrimination based on information derived from genetic testing.

- On May 25, NASA's *Phoenix* lands on the Martian north pole on a quest to learn more about the planet's surface, including whether or not it contains frozen water and possibly organic-based compounds.

- In July, Google indexes one trillion pages.

- On July 31, the *Phoenix* Mars lander detects water in a Martian soil sample using its onboard Thermal and Evolved Gas Analyzer (TEGA).

- In December, surgeons at the Cleveland Clinic in Ohio perform the world's first near-total facial transplant surgery.

- In December, the Federal Communications Commission (FCC) defines basic broadband as data transmission that exceeds speeds of 768 kilobits per second.

- In December, 26 percent of the world's population uses the Internet and surfs the World Wide Web.

- In December Google's assets total approximately $40.5 billion.

- In December, Twitter claims more than 100 million users worldwide.

- In December, online encyclopedia Wikipedia claims more than 13 million articles.

2009

- Toshiba releases its own Blu-ray Disc player.

- Amputee Pierpaolo Petruzziello learns to control a biomechanical hand and becomes the first person to make complex movements with a robotic limb by using his thoughts only.

- On January 21, Steven Chu is sworn in as the twelfth U.S. secretary of energy.

- In February, scientists clone a bucardo, an extinct subspecies of the Spanish ibex, from preserved skin tissue. It dies only minutes after being born.

- In March, President Barack Obama overturns President Bush's policy on stem-cell research, allowing the National Institutes of Health to fund research on embryonic stem cells beyond the previously allotted sixty cell lines.

- In April, the World Health Organization announces the emergence of a novel influenza virus called H1N1.

- In June, the Centers for Disease Control and Prevention (CDC) report that more than 25 million doses of Gardasil, the HPV vaccine, have been distributed in the United States.

- On June 12, full-power television stations in the United States broadcast in analog for the last time.

- On June 18, NASA launches its Lunar Crater Observation and Sensing Satellite (LCROSS) as part of a double mission including the Lunar Reconnaissance Orbiter (LRO) to see if water exists on the Moon.

- In August, Jamie Elsila at NASA's Goddard Space Flight Center in Greenbelt, Maryland, announces that her team has found glycine, an amino acid, in the tail of a comet in outer space.

- In October, San Diego Zoo spokesperson Yadira Galindo announces that California condors have made a comeback.

- On October 1, scientists announce the discovery of Ardi, a 4.4-million-year-old fossilized skeleton that may be an ancestor of modern humans.

- On October 9, NASA's LCROSS is intentionally crashed into the permanently shadowed region of Cabeus crater near the Moon's south pole, followed by a *Centaur* rocket to determine if water is present on the Moon's surface.

- On October 24, President Obama declares the swine-flu pandemic (H1N1) a national emergency.

- On November 13, NASA announces the discovery of water on the Moon.

- In December, federal health officials estimate that ten thousand Americans have died of the swine flu since April.

- On December 7–18, representatives from more than 193 countries convene in Copenhagen, Denmark, for the UN Climate Change Conference.

"Once Again, Scientists Say Human Genome Is Complete"

Newspaper article

By: Nicholas Wade

Date: April 15, 2003

Source: Wade, Nicholas. "Once Again, Scientists Say Human Genome Is Complete." *New York Times*, April 15, 2003. www.nytimes.com/2003/04/15/science/once-again-scientists-say-human-genome-is-complete.html? scp=12&sq=human+genome&st=nyt (accessed on March 23, 2013).

About the Newspaper: The *New York Times* was founded in 1851 as a concise, four-page summary of daily news items. News mogul Adolph S. Ochs acquired the paper in 1896, expanding its scope and size. By the turn of the twentieth century, the *New York Times* was the pre-eminent U.S. newspaper, acclaimed for its objective reporting of "All the News That's Fit to Print." In 1905, the popularity and importance of the paper was memorialized by the City of New York, which called its new public square "Times Square," in honor of the newspaper. The paper's investigative reporting on official and political affairs has always been a trademark, garnering the journalism staff more than one hundred Pulitzer Prizes for its coverage of wars and governments—most notably for its publication of the "Pentagon Papers," leaked documents attesting to the mishandling and uncertainty of the Vietnam War. The *New York Times* remains the nation's most prestigious and important newspaper, and it continues to be owned and operated by descendants of Ochs.

INTRODUCTION

The human genome is the entirety of human genetic information. It is contained in the deoxyribonucleic acid (DNA) found in the nucleus of every human cell and, in much smaller quantities, in human mitochondria. Cellular consists of twenty-three chromosomes, each of which is composed of fifty to three million pairs of nucleobases, known as base pairs. Nucleobases—the compounds adenine, thymine, cytosine, and guanine—are the fundamental building blocks of genetic material and, thus, most organic life. They are capable of forming flexible, strong hydrogen bonds with one another (although adenine and thymine can only pair with each other, as with cytosine and guanine), facilitating the formation of DNA into its customary double-helix structure.

A human haploid (reproductive) cell contains approximately three billion base pairs, and any other human cell contains twice that amount.

Each chromosome contains long stretches of base pairs, known as genes, that operate as the "instruction manual" for the thousands of cellular and biological functions that take place in the human body each second. Genes direct cells on how to build and maintain themselves, how to construct proteins (the compounds responsible for conducting most tasks within the cell), and what functions to perform. Genes determine every conceivable aspect of a human's physiology, from the visible (hair color, facial proportions) to the visually undetectable (blood type, predisposition to certain medical conditions), and they serve as the means by which parents transmit their genetic traits to their children. Every chromosome contains hundreds or thousands of genes, to form a total of approximately 20,500 in normally developed humans.

Although genes only comprise about 2 percent of the human genome—most of the rest performs a variety of functions related to storing, translating, protecting, and carrying out the directions of the genes—they are responsible for many of humanity's most painful, tragic, and horrible afflictions. Certain mutations of specific genes can cause the genes to malfunction, issuing improper directions or failing to perform their duty in the standard fashion, producing the myriad genetic disorders that affect humans. Over four thousand genetic disorders, such as Marfan syndrome, cystic fibrosis, and hemophilia, are caused by mutations in single genes. Others, like asthma and multiple sclerosis, are produced by the confluence of several genetic mutations in an individual. Understanding the human genome is the key to better understanding and treating genetic disorders.

In recognition of this fact, and the universal benefit of combatting genetic disorders, the United States National Academy of Sciences suggested in 1988 that the federal government sponsor a research program with the goal of achieving complete understanding of the human genome. This was to be accomplished through a massive, concerted effort to identify and locate all of the genome's genes and to discern the exact sequence of its billions of nucleobase pairs. The proposal was approved by the U.S. National Institutes of Science (NIS) and the Department of Energy (DOE), and a plan was formulated. The NIS established the National Center for Human Genome Research, where a team of researchers was assembled. It was decided that it would require fifteen years and $3 billion for the geneticists to catalogue the whole human genome. In conjunction with the newly formed International Human Genome Sequencing Consortium, which represented research facilities and universities in Japan, China, France, Germany, and the United Kingdom, the scientists set to work in October 1990.

Using a process known as shotgun sequencing, researchers affiliated with the Human Genome Project made quick advancements toward their goals. Internet and computational technology was undergoing a period of rapid development, allowing genome researchers increasingly faster, more efficient, more accurate tools for conducting and sharing their findings. The project continually attracted new sources of funding and new research contributions, both helped by the initiative's practices of publishing updated results daily and encouraging the free, open exchange of research to accelerate progress.

In 1998 a geneticist named Craig Venter, famous for having led the first successful attempt to sequence the entire genome of a living organism (*H. influenza*), founded Celera Genomics, announcing his own, privately funded program to decode the human genome. Venter's project would cost only $300 million, he said, and would be conducted in a single facility by a single team of scientists. Proponents of the Human Genome Project were briefly concerned by Celera's speedy progress, which relied on a different technique (pairwise end sequencing) to examine genetic information, when he admitted his plans to patent the genes he discovered, as well as the genome itself if he were to complete it before the Human Genome Project. Fortunately for modern medicine, Celera lost momentum, especially when Human Genome Project researchers started employing the pairwise end sequencing process.

On June 26, 2000, the International Human Genome Sequencing Consortium announced that the Human Genome Project had produced a "working draft" of the human genome. The draft, which was not published until February 2001, covered 90 percent of the total genome and had an error rate of 1 base pair per 1,000, but still contained approximately 150,000 gaps between sequenced areas. Then, on April 14, 2003, the "essentially finished" version of the genome was announced to much fanfare. This updated genome, presented as the product of the Human Genome Project's definitive success, covered over 99 percent of the genome, with fewer than four hundred gaps yet to be sequenced and an error rate of less than one error per ten thousand base pairs. Having declared their mission successful, Human Genome Project researchers turned their attention to identifying the

functions and known variations of the thousands of genes they had located.

SIGNIFICANCE

It is difficult to overstate the significance of the Human Genome Project in the field of medicine. The complete, sequenced genome allowed medical researchers to develop a deeper understanding of the human body's functions. The genome gave doctors the information necessary to research the mechanisms and genetic sources of genetic diseases, promising to result in the development of new therapeutic procedures for managing, treating, and even preventing genetic disorders through gene-targeting. Other diseases that are not genetic but are influenced by genetics, such as Alzheimer's and several forms of cancer, were also made easier to study by the completion of the human genome. As research continues to be conducted on the variations and functions of human genes, medicine will become increasingly personalized—genetic diagnostics will be employed to determine the health needs of an individual based on their genetics and to determine which drugs will be the most effective for them.

The Human Genome Project also had considerable implications in other disciplines besides medicine. Evolutionary studies received the completed human genome as a boon to productivity, as it allows scientists the ability to study the emergence of different human traits by examining the genes associated with them. It was also made possible for scientists to compare human genomes with those of other primates to determine the exact nature of the human evolutionary divergence. The technologies developed to sequence the human genome can be used to study the genetic composition of any organism, opening new possibilities for the study of biological evolution. Also, the inexpensive genetic tests made possible by the Human Genome Project saw immediate use by prospective parents, who used them to determine if their coupling would produce children with a predisposition to certain diseases or genetic abnormalities.

Perhaps the most noteworthy aspect of the Human Genome Project was the manner in which it was conducted. Never before had the scientific world witnessed the level of international, interdisciplinary, inter-organizational collaboration that was displayed by the Project. It was also unprecedented in scope, involving unknown thousands of researchers and billions of man-hours over the course of thirteen years. As scientific endeavors become more ambitious and more expensive, the cooperative, team-oriented model of research pioneered by the Human Genome Project will likely become the standard, rather than the exception.

James Watson (left) and Francis Crick discovered the structure of DNA in 1953. © BETTMANN/CORBIS.

"ONCE AGAIN, SCIENTISTS SAY HUMAN GENOME IS COMPLETE"

SYNOPSIS: In this article, the author discusses the announcement that the entire human genome has been sequenced, and what that means.

The human genome is complete and the Human Genome Project is over, leaders of a public consortium of academic centers said today.

"We have before us the instruction set that carries each of us from the one-cell egg through adulthood to the grave," Dr. Robert Waterston, a leading genome sequencer, said at a news conference here at the National Institutes of Health.

Their announcement marked the end of a scientific venture that began in October 1990 and was expected to take 15 years.

Today's finishing date, two years ahead of schedule, was timed to coincide with the 50th anniversary of the discovery of the structure of DNA by Dr. James D. Watson and Dr. Francis Crick. Their article appeared in the April 25, 1953, issue of *Nature*.

Dr. Watson, who became the first director of the Human Genome Project at the institutes, was at a conference here today to celebrate the genome's completion. He had sought that goal, he said, realizing that a family member's illness would never be treatable "until we understand the human program for health and disease."

A "working draft" of the human genome sequence was announced with much fanfare three years ago in a White House ceremony. But at that stage the Human Genome Project had completed only 85 percent of the genome and its commercial rival, the Celera Corporation, using the project's data as well as its own, had attained

Genome scientists (left to right) Eric Lander, Robert Waterston, James Watson, and Francis Collins celebrate the announcement of the sequencing of the human genome, February 12, 2001. © STEPHEN GAFFE/GETTY IMAGES.

somewhat more. The project's draft was not a thing of beauty. It consisted of thousands of short segments of DNA, whose order and orientation in the full genome was largely unknown.

Three years later, the international consortium of genome sequencing centers has now put all the fragments in order and closed most of the gaps, producing an extensive and highly accurate sequence of the 3.1 billion units of DNA of the human genome.

The data, perceived as the foundation of a new era of medicine, will be posted for free on genetic data banks. Celera, whose data are available by subscription, never intended to carry its draft genome to completion.

The working draft of three years ago contained most human genes and was useful for researchers seeking a specific gene. But up to a year ago biologists said they often had to do considerable extra sequencing work on the DNA regions they were interested in.

The completed genome announced today is far more accurate. It can be used out of the box, so to speak, without extra resequencing. The genes and other important elements of the genome are now almost all in their correct position, a vital requirement for researchers seeking to locate a gene that contributes to disease....

The Human Genome Project was originally projected to cost a total of $3 billion. Money spent by the National Institutes of Health and the Department of Energy since the beginning of the project has come to $2.7 billion, but that does not include spending by the Sanger Institute and other foreign collaborators.

The total spending of the Human Genome Project includes pilot projects like sequencing the roundworm and fruit fly genomes. No exact figure was given at today's press conference for sequencing the human genome specifically. But the Sanger Institute has spent 150 million pounds, or about $235 million, to sequence

30 percent of the genome, and on that basis would have required 500 million pounds, or $786 million at the current rate of exchange, to do all of it.

Though the Human Genome Project has been declared completed, the genome sequencing centers will not go out of business. They have switched to decoding the genomes of other species, and to exploring variations in the human genome.

Obtaining the sequence of the human genome is a first step. Biologists must now annotate it, or identify the regions of DNA that hold the genes and their control elements. Next come tasks like discovering the variations in DNA sequence that contribute to disease in different populations, defining the proteins produced by each gene, and understanding how the proteins in each cell interact in a circuitry that controls the operation of the genome.

FURTHER RESOURCES

Books

McElhenny, Victor K. *Drawing the Map of Life: Inside the Human Genome Project*. New York: Basic Books, 2010.

Palladino, Michael A. *Understanding the Human Genome Project*. San Francisco: Benjamin Cummings, 2005.

Web Sites

"All About the Human Genome Project." *National Human Genome Research Institute*. www.genome.gov/10001772 (accessed on March 23, 2013).

"Human Genome News." *Oak Ridge National Laboratory*. www.ornl.gov/sci/techresources/Human_Genome/publicat/hgn/hgn.shtml (accessed on March 23, 2013).

"Human Genome Project Information." *Oak Ridge National Laboratory*. www.ornl.gov/sci/techresources/Human_Genome/home.shtml (accessed on March 23, 2013).

"Rover Unfurls, Opening New Stage in Exploration"

Newspaper article

By: John Noble Wilford

Date: January 5, 2004

Source: Wilford, John Noble. "Rover Unfurls, Opening New Stage in Exploration." *New York Times*,

January 5, 2004. www.nytimes.com/2004/01/05/us/rover-unfurls-opening-new-stage-in-exploring-mars.html?src=pm (accessed on March 23, 2013).

About the Newspaper: The *New York Times* was founded in 1851 as a concise, four-page summary of daily news items. News mogul Adolph S. Ochs acquired the paper in 1896, expanding its scope and size. By the turn of the twentieth century, the *New York Times* was the pre-eminent U.S. newspaper, acclaimed for its objective reporting of "All the News That's Fit to Print." In 1905, the popularity and importance of the paper was memorialized by the City of New York, which called its new public square "Times Square," in honor of the newspaper. The paper's investigative reporting on official and political affairs has always been a trademark, garnering the journalism staff more than one hundred Pulitzer Prizes for its coverage of wars and governments—most notably for its publication of the "Pentagon Papers," leaked documents attesting to the mishandling and uncertainty of the Vietnam War. The *New York Times* remains the nation's most prestigious and important newspaper, and it continues to be owned and operated by descendants of Ochs.

INTRODUCTION

Interest in Mars dates back to the 1600s and begins with the invention of the telescope. Interplanetary journeys are complex, riddled with obstacles and challenges. Given this fact, exploration of the planet has historically been characterized in part by a high rate of failure.

Russia and the United States have been the two main contenders in the race to discover more about the Red Planet (a nickname given for its reddish appearance, which is a result of a high content of iron oxide on the planet's surface). The first true exploration of Mars was attempted in the 1960s, when a Soviet unmanned spacecraft later referred to as *Marsnik* launched in October 1960. This was followed by two more failed missions in 1962 and one the same year that, though it never reached Mars, managed to send sixty-one radio transmissions that provided scientists with a great deal of interplanetary data. Two Soviet probe launches in 1964 failed, and two more in 1969 followed suit. The following decade proved to be much the same for Russia. Probe and orbiter missions failed, but more data, including images, was collected

U.S. exploration was more successful. The *Mariner* program of 1964 consisted of two spacecraft, one launched on November 5, the other on November 28. The first mission failed, but *Mariner 4* completed a seven-and-a-half-month voyage, which provided the first close-up photos of the Red Planet. The combination of photos and data allowed scientists to determine significantly more accurate information. For example, they realized the surface was covered with impact craters. They found no radiation belts or magnetic field, and they could estimate atmospheric pressure and temperatures. The National Aeronautics and Space Administration (NASA) sent two more *Mariner* probes, both of which reached Mars in 1969. The next two spacecraft in the program were identical spacecraft whose mission was to orbit Mars. *Mariner 8* was lost in a launch failure, but *Mariner 9* launched successfully in May 1971 and became the first artificial satellite of Mars. The data collected again significantly enhanced what scientists were able to know about Mars.

The *Viking* program—consisting of two orbiters and two landers—launched in 1975 and credited America with the first landing on Mars. From that mission, NASA learned that the planet consisted of deep valleys resulting from flooding, and had streams in the southern portion, suggesting rain might once have fallen. After the *Viking* program, Mars exploration took a back seat to NASA's space shuttle program, which saw the tragic fatal mission of the *Challenger* in 1986. It would be 1992 before exploration began again, and the Mars *Observer* orbiter was a failure. In 1996, the Mars *Global Surveyor* was launched and became the first fully successful mission to Mars in two decades. It completed its primary mission on January 31, 2001. The Mars *Pathfinder* landed on Mars on July 4, 1997. Its wheeled robotic rover, nicknamed Sojourner, was the first to operate on the planet's surface.

Exploration continued, and in June 2003, NASA launched its Mars Exploration Rover Mission (MER). The mission included twin rovers, *Spirit* and *Opportunity*. The former landed on Mars on January 4, 2004, for what was planned to be a three-month mission, and John Noble Wilford's *New York Times* article captures the mood of excitement and hope that accompanied the mission.

SIGNIFICANCE

Three months turned into six years, and the *Spirit* traveled more than twelve times the goal NASA had set for the mission when it covered 4.8 miles, or 7.73 kilometers. MER project manager John Callas explained, "Our job was · to wear these rovers out exploring, to leave no unutilized capability on the surface of Mars, and with *Spirit*, we have done that." NASA officially ended the twin-rover mission on May 24, 2011, though it then turned its focus to the other, now single rover, *Opportunity*. It had lost communication

with *Spirit* on March 22, 2010, and subsequent efforts to reach it failed.

The mission was full of firsts. *Spirit* made history as it summited a hill on Mars, the first robot to do so. The robot's right front wheel became immobile in 2006 as it got stuck in a sandhill, yet it journeyed another half-mile. The little rover that could sent home more than 124,000 images, some of them having the distinction of being the highest color resolution images ever taken on another planet. While on Mars, it prepared rock targets and other surfaces for inspection with spectrometers and a microscopic imager. One of the most major discoveries resulted from *Spirit*'s broken wheel. As it dragged itself through the planet's white soil, the rover's spectrometers showed the particles to be nearly pure silica. Steve Squyres, principal investigator for both rovers, explained the importance of this discovery. "It showed that there were once hot springs or steam vents at the *Spirit* site, which could have provided favorable conditions for microbial life." The rover also showed that Mars was also once a place of violent volcanic eruptions where water and hot rock interacted. This image painted a picture in direct opposition to the conditions of Mars in the twenty-first centry—cold and dry.

Spirit's mission was considered by NASA to be nothing more than geologic in nature, but it turned out to be so much more. Squyres described the rover's experiment as "humanity's first real overland expedition across another planet. *Spirit* explored just as we would have, seeing a distant hill, climbing it, and showing us the vista from the summit. And she did it in a way that allowed everyone on Earth to be part of the adventure."

■ PRIMARY SOURCE

"ROVER UNFURLS, OPENING NEW STAGE IN EXPLORING MARS"

SYNOPSIS: NASA's robotic rover *Spirit* lands on Mars to begin a geologic experiment that scientists hope will reveal a Mars they have never seen before.

The robotic rover *Spirit* is on the surface of Mars, its arrival Saturday night the suspenseful beginning to a new stage in the exploration of the geology and perhaps biology of the planet that has long fascinated its neighbors on Earth.

Relieved by their long-awaited success, flight controllers and scientists became increasingly ecstatic on Sunday as the 400-pound *Spirit* raised its camera and antenna mast and began transmitting black-and-white picture postcards of its landing place on a broad plain in Gusev crater, near the Martian equator.

The Mars rover *Spirit* examines rocks inside Gusev Crater, October 10, 2007. © AP IMAGES/NASA.

The first successful landing on Mars since 1997 had touched down almost exactly on target. At last, for NASA officials and engineers the memory of the embarrassing failure of the Mars Polar Lander in 1999 had been exorcised. Their spacecraft was on Mars, standing upright and facing south.

All around the arid surface were rocks that scientists suspected once held an ancient lake. But no boulders were in sight that could be impediments to the six-wheel rover's movements. Whirling dust devils left tracks where they had scoured the surface, exposing underlying rock. Nature, it seemed, had thoughtfully cleaned off the rocks for the robotic visitor.

Some of the rocky, pitted surface made flight controllers shudder. A touchdown a few feet one way or the other could have ended much less happily. But some of the spots appealed to scientists as places the rover may be sent to investigate. A depression more than 60 feet in the distance tantalized geologists. And beyond a scattering of craters were low hills on the far horizon.

A mosaic image of the Mars rover *Spirit* as it approaches the surface of Mars. © AP IMAGES/NASA-JPL.

"We hit the sweet spot," exclaimed Dr. Steven W. Squyres of Cornell, the mission's principal science investigator. "We are in the place we absolutely wanted to be in Gusev crater."

From an analysis of pictures the spacecraft took as it was descending to the surface, scientists and navigation engineers determined that *Spirit* landed close to the center of its target, an ellipse about 42 miles long and 3 miles wide. Gusev (pronounced GOOSE-ev) is a 4-billion-year-old crater about the size of Connecticut.

"It may be a dry lake bed," Dr. Squyres said, "but it's really been chewed up by cratering."

With more of its instruments and antennas deployed and checked out, the spacecraft began taking some color pictures Sunday. But the photographs were not expected to be transmitted to Earth and made public until Monday. The color pictures are to be pieces of a panoramic mosaic of the landing site in three-dimensional color. The mosaic, Dr. Squyres said, "will be a truly spectacular image."

Jennifer Trosper, the mission manager at the Jet Propulsion Laboratory here, said it would be another nine days before the rover rolled into action for at least three months of surface exploration. There are tests to perform, batteries to charge with solar energy and pictures to be studied in planning the first traverses over the alien topography. The rollout delay was expected.

Matt Wallace, an engineer planning the rover's surface operations, said that an immediate goal was to establish direct communications between *Spirit* and Earth with the craft's more powerful antennas, which are capable of high-speed radio transmissions of data and pictures. Most of the early transmissions have been relayed through two spacecraft orbiting Mars, Mars *Global Surveyor* and Mars *Odyssey*.

Flight engineers also wanted time to analyze *Spirit*'s descent and landing data to see if there were lessons to be learned and procedures to alter before the next attempt to land on Mars, on Jan. 24. A twin of *Spirit*, a rover named *Opportunity*, is scheduled to touch down on the opposite side of the Martian equator, in a region called Meridiani Planum.

The two spacecraft in the $800 million mission were sent to two different regions for a single purpose: to study the planet's rocks and sediments for signs that Mars once had an abundance of water and could have harbored some forms of life. From earlier photography, the Gusev site appears not only to be a dried lake bed but also to have a drainage valley running into and out of the crater. The Meridiani basin appears to be rich in gray hematite, an iron oxide mineral that usually forms in association with water.

The three previous landing successes were two *Viking* spacecraft in 1976 and Mars *Pathfinder*, with its robotic rover, *Sojourner*, in 1997. When the Mars Polar Lander disappeared trying to touch down near the Martian southern polar region two years later, the loss prompted a management shake-up at the Jet Propulsion Laboratory and cancellation of a landing that had been scheduled for 2001.

More money and more rigorous testing went into the current missions. The rovers are about 15 times larger than *Sojourner*. Each is capable of traveling about 125 feet a day; *Sojourner* managed little more than a daily three feet.

But first *Spirit* had to reach the Martian surface in one piece. The seven-month flight from Cape Canaveral, Fla., was smooth. It was the final six minutes that filled the control center here with apprehension.

"It was nerve-racking," said Rob Manning, the manager of descent operations.

Navigation engineers had good news: *Spirit*'s aim on Mars was almost perfect, requiring no last-day course corrections. A dust storm on the other side of Mars from the Gusev crater was slightly raising the heat of the global atmosphere, making it somewhat thinner. Flight controllers released the parachute slightly earlier to give it more time to brake its descent.

It was afternoon at the Gusev landing site when *Spirit* made its first move 15 minutes before touchdown. The craft cast off the module that supported its operations during the cruise from the Earth. Then *Spirit* turned so that its heat shield faced the angle of descent and maximum frictional temperatures.

Meanwhile, *Spirit* was being reeled in by Martian gravity, reaching a maximum speed of more than 12,000 miles an hour. Its on-board computer was in complete charge. Between Earth and Mars, one-way radio signals take almost 10 minutes.

Spirit plunged into the upper Martian atmosphere at an altitude of 73 miles, with six minutes to touchdown. The landing site was 437 miles downrange....

About two minutes to touchdown, the parachute opened at an altitude of 5.3 miles. Signals from the craft indicated it was decelerating as expected and that the parachute had indeed deployed. The heat shield was jettisoned. Then the rover's cocoon of airbags inflated, with only eight seconds to touchdown. Radar locked on the surface, and retrorockets fired final braking thrusts.

Then the moment came at 11:35 p.m. Eastern time on Saturday. There was no immediate signal from *Spirit*. That was expected, but still a cause for anxiety. Then the commentator in mission control reported, "We have signs of bouncing on the surface of Mars."

Later, pouring Champagne, Sean O'Keefe, head of the National Aeronautics and Space Administration, was jubilant. "This is a big night for NASA," Mr. O'Keefe said. "We are on Mars."

FURTHER RESOURCES
Books
Clancey, William J. *Working on Mars: Voyages of Scientific Discovery with the Mars Exploration Rovers.* Cambridge, MA: MIT, 2012.

Hubbard, Scott. *Exploring Mars: Chronicles from a Decade of Discovery.* Tucson: University of Arizona Press, 2012.

Web Sites
Kremer, Ken. "Opportunity Rover Heads for Spirit Point to Honor Dead Martian Sister; Science Team Tributes." *Universe Today*, June 12, 2011. www.universetoday.com/86429/opportunity-rover-heads-for-spirit-point-to-honor-dead-martian-sister/ (accessed on March 23, 2013).

"Spirit and Opportunity." *NASA.* www.nasa.gov/mission_pages/mer/(accessed on March 23, 2013).

Webster, Guy. "NASA's Spirit Rover Completes Mission on Mars." *NASA*, May 25, 2011. www.jpl.nasa.gov/news/news.php?release=2011-160 (accessed on March 23, 2013).

"Hybrid Vehicle Registrations Jump"

Web site article

By: Associated Press

Date: April 22, 2004

Source: Associated Press. "Hybrid Vehicle Registration Jumps." *NBC News*, April 22, 2004. www.nbcnews.com/id/4799185/ns/us_news-environment/t/hybrid-vehicle-registrations-jump/#.UUenVFeweqh (accessed on March 23, 2013).

About the Organization: NBCNews.com was founded in 1996 as a partnership between NBCUniversal, Microsoft, and the cable news network MSNBC. Originally called MSNBC.com, the name changed on July 14, 2012, the same day that Microsoft sold its controlling share back to NBC. By 2009, NBCNews.com was ranked first among global news sites in terms of most unique visitors, a rank it had held for twelve consecutive months. Unlike the MSNBC cable channel, which is considered liberal in its content, NBCNews.com is held to be one of the more objective news portals in the industry.

INTRODUCTION

Although the idea of combining gasoline and electric motors is commonly believed to be a relatively new concept, it was, in fact, an idea first explored in the late nineteenth century by twenty-three-year-old Ferdinand Porsche, who eventually gained fame for designing the Volkswagen and the highly coveted sports car. He was a man before his time, however, and the world simply was not ready to accept the idea of a hybrid vehicle. In 1975, a division of American Motors began delivering electric vans to the U.S. Postal Service for testing. That same year, the U.S. Energy Research and Development Administration launched a program to advance electric and hybrid technology. This program was in direct response to the oil crisis of the early 1970s, when the price of gas skyrocketed as a result of the Arab oil embargo. After spending in excess of $20 million in research and development between 1977 and 1978, General Motors announced that it could manufacture electric vehicles by the mid-1980s.

The 1980s were years of continuous research, but it was not until 1993, under the Clinton administration, that government took a direct, active role in furthering the research and development of hybrid vehicles. Partnership for a New Generation of Vehicles (PNGV) was launched in 1993, and the government began working with the American auto industry to invent a car that would operate at up to eighty miles per gallon. It took several years and billions of dollars, but PNGV introduced three prototypes for their miracle car. All three were hybrids, that is, they ran on a combination of electricity and gas.

Toyota was not involved in PNGV but instead worked in secrecy to develop a hybrid car. In 1997, the Prius was introduced in Japan; sales that first year reached almost eighteen thousand. Honda introduced to America its first hybrid in 1999. The two-door Insight had mileage ratings of 61 mpg in the city and 70 mpg on the highway. It won several awards and paved the way for acceptance of the Toyota Prius when it was introduced in the summer of 2000 as the first four-door hybrid. Despite the fact that the ride was jerky and it required thirteen seconds to reach 60 mph, sales were higher than Toyota had hoped: Sales for five months of the $19,995 car exceeded fifty-five hundred. Better still was the recognition the hybrid got when *AutoWorld* magazine announced it as running on one of the "10 best engines of 2001." Even more important, the Prius was hailed as the "Best Engineered Car of 2001" by *Automotive Engineering International*, the official publication of the Society of Automotive Engineers. The time of the hybrid had arrived.

Sales of the Prius increased a remarkable 180 percent in 2001 as Toyota reported selling more than 15,500. That number jumped another 29 percent in 2002, with reported sales of more than twenty thousand in 2002. Second-generation 2004 Prius was announced in 2003 at the New York Auto Show. Despite its popularity, the sticker price remained unchanged from the original sticker price of $19,995. As the NBCNews article indicated, Americans began to view the hybrid less as a novelty and more as a smart investment as economic conditions worsened and the number of options and choices improved.

SIGNIFICANCE

As the article predicted, America had a wider array of choices in 2005. In addition to Honda and Toyota, hybrids were manufactured and offered by Ford, Lexus, and Mercury. As the decade rolled on, more makes and models were introduced to the market, and sales continued to climb.

The government did, in fact, begin offering tax credits to those who purchased hybrid gas-electric cars. Part of the Energy Policy Act of 2005, signed into law by President George W. Bush, allowed hybrid car buyers to claim a tax credit ranging between $3,400 and $4,000. That incentive expired on January 1, 2011; however, it was replaced with a combination of credits on both local and national levels. Taken together, the new incentives—up to $7,500 at the federal level, another $2,000 toward the purchase of charging-equipment installation, and $5,000 (in California)—these credits represent the largest incentive ever offered to consumers of "green" vehicles.

Hybrids continued to sell throughout the rest of the decade, though sales in 2009 decreased by 8 percent from 2008. America registered 265,501 hybrid cars (290,272 were actually sold) in 2009, more than any other country in the world. Los Angeles was the top market, followed closely by New York. Hybrid gas-electric vehicles captured 2.8 percent of the total market share that year.

The Honda Civic Hybrid, which runs on both gas and electricity, shown in April 2002. © AP IMAGES/ROBERT F. BUKATY.

PRIMARY SOURCE

"HYBRID VEHICLE REGISTRATION JUMPS"

SYNOPSIS: Americans are gradually warming to hybrid cars and can expect more choices in the near future.

Americans are opting more for vehicles with environmentally friendly gasoline-electric hybrid engines, new statistics show, and that trend is expected to continue because of high gas prices and a growing number of hybrid models.

U.S. registrations for hybrid vehicles rose to 43,435 last year, a 25.8 percent increase from 2002, according to figures from R. L. Polk & Co., a firm that collects and interprets automotive information.

California had the most registrations at 11,425, followed by Virginia, Florida and Washington.

"People are buying hybrids because of mileage benefits and environmental concerns," said Lonnie Miller, director of Polk's analytical solutions unit. "With the rising cost of gas, hybrid registrations will likely increase in 2004."

Annual Growth of 89 Percent Since 2000

Since 2000, hybrid sales in the United States have grown at an average annual rate of 88.6 percent, Polk said, but they account for only a fraction of total vehicles sold. Full-year U.S. sales for 2003 were 16.7 million.

Hybrids draw power from two energy sources, typically a gas or diesel engine combined with an electric motor. For now, the only versions available in the United States are small cars made by Honda Motor Co. and Toyota Motor Corp., but nearly every automaker is investing in hybrid technology.

Honda's hybrid Civic accounted for 50 percent of the registrations last year, slightly ahead of the Toyota Prius, Polk said. Both cars get more than 45 miles per gallon.

Hybrid sales so far this year have been mixed.

Toyota sold 9,918 Prius models through March, 62.4 percent more than it sold in the same period last year, according to Autodata Corp. Toyota was the first in the world to commercially mass-produce and sell hybrid cars with the Prius in 1997.

Honda said it set a monthly sales record in March for the hybrid Civic, though first-quarter sales were off from a year ago—5,982 versus 6,494.

Because of the relatively new technology, the hybrid Civic costs about $2,000 to $3,000 more than a comparable non-hybrid Civic, the automaker said.

More Choices Coming

Hybrid choices will increase. Ford Motor Co. is set to introduce a hybrid version of its compact Escape sport utility vehicle this summer, and luxury brand Lexus also plans a hybrid SUV. Honda plans to introduce a hybrid version of its midsize Accord passenger car this year.

Ford has said the hybrid system in the front-wheel-drive Escape allows the vehicle to get 35 to 40 miles per gallon in city driving, compared with 20 miles per gallon in a 2005 Escape with a V6 engine. It also plans another hybrid SUV and midsize sedan in the next few years.

Having more choices will make the hybrid vehicles more popular, Miller said.

Ford chairman and chief executive Bill Ford has said the federal government should offer tax breaks of about $3,000 or perhaps boost taxes on gasoline to spur consumer interest in hybrids.

Already, officials in some states have successfully pushed for incentives to make buying more energy-efficient vehicles more appealing. Others are trying.

Frank Hornstein, a state representative in Minnesota who drives a Civic hybrid, has introduced legislation that would give state residents a sales tax exemption for buying certain hybrid vehicles.

While one state senator has called the legislation social engineering, Hornstein said he believes Minnesota should promote the technology even if it means roughly $1 million a year in lost revenue, as the state estimates.

"The cost is somewhat minimal," he said. "The state should say: We think this is a good thing and we want to let the auto industry know that we'd like to see more of it."

FURTHER RESOURCES

Books

Anderson, Curtis, and Judy Anderson. *Electric and Hybrid Cars: A History.* Jefferson, NC: McFarland & Co., 2004.

Web Sites

Berman, Bradley. "December 2009 Dashboard: Year-End Tally." *Hybrid Cars*, January 20, 2010. www.hybridcars.com/december-2009-dashboard/ (accessed on March 23, 2013).

Berman, Bradley. "Hybrid Car Tax Credits: Incentives Fade into Memory." *Hybrid Cars*, February 7, 2011. www.hybridcars.com/federal-incentives/ (accessed on March 23, 2013).

Berman, Bradley. "When Old Things Turn Into New Again." *New York Times*, October 24, 2007. www.nytimes.com/2007/10/24/automobiles/autospecial/24history.html?_r=0 (accessed on March 23, 2013).

Taylor, Alex, III. "The Birth of the Prius." *CNN Money*, February 24, 2006. http://money.cnn.com/magazines/fortune/fortune_archive/2006/03/06/8370702/index.htm (accessed on March 23, 2013)

"Toyota Prius Chronological History." *Toyoland.com.* www.toyoland.com/prius/chronology.html (accessed on March 23, 2013).

"The Outsourcing Bogeyman"

Magazine article

By: Daniel W. Drezner

Date: May/June 2004

Source: Drezner, Daniel W. "The Outsourcing Bogeyman." *Foreign Affairs*, May/June 2004. www.danieldrezner.com/policy/outsourcing.htm (accessed March 24, 2013).

About the Author: Daniel W. Drezner was a conservative libertarian assistant professor of political science at the University of Chicago and the author of *The Sanctions Paradox: Economic Statecraft and International Relations.* He went on to become a professor of international politics at the Fletcher School of Law and Diplomacy at Tufts University, a blogger, and a commentator, and he authored several more books and many op-ed pieces in major publications.

INTRODUCTION

An already weakening American economy was further battered by world markets' anxious response to the uncertainty caused by the September 11, 2001, terrorist attacks on the United States. As fear and anxiety replaced the confidence and enthusiasm of the 1990s' robust economy, business slowed still more, hiring contracted, and large numbers of Americans began to lose their jobs. With no end in sight to the economic contraction, citizens and business owners looked to government officials to explain the cause of their pain.

Because 2004 was a presidential election year, politicians felt pressured to come up with plausible explanations. However, twenty-first-century economics is a global affair, making it far more complicated than already-complex national economics. Add to that the fact that economics is an inexact science, based on both hard data and subjective interpretation, and it is not difficult to understand why there are few people—including professionals who devote themselves to it full time—who truly comprehend how economics works. Still, responding to their constituents' needs is a large part of politicians' jobs, so they must find a way to do so. In this case, they had to find a plausible explanation for a situation that—even a decade later—was ongoing, with no unassailably definitive cause.

This article offers one informed explanation of the dilemma. It is written by a self-described "conservative libertarian" and reflects those worldviews.

SIGNIFICANCE

Foreign outsourcing or offshoring of American jobs has happened at some level at least since the end of World War II (1939–45), when American manufacturers especially saw economic benefit in moving labor-intensive functions to Japan and other Pacific Rim countries recovering from depleted wartime economies by offering cheap labor and business-friendly regulatory climates. However, technological advancements around the turn of the twenty-first century allowed companies to effectively outsource many more service jobs than was previously possible, to achieve great labor and other cost savings. It eventually became a large enough movement to be seen by many as disruptive to the overall American economy.

U.S. business publications and experts began talking about this movement almost immediately, but it was not until the presidential election campaign of 2004 that the debate became significant and very public, now including politicians, business owners, and regular citizens.

Proponents of outsourcing say it saves companies money, allowing them to open up more higher-level job opportunities for Americans. They believe this practice engenders substantial net gains to the U.S. economy by creating more domestic buying power, cheaper imports, and stronger exports to countries who gain buying power through the jobs attained in the process.

Opponents of the practice argue that hiring people in foreign countries instead of Americans, and sending business processes and assets such as equipment there, affects the U.S. economy negatively. This practice used to impact only skilled and semi-skilled workers, but as technology advanced, even white collar professionals were being displaced. Outsourcing's detractors argue that the loss of these jobs will be permanent, causing the American worker and economy to lose competitive advantage to other countries forever.

The fact is that it is nearly impossible to tug on one single thread of the global economic fabric and identify the result as the definitive cause of any larger unraveling. Nearly a decade after this article was written and five years after a disastrous financial meltdown caused by high-level banking scandals, the U.S. economy remained weak and outsourcing was still going on. However, more than a few large companies were beginning to move some of their outsourced processes back to the United States, in response to customer service complaints and other unforeseen issues. Though initially countries to which American jobs had been outsourced saw economic gains, overall global economic conditions in the early 2010s remained barely steady or in decline.

Despite a plethora of arguments for and against outsourcing, the jury was still out on whether the practice was, on the whole, a positive or negative influence on the American economy. This situation did prove one tenet of the argument made in this article: That short-term anecdotal evidence, at least as far as economics is concerned, is unreliable as an indicator of long-term conditions.

PRIMARY SOURCE

"THE OUTSOURCING BOGEYMAN"

SYNOPSIS: In 2004, an extended period of economic slowdown had Americans worried. Many were losing their jobs, and everyone wanted to know what was causing the recession. Because economics is an inexact science comprising many complex factors, few truly understand how it works, especially as the world's economies become more intertwined. Bombarded by burgeoning amounts of information every day, Americans tend to prefer brief, encapsulated, "sound bite" explanations of such issues. One particular economic issue of the early 2000s deeply affected by this kind of surface treatment was employment outsourcing. This later became known as "offshoring," to distinguish the sending of a business process outside of a company to a third-party American firm or individual (outsourcing) from the sending of that business process to either an outside firm or a separate division of the same firm located outside the United States (offshoring). This article explains—in the context of the 2004 definition of outsourcing—why such economic shorthand can be misleading, and it argues against the dangers of making important business and political decisions based on anecdotal evidence where global economics is concerned.

THE TRUTH IS OFFSHORE

When a presidential election year coincides with an uncertain economy, campaigning politicians invariably invoke an international economic issue as a dire threat to the well-being of Americans. Speechwriters denounce the chosen scapegoat, the media provides blanket coverage of the alleged threat, and legislators scurry to introduce supposed remedies.

The cause of this year's commotion is offshore outsourcing—the alleged migration of American jobs overseas. The depth of alarm was strikingly illustrated by the firestorm of reaction to recent testimony by N. Gregory Mankiw, the head of President George W. Bush's Council of Economic Advisers. No economist really disputed Mankiw's observation that "outsourcing is just a new way of doing international trade," which makes it "a good thing." But in the political arena, Mankiw's comments sparked a furor on both sides of the aisle. Democratic presidential candidate John Kerry accused the Bush administration of wanting "to export more of our jobs overseas," and Senate Minority Leader Tom Daschle quipped, "If this is the administration's position, I think they owe an apology to every worker in America." Speaker of the House Dennis Hastert, meanwhile, warned that "outsourcing can be a problem for American workers and the American economy."

Critics charge that the information revolution (especially the Internet) has accelerated the decimation of U.S. manufacturing and facilitated the outsourcing of service-sector jobs once considered safe, from backroom call centers to high-level software programming. (This concern feeds into the suspicion that U.S. corporations are exploiting globalization to fatten profits at the expense of workers.) They are right that offshore outsourcing deserves attention and that some measures to assist affected workers are called for. But if their exaggerated alarmism succeeds in provoking protectionist responses from lawmakers, it will do far more harm than good, to the U.S. economy and to American workers.

Should Americans be concerned about the economic effects of outsourcing? Not particularly. Most of the numbers thrown around are vague, overhyped estimates. What hard data exist suggest that gross job losses due to offshore outsourcing have been minimal when compared to the size of the entire U.S. economy. The outsourcing phenomenon has shown that globalization can affect white-collar professions, heretofore immune to foreign competition, in the same way that it has affected manufacturing jobs for years. But Mankiw's statements on outsourcing are absolutely correct; the law of

comparative advantage does not stop working just because 401(k) plans are involved. The creation of new jobs overseas will eventually lead to more jobs and higher incomes in the United States. Because the economy—and especially job growth—is sluggish at the moment, commentators are attempting to draw a connection between offshore outsourcing and high unemployment. But believing that offshore outsourcing causes unemployment is the economic equivalent of believing that the sun revolves around the earth: intuitively compelling but clearly wrong.

Should Americans be concerned about the political backlash to outsourcing? Absolutely. Anecdotes of workers affected by outsourcing are politically powerful, and demands for government protection always increase during economic slowdowns. The short-term political appeal of protectionism is undeniable. Scapegoating foreigners for domestic business cycles is smart politics, and protecting domestic markets gives leaders the appearance of taking direct, decisive action on the economy.

Protectionism would not solve the U.S. economy's employment problems, although it would succeed in providing massive subsidies to well-organized interest groups. In open markets, greater competition spurs the reallocation of labor and capital to more profitable sectors of the economy. The benefits of such free trade—to both consumers and producers—are significant. Cushioning this process for displaced workers makes sense. Resorting to protectionism to halt the process, however, is a recipe for decline. An open economy leads to concentrated costs (and diffuse benefits) in the short term and significant benefits in the long term. Protectionism generates pain in both the short term and the long term.

THE SKY IS FALLING

Outsourcing occurs when a firm subcontracts a business function to an outside supplier. This practice has been common within the U.S. economy for some time. (Witness the rise of large call centers in the rural Midwest.) The reduction of communication costs and the standardization of software packages have now made it possible to outsource business functions such as customer service, telemarketing, and document management. Other affected professions include medical transcription, tax preparation, and financial services.

The numbers that are bandied about on offshore outsourcing sound ominous. The McKinsey Global Institute estimates that the volume of offshore outsourcing will increase by 30 to 40 percent a year for the next five years. Forrester Research estimates that 3.3 million white-collar jobs will move overseas by 2015. According to projections, the hardest hit sectors will be financial services and information technology (IT). In one May 2003 survey of chief information officers, 68 percent of IT executives said that their offshore contracts would grow in the subsequent year. The Gartner research firm has estimated that by the end of this year, 1 out of every 10 IT jobs will be outsourced overseas. Deloitte Research predicts the outsourcing of 2 million financial-sector jobs by 2009.

At first glance, current macroeconomic indicators seem to support the suspicion that outsourcing is destroying jobs in the United States. The past two years have witnessed moderate growth and astonishing productivity gains, but overall job growth has been anemic. The total number of manufacturing jobs has declined for 43 consecutive months. Surely, many observers insist, this must be because the jobs created by the U.S. recovery are going to other countries. Morgan Stanley analyst Stephen Roach, for example, has pointed out that "this is the first business cycle since the advent of the Internet—the enabler of a new real-time connectivity to low-cost offshore labor pools." He adds, "I don't think it's a coincidence that this jobless recovery has occurred in such an environment." Those who agree draw on anecdotal evidence to support this assertion. CNN's Lou Dobbs routinely harangues U.S. companies engaged in offshore outsourcing in his "Exporting America" series.

Many IT executives have themselves contributed to this perception. When IBM announced plans to outsource 3,000 jobs overseas this year, one of its executives said, "[Globalization] means shifting a lot of jobs, opening a lot of locations in places we had never dreamt of before, going where there's low-cost labor, low-cost competition, shifting jobs offshore." Nandan Nilekani, the chief executive of the India-based Infosys Technologies, said at this year's World Economic Forum, "Everything you can send down a wire is up for grabs." In January testimony before Congress, Hewlett-Packard chief Carly Fiorina warned that "there is no job that is America's God-given right anymore."

That last statement chills the blood of most Americans. Few support the cause of free trade for its own sake, out of pure principle. The logic underlying an open economy is that if the economy sheds jobs in uncompetitive sectors, employment in competitive sectors will grow. If hi-tech industries are no longer competitive, where will new jobs be created?

INSIDE THE NUMBERS

Before answering that question, Americans need to separate fact from fiction. The predictions of job losses in the millions are driving the current outsourcing hysteria. But it is crucial to note that these predictions are of gross, not net, losses. During the 1990s, offshore outsourcing was not uncommon. (American Express, for one, set up

back-office operations in India more than a decade ago.) But no one much cared because the number of jobs leaving U.S. shores was far lower than the number of jobs created in the U.S. economy.

Similarly, most current predictions are not as ominous as they first sound once the numbers are unpacked. Most jobs will remain unaffected altogether: close to 90 percent of jobs in the United States require geographic proximity. Such jobs include everything from retail and restaurants to marketing and personal care—services that have to be produced and consumed locally, so outsourcing them overseas is not an option. There is also no evidence that jobs in the high-value-added sector are migrating overseas. One thing that has made offshore outsourcing possible is the standardization of such business tasks as data entry, accounting, and IT support. The parts of production that are more complex, interactive, or innovative—including, but not limited to, marketing, research, and development—are much more difficult to shift abroad. As an International Data Corporation analysis on trends in IT services concluded, "the activities that will migrate offshore are predominantly those that can be viewed as requiring low skill since process and repeatability are key underpinnings of the work. Innovation and deep business expertise will continue to be delivered predominantly onshore." Not coincidentally, these are also the tasks that generate high wages and large profits and drive the U.S. economy.

As for the jobs that can be sent offshore, even if the most dire-sounding forecasts come true, the impact on the economy will be negligible. The Forrester prediction of 3.3 million lost jobs, for example, is spread across 15 years. That would mean 220,000 jobs displaced per year by offshore outsourcing—a number that sounds impressive until one considers that total employment in the United States is roughly 130 million, and that about 22 million new jobs are expected to be added between now and 2010. Annually, outsourcing would affect less than .2 percent of employed Americans.

There is also reason to believe that the unemployment caused by outsourcing will be lower than expected. Gartner assumed that more than 60 percent of financial-sector employees directly affected by outsourcing would be let go by their employers. But Boston University Professor Nitin Joglekar has examined the effect of outsourcing on large financial firms and found that less than 20 percent of workers affected by outsourcing lose their jobs; the rest are repositioned within the firm. Even if the most negative projections prove to be correct, then, gross job loss would be relatively small.

Moreover, it is debatable whether actual levels of outsourcing will ever match current predictions. Despite claims that the pace of onshore and offshore outsourcing

Despite an 11-percent decrease in manufacturing employment in the United States from 1995 to 2002, a corresponding increase did not occur globally: China, for instance, saw a 15-percent decrease during that same time period. © FOCUSCHINA/ALAMY.

would quicken over time, there was no increase in 2003. In fact, TPI Inc., an outsourcing advisory firm, even reports that the total value of business process outsourcing deals in the United States fell by 32 percent in 2003.

There is no denying that the number of manufacturing jobs has fallen dramatically in recent years, but this has very little do with outsourcing and almost everything to do with technological innovation. As with agriculture a century ago, productivity gains have outstripped demand, so fewer and fewer workers are needed for manufacturing. If outsourcing were in fact the chief cause of manufacturing losses, one would expect corresponding increases in manufacturing employment in developing countries. An Alliance Capital Management study of global manufacturing trends from 1995 to 2002, however, shows that this was not the case: the United States saw an 11 percent decrease in manufacturing employment over the course of those seven years; meanwhile, China saw a 15 percent decrease and Brazil a 20 percent decrease. Globally, the figure for manufacturing jobs lost was identical to the U.S. figure—11 percent. The fact that global

manufacturing output increased by 30 percent in that same period confirms that technology, not trade, is the primary cause for the decrease in factory jobs. A recent analysis of employment data from U.S. multinational corporations by the U.S. Department of Commerce reached the same conclusion.

What about the service sector? Again, the data contradict the popular belief that U.S. jobs are being lost to foreign countries without anything to replace them. In the case of many low-level technology jobs, the phenomenon has been somewhat exaggerated. For example, a Datamonitor study found that global call-center operations are being outsourced at a slower rate than previously thought—only five percent are expected to be located offshore by 2007. Dell and Lehman Brothers recently moved some of their call centers back to the United States from India because of customer complaints. And done properly, the offshore outsourcing of call centers creates new jobs at home. Delta Airlines outsourced 1,000 call-center jobs to India in 2003, but the $25 million in savings allowed the firm to add 1,200 reservation and sales positions in the United States.

Offshore outsourcing is similarly counterbalanced by job creation in the high-end service sector. An Institute for International Economics analysis of Bureau of Labor Statistics employment data revealed that the number of jobs in service sectors where outsourcing is likely actually increased, even though total employment decreased by 1.7 percent. According to the Bureau of Labor Statistics "Occupation Outlook Handbook," the number of IT-related jobs is expected to grow 43 percent by 2010. The case of IBM reinforces this lesson: although critics highlight the offshore outsourcing of 3,000 IT jobs, they fail to mention the company's plans to add 4,500 positions to its U.S. payroll. Large software companies such as Microsoft and Oracle have simultaneously increased outsourcing and domestic payrolls.

How can these figures fit with the widespread perception that IT jobs have left the United States? Too often, comparisons are made to 2000, an unusual year for the technology sector because Y2K fears and the height of the dot-com bubble had pushed employment figures to an artificially high level. When 1999 is used as the starting point, it becomes clear that offshore outsourcing has not caused a collapse in IT hiring. Between 1999 and 2003, the number of jobs in business and financial operations increased by 14 percent. Employment in computer and mathematical positions increased by 6 percent.

It is also worth remembering that many predictions come from management consultants who are eager to push the latest business fad. Many of these consulting firms are themselves reaping commissions from outsourcing contracts. Much of the perceived boom in outsourcing stems from companies' eagerness to latch onto the latest management trends; like Dell and Lehman, many will partially reverse course once the hidden costs of offshore outsourcing become apparent.

If offshore outsourcing is not the cause of sluggish job growth, what is? A study by the Federal Reserve Bank of New York suggests that the economy is undergoing a structural transformation: jobs are disappearing from old sectors (such as manufacturing) and being created in new ones (such as mortgage brokering). In all such transformations, the creation of new jobs lags behind the destruction of old ones. In other words, the recent recession and current recovery are a more extreme version of the downturn and "jobless recovery" of the early 1990s—which eventually produced the longest economic expansion of the post–World War II era. Once the structural adjustments of the current period are complete, job growth is expected to be robust. (And indeed, current indicators are encouraging: there has been a net increase in payroll jobs and in small business employment since 2003 and a spike in IT entrepreneurial activity.)

Offshore outsourcing is undoubtedly taking place, and it will likely increase over the next decade. However, it is not the tsunami that many claim. Its effect on the U.S. economy has been exaggerated, and its effect on the U.S. employment situation has been grossly exaggerated.

THE UPSIDE OF OUTSOURCING

To date, the media's coverage of outsourcing has focused on its perceived costs. This leaves out more than half of the story. The benefits of offshore outsourcing should not be dismissed.

The standard case for free trade holds that countries are best off when they focus on sectors in which they have a comparative advantage—that is, sectors that have the lowest opportunity costs of production. Allowing countries to specialize accordingly increases productivity across all countries. This specialization translates into cheaper goods, and a greater variety of them, for all consumers.

The current trend of outsourcing business processes overseas is comparative advantage at work. The main driver of productivity gains over the past decade has been the spread of information technology across the economy. The commodification of simple business services allows those benefits to spread further, making growth even greater.

The data affirm this benefit. Catherine Mann of the Institute for International Economics conservatively estimates that the globalization of IT production has boosted U.S. GDP by $230 billion over the past seven years; the globalization of IT services should lead to a similar increase. As the price of IT services declines, sectors that have yet to exploit them to their fullest—such as construction and health care—will begin to do so, thus lowering their cost of production and improving the quality of their output. (For example, cheaper IT could one day save lives by reducing the number of "adverse drug events." Mann estimates that adding bar codes to prescription drugs and instituting an electronic medical record system could reduce the annual number of such events by more than 80,000 in the United States alone.)

McKinsey Global Institute has estimated that for every dollar spent on outsourcing to India, the United States reaps between $1.12 and $1.14 in benefits. Thanks to outsourcing, U.S. firms save money and become more profitable, benefiting shareholders and increasing returns on investment. Foreign facilities boost demand for U.S. products, such as computers and telecommunications equipment, necessary for their outsourced function. And U.S. labor can be reallocated to more competitive, better-paying jobs; for example, although 70,000 computer programmers lost their jobs between 1999 and 2003, more than 115,000 computer software engineers found

Employees of 24/7 Customer, a customer support company based in Bangalore, India, take calls for U.S. and British companies in March 2004. © BRIAN LEE/CORBIS.

higher-paying jobs during that same period. Outsourcing thus enhances the competitiveness of the U.S. service sector (which accounts for 30 percent of the total value of U.S. exports). Contrary to the belief that the United States is importing massive amounts of services from low-wage countries, in 2002 it ran a $64.8 billion surplus in services.

Outsourcing also has considerable noneconomic benefits. It is clearly in the interest of the United States to reward other countries for reducing their barriers to trade and investment. Some of the countries where U.S. firms have set up outsourcing operations—including India, Poland, and the Philippines—are vital allies in the war on terrorism. Just as the North American Free Trade Agreement (NAFTA) helped Mexico deepen its demo-cratic transition and strengthen its rule of law, the United States gains considerably from the political reorientation spurred by economic growth and interdependence.

Finally, the benefits of "insourcing" should not be overlooked. Just as U.S. firms outsource positions to developing countries, firms in other countries outsource positions to the United States. According to the Bureau of Labor Statistics, the number of outsourced jobs increased

from 6.5 million in 1983 to 10 million in 2000. The number of insourced jobs increased even more in the same period, from 2.5 million to 6.5 million.

POLITICAL ECONOMY

When it comes to trade policy, there are two iron laws of politics. The first is that the benefits of trade diffuse across the economy, but the costs of trade are concentrated. Thus, those made worse off by open borders will form the more motivated interest group. The second is that public hostility toward trade increases during economic downturns. When forced to choose between statistical evidence showing that trade is good for the economy and anecdotal evidence of job losses due to import competition, Americans go with the anecdotes.

Offshore outsourcing adds two additional political pressures. The first stems from the fact that technological innovation has converted what were thought to be nontradeable sectors into tradeable ones. Manufacturing workers have long been subject to the rigors of global competition. White-collar service-sector workers are being introduced to these pressures for the first time—and they are not happy about it. As Raghuram Rajan and Luigi Zingales point out in "Saving Capitalism From the Capitalists," globalization and technological innovation affect professions such as law and medicine that have not changed all that much for centuries. Their political reaction to the threat of foreign competition will be fierce.

The second pressure is that the Internet has greatly facilitated political organization, making it much easier for those who blame outsourcing for their troubles to rally together. In recent years, countless organizations—with names such as Rescue American Jobs, Save U.S. Jobs, and the Coalition for National Sovereignty and Economic Patriotism—have sprouted up. Such groups have dispro-portionately focused on white-collar tech workers, even though the manufacturing sector has been much harder hit by the recent economic slowdown.

It should come as no surprise, then, that politicians are scrambling to get ahead of the curve. During the Democratic primary in South Carolina—a state hit hard by the loss of textile jobs—billboards asked voters, "Lost your job to free trade or offshore outsourcing yet?" Last Labor Day, President Bush pledged to appoint a manufacturing czar to get to the bottom of the outflow of manufacturing positions. In his stump speech, John Kerry bashes "Benedict Arnold CEOs [who] send American jobs overseas."

Where presidential candidates lead, legislators are sure to follow. Senator Charles Schumer (D-N.Y.) claimed in a January "New York Times" op-ed authored with Paul Craig Roberts that because of increased capital mobility, the law of comparative advantage is now null and void. Senator Tom Daschle (D-S.D.) has observed, "George Bush says the economy is creating jobs. But let me tell you, China is one long commute. And let me tell you, I'm tired of watching jobs shift overseas." Senator Christo-pher Dodd (D-Conn.) and Representative Nancy Johnson (R-Conn.) are sponsoring the USA Jobs Protection Act to prevent U.S. companies from hiring foreign workers for positions when American workers are available. In February, Senate Democrats announced their intentions to introduce the Jobs for America Act, requiring compa-nies to give public notice three months in advance of any plan to outsource 15 or more jobs. In March, the Senate overwhelmingly approved a measure banning firms from federal contracts if they outsource any of the work overseas. In the past two years, more than 20 state legislatures have introduced bills designed to make various forms of offshore outsourcing illegal.

SPLENDID ISOLATION?

There are clear examples of jobs being sent across U.S. borders because of U.S. trade policy—but not for the reasons that critics of outsourcing believe. Consider the example of candy-cane manufacturers: despite the fact that 90 percent of the world's candy canes are consumed in the United States, manufacturers have sent much of their production south of the border in the past five years. The attraction of moving abroad, however, has little to do with low wages and much to do with protectionism. U.S. quotas on sugar imports have, in recent years, caused the domestic price of sugar to become 350 percent higher than world market prices. As candy makers have relocated production to countries where sugar is cheaper, between 7,500 and 10,000 workers in the Midwest have lost their jobs—victims not of outsourcing but of the kind of protectionism called for by outsourcing's critics.

A similar story can be told of the steel tariffs that the Bush administration foolishly imposed from March 2002 until December 2003 (when a ruling by the World Trade Organization prompted their cancellation). The tariffs were allegedly meant to protect steelworkers. But in the United States, steel users employ roughly 40 times more people than do steel producers. Thus, according to estimates by the Institute for International Economics, between 45,000 and 75,000 jobs were lost because higher steel prices made U.S. steel-using industries less competitive.

These examples illustrate the problem with relying on anecdotes when debating the effects of offshore out-sourcing. Anecdotes are incomplete narratives that fail to capture opportunity costs. In the cases of steel and sugar, the opportunity cost of using protectionism to save jobs was the much larger number of jobs lost in sectors rendered less productive by higher input prices. Trade protectionism amounts to an inefficient subsidy for uncompetitive sectors of the economy, which leads to higher prices for consumers and a lower rate of return for investors. It preserves jobs in less competitive sectors while destroying current and future jobs in sectors that have a comparative advantage. Thus, if barriers are erected to prevent offshore outsourcing, the overall effect will not be to create jobs but to destroy them.

So if protectionism is not the answer, what is the correct response? The best piece of advice is also the most difficult for elected officials to follow: do no harm. Politicians never get credit for inaction, even when inaction is the best policy. President George H. W. Bush, for example, was pilloried for refusing to follow Japan's lead by protecting domestic markets—even though his refusal helped pave the way for the 1990s boom by letting market forces allocate resources to industries at the technological frontier. Restraint is anathema to the political class, but it is still the most important response to the furor over offshore outsourcing. As Robert McTeer, president of the Federal Reserve Bank of Dallas, said when asked about policy responses to outsourcing, "If we are lucky, we can get through the year without doing something really, really stupid."

The problem of offshore outsourcing is less one of economics than of psychology—people feel that their jobs are threatened. The best way to help those actually affected, and to calm the nerves of those who fear that they will be, is to expand the criteria under which the Trade Adjustment Assistance (TAA) program applies to displaced workers. Currently, workers cannot apply for TAA unless overall sales or production in their sector declines. In the case of offshore outsourcing, however, productivity increases allow for increased production and sales—making TAA out of reach for those affected by it. It makes sense to rework TAA rules to take into account workers displaced by offshore outsourcing even when their former industries or firms maintain robust levels of production.

Another option would be to help firms purchase targeted insurance policies to offset the transition costs to workers directly affected by offshore outsourcing. Because the perception of possible unemployment is considerably greater than the actual likelihood of losing a job, insurance programs would impose a very small cost on firms while relieving a great deal of employee anxiety. McKinsey Global Institute estimates that such a scheme could be created for as little as four or five cents per dollar saved from offshore outsourcing. IBM recently announced the creation of a two-year, $25 million retraining fund for its employees who fear job losses from outsourcing. Having the private sector handle the problem without extensive government intervention would be an added bonus.

THE BEST DEFENSE

Until robust job growth returns, the debate over outsourcing will not go away—the political temptation to scapegoat foreigners is simply too great.

The refrain of "this time, it's different" is not new in the debate over free trade. In the 1980s, the Japanese variety of capitalism—with its omniscient industrial policy and high nontariff barriers—was supposed to supplant the U.S. system. Fifteen years later, that prediction sounds absurd. During the 1990s, the passage of NAFTA and the Uruguay Round of trade talks were supposed to create a "giant sucking sound" as jobs left the United States. Contrary to such fears, tens of millions of new jobs were created. Once the economy improves, the political hysteria over outsourcing will also disappear.

It is easy to praise economic globalization during boom times; the challenge, however, is to defend it during the lean years of a business cycle. Offshore outsourcing is not the bogeyman that critics say it is. Their arguments, however, must be persistently refuted. Otherwise, the results will be disastrous: less growth, lower incomes—and fewer jobs for American workers.

FURTHER RESOURCES
Books

Dobbs, Lou. *Exporting America: Why Corporate Greed Is Shipping American Jobs Overseas.* New York: Business Plus/Hachette, 2006.

Hira, Ron, and Anil Hira. *Outsourcing America: The True Cost of Shipping Jobs Overseas and What Can Be Done About It.* New York: Amacom, 2008.

Web Sites

Ahmed, Syud Amer. "Outsourcing and US Manufacturing Employment." *World Bank Development Research Group.* Originally presented at the Tenth Annual Conference on Global Economic Analysis (June 2007). www.gtap.agecon.purdue.edu/resources/download/4486. pdf (accessed on March 24, 2013).

Matthews, Merrill. "Companies 'Outsource' Because That's Where the Sales Are." *Forbes*, July 20, 2012. www. forbes.com/sites/merrillmatthews/2012/07/20/companies-outsource-because-thats-where-the-sales-are/ (accessed on March 24, 2013).

"Outsourcing: Where's Uncle Sam?" *Bloomberg Businessweek*, February 2007. www.businessweek.com/debateroom/ archives/2007/02/outsourcing_wheres_uncle_sam.html (accessed February 8, 2013).

Pearlstein, Steven. "Outsourcing: What's the True Impact? Counting Jobs Is Only Part of the Answer." *Washington Post*, July 1, 2012. http://articles.washingtonpost.com/ 2012-07-01/business/35486822_1_inventory-control-mitt-romney-lenovo (accessed on March 24, 2013).

Wolverson, Roya. "Renewing America: Outsourcing Jobs and Taxes." *Council on Foreign Relations.* www.cfr.org/ united-states/outsourcing-jobs-taxes/p21777 (accessed on March 24, 2013).

"Researchers Recover T. Rex Tissue"

Web site article

By: Associated Press

Date: March 24, 2005

Source: Associated Press. "Researchers Recover T. Rex Tissue." *Wired*, March 24, 2005. www.wired.com/ science/discoveries/news/2005/03/67014 (accessed on March 23, 2013).

About the Web site: *Wired.com* is the Web extension of *Wired* magazine, a popular technology, culture, and business magazine that was launched in 1993. The magazine was one of the earliest and most prominent U.S. publications to cover the emerging Internet and related technologies, and it has since built on its success to become one of the world's most popular technology magazines, providing exclusive previews of breakthroughs in fields like medicine, computing, biology, and consumer electronics. *Wired.com* was innovative in its own right, being noted as one of the first print-publication-affiliated news sites to provide additional, Web-specific content not featured in the magazine itself.

INTRODUCTION

The first *T. rex* fossil ever discovered consisted of two partial vertebrae and was unearthed in 1892 in South Dakota by paleontologist Edward Drinker Cope. Barnum Brown discovered fragments of the gigantic dinosaur in 1902 and then again in 1908, both times in Montana. Discoveries of the beast were rare, and none were ever complete. In 1942, a skull was found, again in Montana, and a crew from the Natural History Museum of Los Angeles County uncovered the largest *T. rex* skull ever found to date in 1966. Throughout the 1980s, various digs revealed skulls and partial skeletons, always in South Dakota, Montana, or Alberta, Canada.

Because they were never found with complete skeletons, the discovery of *T. rex* was always exciting. One particularly thrilling excavation was that of Black Beauty, found in 1980 in a riverbank by a young boy named Jeff Baker. Found and displayed in Alberta, Black Beauty was named for the color of its bones, and it is the smallest of all known specimens.

Montana rancher Kathy Wankel discovered a *T. rex* specimen in Hell Creek. Now on exhibit in the Museum of the Rockies in Bozeman, Montana, the specimen was almost 90 percent complete and included the skull. Several more fossils were discovered throughout the decade, but the 1990s proved to be the decade for the most impressive *T. rex* findings. Nearly twice as many dinosaurs were excavated in the 1990s than in all the previous years put together. Three of the most complete *T. rex* skeletons on display even in the twenty-first century were found in 1990 and 1991, and the world of paleontology became more controversial as the decade progressed. Legal rights to bones became a source of contention as regular citizens—as opposed to professional paleontologists—accidentally or otherwise unearthed these dinosaur fossils.

But the world of paleontology was turned on its head with the discovery of fossils in 2005, again in Montana. From the fossils, scientist Mary Schweitzer and colleagues were able to recover what they believed to be soft tissue from a femur of a *T. rex*.

SIGNIFICANCE

No one could have predicted the firestorm that ensued after the discovery of what looked to be dinosaur tissue. Schweitzer was attacked from both the scientific community and the Christian faction known as "young creationists."

After repeated and various testing revealed the same results time and again, Schweitzer and several colleagues announced in April 2007 that seven preserved fragments of protein had been found in sample MOR 1125. Five of those fragments closely matched sequences of collagen found in birds—chickens. Suddenly, headlines appeared calling the *Tyrannosaurus rex* a chicken. While startling to people outside the scientific community, this relationship was not altogether unusual to researchers and paleontologists. The relationship between dinosaurs and chickens had long been theorized, and this was the first molecular confirmation of the suspicion. In addition, the discovery provided the first evidence that protein could survive even one million years.

Just over one year after publication of their findings, researchers began publicly doubting the quality of the data. They had difficulty believing collagen could survive for sixty-eight million years, especially given that the sample found was still partially intact. One particularly scathing critic was Pavel Pevzner, a computational biologist at UC San Diego. He ridiculed the quality of work of Schweitzer's research partner, John Asara. The mass spectrometry expert was the scientist who claimed that the fragments were collagen, and Pavzner debunked his findings as "a joke."

The root of the controversy lay in the difference between computational and traditional biological research. There are those scientists who believe that microscopic slides provide a more accurate piece of evidence than do digital processes like spectrometry. Used for decades to help identify the molecular makeup of compounds, the process became more heavily relied upon in more recent years.

Criticism of Asara's lab procedures and findings intensified, and the situation was compared to a similar one that took place in 1994, when scientists claimed to have discovered dinosaur DNA but in fact what they had seen in their work was the result of laboratory contamination. Asara could have answered his critics by releasing the spectra, but he refused. In a community where results are authenticated by peer review and investigation of research, this was not a choice that inspired confidence in the scientist. When the criticism became too much, Asara finally made his research available for scrutiny when he posted 48,216 spectra online in 2008.

It took just two weeks for two scientists to debunk Asara's findings. After downloading the spectra to run their own algorithms, Martin McIntosh and Matthew Fitzgibbon discovered a match not to collagen, but to a hemoglobin peptide found in ostriches. The confusion between the two findings was the result of lab contamination. Yet Schweitzer remained firm in her conviction that she had found evidence of collagen using traditional biological methods, in her own lab, on samples that no one else had ever worked with.

In May 2009, Asara and Schweitzer published a paper with more than twelve other authors indicating that they had replicated their protein experiments on a different bone fragment. This one came from an eighty-million-year-old hadrosaur, a different species, but also found in Montana, this time in 2007. The duo used more rigorous controls and even implemented Pevzner's high standards for statistical analysis. Again, the protein fragments were similar to bird collagen. But there was a surprise: They lined up even more closely with the *T. rex* peptides reported by Asara back in 2007. Research continued into the next decade.

PRIMARY SOURCE

"RESEARCHERS RECOVER T. REX TISSUE"

SYNOPSIS: Paleontologists uncovered what was believed to be soft tissue from a 70-million-year-old *T. rex*, and scientists hoped to get a better understanding of how the dinosaur lived.

For more than a century, the study of dinosaurs has been limited to fossilized bones. Now, researchers have recovered 70-million-year-old soft tissue, including what may be blood vessels and cells, from a *Tyrannosaurus rex*.

If scientists can isolate proteins from the material, they may be able to learn new details of how dinosaurs lived, said lead researcher Mary Higby Schweitzer of North Carolina State University.

"We're doing a lot of stuff in the lab right now that looks promising," she said in a telephone interview. But, she said, she does not know yet if scientists will be able to isolate dinosaur DNA from the materials.

It was recovered dinosaur DNA—the blueprint for life—that was featured in the fictional recreation of the ancient animals in the book and film *Jurassic Park*.

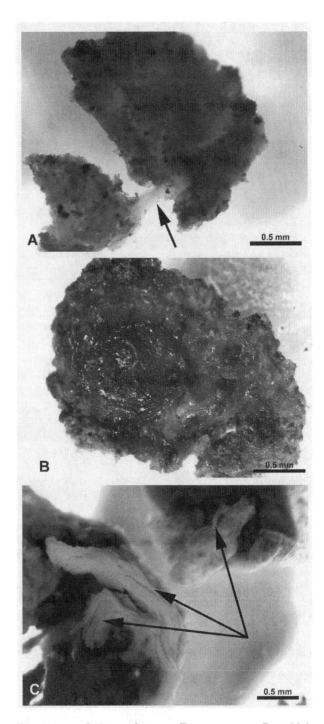

Fragments of tissue from a *Tyrannosaurus Rex* thigh bone. © EPA/CORBIS.

The soft tissues were recovered from the thighbone of a *T. rex*, known as MOR 1125, that was found in a sandstone formation in Montana. The dinosaur was about 18 years old when it died.

The bone was broken when it was removed from the site. Schweitzer and her colleagues then analyzed the material inside the bone.

"The vessels and contents are similar in all respects to blood vessels recovered from … ostrich bone," they reported in a paper being published Friday in the journal *Science*.

Because evidence has accumulated in recent years that modern birds descended from dinosaurs, Schweitzer said she chose to compare the dinosaur remains with those of an ostrich, the largest bird available.

Brooks Hanson, a deputy editor of *Science*, noted that there are few examples of soft tissues, except for leaves or petrified wood, that are preserved as fossils, just as there are few discoveries of insects in amber or humans and mammoths in peat or ice.

Soft tissues are rare in older finds. "That's why in a 70-million-year-old fossil it is so interesting," he said.

Matthew Carrano, curator of dinosaurs at the Smithsonian's National Museum of Natural History, said the discovery was "pretty exciting stuff."

"You are actually getting into the small-scale biology of the animal, which is something we rarely get the opportunity to look at," said Carrano, who was not part of the research team.

In addition, he said, it is a huge opportunity to learn more about how fossils are made, a process that is not fully understood.

Richard A. Hengst of Purdue University said the finding "opens the door for research into the protein structure of ancient organisms, if nothing else. While we think that nature is conservative in how things are built, this gives scientists an opportunity to observe this at the chemical and cellular level." Hengst was not part of the research team.

John R. Horner, of the Museum of the Rockies at Montana State University, said the discovery is "a fantastic specimen," but probably is not unique. Other researchers might find similarly preserved soft tissues if they split open the bones in their collections, said Horner, a co-author of the paper.

Most museums, he said, prefer to keep their specimens intact.

Schweitzer said that after removing the minerals from the specimen, the remaining tissues were soft and transparent and could be manipulated with instruments.

The bone matrix was stretchy and flexible, she said. Also, there were long structures like blood vessels. What appeared to be individual cells were visible.

She did not know if they were blood cells. "They are little round cells," Schweitzer said.

She likened the process to placing a chicken bone in vinegar. The minerals will dissolve, leaving the soft tissues.

The research was funded by North Carolina State University and grants from N. Myhrvold and the National Science Foundation.

FURTHER RESOURCES
Books
Larson, Peter L., and Kenneth Carpenter, eds. *Tyrannosaurus Rex, the Tyrant King*. Bloomington: Indiana University Press, 2008.

Web Sites
Ratcliffe, Evan. "Origin of Species: How a *T. Rex* Femur Sparked a Scientific Smackdown." *Wired*, June 22, 2009. www.wired.com/medtech/genetics/magazine/17-07/ff_originofspecies?currentPage=all (accessed on March 23, 2013).

Webster, Donovan. "The Dinosaur Fossil Wars." *Smithsonian*, April 2009. www.smithsonianmag.com/science-nature/The-Dino-Wars.html (accessed on March 23, 2013).

Zimmerman, Kim Ann. "Tyrannosaurus Rex: Facts About *T. Rex*, King of the Dinosaurs." *Live Science*, October 10, 2012. www.livescience.com/23868-tyrannosaurus-rex-facts.html (accessed on March 23, 2013).

"Cookie Monsters"

The innocuous text files that Web surfers love to hate

Web site article

By: Adam L. Penenberg

Date: November 7, 2005

Source: Penenberg, Adam L. "Cookie Monsters." *Slate*, November 7, 2005. www.slate.com/articles/technology/technology/2005/11/cookie_monsters.html (accessed on March 24, 2013).

About the Publication: *Slate* is an online culture magazine that covers a diverse range of subjects, particularly current matters of public interest. The magazine was founded in 1996 under the ownership of Microsoft Corporation and quickly developed a significant audience. In 2004, the Washington Post Company acquired *Slate*. Under its new ownership, the magazine diversified its offerings to include image galleries, podcasts, and longer articles. The expanded site proved so successful that the Washington Post Company established

The Slate Group, an online-publication management company.

INTRODUCTION

Cookies, also known as "browser cookies," "HTTP cookies," or "Web cookies," are a type of device used by many Web sites to record certain data about individual users. A cookie consists of a small, encoded text file that is inserted by a Web site into the memory of a user's computer. Every time the user revisits the site that installed the cookie, the site decrypts the text file to determine information about the user, such as login status, preferences, page views, and saved settings. Typically, cookies are active only on the site that installed them on a user's Web browser—a cookie placed by site A will not be able to collect information about a user's activity on site B. An exception to this standard is third-party cookies, which are placed by digital advertisers to determine which ads an individual responds to and what their interests are, so as to better tailor ads to their consumer habits. Such "tracking cookies" activate whenever a browser on which they are installed visits a site that hosts ads by the same advertiser that placed the cookies.

Although they may sound ominous, cookies play an integral role in the modern Web. Hypertext Transfer Protocol (HTTP), the computational foundation that governs the operation of the World Wide Web, is inherently stateless—each request sent from a browser to a server is executed independently from all others. Cookies were developed as a simple tool for browsing sessions to persist beyond single host-client interactions, so that Web users could retain the state of a site even after leaving it or moving to a different page within the same site. For instance, an online-shopping site like Amazon.com might place a cookie on users' computers to record their login information, store their billing and shipping information, maintain a "shopping cart" so that users can purchase multiple items in a single transaction, and to record the items users search for to provide better, more relevant purchase suggestions.

Normal first-party cookies are only decipherable by the Web site that placed them and thus cannot be read or accessed by anyone except their originator (with the exception of highly skilled hackers). They provide an important, useful function that benefits both users and Web site operators immensely. Third-party cookies, however, serve a more sinister purpose. When a webpage is queried and loaded, cookies embedded in advertisements hosted on that page are placed on the computer that sent the request, in addition to the standard first-party cookies placed by

the page. Once deposited, such unsolicited cookies become active each time the computer visits a site that hosts content from the same advertiser, storing an ever-increasing amount of information on the user's browsing habits, interests, favorite Web sites, purchase habits, demographics, and reaction to advertising. Theoretically, compiling this data allows advertisers to customize the content of its ads to individual users, or to determine which Web locations are best suited to carry different ads (practices known as behavioral targeting).

During the early 2000s, consumer activist groups and Internet privacy advocates brought tracking cookies to the attention of the general public, warning that they represented a serious threat to the privacy and security of Web users. Because tracking cookies record so much information about their subjects, it was warned, advertisers could potentially match an individual's real-world identity with the profile compiled from the cookies. A single cookie could accomplish this feat: It could be placed on a person's computer from a shopping site, recording their purchases; activate on a local listings site, recording their residential information; and then activate again on a social networking site, recording their profile's unique URL. It would be simple for a data analyst to extract all this information when examining the cookie and to piece it together.

Web users were also cautioned that even first-party cookies were not entirely safe. Skilled hackers are capable of intercepting the transmission of cookies and extracting saved usernames and passwords, allowing them to gain access to sensitive information. Cookies are also susceptible to imitation, in which a hacker copies the signature of the cookie so that a Web site is tricked into thinking it is communicating with a different computer than it actually is. Upon learning about the potential hazards of cookies, the public reacted strongly—some set their browsers to block all cookies, others avoided all sites that used them (a category that includes almost every major site on the Web), and some demanded the abolition or regulation of them.

SIGNIFICANCE

Fortunately for the World Wide Web, the use of cookies prevailed despite the public distrust surrounding them, which was based primarily around a general misunderstanding of what they do and how they work. Experts appeared on television to assure those concerned that cookies are not programmable, do not spy on every move a person makes, cannot carry viruses, and cannot access the information stored on a computer. Antivirus programs adopted the option to root out and remove third-party cookies, even though they pose no threat to a system's operational integrity. Web users generally grew savvier to the nuances of cookies, many opting to block only tracking cookies or to periodically delete all of their cookies.

Advertisers, distressed by the dwindling supply of analyzable data, concocted a novel solution. By exploiting an obscure function of Adobe Flash Player (a near-ubiquitous multimedia program found on more than 90 percent of personal computers), advertisers continued to place tracking cookies on computers, albeit as a slightly different iteration called "local shared objects." Local shared objects perform the exact same function as traditional cookies, except that they cannot be blocked, viewed, or removed without significant technical knowledge. The development and implementation of local shared objects did not draw significant public attention, negative or otherwise.

Ultimately, cookies illustrate the complicated nature of the relationship between the Web and its users. As the 2000s progressed, the Internet developed an increasingly central role in the lives of U.S. citizens, as it became common to store tax and financial information, personal correspondences, credit card information, phone numbers, home addresses, and private media online. The importance of protecting such information from hackers and identity thieves presented a continuous series of new challenges and problems for Web users, who were constantly being alerted to new threats—malware, viruses, worms, spyware, adware, remote infiltration, and so on—each demanding new security measures to avoid. Though the idea of having their online activity recorded by cookies may have bothered many, it was eventually accepted as a necessary aspect of a Web in which ad revenue allows most sites to offer their services for free.

PRIMARY SOURCE

"COOKIE MONSTERS"

SYNOPSIS: In this article, the author explains the function of browser cookies and the public distrust of them.

Slate uses cookies. So do the *New York Times*, the *Washington Post*, and almost every media site on the net. Popular blogs like Daily Kos and Powerline have embraced them. Google and Yahoo! dispatch them to better target ads. Retailers like Amazon rely on them to fulfill orders. Even Sesame Street deploys them on its Web site.

Cookies are simply text files sent by a Web site to your computer to track your movements within its pages. They're something like virtual license plates, assigned to your browser so a site can spot you in a sea of millions of visitors. Cookies remember your login and password, the products you've just bought, or your preferred color scheme. Sites that ask you to register use cookies to target advertising—someone who claims an annual salary of $35,000 might see ads for Boca Burgers rather than foie gras.

Though cookies make navigating the Web profoundly easier, those who deploy them have done a lousy job at promoting their utility. The result is that lots of people don't trust them. Many surfers erase cookies frequently or refuse them entirely, blaming them for everything from spying, to identity theft, to slow Internet connections. A slew of security products lump them in with spyware, viruses, and other nasties and promise to snuff them out at no extra charge.

Cookies are not software. They can't be programmed, can't carry viruses, and can't unleash malware to go wilding through your hard drive. Only the Web site that sent you the cookie can read it. As soon as you leave a site, its cookie sits dormant, waiting for your return.

The exceptions are third-party cookies—also known as "tracking cookies"—placed by an entity (usually a marketing or advertising company) that's interested in tagging visitors. Often they make sure a user won't be hit with the same ad twice; others guarantee that someone who says they have an interest in sports gets different ads than someone who likes gadgets. But third-party cookies could also be used to compile a dossier of surfing habits. Say you visit a Web site with cookies served by a marketing company like DoubleClick. The cookie it dispatches will come alive every time you visit another site that does business with DoubleClick. That means it could track you over dozens of sites, logging every article you read, every ad you click on, and every gadget and gizmo you buy without your knowledge or approval.

What makes many people uneasy is the potential for DoubleClick or a similar firm to match a user's e-mail, home address, and phone number to his surfing history. How do we know the company won't use this information for purposes other than advertising and marketing? All we have is its word that it won't "attempt to know the real-world identity of the owner or user of a computer's browser." DoubleClick was pummeled six years ago when it announced its intent to create a database of consumer profiles that would include names, addresses, and online purchase histories. After public outcry and a class-action suit (which was settled in 2002), DoubleClick did an about-face and said it had made a huge mistake.

Still, the potential for marketers—which in lieu of governmental oversight regulate themselves—to abuse their position as third-party ad servers is the prime reason why all cookies have been demonized. The bad reputation of cookies has contributed to the formation of an entire industry that's based on snuffing out potential threats on consumer desktops. The more threats they find, the more valuable their product. It's funny, then, that many of the same companies that demonize cookies—McAfee, SpyWare Doctor, and STOPzilla—toss them at you when you visit their Web sites.

So, what would happen if the king of the Internet magically banned cookies tomorrow? Much of the Web would cease to exist. Ad-supported sites like *Slate* would either go under or start charging you to visit—without a way to gauge how many people have looked at an ad, online advertisers would pull the plug. And instead of aiding privacy, the death of cookies might very well stifle it. Many Web sites would require more frequent registration—you'd have to log in every time you visited the *New York Times*, since the site wouldn't remember you. And forget about shopping online.

The Web often feels like a free medium, where you can read anything you want free of charge. What keeps it cheap and convenient, though, is that it's an advertisers' medium. At the same time that ad revenue allows companies to serve content free of charge, consumers have unprecedented control over how they consume ad content, both online and offline. Just like you can TiVo shows and skip the commercials, you can block pop-up ads, filter junk e-mail, and corral cookies. Every major browser (Internet Explorer, Safari, and Mozilla Firefox) lets you customize your cookie consumption to accept them from sites you trust, reject them from parties you don't, or block them entirely.

Marketers don't fear that the government will ban or restrict cookies some day. After heavy lobbying they managed to secure an amendment to the Securely Protect Yourself Against Cyber Trespass Act that would exempt cookies from any spyware legislation that passes in the House. Instead, they are afraid that consumers will continue to delete them, which could put a major dent in advertising revenue and undermine the economics of boatloads of sites. If they want to avoid this ignominious end, the marketers who depend on cookies had better figure out a way to market the cookies themselves. A good place to start is to abolish third-party cookies. Only then can they put the focus on the miraculous text files that let you shop and read newspapers with the greatest of ease.

FURTHER RESOURCES

Books

Acquisti, Alessandro, Stefanos Gritzalis, Costos Lambrinoudakis, and Sabrina di Vimercati, eds. *Digital Privacy: Theory, Technology, and Practices*. Boca Raton, FL: Auerbach Publications, 2007.

Web Sites

"Cookies." *Electronic Privacy Information Center*. http://epic.org/privacy/internet/cookies (accessed on March 24, 2013).

"Fact and Fiction: The Truth About Browser Cookies." *LifeHacker*. http://lifehacker.com/5461114/fact-and-fiction-the-truth-about-browser-cookies (accessed on March 24, 2013).

Singel, Ryan. "You Deleted Your Cookies? Think Again." *Wired*, August 10, 2009. www.wired.com/business/2009/08/you-deleted-your-cookies-think-again (accessed on March 24, 2013).

"The Web Privacy Manifesto." *PBS*. www.pbs.org/mediashift/2007/11/the-web-privacy-manifesto330.html (accessed on March 24, 2013).

" 'Significant Amount' of Water Found on Moon"

Web site article

By: Andrea Thompson

Date: November 13, 2009

Source: Thompson, Andrea. "'Significant Amount' of Water Found on Moon." *Space.com*, November 13, 2009. www.space.com/7530-significant-amount-water-moon.html (accessed on March 24, 2013).

About the Web site: Space.com is a news Web site dedicated to providing coverage of "astronomy, skywatching, space exploration, commercial spaceflight, and related technologies." The site was founded in 1999 by Lou Dobbs, previously well-known as a congenial CNN news anchor, and his business partner, Rich Zahradnik. Although the site faltered in its early years of operation, it eventually acquired several of its competitors and assumed the position of premier space-related news provider. Space.com benefits from the employment of a full-time reporting staff and frequent contributions from noteworthy figures relevant to the fields of space exploration and astronomy.

INTRODUCTION

The presence of water on Earth's Moon has been a subject of speculation and debate in the astronomical community since 1960, when scientists first theorized that the freezing, perpetually shadowed craters located near the lunar poles could harbor frozen water.

Although the Sun's rays would quickly decompose any amount of liquid water or water vapor found on the Moon's surface, this theory held, the slight tilt of the lunar rotational axis—approximately 1.5 degrees— produced enough permanently dark area near the poles that, if it were somehow deposited in them, frozen water could conceivably stay that way for billions of years, unaffected by solar heat. Water was also conjectured to exist as individual particles chemically bound to minerals on the lunar surface. These hypotheses could not be tested, however, until the first humans set foot on the Moon in 1969, even after which it took almost fifty years to reach a definitive conclusion.

Part of the goal of every U.S. mission to the Moon, including the manned *Apollo* missions, has been to test for the presence of water. The first widely accepted observation of such came in 1994, when the U.S. military probe *Clementine* detected icy, rather than rocky, surfaces inside craters near the lunar south pole. In 1998, the National Aeronautics and Space Administration's (NASA) lunar *Prospector* probe detected a concentration of hydrogen being emitted from the Moon's polar regions, suggesting the presence of water (although the phenomenon could also be attributed to the presence of other hydroxyl chemical groups besides water on the lunar surface). Throughout the 2000s, a series of lunar observation projects—including NASA's *Deep Impact* spacecraft, Japan's *Kaguya* probe, and India's *Chandrayaan-1* probe—made contradictory observations of the Moon's composition, making it difficult for researchers to reach a conclusive consensus on the presence of lunar water.

In an effort to eliminate this confusion, NASA initiated its first mission to the Moon in more than ten years, consisting of two spacecraft. The first, called the Lunar Reconnaissance Orbiter (LRO), was a robotic craft designed to enter the Moon's orbit and compile a detailed, three-dimensional map of the entire lunar surface. The other craft was named the Lunar Crater Observation and Sensing Satellite (LCROSS); it was designed for the single function of determining the presence of water in the southern polar region of the Moon. This was to be accomplished by deliberately colliding the used upper stage of the launch rocket, called the Centaur stage, into the Cabeus crater, located near the Moon's south pole. LCROSS would then follow the Centaur stage, travelling through the plume of lunar debris caused by the collision to collect and relay data regarding the impact and the chemical composition of the ejected particles. The LCROSS vehicle carried nine observational instruments, including cameras, spectrometers, and a photometer. LCROSS and LRO were launched on June 18, 2009, aboard an Atlas V rocket, and on October 9, the Centaur rocket stage was crashed into Cabeus, followed four minutes later by LCROSS.

SIGNIFICANCE

Following analysis of the data provided by LCROSS, NASA scientists announced on November 13, 2009, that both the vapor plume and low-lying debris cloud caused by the Centaur stage's impact of the Cabeus crater displayed abundant evidence of water content. Researchers proclaimed that the portion of the crater impacted appeared to contain approximately 1 percent water ice, enough to be considered statistically significant. The primary confirmation of water on the moon came from spectrometer data collected by LCROSS, which indicated that the material ejected from the crater included tiny, crystalline particles of frozen water, as well as hydroxyl groups. Although more analysis was required to determine the water's origins and behavior, the LCROSS findings were heralded as conclusive verification that the Moon contains water.

The primary significance of lunar water is its potential to enable human colonization of the Moon, one of NASA's major long-term goals. If existent in sufficient quantities, the presence of water on the Moon would drastically improve the viability of this goal, as it could be harvested to provide drinking water and used to grow crops. Water could also be disassembled into its constituent chemicals—hydrogen and oxygen—to provide breathable oxygen, oxides for fertilizer, and even the hydrogen used to manufacture rocket fuel. This would eliminate the cost of transporting such materials from Earth to the Moon, which would be incredibly expensive. Lunar ice can also be studied to provide insight into the geological history of the Moon and, by extension, the prevalence of space debris like comets and meteors in the younger period of our solar system. Although continued investigation is required, the tentative findings of LCROSS hold great promise for the future of human lunar exploration.

PRIMARY SOURCE

"'SIGNIFICANT AMOUNT' OF WATER FOUND ON MOON"

SYNOPSIS: In this article, the author reports on NASA's announcement that water has been detected on the Moon and explains the significance of this discovery.

It's official: There's water ice on the moon, and lots of it. When melted, the water could potentially be used to drink or to extract hydrogen for rocket fuel.

NASA scientists announced in November 2009 that water had been found on the Moon. © AP IMAGES/NASA.

NASA's LCROSS probe discovered beds of water ice at the lunar south pole when it impacted the moon last month, mission scientists announced today. The findings confirm suspicions announced previously, and in a big way.

"Indeed, yes, we found water. And we didn't find just a little bit, we found a significant amount," Anthony Colaprete, LCROSS project scientist and principal investigator from NASA's Ames Research Center at Moffett Field, Calif.

The LCROSS probe impacted the lunar south pole at a crater called Cabeus on Oct. 9. The $79 million spacecraft, preceded by its Centaur rocket stage, hit the lunar surface in an effort to create a debris plume that could be analyzed by scientists for signs of water ice.

Those signs were visible in the data from spectrographic measurements (which measure light absorbed at different wavelengths, revealing different compounds) of the Centaur stage crater and the two-part debris plume the impact created. The signature of water was seen in both infrared and ultraviolet spectroscopic measurements.

"We see evidence for the water in two instruments," Colaprete said. "And that's what makes us really confident in our findings right now."

How much?

Based on the measurements, the team estimated about 100 kilograms of water in the view of their instruments (the equivalent of about a dozen 2-gallon buckets) in the area of the impact crater (about 66 feet, or 20 meters across) and the ejecta blanket (about 60 to 80 meters across), Colaprete said.

"I'm pretty impressed by the amount of water we saw in our little 20-meter crater," Colaprete said.

"What's really exciting is we've only hit one spot. It's kind of like when you're drilling for oil. Once you find it one place, there's a greater chance you'll find more nearby," said Peter Schultz, professor of geological sciences at Brown University and a co-investigator on the LCROSS mission.

This water finding doesn't mean that the moon is wet by Earth's standards, but is likely wetter than some of the driest deserts on Earth, Colaprete said. And even this small amount is valuable to possible future missions, said Michael Wargo, chief lunar scientist for Exploration Systems at NASA Headquarters.

Scientists have suspected that permanently shadowed craters at the south pole of the moon could be cold enough to keep water frozen at the surface based on detections of hydrogen by previous moon missions. Water has already been detected on the moon by a NASA-built instrument on board India's now defunct *Chandrayaan-1* probe and other spacecraft, though it was in very small amounts and bound to the dirt and dust of the lunar surface.

Water wasn't the only compound seen in the debris plumes of the LCROSS impact.

"There's a lot of stuff in there," Colaprete said. What exactly those other compounds are hasn't yet been determined, but could include organic materials that would hint at comet impacts in the past.

More questions

The findings show that "the lunar poles are sort of record keepers" of lunar history and solar system history because these permanently-shadowed regions are very cold "and that means that they tend to trap and keep things that encounter them," said Greg Delory, a senior fellow at the Space Sciences Laboratory and Center for Integrative Planetary Sciences at the University of California, Berkeley. "So they have a story to tell about the history of the moon and the solar system climate."

"This is ice that's potentially been there for billions of years," said Doug Cooke, associate administrator at Exploration Systems Mission Directorate at NASA Headquarters in Washington, D.C.

The confirmation that water exists on the moon isn't the end of the story though. One key question to answer is where the water came from. Several theories have been put forward to explain the origin of the water, including debris from comet impacts, interaction of the lunar surface with the solar wind, and even giant molecular clouds passing through the solar system, Delory said.

Scientists also want to examine the data further to figure out what state the water is in. Colaprete said that

based on initial observations, it is likely water ice is interspersed between dirt particles on the lunar surface.

Some other questions scientists want to answer are what kinds of processes move, destroy and create the water on the surface and how long the water has been there, Delory said.

Link to *Chandrayaan?*

Scientists also are looking to see if there is any link between the water observed by LCROSS and that discovered by *Chandrayaan-1*.

"Their observation is entirely unique and complementary to what we did," Colaprete said. Scientists still need to work out whether the water observed by *Chandrayaan-1* might be slowly migrating to the poles, or if it is unrelated.

Bottom line, the discovery completely changes scientists' view of the moon, Wargo said.

The discovery gives "a much bigger, potentially complicated picture for water on the moon" than what was thought even just a few months ago, he said. "This is not your father's moon; this is not a dead planetary body."

Let's go?

NASA plans to return astronauts to the moon by 2020 for extended missions on the lunar surface. Finding usable amounts of ice on the moon would be a boon for that effort since it could be a vital local resource to support a lunar base.

"Water really is one of the constituents of one of the most powerful rocket fuels, oxygen and hydrogen," Wargo said. . . .

FURTHER RESOURCES
Web Sites

Crotts, Arlin. "Water on the Moon, I. Historical Overview." *Astronomical Review* 6, no. 8 (2011). www.astroreview.com/upload/3419/WateronTheMoonI.HistoricalOverviewOct.2011.4-20.pdf (accessed on March 24, 2013).

"Ice on the Moon" *NASA*. nssdc.gsfc.nasa.gov/planetary/ice/ice_moon.html (accessed on March 24, 2013).

"LCROSS Project Site." *NASA*. www.lcross.arc.nasa.gov (accessed on March 24, 2013).

"LRO/LCROSS Press Kit." *NASA*. www.nasa.gov/pdf/360020main_LRO_LCROSS_presskit2.pdf (accessed on March 24, 2013).

"Missions to the Moon." *Planetary Society*. www.planetary.org/explore/space-topics/space-missions/missions-to-the-moon.html (accessed on March 24, 2013).

Chronology 526

Chronology

Important Events in Sports, 2000–2009

2000

- On January 4, the #1-ranked Florida State Seminoles win the college football Bowl Championship Series (BCS) national title at the Nokia Sugar Bowl in New Orleans, beating #2-ranked Virginia Tech Hokies 46–29.

- On January 30, the National Football League (NFL) St. Louis Rams defeat the Tennessee Titans 23–16 in Super Bowl XXXIV in the Georgia Dome in Atlanta. The game comes down to the last play with Titans wide receiver Kevin Dyson being stopped on the Rams' one-yard line.

- On April 3, the Michigan State Spartans defeat the University of Florida Gators 89–76 to win the National Collegiate Athletic Association (NCAA) Division I Basketball Championship.

- On June 10, the New Jersey Devils take the Stanley Cup, four games to two, over the Dallas Stars, winning the decisive game 2–1 in double overtime.

- On June 17, the Louisiana State University Tigers win the College World Series by defeating the Stanford University Cardinal 6–5.

- On June 19, the Los Angeles Lakers defeat the Indiana Pacers 116–111 in the National Basketball Association (NBA) finals, winning the series four games to two, for their first title in twelve years.

- On July 8, Venus Williams defeats Lindsay Davenport in women's singles tennis (6–3, 7–6), earning her first Grand Slam title. She and her sister Serena win the women's doubles title. Pete Sampras wins on the men's side, his thirteenth Grand Slam title.

- On July 23, Lance Armstrong captures his second of seven consecutive Tour de France wins.

- On August 12, Evander Holyfield beats John Ruiz in twelve rounds by unanimous decision to become the first boxer in history to hold four world heavyweight championship titles.

- On August 27, the Houston Comets of the Women's National Basketball Association (WNBA) complete a two-game sweep of the New York Liberty with a 79–73 overtime victory to win the championship series; it is their fourth consecutive title.

- On September 15, the 2000 Summer Olympics open in Sydney, Australia. Marion Jones wins three gold and two bronze medals, becoming the only female track-and-field athlete to ever win five medals in a single Olympics. (She later forfeits her medals because of steriod use.) U.S. athletes take home a total of 107 medals, including 40 golds.

- On October 1, a central drug-doping monitoring body, the U.S. Anti-Doping Agency, begins operation for American athletes.

- On October 15, the Major League Soccer (MLS) Kansas City Wizards defeat the Chicago Fire 1–0 to win the MLS Cup.

- On October 26, in the first postseason "Subway Series" in nearly half of a century, the New York Yankees claim the Major League Baseball (MLB) title by defeating the New York Mets 4–2, taking the World Series four games to one.

2001

- On January 3, the #1-ranked Oklahoma Sooners defeat the #2-ranked Florida State Seminoles 13–2 in the FedEx Orange Bowl to claim the college football national title.

- On January 28, Super Bowl XXXV takes place in Tampa, Florida; the Baltimore Ravens defeat the New York Giants 34–7.

- On February 3, the XFL, an eight-team professional football league founded by Vince McMahon of the World Wrestling Federation, plays its first game. Due to its inability to attract a large audience, the league lasts only one season.

- On February 18, National Association for Stock Car Auto Racing (NASCAR) driver Dale Earnhardt dies in an accident in the final lap of the Daytona 500. Michael Waltrip wins the race.

- On March 14, Doug Swingley wins his second Iditarod dogsled race, covering the distance from

Anchorage to Nome, Alaska, in just under nine days and twenty hours.

- On April 2, the Duke University Blue Devils win their third Division I Basketball championship by defeating the University of Arizona Wildcats 82–72.

- On April 8, Tiger Woods wins his second Masters Golf Tournament in Augusta, Georgia, becoming the first golfer in history to hold all four of golf's major titles at the same time.

- On May 29, disabled golfer Casey Martin, suffering from Klippel-Trenaunay-Weber syndrome, a progressive and untreatable circulatory disorder in his right leg, wins a ruling by the U.S. Supreme Court that he can participate on the professional tour using a motorized cart.

- In June, Major League Lacrosse opens play with six professional teams.

- On June 9, the Colorado Avalanche defeat the New Jersey Devils 3–1 in game seven of the Stanley Cup finals.

- On June 15, the Los Angeles Lakers defeat the Philadelphia 76ers 108–96, winning the NBA finals in five games.

- On June 16, the University of Miami Hurricanes win the College World Series, defeating the Stanford University Cardinal 12–1.

- On August 1, Minnesota Vikings offensive lineman Korey Stringer dies from heatstroke during practice; his death leads to discussions and changes in athletic practices held during periods of extreme heat.

- On September 1, the WNBA Los Angeles Sparks defeat the Charlotte Sting 82–54 to capture the league championship, two games to none.

- On September 8, Venus Williams wins her second consecutive U.S. Open, beating her sister Serena (6–2, 6–4), marking the first Grand Slam final competition between siblings in more than a century. The match is also the first time a women's final has been televised in prime time.

- On September 20, the University of South Carolina Gamecocks defeat the Mississippi State Bulldogs 16–14 in the first Division I football game following the September 11 terrorist attacks.

- On September 25, former Chicago Bulls star Michael Jordan signs a contract to join the Washington Wizards; he returns to the NBA after more than three years in retirement.

- On October 7, San Francisco Giants outfielder Barry Bonds hits his seventy-third home run, setting a new record for most home runs in a single season.

- On October 21, the San Jose Earthquakes defeat the Los Angeles Galaxy, 2–1 in overtime, to win the MLS Cup.

- On November 4, in a dramatic game seven of the World Series, the Arizona Diamondbacks become the youngest franchise to win the title with a bottom-of-the-ninth walk-off hit, defeating the New York Yankees 3–2. Dubbed the "November Series," as the series did not begin until October 28 because of regular-season postponements after the September 11 terrorist attacks, it is the latest start to the series in MLB history.

- On December 14, George O'Leary, former football coach at Georgia Tech, resigns five days after being hired by the University of Notre Dame because of a falsified resume.

2002

- On January 3, the #1-ranked University of Miami Hurricanes defeat the #2 University of Nebraska Cornhuskers in the Rose Bowl BCS National Championship game 37–14.

- On February 3, the New England Patriots defeat the St. Louis Rams 20–17 in Super Bowl XXXVI in New Orleans, Louisiana.

- On February 8–24, amid allegations of cheating by French figure skating judge Marie-Reine Le Gougne in the XIX Winter Olympic Games in Salt Lake City, a second gold medal in the freestyle pair competition is awarded to Canadian duo Jamie Sale and David Pelletier. American athletes win ten gold medals, along with thirteen silver and eleven bronze. Sarah Hughes wins the gold in women's figure skating over favored countrywoman Michelle Kwan. One emerging star for the Americans is short-track speedskater Apolo Ohno, who wins a silver medal and a gold.

- On February 17, Ward Burton wins the Daytona 500.

- On February 17, Baltimore Orioles pitcher Steve Bechler dies in Florida of heatstroke. He had been taking weight-loss pills Xenadrine RFA-1 (containing ephedra).

- On April 1, the NCAA Men's Division I Basketball Tournament is won 64–52 by the University of Maryland Terrapins over the Indiana University Hoosiers.

- On April 14, Tiger Woods wins his third Masters.

- On May 30, nine mountaineers fall into a crevasse on Mount Hood, Oregon; three climbers are killed. A military helicopter sent to rescue them crashes on the mountainside, resulting in injuries to six members of the crew.

- On June 8, Lennox Lewis knocks out Mike Tyson in the eighth round, firmly establishing Lewis as the dominant heavyweight boxing champion.

- On June 8, War Emblem stumbles at the start of the Belmont Stakes race, denying him a shot at the horse-racing Triple Crown. The third jewel is won by Sarava at 70–1 odds.

- On June 12, the Los Angeles Lakers capture their third consecutive NBA championship title, taking the last game 113–107 and sweeping the New Jersey Nets in four games.

- On June 13, the Detroit Red Wings win their tenth Stanley Cup with a 3–1 victory over the Carolina Hurricanes, taking the series four games to one.

- On June 22, the University of Texas Longhorns defeat the South Carolina Gamecocks 12–6 in the College World Series, the last time a winner-take-all final game format is used.

- On July 6, Serena Williams takes back the family title, beating sister Venus in straight sets (7–6, 6–3) for her first Wimbledon championship.

- On July 9, the MLB All-Star game goes into the eleventh inning tied 7–7; the game ends that way because of limited rosters.

- On August 25, a team from Louisville, Kentucky, wins the Little League World Series.

- On August 30, a last-minute labor-contract agreement is reached by MLB negotiators to avoid a players' strike. This new contract marks the first time players agree to mandatory, random testing for performance-enhancing drugs.

- On August 31, the Los Angeles Sparks win their second WNBA championship, defeating the New York Liberty 69–66.

- On October 20, in a double-overtime win, the Los Angeles Galaxy defeat the New England Revolution to win the series 1–0 to capture the MLS Cup.

- On October 27, in an interstate matchup between two wild-card teams, the Anaheim Angels defeat the San Francisco Giants 4–1 in the seventh game of the World Series. It is the first championship for the Angels.

2003

- On January 3, the #2 Ohio State Buckeyes upset the #1-ranked University of Miami Hurricanes at the Tostitos Fiesta Bowl BCS National Championship game, winning 31–24 in the second overtime.

- On January 26, the Tampa Bay Buccaneers, led by head coach Jon Gruden, defeat the favored Oakland Raiders 48–21 in Super Bowl XXXVII, for their first-ever title. Gruden left his coaching position at Oakland the year before to coach the Tampa team.

- On February 16, Michael Waltrip wins his second Daytona 500.

- On March 28, American figure skater and two-time Olympic medalist Michelle Kwan wins her fifth World Figure Skating Championship title in women's singles.

- On March 30, at the 2003 Kraft Nabisco Championship thirteen-year-old Michelle Wie, daughter of Korean immigrants, ties for ninth place, making her the youngest player to earn a Ladies Professional Golf Association (LPGA) cut. Later the same year, Wie becomes the youngest person to win a United States Golf Association (USGA) adult event.

- In April, Aron Ralston of Aspen, Colorado, is trapped by a falling boulder while hiking Utah's Bluejohn Canyon; unable to free himself, after five days he amputates his arm and walks to safety.

- On April 4, Chicago Cubs outfielder Sammy Sosa becomes the eighteenth player in MLB history to hit five-hundred career home runs, in a game against the Cincinnati Reds.

- On April 7, the Syracuse University Orangemen defeat the University of Kansas Jayhawks 81–78 to capture the NCAA Men's Division I Basketball Tournament.

- On May 11, Texas Ranger Rafael Palmeiro becomes the nineteenth member of the five-hundred home run club in a game against the Cleveland Indians.

- On June 3, while playing against the Tampa Bay Rays at Wrigley Field, Chicago Cubs slugger Sammy Sosa's bat explodes, revealing that it had cork inserted into the barrel.

- On June 7, Funny Cide is denied the Triple Crown at the Belmont Stakes when he is beaten by Empire Maker.

- On June 9, in game seven of the Stanley Cup finals the New Jersey Devils shut out the Mighty Ducks of Anaheim 3–0, winning their third cup.

- On June 15, the San Antonio Spurs win their second NBA Championship, defeating the New Jersey Nets 88–77 to win the title in six games.

- On June 23, in the first three-game championship round, the Rice University Owls defeat the Stanford University Cardinal in the College World Series, taking the final game 14–2.

- On July 6, Los Angeles Lakers star Kobe Bryant is arrested amid allegations of sexual assault; he is formally charged at the end of the month. The charges are later dropped when the victim expresses her unwillingness to testify.

- On July 21, Baylor University basketball player Carlton Dotson is charged with murdering teammate Patrick Dennehy, whose body was discovered near Waco, Texas. Dotson pleads guilty the following year and is sentenced to thirty-five years in prison. Revelations of drug abuse, recruiting problems, and other problems result in the firing of the team coach and NCAA sanctions being placed on the school.

- On August 25, Pete Sampras retires at the age of thirty-two, having won fourteen Grand Slam tennis titles.

- On September 3, federal agents raid Bay Area Laboratory Co-operative (BALCO) office in search of evidence of steroid misuse in sports. Many important stars, including Barry Bonds (baseball), Bill Romanowski (football), and Marion Jones (sprinter) are tied to the company.

- On September 14, Jamal Lewis of the NFL Baltimore Ravens rushes for 295 yards against the Cleveland Browns, setting a new single-game rushing record.

- On September 16, the Detroit Shock win their first WNBA title, defeating the Los Angeles Sparks 83–78 to take the series two games to one.

- On October 14, during the sixth game of the NLCS a fan in the left-field bleachers at Wrigley Field prevents Moises Alou of the Chicago Cubs from catching a fly ball in the eighth inning, and the Florida Marlins go on to score eight runs in the inning for an 8–3 win. The fan becomes a hated figure in Chicago, as in the following game the Marlins eliminate the Cubs from World Series contention.

- On October 25, the Florida Marlins surprise the New York Yankees at Yankee Stadium with a 2–0 defeat in game six of the World Series, winning their second title in seven years.

- On November 16, Denver Broncos tight end Shannon Sharpe catches his sixty-first touchdown reception, a new record for his position. He caught three touchdowns in the game that day against the San Diego Chargers.

- On November 23, the San Jose Earthquakes defeat the Chicago Fire 4–2 to win the MLS Cup.

- On December 4, Barry Bonds is one of several professional athletes to testify before a federal grand jury in the BALCO hearings; Bonds admits to having used a clear substance and cream but denies knowing that it was steroids.

- On December 15, in a game against the Cleveland Browns, Indianapolis Colts wide receiver Marvin Harrison breaks Herman Moore's single-season record for receptions; he finishes the year with a record 143 catches.

- On December 28, San Diego Chargers running back LaDainian Tomlinson becomes the first NFL player to rush for one thousand yards and catch one hundred passes in the same season.

2004

- On January 4, the Louisiana State University Tigers, ranked #2, defeat the #1-ranked University of Oklahoma Sooners 21–14 in the Nokia Sugar Bowl National Championship Game.

- On January 10, Hawaiian surfer and windboarder Pete Cabrinha rides a specially designed surfboard on a seventy-foot wave off the coast of Maui, the largest wave ever ridden according to the *Guinness Book of World Records*.

- On February 1, in an exciting game in which 37 of 61 total points are scored in the fourth quarter, the New England Patriots defeat the Carolina Panthers 32–29 in Super Bowl XXXVIII. Patriots quarterback Tom Brady, Most Valuable Player (MVP), sets a Super Bowl record with thirty-two pass completions in the game.

- On February 12, Attorney General John Ashcroft hands down a forty-two-count indictment against four men involved in the BALCO steroids scandal. All four will plead not guilty to the charges.

- On February 15, Dale Earnhardt Jr. wins his first Daytona 500, three years after the death of his father on the same track.

- On February 16, MLB player Alex Rodriguez (traded from the Texas Rangers) joins the New York Yankees, moving from shortstop to third baseman.

- On March 16, Alaskan Mitch Seavey wins the Iditarod.

- On April 5, the Connecticut University Huskies defeat the Georgia Tech Yellow Jackets 82–73 to win the NCAA Division I Basketball championship.

- On April 11, Phil Mickelson wins his first Masters at Augusta, Georgia.

- On May 4, shot-putter Kevin Toth is banned from competition for steroid use and loses his 2003 U.S. championship. Two weeks later sprinter Kelli White accepts a similar sentence.

- On May 18, Arizona Diamondbacks pitcher Randy Johnson pitches a perfect game against the Atlanta Braves.

- On May 30, Buddy Rice wins the Indianapolis 500.

- On June 5, Smarty Jones falls short of earning the Triple Crown; the winner of the Belmont Stakes is Birdstone.

- On June 7, the Tampa Bay Lightning secure their first Stanley Cup in game seven of the NHL finals, beating the Calgary Flames 2–1.

- On June 15, the Detroit Pistons defeat the Los Angeles Lakers 100–87, capturing the NBA championship four games to one.

- On June 26, the Washington Capitals pick Alexander Ovechkin in the first selection of the 2004 NHL draft, but the 2004–2005 lockout means he does not play until the 2005–2006 season.

- On June 28, the California State University Fullerton Titans defeat the University of Texas Longhorns 3–2 to win the College World Series.

- On July 14, center Shaquille O'Neal is traded by the Los Angeles Lakers to the Miami Heat in exchange for forwards Lamar Odom, Caron Butler, Brian Grant, and a future first-round draft pick.

- On July 17, runner Regina Jacobs receives a four-year ban from competition for steroid use.

- On August 13–29, U.S. athletes (along with those from 201 other countries) participate in the Summer Olympics held in Greece. Americans take home 103 medals (35 gold, 39 silver, and 29 bronze).

- On August 21, swimmer Michael Phelps wins his eighth medal at the Athens Summer Olympic Games, tying the record for medals won in a single Olympics.

- On September 14, the NFL fines three Oakland Raiders players for using the steroid tetrahydrogestrinone (THG).

- On September 16, the Seattle Storm defeat the Connecticut Sun 74–60, winning the WNBA title two games to one.

- On September 17, Barry Bonds hits his seven-hundredth career home run, making him only the third player in MLB history to do so.

- On October 19, sprinter Alvin Harrison is banned from competition for four years for steroid use.

- On October 27, the Boston Red Sox defeat the St. Louis Cardinals 3–0 to complete a four-game sweep of the World Series, ending their eighty-six-year streak without winning the title.

- On November 14, D.C. United defeats the Kansas City Wizards 3–2 to win the MLS Cup.

- On November 19, with less than a minute to play in an NBA game between the Detroit Pistons and Indiana Pacers, a fight breaks out on the court that escalates to a brawl including players and fans and forces officials to end the game with time remaining.

- On December 2, New York Yankees outfielder Jason Giambi admits to steroid and hormone use and implicates Barry Bonds.

- On December 10, sprinter Michelle Collins receives an eight-year ban from track competition; it is later reduced to four after she agrees not to appeal.

- On December 26, Indianapolis Colts quarterback Peyton Manning breaks Dan Marino's single-season touchdown pass record when he throws his forty-ninth in a game against the San Diego Chargers.

2005

- On January 4, the University of Southern California (USC) Trojans easily clinch the BCS title in a 55–19 rout over the Oklahoma Sooners in the FedEx Orange Bowl, leaving lingering questions about the matchup. (In 2010 the win by the Trojans was vacated because they had used an ineligible player, Reggie Bush.)

- On January 17, *The Ultimate Fighter*, an Ultimate Fighting Championship (UFC) sponsored reality competition show featuring aspiring mixed-martial-arts fighters, debuts on SpikeTV.

- On February 6, in Jacksonville, Florida, the New England Patriots beat the Philadelphia Eagles 24–21 in Super Bowl XXXIX, their third title in four years.

- On February 16, in an unprecedented move, NHL commissioner Gary Bettman cancels the 2004–2005 season, which had never begun because of an ongoing labor dispute over salary caps; it marks the first time a professional sports league in North America lost an entire season because of failed labor negotiations.

- On February 20, Jeff Gordon wins his third Daytona 500.

- On March 7, Steve Fossett becomes the first person to fly around the world on a nonstop solo trip; he also sets records circumnavigating the globe by sailboat and balloon.

- On March 12, Bode Miller wins his first Alpine Skiing World Cup.

- On March 17, Mark McGwire, Jose Canseco, Curt Schilling, Sammy Sosa, Rafael Palmeiro, and Frank Thomas appear before the House Oversight and Government Reform Committee to testify on steroids in baseball.

- On April 4, Coach Roy Williams and the University of North Carolina Tar Heels grab a 75–70 victory over the University of Illinois in the NCAA men's basketball championship; the victory marks the team's fourth overall title and first since 1993.

- On April 4, the MLB Washington (D.C.) Nationals (formerly the Montreal Expos) begin play. Two days later they earn their first victory.

- On April 10, Tiger Woods wins his fourth Masters title, defeating Chris DiMarco in a playoff.

- On June 11, boxing legend Mike Tyson announces his retirement from the sport.

- On June 23, the San Antonio Spurs beat the defending champion Detroit Pistons 81–74 in the decisive seventh game of the NBA finals.

- On June 27, the University of Texas Longhorns win the College World Series over the University of Florida Gators with a final game 6–2 victory.

- On July 2, Venus Williams reclaims her Wimbledon title, beating Lindsay Davenport (4–6, 7–6, 9–7) in the longest women's final to date.

- On July 15, BALCO owner Victor Conte and weight trainer Greg Anderson plead guilty to distributing steroids and are given short prison sentences.

- On July 22, the NHL and its players reach a collective-bargaining agreement that ends the lockout and allows the sport to resume for the 2005–2006 season.

- On July 24, Lance Armstrong wins his seventh consecutive Tour de France and announces his retirement from professional cycling.

- On August 28, a team from Ewa Beach, Hawaii, wins the Little League World Series.

- On September 20, in a playoff series expanded to the best of five games, the Sacramento Monarchs defeat the Connecticut Sun 62–59 to earn the WNBA title three games to one.

- On October 6, seventeen members of the NFL Minnesota Vikings team participate in a wild party involving prostitutes aboard a boat on Lake Minnetonka. Several players are charged with indecent conduct; a new code of conduct is implemented by the team; and fines, suspensions, and service duties are imposed.

- On October 26, the Chicago White Sox defeat the Houston Astros 1–0 to complete a sweep and win their first World Series since 1917.

- On November 13, the Los Angeles Galaxy defeat the New England Revolution 1–0 in overtime to win their second MLS title of the decade.

- On December 10, University of Southern California tailback Reggie Bush wins the Heisman Trophy by an overwhelming majority, securing the second-most votes in history.

- On December 11, St. Louis Rams running back Marshall Faulk sets the all-time receiving record for a player at his position in a game against the Minnesota Vikings. He will end his career with 6,875 receiving yards.

2006

- On January 4, the Texas Longhorns beat the USC Trojans in the BCS Championship Rose Bowl 41–38.

- On February 5, the Pittsburgh Steelers win Super Bowl XL, defeating the Seattle Seahawks 21–10 at Ford Field in Detroit. Steelers running back Willie Parker sets a new Super Bowl record with a seventy-five-yard run for a touchdown.

- On February 10–26, the XX Winter Olympics are held in Turin, Italy. U.S. athletes win nine gold, nine silver, and seven bronze medals.

- On February 14, Bode Miller is disqualified for missing gates in the Alpine combined event at the Winter Olympics. Teammate Ted Ligety wins the event.

- On February 19, Jimmie Johnson wins the Daytona 500.

- On February 24, the United States wins its first medal in curling, a bronze, in the Winter Olympics.

- On March 16, Jeff King wins the Iditarod.

- On April 3, the NCAA Men's Basketball title goes to the University of Florida Gators with their 73–57 win over the University of California, Los Angeles (UCLA) Bruins.
- On April 9, Phil Mickelson wins his second Masters.
- On May 28, Barry Bonds passes Babe Ruth with home run #715; he is now second only to Hank Aaron.
- On May 28, Sam Hornish Jr. wins the Indianapolis 500.
- On June 19, the Carolina Hurricanes defeat the Edmonton Oilers 3–1 to win the Stanley Cup in seven games.
- On June 20, the Miami Heat defeat the Dallas Mavericks 95–92 in the NBA finals, winning their first championship four games to two.
- On June 26, the Oregon State University Beavers win the College World Series by defeating the University of North Carolina Tar Heels 3–2.
- On July 23, Floyd Landis wins the Tour de France. Four days later Landis fails his drug test, making second-place finisher, Oscar Pereiro, the new winner (only the second time in history that the winner is disqualified).
- On August 10, Jamie M. Gold wins $12 million in the World Series of Poker, playing in the No Limit Hold'em Championship.
- On August 28, a team from Columbus, Georgia, wins the Little League World Series.
- On September 9, the Detroit Shock earn their second WNBA crown with a 80–75 victory over the Sacramento Monarchs, taking the series three games to two.
- On October 11, Yankees pitcher Cory Lidle is killed in a plane crash.
- On October 27, the St. Louis Cardinals defeat the Detroit Tigers 4–2 to win their tenth World Series title, four games to one.
- On November 12, after playing to a 1–1 tie, the Houston Dynamo defeat the New England Revolution in penalty kicks to win the MLS Cup.

2007

- On January 8, the University of Florida Gators defeat the Ohio State Buckeyes 41–14 in the BCS title game held in Glendale, Arizona.
- On January 11, British star David Beckham signs a five-year contract said to be for $280 million to play soccer for the Los Angeles Galaxy.

- On February 4, quarterback Peyton Manning leads the Indianapolis Colts to a 29–17 Super Bowl XLI victory over the Chicago Bears. Tony Dungy becomes the first African American coach to win a Super Bowl.
- On February 18, Kevin Harvick wins the Daytona 500.
- On March 13, Lance Mackey wins his first Iditarod.
- On March 27, the owners of UFC agree to buy out their rival Pride Fighting Championships.
- On April 2, the University of Florida Gators repeat as NCAA Men's Division I champions by defeating the Ohio State Buckeyes 84–75.
- On April 8, Zack Johnson wins the Masters.
- On April 11, all charges are dropped against three Duke University lacrosse players who had falsely been accused of the rape and assault of a stripper at a party in March 2006; the prosecuting attorney is disciplined and disbarred. The team coach had been fired and the remainder of the season canceled; players are given an additional year of eligibility by the NCAA.
- On May 25, NHL Phoenix Coyotes assistant coach Rick Tocchet pleads guilty to running a gambling racket, allegedly with Mafia connections.
- On June 6, the Anaheim Ducks defeat the Ottawa Senators 6–2 in game five to win the Stanley Cup.
- On June 14, the San Antonio Spurs sweep the Cleveland Cavaliers in four games to win the NBA Championship, taking the final game 83–82.
- On June 24, the Oregon State University Beavers repeat as champions of the College World Series by again defeating the University of North Carolina Tar Heels, winning the final game 9–3.
- On July 9, NBA referee Tim Donaghy, a thirteen-season veteran, resigns after allegations he bet on games in which he was officiating. He earns jail time on federal charges.
- On July 21, David Beckham plays in his first game with the Los Angeles Galaxy.
- On August 7, Barry Bonds hits home run #756, passing Aaron's record.
- On August 26, a team from Warner Robins, Georgia, wins the Little League World Series.
- On September 3, Steve Fossett fails to return from a flight over Nevada; the search for the sixty-three-year-old sailor and aviator is unsuccessful until late 2008 when his remains are located.

- On September 16, the Phoenix Mercury deny the Detroit Shock their third WNBA crown, taking the title three games to two with a 108–92 victory.

- On October 5, track star Marion Jones pleads guilty to lying to federal agents about her steroid use and forfeits all titles and results dating back to September of 2000, which includes her five medals at the 2000 Summer Olympics in Sydney.

- On October 28, the Boston Red Sox sweep the Colorado Rockies in four games, taking the final game 4–3, to win the World Series, their second title in four years and seventh overall.

- On November 15, Bonds is charged with perjury and obstruction of justice in relation to the federal inquiry into steroid use in professional sports.

- On November 18, in a rematch from the previous championship, the Houston Dynamo defeat the New England Revolution 2–1 to win the MLS Cup.

- On November 21, one hundred skydivers achieve a world record for a canopy formation (a stacking formation with a diver's feet touching the next person's parachute) over Lake Wales, Florida.

- On December 2, the United States wins its thirty-second Davis Cup in tennis with a victory over the Russian team.

2008

- On January 7, the #2 Louisiana State University (LSU) Tigers defeat the #1 Ohio State Buckeyes 38–24 in the BCS championship game held at the Louisiana Superdome in New Orleans.

- On February 3, Eli Manning and the New York Giants shock the previously undefeated New England Patriots 17–14 in Super Bowl XLII. Manning is named MVP, an honor given to his brother the year before, making them the first brothers to win Super Bowl MVPs.

- On February 17, Ryan Newman wins the Daytona 500.

- On March 15, Bode Miller wins his second Alpine Skiing World Cup; Lindsey Vonn wins the women's World Cup (she repeats in 2009).

- On April 7, the University of Kansas Jayhawks defeat the University of Memphis Tigers 75–68 to garner the NCAA Division I Men's Basketball crown.

- On April 20, Danica Patrick wins the Indy Japan 300, making her the first woman to win an Indy Car race.

- On June 4, the Detroit Red Wings defeat the Pittsburgh Penguins 3–2 to win the Stanley Cup in six games.

- On June 7, Da'Tara denies the formerly unbeaten Big Brown the Triple Crown at the Belmont Stakes.

- On June 17, the Boston Celtics defeat the Los Angeles Lakers 131–92 to win the NBA championship in six games.

- On June 25, Fresno State becomes the lowest-ranked team ever to win the College Baseball World Series, beating the heavily favored University of Georgia Bulldogs 6–1.

- On July 5, Venus Williams wins her fifth Wimbledon, defeating sister Serena (7–5, 6–4).

- On August 8–24, the Summer Olympics are held in Beijing, China. American athletes win 110 medals (36 gold, 38 silver, and 36 bronze).

- On August 16, Michael Phelps wins his eighth gold medal of the 2008 Summer Olympics, marking a new record for gold won in a single Olympics.

- On August 24, a team from Waipio, Hawaii, wins the Little League World Series.

- On September 7, Serena Williams wins the U.S. Open, defeating Jelena Kovic (6–4, 7–5).

- On October 5, the Detroit Shock win their third WNBA title in a three-game sweep over the San Antonio Silver Stars, taking the final game 76–60.

- On October 27, the Philadelphia Phillies defeat the Tampa Bay Rays 4–3 in game five to win the World Series.

- On November 23, the Columbus Crew defeat the New York Red Bulls 3–1 to win the MLS Cup.

- On December 6, Oscar De La Hoya loses to Manny Pacquiao in the eighth round of a boxing match touted "The Dream Match."

2009

- On January 8, quarterback Tim Tebow and the University of Florida Gators defeat the Oklahoma Sooners 24–14 in the BCS championship game in Dolphin Stadium in Miami, Florida, winning their second championship in three years.

- On February 1, the Pittsburgh Steelers defeat the Arizona Cardinals 27–23 in Super Bowl XLIII held in Raymond James Stadium in Tampa, Florida.

- On February 5, Michael Phelps is suspended for three months from professional swimming for smoking marijuana.

- On February 15, Matt Kenseth wins the Daytona 500.

- On April 6, the University of North Carolina Tar Heels win their second basketball championship of the decade by defeating the first winner in the decade, the Michigan State Spartans.

- On April 14, Oscar De La Hoya announces his retirement from boxing.

- On April 22, extreme kayaker Tyler Bradt performs a 186-foot drop off Palouse Falls, Washington.

- On May 2, a thunderstorm knocks down the roof of the Dallas Cowboys practice facility, injuring twelve (one with a broken back).

- On May 24, Danica Patrick finishes third in the Indianapolis 500, the highest-ever finish for a female driver.

- On June 12, in a rematch of the previous year's Stanley Cup, the Pittsburgh Penguins defeat the defending champion Detroit Red Wings four games to three, winning the climactic game 2–1.

- On June 14, the Los Angeles Lakers defeat the Orlando Magic 99–86 to win the NBA title in five games; this appearance is the Lakers' thirtieth in the finals, more than any other team, and their fourth championship of the decade.

- On June 24, the U.S. men's soccer team shocks the world when it upsets Spain (the top-rated team) at the Fédération Internationale de Football Association (FIFA) Confederations Cup. Four days later they lose 3–2 to the Brazilians for a second-place finish.

- On June 24, the Louisiana State University Tigers defeat the University of Texas Longhorns 11–4 to win the College World Series.

- On July 4, Serena Williams is back on top, defeating her sister and defending champion Venus (7–6, 6–2) to earn her third Wimbledon title.

- On July 23, Chicago White Sox pitcher Mark Buehrle throws a perfect game at the Tampa Bay Rays.

- On August 9, the Phoenix Mercury take the five-game series with a 94–86 victory over the Indiana Fever to win the WNBA title. The first game of the title series was the highest scoring (120–116) in WNBA history.

- On August 10, North Carolinian Rikki Cunningham plays a record 4,026 minutes of marathon billiards in a charity event.

- On August 25, a team from Chula Vista, California, wins the Little League World Series.

- On September 20, the Dallas Cowboys play their first regular season game in the new Cowboys Stadium, drawing an NFL regular-season record 105,121 fans.

- On September 29, *Forbes* magazine announces that Tiger Woods is the first athlete to earn $1 billion in career earnings.

- On October 8, the United Football League (UFL) debuts with a game between the Las Vegas Locomotives and California Redwoods.

- On November 4, the New York Yankees defeat the Philadelphia Phillies 7–3, winning the World Series four games to two, giving the Yankees a total of twenty-seven titles, more than any other North American professional sports franchise.

- On November 22, the MLS Cup is captured by Real Salt Lake in penalty kicks over the Los Angeles Galaxy, after playing to a 1–1 tie.

- On November 27, Tiger Woods is injured in a car crash outside his home.

- On December 11, amid public accusations of infidelity and marital problems, Woods announces that he will take a temporary leave of absence from professional golf.

- On December 21, NASCAR driver Jimmie Johnson, winner of four consecutive championships, is named the Associated Press (AP) Male Athlete of the Year, the first race-car driver to ever win this award.

"One More Title"

Williams sisters take women's doubles

Magazine article

By: *Sports Illustrated*

Date: July 10, 2000

Source: "One More Title." *Sports Illustrated*, July 10, 2000. http://sportsillustrated.cnn.com/tennis/2000/wimbledon/news/2000/07/10/williams_doubles_ap/#more (accessed on March 24, 2013).

About the Publication: *Sports Illustrated* is an American magazine dedicated to athletic competition, primarily professional sports. The magazine's current incarnation, which began publication in 1954, was the first to provide weekly coverage and news of spectator sports, rather than traditional "lifestyle" content. It quickly became the leading publication in its field, becoming so influential that it prompted sporting arenas to adopt new designs to accommodate *Sports Illustrated*'s cameras. The magazine's most famous features are its annual "Sportsman of the Year" awards and swimsuit editions.

INTRODUCTION

Athletic sibling superstars are unusual. Football has had Peyton and Eli Manning; baseball had Joe, Vince, and Dom DiMaggio. Phil and Tony Esposito excelled in the National Hockey League, and the world of tennis was ruled by Venus and Serena Williams. Venus, the older of the two sisters, burst on the professional circuit in 1994 at the age of fourteen. Sister Serena made a name for herself in 1995 by turning pro at the age of thirteen. Both women were respected singles players from the start, but a true powerhouse was born when they combined talent and skill to compete as doubles partners on the court.

Venus won the first of her singles titles when she was just seventeen years old, in 1998. It was the IGA Tennis Classic, and Williams was ranked number 14 at the time. The victory brought her $27,000 and a much-coveted win against top seed and second-ranked competitor Lindsay Davenport. Thirty minutes after her match, Venus returned to the court, this time with Serena, to clinch their first doubles title.

Serena seemed to find her footing in 1999. That was the year she won her first Grand Slam singles title. The Grand Slam is comprised of four major tournaments: the Australian Open, the French Open, Wimbledon, and the U.S. Open.

Although the sisters played singles separately and doubles together, they also frequently competed against one another. The 2000 Wimbledon match featured in this *Sports Illustrated* article was particularly important because Serena was favored to win the match against her sister, but Venus surprised everyone by taking the victory. Not only did she win Wimbledon, she claimed the first Grand Slam singles title of her career. That same year, Venus took the Gold medal at the Summer Olympics, and the sisters won Gold in their Olympic doubles match as well.

SIGNIFICANCE

Venus and Serena Williams continued their tennis careers, which were still going strong in 2013. Separately, their careers are remarkable. Taken together, their achievements are staggering. Serena is considered by many to be the greatest female tennis player of all time, and by 2013, she had fifteen Grand Slam singles titles to her name; sister Venus had seven, and together the women captured thirteen major doubles titles and three Olympic Gold medals.

The sibling athletes know one another's weaknesses and strengths, and they respect one another's prowess. Serena is certainly the more dominant singles player, but she readily admitted to *USA Today* that Venus is the more accomplished doubles player. "She serves first. She's been the leader since we played back in the '80s when we were juniors. I'm not comfortable being the leader; I don't want to be the leader."

Their athletic ability is not the only thing the Williams sisters are known for. In 2001, the sisters were playing the Indian Wells tournament, now known as the BNP Paribas Open, in Indian Wells, California. Four minutes before the sisters were to face off in a semi-finals singles match, Venus pulled out of the match, citing a knee injury. Disappointed and angry, fans booed loudly, something uncommon at a tennis match. When Serena played opponent Kim Clijsters the following day, the crowd yelled at her with a determination borne of disdain, not anger. Serena beat Clijsters for the trophy, and the sisters vowed to never play Indian Wells again. They went on record time and time again as saying that in addition to the catcalls and booing, tennis fans abused them with racial epithets. As of 2013, the boycott was still active. Without playing Indian Wells, a tennis player cannot be a member of the American Tennis Association. Furthermore, she can be fined for not participating in that tournament. But the sisters remained steadfast in their decision. Indian Wells continued to be a major event, but it never again had the privilege of hosting Serena or Venus Williams.

The Williams sisters—Venus (left) and Serena—raise their championship trophy after winning the Women's Doubles match at Wimbledon, July 10, 2000. © AP IMAGES/JYTTE NIELSEN.

Neither athlete seemed to have suffered for having boycotted one tournament. Both have been ranked number 1 in singles and doubles. Serena's prize money was nearly $42.5 million as of 2013, the highest of any woman athlete of all time. Venus's earnings of nearly $29 million made her the second-highest prizewinner in the history of women's sports. And neither showed any sign of slowing down.

■ **PRIMARY SOURCE**

"ONE MORE TITLE"

SYNOPSIS: The competitive and popular Williams sisters dominated Wimbledon in 2000.

The Williams sisters' dominance at the 2000 Wimbledon Championships continued on Monday, as Venus Williams followed her victory in Saturday's women's singles final by teaming with sister Serena to win the women's doubles title.

The Williams sisters beat Ai Sugiyama and Julie Halard-Decugis 6–3, 6–2.

It's the first time in history that sisters have won the Wimbledon doubles title.

"It's great because it's the millennium Wimbledon," Venus said. "There won't be another millennium Wimbledon for another millennium."

The 70-minute victory gave the Williams siblings their third Grand Slam doubles title. They also won the 1999 U.S. Open and French Open.

The sisters have also won two Grand Slam mixed doubles titles apiece. Counting Serena's singles victory at the 1999 U.S. Open, the pair now hold a total of nine Grand Slam championships.

"We're both going to try to get as much as we can," Venus said.

"We're both really greedy," Serena said.

The doubles final was postponed to Monday because of rain which extended the men's final—won by Pete Sampras over Patrick Rafter—to dusk Sunday.

It's the first time Wimbledon was extended to the third Monday since 1996. That year, the women's doubles final was played on the extra day, with Martina Hingis becoming the youngest Wimbledon champion of all time, at 15 years and 282 days.

Venus Williams, 20, and Serena, 18, have no doubles ranking because they were injured and played so little together this year. They needed a wild card to enter Wimbledon.

Their biggest problem Monday was waking up on time.

The sisters had attended the champions dinner Sunday, both wearing sleeveless gowns, and didn't get back to their rented house until after midnight. Their father, Richard Williams, had flown home to Florida earlier Sunday.

"I said, 'Serena, you have to go to bed as soon as possible,'" Venus said.

"She took over as a parent," Serena said.

Their mother, Oracene, who did not come to Wimbledon, called Monday morning.

"I was somewhat in a coma," Venus said. "It was 8:30. We went to bed at 2. I couldn't think. I told her I'd call her back."

Seeded No. 8, the sisters overwhelmed their fourth-seeded opponents with unreturnable serves and powerful volleys. They slapped hands after each point, win or lose, and whispered tactics to each other between points.

From 3–2 down in the first set, the Williams team won eight straight games and 10 out of the last 12. The match ended with Serena drilling an ace.

After the sisters hugged each other, they accepted the winner's trophy and held it aloft as they paraded around Centre Court to a standing ovation from the near capacity crowd.

There was a carnival atmosphere in the stadium. Fans did the wave at the end of the first set, with guests in the Royal Box joining in.

At several stages, spectators shouted, "C'mon sisters!"

Centre Court tickets for Sunday were valid for Monday's play, while tickets were available to the general public for the discount price of 5 pounds ($7.50), with proceeds going to a children's charity.

There were long queues outside the All England Club, with an estimated 3,000 people lined up for tickets in the early morning for the so-called "People's Monday" match.

"It was such a bargain that we couldn't resist," said Jean Neafcy, who traveled with her husband, Eddie, from Mayfield, 30 miles (50 kms) south of London. "It is nice to be part of the occasion, too.

"The Williams girls are such big stars it will be a treat to see them. They have brought in a new era in women's tennis, something really sensational."

Serena said: "People here really support the sport from the first day. The stadium is packed to the last day. This is not like America, where they come only for the finals or semifinals. It's really different here."

With her 6–3, 7–6 (7–3) victory over Lindsay Davenport in Saturday's final, Venus became the first black women's champion at Wimbledon since Althea Gibson in 1957–58.

Venus was playing in only her fourth tournament this year after being sidelined for six months with tendinitis in both wrists. Serena had a two-month layoff with tendinitis in her knee.

"It's really amazing for us to come back like this," said Serena, who lost to Venus in the semifinals. "People are going to practice harder to beat us. But you know what? We are too. We mean business.

"We can do a lot better. We're not playing our best tennis right now. There's a lot of room for improvement."

The sisters are determined to compete for the No. 1 ranking.

Venus will move up to No. 3 this week behind Martina Hingis and Davenport, tying her career best. Serena will rise to No. 7.

"We're on our way," Venus said. "We believe in ourselves. I don't think I'll be able to attain No. 1 this year. It's going to be tough. But next year, I definitely have the opportunity starting at the Australian Open."

FURTHER RESOURCES
Web Sites

Associated Press. "Williams Sisters Do Double Duty in Melbourne." *USA Today*, January 20, 2013. www.usatoday.com/story/sports/tennis/2013/01/20/australian-open-venus-williams-serena-williams-doubles/1849243/ (accessed on March 24, 2013).

Buckley-Shaklee, Ryan. "SFC's Top Ten Professional Sibling Athletes of All Time." *Sports Fix Chicago*, July 9, 2012. http://sportsfixchicago.com/2012/07/09/sfcs-top-ten-professional-sibling-athletes-of-all-time/ (accessed on March 24, 2013).

Corbett, Merlisa Lawrence. "Williams Sisters' Boycott Taints Indian Wells Tennis Tournament." *Yahoo! Sports*, March 7, 2013. http://sports.yahoo.com/news/williams-sisters-boycott-taints-indian-wells-tennis-tournament-175500266--ten.html (accessed on March 24, 2013).

Doping in Baseball

Introduction to *Juiced: Wild Times, Rampant 'Roids, Smash Hits, and How Baseball Got Big*

Book excerpt

By: Jose Canseco

Date: 2005

Source: Canseco, Jose. "Introduction." *Juiced: Wild Times, Rampant 'Roids, Smash Hits, and How Baseball Got Big*. New York: Harper, 2005.

About the Author: Jose Canseco took Major League Baseball by storm in the 1980s. His athletic prowess was unmatched in terms of speed and power, and he became the first player in history to hit more than forty home runs and steal more than forty bases in a single season. Canseco was one of the first super-athletes, those players who combined unheard-of ability with high salaries and luxurious lifestyles.

"Charlie Brown's Doping"

Editorial cartoon

By: Steve Kelley

Date: 2004

Source: Kelley, Steve. "Charlie Brown's Doping." *Cartoonist Group*, 2004. www.cartoonistgroup.com/store/add.php?iid=6895 (accessed on March 24, 2013).

About the Cartoonist: Steve Kelley began his cartooning career in 1981 at the *San Diego Union Tribune*. He was a Pulitzer Prize finalist in the editorial cartooning category and left the *Tribune* two years later under controversy for a cartoon he submitted to his editors that they did not approve for publication. From there he took a job with the *New Orleans Times-Picayune*. During his tenure there, he and fellow cartoonist Jeff Parker collaborated to produce a comic strip called *Dustin*, which debuted in 2010. The strip was awarded Best Newspaper Comic Strip by the National Cartoonists Society that same year. Kelley left his job at the newspaper in 2012 as part of budget cut-backs.

INTRODUCTION

In the late nineteenth century and early twentieth century, baseball was considered America's pastime. It was a wholesome way for a family to spend a day together, and the low cost of admission to the ballpark made the game accessible to most people. The term "national pastime" was first used in 1850 by savvy public relations men who wanted to link, in the minds of Americans, the sport of baseball with health and well-being. Its popularity continued to grow through the decades as athletes became more evolved in terms of ability and equipment—and rules—became more streamlined.

As baseball became more competitive, players looked for that "edge" that would make them better than the next guy. Physical performance enhancers were not new. Athletes in Ancient Greece and Roman gladiators used them to improve their performances. In the late 1970s and early 1980s, anabolic steroids came into fashion. These drugs are synthetic compounds of hormones, usually testosterone, that build muscle and increase strength fast. Side effects are serious and sometimes permanent. In men, they can shrink the testicles and reduce sperm count. Sterilization is not uncommon. Other side effects include but are not limited to hair loss, high blood pressure, high cholesterol, heart attack or stroke, uncontrollable rage, and delusions. For athletes whose livelihoods depended upon being competitive, these outcomes were a small price to pay for being the best they could be.

The 1980s was the decade many consider to be the beginning of the Steroid Era in baseball. Whereas in the 1970s, steroids could be easily obtained, the 1981 Food, Drug and Cosmetic Act required a physician's prescription for steroids, and they could be used for medicinal purposes only. But the black-market manufacturing and sales of steroids thrived in the 1980s, and those athletes who wanted to find them, did. Jose Canseco was one of the earliest to use them, and in his 2006 memoir, *Juiced: Wild Times, Rampant 'Roids, Smash Hits, and How Baseball Got Big*, he unapologetically confessed to doping. Moreover, he claimed in his book that 85 percent of professional baseball players doped. It was a serious issue, and one that was only going to get worse.

Cuban-born Canseco was an outfielder and designated hitter who was drafted by the Oakland A's in 1982. He debuted in the Major Leagues in 1985 after winning the Baseball America Minor League Player of the Year Award. He followed that with the American League's Rookie of the Year award, based on 33 home runs and 117 runs batted in. Together with another rookie named Mark McGwire, Canseco formed a nearly unbeatable duo known as the Bash Brothers. It was the beginning of what would be a remarkable and distinguished career. Canseco retired in 2002.

PRIMARY SOURCE

"Charlie Brown's Doping" Editorial Cartoon

SYNOPSIS: A more light-hearted approach to the heavy issue of steroid use in baseball. STEVE KELLEY EDITORIAL CARTOON USED WITH THE PERMISSION OF STEVE KELLEY AND AND CREATORS SYNDICATE. ALL RIGHTS RESERVED.

Juiced provides an insider's perspective on the game of baseball and the illegal world of doping. The book's tell-all, tabloid style of writing does not overshadow the serious nature of the scandal. Cartoonist Steve Kelley's "Charlie Brown's Doping" editorial cartoon juxtaposes the innocence of child-hood with the seriousness of the offense for a unique, if not dismaying, look at America's pastime.

SIGNIFICANCE

Although Canseco bragged about his steroid abuse in his 2006 memoir, the love affair did not last forever. A 2010 interview with ESPN had him blaming steroids for ending his career prematurely, causing his financial troubles, and leaving him sterile. Referring to himself as a "modern day Frankenstein," the former MLB player said he had been ostracized from baseball and his former teammates. After writing *Juiced* and the sequel, *Vindicated* (2008), Canseco claimed his life fell apart. "I definitely regret getting involved with steroids in any way, shape or form. . . . I have been living a life of basically terror ever since my book 'Juiced' came out. Whether it be emotionally, financially, it is just terrible." Canseco, unable to find work, was spending his retirement trying to break into acting and making a nominal income in boxing, martial arts, and independent baseball leagues.

Despite the ban of steroids in baseball in 1991, there was no mandatory testing. Both officials and fans turned a blind eye as players like Mark McGwire and Sammy Sosa maintained unbelievable statistics. Critics remained vocal about doping, and the medical community joined them as they publicly decried the severity of steroids' side effects. As studies reflected an

Jose Canseco of the Boston Red Sox swings a bat in the dugout during a game on September 11, 1995. © GREGG NEWTON/CORBIS.

like his peers, lied about it, even in testifying before a grand jury in the government investigation of Bay Area Laboratory Co-Operative (BALCO). BALCO was found guilty of supplying athletes from a number of sports with a then-undetectable steroid nicknamed "the Clear." In September 2003, a number of federal government agencies raided the BALCO facilities and found a register listing customers' names. Bonds's name was included in the record, along with many others. On November 15, 2007, Bonds was indicted for perjury and obstruction of justice. He was convicted in April 2011 for obstruction of justice. His career ended in 2007 with a final record of 762 home runs.

Although tales of doping had become commonplace, things had quieted down for a while after the BALCO scandal. But on January 29, 2013, news broke that some Major League players were linked to new incidents of steroid use. Among the alleged users was New York Yankee all-star Alex Rodriguez, who had already admitted to doping from 2001 to 2003. The new report stated that Biogenesis, a South Florida clinic, had been providing specific players with "human growth hormone, testosterone, specially-designed drug cocktails and other performance-enhancing substances." The investigation into the clinic also revealed that Rodriguez continued using steroids even after his confession. If proven, he faced suspension.

Doping, it seemed, had not gone away afterall.

increase in teen use of steroids throughout the 2000s, public concern and awareness increased.

Limited testing measures were reluctantly agreed to by baseball players and their managers in 2002, and in 2004, President George W. Bush made headlines when he condemned the use of steroids in his State of the Union address. In the wake of stricter standards, major league players were subjected to drug testing, and twelve were suspended for ten days each. That same year, a number of the league's top players—including Canseco, McGwire, Alex Rodriguez, Sosa, Rafael Palmeiro, and Curt Schilling—were called to testify to Congress about their steroid use. Everyone but Canseco claimed innocence, but all were later found guilty or admitted to using steroids.

Steroid use in baseball was rampant throughout the 2000s and into the following decade. One of the most controversial cases involved Barry Bonds, a seven-time National League Most Valuable Player and home-run god. Bonds was accused of doping and,

INTRODUCTION TO *JUICED: WILD TIMES, RAMPANT 'ROIDS, SMASH HITS, AND HOW BASEBALL GOT BIG*

SYNOPSIS: Jose Canseco admits to using steroids and predicts that doping will one day be the norm in all sports.

These past few years, all you had to do was turn on a radio or flip to a sports cable channel, and you could count on hearing some blowhard give you his opinion about steroids and baseball and what it says about our society and blah blah blah. Well, enough already. I'm tired of hearing such short-sighted crap from people who have no idea what they're talking about. Steroids are here to stay. That's a fact. I guarantee it. Steroids are the future. By the time my eight-year-old daughter, Josie, has graduated from high school, a majority of professional athletes—in all sports—will be taking steroids. And believe it or not, that's good news.

Let's be clear what we're talking about. In no way, shape, or form, do I endorse the use of steroids without

Former major league baseball star Jose Canseco testifies during a hearing on the use of steroids in baseball on Capitol Hill, March 17, 2005. © AP IMAGES/GERALD HERBERT.

proper medical advice and thorough expert supervision. I'll say again: Steroids are serious. They are nothing to mess around with casually, and if anything, devoting yourself to the systematic use of steroids means you have to stay away from recreational drugs. I was never into that stuff anyway, cocaine and all that, but if you're going to work with steroids, you have to get used to clean living, smart eating, and taking care of yourself by getting plenty of rest and not overtaxing your body.

I'm especially critical of anyone who starts playing around with steroids too early, when they are barely old enough to shave and not even fully grown yet. Your body is already raging with hormones at that age, and the last thing you want to do is wreak havoc with your body's natural balance. If you want to turn yourself into a nearly superhuman athlete, the way I did, you need to wait until you have matured into adulthood. That way your body can handle it. And you shouldn't fool yourself into thinking all you need to do is just read a few articles on steroids, either. What you need to do is to absorb every scrap of

information on the subject—to become on an expert on the subject, the way I did.

We're talking about the future here. I have no doubt whatsoever that intelligent, informed use of steroids, combined with human growth hormone, will one day be so accepted that everybody will be doing it. Steroid use will be more common than Botox is now. Every baseball player and pro athlete will be using at least a low level of steroids. As a result, baseball and other sports will be more exciting and entertaining. Human life will be improved, too. We will live longer and better. And maybe we'll love longer and better, too.

We will be able to look good and feel strong, fit bodies well into our sixties and beyond. It's called evolution, and there is no stopping it. All these people crying about steroids in baseball now will look as foolish in a few years as the people who said John F. Kennedy was crazy to say the United States would put a man on the moon. People who see the future earlier than others are always feared and misunderstood. The public needs to be informed about the reality of steroids and how they have affected the lives of many star baseball players, including me. Have I used steroids? You bet I did. Did steroids make me a better baseball player? Of course they did. If I had it all to do over again, would I live a steroid-enriched life? Yes, I would. Do I have any regrets or qualms about relying on chemicals to help me hit a baseball so far? To be honest, no, I don't.

We humans beings are made up of chemicals. High school chemistry students learn to recite "CHOPKINS CaFe," which is all the chemical elements that make up the human body: carbon, hydrogen, oxygen, phosphorous, potassium, iodine, nitrogen, sulfur, calcium, and iron. Maybe it bothers some people to think of our bodies as just a collection of those elements, but I find it comforting.

I like studying the body and how it works. I like knowing all about what makes us stronger and faster. If you learn about the chemicals that make up life, and study the hormones coursing through our bloodstreams that give our bodies instructions, you can learn how to improve your health through controlled use of steroids. And you can do it safely.

Yes, you heard me right: Steroids, used correctly, will not only make you stronger and sexier, they will also make you healthier. Certain steroids, used in proper combinations, can cure certain diseases. Steroids will give you a better quality of life and also drastically slow down the aging process.

If people learn how to use steroids and growth hormones properly, especially as they get older—sixty, seventy, eighty years old—their way of living will change completely. If you start young enough, when you are in your twenties, thirties, and forties, and use steroids properly, you can probably slow the aging process by fifteen or twenty years. I'm forty years old, but I look much younger—and I can still do everything the way I could when I was twenty-five.

When I talk in detail about steroids and how I single-handedly changed the game of baseball by introducing them into the game, I am saying what everyone in baseball has known for years. To all my critics, to everyone who wants to turn this into a debate about me, Jose Canseco, let me quote my favorite actor (besides Arnold Schwarzenegger, that is) and say: You can't handle the truth.

That is the story of baseball in recent years. Everyone in the game has been hoping the lie could last as long as possible. They wanted steroids in the game to make it more exciting, hoping they would be able to build its popularity back up after the disastrous cancellation of the 1994 World Series. So when I taught other players how to use steroids, no one lifted a finger to stop me. When I educated trainers and others on how to inject players with steroids, there was nothing standing in my way. Directly or indirectly, nearly everyone in baseball was complicit.

How do I know that? I was known as the godfather of steroids in baseball. I introduced steroids into the big leagues back in 1985, and taught other players how to use steroids and growth hormone. Back then, weight lifting was taboo in baseball. The teams didn't have weight-lifting programs. Teams didn't allow it. But once they saw what I could do as a result of my weight lifting, they said, "My God, if it's working for Jose, it's gotta work for a lot of players."

So all of a sudden ballparks were being built with brand-new, high-tech weight-lifting facilities, and at the older ballparks they were moving stuff around and remodeling to make room for weight rooms. I definitely restructured the way the game was played. Because of my influence, and my example, there were dramatic changes in the way that players looked and the way they played. That was because of changes in their nutrition, their approach to fitness and weight lifting, and their steroid intake and education.

If you asked any player who was the one who knew about steroids, they'd all tell you: Jose Canseco.

Who do you go to when you want information on steroids?

Jose Canseco.

Who do you go to if you wanted to know if you were using it properly?

Jose Canseco.

If you picked up this book just for a few juicy tales about which players I've poked with needles full of steroids, or what it was like when Madonna sat on my lap and asked me to kiss her, that's fine with me. I've lived a colorful life and people have always been curious about the things I've done. If you want to flip through the chapters looking for the highlights, I have no problem with that (as long as you pay the cover price, of course).

But let me be clear that I'm writing this book for people who are ready to think for themselves. That's all I'm asking. Hear me out, listen to what I have to say about baseball and other things, and come to your own conclusions. That might sound easy, but believe me, coming to terms with a true picture of what has been going on in baseball in the past ten years or so might not be what you really want.

Do I expect some skepticism from people? Of course I do. I've made some mistakes in the past. I've made mistakes in my personal life, and I've made mistakes in public, too. There have been times when I spoke out without realizing how my comments might sound to people.

That's all water under the bridge. Now, I'm looking to the rest of my life, not dwelling on what might have been.

I'm telling the truth about steroids in this book because someone has to do it. We're long overdue for some honesty and, as any ballplayer will tell you, I know the real story of steroids in baseball better than any man alive. I'm also in a position to tell you the truth because I no longer have any ties with Major League Baseball. I'm my own man and always have been.

Back when I first started using steroids, I tracked down as many books as I could find on the subject, as I studied the science behind steroids. I started becoming something like a guru. I wanted to know everything about each steroid and what it did, especially pertaining to athletes and sports and baseball. Could it make me faster? Could it make me stronger? Could it make me injury-free? I started experimenting on myself, using my own body to see what steroid could do what. Today, I probably know more about steroids and what steroids can do for the human body than any other layman in the world.

I believe every steroid out there can be used safely and beneficially—it's all a question of dosage. Some steroids you cycle off and on, depending on the dose. You just have to make sure you give your liver enough time to filter them out. There are other steroids that have very low toxicity levels. Those can be taken continuously by most healthy people. It just depends. Growth hormone? You can use that all year round. Same thing with your Equipoise, your Winstrols, your Decas—taken properly, those are all fine all year round. But something like Anadrol, and some high doses of testosterone—those have to be moderated, taken more selectively. This is all important because when ballplayers talk about steroids, they really mean a combination of steroids and growth hormone, and that requires some serious planning if you don't want to get in trouble. . . .

■ PRIMARY SOURCE

"CHARLIE BROWN'S DOPING"

See primary source cartoon.

■

FURTHER RESOURCES

Books

Bryant, Howard. *Juicing the Game: Drugs, Power, and the Fight for the Soul of Major League Baseball.* New York: Penguin, 2005.

Fainaru-Wada, Mark, and Lance Williams. *Game of Shadows: Barry Bonds, BALCO, and the Steroids Scandal That Rocked Professional Sports.* New York: Penguin, 2006.

Web Sites

Fish, Mike. "Canseco: Steroids Are Overrated." *ESPN*, June 2, 2010. http://sports.espn.go.com/mlb/news/story?id=5244705 (accessed on March 24, 2013).

Fitzpatrick, Laura. "A Brief History of Steroids." *Time*, January 13, 2010. www.time.com/time/health/article/0,8599,1953229,00.html (accessed on March 24, 2013).

Nightengale, Bob. "Report: Alex Rodriguez, Others Linked to Doping, Florida Clinic." *USA Today*, January 29, 2013. www.usatoday.com/story/sports/mlb/2013/01/29/mlb-drugs-alex-rodriguez-miami-new-times-nelson-cruz-gio-gonzalez/1874203/ (accessed on March 24, 2013).

Wenner, Kathryn S. "Not Funny." *American Journalism Review*, July/August 2001. www.ajr.org/Article.asp?id=960 (accessed on March 24, 2013).

"Racing to Victory, and Leaving the Men and the Doubters Behind"

Newspaper article

By: Dave Caldwell

Date: April 21, 2008

Source: Caldwell, Dave. "Racing to Victory, and Leaving the Men and the Doubters Behind." *New York Times*, April 21, 2008. www.nytimes.com/2008/04/21/sports/othersports/21patrick.html (accessed on March 24, 2013.)

About the Publication: The *New York Times* was founded in 1851 as a concise, four-page summary of daily news items. News mogul Adolph S. Ochs acquired the paper in 1896, expanding its scope and size. By the turn of the twentieth century, the *New York Times* was the preeminent U.S. newspaper, acclaimed for its objective reporting of "All the News That's Fit to Print." In 1905, the popularity and importance of the paper was memorialized by the City of New York, which called its new public square "Times Square," in honor of the newspaper. The paper's investigative reporting on official and political affairs has always been a trademark, garnering the journalism staff more than one hundred Pulitzer Prizes for its coverage of wars and governments—most notably for its publication of the "Pentagon Papers," leaked documents attesting to the mishandling and uncertainty of the Vietnam

War. The *New York Times* remains the nation's most prestigious and important newspaper, and it continues to be owned and operated by descendants of Ochs.

INTRODUCTION

Danica Patrick was born on March 25, 1982, in Beloit, Wisconsin, and raised in Illinois. She developed an interest in go-kart racing at a young age and began competing in the sport when she was ten years old. With the support of her parents, Patrick set out for England when she turned sixteen, where she raced in the British National Series. In 2002, Patrick's success in the British kart circuit earned her a spot on the Rahal Letterman Racing team back in the United States. She proved exceptionally talented in the IndyCar circuit, competing in the Barber Dodge Pro Series and the Toyota Atlantic Championship, in which she claimed an overall fourth-place season. In 2005, Patrick stepped up to the Indy Racing League (IRL) IndyCar Series, becoming the fourth woman to compete in the Indianapolis 500 since the race's inception. She started and finished in fourth place during that race, the highest placement ever achieved for a woman. The IRL named her Rookie of the Year for the 2005 season.

After another year competing for Rahal Letterman, Patrick signed to Andretti Green racing in 2007, receiving sponsorship deals from cell phone company Motorola, XM Radio, and Internet domain registration provider Go Daddy. The following year, Patrick became the first woman to win an IRL series race when she placed first in the Indy Japan 300, held at the Twin Ring Motegi in Motegi, Japan. She finished that year's series sixth overall. In 2009, Patrick finished third in the Indianapolis 500 and finished the season fifth overall, the best ever attained by a female driver. In subsequent seasons, Patrick raced in both the IRL and NASCAR, making her one of a small number of women to compete in the stock car series.

SIGNIFICANCE

Patrick's unprecedented success as a female competitor in an overwhelmingly male-dominated sport launched her into the public spotlight. The diminutive, attractive racer's likeness became a common presence in advertising and endorsement—her titillating commercial for Go Daddy was the most-watched and highest-rated advertisement of the 2009 NFL Super Bowl. Patrick became a staple of television, appearing on a number of Spike TV programs and appearing on *The Late Show with David Letterman* and *Late Night with Conan O'Brien*. She was also featured in episodes of *CSI: NY* and *The Simpsons*, as well as the music video for rapper Jay-Z's song *Show Me What You Got*.

Patrick served as an inspiration for female athletes and living evidence of the ability of women to compete in motorsports. In addition to her appearance in multiple *Sports Illustrated* swimsuit editions, the driver graced the cover of the magazine (and several others) after her 2008 win in Japan. She used her popular visibility and a portion of her race winnings to become the celebrity spokesperson of the chronic obstructive pulmonary disease awareness nonprofit Drive4COPD. After 2010, Patrick's success in professional car racing began to wane, but she had already created a lasting legacy by demonstrating the potential for female drivers to defeat their male counterparts.

PRIMARY SOURCE

"RACING TO VICTORY, AND LEAVING THE MEN AND THE DOUBTERS BEHIND"

SYNOPSIS: This article describes Danica Patrick's rise to glory in American car racing.

When a 23-year-old rookie named Danica Patrick became the first woman to lead the Indianapolis 500 three years ago, she raised the tantalizing possibility that in a male-dominated American sport, a woman might for the first time stand in victory lane.

Patrick eventually finished fourth in that race, but she quickly became a phenomenon. Companies embraced her willingness to market her good looks, and babies began emerging from maternity wards with the name Danica. But along with her celebrity came a question: When would she win?

It was answered Sunday in Motegi, Japan, where Patrick, now 26, became the first woman to win an Indy car race. She defeated the two-time Indy 500 winner Hélio Castroneves by nearly six seconds in the Indy Japan 300.

"I feel way too young to be giving life advice, but this is a great platform to have," Patrick said Sunday night in a telephone interview from Los Angeles, where she had landed after a virtually sleepless flight from Japan. "This reaches outside racing. This is about finding something you love to do, and following through with it."

Besides saying thanks, Patrick said she was unable to say much more to her crew amid her tears immediately after the race. Back in Los Angeles, she again became emotional when she relived her long road to victory.

"It's going to be nice not to have to answer those questions anymore," she said. "They were just so hard to answer, because I believed in myself. I just didn't know when it was going to happen."

Danica Patrick hoists her trophy in celebration after winning the Indy Japan 300 race in Motegi, Japan, April 20, 2008. © AP IMAGES/SHUJI KAJIYAMA.

There was a time when Patrick could not have competed in Sunday's race. A few years before Janet Guthrie, an aerospace engineer and road racer, became the first woman to qualify for the Indy 500 in 1977, women were not allowed in the press box, the garage area or the pits.

As Guthrie wrote in "Life at Full Throttle," an account of her career in racing, women were dismissed as lacking the strength, endurance and emotional stability to compete against men. Even a driver with Guthrie's credentials as a road racer was seen as dangerous.

"A woman might be a reporter, a photographer, a timer/scorer, she might own the race car—but she couldn't get near it at any time for any reason," Guthrie wrote. "A woman on the track itself was unthinkable."

On Sunday, Guthrie showed little surprise at Patrick's victory.

"Anybody who didn't think she had a chance of winning just hasn't been paying attention," Guthrie, 70, said in a telephone interview from her home in Aspen, Colo. "She's been in the hunt for a long time. It was just a matter of time, as far as I'm concerned."

Guthrie then said, "I absolutely hope this will put all of the naysayers to rest."

For Patrick, the naysayers' chorus had grown increasingly loud as her winless streak wore on. A year ago, in search of a stronger team, Patrick jumped from the IndyCar Series team co-owned by the talk-show host David Letterman to the team co-owned by Michael Andretti, the former racer who is the son of Mario Andretti.

Michael Andretti said he believed the diminutive Patrick, 5 feet 2 inches and 100 pounds, had the skill and desire to win regularly. He provided her with a powerful race car and with his team's expertise, which helped her win the race Sunday at Twin Ring Motegi, a mile-and-a-half oval.

When Patrick burst on the racing consciousness three years ago, she brought with her an extensive racing background. Her father was a racer who introduced his daughter to driving at a young age. At 16, Patrick moved to Europe, alone, to compete.

By 2005, the combination of her promise on the track and her willingness to capitalize on her looks—her biography in the 2008 IndyCar Series media guide includes a photograph of her in a white bikini—soon had marketers clamoring for her.

An IndyCar Series official said in 2006 that Patrick's merchandise outsold that of any other driver, 10 to 1. The series said that the name Danica jumped to No. 352 from No. 610 on the list of most popular baby names from 2005 to 2006. Patrick was in a Super Bowl advertisement this year for Godaddy.com. Expectations became heavy.

Before she drove her car to victory lane, she said Sunday night, she was unable to speak because, "it was an indication of how much had been on my mind—how long it had been since the start of my IndyCar career."

Patrick said her team tried to conserve fuel from the first laps of Sunday's race. When three drivers running at the front of the pack had to make pit stops for fuel in the final 10 laps of the 200-lap race, she charged into second place, behind Castroneves.

Castroneves had enough fuel to finish the race without making a pit stop, but he had to conserve what little he had. Patrick, who lost the 2005 Indy 500 because she had to stretch her fuel supply, took the lead with two laps left on Sunday and won easily.

"In recognition of Danica's talents, she did a good job," Castroneves said in a postrace news conference. "She passed me fair and square. I didn't have enough fuel, even if I wanted to, to fight with her."

Next month, Patrick will return to the Indianapolis 500. The competition at this year's race is expected to be much tougher after a merger in the off-season with Champ Car, another open-wheel racing series.

"I think Danica is such a fantastic person and I'm thrilled for her that the monkey is finally off of her back," Michael Andretti said after the race. "We have all believed in her, and she proved today that she is a winner. Frankly, I think this is the first of many."

Another woman on the IndyCar circuit, Sarah Fisher, 27, has formed her own race team. She did not race Sunday in Japan but has said she hopes to drive in the Indy 500, among other races. Fisher said Patrick's triumph made Sunday a memorable day not only for drivers and open-wheel-racing fans, but for women.

"Today marks the celebration for all of us who have chipped away at the barriers that many women have faced in fields that are dominated by men," Fisher said in a statement. "To finally have a female win an open-wheel race is simply a progression of what Janet Guthrie started."

FURTHER RESOURCES

Books

Morton, Laura, and Danica Patrick. *Danica—Crossing the Line.* New York: Touchstone, 2007.

Web Sites

"Danica Patrick." *Bio.* www.biography.com/people/danica-patrick-201312 (accessed on March 24, 2013).

"Danica Patrick." *Danica Racing.* www.danicaracing.com/#3 (accessed on March 24, 2013).

"Danica Patrick." *ESPN.* http://espn.go.com/racing/driver/_/id/697/danica-patrick (accessed on March 24, 2013).

"Lance Armstrong Rides Again"

Magazine article

By: Douglas Brinkley

Date: September 9, 2008

Source: Brinkley, Douglas. "Lance Armstrong Rides Again." *Vanity Fair*, September 9, 2008. www.vanityfair.com/culture/features/2008/09/armstrong200809 (accessed on March 24, 2013).

About the Publication: First published as a men's fashion magazine in 1913 under the name *Dress and Vanity Fair*, the periodical thrived throughout the 1920s until the Great Depression swept America and forced the publication to merge with *Vogue* in 1935. Condé Nast revived the magazine in 1983 and it became known for its controversial photography as well as hard-hitting journalism. In the twenty-first century, *Vanity Fair* publishes all things having to do with pop fashion and society.

INTRODUCTION

Lance Armstrong was born September 18, 1971, and began his professional cycling career in 1992 with the Motorola team. He won several major competitions, including the 1993 World Championship, before being diagnosed with testicular cancer in 1996. The disease spread to his brain and lungs, but after surgery and intensive chemotherapy treatments, he was deemed cancer-free in February 1997. That same year, he founded the Lance Armstrong Foundation, an organization designed to inspire and empower cancer survivors and their families. Renamed the Livestrong Foundation, it initially supported cancer research but began phasing out that aspect of activity in 2005. Livestrong raised in excess of $100 million and, in collaboration with Nike, launched the Livestrong wristbands that became a global phenomenon. By the end of 2012, more than eighty-four million yellow wristbands had been distributed.

Armstrong renewed his cycling training by January 1998 and signed a contract with U.S. Postal, a team for which he raced from 1998 to July 2005. On July 24 of that year, Armstrong officially retired after claiming his seventh Tour de France victory. Along the way, Armstrong was consistently accused of taking steroids to enhance his physical performance. He repeatedly and vehemently denied these charges.

On September 9, 2008, Armstrong announced his return to competitive cycling, this time with the RadioShack team. His goal, he claimed, was to raise awareness of cancer as a global burden. Journalist Douglas Brinkley's *Vanity Fair* article was published on the same date as Armstrong's surprising announcement.

SIGNIFICANCE

Armstrong did not win the 2009 Tour de France, but finished in third place. That loss would turn out to be the least of his problems when, on April 30, 2010, former teammate Floyd Landis emailed cycling officials to accuse Armstrong of extensive doping and cover-up. On May 20, the *New York Times* reported that Armstrong and other member of Team US Postal had been accused of doping by Landis. Armstrong again denied the accusations, but in September, the wife of a former teammate told federal agents that while visiting Armstrong in the hospital while he was recovering from surgery, he admitted to using performance-enhancing drugs. A January 24, 2011, *Sports Illustrated* article reported that Armstrong had been cited by teammates as the instigator of the team's doping program dating back to the mid-1990s. Again, Armstrong denied the allegation, but because his team was sponsored by a government agency, a federal investigation was required.

After further allegations of steroid use by former teammates of Armstrong, the investigation by federal agents was abruptly dropped in February 2012 for reasons that were not revealed. But on June 12, Armstrong was charged with doping and trafficking of drugs by the U.S. Anti-Doping Agency (USADA). He was suspended from competition and banned from participating in any triathlons. The official report sent to Armstrong revealed that the USADA had concerns over blood samples from the athlete dating back to 2009 and 2010 because they showed evidence of blood "manipulation"—doping.

Armstrong filed a lawsuit against the USADA in an attempt to stop them from further charging him. That suit was thrown out of court, as was a second one he filed. By August 2012, Armstrong had made the decision not to fight the accusations any longer. On August 23, he publicly announced his decision, but continued to deny his guilt. By avoiding arbitration, the cyclist was stripped of all his wins and banned from the sport of competitive cycling forever. History will not show that he ever won any of his races, and in October, he resigned as chairman of Livestrong to spare the charity from the continuing controversy. Weeks later, he stepped down from the foundation's board of directors.

In January 2013, Armstrong appeared in a televised interview with Oprah Winfrey and confessed to doping. Although most Americans by that time had suspected his guilt, the admittance was a surprise primarily because Armstrong had built a reputation as a somewhat arrogant athlete who sought praise and was known for an attitude of superiority. The USADA issued a one-thousand-page report that accused him not only of doping, but of masterminding one of the most sophisticated doping programs the sport had ever seen.

Armstrong faced a slew of lawsuits after his confession. Sponsors, the federal government, and even a British newspaper that Armstrong had successfully sued for libel years back for publishing an article about his name in connection with doping—all were after money as reparation for losses in the wake of his deceit. With an estimated worth of $125 million in March 2013, Armstrong's potential legal payouts totaled in excess of $106 million. A once-mighty sports hero had crashed, and the damages were still being tallied.

PRIMARY SOURCE

"LANCE ARMSTRONG RIDES AGAIN"

SYNOPSIS: Lance Armstrong talks about his plans to ride in his eighth Tour de France, alleged steroid use, and why his career is not over.

Lance Armstrong greeted me at the front door, barefoot, holding a glass of Cabernet. Though we're neighbors among the rolling hills of Austin, Texas, we're not especially close. Occasionally we bump into each other around town and talk about politics. We are, in other words, acquaintances. So when he invited me to dinner in mid-August—at my instigation—my plan was to discuss the Olympics and his future in Texas politics. Armstrong insisted he had something important he wanted to tell me in confidence.

Since I know Armstrong's disdain for small talk, I was somewhat taken aback when the world's top anti-cancer advocate (and seven-time winner of cycling's premier race, the Tour de France) immediately launched into a diatribe about recent charges in the press—first printed in our local paper, the *Austin American-Statesman*—that he was the single largest consumer of water in town, with most of his habit (222,900 gallons in June alone) going to maintain the greenery around his three-acre estate. He complained that the paper had invaded his privacy zone by splashing across its front page an aerial photo of his Spanish colonial mansion, all 8,000 square feet of it.

"That bothered me, 'cause it's my home," he said, offering up tuna-tartare hors d'oeuvres and pouring generously from an uncorked wine bottle. (In collaboration with a friend, Armstrong has his own boutique label.) In Austin, the eco-capital of Texas, residents tend to favor native plants and wildflowers to the sculpted lawns of the Palm Springs variety. So even though I knew Armstrong to be a fierce competitor, I realized that he'd be riled by winning the "water hog" title. Especially when the item was picked up by the newswires and the blogs.

"It's where my kids roll around in the grass," he told me, "and swim in their pools and throw their footballs and kick their soccer balls." (His ex-wife, Kristin Armstrong, with whom he has remained quite close since their 2003 divorce, lives only a few miles away, so he spends a lot of

Cyclist Lance Armstrong in September 2008. © AP IMAGES/THE CANADIAN PRESS, RYAN REMIORZ.

time with their children, eight-year-old Luke, and Grace and Bella, their six-year-old twins. Armstrong's actually one of the best hands-on fathers I've ever met.) He told me he considered the photo and the article "an invasion. It bothers you when it runs in *The New York Times* and every paper across the United States. I was in Santa Barbara for the summer, and it ran in that local paper. I was thinking, Oh my God. But it gets back to politics. I mean, I think from the mind of Texas media they're already thinking, This guy's planning something political. And so they'll look at your voting record, they'll look at your water bill. If you get into a fight at a bar with a bouncer, they'll write it."

But surely he hadn't asked me to dinner to talk about his plumbing. I began to wonder if, instead, he'd wanted to confide in me—as a historian and a journalist—about his purported plans to run for governor. Word had it that he'd been making the public-appearance rounds and setting his sights on 2010. He has Dallas roots and a ranch in Dripping Springs. While many in Texas have pegged Armstrong as a Republican (one of his advisers is Austin's Mark McKinnon, who has helped burnish the images of both George W. Bush and John McCain), he nonetheless seeks the counsel of John Kerry and has decidedly Democratic leanings.

"What about the rumors," I asked him, "that you'll run for governor?"

He answered slyly, "Down the road, something like that might be possible. Probably in 2014."

My host, who has an interior designer's eye, gave me a quick tour. He's created a home that is immense and fluid, with beautiful dark woods and shades of maroon. The spread, while spectacular, has something of a playground feel: wheeled toys are scattered about as if in Legoland. Here and there, the walls are dominated by museum-quality canvases by Ed Ruscha, colorful minimalist pieces bearing concise slogans—pure and direct and in your face, like Armstrong himself. A few years ago, he said, he'd had a chance encounter with the painter whose work he'd been collecting.

While dining at Chef Melba's in Hermosa Beach, California, Armstrong heard an obnoxious voice, with a thick New Jersey accent, coming from the table behind him: "Hey, kid, what are you gonna do for work this summa?!" Armstrong worried that he had a kook on his hands. "I'm talkin' to you, kid. What are you gonna do?" Armstrong got pissed, he recalled. "I was like ... I think [he's] talkin' to me. So I wheeled around in my chair. It was ... Don Rickles. And I started laughing. Anyway, he's like, 'Meet my friend Ed.'

"And I go, 'Hey, Ed. I'm Lance Armstrong.' And he goes, 'I'm Ed Ruscha.' And I'm like, 'Ed Ruscha?' He's

like, 'Yeah, yeah, yeah.' It was ... crazy. My main guy was having dinner with Rickles. I told him about how much [his paintings] *Speed Racer* and *Safe and Effective Medication* have meant to me."

We moved out to the back terrace, overlooking the surrounding grounds, the gardens, a designer pool nearby. Like a couple of back-fence neighbors, we pulled up lawn chairs to chew over the local news. Armstrong read aloud a retaliatory letter to the editor—a screed, in fact—that he'd drafted but never sent to the *Statesman*. I considered this a wise choice. He'd need the support of his hometown newspaper if he'd ever make a run for the statehouse. Furthermore, the editors had consistently promoted his Austin-based anti-cancer efforts, in glowing fashion, for more than a decade; it was best to cut them slack.

And the talk, as it always must with Lance Armstrong, turned to cancer.

Back in October 1996, after winning two Tour stages, he'd been diagnosed with an aggressive strain of testicular cancer. He had had two surgeries: one to remove a cancerous testicle, another to remove two cancerous lesions on the brain. An additional 8 to 10 golf-ball-size tumors were found in his lungs. He'd been a dead man walking. Seeking the best specialists, some of whom happened to be at Indiana University Medical Center, he underwent a round of B.E.P. chemotherapy (Bleomycin, Etoposide, and Platinol), followed by three rounds of V.I.P. chemotherapy (Ifosfamide, Etoposide, and Platinol). He was only 25 years old and had been given less than a 40 percent chance of survival. Victim Armstrong, however, fought the odds and won, going on to take an unprecedented seven straight cycling crowns. Once a year, now, he does blood tests, his levels normal, though the fears of remission always persist. It's the same test that women use for pregnancy. "Back in '96," Armstrong likes to joke, "I was really, really pregnant!"

As I listened to him, my chief worry was that Armstrong's cancer had returned. Could that be what this dinner was all about? Perhaps he wanted me to be his Boswell, to document his fight going forward. Though he's among the most focused and tightly wound people I've ever encountered (and, paradoxically, one of the most unflaggingly upbeat), he seemed particularly intense that night. His lapis eyes seemed to smolder. He fidgeted with his BlackBerry, a skull emblazoned on its back. His restless hands bespoke surplus energy. (Lance and Kristin often text-message each other XXOO notes.)

My heart sank as I considered what he'd gone through: lost testicle, chemo, baldness; the struggles, the titles, then his choice to return to Austin and retire from racing for good.

I knew a bit of his history as an advocate for others who shared the disease. He'd started the Lance Armstrong Foundation (L.A.F.) in Austin in 1997, a little mom-and-pop organization. Over time, he understood that survivors were sometimes too afraid, psychologically, to talk about cancer, let alone spread the word. So, in 2003, he created LiveStrong, in effect an anti-cancer brand, designed to raise public awareness, largely through a Web site that could act as a gathering place for fellow survivors. Within a decade Armstrong had helped raise $265 million, his organization hosting bike-race fund-raisers across the country, creating survivorship programs, posting medical resource guides online. Like his friend Bono, Armstrong had redefined celebrity leveraging, becoming a regular 365-days-a-year walking-talking Jerry Lewis Telethon. (In Armstrong's last appearance on the Forbes Celebrity 100, in 2005, his estimated annual income was $28 million, largely accrued through endorsements and support from companies such as Nike, Bristol-Myers Squibb, and Trek Bicycles.)

The real breakthrough had come in 2004. Nike came to him with the idea of having people wear plastic yellow LiveStrong wristbands—the color of the jersey worn by each day's leader of the Tour de France. "I thought it was a terrible idea," Armstrong told me. "I didn't think it worked. Seemed like a loser. They were going to give us five million of these bracelets to sell for a dollar. But they also were going to donate a million dollars to kick it off. So I looked at that and went, 'Sweet. We've never had a million-dollar donation. We like that!' I didn't know where we were going to store all of these silly yellow bands."

It was his then girlfriend, rocker Sheryl Crow, whom Armstrong now credits with transforming the bracelets into a national anti-cancer symbol (selling 60 million units and counting). "Sheryl was performing on the *Today* show and started handing them out to kids and people in the audience outside," he recalled. "She was so popular that they took off." (Today, Crow, herself a cancer survivor, wears the yellow.)

Next, Armstrong's entire team volunteered to wear them in the Tour de Georgia. Then, during the pre–Tour de France trials, Nike sold them at roadside stands. "Suddenly you started seeing fans wearing them," Armstrong said. "And then [at] the Olympics in Athens ... the track-and-field event happened. Hicham El Guerrouj wore one. Soon we had a lot of support in Hollywood. And I don't know where people got them. I didn't ask them to wear them. They just got them. You know, little kids see Hillary Duff, and she has a whole arm full of them, and next thing you know teenagers start wearing them." (That year John Kerry, a prostate-cancer survivor, wore one on the campaign trail. "I appeared at a huge rally in Sioux City, Iowa, in May '04," Kerry told me

during the Democratic Convention, in Denver, a week after my dinner with Armstrong. "A woman grabbed me in the rope line and told me a tragic story of her sister's fight against cancer. She handed me a bracelet and I put it on.... It was terrific to remind people that we're not doing enough on the cancer front. We're way, way behind. I didn't care if some Republicans thought it was silly.")

In 2007 Armstrong and L.A.F. got behind a pivotal state initiative, Proposition 15, under the tagline, "Texas Holds the Cure." Largely spearheaded by former executive director of the Texas Chamber of Commerce Cathy Bonner (who had watched her close friend, ex-governor Ann Richards, die from esophageal cancer), the bill appropriates up to $3 billion through general-revenue bonds to support the Cancer Prevention and Research Institute of Texas— the largest such state investment ever.

The first time I had seriously imagined Armstrong as a politician was last May, when he'd appeared before a Senate committee assessing how America battles cancer. He was as electric as C-span gets. And his message couldn't have been clearer. This year, 560,000 Americans will die from cancer, he said (close to the human loss suffered in the entire Civil War). The epidemic claims more than 1,500 citizens a day. Put another way, 1.4 million Americans this year will have a doctor tell them, "You have cancer." More Americans have cancer right now than the populations of Idaho, Montana, Wyoming, North Dakota, South Dakota, and Nebraska combined.

As we sat in our terrace chairs overlooking the manicured vista, Armstrong nervously fingered the yellow band on his wrist. He insisted he had something on his mind. "Something huge," as he put it. I braced for the worst.

Then, in almost robotic fashion, he said, "I'm going back to professional cycling. I'm going to try and win an eighth Tour de France."

For a moment I gaped at him. Was I being punked? (Armstrong would later tell Doug Ulman, the president and C.E.O. of L.A.F., that my eyes bulged into saucers, like some boinged-out character in a Ralph Steadman illustration.) As the news sank in, though, I realized he was deadly serious. I knew from Armstrong's memoir, *It's Not About the Bike*, that his VO2 max (the gauge by which the human body's capacity to transport and use oxygen is measured) is superhuman, his ship-sail lungs uncommonly efficient.

But at age 37? A 2,000-mile, 23-day race, much of it uphill? By next July? I asked him, rather ungraciously, if he wasn't too old to get back into shape that quickly.

He laughed. And he was off and running. "Look at the Olympics. You have a swimmer like Dara Torres. Even in the 50-meter event [freestyle], the 41-year-old mother proved you can do it. The woman who won the marathon [Constantina Tomescu-Dita, of Romania] was 38. Older athletes are performing very well. Ask serious sports physiologists and they'll tell you age is a wives' tale. Athletes at 30, 35 mentally get tired. They've done their sport for 20, 25 years and they're like, I've had enough. But there's no evidence to support that when you're 38 you're any slower than when you were 32.

"Ultimately, I'm the guy that gets up. I mean, I get up out of bed a little slow. I mean, I'm not going to lie. I mean, my back gets tired quicker than it used to and I get out of bed a little slower than I used to. But when I'm going, when I'm on the bike—I feel just as good as I did before."

I wasn't totally buying it. "Are you really 100 percent going to race in the Tour de France?"

"One hundred percent!" he replied. "One hundred percent!"

Over filet-mignon dinner in his library, I realized anew that there is an unhinged directness about Armstrong that is refreshing. No slack, no waste. Just raw essence. He speaks like an old wire-service ticker. And as I listened I gathered that he had two main hurdles in this wild new race—beyond his physical prowess, his age, his health. First, he couldn't just cruise up to the starting line; he would need the approval of the Amaury Sport Organisation (A.S.O.), the governing body that oversees the Tour. Second, two words would now dominate his vocabulary: "transparency" and "authenticity." Nobody would be able to call him a "doper" this time around, no matter how circumstantial or bogus the evidence. Like Carlos Sastre, who won the Tour this past July, Armstrong assured me that he would do whatever it took to become a contender—random blood samples and parameter readings—to prove he was a clean rider. In fact, he said, he'd hired a video crew, which was starting to chronicle his journey to the Tour, including his tests, for a possible future documentary.

Every morning, Armstrong explained, he was up at 5:30 training: riding his bike through the Hill Country, lifting weights, sizing up the European competition, jogging for ungodly miles around Lady Bird Lake. He had hired former pro triathlete Peter Park—a Santa Barbara strength and conditioning coach who owns two California gyms—to whip him into shape. His main cycling coach of nearly 20 years, Chris Carmichael, had now picked up the pace. Meanwhile, Johan Bruyneel, his "directeur sportif," would run and manage his team, developing comprehensive tactics for winning the Tour.

What's more, he said, this was, first and foremost, about cancer. Whatever personal or athletic demons he

was taking on, he would use his return to cycling as a way to spread his message.

By dessert his decision made perfect sense to me. After turning a death sentence into seven yellow jerseys and a national anti-cancer mission, he was cranking it up a notch, to the world stage.

Playing Cassandra, I asked him, pointedly, "What if you fall off your bike?"

He simply flashed me the Look, as Sports Illustrated has called it, a blowtorch stare of cobalt blue. While the Look is meant to unnerve any recipient, which it does, that night it seemed the clearest window into Armstrong's psyche. Here was the resolve that had beaten back cancer more assuredly than chemo. Here was the piercing glare that turned the tables: you need to be better informed about this disease.

Suddenly, I felt like a philistine for having bare wrists.

As I drove home after dinner, the clouds in the Austin sky were inflamed by dry lightning. Only a fool, I thought, would doubt Lance Armstrong's determination to win the Tour de France—arguably sport's most grueling event—yet again.

Early the next morning I phoned him. I asked him to consider giving me his first "comeback" interview, for *Vanity Fair*. Perhaps I would even cover the backstory, in book form. On both accounts he seemed cautiously pleased; my guess is that he'd been scheming for this outcome all along. As we talked, I understood the stakes. As the P.R. drumbeat picked up over the coming months, the exposure for LiveStrong, and the sales of those wristbands, would surely balloon.

Unfortunately, Armstrong told me that any interview would have to wait. With a private plane always at his disposal, he was headed to purchase a home in downtown Aspen, his new headquarters as he began training at high altitudes in conditions simulating the Alps and Pyrenees. From Colorado, he would be on to Philadelphia to participate in a LiveStrong Challenge ride and run. But we quickly arranged a follow-up meeting, back in Austin.

When I arrived at his house the next Sunday, however, I encountered a surreal scene out of *When We Were Kings*—part reality show, part Entourage. I'm still not sure which. Upon entering the compound I was greeted by a small film crew, camera rolling. In cinéma vérité fashion, they were already starting to document Armstrong's road to the Eiffel Tower, and I had unwittingly become part of the narrative. Joining us for dinner was Team Armstrong: L.A.F.'s Doug Ulman, agent Bill Stapleton, L.A.F. executive Morgan Binswanger, business manager Bart Knaggs, and media consultant Mark McKinnon.

Quite clearly, I'd flown right into the spiderweb. Not that I was too surprised. Earlier that afternoon, while

Lance Armstrong talks with fellow cyclists before a cancer research fundraising bike ride in Mont Tremblant, Quebec, September 12, 2008. © AP IMAGES/THE CANADIAN PRESS, RYAN REMIORZ.

reading up on my neighbor, I'd stumbled upon an old CNN clip, which quoted a top cycling journalist: "Armstrong is wary at the best of times, keeping tabs on everyone who keeps tabs on him. I soon came to find out that reporting on Armstrong meant that he was also reporting on you." After a few minutes, I bristled and asked the crew to turn off the cameras.

Then I threw a wrench into the works.

"What if you fall off your bike?" I asked, as I had at our dinner, figuring someone had to be the garden-party skunk. "What if you lose?"

A chorus of rattlesnake hisses came my way. It was clear that I wasn't of their ilk. My naked wrists were noticeable. "I can't believe you asked that," said a disappointed Stapleton, deflated. "We don't go there."

A cardinal rule of Team Armstrong is never to contemplate failure. When the subject is cancer—Ulman is also a survivor—failure is not an option. Winning is far less important than not losing.

By the end of the evening, however, they had agreed to cooperate with a story. And an eager Armstrong wanted to have me start the very next day.

In the morning, I stopped at the sleek L.A.F. headquarters, near downtown Austin. "We're looking for a president who'll provide leadership on the cancer front," Ulman explained, ladling out strong doses of LiveStrong Kool-Aid. "Twelve months from now, if we've done our job, the new president will appoint people to lead this war on cancer. And we'll be holding them accountable for what they agree to do. We need transformative change. Cancer needs a Cabinet-level position or a cancer czar."

Having spent the morning at the foundation, I arrived for my 11:00 am interview, chez Armstrong, 18 minutes late. Lance greeted me at the door, slightly miffed. Punctuality is hugely important to him.

As we settled into the library, I asked him whose advice he had sought as he came to his decision. Three weeks before, he said, among the first two people he brought into the loop were the key women in his life: his mother, Linda Armstrong Kelly (who gave birth to him in Plano, Texas, as a 17-year-old single mother), and his ex-wife, Kristin, a devout Catholic. "I definitely tell my mom everything," Armstrong says. "But my ex-wife is [also] a very important lady to me. She is somebody I'm very close to. When I went to Iraq and Afghanistan to visit the troops last Christmas, I sought her permission. I had her over for dinner and asked her if I could go. She said, "I think you can go but, if for any reason in the next three or four weeks I have doubts or I'm uneasy about this, I'm going to tell you and I'd like you not to go.' And I said, 'No problem.' She prayed for me and felt good about it. And same with this comeback. Essentially, I asked her permission."

. . .

The impetus to come back, he says, sprang upon him quite unexpectedly over the summer, in Colorado. Armstrong had an epiphany on August 9 after placing second at the Leadville Trail 100 Mountain-Bike Race—a 100-mile "Race Across the Sky," which climbs to more than 14,000 feet. That ascent, cycling upward in a crosscurrent, tripped something primal in him. "It wasn't a lightbulb going off," he says, but a realization, combined with a gradual frustration "with the rhetoric coming out of the Tour de France. Not just the Tour on TV but the domestic press, the international press, the pace, the speeds at which participants rode. It's not a secret. I mean, the pace was slow.

"Then Leadville, this kind of obscure bike race, totally kick-started my engine. For me it's always been about the process.... The process of getting there is the best part. You start the season a little out of shape, a little heavy. You get in better shape. You lose some weight. I mean you're just crafting this perfect program. For several weeks I [had] trained [for Leadville] and went riding by myself. Obviously beautiful territory and fresh air, just feeling fit, losing weight, getting strong—living a very healthy lifestyle. I thought, This might be fun to try again."

Armstrong's next Station of the Cross was to get the blessing of his L.A.F. colleagues in Austin. If his homeboys thought the Tour was a bad idea, that'd nix it. He laid it out for them this way: A segment of the population

considered him an "asterisk athlete." They believed the charges—never proven—that during his 1999 Tour de France he had used the endurance-boosting hormone EPO. (In 2006, an independent Dutch investigator, appointed by the International Cycling Union, had cleared him of doping during the 1999 Tour, but rumors, especially in France, had still dogged him.) Armstrong vowed to create a comprehensive anti-doping protocol and to undergo one of the most vigorous testings ever devised for an athlete.

In addition, he promised, "We're going to be completely transparent and open with the press. This is for the world to see.... And everybody was supportive. Bart—because he's my best friend—looked at me like, Do you really want to do this? That was the extent of his skepticism. But everybody else was like, Let's go!"

Behind it all, naturally, was not just a yellow jersey, but that yellow bracelet. He was distressed by America's halfhearted war on cancer. Under the Bush administration, the annual budgets for the National Institutes of Health (N.I.H.) and the National Cancer Institute (N.C.I.) [have] gone down. While America spends approximately $12 billion a month in Afghanistan and Iraq, the entire annual N.C.I. budget is about $5 billion. President Bush, in fact, had had the gall to invite Armstrong to his ranch in Crawford, Texas, to go for a ride—it made a good photo op—only to shy away, in Armstrong's estimation, from ramping up the cancer fight.

Armstrong, though disappointed in the administration, personally likes Bush. "I've known President Bush since '95 or '96," he says. "He was governor. My neighbors knew him and we went over there to his office.... Very likable guy in person. I mean, politics aside—a lot of people obviously don't agree with the politics—but, I mean, the guy is decent."

Armstrong gets somewhat agitated, however, when pushed about whether Bush used him as a patsy. Essentially, Armstrong claims, he was taking a page from the Bono nonprofit playbook: talk to all-powerful people. He shifts the conversation to Bill Clinton. "Look, when President Clinton was in the White House after I won the Tour, I presented him with the yellow jersey and a bike. We had seven minutes, we were told, but I think we stayed about 57. We walked around the Rose Garden, and they have this amazing magnolia tree. Epic. Massive. Huge. And I love magnolias; they're my favorite tree. And I said that's an amazing magnolia. And he just stopped in his tracks. He proceeded to give the whole history of the Rose Garden, the White House, everything he could see. It was unbelievable." The Clinton administration doubled funding to the N.I.H. in the 1990s.

Not pacified by his Clinton spiel, I press him to justify his Crawford bike ride. The Look now kicks in. "Cindy

Sheehan [the anti-war activist, whose son, a G.I., had been killed in Iraq] was there [protesting down the road from the ranch], and suddenly it was advertised—publicized—that I was going to ride there," Armstrong recalls. "We got a lot of calls about my going. 'How are you going to handle Cindy Sheehan?' 'Are you going to tell him to stop the war?' This was August of '05. We went to war in '03. I was in Europe leading up to the war and of course the war was tremendously unpopular in Europe.... I was on the record. I said, 'Listen, bad idea. We've got no business going there. We've got a lot of other stuff we need to solve.'"

Clearly Armstrong was caught in a Catch-22 situation. If he saw Sheehan in person he didn't know if he could enter the Crawford compound in good conscience. But around the same time, Sheehan's mother suffered a stroke, calling Sheehan away from her sit-in. "The anti-war people said, 'You better stop, otherwise you're in trouble.'" Armstrong recalls. "And the White House basically said, If you do stop then you better keep stopping, stay stopped. But you know what? At the end of the day, he's the president of the United States of America. He's the most powerful man in the world, and as a cancer survivor and as a very active advocate you have to go.... And let's not forget: At the end of the lunch I asked him for a billion dollars. I said, 'You need to increase the budget at the National Cancer Institute by a billion dollars, right?'"

When asked if the president ever ponied up, Armstrong says, matter-of-factly, "I never got it." As a consolation prize, though, Karl Rove phoned him; it can't get more depressing than that for a health-care advocate.

For the first time all day, Armstrong leans forward in his armchair, getting worked up. As if crystal-balling, he imagines himself as president, his aides informing him every day that 1,500 Americans have died from the illness. "Imagine if I go to sleep [in the White House] and I wake up the next day and they come in the afternoon and aides say, 'Another 1,500 died today, sir.' I can figure that out. That's a ... problem! So there's 1,500 ... 1,500 ... 1,500 ... I mean, after 20, 30, 40 years of that, people start to take that as just part of the deal. And it shouldn't be.

"If cancer got a whole new name tomorrow and a whole new set of fears associated with it and it had the toll that it does, we would act. Look at all those other things they act upon. Forget war and terror. Look at SARS. Remember the bird flu? Remember all that stuff? AIDS, people freaked. Those were new, scary issues that all of a sudden were going to come jump into your house and ruin your life.

"Obviously," he says, emphatically, "we need health-care reform in the United States. It's not a fair system. A third of the society doesn't have access to decent care. It's not right." He then goes on to outline the emergency measures America needs to put into place, sounding positively Ruschaean: "Prevention. Screening. Detection. Survivorship." But his huge beef—besides governmental lethargy and those pesky tabloids—is tobacco. According to the American Cancer Society, smoking accounts for at least 30 percent of all cancer deaths. "It's the only product you can buy, and if you follow the instructions, it will kill you," says Armstrong. "Twenty-four states and D.C. are now smokefree—we're aiming for all 50."

Somehow, Armstrong has managed to work into his schedule enough downtime to answer thousands of letters from kids with cancer and leukemia, in a personal, non-form-letter way. "These days I've been doing these video messages," Armstrong told me. "I'll sit there with a little camera and record a minute-long video and just give a shout-out to them and e-mail it. They love it. They keep it forever, show it to their family and friends."

The subject swings, inevitably, to the dreaded topic: doping. Another reason Armstrong is entering the Tour is to bury the notion, once and for all, that drugs helped propel him to victory, that his generation of cyclists were deviants. By winning the 2009 Tour, under rigid anti-doping strictures, he believes he'll forever silence the doubters. "You know, when I first came back, in '98, '99, there was a huge revenge factor," he explains. "I was basically just not wanted by the sport. And was kicked out of the French team because I was cancer sick and so I was angry at people. And I was going to come back and prove that a survivor could do that. There's a little of that revenge spirit in me now.

"There's this perception in cycling that this generation is now the cleanest generation we've had in decades, if not forever. And the generation that I raced with was the dirty generation. And, granted, I'll be totally honest with you, the year that I won the Tour, many of the guys that got 2nd through 10th, a lot of them are gone. Out. Caught. Positive Tests. Suspended. Whatever.... And so I can understand why people look at that and go, Well, [they] were caught—and you weren't? So there is a nice element here where I can come with really a completely comprehensive program and there will be no way to cheat."

Armstrong recognizes that the European press may very well be laying in wait for him, hoping he'll fail. "I didn't go out of my way to make friends with the French media," he says. "In fact, I was combative. I was unavailable, arrogant, and I was that way to a lot of them. Anybody who wrote a negative article: Done. Never speak to them again. I won't do that this time. I mean, these daily or weekly [phone conferences]? Everyone's invited. From the bitterest of rivals I've ever had in the pressroom: Get on call. If you've got a question, ask it.... They'll realize that I'm not messing around." The difference this time, he says, is that he won't be flaunting his American-ism in their faces. "The constituency that I represent," he says, "is now cancer survivors."

Lance Armstrong trains on the Spanish Canary Island of Tenerife in December 2008 in preparation for the 2009 Tour de France. © JAIME REINA/AFP/GETTY IMAGES.

Can Armstrong rehabilitate his image with the European press that easily? I was in the Netherlands at the height of the anti-Armstrong frenzy in 2005, and I wonder whether he's in for a fresh wave of pummeling. They smell the stubborn Texan in Armstrong, and it turns them off as much as the Bush doctrine. "Ultimately," he says, "the people like who they like and don't like who they don't like. They make up their own mind. The papers loved to write that I was the most hated athlete in France, but I'm the guy who rides through that kind of [stuff]. They don't sit on the bike with me and so, you know, out of 100 people, did you have 10 people throwin' [stuff] at you, yellin', 'Dopé, dopé'? Yeah. But you had 90 goin', 'Allez Lance! Allez Lance!' I can do the math on that. My approval rating is 90 percent.... I like that.

"Look," he insists, "I plan on holding a press conference [saying] I never cheated. I won seven Tour de Frances, fair and square. I'm going back."

Another obstacle Armstrong faces is having his Tour attempt written off as another Brett Favre-ean resurrection. Second—or third or fourth—acts aren't all that interesting anymore in America. But he insists this is different, since he will get no salary for the 2009 season (although his speaking fees and endorsement deals clearly won't suffer). "Everybody in cycling has a team and takes a team salary," he says. "I am essentially racing for free. No salary. No bonus. Nothing on the line.... This one's on the house. And you know what? At the end of the day, I don't need money.... Not only will I be fine, my kids will be fine, my grandkids will be fine."

Money, however, matters to his foundation. And Team Armstrong claims to have recently made a crucial allegiance with the likes of Bill Clinton, New York City mayor Michael Bloomberg, and several other eminences to be named later, who have plans to announce a global cancer summit, possibly inviting various heads of state to Paris around the time of the Tour. Armstrong insists, "France is an important country, regardless of what people in the red states say—and a good country. So you start there, and obviously you're at the hub of Europe. And you can have tons of involvement from leaders there [and] why wouldn't you have the president of the United States there?" And in two weeks, Armstrong will expound on his anti-cancer program at a Clinton Global Initiative forum in New York City.

While it all sounds rather lofty, it's really the small stuff that Armstrong's starting to sweat. He has begun a regimen of "epic workouts." Because he needs curvy mountain roads to train on (Austin only has hills), he'll be spending a lot of time in the Rockies and Solvang, California, in the coming months. "I'm doing a bunch of core stuff, power stuff in the gym," he says. "Just constantly changing [stuff] up." While Armstrong's exact strategy remains sketchy, he might race in the Amgen Tour of California in February, and the Giro d'Italia in May.

That weekend I watch Armstrong run in the Austin leg of the Nike+ Human Race, held in 25 cities worldwide to benefit L.A.F. and two other charities. The 10-kilometer race in Austin fields about 15,000 runners, who gather at twilight on a summer Sunday. (In 2007, Nike debuted a LiveStrong apparel and footwear line and pledged to donate net profits to the foundation.) Ben Harper performs near the finish line, as thousands of exhausted athletes down Evian, text-message babysitters, talk about grabbing a late dinner at a Whole Foods organic bar. These are Lance's folks—passionate and fit, singing along to "Diamonds on the Inside." Optimism is the prevailing vibe.

Armstrong, true to form, seems disappointed he didn't win the charity race. "I did awful," he says, crestfallen. "But look at Harper. He's in great shape. He wrote the best Katrina song, 'Black Rain.' I asked him to play it at the end." Every few minutes, rather healthy-looking women come over to give Armstrong platonic hugs. "I've got to get to bed soon," he says, almost relieved at the concert's end. "Up tomorrow before dawn."

I ask him what he misses most now that he's in monkish training mode. "Salsa and chips," he says. "That's it."

Two days later, I sit in on an Armstrong workout session in his two-and-a-half-car home garage. Even with the garage door open, it's 100 degrees. The brown indoor-outdoor carpeting makes the setting seem like Wayne's World. Free weights are all around. Dressed in baggy green Nike shorts, Armstrong, shirtless, runs through a sick set of pull-ups, medicine-ball exercises, and crunches, all executed at a rapid pace. Conversation is clipped with grunts and groans. I notice a scar on his upper chest where the catheter was inserted during cancer surgery.

The White Stripes are playing on the stereo. You can feel that music is a fuel to him. "From Lyle Lovett to Led Zeppelin," he says of his musical tastes. "When I'm in the garage, I put on satellite radio, like adult alternative. Elvis Costello, great, you can train with that. The next song might be Bob Dylan, great. Next song might be Coldplay, great. Next song might be Foo Fighters, great. . . . I've got 4,000 or 5,000 songs on my iPod."

Nearby, he has his separate bike garage, where cycles, including kids' bikes, hang from the wall in all shapes and sizes. There's also a 1970 black GTO convertible. He has me pick up a Madone 6.9 black cycle, a custom vehicle for riding around New York. "It's light as a feather," he says, admiringly, lifting it with ease. "Weighs about 13 or 14 pounds, due to the carbon-fiber fork."

Team Armstrong says their leader is asymmetrically negative; that is, on a scale of 1 to 10, if Lance wins the Tour de France, he'll only achieve the status of a two or three. But if he loses, he'll be a minus 1,000. Worst of all, there is no guarantee that the Tour's mandarins at the A.S.O. will allow him to race. Plagued by doping dilemmas, rider departures, team withdrawals, and chronic bickering between participants, the A.S.O. has become hyper-selective about who races. If the A.S.O. balks, there's no telling how low he'll sink.

High on top of his bookshelves, in special alcoves, are his seven blue Tour trophies. Desperately, he wants an eighth. And if for some strange reason the A.S.O. doesn't "invite" Armstrong and his team to the Tour de France, he plans on pleading his case directly to the current French president, Nicolas Sarkozy. "I've already put a call in to him," Armstrong says. "Look it up. He's said strong things about me in the past."

A couple of hours later, I do look it up. And, sure enough, Sarkozy has praised Lance Armstrong. Back in 2003, while serving as French interior minister, Sarkozy commented on how inspired he was that Armstrong had overcome cancer to repeatedly win the Tour de France. Armstrong's courage moved him. There are about eight million cancer deaths in the world annually, and Armstrong is leading the way to a new consciousness about the disease. "If we don't applaud and support him," Sarkozy once said, "who should we applaud and support?"

"I fear failure," Armstrong admits, during a quiet moment. "I have a huge phobia around failure. And that's probably a good thing. The thought of losing this thing— anything—I mean, it could be the Tour, it could be Proposition 15. We're down at the state capitol [and] these guys are debating it back and forth, amending the bill. The thing looks like it's gonna die. I mean, the tension was so high. Doug [Ulman] looks at me and goes [whisper voice], 'Man, this is fun!' And I said 'Doug, it is only fun if we win.' And for me, I think a lot of that stems from just the illness and the diagnosis and the process there. Because failure there is death. Loss there is death. And victory is living. Which people just assume they're going to do. I mean, most people—cancer survivors—don't always assume that. But I was scared. You know, from that point on, I associated loss with death. And so I didn't. It was burned in my mind forever.

"I don't like to lose in anything. Anything."

FURTHER RESOURCES

Books

Armstrong, Lance. *Every Second Counts*. New York: Broadway Books, 2003.

Hamilton, Tyler, and Daniel Coyle. *The Secret Race*. New York: Bantam Books, 2012.

Web Sites

"Lance Armstrong Tells Oprah He Doped to Win." *CBS News*, January 15, 2013. www.cbsnews.com/8301-400_162-57563952/lance-armstrong-tells-oprah-he-doped-to-win/ (accessed on March 24, 2013).

Macur, Juliet. "Armstrong Facing Two More Lawsuits." *New York Times*, March 1, 2013. www.nytimes.com/2013/03/02/sports/cycling/lance-armstrong-is-facing-another-lawsuit.html (accessed on March 24, 2013).

Makitalo, Georgia. "A Timeline of Lance Armstrong's Doping Controversy." *Yahoo! Sports*, August 27, 2012. http://sports.yahoo.com/news/timeline-lance-armstrongs-doping-controversy-155600352.html (accessed on March 24, 2013).

Schrotenboer, Brent. "Lance Armstrong Cuts Ties to Livestrong Board, Resigns from Board." *USA Today*, November 12, 2012. www.usatoday.com/story/sports/cycling/2012/11/12/lance-armstrong-resigns-livestrong-board-of-directors/1699531/ (accessed on March 24, 2013).

"Michael Phelps"

Magazine article

By: Alan Shipnuck

Date: December 8, 2008

Source: Shipnuck, Alan. "Michael Phelps." *Sports Illustrated*, December 8, 2008. http://sportsillustrated. cnn.com/vault/article/magazine/MAG1149362/index. htm (accessed on March 24, 2013.)

About the Publication: *Sports Illustrated* is an American magazine dedicated to athletic competition, primarily professional sports. The magazine's current incarnation, which began publication in 1954, was the first to provide weekly coverage and news of spectator sports, rather than traditional "lifestyle" content. It quickly became the leading publication in its field, becoming so influential that it prompted sporting arenas to adopt new designs to accommodate *Sports Illustrated*'s cameras. The magazine's most famous features are its annual "Sportsman of the Year" awards and swimsuit editions.

INTRODUCTION

Michael Phelps was one of the most successful American athletes of all time and the single most victorious Olympic competitor in the history of the games, claiming a total of seventy-one medals in major swimming competitions around the globe and frequently setting world records in a number of events.

Phelps was born on June 30, 1985, the youngest of three siblings. He grew up in suburban Towson, Maryland. Phelps began swimming competitively when he was seven years old, and by age fifteen he had become one of the youngest swimmers ever admitted to the U.S. Olympic Team. At fifteen years and nine months old, he became the youngest man to set a world swim record by narrowly beating the previous best time in the 200 meter butterfly. Under the tutelage of North Baltimore Aquatic Club coach Bob Bowman, Phelps quickly ascended the ranks of international competitive swimming, and soon found himself competing at the 2002 Pan Pacific Swimming Championships in Yokohoma, Japan. There he claimed the gold medal in the 200 and 400 meter individual medley races and the 4 × 100 meter medley relay (setting a new world record of 51.1 seconds on his leg of the race), and silver medals in the 200 meter butterfly and the 4 × 200 meter freestyle relay.

From that point onward, Michael Phelps' career would be characterized by consistent improvement and success. At the 2003 World Aquatics Championships, held in Barcelona, Spain, the young swimmer surpassed Mark Spitz to claim the record for most world-record times at a single meet, with new best times in the 100 and 200 meter butterfly, the 400 meter individual medley, and two successive 200 meter individual medley races. His incredible showing in Barcelona earned Phelps gold medals in the 200 meter butterfly, the 200 and 400 meter individual medleys, and the 4 × 100 meter medley relay, as well as silver medals in the 100 meter butterfly and the 4 × 200 meter freestyle relay. The following year, Phelps competed at his first Summer Olympic Games, held in Athens, Greece. There, he set a number of Olympic swimming records, most notably in the 400 meter individual medley race, where his time of 4:08.26 was also a world record. He claimed a total of six gold medals at those Games, including the 100 and 200 meter butterfly races, the 200 and 400 meter individual medleys, the 4 × 100 meter medley relay, and the 4 × 200 meter freestyle relay. He also won bronze medals in the 200 meter freestyle and 4 × 100 meter freestyle relay.

Phelps continued improving his times, earning overall victories at the 2005 World Aquatics Championships in Montreal, Quebec, Canada, the 2006 Pan Pacific Swimming Championships in Victoria, British Columbia, Canada, and the 2007 World Aquatics Championships in Melbourne, Australia, frequently breaking his own world records and demonstrating an unparalleled command of the sport. By the time of the 2008 Summer Olympics, held in Beijing, China, Phelps was an icon in the world of competitive swimming, widely acknowledged as the favorite before the games. He became an American popular hero after dominating his competition at the Olympics, winning a record-setting eight gold medals (100 and 200 meter butterfly races, 200 meter freestyle, 200 and 400 meter individual medleys, 4 × 100 and 4 × 200 meter freestyle relays, and 4 × 100 meter medley relay) and earning a number of record times. In one of the most dramatic moments in the history of the modern Olympic Games, Phelps beat a trash-talking Serbian competitor, Milorad Čavić, in the 100 meter butterfly by 0.01 seconds, the slimmest margin of victory ever. Six days later, his incredible split in the 4 × 100 meter medley relay brought the American team from third to first place, and his victory celebration received heavy play in the news.

At the 2009 World Aquatics Championships in Rome, Italy, Phelps predictably triumphed over his competition, claiming five gold medals and one silver and becoming the first person to ever complete the 100 meter butterfly in under fifty seconds. He won

Swimmer Michael Phelps celebrates after placing first in the men's 100m butterfly final during the Beijing Olympics in August 2008. © AP IMAGES/BERND THISSEN/PICCUTRE-ALLIANCE/DPA.

another five gold medals at the 2010 Pan Pacific Swimming Championships in Irvine, California, followed by four gold, two silver, and one bronze at the 2011 World Aquatics Championships in Shanghai, China. With his four gold and two silver medals at the 2012 Summer Olympics in London, United Kingdom, Phelps became the most decorated Olympian ever, with twenty-two total medals. He was the most successful athlete in the Olympics for three consecutive Games, and the athlete with by far the most gold-winning performances—Phelp's eighteen gold medals was double the next-highest record. He announced his retirement from competitive swimming shortly after the conclusion of the London Olympics.

SIGNIFICANCE

As the most successful Olympian of all time, the congenial Michael Phelps was an object of national pride for the United States, a nation that values athletic prowess as a chief virtue. He is credited with renewing public interest in competitive swimming, which had recently lost much of its popularity among American youth to more glamorous, lucrative sports like baseball, basketball, and football. Following the

2008 Olympics, Phelps used his celebrity and sponsorship money to create a number of aquatics-related philanthropic programs, including the Michael Phelps Foundation and the "im" project of the Boys & Girls Club. The goal of such programs is to foster youth involvement in competitive swimming and to provide facilities and equipment for aspiring swimmers.

Like most public figures, Phelps did not entirely avoid controversy. He lost a number of sponsorships after the publication of a photograph depicting Phelps smoking what appeared to be marijuana, and he earned the ire and public condemnation of some concerned parent groups when it was discovered that he was dating a stripper. He was also charged with driving while intoxicated in 2004 after being pulled over while driving his Hummer in Maryland while drunk. Phelps drew more praise than criticism, however, receiving special recognition and commendation from the governments of Maryland and the United States, as well as a special career achievement award from the Olympic Games Committee for his unprecedented performance in the Olympics. He even had a street named after him in his hometown.

Most notably, Phelps revolutionized competitive swimming by destroying time records, earning a total of thirty-nine world records (ten with relay teams). His Olympic and other international achievements were not likely to be replicated ever again, making him one of the most noteworthy athletes in modern history and one of the most celebrated Americans of the 2000s decade.

PRIMARY SOURCE

"MICHAEL PHELPS"

SYNOPSIS: This article describes swimmer Michael Phelps's Olympic domination and subsequent philanthropic activity.

The party of the year in the swimming world took place not in Beijing's Water Cube in August but in a New York City hotel ballroom the week before Thanksgiving. The occasion was the Golden Goggle Awards, the Oscars of the amphibious set, and most of the 43 members of the U.S. Olympic swim team turned out for the splashy event. With their short skirts, high heels and ripped biceps the women were visions of powerful femininity. The dudes wore their tuxedos ironically, with shaggy hair and bow ties askew. Before the awards show began, there was a rip-roaring cocktail hour. The view of midtown Manhattan from the ballroom revealed the grand old Ziegfeld Theatre, which on this night was hosting a red-carpet premiere for the latest overwrought Hollywood drama. Despite the constellation of paparazzi flashes the assembled actors couldn't match the star power at the Golden Goggles.

Mingling with a cocktail crowd that had paid as much as $1,250 a ticket to attend was Dara Torres, swimming's answer to Diane Lane—a woman who only gets better as she gets older. Aaron Peirsol, in a rakish beard, was projecting the most laid-back California cool this side of Owen Wilson. Jason Lezak, with his intensity and receding hairline, called to mind a young Ed Harris. All the assembled team members had starring roles of varying magnitude in the blockbuster swim competition at the Games of the XXIX Olympiad, but as the cocktail hour wore on, the 850 guests began scanning the crowd with increasing anxiety, searching for the one swimmer who was noticeably absent. Finally, an escalating buzz turned into a low roar, announcing the belated arrival of Michael Phelps.

Four beefy security guards couldn't hold off the crowd that instantly engulfed the 23-year-old Phelps. Middle-aged women dripping diamonds elbowed and snarled their way through the masses, desperately seeking his autograph. Teenage boys tugged at Phelps's elbow, hoping to get him to look their way for a snapshot. Phelps is undeniably a superstar now, but it is in the Jimmy Stewart vein—an unassuming everyman with

whom others feel a strong kinship. Despite the surrounding bedlam Phelps, in a custom-made Armani tux, seemed to glide effortlessly through the throng, accommodating as many fans as possible between stops to warmly embrace his Olympic teammates.

Phelps remains an ordinary kid suddenly leading an extraordinary life, and he works hard to maintain some balance. His agents always ensure that there is security on hand to help him navigate big public appearances, but otherwise Phelps likes to travel unencumbered; that morning he had taken a train up from Baltimore by himself, only partially disguised by a droopy, Spitzian mustache that he was overly proud of (and later would be crestfallen to have to shave off to look presentable for the awards show). Phelps sat undisturbed in a commuter car as he fiddled around on a laptop with a Wi-Fi card, and upon arriving in New York he made his way through Penn Station and flagged down a yellow cab on the street without a single autograph request, a 21st-century Mr. Smith arriving in his Washington, with iPod. "You can't stop living your life," he says.

Once the Golden Goggle ceremonies began, Phelps was seated between his mother, Debbie, and his older sister Hilary, who in the Beijing drama were supporting actresses, watched voyeuristically by TV cameras as they lived and died in the stands with every race. The Goggles began with a rousing Olympic highlights package shown on huge screens at the front of the ballroom. "To this day I'm not sure the magnitude of what happened over there has hit me," says Phelps, and here was another chance to relive it. As the unforgettable images from Beijing played out, Debbie rubbed her son's back softly, and she and Hilary and Michael occasionally exchanged long, meaningful glances. By the time the video was over, enough emotion had been summoned that all three Phelpses were blinking back tears.

To the surprise of no one, Phelps collected much of the hardware, accepting the awards for Male Athlete of the Year, Male Performance of the Year and Relay of the Year with heartfelt speeches in which he thanked his family, coach Bob Bowman and his teammates, and expressed how proud he was to wear the Stars and Stripes. But asked later to pick out the highlight of the evening, Phelps didn't hesitate: "Having a relatively peaceful dinner with my mom and sister. That never happens anymore."

No sooner had the awards program ended than a mob of Sharpie- and camera-phone-wielding guests encircled Phelps, knowing this was their last chance to take home a piece of him. When a chair was knocked over in the crush, the hired muscle grabbed Phelps and hustled him out of the building. He didn't even have time to say a proper goodbye to his mom, who looked around the ballroom and wondered aloud, "What just happened here?"

Olympic gold medal champion Michael Phelps arrives at the USA Swimming Foundation Golden Goggles Awards ceremony on November 22, 2009, with his mother, Debbie Phelps (left), and his sister, Hilary Phelps. © AP IMAGES/JASON REDMOND.

What happened is that for eight days in August, Debbie Phelps's son turned the Beijing Olympics into a serialized thriller with nightly installments that played out in prime time. Eight gold medals and seven world records would have been more than enough to secure his stardom, but Phelps's performance was made all the more unforgettable by two images for the ages: his primal scream punctuating an improbable U.S. comeback in the 4 × 100-meter freestyle relay on the second night of coverage, and the heart-stopping, fingertip-bending photo finish in the 100 butterfly for his penultimate gold. In the midst of a contentious presidential election and the first signs of a faltering economy, Phelps brought Americans together by the tens of millions, the TV serving as a portal to a faraway land and the outer limits of athletic achievement.

As a spectator sport swimming has always resided in the margins, and even during the Olympics it is often overshadowed by gymnastics and track. But in China,

Phelps turned his every race into can't-miss television. "The Beijing Olympics was the most watched event in American history," says Dick Ebersol, chairman of NBC Sports, referring to the 215 million U.S. viewers who tuned in over 17 days, "and it was almost entirely because of this wunderkind from Baltimore. What he accomplished transcended sport and became a cultural phenomenon."

With the finals of Phelps's races broadcast live between 10 and 11:30 p.m. Eastern time, "swim hangover" became an acceptable excuse for showing up late for work. And Phelps dominated the daylight hours as well. In office cubicles and dorm rooms and Wi-Fi'd coffee shops tech-savvy sports fans monitored Phelps's early-morning heat results and downloaded his races. During the Games nbcolympics.com logged 1.3 billion page views and 75 million viewings of video clips; among the 10,000 Olympic competitors, Phelps accounted for 20% of all athlete-specific traffic.

Phelpsmania was felt most acutely in the hometown that gave rise to a provincial nickname—the Baltimore Bullet—that he has since outgrown. Baltimore had the highest Olympic television ratings of any market in the country on the night of his first final, and when Phelps swam for his record eighth gold the city's NBC affiliate drew a 59 share. (Three out of every five televisions in the metropolitan area were tuned to the Games.) Phelps's march on history became a communal event: When a Baltimore Ravens preseason game was due to end about half an hour before Phelps's final race of the Games, the club invited fans to stick around M&T Bank Stadium to watch their hero on the JumboTron. Thousands did, and even the baddest man in Baltimore got caught up in the spectacle. "I could feel it in my insides," says linebacker Ray Lewis. "It was amazing to see that, to watch someone who has made their mind up to be that great. It was an electric moment."

Merely watching him wasn't enough for those Baltimore fans who needed something tangible to bring them closer to the story. One supplicant showed up at the Meadowbrook Aquatic Center, where Phelps competed growing up, and asked to dip a vial in the pool, to take home a few ounces of this holy water. Those seeking sustenance flocked to Phelps's favorite greasy spoon, Pete's Grille, where his traditional pretraining breakfast was offered during the Olympics as a $19.95 special: a three-egg omelet, a bowl of grits, three slices of French toast with powdered sugar, three chocolate-chip pancakes and three fried-egg sandwiches with cheese, lettuce, tomato, fried onions and mayo. "Usually it was a group of people who'd order it," says Dave Stahl, the owner of Pete's Grille. "The one guy who tried it by himself complained of pretty serious stomach pain."

Phelps's calorie intake may seem superhuman, and his 6'4", 185-pound body may recall Greek statuary, but fans are also drawn to him by a goofy grin and oversized ears that led to his being called Spock on the school bus. (He was also teased about a slight lisp he still has and is self-conscious about.) Being a prodigy in the pool since an early age did not translate into a carefree life. Diagnosed with attention deficit hyperactivity disorder in sixth grade, Phelps felt embarrassed to have to slink to the nurse's office each day to take his Ritalin. (He weaned himself off the drug, with his doctor's blessing, after a year.) He was also deeply affected by his parents' divorce when he was seven, and ever since he has had only infrequent contact with his father; Fred Phelps, who lives in Baltimore, was not in Beijing.

That Michael Phelps turns out to be imperfect is what made it so easy to think of him as one of us, only with a better dolphin kick. Says Debbie, "Michael was invited into people's homes night after night—into their living rooms, to the dinner table with them, into their bedrooms. They lived with him and his quest, and it became a very personal relationship."

The American public became so smitten with Phelps that NBC announced it will offer the first-ever live coverage of swimming's world championships next summer and also will broadcast the U.S. nationals in '09, '10 and '11. "When Michael was 15, he told me he wanted to change the sport of swimming," says Cathy Lears Bennett, the instructor for Meadowbrook's swim school who taught a seven-year-old Phelps to swim. "It was like, Yeah, right, who told you to say that, kid? But he's always had a vision that swimming could become important to American fans."

It is for elevating his sport—and all of us out of our seats—with a beguiling grace and humility that *SI* honors Phelps with its 55th Sportsman of the Year award. "It was a pretty good year," Phelps said at the Golden Goggles. "Hopefully there's more to come." There is so much more. The 2012 London Olympics beckon, but going forward Phelps's legacy will no longer be measured in medals.

It is 8 AM on a Sunday in north Baltimore, and the deserted streets are buffeted by a bitter November wind. All the kids are inside; no doubt some are still snoozing and others are watching cartoons or playing video games, but in the steamy indoor pool at Meadowbrook six dozen diehards, ages 11 to 19, in LONDON 2012 caps are streaking back and forth, a riot of churning arms and legs creating a cacophony of shouting and splashing. Prowling the pool deck is Bob Bowman, gulping coffee and seemingly monitoring every swimmer at once. To the untrained eye all of the kids look pretty much the same as they turn their laps, but Bowman says, "I can show you which ones are the five-star talents, the four-star, the no-star.... "

He stops to bark at some boys roughhousing on the edge of the pool. After they settle down, Bowman says, "Ten years ago that would have been Michael."

"Pushing kids into the pool? That's nothing," says Phelps. "I got busted for much worse than that."

It was at Meadowbrook in 1996 that Phelps, an unbridled 11-year-old, met his match in Bowman, a onetime college swimmer who was channeling his considerable passion into coaching the competitive team that trained there, the North Baltimore Aquatic Club. Though no one in the Phelps camp likes to use the term, Bowman became a father figure to young Michael, and the importance of that relationship helps explain Phelps's strong feelings for Meadowbrook. "There were a lot of friends and some very good role models for him here," says Lears Bennett, who began teaching at Meadowbrook in '64, when she was 13, and remains the director of its learn-to-swim program. "It was a safe place for him. There was a comfort, a familiarity. He felt good about himself here."

The Bowman-Phelps bond long ago transcended a teacher-student relationship. At the Golden Goggles, as he was accepting his third straight Coach of the Year award, Bowman tried to put into words his feelings for Phelps. When he choked up, he merely patted his heart and it was all he could do to say four words: "Michael, I love you."

Since the Olympics their relationship has taken on another dimension, as they are the only partners in Aquatic Ventures, LLC, which last month took a controlling interest in Meadowbrook and the North Baltimore Aquatic Club. When Bowman left Meadowbrook after the 2004 Athens Olympics to become men's coach at the University of Michigan, Phelps (who had won the first six of his Olympic-record 14 career golds at those Games) followed him, and Ann Arbor remained their training base through Beijing. Afterward, Phelps felt the pull of home, and Bowman followed him back to Baltimore. Meadowbrook is where Bowman will train Phelps for the 2012 Olympics, and they have grand plans for a 78-year-old facility that has a lot of character (a polite way of putting it). "We want to turn it into one of the best places to train in the country," says Phelps. "We want to attract the best swimmers, have the best facilities, the best environment. Bob and I want the best of everything. That's just our personalities."

There is plenty of aesthetic work to be done, but even with a 50-meter outdoor pool that is open from Memorial Day through September, Meadowbrook can't accommodate many new swimmers; there are already 1,000 year-round family memberships and another 500 or

Michael Phelps holds his eighth gold medal in pride at the Beijing Olympics in August 2008. © AP IMAGES/MARK J. TERRILL.

so in the summer. When Phelps resumes serious training next month, he will sometimes find himself in a lane next to kids in swim diapers or seniors trying to loosen up arthritic joints. Locally, there has been a lot of speculation about the possibility of Aquatic Ventures' buying a boarded-up ice rink that abuts the property; knock down the rink and the land would offer Meadowbrook enough space to add a couple of new pools. All Phelps will say is that "there are a million ideas right now, and it is going to take a little time to sort everything out."

But turning Meadowbrook into a destination for elite swimmers is only part of Phelps's vision. Increasing participation rates among kids around the country and expanding their access to the water is one of the primary goals of the nascent Michael Phelps Foundation, the seed money for which came from Phelps's donating the $1 million bonus Speedo gave him for winning his record eight golds. At the Golden Goggles the host USA Swimming Foundation played a video that cited drowning as the second-leading cause of accidental death among five- to 14-year-olds in the U.S. Listening intently, Phelps responded with a few violent shakes of his head that could have been roughly translated as, Not on my watch.

"Hearing that, it's shocking," he says. "It needs to change. The reason I started swimming was water safety, pure and simple. I have a passion for keeping kids safe. My mission is to teach as many as I can to swim. It's not about chasing medals—you never know when you're going to be put in a situation that's life or death."

Phelps has long gravitated toward children. Going back to his early high school years he was a regular celebrity guest at the Boys and Girls Club in Aberdeen, Md. "Children know if you're not being real with them, and they respond to Michael because everything he does is from the heart," says Darlene Lilly, who oversees the Aberdeen club. "A few years ago we had an event to honor him, and he seemed so happy after all the cameras and all the adults left because he got to go into the gym with the kids and play basketball, Foosball and all sorts of games for what seemed like hours."

Perhaps because he was regularly hazed by the older swimmers he competed against—during practice a couple of the bigger boys would toss him from lane to lane like a beach ball—Phelps has a knack for befriending those who might benefit from a little extra attention. He has long been close to Mason Surhoff, 16, who is autistic and who trains at Meadowbrook to swim the 50 and 100 freestyle and 50 back in the Special Olympics. Phelps invented a game in which Mason wears a Velcro belt that attaches to a rubber resistance cord. While a brawny adult stands on one side of the pool holding the end of the cord, Phelps tows Mason to the opposite side. Then Phelps lets the boy go, and Mason shoots across the top of the water shrieking and flapping his arms wildly. "The look on his face, it's beyond priceless," says Phelps. He has also taught Mason how to spritz water out of a pylon by releasing it from the bottom of the pool.

"It's very juvenile stuff, obviously," says Mason's mom, Polly, with a laugh, "but he loves it. His relationship with Michael is very important to him. He takes a long time to warm up to people, and many have a hard time relating to him. His speech, his actions, they're very different, and a lot of people don't know how to react. Michael could care less about all that. He has such a young spirit, and there is a goofiness about him that is so attractive to kids."

Mason is a savant who long ago memorized large swaths of The Baseball Encyclopedia, including the statistics of his dad, B.J., a former major league leftfielder. Now he is committing to memory Phelps's myriad records. Inspired by Mason, Phelps has taped public-service announcements for and donated money to the advocacy group Pathfinders for Autism. At the height of the post-Beijing hysteria Phelps cleared his schedule to model clothing at a Pathfinders benefit in Baltimore.

Reaching out seems to come naturally to a swimmer noted for his vast wingspan. In late 2004 Phelps made his only public misstep when he ran a stop sign in Salisbury, Md., and was charged with DUI. (He pleaded guilty and was sentenced to 18 months' probation.) He confronted the fallout forthrightly, with public apologies and a heartfelt talk at the Aberdeen Boys and Girls Club about taking responsibility for your actions. Not long after the DUI made news, the first Golden Goggle Awards ceremony was held, and NBC's Ebersol received an award to open the night. He did not have prepared remarks, and when he stepped onstage he locked eyes with Phelps, sitting at a table in the front row. They were only casual acquaintances, yet Ebersol dedicated his speech to the young swimmer. "People were being pretty tough on Michael right then, and I said that the swimming world should be proud of him because of his great character," recalls Ebersol. "Yes, he made a mistake, but he took the heat in the same way he wins big races—with class, with dignity, without ego."

By the time Ebersol left the dais, Debbie Phelps was crying and Michael, too, was openly emotional.

A couple of weeks later Ebersol and his sons, Charlie and Teddy, were in a private plane that crashed shortly after takeoff in icy conditions. Fourteen-year-old Teddy was killed, along with two crew members. Ebersol broke his back. At Teddy's funeral in Connecticut, Ebersol was startled to see Phelps, who had flown in from Michigan. That was the beginning of a close friendship. "I'm not a crier," says Ebersol, "but every time he won a race in Beijing, I found myself weeping, because when I think of Michael, I think of my son."

The Olympics also had a powerful resonance for the Hansen family, who live in the Baltimore suburb of Timonium and first came in contact with Phelps in the fall of 2002. Stevie Hansen, then seven, was a promising age-group swimmer who was facing surgery to remove a brain tumor. Through Bowman the family asked if Stevie could meet his idol, and the day before the surgery Phelps went to the Hansens' house. He and Stevie shot hoops in the driveway and compared their favorite junk foods. After the operation, while Stevie was recovering in the hospital, Phelps sent balloons and a basket of deliciously unhealthy treats. The next summer Phelps surprised Stevie by showing up at one of his swim meets, and the boy raced across the pool deck to leap into his hero's arms. Phelps later borrowed a suit and swam the anchor leg in a parents-and-coaches relay.

Stevie would occasionally sit on the edge of the Meadowbrook pool watching Phelps practice, and Phelps kept tabs on the boy after he left for Ann Arbor. Stevie continued to swim even as his body was ravaged by more tumors. In April 2007 his health took a dramatic turn for the worse. Phelps rushed back to Maryland but because of a delayed flight didn't arrive at the Hansen home until after midnight. Stevie was so heavily medicated he couldn't be roused, but Phelps stayed for a couple of hours, talking softly to him while the boy slept. "Michael never let go of his hand the whole time," says Stevie's mom, Betsy. "To see this big, strong guy be so tender, it was just incredibly touching." Before he left, Phelps whispered to Stevie that he would win a medal for him in Beijing, and that he would try to make it a gold.

Stevie died a month later. Phelps went to the memorial service and provided a huge bouquet of flowers in purple, Stevie's favorite color.

As the Hansen family gathered in front of the TV for Phelps's first final in Beijing, the 400 individual medley, the promise from a year earlier was on everyone's mind. "That race was so emotional for us," says Betsy of sitting with her husband, Steve, and their 11-year-old daughter, Grace. "Watching Michael swim to the gold, I just cried and cried the whole time. I was so happy for him, but of course it was bittersweet that Stevie wasn't there to help us cheer for him."

Half a world away someone else also thought of Stevie immediately after the 400 IM. "I had promised him I'd win a medal," Phelps says, "and it meant a lot to me to do it for him."

Grace is a swimmer, too, and a good one. During a recent meet she set personal bests in six of her eight events. If Phelps's goal is to inspire the next generation of swimmers, Grace is proof that he's doing a pretty good job of it. "I got into swimming because of Stevie," she says. "Now I'm motivated to be the best I can be because of Michael."

The recent Thanksgiving holiday was the first since 2004 that Phelps got to enjoy with his family, because while in Ann Arbor he was unwilling to interrupt his training to go home. "Last year was the worst," says Hilary. "We called and he had just gotten back from the pool and was eating takeout Chinese all by himself. It broke my heart."

Besides home cooking, Phelps says the best part of returning to Baltimore is having his mom and two older sisters close enough for spontaneous visits. Hilary, who is single, works for an environmental group in Washington; Whitney, who lives with her husband and two children in Rockville, Md., is a recruiter in finance and accounting. The Phelps clan has always been tight-knit and fiercely loyal, but Michael is leaning on them now more than ever, he says, because "they keep things normal."

Since the Olympics his life has been a blur of nonstop business meetings, corporate engagements and media appearances, highlighted by hosting the season premiere of *Saturday Night Live* on Sept. 13 and being a presenter at the MTV Video Music Awards that same month. Although he is not a natural in front of the camera, Phelps feels he can't say no to too many opportunities. "I do feel an obligation to promote the sport," he says. "It's not even about me. I just think it's cool that a swimmer—any swimmer—is hosting *SNL*."

Though he's used to getting mobbed at swimcentric events such as the Golden Goggles, Phelps has only come to understand the magnitude of his new fame as he has ventured into the wider world over the last few months. "The after-party at the MTV awards was a tent with a thousand people in it," says Phelps's longtime agent, Peter Carlisle. "When Michael walked in, there was this incredible crush. The security people looked a little panicky, and they quickly hustled Michael into the VIP room. There were maybe 100 people in there, and a significant number of them you recognized immediately. Again, same thing—nonstop autographs and pictures. So the security guys grab Michael again and take him to what I guess was the VVIP area. There's about a dozen people in there, and it's definitely A-list: Paris Hilton, the Jonas brothers, Demi Moore, people like that. When we get in there, it's like, Ah, now we can take a breath. Then the same thing happened again. He's just instantly surrounded, and out come the cameras and pens! Michael just looked at me like, 'Man, can you believe this?' It was pretty surreal."

Phelps remains admirably down to earth, but he is not above occasionally cashing in on his new celebrity. Having burned innumerable hours between training sessions playing online poker, he eagerly accepted an offer from the Maloof brothers, the Las Vegas casino magnates, to host him and two dozen friends for an ultimate guys' weekend shortly after Beijing. Along for the ride was Steve Skeen, a friend since fourth grade who now works in his family's construction business in Baltimore. "The whole VIP treatment, that was something new," says Skeen. Phelps usually brings his trademark intensity to the poker table—on another visit to Vegas, in October, he finished ninth in a field of 187 contestants— but accompanied by his entourage he was happy to relax among his admirers, who ranged from cocktail waitresses in Playboy bunny outfits to glistening sunbathers by the pool. "There was definitely more female attention," says Skeen. "Michael is a shy guy in general, but he was having fun with it."

It is a sign of his crossover appeal that Phelps's love life has been chronicled by the mainstream gossip purveyors. In October TMZ.com had a couple of pictures of him squiring a former Miss California USA contestant. Last month *People* (which included him on its recent list of the Sexiest Men Alive) reported that he has been dating a Vegas cocktail waitress, and some racy pictures showing her heavily tattooed torso quickly made the rounds on the Internet. Phelps is embarrassed by this kind of attention, and forcing a laugh at the inevitable follow-up, he says, "I'm single. That's the million-dollar question everyone seems to want answered."

After Phelps won his record eight golds, Carlisle told *The Wall Street Journal* that the accomplishment would be worth $100 million to Phelps in lifetime endorsements. The deals are already rolling in. In addition to his pre-Olympic contracts with AT&T, Hilton, Kellogg's and Omega, Phelps has signed to endorse Disney, Guitar Hero, Hewlett-Packard and Subway among others.

Phelps is extremely loyal to all of his sponsors, but there's no doubt which endorsement he's most excited about. He recently signed with an Italian company that will develop a video game starring his likeness. "How cool is that?" Phelps says, sounding like a big kid, which in many ways he still is. "I grew up playing video games, and I can't say I ever thought I'd see one featuring a swimmer." The game is still in the conceptual stage, but, Phelps says, "it's not going to be just boring laps in a pool; there will be a rescue element and some other things people might not expect."

Even as his business portfolio expands, Phelps's only recent splurge has been new rims and a new grill for his 2007 black Range Rover. Bowman bought Phelps's previous Rover at a deep discount, and the coach says, "I had to de-pimp it. I took off the running boards, lightened the tint on the windows and removed that ridiculous sound system. I didn't really need it to listen to NPR."

In the fall of 2007 Phelps spent $1.7 million on a four-story bachelor pad with expansive views of Baltimore's Inner Harbor, but he is still getting moved in, to say the least. The walls are bare, though a lot of sports memorabilia—his and that of other athletes—is piled up on the floor. He has a mattress but no bed frame, and the rest of the furniture consists basically of a dining table and an old couch. "I would like to trick out the pad," he says in hip-hop inflected patois, "but I haven't been home for more than a few days in a row since the Olympics, so it hasn't happened yet." He has his eye on a five-by-nine-foot flat-screen television that would nearly cover one wall, but his only recent purchases have been junk food in bulk at Costco. (Rice Krispie Treats appear to be a staple of his diet.)

Furnishing the house may pose some challenges, but getting resettled in Baltimore is made easier by a core group of friends that go back to high school and before. By now they're inured to Phelps's success—after all, the guy threw the ceremonial first pitch at a Baltimore Orioles game when he was 15, after becoming the U.S.'s youngest male Olympian in 68 years. "I was on Facebook the other day," says Erin Lears, a lifelong friend and the daughter of Phelps's former swim teacher, "and the top two fan groups were Barack Obama and Michael Phelps. It's like, Huh?" Having grown up swimming with Phelps and watching him compete, Lears was immunized against the Phelps fever that swept the country during the Olympics. "Honestly, it felt like another swim meet to me," she says. "It was just Michael doing his thing. Yet again."

But blasé intimates aside, it is hard to overstate the civic pride Phelps has brought to Baltimore. In October some 30,000 locals turned out in neighboring Towson for a parade in his honor. A few weeks later Ravens quarterback Joe Flacco dressed as Phelps for Halloween. (Lacking the courage to don a Speedo, Flacco went with an Olympic jacket and faux gold medals.) It was three days after the presidential election that the *Baltimore Sun* broke the news of Phelps's new business relationship with Meadowbrook, bumping an Obama story off page one. "Michael is as big a franchise for us as the Orioles or Ravens," says the *Sun*'s assistant managing editor for sports, Tim Wheatley.

It takes the perspective of another Baltimore sports idol and native son to truly explain the ardor. "We're tickled to death he's come home," says Cal Ripken Jr., the Hall of Fame infielder who was born in nearby Havre de Grace, spent 21 seasons with the Orioles and still resides in suburban Baltimore. "Sports has a unique way of branding a city, and Michael has brought that pride. He has become a worldwide symbol of excellence, of achievement, and he's ours. We claim him."

"Baltimore has always had a complex because it's not Washington or New York. It's not even Philadelphia," says Pulitzer Prize–winning writer Richard Ben Cramer, who cut his teeth as a reporter at the *Sun*. "The fans are used to getting snubbed—the Colts left, the Bullets left. A guy like Phelps could have gone Hollywood, but instead he's coming back. People like that. The most important thing to a Baltimore sports fan is fidelity."

"It's a blue-collar, working-class town, so most of the sports heroes are not flashy guys," says Academy Award–winning director Barry Levinson, who has set four of his films in his native Baltimore, including the seminal coming-of-age movie *Diner*. (He also owns a small piece of the Orioles.) "Johnny U, Ripken, Brooks Robinson—they were dedicated to the craft, not flamboyant. They just got it done. Phelps is that kind of athlete. Forget the medals. What people respect about him is that he just shows up every day and does the work. That's what Baltimore is all about."

Emerging from the water after the photo shoot for this story, at the New York Athletic Club in late November,

Phelps said with a smile, "That's the most time I've spent in a pool since Beijing." He meant it, too.

"We were talking before the shoot," said Debbie, "and Michael said, 'I hope they don't make me take my shirt off because I've lost my six-pack. I'm getting fat.' I said, 'Michael, don't talk to me about fat—you still have no butt!'"

The long sabbatical after the Olympics was designed to allow Phelps to have some fun and build his brand, but he also needed to decompress from the crushing pressure of Beijing. "For six years he had been living with the quest for eight golds," says Bowman. "We're both like ER nurses in that we thrive on the stress, but it wasn't until Beijing was over that I think we both realized what a weight that was. I think we could both finally breathe again."

The plan has always been for Phelps to resume training in January, but, he says, "I'm starting to get a little antsy."

"He's already asked me how long it will take to get back to his top level, which is a good sign," says Bowman. "The formula is that it takes two days in the pool for every day you miss. So we're looking at about six months to get back to where he was."

That schedule would have Phelps peaking for the world championships, July 18 through Aug. 2 in Rome. Actually, most of the pressure to be ready for the worlds is coming from Debbie. "My mom has already told me I have to make the team because she wants to go to Rome," says Phelps, rolling his eyes. "I told her I would just send her there on a vacation, but she was like, 'Watching you swim is always part of my vacation.' So now I have to get back in shape."

Ask him if he's afraid that he's lost his edge, and the usually laconic Phelps sits up straight, looks you in the eye and says with some steel in his voice, "When I have to turn the switch back on, I know I can. All I have to do is put my mind to something and that's it, it's done."

If Phelps's dedication is a given in the long run-up to the 2012 Games, there is still some uncertainty about what events he will swim in London. Just as Tiger Woods has won the Masters with three different golf swings, Phelps feels compelled to tinker just to make sure he remains fully engaged. He and Bowman are in agreement that he will drop one race from his Beijing program—the 400 IM, even though Phelps set the world record. He will continue swimming the 200 freestyle and will add a new event, the 100 free. In the months to come Phelps and Bowman will decide between the 100 butterfly or 100 back, and the 200 back or 200 IM, and whether to continue with the arduous 200 butterfly. Throw in the

U.S. swimming star Michael Phelps and his longtime coach, Bob Bowman, in March 2007. © AP IMAGES/MARK BAKER.

three relays, and Phelps should be chasing at least seven more golds in London, although he likes to needle Bowman that he may turn himself into a sprinter so he can add the 50 free, just for the heck of it.

"He can't work any harder," says Bowman. "He can't get much stronger. Maybe he can improve his technique a little, but not much. It's really just change for the sake of change."

Going forward, Bowman says, "I'm totally willing to loosen up. Let's be honest: Michael's place in history is secure. Everything from here on out is just gravy. I'd like for him to enjoy it a little more."

"Yeah, right," says Phelps. "There's absolutely no chance he's going to mellow out. Bob has one speed: Go! I'm the one who knows how to relax, not him."

"Did Michael really say that?" asks Debbie, amused. "Mark my words: All it will take is one so-so meet, and he will be back at it full force. He doesn't know any other way. He never has."

Sometime shortly after New Year's, Phelps will awaken in the wee hours and leave the enveloping warmth of his bed to make the short journey through the freezing city to Meadowbrook, resuming his solitary pursuit of unmatched excellence. "I hate to train alone," he says. "It can be lonely."

But whether or not there is somebody in the lane next to him, Phelps does not swim alone. He is guided by the inspiration of Mason Surhoff and propelled by the memory of Stevie Hansen. Though he can't hear them, the kids at the Aberdeen Boys and Girls Club cheer him on, and somewhere Dick Ebersol still pulls for him. Phelps's friends and his family and the people of Baltimore are with him, as they always have been.

By championing the cause of water safety Phelps could save many lives, and the trajectory of others will be changed merely by his inspirational example. In 2012, when we are deep into another presidential election and facing challenges that have yet to reveal themselves, Phelps will once again unite a nation. He does not swim alone. He swims for all of us.

FURTHER RESOURCES

Books

Abrahamson, Alan, and Phelps, Michael. *No Limits: The Will to Succeed.* New York: Free Press, 2009.

Cazeneuve, Brian, and Phelps, Michael. *Michael Phelps: Beneath the Surface.* Champaign, IL: Sports Publishing, LLC, 2009.

Web Sites

"Michael Phelps." *USA Swimming.* www.usaswimming.org/ DesktopModules/BioViewManaged.aspx?personid= 4beec290-d7ae-483d-a512-36b18a4e022a&TabId=1453& Mid=10312 (accessed on March 24, 2013).

"Michael Phelps Archive." *Baltimore Sun.* www.baltimore-sun.com/sports/olympics/phelps/ (accessed on March 24, 2013).

"Michael Phelps Biography." *Bio.* www.biography.com/ people/michael-phelps-345192 (accessed on March 24, 2013).

"The Takedown"

Magazine article

By: S. L. Price

Date: May 18, 2009

Source: Price, S. L. "The Takedown." *Sports Illustrated*, May 18, 2009. http://sportsillustrated.cnn.com/vault/article/magazine/MAG1155392/4/index.htm#top (accessed on March 24, 2013).

About the Magazine: Founded in 1954 by *Time* magazine publisher Henry Luce, *Sports Illustrated* was the first magazine with a circulation over one million to win the National Magazine Award for General Excellence twice. Though Luce's idea to publish a magazine solely dedicated to sports was a joke among his peers, the visionary called "the most influential private citizen of his day" stayed true to his business intuition and it became the premiere sports magazine, an honor it still holds in the twenty-first century. Owned now by Time Warner, the magazine boasts a circulation of 3.5 million, and its most popular issue is its annual Swimsuit Issue, which accounts for about

7 percent of the magazine's annual revenue, according to *Forbes*.

INTRODUCTION

The early 2000s were transitional years in the sport of men's tennis. Several tennis greats— Americans Pete Sampras (2002) and Andre Agassi (2006) among them—retired, and few newcomers broke into the top ranks. In 2003, Swiss-born Roger Federer won his first Grand Slam singles title at Wimbledon (the Grand Slam consists of four major annual events: Australian Open, French Open, Wimbledon, and U.S. Open); he was just twenty-one years old at the time. Numerous other victories on the court earned Federer the number 2 spot in the world, behind Andy Roddick. The following year, Federer won three Grand Slam singles titles, a first in his career and a feat that had not been achieved since 1988. At the age of twenty-two, Federer finished 2004 ranked number 1 in the world. He maintained that position for four consecutive years. In 2009, he won the French Open and Wimbledon, and many tennis players, both active and retired, considered him the greatest tennis player to ever pick up a racket.

Rafael Nadal played tennis in his native Spain until turning pro at the age of fifteen. Two years later, Nadal made it to round three at Wimbledon. Not since Boris Becker in 1984 had a male reached that level at such a young age. Nadal won the French Open the first four times he played it, and in 2003, he won the Association of Tennis Professionals' Newcomer of the Year Award. The following year, Nadal played the top-ranked Federer at the Miami Masters. It was their first match, and Nadal beat the reigning champ in straight sets, one of only six players to score a victory over Federer that year. The match marked the beginning of a friendly rivalry between the two men, and one in which Nadal would finish the decade as winner.

Throughout the next few years, the rivals shared both victory and defeat. Nadal won his first Grand Slam title in 2005 and defeated Federer in order to do so. They played one another in six matches the following year, and Nadal won four of them. In 2007, the opponents faced off five times, and Federer claimed victory in three of the matches. Nadal won all four matches against Federer in 2008, the same year he won his fourth consecutive French Open title and an Olympic gold medal. For the third year in a row, Nadal and Federer met in the final round of Wimbledon in what was the most anticipated match of their rivalry. They played the longest final round in the history of that tournament (4 hours, 48 minutes),

Tennis rivals Rafael Nadal (left) and Roger Federer greet each other before a tennis match in Qatar on January 4, 2009.
© AP IMAGES.

and Nadal finally won in the fifth set, in the rain, in the dark. The event drew the highest television ratings since 1991 "for a Wimbledon men's final not involving an American," reported ESPN. The relentless Nadal finished the year ranked Number 1.

This back-and-forth rivalry gave neither athlete the edge. Each was known for his own strengths and weaknesses, and each played better on specific court surfaces (Federer on grass and hard, Nadal on clay). Federer, always the more outwardly confident of the two—and older, by nearly five years—refused to publicly acknowledge the possibility that Nadal could one day dethrone him from his Number 1 rank in the world. This *Sports Illustrated* article investigates both the personal and professional aspects of the Federer-Nadal rivalry.

SIGNIFICANCE

The S. L. Price article predicted that Nadal and Federer might meet once again across the net at the 2009 French Open and even declared Nadal the "prohibitive favorite" should that happen. It never did. Nadal lost in the fourth round to Robin Soderling, his first loss at a French Open. Federer walked away the champion of the event after beating Soderling; it was his fourteenth Grand Slam title.

Soon after, Nadal withdrew from another tournament when it was confirmed that he was suffering from tendinitis in both knees. He then withdrew from the 2009 Wimbledon Championship, becoming the first champion not to defend his title in eight years. Federer, predictably, won Wimbledon, and Nadal was unseated from his Number 1 world ranking.

The rivalry continued into the second decade of the twenty-first century, and the end of 2010 found Nadal back on top. His return to the Number 1 ranking made him the third player (behind Ivan Lendl in 1989 and Federer in 2009) to ever regain the top spot after having lost it. Federer finished the 2010 as world Number 2.

PRIMARY SOURCE

"THE TAKEDOWN"

SYNOPSIS: This article explores the rivalry between tennis superstars Rafael Nadal and Roger Federer.

The number that best summed up Roger Federer in his prime? There are plenty to choose from: the record 237 consecutive weeks at No. 1, the 13 major titles, the 10 straight Grand Slam finals and 19 straight semifinals. But let's try this number: zero. Because the most astonishing thing about Federer's four-year run atop pro tennis, from February 2004 to August 2008, may be the difference between his exalted estimation of his own skills and what he actually did. There was none.

For those inclined to deflate the self-adoring, though, Federer didn't present an easy target. His offhand tone imbued the most conceited comments—from the frequent "I was always so talented" to this reading of the crowd at his 2007 U.S. Open matches: "I have the feeling they're watching greatness"—with genial detachment. Hearing Federer speak of himself was like listening to a professor describe, while paring his fingernails, the work of his most brilliant student.

And even if some were irked by such statements, could they really dispute them? Federer was only echoing the tributes of John McEnroe and Rod Laver, who hailed him as the game's new gold standard; Pete Sampras, who predicted that Federer would shatter his record of 14 major singles titles and finish with 19; and Andre Agassi, who in 2005 said Federer "plays a game in a very special way. I haven't seen it before." Everyone agreed: Federer would end up the best male player ever. His talent was indeed extraordinary. Greatness was exactly what we were seeing.

Then, late last spring, all that abruptly changed. Federer woke up in Paris on Sunday, June 8, with history in his grasp. Besides having won 12 Grand Slam titles, he was about to play his third straight final at the French Open, the lone major he had never won. If Federer's career had ended right there, before he faced world No. 2 Rafael Nadal, a convincing case could be made that he had already surpassed Pistol Pete, who never reached one singles final at Roland Garros.

But Federer's career didn't end there. By sundown that day he had suffered the worst loss of his 10-year career, a 6–1, 6–3, 6–0 thrashing. Hardly anyone had seen it coming; though Nadal was the three-time defending French Open champion, Federer had beaten him on clay the year before in Hamburg—by a score that also included a third-set bagel—and had won the Australian Open, the last five Wimbledons and the last four U.S. Opens. "I can beat Nadal on all surfaces: clay, grass, indoor, hard," Federer said in the summer of 2007. "And once you beat a player three or four times, you know you can beat him every single time."

In retrospect that statement marked the first disconnect between the Great One's words and his deeds. Federer hasn't beaten Nadal on clay since. Worse, at last year's Wimbledon, Nadal beat Federer, winner of 65 straight matches on grass, on what amounted to his home court. "A disaster," Federer said after the epic five-set final. He salvaged his year—and maintained a shaky dominion on hard courts—by winning his fifth straight U.S. Open after Nadal was eliminated by eventual finalist Andy Murray. Then, on Feb. 1, Nadal beat Federer again, 6–2 in the fifth set, to win the Australian Open and raise the flag over Federer's last redoubt, asphalt. Federer wept at the trophy ceremony. "God, this is killing me," he said.

It was the tennis equivalent of the British surrender at Yorktown, where an empire retreated and a band supposedly played The World Turned Upside Down. In completing one of the great reversals in sports history, Nadal hadn't just dethroned King Roger, he had harried him all over the world and dismantled his mightiest weapons.

Nadal has now beaten Federer in five straight finals and 13 of their last 19 matches, and if they meet again in the final of the 2009 French Open, which begins on May 24, Nadal will be the prohibitive favorite. What was once a great sports rivalry has turned into a rout. How can Federer be deemed the best ever when he might not be the best of his own era?

But more immediate questions still haven't been answered. How did this takedown happen? What, exactly, did we just see?

It has the feel of classical myth. Twenty-eight years ago the gods decided to create the perfect tennis player, tall and lean and as light on his feet as a blown feather. They gave him everything: great hands, a stiletto serve, ground strokes that the sport's hero, Sampras, called better than his own. The perfect tennis player could speak four languages. He was polite to officials, patient with the media and so gracious in victory that opponents almost didn't mind losing to him. After a while, this began to gall the gods, who are, after all, capricious beings. They don't like to be bored. And, as always, they had given themselves an out.

They had left one small flaw in the perfect tennis player's game. Few could expose it. Indeed, years would pass before anyone realized it existed. The pro tour is dominated by righthanders, whose crosscourt backhands are incapable of generating the speed, spin and high bounce necessary to make the weakness plain; only a lefty's forehand could probe it consistently enough. But it was there, a place high on the backhand side where the perfect tennis player's normally impeccable one-hander,

Switzerland's Roger Federer returns a shot against rival Rafael Nadal in the Madrid Open Tennis tournament, May 17, 2009. © AP IMAGES/ANDRES KUDACKI.

which could absorb the heaviest strokes and counter them with pinpoint accuracy, faltered enough to make him human.

Now the gods just needed a tool. And in Rafael Nadal, they found it. As a 10-year-old in the town of Manacor, on the Spanish island of Majorca, the naturally righthanded Rafa had played two-handed off both wings. But his uncle Toni, a former table-tennis champ and club tennis pro who was also the boy's coach, suggested that he drop a hand while hitting off his left side and, while he was at it, why not just play lefthanded? Rafa liked being coached by his uncle. He did what he was told.

At first the boy hit his strokes fairly flat, and Toni soon realized he needed a bigger weapon. So, recalling his own spin-happy Ping-Pong days, Toni persuaded Rafa to develop what some players call a reverse forehand—in which, instead of swinging the racket across his body and finishing above his right shoulder, he jerks the racket back after striking the ball and finishes above his left—to impart extreme topspin. Thanks to his remarkable racket speed

and to advances in string technology, Rafa was eventually able to hit shots that rotated at an unprecedented 3,200 revolutions per minute (compared with Federer's 2,500), fell inside the lines and, most important, bounced like a frightened jackrabbit, high and away from the perfect player's backhand. The stroke's impact? Eric Hechtman, a hitting partner for both players, says returning Nadal's forehand feels "like you're breaking off your arm."

In 2004 Federer had just risen to No. 1 when he faced the 17-year-old Nadal for the first time, in Miami. Nadal won 6–3, 6–3, and Federer walked off the court puzzled. "I couldn't quite play the way I wanted to," he said. "He doesn't hit the ball flat and hard; it's more with a lot of spin, which makes the ball bounce, bounce high, and that's a struggle I had today. I tried to get out of it but kind of couldn't."

Nadal, in other words, was able to do what no other man could. He made the tour's most elegant player—the one with the cream-colored Wimbledon sport coat and the just-so hair—feel awkward. Nadal forced Federer's backhand far out of its wheelhouse, or what Andy Roddick calls the pocket. "It's a huge advantage for Rafa to be able to pull him off [the court] to his weak side," Roddick says. "And we're talking about a foot differential between being in his pocket and being out of it. Play that enough times? It makes a difference."

Nadal won five of their next six meetings, four of them on clay, and his unyielding nature and breathtaking defensive play lifted him to No. 2 in the world. It wasn't enough. "When I was a kid, I always thought about Wimbledon," Nadal says. "I love that atmosphere. In Wimbledon the Spanish players never did very well. It was a challenge for me." Anyone questioning Nadal's resolve stopped in 2006, after he won his second French Open. The next day he took the Eurostar to London, raced to the Queens Club and practiced two hours on the grass, his grunts resounding into darkness. There was only one man in his way.

"Without question he put a bull's-eye on Federer," says former world No. 1 Jim Courier. "Nadal was Number 2 for how long—160 weeks, the most consecutive weeks at Number 2 for any player? And he wanted to be Number 1. So he found a way to get there."

Toni and Rafa both knew that Rafa's forehand, whose height was lessened by grass and hard courts, couldn't do the job alone. Every dimension of his game had to improve. Toni would list his nephew's deficiencies, stroke by stroke, each time they faced Federer. "He's so much better than you," Toni would say, "but if you believe and work, you can win."

Indeed, it has been easy to reduce Nadal's triumph to mere belief and work, as if he were some implacable primitive: will personified. The truth, however, is that Camp Rafa is a fairly sophisticated operation. A Majorcan trainer, Juan Forcades, oversees Nadal's conditioning. Physical therapist Rafael Maymo spends much of his day taking notes on when and what Nadal eats; when he goes to sleep and when he wakes; how much time he spends hitting forehands, backhands and volleys. Toni, meanwhile, has harped on his nephew's weaknesses so effectively that even in the earliest rounds of last year's French Open, Rafa was scared of losing. Toni reassured him—"You're Number 1 on clay!"—but it didn't matter. "He never relaxes," Toni says. "He's so afraid for every match."

From mid-2006 through '07 Federer took five of his seven matches with Nadal, including both Wimbledon finals, and he seemed to have mastered his young rival at last. But Nadal took a major step by pushing Federer to five sets in the '07 Wimbledon final. As the challenger he had the psychological advantage of chasing, and unlike Federer he was determined to keep adding weapons. To beat Federer on grass and hard courts, Toni and Rafa were methodically upgrading Rafa's game, making it less reliant on defense and more geared to dictating play and conserving energy.

"I had to improve," Rafa says. "Sure, having in front of me one guy like Federer, one complete player, it's always pushing me. But I always believed. I thought, I am young, I can improve a lot of things. Without that, I am Number 2, so if I improve I have a chance to be in the top position."

These days it's fashionable to say that Nadal has climbed inside Federer's head. But he needed a ladder to get there. The first rung: consistently staking out an offensive position, or, as Nadal puts it, "always trying to go more inside the court. That gives me more control of the point, no? Before I was maybe one meter behind the baseline, two meters behind." The second rung: a better serve. In his early years on tour Nadal won most of his points with preposterous saves and sterling shotmaking; his serve was strictly a point starter, a predictable slice on which bold returners such as James Blake feasted. Nadal ranked 51st on the ATP tour in serving in 2004, winning just 77% of his service games. After Roddick beat him in straight sets at that year's U.S. Open, the American star walked off the court thinking, He's not going to crack the top five if that serve doesn't improve.

It did. Nadal's serves, which were then clocked at an average speed of 99 mph, are now traveling an average of 16 mph faster—and he regularly hits the upper 120s on the radar gun. But it wasn't just a matter of hitting the ball harder. In fact, Toni says, one reason Federer had the upper hand in 2007 was that he pushed Rafa to serve with too much velocity, and the speed of Federer's returns threw off Nadal's timing. "So we had to learn other things," Toni says. According to Roddick, Nadal now hits to both sides of the service box on his first and second deliveries. "He can kick it, he can slice it," Roddick says. "You don't really know what's coming." Nadal finished last year ranked No. 1 in the world—and fourth in serving, winning 88% of his service games.

Nadal also greatly improved his backhand. He flattened out the two-hander and sharpened his one-handed slice, learning to use it for defense, changes of pace, approach shots and drop shots. Mesmerized by what Courier calls Nadal's "brutish" style, commentators still portray Federer-Nadal matches as beauty versus beast, matador versus bull. But Nadal's devotion to craft belies that caricature. No one can match Federer for artistry, but Nadal has two attributes just as valuable: imagination and the audacity to use it. "He's by far the smartest player of all," says seven-time Grand Slam champ Mats Wilander. "He's not afraid of changing. With a mind like that? There's no limit."

Spain's Rafael Nadal concentrates during match play against Fernando Verdasco in the Madrid Open Tennis tournament, May 15, 2009. © AP IMAGES/ANDRES KUDACKI.

The results have left Federer demoralized. "To Roger, Nadal's tennis is unorganized: big, loopy topspin forehands, that slice serve, now he's slicing his backhand, he's lefthanded—[it affects Roger] mentally," Wilander explains. "When Roger's in his comfort zone, he's a serious fighter. But when he's not in it, he's not able to fight."

The moment when that became clear couldn't have been bigger. Serving for last year's Wimbledon championship at 8–7, 0–15, with night falling, Nadal ventured as far out of his own comfort zone as possible. He had

stunned everyone by outserving Federer throughout the fifth set, but now he took it a step further. Nadal serve-and-volleyed. Then he did it again, and again, winning two of his three approaches to the net, beating the ultimate all-court player at his own game. Against such nerve Federer crumbled. His final forehand fell short. An era ended.

Strangely enough 2008 might have been Federer's greatest year—better than his 92–5 run in '06, better than the three years in which he won nine majors—because he battled his body from start to finish. A bout of mononucleosis in late 2007 had enlarged his spleen, ravaged his powers of recovery and ruined his off-season training; from the '08 Australian Open on, he played a step slow, which threw off his timing and sent his confidence tumbling. Yet Federer still made the Australian Open semifinals and the French Open final, labored back from two sets down to lose the longest Wimbledon final ever by the slimmest of margins, and won the U.S. Open—Hall of Fame stuff for anyone else.

"Federer was ill all season long, and the story was completely missed," Courier says. "He hid it from everybody because it's his responsibility to not show weakness, and he played through it because of his commitment to the tour. Which was a mistake. Mario Ancic [the Croatian once ranked No. 7] missed more than six months on the tour with a mono bout; it's a serious illness for a high-level performance athlete. Roger needed to get off the tour and get healthy again."

Last October, Federer conceded at last, retiring from a tournament for the first time in 763 matches because of lower back pain. It has continued to bother him, but history won't care. Nadal "shot him through the heart by winning Wimbledon," Courier says. "Roger was not at full tilt, but it doesn't matter, because it changed the energy between them—possibly for the rest of their careers."

Federer's breakdown just before Nadal received the '09 Australian Open winner's trophy was the most obvious sign of the shift, but there had been earlier indications. Asked the day before the final whether he relished another shot at his archrival, Federer said, "Honestly, I preferred the days when I didn't have a rival." Nadal had exhausted himself in a five-hour, 14-minute semifinal the day before, but as soon as the final began, Federer seemed out of sorts. Worse, unlike Nadal when he was No. 2, Federer didn't commit himself to attacking his rival, to shaking him out of his comfort zone. Twice Federer ran around his backhand and staggered Nadal with forehand winners, but he never did that again. "Twice in 4-½ hours?" Wilander asks. "Why not show Nadal something different?"

The answer lies in the regal language always used to describe Federer. Born to rule, he has never been interested in fighting for power; that's why in his current exile he looks less like Napoleon plotting on Elba than like the puzzled Czar Nicholas II waiting for the world to right itself and restore his throne.

This attitude perplexes even Federer's staunchest admirers. Former players, coaches, peers: They all accept that his talent is, as Wilander says, "crazy," but his passive response to Nadal goes against what they've been taught a superstar does when he's down. Muhammad Ali came up with rope-a-dope, an aging Michael Jordan perfected the fadeaway jumper: The great

ones adjust, sending a signal not only to their rivals but also to all the newly emboldened. It's no shock that following Nadal's trail, No. 3 Andy Murray has won six of his last seven matches against Federer, and No. 4 Novak Djokovic has won three of their last five. "What makes me scratch my head," Courier says, "is how Roger doesn't shift."

The remedy most often prescribed for Federer's ailing game is hiring a coach such as Darren Cahill, who once counseled Agassi. Federer toyed with the idea in the off-season, but that he didn't follow up seemed further proof that he's not hearing alarm bells. Others suggest that he serve-and-volley more, or play more doubles to replicate the Olympic preparation that helped him win the gold medal in doubles in Beijing and the U.S. Open singles title last September. But if Federer insists on staying back and winning rallies from the baseline, the consensus is that he must shorten points to save energy for the decisive third and fifth sets he has lately been losing: He has to hit more low, short slices to throw off Nadal's rhythm, and he must put more bite on his flatter strokes.

Federer did that in the Australian Open final, but only when desperate; the instant he felt he had gained the momentum, he went back to the game on which he built his empire—and that Nadal solved long ago. "Roger still feels he's just better [than Nadal]," Courier says. "And, frankly, he's not."

On March 30, at the Sony Ericsson Open at Key Biscayne, Fla., Nadal beat 74th-ranked Frederico Gil 7–5, 6–3, walked off the court and disappeared. Maymo waited in the locker room until Nadal showed 15 minutes later, steaming from a sprint on the elliptical trainer. "I wasn't happy with my play," he said, "so I punished myself."

The next night Federer, soon to be married to his longtime girlfriend and manager, Mirka Vavrinec, with whom he is expecting a child, downplayed the idea that he needs to adjust his game. He said he felt fresh, back in shape at last. "That's been my problem, not really Rafa or Andy or Djokovic," he said. "I feel like I'm about to turn the corner."

Four days later Federer lost to Djokovic in three sets, but more notable was how, down a break in the third, his forehand—once the signature shot of the men's game—deserted him. He danced forward as he had so often, an easy approach shot waiting for him at the T, swung … and dumped the ball into the net. Federer stared at his racket a second, then smashed it on the ground. It made all the highlight shows.

But as the losses piled up over the spring—to Stanislas Wawrinka in Monte Carlo, to Djokovic again in Rome—another image from Key Biscayne came to mind. Following Federer's last win there, after he fielded questions in English, then Swiss-German, someone asked if he could answer a few in Spanish. This is part of tennis's law of succession: The new No. 1's mother tongue becomes a tour lingua franca. Nadal had deciphered the language of Federer's game, but those waiting to see if Federer has the stomach to respond in kind would find nothing encouraging this day.

"I'm not there yet," Federer said, trying to grin. "Maybe in the next life."

FURTHER RESOURCES

Books

Wertheim, L. Jon. *Strokes of Genius: Federer, Nadal, and the Greatest Match Ever Played.* New York: Houghton Mifflin Harcourt, 2010.

Web Sites

Associated Press. "Federer-Nadal Rivalry as Good as It Gets." *ESPN*, July 7, 2008. http://sports.espn.go.com/espn/wire?section=tennis&id=3476650 (accessed on March 24, 2013).

Magowan, Alistair. "Roger v Rafa—the Best Final Ever?" *BBC*, July 7, 2008. http://news.bbc.co.uk/sport2/hi/tennis/7493099.stm (accessed on March 24, 2013).

"LeBron James Shoots for the 'Stars'"

Radio transcript

By: Terry Gross

Date: September 9, 2009

Source: Gross, Terry. "LeBron James Shoots for the 'Stars.'" *NPR*, September 9, 2009. www.npr.org/templates/transcript/transcript.php?storyId=112641310 (accessed on March 24, 2013).

About the Host: Terry Gross was the host and producer of National Public Radio's *Fresh Air* program. Founded in 1975 as a daily three-hour show that aired locally in Philadelphia, *Fresh Air* was expanded in 1987 to an hour-long interview and music program that was broadcast nationally five days a week. Gross heavily researched the people she interviewed ahead of time, and she earned a reputation as a thoughtful, attentive interviewer. Among her thousands of radio guests were Johnny Cash, Elie Wiesel, Nancy Reagan, Jimmy Carter, and Toni Morrison. In 1994, *Fresh Air* won the Peabody Award for its "probing questions, revelatory interviews, and unusual insights."

INTRODUCTION

Born in 1984, LeBron James grew up in poverty in Akron, Ohio. He began playing basketball at the age of nine. By his senior year of high school, James had already been featured on the covers of *ESPN* magazine and *Sports Illustrated*. He also played football while still in high school, but a wrist injury cut short that career. Before that happened, he had been offered a football scholarship to the University of Notre Dame, but chose instead to remain dedicated to basketball.

James went straight to the NBA in 2003 after he was the first pick in the draft by the Cleveland Cavaliers. Late in the season, in a game against the New Jersey Nets, James scored forty-one points and became the youngest player in league history to net forty points in a game. He was just nineteen years old. In 2004, James was named Rookie of the Year for the 2003–2004 season. It was an auspicious start for the 6'8" forward, and James remained with the Cavaliers until 2010.

Even before playing his first NBA game, James had signed a seven-year, $90 million with Nike and launched his own signature shoe line with the corporation. Comparisons to Michael Jordan, another NBA star who was nearly twenty years older than James, became rampant, but it was a comparison James was not comfortable with. "I can't be Mike; I don't want to be Mike.... I am who I am," James told CNN's Rachel Nichols. BleacherReport.com columnist Timothy Rapp pointed out what James was trying to say when he wrote that the two superstars would forever "be linked and compared, and forever ... be fundamentally different players who deserve their own category of greatness." Greatness is what James had proven he had. In the 2007–2008 season with the Cavaliers, James averaged thirty points a game, the highest of his career and enough to win him the honor of being the NBA scoring champion of the year. His lowest was his rookie season, with 20.9 point a game. By the time his seven-year career with the Cavs ended, James had scored a total of 15,251 points. He was Cleveland's all-time leading scorer.

SIGNIFICANCE

"King James" became a free agent in 2010 and was courted by numerous teams. The star took a long time to decide what team he would sign with, and on a July 8, 2010, live televised special called *The Decision*, James announced he would sign with the Miami Heat. His decision was based in large part on the fact that two other free agents—Chris Bosh and Dwyane Wade—also signed with Miami. James reasoned that playing with these men as his teammates would give him a better chance of clinching a championship than if he had stayed with Cleveland. The decision caused an uproar in the world of basketball as James's former Cavs coach publicly denounced his choice. Fans were furious, and other players criticized the decision as cowardly because he was admittedly depending on teammates to shoulder the burden of winning. Many sports analysts condemned the athlete for waiting to make a decision until the last minute and keeping his decision a secret even to the interested coaches, who learned along with the rest of the country what team James had chosen. His free-agency period left James with a reputation as one of the most disliked athletes in professional sports, according to a 2012 public poll conducted by Nielsen and E-Poll Market Research. It was an about-face from the hero-worship that the Ohio native had experienced during his years with Cleveland.

Reputation aside, James had a welcome reception in Miami. Having agreed to a lower salary so that Wade and Bosh could join the team, James knew they had a powerhouse with the trio. He talked with sportswriter Eric Reid in 2010. "When they said we had the possibility of all of us joining together also, I couldn't turn that down." Reid called the Heat "Wade's house, LeBron's kingdom, and Bosh's pit," and called the contract signing "unprecedented."

Even with the lower salary, James was the fourth-highest paid professional athlete on *Forbes* list in 2012. His $13 million salary was about three times lower than his endorsement earnings at $40 million. James was affiliated with Nike, Coca Cola, McDonald's, State Farm Insurance, and several other companies, and he enjoyed the honor of being the NBA's biggest endorsement star. During the 2011–12 season, he became the eighth NBA player to win at least three Most Valuable Player awards during his career, and by 2013, he was back in the favor of fans and breaking more NBA records in scoring.

PRIMARY SOURCE

"LEBRON JAMES SHOOTS FOR THE 'STARS'"

SYNOPSIS: LeBron James plugs his new memoir while reminiscing about his childhood and early NBA career.

This is FRESH AIR. I'm Terry Gross. My guest, LeBron James, has been a sports star ever since he was

NPR *Fresh Air* host Terry Gross. © AP IMAGES/SETH WENIG.

on the cover of *Sports Illustrated* at the age of 17, when he was still in high school. He was the number one NBA draft pick out of high school. At 19, he became the youngest Rookie of the Year in NBA history. That was in the 2003–2004 season. At the end of last season, he was named the NBA's Most Valuable Player. He plays for the Cleveland Cavaliers.

James, who will turn 25 in December, grew up in Akron, and that's where his new memoir, "Shooting Stars," is set. It's about growing up poor, the son of a single mother. And it's about his friendship with the boys who became his teammates in junior high and how they managed to stick together, go to the same high school and become state champions. The book is co-written with Buzz Bissinger, who wrote "Friday Night Lights."

LeBron James, welcome to FRESH AIR. Do you remember the very first time that you dunked?

Mr. LeBRON JAMES (Basketball Player; Co-author, "Shooting Stars"): Yeah, I was in eighth grade, and my middle school every year has a teachers-versus-students game. You know, they play the basketball team. And in warm-ups, I have no idea what got into me, but it was so—it was so electric in this gym. I think this gym holds probably, like—oh, it holds probably, like, I'd say probably about 45 people in there. That's a lot, right, for an eighth-grade game, 45 people?

And, you know, the crowd was, you know, the students was having a great time, and, you know, we got out of school early. And in the warm-ups, I just decided I don't know, I was going to jump as high as I could and try to dunk. And I did it. You know, I went up and dunked the basketball. I don't know what got into me that day. And then when the game started, I got a breakaway and did it again, and the crowd went crazy. And that was, like, one of the best moments of my whole life.

GROSS: You're one of the people who went very suddenly from poverty to wealth. You write in your book, you know, your mother had you when she was 16. Her mother died when you were three. It was hard for your mother to support you. You had to keep moving a lot because of eviction notices and, you know, rent problems. Did you think of basketball as a way out, as more than just a game?

Mr. JAMES: Oh, I think it is more than a game. Basketball, and I think sport period, gives you an opportunity to forget about anything that may be going on in your life, back away from that particular sport that you may be playing. You know, I definitely used the game to get my mind off some of the bad things that may have been going on as a child.

GROSS: Like what?

Mr. JAMES: You know, just things you never want your kids to see, you know, violence and things like that. You never want your kids to see that. So, you know, I used the game of basketball to keep me away from that.

GROSS: Your mother, when she was having a hard time financially, thought it would be best for you if you lived with another family for a while, while she tried to get things together. Tell us a little bit about the Walker family that you did move in with.

Mr. JAMES: It was a great family, you know, and without them, I wouldn't be in this position I am today. You know, they welcomed me like I was one of their sons, and, you know, they already had a son and two daughters. And, you know, to open their arms up and to treat me like I was one of their firstborn, I think, you know, I think that I owe them a lot of credit for what they did.

GROSS: Mr. Walker was a basketball coach. Did you already know him from basketball?

Mr. JAMES: Yeah, I had known him from football first. He was assistant football coach on a Little League

team I had played for first, and then the basketball season came on.

GROSS: So how was it arranged? You know, like, why that family?

Mr. JAMES: I have no idea how it was arranged. You know, my mother just told me I was going to be living with a coach of mine, and, you know, I had never asked my mom why or anything like that. I just—you know, I've always trusted her judgment.

GROSS: Now, how did you meet the three players who, along with you, became known as the Fab Four, three players that you went to junior high and high school with and became real winners together.

Mr. JAMES: Well, I met Little Dru through the same Little League team, through the same league. It's the ARB. It's the Akron Recreation Bureau. And Little Dru, just so happened, played on our rival team. We was the Summer League Hornets, and he played for the Ed Davis Dream Team All-Stars. So we were rivals, and you know, we met through that way. Willie played on my team. He played on the Summer League Hornets with me, and I met Romeo on the football team, where I played before basketball, on the East Dragons.

GROSS: What was it about this group that made you work so well together? Like, what was—describe something about, like, the chemistry on and off the court that made you work like that.

Mr. JAMES: Well, the chemistry off the court is why we were so good on the court. You know, we looked at each other as brothers. I mean, at the time it was the Fab Four. It was myself, Dru, Sian Cotton and Willie McGee, and we, you know, we used that off-the-court friendship, that, you know, going to—I don't know—going to McDonald's together, playing basketball outside together, you know, driving to West Virginia to play in the AAU tournament, you know, things like that. And then when we got on the court, it was, like, okay. This is the easy part.

GROSS: Little Dru was called Little Dru because he was little. He was ...

GROSS: He was, like, 5'3" or something when you were in high school?

Mr. JAMES: Yeah, when we was freshmen. No, that's, that's good for him. When we was freshmen, Dru was about 4'11" ...

GROSS: Whoa.

Mr. JAMES: ...when we were freshmen in high school.

GROSS: Whoa.

Mr. JAMES: When he came off the bench that year, our freshman year, and he was a heck of a shooter. And

LeBron James goes up for the slam dunk during practice at St. Vincent-St. Mary High School in Akron, Ohio, in 2003.
© AP IMAGES/BRUCE SCHWARTZMAN.

you know, anytime you left him open, he for the most part wasn't going to miss, and, you know, he did that from game one all the way to the last game of the season in the state championship.

GROSS: So you, Dru, Willie McGee and Sian Cotton wanted to go to the same high school together so that you could continue to be teammates. And you went to a high school that no one expected you to go to. Everybody expected you to go to—is it pronounced Buchtel?

Mr. JAMES: Buchtel.

GROSS: Buchtel, which you describe as the school of choice for black athletes. It was a public school, but instead you went to a predominately white, Catholic school, St. Vincent's. Would you explain how you ended up, the four of you, going to St. Vincent's?

Mr. JAMES: Well, we ended up going to St. Vincent's because Little Dru at the time, remember I told you he was only about 4'10", 4'11", he didn't think Buchtel was

going to give him an equal opportunity to play for them. And when Dru realized that, you know, he was, like, you know, I'm not going there. He had started going to this Sunday night clinic that our high school coach eventually, Keith Dambrot, was holding. And he'd seen how much confidence he had in Dru, and Dru was like, hey, I'm going to St. V, guys. And it was—it was tough at first, you know, because we knew really nothing but Buchtel at the time.

I mean, we went to all the Buchtel games and all the Buchtel events, the football games, everything, and we were—our minds was going to Buchtel. So you know, when Dru just made that decision, you know, it was difficult for us. But, you know, when we finally sat down and really came together as friends, we was like, hey, we, you know, we need to stick together, and, you know, we're going to let you make this call, Dru. We're going to follow you.

GROSS: Now, you write in your book that some people turned against you when you decided to go to St. Vincent because they thought you were turning your back on the African-American community. Could you describe that period and what your response to that was?

Mr. JAMES: Well, it was difficult. I mean, in the summer of—let me see—I went to—in the summer of '99, I think that was my freshman year. That summer before, you know, in between the eighth grade and ninth grade, you had to—you know, even though we had decided to go to St. V, we were still playing in the black community. We were still playing basketball against those same kids and those same adults that really wanted us to come, you know, to Buchtel. So it was difficult, but I think our friendship and what we had with Coach Drew was way more powerful than anything anybody else had ever said for us or, you know, about us.

GROSS: You started winning and becoming pretty famous when you were in high school. In your junior year, you were the cover story in *Sports Illustrated*, and the headline was: The Chosen One. One of the controversial things from your early life, from your high school years that you write about a little bit in your book, is that when you were 18, for your birthday, while your mother still had no money, and you were still in high school, she bought you a $50,000 Hummer, and got the loan with the money that you were predicted to earn because everybody knew you were going to be an NBA draft. And that was pretty controversial because a lot of people assumed it was, like, an under-the-table gift, a real gift from a shoe company or an NBA team—would've been illegal. But, you know, the loan was investigated by the Ohio High School Athletic Association, and they say it was legit. Why did you need a $50,000 Hummer?

Mr. JAMES: I didn't. It was a gift. I didn't ask for it. My mother felt, you know, I was special. She always wanted to do something special for me. And, you know, she did something that was very legal, got a bank loan and, you know, the bank, you know, just basically (unintelligible) that they would be fully paid back. And, you know, and she bought me that for my birthday. And it was a surprise to me when I seen it in the driveway.

GROSS: You know, the funny thing about that, it's such an odd gift because she's getting you this $50,000 car based on money you're going to earn.

Mr. JAMES: Yeah, I know, huh?

GROSS: You're the one who's going to be paying that loan.

Mr. JAMES: So it was like I'm paying for it myself, huh?

GROSS: Yeah, you're paying for that birthday gift.

Mr. JAMES: At that point, at that particular time, it's the point that count. It's the thought that count. It's the thought that count.

GROSS: So did you have to pay off the loan when you joined the NBA?

Mr. JAMES: Yes, we did. Yes, we did.

GROSS: And did you still have the Hummer by the time the loan was paid off?

Mr. JAMES: Yeah, I still have it.

GROSS: You still have it?

Mr. JAMES: Yeah, I still have it.

GROSS: Was it, like, a keepsake or something?

Mr. JAMES: No, I've changed it a few times and painted it a few times, but I still have it.

GROSS: Are you still driving it, or do you just keep it as a ...?

Mr. JAMES: No, I still drive it every now and then.

GROSS: Mm-hmm. So you won the state national championship your senior year. So the bet paid off. The fact that you and your three friends decided to go to St. Vincent together, it paid off. And then, you know, you were an NBA draft. You joined the Cavaliers when they were in last place. I know you're very fond of Cleveland. You grew up in Akron. Why would you want to join a team that was in last place?

Mr. JAMES: Well, first of all, if you—you know, I had no choice. You know, that's why it's called a draft. They pick who they want, and ...

GROSS: Good point.

Mr. JAMES: ... and things like that. But the fact is, when I was drafted to that team, I felt like I could make

an impact. I felt like I could help. You know, they only won 17 games the year before I got drafted. But, you know, I felt that my talents could help that franchise. And, you know, I think the city of Cleveland has some of the best fans that the world has to see, and, you know, I was happy to go into that experience and take my talents to that team, also.

GROSS: I'm sure it was your dream to be in the NBA. When you go there, how did it compare to what you expected?

Mr. JAMES: It was everything and more. I always wanted to be in the NBA and have a uniform with my name on the back—that say James across the back of the jersey. And I can remember my first NBA game, which we played in Sacramento. And to just be out there and to see the fans and to see, you know, the cameras, and to see my teammates and see the opposing team on an NBA floor in an NBA game, it was, like, wow. It was, like, my, like, please don't pinch me because I know I'm dreaming.

GROSS: Now, Shaquille O'Neal is joining the Cavaliers. So now there's going to be two really dominant, famous players on the team. And everybody's speculating about how you're going to feel about that.

Mr. JAMES: I feel great. You know, this is a team sport, and to add someone like that to the team is great. I mean, he has all the accolades that you could ever want and more as an NBA individual and as a team player. So I'm looking forward to the challenge. I think he adds something to our team that we haven't had, and I can't wait until the season starts so I can get out there and play alongside him.

GROSS: Do you know him? Do you know him well?

Mr. JAMES: Yeah, I know him really well. Yeah, I know his family and his kids. I love his kids. You know, I love him. Man, he's like the godfather in the NBA. If you don't—you know, he's like the Don Corleone. If you don't know him or respect him, then something may happen to you.

GROSS: If you're just joining us, my guest is LeBron James, the NBA's Most Valuable Player, and he's got a new memoir called "Shooting Stars." Let's take a short break here, and then we'll talk some more. This is FRESH AIR.

GROSS: If you're just joining us, my guest is the Cleveland Cavaliers' LeBron James. He was named Most Valuable Player in the NBA this past season, and now he has a new memoir called "Shooting Stars."

Let me ask you: I know—this is just a clothing question. So I ask this as a woman who finds it very difficult to find clothes in my size, which is a problem

Cleveland Cavaliers players LeBron James (left), Mo Williams, and Shaquille O'Neal ham it up for the camera during a photo shoot on October 3, 2009. © AP IMAGES/TONY DEJAK.

I suppose you've had being, like, six-foot—I forget what—eight?

Mr. JAMES: 6'8", yeah.

GROSS: So when you joined the NBA, you were probably able to get your clothes made for you. Is that what you do?

Mr. JAMES: Yes. I don't anymore. I mean, sometimes I do. I mean, I get some suits and things like that tailored, but I can go in the store and sometimes find some clothes.

GROSS: Really?

Mr. JAMES: I can go in the store and find some jeans and find some shirts. I wear true-to-size clothes, though. I don't wear that big stuff a lot of people wear. I wear true to size.

GROSS: Oh, you mean, like, the pants that are—your backside …

Mr. JAMES: Like the 5X, 6X T-shirts and all the pants that's hanging below people …

GROSS: Dragging it on the floor …

Mr. JAMES: Yeah, yeah.

Mr. JAMES: Yeah, I wear, you know, a 2X T-shirt. I wear 40 jeans, and, you know, I wear it just how it's supposed to be worn.

GROSS: All right. You know your one-handed, full-court shot?

Mr. JAMES: Mm-hmm.

GROSS: How'd you develop that?

Mr. JAMES: Um, I don't know. It's just—I guess I'm the chosen one, I guess.

Mr. JAMES: I guess *Sports Illustrated* was right.

GROSS: There you go. Now, describe the feeling of taking a shot, and the ball's, like, circling around the rim and then it, like, falls out instead of going in, and the game's really close.

Mr. JAMES: Now, that's happened multiple times. It's not a pleasant feeling, you know, especially when you feel like that was the one. You know, you shoot the ball. All—basketball players know when that shot feels great, you know, and then the ball gets on the rim, and it plays with the rim, and it just, like, goes in, and then it feels like an imaginary hand punches it back out of the net. That's, like, it's not a really good feeling at all.

GROSS: And I want to ask you about something else controversial that's happened pretty recently. You have something called the LeBron James Skills Academy, and a college student attending the academy dunked on you. And it's been reported that Nike, who was sponsoring this, confiscated—I don't know if it was the cameras or just the videos that captured that moment. And so in some people's minds, that's a symbol of your vanity, that you wouldn't allow that to be seen, and in some people's minds, it's not about you, it's about Nike, and it's a symbol of a form of corporate censorship. What is that incident about to you? What's your version of the story?

Mr. JAMES: It's just about people just looking in—when you have nothing more to write about, sometimes people just look for anything. The summer is dead. No basketball is around, so they need something to talk about.

Nike has a no-videotaping policy. It's simple. I mean, if you have a no-videotaping policy, why are you videotaping? So, you know, the kid, which is—really, he's really good, by the way, kid goes to Xavier. And you know, he caught me slipping a little bit, I guess.

Mr. JAMES: Before that day, you can easily go on YouTube and find me getting dunked on by a few more players in the NBA. And, you know, if you even want to look a little bit more, you can find me even dunking on a few players.

GROSS: Really?

Mr. JAMES: I think that may be possible. You may be able to find that. I don't know.

GROSS: Now, you said that you think what makes your approach to basketball different, like, your approach is based on, like, your mental approach to the game. I'm paraphrasing here, but it was something like that. So what do you mean by that?

Mr. JAMES: That my mental aspect of the game is what?

GROSS: That that's the key to your ...

Mr. JAMES: Oh, it is. I mean, I think the game more than I really play it. I mean, I can play the game pretty good, too. But I really think the game and approach the game mentally more than physically, you know, and that's watching film. That's knowing your opponent's likes and dislikes, his pros and cons, what he like to do, what he don't like to do, who are we playing against this particular team. You know, what do they like to do? What do they don't like to do? And that's the way I approach the game. I feel like skill-wise, I'm going to be okay. Who's going to out-think the game more than the next man in front of him?

GROSS: You know, we've been talking through the interview about the three other friends, teammates, who you went to junior high and high school with. What are they doing now?

Mr. JAMES: Well, my four best friends right now, Dru Joyce is playing professionally in Poland. Romeo Travis is playing professionally in Germany. Sian Cotton is playing football at Walsh University in Canton, Ohio, and also in school. And Willie McGee is getting his—is going to graduate school at the University of Akron and also working with the men's basketball team.

GROSS: Have you watched your friends play in Poland and Germany?

Mr. JAMES: Yes.

GROSS: And are the rules any different there?

Mr. JAMES: No, a lot different, a lot different. Yeah, I've watched them on the Internet. Sometimes, their game is, like, replayed on the Internet. And then there's a Web site I can go to, like eurobasketball.com, and they replay their games, which is pretty cool seeing those guys still play.

GROSS: Tell us about what your mother was like when you were growing up.

Mr. JAMES: My mother was great, very fiery, very demanding—demanding greatness, really, honestly. She was—it just seemed like, it seemed like she had everything in control, even though it seemed like the world may have been coming down on her at times. She never let anything get to her, even in the worst times, the best times. She always stayed calm and collected and made sure that her son was always happy and did whatever it took for me to be happy, and I respect that.

Cleveland Cavaliers guard LeBron James drives past Atlanta Hawks guard Joe Johnson in an NBA game on March 1, 2009. © AP IMAGES/GREGORY SMITH.

I respect that in her not only as a mother but as a friend. As a leader, she set me up for life early on because I was able to notice how great and how calm she was, even when times seemed like they was the worst.

GROSS: You said your mother was demanding. What did she demand of you?

Mr. JAMES: No, she just—no, she never demanded anything out of me. I could just see her fire. She was very, like, demanding to herself. Like, she was going to find a way to make everything be right.

GROSS: When you think back to the fact that she was 16 when you were born, do you see that in a different

light than you did when you were young, just in terms of what she had to deal with at the age of 16?

Mr. JAMES: When you're a kid—right, when you're a kid, you don't really know how young your mother is, or is it that young—too young.

GROSS: Exactly.

Mr. JAMES: You only know that as you get older. You're like wow, my mom was what when she had me? She was really 16 years old? That's a sophomore in high school.

Mr. JAMES: I couldn't imagine having no kid at 16. I mean, I ended up having my first kid at 18, but you know, it was—that's was like—for a woman it has to be more difficult. It's way more difficult than for a man to have his own kid by himself. So that's—she's amazing. She's one in a million, I guess, or in my words, one in a billion these days.

GROSS: Well, thank you so much for talking with us.

Mr. JAMES: Oh, well, thank you. I appreciate it. Thanks for having me.

GROSS: LeBron James' new memoir is called "Shooting Stars." Here's a track called "LeBron's Hammer." It was written and performed by Buckethead and is dedicated to James' 24th birthday. I'm Terry Gross, and this is FRESH AIR.

FURTHER RESOURCES

Web Sites

Heitner, Darren. "LeBron James Reminds the World That He Is Not Michael Jordan." *Forbes*, February 13, 2013. www.forbes.com/sites/darrenheitner/2013/02/13/lebron-james-reminds-the-world-that-he-is-not-michael-jordan/ (accessed on March 24, 2013).

"LeBron James." *Basketball-Reference.com*. www.basketball-reference.com/players/j/jamesle01.html (accessed on March 24, 2013).

"LeBron James." *Forbes*, June 2012. www.forbes.com/profile/lebron-james/ (accessed on March 24, 2013).

Nichols, Rachel. "LeBron James: I'm Not Michael Jordan." *CNN*, February 16, 2013. www.cnn.com/video/#/video/sports/2013/02/16/nichols-lebron-james.cnn (accessed on March 22, 2013).

Rapp, Timothy. "Michael Jordan Breaks Down Blueprint for Defending LeBron James." *Bleacher Report*, February 17, 2013. http://bleacherreport.com/articles/1532988-michael-jordan-breaks-down-blueprint-for-defending-lebron-james (accessed on March 24, 2013).

"Terry Gross." *She Made It*. www.shemadeit.org/meet/biography.aspx?m=31 (accessed on March 24, 2013).

Van Riper, Tom. "America's Most Disliked Athletes." *Forbes*, February 7, 2012. http://www.forbes.com/sites/tomvanriper/2012/02/07/americas-most-disliked-athletes/ (accessed on March 22, 2013).

"With Harsh USC Penalties, NCAA Sends Warning to All Elite Programs"

Magazine article

By: Stewart Mandel

Date: June 10, 2010

Source: Mandel, Stewart. "With Harsh USC Penalties, NCAA Sends Warning to All Elite Programs." *Sports Illustrated*, June 10, 2010. http://sportsillustrated.cnn.com/2010/writers/stewart_mandel/06/10/usc.penalties/index.html (accessed on March 24, 2013).

About the magazine: *Sports Illustrated* is an American magazine dedicated to athletic competition, primarily professional sports. The magazine's current incarnation, which began publication in 1954, was the first to provide weekly coverage and news of spectator sports, rather than traditional "lifestyle" content. It quickly became the leading publication in its field, becoming so influential that it prompted sporting arenas to adopt new designs to accommodate *Sports Illustrated*'s cameras. The magazine's most famous features are its annual "Sportsman of the Year" awards and swimsuit editions.

INTRODUCTION

College and university football recruiting has long been one of those activities where rules are in place, silent assumptions are acknowledged, and behavior most people would consider unethical has largely been ignored. The way it is supposed to work is this: College football coaches scout young recruits—high school boys, mostly. They send the athlete a letter and questionnaire, which marks the first stage of the recruiting process, called "recognition." These questionnaires are then used for the coach to determine how well the athlete fits the college's program in terms of grades, speed, strength, etc. If an athlete's questionnaire satisfies a coach's interest, the recruit advances to the second stage, the "evaluation." This is where the coach attends a game or meets specifically to watch that athlete play. Serious contenders for a college team then get a phone call or home visit from the coach, as well as an invitation for an official visit to the school.

The final step is the offer. Legitimate offers include reasonable terms. Where schools have historically found themselves in trouble is when the "offer" more closely resembles a bribe. Sports history—particularly college football—is full of examples of recruiting scandals. From 2002 to 2010, the University of Miami was allegedly offering recruits an array of incentives not allowed under National Collegiate Athletic Association (NCAA) rules, including prostitutes, cars, and other inappropriate "gifts." The university was not the only one breaking the rules. The NCAA had been simultaneously investigating several other high-profile teams, including Ohio State, Auburn, North Carolina, Georgia Tech, Michigan, and Southern California, the school featured in this *Sports Illustrated* article. The scandalous recruiting practices and habits were not relegated to just these institutions; more schools were suspected of the illegal behavior, but investigations took months and so there had to be a reasonable chance of finding proof before the manpower hours were invested.

In colleges where sports are part of the institution's reputation, where the school is judged by the performance and behavior of its athletes, NCAA infractions are particularly damaging. Florida State, for example, became known as the "Free Shoes University" after it was discovered that agents bought more than $6,000 worth of shoes for its players. In 2009, coach Bobby Bowden was forced to vacate twelve victories due to an academic cheating scandal that included athletes from a number of the school's teams. Arizona State tied with Southern Methodist for having the most infractions (9) each. Florida State coach Charley Pell left his position with a whopping 107 NCAA violations, and coaches at South Carolina provided steroids to their athletes. University of Colorado coach Gary Barnett was forced to resign in 2005 when his recruiting practices proved to include sex, drugs, and alcohol … the list is nearly endless.

SIGNIFICANCE

Recruitment scandals make headlines for a short time while they are being investigated, but their inherent lesson does not keep teams and coaches from committing new violations. CNN sports columnist Terence Moore called the proliferation of scandals epidemic. "For a while, it happened only every few years or so. Now, there rarely is a month, week or day that passes without a big-time program in college football sprinting deep into scandal while daring the National Collegiate Athletic Association (NCAA) to tackle it." Moore, a sports writer with more than three decades under his belt, lamented the situation in 2011 when he claimed "no reason to believe things will improve in big-time college football before the end of the millennium."

Others, including some college athletes, agreed and challenged those in leadership positions to brainstorm on ways to police the recruiting habits. Former Ohio State quarterback-turned-award-winning sports analyst Kirk Herbstreit was a vocal proponent of recruitment reform. "We have to figure out how to try to get college football back to people in charge who generally care about the health of the game and not just about churning kids out to get them ready for the NFL. That's not what college football is all about."

It was a dilemma which, as of the turn of the decade, had no resolution in sight.

■ PRIMARY SOURCE

"WITH HARSH USC PENALTIES, NCAA SENDS WARNING TO ALL ELITE PROGRAMS"

The NCAA has a problem. For years, sports agents, runners and various other third-party sleazeballs have infiltrated their enterprise, buddying up to 14-year-old phenoms at shoe camps, cozying up to corruptible assistant coaches and making a mockery of the organization's stated adherence to "amateurism." For the most part, the pencil pushers in Indianapolis have been powerless to do anything about it.

On Thursday, however, the NCAA found a way to strike back. The Committee on Infractions used its much-anticipated decision on USC's sanctions as a chance to make an example of ex-Trojans stars Reggie Bush and O. J. Mayo, both of whom reaped the benefits of gift-wielding outsiders. Essentially, the committee hammered USC's vaunted football program—13 vacated wins, including its 55–19 Orange Bowl win over Oklahoma; a two-year bowl ban; and 30 docked scholarships—to send a message to schools around the country with similar high-profile stars.

"This case is a window onto a landscape of elite college athletes and certain individuals close to them who, in the course of their relationships, disregard NCAA rules and regulations," reads the introduction to the committee's 67-page report.

The document—most of which mirrors allegations first reported four years ago by Yahoo! Sports about housing, airline tickets, and other benefits given Bush and his family by wanna-be sports agents Lloyd Lake and Michael Michaels and marketing rep Mike Ornstein—shows that USC largely disagreed as to the extent of its culpability in the infractions. On Thursday evening, the school went on the offensive, releasing a redacted version of its original response to the NCAA's allegations in which it questions the credibility of Bush's accusers and disputes the validity of the evidence used to support several of the charges.

Rarely have we seen an NCAA case in which the accused school was so unabashedly defiant toward the investigators. At one point, it accuses the enforcement staff of "pursuing a novel and flawed theory" in defining Ornstein's affiliation with USC. No wonder their February hearing before the Infractions Committee lasted 30 hours.

In response to the sanctions, USC President Steven B. Sample said the school will accept "some" of the penalties but "sharply disagree[s] with many of the conclusions reached by the [committee]." It will be filing an appeal in the coming months. Essentially, the school contends there was nothing more it could have done to

University of Southern California running back Reggie Bush, during an October 2005 football game against Notre Dame. © AP IMAGES/MICHAEL CONROY.

stop the rogue agents and street runners at the heart of this case.

The NCAA's take: Oh yes, you could.

"The real issue here is, if you have high-profile players, your enforcement staff has to monitor those students at a higher level," committee chair Paul Dee said in a teleconference announcing the sanctions. "It's extraordinarily important to recognize that the [players] who are likely to be receiving these kind of interactions with people outside of the institution are the same people who are likely to receive some sort of [financial] reward down the road.

"High-profile players merit high-profile enforcement."

Consider: USC received almost the same exact penalties that Alabama did in 2002 (two-year bowl ban, 21 scholarships) for a case in which the school's own boosters made payments to recruits. The committee even said it "seriously considered the imposition of a television ban" against the Trojans, a penalty it hasn't doled out in more than 15 years.

In other words, in the committee's eyes, USC's failure to monitor a player's relationship with those

seeking to cash in on his future earnings is every bit as serious as Alabama's failure to monitor supporters trying to help secure future wins for their favorite team.

If you're a compliance officer at Florida, Texas or any other school teeming with future first-round draft picks, Thursday's ruling should be sending shivers down your spine. If you happen to be the next great quarterback or point guard in the class of 2010 or '11, be prepared to have your every hand-shake, conversation or Facebook post with anyone outside of the school monitored.

Not that that's remotely plausible.

"Monitoring and regulating human behavior is complex at best, and even more so in a far-flung region like Los Angeles, home to a vast entertainment-sports enterprise," said Sample. But he's still going to try. The school is hiring a consulting group led by former FBI director Louis Freeh to "help us take a fresh look at how we can keep unscrupulous agents and sports marketers away from our student-athletes."

It's good to see USC getting serious now, because there are numerous citations in the NCAA's report that show school officials were careless, if not downright negligent, in their handling of Bush and Mayo. Former coach Pete Carroll, now with the Seattle Seahawks, is never mentioned or cited with any wrongdoing. However, the committee contends running backs coach Todd McNair was quite clearly aware of Bush's relationship with Lake and Michaels yet failed to report it.

(McNair, who was retained by new head coach Lane Kiffin, was given a one-year show-cause penalty, which severely restricts his recruiting activities. USC, for its part, vehemently defends McNair, claiming investigators had flimsy evidence against him.)

In another passage, the committee notes that during the 2005 season, a "journalist" started making inquiries about Ornstein's presence on the sideline during games, which USC's sports information director then relayed to its former compliance director (who had signed off on Bush's previous summer internship with Ornstein), its then-compliance director and faculty athletic representative. The former compliance director pledged to follow up with Bush—but never did.

But that's nothing compared with the astounding carelessness alleged against Athletic Director Mike Garrett in regards to USC's recruitment of Mayo, whose handler, Rodney Guillory, was a known runner whose involvement with former Trojans star Jeff Trepagnier led to his suspension. Sayeth the NCAA:

On October 7, 2006, the director of athletics went to the men's basketball office after receiving an e-mail from a sports reporter looking for a response to a report that [Guillory] was a

University of Southern California athletic director Mike Garrett (right) welcomes new head football coach Pete Carroll to the program on December 15, 2000. © AP IMAGES/ REED SACON.

professional sports agent and involved with [Mayo]. When advised by [Floyd] that [Guillory] had on numerous occasions denied he was an agent or runner, the director of athletics responded, "That's all I need to know," and left the office. No further follow-up was done.

Are you serious?

In its defense, USC claims it "went to extraordinary lengths in its monitoring efforts both before and after [Mayo] enrolled." But then, the school self-imposed its own basketball penalties so it can't be all that indignant about the findings.

In a video response from Seattle on Thursday, a visibly angry Carroll said: "The agenda of the NCAA Infractions Committee took them beyond the facts. The facts don't merit the sanctions."

He may be right.

You'd be hard-pressed to find precedent for a school hit so hard over activities by parties with no association to

the university. It's not unreasonable to think it will find sympathy from the Infractions Appeal Committee, which, in 2003, overturned the second year of Michigan basketball's postseason ban despite four former players taking $616,000 from rogue booster Ed Martin. But such reversals are rare.

If anything, it sure seems the committee is trying to set a new precedent. It's holding USC responsible for the sins of not just Bush and Mayo, Ornstein and Guillory, but all the star athletes and seedy brokers everywhere whose misdeeds go unreported. They spent four years building their case in order to use it as a global deterrent.

"It's time for the NCAA and the universities to come together and elevate the awareness and understand of the vulnerability of athletes and their families," said Carroll. "We need to be proactive in act in every way to protect the college experience for these kids."

It's an admirable goal—but fortunately for him, it's also no longer his problem.

Kiffin, Matt Barkley, Seantrel Henderson and the rest of the 2010 and '11 Trojans are the ones who will pay the price for Bush's misdeeds, while administrators scratch some of Carroll's most memorable accomplishments from the record books.

If you believe the NCAA, this all could have been avoided had USC's athletic director, compliance department and running backs coach done their jobs better five years ago. If you believe USC's defense team, they couldn't have done anything more short of fitting Bush with an ankle monitoring bracelet.

One thing's for certain: After keeping fans waiting in the dark for four years, the NCAA delivered a powerful resolution. But it sure seems the end result was less about the organization punishing USC than it was about flexing its muscle to the rest of the country.

FURTHER RESOURCES
Web Sites

"Are You Really Being Recruited?" *National Scouting Report.* www.nsr-inc.com/athletes/are-you-really-being-recruited. php (accessed on March 25 2013).

Moore, Terence. "The Epidemic of College Football Scandals." *CNN*, August 19, 2011. www.cnn.com/ 2011/US/08/18/epidemic.college.football.scandals/index. html (accessed on March 25, 2013).

Weir, Tom. "A Look at Some of College Football's Biggest Scandals." *USA Today*, August 23, 2011. http://content. usatoday.com/communities/gameon/post/2011/08/miami-hurricanes-ncaa-scandals-football-history/1#.UUofn1eweqg (accessed on March 25, 2013).

General Resources

GENERAL

Batchelor, Bob. *The 2000s (American Popular Culture through History)*. Westport, CT: Greenwood Press, 2009.

Berberoglu, Berch, ed. *Globalization in the 21st Century: Labor, Capital, and the State on a World Scale*. New York: Palgrave Macmillan, 2010.

Campbell, Neil, and Alasdair Kean. *American Cultural Studies: An Introduction to American Culture*. 3rd ed. New York: Routledge, 2011.

Ericson, David F., ed. *The Politics of Inclusion and Exclusion: Identity Politics in Twenty-first Century America*. New York: Routledge, 2011.

Feldman, Jay. *Manufacturing Hysteria: Scapegoating, Surveillance, and Secrecy in Modern America*. New York: Pantheon Books, 2011.

Gerdes, Louise I., ed. *Perspectives on Modern History: 9/11*. Detroit: Greenhaven Press, 2010.

Kerton-Johnson, Nicholas. *Justifying America's Wars: The Conduct and Practice of US Military Intervention*. London & New York: Routledge, 2011.

Roberts, Dorothy. *Fatal Invention: How Science, Politics, and Big Business Re-create Race in the Twenty-first Century*. New York: New Press, 2011.

Schildkraut, Deborah. *Americanism in the Twenty-first Century: Public Opinion in the Age of Immigration*. New York: Cambridge University Press, 2011.

Wee, Valerie. *Teen Media: Hollywood and the Youth Market in the Digital Age*. Jefferson, NC: McFarland, 2010.

Zakaria, Fareed. *The Post-American World: Release 2.0.* New York: Norton, 2011.

THE ARTS

Altshuler, Bruce, ed. *Collecting the New: Museums and Contemporary Art*. Princeton, NJ: Princeton University Press, 2005.

Austerlitz, Saul. *Another Fine Mess: A History of American Film Comedy*. Chicago: Chicago Review Press, 2010.

Bailey, Julius, ed. *Jay-Z: Essays on Hip Hop's Philosopher King*. Jefferson, NC: McFarland, 2011.

Biberman, Matthew, and Julia Reinhard Lupton, eds. *Shakespeare after 9/11: How a Social Trauma Reshapes Interpretation*. Lewiston, NY: Edwin Mellen Press, 2010.

Blake, Casey Nelson, ed. *The Arts of Democracy: Art, Public Culture, and the State*. Washington, DC: Woodrow Wilson Center Press; Philadelphia: University of Pennsylvania Press, 2007.

Booker, M. Keith. *Disney, Pixar, and the Hidden Messages of Children's Films*. Santa Barbara, CA: Praeger, 2010.

Bordman, Gerald, and Richard Norton. *American Musical Theatre: A Chronicle*. 4th ed. Oxford & New York: Oxford University Press, 2011.

Brockett, Oscar G., and Robert J. Ball. *The Essential Theatre*. 9th ed. Boston: Wadsworth, 2008.

Cappucci, Paul R. *William Carlos Williams, Frank O'Hara, and the New York Art Scene*. Madison, NJ: Fairleigh Dickinson University Press, 2010.

Cherbo, Joni Maya, Ruth Ann Stewart, and Margaret Jane Wyszomirski, eds. *Understanding the Arts and*

Creative Sector in the United States. New Brunswick, NJ: Rutgers University Press, 2008.

Cowen, Tyler. *Good & Plenty: The Creative Successes of American Arts Funding.* Princeton, NJ: Princeton University Press, 2006.

Davis, Jessica Hoffmann. *Why Our Schools Need the Arts.* New York: Teachers College Press, 2008.

Day, Nancy. *Censorship, or Freedom of Expression?* Minneapolis: Lerner, 2001.

Dolan, Jill. *Theatre & Sexuality.* New York: Palgrave Macmillan, 2010.

Donoghue, Denis. *Speaking of Beauty.* New Haven, CT: Yale University Press, 2003.

Dorn, Charles, and Penelope Orr. *Art Education in a Climate of Reform: The Need for Measurable Goals in Art Instruction.* Lanham, MD: Rowman & Littlefield Education, 2008.

Franke, Astrid. *Pursue the Illusion: Problems of Public Poetry in America.* Heidelberg: Winter, 2010.

Gabbard, Krin. *Hotter Than That: The Trumpet, Jazz, and American Culture.* New York: Faber & Faber, 2008.

Green, Stanley. *Broadway Musicals, Show by Show.* 6th ed., revised by Kay Green. New York: Applause Theatre and Cinema Books, 2008.

Gussow, Adam. *Journeyman's Road: Modern Blues Lives from Faulkner's Mississippi to Post-9/11 New York.* Knoxville: University of Tennessee Press, 2007.

Ivey, Bill. *Arts, Inc.: How Greed and Neglect Have Destroyed Our Cultural Rights.* Berkeley: University of California Press, 2008.

Johnston, Patricia, ed., *Seeing High & Low: Representing Social Conflict in American Visual Culture.* Berkeley: University of California Press, 2006.

Kassing, Gayle. *History of Dance: An Interactive Arts Approach.* Champaign, IL: Human Kinetics, 2007.

Keyser, Herbert H. *Geniuses of the American Musical Theatre: The Composers and Lyricists.* New York: Applause Theatre and Cinema Books, 2009.

Kidd, Dustin. *Legislating Creativity: The Intersections of Art and Politics.* New York: Routledge, 2010.

Knapp, Raymond. *The American Musical and the Performance of Personal Identity.* Princeton, NJ: Princeton University Press, 2006.

Korza, Pam, Barbara Schaffer Bacon, and Andrea Assaf. *Civic Dialogue, Arts & Culture: Findings from Animating Democracy.* Washington, DC: Americans for the Arts, 2005.

Lazerine, Cameron, and Devin Lazerine. *Rap-up: The Ultimate Guide to Hip-Hop and R&B.* New York: Grand Central, 2008.

Levy, Ellen. *Criminal Ingenuity: Moore, Cornell, Ashbery, and the Struggle between the Arts.* Oxford & New York: Oxford University Press, 2011.

Mason, Jeffrey D. *Stone Tower: The Political Theater of Arthur Miller.* Ann Arbor: University of Michigan Press, 2008.

McCarthy, Kevin F., et al. *A Portrait of the Visual Arts: Meeting the Challenges of a New Era.* Santa Monica, CA: RAND, 2005.

Miller, Angela L., et al. *American Encounters: Art, History, and Cultural Identity.* Upper Saddle River, NJ: Pearson/Prentice Hall, 2008.

Murray, William. *Fortissimo: Backstage at the Opera with Sacred Monsters and Young Singers.* New York: Crown, 2005.

Nel, Philip. *The Avant-Garde and American Postmodernity: Small Incisive Shocks.* Jackson: University Press of Mississippi, 2002.

Paik, Karen. *To Infinity and Beyond!: The Story of Pixar Animation Studios.* San Francisco: Chronicle Books, 2007.

Pruett, David B. *MuzikMafia: From the Local Nashville Scene to the National Mainstream.* Jackson: University Press of Mississippi, 2010.

Saddik, Annette J. *Contemporary American Drama.* Edinburgh: Edinburgh University Press, 2007.

Shay, Anthony. *Dancing across Borders: The American Fascination with Exotic Dance Forms.* Jefferson, NC: McFarland, 2008.

Singer, Barry. *Ever After: The Last Years of Musical Theater and Beyond.* New York: Applause Theatre and Cinema Books, 2004.

Smith, Thomas M. *Raising the Barre: The Geographic, Financial, and Economic Trends of Nonprofit Dance Companies: A Study.* Edited by Bonnie Nichols. Washington, DC: National Endowment for the Arts, 2003.

Spiegelman, Willard. *How Poets See the World: The Art of Description in Contemporary Poetry.* New York: Oxford University Press, 2005.

Stout, Janis P. *Picturing a Different West: Vision, Illustration, and the Tradition of Austin and Cather.* Lubbock: Texas Tech University Press, 2007.

Tepper, Steven J., and Bill Ivey, eds. *Engaging Art: The Next Great Transformation of America's Cultural Life.* New York: Routledge, 2008.

U.S. Congress, House Committee on Education and Labor. *The Economic and Employment Impact of the Arts and Music Industry: Hearing before the Committee on Education and Labor, U.S. House of Representatives, One Hundred Eleventh Congress, First Session, Hearing Held in Washington, DC, March 26, 2009.* Washington, DC: Government Printing Office, 2009.

BUSINESS AND THE ECONOMY

Anderson, Chris. *The Long Tail: Why the Future of Business Is Selling Less of More.* New York: Hyperion, 2006.

Auletta, Ken. *World War 3.0: Microsoft and Its Enemies.* New York: Random House, 2001.

Battelle, John. *The Search: How Google and Its Rivals Rewrote the Rules of Business.* New York: Portfolio, 2005.

Cohan, William D. *The Last Tycoons: The Secret History of Lazard Frères & Co.* New York: Doubleday, 2008.

Dubner, Stephen, and Steven D. Levitt. *Freakonomics: A Rogue Economist Explores the Hidden Side of Everything.* New York: Morrow, 2006.

Ehrenreich, Barbara. *Nickel and Dimed: On (Not) Getting By in America.* New York: Metropolitan, 2001.

El-Erian, Mohamed. *When Markets Collide: Investment Strategies for the Age of Global Economic Change.* New York: McGraw-Hill, 2008.

Fishman, Charles. *The Wal-Mart Effect: How the World's Most Powerful Company Really Works, and How It's Transforming the American Economy.* New York: Penguin, 2006.

Gladwell, Malcolm. *The Tipping Point: How Little Things Can Make a Big Difference.* Boston: Little, Brown, 2000.

Greenspan, Alan. *The Age of Turbulence: Adventures in a New World.* New York: Penguin, 2007.

Lewis, Michael. *Moneyball: The Art of Winning an Unfair Game.* New York: Norton, 2003.

McLean, Bethany, and Peter Elkind. *The Smartest Guys in the Room: The Amazing Rise and Scandalous Fall of Enron.* New York: Portfolio, 2003.

Mezrich, Ben. *The Accidental Billionaires: The Founding of Facebook: A Tale of Sex, Money, Genius, and Betrayal.* New York: Doubleday, 2009.

Reinhart, Carmen, and Kenneth Rogoff. *This Time Is Different: Eight Centuries of Financial Folly.* Princeton, NJ: Princeton University Press, 2009.

Rivoli, Pietra. *The Travels of a T-Shirt in the Global Economy: An Economist Examines the Markets, Power, and Politics of World Trade.* New York: Wiley, 2005.

Schroeder, Alice. *The Snowball: Warren Buffett and the Business of Life.* New York: Bantam, 2008.

Sorkin, Andrew Ross. *Too Big to Fail: The Inside Story of How Wall Street and Washington Fought to Save the Financial System from Crisis—and Themselves.* New York: Viking, 2009.

Stewart, James. *Disney War.* New York: Simon & Schuster, 2005.

Surowiecki, James. *The Wisdom of Crowds: Why the Many Are Smarter Than the Few and How Collective Wisdom Shapes Business.* New York: Doubleday, 2004.

Taleb, Nassim Nicholas. *The Black Swan: The Impact of the Highly Improbable.* New York: Random House, 2007.

Tapscott, Don, and Anthony D. Williams. *Wikinomics: How Mass Collaboration Changes Everything.* New York: Portfolio, 2006.

Wessel, David. *In Fed We Trust: Ben Bernanke's War on the Great Panic.* New York: Random House, 2009.

EDUCATION

Chenoweth, Karin. *It's Being Done: Academic Success in Unexpected Schools.* Cambridge, MA: Harvard Education Press, 2007.

Christensen, Clayton M., Michael B. Horn, and Curtis W. Johnson. *Disrupting Class: How Disruptive Innovation Will Change the Way the World Learns.* New York: McGraw-Hill, 2008.

Cohen, David K., and Susan L. Moffitt. *The Ordeal of Equality: Did Federal Regulation Fix the Schools?* Cambridge, MA: Harvard University Press, 2009.

Cullen, Dave. *Columbine.* New York: Twelve, 2009.

Davies, Gareth. *See Government Grow: Education Politics from Johnson to Reagan.* Lawrence: University Press of Kansas, 2007.

Elmore, Richard F. *School Reform from the Inside Out.* Cambridge, MA: Harvard Education Press, 2004.

Goldin, Claudia D., and Lawrence F. Katz. *The Race between Education and Technology.* Cambridge, MA: Belknap Press of Harvard University Press, 2008.

Grant, Gerald. *Hope and Despair in the American City: Why There Are No Bad Schools in Raleigh.* Cambridge, MA: Harvard University Press, 2009.

Green, Jay P., Greg Forster, and Marcus A. Winters. *Education Myths: What Special Interest Groups Want*

You to Believe about Our Schools—and Why It Isn't So. Lanham, MD: Rowman & Littlefield, 2005.

Hanushek, Eric A., and Alfred A. Lindseth. *Schoolhouses, Courthouses, and Statehouses: Solving the Funding-Achievement Puzzle in America's Public Schools.* Princeton, NJ: Princeton University Press, 2009.

Henig, Jeffrey R. *Spin Cycle: How Research Is Used in Policy Debates: The Case of Charter Schools.* New York: Russell Sage Foundation, 2008.

Hess, Frederick M. *Common Sense School Reform.* New York: Palgrave Macmillan, 2004.

Hirsch, E. D., Jr. *The Knowledge Deficit: Closing the Shocking Education Gap for American Children.* Boston: Houghton Mifflin, 2006.

Howell, William G., and Paul E. Peterson. *The Education Gap: Vouchers and Urban Schools.* Washington, DC: Brookings Institution Press, 2002.

Jacobs, Joanne. *Our School: The Inspiring Idea of Two Teachers, One Big Idea, and the School That Beat the Odds.* New York: Palgrave Macmillan, 2005.

Kahlenburg, Richard D. *All Together Now: Creating Middle-Class Schools through Public School Choice.* Washington, DC: Brookings Institution Press, 2001.

Kohn, Alfie. *The Homework Myth: Why Our Kids Get Too Much of a Bad Thing.* Cambridge, MA: Da Capo, 2006.

Koretz, Daniel M. *Measuring Up: What Educational Testing Really Tells Us.* Cambridge, MA: Harvard University Press, 2008.

Matthews, Jay. *Work Hard. Be Nice: How Two Inspired Teachers Created the Most Promising Schools in America.* Chapel Hill, NC: Algonquin Books of Chapel Hill, 2009.

Meier, Deborah. *In Schools We Trust: Creating Communities of Learning in an Era of Testing and Standardization.* Boston: Beacon, 2002.

Moe, Terry M. *Schools, Vouchers, and the American Public.* Washington, DC: Brookings Institution Press, 2001.

Moe, Terry M., and John E. Chubb. *Liberating Learning: Technology, Politics, and the Future of American Education.* San Francisco: Jossey-Bass, 2009.

Murray, Charles. *Real Education: Four Simple Truths for Bringing America's Schools Back to Reality.* New York: Crown Forum, 2008.

Ouchi, William G., and Lydia G. Segal. *Making Schools Work: A Revolutionary Plan to Get Your Children the Education They Need.* New York: Simon & Schuster, 2003.

Payne, Charles M. *So Much Reform, So Little Change: The Persistence of Failure in Urban Schools.* Cambridge, MA: Harvard Education Press, 2008.

Perlstein, Linda. *Tested: One American School Struggles to Make the Grade.* New York: Holt, 2007.

Ravitch, Diane. *Left Back: A Century of Failed School Reforms.* New York: Simon & Schuster, 2000.

Rothstein, Richard, Rebecca Jacobsen, and Tamara Wilder. *Grading Education, Getting Accountability Right.* Washington, DC: Economic Policy Institute; New York: Teachers College Press, 2008.

Thernstrom, Abigail, and Stephan Thernstrom. *No Excuses: Closing the Racial Gap in Learning.* New York: Simon & Schuster, 2003.

Tough, Paul. *Whatever It Takes: Geoffrey Canada's Quest to Change Harlem and America.* Boston: Houghton Mifflin, 2008.

Williams, Joe. *Cheating Our Kids: How Politics and Greed Ruin Education.* New York: Palgrave Macmillan, 2005.

Willingham, Daniel T. *Why Don't Students Like School?: A Cognitive Scientist Answers Questions About How the Mind Works and What It Means for the Classroom.* San Francisco: Jossey-Bass, 2009.

Yong Zhao. *Catching Up or Leading the Way: American Education in the Age of Globalization.* Alexandria, VA: Association for Supervision and Curriculum Development, 2009.

FASHION AND DESIGN

Adams, Cey, and Bill Adler. *Definition: The Art and Design of Hip-Hop.* New York: Collins Design, 2008.

Beckham, Victoria. *That Extra Half an Inch: Hair, Heels, and Everything in Between.* New York: HarperCollins, 2007.

Black, Sandy. *Eco-Chic: The Fashion Paradox.* London: Black Dog, 2008.

Bright, J. E. *America's Next Top Model: Fierce Guide to Life: The Ultimate Source of Beauty, Fashion, and Model Behavior.* New York: Universe, 2009.

Ching, Francis D. K. *Architecture: Form, Space, and Order.* 3rd ed. Hoboken, NJ: Wiley, 2007.

Elam, Kimberly. *Geometry of Design: Studies in Proportion and Composition.* 2nd ed. New York: Princeton Architectural Press, 2011.

Fletcher, Kate. *Sustainable Fashion and Textiles: Design Journeys*. London & Sterling, VA: Earthscan, 2008.

Foley, Bridget. *Marc Jacobs (Memoirs)*. New York: Assouline, 2004.

Foley, Bridget. *Tom Ford*. New York: Rizzoli, 2004.

Freeman, Hadley. *The Meaning of Sunglasses: And a Guide to Almost All Things Fashionable*. New York: Viking, 2008.

Garcia, Nina. *The Little Black Book of Style*. New York: HarperCollins, 2007.

Garcia, Nina. *The Style Strategy: A Less Is More Approach to Staying Chic and Shopping Smart*. New York: HarperCollins, 2009.

Hancock, Joseph. *Brand/Story: Ralph, Vera, Johnny, Billy, and Other Adventures in Fashion Branding*. New York: Fairchild, 2009.

Hannah, Gail Greet. *Elements of Design: Rowena Reed Kostellow and the Structure of Visual Relationships*. New York: Princeton Architectural Press, 2002.

Koda, Harold, and Kohle Yohannon. *The Model as Muse: Embodying Fashion*. New York: Metropolitan Museum of Art; New Haven, CT: Yale University Press, 2009.

Myzelev, Alla, and John Potvin. *Fashion, Interior Design, and the Contours of Modern Identity*. Burlington, VT: Ashgate, 2010.

Norwood, Mandi. *Michelle Style: Celebrating the First Lady of Fashion*. New York: Morrow, 2009.

Oliva, Alberto, and Norberto Angletti. *In Vogue: The Illustrated History of the World's Most Famous Fashion Magazine*. New York: Rizzoli, 2006.

Owen, Marna. *Animal Rights: Noble Cause or Needless Effort?* Minneapolis: Twenty-First Century Books, 2010.

Polan, Brenda, and Roger Tredre. *The Great Fashion Designers*. New York: Berg, 2009.

Schuman, Scott. *The Sartorialist*. New York: Penguin, 2009.

Selby, Todd. *The Selby Is in Your Place*. New York: Abrams, 2010.

Tate, Sharon Lee. *Inside Fashion Design*. 5th ed. Upper Saddle River, NJ: Prentice Hall, 2004.

The Teen Vogue Handbook: An Insider's Guide to Careers in Fashion. New York: Razorbill, 2009.

Watson, Linda. *Vogue Fashion: Over 100 Years of Style by Decade and Designer*. New York: Firefly, 2008.

Zoe, Rachel, and Rose Apodaca. *Style A to Zoe: The Art of Fashion, Beauty, & Everything Glamour*. Buffalo, NY: Grand Central, 2007.

GOVERNMENT AND POLITICS

Berman, Ari. *Herding Donkeys: The Fight to Rebuild the Democratic Party and Reshape American Politics*. New York: Farrar, Straus & Giroux, 2010.

Bernstein, Carl. *A Woman in Charge: The Life of Hillary Rodham Clinton*. New York: Knopf, 2007.

Brinkley, Douglas. *The Great Deluge: Hurricane Katrina, New Orleans, and the Mississippi Gulf Coast*. New York: Morrow, 2006.

Bush, George W. *Decision Points*. New York: Crown, 2010.

Clarke, Richard. *Against All Enemies: Inside America's War on Terror*. New York: Free Press, 2004.

Coll, Steve. *Ghost Wars: The Secret History of the CIA, Afghanistan, and Bin Laden, from the Soviet Invasion to September 10, 2001*. New York: Penguin, 2004.

Dean, Howard, and Judith Warner. *You Have the Power: How to Take Back Our Country and Restore Democracy in America*. New York: Simon & Schuster, 2004.

Draper, Robert. *Dead Certain: The Presidency of George W. Bush*. New York: Free Press, 2007.

Filkins, Dexter. *The Forever War*. New York: Knopf, 2008.

Frank, Thomas. *What's the Matter with Kansas?: How Conservatives Won the Heart of America*. New York: Metropolitan, 2004.

Heilemann, John, and Mark Halperin. *Game Change: Obama and the Clintons, McCain and Palin, and the Race of a Lifetime*. New York: Harper Perennial, 2010.

Horne, Jed. *Breach of Faith: Hurricane Katrina and the Near Death of a Great American City*. New York: Random House, 2006.

Jones, Seth G. *In the Graveyard of Empires: America's War in Afghanistan*. New York: Norton, 2009.

Lepore, Jill. *The Whites of Their Eyes: The Tea Party's Revolution and the Battle over American History*. Princeton, NJ: Princeton University Press, 2010.

Lewis, Michael. *The Big Short: Inside the Doomsday Machine*. New York: Norton, 2010.

Mayer, Jane. *The Dark Side: The Inside Story of How the War on Terror Turned into a War on American Ideals*. New York: Doubleday, 2008.

McLean, Bethany, and Peter Elkind. *The Smartest Guys in the Room: The Amazing Rise and Scandalous Fall of Enron.* New York: Portfolio, 2003.

National Commission on Terrorist Attacks upon the United States. *The 9/11 Commission Report: Final Report of the National Commission on Terrorist Attacks upon the United States.* New York: Norton, 2004.

Obama, Barack. *The Audacity of Hope: Thoughts on Reclaiming the American Dream.* New York: Crown, 2006.

Packer, George. *The Assassins' Gate: America in Iraq.* New York: Farrar, Straus & Giroux, 2006.

Palin, Sarah. *Going Rogue: An American Life.* New York: HarperCollins, 2009.

Remnick, David. *The Bridge: The Life and Rise of Barack Obama.* New York: Knopf, 2010.

Ricks, Thomas E. *Fiasco: The American Military Adventure in Iraq.* New York: Penguin, 2006.

Rove, Karl. *Courage and Consequence: My Life as a Conservative in the Fight.* New York: Simon & Schuster, 2010.

Sabato, Larry J., ed. *Divided States of America: The Slash and Burn Politics of the 2004 Presidential Election.* New York: Pearson-Longman, 2006.

Scahill, Jeremy. *Blackwater: The Rise of the World's Most Powerful Mercenary Army.* New York: Nation, 2007.

Sorkin, Andrew Ross. *Too Big to Fail: The Inside Story of How Wall Street and Washington Fought to Save the Financial System—and Themselves.* New York: Viking, 2009.

Sullivan, Andrew. *The Conservative Soul: How We Lost It, How to Get it Back.* New York: HarperCollins, 2006.

Toobin, Jeffrey. *Too Close to Call: The Thirty-Six-Day Battle to Decide the 2000 Election.* New York: Random House, 2002.

Traister, Rebecca. *Big Girls Don't Cry: The Election That Changed Everything for American Women.* New York: Free Press, 2010.

Woodward, Bob. *Bush at War.* New York: Simon & Schuster, 2002.

LAW AND JUSTICE

Alexander, Michelle. *The New Jim Crow: Mass Incarceration in the Age of Colorblindness.* New York: New Press, 2010.

Amar, Akhil Reed. *America's Constitution: A Biography.* New York: Random House, 2005.

Barnhart, Bill, and Gene Schlickman. *John Paul Stevens: An Independent Life.* Dekalb: Northern Illinois University Press, 2010.

Benhabib, Seyla. *The Rights of Others: Aliens, Residents, and Citizens.* Cambridge & New York: Cambridge University Press, 2004.

Binder, Sarah A., and Forrest Maltzman. *Advice & Dissent: The Struggle to Shape the Federal Judiciary.* Washington, DC: Brookings Institution Press, 2009.

Chauncey, George. *Why Marriage?: The History Shaping Today's Debate over Gay Equality.* New York: Basic Books, 2004.

Chemerinsky, Erwin. *The Conservative Assault on the Constitution.* New York: Simon & Schuster, 2010.

Dean, John. *The Rehnquist Choice: The Untold Story of the Nixon Appointment That Redefined the Supreme Court.* New York: Touchstone, 2001.

Epstein, Lee, and Jeffrey A. Segal. *Advice and Consent: The Politics of Judicial Appointments.* Oxford & New York: Oxford University Press, 2005.

Finan, Christopher M. *From the Palmer Raids to the Patriot Act: A History of the Fight for Free Speech in America.* Boston: Beacon, 2007.

Friedman, Lawrence M. *A History of American Law.* 3rd ed. New York: Simon & Schuster, 2005.

Garland, David. *Peculiar Institution: America's Death Penalty in an Age of Abolition.* Cambridge, MA: Belknap Press of Harvard University Press, 2010.

Graff, Garret M. *The Threat Matrix: The FBI in the Age of Global Terror.* New York: Little, Brown, 2011.

Hall, Kermit L., ed. *The Oxford Companion to the Supreme Court of the United States.* 2nd ed. Oxford & New York: Oxford University Press, 2005.

Lewis, Michael, et al. *The War on Terror and the Laws of War: A Military Perspective.* Oxford & New York: Oxford University Press, 2009.

Marshall, Thomas R. *Public Opinion and the Rehnquist Court.* Albany, NY: SUNY Press, 2008.

O'Connor, Sandra Day. *The Majesty of the Law: Reflections of a Supreme Court Justice.* Edited by Craig Joyce. New York: Random House, 2003.

O'Connor, Sandra Day, and H. Alan Davis. *Lazy B: Growing Up on a Cattle Ranch in the American Southwest.* New York: Random House, 2002.

Perkinson, Robert. *Texas Tough: The Rise of America's Prison Empire.* New York: Metropolitan Books, 2010.

Pious, Richard M. *The War on Terrorism and the Rule of Law.* Los Angeles: Roxbury, 2006.

Powe, Lucas A., Jr. *The Supreme Court and the American Elite, 1798–2008*. Cambridge, MA: Harvard University Press, 2009.

Richards, David A. J. *The Sodomy Cases: Bowers v. Hardwick and Lawrence v. Texas*. Lawrence: University Press of Kansas, 2009.

Rosen, Jeffrey. *The Supreme Court: The Personalities and Rivalries That Defined America*. New York: Times Books, 2006.

Solis, Gary D. *The Law of Armed Conflict: International Humanitarian Law in War*. Cambridge & New York: Cambridge University Press, 2010.

Stone, Geoffrey R. *Perilous Times: Free Speech in Wartime: From the Sedition Act of 1798 to the War on Terrorism*. New York: Norton, 2004.

Strebeigh, Fred. *Equal: Women Reshape American Law*. New York: Norton, 2009.

Thomas, Clarence. *My Grandfather's Son: A Memoir*. New York: Harper, 2007.

Turow, Scott. *Ultimate Punishment: A Lawyer's Reflections on Dealing with the Death Penalty*. New York: Farrar, Straus, and Giroux, 2003.

Vrato, Elizabeth. *The Counselors: Conversations with 18 Courageous Women Who Have Changed the World*. Philadelphia: Running Press, 2002.

Wittes, Benjamin. *Law and the Long War: The Future of Justice in the Age of Terror*. New York: Penguin, 2008.

LIFESTYLES AND SOCIAL TRENDS

Allan, Stuart. *Online News: Journalism and the Internet*. New York: Open University Press, 2006.

Allen, Ted, Kyan Douglas, Thom Filicia, Carson Kressley, and Jai Rodriguez. *Queer Eye for the Straight Guy: The Fab 5's Guide to Looking Better, Cooking Better, Dressing Better, Behaving Better, and Living Better*. New York: Clarkson Potter, 2004.

Bradley, James, and Ron Powers. *Flags of Our Fathers*. New York: Bantam, 2000.

Clinton, Hillary Rodham. *Living History*. New York: Simon & Schuster, 2003.

Crystal, David. *Txtng: The Gr8 Db8*. New York: Oxford University Press, 2008.

Fine, Doug. *Farewell, My Subaru: An Epic Adventure in Local Living*. New York: Villard, 2008.

Friedman, Thomas L. *Hot, Flat, and Crowded: Why We Need a Green Revolution—and How It Can Renew America*. New York: Farrar, Straus & Giroux, 2008.

Gilmour, David. *The Film Club: A Memoir*. New York: Twelve, 2008.

Gore, Al. *An Inconvenient Truth: The Planetary Emergency of Global Warming and What We Can Do About It*. Emmaus, PA: Rodale Books, 2006.

Iggulden, Conn, and Hal Iggulden. *The Dangerous Book for Boys*. London: HarperCollins, 2006.

Krakauer, Jon. *Where Men Win Glory: The Odyssey of Pat Tillman*. New York: Doubleday, 2009.

Levitt, Steven D., and Stephen J. Dubner. *Freakonomics: A Rogue Economist Explains the Hidden Side of Everything*. New York: Morrow, 2005.

Ling, Rich. *The Mobile Connection: The Cell Phone's Impact on Society*. San Francisco: Morgan Kaufman, 2004.

Menn, Joseph. *All The Rave: The Rise and Fall of Shawn Fanning's Napster*. New York: Crown Business, 2003.

Mezrich, Ben. *The Accidental Billionaires: The Founding of Facebook: A Tale of Sex, Money, Genius, and Betrayal*. New York: Doubleday, 2009.

Obama, Barack. *The Audacity of Hope: Thoughts on Reclaiming the American Dream*. New York: Crown, 2006.

O'Reilly, Bill. *Culture Warrior*. New York: Broadway Books, 2006.

Pollan, Michael. *The Omnivore's Dilemma: A Natural History of Four Meals*. New York: Penguin, 2006.

Powers, William. *Hamlet's BlackBerry: A Practical Philosophy for Building a Good Life in the Digital Age*. New York: Harper, 2010.

Schlosser, Eric. *Fast Food Nation: The Dark Side of the All-American Meal*. New York: Houghton Mifflin, 2001.

Simon, Bryant. *Everything but the Coffee: Learning about America from Starbucks*. Berkeley: University of California Press, 2009.

Steiner, Leslie Morgan, ed. *The Mommy Wars: Stay-at-Home and Career Moms Face Off on Their Choices, Their Lives, Their Families*. New York: Random House, 2006.

Strangelove, Michael. *The Empire of the Mind: Digital Piracy and the Anti-Capitalist Movement*. Toronto: University of Toronto Press, 2005.

Winograd, Morley, and Michael D. Hais. *Millennial Makeover: MySpace, YouTube, and the Future of American Politics*. New Brunswick, NJ: Rutgers University Press, 2008.

THE MEDIA

Ali-Karamali, Sumbul. *The Muslim Next Door: The Qur'an, the Media, and That Veil Thing*. Ashland, OR: White Cloud, 2008.

Alterman, Eric. *What Liberal Media?: The Truth about Bias and the News.* New York: Basic Books, 2003.

Andersen, Robin. *A Century of Media, a Century of War.* New York: Peter Lang, 2006.

Bagdikian, Ben H. *The New Media Monopoly.* Boston: Beacon, 2004.

Barkin, Steve Michael. *American Television News: The Media Marketplace and the Public Interest.* Armonk, NY: M. E. Sharpe, 2002.

Best, Joel. *Damned Lies and Statistics: Untangling Numbers from the Media, Politicians, and Activists.* Berkeley: University of California Press, 2001.

Boehlert, Eric. *Lapdogs: How the Press Rolled Over for Bush.* New York: Free Press, 2006.

Brock, David, and Paul Waldman. *Free Ride: John McCain and the Media.* New York: Anchor, 2008.

Chester, Jeff. *Digital Destiny: New Media and the Future of Democracy.* New York: New Press, 2007.

Clark, Lynn Schofield, ed. *Religion, Media, and the Marketplace.* Rutgers, NJ: Rutgers University Press, 2007.

Cohen, Elliot D., and Bruce W. Fraser. *The Last Days of Democracy: How Big Media and Power-Hungry Government are Turning America into a Dictatorship.* Amherst, NY: Prometheus, 2007.

Croft, Stuart. *Culture, Crisis and America's War on Terror.* Cambridge & New York: Cambridge University Press, 2006.

Croteau, David, and William Hoynes. *The Business of Media: Corporate Media and the Public Interest.* Newbury Park, CA: Pine Forge, 2001.

De Zengotita, Thomas. *Mediated: How the Media Shapes Our World and the Way We Live.* New York: Bloomsbury, 2005.

Dill, Karen E. *How Fantasy Becomes Reality: Seeing through Media Influence.* Oxford & New York: Oxford University Press, 2009.

Durham, Meenakshi Gigi, and Douglas Kellner. *Media and Cultural Studies: Keyworks.* Malden, MA: Blackwell, 2001.

Faludi, Susan. *The Terror Dream: Fear and Fantasy in Post-9/11 America.* New York: Metropolitan, 2007.

Fellow, Anthony R., and John Tebbel. *American Media History.* Belmont, CA: Thomson/Wadsworth, 2005.

Franken, Al. *Lies (and the Lying Liars Who Tell Them): A Fair and Balanced Look at the Right.* New York: Dutton, 2003.

Fritz, Ben, Bryan Keefer, and Brendan Nyhan. *All the President's Spin: George W. Bush, the Media, and the Truth.* New York: Simon & Schuster, 2004.

Gauntlett, David. *Media, Gender and Identity: An Introduction.* London & New York: Routledge, 2002.

Gibson, John. *How the Left Swiftboated America: The Liberal Media Conspiracy to Make You Think George Bush Was the Worst President in History.* New York: Harper, 2009.

Gill, Rosalind. *Gender and the Media.* Cambridge & Malden, MA: Polity, 2007.

Gillmor, Dan. *We the Media: Grassroots Journalism by the People, for the People.* Sebastopol, CA: O'Reilly, 2004.

Gitlin, Todd. *Media Unlimited: How the Torrent of Images and Sounds Overwhelms Our Lives.* New York: Metropolitan, 2001.

Goldberg, Bernard. *Bias: A CBS Insider Exposes How the Media Distort the News.* Washington, DC: Regnery, 2001.

Goodman, Amy, and David Goodman. *The Exception to the Rulers: Exposing Oily Politicians, War Profiteers, and the Media That Love Them.* New York: Hyperion, 2004.

Goodman, Amy, and David Goodman. *Static: Government Liars, Media Cheerleaders, and the People Who Fight Back.* New York: Hyperion, 2006.

Gunther, Richard, and Anthony Mughan. *Democracy and the Media: A Comparative Perspective.* Cambridge & New York: Cambridge University Press, 2000.

Hamm, Theodore. *The New Blue Media: How Michael Moore, MoveOn.org, Jon Stewart and Company Are Transforming Progressive Politics.* New York: New Press, 2008.

Hansen, Mark B. N. *New Philosophy for New Media.* Cambridge, MA: MIT Press, 2004.

Harfoush, Rahaf. *Yes We Did: An Inside Look at How Social Media Built the Obama Brand.* Berkeley, CA: New Riders, 2009.

Harrison, John, and Martin Hirst. *Communication and New Media: From Broadcast to Narrowcast.* New York: Oxford University Press, 2007.

Henderson, David. *Making News: A Straight-Shooting Guide to Media Relations.* Lincoln, NE: iUniverse Star, 2006.

Hess, Stephen, and Marvin L. Kalb, eds. *The Media and the War on Terrorism.* Washington, DC: Brookings Institution Press, 2003.

Hollihan, Thomas A. *Uncivil Wars: Political Campaigns in a Media Age*. Boston: St. Martin's Press, 2001.

Indiana, Gary. *Schwarzenegger Syndrome: Politics and Celebrity in the Age of Contempt*. New York: New Press, 2005.

Ito, Mizuko, et al. *Living and Learning with New Media: Summary of Findings from the Digital Youth Project*. Cambridge, MA: MIT Press, 2009.

Iyengar, Shanto, and Jennifer McGrady. *Media Politics: A Citizen's Guide*. New York: Norton, 2007.

James, Carrie. *Young People, Ethics, and the New Digital Media: A Synthesis from the Good Play Project*. Cambridge, MA: MIT Press, 2009.

Jenkins, Henry. *Convergence Culture: Where Old and New Media Collide*. New York: NYU Press, 2006.

Katovsky, Bill, and Timothy Carlson, eds. *Embedded: The Media at War in Iraq—An Oral History*. Guilford, CT: Lyons, 2003.

Klinenburg, Eric. *Fighting for Air: The Battle to Control America's Media*. New York: Metropolitan, 2007.

Knee, Jonathan A., Bruce C. Greenwald, and Ava Seave. *The Curse of the Mogul: What's Wrong with the World's Leading Media Companies*. New York: Portfolio, 2009.

Levinson, Paul. *New New Media*. Boston: Allyn & Bacon, 2009.

Lind, Rebecca Ann, ed. *Race/Gender/Media; Considering Diversity Across Audience, Content, and Producers*. Boston: Allyn & Bacon, 2004.

MacFarquhar, Neil. *The Media Relations Department of Hizbollah Wishes You a Happy Birthday: Unexpected Encounters in the Changing Middle East*. New York: PublicAffairs, 2009.

Manovich, Lev. *The Language of New Media*. Cambridge, MA: MIT Press, 2001.

Mayer, Jeremy D. *American Media Politics in Transition*. Boston: McGraw-Hill, 2007.

McChesney, Robert W. *The Problem of the Media: U.S. Communication Politics in the Twenty-First Century*. New York: Monthly Review, 2004.

Medoff, Norman J., and Barbara Kaye. *Electronic Media: Then, Now, and Later*. Boston: Allyn & Bacon, 2004.

Moyers, Bill. *Moyers on America: A Journalist and His Times*. Edited by Julie Leininger Pycior. New York: New Press, 2004.

Mueller, James E. *Towel Snapping the Press: Bush's Journey from Locker-room Antics to Message Control*. Lanham, MD: Rowman & Littlefield, 2006.

Nichols, John, and Robert W. McChesney. *Tragedy and Farce: How the American Media Sell Wars, Spin Elections, and Destroy Democracy*. New York: New Press, 2005.

O'Reilly, Tim, and Sarah Milstein. *The Twitter Book*. Sebastopol, CA: O'Reilly, 2009.

Potter, W. James. *11 Myths of Media Violence*. Thousand Oaks, CA: Sage, 2003.

Qualman, Erik. *Socialnomics: How Social Media Transforms the Way We Live and Do Business*. Hoboken, NJ: Wiley, 2009.

Radford, Benjamin. *Media Mythmakers: How Journalists, Activists, and Advertisers Mislead Us*. Amherst, NY: Prometheus, 2003.

Ross, Karen. *Gendered Media: Women, Men, and Identity Politics*. Lanham, MD: Rowman & Littlefield, 2010.

Rozell, Mark J., ed. *Media Power, Media Politics*. Lanham, MD: Rowman & Littlefield, 2003.

Squires, Catherine R. *African Americans and the Media*. Cambridge & Malden, MA: Polity, 2009.

Subervi-Velez, Federico, ed. *The Mass Media and Latino Politics: Studies of U.S. Media Content, Campaign Strategies and Survey Research: 1984–2004*. New York: Routledge, 2008.

West, Darrell M. *The Rise and Fall of the Media Establishment*. Boston: St. Martin's Press, 2001.

Wheeler, Marcy. *Anatomy of Deceit: How the Bush Administration Used the Media to Sell the Iraq War and Out a Spy*. Berkeley, CA: Vaster, 2007.

Wolcott, James. *Attack Poodles and Other Media Mutants: The Looting of the News in a Time of Terror*. New York: Miramax, 2004.

MEDICINE AND HEALTH

Abraham, Thomas. *Twenty-First Century Plague: The Story of SARS*. Baltimore: Johns Hopkins University Press, 2005.

Basting, Anne Davis. *Forget Memory: Creating Better Lives for People with Dementia*. Baltimore: Johns Hopkins University Press, 2009.

Brinker, Nancy G., and Joni Rodgers. *Promise Me: How a Sister's Love Launched the Global Movement to End Breast Cancer*. New York: Crown, 2010.

Clark, David. *Germs, Genes & Civilization: How Epidemics Shaped Who We Are Today*. Upper Saddle River, NJ: FT Press, 2010.

Collins, Michael J. *Hot Lights, Cold Steel: Life, Death and Sleepless Nights in a Surgeon's First Years*. New York: St. Martin's Press, 2005.

Cooper, Thea, and Arthur Ainsberg. *Breakthrough: Elizabeth Hughes, the Discovery of Insulin, and the Making of a Medical Miracle.* New York: St. Martin's Press, 2010.

Doidge, Norman. *The Brain That Changes Itself: Stories of Personal Triumph from the Frontiers of Brain Science.* New York: Viking, 2007.

Drexler, Madeline. *Emerging Epidemics: The Menace of New Infections.* New York: Penguin, 2009.

Engel, Jonathan. *The Epidemic (A Global History of AIDS).* Washington, DC: Smithsonian, 2006.

Graboys, Thomas, and Peter Zheutlin. *Life in the Balance: A Physician's Memoir of Life, Love, and Loss with Parkinson's Disease and Dementia.* New York: Union Square, 2008.

Gupta, Sanjay. *Cheating Death: The Doctors and Medical Miracles That Are Saving Lives against All Odds.* New York: Wellness Central, 2009.

Helfgot, Susan Whitman, and William Novak. *The Match: Complete Strangers, a Miracle Face Transplant, Two Lives Transformed.* New York: Simon & Schuster, 2010.

Jacobs, Lawrence R., and Theda Skocpol. *Health Care Reform and American Politics.* New York: Oxford University Press, 2010.

Kohn, Linda T., Janet M. Corrigan, and Molla S. Donaldson, eds. *To Err Is Human: Building a Safer Health System.* Washington, DC: National Academy Press, 2000.

LeDoux, Joseph. *Synaptic Self: How Our Brains Become Who We Are.* New York: Viking, 2002.

Morris, Charles R. *The Surgeons: Life and Death in a Top Heart Center.* New York: Norton, 2007.

Mukherjee, Siddhartha. *The Emperor of All Maladies: A Biography of Cancer.* New York: Simon & Schuster, 2010.

Petryna, Adriana. *When Experiments Travel: Clinical Trials and the Global Search for Human Subjects.* Princeton, NJ: Princeton University Press, 2009.

Pollan, Michael. *In Defense of Food: An Eater's Manifesto.* New York: Penguin, 2008.

Pollan, Michael. *The Omnivore's Dilemma: A Natural History of Four Meals.* New York: Penguin, 2006.

Ridley, Matt. *Genome: The Autobiography of a Species in 23 Chapters.* Rev. ed. New York: MJF Books, 2011.

Robison, John Elder. *Look Me in the Eye: My Life with Asperger's.* New York: Crown, 2007.

Schwartz, Jeffrey M., and Sharon Begley. *The Mind and the Brain: Neuroplasticity and the Power of Mental Force.* New York: ReganBooks/HarperCollins, 2002.

Servan-Schreiber, David. *Anticancer: A New Way of Life.* New York: Viking, 2008.

Shilts, Randy. *And the Band Played On: Politics, People and the AIDS Epidemic.* 20th anniversary ed. New York: St. Martin's Press, 2007.

Snowdon, David. *Aging with Grace: What the Nun Study Teaches Us about Leading Longer, Healthier, and More Meaningful Lives.* New York: Bantam, 2001.

Taylor, Jill Bolte. *My Stroke of Insight: A Brain Scientist's Personal Journey.* New York: Viking, 2008.

Venter, J. Craig. *A Life Decoded: My Genome, My Life.* New York: Viking, 2007.

RELIGION

Abou El Fadl, Khaled. *The Great Theft: Wrestling Islam from the Extremists.* New York: HarperSanFrancisco, 2005.

Adams, William Y. *Religion and Adaptation.* Stanford, CA: CSLI Publications, 2005.

Andresen, Jensine. *Religion in Mind: Cognitive Perspectives on Religious Belief, Ritual, and Experience.* Cambridge & New York: Cambridge University Press, 2001.

Aslan, Reza. *No God but God: The Origins, Evolution, and Future of Islam.* New York: Random House, 2005.

Bagger, Matthew C. *The Uses of Paradox: Religion, Self-Transformation, and the Absurd.* New York: Columbia University Press, 2007.

Berry, Thomas. *The Sacred Universe: Earth, Spirituality, and Religion in the Twenty-First Century.* New York: Columbia University Press, 2009.

Billington, Ray. *Religion without God.* London & New York: Routledge, 2002.

Blain, Jenny, Douglas Ezzy, and Graham Harvey, eds. *Researching Paganisms.* Walnut Creek, CA: AltaMira Press, 2004.

Boyer, Pascal. *Religion Explained: The Evolutionary Origins of Religious Thought.* New York: Basic Books, 2001.

Bridgers, Lynn. *Contemporary Varieties of Religious Experience: James's Classic Study in Light of Resiliency, Temperament, and Trauma.* Lanham, MD: Rowman & Littlefield, 2005.

Dawkins, Richard. *The God Delusion.* Boston: Houghton Mifflin, 2006.

Dennett, Daniel C. *Breaking the Spell: Religion as a Natural Phenomenon.* New York: Viking, 2006.

Ferrer, Jorge N., and Jacob H. Sherman, eds. *The Participatory Turn: Spirituality, Mysticism, Religious Studies.* Albany: State University of New York Press, 2008.

France, David. *Our Fathers: The Secret Life of the Catholic Church in an Age of Scandal.* New York: Broadway, 2004.

Gelman, Andrew. *Red State, Blue State, Rich State, Poor State.* Princeton, NJ: Princeton University Press, 2009.

Harris, Sam. *The End of Faith: Religion, Terror, and the Future of Reason.* New York: Norton, 2004.

Harris, Sam. *Letter to a Christian Nation.* New York: Knopf, 2006.

Hedges, Chris. *I Don't Believe in Atheists.* New York: Free Press, 2008.

Hick, John. *The New Frontier of Religion and Science: Religious Experience, Neuroscience and the Transcendent.* Basingstoke, U.K. & New York: Palgrave Macmillan, 2006.

Hitchens, Christopher. *God Is Not Great: How Religion Poisons Everything.* New York: Twelve, 2007.

Inglis, Laura Lyn, and Peter K. Steinfeld. *Old Dead White Men's Philosophy.* Amherst, NY: Humanity Books, 2000.

Küng, Hans. *Islam: Past, Present and Future.* Translated by John Bowden. Oxford: Oneworld, 2007.

Lash, John Lamb. *Not in His Image: Gnostic Vision, Sacred Ecology, and the Future of Belief.* White River Junction, VT: Chelsea Green, 2006.

Lytton, Timothy D. *Holding Bishops Accountable: How Lawsuits Helped the Catholic Church Confront Clergy Abuse.* Cambridge, MA: Harvard University Press, 2008.

McClenon, James. *Wondrous Healing: Shamanism, Human Evolution, and the Origin of Religion.* DeKalb: Northern Illinois University Press, 2002.

McGrath, Alister E., and Joanna Collicutt McGrath. *The Dawkins Delusion: Atheist Fundamentalism and the Denial of the Divine.* Downers Grove, IL: InterVarsity Press, 2007.

Neusner, Jacob, Bruce Chilton, and William A. Graham. *Three Faiths, One God: The Formative Faith and Practice of Judaism, Christianity, and Islam.* Boston: Brill, 2002.

Neville, Robert C. *Realism in Religion: A Pragmatist's Perspective.* Albany: State University of New York Press, 2009.

Norris, Pippa, and Ronald Inglehart. *Sacred and Secular: Religion and Politics Worldwide.* Cambridge & New York: Cambridge University Press, 2004.

Patton, Kimberley Christine. *Religion of the Gods: Ritual, Paradox, and Reflexivity.* Oxford & New York: Oxford University Press, 2009.

Rorty, Richard, and Gianni Vattimo. *The Future of Religion.* Edited by Santiago Zabala. New York: Columbia University Press, 2005.

Safi, Omid. *Progressive Muslims: On Justice, Gender and Pluralism.* Oxford: Oneworld, 2003.

Saxton, Alexander. *Religion and the Human Prospect.* New York: Monthly Review, 2006.

Smith, David. *Hinduism and Modernity.* Malden, MA: Blackwell, 2003.

Smullyan, Raymond M. *Who Knows?: A Study of Religious Consciousness.* Bloomington: Indiana University Press, 2003.

Sommerville, C. John. *Religion in the National Agenda: What We Mean by Religious, Spiritual, Secular.* Waco, TX: Baylor University Press, 2009.

Steffen, Lloyd H. *Holy War, Just War: Exploring the Moral Meaning of Religious Violence.* Lanham, MD: Rowman & Littlefield, 2007.

Stenger, Victor J. *God: The Failed Hypothesis: How Science Shows That God Does Not Exist.* Amherst, NY: Prometheus, 2007.

Tippett, Krista. *Speaking of Faith.* New York: Viking, 2007.

Turner, Frederick. *Natural Religion.* New Brunswick, NJ: Transaction, 2006.

Tyler, Aaron. *Islam, the West, and Tolerance: Conceiving Coexistence.* New York: Palgrave Macmillan, 2008.

Ward, Graham. *True Religion.* Oxford & Malden, MA: Blackwell, 2003.

Warren, Rick. *The Purpose Driven Life: What on Earth Am I Here For?* Grand Rapids, MI: Zondervan, 2002.

Whitehouse, Harvey. *Modes of Religiosity: A Cognitive Theory of Religious Transmission.* Walnut Creek, CA: Alta-Mira Press, 2004.

Whitehouse, Harvey, and James Laidlaw, eds. *Religion, Anthropology, and Cognitive Science.* Durham, NC: Carolina Academic Press, 2007.

SCIENCE AND TECHNOLOGY

Aczel, Amir D. *Entanglement: The Greatest Mystery in Physics.* New York: Four Walls Eight Windows, 2002.

Battelle, John. *The Search: How Google and Its Rivals Rewrote the Rules of Business and Transformed Our Culture.* New York: Portfolio, 2005.

Bird, Kai, and Martin J. Sherwin. *American Prometheus: The Triumph and Tragedy of J. Robert Oppenheimer.* New York: Knopf, 2005.

Bodanis, David. *Electric Universe: The Shocking True Story of Electricity.* New York: Crown, 2005.

Bryson, Bill. *A Short History of Nearly Everything.* New York: Broadway Books, 2003.

Buchanan, Mark. *Nexus: Small Worlds and the Groundbreaking Science of Networks.* New York: Norton, 2002.

Carr, Nicholas. *The Big Switch: Rewiring the World, from Edison to Google.* New York: Norton, 2008.

Dawkins, Richard. *The Ancestor's Tale: A Pilgrimage to the Dawn of Evolution.* New York: Houghton Mifflin, 2004.

Deffeyes, Kenneth S. *Beyond Oil: The View from Hubbert's Peak.* New York: Hill & Wang, 2005.

Diamond, Jared. *Collapse—How Societies Choose to Fail or Succeed.* New York: Viking, 2005.

Doidge, Norman. *The Brain That Changes Itself: Stories of Personal Triumph from the Frontiers of Brain Science.* New York: Viking, 2007.

Gilbert, Avery. *What the Nose Knows: The Science of Scent in Everyday Life.* New York: Crown, 2008.

Gilbert, Daniel. *Stumbling on Happiness.* New York: Knopf, 2006.

Gilder, Louisa. *The Age of Entanglement: When Quantum Physics Was Reborn.* New York: Knopf, 2008.

Gore, Al. *An Inconvenient Truth: The Planetary Emergency of Global Warming and What We Can Do about It.* New York: Rodale, 2006.

Gould, Stephen Jay. *Punctuated Equilibrium.* Cambridge, MA: Harvard University Press, 2007.

Grand, Steve. *Creation: Life and How to Make It.* Cambridge, MA: Harvard University Press, 2000.

Green, Brian. *The Fabric of the Cosmos: Space, Time, and the Texture of Reality.* New York: Knopf, 2004.

Hawking, Stephen. *The Universe in a Nutshell.* New York: Bantam, 2001.

Henson, Robert. *The Rough Guide to Climate Change.* London: Rough Guides, 2006.

Holmes, Hannah. *The Secret Life of Dust: From the Cosmos to the Kitchen Counter, the Big Consequences of Little Things.* New York: Wiley, 2001.

Horrobin, David. *The Madness of Adam and Eve: How Schizophrenia Shaped Humanity.* London & New York: Bantam, 2001.

Johanson, Donald C., and Kate Wong. *Lucy's Legacy: The Quest for Human Origins.* New York: Harmony, 2009.

Kaku, Michio. *Parallel Worlds: A Journey through Creation, Higher Dimensions, and the Future of the Cosmos.* New York: Doubleday, 2005.

Kirshner, Robert P. *The Extravagant Universe: Exploding Stars, Dark Energy, and the Accelerating Cosmos.* Princeton, NJ: Princeton University Press, 2002.

Kolbert, Elizabeth. *Field Notes from a Catastrophe: Man, Nature, and Climate Change.* New York: Bloomsbury, 2006.

Kunzig, Robert. *Mapping the Deep: The Extraordinary Story of Ocean Science.* New York: Sort Of, 2000.

Linden, Eugene. *The Winds of Change: Climate, Weather, and the Destruction of Civilization.* New York: Simon & Schuster, 2006.

Marchant, Jo. *Decoding the Heavens: A 2,000-Year-Old Computer and the Century Long Search to Discover Its Secrets.* London: Heinemann, 2008.

McCarthy, Wil. *Hacking Matter: Levitating Chairs, Quantum Mirages, and the Infinite Weirdness of Programmable Atoms.* New York: Basic Books, 2003.

Miller, Arthur I. *Empire of the Stars: Obsession, Friendship, and Betrayal in the Quest for Black Holes.* New York: Houghton Mifflin, 2005.

Mlodinow, Leonard. *The Drunkard's Walk: How Randomness Rules Our Lives.* New York: Pantheon, 2008.

O'Shea, Donal. *The Poincaré Conjecture: The Search of the Shape of the Universe.* New York: Walker, 2007.

Penrose, Roger. *The Road to Reality: A Complete Guide to the Laws of the Universe.* London: Cape, 2004.

Pinker, Steven. *The Blank Slate: The Modern Denial of Human Nature.* New York: Viking, 2002.

Sapolsky, Robert M. *A Primate's Memoir.* New York: Scribner, 2001.

Shubin, Neil. *Your Inner Fish: A Journey into the 3.5-Billion-Year History of the Human Body.* New York: Pantheon, 2009.

Stross, Randall. *Planet Google: One Company's Audacious Plan to Organize Everything We Know.* New York: Free Press, 2008.

Tudge, Colin, and Josh Young. *The Link: Uncovering Our Earliest Ancestor.* New York: Little, Brown, 2009.

Tyson, Neil DeGrasse. *Death by Black Hole: And Other Cosmic Quandries.* New York: Norton, 2007.

Tyson, Neil DeGrasse, and Donald Goldsmith. *Origins: Fourteen Billion Years of Cosmic Evolution.* New York: Norton, 2004.

Venter, J. Craig. *A Life Decoded: My Genome, My Life.* New York: Viking, 2007.

Webb, Stephen. *If the Universe Is Teeming with Aliens . . . Where Is Everybody?: Fifty Solutions to the Fermi Paradox and the Problem of Extraterrestrial Life.* New York: Copernicus Books, 2002.

Wilczek, Frank. *The Lightness of Being: Mass, Ether, and the Unification of Forces.* New York: Basic Books, 2008.

SPORTS

Agassi, Andre. *Open: An Autobiography.* New York: Knopf, 2009.

Amaechi, John, and Chris Bull. *Man in the Middle.* New York: ESPN Books, 2007.

Armstrong, Lance, and Sally Jenkins. *It's Not About the Bike: My Journey Back to Life.* New York: Putnam, 2000.

Assael, Shaun. *Steroid Nation: Juiced Home Run Totals, Anti-Aging Miracles, and a Hercules in Every High School: The Secret History of America's True Drug Addiction.* New York: ESPN Books, 2007.

Boyles, Bob, and Paul Guido. *Fifty Years of College Football: A Modern History of America's Most Colorful Sport.* New York: Skyhorse, 2007.

Bradbury, J. C. *The Baseball Economist: The Real Game Exposed.* New York: Dutton, 2007.

Bradley, Michael. *Big Games: College Football's Greatest Rivalries.* Washington, DC: Potomac Books, 2006.

Browne, David. *Amped: How Big Air, Big Dollars, and a New Generation Took Sports to the Extreme.* New York: Bloomsbury, 2004.

Bryant, Howard. *Juicing the Game: Drugs, Power, and the Fight for the Soul of Major League Baseball.* New York: Viking, 2005.

Butterworth, Michael L. *Baseball and Rhetoric of Purity: The National Pastime and American Identity during the War on Terror.* Tuscaloosa: University of Alabama Press, 2010.

Canseco, Jose. *Juiced: Wild Times, Rampant 'Roids, Smash Hits, and How Baseball Got Big.* New York: ReganBooks, 2005.

Cassuto, Leonard, and Stephen Partridge, eds. *The Cambridge Companion to Baseball.* Cambridge & New York: Cambridge University Press, 2011.

Castle, George. *Baseball and the Media: How Fans Lose in Today's Coverage of the Game.* Lincoln: University of Nebraska Press, 2006.

Cox, Ronald W., and Daniel Skidmore-Hess. *Free Agency and Competitive Balance in Baseball.* Jefferson, NC: McFarland, 2006.

deMause, Neil, and Joanna Cagan. *Field of Schemes: How the Great Stadium Swindle Turns Public Money into Private Profit.* Lincoln: University of Nebraska Press, 2008.

Dempsey, John Mark, ed. *Sports-Talk Radio in America: Its Context and Culture.* New York: Haworth Press, 2006.

Donaghy, Tim. *Personal Foul: A First-Person Account of the Scandal That Rocked the NBA.* Largo, FL: VTI Group, 2009.

Dungy, Tony, and Nathan Whitaker. *Quiet Strength: The Principles, Practices, and Priorities of a Winning Life.* Carol Stream, IL: Tyndale, 2007.

Dure, Beau. *Long-Range Goals: The Success Story of Major League Soccer.* Washington, DC: Potomac Books, 2010.

Dyreson, Mark, and J. A. Mangan, eds. *Sport and American Society: Exceptionalism, Insularity, and "Imperialism."* New York: Routledge, 2007.

Edmondson, Jacqueline. *Venus and Serena Williams: A Biography.* Westport, CT: Greenwood Press, 2005.

Evans, Jeremy. *In Search of Powder: A Story of America's Disappearing Ski Bum.* Lincoln: University of Nebraska Press, 2010.

Fainaru-Wada, Mark, and Lance Williams. *Game of Shadows: Barry Bonds, BALCO, and the Steroids Scandal That Rocked Professional Sports.* New York: Gotham, 2006.

Farrey, Tom. *Game On: How the Pressure to Win at All Costs Endangers Youth Sports, and What Parents Can Do About It.* New York: ESPN Books, 2009.

Foer, Franklin. *How Soccer Explains the World: An Unlikely Theory of Globalization.* New York: HarperCollins, 2004.

Forney, Craig A. *The Holy Trinity of American Sports: Civil Religion in Football, Baseball, and Basketball.* Macon, GA: Mercer University Press, 2007.

Freeman, Sharon T. *African Americans: Reviving Baseball in Inner Cities.* Washington, DC: AAS-BEA, 2008.

Gems, Gerald R. *The Athletic Crusade: Sport and American Cultural Imperialism.* Lincoln: University of Nebraska Press, 2006.

Gerdy, John R. *Air Ball: American Education's Failed Experiment with Elite Athletics*. Jackson: University Press of Mississippi, 2006.

Hawkins, Billy. *The New Plantation: Black Athletes, College Sports, and Predominantly White NCAA Institutions*. New York: Palgrave Macmillan, 2010.

Hogshead-Makar, Nancy, and Andrew Zimbalist, eds. *Equal Play: Title IX and Social Change*. Philadelphia: Temple University Press, 2007.

James, Bill. *The New Bill James Historical Baseball Abstract*. New York: Free Press, 2001.

Johnson, Richard A., and Robert Hamilton Johnson. *The Boston Marathon*. Boston: Arcadia, 2009.

Jones, Tom. *Working at the Ballpark: The Fascinating Lives of Baseball People—From Peanut Vendors and Broadcasters to Players and Managers*. New York: Skyhorse, 2008.

Jozsa, Frank P., Jr. *Baseball, Inc.: The National Pastime as Big Business*. Jefferson, NC: McFarland, 2006.

Jozsa, Frank P., Jr. *Baseball in Crisis: Spiraling Costs, Bad Behavior, Uncertain Future*. Jefferson, NC: McFarland, 2008.

Jozsa, Frank P., Jr. *Major League Baseball Expansions and Relocations: A History, 1876–2008*. Jefferson, NC: McFarland, 2010.

Kluck, Ted A. *Game Time: Inside College Football*. Guilford, CT: Lyons Press, 2007.

Knight, Dawn. *Taliaferro: Breaking Barriers from the NFL Draft to the Ivory Tower*. Bloomington: Indiana University Press, 2007.

Kudlac, Christopher S. *Fair or Foul: Sports and Criminal Behavior in the United States*. Santa Barbara, CA: Praeger/ABC-CLIO, 2010.

Kusz, Kyle. *Revolt of the White Athlete: Race, Media and the Emergence of Extreme Athletes in America*. New York: Lang, 2007.

Lee, Bill, and Richard Lally. *The Wrong Stuff*. New York: Three Rivers Press, 2006.

Lewis, Michael. *The Blind Side: Evolution of a Game*. New York: Norton, 2006.

Lewis, Michael. *Moneyball: The Art of Winning an Unfair Game*. New York: Norton, 2003.

Litos, Michael. *Cinderella: Inside the Rise of Mid-Major College Basketball*. Naperville, IL: Sourcebooks, 2007.

Lockwood, Kathleen. *Major League Bride: An Inside Look at Life Outside the Ballpark*. Jefferson, NC: McFarland, 2010.

Mandel, Stewart. *Bowls, Polls & Tattered Souls: Tackling the Chaos and Controversy That Reign Over College Football*. Hoboken, NJ: Wiley, 2008.

Mandelbaum, Michael. *The Meaning of Sports: Why Americans Watch Baseball, Football, and Basketball, and What They See When They Do*. New York: Public Affairs, 2004.

Manning, Peyton, and Archie Manning. *Manning: A Father, His Sons and a Football Legacy*. New York: Harper, 2000.

Markovits, Andrei S., and Lars Rensmann. *Gaming the World: How Sports are Reshaping Global Politics and Culture*. Princeton, NJ: Princeton University Press, 2010.

Mills, Dorothy Seymour. *Chasing Baseball: Our Obsession with Its History, Numbers, People and Places*. Jefferson, NC: McFarland, 2010.

Moon, Warren, and Don Yaeger. *Never Give Up on Your Dream: My Journey*. Cambridge, MA: Da Capo Press, 2009.

Nguyen, Dat, and Rusty Burson. *Dat: Tackling Life and the NFL*. College Station: Texas A&M University Press, 2005.

Price, S. L. *Heart of the Game: Life, Death, and Mercy in Minor League America*. New York: Ecco/HarperCollins, 2009.

Radomski, Kirk. *Bases Loaded: The Inside Story of the Steroid Era in Baseball by the Central Figure in the Mitchell Report*. New York: Hudson Street Press, 2009.

Reilly, Rick. *Who's Your Caddy?: Looping for the Great, Near Great, and Reprobates of Golf*. New York: Doubleday, 2003.

Ring, Jennifer. *Stolen Bases: Why American Girls Don't Play Baseball*. Urbana: University of Illinois Press, 2009.

Ross, Betsy M. *Playing Ball with the Boys: The Rise of Women in the World of Men's Sports*. Cincinnati: Clerisy Press, 2010.

Ruck, Rob. *Raceball: How the Major Leagues Colonized the Black and Latin Game*. Boston: Beacon Press, 2010.

Schmidt, Mike, and Glen Waggoner. *Clearing the Bases: Juiced Players, Monster Salaries, Sham Records, and a Hall of Famer's Search for the Soul of Baseball*. New York: HarperCollins, 2006.

Simmons, Roy, et al. *Out of Bounds: Coming Out of Sexual Abuse, Addiction, and My Life of Lies in the NFL Closet*. New York: Carroll & Graf, 2006.

Stout, Glenn, ed. *The Best American Sports Writing.* New York: Houghton Mifflin, 2000–2009.

Sullivan, Dean A., ed. *Final Innings: A Documentary History of Baseball, 1972–2008.* Lincoln: University of Nebraska Press, 2010.

Szymanski, Stefan, and Andrew Zimbalist. *National Pastime: How Americans Play Baseball and the Rest of the World Plays Soccer.* Washington, DC: Brookings Institution Press, 2005.

Thompson, Teri, et al. *American Icon: The Fall of Roger Clemens and the Rise of Steroids in America's Pastime.* New York: Knopf, 2009.

Uschan, Michael V. *Serena Williams.* Detroit: Lucent, 2011.

Waltrip, Michael. *In the Blink of an Eye: Dale, Daytona, and the Day That Changed Everything.* New York: Hyperion, 2011.

Williams, Venus, Serena Williams, and Hilary Beard. *Venus & Serena: Serving from the Hip, Ten Rules for Living, Loving, and Winning.* Boston: Houghton Mifflin, 2005.

Woods, Tiger. *How I Play Golf.* New York: Crown, 2000.

Yaeger, Don, and Jim Henry. *Tarnished Heisman: Did Reggie Bush Turn His Final College Season into a Six-Figure Job?* New York: Pocket Books, 2008.

Yost, Mark. *Varsity Green: A Behind the Scenes Look at Culture and Corruption in College Athletics.* Stanford, CA: Stanford University Press, 2010.

Zirin, Dave. *Bad Sports: How Owners Are Ruining the Games We Love.* New York: Scribner, 2010.

Primary Source Type Index

Primary source authors appear in parentheses.

General Index

Page numbers in bold indicate primary sources. Primary sources are indexed under the entry name with the author or authors' name(s) in parentheses.